PHILOSOPHICAL FOUNDATIONS OF HUMAN RIGHTS

PHILOSOPHICAL FOUNDATIONS OF LAW

The *Philosophical Foundations of Law* series aims to develop work at the intersection of legal philosophy and doctrinal law. Volumes in the series gather leading philosophers and lawyers to present original work on the theoretical foundations of substantive areas of law, or central topics in legal philosophy. Together, the essays provide a roadmap of current philosophical work in the field to lawyers and philosophers looking for high quality new work and provide a stimulus for further research by specialists in the area.

ALSO AVAILABLE IN THE SERIES

Philosophical Foundations of Fiduciary Law
Edited by Andrew S. Gold and Paul B. Miller

Philosophical Foundations of the Law of Torts
Edited by John Oberdiek

Philosophical Foundations of Property Law
Edited by James Penner and Henry E. Smith

Philosophical Foundations of the Nature of Law
Edited by Wil Waluchow and Stefan Sciaraffa

Philosophical Foundations of the Law of Unjust Enrichment
Edited by Robert Chambers, Charles Mitchell, and James Penner

Philosophical Foundations of Language in the Law
Edited by Andrei Marmor, Scott Soames

Philosophical Foundations of Criminal Law
Edited by R.A. Duff, Stuart Green

Philosophical Foundations of European Union Law
Edited by Julie Dickson and Pavlos Eleftheriadis

Philosophical Foundations of Discrimination Law
Deborah Hellman and Sophia Moreau

Philosophical Foundations of Human Rights

Edited by
ROWAN CRUFT
S. MATTHEW LIAO
MASSIMO RENZO

OXFORD
UNIVERSITY PRESS

OXFORD

UNIVERSITY PRESS

Great Clarendon Street, Oxford, OX2 6DP,
United Kingdom

Oxford University Press is a department of the University of Oxford.
It furthers the University's objective of excellence in research, scholarship,
and education by publishing worldwide. Oxford is a registered trade mark of
Oxford University Press in the UK and in certain other countries

Published in the United States of America by Oxford University Press
198 Madison Avenue, New York, NY 10016, United States of America

British Library Cataloguing in Publication Data
Data available

Library of Congress Control Number: 2014959956

ISBN 978–0–19–968863–0

Acknowledgements

We are very grateful to our contributors for their excellent work and their patience, and to Alex Flach, Natasha Flemming, Dhanuj S. Nair, and their team at Oxford University Press for their care in seeing the book through to publication. We would also like to thank the UK's Arts and Humanities Research Council for funding a set of workshops on human rights, from which some of these papers emerged. Chapter 11, Joseph Raz's 'Human Rights in the Emerging World Order', is reprinted from *Transnational Legal Theory*, 1 (2010), 31–47. Chapter 31, James Griffin's 'The Relativity and Ethnocentricity of Human Rights', first appeared as chapter 7 of his *On Human Rights* (Oxford University Press, 2008). We thank the publishers for permission to reprint this material.

Table of Contents

PART III. CANONICAL AND CONTESTED
HUMAN RIGHTS

PART IV. HUMAN RIGHTS: CONCERNS
AND ALTERNATIVES

Contributors

Larry Alexander, University of San Diego

Elizabeth Ashford, University of St Andrews

Robert Audi, University of Notre Dame

Charles R. Beitz, Princeton University

Samantha Besson, University of Fribourg

Corey Brettschneider, Brown University

Kimberley Brownlee, University of Warwick

Allen Buchanan, Duke University

Thomas Christiano, University of Arizona

Jiwei Ci, University of Hong Kong

Rowan Cruft, University of Stirling

Katrin Flikschuh, London School of Economics and Political Science

Pablo Gilabert, Concordia University

James Griffin, University of Oxford

Carol C. Gould, City University of New York

Virginia Held, City University of New York

Simon Hope, University of Stirling

Liora Lazarus, University of Oxford

George Letsas, University College London

S. Matthew Liao, New York University

David Luban, Georgetown University

Saladin Meckled-Garcia, University College London

Susan Mendus, University of York

David Miller, University of Oxford

James W. Nickel, University of Miami

Onora O'Neill, University of Cambridge

Fabienne Peter, University of Warwick

Joseph Raz, Columbia University

Massimo Renzo, King's College London

Andrea Sangiovanni, Kings College London

A. John Simmons, University of Virginia

Zofia Stemplowska, University of Oxford

Victor Tadros, University of Warwick

John Tasioulas, Kings College London

Guglielmo Verdirame, Kings College London

Jeremy Waldron, New York University

Jonathan Wolff, University College London

Lorenzo Zucca, Kings College London

Abbreviations

CAT	Convention against Torture and Other Cruel, Inhuman or Degrading Treatment or Punishment
CEDAW	Convention for the Elimination of all Forms of Discrimination Against Women
CERD	International Convention on the Elimination of All Forms of Racial Discrimination
CLS	Christian Legal Society
CRC	Convention on the Rights of the Child
CRL	constitutional rights law
DDA	doctrine of doing and allowing
DRMC	Declaration of the Rights of Man and of the Citizen (France)
ECHR	European Convention on Human Rights
HRFR	human right to freedom of religion
ICC	International Criminal Court
ICCPR	International Covenant on Civil and Political Rights
ICESCR	International Covenant on Economic, Social and Cultural Rights
ICJ	International Court of Justice
ICRC	International Committee of the Red Cross
ICTY	International Criminal Tribunal for the Former Yugoslavia
IHL	international humanitarian law
IHRL	international human rights law
ILHRs	international legal human rights
IMF	International Monetary Fund
LWOP	life sentences without parole
MHRs	moral human rights
MP	means principle
MWC	International Convention on the Protection of All Migrant Workers and Members of their Families
NGO	non-governmental organization
PTSD	post-traumatic stress disorder
PWDC	International Convention on the Protection and Promotion of the Rights and Dignity of Persons with Disabilities
UDHR	United Nations Universal Declaration of Human Rights
UN	United Nations
UPR	Universal Principle of Right
WTO	World Trade Organisation

The Philosophical Foundations of Human Rights

An Overview

Rowan Cruft, S. Matthew Liao, and Massimo Renzo

I. Introduction

Human rights are the distinctive legal, moral, and political concept of the last sixty years. The Universal Declaration of Human Rights (UDHR) was adopted by the Third United Nations General Assembly in December 1948, and became a model for the constitutions of many countries and domestic and international non-governmental organizations (NGOs).[1] Following the UDHR, human rights slowly entered international law through, among others, the European (1950) and American (1969) Conventions and the International Covenants (1966).

Of course the idea of rights held by all in virtue of their humanity can be found long before 1948, for example in the 1776 American Declaration of Independence and the 1789 French Declaration of the Rights of Man and the Citizen. In the guise of 'natural rights'—rights held by people as a matter of natural law—the idea can be found in the influential seventeenth- and eighteenth-century work of Grotius, Pufendorf, Locke, and Kant.[2] Indeed, recent scholarship claims that this idea of natural rights first originated much earlier, either in early medieval thought or before.[3]

---

[1] Johannes Morsink, *Inherent Human Rights: Philosophical Roots of the Universal Declaration* (Philadelphia: University of Pennsylvania Press, 2009), 1.

[2] Hugo Grotius, *The Rights of War and Peace* (1625); Samuel Pufendorf, *On the Law of Nature and of Nations* (1672); John Locke, *Two Treatises of Government* (1689); Immanuel Kant, *The Metaphysics of Morals* (1797). Note that Thomas Hobbes's use of the idea of a 'right of nature' in *Leviathan* (1651) is idiosyncratic: for Hobbes, unlike the other thinkers, a person's 'right of nature' is not a right entailing duties that others must fulfil, but consists rather in the person's liberty, in the state of nature without government, to do whatever she wishes to others in order to preserve her own life (*Leviathan*, Part 1, chs. 13–14).

[3] For discussion of the importance of Gratian's *Decretum* (c. 1140) and of Ockham (1287–1347) and Gerson (1363–1429) in relation to the notion of natural rights, including accounts of the Franciscan debates about property rights, see Brian Tierney, *The Idea of Natural Rights* (Grand Rapids: Emory University Press, 1997) and Annabel Brett, *Liberty, Right and Nature: Individual Rights in Later Scholastic Thought* (Cambridge: Cambridge University Press, 1997). Tertullian's translators find the following from the late second or early third century CE: 'it is a basic human right that everyone should be free to worship according to his own convictions. No one is either harmed or helped by another man's religion' (Maurice Wiles and Mark Santer (eds.), *Documents in Early Christian Thought* (Cambridge: Cambridge University Press, 1975), 227); Larry Siedentop writes 'Here we may find one of the earliest assertions of a basic right, a rightful power claimed for humans as such' (*Inventing the Individual: The Origins of Western Liberalism* (London: Allen Lane, 2014), 78). For a wide-ranging history of the roots of human rights thinking, including the roots of ethical universalism in diverse ancient religions, see Micheline R. Ishay, *The History of Human Rights: From Ancient Times to the Globalization Era* (Berkeley and Los Angeles: University of California Press, 2004).

However, it is worth noticing that whether contemporary human rights are the same as, or are at least a modernized, secularized form of natural rights, is highly controversial.

The specific phrase 'human rights' only became common in English usage in the 1970s.[4] The concept has grown in institutional and rhetorical importance during the last two decades—witness, for example, the embedding of the European Convention on Human Rights (ECHR) in UK law (1998) and the frequent framing of measures to resist terrorism as involving a 'balancing' of the human rights of suspects and potential victims. The concept's centrality has been matched by a significant volume of important empirically oriented sociological work and doctrinally oriented legal work. By contrast, with some exceptions (notably, the work of Maurice Cranston and James Nickel), philosophers in the past were slow to examine human rights as they are conceived in international law and politics.[5] There was growing philosophical work on basic moral or natural rights,[6] and also on the very nature of rights,[7] but much less on the human rights of the emerging human rights movement.

Two recent trends reversed this. First, Rawls put the notion of human rights on the map of contemporary political philosophy by giving them a specific role and definition in *The Law of Peoples* (1999), anticipated first in his Amnesty Lecture of the same title (1993).[8] Some of the ensuing philosophical discussion was primarily about the role of human rights within broader debates about poverty,[9] the justification of

---

[4] See Samuel Moyn's graph of usage of the phrase 'human rights' in Anglo–American news; Moyn, *The Last Utopia: Human Rights in History* (Cambridge, MA: Harvard University Press, 2010), 231.

[5] Maurice Cranston, *What Are Human Rights?* (London: Bodley Head, 1973); James W. Nickel, *Making Sense of Human Rights*, 1st edn. (Berkeley and Los Angeles: University of California Press, 1987). See also Jack Donelly, *Universal Human Rights in Theory and Practice*, 1st edn. (Ithaca: Cornell University Press, 1989).

[6] H.L.A. Hart, 'Are There Any Natural Rights?', *Philosophical Review*, LXIV (1955): 175–91; Alan Gewirth, *Reason and Morality* (Chicago: University of Chicago, 1978) and *Human Rights: Essays on Justification and Application* (Chicago: University of Chicago, 1982); John Finnis, *Natural Law and Natural Rights* (Oxford: Clarendon, 1980); Joel Feinberg, *Rights, Justice, and the Bounds of Liberty* (Princeton: Princeton University Press, 1980); Henry Shue, *Basic Rights: Subsistence, Affluence, and U.S. Foreign Policy*, 1st edn. (Princeton: Princeton University Press, 1980); Judith Jarvis Thomson, *The Realm of Rights* (Cambridge, MA: Harvard University Press, 1990); Hillel Steiner, *An Essay on Rights* (Oxford: Blackwell, 1994).

[7] See the essays in Jeremy Waldron (ed.), *Theories of Rights* (Oxford: Oxford University Press, 1984) and Matthew H. Kramer, N.E. Simmonds and Hillel Steiner, *A Debate Over Rights* (Oxford: Clarendon Press, 1998). See also Neil MacCormick, *Legal Right and Social Democracy* (Oxford: Oxford University Press, 1982); Rex Martin, *A System of Rights* (Oxford: Oxford University Press, 1993); Joseph Raz, *The Morality of Freedom* (Oxford: Clarendon Press, 1986); L.W. Sumner, *The Moral Foundations of Rights* (Oxford: Clarendon Press, 1987); Carl Wellman, *A Theory of Rights: Persons under Laws, Institutions, and Morals* (Totowa, NJ: Rowman and Allanheld, 1985); Alan R. White, *Rights* (Oxford: Clarendon Press, 1984). For the current state of debates on the nature of rights, and the rival 'interest' and 'will' theories, see the introduction and essays by Cruft, Wenar, Steiner, Kramer, and Hayward in the symposium, 'Rights and the Direction of Duties', *Ethics*, 123 (2013).

[8] John Rawls, *The Law of Peoples with 'The Idea of Public Reason Revisited'* (Cambridge, MA: Harvard University Press, 1999); 'The Law of Peoples' in S. Shute and S. Hurley (eds.), *On Human Rights: The Oxford Amnesty Lectures 1993* (New York: Basic Books, 1993), 41–82.

[9] See, eg, Onora O'Neill, *Bounds of Justice* (Cambridge: Cambridge University Press, 2000), Pt II; Thomas Pogge, *World Poverty and Human Rights*, 1st edn. (Cambridge: Polity, 2002); Thomas Pogge (ed.), *Freedom from Poverty as a Human Right: Who Owes What to the Very Poor?* (Oxford: Oxford University Press/UNESCO: 2007).

humanitarian intervention,[10] and other issues of international justice.[11] More recently this debate has become more sophisticated and has expanded to cover a number of other important issues, such as international trade.[12]

Secondly, at the same time influential papers by James Griffin and Charles Beitz were appearing that directly address the question of the nature and justification of human rights.[13] They were followed by a number of other papers, which culminated in the publication of two important books: Griffin's *On Human Rights* (2008) and Beitz's *The Idea of Human Rights* (2009).[14] These books, together with the second edition of James Nickel's path-breaking earlier volume, *Making Sense of Human Rights*, and further work by Jack Donnelly and Carl Wellman,[15] have given significant impulse to the creation of a self-standing debate on the 'philosophical foundations of human rights', ie, a debate in which human rights are not discussed simply as part of wider, more established controversies in political and legal philosophy. More recently, John Tasioulas's writings have played an important role in promoting this debate.[16]

Parallel to these developments, a separate literature has emerged on what has come to be called the 'capabilities approach' to global justice. This debate has its own conceptual framework, developed in the work of Martha Nussbaum and Amartya Sen, but has often overlapped with, and to some extent drawn attention to, issues that have become central in the debate on the philosophical foundations of human rights, such as the idea of a list of minimal goods/opportunities required for a minimally decent life, and the related notion of 'human functioning'.[17]

---

[10] Allen Buchanan, *Justice, Legitimacy, and Self-Determination: Moral Foundations for International Law* (Oxford: Oxford University Press, 2004), esp. ch. 3; see also Buchanan's more recent work including *Human Rights, Legitimacy, and the Use of Force* (Oxford: Oxford University Press, 2010).

[11] An exception is the wide range of essays in David Reidy and Rex Martin (eds.), *Rawls's Law of Peoples: A Realistic Utopia?* (Oxford: Blackwell, 2006).

[12] See, eg, Leif Wenar, 'Clean Trade in Natural Resources', *Ethics and International Affairs*, 25 (2011): 27–39.

[13] James Griffin, 'Discrepancies between the Best Philosophical Account of Human Rights and the International Law of Human Rights', *Proceedings of the Aristotelian Society*, 101 (2001): 1–28; James Griffin, 'First Steps in an Account of Human Rights', *European Journal of Philosophy*, 9 (2001): 306–27; Charles Beitz, 'Human Rights as a Common Concern', *American Political Science Review*, 95 (2001): 269–82.

[14] James Griffin, *On Human Rights* (Oxford: Oxford University Press, 2008); Charles R. Beitz, *The Idea of Human Rights* (Oxford: New York: Oxford University Press, 2009).

[15] James W. Nickel, *Making Sense of Human Rights*, 2nd edn. (Malden, MA; Oxford: Blackwell, 2007); Jack Donnelly, *Universal Human Rights in Theory and Practice*, 2nd edn. (Ithaca: Cornell University Press, 2003); Carl Wellman, *The Moral Dimensions of Human Rights* (Oxford: Oxford University Press, 2011).

[16] John Tasioulas, 'The Moral Reality of Human Rights', in Thomas Pogge (ed.), *Freedom from Poverty as a Human Right*, 75–102; John Tasioulas, 'Towards a Philosophy of Human Rights', *Current Legal Problems*, 65 (2012): 1–30; John Tasioulas, 'On the Nature of Human Rights', in Gerhard Ernst and Jan-Christoph Heilinger (eds.), *The Philosophy of Human Rights* (Berlin: de Gruyter, 2012), 17–60; John Tasioulas, 'Human Rights, Legitimacy, and International Law', *The American Journal of Jurisprudence*, 58(1) (2013): 1–25.

[17] See, eg, Martha Nussbaum, *Creating Capabilities: The Human Development Approach* (Cambridge, MA: Harvard University Press, 2011); Martha Nussbaum, *Women and Human Development: The Capabilities Approach* (Cambridge: Cambridge University Press, 2001); Amartya Sen, 'Rights and Capabilities', in *Resources, Values and Development* (Cambridge: Cambridge University Press, 1984); Amartya Sen, 'Elements of a Theory of Human Rights', *Philosophy and Public Affairs*, 32 (2004): 315–56. Carol Gould's work is in some ways akin to the 'capabilities approach' with its stress on the importance

This volume is the first to survey the growing field of the philosophical foundations of human rights. In this Introduction, we aim to provide a state-of-the-art discussion of the central topics. We discuss four main questions.

1. If there are human rights, what are they? Are they a subset of moral rights? Are they legal rights? Call this the Nature of Human Rights question.

2. What grounds or justifies human rights? Call this the Ground of Human Rights question.

3. Which proposed human rights are real human rights? Should we dismiss some classes of human rights claims as morally, legally or conceptually questionable?

4. Are there human rights at all, or should we embrace the sceptical conclusion that there are no genuine human rights?

We shall examine each in turn, and it will become clear that there is a diversity of positions on each question, with no prevailing philosophical view even on fundamental issues like what a human right is. In our view, there is great value in this diversity: the nature, ground, contents, and existence of human rights are not matters of universally accepted, unchallenged dogma. They are, rather, subjects on which there is a range of competing well-developed positions and this, we suggest, is a sign of the intellectual, cultural, and political fertility of the notion of human rights. Following our discussion of the four central topics, we end with a brief overview of the essays in the volume.

II. The Nature of Human Rights

In addressing the question of the nature of human rights, an intuitive move has been to turn to the notion of natural rights, whose main formulation can found in the writings of Grotius, Pufendorf, and Locke.[18] These are rights that all human beings possess simply in virtue of their humanity and which can be identified simply by the use of ordinary moral reasoning ('natural reason'), as opposed to the sort of conventional reasons created within particular social or institutional contexts. In particular, on this naturalistic conception of the nature of human rights, they are (a) moral rights that (b) all human beings possess (c) at all times and in all places (d) simply in virtue of being human and (e) the corresponding dutybearers are all able people in appropriate circumstances. Hence, John Simmons writes, 'Human rights are rights possessed by all human beings (at all times and in all places), simply in virtue of their humanity.'[19] Similarly, Griffin argues that 'The secularized notion [of a human right] that we were

---

of positive freedom as self-development; see Carol C. Gould, *Rethinking Democracy* (Cambridge: Cambridge University Press, 1989) and *Globalizing Democracy and Human Rights* (Cambridge: Cambridge University Press, 2004).

[18] Tasioulas, 'Human Rights, Legitimacy, and International Law'; Pogge, *World Poverty and Human Rights: Cosmopolitan Responsibilities and Reforms*, 60–5; Aryeh Neier, *The International Human Rights Movement: A History* (Princeton, NJ: Princeton University Press, 2012); A. John Simmons, *Justification and Legitimacy: Essays on Rights and Obligations* (Cambridge: Cambridge University Press, 2001). For the original texts, see the references in n 2.

[19] A. John Simmons, 'Human Rights and World Citizenship: The Universality of Human Rights in Kant and Locke', in *Justification and Legitimacy: Essays on Rights and Obligations* (Cambridge: Cambridge University Press, 2001), 179–96, 185.

left with at the end of the Enlightenment is still our notion today…a right that we have simply in virtue of being human.'[20]

Let us examine why each of these features is deemed a necessary part of the nature of human rights.[21] Consider (a). Why should human rights be pre-legal moral rights as opposed to, for example, legally created rights? Presumably, the thought is that human rights should be capable of criticizing conventional, societal standards rather than just mirror these standards. As Griffin writes, 'the international law of human rights aims, or should aim, at least in part, to incorporate certain extra-legal ethical standards.'[22] Consider (b). The belief that human rights are something that all human beings possess is encapsulated in the UDHR, which states that 'all human beings are born free and equal in dignity and rights.' But why should human rights in fact be something that all human beings possess? Despite their physical, social, and cultural differences, human beings have often been thought fundamentally to have equal moral status.[23] This equality in moral status leads to the idea that all human beings should be afforded the similar kinds of protection that human rights provide, ie, they should all possess human rights. Consider (c). The idea that human rights should exist in all times and in all places stems from the observation that fundamental human nature has not changed significantly since the beginning of human existence. For instance, just as we need food and education today, the same applies to people in Ancient Rome or even to our ancestral cave dwellers. If so, it seems that if we have human rights claims to food and education, these claims should be applicable to people in Ancient Rome as well. Consider (d). Why think that human rights are rights that we have simply in virtue of being human? It is a natural thought that some aspect of human nature is what gives rise to *human* rights. Otherwise, why call them *human* rights? Also, as we shall shortly see, human rights tend to protect aspects of human nature that are fundamental to human existence. Finally, consider (e). Why hold the view that the corresponding duty-bearers of human rights are all able people in appropriate circumstances? Since human rights are universal claims that are applicable at all times and places, some believe that they should place all able people in appropriate circumstances under a duty to provide and/ or protect the right-holders' claims. For instance, Maurice Cranston says, 'To speak of a universal right is to speak of a universal duty…Indeed, if this universal duty were not imposed, what sense could be made of the concept of a universal human right?'[24] Similarly, Alan Gewirth says that 'The universality of a positive [human] right is…a matter of everyone's always having, as a matter of principle…the duty to act in accord with the right when the circumstances arise that require such action and when he then has the ability to do so, this ability including consideration of the cost to himself.'[25]

---

[20] James Griffin, *On Human Rights* 1–2.

[21] For an insightful similar discussion, see Tasioulas, 'On the Nature of Human Rights'.

[22] Griffin, *On Human Rights*, 54. We discuss later (at 18–23 in this essay) those who are critical of the view that human rights must be pre-legal moral rights.

[23] Of course, many—perhaps most—societies through history have not accorded human beings equal moral status (consider patriarchal and slave-holding societies), but for the thesis that a proto-commitment to equal status can be found in many religions and cultures, see Ishay, *The History of Human Rights*, ch. 1.

[24] Cranston, *What Are Human Rights?*, 69.

[25] Alan Gewirth, *The Community of Rights* (Chicago: University of Chicago Press, 1996), 63.

In recent years, all these features of human rights have been contested. Beginning with John Rawls, and defended by, among others Charles Beitz[26] and Joseph Raz,[27] the so-called 'political' conception of human rights offers an alternative view of the nature of human rights. In particular, advocates of this political conception argue that human rights are not based on certain features of humanity; rather, the distinctive nature of human rights is to be understood in light of their role or function in modern international political practice.[28] For instance, Rawls argues that 'Human rights are a class of rights that play a special role in a reasonable Law of Peoples: they restrict the justifying reasons for war and its conduct, and they specify limits to a regime's internal autonomy.'[29] According to Rawls, one of the defining features of human rights is that if a society fails to respect them, then external agents may in certain circumstances be permitted to interfere in its internal affairs, for example, by means of economic or political sanction, or even coercive intervention.[30] Raz also believes that human rights characteristically set limits to a society's internal autonomy.[31] Beitz's view is similar, at least in outline: for Beitz, human rights are defined as safeguarding those individual interests whose protection is distinctively a matter 'of international concern'—as opposed to a merely internal, intra-state matter, say, or a matter of interpersonal morality.[32]

In proposing that human rights should be understood in terms of their role or function in modern international political practice, the political conception directly challenges the idea that human rights include all the rights that we have simply in virtue of being human, ie, criterion (d). In addition, the political conception also challenges other features of the naturalistic understanding of human rights. For example, consider (a), the idea that human rights are a subset of moral rights. Charles Beitz has argued that '[w]e understand international human rights better by considering them *sui generis*.'[33] More recently, Allen Buchanan has argued that many human rights are morally justified legal rights rather than pre-legal moral rights, whereas Samantha Besson is developing the idea that human rights must be at once moral and legal.[34]

Likewise, consider (c). A number of people have argued that it is not the case that all human beings at all times and places would be justified in claiming the human rights currently recognized by international practice. For instance, UDHR, Article 26(1) states that: 'Everyone has the right to education. Education shall be free, at least in the elementary and fundamental stages. Elementary education shall be compulsory. Technical and professional education shall be made generally available and higher education shall be equally accessible to all on the basis of merit.' As Beitz argues, 'It is reasonably clear from examples like [this] that its framers could not have intended the

---

[26] Charles R. Beitz, *The Idea of Human Rights* (Oxford: Oxford University Press, 2009).

[27] Joseph Raz, 'Human Rights without Foundations', in Samantha Besson and John Tasioulas (eds.), *The Philosophy of International Law* (Oxford: Oxford University Press, 2010a), 321–38; Joseph Raz, 'Human Rights in the Emerging World Order', *Transnational Legal Theory*, 1 (2010b), 31–47, reprinted in this volume, ch. 11.

[28] Beitz, *The Idea of Human Rights*, 197.   [29] Rawls, *The Law of Peoples*, 79.

[30] Rawls, *The Law of Peoples*, 81.   [31] Raz, 'Human Rights without Foundations', 328.

[32] Beitz, *The Idea of Human Rights*, esp. 109–17.   [33] Beitz, *The Idea of Human Rights*, 197.

[34] Allen Buchanan, *The Heart of Human Rights* (Oxford: Oxford University Press, 2013); Samantha Besson, *Human Rights as Law* (forthcoming, 2015).

doctrine to apply, for example, to the ancient Greeks or to China in the Ch'in dynasty or to European societies in the Middle Ages.'[35] Similarly, Raz argues that if human beings have the right to education at all times and in all places, 'it follows that cave dwellers in the Stone Age had that right. Does that make sense?...The very distinctions between elementary, technical, professional and higher education would have made no sense at that, and at many other times.'[36] In response, some theorists have argued that human rights are 'synchronically' universal—that is, held by all humans at a given time, or in modern conditions—but not universal across history.[37]

Finally, consider (e). It is becoming the norm to think of human rights as primarily entailing duties borne by one's state or political community. For instance, Beitz argues that 'any plausible view of the justifying purposes of a practice of human rights must be compatible with the fact that the state constitutes the basic unit of the world's political organization.'[38] As he explains, 'a practice of human rights, so conceived, might be described as "statist" in at least two senses: its standards apply in the first instance to states, and they rely on states, individually and in collaboration, as their principal guarantors. This does not mean that human rights impose no constraints on other agents or that only states have responsibilities as guarantors. But the centrality of states to the practice of human rights cannot be denied.'[39] Even theorists who do not support the standard 'political' conception—such as Dworkin, Nickel or Pogge—think that the primary duties entailed by human rights are borne by states.[40] The prevalence of this view is perhaps partly due to the primacy and justiciability of state duties in human rights law.

There are some reasons to believe that the difference between the naturalistic conception and the political conception has been overdrawn.[41] According to the naturalistic conception, human rights are rights that we have simply in virtue of being human, whereas according to the political conception, human rights are rights that set limits to a society's internal autonomy (Rawls and Raz) or rights that the international community has a responsibility to protect in modern societies (Beitz). Are these two features incompatible? One way of seeing that they need not be is to notice that the political conceptions seem to be concerned with the issue of who is responsible for protecting and promoting human rights—that is, the issue of the bearers of responsibilities to uphold or enforce human rights, and the issue of when and how such upholding

---

[35] Beitz, *The Idea of Human Rights*, 57.   [36] Raz, this volume, ch. 11, 224–5.

[37] Raz, this volume, ch. 11; see also Tasioulas, 'On the Nature of Human Rights', 17–59, 31–6.

[38] Beitz, *The Idea of Human Rights*, 128.   [39] Beitz, *The Idea of Human Rights*, 128.

[40] See Pogge, *World Poverty and Human Rights*, 2nd edn., section 2.3 on the importance of 'Official Disrespect'; see also Ronald Dworkin, *Justice for Hedgehogs* (Cambridge, MA: Harvard University Press, 2011), ch. 15, in which human rights are discussed as one form of 'political right', rights that 'we each as individuals have against our state' (328); see also Nickel, *Making Sense of Human Rights*, 2nd edn., 10. Note that these theorists also leave a place for important secondary duties borne by non-state actors including transnational corporations, supranational institutions, NGOs and individuals. For criticism of the 'state-centric' approach, see Cristina Lafont, *Global Governance and Human Rights* (Amsterdam: Van Gorcum, 2013), and further discussion at 24–29 later in the current essay

[41] See, eg, S. Matthew Liao and Adam Etinson, 'Political and Naturalistic Conceptions of Human Rights: A False Polemic?', *Journal of Moral Philosophy*, 9(3) (2012): 327–52; Pablo Gilabert, 'The Capability Approach and the Debate between Humanist and Political Perspectives on Human Rights: A Critical Summary', *Human Rights Review*, 14 (2013): 299–325.

and enforcing is permitted—while the naturalistic conceptions seem to be concerned with what important features of human life ground human rights. Perhaps questions about the grounds and questions about the permitted ways to enforce human rights carry no or few implications for each other, and human rights are simply those rights which are *both* grounded simply in our humanity *and* entail duties with a distinctive international function. It seems in principle possible for one to accept both a naturalistic and political conception of the formal features of human rights. To be sure, advocates of the political conception may respond that they also have views about the grounds of human rights, and we return to this in the next section.

Or, consider the concern that human rights such as the right to education are not timeless. This concern can perhaps be addressed by distinguishing, for example, between the aim and the object of a right, or between 'highest-level' or 'basal' human rights which are universal across time and their specific instantiations at a time.[42] An account like this maintains that the aim of a human right is the goal or end of the human right, and the object of a human right is the means to achieving that goal or end; or it maintains that specific human rights are local constituents or instantiations of, or means for securing, over-arching high-level or basal human rights. On this distinction, the aims of human rights—or the high-level, basal rights—are timeless while the low-level objects of human rights may vary across time, location, and society. Applied to free elementary education, we can say that free elementary education is the object of a human right or is a local specific human right. As such, it makes sense only at a specific time, in a specific location, and in a specific society. By contrast, the aim of the human right to free elementary education—or the high-level, basal universal right standing behind it—is to ensure that human beings acquire the knowledge necessary to be adequately functioning individuals in their circumstances. In this regard, it does not seem odd to say such an aim or high-level right was relevant, important, and applied in the context of cavemen. One concern which this strategy must allay is that it seems to leave comparatively few genuinely timeless high-level human rights, certainly fewer than the many specific human rights found in international law.[43]

As noted earlier, the idea that human rights are possessed by all human beings seems to stem from the thought that all human beings have equal moral status. However, many prominent philosophers have argued that children are not right-holders, thereby suggesting that not all human beings have equal moral status. For instance, both James Griffin and Carl Wellman have argued that infants are not right-holders.[44] One might think that if Griffin's and Wellman's accounts of human rights have this implication, then this is a reason to discount their views.[45] Why then do Griffin and Wellman

---

[42] For the aim/object distinction, see Liao and Etinson, 'Political and Naturalistic Conceptions of Human Rights: A False Polemic?'. For the highest-level/lower-level distinction, see Griffin, *On Human Rights*, 149. For the basal/derived distinction, see Wellman, *The Moral Dimensions of Human Rights*, 28–9. For criticism of the general strategy outlined here, see Tasioulas, 'On the Nature of Human Rights', 31–6.

[43] See Tasioulas, 'On the Nature of Human Rights', 34.

[44] Griffin, *On Human Rights*, 95; Carl Wellman, *Real Rights* (Oxford: Oxford University Press, 1995), 107, 113. For Griffin, the claim is that infants do not hold *human* rights; it is not clear that he rejects the view that infants could hold moral rights other than human rights.

[45] See, eg, Massimo Renzo, 'Human Needs, Human Rights', this volume, ch. 32.

nevertheless insist on claiming that infants are not right-holders? An explanation may be the following: in moral philosophy, writers such as Peter Singer and Jeff McMahan have long challenged the idea that all human beings have equal moral status.[46] For instance, Singer argues that the belief that all human beings have equal moral status is really just a form of prejudice, what he calls speciesism, which he regards as being on a par with sexism and racism. As Singer writes,

> Racists violate the principle of equality by giving greater weight to the interests of members of their own race when there is a clash between their interests and the interests of those of another race. Sexists violate the principle of equality by favouring the interests of their own sex. Similarly, speciesists allow the interests of their own species to override the greater interests of members of other species. The pattern is identical in each case.[47]

To avoid the charge of speciesism, a number of philosophers believe that when we consider the moral status of a particular being, we should meet the Species Neutrality Requirement. This requirement says that an adequate account of right-holding should provide a criterion that does not in principle exclude any being simply on the basis of their species, and further the relevant criterion must be applicable through some objective, empirical method.[48] However, there does not seem to be a relevant empirical attribute that would apply to all and only human beings. The most plausible attributes such as actual sentience and actual agency do not apply to all human beings. For example, some human beings such as anencephalic children and comatose persons lack actual sentience, and many human beings including new-born infants lack actual agency. These human beings would not be right-holders on these accounts. Indeed, holding the view that only actual normative agents can possess human rights, Griffin and Wellman are led to the conclusion that very young children cannot have human rights.[49] Alternatively, some have rejected the Species Neutrality Requirement and defended the importance of membership in the human species.[50]

---

[46] Jeff McMahan, *The Ethics of Killing: Problems at the Margins of Life* (Oxford: Oxford University Press, 2002); Peter Singer, *Animal Liberation*, 2nd edn. (London: Jonathan Cape, 1990).

[47] Singer, *Animal Liberation*, 6, 9.

[48] Joel Feinberg and Barbara Blum Levenbook, 'Abortion', in Tom Regan (ed.), *Matters of Life and Death* (New York: McGraw-Hill, 1993).

[49] Griffin, *On Human Rights*, 92, and see n. 44 above.

[50] Cora Diamond, 'The Importance of Being Human', in David Cockburn (ed.), *Human Beings* (Cambridge: Cambridge University Press, 1991), 35–62; B. Williams, 'The Human Prejudice', in A.W. Moore (ed.), *Philosophy as a Humanistic Discipline* (Princeton: Princeton University Press, 2008), 135–54. For a view that allows all human beings, including very young children, to be rightholders without running afoul of the Species Neutrality Requirement, see S. Matthew Liao, 'The Basis of Human Moral Status', *Journal of Moral Philosophy*, 7 (2010a): 159–79. Note that some theorists are open to the possibility that what we call human rights may turn out to be held by animals as well as humans, on the ground that some animals may be 'persons' just as humans are. See, eg, Buchanan's claim that 'if "humanity" refers to personhood rather than to membership in the human biological species, and if we came to know that there were persons who were not of our biological species, then we might decide that what we have called human rights would be more accurately called persons' rights' (Allen Buchanan, *Beyond Humanity? The Ethics of Biomedical Enhancement* (Oxford: Oxford University Press, 2011), 214).

One further feature of human rights is worth noting here: they are often considered to be of overriding or at least special importance.[51] What exactly this means requires clarification: Do human rights always take priority over other rights and non-rights considerations when they conflict? Are the efforts a duty-bearer should make (or costs they should bear) to avoid violating human rights greater than those they should make to avoid violating other rights and non-rights considerations?[52] Are the efforts we should make to support a human rights culture greater than those we should make towards other goals? Very few theorists conceive human rights as of absolute importance in any of the senses just mentioned. Griffin argues that human rights can sometimes be overridden by other issues of justice as well as other moral values.[53] Similarly, the political conception outlined earlier, while defining human rights by their distinctive sovereignty-defeating importance, need not deny that human rights can be justifiably violated in extreme circumstances. And it is worth noticing that the law also acknowledges this point with the doctrine of proportionality, according to which state interference with non-absolute human rights such as privacy, or freedom of religion is lawful if proportionate to the achievement of a legitimate aim pursued by the state.[54] How to understand this legal doctrine, and whether it is justifiable, are highly contested matters.[55] Equally contested are the implications for what should be done when a legal or moral human right is justifiably violated: is the victim of a justified human rights violation or deficit owed compensation, and in what way should their treatment differ from that of a victim of an unjustified violation or deficit?[56] Some will consider the latter question, with its assumption that human rights violations can be justified at least on occasion, deeply misguided.[57] In sum, the importance of human rights, while often made part of their very definition, is highly contested.

---

[51] Some authors see rights as such, or political rights, as possessing a special importance (eg, Dworkin, *Justice for Hedgehogs*, 328–9). It is especially common to see *human rights* in particular as distinctively important.

[52] For interesting discussion of cases where the issues raised by the first two questions diverge (ie, cases in which the right to the fulfilment of which we should devote the most effort is not the right that takes priority in cases of conflict), see F.M. Kamm, *Morality, Mortality, Vol. II: Rights, Duties and Status* (Oxford: Oxford University Press, 1996), ch. 12. See also Thomson's notion of 'stringency' as defining a right's importance in cases of conflict with other rights and other values (*The Realm of Rights*, 152–8). For discussion focused more specifically on the importance of *human* rights, see Nickel, *Making Sense of Human Rights*, 41–4 and Beitz, *The Idea of Human Rights*, 33–42 and chs. 6, 7, and 8.

[53] Griffin argues that justified punishment is a case of the justified violation of a human right. He defends punishment by writing that 'the demands of justice can sometimes, and to some appropriate degree, outweigh the protection of human rights' (*On Human Rights*, 66).

[54] See George Letsas, 'Rescuing Proportionality', this volume, ch. 17.

[55] Letsas, this volume, ch. 17 and Guglielmo Verdirame, 'Rescuing Human Rights from Proportionality', this volume, ch. 18.

[56] This issue raises questions about the 'specificationist' approach to rights. See John Oberdiek, 'Specifying Rights Out of Necessity', *Oxford Journal of Legal Studies*, 28 (2008), 127–46, and Thomson's argument in *The Realm of Rights*, 91–8. See also Saladin Meckled-Garcia, 'Specifying Human Rights', this volume, ch. 16.

[57] For just one example focused on the absolute impermissibility of torture, see Claudia Card, 'Ticking Bombs and Interrogations', *Criminal Law and Philosophy*, 2 (2008): 1–15.

III. The Grounds of Human Rights

So far we have considered the question of the nature of human rights. This section will be devoted to examining the question of their justification. As will become clear, the two questions are to some extent related. Accepting a certain view of what human rights are will naturally incline us toward a certain family of justificatory theories. But the question of what human rights are and the question of what justifies their existence are clearly distinct. We might agree, for example, that human rights ought to be understood as important moral rights that all human beings possess simply in virtue of their humanity, and yet disagree about which aspects of human nature should ground human rights. In fact, we might agree that this is how the notion of human rights would be justified, and yet reject their existence altogether (just as we might agree that the god of Judaism, Christianity, and Islam has certain features, while rejecting the existence of such a god).[58] In this section we will introduce the main approaches to the justification of human rights.[59]

A. Instrumental justifications

Let us start with the view of those who understand human rights as rights that all human beings have simply in virtue of being human. According to this view, the justification for the existence of a special class of rights called 'human rights' is that they protect certain distinctive features of humanity. The most intuitive way of understanding this view is in instrumental terms: human rights are useful or essential means to realize or further valued features of human lives.[60] But what are these features? Three main answers have been offered to this question in the philosophical debate: one appeals to the notion of agency, one appeals to the notion of the good life, and one appeals to the notion of basic needs. We will consider these three answers in turn, beginning with the first one.

---

[58] Tasioulas, 'Human Rights, Legitimacy, and International Law', 19.

[59] Note that in this section we focus on what we see as the most influential theories in the philosophical literature, and this means that some important approaches—such as consequentialist grounds for human rights—are not discussed (see William Talbott, *Which Rights Should be Universal?* (Oxford: Oxford University Press, 2005) and William Talbott, *Human Rights and Human Well-Being* (Oxford: Oxford University Press, 2010)). It also means that we do not examine in detail the distinction between justifying something as a pre-legal moral right, justifying it as a right suitable for legal implementation at the national level (eg in a constitution, or within criminal law) and justifying it as an *international* legal human right. Buchanan thinks that philosophers have neglected the distinctive forms of justification needed for international legal rights (Buchanan, *The Heart of Human Rights*). We discuss Buchanan's position briefly at the end of this section.

[60] Following Scanlon, we can identify three components that characterize an instrumental justification of rights: '(i) An empirical claim about how individuals would behave or how institutions would work, in the absence of this particular assignment of rights...(ii) The claim that this result would be unacceptable. This claim will be based on valuation of consequences...(iii) A further empirical claim about how the envisaged assignment of rights will produce a different outcome.' T.M. Scanlon, 'Rights, Goals and Fairness', in Waldron, *Theories of Rights*, 137–52. However, it is worth noticing that there might be other ways in which human rights can be grounded teleologically, but non-instrumentally—eg, as instantiations of or constituents of the values that ground them. Some of the writers we discuss (perhaps Finnis or Tasioulas) might challenge our designation of their view as 'instrumental'.

Agency is an obvious candidate for an account of human rights of the sort just described, since agency is considered by many as the distinguishing feature of human beings. The main difference between human and non-human animals seems to be that the former have the capacity to form a conception of a good life and to pursue the conception of the good life they have chosen for themselves. James Griffin argues that it is precisely in these terms that we should understand the notion of human dignity. Having human dignity is having the capacity to choose a plan of life for ourselves and to successfully pursue it without interference;[61] and human rights protect human dignity by protecting this capacity. When these rights are violated, our human dignity is compromised and we are not treated with the respect that is owed to us as human beings.[62]

But while initially appealing, agency-based accounts seem to encounter a number of problems. In particular, they seem to offer a reductive picture of the moral considerations at stake in the justification of human rights. For example, consider the paradigmatic human right not to be tortured. The fact that torture undermines one's agency by undermining one's capacity to decide how to act and to stick to the decision is certainly an important factor in justifying the existence of a human right not to be tortured.[63] But is it the only factor? A number of writers have argued that it isn't, and that other important factors, for example the fact that torture causes great pain, are also important.[64]

This objection becomes even more worrisome once we recall the fact that many human beings, most notably children and the severely mentally disabled, simply lack the capacity to act as autonomous moral agents. If we accept the view that human rights are grounded exclusively in the value of agency, we may be led to conclude that neither group can be said to have human rights. As noted earlier, Griffin himself accepts that his view commits us to the conclusion that while these subjects might have *moral* rights against torture, or at least we might have moral *duties* not to torture these subjects, they cannot be said to have a *human* right against torture.[65]

Again, this conclusion seems problematic. The main concern is that both morality and the law attribute human rights both to children and to the severely mentally disabled. Agency accounts fail to the extent that they are under-inclusive with respect to the class of human rights-bearers.[66] Instead of justifying the existence of rights that all human beings possess *qua* human being, they justify something different: rights that all persons possess *qua* persons ('person' is the term used by Griffin to refer to autonomous moral agents).

---

[61] Griffin calls this 'normative agency'. See *On Human Rights*, ch. 2.

[62] Alan Gewirth argues along similar lines, but his view is, we will suggest below, not best conceived as instrumental. See Gewirth, *Reason and Morality* and *Human Rights: Essays on Justification and Applications*. For an approach somewhat similar to Griffin's, but based on a more demanding and expansive conception of human freedom as self-development, see Gould, *Rethinking Democracy*.

[63] Griffin, *On Human Rights*, 52–3.

[64] John Tasioulas, 'Taking Rights out of Human Rights', *Ethics*, 120 (2010): 647–78, 663–6, S. Matthew Liao, 'Agency and Human Rights', *Journal of Applied Philosophy*, 27(1) (2010): 15–25.

[65] Griffin, *On Human Rights*, 92.

[66] Massimo Renzo, 'Human Rights and the Priority of the Moral', *Social Philosophy and Policy* (forthcoming).

One way to avoid this problem is to take a broader view according to which human rights are grounded in a plurality of goods that are required to have a good life, where agency is simply one of these goods. Other elements of a good life are freedom from great pain, knowledge, deep personal relations, and so on. This approach can be traced to Aristotle's writings, among others. Aristotle gives a penetrating investigation of *eudaimonia* or human flourishing and its connection with 'the good of man'.[67] A flourishing life, for Aristotle, is one characterized by virtuous activity, but virtuous activity will be impaired and harder to exercise if we lack certain fundamental goods.[68]

More recently, a similar approach has been adopted by those who advocate an objective list account of well-being. For example, John Finnis argues that there are certain human ends that are objectively good, by which he means that their value stems not from individuals happening to desire them but from their being basic aspects of human well-being (he calls them the 'basic forms of human good'). These include: life, knowledge, play, aesthetic experience, sociability (friendship), practical reasonableness, and religion.[69] In a somewhat similar vein, James Nickel argues that human rights are grounded in four secure claims: to have a life, to lead one's life, and claims against severely cruel or degrading, and against severely unfair treatment.[70] Likewise, in this volume S. Matthew Liao defends the view that human rights protect the fundamental conditions for pursuing a good life.[71] The justification of human rights, according to these views, is grounded in their being necessary for, or at least in their significantly contributing to or protecting conditions for human well-being.

John Tasioulas also adopts a pluralist approach that grounds the justification of human rights in a wide range of human interests, but his view is more expansive in that it does not identify a specific list of goods or claims from which human rights can be derived. Rather, Tasioulas argues that any interest sufficiently important to ground duties in others to protect, respect or advance the interest in question can justify the existence of a human right provided that (a) this is an interest that we have simply in virtue of our humanity (ie, independently from special roles or positions that we happen to occupy) and (b) the duties generated by the interest are feasible in the relevant socio-historical context.[72]

A potential concern with this approach is that it will produce an over-expansive list of human rights. Human rights typically set some sort of minimum standards: 'the lower limits on tolerable human conduct', rather than 'great aspirations and exalted ideals'.[73] The idea that anything we might require for a good life (including, say, the presence of valuable personal relationships) might be turned into a matter of human

---

[67] Aristotle, *Nicomachean Ethics*. Trans. D. Ross (Oxford: Oxford University Press, 1925), i. 7.
[68] Aristotle, *Nicomachean Ethics*, 1153b 17–19.
[69] Finnis, *Natural Law and Natural Rights*, ch. 4.
[70] Nickel, *Making Sense of Human Rights*, 2nd edn., 61–9. In his contribution to the current volume, Nickel adds personal desert as a further ground that plays a role in the justification of some human rights. Whether Nickel's approach is founded on well-being is debatable, but Nickel writes: 'A unifying idea for these four secure claims is that, perfectly realized, they would make it possible for every person living today to have and lead a life that is decent or minimally good' (62).
[71] S. Matthew Liao, 'Human Rights as Fundamental Conditions for a Good Life', this volume, ch. 3.
[72] See especially John Tasioulas, 'On the Foundations of Human Rights', this volume, ch. 1.
[73] Shue, *Basic Rights*, xi.

rights, would threaten to challenge this widely shared assumption. Of course, the theorists mentioned have responses to this concern. For example, Tasioulas argues that the threshold generated by (a) and (b) is such that his approach is not excessively expansive. And he also draws on dignity as a further ground for human rights which generates additional limits.[74]

Other philosophers have been drawn to a related idea: that we can justify human rights by appealing to a particular class of human needs. At first, the notion of needs might sound like a non-starter for a justification of human rights, since typically the needs we have depend on the adoption of specific goals (for example, 'Ben needs to exercise to be in good shape'),[75] whereas human rights are rights that all human beings have, independently of any specific goals they might have adopted for themselves. However, one can argue that there is a class of needs that all human beings have simply *qua* human beings, and that do not seem to depend on the adoption of any specific goal or plan of life. These include things which are required in order to sustain immediately a physical, corporeal existence (like food, water, and air), but also things that human beings need in order to have a healthy psychological and social life (like a minimum degree of social interaction and a minimum level of recognition). These 'basic human needs' are the needs that are to be fulfilled in order for a person to have a minimally decent life. Human rights are rights that protect the conditions for a minimally decent life, by protecting the opportunity to have these needs met.[76]

The basic needs account might seem appealing insofar as it strikes a middle ground between agency accounts and accounts based on the idea of the good life. We have seen that one concern with the former was its being too narrow in focusing on normative agency as the only justification for human rights, thereby ignoring a number of other important elements that seem to be at play in the justification of central human rights. There are concerns, on the other hand, that good life accounts may be too expansive, as they might turn every component of the good life into a matter of human rights. The basic needs account promises to avoid both problems, since it focuses on the limited class of needs that are of universally essential importance to all human beings.

However, we might wonder whether this class of needs is sufficiently broad to support all the rights that an adequate theory of human rights should intuitively account for. Consider for example civil and political rights, such as the right to equality before

---

[74] For alternative responses to the same concern about over-expansiveness, see Liao's account of the specifically fundamental interests which human rights protect (this volume, ch. 3) and Nickel's framework for getting from his four secure claims to specific rights (*Making Sense of Human Rights*, ch. 5).

[75] Philosophers disagree over whether needs claims are always in the form of 'A needs x in order to y'. David Wiggins, 'Claims of Need', in T. Honderich (ed.), *Morality and Objectivity: A Tribute to J. L. Mackie* (London: Routledge & Kegan Paul, 1985), 149–202; David Wiggins and S. Dermen, 'Needs, Need, Needing', *Journal of Medical Ethics*, 13 (1987): 62–8; Garret Thomson, *Needs* (London: Routledge & Kegan Paul, 1987); and G.E.M. Anscombe, 'Modern Moral Philosophy', *Philosophy*, 33 (1958): 7 all think that some needs claims do not have to take this form, while Brian Barry, *Political Argument* (London: Routledge & Kegan Paul, 1965), 47–9 and Alan White, *Modal Thinking* (Ithaca, NY: Cornell University Press, 1975), 105–7 think that all needs claims necessarily take this form. For consideration of the kind of needs relevant to ethics, see Soran Reader, *Needs and Moral Necessity* (London: Routledge, 2007).

[76] David Miller, *National Responsibility and Global Justice* (Oxford: Oxford University Press, 2007); David Miller, 'Grounding Human Rights', *Critical Review of International Social and Political Philosophy*, 15 (2012): 407–27; Renzo, this volume, ch. 32.

the law or the right to fair trial. Which basic needs do these rights aim to protect exactly? Defenders of the basic needs approach argue that these rights can be vindicated via 'linkages arguments',[77] ie, by showing that their exercise is necessary for, or at least significantly contributes to, meeting fundamental needs such as bodily security or subsistence,[78] but opponents of this view worry that this link might be too thin and indirect to provide a suitable justification for civil and political rights.[79]

Whether needs approaches will be under-inclusive, justifying too few human rights, is debatable. But it is worth noting that in order to avoid being *over*-inclusive each of the positions mentioned so far—agency, good life, and needs views—has to draw on some distinction between fundamental and non-fundamental aspects of agency, of the good life or of needs: not all needs generate human rights, nor all aspects of the good life or of agency. Drawing this fundamental/non-fundamental distinction in a substantive, non-question-begging way is a challenge for each account.[80]

The Capabilities Approach developed by Amartya Sen and Martha Nussbaum has recently been used by Nussbaum in connection with human rights, and it shares many of the features and problems of the needs, well-being, and agency accounts. According to Nussbaum, capabilities are an individual's real opportunities to choose and to act to achieve certain functionings, and functionings are various states and activities that an individual can undertake.[81] Nussbaum argues that the following ten central human capabilities are particularly important, as they are 'entailed by the idea of a life worthy of human dignity': life; bodily health; bodily integrity; senses, imagination and thought; emotions; practical reason; affiliation; relations to other species; play; and control over one's environment.[82] Nussbaum believes that all human beings are entitled to these capabilities and these capabilities form the basis of human rights.[83]

The Capabilities Approach inherits some of the problems we have found with other approaches. To give just one example, like Griffin's agency approach, the Capabilities Approach appears to have difficulty explaining many children's rights.[84] The reason is that many children's rights such as the rights to health care, education, name, nationality, and so on, are concerned with functionings rather than capabilities. Nussbaum tries to deflect this point by arguing that these functionings are important for helping children to develop adult capabilities.[85] But this response ignores the fact that some children will unfortunately not live to adulthood (for example, children with terminal

---

[77] Nickel, *Making Sense of Human Rights*, 87–90.

[78] Miller, *National Responsibility and Global Justice*, 195.

[79] Tasioulas, this volume, ch. 1.

[80] See Tasioulas, this volume, ch. 1, for an attempt to resist this objection by reinterpreting the sense in which human rights are minimal conditions for a good life. The objection is expressed by those who accuse Griffin of facing a 'dilemma' between drawing 'normative agency' too narrowly or too widely (see the essays by Buchanan, Cruft, Reidy and Tasioulas, and Griffin's response, all in R. Crisp (ed.), *Griffin on Human Rights* (Oxford: Oxford University Press, 2014)).

[81] Nussbaum, *Creating Capabilities*, 20–6.   [82] Nussbaum, *Creating Capabilities*, 33–4.

[83] Nussbaum, *Creating Capabilities*, 62. Aspects of Nussbaum's capabilities approach to human rights seem non-instrumental, as when she claims that the approach can be the object of an overlapping consensus (Nussbaum, *Creating Capabilities*, 169): if this potential consensus is the *ground* for human rights on the capabilities approach, then it is not instrumental (see discussion at 20–22 later in this essay).

[84] See Liao, this volume, ch. 3, for additional discussion.

[85] Martha Nussbaum, *Frontiers of Justice: Disability, Nationality, Species Membership* (Cambridge, MA: Harvard University Press, 2006), 172.

cancer) and yet it seems that these children would still have human rights to certain functionings.

In addition to the points mentioned so far, most of the approaches considered face additional challenges: they seem to commit us to the conclusion that anyone whose human rights have been violated is thereby at least likely to fail to possess minimal agency or a minimally decent life or a life worthy of dignity. This conclusion seems problematic because many people, perhaps most people through history, have suffered human rights deficits (for example, by lacking a right to political participation or freedom of religion). There is something unsettling about a theory that delivers the conclusion that a great many human beings do not have agency or a minimally decent life.[86] And Allen Buchanan argues that the *non-discrimination, equal status* provisions in human rights law cannot be captured by agency, well-being or needs approaches, because one can possess a reasonable degree of agency and live a good life with one's needs met while being discriminated against or possessing low-caste status.[87] If this is correct, then equality of status and non-discrimination seemingly should be introduced as a separate ground of human rights. But this move depends, of course, on a highly controversial claim: agency, well-being, needs and capability theorists will have to include non-discrimination as, or as required for, a fundamental aspect of agency or well-being, or a fundamental need or capability.

B. Non-instrumental justifications

It is worth noticing that, despite their important differences, most of the accounts discussed so far share the same structure. They seem to adopt an instrumental mode of justification which proceeds in two steps: first, it identifies a valuable end worthy of protection (for example, the exercise of agency, having a good life, or having the opportunity to meet basic needs); second, it ascribes human rights to individuals because and insofar as possessing these rights contributes to the realization of this end. By contrast, some have offered non-instrumental justifications for human rights. Frances Kamm and Thomas Nagel, for example, argue that we hold human rights as a matter of our basic moral status and that our holding these rights is at least partially independent of whether and how they promote or protect further human values such as agency, needs, freedoms or interests. Thus Kamm writes:

> [T]here may be a type of good that already exists but that would not exist if it were permissible to transgress the right of one person in order to save many lives. This is the good of being someone whose worth is such that it makes him highly inviolable and also makes him someone to whom one owes nonviolation. This good does imply that certain of one's interests should not be sacrificed, but inviolability matters not merely because it instrumentally serves those interests....Inviolability is a reflection

---

[86] This objection is discussed in Rowan Cruft, 'From a Good Life to Human Rights: Some Complications', this volume, ch. 4, and Renzo, 'Human Needs, Human Rights', this volume, ch. 32. For defences, see Griffin, 'Replies', section 5, in Crisp, *Reading Griffin on Human Rights*.

[87] Allen Buchanan, 'The Egalitarianism of Human Rights', *Ethics*, 120 (2010): 679–710; see also Besson, *Human Rights as Law*, ch. 5.

of the worth of the person. On this account, it is impermissible for me to harm the person in order to save many in the accident, because doing so is inconsistent with his having this status.[88]

[F]undamental human rights...are not concerned with protecting a person's interests, but with expressing his nature as a being of a certain sort, one whose interests are worth protecting. They express the worth of the person rather than the worth of what is in the interests of that person. [89]

Accepting this view does not commit us to rejecting instrumental justifications of human rights. It is possible to hold a pluralist position according to which human rights are grounded both in their basic non-instrumental value as outlined by Kamm above, and also in their instrumental role as furthering other values such as agency, or the capacity to have a minimally decent or a good life.[90] Indeed, there are reasons to believe that any justification based on the notion of moral status will need to be supplemented by an instrumental justification, in order to be capable of plausibly determining the precise contents of human rights.[91] This is because there is a wide range of normative structures that could secure humans something like a 'high status', or reflect their 'high worth', including structures in which people hold rights sharply different to those we currently recognize as human rights. For instance, Hobbes's 'right of nature'—the right that each person holds in the state of nature, that allows one to do whatever one judges necessary for one's own survival including attack others[92]—secures its holder with a high status. For bearers of the 'right of nature' are unconstrained by moral demands: my 'right of nature' allows me to try to eat your arm for my supper, if I can get it. By making people so unconstrained, this 'right of nature' arguably confers a higher status on people *as agents*, reflecting a particular sort of 'high worth', than the more demanding set of human rights we currently recognize.[93]

If human rights were grounded wholly non-instrumentally, simply as whatever rights secured us with a high status or reflected our high worth, then it would be

---

[88] Kamm, *Intricate Ethics*, 253–4.

[89] Kamm, *Intricate Ethics*, 271. Compare Thomas Nagel's similar 'status' view in his 'Personal Rights and Public Space', in his *Concealment and Exposure & Other Essays* (Oxford: Oxford University Press, 2002), 31–52l and Rowan Cruft, 'On the Non-Instrumental Value of Basic Rights', *Journal of Moral Philosophy*, 7 (2010): 441–61. See also Warren Quinn, *Morality and Action* (Cambridge: Cambridge University Press, 1994). Compare also dignity-based approaches like that of Nickel (James W. Nickel, 'Poverty and Rights', *The Philosophical Quarterly*, 55 (2005): 385–402, esp. 394–5).

[90] Kamm herself seems keen to adopt this position, since she allows that inviolability can matter in part because 'it instrumentally serves...interests'. On this form of pluralist position, see Cruft, 'On the Non-Instrumental Value of Basic Rights', section VI, and Leif Wenar, 'The Value of Rights', in M. O'Rourke (ed.), *Law and Social Justice* (Cambridge, MA: MIT Press, 2005), 179–209.

[91] This point is well made in Wenar, 'The Value of Rights'.   [92] *Leviathan*, Part 1, chs. 13–14.

[93] This point is made without the reference to Hobbes in Shelly Kagan, 'Replies to My Critics', *Philosophy and Phenomenological Research*, 51 (1991): 919–28, 920. Alternative high-status forms of rights are also conceivable, such as rights which prioritize being saved over not being harmed. See, eg, Kasper Lippert-Rasmussen's imagined status of 'high unignorability' which requires people to harm some in order to prevent more occurrences of similar harms to others (Lippert-Rasmussen, 'Moral Status and the Impermissibility of Minimizing Violations', *Philosophy and Public Affairs*, 25 (1996): 333–51); in one respect, this confers a higher status on people (by making them especially unignorable) than the rights constituting 'high inviolability' which we recognize at present.

unclear why we hold the human rights that we naturally think we do, as opposed to Hobbes's bare 'right of nature' or some other configuration of rights which could also get us a high status. But if human rights are also justified instrumentally because they protect agency or ensure the conditions of a minimally decent or a good life, this might be sufficient to explain why something like the traditional picture of human rights should be favoured over the Hobbesian 'right of nature' or some other alternative.[94]

The view defended by Kamm and Nagel is non-instrumental in that human rights are not justified by appealing to their capacity to promote, protect or further certain valuable ends, but rather by appealing to their role in expressing or reflecting the moral worth of their holders. This however is not the only way to justify human rights in a non-instrumental fashion. According to a different approach, which might be termed 'transcendental', human rights can be justified by appealing to the idea that to be an agent at all, one must conceive oneself and others as bearing human rights. For example, Alan Gewirth, the most prominent defender of this view, argues that in acting for a purpose I cannot but conceive my end as a good, and because my freedom and well-being are necessary conditions for pursuit of whatever end this might be, I have to conceive them as things that others ought to refrain from impeding. Thus, in acting I cannot avoid conceiving myself as holding rights to minimal freedom and well-being; but if so, I cannot avoid conceiving any 'prospective purposive agent' like me as bearing similar rights, as other agents do not seem to be different from me in any relevant respect.[95]

There is much to be said about this argument, but we simply note its transcendental form: it says that given the kind of beings we are, we cannot help but take ourselves and others as rights-bearers—this is, arguably, a *synthetic a priori* belief for Gewirth. In her contribution to the current volume, Flikschuh suggests that a Kantian conception of human rights would similarly take them as something in which we cannot help believing: a 'subjectively necessary reflective idea'.[96] Whether one agrees with either approach, the overall method is very different to the foundationalism of the other approaches mentioned: human rights are not grounded as serving or reflecting certain values. Rather, they are things whose existence we cannot help presupposing.

C. Practice-based justifications

As we have seen, some reject the traditional view according to which human rights are rights that human beings have simply in virtue of being human, and conceive

---

[94] For an attempt to combine an instrumental justification of human rights grounded on basic needs with a non-instrumental one, see Renzo, this volume, ch. 32. John Tasioulas pursues a similar strategy in defending a view that, to use his terminology, appeals both to prudential and deontological notions; see this volume, ch. 1.

[95] An excellent summary of Gewirth's view is given in Gewirth, *The Community of Rights*, ch. 1.

[96] Unlike Gewirth, Flikschuh thinks such an approach makes the concept of human rights 'constitutively indeterminable for us', something akin to the idea of God as Kant presents it. On Flikschuh's account, human rights are concepts we cannot help embracing when we face our task as law makers with no natural authority to coerce others. In this position, we will inevitably see those for whom we make laws as bearers of human rights, and the precise requirements of these rights will inevitably be indeterminable—human rights will thus remind the law maker of the 'moral enormity of public office and authority' (Flikschuh, 'Human Rights in Kantian Mode: A Sketch', this volume, ch. 37, 667).

them instead as rights generated within a specific practice existing at the international level. An adequate theory of human rights, according to these theorists, is a political or institutional theory that aims to provide the best interpretation of the normative principles underlying the international human rights practice as we know it. Hence, the label 'political conception' that is often used to refer to this view.

In making this move for the first time, John Rawls was primarily motivated by the concern that speculations about which particular aspect of humanity can be said to ground human rights inevitably require the employment of ordinary moral reasoning, or what Rawls calls 'comprehensive doctrines'. But according to Rawls, we should not ground human rights on such 'a theological, philosophical or moral conception of the human person',[97] as this may render them unacceptable from the point of view of some 'well-ordered peoples' who hold incompatible religious, philosophical, and moral views.[98] The idea that rights generating this sort of disagreement can be legitimately enforced across different cultures is one that Rawls finds problematic.[99] For this reason, he suggests that we should rather think of human rights as an element of the 'law of peoples'. The law of peoples is a set of principles and norms on which well-ordered peoples from different religious, philosophical, and moral backgrounds can freely agree as the basis for governing their behaviour towards one another, thereby establishing a mutually respectful condition of peace.[100] Human rights are a prominent component of this global normative order. To be sure, well-ordered peoples may disagree about the content of human rights, but they will agree about the role that these rights play in international practice, which for Rawls consists in specifying the limits of justified interference with the internal autonomy of sovereign states. As Rawls puts it, human rights' fulfillment 'is sufficient to exclude justified and forceful intervention by other peoples, for example, by diplomatic and economic sanctions, or in grave cases by military force'.[101]

Not all advocates of the political conception follow Rawls in denouncing the appeal to ordinary moral reasoning. For instance, Raz does not commit himself to the strictures of public reason in discussing the grounds of human rights.[102] Furthermore, both Raz and Beitz stress the ways in which a political conception of human rights can define their function in terms of the limits of sovereignty without making human rights violation a matter for *armed intervention*. Responses to human rights violations can take different forms, including economic and diplomatic sanctions, or even simply formal censure from other states or some international body.[103]

---

[97] Rawls, *The Law of Peoples*, 81.

[98] Rawls, *The Law of Peoples*, 68. For Rawls, 'well-ordered peoples' include liberal peoples and what Rawls calls 'decent peoples', his prime example of which are (to put it roughly) peoples without aggressive aims and with a system of law governed by a common good idea of justice that secures human rights for its members (Rawls, *The Law of Peoples*, 64–8).

[99] We will come back to this problem below, when considering the sceptical concern that human rights are a 'Western' imposition.

[100] Rawls, *The Law of Peoples*, 3–4.   [101] Rawls, *The Law of Peoples*, 80.

[102] Raz, this volume, ch. 11.

[103] See, eg, Beitz, *The Idea of Human Rights*, 121. Note that Rawls also mentions 'diplomatic and economic sanctions' as well as military intervention. See the quotation in the previous paragraph in the main text.

Some theorists worry that the political conception relies too much on the international practice of human rights as we currently know it. One concern is that whether there is a case for international concern or intervention will depend on varying contingent features of the geopolitical order, but the existence of a human right should not depend on these features.[104] In response, adherents of the political conception could argue that they do not make the existence of a human right depend on whether there is an actual, all-things-considered current case for international concern, but on a principled distinction between matters that *may or should* be of international concern (such as torture) and those that *may not or should not* (such as marital fidelity). This distinction should guide actual practice rather than being determined by it. This response might seem unhappy for those, like Beitz, who try to ground human rights in the practice, rather than in free-standing principles about the appropriate nature of the international order.[105] But Beitz and other political theorists could argue that such principles are themselves encoded in or underlie current human rights practice.

A worry is that such a political view seems to rest on the assumption that the international practice of human rights is sufficiently homogeneous as to warrant only one interpretation of its underlying principles. But this assumption is questionable. Most notably, different societies seem to disagree as to which rights are genuine human rights, which might lead to significant disagreement about the contours of the practice, in spite of the more general agreement about the role that human rights should play once they are recognized as such.[106]

To be sure, there is a growing body of documents to which we can point in articulating what the international practice of human rights is, but the problem is that the way in which these documents are to be interpreted is itself open to interpretation. In light of what should this interpretation be carried out? A good interpretation is one that will construct the principles underlying the practice in their best light, but this very idea presupposes the existence of moral standards in light of which the principles can be reconstructed.[107] If so, the appeal to a moral theory that some versions of the political conception intend to avoid seems inevitable after all.[108]

Perhaps this criticism relies on an overstatement of the disagreement about human rights that can be plausibly said to exist in the international practice. According to a second family of practice-based justifications, the distinctive feature of human rights

---

[104] For a subtle version of this point, see Tasioulas, 'On the Nature of Human Rights', 55–6. See also Tasioulas's worry about whether the type of role picked out by the political conception (namely, as marking the limits of sovereignty) 'is really an appropriate basis for withholding the label "human right"' from rights which do not fulfil this role' (56).

[105] Recall Beitz's idea of international human rights as 'sui generis', *The Idea of Human Rights*, 197.

[106] See Victor Tadros, 'Rights and Security for Human Rights Sceptics', this volume, ch. 24.

[107] For an interesting attempt to defend the idea of a critical reconstruction of the practice that is 'immanent to the practice' itself, see Andrea Sangiovanni, 'Justice and the Priority of Politics to Morality', *Journal of Political Philosophy*, 16 (2008): 137–64.

[108] See Miller, *National Responsibility and Global Justice*, 170–2; Laura Valentini, 'In what Sense Are Human Rights Political?', *Political Studies*, 60(1) (2012): 180–94; Massimo Renzo, 'Human Rights and the Priority of the Moral', *Social Philosophy & Policy* (forthcoming), presents a different argument in favour of the conclusion that the appeal to moral considerations is harder to avoid than defenders of the political view acknowledge.

is precisely the fact that they are normative standards about which different cultures can be said to agree, despite the fact that they adopt very different moral and religious views. Instead of focusing on the relationship between the protection of human rights and sovereignty, this view justifies human rights by appealing to the fact they are, in Rawlsian terminology, the object of an 'overlapping consensus' among holders of different conceptions of the good. No matter how different these conceptions of the goods will seem at first, if we look closely enough we will see that there is a substantive agreement about the existence of a class of human rights and about the type of protection that they afford to their holders.[109]

Of course the claim that human rights are morally binding norms, no matter which particular culture we belong to, is one that naturalistic conceptions of human rights will also make. The difference between naturalistic conceptions and overlapping consensus views, however, is profound, and depends on the different role that agreement plays within these two views.[110] According to the former, the fact that different cultures will or should converge on human rights norms, is merely a consequence of the fact that these norms are part of a universal moral order which is binding independently of whether it is accepted or not within a specific culture. According to overlapping consensus views, by contrast, the fact that different cultures could reasonably agree from very different starting points about these norms is precisely what grounds the authority of these norms. Human rights are morally binding in virtue of the fact that they constitute normative standards on which different societies holding different moral and religious views could converge.

However, the 'overlapping consensus' approach runs into a dilemma. Either it is understood as a view about the consensus which exists among *all* societies or it is understood as the consensus that exists only among those societies that adopt a *reasonable* conception of the good.[111] In the former case, the view is basically tantamount to simply denying that there can be any substantive disagreement among different societies about the content and the interpretation of human rights. This move is puzzling not only because it seems to fly in the face of reality, but also because it would avoid the objection of parochialism (or cultural imperialism) not by providing an answer to it, but rather by simply denying the force of the objection (often without providing sufficient evidence in support of its striking conclusion).

If, on the other hand, the overlapping consensus view is interpreted as predicating the existence of consensus only among those societies that qualify as reasonable, a question arises: what are the normative standards in virtue of which the status of 'reasonable society' is granted? Some might worry that these standards will be those typical of a certain brand of liberalism, and that therefore the consensus reached within

---

[109] For discussion of this idea, and some limited, critical endorsement, see the essays in Joanne R. Bauer and Daniel A. Bell (eds.), *The East Asian Challenge for Human Rights* (Cambridge: Cambridge University Press, 1999), especially the essays by Onuma Yasuaki, Charles Taylor, Abdullahi An-Na'im, Norani Othman, Suwanna Satha-Anand, and Joseph Chan. See also Donnelly, *Universal Human Rights in Theory and Practice*, ch. 5. For critical discussion, see Beitz, *The Idea of Human Rights*, ch. 4.

[110] Beitz, *The Idea of Human Rights*, 74.

[111] It should be noted that, while the view is often defended by appealing to the former interpretation (Beitz, *The Idea of Human Rights*, 76), it is the second one that is faithful to the idea of 'overlapping consensus' as formulated in Rawls's work.

this view, far from being genuinely universal, will be limited to those cultures that are an expression of a particular conception of the good.[112] We think this would be too quick: 'reasonable' need not be interpreted as 'liberal'. For Rawls, 'decent' societies include some non-liberal societies.[113] Nonetheless, if consensus is ultimately what grounds human rights, what can justify limiting this to consensus among groups that already meet some prior standard? The worry is that this standard, rather than consensus, is what is ultimately doing the justificatory work.

A third approach to the justification of human rights that takes seriously the role they play within the global practice is the one recently developed by Allen Buchanan, and in a somewhat similar fashion by Samantha Besson.[114] Buchanan and Besson focus on one specific element of the practice, namely, international human rights law. This choice is determined by the fact that this body of law plays a crucial role within the global practice of human rights.[115] But international human rights law, Buchanan notices, is constituted by a number of legal rights and other legal rules which need not be the legal embodiment of corresponding moral rights.[116] Legal rights are norms created by appealing to a number of considerations and goals, only some of which will have to do with the need to protect given moral rights. Indeed, Buchanan argues that some legal human rights, in particular rights to public goods, cannot plausibly be grounded on individual pre-legal moral rights, because legal rights to public goods cannot be grounded solely by what they do for the individual right-holder.[117] Thus we should not see the task of justifying human rights law as requiring a justification for antecedent moral rights which this law reflects. Instead, we can justify a given legal human right by appealing to a plurality of justifications, including how the right serves the interests of people beyond the individual right-holder. Buchanan claims that the many grounds for human rights law include the enhancement of the legitimacy of the state and the provision of a unified legal framework for handling genuinely global problems such as climate change.[118]

Buchanan's approach has several advantages. One is that it offers an ecumenical framework, useable by anyone who wants to defend legal human rights, whether or not they are committed to there being pre-legal moral rights, and whether or not they believe—like 'political' theorists—that certain rights mark a limit to state sovereignty.

Theorists have yet to respond to Buchanan's work in detail, but one central problem is that some of the moral force of human rights law would seem to be lost if one followed Buchanan in denying that the duties entailed by legal human rights were owed

---

[112] John Tasioulas, 'The Legitimacy of International Law', in Besson and Tasioulas, *The Philosophy of International Law* (Oxford: Oxford University Press, 2010a), 97–118.

[113] Rawls, *Law of Peoples*, 64–70.

[114] Allen Buchanan, *The Heart of Human Rights* and 'Why *International Legal* Human Rights?', this volume, ch. 13; Samantha Besson, *Human Rights as Law* and 'Human Rights and Constitutional Law: Patterns of Mutual Validation and Legitimation', this volume, ch. 15.

[115] Buchanan could be charged with overlooking the centrality of non-legal aspects of the practice of human rights, including perhaps especially human rights activism. For an account of the practice which encompasses law, activism, journalism, philosophy, and politics, see James Nickel, 'What Future For Human Rights?', *Ethics and International Affairs*, 28 (2014): 213–23.

[116] Buchanan lists a range of components of international human rights law which do not take the form of rights (*The Heart of Human Rights*, Appendix 1).

[117] Buchanan, *The Heart of Human Rights*, 61. See also the discussion of socio-economic rights in the next section of the current essay.

[118] See especially Buchanan, this volume, ch. 13.

morally to the right-holder, and hence in denying that the violation of a legal human right morally wronged the right-holder. Buchanan plausibly characterizes human rights law as 'a set of universal standards...whose primary purpose is to regulate the behaviour of states toward individuals under their jurisdiction, considered as social individuals, and for their own sakes'.[119] Can we understand a given legal human right as genuinely regulating behaviour *for its holder's own sake* if the corresponding duties are grounded in a way that is fundamentally independent of the moral importance of the right-holder?[120]

IV. Which New Human Rights are Actual Human Rights?

Having discussed the nature and grounds of human rights, we now consider critical approaches. Karel Vasek famously distinguished 'three generations' of human rights: first civil and political rights, secondly social rights and thirdly solidarity rights including group rights and rights to peace and development.[121] The second and third generations are often conceived as new, and are often targets of attack. Whether they are new is controversial. Rights to subsistence, health, and education (to take some from the 'second generation') are not found in the US 1789 Bill of Rights nor in the French 1789 Declaration of the Rights of Man and of the Citizen. But the inclusion of such rights to assistance (sometimes called 'positive' rights) in the UDHR or the 1966 Covenant on Economic, Social and Cultural Rights (ICESCR) was not wholly new. In 1689, Locke wrote that a needy person has 'a right to the surplusage' of others' goods; the later 1793 French Declaration included a similar right; and such claims echoed medieval writers.[122]

---

[119] Buchanan, *The Heart of Human Rights*, 86.

[120] David Luban develops a criticism akin to ours in his contribution to this volume (Luban, 'Human Rights Pragmatism and Human Dignity', this volume, ch. 14). He notes that people would not campaign for (and in that sense 'enforce') legal human rights if they thought they were not reflective of underlying natural moral rights. This could be questioned: perhaps people would campaign on behalf of legal human rights if they thought they reflected important moral considerations which did not take the form of pre-legal moral rights. Nonetheless, if they thought this, such campaigners would not seem to be fighting for human rights *for the sake of right-holders*. An alternative response to Buchanan is to reject his thesis that duties owed morally to someone must be grounded individualistically in what they do for that person. This response allows one to say that some duties grounded in what they do for beings beyond the right-holder are nonetheless owed morally to the right-holder, and reflect her moral rights. For critical discussion, see Rowan Cruft, 'Why is it Disrespectful to Violate Rights?', *Proceedings of the Aristotelian Society*, 113 (2013): 201–24.

[121] Karel Vasek, 'A 30-Year Struggle: The Sustained Efforts to Give Force of Law to the Universal Declaration of Human Rights', *Unesco Courier*, 10 (1977): 29–30. For an excellent subtler taxonomy, see Nickel, *Making Sense of Human Rights*, 2nd edn., 93–5.

[122] John Locke, *First Treatise of Government* (1689), section 42. Tierney writes: 'Around 1200 Alanus held that the poor man did not steal because what he took was really his own *iure naturali*—which could mean either "by natural right" or "by natural law". About the same time another glossator suggested that the person in need "could declare his right for himself"....Finally, the doctrine entered the mainstream of medieval jurisprudence when Hostiensis reformulated it more sharply and included it in his very widely read *Lectura* on the *Decretals*' (Tierney, *The Idea of Natural Rights*, 73). See the discussion in Siedentop, *Inventing the Individual*, 248. Alanus's right, like Locke's 'right to the surplusage', could be taken as a Hohfeldian privilege—that is, as simply the absence of a duty, on the part of the needy person, to refrain from taking the wealthy person's surplus. If so, it differs from the 1948 Declaration, which prima facie appears to grant Hohfeldian claim-rights entailing duties to ensure that needy people are given food, clothing, housing and medical care (UDHR, Article 25). For Hohfeld's distinctions between forms of right, see Wesley N. Hohfeld, *Fundamental Legal Conceptions*, ed. W. W. Cook (New Haven,

Nonetheless, central rights within Vasek's first generation (for example, rights not to be tortured, or against arbitrary arrest and detention) have been subjected to less philosophical criticism than rights from the other generations. The UDHR introduced several rarely seen rights that have been objects of controversy, including the rights to employment, periodic holidays with pay, medical care, social security, and housing. Further, a number of international declarations on children's rights have asserted that children have a right to be loved. Some have also asserted that there is a human right to assisted suicide.[123] And, the Director-General of UNESCO claimed in 1997 that there is a human right to peace. Are all these rights real human rights? For example, is there really a human right to paid holidays? It seems that people may have a human right against being required to work all the time. But do they have a human right that their holidays are paid?[124] Or is there really a right to be loved? Is love something that can be an appropriate object of a duty?[125]

In what follows, we focus on two broad forms of human rights that have been the target of especially frequent criticism: first, positive rights to goods and services (sometimes called socio-economic rights), and secondly, group rights.

A. Socio-economic human rights

One criticism of human rights to goods and services (subsistence, health, education) claims that such rights are absurdly demanding. Nickel, although supportive of these rights, puts the point neatly when he writes that '[c]reating grand lists of human rights that many countries cannot at present realize seems fraudulent to many people'.[126] The thought is that it seems fraudulent to proclaim that, say, each citizen of Mozambique has a right to a decent standard of health care when Mozambique is too poor to provide adequate health care for all its citizens.[127] In fact, the government of Mozambique will

---

Yale University Press, 1964). For discussion of the American and French declarations and their political, polity-founding function, see Moyn, *The Last Utopia*, 23–6.

[123] M.P. Battin, 'Suicide: A Fundamental Human Right?', in M. P. Battin and D. J. Mayo (eds.), *Suicide: The Philosophical Issues* (New York: St. Martin's Press, 1980), 267–85, 267–85.

[124] Carl Wellman points out that although the right to paid holidays is 'an official affirmation by a highly respected international organization, almost everyone has regarded it as suspect', *The Proliferation of Rights: Moral Progress or Empty Rhetoric?* (Boulder, Colorado: Westview Press, 1999), 2. But for a strong defence of it, see Jeremy Waldron, 'Liberal Rights: Two Sides of the Coin' in his *Liberal Rights* (Cambridge: Cambridge University Press, 1993), 1–34, 12–13.

[125] For a negative answer, see Miller, *National Responsibility and Global Justice*, 187, and in more detail Tasioulas, this volume, ch. 1, 59 (though Tasioulas's rejection only targets the existence of positive duties to provide others with romantic love). For an account of a form of love that could be an object of duty, see S. Matthew Liao, 'The Right of Children to Be Loved', *Journal of Political Philosophy*, 14/4 (2006): 420–40; S. Matthew Liao, *The Right to Be Loved* (New York: Oxford University Press, forthcoming).

[126] James Nickel, 'Human Rights', in Edward N. Zalta (ed.), *The Stanford Encyclopedia of Philosophy* (Spring 2014 edn.), available at http://plato.stanford.edu/archives/spr2014/entries/rights-human/. For early expression of this concern, see Cranston, *What are Human Rights?* For a cautious expression of the concern, see Virginia Held, 'Care and Human Rights', this volume, ch. 35. Note that this should be distinguished from Buchanan's concern about such rights: unlike the critics, Buchanan thinks socio-economic human rights can be defended, but only by abandoning an individualistic approach to their justification (*The Heart of Human Rights*, ch. 2).

[127] For discussion, including the relevant figures for health care spending and available income in Mozambique, see Gopal Sreenivasan, 'A Human Right to Health? Some Inconclusive Skepticism', *Aristotelian Society*, Supplementary Volume 86 (2012): 239–65, 245–6. In 2009, average Organisation for

likely have to leave this right unfulfilled for the large majority of its citizens. Calling it a right can therefore seem a sham: the right does not secure health care for citizens nor, one might add, does it license citizens to criticize their government or claim compensation for the government's failure to fulfil it, for if the government truly cannot afford to fulfil the right then it is not censurable for failing to do so.

Defenders of human rights to expensive goods and services such as health care sometimes appeal to the fact that there is nothing logically inconsistent about rights or duties that cannot be jointly fulfilled. For example, we might say with Waldron that '[F]or each [citizen of Mozambique], it is *not* the case that his government is unable to secure holidays with pay, or medical care, or education, or other aspects of welfare, *for him*. Indeed, it can probably do so (and does!) for a fair number of its citizens...; rather it is the combination of all the duties taken together which cannot be fulfilled'.[128] Waldron goes on to show that there is nothing incoherent or inconsistent in the existence of a set of jointly unfulfillable rights or duties. Yet although Waldron is correct about the coherence of his position, we might worry that there remains something 'fraudulent' or (as Nickel also suggests) 'farcical' about a set of important rights most of which the duty-bearer will normally have to leave unfulfilled due to lack of resources.[129]

An alternative defence of demanding socio-economic human rights questions the assumption that the right-holder's state or government must be the bearer of the duties entailed by the right. One might, instead, take the duties entailed by a Mozambiquan citizen's human right to health to be borne by the governments of wealthy nations, by wealthy businesses operating in Mozambique, or by wealthy individuals from other parts of the world.[130] There is enough wealth in the world that some allocation of duties will be possible that ensures that most people have most of their socio-economic human rights fulfilled. Of course, the principles allocating duties are controversial, and we return to this later. But to avoid fraudulence or farcicality it looks sufficient to deny that the right-holder's state or government must be the duty-bearer.

Economic Co-operation and Development (OECD) healthcare spending per capita was $3361 (purchasing power parity), while Mozambique's annual per capita gross domestic product was $770 (PPP), and its health spend per capita was $55 (PPP). If human rights are universal, it would seem wrong to say that the standard of health care required by human rights for a citizen of Mozambique is lower than that required by human rights for a citizen of the OECD (though see the discussion of 'progressive realization' later in the main text). If the standard of health care required by human rights is universal across the globe, it seems likely that the relevant standard will be higher than Mozambique can afford: perhaps it will not be more than $770 (PPP), but it will be high enough that if Mozambique fulfilled its citizens' human right to health, there would be insufficient funds left to fulfil other important human rights in Mozambique.

[128] Waldron, 'Rights in Conflict', in his *Liberal Rights*, 203–24, 207–8. We have adjusted the quotation to apply to Mozambique.

[129] As Eddy puts it, 'An uncomfortable implication of [Waldron's] approach is that if there are twenty million people who are at risk of disease, and only enough vaccine for one person, we would have to say that all twenty million people had a right to the vaccine' (Katherine Eddy, 'Welfare Rights and Conflicts of Rights', *Res Publica*, 12 (2006): 337–56, 351). Not inconsistent or incoherent, perhaps, but surely farcical. See Wolff's discussion of the unattractive practical results of enshrining in law a right to health that cannot be fulfilled for all citizens (Jonathan Wolff, 'The Content of the Human Right to Health', this volume, ch. 27, 497–8).

[130] For this approach, see, eg, Charles Beitz, 'The Force of Subsistence Rights', this volume, ch. 30, 546, Charles Jones, 'The Human Right to Subsistence', *Journal of Applied Philosophy*, 30 (2013): 57–72, 65–6, Nickel, *Making Sense of Human Rights*, 2nd edn., 150.

This response may seem to have a significant cost, as it deviates from the practice of human rights in international law. It seems to be a deviation to hold that the *primary* duties entailed by human rights need not be borne by the right-holder's state or government. A less radical alternative holds that duties to provide health care for the Mozambiquan citizen fall on others *if her government cannot provide it*, but the government is still the primary duty-bearer with others secondary. Yet even this less radical view is still a deviation from international practice, if the secondary duties are taken to be enforceable or justiciable rather than 'purely' moral.[131] And to avoid farcically demoting the Mozambiquan citizen's right to something like a 'manifesto' right, it seems that one must see the relevant duties as enforceable or justiciable.[132]

A further option is open to those who wish to defend human rights to goods and services while remaining faithful to the norms of international human rights law. The ICESCR does not designate as 'a rights violator' any state which fails to provide food or health for its citizens. Such a state will still be conforming to the Covenant so long as it is 'tak[ing] steps…to the maximum of its available resources…with a view to *achieving progressively* the full realization' of the Covenant's rights.[133] What this means, one might argue, is that the international legal human right to health or health care is best described as (roughly) a *human right that one's government take available steps towards providing health care for its citizens.* Some argue that the discretion this gives governments means that the socio-economic rights in international law are not genuinely rights at all, but rather goals that governments are legally compelled to pursue.[134] And some think that this conception of socio-economic rights as akin to goals is the morally correct one.[135]

Many see the last position as too weak: health care seems just as important to the individual right-holder as not being arbitrarily detained (say), so why should one have a human right to the latter, but only a human 'right' *that one's government take available steps towards* the former?[136] This concern gains bite when we notice that any right is

---

[131] See the UN's 'Guiding Principles on Business and Human Rights: Implementing the United Nations "Protect, Respect, and Remedy" Framework' for the status of human rights responsibilities borne by businesses.

[132] Imagine a Mozambiquan citizen saying 'Oh yes, I have a human right to health care: my state cannot afford to supply it but the US government (along with other wealthy bodies) has a duty to supply it. Of course this moral duty cannot or should not be made into law, but it is there nonetheless.' A whiff of fraudulence remains. For discussion of Beitz's defence of 'manifesto' rights, see 28 later in this essay and Beitz's essay in this volume, ch. 30.

[133] ICESCR, Article 2, emphasis added.

[134] Wellman, *The Moral Dimensions of Human Rights*, 71. See also James W. Nickel, 'Goals and Rights Working Together?', in Malcolm Langford, Andy Sumner, and Alicia Ely Yamin (eds.), *The Millennium Development Goals and Human Rights: Past, Present and Future* (Cambridge: Cambridge University Press, 2013), 37–48 and Rowan Cruft, 'Human Rights as Rights', in Ernst and Heilinger, *The Philosophy of Human Rights*, 129–58.

[135] See Nickel's claim that 'treating very demanding rights as goals has several advantages. One is that proposed goals that exceed one's abilities are not as farcical as proposed duties that exceed one's abilities….Another advantage is that goals are flexible; addressees with different levels of ability can choose ways of pursuing the goals that suit their circumstances and means' (Nickel, 'Human Rights'). Note that we can explain why we still call socio-economic human rights 'rights' even though they are really goals. If *the individual's* interests, autonomy or well-being are the ground for her government's adopting her health or subsistence as among its important goals, then these goals' grounds have a right-like individualistic structure, a structure in which the individual is foregrounded (Cruft, 'Human Rights as Rights', 151–5).

[136] For this form of argument, see eg, Jones, 'The Human Right to Subsistence'. Elizabeth Ashford's essay in our volume can be read this way, if 'importance' is understood in the 'basic' sense as a pre-requisite

expensive to institutionalize, including rights against torture or arbitrary detention.[137] Why pick out socio-economic rights as especially problematic here? Indeed, one way to address the objection is empirical: one could question whether institutionalizing grand lists of socio-economic rights really is fraudulently expensive for individual states.[138] Taking this route, one could also question the controversial interpretation of the international legal human right to health given in the preceding paragraph: perhaps it really is a right to a certain standard of health care, and the 'progressive realization' doctrine refers only to what states must do if, exceptionally, they cannot fulfil this right. This is a more standard way to interpret the right.

In addition to the burdensomeness objection to human rights to goods and services, a second objection maintains that independently of their *cost*, human rights to goods and services are problematic because prior to institutional allocation, it is indeterminate who bears the duties to fulfil them. As Onora O'Neill argues,

> [T]he correspondence of universal liberty rights to universal obligations is relatively well-defined even when institutions are missing or weak. For example, violation of a right not to be raped or a right not to be tortured may be clear enough, and the perpetrator may even be identifiable, even when institutions of enforcement are lamentably weak. But the correspondence of universal rights to goods and services to obligations to provide or deliver remains entirely amorphous when institutions are missing or weak.[139]

Note that the complaint is not merely *epistemic*: it is not that it is hard to know who bears what duties correlative to pre-institutional socio-economic human rights. Nor is the complaint our first worry, that the relevant duties are absurdly *burdensome* for impoverished states. O'Neill is, rather, concerned that there is no determinate answer to the question of who bears what duties in the case of pre-legal socio-economic human rights, rights that should guide the creation of laws.[140]

In response to O'Neill's objection, one could argue that there are genuine principles that allocate the duties correlative to socio-economic human rights. Proposals in the literature include Barry's contribution principle (which says agents who 'merely suspect' that they have contributed to the existence of acute deprivations—in terms of

---

for other rights (Ashford, 'A Moral Inconsistency Argument for a Basic Human Right to Subsistence', ch. 29. See also Beitz's essay, this volume, ch. 30, and Shue, *Basic Rights*).

[137] S. Holmes and C. Sunstein, *The Cost of Rights: Why Liberty Depends on Taxes* (New York: W. W. Norton, 1999).

[138] We can conceive the argument that Cuba has institutionalized socio-economic rights at the expense of civil and political rights. If this is possible for a fairly low-income state like Cuba, might it not be possible for other low-income states? Why prioritize the civil and political rights instead? Of course, many will find good answers to the latter question, but we could also ask whether there is really a trade-off here. Some might see it as absurd to claim blithely that almost the full range of human rights is affordable for almost any human society, but we see some attractiveness in the claim. The argument will appeal to humans' resourcefulness; the argument would then run that where the full range is unaffordable, this will most likely be due to external interference (eg, fraudulent trade, colonial oppression).

[139] Onora O'Neill, *Bounds of Justice* (Cambridge: Cambridge University Press, 2000), 105. See also O'Neill, 'Response to John Tasioulas', this volume, ch. 2.

[140] The objection only works, of course, if one takes human rights to goods and services to be pre-institutional rights, rights that institutions should reflect. But as our discussion of the nature of human rights showed, this is the mainstream view of at least the central or basal human rights, even among those who adopt the 'political' conception.

health or education, say—bear duties to alleviate them),[141] Kamm's principles about the importance of proximity (which claim that we bear greater responsibility to alleviate suffering the nearer we or our means are to the suffering person or the threat to them),[142] Miller's 'connection theory' of responsibility (which proposes 'six ways in which remedial responsibilities [for example, duties to provide health care, housing or education] might be identified' and allocated, including to those who cause the deprivation, to those who benefit from it, to those capable of alleviating it, and to those sharing community with the suffering person)[143] or Wenar's least-cost principle (which says that 'the agent who can most easily avert the threat [for example, by delivering subsistence supplies] has the responsibility for doing so—so long as doing so will not be excessively costly').[144] If any one of these proposals is correct, then the allocation and content of duties correlative to pre-institutional human rights to goods and services seems determinate.

Perhaps this shows excessive faith in the principles listed: are they at all plausible? And will they really pick out determinate duty-bearers with defined duties?[145] Many of the proposals deviate from the legal norm that the primary duty-bearer will be the right-holder's state or government. An alternative is to return to the notion that such human rights set *goals* rather than entailing determinate duties.[146] Or a different approach again is to argue that pre-institutionally, human rights to goods and services entail universally borne *duties to institutionalize*, rather than duties to provide the relevant goods and services: they entail duties to make a determinate allocation of duties.[147] In a sense, this is Beitz's view when he defends the idea that some human rights to goods and services can be acceptably conceived as 'manifesto' rights in Feinberg's sense. Beitz suggests that even when a socio-economic human right entails no *determinate* or *fulfillable* duties to supply its substance (to roll together both our objections), nonetheless such a right 'count[s] in favor of actions by which an agent can help establish conditions in which those deprived, or their successors, could enjoy the substance of the right in future'.[148] To avoid the earlier charge of 'fraudulence' or 'farcicality', much will turn on the stringency, determinacy, and justiciability of this reason to 'help establish conditions' for delivering the right's object.

---

[141] Christian Barry, 'Applying the Contribution Principle', *Metaphilosophy*, 36 (2005): 210–27.

[142] Kamm, *Intricate Ethics*, chs. 11 and 12; see 377 for a summary of her claims about our intuitions.

[143] Miller, *National Responsibility and Global Justice*, 99–107.

[144] Leif Wenar, 'Responsibility and Severe Poverty', in Pogge, *Freedom from Poverty as a Human Right*, 255–74, 260.

[145] One could also re-run O'Neill's point with a more epistemic focus: because we do not *know* what duties are entailed by human rights in a pre-institutional context, asserting such rights is pointless or maybe even incoherent (see O'Neill, *Bounds of Justice*, 105, the paragraph following the quotation in the main text). There is also an epistemic aspect in her 'Reply to John Tasioulas', this volume, ch. 2, 77–8. Even if we do grasp the relevant principles allocating duties, we might not know this.

[146] See n 135. See also, for rejection of the Hohfeldian idea that a human right only exists when its correlative duties exist, John Tasioulas, 'The Moral Reality of Human Rights', in Pogge, *Freedom from Poverty as a Human Right*, 75–102.

[147] This is one way to read Pogge's idea that any human right to X imposes pre-institutional duties on all citizens to organize society so that 'all its members have secure access to X' (Pogge, *World Poverty and Human Rights*, 2nd edn., 70).

[148] Beitz, *The Idea of Human Rights*, 121, and this volume, ch. 30. See also Feinberg's discussion of subsistence rights in *Rights, Justice, and the Bounds of Liberty*, 153.

It is very important to see that there is powerful pressure to make one or other of the solutions just sketched work. This is because there are strong reasons in favour of human rights to goods and services, despite the doubts outlined. Health care, subsistence, and education are basic needs or interests, and essential to the individual's autonomy.[149] Further, meeting these needs as a matter of right also seems necessary to ensure full respect for *other* well-grounded human rights, or for the values that ground them. For example, following Shue, Ashford shows that meeting these needs is necessary to prevent one's being exploited by someone who offers one a 'subsistence exchange contract' in which one sacrifices one of one's other rights in return for subsistence.[150]

B. Group human rights

Along with socio-economic rights, group human rights are a frequent target of specific criticism. We can distinguish two types of group human right. One is a human right held by an individual on the basis of his or her membership of a particular group. Examples include the distinctive rights one holds as a woman, a child, or a member of a minority group.[151] The second type is a human right held by a group. An example is a people's right to self-determination.[152]

Doubts about the general notion of individually held, group-differentiated rights tend not to challenge the moral justification of such rights, but simply to question their designation as 'human rights'. In what sense can my distinctive rights as a woman, a child, or a member of an oppressed minority be rights that are held universally by all humans, including those who are not women, children, or members of minorities? Nickel proposes the following test: a group-differentiated, individually held right can legitimately be called a human right 'if it is derivable (using plausible additional premises) from a universal human right'.[153] On this basis, Nickel suggests that we can and should take, for example, women's rights to prenatal care as human rights because '[s]tanding behind the right to prenatal care during pregnancy is the universal right to basic medical care. The right to prenatal care necessary to the health and survival of mothers and babies is derivable from that general right'.[154]

---

[149] See, eg, the essays by Ashford, Beitz, Brownlee, Griffin, Held, Liao, Renzo, Tasioulas, and Wolff in this volume.

[150] Ashford, 'A Moral Inconsistency Argument for a Basic Human Right to Subsistence'; Shue, *Basic Rights*. Whether this should be understood as the claim that respect for a right to subsistence is necessary to avoid *violating* other human rights, or whether instead respect for a right to subsistence is necessary for respect for *the values grounding* other human rights, is an important issue. See the debate between Ashford and Beitz in this volume (chs. 29 and 30).

[151] Consider 'the right of the child who is separated from one or both parents to maintain personal relations and direct contact with both parents on a regular basis' (Convention on the Rights of the Child, Article 9). See J.T. Levy, 'Classifying Cultural Rights', in Ian Shapiro and Will Kymlicka (eds.), *Ethnicity and Group Rights (Nomos 39)* (New York: New York University Press, 1997) for a helpful taxonomy of group-differentiated rights.

[152] See the first Article in both Covenants: 'All peoples have the right of self-determination'.

[153] Nickel, *Making Sense of Human Rights*, 2nd edn., 163.

[154] Nickel, *Making Sense of Human Rights*, 2nd edn., 162. A different strategy for explaining group rights maintains that, say, my right, as a child, to maintain contact with my parents is a human right because it can be reconceived as a universal right that takes a conditional form: the universal right to

In explaining why individually borne, group-differentiated rights are sometimes human rights, this strategy resembles the explanation (in terms of 'aim' and 'object' or 'higher-level'/'basal' and 'lower-level') offered for why some rights that seem highly specific to modern conditions, such as the right to the availability of higher education, can nonetheless qualify as human rights.[155] In both cases, a non-universal right is deemed a human right because it is derivable from a universal human right—or more controversially (and this goes beyond Nickel's proposal), because it is derivable from some universal value (autonomy, well-being, needs) that grounds universal human rights.

Contrary to this approach, some theorists suspect that many fundamentally important rights and other moral concerns fail Nickel's test, or our extended version of it. Or alternatively they argue that defending particular individuals' rights via this derivation from universal rights is misleading or distorting. For example, some feminist theorists question the derivation of specific women's rights to prenatal care from universal rights to health care. Lucinda Joy Peach outlines the general position thus: 'Cultural feminists generally stress the significance of differences between men and women and among women....Cultural feminists are, then, skeptical about the value of subsuming all "women" under the concept of "human" as the latter has been defined in international human rights law'.[156] We return to these concerns in discussing anti-universalist and feminist criticisms of human rights in the next section.

Many critics of group human rights are more exercised by the second type: human rights held by groups, rather than human rights held by individuals in virtue of their membership of a group. Some theorists doubt the very existence of pre-legal, moral rights *held by groups*.[157] These theorists suggest that many of the group rights that we want to call human rights are best understood as in some sense reducible to or shorthand for pre-legal moral rights held by individuals: the right ascribed to the group is not fundamental. For example, Griffin suggests that the legal group right to national sovereignty is reducible to individually held rights of the nation's members, including the individual 'right to autonomy (not to have our major decisions taken for us)

---

maintain contact with one's parents if one is a child. This strategy is suspect, partly because any right whatsoever can be converted into a universal right by this process. Eg, my morally justified right, based in university regulations, to timely submission of essays by my students can be taken as the universal right *to timely essay submission if one is a lecturer in institution X*. (For a sophisticated discussion and further argument against this strategy, see Jeremy Waldron, *The Right to Private Property* (Oxford: Oxford University Press, 1988), 117–20). Nickel's strategy is superior because it is more discriminating: at least at first glance, it does not permit all rights to be converted into universal rights.

[155] See p. 8 above. Also, for the case of education in particular, see Raz, this volume, ch. 11.

[156] Lucinda Joy Peach, 'Are Women Human? Feminist Reflections on "Women's Rights as Human Rights"', in David A. Reidy and Mortimer N.S. Sellers (eds.), *Universal Human Rights: Moral Order in a Divided World* (Lanham, MD: Rowman and Littlefield, 2005), 81–108, 90. For doubts about rights 'related to reproduction and childbearing' in particular, see Peach, 'Are Women Human?', 91.

[157] Careful and limited versions of this position are evident in Griffin, *On Human Rights*, ch. 15 and Wellman, *The Moral Dimensions of Human Rights*, 67–8. Unlike these authors, Nickel is happy to accept that groups can hold genuine pre-legal moral rights; he just doubts that they should be called 'human rights'. Group rights are for him 'not human rights in the standard sense because they are not rights that people simply have as humans rather than as members of some state or group. This is not to deny, however, that group rights may appropriately be included in human rights treaties and in other areas of international law. Nor does it deny that [g]roup [r]ights may sometimes be justifiable by reference to the same sorts of considerations as justify human rights' (Nickel, *Making Sense of Human Rights*, 2nd edn., 164).

and...right to liberty (not to be blocked from carrying out our decisions)'.[158] Similarly, Wellman claims that 'the legalization of the right of peoples to self-determination serves to protect the moral human rights to liberty and equitable treatment of individual persons'.[159]

Whether to follow these sceptical authors will be determined, in part, by one's conception of what human rights are and what grounds them. Those who conceive human rights primarily in terms of their function within the contemporary international order will have good reason to make space for group rights of both the types we have discussed, given their centrality to this international order. As Beitz notes in relation to women's rights, '[i]f...one regards human rights functionally, as elements of a practice whose purpose is to elevate certain threats to urgent interests to a level of international concern, then the conceptual objection [to group rights] can be sidestepped'.[160] But, importantly, we have seen that even those who take human rights simply to be those universal rights all humans hold in virtue of being human can find a space—albeit a derivative one—for group rights as a special class within lists of human rights: as derived from universally held individual human rights or their grounds. Accommodating group rights in a non-derivative way is more challenging.

V. Are There Any Genuine Human Rights?

We have examined particular concerns about specific human rights. Yet, despite the popularity of human rights discourse, one sometimes encounters wholesale doubts about human rights as such. We consider four lines of criticism in this section.

A. Human rights as problematically 'Western'

Perhaps the most common attack is that human rights express a 'Western' (or, more precisely, a Western European and North American, or perhaps a capitalist, or a Northern, or an affluent) moral and legal order unfit for imposition as a universal standard around the world. This is sometimes expressed as criticism of the inclusion of certain particular rights within international practice.[161] But it is also sometimes expressed as an attack on the very idea of human rights.[162]

In its most straightforward form, the claim is that although many people believe that there are some rights held universally by every human being, this is a mistake: human

---

[158] Griffin, *On Human Rights*, 274.

[159] Wellman, *The Moral Dimensions of Human Rights*, 67. See also, Jeremy Waldron, 'Two Concepts of Self-Determination', in Besson and Tasioulas, *The Philosophy of International Law*, 357.

[160] Beitz, *The Idea of Human Rights*, 189.

[161] Some of Lee Kuan Yew's criticism of human rights maintains that certain 'Asian values' can have the status of human rights—eg, a right to economic development. He simply questions the inclusion of, or the priority given to, rights to political participation (see the discussion in Bauer and Bell, *The East Asian Challenge for Human Rights*, esp. 4–7).

[162] See Makau Mutua's claim that 'the globalization of human rights fits a historical pattern in which all high morality comes from the West as a civilizing agent against lower forms of civilization in the rest of the world' (Makau Mutua, *Human Rights: A Political and Cultural Critique* (Philadelphia: University of Pennsylvania Press, 2002), 15); see also his claim that human rights discourse involves conceiving the activist as 'Saviour' of third-world 'Victims' of violations by local 'Savages' (Mutua, *Human Rights*, ch. 1).

rights adherents are misled by their specific, parochial 'Western' moral outlook. One ground for this critique is relativism: according to different versions of this view, one's society or one's culture or one's own view 'is the sole source of the validity of a moral right or rule'.[163] On the 'social' version of this view, humans from a society that lacks the concept of human rights, or that considers human rights claims invalid, will lack valid, binding human rights, even if such rights are present in international law; or alternatively they will only hold human rights relative to 'Western' societies, not relative to their own standpoint.[164] If the members of this society lack such rights or only hold them relative to a 'Western' standpoint, then genuinely universal morally valid human rights seem not to exist, for such rights are meant to obtain objectively for all humans, no matter the kind of society in which they live or the standpoint from which they are viewed.

Standard responses to the relativist include the claim that rejection of human rights by some cultures or groups could be an error, perhaps based on some mistaken factual or metaphysical beliefs—rather than involving the non-existence of human rights 'for that culture'. A related response notes that if an evaluative concept, such as 'human rights', has arisen in one culture, this is not in itself ground to doubt that it refers; there might well be human rights—either rights borne by humans in virtue of their humanity, or rights that mark issues of international concern—even if the concept is a Western product.[165] After all, to the extent that it was first understood by Newton, the law of universal gravitation is a Western discovery, but this does not compromise its universal validity. A further response notes that some human rights might conflict with each other and might conflict with other values, and some of these conflicts might involve irresolvable incommensurability: incommensurability which can be mistaken for 'relativity to a culture' or 'relativity to a framework'. Griffin makes subtle versions of these and additional anti-relativist points.[166]

A different ground for taking the 'Western' origins of human rights to undermine their existence stems not from *relativism*, but from consideration of the *diversity* of forms of human life, human flourishing and good lives. Human rights, many believe, are supposed to help support right-holders in living a minimally good life.[167] But what if there are a great many ways to live a minimally good life, which share none but the most abstract of features (for example, involving some lifespan, some action)? Any substantive list of rights will then seem to favour a particular form of minimally good life over alternatives.[168] One option is to make human rights very abstract, perhaps no more than a right to 'a minimally good life'.[169] But to do this is, one might think, to

---

[163] Jack Donnelly, *Universal Human Rights in Theory and Practice*, 2nd edn., 89–90.

[164] See the claims in the American Anthropological Association, 'Statement on Human Rights', *American Anthropologist*, 49 (1947): 539–43.

[165] Griffin, *On Human Rights*, 133–4; Nickel, *Making Sense of Human Rights*, 2nd edn., 171–2.

[166] See Griffin, 'The Relativity and Ethnocentricity of Human Rights', this volume, ch. 31. See also Nickel, *Making Sense of Human Rights*, 2nd edn., ch. 11; Donnelly, *Universal Human Rights in Theory and Practice*, 2nd edn., chs. 4-7; Renzo, 'Human Needs, Human Rights', this volume, ch. 32.

[167] How to understand 'minimally' is a matter for debate, of course.

[168] For an argument of this type for the view that human rights to liberty in particular protect a narrow conception of liberty, see Jiwei Ci, 'Liberty Rights and the Limits of Liberal Democracy', this volume, ch. 33.

[169] This could be seen as an (absurdly) extreme version of the distinction between aim and object, or 'higher-level'/'basal' and 'lower-level' rights discussed earlier.

give up on the notion of human rights. Certainly it involves a sharp deviation from the numerous, specific rights found in international human rights documents.

In response, theorists often highlight the shared, universal aspect of the goods they think human rights protect. Defenders of minimalist approaches, such as those that ground human rights on basic needs or fundamental conditions, or capabilities, for example, typically argue that the claim that human beings need things like food, shelter or a minimum level of health does not depend on adopting some controversial metaphysical view about human nature or a particular conception of the good. Meeting basic needs or having certain capabilities or fundamental conditions is indeed a precondition for the pursuit of any conception of the good.[170] Whether this move is convincing is a matter for debate.

A second concern raised under the umbrella of 'Western moral imperialism' is that it is *illegitimate* to enforce human rights within societies which do not recognize them, and perhaps even illegitimate to criticize such societies. The worry is that legitimate enforcement of a right or criticism of a society requires that those subject to such enforcement or criticism accept or could recognize as good reasons the grounds for the enforcement or criticism. Coupled with the premise that those living in societies conceptually distant from the 'West' in which human rights thinking originated do not and cannot recognize or accept human rights as a ground for enforcement or criticism, some theorists reach the conclusion that such enforcement or criticism is unjustified.[171] Note that this concern is not alleviated by the anti-relativist points mentioned earlier, and that is perhaps one reason why such responses sometimes seem crass. To show that 'the West' is right about the existence of human rights is not to show that 'the West', or indeed anyone, can legitimately enforce such rights worldwide.

There are two versions of the concern about legitimacy. For those who adhere to the naturalistic view that human rights are the moral rights humans hold simply in virtue of being human, the worry is simply as stated above: human rights cannot be legitimately enforced worldwide. By contrast, because the political conception defines human rights as those whose violation pro tanto legitimates some enforcement internationally, for adherents of the political conception the worry is that there are no genuine human rights, even if there are universal moral rights.

In response to this worry in either form, one can question the premise that human rights are justifiable only in 'Western' terms: this response has been pursued in very different ways by Rawls, An-Na'im, Cohen, Donnelly, and Taylor, as well as several authors in this volume.[172] Or one can question the claim that legitimate enforcement requires that

---

[170] See the sketches of the needs, fundamental conditions, and capability approaches in section III earlier.

[171] Griffin considers this in the later sections of 'The Relativity and Ethnocentricity of Human Rights', as does Renzo in 'Human Needs, Human Rights'. There are also suggestions of this thought in Ci, 'Liberty Rights and the Limits of Liberal Democracy' and in Simon Hope, 'Human Rights Without the Human Good? A Reply to Jiwei Ci', this volume, ch. 34.

[172] Rawls, *The Law of Peoples*, 78–81; Abdullahi A. An-Na'im, 'The Cultural Mediation of Human Rights: The Al-Arqam Case in Malaysia', in Bauer and Bell, *The East Asian Challenge for Human Rights*, 147–68; Joshua Cohen, 'Minimalism About Human Rights: The Best We Can Hope For?', *Journal of Political Philosophy*, 12 (2004): 190–213; Donnelly, *Universal Human Rights in Theory and Practice*, 2nd edn., ch. 5; Charles Taylor, 'Conditions of an Unforced Consensus on Human Rights', in Bauer and Bell, *The East Asian Challenge for Human Rights*, 124–46. See the essays by Miller, Griffin, and Renzo in this

those subject to such enforcement in some sense accept or could recognize as good reasons the grounds for the policy of enforcement.

Adherents of the naturalistic approach could also embrace the anti-enforcement conclusion but deny that it undermines human rights discourse: perhaps many human rights are not universally enforceable but are genuine human rights nonetheless. To support this point, one could note that some human rights seem by their very nature unsuited to enforcement. For instance, consider the idea of a human right to respect. Is the right to respect something that is enforceable? If not, rather than giving up the idea of a right to respect, perhaps we should rethink our commitment that human rights require (or typically require) enforceability.[173]

B. Marxist criticisms of human rights

Marx was trenchant in his criticism of rights and human rights.[174] One strand of criticism concerns the distinction between a 'public' and a 'private' sphere. A person's particular constitutional rights define that person's public status vis-a-vis fellow citizens; and the person's human rights arguably define the person's public status vis-a-vis other humans, including non-citizens and aliens.[175] Public matters can be objects of legitimate concern and action by others within the relevant public sphere, while private matters cannot, even if—as in the case of infidelity to one's life partner, say—they involve wrongs.

Now, Marx can be interpreted as arguing that this distinction between private and public matters conceals injustice and alienation. For example, considered as right-holders, an impoverished worker and a wealthy company owner who agree a wage contract possess equal status in the public sphere. They possess a similar status as equal bearers of rights to contract, vote within a democracy, to the protection of law, and so on. But, so the Marxist contends, this appearance of equal status created by the concept of rights is an illusion which hides the often unjust social forces determining economic and political events, and hides the ways in which human life is stunted under capitalism.[176] Many Marxists go further and maintain that it is

---

volume, chs. 12, 31, and 32, respectively. Note also the discussion of 'overlapping consensus' views earlier in this introductory essay.

[173] Finally, even if human rights could in principle be 'enforced' for or on a particular group, 'Western' nations might well—due eg to colonial oppressive actions, or unfair trade wars—have lost their standing to perform this enforcement.

[174] See especially Karl Marx, 'On the Jewish Question', reprinted in David McLellan (ed.), *Karl Marx: Selected Writings*, 2nd edn. (Oxford: Oxford University Press, 2000), 46–70. The essay was originally written in 1843 for the *Deutsch-französische Jahrbücher*.

[175] If the 'political' conception is correct, then this 'public' aspect is built into the very notion of a human right: it is a right that is in some sense 'everyone's business'. If the 'naturalistic' conception is correct, human rights arguably need not be limited to the public sphere: one might have some 'private' human rights that should not be matters of public concern, such as a right that one's spouse be faithful to one or that one not be lied to by one's friends (see Gewirth, *Human Rights: Essays on Justifications and Application*, 56; Sen, *Development as Freedom*, 210; Wellman, *The Moral Dimensions of Human Rights*, 36–9; Tasioulas, 'On the Nature of Human Rights'). Nonetheless, many 'naturalistic' theorists deny that there can be 'private' human rights (see eg, the final section of Roger Crisp, 'Human Rights: Form and Substance' in Crisp, *Griffin on Human Rights*).

[176] See, eg, Marx's claim that 'Right by its very nature can consist only in the application of an equal standard; but unequal individuals (and they would not be different individuals if they were not unequal)

precisely rights' function to shield injustice and legitimate capitalist alienation and exploitation. On this view, human rights have emerged under capitalism because they help to uphold it.[177]

However, a defender of human rights could argue that the status they create, and the public/private distinction it articulates, can work to hide injustices and legitimate alienation and exploitation only if one misconceives the particular human rights people hold. Thus one response to Marx claims that the contemporary human rights regime, with its new socio-economic and group rights, gives people an equal status that, if respected, would ensure that each person leads a minimally decent human life. A more radical but still rights-friendly response is that, with appropriate far-reaching additional rights or further norms, the human rights regime could play a useful or necessary part in giving people a proper equal status even if it does not at present.[178]

Neither response is Marx's own. For Marx, human rights as such are the problem, not the particular rights we include on our list:

[N]one of the so-called rights of man goes beyond egoistic man, man as he is in civil society, namely an individual withdrawn behind his private interests and whims and separated from the community. Far from the rights of man conceiving of man as a species-being, species-life itself, society, appears as a framework exterior to individuals, a limitation of their original self-sufficiency. The only bond that holds them together is natural necessity, need and private interest, the conservation of their property and egoistic person.[179]

One concern here is that the very idea of rights focuses on the right-holder as 'egoistic man'. This could be paraphrased as the worry, shared with some conservatives, that to think of oneself as a right-holder is to think of oneself as entitled to certain benefits, and is thereby to overlook the duties one owes to others. In Marx's version, the concern is primarily about how rights make society 'appear as a framework exterior to' the right-holder. By separating out 'oneself' and 'society' in how one thinks about oneself, rights thereby prevent people thinking of themselves in the manner appropriate to their communal 'species-being'.

---

are measurable only by an equal standard in so far as they are brought under an equal point of view, are taken from one definite side only' (Marx, 'Critique of the Gotha Programme', reprinted in McLellan, *Karl Marx: Selected Writings*, 2nd edn., 610–16, 615). The view that Marx took rights to shield *injustice* is controversial, and depends on vexed interpretative questions about whether Marx saw capitalism as unjust (for a good summary of the issues, see Steven Lukes, 'Justice and Rights', in Alan Ryan (ed.), *Justice* (Oxford: Oxford University Press, 1993), 164–84). The claim that Marx took rights to hide and legitimate *alienation* and *exploitation* is less controversial.

[177] See, eg, G.A. Cohen, *Karl Marx's Theory of History: A Defence* (Oxford: Clarendon Press, 1978). See Marx's claim that 'The ideas of the ruling class are in every epoch the ruling ideas, ie, the class which is the ruling material force of society is at the same time its ruling intellectual force' (Marx, *The German Ideology*, reprinted in McLellan, *Karl Marx: Selected Writings*, 2nd edn., 175–208, 192).

[178] See the discussion of socio-economic rights in the previous section. In this volume (ch. 33), Ci offers a critical voice against the approach which tries to defend the current regime: Ci argues that the liberty rights enshrined in human rights practice are compatible with inequalities that stunt individual self-determination. For the more radical but still rights-friendly response, see Carol C. Gould, *Rethinking Democracy* and also *Globalizing Democracy and Human Rights* (Cambridge: Cambridge University Press, 2004).

[179] Marx, 'On the Jewish Question', 61.

Some defences of human rights reject this concern head-on, highlighting the value of an individualistic self-conception.[180] A further promising response asks whether the Marxist critique is primarily targeted at how *thinking of oneself as a right-holder* can tend to make one think in an excessively individualistic way, rather than targeted at rights themselves. As Waldron notes in relation to a similar communitarian criticism of rights, human rights are useful as 'something to fall back on if an attachment [for example, to one's society, or one's culture] fails'.[181] This is true even if it is distorting to focus solely on one's status as a right-holder. One can concede to the Marxist and the communitarian that humans are very much more than holders of human rights, and indeed very much more than holders of any sort of rights; so focusing solely on one's status as a right-holder will be distorting. But this is compatible with the thesis that we are nonetheless right-holders, and that to deny this is also distorting, and overlooks claims we can make if our communitarian, personal or private attachments fail. An additional response notes how many of our rights protect social or communal aspects of right-holders, rather than protecting right-holders as lone individuals. A related point is articulated by Gould when she observes that human rights 'come into being as claims each has on the others and hence exist as rights only in such a social framework of recognition'.[182]

C. Feminist concerns about human rights

Concern about the distorting individualism of a focus on rights is equally present in feminist criticisms of human rights. There is a rich diversity of such criticism; Reilly lists some of the positions as follows:

> Simply put, anti-universalist feminist critics across the philosophical spectrum challenge dominant Western-centric, neo-liberal, male-defined and otherwise biased interpretations of supposedly universal norms (human rights, equality, rule of law, etc.) and their role in perpetuating practices that systematically disadvantage women and marginalized groups in society. This includes, for example, a public-private divide that conceals private abuses of power; atomistic individualism that privileges rights to private property and profit-making over rights to development, health, welfare and so on; failures to recognize and address inequalities flowing from structural disadvantage and oppression, including global inequalities; 'impartialist reasoning' that often serves male-defined interests (e.g. failures of justice systems in rape cases); and cultural and political processes of false universalization wherein the perspectives of a hegemonic grouping become *the* particular worldview from which universal norms are formulated and imposed on less dominant groups in society, including

---

[180] See Siedentop, *Inventing the Individual* and Feinberg's defence of rights as allowing individuals to make demands upon each other simply qua individuals ('The Nature and Value of Rights' in *Rights, Justice, and the Bounds of Liberty*, 143–58). For critical discussion of the varied forms of individualism, see Steven Lukes, *Individualism* (Oxford: Blackwell, 1973).

[181] Jeremy Waldron, 'When Justice Replaces Affection: the Need for Rights', in his *Liberal Rights*, 370–91, 391. Note that Waldron considers himself to be addressing Marx along with contemporary communitarians (382–5).

[182] Gould, *Globalizing Democracy and Human Rights*, 144. For more on the way that human rights are not individualistic, see Gould, 'A Social Ontology of Human Rights', this volume, ch. 9.

women and minorities. Postmodern and post-structural thinkers are particularly trenchant in their rejection of universal norms—viewing them as modernist, totalizing narratives that are deeply implicated in a complex of dominating and oppressive practices.[183]

Some of the criticisms listed have already been discussed, for example, concerning the downgrading of 'rights to development, health, welfare' or concerning the dangers of universal norms enforceable worldwide;[184] but it is important to note their intersection with specific feminist concerns. Even if some of the attacks on human rights—as 'Western' constructions or as excessively demanding, say—can be dismissed when expressed in the terms considered earlier in this Introduction, their articulation from a feminist perspective could be harder to dismiss. In what follows, we focus on problems generated by the public-private distinction, and on criticism arising from the ethics of care. But we do not thereby deny the importance of the other, related criticisms.[185]

Initially it is worth noting, as Reilly's list makes clear, that not all feminist criticisms target the very existence of human rights. Feminist concerns are unlike the others discussed in this section, in that many feminists do not take themselves to be criticising human rights as such (although some do).[186] Many feminists defend human rights, but argue that significant work is needed to ensure that they are construed in an appropriately non-patriarchal way. Much criticism is aimed at our current international legal system, or at the general idea that human rights are best expressed and enforced through law.[187] Others defend human rights but argue for the parallel and equal importance of moral and political considerations that go beyond rights.[188]

A specific feminist concern about the expression of human rights in law focuses on the fact that human rights entail primary legal duties for states. Thus MacKinnon writes:

> States are the only ones recognized as violating human rights, yet states are also the only ones empowered to redress them. Not only are men's so-called 'private' acts against women left out; power to act against public acts is left exclusively in the hands of those who commit those acts.[189]

Part of the concern here is, as in Marx, with the very idea of a public/private distinction: such a distinction can hide or legitimate domestic violence, rape, abuse, and patriarchal coercion and tyranny, as well as injustices in our distribution and conception of domestic labour including child-rearing. Proposed responses range from a

---

[183] Niamh Reilly, *Women's Human Rights* (Cambridge: Polity 2009), 3.

[184] See 24–29 and 31–34 earlier in this essay.

[185] In focusing on the public–private distinction and the ethics of care, we follow Gould, *Globalizing Democracy and Human Rights*, 143.

[186] For someone who is critical but also supportive of human rights, see Virginia Held, this volume, ch. 35.

[187] See what Lucinda Joy Peach calls the 'liberal feminist defence' of human rights, and the critical edge this brings to aspects of contemporary human rights practice (Peach, 'Are Women Human?', 86–9). See also Held, this volume, ch. 35, and Catharine A. MacKinnon, 'Crimes of War and Crimes of Peace', in Shute and Hurley, *On Human Rights*, 84 and 97.

[188] Held, this volume, ch. 35.

[189] MacKinnon, 'Crimes of War and Crimes of Peace', 93.

radical rejection of the public/private distinction to an attempt to delineate a narrower private sphere, within which serious harms cannot be tolerated.[190]

In principle, even the radical move seems compatible with human rights: one way to make this move would be to introduce a range of justiciable legal human rights within what has traditionally been thought of as the private sphere.[191] But many feminists would be troubled by this simplistic recourse to law as the solution. One source of this concern, a source which also drives some feminist concerns about the universality of human rights, is derived from the ethics of care. This conception of ethics is built on Gilligan's work on gendered modes of moral development and Noddings's focus on the importance of specific relationships of care.[192] Held summarizes some of its key features thus:

> The ethics of care rests on a conception of persons as relational and interdependent, and on an appreciation of the values of care embedded in practices of care...Attending to care and its practices brings to the fore such values as empathetic understanding, sensitivity to the needs of others and especially, responsiveness to such needs...Care seeks to meet effectively, and with sensitivity and respect, the actual needs of embodied persons located in actual contexts. It appreciates and relies on the caring emotions and rejects the view of the dominant theories that morality must be based only on ideal, abstract, impartial principles recognizable by reason.[193]

This approach to ethics can generate criticisms of human rights law, as including too few 'rights to be cared for', such as rights to health care and other 'welfare' rights or, more controversially, children's rights to be loved.[194] It can generate criticisms of law as a means for delivering care, for example on the ground that legal reasoning is too algorithmic to enable contextually specific caring responses, and on the ground that law cannot require the kind of emotional response that caring involves.[195]

Note that the latter point is not simply that law should not require certain emotional responses, but also that sometimes an appropriate emotional response may be impossible if it is required by duty (legal or moral). For example, there is the concern that if one tried to love someone else romantically because the law demanded it, what one would end up with would not be romantic love. There may be conceptual as well as empirical limits to what duty can require.[196]

---

[190] For the latter, see Gould, *Globalizing Democracy and Human Rights,* 148.
[191] Some liberal thinkers seem willing to do this with respect to non-justiciable human rights: thus Gewirth countenances a right not to be lied to by one's friends, and Sen affirms a human right to a say in important family decisions (see references at n 175 earlier). But neither conceives these as justiciable rights enforceable by law.
[192] See Carol Gilligan, *In a Different Voice: Psychological Theory and Women's Development* (Cambridge, MA: Harvard University Press, 1982); Nel Noddings, *Caring: A Feminine Approach to Ethics and Moral Education* (Berkeley: University of California Press, 1984).
[193] Held, this volume, ch. 35, 630.
[194] On socio-economic rights and feminism, see Held, this volume, ch. 35; on the right to be loved, see Liao, *The Right to Be Loved.*
[195] On women's socio-economic rights, see Gould, *Globalizing Democracy and Human* Rights, 149–51. On children's rights, see David Archard, *Children: Rights and Childhood,* 2nd edn. (London: Routledge, 1993), esp. 118–23. On the limits of the law, see eg, MacKinnon, 'Crimes of War, Crimes of Peace', 97–8, Peach, 'Are Women Human?', 91; Held, this volume, ch. 35.
[196] See note 125 earlier in this Introduction.

This line of argument has been developed, by some proponents of the ethics of care, into much more radical criticisms of the existence of human rights as moral rights, criticisms that bite independently of whether human rights should be legalized. On one version, the very idea of rights stands in opposition to care. For rights specify what I can demand as my entitlement. This notion that some service can be demanded and must be supplied as a matter of entitlement is, it is claimed, in sharp tension with the idea that the service will or can be provided as a matter of care. Care involves a directed concern for the specific recipient, and this type of concern can seem either impossible or at least extremely difficult to supply as a response to an entitlement.[197]

In addition, the idea of *human* rights introduces the idea of demands I can make simply in virtue of my falling within the general category, 'human'. Again, this can seem in tension with the idea of caring as a concern for an individual in all their particularity and context. Is it really possible to care for you 'as a human', as opposed to as the specific embodied being you are?

Many adherents of the ethic of care do not make these radical criticisms, because they think care is compatible with or even conceptually bound up with rights.[198] Yet even such rights-friendly theorists often see care as an extremely important, historically overlooked complement and corrective to a narrow, legalistic approach to human rights.

D. Human rights as problematically unenforced

The final brand of concern about human rights which we consider dates back at least to Bentham.[199] It is a doubt about any kind of pre-legal right, human or natural. Recently, the view has been expressed by Raymond Geuss who argues, like Bentham, that rights do not exist unless they are actually enforced, and he adds that international law in territories whose governments do not recognize human rights does not normally qualify as appropriately 'enforced'. Geuss writes:

> Either there is or there is not a mechanism for enforcing human rights. If there is not, it would seem that calling them 'rights' simply means that we think it would (morally) be a good idea if they were enforced, although, of course, they are not. A 'human right' is an inherently vacuous conception, and to speak of 'human rights' is a kind of puffery or white magic.[200]

[197] On the idea of rights as entitlements, see Feinberg, 'The Nature and Value of Rights'. Tensions between notions of entitlement or right and care can be found in Gilligan, *In a Different Voice* and Noddings, *Caring*.

[198] See, eg, Gould, *Globalizing Democracy and Human Rights*, 143–7; Held, this volume, ch. 35.

[199] Jeremy Bentham, 'Anarchical Fallacies', in Jeremy Waldron (ed.), '*Nonsense Upon Stilts': Bentham, Burke, and Marx on the Rights of Man* (London: Methuen, 1987). This was originally written in response to the 1789 French Declaration of the Rights of Man and of the Citizen.

[200] Raymond Geuss, *History and Illusion in Politics* (Cambridge: Cambridge University Press, 2001), 144. A similar view—that rights only exist when in some sense socially recognized or enforced—is found in various forms in 'rights externalists': see Derrick Darby, 'Rights Externalism', *Philosophy and Phenomenological Affairs*, 68 (2004): 620–34; Martin, *A System of Rights*. See also Susan James, 'Rights as Enforceable Claims', *Proceedings of the Aristotelian Society*, 103 (2003): 133–47.

Geuss goes on, using the case of Indonesia, to argue that the international law of human rights is not currently enforced universally, and that if it were this would be 'the invention of a new set of positive "rights" rather than the emergence into visibility of a set of natural human rights that already existed'. [201]

In our view, the actual enforcement condition on rights which appeals to Geuss and Bentham, and to 'rights externalists' including Darby, Martin, and James, cannot be motivated.[202] We frequently refer to unenforced rights. Consider the legal right not to have eggs and flour thrown at one's windows. This is violated by many citizens in places where Hallowe'en is celebrated, and the police and courts rightly do not pursue enforcement. Or consider black citizens' rights to political participation in apartheid-era South Africa. People frequently conceive this as a violation of moral right by the apartheid government, rather than the mere absence of a morally desirable legal right.[203] It is unclear to us why *rights in particular,* as opposed to other moral norms (for example, those requiring the pursuit of moral goals) or legal requirements (for example, tax rules) must be enforced in order to be genuine.

VI. The Structure of the Volume

This volume is the first to offer a comprehensive set of essays on the fast-growing field of the philosophical foundations of human rights. It contains thirty-eight essays, all but two of which are original, and is divided into four sections: first on human rights' foundations, secondly, on human rights in law and politics, thirdly, on a range of canonical and contested human rights and fourthly, on concerns about and alternatives to human rights.

In each section we have sought chapters covering a broad range of positions including both established views and new insights. For instance, within the section on human rights foundations, the venerable ideas that human rights are grounded on human interests and on human dignity are discussed in detail (Tasioulas; O'Neill; Liao; Cruft; Waldron; Simmons; Gould; Gilabert), as is the newer idea that some human rights are grounded on personal desert (Nickel; Stemplowska). In the section on human rights in law and politics, the vexed questions of the relationship between human rights and international law, and the relationship between domestic legal systems and inter- and supranational law are discussed (Raz; Miller; Buchanan; Luban; Besson; Meckled-Garcia; Letsas; Verdirame). In the section on canonical and contested human rights, particular central human rights, including such traditional civil rights as free speech (Brettschneider; Alexander), religion (Zucca; Audi), and security (Lazarus; Tadros), are examined along with work on the status of more controversial human rights

---

[201] Geuss, *History and Illusion in Politics*, 145.   [202] See n 200.

[203] Whether rights must be *enforceable* (either in the sense of it being *possible* to enforce them, or *permissible* to do so) if not *actually enforced* is much more debateable. For the view that it is definitive of rights (and not just *human* rights) that it is morally permissible to demand their fulfilment, where demanding involves a request that can permissibly be backed up by force, see John Skorupski, *The Domain of Reasons* (Oxford: Oxford University Press, 2010), 307–13. For discussion of unenforced legal rights, see Matthew H. Kramer, 'Getting Rights Right', in Kramer (ed.), *Rights, Wrongs, and Responsibilities* (Basingstoke: Palgrave, 2001), 28–95, 65–73.

including self-determination and democracy (Christiano; Peter) and such 'socio-economic' rights as health (Wolff; Brownlee) and subsistence (Ashford; Beitz). In the final section, familiar but important concerns about the ethnocentric nature of human rights (Griffin; Renzo), and about the extent to which human rights need supplementing by a care ethics (Held; Mendus), are considered, while new Kantian and other strands of criticism of human rights are also introduced (Flikschuh; Sangiovanni; Ci; Hope). It is worth noting that none of the essays in this final section is strictly critical of human rights as such; rather they offer alternative perspectives, interpretations, and supplements. Many of the chapters in the two central sections—on human rights in law and politics, and on canonical and contested human rights—focus on quite specific issues such as proportionality or religion. We have chosen the particular range of issues both for its intrinsic interest and because as a whole the chapters give the reader a broad grasp of the diversity of challenges facing an overarching account of the foundations of human rights.

We have pursued a dialogic approach in assembling our chapters.[204] They fall into pairs, with the second chapter in each pair written in part as a response to the first. In some cases authors take the opportunity to develop their own position while in others a detailed response is offered. In our view, this dialogical approach is particularly important for a survey volume of this type. We want to make clear that such a survey cannot 'tell' the reader what the philosophical foundations of human rights are. Human rights foundations are too contested for this. Indeed, what it is for human rights to have foundations is contested, as is the metaphysical nature of human rights. For these reasons, we believe an accurate introduction must involve a diversity of voices. In addition, we believe the dialogic approach offers a particularly strong way to enable the reader to learn about and engage with the philosophical foundations of human rights.

We believe the range demonstrates the breadth and value of philosophical theorizing about human rights.[205]

---

[204] The model for us has been Samantha Besson and John Tasioulas's volume, *The Philosophy of International Law*. Besson and Tasioulas in turn cite the annual supplementary volume of the *Proceedings of the Aristotelian Society* as an inspiration (Besson and Tasioulas, 'Introduction', *The Philosophy of International Law*, 1–27, 19).

[205] Many thanks to Simon Hope, Jim Nickel, Andrea Sangiovanni, and John Tasioulas for helpful comments on a draft of this Introduction.

PART I

HUMAN RIGHTS' FOUNDATIONS

1

On the Foundations of Human Rights

John Tasioulas

I. Foundations Without Foundationalism

The nature of human rights, the subject we are talking about when we invoke this globally resonant category of practical standards, is a distinct matter from their foundations or grounds. On the former question there is disagreement as to the merits of the orthodox view, according to which human rights are moral rights possessed by all human beings simply in virtue of their humanity.[1] Even for those with orthodox sympathies, however, the question of grounds remains to be faced: what are the conditions that make it the case that anything is a right of this kind, and are they ever satisfied?[2] At most, orthodoxy about the nature of human rights is committed to the thesis that the satisfaction of the relevant conditions is a matter for natural reason and hence underwrites the objective truth or correctness of positive human rights claims. But the nature of those conditions is notoriously the subject of deep and persistent disagreement. Some philosophers echo contemporary human rights instruments by presenting human dignity as the foundation, others appeal to a schedule of basic human needs or universal interests, yet others to the value of personhood or some combination of these factors. And of course there are still those who insist, against all secular doctrines of the kind just listed, that a compelling grounding of human rights is inescapably theistic in character.

I distinguish the contention that human rights have *foundations*, a version of which I defend in this chapter, from certain *foundationalist* deformations it is liable to undergo. Foundationalism, which elaborates erroneously on the bare orthodox thesis that human rights have objective grounds, comes in both meta-ethical and normative versions. Meta-ethical foundationalists offer defective accounts of what objectivity is, how it is secured, or the nature of its implications. One example is the naturalist thesis that the objective grounding of human rights consists in their being logically derivable exclusively from an array of value-neutral facts about human nature or a metaphysical human essence. Another is the historicist

---

[1] For a defence of orthodoxy, see J. Tasioulas, 'On the Nature of Human Rights', in *The Philosophy of Human Rights: Contemporary Controversies*, ed. G. Ernst and J-C Heilinger (Berlin: Walter de Gruyter, 2012), 17–59.

[2] I speak interchangeably of the foundations or grounds or basis or justification of human rights throughout this chapter. In each case, I am concerned with what it is that makes it the case that something qualifies as a human right on an orthodox construal. This constitutive issue is distinct from, although also related to, the epistemic one of finding reasons for believing that X is or is not a human right. One may have good reasons for such a belief without being in possession of an account of the foundations of human rights.

thesis that the objectivity of human rights endows them with sufficient psychological and social efficacy to render probable their eventual historical triumph. In his well-known Oxford Amnesty lecture, Richard Rorty foisted both naturalism and historicism on objectivist believers in human rights, doing so as a prelude to insisting that the quest for foundations, so understood, has become a hindrance in sustaining a culture of human rights.[3]

Rorty's mistake was to conflate foundations and foundationalism. Neither the naturalist nor the historicist theses are entailed by the commitment to objectivity. The considerations that ground human rights may themselves belong within the normative domain; for example, they may be inherently reason-giving considerations about the elements of a good human life or the equal moral status of all humans. Moreover, these evaluative considerations may even be thought of as natural facts, provided we have a suitably expansive understanding of the natural realm, one that does not limit natural facts to those that do explanatory work within the natural sciences. This expansive understanding might emerge out of a conception of objectivity according to which objective qualities are those that possess explanatory power; in particular, those qualities that can figure in vindicatory explanations of a certain kind. Thus, justice is on one reckoning an objective property if the best explanation of someone coming to believe the proposition 'Slavery is unjust' can be one that leaves no room for the denial that slavery is unjust. But the claim that objective qualities figure in such vindicatory explanations is categorically distinct from the historicist prediction that they will effect a general convergence of belief on the moral truth.[4]

The normative version of foundationalism consists in the general idea that the values that ground human rights are somehow importantly distinctive in character. This can be made more precise by reference to the role of human interests or the components of a good human life. Paradigmatic human rights seemingly protect an array of human interests. For example, torture attacks our interests in life, health, and freedom from pain, it is corrosive of our capacity for autonomous decision making and our ability to form and sustain intimate relationships. It is a natural inference to conclude that the human right not to be tortured owes its very existence, in crucial part, to the fact that it systematically protects these interests of the right-holder. Moreover, it is equally natural to suppose that human rights share this grounding in human interests with many other standards of inter-personal morality. Normative foundationalism denies the antecedently plausible assumption that human rights are anchored in a profile of universal human interests. In extreme versions, it holds interests to be irrelevant to at least the primary grounding of human rights, whereas in moderate versions, only a narrowly restricted sub-set of human interests plays a grounding role.

Two forms of moderate foundationalism—agency-based and needs-based accounts of human rights—come under scrutiny at the very end of this chapter (section IV). Here I will only make some brief observations about extreme normative foundationalism

[3] R. Rorty, 'Human Rights, Rationality and Sentimentality', in S. Shute and S.L. Hurley (eds.), *On Human Rights: The Oxford Amnesty Lectures, 1993* (New York: Basic Books, 1993), 111–34.

[4] D. Wiggins, *Ethics: Twelve Lectures on the Philosophy of Morality* (London: Penguin Books), chs. 11–12.

prior to outlining a non-foundationalist account of the grounds of human rights (in sections II and III). The least interesting forms of extreme foundationalism, from the perspective of our concern with human rights, are those that present morality in its entirety as having a grounding that is totally independent of interests. On such views, usually referred to as 'deontological', there is nothing distinctive about human rights, among moral standards generally, in not being grounded in interests. The more interesting versions allow that interests may ground some moral standards, but maintain that human rights have a sufficient basis in considerations other than human interests. There are at least two, distinct but complementary, routes to this insistence. The first, positive route, finds compelling the idea that human rights are grounded in a value that is not an interest or itself interest-based. The second, negative route, rejects the grounding of human rights in interests as misguided because it fails to capture the distinctive role of human rights within moral thought.[5]

Negative pathways to extreme foundationalism must appeal to some feature of interests that disable them from figuring in the primary grounding of human rights. The most commonly invoked feature is an inability to capture the resistance to being defeated in the context of all-things-considered practical judgments that is supposed to characteristize human rights. So, for example, torturing one innocent individual in order to prevent three other innocent individuals from being tortured is ruled out by a proper appreciation of the normative force of the right not to be tortured. Acknowledgement of this resistance to trade-offs is supposed to be compatible with accepting that an obligation associated with a human right may be defeated in order to avert a sufficiently disastrous outcome. Why might human rights, conceived as grounded in human interests, be thought to lack the resistance to trade-offs (against other rights, and against other values) that is supposed to be characteristic of human rights?

One answer begins by interpreting theories that seek to *ground* human rights in interests as *identifying* them with the latter. If this interpretation is sound, then the extreme foundationalist's objection is cogent. Human interests—even our most urgent interests, such as the avoidance of imminent death—can be impaired or neglected in all sorts of ways without any wrong being committed, let alone one that has the character of a rights violation. Hence, the claims of interests in practical reason are more vulnerable to defeat than those of rights, since the latter inherently involve counterpart duties, and duties are characterized by two features that confer upon them a greater resistance to trade-offs. On the one hand, non-compliance with a duty is a form of moral wrongdoing which, subject to justification or excuse, makes appropriate a range of negative responses, such as blame and guilt; on the other hand, duties are exclusionary in force, putting out of normative play *some* countervailing reasons that would otherwise apply. However, this route to extreme foundationalism proceeds on a false assumption. Grounding human rights in the interests they serve is not the

---

[5] Both routes are travelled in Thomas Nagel's 'Personal Rights and Public Space': 'Rights form an essential part of any moral community in which equality of moral status cannot be exhaustively identified with counting everyone's interests the same as a contribution to an aggregate collective good whose advancement provides the standard of moral justification', T. Nagel, 'Personal Rights and Public Space', in *Concealment and Exposure and Other Essays* (Oxford: Oxford University Press, 2002), 33–4.

same as identifying them with (some class of) the latter. The content of a human right is the content of its associated duties, not of the interests that ground those duties. The key question for an interest-based account of human rights is whether, and the extent to which, an individual's interests generate duties. It follows that not all of the ways in which an interest may be impaired are violations of duties grounded in those interests.

An alternative way of travelling the negative route is by means of the claim that interest-based theories, even if they do not strictly equate human rights with interests, nonetheless explain their normative significance largely in terms of the interests they protect. But, the argument goes, this explanation is incompatible with the resistance to trade-offs characteristic of rights, because the normative significance of interests reduces to the maximization of their fulfilment within some aggregative calculus in which the right-holder's interests are bundled together along with those of others. Hence, an interest-based account of the right against torture would be committed, other things being equal, to endorsing the torture of one innocent person in order to prevent the torture of three others. Again, we should reject the original assumption about the shape inevitably assumed by an interest-based account of human rights. There is no compelling reason to suppose that a logic of maximizing their aggregate fulfilment is the (only) appropriate moral response to interests. We can understand morality, or some segment of it, as teleological—as grounded in advancing, protecting, and respecting human interests—without adopting a consequentialist or maximizing interpretation of the proper moral response to interests. And it is clear that leading proponents of interest-based accounts of rights do not regard those rights as generated by a background principle mandating the aggregate maximization of interests; indeed, some reject the very idea that such a principle forms part of morality, because it is strictly speaking incoherent.[6] Conversely, of course, many who accept a consequentialist/maximizing principle also seek to subsume non-interest-based considerations under it, including rights conceived as grounded independently of interests. If they are correct, the retreat from interests is no defence against the supposed perils of consequentialist maximization.

Extreme foundationalism may, instead, be motivated principally by the identification of a value, or set of values, that seems to be a promising candidate for grounding human rights, but which apparently does not have the shape of an interest. For many writers, the value of freedom meets this specification. They argue that freedom is the exclusive positive grounding of human rights, but that it is not an element of the good life, in that the reasons for valuing freedom do not include the intrinsic contribution that it makes to how well a person's life goes for them. Amartya Sen, for example, asserts that many of the freedoms protected by human rights—such as the freedom to play trivial games or participate in political demonstrations—do not serve our interests.[7] But there is a strong case for treating play, even as exemplified by the playing of computer games, as a prudential value.[8] Why should there not also be value in being given the opportunity to *choose* to engage in play? A confusion to guard against in this

---

[6] Eg, J.M. Finnis, *Natural Law and Natural Rights* (Oxford: Oxford University Press, 1980) and J. Raz, *The Morality of Freedom* (Oxford: Oxford University Press, 1986).

[7] A. Sen, *The Idea of Justice* (Cambridge, MA: Harvard University Press, 2009), 376–9.

[8] J. Tasioulas, 'Games and the Good', *Proceedings of the Aristotelian Society*, sup. vol. 80 (2006), 237–64.

vicinity is that of conflating what *generally* serves our well-being in *some* respect with that which will best serve our *overall* well-being in any *particular* case. This confusion is courted by Sen's case of the 'game maniac'. Even if we agree that his overall well-being is not enhanced by playing a computer game (he would be better off reading a serious newspaper instead), we can still hold fast to the thought that an aspect of his well-being (ie, freedom) is served by having the opportunity to play the game. The case of political protest is rather more troublesome, since here the choice is not to engage in the realization of some other prudential value, but in the promotion of the unmistakably *moral* value of justice. Is the notion of an interest unduly stretched by the claim that someone's interests are served through being able to participate in a demonstration against an unjust war? Now, it certainly is true that he need not be *motivated* by his self-interest in taking part in the demonstration; ideally, he should be motivated by a concern for justice. But, as Joseph Raz has put it, well-being consists in the wholehearted and successful engagement in worthwhile pursuits,[9] and one of the ways in which a pursuit can be worthwhile is by advancing the cause of justice.

The foregoing hardly amounts to a refutation of non-prudential interpretations of freedom. However, two additional observations are worth making. The first is that such interpretations are sometimes the product of an unduly restrictive understanding of well-being in general. If the intrinsic components of a good human life are given a subjectivist interpretation, as essentially consisting in mental states such as pleasure or in the fulfilment of mental states such as desires of preferences, then the exclusion of freedom from the prudential domain is plausible. We value freedom in ways that do not match this subjectivist construal; for example, we value people's freedom to make life choices even if external interference would promote better outcomes so far as their happiness or preference-satisfaction is concerned. The problem, however, is that the subjectivist interpretation of well-being is not only highly contestable but also deeply flawed. This leaves open the possibility of including freedom—which centrally involves making and pursuing life-shaping choices from a range of worthwhile options—alongside other objective goods such as knowledge, friendship, accomplishment, and play. The second observation is already implicit in the previous sentence. If freedom as a value is constrained by the value of the options to be chosen and pursued—so that preventing someone fulfilling their desire to be tortured, maimed or publicly humiliated is not a genuine restriction of their freedom, as these activities do not embody even minimally worthwhile options—then insisting on the non-prudential character of freedom is a futile way of expelling interests from the foundations of human rights, since the value of those options will itself often turn on prudential judgments.

An even more widely credited candidate for the role of non-prudential foundation of human rights is human dignity, which I take to designate an intrinsically valuable moral status inhering in being human, a status that is shared equally by all human beings, elevating them above non-human animals, but whose normative significance is graspable independently of the interests of the human beings who possess it. For some philosophers, the status of human dignity essentially consists in the possession

---

[9] Raz, *The Morality of Freedom*, ch. 12.

of a series of universal moral rights, a thesis that expresses what they take to be the fundamental and non-derivative character of those rights. Others reply that the amorphous notion of human dignity is in fact best understood in terms of our capacity to realize one aspect of the human good—freedom itself (see section IV). By contrast, I argue in section II that there is a compelling interpretation of human dignity according to which it *is* a moral status, not a prudential value among others, but that this status does not consist in possession of a schedule of rights. Moreover, although human dignity lies at the foundations of human rights, it does not by itself exhaust those foundations; instead, human dignity characteristically operates in intimate union with a profile of universal human interests in generating human rights. Contrary to extreme foundationalists, my contention is that the foundations of human rights, like those of morality generally, are characterized by a value pluralism that embraces both moral and prudential elements. Human rights are grounded in the universal interests of human beings each and every one of whom possesses an equal moral status arising from their common humanity.

II. Dignity and Interests

Before addressing the role of human dignity, let me begin with a highly schematic explanation of how human rights are grounded within a broadly interest-based account of moral rights.[10] On such an account, a right exists if an individual's interest in the object of the putative right (for example, freedom from torture, access to health care, opportunities for political participation) has the requisite sort of importance to justify the imposition of duties on others variously to respect, protect or advance that interest by securing to that individual the object of his right. Human rights are rights that all human beings possess simply in virtue of their humanity; on an interest-based account, they are rights grounded in universal interests that generate duties on the part of others. Although it would be pleasingly symmetrical, there is no implication that the duties must also be universal, ie, that all persons bear the duties correlative to the human rights enjoyed by all.

Now, even within an interest-based account there are a variety of potential ways of justifying a human right. One strategy is essentially derivative. It begins by justifying certain other human rights, for example, rights to free speech and an adequate standard of living, and then derives other more specific rights, such as rights to political advocacy or food, from them. But human rights can also be given an independent justification not derived from prior human rights. Let me propose, therefore, the following schema as the basic argument for establishing the existence of a human right:

   (i) For all human beings within a given historical context, and simply in virtue of their humanity, having X (the object of the putative right) serves one or more of their basic interests, for example, interests in health, physical security, autonomy, understanding, friendship, achievement, play, etc.

---

[10] For a classic exposition of the interest-based theory of individual moral rights, to which I am indebted, see Raz, *The Morality of Freedom*, ch.7.

(ii)   The interest in having *X* is, in the case of each human being and simply in virtue of their humanity, pro tanto of sufficient importance to justify the imposition of duties on others, for example, to variously protect, respect or advance their interest in *X*.

(iii)   The duties generated at (ii) are feasible claims on others given the constraints created by general and relatively entrenched facts of human nature and social life in the specified historical context. Therefore:

(iv)   All human beings within the specified historical context have a right to *X*.

Something is an interest of a person if its fulfilment enhances an aspect of their well-being; in other words, it makes that person's life better in some respect, for the person living it, than it would have been but for the fulfilment of that interest. As observed earlier, there is no implication that the fulfilment of the interest makes the person's life better overall than it otherwise would have been. For example, playing cricket may make my life better in one respect than otherwise it would have been, but my overall well-being might be diminished as a result because I forego other, more valuable activities. For an interest-based approach to rights, the operative question is whether any particular interest of ours—any aspect of our well-being—suffices to generate duties on others to respect or protect that interest. The result that we sometimes achieve a lower overall level of well-being than would have been the case had we not exercised our rights (or not exercised them in some particular way) is perfectly compatible with this interest-based view of rights.

The universal interests referred to in (i) are *objective, standardized, pluralistic, open-ended*, and *holistic* in character. By *objective*, I mean that the interests are interests of human beings whether or not they are believed by them to be interests of theirs and whether or not they actually desire their fulfilment or would do so were they fully informed of certain non-evaluative facts. Describing them as *standardized* indicates that in their specification one may abstract from some variations among individuals by focusing on the standard case of an ordinary human being living in a modern society. Hence, for example, we can regard personal achievement—engaging in difficult activities in such a way as to merit admiration—as a universal human interest, notwithstanding the fact that some individuals may not share this interest, such as those whose idiosyncratic psychological make-up effectively precludes them from engaging in challenging enterprises. There is a *plurality* of interests in play at the level of (i). This means that our basic interests cannot be reduced to some single overarching value, as in the hedonist's attempt to reduce all prudential value to pleasure. Moreover, given this plurality of basic interests, the basic schema does not limit itself to drawing on only one type of basic interest, such as our interest in autonomy. What is envisaged is a flexible, many-faceted approach to the grounding of human rights, whereby more than one interest, or combination of interests, grounds the existence of any given right. The list of interests is *open-ended* rather than definitively established once-and-for-all. In light of their objectivity, we must allow for the possibility that, on further reflection, new interests need to be added. This means that the background account of prudential value that I am drawing on here is one usually referred to as an 'objective list' theory

of the good.[11] Because its emphasis on an open-ended plurality of grounding interests is its most distinctive feature, I will refer to the basic schema as the core of a
pluralist account of the grounds of human rights.

In coming to understand the nature of universal human interests, we need to grasp
their holistic character, the way they bear important non-instrumental relations to
each other, so that an interest's nature and significance is partly determined by its
location within a broader web of prudential values. In order to grasp fully the significance of a value such as friendship, for example, we have to understand the special
concern that friends have for each other's welfare, and this brings into play elements of
the good life other than friendship itself. Equally, to appreciate what genuinely counts
as an achievement, we need some fix on the idea of what makes a goal valuable, and
often this will involve the way it furthers elements of human well-being other than
achievement itself. Indeed, at a further level of complexity, we must also register the
way in which prudence and morality inter-penetrate, so that even basic prudential values, such as friendship, are structured by recognizably moral concerns. But even if the
full specification of prudential interests characteristically has a moral dimension, we
must take care for the purposes of the basic schema not to presuppose the very human
right whose existence we are seeking to determine. More generally, we can insist on a
specification of the interest such that the significance accorded to its moral dimension
is primarily self-regarding (for example, how being able to discharge my responsibilities as a parent enhances *my* life).

It is worth elaborating on this point about holism in relation to the prudential value
of freedom—by which I mean the value of exercising one's rational capacities in choosing and pursuing worthwhile goals from a suitably broad range of options.[12] This is
because of the uniquely intimate relation that some theorists have posited between
freedom and human rights. Let us consider, somewhat artificially, both directions of
penetration in turn. As noted earlier, freedom involves being able to choose and pursue what one takes to be worthwhile goals; but there are evaluative constraints on what
is plausibly treated as a goal of this sort. Some of this evaluation will be non-prudential
in character; it will relate to non-prudential goods such as justice and beauty; some of
it will be prudential, referring to other prudential goods such as knowledge, friendship, and so on. Contrast with these goods the freedom to drive the wrong way down a
one-way street or to torture people for fun, neither of which are valuable goals. Hence,
one way of enhancing people's freedom is by increasing the number of their options
that are valuable in these various ways. By contrast, multiplying trivial or morally
depraved options does not enhance their freedom.

Second, freedom is often implicated in our engagement with other values, transforming their nature and significance in the process. Pursuit of deep personal relations, or achievement, takes on a different aspect when these activities embody the
free choice of individuals. It is difficult to deny, for example, that the value of deep

---

[11] Versions have been defended by Finnis, *Natural Law and Natural Rights*, J. Griffin, *Value Judgement:
Improving our Ethical Beliefs* (Oxford: Oxford University Press, 1996), and M. Nussbaum, *Women and
Human Development: The Capabilities Approach* (Cambridge: Cambridge University Press, 2000).

[12] By 'freedom' I mean to refer compendiously to the two values that James Griffin separates out as 'autonomy' and 'liberty', although I speak more broadly of 'worthwhile goals' than 'conceptions of the good life'.

personal relations can be realized even within a relationship which has not been freely embarked upon, and which cannot be freely exited, such as an arranged marriage. Yet the romantic ideal of marriage as a voluntary union transforms and enhances the value of the ensuing relationship. Even something as rudimentary as the conditions for preserving one's animal being—such as our interest in adequate nutrition—acquires a different character through the exercise of our capacity to choose what and how to eat and with whom.[13] Some have even advanced the sweeping conjecture that autonomous engagement with other values is in general a necessary condition of their contributing intrinsically to our well-being.[14] This seems plausible in some cases: it is questionable, for example, that forcing a person to engage in religious observances makes any intrinsic contribution to their welfare. But it is less plausible in others: even a forced marriage, one that neither party can exit without incurring severe social censure, may realize the good of friendship, and similarly an unwilling pupil's life may be enhanced by the knowledge he is forced to acquire. So, we can register the special, pervasive significance of freedom without endorsing this additional claim.

This pervasive significance of freedom also emerges in the way that many human rights protect our ability to make choices from a range of valuable options, including the choice not to take up any of these options. The right to marry and have a family does not simply entitle one to get married and have a family but to choose whom one marries or whether one gets married or has a family at all; likewise, the right to freedom of religion protects not only one's choice of religious affiliation, from a very broad range, but also the choice to reject any such affiliation. The nature and extent of the contribution made by freedom to the existence and content of human rights will naturally differ from one right to another. For example, although the right to work may include a right to some degree of choice from a range of occupational options, it may not include, as in the case of the right to marry or to freedom of religion, a right to abstain from any work at all. The content of the right not to be tortured, by contrast, may be totally inattentive to the choices of the right-holder.

It might be thought that the pluralist's basic justificatory schema offers an account of the grounds of human rights that dispenses with any reliance on the controversial notion of human dignity. Although this might be perceived as a merit of the approach, interpreting it in this way is a mistake. The interests on which the pluralist account draws are always the interests of individual human beings, and understanding their normative significance requires that we grasp the intrinsically valuable status equally possessed by all human beings, one grounded in the fact that they are humans. What emerges is a form of the interest-based theory which regards the interests in question as generative of human rights in crucial part because they are the interests of human beings who possess equal moral status: human dignity and universal human interests

---

[13] The Aristotelian idea that even humans' 'animal' functions and needs are transformed by the distinctively human capacity to pursue them through the use of reason and in community with others, which is also a prominent theme in the writings of Marx, has been helpfully emphasized by Martha Nussbaum in *Women and Human Development*, 71ff.

[14] Thus, it has been argued that 'nothing counts as an accomplishment…unless it is one's own choosing…Understanding, in the relevant sense, can only be autonomous', J. Griffin, *On Human Rights* (Oxford: Oxford University Press, 2009), 151.

are equally fundamental grounds of human rights, characteristically bound together in their operation.[15]

What it is to be a human being, the ontological basis of human dignity, is an inexhaustible topic. But in broad outline it consists in the fact that humans belong to a species which is in turn characterized by a variety of capacities and features: a characteristic form of embodiment; a finite life-span of a certain rough duration; capacities for physical growth and reproduction; psychological capacities, such as perception, self-consciousness, and memory; and, specifically rational capacities, such as the capacities for language-use, for registering a diverse range of normative considerations (including evaluative considerations, prudential, moral, aesthetic, and others besides), and for aligning one's judgments, emotions, and actions with those considerations. Call this the human nature conception of human dignity, insofar as it grounds the value of human dignity in the characteristic elements that constitute human nature. It is worth observing that, complex and elusive as they are, the heterogeneous facts listed here can be gleaned by a phenomenology of human life that does not obviously implicate scientific or metaphysical conjectures about an underlying, historically invariant human nature or essence.

Two significant implications of this conception of human dignity are worth highlighting. First, it consists in an equality of basic *moral* status among human beings, affirming a fundamental level of moral regard at which they enjoy an equal importance as human beings. It does not, in itself, consist in any claim about the social, political or legal status that should be conferred upon them.[16] Indeed, historically, defenders of human dignity, or the basic moral equality of human beings, such as the Stoics, Aquinas, Locke, and Kant, have espoused some strikingly inegalitarian doctrines regarding social, political, and legal status, ranging from the exclusion of women from political participation to the acceptance of some form of slavery. But even if these practices are inconsistent with human dignity, this can only be shown by

---

[15] George Kateb has also defended a structurally similar grounding of human rights in which two elements—the 'existential' element of equal individual status (one of the aspects of human dignity, along with the stature of the human species) and the 'moral' element of minimizing pain and suffering—operate together, each 'doing indispensable work', G. Kateb, *Human Dignity* (Cambridge, MA: Harvard University Press, 2011), 39. I differ from him in my characterization of the two grounding elements. For me, the recognition of the equal dignity of each individual is itself a moral notion. Kateb, however, construes morality as essentially concerned with pain and suffering, which has the unfortunate consequence that other universal interests, beyond the avoidance of pain and suffering, are not given their due in the foundations of human rights. Rather closer to my view is the account of human dignity, and its relationship to human rights, advanced by 'new natural law' theorists, eg, J. Finnis, *Aquinas: Moral, Political, and Legal Theory* (New York: Oxford University Press, 1998), 176–80 and 'Equality and Differences', *Solidarity: The Journal of Catholic Social Thought and Secular Ethics*, 2 (2012), 1–22, and P. Lee and R.P. George, 'The Nature and Basis of Human Dignity', *Ratio Juris*, 21 (2008), 173–93. But there are also some important differences, among them: I separate much more sharply the attribution of the status of human dignity from the attribution of human rights and I do not treat possession of a rational nature as a necessary condition for the capacity to have moral rights, hence allowing for the possibility that non-human animals may have rights.

[16] This distinction is marked by Rawls, who insists on the difference between 'equality as it is invoked in connection with the distribution of certain goods, some of which will almost certainly give higher status or prestige to those who are more favoured, and equality as it applies to the respect which is owed to persons irrespective of social position', J. Rawls, *A Theory of Justice* (Oxford: Oxford University Press, 1999), 447.

means of a substantive argument that draws out the social and other implications of that underlying moral status. The claim of human dignity is not in and of itself a claim about any such social status, just as human rights may have political implications, but are not themselves inherently political claims.[17] Second, the possession of this status is contingent on the possession of a human nature. The value of human dignity is therefore equally shared by human beings despite other ethically salient differences among them, such as those that bear on matters of personal desert or virtue. Someone with profoundly underdeveloped or impaired rational capacities (for example, a newborn baby or a sufferer of advanced senile dementia) has this status no less than someone with exceptional intellectual capacities (a scientific genius), since both equally share a human nature, and the same applies to someone who has neglected the development of their capacities or committed wrongs against others. What matters, so far as human dignity is concerned, is that they all equally belong to a species that has certain characteristic features and capacities.

Of course, considerably more needs to be said about the content, and ontological basis, of human dignity. Here I indicate only two key respects in which it operates within the basic schema. It is a presupposition of that schema that human beings have the capacity to possess moral rights. As Joseph Raz has argued, a necessary condition for any individual's capacity to have rights, leaving aside artificial agents such as corporations, is that their existence and well-being have intrinsic and non-derivative value.[18] Beings with the capacity to possess rights are in this way sources of ultimate moral concern. Now, the value of human dignity is one way, albeit not the only way, of satisfying this general condition for rights-bearing capacity. Beings who belong to the human species are one type of being with the capacity to possess rights. Their existence and welfare has intrinsic or non-instrumental value, rather than merely having value in virtue of their causal consequences; and this intrinsic value is not exhausted by the constitutive role they play in sustaining the existence or advancing the interests of some other being. Human beings matter in themselves, and so satisfy a necessary condition for possessing rights, whereas entities such as the collection of water molecules or the man-made receptacle in which they are contained do not. Second, if we understand the interests on which human rights are grounded as belonging to individuals who share equally in the status of human dignity, we can start to make sense of the characteristic resistance to trade-offs displayed by human rights. If human beings matter in themselves, as sources of ultimate moral concern, each potentially with their own life to lead, then it is a travesty simply to 'detach' their interests from them with a view to maximizing the overall fulfilment of interests across persons. The individuals with these interests count in themselves and not because the satisfaction or frustration of their interests is ultimately assimilated to some overarching aggregative concern.

Like universal human interests, basic human dignity is a ground for human rights but is not itself to be identified with human rights. Instead, the value of human dignity

---

[17] cf Jeremy Waldron's recent conjecture that human dignity is principally a juridical notion that attributes to all human beings a 'high-ranking legal, political, and social status', J. Waldron, *Dignity, Rank, and Rights* (Oxford: Oxford University Press, 2012), 47.
[18] Raz, *The Morality of Freedom*, 176–80.

forms part of the indispensable moral background to the vindication of such rights. That the idea of equal human dignity is distinct from the human rights it grounds emerges by reflecting on the case of the liberal racist. This could be someone whose attitudes and behaviour unmistakably express the fact that they do not regard blacks as of equal moral worth to whites, perhaps because of a racist upbringing, but who disowns these racist attitudes and does nothing that we should be inclined to describe as a human rights violation. Instead, his lack of respect for blacks is revealed by distress at the prospect of one of his children marrying a black person or frostiness towards his black neighbours. In neither case, however, would it make obvious sense to regard this individual as breaching anyone's rights in virtue of his racist attitudes and behaviour.

That human dignity is a ground of human rights, as of interpersonal morality in general, does not prevent it from playing a more prominent role in the shaping of some moral standards, including some human rights, as compared with others. This is because some moral standards are more directly protective of equal human status than others. One type of case consists of moral prohibitions against the discriminatory treatment of various classes of people—women, gays, ethnic and religious minorities, the poor—insofar as it reflects the odious idea that, simply in virtue of belonging to these classes, such people do not 'count' morally as much as others. Another type of case is those norms that prohibit certain forms of degrading or humiliating treatment of the sort that is sometimes aptly described as reducing humans to the level of non-human animals. However, in neither of these cases need we suppose that human dignity is the only operative value in grounding the relevant moral standard. If some standards are exclusively grounded in the value of human dignity, they are most likely to be those prohibiting certain kinds of purely symbolic wrong—attitudes and conduct that give expression to the idea that certain people lack equal human dignity without threatening their interests. Plausibly, such a wrong is committed when neo-Nazi thugs desecrate a Jewish cemetery, giving vent to their belief in the sub-human status of the people buried there. But it is hardly a coincidence that arguably no human rights violation is perpetrated in this case and the reason for this is the difficulty of regarding the dead as having interests capable of being harmed.[19] There is no compulsion to resolve the question either way, however. The key point is that human dignity has an indispensable role in justifying human rights, but that it characteristically plays this role in intimate alliance with universal human interests. We should reject as false the choice between a status-based or dignitarian account of human rights and an interest-based account.

III. The Threshold

A vital feature of an interest-based account of human rights, along the lines of the pluralist theory sketched in the previous section is that it does not equate human

---

[19] For a related discussion of human dignity and the treatment of human corpses, see M. Rosen, *Dignity: Its History and Meaning* (Cambridge, MA: Harvard University Press, 2012), ch. 3. However, I think that Rosen concludes too quickly that human dignity is not foundational for human rights, partly because he considers it as an exclusive basis for such rights and does not entertain the possibility that it characteristically performs its grounding role in tandem with universal human interests.

rights either with the universal interests of human beings or with the principle that they possess an equal share in human dignity. Most fundamentally, this is because the pluralist approach offers a claim about the *grounding* of human rights, not a *semantic* claim about the concept of human rights. Still, it might be thought that the link it asserts between interests and rights is so immediate that the right in effect consists in the interest, with the result that infringing the former straightforwardly amounts to impairing the latter.[20] But this is a gross caricature of the interest-based approach. Instead, as premises (ii) and (iii) of the basic schema make clear, any universal interests of human beings must first pass a crucial threshold before a human right is generated. The threshold requires an affirmative answer to the question: do the specified universal interests of human beings, all of them bearers of equal moral worth, generate in the case of each and every one of them duties to secure the object of the putative right? And duties are here to be understood as moral reasons of a special kind: categorical, exclusionary, and subject to an array of moral responses—such as blame, guilt, etc—in light of their violation. If the answer is affirmative, then there is a human right to that object. Although the precise allocation and specification of the duties may be subject to legitimate variation from case to case, it is the fact that the self-same object—for example, a certain level of access to health care or a certain degree of freedom to express one's political and religious beliefs—is to be secured as a matter of duty for all that justifies the assertion of a unitary human right. It is their having crossed this threshold that distinguishes human rights from a mere shopping list of valuable 'goals'.

It is doubtful, however, that there is a great deal that can be helpfully said, at the abstract level at which philosophers customarily operate, about the threshold at which universal interests give rise to duties to deliver the objects of putative rights. As we should expect, philosophy is best confined to articulating the variety of considerations that bear on the question of the threshold and the relations among them, rather than striving to offer a litmus test that would enable us to dispense with any resort to contestable judgments. Moreover, we should acknowledge that at the level of pure moral reasoning, there may be an ineliminable indeterminacy in the deontic content of any given right, even one we are confident exists, so that the formulation of a practically workable standard will require us to supplement such reasoning with positive legal norms or social conventions. This indeterminacy characterizes moral norms quite generally and is hardly unique to human rights.

With these caveats in mind, we can shed some light on the nature of the threshold by distinguishing two parts (premises (ii) and (iii)), the first of which relates to the existence of a pro tanto case for a duty, the second of which affirms or rejects that case in light of the supposed duty's feasibility. The two stages are meant to register two

---

[20] cf G.A. Cohen's comment on Raz's interest-based theory of rights: '[T]he justification of the right by the interest is so immediate on this different and nonaggregative view that it would seem bizarre to say that honouring the right is a matter of justice but satisfying the interest is not', G.A. Cohen, *Rescuing Justice and Equality* (Cambridge, MA: Harvard University Press, 2008), 290. As argued later, the self-same interest, eg, in health, may be set back in ways that involve a rights violation (eg, by not providing a person with an adequate standard of health care) and in ways which do not (eg, by not providing that person with the highest attainable standard of health care).

broad categories of obstacles to the derivation of a duty from the relevant set of interests, which might be called internal and external respectively. At stage (ii), a pro tanto case for the existence of a duty depends on the absence of certain internal impediments to such a duty. They are internal obstacles just in the sense that they do not take into consideration any interests beyond those of the putative right-holders (and only their interests *qua* right-holders, prescinding from the question of how the recognition of the right may affect them as a potential duty-bearers). One such obstacle is that the object of the supposed right cannot be secured to the right-holder, because it is impossible to do so. The impossibility may be logical, metaphysical or empirical (in the specified socio-historical context). Thus, there is no right to be both alive and dead at the same time, no right to give birth irrespective of one's sex, and no right to inter-galactic space travel.

In determining what is *possible* for these purposes, we ask what is generally compossible by way of duty-fulfilment in the case of all supposed right-holders. Here we depart from Jeremy Waldron's suggestion that, in justifying rights claims, one need consider only whether the fulfilment of any given individual's right, taken in isolation, is possible. Addressing familiar objections to 'welfare rights' that invoke insufficient resources and capabilities to satisfy the positive duties such rights would impose, Waldron observes:

> The problems posed by scarcity and underdevelopment only arise when we take all the claims of right together. It is not the duties in each individual case which demand the impossible (as it would be for example, if we talked about a right to happiness); rather it is the combination of all the duties taken together that cannot be fulfilled. But one of the important features of rights discourse is that rights are attributed to individuals one by one, not collectively or in the aggregate.[21]

Waldron is correct that the positive case for a human right stems from the normative significance of each person's interests considered individually, rather than some aggregative function of many persons' interests. This is the vital non-aggregative dimension of the interest-based approach that is often ignored by its deontological critics. But given that the rights in question are supposedly *human rights*—rights possessed by all human beings simply in virtue of their humanity—their being possessed by any one human being must be compatible with their being simultaneously possessed by all others within the specified socio-historical context. Hence, the fulfilment of all their rights, through compliance with the counterpart duties, must be generally compossible (although this general constraint leaves open the possibility of practical conflicts involving unfulfillable rights in specific circumstances). Therefore, on the grounds of impossibility, we can rule out a right to live in luxury, construed as imposing a positive duty to provide the right-holder with all the trappings for a luxurious lifestyle, since given limited material resources, this is not possible for all. But it is highly likely, on this basis, that we can affirm a right to an *adequate* standard of living and many other standard welfare rights. Moreover, this conclusion leaves it open that, *qua* members of

---

[21] J. Waldron, 'Rights in Conflict', in his *Liberal Rights: Collected Papers 1981–1991* (Cambridge: Cambridge University Press, 1993), 208.

particular polities, rather than simply in virtue of their humanity, some people may have a right to a more-than-adequate standard of living.

Another internal limit to the existence of human rights relates to cases of what might be called *evaluative* impossibilities. Here, the very idea of having a *duty* to deliver the relevant object of the putative right seems inappropriate in terms of the the right-holder's own interests. The starkest case is one in which imposing a duty would destroy the value of the object of the right to the right-holder. Consider, for example, the way in which our interests are served by being the object of another's romantic love. Can this interest generate a positive duty on the part of others to love us romantically? Any such duty is incompatible with the way in which romantic love enhances our lives. Romantic love is one of the valuable aspects of human life regarding which the notion of a duty to bestow it, and the kind of moral assessment such a duty entails, is inherently out of place. It is not merely that feelings of romantic love are not manifestly subject to control by their subjects. After all, a modern-day equivalent of Puck's potion in *A Midsummer Night's Dream* might be invented, a drug that could bring about romantic feelings towards pre-determined persons. Rather, the idea is that the way romantic love serves our interests is inconsistent with its being motivated by, or properly subject to, critical evaluation in terms of a moral duty to experience it towards specified persons. Romantic love is valuable as a freely bestowed gift, a spontaneous expression of the lover's own deepest desires, rather than something one is obligated to deliver. Another way of putting it would be to say that the recognition of such a duty would be self-defeating, seeking to deliver the object of the putative right by eliminating a feature inextricably bound up with the distinctive value possessed by that object. In making romantic love an object of duty, and moreover one that can be demanded by right, we do violence to its nature: the supposed right-holder stands to receive only the pitiful simulacra of such love rather than the genuine article.

Other cases in which the right-holder's interests themselves bar the recognition of a *duty* to deliver the object of a putative right do not rely on the idea that the duty is constitutively self-defeating in undermining the value to the right-holder of the object of his supposed right. Consider, for example, the claim that there is a human right to the highest attainable standard of mental and physical health, one that includes a positive duty to ensure that the right-holder enjoys this formidably robust level of health. Now, such a right might be ruled out on the simple grounds of impossibility: if the highest attainable standard is construed as an absolute standard, then it may be empirically impossible to bring all people, irrespective of their genetic make-up, up to this very high level of health. One might respond by relativizing the standard of health, so that it is taken as the highest attainable standard of health for each and every person in light of their particular genetic constitution. But even such a right might be precluded, because a duty to deliver its object would be incompatible with the interests in autonomy of the right-holder. This is because it would validate repeated interventions in the latter's life—overriding his will on health-affecting choices such as diet, occupation, leisure activities, and so on—that constitute an unacceptable curtailment of his autonomy. At best, it would seem, we could affirm a right of access to the highest attainable standard of mental and physical *health care*, rather than health itself, leaving it in significant part to the discretion of the right-holder (within certain limits) whether or not to avail themselves of such care.

But even if a putative duty does not fall at the hurdles of impossibility or internal principled objections of the sort we have just canvassed, the case for it may still be defeated at the second level, at which we register the implications of the supposed right on the interests of duty-bearers and on other values. Let us subsume these implications under the heading of 'burdensomeness'. What is in question is the joint feasibility of the supposed duties generated severally by each and every supposed right-holder. Consider again the supposed human right to the highest attainable standard of physical and mental health care. A duty to provide this seems neither obviously impossible to deliver nor unsupported by the interests of the putative right-holder *qua* right-holder, whether his interests in health care itself or more generally. So, a pro tanto case for the existence of a duty to deliver this object, arising from the interests of each and every human being, may well survive the first stage of the threshold. But now at the second stage we ask whether this duty is excessively burdensome. Is the case for recognizing it defeated because the supposed duty imposes excessive burdens on potential duty-bearers, in terms of other values, including excessive sacrifices in our ability to fulfil other human rights? It seems unlikely that a human right to the highest attainable standard of health care can be sustained on the grounds of feasibility. Any duty of health care that arises from our interests in it, therefore, will be considerably less demanding than the readings of 'highest attainable' canvassed so far. Something similar may be said of a positive duty of romantic love, even if I was mistaken in claiming that a pro tanto case could not be made for its existence.

At this point it is worth underlining the significance of the fact that the interests in question are not free-floating, but are rather the interests of beings with an equal share in human dignity. Two features ultimately trace back to this crucial fact. The first is that we cannot determine whether or not a putative right exists by means of a cost–benefit analysis that simply aggregates across persons. We cannot, for example, argue that there is a human right to be able compulsorily to acquire essential human organs if one is in need of a transplant, on the grounds that such a right maximizes interest-fulfilment overall. This would be to treat human beings as merely the 'locations' at which various interests are fulfilled or unfulfilled, ignoring the fact that, as humans, they merit a kind of respect that is far more exacting than the subsumption of their interests within an overarching aggregative function. Second, in assessing the costs associated with a putative right for the purpose of determining its existence, we should accord no weight to those costs that are in some significant sense attributable to mistaken moral beliefs on the part of would-be duty bearers. Among the most egregious cases are those in which the mistaken beliefs involve a denial of the equal dignity of the putative right-holders.

So, for example, there is a sense in which the rights not to be discriminated against on the grounds of race or sexual orientation may be 'costly' to people with racist or homophobic outlooks. Such people may be outraged at the prospect of black children attending the same school as their own children, or of gays being employed to teach their children. But these attitudes and beliefs are typically premised on a deep moral error—the inherent inferiority of blacks and gays—and should therefore be disregarded in determining whether a human right to non-discrimination exists. The alternative would be to put the existence of human rights at the mercy of warped beliefs that are inconsistent with the ethical considerations those rights are supposed to reflect. Accepting this second point is entirely consistent with factoring the excluded costs into an all-things-considered decision regarding whether, and to what extent, to demand compliance with those rights or embody them in law. So, if the homophobes are so hostile to the prospect of openly homosexual teachers that they are prepared to bring down the entire education system, rather than have their prejudices thwarted, the all-things-considered best course is not to insist on the strict implementation of the right to non-discrimination. This is a case in which the relevant human right is justifiably infringed with consequent obligations of apology and reparation. In this way, we preserve the important distinction between considerations that bear on the existence of human rights, and those that do not but which, given unfortunate circumstances, may lead to the demands of those rights being compromised or defeated in all-things-considered practical deliberation.

This general way of conceiving the threshold between interests (of beings of equal moral dignity) and human rights has two consequential advantages. First, it helps to account for the way in which human rights evolve over time. In making judgments of empirical possibility and burdensomeness, at respectively the first and second stages of the threshold test, reference is made to the socio-historical conditions that have been specified as the background to any attempt to deploy the pluralist approach. This means that our assessments as to empirical possibility and burden may quite properly shift over time, especially with the growth in our knowledge and the development of new technologies, modes of social and economic organization, and so on. Hence, there may now be a human right to positive assistance in reproduction, including access to IVF treatment, which did not exist prior to the development of IVF technology (or prior to the point at which its development became feasible). This gives us one benign interpretation of at least some of the 'proliferation' of human rights claims over the years. Equally, it enables us to see how, in light of the potential effects of population growth or climate change on our ability to serve people's interests, some existing human rights may eventually cease to apply to future generations.

Second, it helps us make sense of the idea that rights have a special *directed* quality, in that violations of them constitute the *wronging* of a specific individual, ie, the right-holder. Although we may all be legitimately aggrieved at wrongdoings committed against anyone, we recognize that the person whose right has been violated is legitimately aggrieved in a special way. This special standing manifests itself in the fact that some emotional responses, such as resentment, are paradigmatically if not exclusively responses available to victims of rights violations, and also in the fact that the victim of a rights violation has certain moral powers over the wrongdoer, such as the granting of forgiveness or, in some cases, the power to waive performance of the duty associated with the right. What the directedness of the right ultimately comes down to, on the interest-based view, is the fact that its counterpart duty has its source exclusively in the interests of the right-holder. This means that only the interests of the right-holder, and not anyone else's interests, need to be invoked as part of the positive case for the right's existence. It is a wronging of *him* insofar as the duty violated owes its existence exclusively to his interests as a being of equal moral status.

Consider, by contrast, 'imperfect' duties, such as those of charity, which lack a right-holder. Judges may have a duty to be merciful in sentencing, but we should not normally say that a properly convicted criminal has a *right* to merciful treatment, ie, to be punished less severely than he deserves given the gravity of the offence he has committed. The reason for this is that his interest in such leniency is not sufficient to generate a duty to show him mercy given the pre-existing duty of retributive justice to inflict a deserved punishment.[22] Still, there may yet be a sound case for a duty of mercy, one that affords a compelling basis for tempering the demands of justice in particular cases, but it will have to draw on considerations that go beyond the benefit to the wrongdoer, such as the way in which various aspects of the common good are advanced by showing mercy to certain categories of criminals, for example, those who have already repented of their wrongdoing. Compare the right not to be subjected to a sentence in excess of that which is deserved in light of the gravity of one's wrongdoing. This is a strong candidate for recognition as a human right precisely because the interests of the offender in avoiding such punishment arguably generate duties that pre-empt or exclude, at least in the standard cases that bear on the content of the duty, many of the social benefits of inflicting it, such as those of incapacitation or general deterrence.

We can now appreciate the deceptive simplicity of some of the slogans in terms of which the interest-based approach to (human) rights has been presented, both by critics and defenders. Thus, it is a mistake to suppose that the pluralist's basic schema depends upon the idea that a right will be generated by an interest provided only that the interest in question is in some independent sense 'important'.[23] Few things, after all, can claim to be more 'important' to our flourishing than romantic love. But the notion of 'importance' here is not only rather amorphous, it also bears no suitable rights-generative interpretation. Instead, the interest must have a very specific *kind* of moral importance, namely, it must be capable of generating a duty, as partially explained by premises (ii) and (iii)—and, since we are speaking here of human rights, it must be a duty in the case of each and every human being simply in virtue of their humanity.

We should also handle with care the seductive idea that interest-based accounts regard human rights as securing the 'conditions of a minimally good life' rather than a good life itself.[24] This slogan contains a grain of truth. Whether or not we achieve a

---

[22] See J. Tasioulas, 'Punishment and Repentance', *Philosophy*, 81 (2006), 279–322. The situation here is potentially rather complex; as Raz indicates, sometimes the systematic presence of conflicting reasons may not undermine the existence of the right but, instead, qualify its content: 'Where the conflicting considerations override those on which the right is based on some but not on all occasions, the general core right exists but the conflicting considerations may show that some of its possible derivations do not', *The Morality of Freedom*, 184.

[23] cf K. Eddy, 'On Revaluing the Currency of Human Rights', *Politics, Philosophy, and Economics*, 6 (2007): 307–28, 314.

[24] See J. Nickel, *Making Sense of Human Rights* (Oxford: Blackwell, 2007), 138: 'Human rights are not ideals of the good life for humans; they are rather concerned with ensuring the conditions, negative and positive, of a minimally good life'.

good life is to a significant degree down to our own attitudes, choices, and conduct, but whether our human rights are respected is fundamentally a matter of whether others comply with the duties corresponding to those rights. But the slogan is misleading insofar as it suggests that we need an independent grip on the 'conditions of a minimally good life' in order to identify which putative human rights meet the threshold requirements set out in premises (ii) and (iii). On the contrary, the explanation goes in the opposite direction: human rights are such 'minimum conditions' precisely in virtue of satisfying, inter alia, the demands of (ii) and (iii). They are those conditions of a good life that can, in the case of everybody, be demanded as of right simply in virtue of our humanity. The alternative reading would leave an interest-based account vulnerable to the accusation that it is incapable of validating prominent elements of the contemporary human rights culture, such as anti-discrimination rights. This is because we can intelligibly interpret the phrase 'conditions of a minimally good life' in ways that fall short of encompassing many of these rights. For example, one can enjoy a recognizably 'good life' despite being legally excluded, on the grounds of sex or religious creed, from occupying major public offices or openly expressing one's political beliefs.[25] But this complaint gets matters back-to-front. The only sense of 'minimum conditions' properly operative here is that given by the threshold from interests to duties; it therefore remains an open question to what extent anti-discrimination rights satisfy the criteria it imposes.

IV. Beyond Freedom and Necessity

The idea that human rights reflect certain minimal conditions or aspects of a good life, specifiable in advance of the operation of the threshold, is not so easily laid to rest. It informs two interest-based approaches to the grounding of human rights that are major rivals to the pluralist theory—the agency and needs theories. The agency theory restricts the human rights-generative interests to those in freedom or normative agency, while the needs theory confines them to basic human needs. Hence an extra test is introduced at the level of the input in premise (i) on the grounds that a plurality of objective and universal human interests—although in some sense undeniably important—does not adequately reflect the distinctive significance characteristic of human rights.[26] One consequence of this failure, according to agency and needs theories, is that the pluralist approach countenances more human rights norms than is desirable either in terms of the desiderata of fidelity to the wider human rights culture or ensuring the non-parochial character of our approved schedule of human rights.

James Griffin's *On Human Rights* is the most significant contemporary statement of the agency theory. It grounds the existence of human rights exclusively in the value

---

[25] See the critique of Nickel's theory along these lines in A. Buchanan, 'The Egalitarianism of Human Rights', *Ethics*, 120 (2010), 679–710.

[26] This is a widely shared intuition; e.g., Nickel insists that human rights norms enjoy 'importance' or 'high priority' because they protect 'things that are central to a decent life as a person', *Making Sense of Human Rights*, 70. Griffin, too, writes: 'There is a minimalist character to human rights, which different writers will explain in different ways. I explain it as coming from human rights' being protections not of a fully flourishing life but only of the more austere life of a normative agent', *On Human Rights*, 53.

of possessing, and being able reasonably effectively to exercise, the capacity for personhood or normative agency. Normative agency is in turn decomposed into the values of autonomy, liberty, and the minimum material provision that they require.[27] As for the needs theory, we may take David Miller's lucid formulation as our focus. It grounds human rights in *basic* human needs: conditions that human beings everywhere require in order to avoid harm, ie, to be able live a 'minimally decent life' in whichever society they happen to belong.[28]

A problem that arises for both theories, however, is that it is hardly obvious that we have a determinate grasp of the kind of 'minimalism' they claim to secure. For example, prescinding from the sorts of considerations set out in (ii) and (iii), how do we begin to identify the culturally universal conditions of a 'decent life'? What makes it the case, for example, that freedom of movement counts as such a condition but democratic political participation does not? And even if we agree with Miller that education is a condition of a decent life, how do we decide whether this means only basic primary education or extends to secondary and even tertiary education? Similarly, in the case of Griffin's agency theory, some critics have discerned a supposedly fatal ambiguity in his characterization of personhood. Sometimes this seems to consist in the bare capacity for intentional action together with some measure of its successful exercise, in which case even a slave's life could realize it. At other times, a richer conception of 'normative agency' is at work, one that requires the presence of a diverse array of genuinely valuable options from which to choose in shaping the contours of one's life, and enough liberty and material wherewithal to makes one's choices effective.[29] Whatever the merits of these objections, we should not simply take for granted that the 'minimalism' of either theory is well-defined. But even on the assumption that it is, serious difficulties remain.

---

[27] 'Human rights can then be seen as protections of our human standing or, as I shall put it, our personhood. And one can break down the notion of personhood into clearer components by breaking down the notion of agency. To be an agent, in the fullest sense of which we are capable, one must (first) choose one's own path through life—that is, not be dominated or controlled by someone or something else (call it "autonomy"). And (second) one's choice must be real; one must have at least a certain minimum education and information. And having chosen, one must then be able to act: that is, one must have at least the minimum provision of resources and capabilities that it takes (call all of this "minimum provision"). And none of this is any good if someone then blocks one; so (third) other must also not forcibly stop one from pursuing what one sees as a worthwhile life (call this "liberty")', Griffin, *On Human Rights*, 32–3. Although Griffin describes his theory as 'trinist', appealing to the three values of personhood: autonomy, liberty, and minimum provision (at 51), it is probably best to regard it as dualist, since minimum provision is invoked only as a condition for realizing the other two values.

[28] '[W]e prove that something is a human right by showing that right fulfils the [basic] needs of the right-holder...Basic needs...are to be understood by reference to this idea of a decent human life. They are the conditions that must be met for a person to have a decent life given the environmental conditions he faces. The list of such needs will include (but not be exhausted by): food and water, clothing and shelter, physical security, health care, education, work and leisure, freedoms of movement, conscience, and expression', D. Miller, *National Responsibility and Global Justice* (Oxford: Oxford University Press, 2008), 184.

[29] Such an equivocation is identified by Joseph Raz, 'Human Rights without Foundations', in S. Besson and J. Tasioulas (eds.), *The Philosophy of International Law* (Oxford: Oxford University Press, 2010) and Buchanan, 'The Egalitarianism of Human Rights'. My own view is that there is a charitable interpretation of Griffin's theory, according to which the austere interpretation of personhood is the condition for possessing human rights, while human rights protect both that capacity *and* its reasonably effective exercise.

To appreciate these difficulties, we can begin by noting that the agency and needs theories can both be interpreted in either of two broad ways. First, they are amenable to an essentially reductive interpretation, one that identifies human rights with the values of normative agency or basic needs. But this interpretation faces all the grave problems that arise for reductive views whose account of the nature of human rights does not treat them as a sub-class of moral rights in general.[30] In disregarding or downplaying the fact that human rights are rights, both theories on this interpretation would fail to capture the distinctive moral character of human rights discourse. One manifestation of this is that the reductive interpretation of both would lead to their countenancing a massive proliferation of 'human rights'. For example, provided some medical operation or cure was needed to save someone's life, and so was a basic need of theirs or indispensable to preserving their status as a normative agent, there would be a 'human right' to it, in spite of its potentially exorbitant cost.

So, we should adopt the second interpretation of the two theories, according to which human rights come into being only once the significance of the underlying needs or agency values crosses a threshold akin to (ii) and (iii) of the basic schema. This is broadly consonant with Griffin's claim that human rights characteristically—but not always[31]—have a *dual* foundation: in normative agency or personhood and 'practicalities'. These practicalities are a heterogeneous group of considerations that shape the content of a human right so it can be 'an effective, socially manageable claim on others'.[32] Griffin's account of practicalities is disappointingly terse, but it is endorsed, and helpfully elaborated upon, by Miller in such a way as to bring it rather close to premises (ii) and (iii) of the basic schema.[33] Let us proceed, then, on the basis that the restricted input of the agency and needs theories must be conjoined with a threshold—the broad equivalent of premises (ii) and (iii)—in generating human rights.

Does the fact that the pluralist approach allows universal interests, not just basic needs or interests in normative agency, to play a human rights-grounding role render it inferior to either the agency or needs theories? Prima facie, it would seem odd to suppose that it does. After all, assuming that universal interests beyond the category of basic needs or agency values are capable of satisfying the threshold requirements of (ii) and (iii), so that in the case of each human being they generated duties to serve those interests in various ways, what would justify withholding the description 'human right' from the resultant universal rights? In particular, what sense would there be in maintaining a bifurcated account of universal moral rights, one that turned on the prudential basis of the respective universal rights?[34] But rather than rest content with shifting the burden of proof onto agency and needs theorists, let me instead outline some of the ways in which the parsimoniousness of these theories makes them less attractive than the unrestricted pluralist approach.

---

[30] See Tasioulas, 'On the Nature of Human Rights'.
[31] Griffin, *On Human Rights*, 37. This qualification has to be dropped on the second interpretation.
[32] Griffin, *On Human Rights*, 38.
[33] Miller, *National Responsibility and Global Justice*, 186–94.
[34] In recent work, however, David Miller takes for granted as a 'fundamental intuition' the proposition that only needs can ground moral rights generally, see D. Miller, 'Grounding Human Rights', *Critical Review of International Social and Political Philosophy*, 15 (2012), 207–27, 422.

The first problem with the agency and needs theories is one of fidelity, and concerns their inability to vindicate certain key human rights. For example, Miller's theory is unable to encompass human rights that reflect vital interests, but which arguably do not plausibly protect basic human needs. Consider, for example, his treatment of religious freedom. Here, the operative basic need is freedom of conscience—'not being forced to live according to values that you cannot endorse, and that you may find repugnant'.[35] Leave aside the problematically subjective formulation of this supposed need—after all, what if I find laws enforcing moral prohibitions against murder and theft 'repugnant'? The key point is that according to Miller himself it generates a rather limited protection of religious freedom: it prevents one being forced to adopt religious practices or espouse religious beliefs that one does not endorse, but does not extend to the right to proselytize or establish a church.[36] The resultant freedom is modest compared to the extensive religious freedom many believe to be protected by the human right of freedom of conscience (or religion). Similar considerations apply to human rights prohibiting discrimination on the grounds of sex, religion, and political creed. For example, a society that excluded women or members of religious or political minorities from holding public office might not thereby imperil the satisfaction of their basic needs, even if in doing so it acts detrimentally to their interests.[37] By contrast, a pluralist is free to exploit the rights-generative power of all universal human interests within the discourse of human rights. In the case of Griffin, the problem with fidelity arises not so much in the grounding of standard rights, but in securing their scope of application. As interpreted by Griffin, the agency theory attributes human rights to human beings only to the extent that they have the actual rather than merely the potential capacity for normative agency. As a result, newborn babies and those suffering from profound mental disabilities are excluded from the scope of human rights protection. Griffin regards these exclusions as welcome confirmations of the determinateness of sense secured by his theory: we can mobilize other vocabulary, that of cruelty, murder, etc, to characterize the moral wrong in these cases.[38] But, on the one hand, this seems to confuse determinateness with parsimoniousness; and, on the other hand, it appears to exact a serious cost in fidelity to ordinary modes of thought that have a strong grip on us, such as the idea that torturing babies violates their human rights. The pluralist, by contrast, is better placed to extend the protection of at least some human rights, such as the right not to be tortured, to human beings who are not agents, because it can appeal directly to their non-agency interests, such as the avoidance of pain.

But perhaps the deepest difficulty for both theories concerns not their inability to ground standard human rights, in terms of content and scope, but the counter-intuitively circuitous and precarious justifications they offer for many such rights. There is no human right more paradigmatic than the right not to be tortured. In conformity

---

[35] Miller, *National Responsibility and Global Justice*, 196.
[36] Miller, *National Responsibility and Global Justice*, 196.
[37] Miller, 'Grounding Human Rights', 421, where he claims that the need for recognition does not ground a 'strong, universal, right of non-discrimination', since it can be met by securing recognition for people as members of 'status groups'.
[38] Griffin, *On Human Rights*, ch. 4.

with common sense, this right can be defended within the pluralist account as resting directly, but not exclusively, on the victim's interest in avoiding severe pain. By contrast, for the agency theorist, the pain of torture can only bear indirectly on the justification of that right, ie, insofar as it impacts adversely on our personhood by 'render[ing] us unable to decide for ourselves or to stick to our decision'.[39] The point extends to not quite so paradigmatic human rights, such as those to education, work, and leisure (resting, in key part, on our interests in knowledge, accomplishment, and play, respectively). To this a pluralist may add the *ad hominem* observation that Griffin's rich understanding of personhood values—the way in which he conceives of autonomy as the capacity to choose among *intelligible* conceptions of a worthwhile life, and of liberty as the unimpeded pursuit of such choices—already implicates judgments about human interests beyond strictly those of normative agency. Consider, by way of illustration, Griffin's heavy reliance on the values of deep personal relations and accomplishment when vindicating a human right to same-sex marriage.[40] The pluralist account therefore elaborates a tendency already latent in Griffin's agency, but one which is disguised by his official commitment to an agency theory of human rights.

The needs theory also gives counter-intuitively roundabout and precariously contingent justifications of standard human rights norms. Many classic civil and political rights cannot be plausibly grounded directly in basic intrinsic needs; instead, they will have to be given a derivative justification in terms of securing *other* human rights, such as the right to bodily security, which do enjoy a direct grounding in such needs.[41] Such derivative groundings of key human rights not only rely on often controversial empirical premises, for example, that rights to political participation or a fair trial are as a contingent matter 'necessary' to guarantee rights of bodily security or subsistence, etc. They are also strikingly counter-intuitive insofar as they deny that rights of the former sort can be made to stand on their own feet, justifying them instead exclusively as means for securing other rights that do possess a direct grounding in basic needs. Surely political rights 'matter' independently of how they serve rights to bodily security, subsistence, etc, and their so mattering should at least in principle count in favour of their status as human rights. The pluralist's basic schema for grounding human rights, by contrast, allows greater scope for the possibility of a non-derivative grounding of classic civil and political rights by lifting the embargo on invoking interests that are not basic needs. We can therefore appeal to our interests in autonomy and communal identification, for example, in order to ground civil and political rights.

We may conclude by reflecting on two possible rejoinders on behalf of the agency and needs theories. An agency theorist might challenge the claimed superiority of

[39] Griffin, *On Human Rights*, 52.   [40] Griffin, *On Human Rights*, 163–4.

[41] 'It is clear that (intrinsic) needs can only play an indirect role in justifying most civil and political rights. If we start from the conditions that human beings everywhere require to avoid harm, then although we can move directly to rights such as bodily security and freedom of movement, other rights will prove to be important only as secondary protections for these more basic conditions. Political rights, for example, will matter if it can be shown that the possession and exercise of these rights is necessary in order to guarantee rights to bodily security, subsistence, and so forth'. Miller, *National Responsibility and Global Justice*, 195. See also Miller, 'Grounding Human Rights', 421–2.

pluralism on the grounds of both fidelity and distinctive importance. Thus, Griffin contends that something like an unrestricted, interest-based approach would be excessively permissive, conniving at human rights 'proliferation' by promoting a bloated conception of human rights that threatens to 'fill most of the domain of well-being'.[42] If well-grounded, this would be a powerful objection; but Griffin does little to substantiate his claim. After all, the pluralist's basic schema offers a framework aimed precisely at drawing a genuine distinction between human interests, on the one hand, and what they entitle all of us to as a matter of right, on the other. To say, as Griffin does, that pluralism 'undermines our belief that we have a human right to material and cultural resources only up to a minimum acceptable level beyond which they are *not* a matter of right' is simply to reject, without argument, the efficacy of premises such as (ii) and (iii) in establishing this distinction. But, as we have already noted, such a denial would be devastating for Griffin's own theory, since it too presupposes something like the threshold embodied by those two premises.[43]

Perhaps Griffin's real objection is a simpler one of infidelity. He may believe that pluralism countenances as 'human rights' a whole host of entitlements that have never appeared in the canonical human rights documents and, in Griffin's case, form no part of the 'Enlightenment' human rights tradition. This is one way of reading his case of the callous spouse: 'One partner in an unsuccessful marriage, for example, might treat the other coldly and callously, and the suffering caused the second partner over the years might mount up into something much worse than a short period of physical torture. The first partner, however, simply by being cruel, does not thereby violate the second's human rights'.[44] Now, it would certainly be odd to claim that we can give a *full* explanation of the wrongness of such behaviour solely by appealing to the violation of human rights. But the pluralist is committed to no such claim. On the contrary, there will be values, and even rights, violated by cruelty and cold indifference within marriage which are not recognizably *human* rights. This is because their existence arises from the fact that the spouses are parties to a special relationship, rather than being rights possessed simply in virtue of our humanity.

A pluralist might stop there, and simply deny that the callous spouse case, as described by Griffin, involves any human rights violation. More plausibly, he might venture a somewhat more complex explanation. There may indeed be a human right against being subject to cruel treatment, and some forms of cruelty within marriage may constitute a violation of it. But it does not follow that all the rights that the spouses have against each other not to be subject to cruel treatment are themselves human rights, even if their violation is a way of violating the broader right, which is a human right. This is because they do not have the former rights simply in virtue of

---

[42] Griffin, *On Human Rights*, 55.

[43] That the agency theory requires such a threshold is something Griffin occasionally acknowledges, eg, 'The place where we fix the limits of these demands [of duties corresponding to human rights] is not easy either to decide or defend. But, again, this is not a problem special to human rights', *On Human Rights*, 106. But precisely the same point is available to the pluralist, as Griffin elsewhere implicitly acknowledges, *On Human Rights*, 47.

[44] Griffin, *On Human Rights*, 52. For a helpful discussion of this and other cases invoked by Griffin against a more pluralist interest-based grounding of human rights, see S. Matthew, 'Agency and Human Rights', *Journal of Applied Philosophy*, 27 (2010), 15–25.

their humanity, but in part because of the special relationship of marriage. The situation is comparable to the way in which the denial of a vote to a citizen of a democratic society may be a violation of their human right to political participation, even though there is no *human right* to vote as such.[45] Moreover, there are other considerations at stake in a case of marital cruelty—considerations such as mutual trust, personal love, and the significance of a commitment to a shared life—that go beyond anything contemplated by the discourses either of human rights or rights more generally, but which are germane to the wrongfulness of the callous spouse's conduct.

Compare Griffin's analysis. He claims a human rights violation will only emerge at the point at which the culpable spouse's behaviour 'starts to undermine the other's ability to function as an agent'.[46] This is because, according to Griffin, the break in the spectrum between something impacting on one's well-being, on the one hand, and generating a (human rights-based) duty, on the other, is marked by the point at which the values of normative agency are implicated. But as we have already seen in rejecting the reductive interpretation of the agency theory, this claim is mistaken. The mere fact that agency values are in play—and are even seriously threatened—in any given situation does not entail the existence of a right of any kind. Such a right will arise only if the significance of the values in that sort of case satisfies a threshold akin to premises (ii) and (iii). But a threshold of this sort is common ground between the pluralist and the agency theories. We should not, as Griffin is prone to do, conflate 'minimalism' at the level of prudential input (premise (i)) and insistence on a threshold at which any prudential values general rights (premises (ii) and (iii)). With that conflation skirted, the agency theory's relatively parsimonious account of the prudential basis of human rights stands revealed as not only under-motivated but also as distortive of the moral significance of human rights.

The objection from the needs theorist travels in the opposite direction: it accuses pluralism of *excessive* fidelity to existing human rights practice, at least in the large number of norms it seems prepared to countenance as genuine human rights. But—the response goes—many of these norms cannot be given a non-parochial justification. The needs theory, by contrast, is able to pick out from the general class of universal moral rights those that can be justified to all people, irrespective of cultural variations, because they are grounded in needs that all people have independently of which particular society they inhabit.

The problem with this line of argument centres on Miller's interpretation of the non-parochialism desideratum. If the kind of justification it calls for is one that purports to issue in an objectively true conclusion, then it seems that pluralism satisfies it, provided that the interests it appeals to in generating human rights are genuinely interests of all human beings irrespective of the particular society to which they belong. Now, there is room here to debate such questions as whether, in fact, all human beings simply in virtue of their humanity, and living in broadly modern circumstances, have interests that would directly justify a right of democratic political participation or extensive religious freedom. The important point is that nothing in the non-parochialism desideratum, interpreted as requiring an objective vindication

---

[45] Tasioulas, 'On the Nature of Human Rights', 39. [46] Griffin, *On Human Rights*, 56.

of human rights norms, necessitates the restriction of the grounds of human rights to basic needs.

However, Miller clearly regards the non-parochialism desideratum as involving more than a bare insistence on objectivity. Human rights must be capable of being justified *to* members of all diverse cultures, which means that the justification is one that 'connects to beliefs that they already hold'.[47] Now, it is far from obvious what sort of connection is contemplated here; however, it suffices to note two major problems for Miller's own version of this proposal. First, there is a serious risk that it may backfire. After all, it is arguable that many of the supposed basic needs he lists are not regarded as such by members of some cultures—or at least not in a way that extends equally to all human beings, whether male or female, believers or non-believers, and so on. Why suppose, for example, that a prohibition on female genital mutilation protects a basic need, given widespread cultural adherence to the practice?[48] Second, even if something like Miller's subjectivist constraint on justification can be stated in a cogent, non-self-undermining way, the question remains, why it should bear on the ultimate grounds of human rights. A natural alternative is to treat it as operating downstream from the question of grounds, playing an important role in guiding our judgments about the extent to which objectively grounded human rights should be established in international law or whether, and in what way, it is appropriate to enforce or more generally seek to implement those rights.

V. Conclusion

Human rights—understood as moral rights possessed by all human beings simply in virtue of their humanity—are grounded in the universal interests of their holders, all of whom possess the equal moral status of human dignity. This is a two-level pluralist account of the grounding of human rights, since it appeals to both moral (equal human dignity) and prudential (universal human interests) considerations, and allows a plurality of human interests to play a grounding role. One consequence of this view is that the distinctive character of human rights is given by their nature as universal moral rights and not by the underlying values that ground them. The idea that the special character of human rights involves a highly distinctive grounding, as developed in different ways by extreme and moderate foundationalists, should be discarded as an obstructive fantasy that has been projected by philosophers onto human rights morality.

---

[47] Miller, *National Responsibility and Global Justice*, 165.
[48] Miller, 'Grounding Human Rights', 424.

2

Response to John Tasioulas

Onora O'Neill

I. Justifying Human Rights

On first consideration the project of devising a philosophical justification for human rights looks quite odd. Human rights have a specific and recent origin, and the schedule of rights declared in the *Universal Declaration of Human Rights* of 1948 reflects the contingencies of that history. Those who framed the Declaration drew on earlier arguments for conceptions of natural rights and of the rights of man, but what they produced reflects a specific historical situation. The Declaration is a central part of the post-WWII settlement and the institutional structures it established. The rights declared were to be acknowledged by the accession of states to the United Nations, and later by their ratification of the more specific rights set out in the human rights Covenants of the late 1960s. It seems that the answer to the question "Why are human rights binding?" might be simply that the states of which we are citizens have agreed to them. This "justification" assumes the authority of states, and assumes that the relevant exercises of that authority have taken place. It brackets questions about any deeper normative justification of the standards that are set out in the human rights documents.

Nevertheless, the thought that human rights are no more than the assertions and standards of a particular historical moment, to which states have committed themselves (at least for the time being) is widely rejected. For better or for worse, human rights are seen as formulating valid moral claims that human beings can make on one another, and in particular on states and their institutions and officials, even (or especially) when existing institutional structures fail to protect or secure those claims. When the citizens of rogue states are tortured or imprisoned without trials or deprived of their livelihoods, nobody says in justification that those states have not signed up to human rights, or (a common situation) that they have signed up but taken no effective steps to secure or implement the standards to which they signed up. Human rights are typically seen as "moral rights possessed by all human beings simply in virtue of their humanity".[*] So like earlier proponents of natural rights or of the rights of man, the proponents of human rights face a deeper and more difficult justificatory task. John Tasioulas addresses this deeper task.

If human rights are standards that law and public policy *ought* to secure and enforce—if they are normative for state action and legislation—a demand for deeper justification is entirely reasonable. Accession and ratification do not provide deep justifications: rather they are the first (and *only* the first) steps towards implementation. If those steps were all that lies behind human rights, then human

---

[*] John Tasioulas, 'On the Foundations of Human Rights', this volume, ch. 1, 45. All subsequent references to ch. 1 appear parenthetically in the text.

rights would be on a par with other matters of international agreement or legal enactment, and could be rescinded or amended by subsequent international agreement or legislative enactment. Although there are those who try to suggest that any deeper justification is now otiose because human rights have been widely accepted, or because the more specific conventions on human rights of the late 1960s have been widely ratified by the states party, this strategy evades rather than meeting the demands of normative justification.

Tasioulas begins his rich discussion of the justification of human rights by characterising his aim as that of providing "foundations without foundationalism" (45–50). The point of this distinction is to maintain that justification is needed and not redundant, but not to assume that there is some specific type of foundational consideration that can justify all human rights claims. Tasioulas characterizes the justification that he offers as "a two-level pluralist account of the grounding of human rights, since it appeals to both moral (equal human dignity) and prudential (universal human interests) considerations, and it allows a plurality of human interests to play a grounding role" (70). His approach may seem unconvincing to those moral realists who take it that justification must fail unless it traces human rights back to basics of a single, canonical type. However, Tasioulas does not take such moral realists head on in this paper.

II. Arguments for Plural Justification

Much of the paper is devoted to showing that an adequate justification of human rights must appeal to a plurality of considerations, and in particular that it cannot rest solely on appeals to the importance of protecting human interests.

Tasioulas's discussion of the limitations of appeals to interests seems to me convincing. Although he accepts the idea that normative justifications, including justifications of rights, need to take serious account of human interests, he argues that appeals to human interests *on their own* would fail to secure the sort of "resistance to trade-offs" that is characteristic of rights (70). Rights cannot be "identified" with interests, even with basic interests, because "[h]uman interests—even our most urgent interests, such as the avoidance of imminent death—can be impaired or neglected in all sorts of ways without any wrong being committed, let alone one that has the character of a rights violation". This consideration tells not only against would-be justifications of rights that "identify" or equate them with interests, but against more guarded positions that seek to justify human rights solely as means to protect and realize (basic) human interests. Interests often go beyond rights: we may have an interest in acquiring another's possessions, or in being the object of another's romantic love, but rights to neither. And rights often go beyond interests: everyone may have rights to freedoms of speech or association, but some individuals may have little or no interest in either, for example if they lack capacities to communicate or to associate with others. More generally, the fact that the interests of a given person may not be wholly compossible, and that the interests of distinct persons are rarely if ever wholly compossible, are sufficient to show that interests constantly have to be traded off against one another. This indeed shows that *by themselves* interests cannot offer a plausible grounding for rights, where trade-offs are generally suspect.

III. From Rights to Duties

But if interests alone cannot justify human rights, what are the alternatives? Should human rights be grounded in the demands of human freedom, of human agency, of human needs or human dignity? Or in all of these?

Tasioulas begins by asking what gives rights their resistance to trade-offs. Some might think that this is simply a definitional matter: a right is a claim that is not automatically defeated by pointing to interests that would be damaged by failure to respect that claim. Tasioulas points out that that "the claims of interests in practical reason are more vulnerable to defeat than those of rights, since the latter inherently involve counterpart duties, and duties are characterized by two features that confer upon them a greater resistance to trade-offs" (47). The first of these features is the incompatibility between rights and aggregating views of the interests that rights are taken by some to protect, and the second is the "equal dignity of the putative right-holders" (60). I agree that the indispensable link between rights and duties is the crucial step in understanding why rights cannot be wholly, let alone merely, responsive to interests, and that this reflects the fact that violations of duties are a general form of wrongdoing (48), and that duties are "exclusionary in force, putting out of normative play *some* countervailing reasons that would otherwise apply" (47).

It seems to me to follow that any approach to justifying human rights will have to consider what can be said about the counterpart duties. Any justificatory potential that may be derived from appeals to freedom, agency, needs or dignity must take seriously the fact that there can be no rights unless some configuration of counterpart duties that could realise or secure them is possible.

Tasioulas develops his justification of human rights by way of a (lightly historicized) justification of moral rights, in which the part played by interests is combined with a requirement to acknowledge the status (the dignity, the moral worth) of all humans and the consequent need to justify any imposition of duties on others. He formulates this position schematically as follows (50–51):

(i) For all human beings within a given historical context, and simply in virtue of their humanity, having X (the object of the putative right) serves one or more of their basic interests, for example, interests in health, physical security, autonomy, understanding, friendship, achievement, play, etc.

(ii) The interest in having X is, in the case of each human being and simply in virtue of their humanity, pro tanto of sufficient importance to justify the imposition of duties on others, for example, to variously protect, respect or advance their interest in X.

(iii) The duties generated at (ii) are feasible claims on others given the constraints created by general and relatively entrenched facts of human nature and social life in the specified historical context. Therefore:

(iv) All human beings within the specified historical context have a right to X.

This schema is supplemented by an open-ended account of a plurality of grounding interests, which is both more abstract than, and in my view more plausible than, some attempts to list basic human interests. (However, I shall not discuss Tasioulas's critical discussions of attempts to justify human rights by appealing either to basic needs or interests, or to the requirements of agency, in any detail.) Tasioulas's own proposal is that the list of grounding interests relevant to justifying human rights should be *"objective, standardized, pluralistic, open-ended* and *holistic* in character"* (51). This approach allows that human interests, and with them the configuration of human rights that they can help justify, may change across history.

This approach has, moreover, to show *which* interests are of sufficient importance to justify the imposition of duties on others. How is this to be done? Would not a requirement to judge whether an interest is of sufficient importance to justify the imposition of duties on others return us to the impossible task of trying to rank interests, while lacking a metric for doing so or for trading them off against one another? To what extent does A's interest in health justify limiting B's physical security? To what extent does C's interest in friendship justify limiting D's right to autonomy? How far can E's interest in food and sustenance justify limiting F's right to achievement? When all goes well and in the absence of scarcity and conflict, it may seem that a system of rights can protect and secure all or most interests for everybody. But at many times not everything goes well; and even when it does, we need both to judge which interests are of sufficient importance to justify the imposition of duties, and which are not, and to understand which duties are to be met by which others.

Tasioulas poses the central question: "For an interest-based approach to rights, the operative question is whether any particular interest of ours—any aspect of our well-being—suffices to generate duties on others to respect or protect that interest" (51). I think this quite radical question is the right question to ask: for once we take the moral standing of human beings seriously; any imposition on human beings of duties to respect or protect others' interests requires justification. But how is his question to be answered? One response (which, like him, I would set aside) would be to say that a justification of human rights need not (perhaps cannot) generate an account of others' duties because these will only be made determinate once human rights are institutionally secured. It is true that a *fully* determinate account of others' duties to respect and secure rights will only emerge as duties are institutionalized: but we cannot even tell what we should aim to institutionalize without first saying something about the counterpart duties and their bearers that does not depend on but rather can guide institutionalization. The thought that duties come into the picture only *after* or *through* the construction of the institutions that deliver determinate versions of them at a particular time and place evades rather than settles the fundamental issues about the normative justification of human rights. It fails to address Tasioulas's operative question about identifying *which* interests can or should generate duties on others to respect or protect that interest (51). In effect it concedes that the allocation of duties will not be supported by any deep form of justification, but simply by historical or other contingencies.

IV. Rights and Feasible Duties

There are, I believe, two distinct questions to be addressed. The first asks only how are we to tell when "the specified universal interests of human beings, all of them bearers of equal moral worth, generate in the case of each and every one of them duties to secure the object of the putative right" (57)? A further question asks not merely *which* interests have sufficient importance to generate counterpart duties for someone or other, but *who* holds which counterpart duties. Tasioulas deals with the first of these questions, and I shall discuss it in this section. In the last section of this paper I shall offer some comments on the second question, on which he says much less.

Tasioulas approaches the first question, by aiming to show what "distinguishes human rights from a mere shopping list of valuable 'goals'" (57). The basic feature that makes human rights more than a set of goals is, he suggests, that all right-holders have equal moral worth. Human rights are not the rights of some privileged class of humans, but of all human beings. The premise of the equal status or dignity of all persons has large implications, and most fundamentally requires that any human right be one that could be held by all. It is the reason for thinking of human rights as universal, as held by each and every human being.

One argument to this conclusion is based on premise (ii) of Tasioulas's schematic argument for rights, in which he claims that there is no *pro tanto* case for any duty whose performance would be impossible in the face of "internal impediments". Such internal impediments or impossibilities might be logical, metaphysical or empirical. They offer, for example, a basis for concluding that there can be no right to be both alive and dead at the same time, no right to give birth irrespective of one's sex, and no right to inter-galactic space travel (58). Nobody would think that there can be duties to perform the impossible, or that any of these could be human rights. There may be other disagreements about the full implications of "*ought* implies *can*", but not about this central implication.

This line of thought about the feasibility of rights being held by all leads further if we focus not on the task of respecting or securing rights for a particular person, but on that of respecting or securing them for all others. Tasioulas poses the question: "what is generally compossible by way of duty-fulfilment in the case of all supposed right-holders?" (58). He points out that "given that the rights in question are supposedly *human rights*—rights possessed by all human beings simply in virtue of their humanity—their being possessed by any one human being must be compatible with their being simultaneously possessed by all others within the specified socio-historical context" (58). Consequently there cannot, for example, be rights to live in luxury, although there can (in favourable times) be rights to an "adequate standard of living". This point can be generalized: there cannot be rights to positional goods, since by definition they cannot be procured for all. There are no rights to win, no rights to come first, no rights to have a greater than average income, no rights to live the longest or to be the strongest, and no rights for all children to be above average. Equally, there can be no rights to states of affairs which cannot be delivered for all, such as the enjoyment of good health, but at most rights to health care.

In a third step Tasioulas then suggests that premise (iii) of his basic scheme requires rights to be limited because duties to respect and secure them must make claims that are feasible for the relevant duty-bearers. We must take account of the "joint feasibility of the supposed duties generated severally by each and every supposed right-holder" (60). As an illustration of this point he suggests that the duties that would be implied by a right to "the highest attainable standard of health care" would be excessively burdensome, and that any feasible right to health care will not justify duties that impose this level of burden on others. An advantage of this approach, to which he points, is that it is sensitive to the fact that our assessments of what is feasible may have to change over time, so that we may come to acknowledge rights to action that used not to be feasible (for example, rights to reproductive assistance, or advanced cancer treatments) or cease to think that there can be rights as extensive as we formerly assumed, where the counterpart duties have ceased to be feasible (for example, because of climate change or population growth). This lightly historicised view, it seems to me, puts a plausible distance between claims that human rights are universal and claims that our Stone Age ancestors, or our pre-modern predecessors, or future generations, must have had or will have the very same rights as we do today. (This, of course, leaves many questions about intergenerational justice unanswered.)

V. Who Owes What to Whom?

Although Tasioulas argues that the duties that correspond to any supposed human right must themselves be not only possible but compossible, indeed feasible for duty-bearers at a given time and place, there is a good deal more to be said about these matters. The way in which he poses the question leads him to consider the compossibility for duty-bearers taken together to respect or secure a given right for all supposed right-holders, but not the compossibility for each duty-bearer of discharging any given right, or indeed a wide range of rights, for a plurality of right-holders. He does not extend his comments on compossibility to consider the range of burdens on duty-bearers who face many (supposed) claims of right.

To say more it is useful to distinguish the case of liberty rights from other rights. In making that distinction I do not mean to suggest either that liberty rights are more important than other rights, or that all of the duties that arise if liberty rights are to be respected and secured will be "negative" duties to refrain from action. Evidently, the duties that arise if liberty rights are to be enforced by the police and the courts will not all be "negative" duties: some duties that are needed to secure liberty rights are positive, have to be allocated to those holding specific roles, and are expensive. However, at the core of these duties there are duties to respect others' liberties, and these first-order duties fall equally on all. Your right to freedom of speech (however configured) is compromised if there is anyone who has no duty to respect it; your right to freedom of movement (however configured) is compromised if there is anyone who has no duty to respect it. A more traditional way of making this point would be to say that if anyone is "above the law", others' liberties will be compromised or incomplete. In the case of liberty rights it matters hugely not only that all have the same rights, but that all have the necessary counterpart duties to respect them. We cannot fully appreciate the weight of Tasioulas's claim that duties must be jointly feasible for duty-bearers unless we look not only at the duties "generated severally by each and every supposed right-holder" but also at the duties "held concurrently by each and every supposed duty-bearer".

Fortunately, this does not lead to distinctive problems in judging the compossibility of meeting the duties that are the counterparts to liberty rights. Although it may be exacting to identify the optimal way to configure each liberty right, or a complete and compossible set of liberty rights, for a given society at a given time in its history, with its distinctive opportunities and limitations, the first-order duties that are the counterparts to each compossible configuration of liberty rights will also be compossible. Since compossible liberty rights require specific forms of forbearance or restraint, they will not require action that burdens duty-bearers (although conflicts between duties are always possible): there is not a problem of principle in refraining at one and the same time from injury, perjury, and defamation of others, indeed of all others. Although there are many ways to configure compossible interpretations of rights to privacy and rights to freedom of expression, each requiring specific forms of restraint and forbearance, each will define a compossible set of counterpart duties. Here the compossibility of the rights is matched by the compossibility of the counterpart duties.

However, judging the compossibility of duties that are the counterparts to rights to goods or services (the term "welfare rights" is too narrow and something of a misnomer) is a less tractable matter. The counterpart duties to rights to goods and services require "positive" action of specified sorts by some, and not only forbearance or restraint by all. Here aspects of duties have to be allocated to specified and (it is to be hoped!) competent duty-bearers. In this respect rights to goods and services differ from liberty rights. While it is true that enforcing or guaranteeing rights of either sort needs positive enforcing action by specified institutions and office-holders, rights to goods and services also require some effective allocation of first-order duties if others' rights are to be secured. Consequently rights to goods and services are often indeterminate in the absence of institutionalisation that allocates the relevant duties.

One corollary is that while violators of liberty rights can in principle be identified even where there is no effective way to hold them to account or to enforce compliance—Amnesty International often does so with zeal!—violators of rights to goods or services cannot be identified in the same way. *Whose* dereliction of duty leaves a child or a village in a distant part of the world lacking food, or elementary health care, or clean water, or education? There may be many who could have ensured that (some of) these rights were met, but if the duties to meet them were not allocated to anybody in particular, it seems that the duty lies with nobody, and that nobody is at fault for failing to provide. In such cases—alas, all too common—right-holders can claim goods and services to which they are supposedly entitled only if tasks and roles have been defined and allocated to (competent) duty-bearers. Unsurprisingly, we find that where rights to goods and services are not met, accusations often gesture towards violators in imprecise and ineffective terms: the fault is said to lie with governments (which may or may not have the relevant capacities); with "the international community", with "civil society", with "corporations".

The problem, it seems, is that in the case of rights to goods and services we cannot assess the "joint feasibility of the supposed duties" unless we already know on whom those duties are to fall, what capacities they have, and what other duties they are simultaneously to carry, that may shape or restrict their capacities to carry the relevant "supposed" duties. Here, I believe, it may be useful to reverse perspectives and to consider not the compossibility of rights, but the compossibility of duties. This is complicated, but realistic. Any configuration of human rights that can be held by all, must pay attention not only to the "joint feasibility of the supposed duties generated severally by each and every supposed right-holder", but to the "joint feasibility of the supposed duties falling on each and every duty-bearer". There may be a number of distinct configurations of rights and duties—of normative requirements—that meet both of these feasibility constraints, but taken together they may offer a promising and powerful, though perhaps not a complete, justification both of human rights and of their counterpart duties.

3

Human Rights as Fundamental Conditions for a Good Life

S. Matthew Liao

I. Introduction

Human rights can offer powerful protection to those who possess them. As such, human rights are frequently invoked in contemporary political discourses. At the same time, many people question whether many purported human rights claims are genuine human rights. For example, the United Nations Universal Declaration of Human Rights (UDHR) lists such rights as the right to employment and periodic holidays with pay. Or, some claim that there is a human right to assisted suicide.[1] Also, many international declarations on the rights of the child proclaim that children have a right to be loved.[2] And, more recently, the Director-General of UNESCO announced that there is a human right to peace. Are all these claims genuine human rights?

To determine whether a human rights claim is genuine or not, we need a *substantive account* of human rights, that is, an account that tells us what human rights we have and why we have these rights.[3] But what gives content to a substantive account of human rights? In this paper, I offer a new answer: human beings have human rights to what I call the fundamental conditions for pursuing a good life. I call this the Fundamental Conditions Approach. To articulate and defend this approach, I shall do five things. First, I shall explain what I mean by the fundamental conditions for pursuing a good life and why human beings have human rights to these conditions. Second, I shall demonstrate how this approach can explain many of the rights found in the UDHR. At the same time, I shall illustrate how this approach can explain why some of the claims in the UDHR are not genuine human rights. Third, James Griffin has argued that the notion of agency should ground human rights.[4] I shall explain how Griffin's Agency Approach differs from the Fundamental Conditions Approach and why the Fundamental Conditions Approach should be preferred. Fourth, my appeal to the notion of a good life will prompt others to think of Martha Nussbaum's Central Capabilities Approach, which, like the Fundamental Conditions Approach, is in part

---

[1] Margaret P. Battin, "Suicide: A Fundamental Human Right?," in Margaret P. Battin and D.J. Mayo (eds.), *Suicide: The Philosophical Issues* (New York: St. Martin's Press, 1980), 267–85.

[2] S. Matthew Liao, "The Right of Children to Be Loved," *Journal of Political Philosophy,* 14(4) (2006): 420–40.

[3] James Griffin, "Towards a Substantive Theory of Rights," in Raymond G. Frey (ed.), *Utility and Rights* (Oxford: Blackwell, 1984), 137–60.

[4] James Griffin, *On Human Rights* (Oxford: Oxford University Press, 2008).

Aristotelian in spirit.[5] My complaint with the Central Capabilities Approach as a substantive account of human rights is that it cannot adequately explain a significant number of human rights.

Finally, the Fundamental Conditions Approach (along with Griffin's Agency Approach and Nussbaum's Central Capabilities Approach) assumes that human rights are those that we have simply in virtue of being human. It therefore belongs to what might be called a Naturalistic Conception of human rights.[6] In recent years, a new and purportedly alternative conception of human rights, the so-called Political Conception of human rights, has become increasingly popular. The Political Conception has been defended by, among others, John Rawls,[7] Charles Beitz,[8] and Joseph Raz.[9] According to the Political Conception, the distinctive nature of human rights is to be understood in light of their role or function in modern international political practice.[10] Proponents of the Political Conception believe that the Naturalistic Conception "tend[s] to distort rather than illuminate international human rights practice"[11] and should therefore be rejected in favor of its Political counterpart. Since my aim here is to develop what I take to be the correct substantive account of human rights, it will be helpful to discuss the Political Conception of human rights. On behalf of the Natural Conception, I shall argue, among other things, that the theoretical distance between the Naturalistic Conception and the Political Conception is not as great as it has been made out to be.

Here it is worth making explicit an assumption that I make but do not defend, namely, I assume that there are positive rights. A person has a positive right if the person is entitled to the provision of some good or service, for example, a right to welfare assistance; and a person has a negative right if the person is entitled to non-interference, for example, a right against assault. Although some people have claimed that there are only negative rights,[12] many others have put forward strong arguments in favor of positive rights.[13] Given this, and given that what I take to be the main competitors to the Fundamental Conditions Approach such as Griffin's Agency Approach and Nussbaum's Central Capabilities Approach all accept that there are

---

[5] Martha C. Nussbaum, "Capabilities and Human Rights," *Fordham Law Review,* 66(2) (1997): 273–300; Martha C. Nussbaum, "Capabilities as Fundamental Entitlements: Sen and Social Justice", *Feminist Economics,* 9(2–3) (2003): 33–59; Martha C. Nussbaum, *Frontiers of Justice: Disability, Nationality, Species Membership* (Cambridge: Belknap Press, 2006); Martha C. Nussbaum, *Creating Capabilities: The Human Development Approach* (Cambridge: Belknap Press, 2011).

[6] What I am calling the Naturalistic Conception has, among other things, also been called the "orthodox" view (Charles R. Beitz, "Human Rights and the Law of Peoples," in Deen Chatterjee (ed.), *The Ethics of Assistance: Morality and the Distant Needy* (Cambridge: Cambridge University Press, 2004); John Tasioulas, "Taking Rights out of Human Rights," *Ethics,* 120 (2010): 647–78).

[7] John Rawls, *The Law of Peoples: With "The Idea of Public Reason Revisited"* (Harvard: Harvard University Press, 1999).

[8] Charles R. Beitz, *The Idea of Human Rights* (Oxford: Oxford University Press, 2009).

[9] Joseph Raz, "Human Rights without Foundations," in Samantha Besson and John Tasioulas (eds.), *The Philosophy of International Law* (Oxford: Oxford University Press, 2010a), 321–38; Joseph Raz, "Human Rights in the Emerging World Order," *Transnational Legal Theory,* 1 (2010b): 31–47.

[10] Beitz, "Human Rights and the Law of Peoples," 197.

[11] Beitz, "Human Rights and the Law of Peoples," 198.

[12] Jan Narveson, *The Libertarian Idea* (Philadelphia: Temple University Press, 1988).

[13] See, eg, Henry Shue, *Basic Rights: Subsistence, Affluence, and U.S. Foreign Policy,* 2nd edn (Princeton: Princeton University Press, 1996).

positive rights, I shall not try to defend this assumption here.[14] My argument can therefore be understood in conditional terms, namely, conditional on the existence of positive rights, human rights should be seen as grounded in the fundamental conditions for pursuing a good life.

II. The Fundamental Conditions Approach

To start, let me explain what I mean by a good life and the fundamental conditions for pursuing it. I shall then explain why human beings have human rights to these fundamental conditions.

As I see it, a characteristically good human life, or a good life, for short, is one spent in pursuing certain valuable, basic activities. "Basic" activities are activities that are important to human beings *qua* human beings' life as a whole. Sunbathing, for example, is an activity, but is not a basic activity, because a human being *qua* human being's life as a whole is not affected if one does not go sunbathing. In addition, activities that are very important to an individual human being's life as a whole may nevertheless not be basic activities, because these activities may not be important to human beings *qua* human beings' life as a whole. For instance, being a professional philosopher is very important to my life as a whole. But being a professional philosopher is not a basic activity because it is not an activity that is important to human beings *qua* human beings' life as whole. Similarly, an individual may devote her entire life to the betterment of those in need. This is without a doubt a very moral activity and may also be very important to this individual's life as a whole. But it is not a basic activity, as I understand it, because, again, it is not an activity that is important to human beings *qua* human beings' life as whole. Finally, basic activities are ones that if a human life did not involve the pursuit of any of them, then that life could not be a good life. In other words, a human being can have a good life by pursuing just some, and not all, of the basic activities. Some of the basic activities are as follows: deep personal relationships with, for example, one's partner, friends, parents, children; knowledge of, for example, the workings of the world, of oneself, of others; active pleasures such as creative work and play; and passive pleasures such as appreciating beauty.[15]

It is worth noting that a good life, as I understand it, is not the same thing as an excellent life. An excellent life may require one to have certain accomplishments such as discovering a cure for cancer or having climbed Mount Everest, whereas a good life, as I understand it, does not. My understanding of a good life is closer to what might be called a "minimally decent life." But whereas the idea of a "minimally decent life" is often not explicated, I explicitly understand a good life in terms of pursuing the basic activities and I detail what some of these basic activities are.

From these basic activities, we can derive the contents of the fundamental conditions for pursuing a good life. The fundamental conditions for pursuing a good life

---

[14] See, eg, James Griffin, "Welfare Rights," *The Journal of Ethics*, 4 (2000): 27–43; Nussbaum, *Frontiers of Justice*, 286.

[15] A way to identify what the basic activities are is through a mixture of empirical research from, eg, anthropological and sociological studies, and normative theorizing, using something like the method of reflective equilibrium.

are various goods, capacities, and options that human beings *qua* human beings need, whatever else they (*qua* individuals) might need, in order to *pursue* the basic activities. For example, the fundamental goods are resources that human beings *qua* human beings need in order to sustain themselves corporeally and include such items as food, water, and air. The fundamental capacities are powers and abilities that human beings *qua* human beings require in order to pursue the basic activities. These capacities include the capacity to think, to be motivated by facts, to know, to choose an act freely (liberty), to appreciate the worth of something, to develop interpersonal relationships, and to have control of the direction of one's life (autonomy). The fundamental options are those social forms and institutions that human beings *qua* human beings require if they are to be able to exercise their essential capacities to engage in the basic activities. Some of these include the option to have social interaction, to acquire further knowledge, to evaluate and appreciate things, and to determine the direction of one's life. The difference between the fundamental goods and the fundamental options is that the former focuses on the internal, physical conditions for pursuing a good life whereas the latter focuses on the external, environmental conditions for pursuing a good life.

Having the fundamental conditions for pursuing a good life of course cannot guarantee that an individual has a good life; no condition can guarantee this. Rather, these goods, capacities, and options enable human beings to *pursue* the basic activities. Also, these fundamental conditions are intended to provide human beings with an *adequate range* of fundamental goods, capacities, and options so that they can pursue those basic activities that are characteristic of a minimally decent human life. Now many of the fundamental conditions are all-purpose conditions in that they are needed whatever basic activity one aims to pursue. For example, all human beings need food, water, the capacity to think, and the capacity to determine the direction of their lives, whatever basic activity they aim to pursue. But it is possible that some fundamental conditions are needed just for pursuing particular basic activities. For instance, it is possible that the capacity to develop deep personal relationships is needed only if one aims to pursue deep personal relationships. Suppose that this is the case. We can leave it open whether a particular individual will make use of all the fundamental conditions when pursuing a particular kind of good life. This individual's having all the fundamental conditions means that this individual would still have access to an adequate range of goods, capacities, and options to pursue those basic activities that are characteristic of a minimally decent human life. This could become important if, for example, this individual changed his/her mind about pursuing a particular kind of good life. Finally, owing to space, I shall not be able to say much about *how much* of the fundamental conditions human beings need in order to pursue the basic activities and what one should do when one can only promote some, but not all, of these conditions in a given society. All too briefly, my view is that human beings need *enough* of these fundamental conditions in order to pursue the basic activity; that when one can only promote some, but not all, of these conditions in a given society, what one should do will depend on the context but that there are likely to be determinate answers; and that the ultimate goal of a given society is to devise policies that would ensure that every person has enough of these conditions.

My notion of the fundamental conditions for pursuing a good life bears some similarities to Rawls's notions of primary goods, which are goods that all individuals are presumed to want, whatever else they may want.[16] So let me briefly highlight some of the differences. One difference is that Rawls is interested in *social* rather than *natural* primary goods, where, for Rawls, social primary goods include such things as rights, liberties, powers and opportunities, income and wealth, and a sense of self-respect, while natural primary goods include such things as health, vigor, intelligence, and imagination.[17] By contrast, as I conceive it, the fundamental conditions for pursuing a good life would include some natural primary goods such as health. Another difference between the two is that a person who is severely handicapped may have all the primary goods (income, wealth, liberties, and so on) and still not have all the fundamental conditions for pursuing a good life, because he may lack certain capacities necessary to pursue the basic activities.

In my view, these fundamental conditions for pursuing a good life ground human rights because having these conditions is of fundamental importance to human beings, and because rights can offer powerful protection to those who possess them. The former is true because if anything is of fundamental importance to human beings, then pursuing a characteristically good human life is; pursuing a good life is the first and foremost aim of most human beings. And it seems clear that if we attach a certain importance to an end, we must attach this importance to the (essential) means to this end. For example, if we care about making a cake, then we must care about the (essential) ingredients that would enter into making this cake such as flour, water, sugar, eggs, and raising agents. Losing any of these essential ingredients is tantamount to losing the cake itself. Given this, since pursuing a good life is of fundamental importance to human beings, having the fundamental conditions for pursuing a good life must also be of fundamental importance to human beings.

That rights can offer powerful protection to those who possess them is well known.[18] By their nature, rights secure the interests of the right-holders by requiring others, the duty-bearers, to perform certain services for the right-holders or not to interfere with the right-holders' pursuit of their essential interests. In addition, at least on certain structural accounts of rights, rights typically prevent the right-holders' interests that ground rights from being part of a first-order utilitarian calculus.[19] This means that if a right-holder has a right to something, V, then typically no non-right claims can override the right-holder's right to V. Finally, as some writers have pointed out, because the right-holders are entitled to these services as a matter of rights, this means that the right-holders can simply expect the services without requesting them.[20] Given the strong protection that rights can offer to the right-holders, and given the importance

[16] John Rawls, *A Theory of Justice* (Oxford: Oxford University Press, 1971).
[17] Rawls, *A Theory of Justice*, 62.
[18] Rights could also have non-instrumental importance in addition to having instrumental importance.
[19] See, eg, Ronald Dworkin, *Taking Rights Seriously* (London: Duckworth, 1977); Robert Nozick, *Anarchy, State and Utopia* (Oxford: Blackwell, 1974).
[20] Joel Feinberg, "The Nature and Value of Rights," in Elsie L. Bandman and Bertram Bandman (eds.), *Bioethics and Human Rights: A Reader for Health Professionals* (Boston: Little, Brown, 1970), 19–31.

of having these fundamental conditions to human beings, it seems reasonable that human beings have rights to these fundamental conditions. If this is correct, this provides us with a justification for the idea that human beings have human rights to the fundamental conditions for pursuing a good life.

III. Rights in the United Nations and the Fundamental Conditions Approach

The Fundamental Conditions Approach can explain why many of the rights in the UDHR are genuine human rights, and it also has the resources to exclude some of the claims in the UDHR as genuine human rights.

Consider the right to life, liberty and security of person (Article 3). Whatever else human beings (*qua* individuals) need, they (*qua* human beings) need life, liberty, and security of person in order to pursue the basic activities. If they are not alive; if they cannot freely choose to act to some degree; or if the security of their person is not guaranteed, they cannot pursue the basic activities. Given this, on the Fundamental Conditions Approach, human beings would have human rights to life, liberty, and security of person.

Or, consider the right to recognition everywhere as a person before the law (Article 6); the right to equal protection before the law (Article 7); the right against arbitrary arrest, detention or exile (Article 9); the right to a fair and public hearing (Article 10); and the right to be presumed innocent until proven guilty (Article 11). These are things that human beings (*qua* human beings) need whatever else they (*qua* individuals) might need in order to pursue the basic activities. In particular, when we pursue the basic activities, conflicts with others are bound to arise. If and when such conflicts arise, we need guarantees that we would be treated fairly and equally. Fair trial, presumption of innocence, equal protection before the law, and not being arrested arbitrarily serve to ensure that we would be treated fairly and equally. As such, they are things that human beings (*qua* human beings) need whatever they (*qua* individuals) might need in order to pursue the basic activities. As such, the Fundamental Conditions Approach can explain why there are these human rights.

Finally, consider the right to freedom of thought, conscience and religion (Article 18), the right to freedom of opinion and expression (Article 19), and the right to freedom of peaceful assembly and association (Article 20). As we said earlier, one of the fundamental conditions for pursuing a good life is being able freely to choose to pursue the basic activities. In order freely to choose to pursue the basic activities, one must have freedom of expression, thought, religion, and association. On the Fundamental Conditions Approach, human beings would have human rights to freedom of thought, expression, religion, and association.

At the same time, the Fundamental Conditions Approach would exclude some of the claims in the UDHR as genuine human rights. To give one example, consider the right to periodic holidays with pay (Article 24). Is there such a human right? On the Fundamental Conditions Approach, the important question to ask is whether paid holidays are a fundamental condition for pursuing a good life. That is, are paid holidays something that human beings (*qua* human beings) need whatever else they (*qua* individuals) might need in order to pursue the basic activities? There is no doubt that human beings need some rest and leisure in order to pursue the basic activities. Without time for leisure, human beings would not have sufficient time to pursue the basic activities. Given this, some amount of leisure, in the form of holidays, is a fundamental condition for pursuing a good life. However, it does not seem that *paid* holidays are a fundamental condition for pursuing a good life, because it seems that human beings can pursue the basic activities even if their holidays are not paid. It might be thought that if holidays were not paid, then some people would not be able to afford to take holidays. But this seems to conflate a person's right to certain minimum welfare, which he has, with a right to paid holidays. If a person cannot afford to take time off work unless his holidays are paid, this person has a human right to certain minimum welfare assistance. But he does not have a human right to paid holidays, because paid holidays are not a fundamental condition for pursuing a good life. Note that while there may not be a human right to paid holidays, this does not mean that there could not be a legal right to paid holidays. It goes without saying that there are other sources of normativity besides human rights (for example, considerations of justice and/or equality) and some of them may ground social goods such as paid holidays.

IV. Why Not Just Agency?

In *On Human Rights* and in a series of articles, Griffin has argued that the notion of agency should determine the content of human rights.[21] Griffin writes,

> What seems to me the best account of human rights is this. It is centred on the notion of agency. We human beings have the capacity to form pictures of what a good life would be and to try to realize these pictures. We value our status as agents especially highly, often more highly even than our happiness. Human rights can then be seen as protections of our agency—what one might call our personhood.[22]

By agency, Griffin means our autonomously choosing a conception of a worthwhile life (autonomy), our being at liberty to pursue this conception (liberty), and our having minimum material provision and education.[23]

There is much to be said in favor of Griffin's Agency Approach. For one thing, agency is clearly of great importance to human beings. Without some of it, human beings would not be able to bring about any actions at all, let alone actions necessary for a moral and purposeful life. Given this, it seems highly appropriate to protect it with human rights, which offer strong protections for its possessors.[24] Also, the

---

[21] Griffin, *On Human Rights*; James Griffin, "Welfare Rights," *The Journal of Ethics* 4: 27–43; J. Griffin, "Discrepancies between the Best Philosophical Account of Human Rights and the International Law of Human Rights," *Proceedings of the Aristotelian Society,* CI (2001a): 1–28; James Griffin, "First Steps in an Account of Human Rights," *European Journal of Philosophy,* 9(3) (2001b): 306–27. This section draws on S. Matthew Liao, "Agency and Human Rights," *Journal of Applied Philosophy,* 27(1) (2010): 15–25.

[22] Griffin, "Discrepancies between the Best Philosophical Account of Human Rights and the International Law of Human Rights," 4.

[23] Griffin, "First Steps in an Account of Human Rights," 311.

[24] Griffin, "First Steps in an Account of Human Rights," 313.

Agency Approach does appear to be able to help us determine which human rights are real. For example Griffin's derivation of rights such as the right to life and the right to freedom of expression using the notion of agency seems plausible.[25]

This said, Griffin's Agency Approach also faces a number of issues.[26] I shall discuss two in order to highlight the difference between Griffin's Agency Approach and the Fundamental Conditions Approach. First, there is an issue of whether agency should be the sole ground for human rights.[27] To understand this concern, it is useful to begin by pointing out that Griffin has what might be called a *wide* notion of agency, because he holds that agency is valuable only in the context of a good, flourishing life. In contrast, a narrow notion of agency would regard agency as being valuable in and of itself regardless of how it might contribute to a good, flourishing life. As Griffin says, autonomy and liberty, the two core values that make up his notion of agency, are "elements of a good life…features that characteristically enhance the quality of life," but they do not exhaust all the elements of a good life—other elements include freedom from great pain, accomplishing something in the course of one's life, understanding certain moral and metaphysical matters, deep personal relations, and so on. [28]

However, given that Griffin holds that agency is valuable only in the context of a good, flourishing life and given that he accepts that in addition to agency, there are other elements of a good life such as freedom from great pain, understanding, deep personal relations, and so on, which can be used indirectly to shape agency, this raises the question of whether agency should be considered the sole ground for human rights. For example, consider the paradigmatic human right not to be tortured. The fact that torture undermines one's agency by undermining one's capacity to decide and to stick to the decision is certainly an important factor in deciding that torture violates a human right.[29] But it seems that another important factor in deciding that torture violates a human right is that it causes great pain. Griffin insists though that the notion of agency by itself can adequately explain such human right as the right against torture.[30] So let us consider his arguments.

---

[25] See Griffin 2008, chs. 12 and 13.

[26] For an excellent discussion of some of the problems that Griffin's approach might face, see John Tasioulas, "Human Rights, Universality and the Values of Personhood: Retracing Griffin's Steps," *European Journal of Philosophy,* 10(1) (2002): 79–100.

[27] Lest this lead to confusion, let me note that Griffin does mention a second ground for human rights, what he calls practicalities, which, as he explains, help to make the content of a particular human right "determinate enough to be an effective guide to behaviour…" (*On Human Rights*, 37–9). For my purpose, we can leave this aside, because I am interested in standalone grounds for human rights, that is, those grounds that are not parasitic on other grounds for human rights. For example, since the role of practicalities is to make human rights that are grounded in some other way, eg, agency, more determinate, practicalities are parasitic on other grounds for human rights, and are therefore not standalone grounds for human rights. In fact, the requirement of practicalities seems to be a reasonable requirement for any standalone ground for human rights, since any standalone ground for human rights should be determinate enough to be an effective guide to behavior. Hence, when I claim that Griffin believes that "agency is the sole ground for human rights," I am taking him to be holding the view that agency is the sole standalone ground for human rights, which I believe he does. Also, when I investigate whether there could be other grounds for human rights, I am interested in whether there could be other standalone grounds for human rights. To save words though, I shall leave out the word "standalone" throughout the rest of the paper.

[28] Griffin, *On Human Rights*, 36.   [29] Griffin, *On Human Rights*, 52–3.

[30] As another example, while education is important for autonomy, it seems that the value of understanding is also sufficiently important to human life that it could provide its own independent

According to Griffin:

> Torture has characteristic aims. It is used to make someone recant a belief, reveal a secret, "confess" a crime whether guilty or not, abandon a cause, or do someone else's bidding. All of these characteristic purposes involve *undermining someone else's will, getting them to do what they do not want to do or are even resolved not to do* [emphasis added].[31]

Griffin then offers two arguments to support his claim that the human right against torture can be adequately explained by the notion of agency alone.

First, Griffin accepts that when asked what is wrong with torture, the obvious response is that it causes great pain. However, he argues that causing pain cannot be why torture violates a human right, because there are many cases of one person's gratuitously inflicting great pain on another that are not a matter of human right violation. For example, consider

> **Callous Partner:** There is an unsuccessful marriage in which the first partner treats the second partner callously, and the suffering endured by the second partner over the years is arguably worse than a short period of physical torture.[32]

Griffin argues that in this case, the first partner, simply by gratuitously inflicting great pain on the second partner, does not thereby violate the second partner's human right.

Second, Griffin argues that undermining someone else's agency without causing great pain is sufficient for there to be a human right violation in other cases. For example, consider

> **Truth Drug:** Instead of torture, one uses truth drugs to extract secrets.[33]

Griffin argues that while Truth Drug does not involve inflicting pain, it does involve undermining an individual's agency, which he believes amounts to a human right violation. As he says:

> We could not call [Truth Drug] "torture" because it is essential to "torture" that the infliction of great pain be the means. But what concerns us here is whether the painless chemical destruction of another person's will raises any issues of human rights. And it does. It does because painless domination is still a gross undermining of personhood.[34]

Since causing great pain is not sufficient for the existence of a human right against torture, and since undermining agency in, for example, Truth Drug is sufficient for the existence of a human right violation, according to Griffin, this shows that the notion of agency, and not, for example, causing great pain, is what explains the existence of a human right against torture.

Let me start with Griffin's second argument. Truth Drug may show that undermining agency sometimes violates a human right, but it does not show that undermining

---

contribution to the existence of a human right to education. If so, it could also be asked whether Griffin's notion of agency should be the sole explanation for such human right as the right to education.

[31] Griffin, *On Human Rights*, 52.   [32] Griffin, *On Human Rights*, 52.
[33] Griffin, *On Human Rights*, 53.   [34] Griffin, *On Human Rights*, 53.

agency always violates a human right. Recall that Griffin understands undermining someone's will or agency as "getting them to do what they do not want to do or are even resolved not to do." But suppose that I entice you with the possibility of great pleasure in order to get you to do something that you do not want to do or are even resolved not to do. For instance, I offer you lots of money so that you would eat large worms—something you do not want to do or are even resolved not to do.[35] In such a case, I may have undermined your agency but this would hardly constitute a case of human right violation. If so, while causing great pain may not always be a sufficient condition for the violation of a human right in all cases, neither is undermining an individual's agency.[36]

However, suppose I am wrong and enticing you with the possibility of great pleasure in order to undermine your agency is a case of a human right violation. Still, this does not seem to be the same kind of human right violation as torture is, which involves inflicting great pain. In other words, the Agency Approach faces the question of explaining how undermining agency through extreme pain might be significantly different from undermining agency through great pleasure.

Griffin's first argument at best shows that causing great pain is not a sufficient condition for the violation of a human right. It does not undermine the idea that causing great pain is necessary for explaining why torture violates a human right. One significant difference between torture and Callous Partner is that in the latter, the second partner typically can leave the marriage, whereas in the case of torture, the individual being tortured typically cannot leave the torture chamber. That the second partner can leave the marriage may explain why in this case, there is not a human right violation, despite the psychological torment the second partner has to endure. Consider instead two couples whose second partners could not leave the marriages (as for example in some cases of forced, arranged marriages). In the case of the first couple, the second partner was treated lovingly and respectfully by the first partner. In the case of the second couple, the second partner was subjected to a long period of psychological torment by the first partner. It seems plausible that both cases involve human right violations in virtue of the fact that the second partner could not leave the marriage. But it seems that there was an additional form of human right violation with respect to the second couple in virtue of the fact that the second partner was subjected to a long period of psychological torment.

---

[35] It might be thought that offering someone a large sum of money so that she would do something she does not want to do or are even resolved not to do does not undermine her agency, since she has chosen to accept the offer. Two comments. First, this is not how Griffin understands what it means to undermine someone's agency. As said earlier, for Griffin, getting someone to do what she does not want to do or are even resolved not to do is sufficient to undermine that person's agency. Second, there are numerous examples in which it seems that a person's agency has been undermined even though the person has chosen to accept an offer. For instance, the practice of paying subjects large sum of money so that they would sell body parts, eg, oocytes or organs, or participate in medical research, arguably undermines their agency even though these individuals would have chosen to accept the offer. This may explain why a number of people believe that such a practice is a form of undue inducement.

[36] Or, consider another example suggested by an anonymous reviewer: Suppose I decorate your work environment with images of enticing sweets, none of which you notice, but together they give you the idea that you would like a donut break and this prompts you to go to the cafeteria. It seems that I have undermined your agency, but it does not seem that I have violated your human rights.

Moreover, the kind of torture that Griffin has in mind, where one causes great pain in order to undermine the victim's capacity to decide and to get the victim to give up information, is what might be called Instrumental Torture. Another kind of torture, call it Intrinsic Torture, involves causing extreme pain just for the sake of causing extreme pain. Since Intrinsic Torture does not aim at undermining the victim's capacity to decide and stick to a decision, it involves less agency-related violations. Even so, it would still be a human right violation. If this is right, it seems that causing extreme pain would play an even more significant and necessary role in explaining why there is still a human right violation in Intrinsic Torture. If all of this is right, Griffin has not yet shown that the notion of agency can by itself explain the human right against torture.

The second issue regarding Griffin's Agency Approach is as follows: Griffin resists allowing the other elements of a good life to ground human rights because he is concerned that permitting these elements directly to determine the content of human rights would lead to the case that all the necessary elements of a good life would determine the content of human rights, which Griffin believes, would cause the language of rights to become redundant, diluting the discourse of rights. As Griffin writes:

> If we had rights to all that is needed for a good or happy life, then the language of rights would become redundant. We already have a perfectly adequate way of speaking about individual well-being and any obligations there might be to promote it.[37]

Call this the Redundancy Objection.

Griffin is certainly correct that there is no human right to everything necessary for a good life. Suppose that sailing is my passion in life, and, hence, having a yacht is a necessary condition for me to pursue a good life. It would not follow that I have a human right to a yacht. However, the Fundamental Conditions Approach also has resources to block the Redundancy Objection. To see this, note that the Fundamental Conditions Approach would include all the essential agency considerations in Griffin's Agency Approach. In addition, it would allow fundamental, but non-agency, considerations such as freedom from great pain also to determine the content of human rights. The Fundamental Conditions Approach can straightforwardly exclude as being a valid human rights claim my need to have a yacht because such a need is not a fundamental condition for pursuing a good life. Indeed, it is not something that human beings (*qua* human beings) need whatever else they (*qua* individuals) might need in order to pursue the basic activities.

Lest Griffin wish to criticize the notion of "fundamental" conditions and argue that one cannot draw a meaningful distinction between these conditions and all the necessary elements of a good life, let me explain why Griffin's Agency Approach too requires something like the notion of "fundamental conditions" if it is to be plausible.

---

[37] Griffin, *On Human Rights*, 34.

Recall that Griffin's main concern against broadening the ground for human rights is that he believes that there is no human right to everything necessary for a good life. For example, I do not have a human right to a yacht, even if having a yacht is a necessary condition for me to have a good life. But a similar worry could be raised regarding Griffin's Agency Approach, namely, there is no human right to every *agency* consideration that is necessary for a good life. Continuing with the yacht example, developing the agentic capacity to sail a yacht may be necessary for me to have the necessary agentic capacity for a good life, but I do not have a human right that someone help me acquire this capacity. To prevent the Agency Approach from having such an implication, it seems that Griffin would need something like the notion of "fundamental" conditions, which would restrict agency considerations to only those that human beings (*qua* human beings) need whatever else they (*qua* individuals) might need.

In other words, we can distinguish between *agency interests* and *non-agency interests*, where the former kinds of interests are derived from considerations such as autonomy and liberty, and the latter kinds of interests are derived from other elements of a good life such as freedom from pain, understanding, and so on. In addition, we can distinguish between *fundamental interests* and *secondary interests*, where fundamental interests are things that human beings (*qua* human beings) need whatever else they (*qua* individuals) might need in order to pursue a good life (that is, they are the fundamental conditions for pursuing a good life), and secondary interests are things that human beings need in order to pursue a good life. These two sets of distinctions give us four kinds of interests: fundamental agency interests, fundamental non-agency interests, secondary agency interests, and secondary non-agency interests—see Table 3.1.

On this typology, Griffin's claim is that only fundamental agency interests should ground human rights, whereas on the Fundamental Conditions Approach, fundamental non-agency interests could also ground human rights. One should see that Griffin's Redundancy Objection need not apply to the Fundamental Conditions Approach because the Fundamental Conditions Approach can exclude secondary non-agency interests as grounds for human rights. More pertinently, the point I am making here is that if Griffin were to criticize the notion of fundamental conditions, then he would be unable to block secondary agency interests from grounding human rights. Accepting that secondary agency interests could ground human rights would run counter to Griffin's aim to restrict the content of human rights. Hence, Griffin's arguments do not rule out the possibility of a wider account of human rights, which would draw on the notion of agency as well as other elements of a good life.

Table 3.1

	Agency interests	Non-agency interests
Fundamental interests	fundamental agency interests	fundamental non-agency interests
Secondary interests	secondary agency interests	secondary non-agency interests

V. Why Not Just Capabilities?

Key to Nussbaum's Central Capabilities Approach are the notions of capabilities and functionings, where capabilities are an individual's real opportunities to choose and to act to achieve certain functionings, and functionings are various states and activities that an individual can undertake.[38] To illustrate, compare a person who is robbed at gunpoint and told "your money or your life" and a person who voluntarily gives money to someone on the street. The two individuals may have the same functioning as they are both engaging in the activity of giving money away. However, they do not have the same capability, because the individual who voluntarily gives money can choose not to do so, while the individual who is robbed at gunpoint does not have the choice.

According to Nussbaum, not all capabilities are good or important. For instance, being able to be cruel is neither good nor important.[39] Nussbaum argues that the following ten central human capabilities are particularly important, as they are "entailed by the idea of a life worthy of human dignity": life; bodily health; bodily integrity; senses, imagination and thought; emotions; practical reason; affiliation; other species; play; and control over one's environment.[40] Nussbaum believes that all human beings are entitled to these capabilities and these capabilities form the basis of human rights.[41] In particular, to have human dignity, Nussbaum argues that each human being must have enough of each of these capabilities.[42] Moreover, according to Nussbaum, these capabilities generate constraints that political institutions must meet if they are to be minimally just.[43] Following Rawls, Nussbaum is particularly keen to argue that her list of the ten central capabilities can be the object of an overlapping consensus among citizens who otherwise have different comprehensive views.[44]

The hallmark, and indeed the strength, of Nussbaum's Central Capabilities Approach is its emphasis on our opportunities to choose to do certain things rather than on what we actually choose to do. For instance, with respect to political participation and religious practices, Nussbaum rightly argues that it is the capability or opportunity to engage in such activities that is the appropriate social goal. The Fundamental Conditions Approach too recognizes the importance of being able effectively to choose to do certain things. As noted earlier, one of the fundamental conditions for pursuing a good life is *being able freely to choose* to pursue the basic activities.

My concern with the Central Capabilities Approach as an account of human rights is that a significant number of human rights cannot be adequately explained in terms of capabilities.[45] For instance, capabilities do not seem adequate for explaining what

---

[38] Nussbaum, *Creating Capabilities*, 20–6.   [39] Nussbaum, *Creating Capabilities*, 28.
[40] Nussbaum, *Creating Capabilities*, 33–4.   [41] Nussbaum, *Creating Capabilities*, 62.
[42] Nussbaum, *Creating Capabilities*, 36.   [43] Nussbaum, *Creating Capabilities*, 168.
[44] Nussbaum, *Creating Capabilities*, 169.
[45] One could also quibble with Nussbaum's list of central capabilities. For instance, is being able to live with concern for and in relation to animals and plants really a central human capability without which a human life would be undignified? Suppose that it were possible for human beings to live on Mars (or some other planet). Suppose that Mars did not have other animals and plants. Suppose that some human beings were to migrate to Mars. Would the lives of these human beings be undignified because these

might be called status rights, which are rights that protect our moral status as persons. For instance, in the UDHR, the right to recognition everywhere as a person before the law (Article 6); the right to equal protection before the law (Article 7); the right against arbitrary arrest, detention or exile (Article 9); the right to a fair and public hearing (Article 10); the right to be presumed innocent until proven guilty (Article 11) are all status rights, as they protect our moral status as persons.

Capabilities do not seem particularly well suited to explain these rights, because if they were able to explain these rights, it would imply that one can sometimes choose not to exercise these rights, since capabilities are concerned with our real opportunities to choose. But it does not seem that one can sometimes choose whether or not to exercise these rights. For instance, it does not seem that one can sometimes choose not to be recognized everywhere as a person before the law; choose not to have equal protection before the law; choose to be arrested arbitrarily; choose to have an unfair hearing; and choose to be presumed guilty.

Nussbaum does say that

> [o]nly in the area of self-respect and dignity itself do I think that actual functioning is the appropriate aim of public policy. Suppose a state were to say, "We give you the option of being treated with dignity. Here is a penny. If you give it back to us, we will treat you respectfully, but if you prefer, you may keep the penny, and we will humiliate you." This would be a bizarre and unfortunate nation, hardly compatible, it seems, with basic justice. We want political principles that offer respect to all citizens, and, in this one instance, the principles should give them no choice in the matter.[46]

So Nussbaum might grant that capabilities cannot adequately explain status rights, but she might argue that status rights represent only a small fraction of the total number of human rights that exist. However, this response is unpersuasive because, as we have seen, a significant number of human rights are status rights; Articles 6, 7, 9, 10, 11 of the UDHR all contain status rights. Hence, once Nussbaum accepts that capabilities cannot adequately explain status rights, she must also accept that capabilities cannot adequately explain a significant number of human rights.

In addition to status rights, capabilities also cannot adequately explain many children's rights because many children's rights are concerned with functionings rather than capabilities. For example, children have rights to health care, education, name, nationality, to be protected from economic exploitation, and so on. These rights are best understood as rights to certain functionings rather than rights to certain capabilities. Nussbaum concedes this. As she says, "For children, however, functioning may be made the goal in many areas."[47] Nussbaum does try to minimize the impact of this point on her theory by arguing that these functionings are important for helping children to develop adult capabilities.[48] However, this response ignores the fact that some children will unfortunately not live to adulthood (eg, children with terminal

---

human beings would not be able to live with concern for and in relation to animals and plants? It does not seem so. Moreover, if human rights were grounded in capabilities, it does not seem that these human beings would be deprived of key human rights.

[46] Nussbaum, *Frontiers of Justice*, 172.   [47] Nussbaum, *Frontiers of Justice*, 172.
[48] Nussbaum, *Frontiers of Justice*, 172.

cancer). Nevertheless, it seems that these children would still have human rights to certain functionings. If so, this further supports the point that these rights are best understood as rights to certain functionings rather than rights to certain capabilities.

Here it may be useful to point out that in contrast, the Fundamental Conditions Approach can explain these rights. I have previously already shown how the Fundamental Conditions Approach can explain status rights. Here let me explain how the Fundamental Conditions Approach can explain many of the rights that children have. I shall not attempt to be exhaustive. Consider for example children's right to health care and education. Children need to be healthy in order to pursue the basic activities, and to be healthy they need to have access to basic health care. Hence, having access to basic health care is a fundamental condition for pursuing a good life. Similarly, education is a fundamental condition for pursuing a good life because children need to acquire the basic knowledge to be adequately functioning individuals in their society, and to acquire such knowledge, they need some kind of education. Given that health care and education are fundamental conditions for children to pursue a good life, on the Fundamental Conditions Approach, children would have a right to health care and education.

Consider also the right to have a name and a nationality. Having a name and a nationality is a fundamental condition for pursuing a good life because to pursue the basic activities, children need to know that they are unique individuals deserving of equal respect, and to know this, they need to have their own identity. In modern societies, having a name and a nationality gives one one's own identity. Hence, having a name and nationality is a fundamental condition for children to pursue a good life. On the Fundamental Conditions Approach, children would have the right to have a name and a nationality.

Given that a significant number of human rights cannot be adequately explained in terms of capabilities and given that the Fundamental Conditions Approach can readily explain these rights, this is a reason to prefer the Fundamental Conditions Approach over the Central Capabilities Approach.

VI. Why Not the Political Approach?

As I said at the outset, proponents of the Political Conception believe that the Naturalistic Conception of human rights should be rejected in favor of its Political counterpart. I have also said the Fundamental Conditions Approach is a Naturalistic Conception. Since my aim here is to develop the correct substantive account of human rights, it will be helpful to say something about the Political Conception. Owing to lack of space, I shall not attempt to give a full defense of the Naturalistic Conception. But I shall do three things.[49] First, I shall argue that Naturalistic Conceptions can accommodate one of the most salient concerns that proponents of the Political Conception have raised about them. Second, I shall demonstrate that the theoretical distance between Naturalistic and Political Conceptions is not as great as it has

---

[49] This section draws on S. Matthew Liao and Adam Etinson, "Political and Naturalistic Conceptions of Human Rights: A False Polemic?," *Journal of Moral Philosophy*, 9 (2012): 1–26.

been made out to be. Third, I shall point out that a Political Conception, on its own, lacks the resources necessary to determine the substantive content of human rights. If I am right, not only should the Naturalistic Conception not be rejected, the Political Conception is in fact incomplete without the theoretical resources that a Naturalistic Conception characteristically provides.

To start, it will be helpful to provide an overview of different ways of understanding the Political Conception.

A. Political conceptions of human rights

According to Rawls, "Human rights are a class of rights that play a special role in a reasonable Law of Peoples; they restrict the justifying reasons for war and its conduct, and they specify limits to a regime's internal autonomy."[50] More specifically, a society's observance of human rights is necessary for the society to be a member "in good standing in a reasonably just Society of People" and is "sufficient to exclude justified and forceful intervention by other peoples."[51] Human rights, Rawls tells us, are "Necessary conditions of any system of social cooperation. When they are regularly violated, we have command by force, a slave system, and no cooperation of any kind."[52] Moreover, if a society fails to observe human rights, then, according to Rawls, it cannot complain if external agents interfere in its internal affairs, for example, by means of economic or political sanction, or even coercive intervention.[53]

Raz agrees with Rawls's idea that human rights characteristically set limits to a society's internal autonomy.[54] But Raz's account differs from Rawls's in two main respects. First, Raz argues that while human rights are primarily rights against states, human rights can be held against international agents and organizations of all sorts, including individuals, groups, corporations, and other potential violating domestic institutions.[55] Second, Raz argues that Rawls fails to distinguish between the limits of sovereignty and the limits of legitimate authority.[56] Rawls holds that human rights are necessary conditions of any system of social cooperation, and he believes that conditions of social cooperation can determine the limits of sovereignty. But Raz argues that not every action that exceeds a state's legitimate authority can be a reason for interference by other states. For instance, a state can sometimes be protected from external interference even if it lacks internal legitimacy (for example, if the external agents are themselves biased and corrupt). If so, the conditions of social cooperation alone cannot determine the limits of sovereignty.

Beitz argues that the current role of human rights in international political practice extends beyond that of the (pro tanto) justification of foreign interference or intervention.[57] In particular, it encompasses the broader role of guiding practical judgments about international responsibility or concern. For instance, there is a broad

---

[50] Rawls, *The Law of Peoples*, 79.   [51] Rawls, *The Law of Peoples*, 80.
[52] Rawls, *The Law of Peoples*, 68.   [53] Rawls, *The Law of Peoples*, 81.
[54] Raz, "Human Rights without Foundations," 328.
[55] Raz, "Human Rights without Foundations," 329.
[56] Raz, "Human Rights without Foundations," 330–2.
[57] Beitz, *The Idea of Human Rights*, 101.

range of non-coercive political and economic measures that states and international organizations can use to influence the internal affairs of societies where human rights are threatened, measures that are better classified as assistance than interference. Moreover, Beitz observes that human rights are also justifications for individuals and non-governmental organizations to engage in reform-oriented political action. In short, Beitz believes that from the perspective of a theory's attempting to explain the current international practice of human rights, it would be better to take a broader view of the international role of human rights than Rawls's narrower view.

B. The concern about timelessness

Proponents of the Political Conception have expressed a number of concerns regarding the Naturalistic Conception. The one I shall discuss here is the concern about Timelessness. Beitz and others have observed that, on a Naturalistic Conception, human rights seem to be "timeless—all human beings at all times and places would be justified in claiming them."[58] However, they argue that it is not the case that all human beings at all times and places would be justified in claiming the human rights currently recognized by international practice. For example, consider the right to education, in Article 26 (1) of the UDHR, which states that:

> Everyone has the right to education. Education shall be free, at least in the elementary and fundamental stages. Elementary education shall be compulsory. Technical and professional education shall be made generally available and higher education shall be equally accessible to all on the basis of merit.

Raz points out that if people have a right to education simply in virtue of their humanity, "it follows that cave dwellers in the Stone Age had that right. Does that make sense?... The very distinctions between elementary, technical, professional and higher education would have made no sense at that, and at many other times."[59]

Beitz argues further that international human rights are intended to play a role in a certain range of societies:

> Roughly speaking, these are societies that have at least some of the defining features of modernization: for example, a minimal legal system (including a capability for enforcement), an economy that includes some form of wage labor for at least some workers, some participation in global cultural and economic life, and a public institutional capacity to raise revenue and provide essential collective goods.[60]

Echoing this sentiment, Raz argues that human rights are "synchronically universal," by which he means that all people alive today have them.[61] If it is essential to Naturalistic Conceptions such as the Fundamental Conditions Approach that human rights are timeless, but if it is the case that human rights as found in international practice are not timeless, then this seems to call into question the plausibility and validity of Naturalistic Conceptions.

---

[58] Beitz, "Human Rights and the Law of Peoples," 198; Beitz, *The Idea of Human Rights*, 57.
[59] Raz, "Human Rights in the Emerging World Order," 40.
[60] Beitz, *The Idea of Human Rights*, 56–7.
[61] Raz, "Human Rights in the Emerging World Order," 41.

In response to this concern, it seems that at least some of the rights that can be found in the UDHR are indeed timeless. For example, consider the human right against torture. There seems to be good reasons to believe that even cavemen had a human right not to be tortured. The same can be said regarding the rights not to be murdered, enslaved, and so on.

Second, recall that when Beitz says that international human rights are intended to play a certain role in modern societies, he takes this to mean societies that have a minimal legal system, an economy that includes some form of wage labor for at least some workers, some participation in global cultural and economic life, and so on. However, there are over a hundred un-contacted tribes in the world today, that is, tribes that have no contact with the outside world.[62] It seems doubtful that all of these tribes have the defining features of modernization that Beitz speaks of, such as "some participation in global cultural and economic life." Should we draw the conclusion that members of these tribes do not have human rights? Such a conclusion seems dubious. If so, why should we not accept that human rights can also apply to past societies that similarly lacked features of modernization?

The same point can be made against one of Raz's reasons for rejecting the idea that human rights are timeless. Raz argues that since many of the most uncontroversial human rights appeal to institutions and make use of distinctions (for example, the distinction between elementary, technical, professional, and higher education) that could not possibly apply in Stone Age societies, it is senseless to think of such rights as timeless. But such institutions and distinctions also fail to apply in the case of present-day un-contacted tribes. And so, by his own reasoning, Raz would have to admit that members of these tribes do not have, say, the human right to elementary education. But if Raz accepts that members of un-contacted tribes do not have some human rights, it seems that he would have to abandon his claim that human rights are synchronically universal, by which he means that *all* people alive today have them.

Third, there are plausible ways of explaining how there could be contemporary human rights such as the right to elementary education without abandoning the claim that human rights are timeless. For instance, we can distinguish between the aim and the object of a right. The aim of a human right is the goal or end of the human right, and the object of a human right is the means to achieving that goal or end. The proposal is that the aims of human rights are timeless while the objects of human rights may vary across time, location, and society. As long as we are clear that when we say that human rights are timeless, we are referring to the aims of human rights, then the puzzle just articulated should disappear.

To illustrate, consider the human right to free elementary education. We could say that free elementary education is the object of a right. As such, it makes sense only at a specific time, in a specific location, and in a specific society. By contrast, the aim of the right to free elementary education is to ensure that human beings acquire the knowledge necessary to be adequately functioning individuals in their circumstances, and it does not seem odd to say such an aim was relevant, important, and applied in the context of cavemen. In other words, while cavemen would not have had a right to

---

[62] http://www.survivalinternational.org/uncontactedtribes.

free elementary school education, it does not seem odd to think that the *aim* of that right did have normative force in their circumstances, and that it would have generated a different, but similar, object of right for cavemen, for example, the right to be educated (in a basic way) about how to hunt and gather, assuming that such instruction could feasibly be provided to them. Hence, as long as we are clear that when we say that human rights are timeless, we are referring to the aims of human rights, then the puzzle should disappear.

C. Formal compatibility

I shall now argue that the theoretical distance between these two conceptions is actually not as great as it has been made out to be. To see this, consider the *formal* features of both conceptions. According to the Naturalistic Conception, human rights are rights that we have simply in virtue of being human. And, according to the Political Conception, human rights are rights that set limits to a society's internal autonomy (Rawls and Raz) and/or rights that the international community has a responsibility to protect in modern societies (Beitz). Are these two formal features incompatible? One way of seeing that they need not be is to notice that the formal features of Political Conceptions seem to be concerned with the issue of who is responsible for protecting and promoting human rights—that is, the issue of the *duty-bearers* of human rights—while the formal features of Naturalistic Conceptions seem to be concerned with what *grounds* human rights. Since questions about the grounds and questions about the duty-bearers of human rights are non-overlapping or, at least, need not overlap, it is in principle possible for one to accept both a Naturalistic and Political Conception of the formal features of human rights.

To flesh this point out, let us consider what advocates of Naturalistic Conceptions have actually said about the issue of duty-bearers. For example, D.D. Raphael argues that:

> The expression "a universal moral right" may be used in a stronger sense or in a weaker sense. In the stronger sense it means a right of all men against all men; in the weaker sense it means simply a right of all men, but not necessarily against all men. In the weaker sense, all men may have a right which is, for each of them, a right against some men only.[63]

To keep the discussion simple, let us focus on the:

Strong Sense: Human rights are rights against all able persons and agents in appropriate circumstances.

Is Strong Sense incompatible with a Political Conception, according to which human rights first and foremost set limits to a society's internal autonomy (Rawls and Raz) and/or are rights that the international community has a responsibility to protect in modern societies (Beitz)? The two formal features can in principle be compatible given that "all able persons and agents in appropriate circumstances" can be read as an abstract statement about who the duty-bearers of human rights are, and that "the

---

[63] D. D. Raphael, "Human Rights, Old and New," in D. D. Raphael (ed.), *Political Theory and the Rights of Man* (London: Macmillan, 1967), 65.

state and/or the international community in modern societies" can be read as a more specific formulation of who such duty-bearers are. Indeed, supposing that the relevant "appropriate circumstances" are those of modernity, if one were to ask advocates of the Naturalistic Conception who the "able persons and agents" in modern societies are, it seems likely that they would accept that it is first and foremost the state and/or the international community that are the relevant "able persons and agents." But if advocates of these two Conceptions would come to the same conclusions about who the relevant duty-bearers of human rights are, this suggests that the two Conceptions can be compatible in this respect.

D. Formal and substantive accounts of human rights

Finally, I argue that Naturalistic and Political Conceptions are not only in principle formally compatible, but that, in fact, the Political Conception is incomplete without the theoretical resources that a Naturalistic Conception characteristically provides. To see this, it is useful to distinguish between a *formal* and a *substantive* account of human rights. A formal account provides criteria for distinguishing human rights claims from those that are not human rights claims. A substantive account, by contrast, provides criteria for generating the content of human rights. A Naturalistic Conception typically provides us with not just a formal, but also a substantive, account of human rights. In this respect, the Fundamental Conditions Approach is a substantive account of human rights. By contrast, the Political Conception tends to provide us with only a formal account of human rights. This is clearest in Beitz's account. Beitz does not provide a list of human rights that we have, but instead proposes what he calls a "model" of such rights, which has three key elements:[64]

(i) Human rights protect urgent individual interests against standard threats that one might find in the modern statist global order.

(ii) Human rights apply in the first instance to the political institutions of states.

(iii) Human rights are matters of international concern. A state's failure to carry out its responsibilities may be a reason for "second level" agents such as the international community to hold the state accountable for carrying out these responsibilities, to assist the state if the state lacks capacities to carry out these responsibilities, and to interfere in the state if the state is unwilling to do so.

Beitz's account surely provides us with criteria for distinguishing human rights claims from those that are not human rights claims. To keep things simple, consider (i). According to (i), if something is a human right, then it will protect some urgent individual interest. And if something is not an urgent individual interest, then it will not be protected by a human right. The notion of an urgent individual interest therefore tells us something about the formal features of human rights, but it is unclear what substantive human rights would follow from this notion. Similar things can be said regarding (ii) and (iii).

---

[64] Beitz, *The Idea of Human Rights*, 109.

The same can be said about Raz's version of the Political Conception. Raz also does not provide a list of human rights that we have, but he proposes the following three steps as a way to determine whether something is a human right:[65] a human right exists if:

(a) there is an individual interest that is sufficient to establish an individual moral right;

(b) states are to be held duty bound to respect or promote this interest; and

(c) states do not enjoy immunity from interference should they fail to respect or promote this interest.

Raz's three-step program would, for example, exclude (from the category of interests protected by human rights) interests that cannot ground individual moral rights or interests that states have no duty to protect or promote. But, again, it is unclear what human rights would follow from this program. So Raz's account also does not give us a substantive account of human rights.

Rawls does provide us with a list (albeit a very short one) of human rights, but in any case it remains unclear whether Rawls's account provides us with more than a formal account of human rights. To see why, recall that for Rawls, one of the main roles of human rights is to set limits to a society's internal autonomy. This provides us with a criterion for distinguishing human rights claims from those that are not human rights claims. In particular, it says that if something, X, is a human right, then X will set limits to a society's internal autonomy. And if an individual right, Y, does not set limits to a society's internal autonomy, then Y is not a human right. However, it is unclear what human rights will follow from this criterion. And so it does not provide us with a substantive standard with which we can determine the content of human rights.

However, Rawls also claims that human rights are "necessary conditions for any system of social cooperation." So it might be thought that Rawls intended the notion of social cooperation to serve as such a substantive criterion. But this interpretation of Rawls faces two difficulties. First, the idea that X (a set of human rights) is a necessary condition for Y (a system of social cooperation) is not equivalent to the idea that X is based on, or grounded in, Y, and it is the latter sort of relationship that is required for something to serve as a substantive criterion. Compare: the idea that air is a necessary condition for agency is not equivalent to the idea that air is based on, or grounded in, agency; the latter does not even make very much sense. Hence, the claim that human rights are necessary conditions for social cooperation is not the same as the claim that human rights are based on, or grounded in, social cooperation. Given this, the fact that Rawls has claimed the former does not mean that he has claimed the latter. And since the latter is what is required for something to serve as a substantive criterion, the fact that Rawls has not claimed the latter means that it is unclear that Rawls intended the notion of social cooperation to be a substantive criterion.

Second, even if Rawls did intend for the notion of social cooperation to be a substantive criterion, it does not seem to be a plausible one. Not all societies that fail

---

[65] Raz, "Human Rights without Foundations," 336.

to respect the human rights that Rawls lists command by force.[66] For instance, it is implausible to think that communities that do not recognize personal private property (one of Rawls's human rights) must command by force. Moreover, it is unclear how one derives the right to personal property from the notion of social cooperation. Hence, a substantive account of human rights based on the notion of social cooperation seems to be fraught with difficulties.

It might be said that the Political Conception was never intended to answer the sort of substantive questions that I have accused it of failing to address. However, if this is right and, in fact, the Political Conception, as a formal account of human rights, leaves the important problem of generating the content of human rights out of view, then the Political Conception is incomplete. Accordingly, it may very well look to Naturalistic Conceptions such as the Fundament Conditions Approach as a source for generating a substantive account of human rights.

VII. Conclusion

In this chapter, I argued that human rights should be grounded in the fundamental conditions for pursuing a good life. I showed how this Fundamental Conditions Approach can explain why many of the rights in the UDHR are indeed human rights, and also how this approach can rule out some of the claims in the UDHR as genuine human rights. I also distinguished the Fundamental Conditions Approach from Griffin's Agency Approach and Nussbaum's Central Capabilities Approach by arguing, among other things, that Griffin's approach cannot adequately explain the right against torture and that Nussbaum's approach cannot adequately explain status rights and many children's rights.

I further defended the Fundamental Conditions Approach as a Naturalistic Conception of human rights against the Political Conceptions of human rights by (a) arguing that the distinction between the aim and the object of a right can explain how human rights can be timeless even if many of the human rights proclaimed in international declarations do not appear to be so; (b) showing that Naturalistic and Political Conceptions can in principle be compatible at the formal level because the formal features of Political Conceptions seem to be concerned with the issue of who is responsible for protecting and promoting human rights, while the formal features of Naturalistic Conceptions seem to be concerned with what *grounds* human rights; and (c) arguing that the Political Conception tends to offer only a formal account of human rights, which means that a Political Conception is, on its own, incomplete, and may very well look to a Naturalistic Conception to provide what it is missing, ie, a substantive account of human rights. If all of this is right, the Fundamental Conditions Approach offers a real and coherent alternative to existing approaches to human rights and deserves further study in the debate regarding the grounds of human rights.[67]

[66] Raz, "Human Rights without Foundations," 330.

[67] I would like to thank Rowan Cruft, Massimo Renzo, Rob Shaver, Daniel Khokhar, Carolyn Plunkett, Andrew Franklin-Hall, Nic Southwood, Collin O'Neil, Christian Barry, Daniel Nolan, Rachael Briggs, Rahul Kumar, Kerah Gordon-Solmon, Meena Krishnamurthy, Christine Sypnowich, Adrian Currie, and audiences at the Australian National University, the Queen's University, Kingston, and the University of Manitoba, for their helpful comments on earlier versions of this paper.

4

From a Good Life to Human Rights

Some Complications

Rowan Cruft

It is natural and appealing to ground human rights in their relation to the good life. Yet many people—perhaps the majority of humans across history—have suffered either from human rights violations (for example, as slaves) or at least from what we might term human rights 'deficits' (for example, those who live or lived in societies that restrict religious worship and political participation). It would be odd, I think, if human rights theory classified every one of these people as unable to attain a good life. While some might well have had their lives blighted by the violations suffered, not all will and some will have recovered following violation, or even found meaning in the violation itself, as a martyr for example.[1] So respect for a person's human rights cannot be necessary for that person to have a good life. In addition, many people whose human rights are recognized and respected fail to live good lives due, for example, to miserable personal relationships, thwarted ambitions or major illnesses. So respect for a person's human rights cannot be sufficient for that person to have a good life either. Maybe respect for human rights tends to make a good life more likely, but that could be questioned.

Nonetheless, it would be odd if there was no important relationship between a person's human rights and their living a good life. Without such a relationship, the power and appeal of human rights would be significantly diminished. One of the virtues of Liao's account is that it brings out clearly the complexity of the relationship between human rights and a good life, while still taking the good life as the ultimate ground for such rights. In sections I to IV that follow, I examine Liao's account in order to show that to deliver a standard list of human rights, Liao has to endorse a somewhat controversial liberal commitment to the importance of *a range* of ways of pursuing a good life—and to a somewhat technical notion of *pursuit*. An alternative that avoids these commitments makes the relation between human rights and the good life weak in a way that threatens human rights' special status. At the end of the essay (section V), I show that human rights' recognition-independence means that their grounding cannot proceed in a straightforward way from the value of what they protect: an explanation is needed for why this value grounds rights even when they will not help to secure it. There is a risk that this explanation will leave the good life defined in part as a life

---

[1] This is not to romanticize suffering. For a case where a violation contributes to a life's success in a sense, see Griffin's discussion of Solzhenitsyn (James Griffin, *On Human Rights* (Oxford University Press, 2008), 46–7).

in which independently grounded human rights are respected, rather than grounding such rights on a separately conceivable notion of the good life. My points do not undermine approaches, like Liao's, which ground human rights on a good life; my aim is rather to sketch the key challenges for such approaches to overcome.

I. The Initial Appeal of Grounding Human Rights in a Good Life

Liao argues that human rights protect the goods, capacities, and options which are necessary for human beings to be able to pursue the basic activities that are important for a good life. A good life, for Liao, means a 'minimally decent life', where this is a life involving 'certain valuable, basic activities'. These basic activities, of which we must enjoy at least some if we are to have a good life, include 'deep personal relationships', 'active pleasures such as creative work and play', and 'passive pleasures such as appreciating beauty'.[2] For Liao, a good life need not be an excellent or flourishing life; rather, it is 'minimally' good.

The claimed link between human rights and a minimally good life is appealing. Surely the reason I have human rights is in order to provide some protection for the minimal quality or success of my life, to try to ensure that my life is not blighted. Many theorists—especially those who regard human rights as modern forms of 'natural' or 'basic' rights—similarly ground human rights by their relation to the good life: Tasioulas grounds human rights in part on their holders' interests and he takes an interest, in Raz's words, as an 'aspect of well-being'; Miller's needs-based approach understands right-grounding needs by their relation to harm, which we could understand as a set-back to a good life; a similar link between needs and a good life could be developed in interpreting Renzo; Liao examines Nussbaum's capabilities approach as a rival that derives human rights from a conception of a good life; and even Griffin, who grounds human rights in 'normative agency', can plausibly be read as grounding human rights on one specific aspect of a good human life.[3]

Liao's account is unusual for keeping the good life to the fore,[4] and this is helpful. Liao's concept of the 'fundamental conditions for a good life' seems attractively

---

[2] S. Matthew Liao, 'Human Rights as Fundamental Conditions for a Good Life', this volume, ch. 3, 81.

[3] John Tasioulas, 'On the Foundations of Human Rights', this volume, ch. 1 (the quotation from Raz is in Joseph Raz, *The Morality of Freedom* (Oxford University Press, 1986), 166); David Miller, 'Grounding Human Rights', *Critical Review of International Social and Political Philosophy*, 15(4) (2012): 407–27, and 'Joseph Raz on Human Rights: A Critical Appraisal', this volume, ch. 12; Massimo Renzo, 'Human Needs, Human Rights', this volume, ch. 32; Martha Nussbaum, *Creating Capabilities: The Human Development Approach* (Harvard University Press, 2011). James Griffin distances his approach from the notion of a good life (*On Human Rights*, 34), but see Liao, 'Human Rights as Fundamental Conditions for a Good Life', 86–90, for an explanation of the link between Griffin's approach and the good life. Note that adherents of the 'political' approach to human rights also include a link with the good life: see Beitz's grounding of human rights in 'urgent individual interests' (Charles R. Beitz, *The Idea of Human Rights* (Oxford University Press, 2009), 109) and Raz's conception of human rights as rights and hence, in his terms, as grounded in interests (Joseph Raz, 'Human Rights in the Emerging World Order', this volume, ch. 11).

[4] Nussbaum is similar in this respect.

broader than Griffin's grounding notion of normative agency. Liao argues that conditions necessary for human beings' pursuing the basic activities but which were not necessary for normative agency would nonetheless be plausible grounds for human rights, due to the great importance to a good life of pursuing the basic activities. And Liao similarly argues that his approach can ground status rights and children's rights to good parenting and education (because, he argues, an appropriate status and upbringing are essential to one's being able to pursue some of the activities central to a good life) while Nussbaum's approach cannot easily accommodate rights protecting these aspects of a good life because they are 'best understood as rights to certain functionings rather than rights to certain capabilities'.[5] In addition, Liao's position seems helpfully narrower than Tasioulas's pluralist interest-based approach. For Tasioulas human rights are grounded in the interests and dignity of human beings. The interests which ground human rights, for Tasioulas, are those sufficiently important to generate duties despite the burdens they impose, and that ground rights borne universally by all humans in virtue of their humanity.[6] One might worry that there is little substantive material in Tasioulas's account (beyond the notions of dignity and the 'in virtue of one's humanity' clause) that can bind together or limit the grounds for human rights. The account might thus seem unhelpfully broad,[7] and also difficult to operationalize. By contrast, Liao's approach gives the practitioner a neat, substantive, and seemingly narrow test for whether something is a human right: does it protect one among an adequate range of the conditions whose obtaining is necessary if the right-holder *qua* human being is to be able to pursue one or more basic activities?

II. The Intricacy of the Relationship Between Human Rights and a Good Life

Liao's account uses five concepts—italicized and numbered here—that make the link between human rights and the minimally good life intricate: for Liao, human rights protect (1) an *adequate range* of the (2) *fundamental conditions* that (3) *human beings qua human beings* need in order to (4) *pursue* the (5) *basic activities*. I discuss them in reverse order.

On the relation between the good life and *basic activities*, Liao writes:

[A] characteristically good human life, or a good life, for short, is one spent in pursuing certain valuable, basic activities. 'Basic' activities are activities that are important to human beings *qua* human beings' life as a whole. Sunbathing, for example, is an activity, but is not a basic activity, because a human being *qua* human being's life as a whole is not affected if a human being does not go sunbathing. In addition, activities that are very important to an individual human being's life as a whole may nevertheless not be basic activities, because these activities may not be important to human beings *qua* human beings' life as a whole. For instance, being a professional

---

[5] Liao, 'Human Rights as Fundamental Conditions for a Good Life', 92.
[6] Tasioulas, 'On the Foundations of Human Rights'.
[7] Tasioulas would question this charge. See his points about the limits on the interests which can ground human rights, Tasioulas, 'On the Foundations of Human Rights', Section III.

philosopher is very important to my life as a whole. But being a professional philosopher is not a basic activity because it is not an activity that is important to human beings *qua* human beings' life as a whole. [...] Some of the basic activities are as follows: deep personal relationships with, for example, one's partner, friends, parents, children; knowledge of, for example, the workings of the world, of oneself, of others; active pleasures such as creative work and play; and passive pleasures such as appreciating beauty.[8]

Liao makes clear that a life can be a good life even if it does not contain all the basic activities together. This is plausible: one can have a minimally good life without deep personal relationships, so long as other valuable activities take their place; similarly, I suspect one can have a minimally good life without passive pleasures. So the basic activities are not individually necessary conditions for a minimally good life. They are, rather, disjunctively necessary: important activities such that a life totally devoid of them all could not be a minimally good life.

Liao says that human rights protect the conditions for *pursuit* of the basic activities.[9] One can pursue such activities, and thus pursue a good life, without succeeding—for example by pursuing a personal relationship which fails. Perhaps one can sometimes also fall into a basic activity without pursuing it: maybe personal communion with god is not something one can pursue, but something that is bestowed on one if one is lucky. I am unsure about the latter point, but certainly Liao is committed to the former: pursuit is a precondition for rather than a guarantee of one's engaging successfully in a basic activity.

Liao conceives human rights as protecting the conditions for *humans qua humans* to pursue the basic activities. *Qua* individual in a particular context, I might—in order to pursue a particular basic activity—need rather more than what human rights provide. For example, I might need something idiosyncratic: a very sharp eye in order to join the shooting team (my only chance of fellowship), a tiddlywinks set (my only chance of play). Liao makes clear that my human rights protect only what humans need *qua humans* to pursue the basic activities: this will often differ from what a particular contextually situated individual human needs.[10]

For Liao, human rights protect the *fundamental conditions* for a human *qua* human to pursue the basic activities. These 'fundamental conditions' are necessary conditions, and Liao notes that they will include goods, capacities, and options. While some of these fundamental conditions (perhaps absence of torture) will be 'all purpose means' essential for a human *qua* human to pursue *any basic activity at all rather than none*, others (perhaps the guarantees of fair and equal treatment that Liao mentions) will be necessary conditions for a human *qua* human to pursue *some particular basic activities* and will not be necessary for the pursuit of different basic activities.[11]

---

[8] Liao, 'Human Rights as Fundamental Conditions for a Good Life', 81.
[9] Liao, 'Human Rights as Fundamental Conditions for a Good Life', 81-3
[10] See Liao's claim that '[t]he fundamental conditions for pursuing a good life are various goods, capacities, and options that *human beings (qua human beings) need, whatever else they (qua individuals) might need*, in order to pursue the basic activities' (Liao, 'Human Rights as Fundamental Conditions for a Good Life', 81–2 emphasis added).
[11] Liao, 'Human Rights as Fundamental Conditions for a Good Life', 82.

Finally, Liao adds:

> [An] individual's having all the fundamental conditions means that this individual would still have access to an *adequate range* of goods, capacities, and options to pursue those basic activities that are characteristic of a minimally decent human life. This could become important if, for example, this individual changed his/her mind about pursuing a particular kind of good life.[12]

Thus for Liao an individual's human rights protect an *adequate range* of the fundamental conditions for a human *qua* human to pursue basic activities. Even if I have chosen a basic activity to which some human rights violations seem irrelevant—for example, suppose I am able to pursue my ascetic religious convictions by fasting within a regime that would have starved me anyway—Liao's approach still requires that an adequate range of the goods, capacities, and options necessary for a human *qua* human to pursue basic activities be open to me. Such an adequate range will include the option to eat, even though I have not chosen this.

Liao has moved five steps away from the problematic thesis that respect for any one human right is necessary if the particular right-holder is to live a good life. These moves give us a link between human rights and the right-holder's living a good life, while allowing (i) that many people whose rights are respected will fail to live good lives either because their *pursuit* of basic activities fails or because to pursue these activities they need more in their context than simply what a *human qua human* needs. It also allows (ii) that many people whose rights are violated will still live good lives because despite being denied the conditions necessary to pursue *some* basic activities, they have nonetheless been able successfully to pursue *others*. It might also allow that some people whose rights are violated will nonetheless live good lives by means other than *pursuit* of the basic activities, such as by 'falling into' such activities without pursuing them—though this is controversial. Furthermore, although this is not delivered directly by the five steps I have identified in Liao, it seems likely that Liao would also want to allow that in some cases a person whose rights are violated will nonetheless live a good life because the violation (for example, torture from which one manages to recover) only made impossible pursuit of a basic activity *at a time*, rather than across the right-holder's lifetime.

One might think that Liao's approach also allows victims of rights violations to have lived good lives on the related ground that for Liao human rights offer 'powerful protection'[13] for the fundamental conditions, and such protection is not strictly *necessary* for the fundamental conditions to obtain, and hence these conditions can sometimes continue to obtain even when the protection has been violated. I discuss this possibility in section IV. Before this discussion of *how* human rights protect what they protect, I assess Liao's view of *what* human rights protect (namely, the fundamental conditions for a human's pursuit of the basic activities).

---

[12] Liao, 'Human Rights as Fundamental Conditions for a Good Life', 82 (emphasis added).
[13] Liao, 'Human Rights as Fundamental Conditions for a Good Life', 83.

III. What Human Rights Protect: The Good Life and Liao's Additions

What makes for a minimally good life—in Liao's terms, what should count as a basic activity—is controversial. Someone committed to the importance of feudal social roles might claim that serfs serving generous lords had a minimally good life; others will disagree. For Liao what is needed is not simply to determine which actual lives have been minimally good, nor what a historically typical minimally good life has involved. Liao's reference to the conditions needed *qua human* for pursuing the basic activities makes clear that he has in mind the kind of minimally good life that our human nature makes possible. Similarly, Tasioulas's right-grounding 'basic interests' will need to be defined by the forms of well-being that our human nature makes possible, and the components of Griffin's 'normative agency' will be determined by what is humanly possible. Such approaches are needed if we are to ground human rights with a critical edge: rights that protect conditions such as political participation, which most actual humans leading actual minimally good lives have failed to attain.

There are epistemic difficulties in deciding whether a given concrete individual has had a minimally good life: we cannot always trust her own judgement on the matter, nor the judgement of third-party expert observers (anthropologists, biologists, sociologists), though such judgements are clearly relevant. These difficulties are magnified when considering the forms of good life that our human nature makes possible: there are risks of conservative bias (for example, human possibilities that are rarely or never played out in actuality might be overlooked) and of a circularity in which entrenched conceptions of what our rights are (for example, the belief in an asymmetry between rights to assistance and rights to non-interference) infect our view of the possible good lives for humans. Some theorists will reject the idea that there are any unifying features to what is picked out by 'the forms of good life possible for humans'.

I do not at present feel I can do much more than report my uncertainty about whether confidence on this issue is justified.[14] Nonetheless, it is not clear to me that such concerns threaten Liao's approach *in particular*, nor related approaches like that of Griffin, Miller, Nussbaum or Tasioulas. Our grasp on which forms of minimally good life our nature makes possible is perhaps shaky and views on the matter will be contestable, but I suspect the same is true of alternative fundamental grounds for human rights—for example, what we cannot help presupposing as agents,[15] or what would be agreed by hypothetical contractors—and of other areas of moral and political importance such as the nature of legitimate authority.

---

[14] For confident responses to the worry, see—among many others—Griffin, 'The Relativity and Ethnocentricity of Human Rights', this volume, ch. 31 and Massimo Renzo, 'Human Needs, Human Rights', this volume, ch. 32. For those who are more concerned that there is no unity to the very wide range of forms of good human life, see for example Simon Hope, 'Human Rights without the Human Good? A Reply to Jiwei Ci', this volume, ch. 36, and his use of Clifford Geertz, *Local Knowledge* (Basic Books, 1983).

[15] See Alan Gewirth's approach to human rights (*Reason and Morality* (University of Chicago Press, 1978)).

A further question concerns Liao's claim that human rights protect *an adequate range* of fundamental conditions for a minimally good life. If the importance of living a minimally good life is what ultimately grounds human rights, insisting on providing an 'adequate range' of ways to enable pursuit of such a life can seem unmotivated.[16] For example, what should Liao say to a repressive regime which claims that, despite the limitations it imposes on freedom of speech, assembly, and political participation, nonetheless most of its members succeed in living minimally good lives, because most members successfully pursue other life-enhancing basic activities including meaningful employment and personal relationships?[17] Liao mentions the possibility that individuals will change their pursuits in such a way that new activities will become central to their having a good life, and perhaps he would claim that by repressing these possibilities for change, the relevant regimes fail properly to respect the good lives of their subjects. But a repressive regime might be correct in predicting that very few of its subjects will wish to engage in the political activities it represses, and it could add that it will take measures to prevent people choosing to engage in such activities. If individuals' having *minimally good lives* is ultimately what grounds human rights, then why should such a regime recognize the civil and political human rights which its subjects do not and will not need for a minimally good life?

By keeping the good life to the fore, Liao makes these questions more pressing than they are for theorists like Tasioulas who pick out particular basic human interests as meriting protection without grounding their importance directly in their relationship to the good life—though a version of the charge could be developed against Tasioulas if one takes the importance of basic interests to derive from their role in a good life. Renzo suggests that such a charge can also be pressed against need-based theories of human rights.[18]

One response is to maintain that a person does not really have a minimally good life if she lacks an adequate range of the fundamental conditions for pursuit of the basic activities, even if she is nonetheless able to pursue *some* fulfilling basic activities from within her narrow range of options.[19] This seems quite attractive, but it amounts to what one might call a 'liberal imperialist' classificatory position according to which most inhabitants of repressive regimes, and thus I would suggest most

---

[16] I set aside the question of whether 'adequate' is question-begging, though this could be pressed.

[17] This is one, admittedly disputable, way to understand Lee Kuan Yew's claims about 'Asian values' in relation to his role leading Singapore, and Mahathir Mohamad's similar claims for Malaysia (discussed in Joanne R. Bauer and Daniel A. Bell (eds.), *The East Asian Challenge for Human Rights* (Cambridge University Press, 1999)).

[18] Renzo, 'Human Needs, Human Rights', 580.

[19] Renzo considers and rejects this reponse in discussing Nickel's suggestion that rape denies one a good life ('Human Needs, Human Rights', 580–1). The idea can be read—perhaps mis-read—into Raz's claim that '[a]utonomy is a constitutive element of the good life' (*The Morality of Freedom*, 408), coupled with his conception of autonomy as requiring the availability of a range of valuable options. Nussbaum can similarly be read as claiming that denial of any one of her ten 'Central Capabilities' denies a person 'human dignity and a life worthy of it' (*Creating Capabilities: the Human Development Approach*, 29 and 32–5) Compare also John Finnis's claim that '[i]f a statesman…treats truth or friendship or play or any of the other basic forms of good as of no account, and never asks himself whether his life-plan(s) makes reasonable allowance for participation in those intrinsic human values…, then he can properly be accused…of stunting or mutilating himself and those in his care' (*Natural Law and Natural Rights* (Oxford University Press 1980), 106).

humans throughout history, are classified as lacking a minimally good life. Concern about this position is what motivated my questions at the start of the chapter.

An alternative response maintains that if X is the ultimate ground for human rights then, *whatever X is*—whether it is a minimally good life, agency, needs or something else—there is independent reason to regard human rights as protecting a *range* of the fundamental conditions for a human to be able to pursue X. This independent reason might be humans' status as self-determining agents: because we are self-determining agents, our rights should secure us with a range of ways of pursuing the relevant X. This argument—or any other similarly offering independent support for Liao's *range* requirement—will need careful development to ensure that it generates a grounding for an appropriately wide range of rights for every human being.

The latter approach clearly needs more discussion, but my aim for now is simply to show that Liao and similar theorists will need something like the range requirement and that, to avoid the liberal imperialist position, it will need a grounding distinct from the claim that the relevant range is necessary for the right-holder's having a minimally good life. Such a range requirement thus adds something independent to the grounding of human rights, and the load-bearing role of this addition will seem controversial. Why should regimes committed to their subjects' living minimally good human lives be committed to providing a range of ways of so living? To address such doubters, we need an explanation that goes beyond Liao's claim that a range is helpful for those who change their mind, an explanation that can underpin the need for an appropriately wide range for everyone.

Further concerns can be raised about Liao's idea that human rights protect conditions on the *pursuit* of the basic activities, rather than on the basic activities themselves. What criticisms could be levelled at a regime which made sure its citizens engaged in basic activities by somehow directly providing such activities (and thus directly providing 'good lives'), rather than facilitating their *pursuit*? The answer here is that engaging in an activity without pursuing it is impossible for many basic activities (one cannot simply 'fall into' climbing a mountain without pursuing it; indeed successful *achievements* in general seem impossible if they are not pursued), and that for other activities it significantly diminishes their contribution to the quality of the agent's life (pleasant experiences thrust onto one do less for the quality of one's life than those one successfully pursues).

But if this is correct, then taking the good life—or the basic activities which constitute it—directly as the ground for human rights will already ensure that human rights protect *pursuit*, for such pursuit is an indispensable means or even component of many of these activities. Why, then, insist instead that human rights are grounded only on *pursuit* of the good life, rather than directly on the basic activities which constitute a good life? The direct approach will already give pursuit an appropriate prominence.

This question presses particularly hard when one notes that on an ordinary understanding of the term, 'pursuit' of an activity is rather easily achieved. There is a sense in which many captives in prison are *pursuing* freedom, happiness, and a range of other things, even though their pursuit is futile. Similarly, those denied a political voice will often nonetheless *pursue* political participation. If we take 'pursuit' in its broadest sense, there is not much that a human needs *qua* human in order to *pursue* anything: a will, some lifespan and some awareness might be enough. So even if—as outlined in the previous paragraphs—pursuit is necessary for attaining many aspects of a good life, it is very far from sufficient and simply to protect *pursuit* of the good life is not to protect much. For example, Liao claims that fair and equal treatment in cases of conflict is necessary for a human to be able to pursue the basic activities.[20] But someone denied a fair trial, or imprisoned without trial, can still *pursue* any of the basic activities in a sense. It is just that their pursuit will not get far.

One response takes 'pursuit' in a technical manner as a threshold concept, and denies that prisoners or those denied a fair trial meet the threshold for being genuinely able to *pursue* basic activities in the relevant sense. This approach could forestall my concern, though it would leave one wondering how exactly the relevant technical notion is to be delineated: ideas such as 'effective pursuit' or 'pursuit with a reasonable chance of success' might be helpful. However, the approach seems hard to motivate when one remembers that the alternative—to ground human rights directly on the basic activities which constitute a good life—will already ground rights to pursuit where pursuit is important for the relevant basic activity. But it will ground more demanding rights as well, for actual engagement in basic activities is harder to attain than mere pursuit of them.

I suspect Liao will worry that deleting 'pursuit' from his approach—and thus grounding humans rights as protecting an adequate range of the fundamental conditions for a human *qua* human's *engagement in* the basic activities—will make human rights too demanding, turning them into guarantees of a minimally good life. But as noted earlier, in order to engage in a basic activity, a given individual will often need more in her context than that which a human *qua* human needs, so human rights will not guarantee the possibility of such engagement.[21] Further, a revised Liao-type approach minus 'pursuit' does not claim that there are rights to *every* condition necessary for humans *qua* humans to engage in basic activities. Some conditions might be excluded from the 'adequate range' because they cannot conceptually qualify as objects of rights.[22] Such exclusions, along with the limitation to what *humans qua humans* need, support the thought that deleting 'pursuit' from Liao's approach need not deliver excessively demanding human rights.

IV. How Human Rights Protect their Grounds

My opening concern was how we can ground human rights on the good life without classifying all those suffering human rights deficits as necessarily living a life that is less than minimally good. Liao's intricacies and my proposed adjustments discussed in sections II and III are motivated, in part, as ways of avoiding this problem by denying that human rights are simple necessary conditions for a minimally good life.

---

[20] Liao, 'Human Rights as Fundamental Conditions for a Good Life', 84.

[21] It is notable that Liao appeals to the *human qua human* clause, rather than the notion of *pursuit*, in replying to Griffin's charge that Liao-type approaches generate too many human rights (Liao, 'Human Rights as Fundamental Conditions for a Good Life', 89–90).

[22] See, eg, Tasioulas's argument that one cannot have a right to romantic love, 'On the Foundations of Human Rights', 59 below, and Miller's similar claim, 'Joseph Raz on Human Right: a critical appraisal', 233 below.

But there is an entirely different response to the problem which is often overlooked or covert in the literature. This is to weaken the link between human rights' content and their grounds to a matter of promotion and support. Such an approach maintains merely that human rights *promote, support* or *make more likely* their holder's living a minimally good life. With a weak link of this type, we can happily recognize that sometimes violations of human rights will not make a minimally good life impossible for right-holders, and that respect for human rights will not guarantee them a minimally good life. For failure to supply something that would promote or support X does not make X impossible or unattainable, and supplying it does not gurarantee X. Thus this route allows us to answer my opening question without needing the complications of section II: human rights are grounded as promoting or supporting their holders' living *minimally good lives* (unqualified by section II's complications), even though violating them does not make minimally good lives impossible for right-holders.

Should Liao—or Griffin, Miller, Nussbaum, Renzo or Tasioulas—take this route, making human rights simply *support* or *make more likely* the vital goods that ground them? I think not. The special status of human rights as important rights that legal systems should recognize whether or not they actually do is inconsistent with calling some right a 'human right' when its fulfilment only *tends to further or promote* the realization of the human-rights-grounding value. Such helpful but unnecessary conditions should not be given the status of rights that legal systems *must* recognize, both because this would leave too little space for culturally specific variation in human rights implementation, and because this would mislead us into thinking that helpful but unnecessary conditions bear the same importance as the grounding conditions that justify them and as the rights more directly justified by these grounding conditions.[23]

Instead, Liao is correct to assume that human rights' contents are more closely related to their grounds. In particular, human rights will most directly inherit the importance of their grounds if we can follow Liao in accepting that violation of a human right entails that whatever important thing grounds it has not been supplied to the right-holder by the duty-bearers, and that respect for the right entails that it has been so supplied.[24] This reopens the need for the complications of section II, for as we have seen, violation of a human right does not entail that a minimally good life is unavailable to the right-holder, nor does respect entail that a minimally good life has been achieved. This is why Liao favours grounding human rights on *an adequate range of fundamental conditions for a human qua human's pursuing the basic activities*. If this

---

[23] For a sophisticated discussion of the related issue of the relative importance of rights that offer inessential but useful support to other rights, see James W. Nickel, 'Rethinking Indivisibility: Towards A Theory of Supporting Relations between Human Rights', *Human Rights Quarterly*, 30 (2008): 984–1001. See also Nickel's suggestion that Henry Shue's idea that basic rights are necessary for 'full enjoyment' of other rights grounds basic rights on a merely supportive relationship of the kind considered (Nickel, *Making Sense of Human Rights*, 2nd edn (Blackwell, 2007), 89, discussing Henry Shue, *Basic Rights: Subsistence, Affluence, and U.S. Foreign Policy*, 2nd edn (Princeton University Press, 1996), 21). For different views on the importance of cultural variation in human rights implementation, see Samantha Besson, 'Human Rights and Constitutional Law: Patterns of Mutual Validation and Legitimation' and Saladin Meckled-Garcia, 'Specifying Human Rights', this volume, chs. 15 and 16.

[24] Compare Raz's discussion in 'Human Rights in the Emerging World Order', this volume, ch. 11: at 221, he comes close to defining a right's ground as the value of what it protects.

grounds human rights, then we should accept that violation entails that something within this adequate range is not available for the right-holder, and that respect entails that an adequate range is available. This sounds rather attractive, even though it leaves Liao vulnerable to the problems outlined in section III.

Note that this is not to deny the further attractive thesis (for which Liao can readily make space) that while human rights are grounded on the importance of an adequate range of the fundamental conditions for a human *qua* human to pursue some basic activity, nonetheless human rights also gain support from other goods they deliver, such as the value of thinking of oneself and others as right-holders, and the value of an open society constituted by recognition of human rights.[25]

V. The Relation Between Human Rights' Empirical Results and their Grounding

A difficult question for Liao—and for Griffin, Miller, Nussbaum, Renzo, and Tasioulas—arises from the fact that human rights are recognition-independent. Humans hold them even in societies in which no people, not even the holders themselves, recognize them. For this reason, a human right to X cannot be grounded *in a straightforwardly instrumental way* by the value of X. Nor can it gain support *straightforwardly instrumentally* from the value of one's thinking of oneself or others as holding a right to X, nor from the value of an open society constituted by recognition of human rights—as mentioned in the previous section. It cannot be grounded by its outcomes' value in a straightforwardly instrumental way because, as recognition-independent, the right to X will survive even when none of these outcomes obtain because the right goes unrecognized.

My point here differs from the concern of the previous section. There (section IV), I rejected the thesis that human rights can be grounded as inessential supporters or promoters of their grounds. Now (section V) I outline a difficulty with grounding human rights even as *essential* and *guaranteeing* means for the obtaining of their grounds. The problem is how to make sense of the view that human rights, with their recognition-independent character, are grounded as *means* at all.

Trivial systems of rights are grounded in a simple instrumental way by the value of the outcomes they secure. To take an example used frequently, the important end of efficiency in movement is promoted by people's subjecting their driving and parking to regulations. The duties (not to drive the wrong way down a one-way street, to stop at red lights) and rights (that others will stop at stop signs; that others will not park for longer than they have paid for) are generated by this end in an instrumental way: the duties and rights exist because they help meet the important end of efficiency in movement. If they did not help to meet this end, perhaps because people's psychology changed so that they became totally unmotivated by government attempts

---

[25] See Nickel's discussion of complementary and supporting arguments that can supplement the primary ground for a human right (*Making Sense of Human Rights*, 90). See also Joseph Raz, 'Rights and Individual Well-Being', in his *Ethics in the Public Domain: Essays in the Morality of Law and Politics*, revised edn (Oxford University Press, 1994), 44–59.

to regulate them, then there would be no point in having traffic regulations, and the duties and rights created by traffic regulations would cease to exist.

Unlike traffic regulations, *human rights* and *their* correlative duties would exist even in situations where they were useless or counter-productive as means for making their objects obtain. Suppose we lived in a terrible world in which a group was tortured and excluded. Suppose also that, perhaps due to certain religious beliefs, everyone accepted this as the norm and nobody ever came to think it violated human rights: nobody, not even members of the oppressed group, recognized their rights, and they will never come to recognize them. In such a situation, it looks as though the duties to refrain from torture and to allow political participation have no effects: the rights are useless in the same way that traffic regulations are useless in the example mentioned before. But I maintain that the members of the oppressed group in this case really do have human rights, even if the rights do nothing for the relevant people and never will.

From this I infer that Liao's and related approaches need a further component. Human rights might well be justified partly because, in Liao's words, they offer 'powerful protection', even indispensable protection, for something important like a minimally good life (and Liao might want to add that they also help secure an open society of value to us all, among other goods).[26] But human rights' justification cannot proceed in the straightforward instrumental manner that works for trivial socially created rights like the traffic regulations. Rather, we need an explanation of how we get from the proposition that X is an important ground for rights (in Liao's terms, X is among an *adequate range of the fundamental conditions for a human qua human to pursue some basic activity*) to a recognition-independent right to X, a right that exists even when X and its related values will never obtain.

Appealing to human rights' latent value—their value as rights which, *if respected*, would protect their holders in the manner specified by Liao—cannot provide the missing explanation. For the fact that certain traffic regulations would serve the good life if they were respected does not make such regulations exist under conditions in which they will never be respected: why, then, should a similar fact about human rights make them exist in my nightmare scenario above in which they will never be respected?

Some approaches to this question ground human rights entirely independently of the good life. For example, some take human rights as norms we cannot avoid presupposing if we are agents,[27] as grounded on liberty and equality conceived independently of their role in the good life,[28] or as grounded in dignity or our high worth taken independently of the good life.[29] A particularly problematic conclusion for Liao (and related theorists) would be if such approaches succeeded in grounding

---

[26] Liao, 'Human Rights as Fundamental Conditions for a Good Life', 83, and see n. 25 in the current essay.

[27] Gewirth, *Reason and Morality*.

[28] See, eg, Hillel Steiner, *An Essay on Rights* (Blackwell, 1994).

[29] Thomas Nagel, 'Personal Rights and Public Space', in his *Concealment and Exposure & Other Essays* (Oxford University Press, 2002), 31–52; F. M. Kamm, *Intricate Ethics* (Oxford University Press, 2007), ch. 8.

human rights, and further if a person's living a minimally good life was then defined in part by whether their rights were respected. On such an approach, the minimally good life would ultimately depend on human rights rather than vice versa. This would enable us to explain away the appeal of Liao's position. One could say that there is indeed, as noted in section I, a close relation between a person's human rights and their living a good life: but not because—as Liao claims—human rights are grounded on the good life; rather, there is a partial grounding relationship in the other direction.

If the requisite independent grounds can be found for human rights, then it seems to me fairly likely that the good life will then be defined in part by respect for such rights. Violations of my right to X are an affront to me *qua* violations even when my life would otherwise go successfully without X: consider violations of unneeded but justly acquired property. Such an affront is an effect on the quality of my life in some sense, independently of whether I would ever have used the property in question.

Nonetheless, there are two reasons for Liao to be untroubled by this. First, it is doubtful that violations of a person's human rights will *qua* violations necessarily condemn their victim to a life that is *less than minimally* good. Such a move would entail the liberal imperialist position rejected earlier: the position which classifies most people throughout history as unable to attain a minimally good life. It is more attractive to say merely that violations of human rights must *qua* violations have *some* effect on whether the victim's life is as good as it could be. To avoid the liberal imperialist view we should insulate whether one has a 'minimally good life' from moral affronts caused by human rights violations *qua* violations (or indeed, human rights deficits *qua* deficits)—though the quality of one's life above this minimal level cannot be so insulated.

Secondly, there are major difficulties for each of the good-life-independent approaches to human rights mentioned, though I lack space to go into this here. A seeming 'middle way' is offered by Kamm and Nagel, who claim that there is something good about the existence of human rights independently of whether they are respected or recognized:

> [T]here may be a type of good that already exists but that would not exist if it were permissible to transgress the right of one person in order to save many lives. This is the good of being someone whose worth is such that it makes him highly inviolable and also makes him someone to whom one owes nonviolation. This good does imply that certain of one's interests should not be sacrificed, but inviolability matters not merely because it instrumentally serves those interests....Inviolability is a reflection of the worth of the person. On this account, it is impermissible for me to harm the person in order to save many in the accident, because doing so is inconsistent with his having this status.[30]

Aspects of this passage—the 'good of being someone...'—suggest that bare possession of human rights independently of whether they are recognized is not only

---

[30] Kamm, *Intricate Ethics*, 253–4.

good as such, but good for the right-holder, and I can see the appeal of this position. Possession of human rights makes the miserable situation of those whose rights are forever unrecognized qualify as a *violation*, one in which *they have been wronged*, and *wronged in the way humans can be wronged*. Possession of human rights generates these normative consequences even if nobody recognizes them. It can seem as though it would be even worse if the relevant people were suffering as outlined in my earlier example but this suffering did not count as wronging them: that would be for them to have the status of insects or robots, beings that (I here just assert) cannot be wronged. And it would also be worse for them if their suffering qualified only as wronging them in the way that animals can be wronged.[31]

But these claims are odd. If human rights are necessarily borne by humans, then it seems that by saying their bare existence makes one's life go 'better' one is asserting that it is good for one that the impossible does not obtain—and this is problematic. Even the claim that human rights are merely 'a good' rather than 'good *for* their holders' is odd, because it appears to be the claim that the world is somehow better for the fact that humans hold human rights—but again this looks like asserting that it is good that the impossible (humans lacking human rights) does not obtain.[32]

Perhaps Kamm and Nagel need not be given this reading: in the quotation provided earlier, Kamm is cautious, saying only that 'there *may be* a type of good…' (emphasis added). If we reject this good-based approach, we can still retain Kamm's notion of human rights as reflections or expressions of humans' high worth. This idea can be taken simply to offer an independent account of human rights' grounds, one that should not be understood in terms of the 'good'. But even so taken, Kamm's and Nagel's account has notable limitations when considered on its own: to say simply that human rights are grounded independently of their effects because as bare normative structures they reflect or express humans' high worth is to leave human rights' contents under-determined. Kamm tries to argue that certain specific rights (in particular, constraints on interference with an intricate form of priority over requirements of assistance) constitute an inviolability that is a necessary reflection of humans' high worth.[33] But rights with alternative contents and stringency (for example, rights prioritizing assistance over non-interference) would give us different forms of high worth; if human rights are grounded solely as reflections of our high worth, this leaves it under-determined which particular rights we hold.[34]

In my view, the best reading of the Kamm/Nagel position, and also positions appealing to dignity, is as attempts to provide the supplement needed by approaches like

---

[31] Nagel, 'Personal Rights and Public Space', 37–9.

[32] Thanks to Mike Ridge for first pointing this out to me.

[33] Kamm, *Intricate Ethics*, chs. 8 and 9.

[34] Kasper Lippert-Rasmussen considers a possible world of 'high unignorability' but 'low inviolability' in which agents are required to harm some in order to prevent more occurrences of similar harms to others; in one respect, this world confers a higher status on people (by making them especially unignorable) than a world of 'high inviolability' of the type Kamm considers (Lippert-Rasmussen, 'Moral Status and the Impermissibility of Minimizing Violations', *Philosophy and Public Affairs*, 25 (1996): 333–51, 340–1). Lippert-Rasmussen goes on to consider other alternative high status structures (eg, 'high unsacrifice-ability', 349–50), as does Shelly Kagan in his 'Replies to My Critics', *Philosophy and Phenomenological Research*, 51 (1991): 919–28, 920. See also Rowan Cruft, 'Kamm and Miller on Rights' Compatibility', *Ethical Theory and Moral Practice*, 13 (2010): 393–401.

Liao's: the explanation for why exactly the fact that X is of great importance grounds *recognition-independent* rights to X, rights that persist even when there is no chance of attaining X. For Liao, X refers to an adequate range of the fundamental conditions for a human *qua* human to pursue the basic activities, but the same question arises for Tasioulas (for whom X refers to the basic interests of beings with dignity) or Griffin (for whom X is humans' personhood construed in terms of agency) or Nussbaum (for whom X is the 'Central Capabilities').[35] When X is efficiency in traffic movement, the rights grounded are not recognition-independent. Similarly, I would say that whatever X grounds property rights fails to make them recognition-independent. Perhaps what the Kamm/Nagel and dignity positions highlight is that the X in the case of human rights has a special character such that we should be required to pursue it even when we will not, and indeed even when there is no hope that we will.

But this is just a schematic description of how the Kamm/Nagel or dignity positions could fill the relevant gap. For Liao's view or its cognates to give us a full account of what grounds human rights and of what this tells us about such rights' contents, more must be said. In Liao's terms, the relevant questions will be: why exactly do rights grounded in the importance of an adequate range of the conditions for humans qua humans to pursue the basic activities *reflect or express their holders' high worth or dignity as humans*, in a way that rights with alternative groundings do not? And why does such reflection or expression mean that the relevant rights exist independently of whether they are recognized?[36]

To my mind, the second question is harder. To begin to answer the first, we can note that any right grounded primarily just in what it does for its individual holder *qua* human will reflect or express her intrinsic worth or value as a human: this includes any rights grounded in the manner Liao, Griffin, Nussbaum or Tasioulas specify for human rights. By contrast, a right grounded primarily by what it does for others beyond the right-holder will not express the holder's intrinsic worth: consider a parent's right to child benefit payments, or a pregnant woman's right not to be executed.[37] And a right grounded by what it does for the right-holder *qua* contextually situated individual will not express the right-holder's intrinsic worth *as a human*: consider my right, as a British citizen living in Scotland, to free dental check-ups under the National Health Service.

Yet even if these thoughts can establish that rights grounded in Liao's way will—unlike many other rights—reflect or express their holders' intrinsic high worth as humans, we need to say much more if we are to understand why rights that express this high worth are *recognition-independent*, while rights which do not are not.

---

[35] See n. 3 for references.

[36] Renzo considers similar issues in his chapter. We can rephrase these questions in Renzo's terms: why exactly do actions violating rights grounded on basic needs 'represent the value of the victim as less than the value that she possesses', in a way that rights with alternative groundings do not (Renzo, 'Human Needs, Human Rights', 582)? And why are rights whose violation involves such misrepresentation recognition-independent?

[37] The examples are drawn from Raz, 'Rights and Individual Well-Being', 50. For defence of the thesis that any right which qualifies as a human right must be grounded primarily by what it does for the individual right-holder, see Rowan Cruft, 'Why is it Disrespectful to Violate Rights?', *Proceedings of the Aristotelian Society*, 63 (2013): 201–24, 208.

VI. Conclusion

An approach like Liao's is attractive for anyone who sees human rights as secularized natural or basic rights.[38] I said that my aim was to sketch the key challenges for such approaches to overcome. The three toughest challenges considered are as follows, I think.

First, how exactly can we identify the forms of good life that our human nature makes possible? For Griffin, Miller, Nussbaum, Renzo or Tasioulas, the parallel question is: how can we identify the aspects of agency that define the threshold concept of a 'normative agent', or how can we identify the basic needs, the central capabilities or the basic interests?

Secondly, to avoid making respect for human rights necessary for the right-holder's living a minimally good life, Liao must ground human rights on the importance of the availability of a range of ways of living a good life—a range wider than that range *necessary* for a minimally good life. How can we justify appealing to this range, and in a way that makes it neither too wide nor too narrow? Or for Griffin, Miller, Nussbaum, Renzo or Tasioulas: why does securing a wide range of agency interests, basic needs, capabilities or basic interests matter even when the right-holder is able to live a good life without the full range being secured for her? And what exactly determines the parameters of the appropriate range?

Thirdly, why does the particular X that human rights protect ground recognition-independent rights, rights that persist even when there is no hope of securing X for their holders?

Filling in these gaps would give us a satisfyingly complete theory of human rights as basic or natural pre-legal rights.[39]

[38] And it also seems necessary as at least part of a 'political' account. See n. 3, and Liao, 'Human Rights as Fundamental Conditions for a Good Life', section VI.
[39] Many thanks to Matthew Liao, Antony Duff, Simon Hope, Sandra Marshall and Massimo Renzo for very helpful, patient discussions and argument.

5

Is Dignity the Foundation of Human Rights?

Jeremy Waldron

I. Foundation and Exploration

In this chapter I would like to examine, in part with the eye of a pedant, the proposition that human dignity is the foundation of human rights. That proposition, or something like it, is found in the preambles of the major human rights conventions, and it is quite common too in the rhetoric of scholars addressing the subject of rights. It bears examining for all sorts of reasons: first, on account of the recent revival in the philosophical study of dignity;[1] second, because people continue to disagree about human rights and it is worth looking into any thesis that promises to help us with these disagreements; third, because claims about dignity, if put forward as foundational, may provide a basis for challenging other values or principles that have also claimed to occupy this foundational ground (like the principle of utility, for example);[2] and fourth (and this is a reason that takes us in a different direction) because the very idea of *foundations* for our political ideals has been called in question, and what we find out about dignity may confirm (or refute) the proposition that searching for foundations is more trouble than it is worth.[3]

I hasten to add that I am undertaking this inquiry, not to discredit the concept of dignity, but to clarify its role in human rights theory. Some of the things I will say at various stages may seem critical, even dismissive. But it is not the aim of this chapter to denigrate the idea of dignity in relation to rights. For even if it turns out that a strict understanding of the foundationalist claim cannot be defended, still there may be other ways in which dignity will turn out to be important in our understanding of human rights. Subjecting the foundationalist claim to critical scrutiny may have the side-benefit of revealing some of these.

---

[1] For a sample, see: Jeremy Waldron, "Dignity and Rank," *European Journal of Sociology*, 48 (2007): 201; Michael Rosen, *Dignity: Its History and Meaning* (Harvard University Press, 2012), George Kateb, *Human Dignity* (Harvard University Press, 2011), Christopher McCrudden, "Human Dignity in Human Rights Interpretation," *European Journal of International Law*, 19 (2008): 655. See also the immense volume of thirty-nine essays from a recent conference on human dignity at Oxford: Christopher McCrudden (ed.), *Understanding Human Dignity* (Oxford University Press/British Academy, 2013).

[2] George Fletcher, "Human Dignity as a Constitutional Value," *University of Western Ontario Law Review*, 22 (1984): 178.

[3] See, eg, Richard Rorty, *Contingency, Irony and Solidarity* (Cambridge University Press, 1989), 44–5 and 52–7.

II. The Basic Human Rights Documents

We are told in the preamble to the International Covenant on Civil and Political Rights (ICCPR) that the rights it contains "derive from the inherent dignity of the human person." The International Covenant on Economic, Social and Cultural Rights (ICESCR) says something similar, though both conventions also proclaim that "recognition of the inherent dignity and of the equal and inalienable rights of all members of the human family is the foundation of freedom, justice and peace in the world," as though the two were coordinate principles. We see this second formulation also in the Universal Declaration of Human Rights (UDHR); there it is unaccompanied by the claim of the two conventions that rights derive from dignity.

Are these differences important? The first claim, that "rights derive from the inherent dignity of the human person," seems straightforwardly foundational. It makes it sound as if the whole point of human rights is to protect and promote human dignity, and it would seem to follow that the best way to find out what rights we have is to figure out what the inherent dignity of the human person involves and what is necessary for the protection and promotion of that dignity. The second claim, by contrast, treats rights and dignity as coordinate ideas rather than deriving one from the other: this impression is reinforced in the first article of the UDHR: "All human beings are born free and equal in dignity and rights."

Probably it is a mistake to put too much weight on the logic and detail of any of these preambular formulations. They are intended as prefatory pieces of rhetoric; they are not noted for their philosophical rigor; they probably represent political compromises;[4] and they are not always consistent, at least not to the eye of a pedant. But if we discount them, we should probably discount both formulations; it is not clear that we are entitled just to sweep away one of the formulations because it is inconsistent with what is now *our* idea—rather than something expressed unequivocally in the conventions—namely, that dignity is the foundation of rights.

III. Content Versus Foundation of Rights

Continuing with this purely textual analysis, it is interesting that both covenants also seem to present dignity as part of the content of certain rights. Article 10(1) of the ICCPR says: "All persons deprived of their liberty shall be treated with…respect for the inherent dignity of the human person." (This is similar to the requirement in international humanitarian law that detainees, in particular, be protected from, among other things, "outrages upon personal dignity.")[5] Dignity is also implicated in certain particular claims about socio-economic rights. Article 13(1) of the ICESCR recognizes a right to education and lays it down that "education shall be directed to the full development of the human personality and the sense of its dignity," and, in the UDHR, Article 23(3) proclaims that "[e]veryone who works has the right to just and

---

[4] See Johannes Morsink, *The Universal Declaration of Human Rights: Origins, Drafting and Intent* (University of Pennsylvania Press, 1999), 281ff.

[5] Geneva Conventions, Common Article III.

favourable remuneration ensuring for himself and his family an existence worthy of human dignity." Is the particularity of these claims about dignity consistent with the view that dignity is the general foundation of all human rights?

Some scholars perceive a contradiction here.[6] Others infer that "dignity" must mean different things in these different contexts.[7] I think they are wrong. Suppose dignity is the foundation of our rights and that the role of particular rights claims is to point to what dignity requires in particular areas (speech, worship, privacy, health care, and so on.) For some of these particular areas, it may be well known that dignity requires φ (say, freedom of worship or freedom from torture) and so we talk directly of a right to φ without mentioning dignity. In other areas, there may be no familiar benchmark, so we simply refer to dignity itself as the criterion of what is required: that is what seems to be going on in the UDHR's insistence on "remuneration ensuring...an existence worthy of human dignity." We don't say what the required level of remuneration is: but we point to dignity as a way of pinning it down.

Also, in a set of rights based generally upon dignity, there may be some requirements which engage the dignitarian foundation more or less directly. Prohibitions on "degrading" treatment are like this: they address the most direct and alarming ways in which human dignity might be assaulted—for example, conscious attempts to treat people as having a sub-human status. Consider an analogy. Members of the judiciary have a certain dignity in most legal systems, and it is not implausible to say that marking and protecting that dignity is the foundation of many of the rights that judges have. They have the right to appear in their judicial robes on state occasions and they have, as one national constitution puts it, a right to "remuneration consistent with the dignity of their office..."[8] As well as this, they have right not to suffer direct affronts to their dignity in court; this is the basis of the law on contempt of court. Now the fact that this latter right refers more or less directly to their dignity does not preclude the possibility that judicial dignity is the foundation of *all* their rights. The law forbidding contempt of court engages judicial dignity directly; but it is not all there is to judicial dignity. And something similar may be true for human dignity. We may be able to distinguish between human dignity in general and certain particular rights that protect it explicitly and more or less directly. As we have seen, some of these particular rights are affirmative and some are negative. Both kinds of protection are important, but they are not all there is to human dignity. Dignity's presence as a criterion for determining appropriate treatment may be explicit in some cases and implicit in others. There is no contradiction here and we have not had to assign different meanings to different occurrences of "human dignity" to prevent a contradiction from arising.

---

[6] Luis Roberto Barroso, "Here, There, and Everywhere: Human Dignity in Contemporary Law and in the Transnational Discourse," *Boston College International and Comparative Law Review*, 35 (2012): 331, 357: "It would be contradictory to make human dignity a right in its own, however, because it is regarded as the foundation for all truly fundamental rights and the source of at least part of their core content."

[7] Rosen, *Dignity: Its History and Meaning*, 59–60.

[8] The Constitution of Poland, Article 178(2).

IV. Foundational Pluralism

On the other hand, we should not neglect the possibility that dignity might turn out to be foundational for some rights and not others. Human rights, notoriously, present themselves to us in the form of a list rather than as a unified theory,[9] and a list encourages us (though it does not require us) to think pluralistically about rights. Maybe we should say that there are all sorts of rights, with all sorts of foundations: free speech has one sort of foundation; humane treatment for detainees has a different foundation; the right to education yet another; and so on.[10]

Someone may protest: doesn't the fact that all these rights are presented as *human* rights mean that they must be unified in their grounds by a single theory of what it takes for something to be a right of that kind? Possibly; but the characterization of a set of rights as human rights may mean no more than that they are rights which are properly attributed on a universal basis to all human beings. This presumably means that each of them is based on some fact about human nature. But human nature is multi-faceted and right R_1 may be based on characteristic C (which all humans share), right R_2 may be based on characteristic D (which all humans share), and right R_3 may be based on characteristic E (which all humans share). For these all to be regarded as human rights, it is not necessary for there to be a single theory of humanity—or human dignity—that makes sense of C, D, and E together.

After all, the fact that dignity is important does not mean that other foundation-ish values are not also important. Dignity's importance does not necessarily make it into a master-value, overshadowing every other value that might occupy a foundational role. Some rights may be based directly on liberty or autonomy—without regard to the place those ideas have, in turn, in the analysis of dignity. Some might be based on equality and social justice. Some might be even based indirectly on utility.[11]

Dignity does not figure in the Constitution of the United States, but it is invoked sporadically in American constitutional doctrine. Again this is true of some rights rather than others. It seems to be particularly important with regard to the Eighth Amendment prohibition on cruel and unusual punishment;[12] but one would not expect to see it cited, say, in interpretations of the Third Amendment (the right not have troops quartered in one's home). Even when it is cited in support of Second Amendment matters (the right to bear arms), dignity is cited tendentiously as an *ad hominem* response to the suggestion of liberal justices that only rights protecting "fundamental aspects of personhood, dignity, and the like" are incorporated into the meaning of "liberty" (as against the states) in the Fourteenth Amendment.[13] More generally, it is possible

---

[9] For some reflection on the list-ish aspect, see John Rawls, *Political Liberalism* (Columbia University Press, 1986), 292 and Jeremy Waldron, "Socio-economic Rights and Theories of Justice," *San Diego Law Review*, 48 (2011): 773, 793.

[10] We should also not rule out the possibility that what we regard as one-and-the-same right may have multiple foundations or multiple foundational elements.

[11] It would be a mistake to think that because the trumping logic of rights seems to displace direct utilitarian calculations that therefore utilitarian ideas can have no place at all in a theory of rights.

[12] cf *Trop v. Dulles* 356 U.S. 86, 100 (1958): "The basic concept underlying the Eighth Amendment is nothing less than the dignity of man."

[13] *McDonald v. Chicago* 130 S.Ct. 3020, 3051 and 3055 (2011), Scalia J., concurring.

to read the Bill of Rights without getting any impression that the particular rights are all derived from a single foundation. Nothing in their history suggests that they are. Particularly in circumstances where rights are added over time to a list or bill or charter of rights—in the way that the Thirteenth, Fourteenth, Fifteenth, and Nineteenth Amendments were added to the American Bill of Rights—it is perfectly possible that the concerns that motivated the original list may not be the same as the concerns that motivate the later additions. Certainly many of the non-rights amendments have been added in an ad hoc way, without particular regard to any theoretical unity—the prohibition amendment, elections to the senate, legality of the income tax, reduction of the voting age to 18, and so on. It is perfectly possible that the *rights* listed among the amendments have an ad hoc character as well. I am not actually arguing for this pluralistic approach, but I do not think we can rule it out as a possible reason why dignity seems more germane to some rights than to others.

V. Definitional Difficulties

Potential difficulties with the idea that dignity is the foundation of human rights crop up also from another direction. Perhaps the phrase "human dignity" is too vague to be of any foundational use.

A respected human rights jurist, Oscar Schachter has observed that there is no explicit definition of "human dignity" in any of the charters that invoke it. "Its intrinsic meaning has been left to intuitive understanding," says Schachter, which is hardly satisfactory so far as a foundational role for the concept is concerned: "Without a reasonably clear general idea of its meaning, we cannot easily draw specific implications for relevant conduct."[14] Christopher McCrudden has argued that this lack of definition is not an oversight. Dignity was written into the preambles of the great human rights covenants not to convey any particular meaning, but to operate as a sort of place-holder in circumstances where the drafters wanted to sound philosophical but couldn't agree on what to say.[15]

Outside the area of human rights, commentators have been quite skeptical about the meaning of "dignity." Addressing its use in bioethics debates, Stephen Pinker called it "a subjective squishy" notion and Ruth Macklin observed that "the concept remains hopelessly vague... [T]o invoke the concept of dignity without clarifying its meaning is to use a mere slogan."[16]

On some accounts, the amorphous character of dignity is simply a sign that we are in the early stages of its elaboration: our understanding of its meaning is a work-in-progress. This is not inconsistent with dignity operating as a foundation for rights, for our understanding of human rights, no more than seventy years old in its modern incarnation, is a work-in-progress also. There is still no settled consensus about what it means to say that the right to φ is a human right, apart from the minimum

---

[14] Oscar Schachter, "Human Dignity as a Normative Concept," *American Journal of International Law,* 77 (1983): 848, 849.

[15] McCrudden, "Human Dignity in Human Rights Interpretation," 675–8.

[16] Steven Pinker, "The Stupidity of Dignity," *The New Republic,* May 28, 2008 and Ruth Macklin, "Dignity is a Useless Concept," *British Medical Journal,* 327 (2003): 1419.

claim that it is a right that all humans are now conceived to have. And we still disagree about which rights are human rights. It should not be surprising then that dissensus about rights is associated with indeterminacy in rights' foundations. Building a determinate theory is going to involve work at both levels. On this account, the claim that dignity is the foundation of rights does not point us to a determinate premise. Rather, it instructs us to pay attention to *questions* about dignity in trying to address questions about rights; it implicates the one line of inquiry in the other. For example, in addressing issues about the limits on rights and the possibility of developing concepts like *abuse of rights*, we are invited to explore recent discussions of human dignity that address its moralistic or non-emancipatory character, ideas of human dignity that explore the responsibility that each individual has in respect of the human dignity embodied in his or her person.[17] My point is that these responsibility characterizations of dignity are, at this stage, works-in-progress, just like the idea of responsibility rights that they appear to underpin.[18]

On other accounts, what an observer might see as a definitional mess may be an indication that dignity is in fact a *contested* concept—with reasonably determinate conceptions, opposed to one another, already well crystallized.[19] For there is not just a proliferation of uses of the term "dignity"; there is in modern political philosophy a proliferation of dignitarian theories. There is the Kantian theory based on autonomous moral capacity, there is the Catholic theory based on humans' being created in the image of God, there is a theory developed by me and others about dignity as a status rather than a value (more of this later), and there is the theory of dignity developed by Ronald Dworkin in *Justice for Hedgehogs*.[20] These rival accounts confront one another, and the cacophony of contestation may make us despair that there is any common ground to act as a rights foundation. At least one scholar has argued that if we treat dignity as the foundation of rights, we are likely to end up with different conceptions of rights matching different conceptions of dignity. This, she suggests, may already be happening so far as constitutional alternatives on the two side of the Atlantic are concerned.[21]

Of course this won't be the first time that foundational ideas in political theory have presented themselves as contested concepts. Contestation about the meaning of *liberty* is notorious.[22] *Democracy* was cited as a paradigm case of an essentially contested

[17] See, eg, Stephanie Hennette-Vauchez, "A Human Dignitas? The Contemporary Principle of Human Dignity as a Mere Reappraisal of an Ancient Legal Concept," *International Journal of Constitutional Law*, 9 (2011): 32.

[18] Jeremy Waldron, "Dignity, Rights, and Responsibilities," *Arizona State Law Journal* 43 (2011): 1107.

[19] For the idea of well-defined conceptions in relation to a contested concept, see Ronald Dworkin, *Taking Rights Seriously* (Harvard University Press, 1977), 134–6. See also McCrudden, "Human Dignity in Human Rights Interpretation," 679–80.

[20] Immanuel Kant, *Groundwork of the Metaphysics of Morals*, ed. Mary Gregor (Cambridge University Press, 1997), 42–6; John Paul II, *Evangelium Vitae* (25 March 1995); Jeremy Waldron, *Dignity, Rank, and Rights* (Oxford University Press, 2012), 30–6; Ronald Dworkin, *Justice for Hedgehogs* (Harvard University Press, 2010), 202–14.

[21] See Neomi Rao, "On the Use and Abuse of Dignity in Constitutional Law," *Columbia Journal of European Law*, 14 (2008): 201 and Neomi Rao, "Three Concepts of Dignity in Constitutional Law," *Notre Dame Law Review*, 86 (2011): 183.

[22] Isaiah Berlin, "Two Concepts of Liberty," in his collection *Four Essays on Liberty* (Oxford University Press, 1969), 118.

concept, by the philosopher who introduced us to that latter idea.[23] And *equality* and *the rule of law* have both in their time presented contestation as their leading definitive characteristic.[24] Presenting these values as foundational raises the stakes in the contestation about how they are properly conceived. It should be no surprise that contestation about the proper meaning of dignity has increased since people began taking seriously the foundational claims presented in the preambles of the great human rights charters.

VI. Do Human Rights Actually Need a Foundation (Like Dignity)?

On the other hand, the difficulty in defining the word "dignity" raises the question of whether we actually need a foundational theory for our commitment to human rights. Are we better off with such a foundation or are we worse off because we have now entangled rights (about which we were once reasonably clear) with an allegedly foundational idea which poses more problems than it seems to be worth? As George Kateb puts the point (though he does not actually endorse it),

> [W]hatever was the case some centuries ago, the defense of rights at present requires little theoretical articulation. Why make trouble by defending rights at length and make worse trouble by claiming that human dignity is the basis, or part of the basis, for human rights? Theoretical defense invites philosophical skepticism, which is sometimes useful to stimulate thought, but there is these days not very much theory, though there is some, that comes out and says that human rights are, in Jeremy Bentham's phrase, "nonsense upon stilts," and that the idea of human dignity adds yet more nonsense.[25]

From a number of pragmatic points of view, this position might sound sensible. If our pragmatism is just a matter of the outcomes that we are trying to promote as human rights activists, then probably we should concede that foundationalism, particularly dignitarian foundationalism, is more trouble than it is worth. We should just get on with sending money to Amnesty International, etc. Again, if our pragmatism is that of bottom-line lawyering, then we may not find propositions about the foundational status of dignity much use either. On no account are such propositions likely to generate clear and compelling lines of legal argument for particular rights claims. Lawyers and judges will disagree back and forth about the alleged foundational premise, they will disagree about its character and its definition, and they will certainly disagree about how to draw inferences from it and about what its bottom-line implications are. It is not at all clear that this tangle of disagreements represents any improvement on an environment for legal rights lawyering that is bereft of philosophical foundations.

---

[23] W.B. Gallie, "Essentially Contested Concepts," *Proceedings of the Aristotelian Society*, 56 (1955–56), 167, 168 and 183.

[24] See Ronald Dworkin, "What is Equality? I and II," *Philosophy and Public Affairs*, 10 (1981): 185 and 283 and Jeremy Waldron, "Is the Rule of Law a Contested Concept (in Florida)?" *Law and Philosophy*, 21 (2002): 137.

[25] Kateb, *Human Dignity*, 1–2.

But foundations are not inquired into for their pragmatic benefits. Sometimes they are pursued just for the sake of better understanding, where "better" means "deeper," not "more practically effective." Quantum physics is the foundation of our understanding of material nature; and although a case could be made that for all sorts of practical purposes we have a much clearer grasp of the nature and behavior of ordinary middle-sized objects than we do of sub-atomic particles, still we are led intellectually into the sub-atomic world for a level of understanding that is deeper than that. And even if quantum physics offers more in the way of questions rather than answers, we believe that posing those questions and wrestling with them is the best way to understand how the material world really works. Something similar may be true of foundationalism in moral and political theory. Even if our foundational inquiries do not promise to yield any sort of litmus test for assessing rights claims, still the questions we face in pursuing these inquiries help to deepen and enrich our understanding of human rights. I think this is true of value-inquiry generally; it is certainly true of what Richard Primus has called the "resurgence of normative foundationalism" in the study of rights.[26] Legal theorists do not pursue foundational inquiries just in order to equip their more practical-minded colleagues with impressive sounding arguments that will work in the courtroom. They pursue them because it is intrinsically important to have a deep and abstract as well as a surface-level and practical understanding of these rights that we claim to take so seriously.

None of this shows, of course, that human dignity is the sort of foundation we are looking for, in pursuit of this deep understanding. Dignity might be a cul-de-sac in this foundational enterprise. But I do not think it should be dismissed out of hand on the grounds that, pragmatically speaking, it is more trouble than it is worth.

The same point can be put another way. We did not invent the concept of dignity to be immediately useful. It has emerged anyway as an apparently important idea in ethics and political philosophy. We cannot reverse and we should not ignore the heritage of moral theology, natural-law theorizing, and Kantian philosophy that has put this idea in front of us. Some philosophers claim that dignity adds little to concepts that are already reasonably well-understood, like autonomy and respect for persons.[27] They may be right. But we would be unwise to dismiss dignity unless we were sure that it neither added anything to nor modified our understanding of those other concepts.[28] Being (so to speak) stuck with this concept by the legacy of our moral and political philosophy, it is incumbent on us to explore its content and its relations to other moral ideas. I don't pretend there are easy answers here: the legacy of our discipline has given us something of a conundrum to unravel rather than a conception already resplendent in its clarity.

Not only that, but whether we like it or not, a more recent heritage—this time a heritage of human rights proclamations—has saddled us with claims about dignity's foundational role to explore. Those of us who want to explore the connection between

---

[26] Richard A. Primus, *The American Language of Rights* (Cambridge University Press, 1999), 178–9.
[27] See Macklin, "Dignity is a Useless Concept," and Pinker, "The Stupidity of Dignity."
[28] Neither Macklin nor Pinker presents anything other than a bare assertion that the meaningful content of "dignity" is exhausted by reference to autonomy and one or two of the respect-based requirements of medical ethics.

dignity and human rights did not make that connection up. The world (as it were) committed itself to claims about a foundational connection between dignity and human rights. Those claims might turn out to be false, misconceived, confused, or merely rhetorical. The skeptics may be right when they say it is mere decoration in the great charters, or a place-holder to conceal intractable controversy. But we cannot be sure of this in advance. Anyway, for those who practice philosophy, there is no option but to explore these claims. The fact that good-hearted men of action may have other priorities does not affect the philosopher's mission. It is often our job, in the great division of labor, to explore claims like this long after a more pragmatic-minded person has thrown up his hands and gone back out into the field. The exploration may be undertaken in a moderately skeptical spirit (as mine is, in this chapter). But it needs to be undertaken nevertheless in good faith.

VII. What is a Foundation?

Part of this exploration involves asking: what is it, anyway, for something to be the *foundation* of rights? Are foundational claims just symbolic? Is this foundational claim just a claim about dignity's importance?—for example, the proclamation of "human dignity as a right so fundamental that no decent society, or legal system, would deny it strong protection."[29] Or is there a real sense in which dignity may be regarded as "the fountainhead from which the equal rights of man follow"?[30]

The idea of foundations can be understood in many ways. I am going to explore (and apply to the relation between dignity and rights) four possible accounts of what it might mean to say that one concept, α, is the foundation of another concept, β. It might mean that

(i) as a matter of history and genealogy, β was generated out of α;

(ii) α is the source of β, in the way that the application of one legal proposition may be the source of the validity of another;

(iii) β can be derived logically from α, either deductively or with the help of empirical premises; or

(iv) α throws some indispensable light on β or helps in the interpretation of β.

As we pursue these possibilities for {α = human dignity, β = human rights}, it is probably worth noting that the β-term, human rights, might also be understood in different ways. Not only are there still substantive disagreements about the content and character of human rights, but the idea of foundations might engage with human rights at a number of different levels. "Human rights" might be understood to describe a concept, a list of rights, and a practice of asserting and applying them; and the concept,

---

[29] This phrase is taken from Norman Rosenberg, *Dignity, Rights, and Recent Legal Scholarship, American Quarterly*, 45 (1993): 429, 430 (reviewing Michael J. Meyer and W. A. Parent (eds.), *The Constitution of Rights: Human Dignity and American Values*).

[30] Yehoshua Arieli, "On the Necessary and Sufficient Conditions for the Emergence of the Doctrine of the Dignity of Man and his Rights," in D. Kretzmer and E. Klein (eds.), *The Concept of Dignity in Human Rights Discourse* (Kluwer Law International, 2002), 1, 8.

the list and the practice, may be understood in moral or legal terms. Accordingly, what human dignity is supposed to be foundational to (or for, or of) may vary depending on whether we claim it to be foundational vis-a-vis a moral or legal proposition, a moral or legal concept or theory, or a moral or legal practice. My pedantry in these matters usually knows no bounds, but I will not explore these variations systematically. As we consider options (i) through (iv), I hope it will be clear which level of human rights talk I am engaging.

A. Origins and genealogy

When people say that human rights are based on human dignity, one possibility is that they mean that our discourse of human rights grew out of a pre-existing discourse about human dignity. The claim would be that the latter is foundational in a genealogical sense, that the prevalence or power of talk about human dignity helps us explain, in an historical way, where our ideas about human rights came from. The genealogy of human rights talk is an important topic: it is an interesting task in the history of ideas to relate it to much earlier talk of natural rights, and to explain why, when the notion of natural rights lay fallow or discredited in many circles for more than a hundred years (roughly from the end of the eighteenth until mid-way through the twentieth century), it was so easily revived under this new label.[31]

There was certainly a pre-existing discourse of human dignity before the emergence of human rights talk in its modern form. But, as Oscar Schachter has argued, it is implausible to suppose that human rights grew out of the discourse of dignity:

> The Helsinki Final Act declares in Principle VII that all human rights and fundamental freedoms "derive from the inherent dignity of the human person." This statement should be understood in a philosophical rather than historical sense. As history, it would probably be more correct to say the opposite: namely, that the idea of dignity reflects sociohistorical conceptions of basic rights and freedoms, not that it generated them.[32]

No doubt existing dignity discourse had some effect on the way in which human rights discourse emerged. But it would be wrong to treat the former as the historical precursor of the latter. And in many respects, the reverse story seems more plausible, as Schachter suggests. Our modern dignity discourse owes more to the human rights discourse that has emerged since 1948 than the latter owes to the former.

B. Source and legitimacy

In a recent essay, Klaus Dicke has suggested that in the UDHR "the dignity of human beings is a formal transcendental norm to legitimize human rights claims."[33] This

---

[31] See, eg, Jeremy Waldron, "The Decline of Natural Right," in Allen Wood and Songsuk Susan Kahn (eds.), *The Cambridge History of Philosophy in the Nineteenth Century* (Cambridge University Press, 2012), 62, and Samuel Moyn, *The Last Utopia: Human Rights in History* (Harvard University Press, 2012).

[32] Schachter, "Human Dignity as a Normative Concept," 853.

[33] Klaus Dicke, "The Founding Function of Human Dignity in the Universal Declaration of Human Rights" in Kretzmer and Klein (eds.), *The Concept of Dignity in Human Rights Discourse*, 111, 118.

terminology is rather opaque but Dicke seems to be invoking a Kelsenian idea. Just as the *"grundnorm"* of a legal system—the norm that says that the provisions of the highest constitution are to be respected—is the source of legal validity and, in that sense, of legitimacy in that system for all statutory and regulative norms,[34] so a norm regarding human dignity might be an ultimate source for the legitimacy of human rights norms. The validity of a statute derives from the constitutional norms that empower a given legislature and lay down the basic procedures for enactment; and, on Kelsen's account, in order to preclude unanswerable questions about where the validity of the relevant constitutional provisions derive from, we *posit* a final and transcendental norm to underpin the validity of the constitution, rather than trying to locate a still higher positive norm (say, the empowering statute of a former colonial power) to validate it. In a moment, I shall say something about the difference between this story, which concerns what Kelsen called the "dynamics" of a legal system, and the sort of story that I suspect Dicke has in mind, which seems to have more in common with what Kelsen called the "static" derivation of one norm from the content of another.[35]

But first let us explore what could possibly be meant here. Dicke presumably does not want to deny the status of the great human rights covenants as sources of law, valid on account of their signature and ratification by a large number of countries. But I think he wants to deny that persons have the rights mentioned in those covenants just because the ICCPR, for example, was enacted as a multi-lateral treaty. The ICCPR on his account does not create the rights; it recognizes and proclaims the rights that humans already have. Why is the invocation of human dignity a way of saying this, or what does it add to this? Dicke believes that the invocation of human dignity is a reference to the special nature of human beings, their inherent worth, which explains why they really do have the rights that the covenants proclaim, prior to and independent of the positive law proclamation.

Oscar Schachter seems to infer something similar, at least in a negative way: "as a philosophical statement, the proposition that rights derive from the inherent dignity of the person ... implies that rights are not derived from the state or any other external authority."[36] Again, Schachter, one of the first generation of great human rights jurists, need not be interpreted here as denying the authority of positive international law. He is merely insisting on the "suprapositive" element that lies behind the law's recognition of these rights.[37] More affirmatively, the invocation of dignity may suggest that there is a suprapositive explanation for our according the importance to human rights that we do, for our insistence on their universality, inalienability, and non-forfeitability. It is not simply a matter of our having decided to create positive law in this form; our creation of laws with these features presents itself as an affirmative response to facts about human specialness that we recognize in our ethical talk of human dignity.

I think this is about as far as I can take this version of the foundational claim. I suppose one could go a step further and say that the legitimacy of our human rights law is

---

[34] Hans Kelsen, *Pure Theory of Law*, trans. Max Knight (University of California Press, 1967), 198–205.
[35] Kelsen, *Pure Theory of Law*, 108ff.
[36] Schachter, "Human Dignity as a Normative Concept," 853.
[37] For "suprapositive element," see Gerald Neuman, "Human Rights and Constitutional Rights: Harmony and Dissonance," *Stanford Law Review*, 55 (2003): 1863.

derived from a higher law respecting human dignity—God's law, for example, or some natural law conception. Certainly the belief in such a higher law explains the positive law-creating actions of many who drafted and subscribed to the human rights cove-nants. But I think this is better conveyed by saying, as I said in the last paragraph, that the covenants represent themselves as positive law responses to suprapositive ideas, rather than that the legitimacy or validity of human rights norms can be traced to non-positive law. Some will concede the point readily enough so far as legal validity is concerned; like me they may be unable to make good sense of Dicke's implicit compar-ison of the value of human dignity with a Kelsenian *grundnorm*. But "legitimacy" is a looser term—it can mean anything from legal validity through popular acceptance to moral appeal. If it means "moral appeal," then, yes, we can say that the legitimacy of human rights ideas owes a lot to the legitimacy of dignitarian ideas (and vice versa).

In his legal theory, Hans Kelsen distinguished between the dynamics and the statics of a legal system.[38] In a dynamic sense, validity is a matter of higher laws empowering the making of laws or legal orders at a lower level. The constitution empowers legisla-tors; they enact statutes which empower municipal authorities; municipal authorities enact ordinances which empower local magistrates to condemn this or that dilapi-dated house.[39] A static analysis, on the other hand, is a relation between legal proposi-tions which is more like derivation than like empowerment and enactment. A static analysis will show why if wounding is wrong, then stabbing is wrong: the idea of stab-bing is already comprised in the more general idea of wounding and the connection is established more or less by deduction.[40] I think the Dicke approach unhelpfully blurs this distinction between static and dynamic approaches. But of course, this does not mean that a static analysis of the relation between human dignity and human rights is impossible. Maybe one *can* be derived from the other; it is to this possibility that we now turn.

C. A genuine basis for derivation

The sense of "foundation" that promises the most is the suggestion that knowing what the foundation of rights is would enable us to generate or derive human rights claims. We could then build up an account of human rights on a more rigorous basis than the list of rights given in a legal charter; and this foundationalism would also provide a sort of litmus test for assessing what people say about human rights. People make all sorts of suggestions as to what rights we have or what human rights there are: a foun-dation of the kind now being contemplated would give us a basis on which we could test such claims, by looking to see whether the content of a given claim could indeed be derived from the foundation.

Of course this foundational power could not be bought cheaply. Slight variations in the way the foundation is specified—variations in our conception of dignity, for example—might lead to significant differences in the claims about rights that are generated or certified by this method. People will be tempted to rig their conception

---

[38] Kelsen, *Pure Theory of Law*, 195–8.   [39] Kelsen, *Pure Theory of Law*, 221–8.
[40] Kelsen, *Pure Theory of Law*, 195.

of the foundational value so that it generates the kinds of rights claims they already favor; and antagonists will stand ready to accuse rights theorists of doing this. In other words, this foundational approach does not ease the burden involved in the defense of particular claims about human rights. Instead it shifts the burden to the foundational level, by implying that that is the level at which rights controversies really arise. Still, in the spirit of the way we have been proceeding, this shifting of controversies is not necessarily disreputable. It may be sensible and illuminating to relocate our controversies about human rights in this way. Perhaps we will be better able to see what is at stake in the assessment of (say) claims about socio-economic rights, by seeing the distinctive form of dignity-foundation that is needed to generate rights of this kind.

Formally, the sort of derivations I have in mind are going to be partly deductive and partly empirical. On a deductive approach, we begin with our conception of the foundational value—say, human dignity—and we unpack it analytically to see what it involves.

James Griffin's argument in *On Human Rights* is an example. Griffin begins with "the dignity of the human person" and he argues that that idea is best understood in terms of the importance of normative agency in the life of a human being.[41] The value of the normative agency of a human being discloses itself in that being's autonomy, that is, in her ability to determine for herself what the shape of her life will be and what it is for her life to go well.[42] And that ability in turn requires liberty in certain key areas—indeed certain basic rights embodying liberty, to guarantee that the person in question is the one who makes the key decisions about her life without coercive interference. Griffin believes we can also infer from the importance of autonomy that the key choices must be educated choices and must be made from an array of meaningful available options.[43] All of this, I think, is supposed to be established more or less analytically, with dignity being constituted by normative agency, with normative agency being characterized definitionally by autonomy, and with various forms of negative and positive liberty being derived from what is necessary to protect autonomy. And of course it can be challenged by someone who denies that dignity is the foundation of human rights, or that dignity (if it *is* the foundation) is connected successively to the value of normative agency, the importance of autonomy, and the right to liberty, in the way that Griffin argues.

Some of the derivations that Griffin has in mind are mediated in part by empirical premises. (These operate, presumably, as minor premises, with dignitarian propositions or propositions deduced from or associated constitutively with dignitarian propositions as major premises.) So they too are open to challenge—but now empirical challenge as well as analytic challenge. In his argument that human rights include certain welfare rights, Griffin suggests that there may be points about what is needed to protect and promote autonomy that cannot be established *a priori* but only by observation of how autonomy flourishes or withers in particular kinds of political economy. He says that not all arguments for welfare rights are of this character—"There are forms of welfare that are empirically necessary conditions of a person's being

---

[41] James Griffin, *On Human Rights* (Oxford University Press, 2008), 152.
[42] Griffin, *On Human Rights*, 150–1.   [43] Griffin, *On Human Rights*, 159–69.

autonomous and free, but there are also forms that are logically necessary."[44] Still a rights foundationalist has to be ready to work both sides of this street.[45]

I have gone on at length about Griffin's theory because it illustrates, better than any other, what might be involved in this third, most robust kind of rights foundationalism. I do not mean either to endorse it or to criticize it. I do think it is important to see it as one account among several of what it means to say that something like dignity lies at the foundation of human rights.

D. The key to interpretive understanding

The approach we have just been considering envisages the foundation of rights as a very abstract major premise from which we derive particular rights, perhaps also with the help of minor empirical premises. We start with the foundation and we generate rights out of that. An alternative approach would be more inductive or "bottom-up," and goes as follows.[46]

We begin with an understanding of the rights we have—maybe not a complete or fully elaborated understanding, but something like one of the lists of human rights that is already widely accepted. And then we try to make sense of that, perhaps by considering the values that would have to be presupposed in order for *this* list of rights to be sensible. We may try to hook up with the approach described in section C by first asking what would have to be postulated as a foundation in order to generate all or most of the items on our list, and then treating the value that we have postulated as a major premise for the formal derivation of what we had assumed as our rights already. Or the bottom-up approach may be looser than that. We might think of the postulated value as helping us make sense of the rights on our list, whether we then go on to assign a formally foundational role to it or not. Michael Rosen says this about the connection between human dignity and human rights:

> Human rights are obviously deeply puzzling—almost everyone nowadays professes commitment to them, yet few people would claim that they had a good, principled account of what they are and why we have them. Could a modern understanding of dignity meet that need?[47]

Giving a good, principled account of what rights we have and why we have them need not involve linear derivation on the model outlined in section C. Understanding why we have human rights involves understanding the point of the rights we have. But

---

[44] Griffin, *On Human Rights*, 180.

[45] If I read him rightly, Arthur Chaskalson, "Human Dignity as a Constitutional Value," in Kretzmer and Klein (eds.), *The Concept of Dignity in Human Rights Discourse*, 133, 135, gives the impression that the whole of the dignitarian case for rights is instrumental. He says that having introduced dignity into the picture, the idea is that all of the remaining rights "can be analyzed and defended as being necessary for the protection or promotion of human dignity." But this may be to ignore the constitutive and deductive element.

[46] I owe the distinction between top-down and bottom-up approaches in this context, to Griffin, *On Human Rights*, 29–30. Griffin claims that his own account is a bottom-up account, but I think this is misleading in light of the great emphasis he gives to premises of personhood, dignity, and normative agency at 30–48 and 149–58.

[47] Rosen, *Dignity*, 54.

again, the point of rights need not be understood in a rigidly teleological sense—a sense that would license the derivation of other rights from a statement of the *telos*. The sort of understanding I have in mind in this section (D) may be loosely oriented to a class of human rights that is in some sense given, and our understanding of it need not be conceived in a way that permits any expansion of the list of rights beyond what we started with. This of course is definitely the case when human rights are understood as *legal* rights. We cannot always show that something is law by showing that it can be derived from what seems necessary for understanding other legal propositions.

Still, the fact that rights have a legal presence (in constitutional law or in human rights law) does not obviate the need for an understanding of the kind I am talking about. Even our most clearly established rights may still be bewildering. As Ronald Dworkin put it,

> The institution of rights against the government is not a gift of God, or an ancient ritual, or a national sport. It is a complex and troublesome practice that makes the government's job of securing the general benefit more difficult and more expensive, and it would be a frivolous and wrongful practice unless it served some point. Anyone who professes to take rights seriously, and who praises our government for respecting them, must have some sense of what that point is. He must accept, at the minimum, one or both of two important ideas. The first is the vague but powerful idea of human dignity. This idea, associated with Kant, but defended by philosophers of different schools, supposes that there are ways of treating a man that are inconsistent with recognizing him as a full member of the human community, and holds that such treatment is profoundly unjust. The second is the more familiar idea of political equality. This supposes that the weaker members of a political community are entitled to the same concern and respect of their government as the more powerful members have secured for themselves, so that if some men have freedom of decision whatever the effect on the general good, then all men must have the same freedom. I do not want to defend or elaborate these ideas here, but only to insist that anyone who claims that citizens have rights must accept ideas very close to these.[48]

We need not accept Dworkin's account of the alternatives to appreciate the point that he is making. What we need—and what we sometimes loosely call a "foundation"—is a way of understanding the point of rights that will help us interpret particular rights provisions as well as help us determine the spirit in which we should proceed in advancing rights-based claims, as well as the way in which we deal with possible conflicts of rights and the question of their limitation.[49]

If dignity were treated as the foundation in the sense of this section (D), it might have a greater or a lesser impact depending on how robust the conception of dignity was taken to be. In the *German Airliner Case*, the German Constitutional Court considered the right to life in the context of a statute that would empower the armed forces to shoot down a passenger plane in a 9/11 type of situation. The Court insisted on viewing the right to life through the lens of dignity and since it was using a strongly

[48] Ronald Dworkin, *Taking Rights Seriously* (Harvard University Press, 1977), 198.
[49] For a good account of how dignity works to structure our understanding of legal rights, see Barroso, "Here, There, and Everywhere."

Kantian notion of dignity, it was able to insist that the innocent passengers and crew of the airliner could not be destroyed simply to save the lives of a greater number of other innocent people (for example, in a building targeted by the hijackers).[50] On a less robust conception of dignity, however, approach (D) might simply indicate that we are to take individuals and their autonomy seriously in interpreting rights and not treat them as heuristics for the advancement of the general good. It would not tell us much more than that.

VIII.　Foundations and Characteristics

The looser our approach to the alleged foundational role of dignity, the more we need to be alert to another possible worry. We need to be alert to the fallacy of mistaking a feature common to all rights for something that plays one of these foundational roles.

This often happens with rights on account of their rather complex formal structure. The idea of a right (let alone a human right) is a not a simple one. In the discourse of rights, a given content is not just presented normatively; it is presented in a particularly demanding normative mode. The demand is peremptory and the demand is for the securing not just the adventitious satisfaction of the norm. Moreover, the demand is presented in a way that relates it essentially to the interests and perhaps also to the choices of an individual. Finally, if we are talking about human rights, we are also talking about equality—that is, we are talking about rights that are held equally, rights such that if any person has them, then everybody has them.

These features of human rights can be established by analysis. They are important and their ubiquity might lead us to mistake them for foundational elements. But though they are structural components characteristic of all rights, it is a mistake to infer anything foundational on this basis.

For example, on some approaches, having a right means being able to control another's duty by one's choice.[51] This is not the place to discuss the detail of the "Choice Theory" of rights, beyond saying that even if the theory were true, it would be wrong to infer that free choice is therefore the foundation of rights or that rights exist in order to protect and promote autonomy. I do not mean that these latter claims are false; I mean rather that this formal move is not the right sort of way to establish such foundational claims. The substance of a given right might have nothing to do with freedom: it may be a human right to health care for example. All that the Choice Theory implies is that even for a right like this (which does not directly concern liberty), the right-bearer has the privilege of choosing whether the duty-holder is held liable for a breach. It is up to her (her choice) whether a law-suit is brought. That is not enough to establish a foundation in liberty for the right to health care.

---

[50] *Bundesverfassungsgericht*, 15 February 2006, 115 BVerfGE 118, at §122: "By their killing being used as a means to save others, they are treated as objects and at the same time deprived of their rights; with their lives being disposed of unilaterally by the state, the persons on board the aircraft, who, as victims, are themselves in need of protection, are denied the value which is due to a human being for his or her own sake."

[51] For the "Choice Theory" of rights, see H.L.A. Hart, "Are There Any Natural Rights?" in Jeremy Waldron (ed.), *Theories of Rights* (Oxford University Press, 1984), 77.

For a second example, consider that it is often supposed to be a feature of rights that they must *secure* the goods or freedoms that they promise, not just bring them about adventitiously. I do not have a legal right to φ unless φ is in some way guaranteed to me beyond the day-to-day vicissitudes of public policy. But again we should not make too much of this, at least for foundational purposes. From the fact that security (of some interest or liberty) is what one demands when one demands one's rights, we cannot infer that all rights are *based* on security. Those who make this inference use it sometimes as a basis for saying that civil liberties cannot be set up against security or against the activity of the security state, because they are all in the end dependent on security.[52] There may be something to this if it is meant in the spirit of Henry Shue's claim that one cannot enjoy one's rights except in circumstances of security.[53] But it is not persuasive if the inference is drawn simply from the fact that it is the point of rights to establish the goods or freedoms they protect securely.

A third example involves equality. If there are any human rights, they are presumably to be secured to all humans equally. But that doesn't license us to say that equality is the *foundation* of all rights, though again there may be independent arguments to that effect.[54] Nor does it license us to make the more foundational-sounding claim that it is the point of human rights to see that all persons are treated as equals.

Might the claim that dignity is the foundation of human rights be based on an analogous mistake? It may be. It is sometimes said that there is a certain dignity just in being a right-holder. Joel Feinberg who has long insisted on the importance of the analytic point that exercising a right means making a claim has suggested that "what is called 'human dignity' may simply be the recognizable capacity to assert claims. To respect a person, then, or to think of him as possessed of human dignity simply is to think of him as a potential maker of claims."[55] This is a relatively weak conception of dignity and even if it is implicated with rights in the way Feinberg suggests, it cannot plausibly be regarded as foundational for rights. It is just one of the features that all rights possess.

IX. Dignity as a Status

Sometimes it is said—correctly in my view—that dignity is a status-concept, not a value-concept.[56] If we think carefully about status, it may seem that this opens up yet another possibility for a mistake about dignity's alleged foundational role.

---

[52] For discussion of this misconception, see Liora Lazarus, "Mapping the Right to Security," in Benjamin Goold and Liora Lazarus (eds.), *Security and Human Rights* (Hart Publishing, 2007), 325. See also Jeremy Waldron, "Safety and Security," *Nebraska Law Review*, 85 (2006): 454 (reprinted in Jeremy Waldron, *Torture, Terror and Trade-Offs: Philosophy for the White House* (Oxford University Press, 2010), 111).

[53] Henry Shue, *Basic Rights: Subsistence, Affluence, and U.S. Foreign Policy* (Princeton University Press, 1980). See the discussion in Jeremy Waldron, "Security as a Basic Right (after 9/11)," in Charles Beitz and Robert Goodin (eds.), *Global Basic Rights* (Oxford University Press, 2009), 207 (reprinted in Waldron, *Torture, Terror, and Trade-Offs*, 166).

[54] See, eg, Dworkin, *Taking Rights Seriously*, 272–8.

[55] Joel Feinberg, "The Nature and Value of Rights," *Journal of Value Inquiry*, 4 (1970): 243, 252.

[56] For argument to this effect, see Jeremy Waldron, *Dignity, Rank and Rights* (Oxford University Press, 2012), 57–61.

In law, a status is a particular package of rights, powers, disabilities, duties, privileges, immunities, and liabilities accruing to a person by virtue of the condition or situation they are in. Bankruptcy, infancy, royalty, being an alien, being a prisoner, being a member of the armed forces, being married—these are all statuses, each of them comprising its particular package of rights, powers, etc. In Britain, the monarch has distinctive powers and duties; in most countries, a bankrupt has distinctive disabilities; so do convicts (often they cannot vote, for example); a serving member of the armed forces has distinctive duties and a few distinctive privileges; and infants have few, if any, of the legal rights and powers that adults have; and so on. In all these cases, the status word operates rather like an abbreviation for the list of rights, powers, etc. that a person in one of these situations has. We could, if we liked, laboriously spell out each of these incidents. For infancy, we could say: (a) if X is under eighteen, then X has the right to support from X's parents; and (b) if X is under eighteen, then X does not have the power to enter into certain contracts; and so on. Or, for bankruptcy, we could say: (a) if Y's liabilities have been adjudged to exceed his assets or he does not have the wherewithal to pay his debts as they fall due, then he is forbidden from incurring any further debts; and (b) if Y's liabilities have been adjudged to exceed his assets or he does not have the wherewithal to pay his debts as they fall due, then he is entitled to protection from his creditors; and so on. But instead we summarize all this information by saying that in law X is an infant and Y is a bankrupt, and our understanding of the technical legal meanings of those terms—bankruptcy and infancy, respectively—carries with it knowledge of the details of the legal position that people with this status are in.

It can easily appear that the status term does not introduce any new information. John Austin thought this. As he wrote in his *Lectures on Jurisprudence*, "[t]he sets of rights and duties, or of capacities and incapacities, inserted as status in the Law of Persons, are placed there merely for the sake of commodious exposition."[57] A status term, he said, is "an ellipsis (or an abridged form of expression)," purely a matter of expository convenience.[58] It is nothing but an abbreviation, a "device of legal exegetics."[59]

If all this is true, and if dignity is a status, then it will be a mistake—a sort of category mistake—to talk of dignity as the foundation of rights. Instead, we may say that dignity is a status that *comprises* a given set of rights. The old notion of *dignitas* was like this: the *dignitas* of a noble was a different status from the *dignitas* of a priest and the difference consisted simply in the detail of the rights associated, respectively, with the status of nobility or the status of being in holy orders. And so too, perhaps, with our notion of human dignity. To say of an entity that it has the status of human dignity is certainly to imply that it has human rights.[60] But that is because human dignity as

---

[57] John Austin, *Lectures on Jurisprudence, or The Philosophy of Positive Law*, 5th edn, ed. Robert Campbell (John Murray, 1885), vol. II, Lecture XL, 687–8.

[58] Austin, *Lectures on Jurisprudence*, 700.

[59] This is the rendering of Austin's position in C.K. Allen, *Legal Duties and Other Essays in Jurisprudence* (Oxford: Clarendon Press, 1931), 34.

[60] Some jurists maintain that, strictly speaking, the status of a human person is a sort of oxymoron. R.H. Graveson, *Status in the Common Law* (Athlone Press, 1953), 2, defines "status" as "a *special* condition of a continuous and institutional nature, *differing from the legal position of the normal person*,

a status term is just a short way of conveying that information. Like every other status term, it abbreviates a list of rights. We do not have human rights because we have human dignity; our having human dignity *is* our having human rights. This is what one might think.

But perhaps this is not the end of the matter. On Austin's view, a status term is *just* an abbreviation for a list of rights, powers, disabilities, duties, privileges, immunities, and liabilities. But perhaps it is also worth insisting that the list is not arbitrary; it is supposed to be a list that *makes sense* relative to some *underlying idea* that informs the status in question. And the meaning of the status term embraces this idea as well.[61] In the example of infancy, propositions (a) and (b) are not arbitrary legal propositions. Each of them makes sense in terms of the underlying idea that human children are much less capable of looking after themselves and much more vulnerable to depredation or exploitation by others than adults are. And they make sense *together*, as a package, in response to that idea—ie, they make sense jointly as well as severally. The underlying idea—that being an infant (in the ordinary-language meaning of that term) requires special solicitude from society—is what makes sense of infancy in its technical legal meaning. We can say something similar about bankruptcy, alienage, royalty, being a prisoner, and all the other status terms I mentioned. Each of them is not just an abbreviation of a list of legal "if-then" propositions; it packages a list of propositions deemed to make sense, jointly and severally, in virtue of a certain underlying idea about a particular circumstance or vicissitude of the human condition.

This is not just a matter of each item (in the list abbreviated by a given status) having some rationale.[62] It is a matter of their having a common rationale which explains how the various rights, duties, and so on hang together, ie, the underlying coherence of the package. So, for example, the contractual incapacities of infants are understood in relation to the duties of their parents to make the provision for them that for most of us is made by our own ability to enter into contracts. Because an infant lacks contractual capacity, someone else must make provision for them. Abstracted from the

---

which is conferred by law... whenever a person occupies a position of which the creation, continuance or relinquishment and the incidents thereof are a matter of sufficient social concern." I disagree with this: it compares unfavorably with Roman law notions, which included, as one status among others, the status of the ordinary free man.

[61] Austin was not unaware of this account. He associated it with the work of his own mentor Jeremy Bentham, and he offered rare criticism of the master in this regard, at Austin, *Lectures on Jurisprudence*, 690, complaining that "Mr. Bentham... appears to me to be inconsistent and obscure in all he says on the subject."

> It is remarkable that Bentham (who has cleared the moral sciences from loads of the like rubbish) adopts this occult quality under a different name. In the chapter in the *Traités de Législation*, which treats of États (or of status or conditions), he defines a status thus: *Un état domestique ou civil n'est qu'une base idéale, autour de laquelle se rangent des droits et des devoirs, et quelquefois des incapacités.*

Austin, *Lectures on Jurisprudence*, 699. Austin is quoting from a work we know now as Jeremy Bentham, *The Theory of Legislation*, ed. C.K. Ogden (Kegan Paul, Trench, Trubner & Co., 1931), but which in Austin's day was published only in French.

[62] I do not just mean someone's particular opinion as to why a given set of legal provisions is justified. I mean something more like a legally established justification—like a legally recognized purpose or policy—something which is not just present in politics to persuade people that the law is good and right, but rather suffuses the law itself with a sense of purpose.

whole package, a given incident of a given status may not make much sense. But, in the package, it makes sense in relation to the underlying idea which it shares with all the other incidents.

Accordingly, if human dignity is a status, then we should say that it comprises not just a set of human rights, but an *underlying idea* which explains both the importance of each of these rights in relation to our being human and the importance of their being packaged together in this regard. If this is so, then the objection we considered early on in this section is a mistake. It is wrong to criticize a claim that dignity is the foundation of rights by saying that all that dignity does is abbreviate a set of rights. It doesn't just abbreviate them, it refers to the idea that underlies and unifies them.

X. The Grounds of Dignity

My aim in this chapter has been to explore some of the difficulties that might seem to stand in the way of a claim that rights are derived from dignity or that human dignity is the foundation of human rights. One last objection needs to be entertained.

When we say that dignity is the foundation of human rights, we often give the impression that dignity is an irreducible value, that we have burrowed deep below the rights that are recognized in the familiar human rights charters, and that once we burrow down to dignity, it is not necessary to go any further. But when dignity is discussed in other settings, it is often accepted that dignity is an idea with foundations of its own and that it is sensible to ask what dignity is based on and from what features of the human person or the human species human dignity is derived. For example, some say that our dignity consists in God's claim upon us, or our being created in His image.[63] Others say, with Kant, that our dignity is based on the metaphysical significance of our possession of moral capacity, the ability to act on principle even when every empirical impulse or inclination, every sentiment, and every element of self-interest pressures us to the contrary.[64] Others say that dignity is based on our ordinary non-metaphysical ability to take responsibility for our lives and our recognition of similar abilities in others.[65] Others still, say it is rooted partly in the specialness of the human species, of which every individual partakes *qua* human even if he or she does not actually share the qualities and achievements that distinguish the species.[66] As I said in section V, a rights theorist's foundational claim about dignity directs us, not to a clear conception, but to questions and controversies about that idea—questions and controversies that can't be answered without going much deeper than the alleged foundation itself.

Is this a problem—that our alleged foundational idea turns out to be in quest of foundations for itself? I don't think so. That X is a foundation for Y may be a relative rather than an absolute claim; the claim is that X illuminates Y in an interesting

---

[63] For the former conception, see Jürgen Moltmann, *On Human Dignity: Political Theology and Ethics* (Fortress Press, 1984). For the latter, see Jeremy Waldron, "The Image of God: Rights, Reason, and Order," in John Witte and Frank Alexander (eds.), *Christianity and Human Rights: An Introduction* (Cambridge University Press, 2010), 21.

[64] Kant, *Groundwork of the Metaphysics of Morals*, 42–6.

[65] Dworkin, *Justice for Hedgehogs*, 202–14.   [66] See Kateb, *Human Dignity*, 174ff.

way or that claims like Y can be derived from X; it is not necessarily a claim that X is rock-bottom, as it were. It does not preclude the possibility of there being an even deeper value W that in turn illuminates X or from which conceptions like X can be derived. I suppose it might mean that, strictly speaking, dignity is redundant: one could just go all the way down to the deepest foundational idea, bypassing dignity en route. But this would sell short the role of dignity in organizing and explaining the relation between rights, on the one hand, and certain distinctive aspects (and not others) of the deepest foundational idea.

Alternatively, we may use the framework discussed in the previous section to convey the thought that the invocation of dignity points not just to the rights that constitute a particular status but to the underlying idea that unifies them. That underlying idea may be thought of as what dignity ultimately amounts to or as what dignity is ultimately based on or as what the rights that dignity comprises are ultimately based on. It might even convey the idea that dignity and rights are co-foundational, which will be unsurprising if the grammar of dignity is that of a status concept, along the lines I set out in section IX. It is probably wise not to be too fussy about this. Section IX dealt with status in a technical legal way. But moral philosophers and others use status—particular in relation to dignity—in a much looser sense. Once we understand that the technical analysis does not disclose any insuperable objection to talk of dignity (the status) as a foundation for the rights it comprises, then we can afford to be accommodating of the looser sense and relatively indiscriminate as between the models indicated in sections A to C.

I said at the beginning of this chapter that my aim was to explore the claim that human rights are based on human dignity, not with a view to refuting the claim, but in order to see what obstacles the claim might face. The claim is often made loosely; sometimes it is barely more than a piece of decorative rhetoric. Other times, it seems to convey a quite precise (and controversial) proposition. I don't want to make a fetish of precision; part of the point of my analysis is to see where we can afford loose talk in this regard and where it is important to tighten up the claim about the relation between dignity and rights. Philosophers tend to think that precision is always important; but they have known since Aristotle that that may not always be wise.[67] Sometimes the quest for precision blinds us to certain insights that we can as yet only formulate haltingly; sometimes it blinds us to the importance of pursuing certain questions (and linking them to other questions) even when there is not yet an answer in sight.

It has not been my intention to defend any particular version of the claim that human dignity is the foundation of human rights. For what it is worth, I think some such claim is true and helpful. Mostly I have wanted to see whether there is room for any such claims. I think there is; there are all sorts of pitfalls and fallacies, but the propounding of a foundational relation between human rights and human dignity is not always a matter of confusion.

---

[67] Aristotle, *Nichomachean Ethics*, Bk. I, ch. 3 (1094b13).

6

Human Rights, Natural Rights, and Human Dignity

A. John Simmons

I. Foundations for Human Rights

The Universal Declaration of Human Rights (UDHR), in its preamble, famously recognizes "the inherent dignity...and the equal and inalienable rights of all members of the human family." And it suggests in Article 1 an intimate relationship between human dignity and human rights: "All human beings are born free and equal in dignity and rights." The International Covenant on Civil and Political Rights (ICCPR) appears to identify a more precise relationship between these ideas, suggesting that the human rights it names "derive from the inherent dignity of the human person." Such claims, of course, suggest the possible appropriateness of a certain sort of philosophical project, a sort of project that has not been uncommon in the literature on human rights. Begin by analyzing the idea of inherent human dignity, possessed equally by all. Then show how the moral importance of human dignity can serve as a foundation—or at least as a more basic ground—for a set of universal moral rights for human beings. Finally, determine which specific human rights are implied by this foundation. The resulting list of *moral* human rights might then be compared to the Declaration's list, or to some other list containing more recent additions from other important documents. We could then affirm these lists, correct them (by subtraction, by addition, or both), or simply note (and possibly try to explain or justify) any differences between our well-grounded set of moral human rights and the positive rights affirmed in human rights law.

A related, but more historically based (and equally familiar) philosophical project might also be suggested by the Declaration's appeal to the "equal and inalienable" rights of human persons. While the power, urgency, and frequency of appeals to human rights is, of course, a relatively recent phenomenon, largely motivated by the moral horrors perpetrated during (and surrounding) the Second World War, the historical origins of human rights thought runs back at least to classical natural rights theory. So it might seem sensible to trace the idea of human rights back to its roots in natural rights theory and in its deployment in the great rights manifestos of the eighteenth century (such as the French Declaration of the Rights of Man and Citizen). We could then try to understand the idea of a human right in terms of its growth out of the *natural* rights tradition, seeing what kinds of natural rights might count as genuinely human rights, and perhaps then again affirm, correct, or justify the Declaration's (or some other document's) enumeration of human rights.

The first sort of project, whatever its initial appeal or the apparent support it enjoys in (some of the) key historical human rights documents, might nonetheless prove to be misguided in one of a variety of ways. Perhaps the idea of human dignity is not best understood as the proper *foundation* of a theory of human rights at all, or even as something (more basic but not foundational) from which human rights can be derived. While human rights and human dignity might be intimately related in some way, the relationship between them might not be one of moral conclusion to more basic or foundational moral idea. Or perhaps the problem with *either* sort of philosophical project runs deeper than that. It might be a mistake to suppose that a theory of human rights is a better or more fully justified theory when it is made to rest on such deep and naturalistic foundations as an account of human dignity or a theory of natural rights. Such a foundational approach might yield a distorted, rather than an illuminating, understanding of human rights. This essay will briefly explore in turn each of these possible avenues of criticism of familiar foundational projects in the theory of human rights.

II. Waldron on Foundations

Jeremy Waldron, in his chapter, "Is Dignity the Foundation of Human Rights?" (this volume, chapter 5), builds upon the more general exploration of the idea of human dignity pursued in his 2009 Tanner Lectures ("Dignity, Rank, and Rights").[1] This new chapter focuses more specifically on the claim "that human dignity is the foundation of human rights" (117), a position familiar to us not only from the language of important human rights conventions, but as well from the rhetoric employed in discussing them and from various more philosophical theories of human rights. The conventions themselves, as Waldron rightly notes, utilize the idea of human dignity in no consistent role, referring to it sometimes as if it were the (or a) foundation of human rights claims, but other times apparently employing it in other ways, including using it as (or in) the content of particular human rights. Waldron's take on this is in part to observe, again correctly, that the mere fact that some of the listed human rights appear to protect human dignity "explicitly and more or less directly" while others do not is not inconsistent with dignity nonetheless being the foundation for all human rights (119); nor is it inconsistent with the existence of multiple foundations for these different rights (120–1). Attending to the conventions, in short, reveals no clear or consistent stance on either what it might mean for human dignity to be the foundation of human rights or whether a foundational role is the best way to understand human dignity's relation to all human rights.

Waldron instead examines these questions by utilizing distinctions between four ways in which one concept (such as human dignity) might be the foundation of another (such as human rights). The foundational relationship could be understood in terms of (i) one concept arising from another as a matter of "history and geneology", (ii) one serving as the source of the validity or legitimacy of the other, (iii) one being logically

---

[1] Unless otherwise stated, subsequent in-text references refer to Waldron, this volume, chapter 5. The Tanner lectures are published in Jeremy Waldron, *Dignity, Rank, and Rights*, ed. M. Dan-Cohen (Oxford: Oxford University Press, 2012), 13–76.

derivable from the other (perhaps with the addition of certain empirical premises), or (iv) one concept throwing "some indispensable light" on the other (125).

While "historical genesis" arguments are not the kind of argument that most philosophers would take to reveal the normative "foundations" of concepts—rather than, say, merely their historical source or origin—I think Waldron is still right to mention such arguments. After all, few of those who discuss and work to promote human rights are philosophers, and the order of things in the history of ideas may well be exactly what many have in mind in talking about human dignity being the foundation of human rights. Even understood as a mere claim in the history of ideas, however, the claim that dignity is foundational for human rights is not very plausible (126). Waldron's second conception of "foundationality" is more obscure, but it involves comparing the importance of human dignity (as the source of the legitimacy of human rights claims) to a Kelsenian *grundnorm* (as the source of validity of all other norms in the legal system). I can add nothing to Waldron's skeptical treatment of this approach.

In any event, it is only the third and fourth notions of a foundation that remain actively in play in Waldron's discussion of the matter, with the third being what philosophers and legal/political theorists no doubt mostly have in mind when they speak of foundations, but the fourth seeming to Waldron to more accurately characterize the relationship between human dignity and human rights. The kind of logical derivation that Waldron imagines being provided on the third approach is one that is "partly deductive and partly empirical" (129), with the "deductive" portion involving an analytical "unpacking" of the foundational value—in this case, the value of human dignity. That unpacking would yield various value propositions, which would then serve as major premises in syllogistic arguments to conclusions about human rights. The intermediate minor premises would be empirical claims (presumably about the kinds of guarantees that would be necessary for human dignity to be realized in the world). Waldron takes James Griffin's theory of human rights to be an example of this third approach to showing that human dignity is the foundation for human rights, with Griffin's ideas about the importance of "normative agency" (and about what normative agency involves) constituting the relevant analytical unpacking of the concept of human dignity.

While I have my doubts about how well Griffin's account actually exemplifies the (third) approach Waldron describes, such doubts may have no real impact on Waldron's project in this chapter, since Waldron says that he intends neither "to endorse [Griffin's account] [n]or to criticize it" (130). Indeed, Waldron appears never to argue that there is any general reason to reject foundational derivations of his third sort, Griffin's or any other. He maintains only that we "need not" understand the point of (human) rights in such "a rigidly teleological sense" (131). Waldron then proceeds to propose a different, fourth, "foundational" model. As far as I can see, though, the truth of Waldron's preferred fourth ("indispensable light") approach—in which human dignity is viewed as a special kind of normative status—is not inconsistent with the validity and soundness of any of a wide range of possible "logical derivations" of human rights (of Waldron's *third* sort). For there to be any inconsistency between the third and fourth approaches, I think, we would have to understand the particular status of human dignity (or understand all statuses) in a special, and I think implausible, way. So even if we think "logical derivations" of the third sort need not conform very closely to Waldron's model of them—perhaps by proceeding without the sharp, syllogistic separation of value and empirical premises that Waldron imagines, or by regarding human rights as more inclusively (and less teleologically) connected to the foundational value—none of that may matter much if Waldron's approach is simply consistent with those foundational "logical derivations".

There is, however, one difference between Waldron's preferred account (of the relation of human dignity to human rights) and foundational accounts of his third sort that *might* make them genuinely inconsistent with one another. It is mentioned by Waldron almost in passing. Derivations of the third sort, Waldron suggests, "would license the derivation of other rights from a statement of the *telos*"—that is, from the relevant understanding of the goal or "the point of the rights we have" (131). So, for instance, Griffin's understanding of the point of human rights (in terms of their relation to normative agency) would, in Waldron's view, "license" the derivation of other human rights, in addition to those on the list of rights with which we begin. Waldron's preferred (fourth) strategy, however, would understand the point of human rights in a way that is "loosely oriented to a class of human rights that is in some sense given" and that does not permit "any expansion of the list of rights beyond what we started with" (131).

Waldron's use of "loosely" and "in some sense" makes it difficult to be certain how seriously we are to take these ideas, but the general line of thought nonetheless seems reasonably clear. Human rights "have a legal presence (in constitutional law or in human rights law)", and there are (or we can make) lists of those rights that are implicated in that legal presence. The lists constitute (provisionally?) fixed points in a proper approach to understanding human rights. While this fact does not "obviate the need for an understanding" of the point of those rights (131)—that is, it does not eliminate the need to see which ideas are necessary to make sense of those particular rights being grouped together on those lists—it does argue against understanding their point in a way that would justify our simply adding or subtracting rights from that set of fixed points wherever the perceived point of human rights might seem to indicate the need for this. This kind of criticism of the third model of foundational arguments is not unfamiliar. Charles Beitz, for instance, complains about the fact that "naturalistic views" (like Cranston's or Griffin's) "can yield skeptical conclusions about the scope and content of international doctrine".[2] There is a *practice* of human rights to attend to in our theorizing about human rights.

It is easy to see how the spirit of Waldron's account is partly driven by the fact that the practice of human rights presents those rights "to us in the form of a list rather than as a unified theory" (120). If Waldron is right "that dignity is a status-concept, not a value-concept", then we should think of dignity, like other statuses, as "a particular package" of rights and responsibilities" that a person has in virtue of his position or situation (134)—in this case, in virtue of his being human. Human dignity is both a shorthand term for the list of human rights we find in human rights practice and includes the "*underlying idea* that informs the status in question" (135). Human

---

[2] Charles R. Beitz, *The Idea of Human Rights* (Oxford: Oxford University Press, 2009), 50.

dignity includes the "common rationale" that explains how the human rights on the list "hang together" or cohere, that explains why they belong together on one list (135). So it is "a mistake—a sort of category mistake—to talk of dignity as the foundation of rights. Instead, we may say that dignity is a status that *comprises* a given set of rights" (134).[3] Waldron actually puts his point somewhat differently in his Tanner Lectures: "a status account will present dignity (however defined) as foundation-*ish* (or, as we might say, foundation-*al*) but it may not be a foundation in the simple way that (for example) the major value-premises of a consequential argument are a foundation of everything else in the consequentialist's moral theory".[4] Given that Waldron allows in closing that some "version of the claim that human dignity is the foundation of human rights" is "true and helpful" (137), perhaps this latter way of putting his point is truer to his intentions than the former.

Lists of things (including, perhaps, things like human rights) do, of course, typically suggest their own unifying rationales, their implicit reasons for collecting together distinct items under one heading. My grocery lists, to-do lists, and wish lists all unify diversity according to certain (usually transparent) ends or purposes. And within those lists, there may be further divisions of items, again unified by some sub-purpose—as when my grocery list includes some items for hygiene, some for cooking, and some for eating-without-cooking. Lists of human rights usually appear similarly to include various sub-groups with their own rationales, all unified under one common purpose. So some human rights seem chiefly to be aimed at promoting or protecting individual welfare, with others providing for personal security, due process, individual liberty, political equality, group welfare, and so on. Each category of right may have its own distinctive sub-rationale, or multiple groups may share the same one—such as protection from living in fear, in pain, or in desperate need, protection of one's ability to pursue relationships and projects that make life worthwhile, or protection from being treated as a mere pawn in the power games of others. All might be aspects of what is necessary to live a "fully human" life, the life of a "human person" (as opposed to the life of a mere human animal), or a "life of dignity". Protecting and facilitating human dignity might thus serve as the overall rationale for some list of human rights, unifying the (themselves unified) sub-groups of human rights. Perhaps something like this is what Dworkin has in mind in characterizing dignity as a "portmanteau description",[5] a portmanteau being a bag that, as it were, unifies separate (but themselves unified) compartments.

---

[3] As opposed, eg, to Feinberg's view of dignity as the *capacity to claim* such rights: "respect for persons...may simply be respect for their rights; and what is called 'human dignity' may simply be the recognizable capacity to assert claims." (from "The Nature and Value of Rights", in Joel Feinberg, *Rights, Justice, and the Bounds of Liberty* (Princeton: Princeton University Press, 1980), 151).

[4] Waldron, *Dignity, Rank, and Rights*, 21.

[5] Dworkin, however, appears to be concerned with "unifying" rather different items than I am discussing here: "I use dignity as an organizing idea...to collect widely shared ethical principles under one portmanteau description". For Dworkin "dignity requires self-respect and authenticity." "Someone lives well when he senses and pursues a good life for himself and does so with dignity: with respect for the importance of other people's lives and for their ethical responsibility as well as his own" (Ronald Dworkin, *Justice for Hedgehogs* (Cambridge, MA: Harvard University Press, 2011), 205, 204, 419).

So suppose for a moment that human dignity is in fact best understood as a special status (enjoyed by all humans) that comprises a particular list of human rights along with that list's guiding rationale. Two further questions seem appropriate. First, exactly what kind of status for humans is being asserted in putting forward this list of human rights (along with human dignity as that list's guiding rationale)? Second, is there any good reason to think of that list of rights as fixed or "given"?

Waldron answers the first question in his Tanner Lectures. The idea of human dignity, he suggests, is the idea of humans enjoying the highest possible status, "comparable to a rank of nobility—only a rank assigned now to every human person, equally without discrimination: dignity as nobility for the common man."[6] "We are all chiefs; there are no Indians...High status can be universalized and still remain high".[7] Here Waldron brings together his ideas on the importance of human rights, the idea of human dignity as a status-concept, and the fact that the word "'dignity' has resonances of something like noble bearing."[8]

In these claims it seems to me that Waldron over-reaches a bit. Our ordinary notion of dignity does indeed convey something like a sense of "noble bearing"; but the "nobility" at issue here is surely less the bearing of one who enjoys aristocratic privileges, and more the bearing of someone who is simply upstanding, independent, imposing. A dignified demeanor is one that is self-assured, uncorrupted, and healthy, bowing and scraping to none, strong in adversity—like the "noble savage" ("le bon sauvage") of seventeenth- and eighteenth-century romantic drama and literature. When we think of the popular origins of human rights discourse—for instance, in the process by which the French Declaration flowed from the French and American Revolutions—it seems clear that "leveling down" was being taken as seriously as "leveling up". The exalted statuses of nobility and kings (as "little gods") were as much the target for attack as were the degraded statuses of serf and peon and peasant. The sturdy yeoman seems a better model for the dignified bearer of human rights than does the blood nobility.[9] To take a more recent example: Huey Long's populist campaign slogan may have been "every man a king", but this was carefully followed by the qualifier "but no one wears a crown". Perhaps human dignity does capture the idea of a standing for humans that is above that of all other creatures, but it seems to convey that superiority with more modesty and restraint than is typical of king or earl.

Even granting Waldron his associations between dignity and noble rank, however, is there good reason to suppose that the list of human rights in which that rank (partly) consists is more or less fixed, resisting "expansion"? It is hard to see why we should be persuaded of this, at least if we follow Waldron in viewing the status of human-right-holder as including that position's guiding rationale, as including the

---

[6] Waldron, *Dignity, Rank, and Rights*, 22.   [7] Waldron, *Dignity, Rank, and Rights*, 60.
[8] Waldron, *Dignity, Rank, and Rights*, 21.
[9] This appears to be one of the common themes in the critical responses that were recently published along with Waldron's lectures, especially in those by Michael Rosen and Don Herzog. Waldron's reply is to concede that while we may not want human dignity to "be associated with the old arrogance of nobility,...we will expect it to be associated with a furious sense of one's rights and a willingness to stand up for them as part of what it means to stand up for what is best and most important in oneself" (*Dignity, Rank, and Rights*, 145).

ideas that give the list of human rights their unity and point. Acknowledging that a list of rights is not a mere plurality—acknowledging that there is a clear point to gathering those rights together while excluding others—may not logically commit one to any position on the subject of whether that justifying point can require (or permit) the inclusion on that list of additional, originally neglected items. But such an acknowledgement surely at least *suggests* that view. Other kinds of lists, along with their unifying rationales, surely call for or permit such expansion (as when I simply remember or discover another thing that needs to be purchased or done, and so needs to be added to my lists). Only, I think, if we suppose that the status of human dignity is not a general *normative* status at all, but only a legal status, would we be inclined to suppose that the list justifiably resists expansion—and only even then if we think of legal status in an especially narrow and implausible way. Other kinds of legal status grow and evolve as social facts change or become clear, or as prejudices narrow or dissolve. Even a determinedly practice-based approach to human rights can "achieve some critical leverage on the practice as we observe it".[10]

If a proper understanding of the status of human dignity might itself "license derivations" of additional human rights for our list, however, then there is no obvious inconsistency involved in both accepting Waldron's very plausible analysis of human dignity and at the same time pursuing foundational projects of Waldron's third sort ("logical derivations", such as Griffin's). The concept of human dignity might both serve as Waldron's fourth sort of foundation, by casting "indispensable light" on the concept of human rights, and at the same time serve as the (third kind of) foundation from which flow arguments that have as their conclusions either our original list of human rights or that list with additions to or subtractions from it. Perhaps Waldron never really intends to deny this possibility, as he appears to do when trying to contrast the third and fourth approaches to human dignity as the foundation of human rights. He is certainly prepared to allow that human dignity might itself rest on deeper foundational ideas or that it and other ideas might be co-foundational (137). But perhaps he is also willing to accept the possibility of consistent, dual roles for the concept of human dignity in two different types of "foundational" approaches.

My own view is that a full defense of the importance of human rights does, indeed, require deep foundations, not just something "foundation-ish". And, as we saw at the start, we might look for such deep foundations not only in possible conceptual connections between human dignity and human rights, but also in the historical connections between human rights theory and natural rights theory. Where Waldron rightly dismisses the idea that thought about human dignity served as the historical "foundation" of human rights thought, it is clearly much easier to defend the idea of a strong historical connection between human rights thought and earlier *natural rights* thought. As we've seen, of course, mere historical genesis (historical origin or source) is not what we theorists normally have in mind when we speak of "foundations". But the connection between human rights thought and natural rights theory might be far stronger than one of mere historical genesis. Human rights might be not just historically tied to natural rights; they might *be* natural rights, or, rather, they

---

[10] Beitz, *The Idea of Human Rights*, 106.

might be one distinctive and important class of natural rights. The "deep foundations" of human rights theory would then be simply identical to the foundations of natural rights theory.

III. Naturalistic Theories of Human Rights

What would claiming that "human rights are natural rights" amount to? Suppose we define natural rights as those moral rights (a) that could be possessed by persons in a state of nature and (b) whose grounds (or justifications) are not merely conventional.[11] Human rights, if we understand them (in the standard fashion) as *universal* rights— that is, as rights necessarily possessed by all (and only) human beings—would then be those natural (non-conventional) moral rights that not only could be but must be possessed by humans, not only in a state of nature but in all other "non-natural" conditions as well. Human rights must be "innate" rights (ie, rights enjoyed from the moment that human life begins) and rights that cannot be lost—by alienation or renunciation (ie, through voluntary choice), by forfeiture (through negligence or wrongdoing), or by prescription (either through governmental "acts of prescription" or through long passages of time without enforcement).

There is, I believe, a strong case that can be made for the view that, strictly speaking, there are no human rights, so understood, either because biological humans who lack even minimal cognitive and affective potential do not hold such rights (so that per-haps only "human persons", but not all "human beings" or "members of the human family," possess human rights),[12] or because no such rights are *in principle* inalienable or nonforfeitable (even if they may not *routinely* be either alienable or forfeitable). But it might well also be true that certain natural rights are *nearly* universal—that is, innately possessed by nearly all biological humans and alienable or forfeitable only in extraordinary cases. And if that is true, then *declarations* of human rights and human rights conventions probably ought to describe and enforce the most basic moral rights of persons *as if* they were truly universal human rights, if only to guard against the amply demonstrated human propensity for conceiving of and treating those who are different as *sub-human* (and so as morally vulnerable to segregation, confinement, exploitation, or extermination).[13]

Further, if there *are* natural moral rights that are both innate and cannot be lost (or that are *nearly* so), the likely candidates for inclusion in this category will make a familiar and a naturally unified list. People do terrible things to others, and in doing so they forfeit rights that they formerly possessed. May they forfeit *all* rights by such acts (as Locke seemed to believe, suggesting that committing great enough wrongs reduces one to the moral status of a dangerous lower animal)? Perhaps (as Locke might

---

[11] I defend this understanding of natural rights in A. John Simmons, *The Lockean Theory of Rights* (Princeton: Princeton University Press, 1992), 89–91.

[12] The important human rights documents appear to use these terms more or less interchangeably.

[13] This may be true even with respect to particularly clear cases of biological humans who lack all cognitive capacities. Declaring the universality of legal human rights effectively draws the line (between right-holders and non-right-holders) in a place sufficiently clear to discourage most agenda-driven rationalizations for cruel and inhumane treatment of fellow humans.

have been persuaded to concede and as the US Bill of Rights suggests) a doer of terrible wrongs forfeits his right not to be killed, but not his right not to be tortured, his right not to be killed in degrading or humiliating ways, his right not to be hunted for sport or punished for the entertainment of others, and so on. Similarly, people are often thoughtless or imprudent in alienating their rights (for instance, in losing needed funds or their return tickets while visiting a casino). May people thus alienate (or risk alienating) *all* of their *moral* rights? If we think not, surely the best candidates for inalienability would again appear to be moral rights whose legal analogues in US law have that same property—such as the inalienable legal right not to be held as a slave (or perhaps the right not to be killed or the right to the satisfaction of our most basic needs).

In short, the natural rights that seem likeliest to qualify as universal human rights (because they are neither forfeitable nor alienable) are precisely those rights possession of which we might naturally say is necessary for living (or dying) with appropriate human dignity. The best arguments for human rights foundations in natural rights theory, then, seem bound to return us to that same idea of human dignity that is explored (and analyzed as a status-concept) by Waldron. Whether we begin from the "top", with a list of legally established human rights (accompanied by their unifying rationale), or begin from the "bottom", by thinking about those innate natural rights that seem least likely to be alienable or forfeitable, our arguments appear to converge on the same conclusions. So if, as I've argued, there is no genuine inconsistency between Waldron's preferred approach and an approach starting from the foundations of natural rights theory, the two approaches may be not only logically consistent but mutually supportive.

None of this, of course, constitutes an argument that human rights are best understood as a special category of natural rights. The arguments at the foundations of natural rights theory (however we might best develop them) may be thought to simply fail. Or a general moral skepticism, a more targeted skepticism about non-conventional bases for morality, or a still more targeted skepticism about the possibility of natural moral *rights* might be thought to derail natural rights theory from the start. While I believe that these forms of skepticism about natural rights are in the end indefensible—and that plausible arguments for natural rights foundations are in fact available to us—the past few decades of political philosophy/theory have been more centrally devoted to avoiding than to resolving such debates. And that same strategy of avoidance has, of course, been deployed in discussions of *human* rights, due largely to the influence of Rawls' account of human rights in *The Law of Peoples*.

Rawls does not include in his discussion of human rights any real critique of "foundational" projects that approach human rights through an analysis of human dignity or through a theory of natural rights; but a kind of critique is, of course, implicit in his re-deployment in *The Law of Peoples* of the basic argumentative structure of *Political Liberalism*, with its rejection of appeals to "comprehensive" moral views as foundations for a theory of justice. The critique does not, however, in either case take the form of real skepticism about foundational projects in value theory. Rawls famously denies that the arguments of *Political Liberalism* (and, by implication, the subsequent arguments of *The Law of Peoples*) rest on such skepticism.[14] Rather, the conception

---

[14] John Rawls, *Political Liberalism* (New York: Columbia University Press, 1993), 62–3.

of justice defended in *Political Liberalism* is understood by Rawls as a *political* conception, just as the theory of human rights in *The Law of Peoples* is intended to be a *political* conception of human rights. Human rights are simply the "urgent" rights that must be respected in a society for it to count as a "system of social cooperation", and so for that society to be a candidate for inclusion in (and non-intervention within) a stable, international Society of Peoples.[15] Similarly, justice as fairness (in *Political Liberalism*) is that conception of justice on which might be achieved a stable overlapping consensus (in a liberal society) among proponents of competing comprehensive conceptions of the good.

The philosophical quest for deep foundations (for a theory of human rights or a theory of justice) may be an interesting one, but completing it is, in Rawls' view, unnecessary for doing the philosopher's work in political and legal philosophy. The human rights acknowledged in Rawls' Law of Peoples "do not depend on any particular comprehensive religious doctrine or philosophical doctrine of human nature;" but "still, the Law of Peoples does not deny these doctrines".[16] The Rawlsian "political" approach to these basic problems in political and legal philosophy, if it is to remain *genuinely non-committal* on questions about deep philosophical foundations, thus appears to leave open the following disturbing possibility: that a demonstrably true or valid "comprehensive doctrine" might have implications for an account of social justice or human rights that directly conflict with the "reasonable" content of the "political" conceptions of justice or human rights. Only a Rawlsian conviction that reasonableness trumps truth in political philosophy—so that true comprehensive views must be reasonable, acknowledging the political conceptions as "modules" attaching to and modifying those views—seems to stand in the way of our being forced to choose between a true theory of human rights and a thinner, but reasonable, political conception of human rights. Those of us who are reluctant to follow Rawls in that conviction are not likely, I think, to be persuaded to simply embrace his political conception of human rights, at best allowing that there are two kinds of (or two ways of thinking about) human rights.

More recently, however, Charles Beitz has argued for a related, "practical" conception of human rights (that he regards as "implicit" in Rawls' view) in a way that might appear to close off such an option. Rather than simply pursuing a strategy of avoidance, Beitz has advanced a more systematic case against all theories of human rights that are "naturalistic" in form—including, particularly, those theories (of the sorts under consideration here) that begin with the idea of human dignity or with a theory of natural rights. The contemporary practice of human rights, he argues, has made appeals to such foundations (for human rights claims) not only obsolete, but seriously misleading. I will here briefly focus our attention just on Beitz's arguments against the idea (suggested earlier) that human rights are natural rights.

Chapter 3 of Beitz's *The Idea of Human Rights*, an extended critique of naturalistic conceptions of human rights,[17] cites as an example of such conceptions my own

---

[15] John Rawls, *The Law of Peoples* (Cambridge, MA: Harvard University Press, 199), 68, 79–80.

[16] Rawls, *The Law of Peoples*, 68.

[17] The accounts of human rights defended by Maurice Cranston, James Griffin, and Amartya Sen and Martha Nussbaum come in for the bulk of Beitz's attack.

characterization of human rights as "those natural rights that are innate and that cannot be lost".[18] Beitz then summarizes his more general understanding of such views as follows:

> Naturalistic conceptions regard human rights as having a character and basis that can be fully comprehended without reference to their embodiment and role in any public doctrine or practice. According to such a view, the "human rights" of international doctrine derive their identity and authority from this more basic level of value.[19]

Beitz's most general complaint about such naturalistic views (aside from the difficulties involved in characterizing them precisely) is that "our understanding of international human rights is distorted rather than helped by conceiving them on the model of natural rights".[20] Human rights are "unlike natural rights in not presupposing any one view about their basis or justification".[21] And, again unlike natural rights, for some human rights we cannot "conceptualize them as existing in a condition where there are no institutions" (since they presuppose certain institutional structures),[22] nor can we think of them as "timeless" (since they are clearly framed with modern and modernizing societies in mind).[23] Finally, where modern natural rights theories "were primarily attempts to formulate constraints on the use of a government's coercive power in circumstances of religious and moral diversity…, the motivating concern of international human rights is evidently broader" (being "an effort to identify the social conditions necessary for the living of dignified human lives").[24]

While Beitz does not think these arguments "add up to a refutation of naturalistic theories",[25] he regards them as "sufficiently discouraging"[26] to justify moving on to other possible approaches. The view he ultimately defends, as his favored alternative, is a "practical" approach that "tries to grasp the concept of a human right by understanding the role this concept plays within" the global ("discursive and political") practice of human rights.[27] Beitz attempts to reply to the obvious objections to such practice-based analyses—namely, that they reduce human rights claims to nothing more than "complicated sociological facts" and give "too much authority to the status quo"—by distinguishing, first, between "conceptualizing" human rights and explaining their reason-giving force, and, second, by distinguishing between "the details of present practice" and the roles of human rights claims within the best understanding of such a practice.[28] Beitz's disagreement with Rawls' approach seems to lie primarily in a difference concerning the best way to understand the roles of human rights in global practice.

---

[18] A. John Simmons, "Human Rights and World Citizenship: The Universality of Human Rights in Kant and Locke", in *Justification and Legitimacy* (Cambridge: Cambridge University Press, 2001), 185.
[19] Beitz, *The Idea of Human Rights*, 49–50.   [20] Beitz, *The Idea of Human Rights*, 50–1.
[21] Beitz, *The Idea of Human Rights*, 54.   [22] Beitz, *The Idea of Human Rights*, 55.
[23] Beitz, *The Idea of Human Rights*, 57–8.   [24] Beitz, *The Idea of Human Rights*, 57.
[25] Beitz, *The Idea of Human Rights*, 71.   [26] Beitz, *The Idea of Human Rights*, 96.
[27] Beitz, *The Idea of Human Rights*, 8.
[28] Beitz, *The Idea of Human Rights*, 104–6. These distinctions do not, I should note, actually suffice to answer these most fundamental concerns about any practice-based account of human rights. But I will not further pursue that problem here.

I believe that Beitz here underestimates the difficulties involved in giving a clear and uncontroversial account of the purposes and trajectories of human rights claims in domestic and international politics,[29] as do others who defend "practical" or "political" approaches to human rights.[30] But I will confine my attention here to a different problem for Beitz's position: namely, its dramatic underestimation of the resources available to a plausible "naturalistic" theory of human rights—in this case, the kind of natural rights theory of human rights that we've been considering. Beitz's criticisms of such a theory, remember, concern (1) two ways in which it distorts our understanding of the point of human rights claims in actual practice (by presupposing a single justification for them and by misunderstanding their "motivating concerns") and (2) two conceptual bars to natural rights serving as the basis for the human rights of actual practice (since many human rights cannot be understood as either "pre-institutional" or "timeless").

Both criticisms of natural rights accounts in (1) seem to me inapt. Whether or not human rights practice presupposes one (or any) justificatory foundation for all human rights claims is at best unclear. Some of the important human rights conventions, as we've seen, do in fact suggest derivations of human rights from more foundational ideas (or co-derivation of human rights along with related ideas). What the conventions seem pretty clearly to be intent on avoiding is any reference to possible *religious* foundations for human rights claims, for obvious reasons. But it is not at all plain from their language that the central human rights documents (or the actual practice of human rights law) are intent on ruling out all secular and (for that reason) more universally accessible possible foundations for human rights claims—such as "deep" ideas of human dignity or natural rights.

Further, Beitz's point about the "breadth" of the "motivating concerns of international human rights"—compared to the narrower concerns of historical natural rights theories—seems, by itself at least, a non sequitur. The fact that particular kinds of social concerns were in the minds of their authors is far from conclusive in identifying the true characters of either philosophical theories or legal conventions. Natural rights theory, while emerging historically amid concerns to constrain tyrannical princes and centrally concerned with identifying the moral limits on their coercive powers, can (and does) still have direct relevance for other kinds of social concerns—such as the necessary conditions for living a "dignified human life". Author preoccupations do not define theoretical reach. Locke's theory of natural rights, for instance, was developed in the shadow of deep fears about the coercive imposition of Catholic rule (through the king's subservience to the Pope or through dealings with the Catholic king of France); but later uses of very closely related views (such as those appealed to

---

[29] See, for instance, Allen Buchanan's discussion of "political theories" of human rights ("Human Rights", in D. Estlund (ed.), *The Oxford Handbook of Political Philosophy* (Oxford: Oxford University Press, 2012), 284–7.

[30] See, eg, Joseph Raz's defense of a political approach, in which he advances (largely without argument) the view that the practice-based role of human rights claims is to "set limits to the sovereignty of states" ("Human Rights Without Foundations", in S. Besson and J. Tasioulas (eds.), *The Philosophy of International Law* (Oxford: Oxford University Press, 2010), 328.

by Jefferson and some of the other American Founders) drew on the theory's resources to justify protests against perfectly secular political tyranny.

Consider next Beitz's claims that the timeless and pre-institutional character of natural rights makes them an impossible conceptual "fit" with many acknowledged human rights (and, as such, an impossible foundation or basis for all human rights). We might, with Allen Buchanan, try to blunt the force of this criticism by arguing that, despite natural rights being pre-institutional in nature, "an attempt to realize them in a system of international legal rights will need to take existing institutions into account".[31] I think, however, that a more direct response to Beitz (on behalf of a natural rights theory of human rights) is possible here. Even if we understand natural rights as I've suggested—as "timeless" rights that can be possessed in a pre-institutional condition—there are still at least two ways in which such natural rights might nonetheless be directly concerned with institutional forms (despite their being "pre-institutional") and be directly concerned with distinctive features of (and threats to) modern or modernizing societies (despite their being "timeless").

The "two ways" that I have in mind correspond to the two traditions of natural rights thought. The Kantian tradition is committed to only one innate natural right: the right to the maximal freedom (from constraint by the choices of others) consistent with a like freedom for all. But this one innate right includes, on the Kantian view, the right to be in civil society with others, governed by those institutions necessary to realizing all of the social conditions for full freedom.[32] It is, in short, a natural right (held against all others) to be collectively subject to an institutional structure that effectively administers justice (by determining and enforcing our rights). Contemporary Kantians fill out this basic argument with a suitably contemporary and democratic conception of what is required for social justice to be effectively administered. Suppose, for instance, that we determine that some theory of justice (perhaps Rawls' theory) is defensible. Then the Kantian argument justifies a natural right to as much specific institutional content as is implied by that theory. And this natural right can still plausibly be characterized as both timeless and necessarily possessed by all. Further, since it is a right to *effective* justice-administering institutions, it is a right to suitably different institutions in different historical settings—including rights to appropriately modern institutions (which will counter modern threats) in modern societies. And if, as I believe, the best account of what makes an institutional structure just will yield not merely domestic requirements, but also requirements regarding how societal institutions are oriented toward those outside societal borders, such arguments will have straightforward implications for the international institutions that are sometimes directly referred to in modern human rights practice.

Consider now the second "way", that of the Lockean natural rights tradition. Lockean accounts of natural rights focus primarily on broad rights to self-government and more limited rights to positive assistance from others. Lockeans, unlike Kantians, thus do

---

[31] Buchanan, "Human Rights", 286. Here, Buchanan suggests that Beitz's criticism would only be effective against views that "*identify* legal human rights with moral rights understood as preinstitutional rights". I'm not certain that I understand how such an identification is even conceptually possible.

[32] See my discussion of Kant's position in Simmons, "Human Rights and World Citizenship", especially 188–9.

not acknowledge natural rights to the cooperative provision of justice-administering institutions. We may join with others to create such institutions, where all agree to do so; but none is naturally entitled to others' participation in such an endeavor. The Lockean tradition does, however, defend a natural right not to be non-consensually subjected to (even just) political/legal institutions, as well as a natural right to reparation for such wrongs. And implied by such rights (to be free of involuntary subjection and to have such wrongs repaired) is the natural right that others at least try to *minimize* the wrongs they do to us.

In the modern world, most of us have been subjected without our consent to political, legal, and economic institutions that deeply affect our life prospects (and prospects for self-government), institutions that are extremely wide-reaching and straightforwardly coercive. Being subjected at birth to the basic structures of our societies is not a way of our choosing anything. It thus, in my view, constitutes a violation of our natural rights, a wrong that, if it will not be fully repaired (as seems extremely likely), must at least be minimized. And the obvious path to minimizing that wrong (in a society that inevitably will not fully correct that wrong) is to subject people only to institutions that treat them as fairly as is possible (in the context of a coercively imposed and maintained system). So Lockean natural rights theory can in fact defend the very same kind of natural right to a fully just institutional structure that flows more directly, as we've seen, from Kantian natural rights theory—though that natural right is now conceived of as a remedial right for the many non-consenting residents of modern societies. And the right in question can thus have precisely the same institutional and historically sensitive contents as the Kantian version of that right. While this right is admittedly, on the Lockean version of it, not strictly "timeless" or necessarily possessed by all humans, the historical pervasiveness and duration of the practice of non-consensually subjecting persons to political authority makes it virtually so. Here, I think, the Lockean theory actually follows a line of argument suggested, but never completed, in Rawls' early efforts to explain the force of his own theory of justice.[33]

Such arguments for natural rights to institutional provision (or institutional restraint) may at first seem not to yield rights to sufficiently specific institutions to match (or to justify) the institutional content of human rights claims in actual practice. Indeed, Beitz's objection to such natural right arguments appears to be precisely that they must surrender either their claim to genuine "naturalness" or their claim to justify rights to "an extended catalog" of institutional arrangements.[34] But, to be fair, the institutional content of the global practice of human rights is not, for the most part, itself very specific; and some cases of well-known human rights claims that *are* very specific about institutional requirements are precisely the cases that arouse the most skepticism *within* that practice. In any event, Beitz's own examples of human

---

[33] "No society can, of course, be a scheme of cooperation which men enter voluntarily in a literal sense; each person finds himself placed at birth in some particular position in some particular society, and the nature of this position materially affects his life prospects. Yet a [just society] comes as close as a society can to being a voluntary scheme…" (John Rawls, *A Theory of Justice* (Cambridge, MA: Harvard University Press, 1971), 13).

[34] Beitz, *The Idea of Human Rights*, 56.

rights with institutional content—human rights to political asylum, to political participation, and to free elementary education[35]—can be easily derived from *either* of
the kinds of natural rights arguments sketched earlier (by straightforward appeal to
the justice-based requirements for institutions that secure international and domestic
freedom and equal opportunity).

Natural rights accounts of human rights, then, are far more flexible (and hence far
more promising) than Beitz's critique of them suggests. Perhaps natural rights theory
cannot yield an account of human rights according to which they are strictly universal (ie, held by all or only biological human beings). But many other kinds of theories of human rights reach that same conclusion. If I am correct, though, a natural
rights account can capture the modern and institutional characters displayed by some
human rights claims, while still conceiving of the rights at issue as suitably timeless
and pre-institutional. And, as we've seen, a natural rights account can capture the orientation of modern human rights practice toward identifying "the social conditions
necessary for the living of dignified human lives". Indeed, one of the theory's great
virtues is its ability to give appropriately "deep" content to the idea of human dignity
that guides and unifies the lists of human rights that practice has produced. We do far
better in understanding human rights, I think, to continue to pursue and criticize the
arguments of natural rights theories than we do in trying to justify remaining neutral
in such debates or in constructing blanket (and necessarily distorting) rejections of all
"naturalistic" theories of human rights. In the end, I suppose, we might all come to
agree that the foundational arguments of natural rights theory are in some way fatally
flawed, or that they cannot constitute the basis of a satisfactory theory of human
rights. But this has not yet been convincingly shown. The game, I think, is still afoot.

---

[35] Beitz, *The Idea of Human Rights*, 55.

7

Personal Deserts and Human Rights

James W. Nickel

Personal moral desert can make it permissible, appropriate, and even obligatory for benefits, burdens, and penalties to be given to or imposed on people on the basis of the moral quality of their individual behavior and/or character. Could (or do) personal moral deserts play a role in the justification and shaping of human rights? And if so, what form could (or does) that role take? Human rights theorists (including me) have generally assumed that in order to give an adequate account of the values and norms underlying human rights it is not necessary to mention desert. This chapter challenges that assumption.

It is easy to construct nightmare scenarios purporting to show that taking deserts seriously in the realm of human rights would be destructive. In these scenarios some people have their rights suspended or permanently forfeited for bad behavior, the undeserving have their rights trimmed and the virtuous have their rights enlarged, and the universality and egalitarian character of human rights are greatly diminished.[1]

It would be good to know if personal deserts are or should be operative in the realm of human rights, and if so, whether anything like these scenarios would follow. And if these consequences do not follow, it would be good to have some idea of what keeps this from happening. Is it that desert is not a very powerful norm? Is it that other values and norms fully or partially block considerations of desert from playing a strong role? Or is it that desert is too hard to administer fairly and consistently? This chapter is a start, but only a start, at answering these questions.

James Griffin included a brief discussion of deserts and human rights in his recent book, *On Human Rights*.[2] As a theorist who proposes to base all moral human rights on autonomy or "normative agency," Griffin denies that considerations of desert contribute to the justification or shaping of human rights. He allows, however, that desert may play a role from the outside when rights are being applied. Discussing the case of a person needing an organ transplant whose need stems from his own bad behavior, Griffin allows that "fault must have weight at least as a tie-breaker." He continues: "If I am clearly undeserving and you thoroughly deserving, but we are regarded by the hospital as having equal claim on the next [organ] available for transplant, you may protest that the way the hospital decides priorities is unfair."

If considerations of desert were operative in the realm of human rights, and if the result was to make the undeserving less eligible to have or use particular rights,

---

[1] On the universal and egalitarian character of human rights see James W. Nickel, *Making Sense of Human Rights*, 2nd edn. (Oxford: Blackwell Publishing, 2007), 7–14, 35–82.
[2] James Griffin, *On Human Rights* (Oxford: Oxford University Press, 2008), 184–5.

this would be incompatible in Griffin's view with the universality of human rights. He says that "a restriction to the deserving cannot be written into the human right itself…" because such a restriction "is incompatible with the "universality of the class of right-bearers." I criticize this claim in this chapter. I argue as well that the role of considerations of desert in the realm of human rights is sometimes positive (contributing to the justification of some human rights) as well as negative (providing justifications for limitations on some people's rights).

The question of the role of desert in justifying human rights applies both to moral human rights and to legal human rights. In the case of legal human rights we can ask what their moral grounds are and whether they include considerations of moral personal desert. For present purposes I will draw my guidance concerning the content of human rights from international law, and particularly from the International Covenant on Civil and Political Rights (ICCPR) and the International Covenant on Economic, Social and Cultural Rights (ICESCR).[3] The attraction of legal rights for my purposes is that they have canonical formulations and areas of established content. Although I do not believe that there is a one-to-one relationship between legal human rights and moral human rights, all of the legal rights I mention are ones that can plausibly be held to be moral rights as well.

I. Personal Moral Deserts

To think about what considerations of desert imply for human rights we need a view of what those considerations are and how they operate. This section offers a sketch.

The concept of deserving something is used in a wide variety of areas. We say that a potential student deserves to be admitted because she has the highest grades and test scores, that an exceptionally good painting in a competition deserves to win First Prize, and that areas of natural beauty deserve to be preserved.[4] I am interested only in one important slice: the deserts that individual persons have that are due to the moral features of their actions, states of character, and harmful wrongs suffered.[5]

Because people are agents who choose, plan, deliberate, and act, we often respond to the beneficial or harmful changes their actions bring about in the world with attributions of responsibility and praise or blame.[6] As agents, people's deserts can be due to the particular actions they perform (as when a person performs a lifesaving rescue or commits a crime) or to their characters as seen in the high or low level of moral virtue

---

[3] United Nations, International Covenant on Civil and Political Rights, and International Covenant on Economic, Social, and Cultural Rights (both 1966).

[4] These statements about non-moral desert often fit or mimic the generic pattern for desert statements about personal moral desert that is described later.

[5] Important sources on the idea of desert include: Joel Feinberg "Justice and Personal Desert," in *Doing and Deserving* (Princeton, NJ: Princeton University Press, 1970); Fred Feldman, *Utilitarianism, Hedonism, and Desert* (Cambridge: Cambridge University Press, 1997); Shelly Kagan, *The Geometry of Desert* (Oxford: Oxford University Press, 2012); Louis Pojman and Owen McLeod (eds.), *What Do We Deserve?* (New York: Oxford University Press, 1997); and George Sher, *Desert* (Princeton, NJ: Princeton University Press, 1987).

[6] See Samuel Scheffler, 'Responsibility, Reactive Attitudes, and Liberalism in Philosophy and Politics,' *Philosophy and Public Affairs*, 21 (1992): 299–323, and Stephen Munzer, *A Theory of Property* (Cambridge: Cambridge University Press, 1990), 255–6.

that their actions generally display. An action or character trait that makes someone deserving of something is often called the "desert basis." It is a fact about or evaluation of a person that is the starting point for deliberation about what they deserve. Abe may deserve praise for the high level of moral virtue that he has displayed in his attitudes and actions over many decades (a sort of career achievement award). Juanita may deserve gratitude from Carolina for concern, emotional support, and assistance during Carolina's recent battle with cancer. Bernard may deserve legal punishment for the financial fraud that he recently perpetrated.

Desert bases can be about good or bad behavior and vary in their strength, in how much by way of good or bad treatment they make appropriate. If Carolina decides that words of appreciation alone would not be sufficient as an expression of appreciation to Juanita for what she did, and that a gift is required as well, then she has to decide the size and nature of the gift. To determine what Bernard deserves for his recent crime we need to know the nature and size of the fraud.

Desert bases can be things that one has not done (omissions). If Paul did not steal Fred's motorcycle then he should not be punished for the theft because such punishment would be disproportionate to his innocence. For another example, imagine that Zelda agrees to mow Elmer's lawn for a fee. If Zelda shows up and mows the lawn we can say that she deserves payment for this work. If Zelda never actually mows the lawn or brings it about that the lawn is mowed we can conclude that Zelda does not deserve payment from Elmer for lawn mowing (Zelda might, of course, nevertheless deserve payment from Elmer for doing some other job). Not mowing is the desert basis for not deserving pay-for-mowing.

Some humans lack the ability to generate desert bases through their actions. For example, very young children's agency and moral capacities are so little developed that they may lack desert bases entirely—or at least only have passive ones like "innocent" or "harmed by parental negligence."

To be complete, a statement about what someone deserves has four blanks or variables that must be specified. First, we need to specify the party who deserves something. Second, we need to specify the desert basis, what it is about the party identified that makes them deserving in this context. Third, we need to specify *what* the person deserves by way of good or bad treatment. Finally, we need to identify the party who is called upon or permitted to deliver this treatment. In the pattern,

P1 deserves T from P2 in virtue of having DB

P1 is a person who deserves something, T is some treatment or state of affairs that is deserved, P2 is a person who is permitted or obligated to give or impose T, and DB is the desert basis. The desert relation puts these elements together and asserts that T in its size and nature is permissible or required in light of DB for P2 to give to or impose on P1.[7] This is the proportionality aspect of desert. Both T and DB must admit of degrees so that more or less of T can be proportional to more of less of DB.

---

[7] This schema will need one or more temporal variables as well. One can deserve something at a particular time but later cease to deserve it because of one's behavior in the interim. On this see Kagan, *The Geometry of Desert*, 11–12. Further, we make desert statements in the past tense. An example is "My late brother never got the promotion he deserved."

Some theorists leave the P2 variable out of such an analysis because there seem to be meaningful desert statements in which no second party needs to be or is available to be mentioned. One example is where Martina already has what she deserves (a happy and financially comfortable retirement, say) and someone remarks that it is well deserved because of her virtue and hard work over a lifetime. Here the question of someone *giving* Martina a happy and comfortable retirement does not arise. Another example is where a notorious pirate, Pierre, is operating on the high seas outside the territorial boundaries of any country. Pierre may deserve to be caught and imprisoned but we may nevertheless be unsure about which persons or governments if any are permitted or required to attempt to administer this treatment. In spite of these cases, second parties often play very important role in considerations of desert and I think that it is therefore best to include them in our generic pattern for desert statements.

Because a desert statement like the one in the pattern above includes "...in virtue of having DB," it already points to a reason for permitting or requiring T. Proportionality between DB and T is central to the idea of desert—even though there are cases in which very rough proportionality is the best we can hope to achieve. One way to find areas where desert is at work is to look for areas where proportionality judgments are being made between something about a person and some treatment or state of affairs. If one says that "P1 ought to receive T because of F," where "F" is some fact about P1's actions or character, this could be a desert statement if proportionality between T and F is explicitly or implicitly asserted. But it could also fail to be a desert statement if F is not a desert basis requiring proportionality but rather involves some other relation between T and F. Examples of the latter are that T would be useful to P1 in light of F or that T is required in order to treat P1 equally with other people who are F.

Judgments about what people deserve are often difficult to make if we care about getting it right. We rightly worry that we don't know enough about P1 and his or her desert basis (is P1 a competent moral agent, what were P1's intentions, what exactly did P1 do, and were there mitigating circumstances?). And we worry about the nature and scale of T (how can we know how big an award or how severe a punishment is appropriate to P1's DB?).

In cases where T is of substantial value or disvalue to P1, responding appropriately to P1's deserts regarding T is sometimes a type of justice, of giving P1 what is due. If the criminal justice system gets it wrong in Bernard's case and gives him a large punishment when he only deserves a small one then a major injustice is done.

Considerations of moral desert yield conclusions of varying modalities (permissions versus duties) and strengths (high versus medium or low priority in competition with other considerations). Sometimes these considerations merely give a person permission to give a person the treatment he or she deserves, and sometimes they yield both a permission and a duty to do so. Henry's extreme rudeness to Irma may give her permission to reprimand him without making her doing so obligatory. The permission one gets in such cases is not unlimited; proportionality determines how far Irma can go in criticizing Henry. Permissions to respond to people's deserts are far more common than duties to do so, but there are plenty of cases where considerations of desert yield moral duties to respond with appropriate treatment.

The strength of permissions and duties to respond to someone's desert may be fortified in some cases by the usefulness of praising virtuous people like Abe and Juanita, reprimanding rude people like Henry, and punishing criminals like Bernard. In such cases responses to desert are both fitting and useful.

The ways in which one person is "called upon" by another person's desert seem complicated. Carolina had a desert-based duty to Juanita because she was the beneficiary of Juanita's kind assistance. And Irma had permission to reprimand Henry because he was rude *to her*. In other cases, however, a person's desert basis may generate permissions for everyone to respond to him or her. Perhaps anyone who can is permitted to punish Pierre the pirate. Recall Locke's idea that in the state of nature everyone is at liberty to punish crimes, including crimes against other people. And which agents have duties to respond to deserts with appropriate treatments may depend on local institutional arrangements. Locke thought that entering civil society required turning over the punishment of crimes to government.[8]

Duties to respond appropriately to deserts can be discharged by appropriate responses from the parties. After Carolina has thanked Juanita profusely and offered a small but thoughtful gift she can think of the matter as settled. She has done what it was fitting for her to do, and Juanita has gotten what she deserved. Similarly, when the system of criminal law has subjected Bernard to an appropriate amount of time in prison, and he has given appropriate apologies and compensation to the victims of his crimes, he (and we) can think of his negative deserts for these crimes as having been discharged. His "debt" has been paid. And in his case, the government has met its responsibility to punish with criminal sanctions persons who have severely negative deserts based on criminal behavior.

When not discharged, deserts can continue for an extended period to generate permissions and duties. When Lee's negligence or wrongdoing introduces a large disproportion between what Irving deserves and what he receives, measures to remedy that disproportion are called for during an extended period after the negligence or wrongdoing.

II. Qualifications to Human Rights Based on being Undeserving

A widely accepted feature of human rights is that people have them just by being persons. All people, not just the best behaved, qualify for a set of basic rights. This is, of course, a broad or abstract feature of human right and it requires specification as we move from abstract ideas to particular rights such as freedom of movement and political participation. As we make this transition, considerations of desert, as well as other norms, may introduce opposing tendencies. If desert plays, or were to play, a big role in shaping human rights then the possession and/or operability of those rights could vary with individual deserts.

Personal moral deserts often help determine whether people should receive wages and other rewards, whether or not people should be punished with fines or

---

[8] John Locke, *Second Treatise of Government* (1690), sections 7–13.

imprisonment, and whether people are appropriately esteemed or despised. Because of this it would be surprising if the restrictions of rights to the deserving applied only to welfare rights. My research suggests that the place where we find the most desert-based restrictions to human rights is in rights to the fundamental freedoms and to political participation.

Consider the right to freedom of movement and residence as found in ICCPR Article 12. It says that "1. Everyone lawfully within the territory of a State shall, within that territory, have the right to liberty of movement and freedom to choose his residence" and "2. Everyone shall be free to leave any country, including his own." People serving prison terms for crimes for which they were justly convicted do not qualify for this right during their incarceration (and not fully afterwards while they are on parole). It seems plausible that part of the justification for qualifying their right to freedom of movement is that people who are justifiably in prison for crimes have undischarged negative deserts and that responding appropriately to those deserts requires, in many cases, restricting the liberty of movement of persons as part of their punishment. Since prisoners cannot have much freedom of movement, they cannot engage in forms of political expression and protest that require assembling with others or going to a particular place. Thus these qualifications apply not just to freedom of movement but also to freedom of assembly and freedom of expression.

Perhaps this example is not conclusive because it can be argued that these qualifications to the fundamental freedoms are based not on desert but on what is necessary to protect people's security against crime. Perhaps the next example is more persuasive in this respect.

ICCPR Article 25 says that "Every citizen shall have the right and the opportunity...to have access, on general terms of equality, to public service in his country." This does not mean that every person gets to be a public official for two minutes; rather, it means that citizens of appropriate age have the right to be considered for appointment to public office within a fair selection process or election. People cannot be excluded from public service because they are impoverished, female, or members of an unpopular minority. Persons who have been justly convicted of serious crimes are frequently disqualified from serving in public office while serving time in prison for their crime, and if their crime was serious enough may be permanently disqualified from being a lawyer or judge. Considerations of desert yield the permission to impose such disqualifications. They are not necessary consequences of being in prison (as is limited freedom of movement and residence) since in many cases a person in prison could do her job as a city commissioner, say, if she were allowed easy access to visitors and provided with phones, internet, and video equipment that would allow her to participate virtually in meetings outside the prison. If Kim, an elected city commissioner who has been justly convicted of taking bribes and sent to jail, demands these privileges and services so that she can perform her elected role, officials could—and hopefully would—refuse on the grounds that persons justly convicted of serious crimes are ineligible for public office at least until their negative deserts have been discharged.

At this point the worry about such restrictions being incompatible with the universality of human rights comes back into play. How is the permissibility of denying some people access to political participation to be reconciled with everyone's having a right to such participation? One path to reconciliation is to write into the scope of the right an exception that temporarily excludes from participation persons who are being justly punished for crimes. We would then say that Kim, like everyone else, has the right to political participation but that she falls under one of its exceptions.

Another path to reconciliation says that the universality of human rights is an abstract idea that requires considerable specification and qualification before it is ready to work reliably at the stage where rights are being applied to actual persons and situations. Here we might draw a distinction between exceptions to the scope of a right and qualifications concerning who has it. A human right may have exceptions to its scope while applying to and being claimable by the entire human population. For example, the human right to freedom of religious practice has an exception excluding human sacrifices, but the right is held by the entire human population (or at least that part of it capable of choosing religious beliefs and practices; perhaps it is not held by infants). Let's say that *exceptions* apply to the scope of the right, to what it permits or protects. In contrast, let's say that *qualifications* apply to who can successfully invoke the right in his or her own case. Qualifications use personal characteristics to make a universal right available to only part of the human population.

Not all qualifications in this sense are based on desert. The right to medical care, for example, is need-based. Everyone has the right but they only get to exercise it when they have a medical problem or are scheduled for periodic check ups. A qualified human right begins by saying that "Everyone has the right to..." but before it finishes it states qualifications that exclude some people from having or being able to use the right temporarily or permanently. Most human rights do not simply deliver a uniform freedom, protection, or good to everyone, or even everyone willing to accept these things. Qualifications may say, for example, that everyone has the right to freedom of movement and residence *unless* they are young children, are serving in the military, or are attempting to enter or reside in a country in which they are not citizens and do not have authorization for entry and residence. Considerations of desert add to this list "unless at present they are justly imprisoned for a crime of which they have been duly convicted."

A number of the human rights in international treaties seem to have only qualified universality. Although formally rights of everyone, their operability in one's case requires that one have some sort of need and willingness to consent (the right to medical care), vulnerability (the right to a fair trial when accused of a crime), ability (the right to serve in public office), or desert. Consequently, we cannot say that putting desert-based qualifications on human rights would so undermine their universality as to make them farcical unless we are prepared to say that the qualifications that we already accept for many international human rights on grounds other than desert also make those rights farcical. The universality of specific human rights is more qualified than one might initially expect.

My suggestion, then, is that we have at least two ways of reconciling desert-based restrictions on the application of human rights with the universality of those rights. The first writes an exception into the scope of the right, and the second weakens the meaning of universality as we move from abstract to specific rights.

III. The Positive Role of Desert in the Realm of Human Rights

Considerations of desert can do more than impose qualifications for the undeserving. They also help justify and shape some human rights. In this section I again proceed by identifying some human rights that seem to be supported by considerations of desert. Some but not all of these pertain to crimes and punishments.

A. The right of the innocent against punishment

The desert basis for criminal punishments is having committed a crime. People who have committed no crimes do not deserve to be punished for crimes (although they might deserve to be criticized or penalized for other moral failings). In relation to criminal punishments their desert basis is zero. Criminal punishments that involve large fines and/or long-term imprisonment have the potential to be seriously harmful and unjust if erroneously imposed. Perfection in allocating punishments to the guilty is unavailable to humans, even when trials are carefully conducted and due process rights respected. Still, a human right of innocent persons against intentional or negligent criminal punishments is strongly supported by considerations of desert. This right protects against one of the most severe forms of disproportionality between desert basis and treatment. Due process rights are means of preventing the punishment of the innocent and hence receive some indirect support from considerations of desert.

B. The right against grossly disproportionate punishments

Almost as bad as punishing the innocent is punishing with very severe criminal punishments a person who has committed a minor crime. Considerations of desert require proportionality and condemn large departures from it. Human rights requiring that punishments be proportional to crimes committed seem to be at least partially desert-based. Although these rights are universal, individual variations in regard to innocence and levels of criminal guilt lead to different specific prescriptions for different people.

An explicit proportionality clause is not found in the European Convention or in the ICCPR (although judges have found a foothold for it in the requirement that punishments not be cruel).[9] The recent European Charter of Fundamental Rights in the Treaty of Lisbon sets it out explicitly, however, in Article 49.3: "The severity of penalties must not be disproportionate to the criminal offence." This principle is also clearly present in ICCPR Article 6 which sets out the right to life. Section 6.3 says that: "In countries which have not abolished the death penalty, sentence of death may be imposed only for the most serious crimes in accordance with the law in force at the

---

[9] See Dirk van Zyl Smit and Andrew Ashworth, "Disproportionate Sentences as Human Rights Violations," *Modern Law Review*, 67 (2004): 541–60.

time of the commission of the crime..." Execution, as one of the most severe punishments, may only be used—if at all—for the most serious crimes.

C. Remedies for violations of human rights

Being a victim of a serious and harmful moral wrong is a desert basis that calls for some sort of compensation or remedy. I do not mean to assert that all plausible claims to compensation are matters of desert. Grounds for compensation are wider than this. Nevertheless, some claims to compensation are claims to what is deserved. If Bernard takes Hilda's savings into his fraudulent "investment fund" and spends the money on a yacht, when Bernard's wrongful conduct is revealed Hilda deserves repayment. Other desert-based compensation decisions may involve desert-for-fault in an accident. Being at fault for an accident can make it permissible for the party at fault to be required to pay the costs of the accident.

Negligent and intentional violations of human rights are generally serious and harmful moral wrongs and hence call for compensation or some other form of remedy. ICCPR Article 2.3 sets out a right to a remedy for human rights violations that individuals have suffered: "[A]ny person whose rights or freedoms as herein recognized are violated shall have an effective remedy, notwithstanding that the violation has been committed by persons acting in an official capacity." Further, ICCPR Articles 9 and 14 require, respectively, compensation for unlawful arrest and detention and compensation for convictions that are shown conclusively to be miscarriages of justice.

Compensation partially removes the disproportionate loss suffered by an innocent person who is unjustly arrested, detained, convicted, or punished. Remedies include not only stopping the violation if it is still occurring but also attempting to undo or compensate for wrongs and harms suffered in the past. Suppose that a judge decides on appeal that an imprisoned person, Ivana, is innocent and orders her to be released but that prison officials negligently fail to release her. When Ivana again appeals to the courts for release she can very plausibly say that as an innocent person she deserves her freedom, that prison officials are failing to give her the freedom that is her due. Considerations of desert come into play in a case like this, requiring that innocent persons not be subject to continued punishment after their innocence has been certified. For the innocent, any size of punishment is disproportionately large.

D. Work and wages

If income is mainly provided through wages or salaries for work, a right to fair wages protects people against nonpayment and earnings that are low to the extent of being grossly disproportionate to labor and contribution. The ICESCR deals with work in Articles 6 to 8. Article 7 deals with "just and favorable conditions of work" and sets out at 7 A (i) a clear proportionality principle. Countries ratifying the treaty are to ensure "[f]air wages and equal remuneration for work of equal value..." Fairness here is taken to require that women be guaranteed "equal pay for equal work."[10] People vary greatly in the value of the work they perform or can perform, and the kind of fairness required here is proportionality. The proportionality is both vertical (if one improves the value of one's work substantially this should improve the size of one's wage) and horizontal (different people doing work of the same value should receive roughly the same wage). The value of work is difficult to estimate so we cannot expect that the application of this principle will be precise. Further, the value of the work a person can do depends partially on cooperation from others and on available materials, tools, and technology.

We speak of the wages from work as "earnings" and "compensation." In the ideal scenario, Zelda makes a contribution through work and the beneficiaries compensate her with wages that are roughly equal to the value of her contribution. ICESCR Article 15.1(c) applies this idea to people who do creative work. It says that participating countries "recognize the right of everyone:... To benefit from the protection of the moral and material interests resulting from any scientific, literary or artistic production of which he is the author."

IV. If the Principle of Desert is Operative within the Realm of Human Rights, Why isn't its Influence Stronger?

In previous sections I have argued that considerations of desert not only qualify some human rights but also provide significant justificatory support for some human rights. The question to be addressed here is why desert's role is not even larger. If it is already within the realm, why isn't it in total command? Why, for example, aren't more human rights subject to desert-based qualifications?

A. Considerations of desert have weak normative force

One possible explanation is that considerations of desert are just not very strong, even in the cases where they are strongest. On this view these considerations are simply not in the same league as norms such as the right to life, the right to lead one's life, welfare, rights against severe cruelty and unfairness, and rights to moral and social equality. I am inclined to this view, and think that considerations of desert are frequently middleweight considerations. They are often outweighed by other norms and seem to play a large role in government and policy only when running in tandem with and imposing only mild limits on stronger norms such as security and welfare. Still, the normative force of considerations of desert should not be underestimated. They can generate duties and not just permissions (and permissions can be very significant). And violations of the duties they generate can be substantial moral and legal wrongs. For example, suppose that a homeowner, Kevin, engages a day laborer, Leonidas, for a week of work in Kevin's rock garden. Leonidas works hard and well for the entire week and then asks for his wages. Kevin, knowing that Leonidas is undocumented and therefore unlikely to seek legal remedies, falsely says that his work was inadequate and pays him for only one day.

---

[10] See also United Nations, Convention on the Elimination of Discrimination against Women (1979), Article 11.d.

B. Desert's application is information and judgment intensive

Assessing and responding appropriately to people's desert bases is far from easy. This makes the application of the considerations of desert expensive to administer and prone to mistakes. One difficulty is that it is that the characteristics that form the basis for some reward or punishment are often matters of controversy. For example, is the basis for fair wages expending effort at work, making a relevant contribution through one's work, or both? And even if we can agree that both contribution and effort are relevant to fair wages, how do we combine and weigh them?

Another difficulty is that high-quality administration of deserts is information intensive. Finding out someone's levels of effort and contribution on the job requires observation, evaluation, and record keeping over an extended period. This is, of course, something that many employers do, but it is expensive and difficult.

Further, judging proportionality is difficult, contextual, and frequently comparative. Even when we know that a particular carpenter, Marvin, is highly skilled, works hard, and produces good results, it is still hard to know what wages are appropriate for him without appealing to what similar workers are paid in local labor markets. Because proper use of the considerations of desert typically requires judgment at many points, error and abuse are serious possibilities. I do not think that this is fatal to the use of considerations of desert, but it does help to explain why norms that are simpler to use sometimes prevail.

Consider an example. Crudely, the human right to health has at least three parts with somewhat different grounds and appropriate distributive principles. The first part is public health measures such as clean water, sanitation, and vaccinations. Here public goods are being created that to be enjoyed by most must be enjoyed by all. Even prisoners must be included if they are not to be sources of danger to the general population. The second part contains parts of health care that are relatively inexpensive but produce very valuable results for people's health and productivity. These would include care for mothers and infants, antibiotics, and low-cost treatments for broken bones and other injuries. Given how mistake-prone and information- and judgment-intensive administering these services on the basis of desert would be, it is simply too much trouble. The third part of the right to health is high-cost treatments and therapies that possibly could be administered partially on the basis of personal desert—and that, in cases of competition for scarce resources such as organs for transplant, sometimes in fact are. But even here other distributive principles that are need- or welfare- or dignity-based compete with the considerations of desert and often win.

C. Most people's deserts are the same or similar in many areas

It is incorrect to assume that desert bases always vary among persons. There are treatments in regard to which everyone has the same deserts because those treatments are ones that no one deserves. When everyone has the same desert bases the resulting prescription is equality. Further, even in areas where people's desert bases vary most people's deserts are fairly similar. Desert bases, like other human characteristics, probably form a bell curve. A few people are exceptionally virtuous in their character and actions, and in the other tail of the bell curve a few people are exceptionally lacking in virtue and behave very badly. Most of us, however, are average or not too far from it and hence are bunched in the fat middle. As morally average or even mediocre, our desert bases are not large or interesting enough to make imperative desert's operation in the realm of human rights.

D. Giving government a large role in monitoring and recording people's desert bases risks turning it into Big Brother

People that I tell about this essay often respond with worries about who is going to monitor and judge everyone's deserts. They think it is dangerous to give governments a job that only an all-knowing and wise God could perform well. Decisions that are information- and judgment-intensive are often abuse prone. And this worry becomes especially intense if the enjoyment of our most basic rights becomes conditional on government decisions about what we deserve.

One response to this worry is to remind ourselves that all of the world's governments use law and threats of legal sanctions to govern, to collect taxes, to protect their citizens, and to implement human rights. Law enforcement requires monitoring people's actions to see if they are in compliance with the law. In particular, the criminal law in every country prohibits actions such as murder, rape, theft, and fraud that provide the bases for negative deserts. Consequently, every government monitors these bases to some extent. The criminal law is indeed one of the most dangerous parts of government but over the centuries humans have developed means such as due process rights of limiting its dangers and those means are now prescribed by international human rights. Further, investigations of the bases of people's deserts can be conducted in response to individual complaints or lawsuits. In this way the attention of government officials can be directed to the desert bases of some people without governments having to monitor everyone's behavior.

Secondly, many believe that besides legal human rights there are also moral human rights, and that these moral rights pertain to interpersonal relations and not just to what governments should do. For example, Griffin's view of human rights is worked up within philosophical ethics and deals with rights against other persons as much as with rights against governments. Claims about what governments can and should do say little about whether the considerations of desert can influence *moral* human rights that operate in the realm of interpersonal relations.

Finally, considerations of desert do not just present dangers; they also justify protections. As we saw in rights against punishing the innocent, rights against punishments that are disproportionately severe, rights to remedies for violations of human rights, and rights to wages that are not disproportionately small in relation to work and contribution, considerations of desert help justify some important protections.

V. Conclusion

Normative considerations, like actors, can play bigger or smaller roles in a production. In human rights theory, considerations of personal desert could play a starring role (although this seems unlikely), a major role along with some bigger stars, a significant but modest role, or a very minor role. I have attempted to show that principles of desert can and do play a significant but modest role in the realm of human rights. Not only do considerations of desert justify qualifications and limits to rights; they also provide justifications for human rights protections against disproportionate treatment in areas where proportionality between desert basis and treatment is required. If my arguments are plausible, quick and undefended dismissals of desert from human rights theorizing should no longer be acceptable.

8

Can Moral Desert Qualify or Justify Human Rights?

Zofia Stemplowska

I. Introduction

A person is morally deserving of some treatment when this is the morally fitting response to her desert basis.[1] The thought here is that such a 'fitting' response is intrinsically valuable and it is impersonally valuable—ie, it is valuable even if it does not benefit anyone.[2] Thus a world in which everyone is treated as they deserve would be in one respect better than a world in which the same people were all better off undeservedly. The idea of moral desert requires that only the features that can form the basis for moral appraisal qualify as desert bases. Typical candidates, all embraced by Nickel (this volume, Chapter 7), include a person's actions, attitudes, and character. For example, we may think that a wrongdoer who commits a crime deserves to be imprisoned while an honest lawyer deserves to be rewarded for her work.[3]

Can personal moral desert, as Nickel argues, qualify the scope of (some) human rights and play a role in justifying (some) human rights? That is, can the treatment that a person deserves amount to the withdrawal of a human right or conferring of reward as a matter of human right? A right is *qualified* when there are restrictions based on personal features regarding who can hold it. As Nickel puts it, '[q]ualifications use personal characteristics to make a universal right available to only part of the human population' (159). So if desert affects who is entitled to a given human right X, then

[1] I am grateful for comments to Matthew Clayton, Ben Jackson, S. Matthew Liao, and Andrea Sangiovanni as well as to the participants of the Warwick–Oxford joint seminar on human rights, May 2013.
[2] More would need to be said to distinguish responses that are appropriate in terms of desert from those that are appropriate in terms of, say, fairness, but I hope an intuitive understanding of the former will suffice to highlight my disagreement with Nickel.

[3] Unless otherwise stated, subsequent in-text references refer to Nickel, this volume, chapter 7. Nickel (this volume, ch. 7) adds 'harmful wrongs suffered' (154) as a desert basis. Later in the text, he offers an example: 'If Bernard takes Hilda's savings into his fraudulent "investment fund"…Hilda deserves repayment' (161). But clearly Hilda is entitled to repayment simply because the money was hers; she is entitled to it even if she does not deserve it because, say, she knew what Bernard was doing all along (even though she did not consent to it). This shows that desert is not necessary for Hilda's right to repayment; I do not think it is sufficient either (see section III). Nickel also adds 'innocence' as a desert basis, arguing that even in those who 'lack the ability to generate desert bases through their actions' (156) it is a 'passive' desert base. I do not see how being wronged, suffering or innocence can count as moral desert bases. Rather, I agree with David Miller that desert is 'on the basis of an activity or performance' that is 'in the relevant sense' the agent's—ie, she is responsible for it (David Miller, *Principles of Social Justice* (Harvard University Press, 1999), 133). Miller's own focus is not merely on moral desert, which affects how he understands 'performance' but I side-step this debate here; my focus throughout, like Nickel's, is on moral desert.

this human right is qualified in a way that excludes some people from the domain of holders of X, even if they are still in need of the protection that the right is meant to deliver.[4] The worry with qualifying human rights is that it might stop them from being *human* rights—ie, universal and crucial rights that humans are entitled to simply in virtue of being human (or, to avoid speciesism, persons are entitled to simply in virtue of being persons).[5] As Nickel puts it, desert-based qualifications might conflict with or diminish 'the universality and egalitarian character of human rights' (153).

Nickel acknowledges this worry about desert-based qualifications, but defends them nonetheless. He thinks that they arise when we move from 'abstract ideas to particular rights' (157) and observes that '[a] number of human rights in international treaties seem to have only qualified universality [on various grounds: need, consent, vulnerability, ability]' (159). Therefore, he suggests, adding desert to the list of grounds for qualification does not make much difference: 'we cannot say that putting desert-based qualifications on human rights would so undermine their universality as to make them farcical unless we are prepared to say that the qualifications that we already accept for many international, human rights on grounds other than desert also make those rights farcical' (159).

Rights are *justified* with reference to desert when desert considerations 'support' (160) the granting of the right or its shape. Here I take 'supporting' to mean more than just that considerations of desert point in the same direction as some other considerations—for example, fairness—that actually give rise to a right of a given shape; rather desert justifies the right when the considerations support the right by actually bearing on the presence and shape of the right. Again, as Nickel puts it, 'Personal moral deserts often help determine whether people should receive wages and other rewards, whether or not people should be punished with fines or imprisonment, and whether people are appropriately esteemed or despised' (158). He argues that deserts help determine that we should get these things as a matter of right.

But although, for Nickel, desert plays both the qualifying and justifying roles, he adds that it is, nonetheless, only a 'middleweight' consideration (162). That is, although desert provides a 'significant justificatory support for some human rights' (162), he adds that he is '…inclined to the view' that considerations of desert 'are simply not in the same league' as norms such as the right to life—they 'seem to play a large role in government and policy only when running in tandem with and imposing only mild limits on stronger norms such as security and welfare' (162).

In what follows, I will challenge both of the suggestions advanced by Nickel regarding desert's role in the geography of human rights—that it can qualify and that it can justify them. In sections II and III I will attempt to offer alternative explanations for

---

[4] I am a supporter of the interest theory of rights and think of human rights as protecting the fundamental (basic, essential) interests that humans have; a protection that they qualify for simply in virtue of being human. But rights grant protections even on the will and status theories of rights and what I say here applies beyond the interest account.

[5] In what follows I understand human rights as rights that persons enjoy in virtue of being persons (whatever account of personhood we may wish to adopt), ie, they don't need to be earned by them. I add that the rights be crucial since I think debates over crucial rights of persons matter the most. This move will become significant in the final section of the chapter. For a criticism of the whole category of human rights see Victor Tadros's essay in this volume (ch. 24).

the examples that Nickel uses to bolster his intuitive case. In the concluding section IV, I will outline a more general reason why we might be sceptical of desert bearing on any aspect of human rights.

Unless otherwise indicated, for simplicity, whenever I refer to rights I will mean human rights. Nickel's focus in his chapter is on human rights that, by and large, are both legal and moral. Here I consider only the relationship between desert and moral human rights, leaving aside the complication of when moral rights should be legalized.[6]

II. Can Desert Qualify Human Rights?

So which rights are meant to be qualified by desert? The main example offered by Nickel is that of political human rights such as the right to free movement, to freely associate, to stand for office. As he explains, 'the place where we find the most desert-based restrictions to human rights is in rights to fundamental freedoms and to political participation' (158). For example, according to Nickel, those engaging in criminal activity punishable by prison are not deserving of the right to free movement and the right to run for office. He explicitly states that the reason the right to run for office is withdrawn is not merely logistical: while it is hard to discharge the duties of one's office while one is in prison it is not impossible to arrange prison in such a way as to make it easier (158).

I will look at the two key rights—to run for office and to free movement—in turn. But first, to make progress, let me distinguish between a direct and indirect role that desert could, in principle, play in qualifying human rights. A right is qualified by desert directly when withholding or granting of the right is the object of the deserved treatment. For example, desert's role is direct when the reason we withhold the right to run for office from you is because your action makes you undeserving of it. By contrast, a right is qualified by desert indirectly when the desert basis gives rise to some treatment/property Y that in turn affects one's holding of the right but it is Y that gives rise to changes in the person's standing vis-a-vis the right. For example, desert's role is indirect when the reason we withhold the right to run for office from you is because you are in prison, and it would therefore be impossible for you to perform the job properly, but we do not withhold the right because you do not deserve it (even if we put you in prison on account of what you deserve). I take it that only the direct role for desert should count as a genuinely desert based qualification on human rights.

A. The right to run for office

Nickel's example of losing the right to stand for political office appears to be a case of desert's direct role in shaping human rights. But this appearance is misleading. After all, we do not say that a person cannot run for political office simply because

---

[6] I put aside Nickel's discussion of how to respond to epistemic and practical worries that arise should desert turn out to play the roles Nickel identifies for it. That said, I am of the view that should desert really matter in the way Nickel suggests, then the difficulties in ascertaining and administering desert should lead us far less readily than he suggests to abandon it. That is, if desert really matters then the fact that, say, it's hard to know who deserves what, does not make it a neutral position to not pay any attention to it.

she is undeserving (for example, vicious people or people who acted viciously but non-criminally, can do so even though they clearly do not deserve the chance). Rather, a person cannot run for office because she has a criminal conviction. Even a person who clearly deserves the chance to run for office might justifiably lose the right to do so if she had a criminal conviction. Think here, for example, of a person who commits a victimless crime in order to bring about an unambiguously good (even if only in comparison to the alternative) outcome. For example, a woman might engage in illegal prostitution to stop her underage sister from needing to do so. We may think, in such a case, that although she still deserves the chance to run for office, she is not entitled to it because only those who observe the law are.

Of course, this would only show that being deserving of the right to run for office is neither sufficient nor necessary to have the right; it does not show that being *unde*serving might not bear on losing the right. But here again we do not need to appeal to considerations of desert to account for the judgment that criminals lose the right to run for office. For example, criminals may be thought to lack the necessary competences for serving others in accordance with the rule of law: after all, they failed to uphold it.[7] Or we may think that although some criminals do not lack such competences, it is too hard to tell which of them do and which do not. Notice that this would be a future-oriented judgment about likely competences of the office holders and so it would not be a desert judgment.[8] Given the existence of such alternative explanations for our intuitions about the right, Nickel does not say enough to show that the qualification on the human right to run for office is desert-based.

The above discussion presupposes that some qualifications on the right to run for office are acceptable, even if I disagree with Nickel regarding its grounds. This brings us back to the more general question of whether any qualifications on human rights are acceptable or whether they amount to an unacceptable attack on the universalism of human rights.

One possible way of explaining why some qualifications are acceptable in the case of criminal conduct is to appeal to the fact that criminal conduct is avoidable. The right to run for office then is only lost if you perform an avoidable action. This means that the loss of the right is a matter of voluntary (even if not necessarily deliberate) choice. And we do not think that people lack the right to run for office if they have first to fill in a simple form indicating intent, especially if help is available with the form filling. Those who do not submit the form would forfeit the right to run, but it would be inaccurate to describe the right as qualified in a way that genuinely excluded them from its scope.

This answer might be too quick. As a matter of horrible fact, not everyone is reasonably able to avoid criminal conduct. As *Oliver Twist* and the Australian movie *Animal Kingdom* illustrate, sometimes there may be no clear way out. Similarly, in a society with high illiteracy rates or without a common language, the requirement to fill in a form in the single official language of the state in order to be able to run for office may be rightly seen as a qualification on the human right to run for office. Suppose,

---

[7] Of course, so do the very selfish or the very stupid, but the criteria for determining who falls into these latter categories may be too controversial or too hard to apply.

[8] Miller, *Principles of Social Justice*.

then, that we accept that the qualification is, in some cases, genuinely exclusionary. Qualifying the right to run for office may still, as Nickel suggest, be justified given some instances of criminal conduct. Unlike Nickel, however, I think that what justifies it are not backward-looking desert considerations. Rather, in the specific case of the right to run for office, we need to balance the interest to be able to run for office that normally gives rise to the right with the interest to live in a society governed by the rule of law dedicated to protecting everyone's essential interests. If so, then what justifies the qualification are forward-looking reasons relating to the balancing of the above mentioned interests. That is, once everyone's interests are taken into account we may be justified in qualifying the right to run for office.

Ultimately, there are alternative explanations of the qualification of the right to run for office. I hope to have shown that desert is not necessary to qualify the right. I did not establish that it is also insufficient even in cases when, for example, a law has been broken[9] but I think that the idea of qualifications grounded in forward-looking reasons that balance everyone's interests fits better with the idea of universal human rights than the idea that human rights are qualified by backward-looking desert considerations.

B. The right to free movement

Let me then turn to another of Nickel's examples of what he believes is a desert-qualified human right. He argues that desert qualifies the right to free movement/the right not to be imprisoned (in what follows, I won't distinguish between these two formulations of the right, even though there are contexts in which such a distinction would matter). Is this right qualified due to desert?

Again, Nickel does not say enough to explain why we should think that it is desert in particular that qualifies the right. There are reasons, however, to be sceptical. First, we know that desert is not necessary to qualify the right to free movement since some people with severe mental disabilities lose it without deserving to. Second, it is not clear that considerations of desert are sufficient to do so. After all, even in cases where considerations of desert do point towards confinement, the right might be lost for non-desert reasons—for example, due to forward-looking reasons (protection) or even due to backward-looking reasons that are not, however, reasons of desert: for example, imprisonment might be a form of showing respect for the rights of those who had been victimized. Thus we may think that imprisonment is justified provided that people have had a good enough (even if imperfect) opportunity to avoid it and provided that it is needed to protect others from serious harms or costs.[10] Consider an analogy. Suppose I have a right to be fed when I lack the resources to purchase food. We may accept this but still believe that such a right does not include the right to be fed when I deliberately and repeatedly burn the resources I am offered. In this case, I do not deserve the money to buy food and yet it is not because of considerations of

---

[9] That is, although desert alone could not do the trick, desert jointly with law-breaking could, perhaps, be sufficient to qualify the right.

[10] T.M. Scanlon, *What We Owe to Each Other* (Harvard University Press, 1998), ch. 6.

desert but due to considerations of avoidability plus fairness, given scarce resources, that lead us to curtail the right, not my desert.[11] Suppose scarcity was absent and so the issue of fair distribution did not arise. If so, desert alone should not lead us to curtail the right. Similarly, we may think that the right to free movement is curtailed due to considerations of avoidability and fairness (towards the victims) rather than desert, even though the imprisonment also happens to be deserved.[12] Moreover, the mere fact that imprisonment tracks a blameworthy *action* (criminal wrongdoing), which is, in principle, a candidate desert base, does not mean that it is the action understood as a desert-base that qualifies the right against imprisonment. It may instead be the fact that the action constitutes wasteful or unfair conduct that makes a given response appropriate. If you burn your share of resources, you may not be entitled to compensation not because you do not deserve it (though you do not) but because we only need to provide you with one (or two or three) chances to fare well.[13]

The more general problem with Nickel's use of the right against imprisonment example is that it relies, without support, on a rather controversial theory of punishment. The theory, as far as it can be reconstructed from his chapter, resembles simple desert retributivism, the view that punishment (or, in this case, confinement) is justified when and because it is deserved. But, as McDermott, Tadros, and others have shown, it is implausible to believe that we can imprison people—that people lose the right not to be imprisoned—simply because they deserve to be in prison.[14] To name just two problems in passing, as Tadros has argued, if desert had such normative power, it would be hard to see why people could not accumulate positive desert that would protect them from imprisonment. Moreover, it would be hard to avoid the following problem: if I know you are about to be miserable (or falsely imprisoned), I have a reason to encourage you to commit a crime so that the suffering is more fitting.[15] But it's unclear that we can make sense of such a reason.

C. Desert-based qualifications

Finally, let me return to the more general worries about desert-based qualifications on human rights (I will revisit this problem once more in the final section). Specifically, consider one of Nickel's defences of the appropriateness of qualifying human rights on grounds of desert with reference to the claim that we already qualify human rights anyway. That is, Nickel sees desert-based qualifications as simply extending the list of other qualifications he identifies, namely those grounded in need, consent,

---

[11] Zofia Stemplowska, 'Responsibility and Respect', in Carl Knight and Zofia Stemplowska (eds.), *Responsibility and Distributive Justice* (Oxford University Press, 2011).
[12] Nickel acknowledges that we may think that 'these qualifications to fundamental freedoms are based not on desert but on what is necessary to protect people's security against crime' (158).
[13] The difference between desert and responsibility might also explain why in the example of an organ shortage used by Nickel (153), we would use prior conduct as a tie-breaker regarding who should get the transplant. It need not be desert that matters.
[14] Daniel McDermott, 'Desert, Rights and Justice', unpublished paper—henceforth page references given refer to the pagination of the paper; Victor Tadros, *The Ends of Harm* (Oxford University Press, 2011).
[15] Tadros, *The Ends of Harm*, 70–1.

vulnerability or ability. But all these qualifications are not equally problematic from the viewpoint of the universality of human rights. Consider the qualifications due to need and vulnerability first. They do not have the effect of excluding anyone from the protection that the right is meant to afford. Suppose that the human right to be fed when starving is qualified in the sense that it applies only to those who are starving and so in desperate need of food. Still, anyone who is starving, no matter who they are or what they did, is entitled to be fed. So if we think of human rights as offering protection to people, anyone in need of the protection continues to get it (or, rather, continues to be the holder of the right to get it).

Similarly, it is not clear that consent-based qualifications exclude anyone in an unacceptable way from the right since, here again, the protection is not simply withdrawn. Therefore, the person who fasts rather than starves or the person who alienates her human rights may still be seen as someone who had been given the exact same rights as everyone else and none have been withdrawn against her will.

What of ability-based qualifications, that is the withholding of a right from those who lack certain abilities? Such qualifications do seem genuinely exclusionary, like the desert-based ones, and perhaps even more so since ability is more readily unavailable to some than appropriate desert bases, due to no choice of their own. But then the list of ability-qualified human rights seems rather short. We might think that even the most mentally disabled people are entitled to marry or have jobs just as long as they can formulate a coherent desire to do so. Where we do qualify their rights, we do it in order to balance their interests (indeed, sometimes in a paternalistic way to protect them) and the interests of others. Thus ability-based qualifications may in fact allow us to balance better all the essential interests at stake. The same rationale cannot be offered for desert-based qualifications since their point is to give people what they deserve rather than what best balances the interests of those involved. All in all, therefore, we could accept non-desert grounds for qualifying human rights without thereby being committed to welcoming desert-based qualifications.

III. Can Desert Justify Human Rights?

The second role Nickel identifies for desert is that of justifying human rights.[16] In what follows I will assume that desert justifies a right when it either gives rise to it (the right to be paid for work) or gives it a specific shape (the right to be paid P for work W). Since, depending on how we individuate rights, the second description can collapse into the first, in what follows I will refer to giving rise and shaping rights interchangeably.

Nickel offers a range of examples to support his claim, of which perhaps the most prominent is that of the right to be rewarded for one's contribution. I will argue that alternative desert unrelated reasons might account for the examples used by Nickel and that, since he does not explore them, we are left without a persuasive reason to

---

[16] Here his examples include the right of the innocent not to be punished. I do not see why we need to, or can, appeal to desert to assert this right so I put this aside. For an interesting discussion of innocence and desert see Tadros, *The Ends of Harm*, ch. 14.

believe that desert really plays the role Nickel suggests. Consider then the following scenario (162).

> [S]uppose that a homeowner, Kevin, engages a day labourer, Leonidas, for a week of work in Kevin's rock garden. Leonidas works hard and well for the entire week and then asks for his wages. Kevin, knowing that Leonidas is undocumented and therefore unlikely to seek legal remedies, falsely says that his work was inadequate and pays him for only one day.[17]

We can all agree that, given certain plausible background assumptions, Leonidas has been treated unjustly and his right to a just reward has been violated. The difficulty with the example, however, is that it cannot establish the importance of desert to this conclusion since the (explicit or implicit) promise of payment for the full week given to Leonidas by Kevin as he engages him is itself sufficient to generate the right to be paid for the full week rather than just one day. Since this example cannot establish that desert is operative in what does the work here, consider an alternative scenario. Suppose that Kevin mentions to Leonidas that he would like his rock garden resculpted but does not give an even implicit promise of paying for such work. Leonidas, nonetheless, works for a week to improve the garden, delivering beautiful results that please Kevin who concludes that Leonidas is certainly deserving of reward. Still, without a contract or an even implicit promise of employment, Leonidas's desert is insufficient to generate a right to be paid.[18]

It might be objected that we should not be too quick to generalize from this case to the conclusion that desert cannot justify the right to fitting reward for work: even if desert alone cannot generate the right to be paid, it could still give rise to the right to be paid the appropriate amount once the right to be paid arises in the first place on some other grounds. Thus, the argument would go, those employed through contract or promise cannot, on pain of rights violation, be paid exploitative wages or indeed wages that are not fitting with their desert. As Nickel explains, '[o]ne way to find areas where desert is at work is to look for areas where proportionality judgments are being made between something about a person and some treatment or state of affairs' (156).[19]

However, even the suggestion that desert generates a right to a proportionate wage seems implausible in light of other considerations that must be accommodated. It would, of course, be wrong of me, barring special circumstances, to employ you on wages that would be widely—or even narrowly—out of proportion with your stellar desert but, assuming these are the terms (that were consented to under fair conditions),

---

[17] Nickel offers one other case: '[I]magine that Zelda agrees to mow Elmer's lawn for a fee. If Zelda shows up and mows the lawn we can say that she deserves payment for this work' (155).

[18] Daniel Butt, in the context of a different debate, has come up with a more complicated case, which adapted for my purposes, might go as follows: suppose you had engaged someone else to sculpt your rock garden while your neighbour engaged Leonidas. However, following a mix-up for which no one bears any responsibility, Leonidas did work in your garden, while the person you engaged worked in your neighbour's garden. I agree that in such a case, you may be required to pay Leonidas despite not even implicitly promising to do so. However, this is because of worries we may have about free-riding and advantage taking rather than because of Leonidas's desert. cf Daniel Butt, "'A Doctrine Quite New and Altogether Untenable': Defending the Beneficiary Pays Principle", *Journal of Applied Philosophy*, 31 (2014): 336–48.

[19] Though he admits that such a discovered statement of proportionality 'could also fail to be a desert statement' involving instead 'some other relation' (156).

your desert does not create an entitlement to a higher wage. Or, to adapt an example from Daniel McDermott, if suddenly everyone in a given factory becomes deserving of higher rewards—they work extremely hard while also, in their spare time, saving the factory from calamities not of their own making—it still does not follow that they thereby become entitled to them.[20] The factory owner may have or can make other commitments for his or her resources, including serving her own interests, and changes in people's desert levels should not be allowed to wreak havoc with this.

There is a further problem with Nickel's specific linking of contribution (as a desert basis) to reward (as the deserved treatment) owed as a matter of right. First, it is not clear that 'contribution' as such, rather than effort or intelligent input in particular, can be a proper desert basis. What if I mowed the lawn while sleep-walking? I would have made a contribution, but I would not be morally deserving of reward. Similarly, what if my contribution was a fluke? For example, suppose you and I signed up to go looking for a missing cat. You dutifully check the back gardens, while I sneak off to a café and, to everyone's surprise, find the cat under the table.[21] Because my contribution again bypasses my moral agency (I did not even try to contribute), it does not seem like a good candidate for a moral desert basis.

However, even if Nickel were to respond by linking reward to effort, it would still be unclear that it is desert that drives our intuitions about the appropriateness of the rightful reward. An alternative explanation might be that of agent responsibility (or choice), where the reward is due to the person who is agent responsible for the outcome—ie, she is the author of the action that foreseeably leads to the outcome. On this view, it is agent responsibility rather than desert that makes the reward appropriate as a matter of right. To see that agent responsibility is operative this way consider the following. Suppose that you work hard to finish a project because you reasonably believe that a completed project will lead to the destruction of the company (for example, you heard the arch enemy of the company promised to set fire to it on completion of the project). Because you completed the project, you are due the reward for the job even though it is unclear that you are also deserving of it (except, perhaps, in some narrow sense). It is also agent responsibility that in my view accounts for another of Nickel's example. He claims that '[b]eing at fault for an accident [and thus undeserving] can make it permissible for the faulty party to be required to pay the costs of the accident' (161). But more needs to be said to establish that it is desert and not responsibility that does the work. If I crash your car to avoid hitting a dog, I still owe you compensation, since I am responsible for the crash, but it is not clear that I did anything morally wrong and that desert has anything to do with my duty to compensate.

So far I have only suggested that alternative explanations might account for our intuitions in Nickel's examples. In the following, final section, I will outline a more general reason why we should be sceptical of desert's ability to justify human rights.

---

[20] McDermott, 'Desert, Rights and Justice'.
[21] This example is adapted from David Miller's discussion of market socialism, 'G.A. Cohen and Our Unfinished Debate', *Politics Philosophy and Economics*, 13 (2014): 119–39.

IV. Desert and Human Rights

We can distinguish between the realm of rights and the realm of the good and, following McDermott, assign desert to the latter (162 and elsewhere).[22] Claims about desert can be understood as claims about what it is good for people to have. Claims about rights are about what we must give them. I will not be able to establish here in the remainder of this chapter that this picture is correct but I hope to offer some reasons for finding it attractive.

Notice that this picture allows us to make sense of our reactions in the reward cases described earlier, in which the deserving do not get the reward they deserve. We can consistently think that the lawn, rock garden, and factory owners, barring countervailing considerations, ought to pay their workers what they deserve—in the sense that it would be good if they did and bad if they did not—but still believe that the workers do not have the human right that they be so paid.

Two other examples, adapted from Feinberg and McDermott, illustrate this bifurcation of rights and desert. Imagine that a father of two sons—one, a virtuous do-gooder, Good, and one, a vicious evil-doer, Bad—leaves his estate, in his will, to Bad. Suppose he does it while knowing that Good is good and Bad is bad. Barring other considerations, he certainly ought not to have done it. But it was his right to do it and Bad now has the right to the estate: Bad must get it. Had the father left the estate to Good, Good would have been entitled to it and it would also have made the outcome better, since it would be deserved reward. But even then, clearly, desert would not have been the reason why Good must get the farm. It would not be the reason, even if the reason the father left the farm to Good was because Good was deserving. Similarly, in Feinberg's case of running for office, entitlement and desert can easily come apart. A candidate running the honest campaign deserves to win but the candidate who actually wins the vote, even if—short of criminal activity—he lied and manipulated, is the one who has the right to the office.

Why should we think of rights and desert as part of two different normative registers? For McDermott, we should think of desert as a consideration of the good rather than the right because of 'the liberal commitment to the moral equality of persons' (23). Rights capture this moral equality and for this reason should not be moulded to fit round desert considerations. Desert considerations force us to group people into deserving and undeserving, good and bad, and work at cross-purposes with our commitment to moral equality.

Notice that even if we resist McDermott's conclusion that *all* rights should reflect our liberal commitment to the moral equality of persons, surely we should accept that this, at least, is the role of human rights.[23] After all, there are two features in standard accounts of human rights. First, human rights are rights we all have in virtue of being

---

[22] Joel Feinberg distinguishes between desert and rights as being part of a different 'ethical vocabulary' ('Justice and Personal Desert', in Joel Feinberg, *Doing and Deserving* (Princeton University Press, 1970), 86; quoted in McDermott, 'Desert, Rights and Justice', 2).

[23] This is compatible with the picture of human rights according to which human rights differ (implausibly) between different political communities; in such a case, their role is to assert the moral equality of those who belong to the same political community.

human or in virtue of being persons (of course, this feature cannot be assumed since this is what is at stake in the debate over the role of desert). Second, they are rights that protect what is essential for those who qualify to be their recipients. Enjoying protection from lethal threats, avoiding malnutrition, having access to basic education, being paid the living wage, having a job, being able to rest, etc, are all essential interests for persons (and must be protected or even provided for subject to satisfying other essential interests). The more essential the interest, the more important it is that this interest is met equally for all (ie, the more essential the interest at stake, the less acceptable it is if only some have it met, at least when such an uneven distribution is morally avoidable). This explains why we should resist desert-based qualifications on human rights.

It may seem that we should also, therefore, reject ability-based qualifications. However, as I argued earlier, ability-based qualifications may in fact allow us to meet better our other essential interests and, for this reason, I am prepared to accept the ability-based qualification on some political rights (and perhaps other human rights). The same rationale cannot be offered for desert-based qualifications. For example, the interest that we be given our just deserts in remuneration does not seem half as important as the interests that normally ground human rights and so we may be skeptical that human rights would be needed to protect it. Nickel may be thought to acknowledge this himself when he calls desert a middleweight consideration. In my view, this rules out desert as a good ground for justifying human rights.

I conclude by briefly considering a challenge that arises because we are all familiar with entitlements that are deliberately designed to track desert. For example, medals and honours are to be given to the deserving and, given this, the deserving may have, for example, the right that the undeserving do not receive them. In response notice, first, that it is not clear that we should set up such entitlements in the first place. Would it be wrong to scrap honours? Second, even if we should set up such schemes, it is not the case that we must set them up. If the courageous in battle are never rewarded with medals, can they object that their rights have been violated? Finally, even if it were the case that some rewards for the deserving, or punishment for the undeserving, must be put in place, it is still unclear that we should see such requirements as a matter of human (in the sense of crucial) rights.[24]

All in all, I think that the intuitiveness of the examples offered by Nickel to support his case can be explained without invoking desert as a consideration that can qualify and justify human rights. We also have a more general reason to resist Nickel's suggestion that desert can do either: if human rights are to protect the essential interests we have as persons, then they should protect them just as long as we remain persons with such interests. Allowing desert to qualify or justify human rights would weaken human rights and, given that alternative considerations can account for our intuitions about, for example, the rights of prisoners, it would not deliver anything essential to make sense of our moral landscape.

---

[24] McDermott, 'Desert, Rights and Justice' 49, fn 12. cf Samuel Scheffler, 'Justice and Desert in Liberal Theory' in his *Boundaries and Allegiances* (Oxford University Press, 2001) and Samuel Scheffler, 'Distributive Justice and Economic Desert', in Serena Olsaretti (ed.), *Desert and Justice* (Oxford University Press, 2003).

9

A Social Ontology of Human Rights

Carol C. Gould

I. Introduction

The individualism of human rights has been regarded as both their strength and their weakness. As claims that individuals can make against the state and even perhaps against all other individuals for their fulfillment, these rights centrally appeal to an important notion of the inviolability of persons. Further, as pertaining to each individual simply in virtue of that person's humanity, such rights have a universalistic, and in this respect an egalitarian, dimension, stretching in a cosmopolitan way across time and place. Nonetheless, this strength has at the same time been held to constitute a profound weakness in the very conception of a human right. Insofar as such rights assert basic claims of each individual against others, an emphasis on human rights is thought to neglect our social nature, and the need for social cooperation for the achievement of most human goods. This putative asociality would also divert attention from the problematic power relations and forms of oppression that most urgently need to be redressed in contemporary forms of society.

In this chapter, I will consider the philosophical basis for human rights and argue—in contrast to such views—that human rights are in important ways based on sociality and are themselves fundamentally social or relational conceptions, in ways that existing interpretations of them most often fail to recognize. Such relationality at the root of human rights will be seen to go beyond the correlativity of rights to duties or of rights to responsibilities. Further, when properly interpreted, the fulfillment of human rights, when understood in connection with the central norm of equal freedom, is implied by any critique we might give of domination and exploitation. The recognition of human rights, I suggest, can foster social cooperation while at the same time preserve an important regard for individuality. In order to develop these sizeable claims, I will appeal to what I have previously called social ontology[1] and show its import for our understanding of human rights norms.

---

[1] I originally used this term and elaborated a conception of social ontology in a short course on *Marx's Social Ontology* at the Graduate Center of the City University of New York in 1975, and subsequently in the book of the same title (Carol C. Gould, *Marx's Social Ontology* (Cambridge, MA: The MIT Press, 1978)). A work that influenced me in constructing the term was Lukacs's *Zur Ontologie des gesellschaftlichen Seins*, 3 vols. (Neuwied: Luchterhand, 1971–73). It has recently come to my attention that the term social ontology was used by Joseph Gittler in 1950 in "Social Ontology and the Criteria for Definitions in Sociology," *The Midwest Sociologist*, 13(1) (1950): 8. In recent decades, the term, as well as the general project to which it refers, has become a commonplace in social philosophy. It has, of course, been variably interpreted, from views that seek to place sociality in the context of material factors to more phenomenological approaches. My own account takes social ontology as a theory of the nature of social reality, in terms of its basic entities, relations, and processes, and operates within an experiential or phenomenological framework. It is to be understood as a regional ontology rather than as a metaphysical theory.

In proposing this revisionist understanding of the philosophical basis of human rights, the investigation that follows will go beyond understanding these rights as primarily legal ones that hold against nation-states. The account will focus on their fundamental moral and social dimensions, which I believe can also serve to provide guidelines for interpreting and expanding existing legal notions of human rights. Within the moral sphere itself, it will be evident that we need to go beyond the idea, originally powerfully articulated by Henry Shue, that "human rights are the morality of the depths."[2] Rather, the suggestion will be that these norms can and should play a much broader role within social and political life. Further, while traditional views most often take human rights to protect individuals against grave wrongs perpetrated against them by their own nation-states or their governments, for example, in the case of torture or the abrogation of freedom of speech or unreasonable search and seizure, the perspective here follows recent developments in political philosophy that take human rights to require wider-ranging institutional structures (including economic, as well as political, ones), along with transnational, rather than strictly national, institutions, if the rights are to be adequately fulfilled.

Likewise, human rights will be understood to range over a variety of economic and social rights, as well as civil and political ones. The Universal Declaration of Human Rights provides a useful starting point for this sort of broad legal/moral account (despite its unsystematic and rather too extensive list), and many theorists have followed its approach by regarding the various enunciated rights as mutually interdependent. On this issue, I will instead maintain the distinction I introduced in previous work between basic and nonbasic human rights, keeping in mind that the latter remain essential, if not primary.[3] (This distinction between basic and nonbasic human rights makes a human rights framework considerably more practicable than if all the rights are taken as wholly interdependent.)

In what follows, I will delineate key features of my own approach by way of a critical review of a few of the prominent accounts of human rights, focusing on how those accounts either incorporate or fail to adequately incorporate a conception of human sociality. Specifically, I will raise some concerns about the otherwise strong agency approaches of James Griffin and Alan Gewirth, which, I suggest, at important junctures end up not being social enough, and I will consider my own alternative in relation to theirs. I will then turn to two (disparate) approaches that emphasize sociality or certain social and legal practices as at the basis of human rights—those of Jürgen Habermas and of Charles Beitz—but will suggest that these views are (in different ways) ultimately unable to give an account of human rights as well-supported and fully universalist norms.

---

[2] Henry Shue, *Basic Rights* (Princeton: Princeton University Press, 1980).

[3] Carol Gould, *Rethinking Democracy: Freedom and Social Cooperation in Politics, Economy, and Society* (Cambridge: Cambridge University Press, 1988), ch. 7; Carol Gould, *Globalizing Democracy and Human Rights* (Cambridge: Cambridge University Press, 2004), chs. 1 and 9; Carol Gould, "Approaching Global Justice through Human Rights: Elements of Theory and Practice," in *Global Justice and International Economic Law*, ed. Chi Carmody, Frank Garcia, and John Linarelli (Cambridge: Cambridge University Press, 2012), 27–43.

These critical considerations pose two large and difficult problems for the alternative account proposed here. First, and rather generally, how is it possible to preserve notions of agency and individuality while giving a stronger account of the interdependence of individuals? And second, how is it possible to give a universalist account that nonetheless recognizes varying historical and cultural understandings of human rights? Although these questions are too large to be adequately dealt with in the short frame of this essay, I will point to some directions for their resolution. First, my suggestion will be that an effective constructive account will need to operate with a more open and relational conception of agency than on existing views. And second, it will need to add a conception of what I have called *concrete universality* to the abstractly universal approaches to human rights that have been traditionally advanced as their foundation. The challenge in that connection is to develop a view that gives weight to social practices without making human rights relative to existing, and perhaps pernicious, practices. I suggest that what I have called a "quasi-foundational" social ontological (though not "metaphysical") perspective is best able to mediate between the various desiderata of agency and relationality, and between historicity and normativity. Although I will not be able to fully articulate this basis here, I hope to sketch some of its features as a springboard for further research.

II. Strongly Individualist Accounts of the Basis for Human Rights

One theory that aims to provide a foundation for human rights is that of James Griffin in his *On Human Rights*. Griffin regards his approach as a "bottom up" one, inasmuch as it reflects on human rights as they are conceived in law and society and as they have historically come to be recognized since the Enlightenment. His theory articulates a conception of individual "personhood" as the justificatory core of the human rights idea, and he articulates this in terms of a conception of "normative agency," and as involving autonomy, liberty, and a minimum provision of goods necessary for such agency. The main notion is that persons are agents in having "a conception of a worthwhile life" (which is to be distinguished from having a single "plan of life"). In Griffin's terms, "what we attach value to, in this account of human rights, is specifically our capacity to choose and to pursue our conception of a worthwhile life."[4] He regards such normative agency as typical of adult human beings, and stipulates that children are only potential agents in this sense, while some disabled adults lack even that potential. Thus human rights on his view pertain to normative agents in this rather restrictive sense. Griffin suggests that limiting human rights in this way avoids the indeterminateness that has afflicted alternative accounts of them, as well as their inflation in some recent discourse to cover the entire moral realm. Of course, children and disabled adults have other moral rights, but not human rights (though he acknowledges that children could also plausibly be held to have human rights, although he opts for the view that they lack them).[5]

[4] James Griffin, *On Human Rights* (Oxford: Oxford University Press, 2008), 45.
[5] Griffin, *On Human Rights*, ch. 2.

There are several issues to focus on in Griffin's account. The most obvious one, though not the most central to the theme of this chapter, is his restriction of human rights to a subset of humans (in a way reminiscent of Kant's account of moral personhood). Griffin's exclusionary account strikes me as problematic, since it loses the very force of the notion of the human that makes human rights norms such powerful instruments of social and legal change worldwide (at least potentially, given that this power is far from fully actualized). While it is true that boundary and extension issues inevitably arise with notions of the human, it seems clear that human rights, in their root conception, should pertain to all and only humans. I think we need to take an inclusionary approach such the conception of human rights sees them as fundamentally applying to children and to adults with disabilities, and in short, to all humans from birth to death. It is beyond the scope of this essay to go into the issues surrounding who or what to call potential persons, but I think that Griffin goes astray in regarding children as only potential persons, rather than restricting this latter notion to embryos and fetuses. Even small babies display a sort of agency, though not the rich sense of normative agency that Griffin feels grounds human rights norms, in which such agents must have a "conception of a worthwhile life."

Significant for our purposes, here, is this high-level conception of personhood itself and the interpretation it gives of agency. Any account that builds a notion of "having a conception" into the basic idea of human agency is bound to exclude some humans. Having a conception of a good life is a fairly developed accomplishment. Moreover, the formulation itself seems distinctively liberal individualist in a way that is not obviously cross-cultural.

Yet, in some other important ways, Griffin's account is consonant with the one I gave of agency and human rights in my own *Rethinking Democracy* of 1988.[6] I believe that a comparison of the approaches would be helpful to delineate some important similarities but also differences. My own view of agency and its conditions, I have claimed, is better able than Griffin's to support our attribution of human rights to all humans from birth to death, and also offers a more social account than Griffin's own, as well as one that is more open to the full range of human action and cultural expression. We can note that Griffin's emphasis on the high-level notion of normative agency does enable him to incorporate some of the richness and multiplicity of contemporary human rights norms, which more minimal accounts of agency open to all humans (for example, those emphasizing negative liberty) would seem not to support. Thus because Griffin's approach includes the conditions for people to pursue their conception of the good, it requires not only basic civil and political rights, but also rights to a level of welfare. However, I think there is a better way of keeping human rights open to all humans while at the same time making room for this multiplicity of human rights, including the more demanding ones included in the UDHR.[7] In the course of the subsequent discussion here, I will point to that approach, elaborated in my previous work, including my *Globalizing Democracy and Human Rights* (2004). It

---

[6] Gould, *Rethinking Democracy*, especially chs. 1, 3, and 7.

[7] This is not to say that all those rights are always optimally formulated in the international documents and not open to future reinterpretation or revision.

is an approach that distinguishes basic agency, taken in an open and inclusive sense, from the development or flourishing of this agency, but at the same time ties these two aspects of agency together. Such an account is able to support a useful distinction between basic and nonbasic (though still essential) human rights. I also suggest that this sort of approach enables us to accommodate the important emphasis on both freedom and dignity that pervades the international human rights documents.

My account of agency with its accompanying understanding of human rights is developed most fully in *Rethinking Democracy*, on the basis of a social ontology of what I call "individuals-in-relations," a conception I introduced originally in *Marx's Social Ontology*.[8] This conception of agency appeals to a norm of positive freedom, interpreted in a different way from the notion of positive liberty that liberals like Isaiah Berlin were at pains to criticize. I distinguish a basic sense of agency characteristic of human beings, and consisting in intentionality or choice as a feature of human action, from the exercise of this agency in the development of capacities or the realization of long-term projects or goals. The first sense is not to be taken as restricted to purely conscious or conceptual activity but I suggest is evident in human life activity as a mode or way of being. I characterize the latter sense of agency in terms of a notion of self-development (or self-transformation, in more recent work), which can take both individual and collective forms, and emphasize that such self-transformation is a process that transpires over time. If we say that basic agency involves intentional action or choices, we can see that self-development presupposes this capacity for choosing. However, beyond this, a process of self-development (or "freedom to" and, in this sense, positive freedom) requires that choices be effective and involves also the cultivation of capacities. For this agency to be effective, a set of concrete conditions are needed, including both freedom from constraints on one's choices (including the negative liberties and also freedom from domination), as well as the positive availability of what I have called enabling conditions of action (both material and social).[9] I have suggested that human rights specify these necessary conditions of action. Where these are conditions for any human life activity whatever (for example, security of the person, subsistence, and liberty), we have basic human rights, which presumably should have priority for fulfillment. Beyond this, the essential conditions for fuller flourishing or for self-development constitute the nonbasic, though still important, human rights.[10]

The distinctive advantage of this view, versus that of Griffin, is that the notion of basic agency is open and inclusive whereas his is exclusionary. Inasmuch as choice or intentionality is taken as characteristically human, it applies to humans as a class and thus can more easily support the universality necessary for an adequate conception of human rights. Nonetheless, the account here also emphasizes that this bare capacity of choice is insufficient without the conditions for its exercise. It articulates a richer conception of freedom as self-development or self-transformation of persons (including

---

[8] Gould, *Rethinking Democracy*, especially chs. 1 and 2; Gould, *Marx's Social Ontology*, especially ch. 1.
[9] For a fuller discussion of this distinctive sense of agency and of self-development, including the limits there may be on it, see Gould, *Rethinking Democracy*, especially ch. 1.
[10] My earlier account of human rights as basic and nonbasic was given in Gould, *Rethinking Democracy*, ch. 7, and Gould, *Globalizing Democracy and Human Rights*, especially ch. 1.

the development of capacities and realization of goals), understood as a "normative imperative" posited in free human activity at the more basic level. Griffin, by contrast, is forced to introduce a single, high-level, notion of personhood as the justification for human rights, inasmuch as he sees that many of those rights are rather demanding and involve a complex exercise of capacities. Unfortunately, as we have indicated, Griffin is thereby forced to exclude a large number of humans from having human rights, including not only infants, but also children, as well as many people with disabilities. My account, by contrast, takes the basic conception of human agency as what we recognize when we say that human beings have human rights, but also holds that such agency must be cultivated or elaborated in the course of our lives, which requires a substantial set of conditions.[11] Unlike in Berlin's account, however, these conditions are not just externally necessary for the achievement of freedom, but are integral to this overall conception of positive freedom itself, since human action always operates on such conditions, or takes place within them.

As I have indicated, among these conditions are social requirements of freedom from domination and oppression, as well as the need for recognition and the provision of care, welfare, and education over the course of a life. Thus the account here is able to make room for both traditional civil and political rights, and the newer social, economic, and cultural rights. The requirement for people to be free from constraint supports both liberty and non-domination, while the broader emphasis on freedom in the positive sense goes beyond security of the person as customarily understood to encompass also the newer requirements for what has been called human security. We can suggest too, but without elaborating it here, that these human rights can be construed as conditions for dignity as well, given the close connection between the notion of agency, taken as free in the twofold sense discussed here (namely freedom as the capacity of choice and its development in forms of flourishing) and the understanding of dignity in the human rights documents. The latter goes beyond respect for purposes to an appreciation of the conditions that make people's lives bearable and indeed potentially flourishing.

It is worth noting as well that the distinction between conditions necessary for human life activity in an ongoing manner and those required for its flourishing, including in diverse social and political contexts, helps to clarify how basic human rights apply to all humans in roughly similar ways, while political and social rights can reasonably take more specific forms (as they do in the international documents) and also can vary to a degree in their application in diverse forms of social and cultural organization. Taking human rights to include both primary (basic) and secondary (nonbasic) rights has the further advantage of retaining the highest urgency for the protection and provision of the basic conditions for life and liberty, while also including among the human rights themselves certain important conditions that are often relegated to optional status as merely civil matters, to be decided by particular nation-states. In this way, this approach explicitly seeks to push human rights theory

---

[11] While Griffin is able to recognize a number of demanding human rights as well (though not all of them in the UDHR), my suggestion here has been that he is able to do so so only by positing an overly restrictive basis for human rights, in his account of personhood.

and practice to go beyond a minimalist account and to devise ways of institutionaliz-ing the richer set of rights pointed to in the UDHR and other documents. Yet, the dis-tinction between most urgent rights and other of the human rights also suggests how their fulfillment can proceed in a practicable and effective way.

The central understanding of individuals as interdependent proposed in this approach, that is, understood as individuals-in-relations, leads not only to differences in what are taken to be human rights (that is, in the list of such rights), but also affects the basic justification that can be given of human rights, which here appeals to a norm of equal freedom and the conditions needed for making freedom effective. In this proposed approach to justification, we can see a distinction not only from Griffin's theory, but also from that of Alan Gewirth, to whose approach the view here is similar in some ways (particularly in interpreting rights in terms of the necessary conditions for agency).

In his influential approach to justifying human rights, as presented in his *The Community of Rights* and elsewhere, Gewirth formulates an argument for human rights as moral rights to freedom and well-being, which he thinks each agent must recognize in others on pain of logical inconsistency. Without reviewing the argument in detail, or the various criticisms that have been advanced against it, we can note that Gewirth operates with a conception of people as "prospective purposive agents" who act for goals that they regard as good.[12] He holds that they must claim for them-selves freedom and well-being as necessary conditions of their action. Gewirth fur-ther argues that this "must" supports a claim on the part of agents to their having a right to these conditions. Beginning from this prudential perspective of a single agent, Gewirth believes that we can universalize this claiming in that it is a matter of logi-cal consistency that any other agent, similar in all relevant respects, would equally require these conditions. Gewirth suggests that this universalization yields a moral perspective in which all other human beings also have rights to freedom or well-being, as human rights.

Gewirth tends to think that these rights do not apply to infants or to people who are severely cognitively disabled, which is a problem for his view. Although his account of purposive activity is somewhat less demanding than Griffin's, it nonetheless is more robust than the emphasis on choice or intentional activity as a basis for universal rec-ognition that I suggest. But apart from this, the justification Gewirth offers differs at crucial points from the one I would give. Gewirth has been criticized especially for the transition he makes from "must" in the prudential perspective of the agent in which the agent must (ie, needs to) have freedom and well-being as conditions to the idea that the agent has rights to these conditions in that it is not permissible for others (seemingly a different sense of must) to interfere or that they have duties not to inter-fere.[13] Equally problematic for my purposes is Gewirth's move from the prudential to the moral perspective. That is, universalizing my claiming freedom and well-being as

---

[12] Alan Gewirth, *The Community of Rights* (Chicago: University of Chicago Press, 1998), 16–19.
[13] See James Nickel and David A. Reidy, "Philosophical Foundations of Human Rights" (11 July 2009). Available at http://papers.ssrn.com/sol3/papers.cfm?abstract_id=1432868. See also Jamie Lindsay, "Gewirth's Argument to the Principle of Generic Consistency" (unpublished manuscript).

rights might only amount to the idea that I recognize that others will likewise claim freedom and well-being, but not yet amount to their having a right to those conditions of action.[14]

The account I gave in *Rethinking Democracy* proceeds rather differently. It argues that the moral perspective requires a stronger and pre-existing commitment to the sociality of individuals if the requisite rights are to be generated. It proposes not only that people are agential in the open sense specified earlier but also that they are fundamentally interdependent. The social ontology of individuals-in-relations sees these relations as constitutive of individuals in the sense that they become who they are in and through these relations, to put it in quasi-Hegelian terms. But it crucially differs from holistic social accounts, in which individuals are wholly constituted by their relations or by the community of which they are a part, inasmuch as I locate the power of change as arising from individuals as agents. That is, individuals remain capable of choosing and changing their relations (though often only through collective rather than individual action), but are then formed or constituted by these relations (as well as by previous ones).

In my view, the process of recognizing other human beings as basic agents (ie, recognizing them as manifesting intentional activity) is already a feature of everyday experience. It is evident, for example, in the reciprocity of greetings ("Hello, how are you?" "I'm fine thanks, how are you?") and in such elementary experiences as avoiding bumping into each other on the street (by meeting the other's glance and moving in an appropriate direction), which Goffman called "vehicular interaction." It is also evident in the reciprocity of discourse, as Habermas has emphasized. The basic forms of equality and reciprocity posited in these customary and practical (and most often embodied) interactions, whether verbal or not, are elaborated in other forms of reciprocity, including widespread instrumental ones (for example, "tit for tat," or exchange for mutual benefit), along with more robust social forms of reciprocal respect and the reciprocity involved in group action oriented to shared goals, and ultimately in forms of genuinely mutual aid.[15] I suggest that such stronger forms of recognition of others as equals are previsioned in the elementary practices of everyday life, which involve reciprocally regarding others as agents, at least in the basic sense, that is, as choosers who manifest intentionality in their life activity (but who do so in diverse ways).

Needless to say, elementary experience can also include forms of misrecognition, in which denigrating views of others are often built into our ordinary interactions as well. Thus it is certainly possible to internalize and to manifest attitudes that stereotypically downgrade others or display oppressive attitudes of other sorts. In extreme cases, we can almost convince ourselves that the others are no better than animals or things to dispose of, or more weakly and commonly, are simply instrumental to our purposes. So I do not wish to imply that ordinary experience

---

[14] Nickel and Reidy, "Philosophical Foundations of Human Rights."

[15] Carol C. Gould, "Beyond Causality in the Social Sciences: Reciprocity as a Model of Non-Exploitative Social Relations," in *Epistemology, Methodology and the Social Sciences: Boston Studies in the Philosophy of Science*, Vol. 71, ed. R.S. Cohen and M.W. Wartofsky (Boston and Dordrecht: D. Reidel, 1983), 53–88.

is fully egalitarian by any means. Actual relations of oppression and domination can inform that experience and our modes of perception so that we grasp others as lesser, in very immediate and almost automatic ways. However, it seems to me that the basic idea of recognizing the other as a human being is evident in germ despite that fact. As Hegel early observed in his master–servitude account along somewhat similar lines, the master cannot succeed in subordinating others whom he regards as not fully human in a way that is satisfying (precisely because in their subjugated state they are regarded as lesser and unworthy, and thus incapable of fully recognizing the master as free).[16]

However, beyond the basic recognition of others in ordinary experience, we can come to see that the choice or intentional activity that grounds it is insufficient or ineffective without access to the conditions that support the development of people's various capacities and the realization of longer-term goals, as well as the cultivation of relationships (what I have called positive freedom). Taken without these conditions, choice remains bare or abstract, without consequence. This recognition of the importance of the conditions for effective freedom is not just a rational matter. Instead, in virtue of our interdependence and embodiment, we each necessarily and *ab initio* make social claims on others for the fulfillment of these conditions. As noted, these conditions include recognition itself (and freedom from domination), care, and education, as well as material conditions such as adequate food, shelter, and the means of work. Although the argument would be more complicated, I would suggest that the social claiming could be extended to the ability to participate in matters that concern groups or collectivities and ultimately to political decision making itself.

But what supports the validity of these claims that we make on each other, ie, their moral status as valid claims or rights? My suggestion is that we cannot get to this dimension of rightness by supposing that we reason from what we need as individuals with specific goals at which we aim to what others similarly situated need (seemingly involving an argument by analogy), along Gewirthian lines. This would yield only the observation that others make similar claims rather than that they have valid claims, although the recognition of equal status implied in that argument is an important feature of it and needs to be retained. Moreover, the Gewirthian argument appears to mistakenly suppose that the individual's interests and goals, as well as the conditions for action can be identified in this elaborated form prior to the recognition of other individuals, whereas in fact the individual in this strong sense (which goes beyond bare choice and intentionality) is already socially constituted. Instead, I think we recognize the basic agential power in others, which is equally characteristic of each of them. Beyond basic agency, we can come to recognize that the agency of each is

---

[16] G.W.F. Hegel, *Phenomenology of Spirit*, trans. A.V. Miller (Oxford: Oxford University Press, 1977), 111–19 ("Independence and Dependence of Self-Consciousness: Lordship and Bondage"). For Hegel, the achievement of mutual rather than one-sided recognition was a product of a historical development. In the account in this essay, reciprocal recognition is understood as posited in germ in certain everyday practices, though it remains far from a robust recognition of each as free and is consistent with the prevalence of forms of domination.

inadequate without access to conditions and without the elaboration of social support through systems of mutual aid that we all need and that shape us, whether in particularistic or more universal ways.

The argument for equally valid claims here, ie, prima facie equal rights of access to the conditions (following Feinberg's account of rights as valid claims) therefore involves several features beyond those appealed to in Gewirth's account: (1) the idea that our experience as agents is already normative, that is, endowed with values and value endowing. More precisely, on my view this agential power is a source of value and this agency also affirms itself as valuable in the process of self-transformation or self-development. In this sense, the social ontology pointed to here is already normative. But (2) this creative and valuing agency is also interactive and socially constituted. It is essentially open to others and expresses our need for and dependence on each other. Such interdependence and mutual neediness involve elements of both inter-constitution through processes of recognition and the necessity for collective rather than only individual action for the realization of many aims and goals. (3) The everyday recognition of basic agency as free and thus as equal in a minimal sense is the germ of the elaborated recognition that each must not be dominated or oppressed, if their capacities are to be developed, their goals realized, and their relationships allowed to flourish. Such freedom from domination and the positive freedom to transform ourselves (individually or in common activity with others) involve claims we make on each other both for recognition of our agency and for the positive provision of means of action. (4) Given the importance not only of interdependence but also embodiment, a set of such means or conditions of action, including basic life and liberty and extending to means of subsistence and other social and economic factors, are needed by each and realizable only jointly.

From these various presuppositions, then, we can see that people can be said to make not only claims but also valid claims on others for the fulfillment of the basic conditions of action. This follows from the normative fact of their equal (basic) agency and from the deep features of mutual neediness and embodiment. In contexts in which there is a need to recognize and adjudicate among the various claims that each makes on others, we can recognize that no one has more of a claim on these conditions for action than any other (by virtue of the equality of their basic agency ingredient in their human status) and they each need to be free from domination for self-transformation (individually or collectively). Their sociality signifies that they necessarily depend on each other and are inter-constituting, such that their agency is what it is only in a social context of cooperation (whether implicit or explicit). Inasmuch as they are equally agents, where this agency is valuable and where it operates necessarily through structures of interdependence, no one has a right to dominate others and they equally require access to the conditions of self-transformation, material and social. The value of access to the conditions arises from the value of the free agency as such, which though recognized in germ, that is, in its basic forms, necessarily aims at further transformation and development by way of institutional structures of interdependence (and especially economic and political institutions, at least in modern forms of society), as well as particularistic forms of care.[17] In my view, while the features of agency and interdependence are given in the basic structure of experience and obtain elemental recognition there, in order that these features can come to be widely acknowledged to extend to the broad requirements of universal human rights, historical processes of development are required.

For the various reasons just given, the normativity of equal claims such as is involved in human rights as moral and ultimately as legal rights cannot therefore be derived simply from a first person perspective coupled with a process of reasoning about its universality, as in Gewirth's account. Rather it only seems to be derivable in this way if we abstract from the feature of interdependence, which, like that of free activity, is a fundamental aspect of human action and interaction. Recognizing interdependence, however, does not mean that the power of agency, evident in ordinary experience and developed over time, can be reduced to any particular set of social relations; rather, it is also capable of transforming the very conditions of agency—material and social—though often only jointly with others. (Of course, this is not to say that this transformation is bound to occur, only that it is a possibility or potentiality of human action.) We can observe too that reason plays a role in this recognition of the equal agency of each, as Gewirth emphasizes, but that empathy and solidarity are also important, both as aspects of such processes of recognition, and in the emergence and development of individuality itself.

On the view presented here, then, the equality of agents can be seen to be the reverse side of the critique of domination or oppression. In order to be able to criticize the latter forms, we need the recognition of the value of agency and of its status as a characteristic feature of humans. I have suggested that when human activity is seen as free human activity, as presupposing both intentionality and its elaboration in processes of capacity formation, realizing individual and collective ends, and cultivating relationships, we can find a basis for the critique of misrecognition and of one-sided forms of recognition. However, such equal agency has hardly been overtly acknowledged in any more than the barest and implicit forms. Even in contemporary societies, there is regrettably considerably more oppression, domination, or exploitation, than equal treatment or reciprocal recognition of agency. This raises for us the need to articulate how the relevant human rights norms are related to social and historical practices, and to further develop the social aspects of human rights and more generally the ways they can be said to be relational.

III. Social and Practice-oriented Conceptions of Human Rights

I would like now to briefly turn to the more social account of human rights found in Jürgen Habermas and to the practice-oriented one advanced by Charles Beitz. I want

---

[17] Each recognizes the equality of the others implicitly in perceiving the other human being as a (minimal) agent. This recognition is itself mutual (though barely so), in the features noted in ordinary experience. On this basis, equality can come to be articulated more fully as a value. Thus it should not be framed as a matter of reasoning from one's own case where the fully formed individual agent already recognizes the need for the conditions of agency. It involves also a reflection on the reciprocity and recognition in ordinary experience as well as by seeing the other as an agent. It is grounded, however, in their actually being agents, that is, phenomenologically.

to consider some of the implications of their approaches for the question of the basis of human rights, as well as to take note of the differences of the account proposed here from theirs.

In Habermas's relatively late magnum opus, *Between Facts and Norms*, human rights are given an importance beyond that found in his earlier works.[18] In a way that partly contrasts with the approach here, Habermas conceives of human rights as emerging in the sphere of law rather than morality. I propose instead that human rights as fundamental normative claims of each on others ground human rights as legal rights. But these are not moral rights in Habermas's sense, taken as strictly individualistic duties towards others. Rather, I want to interpret these basic claims in social terms, though still normative ones. In Habermas's conception, while law and politics are capable of being organized normatively in terms of the discourse principle, that legal–political sphere, as including both democracy and rights, is now understood as separate from the moral domain. For Habermas (at least in *Between Facts and Norms*), as in prevailing understandings of human rights, the classic rights of life, liberty, and property pertain to citizens within a democracy, and he sees these rights as coming into being along with popular sovereignty or political autonomy itself. Popular sovereignty, for Habermas, gives his core discourse principle a legally institutionalized form, which is at the same time the "logical genesis of rights."[19] According to Habermas, "This system [of rights] should contain precisely the rights citizens must confer on one another if they want to legitimately regulate their interactions and life contexts by means of positive law." He refers to such rights as "conditions for a discursive exercise of political autonomy."[20]

In this way, for Habermas, human rights hold against nation-states, as in the classical models, though they presumably could be constitutionalized at supranational levels as well. On such an interpretation, however, it is not clear how they can gain a fully universalist dimension as rights of everyone worldwide, which seems to me to be a great strength of this concept, along with their resulting transnational critical dimension. Habermas indicates that the rights will to a degree be specific to each political community. While this allows for some helpful diversity of interpretation and application, it does not explain their transnational or fully cosmopolitan dimension. Clearly, Habermas is concerned to emphasize a postmetaphysical justification for rights, and to eschew any notion of them as natural, or even as necessarily founded in structural features of human action. But given their tie to legality and democracy in his view, it remains unclear what their basis or justification is beyond the requirement that they are required by formal and procedural principles of law and democratic discourse. Habermas's guidance is to say that they arise from "applying the discourse principle to the general right to liberties—a right constitutive of the legal form as such."[21] Inasmuch as they accord with the discourse principle, these rights are understood to arise in a communicative and socially interactive context, and, as

---

[18] Jürgen Habermas, *Between Facts and Norms: Contributions to a Discourse Theory of Law and Democracy,"* trans. William Rehg (Cambridge, MA: MIT Press, 1996), especially ch. 3.
[19] Habermas, *Between Facts and Norms*, 121.   [20] Habermas, *Between Facts and Norms*, 122.
[21] Habermas, *Between Facts and Norms*, 121.

he says, concomitantly with political autonomy, as two sides of the same coin, so to speak. His account is thus a social one, but one in which rights are taken as emerging in post-conventional legal contexts, and pertaining primarily to nation-states. Aside from not doing justice to the cosmopolitan appeal of human rights, this view cannot account for the urgent need to fulfill human rights precisely where states are weakest or even absent.[22]

Like many other theorists, Habermas understands human rights as primarily civil and political rights, which is not surprising given that he sees human rights as tied to political democracy and political autonomy. Partly as a consequence, his view treats economic and social rights as secondary, and they come in as conditions for effective political democracy. This reflects a common, though I think mistaken, view of social and economic rights, as required for the sake of political equality, rather than for fulfilling basic human needs. It is partly to accommodate the latter requirement, now recognized in many countries worldwide, that I think we have to introduce a more general and fundamental conception of human rights.

The sociality of Habermas's view more generally, arises primarily from the way it connects law to the Discourse principle, that is, the principle that "[j]ust those action norms are valid to which all possibly affected persons could agree as participants in rational discourses."[23] What human rights norms protect are both liberties and political rights that are important to citizens within a democratic state and which they can discursively justify to each other, in a way required by their communicative freedom in that context. The conditions of discourse are expressed in historically changing forms, however, rather than being understood as protections of fundamental agency, taken apart from or prior to or other than this discursive context, which Habermas understands here as a specifically legal one. In this way, Habermas's view contrasts with the standard liberal view, which presupposes individual agency as fundamental.

With his emphasis on communication, whether understood in "quasi-transcendental" or in a wholly non-foundationalist fashion, Habermas's view is on the side of those who emphasize the justifications or rational arguments we can give each other to be fundamental.[24] Indeed, Habermas seems to see the rights themselves as emerging in an historical context, and thus capable of a reconstructive account. This contrasts with an account of human rights as conditions for human life activity or agency and as involving centrally the fulfillment of needs, including bodily ones. Habermas's approach also privileges one dimension of social practice and interaction, namely communication and discourse, and delimits that to the legal and political domain. In contrast, I seek to build on more recent expanded interpretations of human rights as centrally including social and economic rights that address our embodied and relational existence. I see their basis not only in discourse, communication, and justification, but in the fundamental social claims we make on each other to cooperate to meet needs and common goals, as well as in our caring relations with each other. In such contexts, we

---

[22] cf Jeffrey Flynn, "Habermas on Human Rights: Law, Morality, and Intercultural Dialogue," *Social Theory and Practice*, 29(3) (July 2003): 431–57.

[23] Habermas, *Between Facts and Norms*, 107.

[24] See also Rainer Forst, "The Justification of Human Rights and the Basic Right to Justification: A Reflexive Approach," *Ethics*, 120(4) (July 2010): 711–40.

recognize each other as agents, but not only as individualized but as socially intercon-
stituting, expressing our mutual dependence.

Despite its great strengths, then, a Habermassian account is limited in the ways
described. I have elsewhere focused on the exclusionary aspects of a view that privileges discourse in this way, and have suggested difficult sorts of circularity that are evident in discursive approaches to justifying norms.[25] An implication for human rights,
however, is that the freedom and equality of participants in discourse (or politics) are
not seen as independently required by their agency but as justified as conditions for
discourse (and more specifically in the context of law). But it is then unsurprising that
the norms that emerge in such discursive contexts would turn out to include the very
freedom and equality already presupposed in discursive practices themselves.

An alternative practice-based account of human rights is advanced by Charles Beitz
in his influential book *The Idea of Human Rights*.[26] Without elaborating his theory
here, we can note that at least relative to the moral individualist views considered
earlier, his account is rather deflationary, and emphasizes the contemporary practice
of human rights enunciation and protection in the context of international relations.
Beitz presents a model of that practice, understanding human rights as the protection
by nation-states of important human interests as a matter of international concern.
The account articulates human rights in terms of the norms ingredient in that practice, with attention focused on the way human rights operate in that international
domain, in a way that is consonant with Rawls' approach if not directly parallel to
his. But there is also, perhaps inevitably, an appeal to notions of fundamental human
interests, which we will presumably agree on cross-culturally, though Beitz seeks to
distance himself from agreement views in the first part of his work, along with giving
criticisms of what he terms naturalistic approaches that elaborate contemporary versions of natural rights theory.[27]

The restriction to contemporary international human rights practice lends the
account specificity but also raises questions concerning whether such an approach can
retain the important critical and normative edge of human rights as fully cosmopolitan norms. Beitz holds that these norms do preserve that edge, as is evident in his discussions of their role as calling for the elimination of global poverty and in requiring
women's human rights. But I suggest that they do so for him by way of his tacit appeal
to notions of fundamental interests and that this is comparable to such appeals in
more foundational approaches to human rights. Moreover, the discussion sometimes
seems simply to posit the priority of contemporary human rights practice and the
norms ingredient in it, in a way similar to Rawls's notion that these are essential elements of global public reason, without constructive arguments as to why they should

[25] See Carol C. Gould, "Democracy and Diversity: Representing Differences," in *Democracy and
Difference: Changing Boundaries of the Political*, ed. S. Benhabib (Princeton: Princeton University Press,
1996), 171–86, and Gould, *Globalizing Democracy and Human Rights*.
[26] Charles Beitz, *The Idea of Human Rights* (Oxford: Oxford University Press, 2009).
[27] For Beitz, agreement views understand human rights as the product of overlapping cultural perspectives and gain their authority from that intercultural agreement. Naturalistic conceptions for him
conceive of human rights as possessed by all humans, simply in virtue of their humanity, rather than as
a matter of legal enactment. Beitz, *The Idea of Human Rights*, 49–50, 73–4.

be taken to have this priority. Certainly, Beitz gives a critique of what he calls naturalistic and agreement views, but it is not clear that the interpretation he gives of those are the strongest existing versions available, particularly of the foundationalist approaches.

In any case, I suggest that the account I propose here is not simply naturalistic in Beitz's terms and certainly does not follow natural rights theory per se. Rather, it aims to combine both given and social understandings of agency and interaction, and also assigns a role to practices, as well as to cross-cultural dialogue. Of course, the practices I draw on are more basic social ones, rather than simply those evident in current international relations and law. I believe that only such a view is capable of guiding the further development of human rights in a way that is relevant to the emerging regionalization in world politics, as well as to controlling the economic forces of globalization in democratic and rights-respecting ways. It remains unclear to me how an analysis of the norms of contemporary practice can have this sort of critical role (beyond holding those who have already subscribed to them to account for these norms). Moreover, it is not clear how, despite its strengths in modeling contemporary practice, such an account can escape a problematic historicism in regard to norms and be able to succeed in providing guidance for future development of either the human rights conception generally or more specific concepts of human rights that articulate features of fundamental human interests.

IV. The Universality of Human Rights

I have questioned whether either of these social or practice-oriented conceptions is able to give sufficient weight to human rights as fundamental protections of individuals. We need an adequate basis for regarding human rights as more than contingent or relative to a given time and place. And we should have reason to expect that human rights will retain their importance even if states became transformed into less state-like entitles, such that these rights give us legitimate claims on others in a more cosmopolitan framework. Thus they cannot be only protections given by our citizenship or our political community, but more fundamentally call on us to devise institutions that may serve to realize them, whether those institutions take the form of states or not.

The question is, then, how an account can be adequately historical and attentive to divergent contexts of practice and the emergence of norms, without at the same time being historicist, such that these norms would be conceived as relative to time and place. As we have seen, this historicism can be a problem for views that place exclusive emphasis on practices, to the degree that they are limited to holding a given practice to the norms implicit in it. Alternatively, procedural approaches to norm discovery may covertly introduce those very norms or values into the process itself and thereby rather too easily achieve the universal range they aspire to. I have suggested that this problem can afflict counterfactual strategies that propose to rely on what people would agree to under ideal conditions, inasmuch as conditions of freedom and equality are implicitly built into these procedures from the beginning. In such cases, it is unsurprising that the same values of freedom and equality become aspects of the norms agreed to under such conditions.[28]

---

[28] See also Gould, *Globalizing Democracy and Human Rights*, ch. 1.

I have instead proposed an explicitly normative basis for human rights, under-standing it as having two interrelated elements—(equal) agency and its elaboration or development, the first referring to a capacity serving as a condition for the second. While agency as a basic existential capacity or power is implicitly recognized in ordinary interaction, it does not merely exist to the degree that it is recognized. As a capacity for change and self-transformation, it is manifest in the intentionality of human action and in our concrete ways of being in the world. Yet, as inseparable from ongoing processes of human life activity, such agency is partly constituted by previous social relations, and by ongoing contexts of shared meanings and practices, which are appropriated and elaborated subsequently in new ways, through concrete responsive and collective relations with others. This agency-in-relations, moreover, develops over time, both in the life of an individual and of a collectivity or cultural group. As a capacity for freedom-in-interdependence with others, such agency may also come to be explicitly recognized in its normative importance in the course of historical development. Its more concrete elaboration in processes of capacity formation and realization of long-term projects can also come to be acknowledged as important aspects of really effective freedom.

The proposed approach, then, has a quasi-transcendental or indeed quasi-foundationalist aspect in its reliance on a norm of equal agency (or more fully equal positive freedom). But the analysis also gives considerable weight to specific social relations as they emerge historically, and particularly the overcoming of relations of domination and exploitation, which in turn enable the fuller and more inclusive recognition of agency. The account thus differs from traditional liberal or transcendental ones in not supposing that agency even as a capacity or mode of being is complete *ab initio*. With historical accounts, it acknowledges the relevance of the method of rational reconstruction of the conditions of emergence of these broader and more universalistic capacities. But I suggest it is not helpful to construe this in terms of what people would counterfactually agree to under ideal circumstances, since the latter does not in my view carry sufficient normative weight, or else it simply tacitly presupposes these very norms of freedom and equality. Such counterfactual approaches are in one sense, then, not normative enough, while in another sense they are too normative. They are not normative enough if they are limited to making a kind of prediction about what people would agree to, or else they are too normative in tacitly appealing to the very norms that are supposed to emerge through the relevant processes of dialogue and discourse. The account given here can, I think, more adequately explain why people should agree to recognize the agency of others and correlatively their human rights, without simply embedding this recognition in processes of interaction or of historical development. Nonetheless, this should also not be taken as traditionally deontological, but is instead based on what I have characterized as an experientially-based normative social ontology.

In this perspective, human rights are emergent in regard to their explicit normative status but should not be reduced to, or seen as merely relative to, existing forms of social life, or to particular stages of social and historical development. The approach attempts to go beyond the abstract universalism of liberalism (or indeed of natural rights conceptions) while avoiding an excessive historicization by making use of the additional notion of *concrete universality*.[29] This conception involves the notion that particular forms of social relations are not merely accidental to individuals as human agents. Instead, it sees individuals as in part constituted by these relations, whether egalitarian ones of reciprocal recognition, or else one-sided relations of oppression, domination or misrecognition. This concrete universality can be usefully tied to what Marx characterized as a historical process of cultivating a many-sided individuality, one that is multiply related to others within particular structurally important forms of relationships and institutions (particularly economic ones).[30] For Marx in the *Grundrisse*, this is a matter of the emergence of a multi-dimensional personality, which is universal in the sense of being open to multiple and wide interactions and constituted by a plethora of such diverse interactions, which Marx sees as for the most part supplanting abstractly universal notions of the human. But while Marx at times conceives of the person simply as the node of a set of relations, in a way comparable to contemporary intersectional analyses, I think it is important to recognize that individuals have the power of agency, whether individually or more often jointly with others, such that they can (at least sometimes) change the conditions of their action, as well as in some ways their agency itself.

Thus, my own view departs from that of Marx in attempting to articulate more fully than he does the relation between an open conception of agency as characteristic of each individual and this universalizing multi-sidedness of persons and their relations, which develops over time. In Marx's trenchant analysis, such elaboration is facilitated by the emergence of a world market along with extensive trading relations, and by an economy that breaks down barriers, in the first instance through capitalist processes themselves. More generally, I think it useful to clarify the role of abstractly universal norms in the context of these constitutive social relations and to more fully consider how such concrete universality is related to those abstract norms. Clearly, the abstractly universal norms have an important critical dimension of their own in positing the equality and universality of individuals as a basis for assessing as deficient the one-sided relations of domination that prevent people from realizing their freedom. But the necessary supplement is a notion of the many-sidedness of the relations that makes it possible for people to become fully aware of these norms and to articulate their ramifications over time. (This many-sidedness can also be seen as part of the notion of positive freedom itself, to the extent that it is understood as a process of the development or flourishing of agency over time.)

The implication for understanding human rights is that they too need to be taken in their concrete elaborations and interpretations across cultures and contexts, and not only as abstractly universal norms. This elaboration involves not only discursive processes of articulating and agreeing to the norms but also concrete constructions of fuller realizations of it, on the ground as it were. This occurs through the cultivation of

---

[29] I introduced this concept, drawing on a notion of it in Hegel, in Carol C. Gould, "The Woman Question: Philosophy of Liberation and the Liberation of Philosophy," *The Philosophical Forum*, V(1–2) (Fall–Winter, 1973–74): 5–44, reprinted in *Women and Philosophy: Toward a Theory of Liberation*, ed. Carol C. Gould and Marx W. Wartofsky (New York: G.P. Putnam's Sons, 1976). I subsequently discussed it at some length in Gould, *Globalizing Democracy and Human Rights*, ch. 2.

[30] Gould, *Marx's Social Ontology*, particularly ch. 1.

specific (many-sided) relationships, for example, of solidarity both within nations and across borders and also through institutional innovation and development. Thus the relevant universality of agency is recognized in germ but only implicitly in basic social practices of reciprocity and it comes to be explicitly acknowledged only as a result of a process of development that can take more inclusive forms over time (though there is no necessity to this). Wider interactions in practice actually serve to construct the conditions for these norms to come to be recognized as fully universal. So the process of this concrete and differentiated universalizing presupposes the form of agency and the implicit reciprocity which supports the abstractly universal norm but practical processes are also conditions for its coming to be recognized more fully as a norm. It is the openness and multi-sidedness of the agency itself and its differentiation that makes possible such norm recognition.

The notion of concrete universality also ties in with the account of sociality as discussed earlier in this chapter. The suggestion was that human rights have a double basis—(1) in agency, understood as a creative power of self-transformation, taken both in individualistic and social forms; and (2) in interdependence as constitutive of this agency, in that the choices and intentions operate in and through a set of given social conditions and relations. Thus, people are not understood as *using* social cooperation in order to meet independently identified goals and aims, but instead their action presupposes cooperative contexts and their self-understandings are already informed by interdependent relations with others. Power is still identified with agency—whether individual or collective—but the context and the form of the agency, as well as the conditions needed to realize projects and develop capacities, are all social. So the idea of human rights as claims potentially on everyone for supporting institutions that can fulfill them can be understood as an expression and generalization of this fundamental interdependence and of the basic claims that we make on each other for the realization of our needs. This is clear in the case of our early claims on those close to us, especially members of our own families, but there is no principled restriction of such social claims to that context. Yet, it would be impractical for all others, including those at a distance, to have to realize our particular needs (and we theirs) and it seems clear that no one can be expected to do so without the intermediation of institutions. Rather, I suggest that human rights are valid claims on others to work to create the institutions that will enable us and others to fulfill human rights. It is in the first place a claim on each other to create relevant structures that will function effectively to fulfill these rights, basic and (eventually) nonbasic.

V. Human Rights and the Conditions for Agency

I have suggested that human rights are justified in terms of their connection to (positive) freedom as a norm ingredient in agency and are understood as specifying the most salient conditions for such agency, including basic and nonbasic conditions. These conditions include both negative ones that require freedom from interference, as well as positive or enabling ones. In these ways, these rights are responsive to both embodiment and sociality, and also presuppose some form of political community with others.

Inasmuch as the agents in question are understood to exist substantially in nature and need to interact with it for their continued existence, economic human rights and especially the right to means of subsistence and to security of the person take on major importance. (Needless to say, to recognize the relevance of material needs in this way does not mean that these very needs are not also socially interpreted and constructed.) Other salient conditions for agency are given in the traditional liberal rights that protect individuals from interference by the government or other authorities. But the view here goes beyond such an emphasis on negative liberty or freedom from interference to call attention to the requirement of freedom from domination or exploitation, omitted from these traditional accounts. It also goes beyond all those negative freedoms to propose the importance of enabling conditions for effective freedom, for example, education, health care, welfare, rights to work, etc., themselves specified in other human rights.

To understand such rights as providing for the conditions for both basic and developed forms of agency is distinct from emphasizing the provision of primary goods or even of resources for goal fulfillment. In a way similar to capabilities approaches, the notion of conditions for action is understood in terms of a conception of development or effective freedom. But unlike some capabilities approaches, the relevant notion of equal positive freedom here eschews any lists of essential capabilities or of functionings. Instead, it makes room only for lists of human rights themselves, and even there it sees them as provisional. Although rights specify necessary conditions of agency, they nonetheless can be variably used and need to be understood in a way consistent with the open conception of freedom advocated earlier. Moreover, the list of human rights can be thought of as somewhat variable for different social and historical contexts, though the basic rights, as conditions for any human life activity whatever, are likely to be relatively stable through time, although subject to different interpretations and elaborations.

Since such lists of basic and nonbasic (though still important) human rights pertain to conditions rather than actual functionings or even exclusively to capabilities, they avoid essentialism as well as the potentially ideological aspect of lists. And although lists of capabilities have certainly proved helpful for assessing a country's (or society's) development, it is not plausible to claim that such lists are definitive for all human development through all time. Lists of human rights, by contrast, somewhat more modestly address not agency itself but its conditions, which can be variably used or appropriated. Thus, the role of ideological bias or one-sidedness is minimized, though probably not eliminated. Further, such lists of human rights are best understood as provisional and as articulated through cross-cultural dialogue. This does not undermine their fundamental character, however, since they are rooted in the features of agency, interdependence, and embodiment. Yet, as conditions, they go beyond abstract goods and resources, in gaining their significance from the uses that people can make of them (a feature also emphasized in capabilities and other positive freedom approaches). In this way, such human rights should be understood as speaking to our shared needs and our potentials for cultivating fuller freedom, both individually and collectively.

10

Human Rights, Human Dignity, and Power

Pablo Gilabert

I. Introduction

This chapter explores the connections between human rights, human dignity, and power. The idea of human dignity is omnipresent in human rights discourse, but its meaning and point is not always clear. It is standardly used in two ways, to refer to (a) a normative status of persons that makes their treatment in terms of human rights a proper response, and (b) a social condition of persons in which their human rights are fulfilled. This chapter pursues three tasks. First, it provides an analysis of the content and an interpretation of the role of the idea of human dignity in current human rights discourse. The interpretation includes a pluralist view of human interests and dignity that avoids a narrow focus on rational agency. Second, this chapter characterizes the two aspects of human dignity in terms of capabilities. Certain general human capabilities are among the facts that ground status-dignity, and the presence of certain more specific capabilities constitutes condition-dignity. Finally, this chapter explores how the pursuit of human rights and human dignity links to distributions and uses of power. Since capabilities are a form of power, and human rights are in part aimed at respecting and promoting capabilities, human rights involve empowerment. Exploring the connections between human rights, capabilities, and empowerment provides resources to defend controversial human rights such as the right to democratic political participation, and to respond to worries about the feasibility of their fulfillment. This chapter also argues that empowerment must be coupled with solidaristic concern in order to respond to unavoidable facts of social dependency and vulnerability. A concluding section identifies some commonalities and differences with the approach to the ontological underpinnings of human rights presented by Carol Gould in her contribution to this volume.

II. Analysis of Uses of "Human Dignity" in the Main Human Rights Documents

A. A brief survey

I focus here on the idea of human dignity in the specific context of human rights practice.[1] A natural starting point for our exploration is the main human rights documents. Their inspection reveals at least eleven points about the use of the idea human dignity.

---

[1] For broader historical explorations see George Kateb, *Human Dignity* (Cambridge, MA: Harvard University Press, 2011) and Michael Rosen, *Dignity* (Cambridge, MA: Harvard University Press, 2012).

(i) Some utterances seem to refer to human dignity as an inherent property of human beings, a status they constantly have rather than one they can achieve. (a) The first sentence of the preamble of the Universal Declaration of Human Rights (UDHR) refers to the "inherent dignity...of all the members of the human family." (b) The fifth sentence expresses "faith...in the dignity and worth of the human person." (c) Article 1 says that "[a]ll human beings are born free and equal in dignity and rights." (d) The second and third sentences of the preambles of both the International Covenant on Economic, Social and Cultural Rights (ICESCR) and the International Covenant on Civil and Political Rights (ICCPR) also refer to human persons' "inherent dignity." The expression also occurs in the first clause of Article 10 of ICCPR and in the first sentence of Article 20 of the Vienna Declaration.

(ii) A statement appears to tell us something about the features in virtue of which human persons have human dignity in the sense referred to in (i): "All human beings are born free and equal in dignity and rights. They are endowed with reason and conscience and should act towards one another in a spirit of brotherhood" (UDHR, Article 1).

(iii) We are told that human rights are "derived" from human dignity. (a) The third sentence of the preamble of both ICCPR and ICESCR refer to the recognition "that these rights derive from the inherent dignity of the human person." (b) The third sentence of the preamble of the Vienna Declaration claims that "all human rights derive from the dignity and worth inherent in the human person."

(iv) Some statements appear to refer to dignity as a more contingent condition or state that human beings may come to enjoy (and this includes certain treatment of them by others). This sense is different from the one considered so far. Examples include reference (a) to "economic, social and cultural rights as indispensable for [persons'] dignity and the free development of [their] personality" (UDHR, Article 22); (b) to "just and favourable remuneration" from work "ensuring for [the worker and their] family an existence worthy of human dignity" (UDHR, Article 23, third clause); (c) to education as being "directed to the full development of the human personality and the sense of its dignity" (ICESCR, Article 13, first clause); and (d) to seeking a treatment of refugees that involves "durable solutions, primarily through the preferred solution of dignified and safe voluntary repatriation" (Vienna Declaration, Article 23, third paragraph).

(v) Some references to dignity seem ambiguous between the senses mentioned in (i) and (iv). An example is the claim that "one of the most atrocious violations against human dignity is the act of torture, the result of which destroys the dignity and impairs the capability of victims to continue their lives and their abilities" (Vienna Declaration, Article 55).

(vi) Some statements intimate a connection between dignity, rights, and social and political power:

  (a) "[A]ll human rights derive from the dignity and worth inherent in the human person, and...the human person is the central subject of human rights and fundamental freedoms, and consequently should be the principal beneficiary and should participate actively in the realization of these rights and freedoms" (Vienna Declaration, Preamble, third sentence).

(b) "[E]xtreme poverty and social exclusion constitute a violation of human dignity and … urgent steps are necessary to achieve better knowledge of extreme poverty and its causes, including those related to the problem of development, in order to promote the human rights of the poorest, and to put an end to extreme poverty and social exclusion and to promote the enjoyment of the fruits of social progress. It is essential for States to foster participation by the poorest people in the decision-making process by the community in which they live, the promotion of human rights and the efforts to combat extreme poverty" (Vienna Declaration, Article 25).

(c) "Men and women have the right to live their lives and raise their children in dignity, free from hunger and from the fear of violence, oppression and injustice. Democratic participatory governance based on the will of the people best assures these rights" (UN Millennium Declaration, Article 6).

(vii) Dignity seems in most cases to be primarily a predicate that applies to individuals. (See, for example, (vi.a)). However, it occasionally appears to apply to collectives. An example includes indigenous people in Article 20 of the Vienna Declaration.

(viii) Some statements emphasize the global scope of the duties to respond to human rights deprivations. Thus (a) the UN Millennium Declaration, in its Article 2, says that "in addition to our separate responsibilities to our individual societies, we have a collective responsibility to uphold the principles of human dignity, equality, and equity at the global level." (b) The global scope of duties correlative to human rights (and thus to human dignity) is a clear corollary of UDHR, Article 28, according to which "[e]veryone is entitled to a social and international order in which the rights and freedoms set forth in this Declaration can be fully realized."

(ix) Not only are some duties correlative to human rights (and thus to human dignity) global in scope (as mentioned in (viii)). Some human rights documents emphasize that also the site of action and responsibility is quite wide, including not only state institutions. (a) A striking example is the Convention for the Elimination of all Forms of Discrimination Against Women (CEDAW), whose claims range over "the political, economic, cultural, civil or any other field" (Article 1). (b) Rene Cassin, one of the drafters of the UDHR, insisted that the duties of individuals and institutions below and above the state are crucial.[2] (c) In its preamble, the UDHR's intention is presented as "a common standard of achievement for all peoples and all nations, to the end that every individual

---

[2] See Mary Glendon, *A World Made New: Eleanor Roosevelt and the Universal Declaration of Human Rights* (New York: Random House, 2001), 93, 113–14. This is why Cassin proposed, just before its adoption, that the title of the Declaration be changed to "Universal Declaration of Human Rights" from "International Declaration of Human Rights." Glendon explains: "The title 'Universal' [Cassin…] later

and every organ of society... shall strive by teaching and education to promote respect for these rights and freedoms and by progressive measures, national and international, to secure their universal and effective recognition and observance."

(x) "Children" are said to be within the scope of dignitarian principles. The text cited in (viii.a) continues: "[W]e have a duty...to all of the world's people, especially to the most vulnerable and, in particular, the children of the world."

(xi) It is important, when we think about human dignity as a status in the sense mentioned in (i), that this status differs from other, specific social statuses. "Everyone is entitled to all the rights and freedoms set forth in this Declaration without distinctions of any kind, such as race, colour, sex, language, religion, political or other opinion, national or social origin, property, birth or other status" (UDHR, Article 2).

B. Conceptual elements and substantive questions

The conceptual structure of the use of the idea of human dignity in human rights discourse surveyed in the previous section is not immediately transparent. But an analysis of it reveals some elements and connections. The elements are the following:

- Human persons' more or less general, constant, or permanent features. (Examples include persons' conscience, reason, and capacity to act in a spirit of brotherhood—see (ii) and (xi).)[3]

- Human persons' human dignity as an inherent property. Let us call this *status-dignity* (see (i)).[4]

- Human persons' various human rights.

- Human persons' condition in which human rights are fulfilled. Let us call this *condition-dignity* (see (iv)).

---

wrote, meant that the Declaration was morally binding on everyone, not only on the governments that voted for its adoption. The Universal Declaration...was not an 'international' or 'intergovernmental' document; it was addressed to all humanity and founded on a unified conception of the human being" (161).

[3] The capacity to act in a spirit of brotherhood must be assumed to exist by the text referred to in (ii), since it says that people "should" act in that spirit, and should, like ought, implies can.

[4] The general idea of dignity as a normative status is that dignity grounds certain kinds of treatment toward those who have it. If X has dignity, then any other person Y ought to treat X in certain respectful and helpful ways. (On the last point see Derek Parfit, *On What Matters*, vol. 1 (Oxford: Oxford University Press, 2011), 241). Furthermore, in our context of discussion, if X has dignity, then X is *entitled* to certain forms of treatment by Y. The relevant forms of treatment owed to X by Y, and the recognition of rights to that treatment, would be a proper response to X's dignity. Now, if X has dignity, then X has some features F such that any other agent Y ought to respond to X-who-has-F by treating X in certain respectful and helpful ways. The appropriate forms of respect and help, and their correlative rights, depend in part on the content of F. Different kinds of dignity depend on the features F that X has and that ground certain proper normative responses (thus, human dignity is broader than the "dignity of office" of a magistrate, since the former depends on general facts about human beings and the latter depends on a specific institutional status—see (xi) in section II.A). In sum, if X has F, then X has status-dignity, which in turn helps ground some of X's rights and some of Y's duties towards X.

- Human persons' duties towards others concerning the fulfillment of their human rights (and thus their dignity in the two senses). (See (viii) and (ix).)
- Human persons' power to control the political process and other aspects of their social life that affect the fulfillment of their human rights. (See (vi).)

How are these elements related? The basic links seem to me to be the following:

1. Human persons have status-dignity in virtue of some of their more or less general, constant, or permanent features.

2. Human persons have human rights because they have status-dignity. (See (iii).)

3. Human rights are those rights the fulfillment of which secures that human persons enjoy a dignified life (condition-dignity).

4. Human persons have duties to respect, protect, and promote the fulfillment of those rights. Such duties may have a wide scope and site.

5. To secure the fulfillment of human rights, human persons require access to various forms of power, and thus they have a right to that access. Some forms of power may be instrumentally significant (to achieve and retain condition-dignity). And some forms of power may be intrinsically significant (their recognition may involve a recognition of capacities that give rise to status-dignity).

I have proposed an analysis of the use of the idea of human dignity in some of the most important documents in human rights discourse. Now, this analysis prompts a set of substantive interpretive questions. What are the features of human beings that give rise to status-dignity? What does that status consist in? How does that status support the existence of various human rights? How are duties to properly respond to status-dignity (by contributing to furthering condition-dignity) to be articulated? What forms of power are instrumentally or intrinsically significant for an account of human dignity and human rights? In the remainder of this chapter I address these questions about how to understand human dignity in human rights practice.

III. Developing a Proposal about How to Understand Human Dignity

A. The role of the idea of human dignity in human rights discourse and practice

How should we develop an account of human dignity? In this section I suggest a general interpretive strategy (III.A), and address the question of the extent to which we should expect the idea of human dignity to be a key for our understanding and justification of human rights (III.B). In the next section I will propose a partial deployment of this strategy.

To make headway in determining what to think about human dignity in the practice of human rights we could ask: What is the role, or point, of invoking the idea of human dignity in the practice of human rights? The content of the idea depends on its function within the practice in which it operates. So, to understand human dignity, we must have a view of what the use of the concept is to accomplish within human rights practice. But before answering this question, we should notice that it could be construed in different ways. I will construe it in terms of what we may call a *deliberative interpretive proposal*, which I see as different both from an *elucidation* and a *stipulation*. An elucidation of a concept within a practice is a description of how agents who participate in the practice understand it. A stipulation of a concept is a recommendation that participants in the practice use it, regardless of whether they have done it already. A deliberative interpretive proposal falls somewhere in between. Like a stipulation and unlike an elucidation, its aim is not fundamentally descriptive. Its aim is deliberative in the sense that it seeks an answer to a question of the form "How am I *to* conceive of human dignity in human rights practice?" This question differs from the elucidatory question "How did, or have, I conceived of human dignity in human rights practice?" A deliberative proposal may recommend an understanding of human dignity that differs significantly from previous or current understandings, and it involves an ethical assessment of the practice. But although it is a proposal, it is not a mere stipulation. Its justification may require some continuity with the previous forms of the practice within whose continuation it is to play a role. It involves an interpretation of the practice, a view of what it has been and how it could be developed. To forestall misunderstandings, I do not say that the interpretation of the practice assumes that it is valuable. The result of the deliberative assessment may well be that the practice must be abandoned altogether. But if the practice is worthy of continuation, then one's understanding of the key normative ideas in it should take into account the valuable materials it itself provides. This is the case with the human rights practice (as opposed to, say, the practice of slavery).[5] When asking how this practice should be shaped from now on, a deliberative interpretive proposal is appropriate. A merely elucidatory answer would risk being unduly conservative, and a merely stipulative answer might turn out to be irrelevant to the practice, or involve a change of subject we would regret.

Now, what desiderata should we have in mind when developing a deliberative interpretive proposal regarding the normative idea of human dignity in human rights practice? In general, we should seek a deliberative reflective equilibrium in which our understanding of human dignity fits well within the set of claims we have reason to make about the content and justification of human rights.[6] I think that at least four desiderata should play a role in this search. First, as we saw, we should seek some level of continuity with the practice if it is valuable. In this chapter I try to honor this desideratum by starting with a survey of the uses of the idea of human dignity in human rights practice (see III.B, and the next paragraph). Second, we should make proposals whose content has intrinsic ethical appeal. As I will go on to argue in the

---

[5] Notice, however, that the normativity of the values on which the ethical assessment of the practice relies does not depend on their having been operative, or accepted in the practice. My account of deliberative interpretive proposals is in some way similar to the "constructive interpretation" approach to practices and normative concepts that Ronald Dworkin proposes in *Law's Empire* (Cambridge, MA: Harvard University Press, 1986), ch. 2. However, I do not simply adopt that approach because it is not fully clear to me how description and evaluation of a practice operate within it. I think it is important to distinguish the questions "What is this practice like?" and "What should this practice be like?" even if they are related.

[6] On deliberative reflective equilibrium see T.M. Scanlon, "Rawls and Justification," in *The Cambridge Companion to Rawls*, ed. S. Freeman (Cambridge: Cambridge University Press, 2003), 139–67.

reminder of this chapter, human dignity should be used to pick out significant values in social life, and to help us articulate and defend morally appropriate responses to them. The practice of human rights is worth pursuing largely because, and to the extent that, it is framed in some such ethically desirable way. Third, and obviously, our proposal should offer a concept that is not intolerably indeterminate. Finally, our proposal should have justificatory power. Our account of human dignity should help us formulate and defend the human rights we have reason to accept.

Let us return to the role of human dignity in human rights practice. We can take our cue from how the idea has operated since the drafting of the UDHR. It has been referred to as perhaps the central substantive normative idea of the human rights project. More specifically, human dignity has been invoked as a shareable normative idea whose role is to help ground and give unity to the human rights project in the face of deep disagreement about fundamental metaphysical and moral principles amongst its supporters.[7] The idea of human dignity is thus architectonic to the practice, and responds to important needs within it. We need an idea that carries compelling moral force, can help us explain what is distinctive and valuable about the human rights practice, and can help us argue about various human rights. We also need that idea to provide a common ground even if different people in turn defend it in different ways on the basis of more fundamental principles that are not shared. (This constitutes the best realistic hope in a world of deep cultural, religious, and moral diversity.) The answer to our original question about the role of human dignity could preserve this role, and be mindful of the circumstances (regarding moral importance and disagreement) that surround it.

We could then develop an understanding of human dignity that captures the basis of human rights, their great importance, and the fact that disagreement on deeper levels of justification exists and is likely to remain. In formulating a more determinate idea, we would do well to signpost both areas of (existing or likely) agreement and disagreement about it. This means that, often, the idea of human dignity will mark a terrain of argument and bounded disagreement. The latter is not futile. Human rights are an *ongoing* project, and greater levels of agreement may be achieved in the future.[8] By identifying areas of disagreement we care about as focal points of debate, we express to each other that we are committed to pursuing the project.

This idea of a terrain of argument is important in defusing the common worry that there is too much disagreement about the idea of human dignity for it be of good use. First, notice that the same could be said about equality and liberty, which we rightly do not think should be dropped from our debates about social justice. These ideas do important justificatory work, which we need to do if our more specific claims are to be better than mere assertion. And dropping them will not solve our disagreements, which are likely to infect any other justificatory ideas we choose to use as substitutes. We do better by taking them as marking important areas of debate in which

---

[7] Christopher McCrudden, "Human Dignity and Judicial Interpretation of Human Rights," *European Journal of International Law*, 19 (2008): 655–724, 675–8; Glendon, *A World Made New*, 146.

[8] Charles Beitz helpfully characterizes the human rights practice as "emergent." Beitz, *The Idea of Human Rights* (Oxford: Oxford University Press, 2009), section 7.

it makes sense to engage. Second, we can recognize that since there is disagreement about deeper moral foundations, whatever agreement about human dignity we reach may be incomplete. For example, a Kantian and a Catholic may agree that human dignity is very important, and that it helps justify human rights. But since they disagree on whether human dignity as a normative status concept applies to beings that are not rational agents (such as a severely cognitively impaired individual or a human fetus), they might disagree on whether (or how) human rights doctrine concerning condition-dignity applies to them. We should acknowledge that this kind of disagreement exists and should not seek to eliminate it by definitional fiat.

B. Human dignity and a broad view of human interests

The idea of human dignity is key to understanding human rights, their basis, and content. An account of human dignity should point us to certain features of human beings that give rise to their status-dignity and are significant in justifying human rights (the fulfillment of which constitutes condition-dignity). But is the idea of human dignity a partial or a systematic key? It would be a systematic key if it is necessary for the justification of all human rights, and it would be a partial key if it is a contributory resource for justifying some but not all human rights. If we think that the former is the correct answer, a question arises about the relation between two common ways of understanding human rights: (a) as flowing from the importance of human dignity; and (b) as flowing from the importance of certain human interests. (a) and (b) might converge on the list of human rights that are justified. If this is so, then the two approaches would be extensionally equivalent, and differences in intension might not, perhaps, be very important. But if (a) and (b) have different implications as to which rights are justified, then we must choose. But what should we prioritize in that choice? Should we preserve the rights that are not justified by one view and invoke the justification of them provided by the other? Or should we preserve the preferred basis of justification and see the alleged rights that do not flow from it as not being human rights?

A way in which we may seek convergence between (a) and (b) is by saying that the former works through the latter: if persons have human dignity, they have human rights whose content involves the protection of their urgent human interests. I favor this approach. But given two common understandings of (a) and (b), this strategy may not seem to work. The features that give rise to status-dignity may not comprise all that is needed to capture some intuitively important human interests. For example, if we think, as many do, that what gives rise to human dignity is human beings' capacity for rational agency, [9] then we will not include some obvious sources of urgent human interests such as the capacity to feel pain. The mismatch seems to arise as follows: when we identify important human interests, we look for normatively relevant general features of human beings without regard as to whether some of these features are also held by

---

[9] See, eg, James Griffin, *On Human Rights* (Oxford: Oxford University Press, 2008). Griffin focuses on the "the capacity to choose and to pursue our conception of a worthwhile life" (calling it "normative agency") (45). For a more pluralist view that captures dignity in terms of various basic claims, see James Nickel, *Making Sense of Human Rights*, 2nd edn. (Oxford: Blackwell, 2007), ch. 4.

other beings, for example non-human animals; in contrast, when we identify human dignity, we look for general features of human beings that differentiate them in normatively significant ways from other beings such as non-human animals.[10] I worry that if we understand human dignity in the way stated in the previous sentence, and we decide to base the justification of human rights on it, we will be left with a less pluralistic evaluative view of human interests than that sentence refers to: the focus would be not on the urgent interests that *all* (or *most*) humans have, but on the subset of them that *only* humans have. We will then be unable to refer to obviously important interests such as avoiding pain when justifying human rights. This is too restrictive.

There are two ways to avoid the unduly restrictive conclusion. One is to construe human dignity as a partial rather than as a systematic key for the articulation of human rights. But this construal would clash with the common view within human rights practice that human rights must be justified by reference to human dignity (see (iii) in section II.A). So we should see whether a less revisionary option is available.[11] One such option would be to find a plausible account of human dignity that is broader than the one mentioned in the previous paragraph. A proposal I favor is the view that a significant basis of humans' status-dignity is a set of very important human capabilities. These capabilities ground interests in the opportunities and abilities to maintain, develop, and exercise them. I will develop this capabilitarian picture in section IV. For now, it is important that the set of important capabilities is plural and broad: it does not only include capabilities for rational (prudential and moral) agency, but also other capabilities, such as to feel pain and pleasure. The latter are important, for example, in a straightforward articulation of some rights to bodily integrity and health care.

Now consider the worry (which may be part of what motivates narrow conceptions of human dignity)[12] that this account, by including the capabilities to feel pain and pleasure, will make us unable to identify specifically human rights. The account will yield rights that some non-human animals would also have. It would be better, in an account

---

[10] Is this true? Presumably, Kantians could think that rationality is something that human beings and other beings, eg, intelligent beings in other planets, could hold. They might just think that as a matter of fact, non-human animals on earth don't have rationality. But that strategy would not be premised on the goal of finding what is distinctive about human beings (which is what I am considering here). It starts with the value of rationality, and then claims that human beings (and any other beings that are rational) qualify as having dignity. In this paragraph I am not discussing that strategy. I find it problematic for the different reason that it has a narrow account of the sources of dignity. I turn to the need for a broader account in the rest of this subsection. I thank Matthew Liao for discussion on this point.

[11] What I proceed to suggest may not succeed at positioning human dignity as a systematic rather than as a partial key for the articulation of human rights. This failure may not affect the proposal regarding the relations between human rights, human dignity, and power that I outline in section IV, which is explicitly presented as partial.

A way to make the view of human dignity as a systematic key less vulnerable is to interpret the common claim that human rights are derived from human dignity as saying that every justification of a human right must draw on human dignity, even if they need not draw *only* on it. Human dignity would then be an idea that is pervasive without being exhaustive: it should figure in all justifications, but not as the only key component. Other values (perhaps different for different rights) might also be invoked.

[12] Another, perhaps related worry motivating narrower conceptions of dignity is that broader conceptions are too indeterminate. See Griffin, *On Human Rights*, 51–6, 88–90. I think that determinateness of sense is important, and mentioned it as the third desideratum of deliberative interpretative proposals in section III.A. But we should also attend to the other important desiderata. If a somewhat less determinate

of *human* rights, to see the basis of *human* dignity as comprising *specifically human* capabilities and interests.

We can respond to this worry in at least three ways, which I present in order of decreasing concessiveness. First, we can give instrumental arguments about the importance of responding appropriately to humans' capability to feel pain and pleasure. An example would be to point out that when people experience extreme pain, they are unable to exercise their specifically human capabilities of rational agency. This response retains the narrow account of human dignity because the not specifically human capabilities or interests are causally but not constitutively relevant for it.

A second response is to point out that people have a specifically human way to experience pain and pleasure. Usually, such experiences have an intentional content that involves some level of linguistic and inferential articulation. This response is less concessive than the previous one because it sees at least some instances of pain and pleasure as constitutive of specifically human life.

I accept the foregoing responses, but I think that we should go further. Consider pain. We also want to recognize the great importance of sheer, animal, pain in our lives, even when it is not articulated in the ways the second response envisages. We want to have arguments for human rights to avoid experiences of such pain that are not merely instrumental but are also based on the recognition of their great intrinsic significance. For example, we do not only want to be able to say: "I shouldn't be beaten up or tortured when I try to express political dissent, because if I am I will be less likely enjoy my right to political participation." We also want to be able to say, more directly: "I am entitled to live without arbitrary impositions of pain." Human rights practice would be severely impoverished if utterances like the last are ruled out as basic (rather than merely derived) moves.

A third response seems then to be called for, in which we take some capabilities that humans have, even when other animals also have them, as among the constituents of what gives rise to the normative status of human dignity. This response is not concessive to the objector, because it denies that human dignity must only be based on features of human beings that are not shared by other beings.

How should one then respond to the likely protest that this account fails to capture *human* rights? By insisting that the not specifically human features included are extremely important to understand what human beings are and have interests in. Even if other animals *also* have them, they are no less human for that. The objector may say: But will we not then have to grant dogs *human* rights to avoid pain? The answer is: Of course not, as dogs' pain is not humans' pain. But it is pain all the same, the objector continues. At this point one must simply say: Surely there are *animal* rights that partly overlap with *human* rights.[13]

An important source of the difficulty here is that the idea of human dignity is sometimes linked with a hierarchical perspective on value. Human dignity must capture

---

proposal fits better the other desiderata than an alternative, more determinate proposal, then we may have all things considered reason to prefer the former. The need for greater determinacy can then be fulfilled through interpretations of dignity in specific contexts.

[13] My account relies on a conjunction: There is a human right to O if (inter alia) this is a right that humans have and O is connected with some of the features F that give rise to status-dignity. Other animals might have some F, and a right to O, but since the right would not be one that humans have, the

the very high worth of human beings in contrast with other, lesser beings (by analogy with the earlier, historical use referring to the dignity of those in higher classes or castes when compared to those in lower ranks).[14] I see the force of this point. But what gives "higher" worth to human beings is not all that gives worth to them: "lesser" sources of the worth of humans are still significant. Thus, the capacity for rational agency may make humans especially significant, but their abilities to feel pleasure and pain are further sources of value. I also see that pressing this line may lead to issues of conflict of interests between humans and non-human animals. But when not utterly tragic (as when we would die unless we kill animals for food), these conflicts may have to be responded to by surrendering, or severely qualifying, humans' alleged entitlement to harm other animals.[15]

IV. Dignity, Power, and Capabilities

A. Rank, status, and power

I present now a more determinate and substantive account of human dignity that addresses the questions mentioned in the last paragraph of section II.B. I should emphasize that this proposal is partial rather than complete. It focuses on foregrounding the significance of social and political power.

Some formulations in the survey in section II.A state intriguing connections between human dignity and social and political power. (vi.a) says that people "should be the principal beneficiary and should participate actively in the realization" of the human rights that derive from their status-dignity. This statement suggests that people should have the power to shape the social processes that fulfill their human rights rather than be merely the passive recipients of it. Empowerment seems to have intrinsic significance. It may also be a constitutive part of the condition in which human rights are fulfilled. (vi.c) says that "democratic participatory governance…best assures" the fulfillment of human rights. Here specifically political empowerment appears to have at least instrumental significance. It may be causally important in the process of human rights fulfillment. How can we make sense of these connections between human rights, dignity, and power?

One possibility is to explore further the notion of dignity as a status. If we look at statements (i) and (xi) we notice an important contrast. Human rights are based on a status-dignity that all human beings possess equally. Such a status differs from more circumscribed ones that might be attached to specific or contingent social positions. In his recent work on the subject, Waldron has accounted for this contrast

---

absurd conclusion that they have a human right to O does not follow. The relevant contrast when shaping our ideas of human dignity and human rights is not between humans and other species, but between what belongs to all humans and what belongs to some by reference to special features such as race, class, and nationality. I thank Rowan Cruft and Massimo Renzo for discussion on these issues.

[14] Jeremy Waldron, "Dignity and Rank," *European Journal of Sociology*, 48 (2007): 201–37; and "Tanner Lectures: Dignity, Rank, and Rights," (Berkeley, April 2009), available at http://papers.ssrn.com/sol3/papers.cfm?abstract_id=1461220.

[15] See Martha Nussbaum, *Creating Capabilities* (Cambridge, MA: Harvard University Press, 2011), 157–63.

by exploring the genealogy of the idea of dignity in relation to the idea of rank.[16] Historically, dignity was first associated with the high rank or nobility of some individuals occupying high positions in hierarchical social structures. But later dignity became associated with all individuals in an egalitarian way. Waldron explores, in particular, the significance of this shift for the development of our view of the nature of juridical institutions. I think that the genealogical link is worth exploring further to reveal the importance of social and political power for dignity and human rights. The inegalitarian and non-universalist use of dignity in the past was directed to agents who had power over others. Thus, the egalitarian and universalist use could be seen as demanding equal empowerment. Such an empowerment, I suggest, would be part of what condition-dignity involves, and it would be a fitting response to people's status-dignity.

Now, we cannot make full sense of condition-dignity as involving equal empowerment if we just think about how to universalize and equalize the earlier entitlements of rank. First, as Waldron recognizes, some entitlements would simply disappear if they were to be universalized (this holds for essentially hierarchical power positions such as being a slave-holder or an aristocrat).[17] Second, in this exercise we would be stuck with the raw materials provided by the hierarchical societies we take as starting points. These may not provide enough information to articulate all the forms of condition-dignity and empowerment that we have reason to recognize. In addition to the formal test (according to which we should recognize only those conditions that survive universalization), we need a more substantive strategy that helps us explain why some candidates make ethical sense, which amongst those that can be universally held are to be accepted, and why power is an important dimension for their articulation.

B. Capabilities, power, and the basis and content of human rights

Why does power matter for dignity? The answer I propose has two components. First, power matters for status-dignity because some forms of it are among the facts that make human beings need and deserve treatment in terms of human rights. Second, power matters for condition-dignity because some forms of it contribute both intrinsically and instrumentally to the fulfillment of human rights. I will argue that these points can be helpfully articulated in the language of capabilities, which is already being used to explore the link between what human beings can do or be and what they should be able to do or be in their social and political life. Because of this link, the capability perspective helps us account for human rights and dignity. Human beings have some capabilities that justify status-dignity, and they should have some capabilities that constitute and secure condition-dignity.

Before unpacking these claims, let me briefly say why the concept of *capability* can be used to articulate various considerations about *power*. The general idea is that we can use the vocabulary of capabilities to capture important issues commonly couched

---

[16] Waldron, "Dignity and Rank".
[17] Waldron, "Dignity and Rank," 224–5, 227–8; Waldron, "Dignity, Rank, and Rights," 32.

in terms of power. This is possible because of the coincidence between the two concepts (or, at any rate, between the aspects of them that I proceed to mention). Let me start by characterizing the notion of capability. As used by defenders of the so-called "capability approach," a capability is a real or substantive (as opposed to merely formal) opportunity or freedom of persons to do or be certain things (ie, to engage in certain "functionings") if they so choose.[18] This notion can be used to capture the concept of agential power in both its general sense and in its specific social and political sense. The general sense is the following: In certain circumstances C, an agent A has power with respect to whether some outcome or state of affairs O occurs to the extent that A can voluntarily determine whether O occurs. The idea is simply that an agent's power is their ability to shape aspects of the world as they choose.[19] As I see it, a capability is an agent's power to do or be certain things. A more specific sense of power concerns social and political settings: here an agent has power to the extent that they can voluntarily shape their social interactions with others, including the decision-making processes through which the outcomes of those interactions are determined. Specific capabilities in social and political life can be identified to capture instances of this dimension of power.

Let us now consider how the idea of capability, by articulating the aforementioned general and specific dimensions of power, can help us make sense of status-dignity and condition-dignity.

(a) Status-dignity. To illuminate the relation between capabilities and status-dignity we can ask: What are the general facts that make our practical attitudes and responses to human dignity desirable and feasible? This question tracks what we may call the *circumstances of human dignity* (by analogy with Rawls's "circumstances of justice").[20] It seems to me that at least part of the answer should refer to some capabilities (ie, some powers) that people normally have.[21] Some valuable basic capabilities are among the features of human beings that ground our view of them as deserving the kind of respect and concern that human rights articulate. These clearly include the capabilities concerning reason, conscience, and solidaristic action (see (ii) in section II.A). Human beings are able to recognize, assess, and act on the basis of reasons. These involve both prudential considerations about how to live a good life and moral considerations about how to show proper respect and concern toward other persons. Human beings can take the initiative and shape their lives (to pursue the good and the right)

---

[18] Amartya Sen, *Development as Freedom* (New York: Anchor Books, 1999), 74–6. Nussbaum, *Creating Capabilities*, 20–5.

[19] This ecumenical characterization does not preempt substantive debates: it may apply to individual or collective agents, allows for degrees of power, includes power over oneself and over others, includes "good" and "bad" ways of exercising power (eg, through rationally convincing someone to do something or through force, coercion or manipulation), includes power over things besides persons (eg, technological power to transform material environments), and includes various possible subjects of power: not just someone's action, but also the formation of their beliefs, desires, and other features and circumstances. For a survey see Steven Lukes, *Power: A Radical View*, 2nd edn. (New York: Palgrave, 2005).

[20] John Rawls, *A Theory of Justice*, rev. edn. (Cambridge, MA: Harvard University Press, 1999), section 22.

[21] Of course, people vary in the extent to which they have these capabilities, but what is crucial for what I proceed to say is that they have them to a sufficient extent. These capabilities are what Rawls calls "range properties" (*A Theory of Justice*, section 77).

in multiple ways. They can imagine alternative forms of personal and social life, and achieve some of them through technological inventions, productive work, and social cooperation. Of course, human beings have other valuable basic capabilities, such as to experience pleasure and to relate cognitively and aesthetically to the world around them.

Referring to the aforementioned valuable capabilities is not enough to explain why the talk of human dignity makes ethical sense. Such talk links to rights and duties, and for these to be practically relevant there must also be some facts that render the development and exercise of the valuable basic capabilities both difficult and feasible. Sources of difficulty include the existence of certain *dis*valuable capabilities—such as to be cruel or domineering—and certain deficiencies regarding the exercise of valuable capabilities—such as indifference or insufficient solidarity. They also include conflicts of interests given material scarcity (so that people find it hard to simultaneously realize their prima facie permissible life-projects when there are not sufficient resources for everyone). Still, if talk of human dignity and rights is to have real practical traction (as it clearly does), circumstances have to be such that important achievements regarding the development and exercise of basic valuable capabilities are accessible. Thus, it should be the case that the operation of the disvaluable capabilities is not always triumphant, valuable capabilities could be extensively deployed, and circumstances of scarcity and conflict can be ameliorated (for example through technical and institutional innovation). Dynamic duties to expand the feasibility of a decent life for all must be possible to fulfill.[22]

(b) Condition-dignity. Human beings are agents with capabilities of prudential and moral reasoning, imagination, knowledge, productive labor, and social cooperation. Given material and social difficulties, they have reason to respond to the existence of these features with respect and concern, by recognizing the status-dignity of each person. Such respect and concern is to be expressed by articulating a set of human rights and duties. The basic valuable capabilities that give rise to status-dignity ground a plurality of human interests whose content concerns the abilities to maintain, develop, and exercise them in desirable and permissible ways. This brings us to the issue of condition-dignity. We can identify various kinds of social conditions in which human dignity is fostered. Human rights practice focuses on the most urgent of them. In general, seeing human rights as supporting capabilities means being concerned with whether people are really able to do and be what they have urgent reason to value.[23] If there is a human right to x, then every human person ought to have the capability to get x.

Now, the existence of specific capabilities involves the presence of social and political empowerment, which is significant both intrinsically and instrumentally. It is intrinsically significant for condition-dignity because it is desirable that the occurrence of states of affairs in which people develop and exercise their capabilities is up to

---

[22] On *dynamic duties* see Pablo Gilabert, "The Feasibility of Basic Socioeconomic Human Rights. A Conceptual Exploration," *Philosophical Quarterly*, 59 (2009): 559–81.

[23] Nussbaum, "Capabilities, Entitlements, Rights: Supplementation and Critique," *Journal of Human Development and Capabilities*, 12 (2011): 23–37, 29–30.

them, ie, that they select and shape them through their choice. Consider labor rights (see (iv.b) in II.A). People should be able to work, but no one should be forced to work. And labor conditions should not be humiliating and degrading, as is often the case in contemporary sweatshops. Social and political empowerment is also instrumentally significant. It makes sense to recognize rights to form and join unions (UDHR, Article 23.4) because they give workers the strength to bargain for labor conditions and remuneration that are not crushing.

If we think of the content of human rights as involving capabilities to engage in valuable functionings, then it is important that people can choose whether to engage in such functionings. This includes being able to articulate, through cooperative exercises of prudential and moral reasoning and inclusive decision making with others, some appropriate solutions to circumstances of conflict of interests (and rights). Such political capabilities, and the empowerment they involve, are significant intrinsically, as their fostering involves a public recognition of people's capacity to judge and choose how to organize their social life. They also matter instrumentally: individuals can use them to prevent domination, oppression, or indifference to their basic interests.[24] People need political power to keep mechanisms of collective decision making responsive to their urgent interests. They also need power to process, in a fair and insightful way, the indeterminacy and the disagreements about rights that exist (and thus engage in the terrain of argument mentioned in section III.A). Political empowerment is a reasonable response to the common tendencies to exclude groups of people from political participation and other social advantages, be self-serving and biased when wielding decision-making power, disagree on moral matters, and have limited knowledge of the needs and views of others.

The points made in the last paragraph help defend democratic rights as human rights. The claim that such rights exist has recently been subject to philosophical challenge.[25] But it is becoming increasingly recognized in the actual international practice of human rights. We already considered points (vi.a) and (vi.c) from the survey in section II.A (see section IV.A). UDHR, Article 21 and ICCPR, Article 25 include very strong statements of political participation rights. And a plethora of grass-roots movements from Latin America and Eastern Europe in the 1980s to the Arab Spring and the Occupy movement in 2011 have framed domestic and global campaigns for democracy in terms of human rights. Rights of political equality make clear sense once we see human dignity as tied to capability and power. When some people are treated as political inferiors their capabilities for reason, conscience, and solidaristic action with their fellow human beings are not properly recognized. Their status-dignity is not respected. And when they lack political equality their condition-dignity is not

---

[24] This also applies at collective levels. (vii) in section II.A intimates the importance of collective self-determination for dignity. Empowerment of political communities in their international relations (or of national minorities within multinational states) deserves attention. This is important when addressing the common worry that human rights are used as an ideological instrument in domestic or international domination. To the extent that political equality exists within and between states, the worry loses force.

[25] Joshua Cohen, *The Arc of the Moral Universe and Other Essays* (Cambridge, MA: Harvard University Press, 2010), 349–72; Pablo Gilabert, "Is There a Human Right to Democracy? A Response to Joshua Cohen," *Revista Latinoamericana de Filosofía Política / Latin American Journal of Political Philosophy*, 1 (2012): 1–37.

appropriately guaranteed. Some are avoidably placed at the mercy of others who are more powerful. The realization of their fundamental civil and socio-economic rights is thus less secure than it would be in a political system that gives them full political standing.

Let me add a cautionary remark about the limits of a treatment of human rights and dignity in terms of empowerment. In addition to identifying the many ways in which persons have or need power to fulfill their human rights, we must also recognize unavoidable restrictions. In politics, in economic affairs, and in personal life, human beings cannot be completely independent. A radical ideal of independence is infeasible. We all depend on the help of others to live a decent life. We may not always be able to reciprocate. Given that some significant differences of social and political power may remain even after profound reforms, we may not always be able to make it prudent (on instrumental grounds) for others who are more powerful to help us. Hence, we should emphasize the importance of solidarity, and cultivate our readiness to give it and receive it. This affects the proper understanding of the nature and content of human rights. Consider, for example, UDHR, Articles 1 and 25. The first refers to the idea of universal "brotherhood," and the second recognizes a right to assistance for those who cannot fully support themselves. Securing human rights requires giving people power. But it also requires that they use it with a spirit of human solidarity. This will not be achieved unless we articulate our commitment to human dignity and human rights in a way that illuminates the passive besides the active dimensions of the human condition. We need moral space for dignified vulnerability and receptivity.[26]

I conclude this section by briefly stating some debts, complementarities, and disagreements regarding the capability approach as developed by Martha Nussbaum. The debts are obvious: I build on Nussbaum's account of human rights as requiring the presence of certain capabilities, and define the latter as she does. I also take some basic capabilities as the ground of human dignity, recognize that there is a plurality of them (including forms of sentience and striving that lie beyond rational agency), and claim that the content of human rights (which identify what is needed for a life worthy of human dignity) includes securing various central capabilities. These central capabilities, as Nussbaum explains, involve a development of basic capabilities into "combined capabilities" that include both agents' internal preparedness to do or be certain things and external material and social conditions that allow them to do so. Nussbaum proposes a valuable list of ten central human capabilities, which, in her account, ground the various human rights. They refer to conditions securing adequate levels of people's capabilities with respect to life; bodily health; bodily integrity; the use of their senses, imagination and thought; the engagement of their emotions; the use of their practical reason; the development of social affiliation; the concerned relation with other species; activities involving play; and the control of their political and material environment.

This chapter advances original points that complement Nussbaum's approach. It provides a direct discussion of the uses of "dignity" in human rights documents, and

---

[26] See also (x) in section II.A. Further, we need this sensitivity to avoid sliding from the connection between dignity and power into a destructive attitude toward the nonhuman natural world. The pluralist view of human interests (introduced in section III.B) can enhance this sensibility.

proposes a deliberative interpretive proposal to articulate their structure and substance. It explores the fruitful connection between capabilities and various issues normally couched in terms of power. Finally, it introduces the idea of the circumstances of dignity, and within them it emphasizes the significance of disvaluable capabilities and the moral dimension of practical reason (ie, the power to be reasonable besides rational).

An important difference with Nussbaum is that I present reference to valuable capabilities as providing only a partial key to articulating human rights. There may be human rights whose content is not best, or fully, captured as securing some capability. An example concerns rights to due process, which are based on independent considerations of fairness. The wrongness of some violations of rights, such as the avoidable failure to make health care available, need not depend on lack of choice by the right-holder (even if that makes them worse). Furthermore, and relatedly, I think that to move from the identification of interests regarding valuable capabilities to the identification of rights we need to deploy a framework of reasoning that systematically factors in the perspective of duty-bearers beside that of right-holders to articulate reasons of feasibility, fairness, and responsibility that contribute to determining whether the interest in having a certain capability links to correlative duties to protect or promote its satisfaction. I think (and argue elsewhere) that moral contractualism would be useful for this task.[27]

V. Some Commonalities and Differences with Gould's Approach

In her contribution to this volume (chapter 9), Carol Gould argues that any conception of human rights must rely on some general view of human beings, that such a view affects the conception's account of the basis and content of human rights, and that we should develop a conception that captures both the active agency and the interdependence of persons in their social life (including the power relations they face or generate). I agree with these points, and in this chapter I provided a fresh articulation and defense of them. I developed the common points by connecting them directly with central aspects of the contemporary human rights practice. The idea of human dignity, which is foundational for that practice, involves both descriptive and normative views of human beings in their social life that can (and as I argued should) be interpreted in a way that captures the importance of power, agency, and solidarity.

My focus on the contemporary human rights practice motivates two possible disagreements. The first concerns the capability approach. Gould shares with that approach the preoccupation with persons' effective freedoms, but she challenges what she sees as an "essentialism" in that approach's identification of lists of capabilities to engage in certain functionings. Such lists, Gould claims, may be useful in specific contexts, but may not work as general pictures of human development. Her focus on

---

[27] I thank Matthew Liao for discussion on these points. See further Pablo Gilabert, "The Capability Approach and the Debate between Humanist and Political Perspectives on Human Rights: A Critical Survey," *Human Rights Review*, 14 (2013): 299–325.

more general conditions of free agency is more ecumenical: it minimizes ideological bias or one-sidedness, leaving specifics for "cross-cultural dialogue." I do not think that this challenge to the capability approach succeeds. The lists of capabilities that approach seeks to identify are explicitly presented as emerging from cross-cultural dialogue, and are open to contestation and revision within it. Furthermore, if we want to generate and justify the various civil, political, and socio-economic human rights of contemporary practice, we cannot avoid making claims about what freedoms are especially significant, and this cannot be done without taking a stance on controversial lists of important goods those freedoms would involve access to (ie, we should appraise certain functionings, and capabilities to achieve them).

I acknowledged the problem of deep disagreement in section III.A. But the best response to it is to engage it directly where it arises, seeking broadly shareable yet substantive pictures of important human capabilities. The second possible difference with Gould's approach concerns how demanding the list of capabilities or freedoms underpinning human rights should be taken to be once we take this disagreement seriously. Gould says that the content of human rights tracks the necessary conditions of agency (construed broadly, including capacity for intentional activities in social contexts). She claims that we should acknowledge both basic human rights securing the bare existence of agency and nonbasic human rights securing the flourishing of it. My worry here is that this picture may miss a distinctive feature of the human rights of contemporary practice, according to which human rights are especially urgent claims. Humanist considerations of justice responding to human dignity, both domestic and global, can go beyond human rights.[28] Although they go beyond ultra-minimal claims to survival and security, human rights do not seem to exhaust what humans owe to each other as a matter of justice. Instead, they mark the most urgent forms of justice, targeting the conditions for a decent rather than a fully flourishing human life for all. Take socio-economic rights. There is a difference between sufficientarian claims against severe poverty and claims to full equality of access to important advantages. We should pursue both. But given the difference in relative urgency, we should not make justification of the former hostage to the success of arguments pertaining to the latter.

---

[28] For exploration of both dimensions see Pablo Gilabert, "Humanist and Political Perspectives on Human Rights," *Political Theory*, 39 (2011): 430–67; and Pablo Gilabert, *From Global Poverty to Global Equality. A Philosophical Exploration* (Oxford: Oxford University Press, 2012). I don't deny that future human rights practice may incorporate more demanding claims. Perhaps it should. Like Gould, I reject conventionalist views of practices. But we could think more lucidly about the changes if we are aware of how they would change our current situation. I thank Laura Valentini for discussion on this point.

PART II

HUMAN RIGHTS IN LAW
AND POLITICS

11

Human Rights in the Emerging World Order

*Joseph Raz**

I will start with some—hopefully truistic—observations about rights, which will lead to a reflection on the role that human rights play in the emerging world order. I say 'the emerging world order', for it seems that we are going through a period of fast transition. If it is sensible to date its beginning to the collapse of the Soviet Union and the Soviet Bloc, then it is clear that its progress is anything but smooth. But I will neither be concerned with analysing the prevailing forces pressing for the remoulding of the shape of our world, nor with predicting its likely future direction. Rather my observations are those of a spectator commenting on one aspect of the process: that concerning the role that claims of individual rights, and the attempts to implement them, play and can usefully play in it.

Recognition and implementation of individual rights are not necessarily the most important aspects of the emerging world order. But there is no denying that its emergence is accompanied by extensive debates about human rights, and intensive efforts to secure their implementation. My discussion of the place of rights in the world order is conducted against the background of this hectic activity. I will use two rights to illustrate some of my points: the right to education and the right to health.

The right to education is recognized in a variety of international treaties. Perhaps the main location is the 1948 Universal Declaration of Human Rights (UDHR),[1] which in Article 26(1) declares:

* Thomas M Macioce Professor of Law, Columbia University, and formerly Professor of The Philosophy of Law, University of Oxford. This article is an expanded and revised version of the lecture I gave at the opening plenary session of the 24th IVR World Congress in Beijing, September 2009, which was entitled 'Human Rights in a New World Order'. I have retained its character as a mostly footnote-free and fluidly structured address. I am indebted to Professor Craig Scott for many comments and suggestions for improving the text. The unrevised 'Human Rights in a New World Order' speech will appear in the IVR proceedings as well as in translation in Chinese. This chapter was first published in 1 *Transnational Legal Theory*, (2010): 31–47 and is reproduced here with permission.

[1] Article 26(2) continues, 'Education shall be directed to the full development of the human personality and to the strengthening of respect for human rights and fundamental freedoms. It shall promote understanding, tolerance and friendship among all nations, racial or religious groups, and shall further the activities of the United Nations for the maintenance of peace' [UDHR] (GA Res 217A (III), UN Doc A/810 at 71 (1948)). Beyond the Universal Declaration, all eight treaties that are considered the core in-force United Nations human rights conventions expressly include rights related to education. See, eg, Article 13 of the International Covenant on Economic, Social and Cultural Rights [ICESCR] (GA Res 2200A (XXI), 21 UN GAOR Supp (No 16) at 49, UN Doc A/6316 (1966), 993 UNTS 3, *entered into force* 3 January 1976); Article 18(4) of the International Covenant on Civil and Political Rights [ICCPR] (GA Res 2200A (XXI), 21 UN GAOR Supp (No 16) at 52, UN Doc A/6316 (1966), 999 UNTS 171, *entered into force* 23 March 1976); Article 28 of the Convention on the Rights of the Child [CRC] (GA Res 44/25, annex, 44 UN GAOR Supp (No 49) at 167, UN Doc A/44/49 (1989), *entered into force* 2 September 1990); Article 10 of the International Convention on the Elimination of All Forms of Discrimination Against Women [CEDAW] (GA Res 34/180, 34 UN GAOR Supp (No 46) at 193, UN Doc A/34/46, *entered into*

Everyone has the right to education. Education shall be free, at least in the elementary and fundamental stages. Elementary education shall be compulsory. Technical and professional education shall be made generally available and higher education shall be equally accessible to all on the basis of merit.

The human right to health appears in Article 12(1) of the 1966 International Covenant on Economic, Social and Cultural Rights (ICESCR):[2]

The States Parties to the present Covenant recognize the right of everyone to the enjoyment of the highest attainable standard of physical and mental health.

My aim is to highlight both the vital importance of individual rights such as the rights to education and health in the world order, and to raise some difficult problems regarding their intellectual foundations, their definitions, and their implementation.

---

force 3 September 1981); Article 5(e)(v) of the International Convention on the Elimination of All Forms of Racial Discrimination [CERD] (660 UNTS 195, *entered into force* 4 January 1969); Article 10 of the Convention against Torture and Other Cruel, Inhuman or Degrading Treatment or Punishment [CAT] (GA Res 39/46, annex, 39 UN GAOR Supp (No 51) at 197, UN Doc A/39/51 (1984), *entered into force* 26 June 1987); Article 30 of the International Convention on the Protection of All Migrant Workers and Members of their Families [MWC] (GA Res 45/158, annex, 45 UN GAOR Supp (No 49A) at 262, UN Doc A/45/49 (1990), *entered into force* 1 July 2003); and Article 24 of the International Convention on the Protection and Promotion of the Rights and Dignity of Persons with Disabilities [PWDC] (GA Res 61/106, Annex I, UN GAOR, 61st Sess, Supp No 49, at 65, UN Doc A/61/49 (2006), *entered into force* 3 May 2008). In several of these treaties, education is also referenced in other articles than the lead right-to-education article cited here.

  [2] Article 12(2) continues:

  The steps to be taken by the States Parties to the present Covenant to achieve the full realization of this right shall include those necessary for:

  (a) The provision for the reduction of the stillbirth-rate and of infant mortality and for the healthy development of the child;
  (b) The improvement of all aspects of environmental and industrial hygiene;
  (c) The prevention, treatment and control of epidemic, endemic, occupational and other diseases;
  (d) The creation of conditions which would assure to all medical service and medical attention in the event of sickness.

The UDHR also included the right to health, in its Article 25 on the right to an adequate standard of living, but it was only with the ICESCR that the right to health was placed in a free-standing article. Alongside the UDHR and ICESCR, five of the other seven core UN human rights treaties expressly include rights related to health. See eg, CRC, Article 24; CEDAW, Article 12; CERD, Article 5(e)(iv); MWC, Article 28; and PWD, Article 25. Neither the ICCPR nor CAT expressly refers to a right to health (other than 'public health' being included at several points in the ICCPR as a legitimate objective on the basis of which various ICCPR rights can be justifiably limited, subject to proportionality analysis). However, health is necessarily implicit in CAT, given the very nature of torture and its effects on health; CAT, Article 1 prohibits the infliction of 'severe pain or suffering, whether physical or mental'. And the Human Rights Committee has long interpreted the right to life in ICCPR, Article 6 to include right-to-health dimensions. As early as 1982, the Human Rights Committee, in its first General Comment on Article 6, indicated that the right to life generated a duty on states to take positive measures including what the Committee expressed as the 'desirab[ility]' that states 'take all possible measures to reduce infant mortality and to increase life expectancy, especially in adopting measures to eliminate malnutrition and epidemics': Article 6 (16th Sess, 1982), Compilation of General Comments and General Recommendations Adopted by Human Rights Treaty Bodies, UN Doc HRI/GEN/1/Rev.6 at 127 (2003). Since then, the Committee has invoked health-related aspects of ICCPR rights in Concluding Observations in relation to various states' human rights performances, eg, with respect to the health consequences of homelessness in Canada in 1999: Concluding Observations of the Human Rights Committee, Canada, UN Doc CCPR/C/79/Add.105 (1999), para 12.

I will advance no firm recommendations, though I hope that my comments help point to the direction in which both theoretical inquiry and political activity can contribute to their solution.

I. On Rights in General

Let me start with some observations about rights in general. My observations are not a general account of the nature of rights. I have written about that before, and the following observations do not qualify that analysis.[3] They point to features that are typical of many rights, and therefore reflection on them helps in considering the role of rights in the international, as well as in the domestic, arenas.

My topic is individual rights, but of course rights can be possessed not only by individuals. States, corporations, and other legal persons also have rights. Since states and corporations are creatures of law, their rights are legal rights. Among legal rights we can distinguish those created by law from those recognized by law. If individuals have a right to free expression, then the legal right to free expression constitutes an adequate or a partial recognition of that prior right—call it a moral right—to free expression. I will ignore possible refinements here. For example, I take recognition to be constituted by the fact that the legal right has the same, or nearly the same, content as the moral right, regardless of whether it was adopted by law in order to give legal effect to the moral right, or for some other reasons. I will also disregard the fact that whether a legal right recognizes a moral right is a matter of degree.

Some rights are created by law. A right to ownership of government bonds, like those bonds themselves, does not exist independently of the law. It is a legal creation. Legally created rights may be moral rights; that is, they may be legal rights that have moral force. Others may lack moral force. Sometimes the law creates new rights when the law-makers intend to recognize an independent right, but fail to do so. And such legally created rights too may be moral rights, that is, have moral force, or fail to be so. Where there is a moral obligation to obey the law, or to obey some parts of the law, rights created by morally binding law have moral force, even if the legislature that created them may have been mistaken in its belief that they recognize independently existing moral rights.

For the rest of this chapter I will ignore legal rights with no moral force. So, when I refer to legally created rights I will be referring to morally valid legally created rights.

The existence of legally created rights teaches us important lessons. First, the (moral) rights that people have can change. As the law creates new ones or terminates the existence of old ones, our (moral) rights change. Second, moral rights can rest on—be justified by—factors other than more basic moral rights.

Let me elaborate on this second point. Legal rights, with moral force, that are created by law (rather than being simply legally recognized moral rights) are likely to be

---

[3] Joseph Raz, 'On the Nature of Rights', *Mind*, 93 (1984): 194. See also Joseph Raz, 'The Nature of Rights', in Joseph Raz, *The Morality of Freedom* (Oxford University Press, 1986), 165ff. The latter chapter is largely identical to the preceding article except for an added treatment of Ronald Dworkin's notion of rights as trumps at 186–92.

justified by considerations other than other moral rights alone, and possibly not to rest on any other moral right at all. For example, the justification of the rights one has in virtue of holding a government bond will include considerations that explain why government bonds are sound commercial instruments, considerations which would relate to the economic functioning of governments, and so on, and not merely, if at all, some antecedent moral rights of the bond-holders. Alternatively or in addition, the justification of the bond-holders' rights will derive from the general obligation to obey the law, resting as it does on the need to secure peaceful government in the country, being again considerations that go beyond any antecedent right of the bond-holder.

Now, some people may say that only moral rights that are legal rights can be justified without being derived from other moral rights. 'Independent' moral rights—that is, ones whose moral status does not depend on being created by the law, or by other social institutions or practices—derive, they say, from other independent moral rights, and ultimately from fundamental moral rights which do not derive from—are not justified by—anything other than themselves. But there is no reason to think that that is so. That is, there is no cogent argument that would show why, if moral rights can arise out of morally significant legal actions, they cannot arise out of morally significant factors of other kinds. And the fact that they need to be morally significant is no restriction on what they are. They are made morally significant by justifying rights if by nothing else.

At most, *some* rights may be basic, in that their justification does not depend on other factors. They are in some sense self-justifying, or their validity is self-evident. I doubt that any rights are basic in that sense. While the argument of my talk does not depend on these doubts being well founded, it does depend on a general way of thinking about rights, which I will now explain. The explanation of this way of thinking about rights will show why my doubts are plausible.

The explanation depends on what I hope are entirely truistic observations. First, it is a common feature of rights that the objects of rights—that is, what one has a right to—are things of value. Normally, the objects will be of value to the right-holders themselves. This truism is to be distinguished from a second one, namely, that having a right is itself something of value to the right-holder. Often, the value of the right depends on the value of the object of the right. Because the right is to something of value, the right itself is of value. The third truism is that the right of one person limits the freedom of other people. Generally speaking, people have a duty not to violate the rights of others. Each right establishes a set of duties, and identifies a set of people who are subject to the various duties. What unites the duties is that they secure (at least to some degree) the right-holder's control over the object of his right. Because (by the first truism) the object of the right is of value to the right-holder, controlling it is also of value. Hence the first and the third truisms yield the second one, that rights have value to those who have them.

However, these truisms need to be qualified. Most rights can be renounced; that is, right-holders can give up their rights, or some aspect of them. Very often right-holders can transfer, by gift or sale or in some other way, their rights to other people. Sometimes the very point and value of the right is in the value of the control over its object combined with the value of the ability to alienate that control, to give it up, or to transfer it. These are the typical cases in which the value of the right is detached from the value of its object to the right-holders. The interest of right-holders in their rights is in their ability to alienate these rights. (There are other exceptions, but we need not dwell on them here.) Let me add just one further word of explanation: the value that the object of the right may have for the right-holder can depend on the moral duties of the right-holder—the value of having property includes the fact that it enables one to meet one's responsibilities towards family members, the environment, and so on.

Given these truisms, we have to wonder about their significance. In particular, could it be that the object of a right's being of value to the right-holder has nothing to do with the justification of the right, with the explanation of why the right-holder has that moral right? Could it be that the fact that having the right is of value to the right-holder has nothing to do with the explanation of why the right-holder has that right? That somehow sounds implausible. The natural explanation is that the fact that the objects of rights are of value is the reason or part of the reason why the right-holders have the right. Of course, people do not have a right to whatever is of value to them. Here the third truism comes into view: rights are grounds of duties on others. The bare fact that something is of value to me does not endow me with a right to it, because it does not in itself establish that other people have a duty to secure me with, or not to interfere with my, possession of it. It would appear that we have a right only if the right entails that the value of having it, or our need for it, is of a kind sufficient to impose duties on some others—more precisely, on at least one other.

The value of the right to its possessor is its ground. It is that value which justifies holding others to be duty-bound to secure or at least not to interfere with the right-holder's enjoyment of the right, and it is only when such duties exist that the right exists. It exists because it gives rise to such duties.

Notice that here I shifted attention from the value of the object of the right to the value of the right to that object. The value of the right depends on the value of the object, but also includes the value of the secure enjoyment of that object. It further includes the exchange value of the right, in the case of rights to alienable interests—that is, the value of the fact that one can pass the right (and the underlying object of the right) to others, such as by way of gift or as part of a trade-off. As I noted earlier, with some rights (for example, many property rights), the main value of having the right is the value of being able to trade it. That value presupposes that the object of the right is of value to someone other than the right-holder. But the object may be of little or no value to the right-holder, for whom the main value is in the ability to sell the right.[4]

Truistic as they may be, the three truisms—that both the right and its object are of value to the right-holder and that the right of one generates the duty of another—do nonetheless prompt the question: why is it that rights are of value to the right-holder and why do they involve duties on others? The explanation is that rights have a special role in our moral universe: they apply to cases where the value of something to a

---

[4] I should repeat that the observations I rely on here are generalizations that allow of exceptions, exceptions which indirectly prove the same general lessons to which I draw attention. For example, some rights invest their holders with control over objects that, far from being valuable, are harmful to them. Here, the right is valuable for its point is to provide the right-holders with control over the source of harm, which enables them to neutralize it.

person is of a kind that warrants holding others duty-bound to respect it or otherwise secure its enjoyment in some ways.

This view of rights is broad enough to allow for a great variety of rights. They can differ in their object, in those on whom the duties to respect the rights fall, and in the nature and scope of those duties, as well as in other respects. So broad is the view that, rooted as it is in truisms, it may appear to say too little to be of interest.

The contrary is the case. In seeing rights as justified by what is of value to the right-holders, this view challenges the view that rights are fundamental. It also exposes one common lacuna in much discussion of human rights. So much of that discussion focuses on the value of the putative right or its object to the right-holder, as if this is sufficient to establish that there is such a right. So often there is little concern to show why others are subject to duties in regard to the putative right or its object. That something is of value to someone does not even begin to establish that I or anyone else has a duty to secure or protect his possession or enjoyment of that thing. A special argument is needed here, and it is all too often missing, an argument which relies on the special character of the value that the right provides.

Before moving on, a fourth truism should be noted. It has to do with the special control right-holders have regarding their rights. What is it? It is often said that right-holders have standing to complain about violations of their rights. Having standing means that the complaint cannot be blocked by saying 'mind your own business', or words to that effect. Such responses are often appropriate. In giving such a response, one refuses to enter into conversation with the person making the complaint, the person alleging that one acted improperly and thus either violated the complainant's right or violated someone else's right. The blocking move—'it is none of your business'— does not deny that one acted improperly, nor does it admit it, nor does it invoke an excuse for one's conduct. It simply denies the standing of the other to engage one on this point (at least in the context in which the complainant seeks engagement), and is a refusal to deal with him about it.

It is true that, subject to exceptions which I will come back to shortly, such a response is unacceptable if the complaint is made by the person whose right—it is claimed—has been violated and is made in an appropriate social or institutional context. But I do not share the views of several writers who made this fact the corner-stone of their theories of rights or even of morality as a whole, writers who looked for a further elusive factor that explains why right-holders have a standing regarding the violation of their rights. To understand my observations later on in the chapter it is important to see where these writers went wrong. So I will say a little more on the subject.

As a matter both of moral principle and of common belief, it seems to me that we are all within our rights in forming views about the morality of the conduct of anyone without restriction. We should not form such views lightly, nor should we form them for some unworthy purpose. But that is true of all our beliefs. It may be particularly unappealing to be the sort of person who makes it his or her business to judge others, whether there is any point or purpose in doing so or not. Nevertheless one is within one's rights in forming such views, so long as one does so responsibly. Similarly, general principles of freedom of expression govern the communication of such views. Again, as with other beliefs, the right to communicate them should not be abused. But it is a universal right. There is no special standing here for people whose views or communications concern their own rights and their actual or possible violation. Indeed it would be a sorry society—including, as I will discuss later, world society—in which no one other than the victim or his close friends is allowed to protest against violations of people's rights.

Notice that the powers of enforcement and protection of rights do not belong exclusively to the right-holder either. All these precepts are widely recognized in the public culture and legal institutions of many countries. Journalists have a right and indeed a duty to uncover right-violations, and report on them. Governments have a right and a duty to protect right-holders; in this context, while some enforcement measures are at the discretion of, or affected by decisions and preferences of, the right-holders, others are not. They are a matter of public concern, and public officials are in charge.

So what is the special standing of the right-holders? Needless to say, the right-holders are most directly affected by respect for or violation of their rights. Therefore their concern is rarely trivial or nosey. That is why they have standing in matters to do with their rights. Other people have standing on the same footing, that is, when their interference has a serious point and expresses a genuine concern in a matter which is either not yet resolved or not yet properly handled. The difference is that, with the right-holders, the concern is almost always serious. Or at least appears serious: true, right-holders can pursue their rights for unworthy reasons, even when no non-trivial interest of theirs is at stake. But it is rare that others will be in a position to know that, and to insist that that is the case.

There is, of course, another way in which right-holders are involved, and it is this other way that seems to be the central factor explaining right-holders' special standing regarding their own rights. Commonly, right-holders have the power to waive their rights—permanently or on some occasions—and that includes the power to suspend the enforcement of their rights on one or more occasions. On occasion, they may prefer that a right not be respected or that its violation shall not be rectified. They can achieve such results by using the power to waive the right, whether generally or in a single instance, and they can waive their right to compensation or other remedies for its violation.

This said, there may be rights which cannot be waived. The rights to some basic freedoms are plausible candidates. But generally rights are (by the third truism) protected by duties on others, which can be—and that is the fourth truism—waived or suspended by the right-holder. It is this power, and not the standing to complain, that is at the core of the special standing of right-holders regarding their own rights.

These truisms, especially the last one, are important to the role of rights in the emerging world order, a subject to which we should now finally turn.

II. The Emerging World Order: Where Do Rights Come In?

When talking of the emerging world order I have in mind the pattern of institutions, treaties and established practices that are emerging under the impact of the economic, social and cultural pressures in a world growing smaller and more inter-dependent through vastly enhanced communication technology. The new world order is in the making. We are in a period of fast changes in many aspects of the international situation, changes whose directions are uncertain. I would not venture to predict, or to recommend a blueprint for, a desirable outcome. My modest aim is to point to some possibilities and difficulties inherent in some of the current trends regarding the role of individual rights. But even that presupposes a certain aware-ness and understanding of those trends, for there is no possibility of sensible recom-mendations based on *a priori* considerations only. They must relate to the reality for which they are intended.

The individual rights discussed and pursued in the international arena are invari-ably human rights. Other rights come in when incorporated in treaties or the consti-tutions of international organizations. Human rights stand in their own right. Their implementation, like that of other legal precepts, requires institutionalization. But when incorporated into law the relevant legal rights are, rightly, considered not to be rights created by law, but ones recognized by law. They are moral rights we have independently of the law, and that is why the law should recognize and enforce and protect them.

But why are they considered to be not only moral rights which the law should respect but moral rights of a special kind, namely, human rights? Briefly put, this is because they are thought to combine exceptional importance and universality. Even though various writers have offered explanations of the first element, that of importance, none seems to me successful either in explaining what is the importance of those rights or in establishing that only important rights can be human rights. In the present chapter, I will ignore this element altogether. What about universality?

The theories that I will call 'traditional' claim that human rights are universal because they are rights every human being has as a human being. That is, being a human being is the ground of possessing those rights. This claim is hard to sus-tain concerning the rights recognized as human rights in international instru-ments in the modern UN Charter era as well as in the more contemporary period of what I am calling the emerging world order.[5] Take my first example, that of a right to education. If people have the right identified by the Universal Declaration as a right to education in virtue of their humanity alone, it follows that cave dwell-ers in the Stone Age had that right. Does that make sense? Recall the language of the Declaration:

> Everyone has the right to education. Education shall be free, at least in the elementary and fundamental stages. Elementary education shall be compulsory. Technical and

---

[5] For longer-standing human rights treaties of the UN Charter era, see the ICESCR, ICCPR, CERD, CEDAW, and CAT. For post-Cold War treaties, see the MWC and the PWDC. In formal terms (date of conclusion and opening for signature of the treaty), the CRC falls exactly on the divide between these two periods, although its formulations would have been largely settled in negotiations prior to the advent of the present 'emerging world order' period. I have elaborated on the critique of the traditional theory and explained in greater detail my own approach in Joseph Raz, 'Human Rights without Foundations', in Samantha Besson and John Tasioulas (eds.), *The Philosophy of International Law* (Oxford University Press, 2010), 321.

professional education shall be made generally available and higher education shall be equally accessible to all on the basis of merit.

The very distinctions between elementary, technical, professional, and higher education would have made no sense at that time, and at many other times. Nor would it make sense to think of any part of education as compulsory. Who was supposed to do the compelling? Clearly the right here recognized is one that applies—if at all—to people who live in conditions not unlike ours. But if so then it cannot be grounded in our humanity alone.

It is plausible to think that the reasoning behind the right to education is that people's ability to have a rewarding, fulfilling life depends on having the skills required to cope with the challenges of life and to take advantage of the opportunities available at the time and in the place where they live or are likely to live. Given the circumstances of life today, that requires formal schooling, and given the political organization of our societies into states, it makes sense to make governments responsible for the provision of education to all. This is a very abbreviated story. The explanation and justification of the right requires considerable amplification. I will omit that.[6]

Some theorists would insist that, even though the right to education recognized in international law today is not a universal human right, it derives from some ur-right which is genuinely universal. I can find no such right. I also believe that the motivation to look for one is misguided. The justification for the existing right to education that I sketched is based on perfectly universal considerations, namely on the importance of the opportunity to have a rewarding life and on the way the chances to have a rewarding life depend on possessing skills to tap the opportunities available in one's place and time. All practical moral conclusions are based on universal considerations applied to specific circumstances. There is nothing special to rights, or to human rights, in that. And the earlier-noted considerations about rights generally have shown that rights do not necessarily derive from other rights. More commonly, and perhaps in all cases, they derive from considerations to do with the value of life in the way my story about the right to education illustrates.

The more plausible claim is that human rights are synchronically universal, meaning that all people alive today have them. Something like that seems to be assumed in contemporary human rights practice. This is of crucial importance, as it expresses the view that human life is valuable unconditionally, a view we tend—I hope—to take for granted, but which is not always observed in practice. So, one crucial contribution of individual rights to the emerging world order is in underpinning its commitment to the value of human life.

There is an additional crucial contribution that human rights make to the emerging world order: the most powerful actors on the international scene are states, big corporations, and at least some international organizations. Human rights are rights of individuals, and as the fourth truism (and the attendant discussion of it earlier in

---

[6] Whichever way the explanation of the grounds of the right is to be augmented it will rely on empirical generalizations about social and political conditions, which, like all such generalizations, are not without exceptions. It is part of the burden of the explanation that the exceptions are not of a character to undermine the existence of the right.

the chapter) says, right-holders have a say in their enforcement, and everyone—every individual or association of individuals—has standing to press for their recognition as demanding protection. This enables the cause of human rights to mobilize concerned individuals, and to generate considerable pressure on states, corporations, and international organizations. As we know, this is indeed what has happened and what is happening. One of the most important transformations brought about by the pursuit of human rights has been the empowerment of ordinary people, and the emergence of a powerful network of nongovernmental as well as treaty-based institutions pressurizing states and corporations (and, to a lesser extent, international organizations) in the name of individual rights. The human rights movement launched a new channel of political action, which continues to be a major corrective to the concentration of power in governmental and corporate hands.

III. Difficulties and Risks

The importance of human rights, I suggested, is in affirming the worth of all human beings, and in distributing power away from the powerful to everyone, including any group or association willing to advocate and promote the interests of ordinary people. But human rights come with an intellectual claim not strictly required for the achievement of those two ends. If we recognize that all human beings can have rights because they are human beings, we already recognize that they all have moral worth. And the distribution of power is an essential feature of rights, not only of human rights. All rights assign to the right-holders power over the object of the rights. Human rights involve the further claim that comes with synchronic universality, the claim that all people alive today have the same human rights.

I should make clear at the outset that I do not intend to criticize this feature of contemporary human rights doctrine. But it is important to understand why it is there. According to traditional human rights theory, with its belief that people have those rights in virtue of their humanity alone, it is obvious why all human beings have exactly the same rights: they are all human beings, and it is just that which endows each one of them with human rights. Theories of human rights which opt only for synchronic universality accept that different people can have different human rights, for they accept that factors other than being human determine which human rights one has. In my example of the right to education, these include the social conditions that make schooling necessary for the opportunity to have a rewarding life, and the political conditions that make it appropriate to hold governments responsible for the provision of education. But if people can have different human rights at different periods, why can it not be the case that people who live today can have different human rights? Why must human rights be synchronically universal?

I believe that there is no principled ground for identifying human rights with synchronically universal rights only. But there are important pragmatic reasons for singling out synchronically universal rights, and letting them inherit the title of human rights, derived from the defunct traditional theory. We single out as human rights those rights respect for which can be demanded by anyone. In particular, inhabitants of one country can address such demands to the governments of other countries regarding those governments' treatment of their own citizens. And those governments cannot block the demands by saying 'this is none of your business'. The ability of states to block interference in their internal affairs, to deny that they are responsible in certain ways to account for their conduct to outside actors and bodies, is what traditionally conceived state sovereignty consists in. But human rights, as they function in the world order, set limits to sovereignty. States have to account for their compliance with human rights to international tribunals where the jurisdictional conditions are in place, and to responsibly acting people and organizations outside the state.

This is the other crucial feature of the way human rights function in the emerging world order.[7] In order to function sensibly in that way—that is, in order to set a limit to state sovereignty—claims about human rights violations, coming from people or organizations outside the state blamed for committing or not preventing those violations, must be capable of rebutting the retort: conditions in our state are different and you are in no position to know what rights inhabitants of our country have, and therefore in no position to interfere in our affairs in the name of those rights. Human rights cannot be subjected to such a response because we identify human rights with those rights that all people living today have in virtue of the common conditions of life today, especially in view of the worldwide broadening and deepening of those conditions in the rapidly evolving circumstances of the emerging world order. That is part of the case for acknowledging that respect for those rights can be demanded by anyone, including people and organizations that have no connection with the country concerned. Because we have those rights in virtue of common conditions of life today, no special knowledge of the circumstances of this country or that are required to know that its citizens have those rights. And that is part of the case for taking them to set limits to state sovereignty, to be rights for whose implementation states are accountable to individuals, organizations, and other states beyond their borders.

The synchronic universality of human rights raises the bar for any claim that any particular human right exists. As I have already intimated, many theoretical writers and political activists ignore the difficulty of the task their advocacy faces because they labour under the illusion that all they need to do is to point to the importance of the alleged right or its object to the putative right-holders. They neglect the need to establish a case for holding others to be under a duty to secure, at least to some degree or in some ways, the right-holders' enjoyment of the rights. I will point to two kinds of difficulties in establishing the case for such a right: difficulties to do with process, and difficulties to do with content.

Let me start with issues of process. I have in mind the question of institutions with legitimate authority to settle controversies regarding the scope of rights, and to enforce respect for them. Not all moral rights should be enforced by law. Respect for various moral rights should be a matter of individual conscience, and subject to voluntary interactions among individuals, free from coercion or from institutional involvement. Human rights are not among those. Needless to say, ideally they should

---

[7] I do not argue for this point. That is, I do not argue that it would be good if human rights did set limits to state sovereignty, or that it is good that they do so. I merely observe that that is a crucial aspect of the way they actually function in today's world.

be respected voluntarily, independently of any institutional involvement. But of all our moral rights only rights that should be respected and enforced by law are identified as human rights. Obviously, injustices are bound to occur if the recognition and enforcement of a right are entrusted to institutions that are inherently biased, lack independence and impartiality, and lack fair procedures, or to ones whose interventions are haphazard and arbitrary.

The vital importance of impartial, efficient, and reliable institutions for administering and enforcing human rights has three implications for arguments about them. First, if there is a human right to something, then there is also a duty to establish and support impartial, efficient and reliable institutions to oversee its implementation and protect it from violations. Second, until such institutions exist, normally one should refrain from attempts to use any coercive measures to enforce the right. We are bound by such caution given the common and serious harms attending use of coercion on the international scene, and the risks that purported enforcement measures are no more than misguided presumptions. Third, if, given the prevailing circumstances, there is no possibility that impartial, efficient, and reliable institutions may come into existence regarding a certain right, then that right is not a human right.

I stated these conclusions in stark form, and, so stated, they are misleading, especially the second and third ones. It is likely, indeed I believe it to be the case, that the picture regarding institutional enforcement is mixed. Within some regions, for example within the Europe of both the Council of Europe and the European Union, there may well be adequate institutions and procedures for the recognition and enforcement of all human rights insofar as respect for them within these regions is concerned, while they may be absent in some other parts of the world. Moreover, some institutional arrangements, like the International Criminal Court, may be launched, and may still exist in an experimental spirit. They are not proven to be impartial, efficient, and reliable. But they may become impartial, efficient, and reliable with time. We should not hesitate to experiment when there are fair chances of success. You will remember that all my reflections are based on the perception that we are in the midst of a flux, a period during which many ideas are tried and only some succeed. That is the only way to make progress in international relations and we should not be fastidious in ways that make success harder. So, in effect my second conclusion is a call for vigilance, for awareness of the crucial importance of having appropriate institutions but also for willingness to be suspicious of enforcement of rights where attempts to enforce them are likely to lead to injustices.

My third conclusion was that, where there is no possibility of fair and reliable enforcement, there is no human right. This is the result of the general approach to rights, and in particular of their dependence on contingent factors. Think of any moral right that should not be enforced by law. The reasons for that will be that it cannot be effectively enforced, or that enforcement will be impossible or counter-productive. The reasons are rooted in the nature of human and social life and institutions. Some may be inseparable from the inescapable conditions of human life while others will be more contingent.

It is important here to remember that the conclusion is not that the right does not exist. It is only that it is not a human right. The contemporary practice of human rights identifies as human rights only those that should be enforced by law. It follows that, while there may be human rights that are not enforced by law and whose existence is the case for just such enforcement, there cannot be human rights that cannot be enforced by law. If enforcement—fair, efficient, and reliable enforcement—is impossible, we should recognize that the right is not a human right, and refrain from calling for its enforcement.

Finally, I want to mention one particular content-related difficulty in establishing that any right is a human right. This difficulty relates to the suspicion that claims—or some claims—of human rights are culturally biased, that they represent an ideological claim that the ideas of the West should prevail across the globe. In a way, this difficulty is not specifically about establishing a duty towards putative right-holders. But in practice this is where the difficulty lies.

Take the right to health, for example. Who could deny that health is of value to the people whose health is in question? Who can doubt that this is a truly universal right, for health has been of value to people for as long as there have been people? Well, things are not that simple. First, it would be silly to think that people really have a right to be healthy, a right which is violated every time they are not healthy. A saner view of the right sees its focus in ICESCR, Article 12(2), with its list of state duties. But states, or governments, are not inter-temporally universal: they did not exist from the beginning of *homo sapiens*. Second, health can be said to have both an intrinsic and an instrumental value. The intrinsic value is that of the sense of physical well-being enjoyed by the healthy. The instrumental value is that health greatly increases one's prospects of having a rewarding life. If not all, at least many forms of ill-health—involving as it does pain, suffering and disability—make fulfilling and satisfying life much harder to achieve, or even impossible.

It seems to me plain that it is the instrumental rather than the intrinsic value of health that is the foundation of the human right to health. That is so because, absent special relations, no one has a duty to secure for me or for any other person a feeling of physical well-being. But they may have such a duty to secure people the opportunity to have a fulfilling life.

But let me return to my main theme: the difficulties of dealing with cultural diversity, as they manifest themselves in the case of a right to health. As we know, the very idea of health is culturally relative. Health relates to functionality, and functionality relates to the type of activities important for normal successful existence in a particular context. The right to health is broad enough to cover the prevention of disability and other disadvantages, and they provide obvious examples of cultural relativity: for example, does infertility or does facial disfigurement constitute a condition the prevention or removal of which is covered by the right to health? Notoriously, the mental conditions constituting mental illness are culturally relative, but so are, in less obvious ways, the conditions we classify as diseases.

There is another difficulty, and I want to highlight it in particular: the right as expressed in the ICESCR is 'to the enjoyment of the highest attainable standard of physical and mental health'. Attainability connotes duties being relative to the economic, social and political circumstances of different countries. But all countries are required to prioritize health. The question is, to what extent? Should health take priority over personal liberty, or commercial freedom? Does the right to health include a duty to prohibit smoking, or other activities damaging to health? Does it include a duty to make more expensive the availability of objects or opportunities engagement with which is risky in order to discourage their use? One can have a special tax on ski resorts, or restrict the production of cars to vehicles that cannot exceed 60 km/h, and so on and so forth.

The plain truth is that we should reject the highest attainable standard test if taken to refer to what is factually attainable. If we take it more sensibly to refer to what is attainable given proper weight to all other considerations, including other moral rights and worthwhile goals, then the content of the right and the extent of required attainment are wide open and raise crucial questions, questions which affect not only the right to health but other rights and values as well.

I hope that everyone would agree that health should not take priority over all else. All of us, to various degrees, find satisfaction and fulfilment in activities that risk our health and life, and sometimes the risk is part of the point of those activities. The crucial point is that different cultures have different, conflicting, and yet reasonable attitudes to such conflicts. There is no single way of striking the balance between health and other concerns. In their lives different individuals strike a different balance, and, in their public policies, different countries strike a different balance. Some ways of neglecting or risking life for other ends are senseless or even wrong. But many different individual attitudes and public policies, though inconsistent with one another, are sensible or at least acceptable.

How can this be reconciled with the fact that we all have the same human rights, that they are synchronically universal? Does it not follow that the inhabitants of Tamil Nadu have a different right to health than the inhabitants of Vermont, not because the two states differ in wealth, but because they act on reasonable but conflicting views of what constitutes the highest attainable standard?

It is no good saying that the formulation of the right in the Covenant allows for it to be relative to such variations. True though this is, it does not help either with the point of principle or with the need to develop a sensitive practice. The difficulty is to make practical sense of the right, to acknowledge both its universality and its sensitivity to cultural variations. The dominant practice of international human rights appears deficient in this regard. Human rights advocates seem more likely to invoke cultural differences to condemn them rather than to acknowledge their validity.

But that is not all: human rights are there to be enforced. They call for authoritative institutions to be in charge of supervising their implementation and for institutions that have responsibility for their implementation. Those institutions—both the implementing institutions and the supervising institutions—will have to take practical decisions that acknowledge the soundness or condemn the unreasonableness or immorality of various cultural attitudes and practices. This raises the point of principle I referred to: the fact that, in acknowledging the human right to health, countries concede the right of international institutions[8] to judge not only their health policies

---

[8] At the moment these include the UN Human Rights Council, specific human rights treaty bodies and, if the state has accepted jurisdiction, the International Court of Justice. But my point is not specific to these institutions. Acceptance of a human right is acceptance that there can be, and should be, international bodies with power to oversee its implementation.

but also their pursuit of other rights and values because, in deciding on the highest attainable level of health, the relevant international institutions must pass judgment over the way different countries compromise between concern for health and the pursuit of other values.

This raises the practically delicate question of 'who decides'. Is it acceptable that international bodies whose office-holders tend to be drawn disproportionately from a few powerful countries should decide about the good sense or otherwise of the practices of countries all over the world?

IV. Concluding Words

I want to conclude with questions rather than answers. I underlined the crucial role human rights play in the emerging world order—first, in expressing the worth of all human beings; second, in placing on the agenda concerns other than those of inter-governmental relations or big business profit; and third, in empowering individuals and voluntary associations in creating an additional channel for exerting influence and affecting the international order. I also underlined some of the difficulties and dangers of human rights practices. In the existing climate they lend themselves to reckless activism, which ignores the fact that rights impose duties and that the case for the existence of the duties has to be established beyond pointing to the value of the right to the right-holder. Furthermore, attempts to implement the rights can do much harm if not entrusted to the care of impartial, efficient, and reliable institutions. Finally, contrary to much current rhetoric, human rights are not absolute, or, at least, most human rights and certainly the two on which my discussion has focused, the rights to education and health, are not absolute: their just interpretation and implementation require sensitivity to cultural diversity and to the validity of other ends.

Such problems exist, even if often to a lesser degree, in the domestic implementation of individual rights. We do not have recipes for solving the problems. We struggle with them over time through a process of public debate, informed by the opinions (rarely unanimous) of professional elites, leading to revisable decisions by authoritative institutions. We need to have something like that in a form suitable to the international arena. We have nothing of the kind, though we have some beginnings that may or may not lead to the development of international authorities and associated processes of the needed kind.

I started by saying that we live in a period of transition with fast changes. It is possible to be optimistic. It is possible to be pessimistic about the direction of things. We should definitely not be complacent.

12

Joseph Raz on Human Rights

A Critical Appraisal

David Miller

The current popularity of human rights talk in legal and political circles has generated a higher level debate among philosophers about how the concept itself should be understood.[1] Unlike the much earlier debate about social and economic rights, and whether they should qualify as human rights proper, this is not primarily about the *substance* of human rights—about what should belong on the list of human rights and what should not. Instead the focus is on the kind of claim one is making when one says that such-and-such is a human right, and on how such claims can be justified; although the answer turns out to have implications for what belongs on the list, this is not the main concern. On one side are those who defend 'humanist' or 'naturalistic' or 'traditional' accounts of human rights; on the other side are those who defend 'political' or 'practical' accounts. Raz places himself, and has been placed by others, in the second camp.[2]

This is how the landscape is usually described, but recently there have been dissenting voices suggesting that the contrast between the two camps is at least overdrawn if not wholly misleading.[3] The dissenters argue that the two perspectives are complementary to one another, and both are necessary for a full understanding of human rights. I am sympathetic to this conciliatory move and will apply it to Raz's essay in this reply. But first it will be helpful briefly to characterize the two allegedly rival accounts of the nature of human rights.

The first, humanist, view holds that the way to understand human rights is to see them as moral rights justified by the role they play in protecting essential human interests. Proponents of this view differ over how these interests should be characterized: some identify a single feature such as 'personhood' which is then used to ground all rights; others argue that human beings have several distinct basic interests, each of them playing some role in the justification of human rights.[4] These disagreements are

[1] I am very grateful to Rowan Cruft and Matthew Liao for their helpful comments on an earlier draft of this chapter.

[2] J. Raz, 'Human Rights Without Foundations', in S. Besson and J. Tasioulas (eds.), *The Philosophy of International Law* (Oxford: Oxford University Press, 2010), and J. Raz, 'Human Rights in the Emerging World Order', this volume, ch. 11.

[3] See especially S. Matthew and A. Etinson, 'Political and Naturalistic Conceptions of Human Rights: A False Polemic?', *Journal of Moral Philosophy*, 9 (2012): 327–52; P. Gilabert, 'Humanist and Political Perspectives on Human Rights', *Political Theory*, 39 (2012): 439–67.

[4] See the ongoing debate between James Griffin and John Tasioulas on this point: J. Griffin, 'First Steps in an Account of Human Rights', *European Journal of Philosophy*, 9 (2001): 306–27; J. Tasioulas, 'Human Rights, Universality and the Values of Personhood: Retracing Griffin's Steps', *European Journal of Philosophy*, 10 (2002): 79–100; J. Griffin, *On Human Rights* (Oxford: Oxford University Press, 2008),

not germane to the discussion of Raz, and I will not pursue them further here. What is more important to notice is that even on the humanist view, the move from essential interests to rights is not straightforward. First, the interest in question has to be one that it makes sense to look to rights to protect. Humanist authors are fully aware that human rights once identified are meant to guide the actions of states. So it would be damagingly pointless to announce rights to have interests fulfilled that states could do nothing to secure—such as the 'right' to love, in the sense of the right to find a partner who loves one in return—no matter how important the interest itself. Second, some regard must be had to the potential cost of enacting a proposed right. Rights impose obligations, and discharging the obligations may require sacrifices of resources or of personal freedom; some of these sacrifices may involve encroaching upon other proposed rights. As a result, a feasibility condition of some sort has to be imposed when interests are being used to ground rights. Again the details are not important at this stage. But we should notice that on the humanist view there is always a gap between human rights themselves and the human interests that are used to justify them, a gap created by recognizing, in broad terms, the role that human rights are meant to play in practical discourse.

Raz calls the theories of human rights he is opposing 'traditional'. This might be misleading if it suggests that modern humanist theories are simply updated versions of the natural rights theories popular in the seventeenth and eighteenth centuries, where rights are attributed to individual persons inhabiting a pre-political state of nature. It is then easy to pillory such theories for their inability to explain many of the rights set out in the leading declarations and charters, rights that make no sense outside the context of the modern state. It is important, therefore, to separate what is essential to humanist theories as a class, namely, that human rights are justified by showing how they serve to protect essential interests of one kind or another, from features that particular members of that class might possess, such as identifying only rights that could be exercised in a state of nature. Raz says:

> The theories that I will call 'traditional' claim that human rights are universal because they are rights every human being has as a human being. That is, being a human being is the ground of possessing those rights. This claim is hard to sustain concerning the rights recognised as human rights in international instruments in the modern UN Charter era...[5]

Three features of this passage are worth our attention. First, although humanist theories do indeed claim that human rights are universal in the sense Raz explains, that, by itself, does not convey anything distinctive about this class of theories. That is, all theories of human rights assert that they are rights a person has simply by virtue of being a human being, as opposed to rights that one has by virtue of meeting some special qualifying condition, such as being the citizen of a particular state. Second,

especially ch. 2; J. Tasioulas, 'Taking Rights out of Human Rights', *Ethics*, 120 (2009–10): 647–78; J. Griffin, 'Human Rights: Questions of Aim and Approach', *Ethics*, 120 (2009–10): 741–60. For my own discussion of Griffin's personhood theory (and my preferred alternative), see D. Miller, 'Personhood versus Human Needs as Grounds for Human Rights', in R. Crisp (ed.), *Griffin on Human Rights* (Oxford: Oxford University Press, 2014).

[5] Raz, 'Human Rights in the Emerging World Order', 224.

it is somewhat misleading to say that being human is the *ground* of human rights, according to the theories we are considering. The ground of human rights is rather the feature, universally possessed by human beings, that justifies these rights, by explaining their practical importance (as we saw, different theories dispute precisely what this feature is). Third, as we have seen, establishing that something is a human right involves more than just showing that it can be given the right kind of grounding, even for humanist theories. Argument of a different kind is needed before we approach the rights contained in the modern charters.

Raz goes on to claim that the logic of 'traditional' theories forces them to concede that even 'cave dwellers in the Stone Age' had human rights such as the right to education. I will return to this claim later. Now I want to introduce the rival, 'political' account of human rights. According to this account, we should understand human rights by beginning with their political function—what they are being used to do. Again, there are different ways of setting out this function. According to Raz, what distinguishes human rights from other rights is that they serve to set limits to state sovereignty:

> Following Rawls, I will take human rights to be rights which set limits to the sovereignty of states, in that their actual or anticipated violation is a (defeasible) reason for taking action against the violator in the international arena, even when—in cases not involving the violation of either human rights or the commission of other offences—the action would not be permissible, or normatively available on the grounds that it would infringe the sovereignty of the state.[6]

This definition is ambiguous in one respect. Does the criterion being proposed for something's being a human right appeal to what are, as a matter of fact, taken to be reasons for taking action against states that infringe their sovereignty? In other words do we look to the behaviour of members of the international community, and examine when they believe they have reasons to intervene in the internal affairs of states (in ways that violate sovereignty)? Or is the issue a normative one? Is the question when outsiders have a *good* (albeit defeasible) reason to intervene, regardless of whether they currently believe that they do? Neither horn of this dilemma is particularly comfortable, as I shall seek to show.

If we ask first what limits to their sovereignty states currently acknowledge, the answer is that this is a disputed question. In general, liberal states recognize more limits than do authoritarian or dictatorial states, which are likely to insist on virtually untrammelled sovereignty. In international law, the tendency has been gradually to enlarge the grounds of intervention over time, with the development of the idea of 'the responsibility to protect' (against large-scale human rights violations).[7] So the answer to our question about which rights are human rights is also going to be disputed, if we look at existing practice, with a secular trend towards extending the range of rights recognized as human rights (by the proposed criterion). But even if history is moving in the right direction from the point of view of the theory, isn't

---

[6] Raz, 'Human Rights Without Foundations', 328.
[7] This development is traced in A. Bellamy, *Responsibility to Protect: The Global Effort to End Mass Atrocities* (Cambridge: Polity, 2009).

there something anomalous about leaving our list of (genuine) human rights hostage to what are regarded at any moment to be grounds for violating sovereignty?

This suggests that we should instead treat the criterion as a normative one: human rights are rights violation of which would *justify* interventions that infringe sovereignty according to some principle. But remember what the direction of the argument is supposed to be here. We begin by working out when it is (defeasibly) justifiable to infringe sovereignty, and then we attach the label 'human rights' to the rights that we discover to be the ones in whose name the infringement would be undertaken. Human rights are the conclusion of the argument, not the premise. Now it may be that those who support 'political' theories have the strong independent intuitions about sovereignty and when it may justifiably be infringed that would be needed to make such theories work. But, speaking for myself (and I suspect for many others), I find that when I think about intervention, I begin by considering the harms that it is meant to prevent. That is, I begin by looking at what I would regard as serious violations of human rights—people being driven from their homes, people being deprived of their means of subsistence, people being severely 'punished' on account of their ethnic or religious identities, etc. Where it looks as though some form of intervention, whether undertaken directly through military action, or indirectly by applying pressure to the rulers of the regime that is carrying out the violations, is likely to curb these harms, I conclude that we have (defeasible) reason to waive sovereignty for the duration of the intervention. The argument moves in the opposite direction. It *begins* with human rights violations, and *ends* with reasons to infringe sovereignty. So to make it, we need to know which rights qualify as human rights in the first place. Admittedly, there are some intermediate steps. Not just any human rights violation is going to count. For instance, restrictions on free speech, or inadequate provision of education, may violate human rights without being sufficiently grave to justify forms of intervention that impinge on sovereignty. But even here, it looks as though drawing the line will call on the resources of a humanist account. We will be asking how severely essential human interests are being sacrificed, whether the damage that is being done is permanent or capable of being reversed, and so forth. The grounds we appeal to will be those that figure in our general theory of human rights.

The challenge, then, for those who want to sit on the second horn of the dilemma is to provide an account of justifiable infringements of state sovereignty that does not already presuppose a theory of human rights.[8] I do not find such an account in Raz. Some of his remarks suggest that he thinks that the moral limits to sovereignty will vary over time, depending not only on the character of the state whose sovereignty is at issue, but also on the likelihood that those that could feasibly intervene will be guided

---

[8] This would not necessarily have to be a complete account of when sovereignty may justifiably be infringed. For instance we might think that a state that continued to pour out large quantities of greenhouse gases in defiance of an international agreement restricting emissions would be liable to have its sovereignty restricted, even though it was not putting basic human interests *directly* at risk. So a complete account might also introduce issues of fairness between states, breaches of international law, and so forth. The point remains, however, that the political account as I am reading it here needs to be able to tell us which instances of states behaving badly towards their citizens can justify outside intervention without openly or tacitly relying on an independent theory of human rights.

by morally sound principles.[9] This has the implication that human rights will expand and contract as the configuration of the international system changes. Evidently, this goes against the idea of formulating a fixed set of human rights that could be codified in a charter. I do not say that a purely political theory of human rights is an impossibility, but it seems to take us far away both from the substance of human rights as they are set down in the main charters, and from the way they are usually understood as bastions that stand firm against the rise and fall of different political regimes. The second horn of the dilemma proves to be no more comfortable than the first.

The obvious way to avoid it is to allow some version of the humanist theory to fill the gap left by the political conception. In other words, we first develop a provisional account of human rights by appealing to essential human interests and specifying the set of rights that would protect these interests most effectively. But then, following Raz's political approach, we identify the subset of these rights that are sufficiently important that their violation would give us a (defeasible) reason to intervene in the state responsible for the violation; these are the ones to which we attach the label 'human rights'. This, then, involves treating humanist and political approaches to human rights as to some degree complementary to one another. They are not, however, interchangeable because the political approach is likely to yield a narrower set of rights. How narrow will depend on the meaning we attach to 'intervention'. If we were to restrict it to armed military intervention, we would almost certainly arrive at a very short list indeed; at the other extreme, if we include robust criticism from outsiders as a form of sovereignty-limiting intervention, then there will be no substantive difference between the two approaches, since anyone who adopts a humanist approach will think that a state that violates human rights as she understands them opens itself to robust criticism at the very least.

Interestingly Raz sometimes suggests a different way of distinguishing human rights from other moral rights. He says 'of all our moral rights only rights that should be respected and enforced by law are identified as human rights'.[10] I take him to be giving a necessary rather than a sufficient condition here, since there are moral rights such as the rights that stem from ordinary contracts that should be legally enforced but are not plausibly counted as human rights. But is it true that it is a mark of a human right that it should be enforced by law, or does this narrow the class of human rights too far?

It is obviously a feature of a morally defensible legal system that it should *respect* human rights, in the sense that it should not require those subject to it to perform actions that violate the human rights of others. It is also true that there are many human rights, such as the right to physical security, to political participation, to non-discrimination, and so forth, that should be legally enforced. But if we think of socio-economic rights, such as the right to subsistence or the right to basic health care, it is much less clear that legal entrenchment, even if it could be made meaningful, is the best approach to securing them. What a state needs to do to fulfil these rights is to make effective public policy; it needs to avoid economic disasters like Mao Tse-Tung's

---

[9] Raz, 'Human Rights Without Foundations', 331.
[10] Raz, 'Human Rights in the Emerging World Order', 228.

Great Leap Forward, and ensure that sufficient resources are devoted to health care, education, and so forth. It is an open question whether the best way to achieve this is to give people legally enforceable rights to receive these goods. Perhaps there will still be some role for the law to allow individual people to take action if they believe they are being unjustly discriminated against when the goods are allocated. But equally there is a danger that the law will intrude upon decisions that are properly political because they involve weighing the most effective use of scarce resources.[11]

A further implication of tying human rights to legal enforceability is explicitly recognized by Raz. Enforceable human rights need appropriate institutions to implement them. But what if such institutions do not currently exist? According to Raz, 'if, given the prevailing circumstances, there is no possibility that impartial, efficient, and reliable institutions may come into existence regarding a certain right, then that right is not a human right'.[12]

This implication is surely troubling. Some of the worst human rights violations (as human rights are normally understood) occur in circumstances of political collapse when the institutions of the state largely cease to function, and there are no formal mechanisms available to provide basic physical security, food, shelter, etc. to perhaps millions of people. The natural response is to say that the human rights of the people affected demand a response, which is likely to take the form of ad hoc provision by outside security forces, aid agencies, and so forth. At this time and place, there is no possibility that impartial, efficient, and reliable institutions will emerge. Of course, taking a much longer perspective, one can hope for a political transformation that would allow this to happen. So the question is how Raz understands 'possibility' in the passage just quoted. On a generous interpretation, which accommodates political change, it will always be possible for suitable institutions to come into existence, even in the most inhospitable places, and so the proposed criterion does not rule anything out. On a narrower interpretation, it seems that in circumstances where human rights most need to be protected (such as those outlined in this paragraph), they lose their status as human rights because legal enforcement is no longer possible. Raz is candid about this: 'If enforcement—fair, efficient, and reliable enforcement—is impossible, we should recognize that the right is not a human right, and refrain from calling for its enforcement.'[13]

I hazard that Raz holds this view because of a legitimate worry (which I share) about the unfettered proliferation of human rights. Our theory of human rights must ensure that only a subset of moral rights (and for that matter only a subset of justice claims) qualify for that status. But I am not convinced that the way to control proliferation is to insist that human rights must be suitable for legal enforcement. Indeed that insistence seems somewhat at odds with another aspect of Raz's account, his claim that the importance of human rights lies 'in affirming the worth of all human beings, and in distributing power away from the powerful to everyone, including any group or

---

[11] For a fuller discussion of the enforceability question, see J. Tasioulas, 'The Moral Reality of Human Rights', in T. Pogge (ed.), *Freedom from Poverty as a Human Right* (Oxford: Oxford University Press, 2007).
[12] Raz, 'Human Rights in the Emerging World Order', 228.
[13] Raz, 'Human Rights in the Emerging World Order', 229.

association willing to advocate and promote the interests of ordinary people'.[14] What Raz sees here, correctly, is that the language of human rights has proved to be an effective vehicle for various civil society groups to press their claims *against* the institutions of the state, in other words to demand policy changes that would better protect the human rights of those they represent. Human rights here serve as political weapons. But what is being demanded is not necessarily that the rights in question should become legally enforceable. Consider an advocacy group speaking on behalf of the homeless. It invokes the human right to shelter and demands that government should make available more homes that poor people can afford to rent, meanwhile perhaps providing temporary accommodation. But it is unlikely to argue that there should be an enforceable legal right to a home: it is not clear what this would mean, or who the right should be claimed from. Nor, to revert to the point made earlier, would such a group suggest that the human right it was advocating was grounds for infringing the sovereignty of the state. One can think that a human right represents an important moral claim that all governments including one's own are obliged to respect without holding any particular view about how this right should be implemented, or whether failure to respect it gives grounds for intervention by outside agencies.

This, however, is to revert to a humanist approach to human rights, so it is time to examine Raz's critique of the approach he calls 'traditional'. Perhaps it suffers from flaws that are more serious still than those we have detected in a (purely) political approach. Raz lays two main charges at its door. One is that it makes human rights 'universal' in an implausible way. The other is that it expands the content of human rights excessively, without paying due attention to how they can be secured. I will consider these in turn.

Raz argues that if human rights are taken to be moral rights that human beings have simply by virtue of their humanity, it would follow that people must have possessed these rights throughout history, going back as far as the Stone Age. Taking the example of the right to education in the form in which it appears in the UN Declaration, he suggests this is implausible.[15] Instead, the human rights we recognize today are a response to the particular conditions of life in modern societies governed by states.

There are two ways to respond to Raz's argument here. The first is to accept that the idea of human rights, like the idea of rights themselves, is relatively modern.[16] The latter idea is generally thought to have emerged in the late Middle Ages. The concepts used in earlier societies were different. So it would be anachronistic to attribute human rights to Stone Age cave dwellers, given that this is not an idea that was available to them. They would of course have had the same essential interests that ground rights in us—they would have needs for food, shelter, protection against bodily assault, and so forth. However it would be possible to devise an ethics for cave dwellers that

---

[14] Raz, 'Human Rights in the Emerging World Order', 226.

[15] The clause reads: 'Everyone has the right to education. Education shall be free, at least in the elementary and fundamental stages. Elementary education shall be compulsory. Technical and professional education shall be made generally available and higher education shall be equally accessible to all on the basis of merit.'

[16] This is the position taken by Tasioulas in 'Human Rights, Universality and the Values of Personhood' and 'Taking Rights out of Human Rights'.

responded to these needs without referring to rights, and this, presumably, is what they did themselves. But this possibility is not an embarrassment for humanist theories, since they do not set out to explain or justify the very idea of rights. What they do is to explain why certain rights should be singled out as human rights, and provide a way of settling disagreements about their content. In other words, if we are going to play the rights game, these are the rights that we should recognize as having the special status of human rights. So according to this first response, asking whether Stone Age cave dwellers had human rights is like asking whether the present King of France is bald: the question simply does not arise.

A different response, more congenial to those who think that if human rights are universal we must be willing to attribute them to every human who has ever lived, is to say that cave dwellers did indeed have human rights, but the form that these rights took is different from the form they take with us. Raz considers such a possibility, but in slightly distorted form. He asks whether there might be universal 'ur-rights' from which contemporary rights such as the right to education could be derived. However I think that the picture here of deriving one right from another right is misleading. It would be better to think in terms of *specification*.[17] We have a general right to education, meaning the right, while growing up, to be equipped with the various intellectual and practical skills that we need to flourish as human beings in whatever social context we find ourselves in, and then this right will be specified in particular ways, depending on what that context is.[18] The degree of specification can vary. The clause from the UN Declaration that Raz cites represents an intermediate level of specification, because it lays out in brief the form that the right to education will take in modern states, states that are sufficiently alike that the various types of education (elementary, professional, etc.) it refers to must be provided in each of them. This is appropriate, since it is modern states that are the primary addressees of the Declaration. In any particular state, the right can be specified more precisely.

In fact, the explanation of the right to education as set out in the Declaration that Raz proceeds to give runs along exactly the lines of a humanist theory: a common human interest is invoked ('the opportunity to have a rewarding life', which 'depend[s] on possessing skills to tap the opportunities available in one's place and time'),[19] and this is shown to require, in the circumstances of contemporary life, the right to state-provided formal schooling, and so forth. This comes as something of a surprise since, as we have seen, Raz's stated view is that the mark of a human right is that it is a right whose violation removes the shield of sovereignty and opens the

---

[17] Variations on this theme can be found in a number of authors. Griffin speaks of different levels of abstraction: see Griffin, *On Human Rights*, 50. Gilabert likewise distinguishes between abstract and specific rights, and suggests that the humanist focus on the former complements the political focus on the latter: see Gilabert, 'Humanist and Political Perspectives', 442–6. Liao and Etinson distinguish between the aim of a right—the underlying purpose for which a right is instituted—and the object of a right—the institution or policy which achieves that aim in a particular setting: see Liao and Etinson, 'Political and Naturalistic Conceptions of Human Rights', 339–41.

[18] As this example shows, the aim is not to boil human rights down to a small number of very abstract rights, but to have a fairly extensive list of freedoms, resources, procedural rights, and so forth, that is still general enough in content to allow for contextual specification.

[19] Raz, 'Human Rights in the Emerging World Order', 225.

offending state to outside interference. Do we believe this about the right to education? Suppose a state failed to make publicly funded technical or professional education available to women. This would be gravely unjust, and grounds for criticism and
protest both inside and outside the state. But would it constitute grounds for interference, if interference is understood to mean coercive interference with the state's
exercise of sovereignty? This, at any rate, is what Raz needs to show if he is to keep to
his 'political' understanding of human rights. But here he seems to proceed just as a
humanist would.

So to conclude on Raz's first objection to humanism, holding human rights to be
universal does not mean attributing modern-style rights to Stone Age cave dwellers.
Either we can say that the question of human rights does not arise for pre-modern
humans—they neither have them nor lack them—or we can attribute to them generic
rights which would need to be variably specified according to local circumstances.
What about the second objection, that a humanist approach will allow human rights
to proliferate unjustifiably?

Raz's argument here, which he applies for example to the theory of human rights
developed by Griffin, is that if we start with some feature of human beings as the
basis of their rights—say their personhood—then whatever turns out to be necessary
to protect that feature will turn into a right. If personhood involves autonomy, for
example, and autonomy requires having a sufficiently wide range of options to choose
between, then human rights will have to expand to cover all of these options. Without
denying that some theories of human rights have been tempted down this primrose
path, it is by no means an inevitable consequence of humanist theories. Here we have
to pay closer attention to how such theories move from their grounding feature to the
resulting set of rights.

The essential starting point here is that although humanist theories do not construe
the point of human rights as narrowly as political theories—they do not see their
purpose merely as one of setting limits to state sovereignty—they nonetheless want
human rights to be rights proper, that is powerful demands that can only be overridden in exceptional circumstances. If they are to retain this force, they must be quite
narrowly construed. So to begin with, when a particular right is specified, it needs to
be shown that the exercise of that right is normally compatible with other members of
the set of human rights.[20] The right must not impose obligations that would infringe
the human rights of those who bore them. Next, the right that is specified must represent the *least demanding* way of protecting the essential interest that grounds it.
Demandingness here is a matter of the general social costs imposed by different versions of a particular right. To illustrate, the right to shelter may require the government to provide adequate housing to all who need it, but the form that the housing

---

[20] 'Normally' has to be inserted here, because a plausible theory of human rights will not entail that
they are strictly compossible under all circumstances. So, eg, if an epidemic with potentially many fatali-
ties breaks out, it may be justifiable to restrict the right to free movement in order to protect the rights
to life and health. But such cases will be rare, if the rights have been properly specified. I have addressed
this issue more fully in D. Miller, *National Responsibility and Global Justice* (Oxford: Oxford University
Press, 2007), ch. 7 and in 'Grounding Human Rights', *Critical Review of International Social and Political
Philosophy*, 15 (2012): 407–27.

takes can be the cheapest possible that does the job. Anything more than this takes us beyond the *human right* to shelter. And third, in the case of rights that serve a primarily protective function—rights whose purpose is to ensure that other rights can be enjoyed in relative security from interference—a judgement must be made about what counts as an adequate level of security, and how accordingly the right should be defined. My human rights include the right to legal counsel if I am charged with a crime, but not the right to the services of the highest-paid barrister in the land.

This does, however, suggest a point of convergence between humanist and political theories. If a humanist theory is to deliver a defensible account of the scope of human rights, it has to take cognizance of the forces that are liable to threaten these rights. Attention to this dimension is a feature of political theories, though it is less prominent in Raz's work than, for example, in the work of Charles Beitz. According to Beitz, 'human rights are requirements whose object is to protect urgent individual interests against certain predictable dangers ("standard threats") to which they are vulnerable under typical circumstances of life in a modern world order composed of states'.[21] This notion of a 'standard threat' is a helpful complement to the approach to human rights sketched earlier, which aims to develop a list of rights that is just sufficient to protect essential interests, and is therefore wary about expanding rights unduly. It might not be obvious why access to legal counsel should count as a human right, until we reflect on the fact that over-zealous police forces are always in danger of bringing prosecutions against innocent people. Being falsely accused of a crime is just the sort of standard threat against which human rights are intended to protect us. So here introducing 'political' elements into our theory of human rights might encourage us to expand the list somewhat, by adding more protective rights, or by extending the scope of some substantive rights on the basis that a narrower scope would allow states to target vulnerable groups.

In short, deciding on the proper scope of human rights always involves a balancing act: on the one side, only listing rights that are essential to protect basic interests, and ensuring that the interests of the right-holder are properly weighed against the interests of others whose freedom and opportunities would be restricted by recognizing the right; on the other side, ensuring that the protection offered is adequate to protect the right-holder from various likely threats that the modern state order creates. Achieving this balance may require drawing upon both the resources found in humanist and those found in political theories.

Raz seems to think that if we begin with the 'traditional' approach, there is no non-arbitrary way to control the expansion of rights. His practical concern is that 'in

---

[21] C. Beitz, *The Idea of Human Rights* (Oxford: Oxford University Press, 2009), 109. Note that picking out states in this way as the main source of the threats against which human rights are meant to guard us does not entail that *only* states are capable of violating them. Although it may at first seem linguistically odd to speak about human rights being violated when one individual person murders or rapes another, this is partly I think because positive legal rights are also being violated, and so we can describe these events in different, but equally valid, ways. And when thinking about what can justifiably be done to individual rights-violators, it may be important to recognize when human rights are at stake and when they are not. I have explored this latter question in 'Are Human Rights Conditional?' in T. Sakurai and M. Usami (eds.), *Human Rights and Global Justice: The 10th Kobe Lectures, July 2011* (Stuttgart: Franz Steiner Verlag, 2013).

the existing climate [human rights] lend themselves to reckless activism, which ignores the fact that rights impose duties and that the case for the existence of the duties has to be established beyond pointing to the value of the right to the right-holder'.[22] As I have signalled already, I share this concern, but do not see it as an unavoidable consequence of the humanist approach. In his critique of Griffin, Raz argues that if we take 'personhood' to be the ground of human rights, it will be impossible to draw a non-arbitrary line to prevent rights expanding to include 'all the conditions of a good life which one person can secure for another'.[23] (For some reason, Raz chooses to ignore Griffin's appeal to 'practicalities' which Griffin intends to serve as a means of restricting this expansionary tendency.)[24] I have tried to show why this does not follow once we see what is involved in moving from the feature that humanist theories light on to ground human rights to the list of rights that eventually emerges. Along the way, I have suggested, these theories can be improved by reflecting on the practical function of human rights in the existing world order, and to that extent drawing inspiration from the initially rival political approach.

Another concern that I share with Raz is the worry that a rigid interpretation of human rights would license international bodies to begin interfering with decisions about priorities that are properly taken at domestic level. He instances the human right to health. But again this is not an unavoidable corollary of a humanist approach. The balancing of interests, referred to earlier, that has to go on before rights are defined, has no one 'correct' answer. There is no canonical way of deciding how many resources should be devoted to health care compared to other social objectives. Instead there is a range of solutions all of which remain compatible with meeting the underlying human need for a healthy life. So the human right to health, as it occurs in the international documents, must be given only a modest degree of specification to allow room for higher levels of specification in particular societies.

Raz's worry here is intensified by his belief, critically discussed earlier, that human rights must be capable of legal enforcement. So he thinks in terms of authoritative international institutions attempting to enforce rights like the right to health in the face of local cultural variation. But I believe this presents the wrong picture. Human rights set standards that states must achieve as far as they are capable (and if they are not, other states may have obligations to offer help), but in the interpretation of these standards they should be allowed a 'margin of appreciation', the term adopted by the European Court of Human Rights to acknowledge justifiable variation in the way that member states interpret the Convention under which it operates. This is true

---

[22] Raz, 'Human Rights in the Emerging World Order', 231.
[23] Raz, 'Human Rights Without Foundations', 326.
[24] See Raz, 'Human Rights Without Foundations', 324, fn 12. I conjecture that Raz may have been misled here by Griffin's description of practicalities as a second *ground* of human rights. Their role according to Griffin is not to ground rights in the sense of justifying them, but to make rights more determinate by considering the practical constraints imposed by familiar features of human life on their content. Although I do not think that Griffin's appeal to practicalities is the best way to accomplish this (see my discussion in 'Personhood versus Human Needs as Grounds for Human Rights'), it is clear that he is alive to the danger that Raz is pointing to. As he says, 'if we had rights to all that is needed for a good or happy life, then the language of rights would become redundant. We already have a perfectly adequate way of speaking about individual well-being and any obligations there might be to promote it' (Griffin, *On Human Rights*, 34).

regardless of who is applying the standards. As Raz sometimes acknowledges, human rights have many uses. They can be appealed to by citizens challenging the policies of their own states, by civil society groups targeting abuses abroad, by states applying pressure to other states, by international organizations criticizing the behaviour of their members, and so forth. The forms of action involved are equally varied. Legal enforcement is neither the only vehicle for promoting human rights, nor necessarily the most important.

13

Why *International Legal* Human Rights?

Allen Buchanan

I. A Neglected But Fundamental Question

Recent philosophical theorizing about human rights is burgeoning. There is one glaring lacuna, however. Philosophers have not identified, much less addressed, one of the most fundamental questions a philosophical theory of human rights must answer: What justification, if any, is there for having a system of *international legal human rights*? Because the system of international legal rights is central to contemporary human rights practice, one must answer that question to know whether the practice is justified. Instead, the focus has been on three different questions: (1) how is the concept of human rights to be analyzed, (2) how are statements about the existence of moral human rights to be justified, and (3) how can moral philosophy be enlisted to criticize or help justify various particular international legal human rights?[1]

Question (1) is poorly framed because it assumes, without warrant, that there is one concept of human rights. Instead, it can be argued that there are at least two: the concept of human rights as general moral rights of all human individuals, regardless of whether they are recognized in positive law, whether domestic or international; and the concept of international legal human rights.[2] The former concept was evident in

---

[1] On question (1) Beitz and others who espouse what is sometimes called a Political (or Practical) view hold that the key to understanding the concept of human rights is to see how claims about human rights function in international human rights practice. They conclude it is part of the concept of human rights that if these rights are violated by a state, then other states have a pro tanto reason to take action against the violator (Beitz) or that violations disable what would otherwise be an appropriate reply by the state to criticism, namely, "it is none of your business" (Raz). On the Political View, the concept of human rights presupposes the state system, or, to put the same point differently, it is part of the concept of a human right that these rights may be asserted against states. Tasioulas rejects the Political View, arguing that the concept of human rights would be applicable in a condition of global anarchy or where a world government existed. To my mind this dispute is a case of ships passing in the night. Political View theorists like Beitz and Raz should simply admit that they are talking about an important feature of the concept of human rights that is central to international human rights practice and acknowledge that the term "human rights" is sometimes used differently, to refer to rights of all humans by virtue of their humanity and in ways that do not presuppose the existence of the state system. (For example, the term was often used this way by abolitionists and feminists in the nineteenth century, before there was serious consideration of states invoking human rights to criticize the behavior of other states). And Tasioulas should simply acknowledge that there is more than one valid use of the term "human rights" and that in international human rights practice it is often used in ways that are captured by the Political View. In international human rights law and practice the term "human rights" sometimes refers to international legal human rights and sometimes to rights that should be incorporated into international human rights law, as in deliberations leading to the creation of new human rights treaties.

[2] Samantha Besson notes that recent philosophical theorizing about human rights has often neglected the centrality of law in human rights practice. "The Human Right to Democracy: A Moral Defense, with a Legal Nuance," in *Souverainete populaire et droits de l'homme, Collection Science et Technique de la*

natural rights thinking in the seventeenth and eighteenth centuries, where it was used to describe the boundaries of state sovereignty and to formulate doctrines of justified revolution; and by the nineteenth century it was deployed conspicuously in the abolitionist and early feminist movements. The latter concept came to prominence with the founding of the modern human rights system at the end of the Second World War and introduced an international legal element that was lacking in the earlier concept. The distinctive idea of the modern human rights enterprise was to create standards, in international law, for how all states are to treat those under their jurisdiction. These international legal standards for states were formulated prominently, though not exclusively, in terms of individual legal rights.

Whether there is one concept of human rights or two is of limited significance. The more interesting question is this: What is the relationship between moral human rights and international legal human rights? A number of theorists assume, rather than argue for, an answer to this question, namely, what I shall call the Mirroring View. According to the Mirroring View, justifying particular international legal human rights (ILHRs) requires showing how they realize corresponding, pre-existing, moral human rights (MHRs).[3] In other words, even when they do not explicitly address the question of how to justify the system of international legal human rights, some philosophers simply assume that to justify it one must first develop a satisfactory theory of moral human rights, because they implicitly subscribe to the Mirroring View.

With respect to question (3), there is a widespread sense that international legal human rights suffer inflation and that proper constraint could be supplied by a sound philosophical theory (the favorite example of supposed inflation being the right to periodic holidays with pay). This makes good sense if one holds the Mirroring View. If international legal human rights are justified by showing how they help realize corresponding, pre-existing moral human rights, then we first need to know what moral human rights there are, in order to know which rights should be included in a system of international legal human rights. And this is true even if not all moral rights are suitable for international legalization. On this view, if there is no moral human right to periodic holidays with pay, then there should be no international legal human right of that description.

Although these three questions are all important, answering them would not answer a different, quite fundamental question: What reasons are there for having a system of ILHRs and are those reasons sufficient? Call this the General Justification Question regarding international legal human rights. Notice that it is different from—and prior to—the question of whether any particular right ought to be included in a system of

---

Societe (Strasbourg: Editions du Conseil de l'Europe 2010), 6–7. Available at http://www.venice.coe.int/docs/2010/CDL-UD%29003-e.pdf).

[3] Allen Buchanan, "Human Rights," in David Estlund (ed.), *Oxford Handbook of Political Philosophy* (Oxford: Oxford University Press, 2012). Theorists who proceed as if they hold the Mirroring View include James Griffin, Christopher Wellman, Carl Wellman, Andrew Altman, David Miller, and Joseph Raz. Rawls explicitly rejects the Mirroring View. Beitz can be interpreted as doing so as well, though he may not, because he mainly concerns himself with the concept of human rights and has relatively little to say about the justification of international legal human rights.

ILHRs ((3) noted earlier). The latter question assumes that having a system of ILHRs is justified and then asks whether this or that right should be included in it.

II. Legal Rights Without Corresponding Moral Rights

Those who assume the Mirroring View fail to consider the possibility that international legal human rights, like many rights in domestic legal systems, can be justifiable even in the absence of a corresponding moral right. For example, there are a number of different moral grounds for having a legal right to health care and the goal of giving legal effect to a moral right to health care is only one of them. Without appealing to a corresponding moral right, the legal right to health care can be justified on the grounds that it prevents great social disutility that would otherwise result from treatable or preventable diseases, that it promotes social solidarity, that it contributes to economic prosperity, and that it is an important ingredient of a decent society. So, it is a mistake to assume that legal rights, if they are justified, must be justified by reference to corresponding moral rights. It is better to focus on the basic idea of the modern human rights movement—the project of creating international legal standards for how states are to treat those under their jurisdiction—to note that these standards are largely, though not exclusively formulated in terms of international legal rights, and then, with an open mind, ask what different sorts of moral justifications might be given for having such a system.

This simple point that justified legal rights do not presuppose corresponding moral rights bears emphasis, because it shows that it is unwarranted to assume that ILHRs are just the embodiment in international law of MHRs and that consequently any international legal right (such as the right to periodic holidays with pay) that does not have a moral counterpart is unjustifiable. From this it follows that a standard form of argument among philosophers working on human rights is wrong-headed: One cannot infer from the fact (or, rather, intuition) that there is no MHR to X, that the inclusion of X in ILHR documents is a case of inflation.[4]

It also shows to be groundless the assumption that a philosophical account of the system of international legal rights is by and large a matter of producing a theory of moral human rights and then leaving the supposedly much less interesting and less philosophical question of their proper implementation to lawyers. Even if they do not explicitly make this last assumption, a number of philosophical theorists of human rights proceed as if they do, because they devote their energies exclusively to producing a moral theory of human rights, ignoring the yawning gap between claims about MHRs and claims about the justification for having a system of ILHRS.

The General Justification Question is also distinguishable not only from the question of whether any particular right should be included in the system of ILHRS, but also from another question: If the answer to the General Justification Question is affirmative, is the *existing* system of international legal human rights justifiable? Call this the Special Justification Question. There might be a justification for having

---

[4] Griffin makes this mistake. James Griffin, *On Human Rights* (Oxford: Oxford University Press, 2008), 191–211.

a system of ILHRS, but the system we have might lack some of the features that figure prominently in that justification. Oddly, when philosophers have gotten beyond the stage of analyzing "the" concept of human rights, they have generally only tried to determine whether or not some particular right is a plausible candidate for inclusion in a system of international legal human rights, without first answering either the General or the Special Justification Questions.

III. The Relevance of History

Beitz offers an explanation of the moral thinking that motivated the creation of the international human rights practice (henceforth, the Practice). Since the system of international legal human rights is central to the Practice, we may read him as offering an explanation of what motivated the creation of that system. Showing the incompleteness of his explanation can point us toward an answer to the General Justification Question.

Beitz says that in the immediate aftermath of the Second World War and the Holocaust there was a widespread conviction of the need for a new set of internationally recognized protections for individuals against harms inflicted by their own states.[5] This characterization does not explain why the chosen remedy took the form of a set of *individual rights*, much less a set of *international legal* individual rights. There were in fact several alternatives for devising constraints on state power to protect individuals, including: (1) a list of duties of states (without correlative rights), (2) a list of group rights (given that the Holocaust and other major atrocities during the war were perpetrated against individuals *qua* members of groups), or (3) a modification of international law that lowered the barriers against interference in what states do within their borders, thus allowing third parties to aid victims in their efforts to protect themselves from the state. Simply saying that the Practice arose in response to a perceived threat posed by states to individuals is clearly insufficient, then, to explain the fact that individual rights are central to the Practice. Nor does it explain why the founders of the Practice agreed that the response to the problem of vulnerability should rely heavily on international law, rather than on other means of implementation.

Elsewhere I have sketched a more adequate explanation of what motivated the founding of the Practice.[6] The basic idea is that the problem to which the creation of the Practice was a response was characterized by the founders much more specifically than Beitz suggests. The point was not just that individuals were vulnerable to harm inflicted by their states. Instead, it was widely assumed that the most serious threat of harm, as evidenced by the massive destruction recently witnessed, was in significant part the result of two distinct features characteristic of fascist/militarist ideology: *radical status inegalitarianism*, the denial that all those usually regarded as human have equal basic moral worth; and *radical collectivism*, the view that the individual is of no significant moral worth on his own account, but rather derives whatever value he has by virtue of his usefulness to or membership in the nation. This more fine-grained diagnosis of the problem points in the direction of a particular solution to it: Developing

[5] Beitz, *The Idea of Human Rights* (New York: Oxford University Press, 2009), 129.
[6] Buchanan, "Human Rights".

a new body of international law that gives equal legal standing to individuals does something to protect them against the threat that their own state will relegate them a status of inferiority and signals that they are objects of international concern in their own right, independently of how their own states may value them.

Focusing only on the problem of making individuals less vulnerable to abuses or harms inflicted by their states overlooks the fact that from the beginning, in the drafting of the Universal Declaration of Human Rights, the founders assumed, in effect, that every state should perform the basic functions of the modern welfare state. So-called positive or welfare rights, not just protections against state-inflicted harms or abuses of government powers, were included from the outset, in the Universal Declaration of Human Rights (UDHR), which was understood to be a precursor to legally binding documents. So, a more accurate characterization of the project is to say that it was the attempt to use international law to set universal standards for how states are to treat those under their jurisdiction, where this encompasses (1) protections against state-inflicted harms or abuses of government power, (2) the affirmation of basic equal status for all, and (3) securing for all the conditions for a decent or minimally good human life, or, alternatively, ensuring that every state performs basic welfare state functions. Most if not all of the rights included in the UDHR and the various human rights treaties that followed it can be seen as performing one or more of these three functions.

IV. Did the Founders of the ILHR System Assume the Mirroring View?

The opening passage of the UN Charter, which preceded the UDHR "…affirms faith in fundamental human rights, in the dignity and worth of the human person…" The UDHR's preamble appeals to "the inherent dignity and…equal and inalienable rights of all members of the human family," states that "human rights should be protected by law," and asserts that "[a]ll human beings are born free and equal in dignity and rights."[7] These are clearly references to moral, not legal rights. The preambles of the International Covenant on Civil and Political Rights (ICCPR) and the International Covenant on Economic, Social, and Cultural Rights (ICESCR) replicate this language almost verbatim. The most straightforward interpretation of this phrasing is that the project of that the UDHR begins is to establish a global practice that realizes, through international law, moral rights of all human individuals that exist independently of that practice itself or any other practice.[8]

---

[7] http://www.un.org/en/documents/.

[8] The preamble also includes the idea that respect for human rights is needed for international security, but it is the idea that human rights are grounded in the inherent dignity or equal worth of the human person that distinguishes the Charter, the UDHR, and the Covenants from traditional international legal discourse, marking the beginning of the modern human rights era. The language of inherent dignity or equal moral worth is also found in the Racism Convention, the Migrants Convention, the Vienna Declaration, the Children's Convention, and the Torture Convention. For a meticulous documentation of the claim that the Practice was founded on the idea of moral rights that all human individuals have equally and on their own account, drawing on the language of the UDHR, the records of the preparatory work of the Human Rights Commission that drafted the UDHR, and the records of the debates on the UDHR in the UN General Assembly, see Johannes Morsink, *The Universal Declaration of Human Rights: Origins, Intent, and Drafting* (Philadelphia: University of Pennsylvania Press, 1999) and Johannes Morsink, *Inherent Human Rights* (Philadelphia: University of Pennsylvania Press, 2009).

This is completely compatible, of course, with the Mirroring View being false. It might turn out instead that, contrary to what the founders thought, the *best* justification for having a system of international legal rights is not that they help realize a set of corresponding moral human rights, either because there are no moral human rights (as Bentham thought) or because other moral considerations in favor of having such a system suffice. Moreover, providing a non-MRH-based justification for ILHRs might be advantageous, if, as some have argued, there are some valid or credible moralities that do not recognize individual moral rights, or moral rights of any kind. A justification for the system of ILHRs that did not rely on the assumption that there are individual moral rights might in that sense be more "exportable," that is, might enjoy wider cross-cultural support.

The possibility that the best justification of the ILHR system would not proceed on the basis of the Mirroring View ought not to be dismissed out of hand, because, as I have already noted, in many cases legal individual rights can be adequately justified by a combination of moral reasons, without showing that they are needed to realize a corresponding moral right. One option worth considering is that even if some ILHRs are best justified by reference to corresponding moral rights, some are justified by other considerations.

V. Reasons for Having a System of International Legal Human Rights

In this section, I outline three distinct justifications for having an international legal system similar to the existing one. Argument One appeals to the benefits that such a system provides. Argument Two justifies the system of international legal human rights by showing that it mitigates a serious flaw of the international legal order that renders it unjustifiable, unless modified: the fact that it confers sovereign powers on states that create great risks for those under their jurisdiction. Argument Three shows that states, and the governments that act as their agents, have a special obligation to support an international legal human rights system because they are the chief beneficiaries of an international order that would be morally unjustifiable without it.

A justification for having a system of international legal human rights must be two-pronged, addressing both the fact that the rights that compose such a system are *international legal* rights and the fact that they are rights *of individuals*. Theorists who situate themselves in the broadly liberal tradition find it obvious that, within the state, legal individual rights can provide valuable protections against abuses of state power and would agree that they are especially valuable for shielding individuals from harms inflicted in the name of ideologies of radical status inegalitarianism and radical collectivism. But more needs to be said about why there is a need for a system of *international* legal individual rights.

A substantial part of the answer lies in an appreciation of both the success and the limitations of domestic constitutionalization of individual rights. At the time of the founding of the Practice, there were a number of examples where domestic bills of rights appeared to be playing a significant role in protecting the equal dignity of individuals.

It is unsurprising, then, that in preparing the first draft of the UDHR, existing domestic bills of rights were surveyed, and that the original Human Rights Commission's members characterized their task as the formulation of an international bill of rights.[9]

If domestic bills of rights were so valuable, why was it thought necessary to formulate an international bill of rights? Instead, why not simply mobilize diplomatic, political, and economic pressure, under the leadership of powerful states that appreciate the importance of constitutional individual rights, to encourage states that lack such protections to remedy this defect?

Argument 1: The benefits of having an ILHR system

There are a number of reasons to opt instead for a system of international legal human rights, corresponding to different valuable functions that such a system can perform. These fall under the seven headings below.

(1) Encouraging and supplementing domestic constitutional bills of rights

Promulgating a list of international legal rights, with corresponding legal obligations on the part of states, especially if it is supported by the authority of the UN—arguably the only international institution with credible pretensions to genuine inclusiveness and global moral standing—could both encourage those societies lacking domestic bills of rights to create them and provide a model for them to emulate. There is evidence that this has indeed occurred, especially in the cases of peoples emerging from colonial domination and former socialist states undergoing liberal democratization.[10] In the case of societies that have incomplete or otherwise defective domestic constitutional rights regimes, a well-crafted international list of rights can encourage improvements. To the extent that the domestic constitutionalization of individual rights is a progressive development, the fact that a system of international legal human rights can assist it counts in favor of having it.

There are other ways in which states might be encouraged to adopt or improve constitutional rights systems, for example, through international declarations or goal-setting exercises that lack the force of international law. The mechanism of international law has two advantages. First, and most obviously, it makes it clear that states have legal obligations to promote certain rights within their jurisdictions, not just that it would be a good thing if they did, while at the same time providing an authoritative initial formulation of what these rights are and, perhaps more importantly, processes for interpreting these obligations that conform to principles of legal reasoning. So far as states give more weight to international legal obligations than to less formal undertakings, the system of international legal human rights is likely to be more effective than non-legal alternatives. Second, when states incur international legal obligations,

---

[9] Mary Ann Glendon, *A World Made New* (New York: Random House, 2001), 56–83; Morsink, *Inherent Human Rights*, 149.

[10] Nancy Flowers (ed.), *Human Rights Here and Now: Celebrating the Universal Declaration of Human Rights* (University of Minnesota Human Rights Center). Available at http://http://www.1.umn.edu/humanrits/edumat/hreduseries/short-history.htum.

this creates the possibility of eventually developing legal institutions that will hold states accountable for fulfilling them.

(2) *Providing back-up for failures of domestic protection of rights*

Even in societies that have comprehensive constitutional individual rights, there can be failures of implementation which a system of international legal rights can help prevent or ameliorate. Societies that generally do a good job of protecting the rights of their citizens sometimes fall short in the case of particular groups—women, racial or ethnic minorities, or gays, lesbians, or transgender people. And in cases of perceived national emergency, as in war or in the wake of dramatic terrorist activity, the rights of all citizens may be imperiled by state action, in the name of national security. In some cases, domestic courts appeal to international legal human rights to justify decisions to prevent or remedy both kinds of failures.[11] The fact that international legal human rights are law, not simply a statement of supposed moral rights, empowers domestic courts to invoke it to correct for lapses in the state's protection of rights.

Even though there may be some differences in domestic and international lists of rights, there is sufficient overlap to make the back-up function significant. That there should be considerable overlap is not surprising, given the fact, noted earlier, that the drafters of the UDHR looked to influential domestic bills of rights for guidance and given that the UDHR and the ICCPR have subsequently influenced the content of many domestic bills of rights.

A system of international legal rights can perform the back-up function even if (i) there are no *international* institutions for enforcement of international legal human rights and (ii) even in cases where no significant *external* pressures can be brought to bear on states when they fall short in implementing their own domestic constitutional rights. With respect to (i), it must be emphasized that most legal enforcement of international legal human rights is not achieved through the actions of international institutions but through the operations of domestic institutions.[12] In states where the judiciary is relatively independent and there is a culture of compliance with its determinations, a court's ruling that the state violates a citizen's international legal human right can result in the state taking corrective action, even in the absence of any possibility of enforcement from outside the state. With respect to (ii), there is impressive evidence that some states respond to pressures from *domestic* groups mobilized under the banner of international legal human rights.[13] So, neither international institutions

---

[11] See, eg, *Dudgeon v. United Kingdom*, 4 Eur. Ct. H.R. 149 (1981), which held that Irish law criminalizing "buggery" between consenting adults violated the right to privacy under Article 8 of the European Convention on Human Rights (ECHR), and UN Human Rights Committee judgment against similar laws in Tasmania (*Toonen v. Australia*, Case No. 488/1992, U.N. Hum. Rts. Comm., 15th Sess., U.N. Doc. CCPR/C/50/D/488/1992 (1994)). For other examples, see Robert O. Keohane, Stephen Macedo, and Andrew Moravcsik, "Democracy-Enhancing Multilateralism," Institute for International Law and Justice Working Paper No. 2007/4 (New York University Law School, 2007).

[12] Henry J. Steiner, Philip Alston, and Ryan Goodman, *International Human Rights in Context: Law, Politics, Morals*, 3rd edn. (Oxford: Oxford University Press, 2008), vii, 1087–222).

[13] Beth A. Simmons, *Mobilizing for Human Rights: International Law and Domestic Politics* (Cambridge: Cambridge University Press, 2009), 112–54.

capable of enforcement nor effective external pressure appear to be necessary for a system of international legal human rights to perform the function of providing back-up for failures in the implementation of domestic constitutional rights.

(3)　*Enhancing the legitimacy of the state*

An institution is legitimate in the normative sense if it has the right to rule (that is, has rightful authority); it is legitimate in the sociological sense if it is widely *believed* to have the right to rule. Sociological legitimacy is normatively important, to the extent that an institution's ability to perform its functions depends on whether it is perceived to exercise rightful authority.

When a system of international legal human rights performs the back-up function just described, it can contribute to the state's legitimacy in the normative sense, given the plausible assumption that the legitimacy of the state depends in part on its at least providing minimally adequate protection of its citizens' human rights. But a system of international legal human rights can also contribute to legitimacy in the sociological sense. If citizens know that when it comes to legal claims they make against their state, the state is not the final arbiter in its own case, this can bolster the belief that the state is legitimate.[14] Thus the public's knowledge that the system of international legal human rights is performing the back-up function can enhance sociological legitimacy. So, to the extent that it is important not only whether the state has the right to rule, but also whether it is recognized to have the right to rule, there is value in having a system of ILHRs.

(4)　*Contributing to better understandings of domestic constitutional rights*

It is a perennial complaint in some quarters that international legal human rights betray a parochial scheme of values and, more specifically, that they are infected by the particular cultural biases of "Western" societies, who are said to have played a disproportionate role in formulating them. Interestingly, those who voice this complaint seem to be unconcerned about the risk of cultural biases in domestic bills of rights. The most influential domestic bills of rights—those that have been most widely imitated in constitutions across a diversity of societies—are the French Declaration of the Rights of Man and the Citizen and the US Bill of Rights. Both of these documents and many of their numerous offspring present the rights they enumerate as *universal rights*, not rights peculiar to people in a particular society. Given that this is so, the question arises as to whether in some cases domestic bills of rights fail to deliver on the promise of universality, and instead exhibit a parochial bias due to the particular historical–cultural context in which they originated.

The existence of a system of international legal human rights can help ensure that domestic bills of rights are not distorted by parochialism if two conditions are satisfied: First, the system exerts significant influence on the original formulation or

---

[14] Stephen Gardbaum, "Human Rights as International Constitutional Rights," *The European Journal of International Law*, 19(4) (2008): 762–5. See also Besson, "The Human Right to Democracy."

subsequent interpretation of the items included in domestic bills of rights, at least in a non-trivial proportion of cases; and second, the system includes effective measures to reduce the risk of parochialism.

I have already indicated that the first condition is satisfied with respect to the existing system of international legal human rights: The UDHR and the ICCPR in particular have influenced the creation of domestic bills of rights in a number of states and, at least in states whose courts recognize the supremacy of international human rights law or look to it as a legitimate interpretative source, international legal human rights influence the interpretation of domestic constitutional rights.

With regard to the second condition, there is abundant evidence that both in its origins and its subsequent development the existing international legal human rights system includes impressive provisions for reducing the risk of parochialism in how human rights are conceived. The strenuous efforts of the drafters of the UDHR to include a wide range of cultural perspectives have been well-documented.[15] Further, there is clear evidence that anti-colonialist (and hence "non-Western") views were not only voiced in the deliberations that led to the drafting but also found their way into the final document, in particular with respect to the unambiguous assertion that the rights therein contained apply to all persons, including those currently under colonial domination[16] and the enunciation of a right of self-determination of *all* peoples.

It would be a mistake, however, to assume that whether the existing system of international legal human rights includes protections against parochialism depends solely or even chiefly on whether such measures informed the drafting of the founding documents. What matters is whether the system subsequently developed institutions and principles that provide creditable protections against parochialism in the ongoing interpretation and re-interpretation of international legal human rights and in particular in the processes by which new human rights conventions are created.[17]

This is precisely what has occurred. The treaty bodies that were established to monitor compliance with the conventions that followed the UDHR were explicitly designed to incorporate diverse points of view and, as the membership of the UN quadrupled through the inclusion of newly liberated colonies, the risks of Western-dominated, parochial understandings of international legal human rights diminished accordingly.

I am not suggesting that the existing understanding of international legal human rights is free of parochial bias.[18] Instead, I am making two more modest points. First, the existing international legal human rights system is institutionally designed to reduce the risk of parochialism. Second, regardless of whether the existing system does a good job of reducing the risk of parochialism, a legal order for the protection of individual rights that is created and developed through the participation of people

---

[15] Glendon, *A World Made New*, 56–83.

[16] UDHR, Article 2 states that "Everyone is entitled to all the rights and freedoms set forth in this Declaration [and that] ... no distinction shall be made n the basis of the political, jurisdictional or international status of the country or territory to which a person belongs, whether it be independent, trust, or non-self-governing or under any other limitation of sovereignty."

[17] Allen Buchanan, "Human Rights and the International Legal Order," *Legal Theory*, 14(1) (2008): 39–70.

[18] For an in-depth assessment of the frequently voiced complaint that the international legal human rights system is biased against collectivistic moralities, see Allen Buchanan, *The Heart of Human Rights* (New York: Oxford University Press, 2013), ch. 7, "The Ethical Pluralist Challenge to Human Rights."

from many cultures should be less prone to parochialism in its understanding of those rights, other things being equal, than one that operates solely within a domestic cultural context. An international legal regime of rights that are explicitly and unambiguously conceived as universal, rather than local, and that includes institutional measures to reduce the risk of parochialism, can provide a corrective for parochial understandings of those individual rights that are intended to be universal in domestic constitutions.

(5) *Supplying resources for improving international humanitarian law*

To a significant degree, international human rights law and international humanitarian law (IHL) have distinct origins and, until very recently, have developed independently from one another. IHL originated in an international order that did not yet view individuals as subjects of international law and that was not yet transformed by the momentous advent of the post-Second World War human rights regime. Hence it is not surprising that IHL has not been framed in the language of individual rights.

To the extent that the statist origins of IHL still influence its content and institutional development, reconceptualizing it in the light of international human rights law would not only help to correct for any statist biases, but also could strengthen its implementation by harnessing it to the resources of the larger human rights movement. The point is not that traditional IHL did not take the well-being of individuals into account at all, but rather that subsuming IHL under the system of international legal human rights would unambiguously convey the message that the most important aim of constraining the conduct of war is to protect individuals, not to benefit states. It would also make absolutely clear that the constraints on war are not conditional on reciprocity in their observance, but are instead grounded in proper regard for all human individuals.

There is evidence that the influence of the existing international legal human rights system has already begun to stimulate progressive developments in IHL, without anything as radical as a merger of the two types of law. For example, the concept of war crimes has recently been expanded to include mass rapes. Rape was recognized as a violation of international legal human rights long before it was seen to fall within the scope of war crimes. Moreover, the effective use of ILHRs discourse by international human rights non-governmental organizations appears to have played a major role in this change. It can also be argued that the 1977 Additional Protocols to the Geneva Conventions strengthen the Conventions by including human rights provisions not previously found in them.[19] Finally, James Nickel has suggested that international legal human rights law has had another, arguably progressive influence on IHL: Conceptualizing the traditional IHL protections as human rights increases their weight in international legal reasoning, making them more resistant to certain trade-offs.[20] These developments have been succinctly summarized by Robert

---

[19] Frits Kalshoven and Lisabeth Zegveld, *Constraints on Waging War: An Introduction to International Humanitarian Law*, 3rd edn. (Geneva: ICRC, 2001), 34.

[20] James Nickel, personal communication, 16 June 2011.

Sloane as follows: [21] "[Modern] IHL signifies a major postwar shift…away from an interstate model grounded solely in simple reciprocity and interstate dynamics and toward a model justified more explicitly by international human rights law's solicitude for the individual and normative commitment to a universal conception of human dignity."

(6) Constituting an individual-centered legal framework for coping with genuinely global problems

As we have seen, the value of having a system of ILHRs depends in large part on whether there are deficiencies in domestic law that such a system can ameliorate. There are two kinds of threats to human welfare that present serious problems for even the more enlightened domestic legal systems. The first is the vulnerability of stateless persons. Domestic constitutions ascribe rights chiefly to citizens. When rights are ascribed to non-citizens, they apply only to those non-citizens within the state's territory. Not surprisingly, domestic constitutions do not affirm rights for stateless persons elsewhere.[22] International legal human rights are ascribed to all individuals, including those who are stateless, irrespective of where they are.

The second problem that domestic rights regimes have difficulty addressing is harms that states individually cannot effectively cope with and for which it would be inappropriate to hold them responsible, in the absence of any voluntarily assumed special international legal obligation. These include harms to health and well-being caused by environmental pollution, but also damage caused by international terrorists or pirates on the high seas. To cope with this second category of threats, states not only need to cooperate, but also to coordinate their cooperation on a single set of legal standards. Framing the standards in terms of international legal human rights not only gives them greater legal weight, but also enlists the impressive political and legal resources of the international human rights movement. Thus, for example, if the more severe harms that may occur as a result of global climate change are conceived as violations of international legal human rights to an adequate standard of living or to health or even to physical security in extreme cases, the efficacy of mobilization to prevent them may be increased.

Both in the case of stateless persons and that of global environmental threats, voluntary solutions may be blocked by the free-rider problem, because averting the threat has the characteristics of a public good. To the extent that obligations under international human rights law are treated as among the most weighty international legal obligations rather than just matters of morally admirable policy or bureaucratic requirements, conceiving of these threats as violations of international legal human rights can help counteract the incentives for free-riding.

---

[21] Robert Sloane, "Prologue to a Voluntarist War Convention," *Michigan Law Review*, 106(443) (2007–08): 483.

[22] Gardbaum, "Human Rights as International Constitutional Rights," 764–5.

(7) Helping to correct an inherent flaw of democracy

It is a virtue of democracy that government officials are accountable to their fellow citizens. That is the good news. The bad news is that the democratic commitment to the accountability of government to citizens tends to produce not just accountability, but near exclusive accountability. Democratic electoral processes and constitutional checks and balances create formidable obstacles to government taking into due account the legitimate interests of anyone who is not a citizen. In other words, democracy has an inherent structural bias toward excessive partiality or, if you will, against cosmopolitanism.[23] This bias is most evident in the case of accountability through periodic elections: Foreigners have no votes.

A system of international legal human rights can provide resources for domestic and transnational groups to exert pressure for domestic government officials to take the rights of foreigners into account and to that extent curtail the structural bias of democracy. From the standpoint of institutional design, a commitment to international legal human rights can be seen as a self-binding mechanism for democratic peoples to help counteract this structural bias of their own constitutional structure. Even those democratic states (if there are any) whose implementation of individual rights for their own citizens is so perfect as to render the back-up function of international legal human rights otiose would still have this reason for supporting a system of international legal human rights.

Argument 2: International legal human rights as a necessary condition for the justifiability of the international order

The traditional, pre-human rights era international legal order conferred impressive—and extremely dangerous—rights and powers on states while at the same time imposing scandalously minimal requirements for statehood or, rather, for what qualifies a group to count as the government representing a state. The international order is often described as "the state system," and until the advent of the modern human rights movement, its norms governed the relationships between states and international law did not even recognize individuals as having rights on their own account. Generally speaking, the international order, at least in its legal structure, treated individuals as if they were of consequence only so far as their well-being affected the interest of states.[24]

The rights of sovereign states conferred by the traditional international order—or perhaps more accurately, the rights that constituted that order—included first and foremost an extremely robust right against interference in the "domestic affairs" of states. Operating behind the "veil of sovereignty," states had great latitude as to how they treated those under their jurisdiction.

---

[23] Note that this point does not assume an extreme cosmopolitan point of view. It only assumes that states should systematically give some independent weight to the well-being and freedom of foreigners, not that they should be given equal consideration.

[24] The humanitarian law of war, which began to develop prior to the modern human rights movement, is an exception to this generalization.

The extremely robust right against interference in a state's "domestic affairs," taken by itself, contributed significantly to the vulnerability of individuals to abusive behavior by their own states. It erected a formidable obstacle to efforts by oppressed people to enlist the help of external agents in combating tyranny. But there were several other norms of the international order that exacerbated the problem of vulnerability. Among the most important are the resource control norm, the borrowing privilege, and the right to limit or completely prohibit immigration.

According to the resource control norm, any government that the rules of the international order recognizes as legitimate has a right to dispose of the natural resources within the state's territory. As Thomas Pogge has pointed out, this norm gives governments virtually blank checks to sell or lease the country's natural resources to the highest bidder, without regard for the well-being of the general population.[25] In brief, the resource control norm confers awesome power over resources without any checks to ensure responsible stewardship.

The borrowing privilege, whose destructive effects are also emphasized by Pogge, empowers states (or, in practice, the governments of states) to borrow, again without any restrictions. The effect of this norm is not only to lessen the incentives for governments to make the country self-reliant in financial matters, but, much worse, it enables irresponsible, inept, or corrupt governments to burden their populations with debts that can extend over generations and pose a formidable obstacle to economic development and the efforts of individuals to improve their lot in life. As with the resource control norm, a formidable power is conferred without provisions to prevent it from being exercised in deleterious ways, in conditions under which it is virtually guaranteed that abuses will occur.

Under the traditional international legal order, states also have a virtually absolute right to prevent foreigners from settling in or even entering their territories, as well as the right to withhold from them the rights usually accorded to citizens. This norm greatly compounds the damaging effects of the preceding three norms, because it makes the option of exit impractical for those whom other states are unwilling to accept. When governments persecute some people within their jurisdiction or abuse all of them, or when they squander resources or pile up mountains of debilitating debts, those who suffer from these actions may find no other country willing to accept them. By weakening the credibility of the threat of exit, the norm that confers the power to prohibit immigration deprives the oppressed of what might otherwise be an effective means of resisting tyranny or at least escaping it.

I have characterized these four norms of the traditional international order as conferring powers, privileges, and immunities on states, but in describing their effects the focus has been on the behavior of governments. This is not a mistake or an equivocation. Although the most basic norms of the international order are formulated in terms of states, they are applied to the behavior of governments, on the assumption that they are the agents through which the state acts. The destructive potential of the four norms of sovereignty noted earlier is exacerbated by a fifth norm, the Principle of

[25] Thomas Pogge, *World Poverty and Human Rights* (Cambridge: Polity Press, 2008).

Effectivity, which determines who counts as the government of a state. According to this principle, all that is required for a group of people to qualify as the government of state is that it exercise effective control over a territory with a relatively stable population and be capable of entering into relationships with other states.[26]

The Principle of Effectivity imposes no normative criteria whatsoever on what counts as a legitimate government. It is simply an instance of the more general principle that might makes right. In a world in which coming to be recognized as the legitimate government of a state means gaining all the powers, rights, privileges, and immunities that accrue to states, especially the right to control resources and the borrowing privilege, the Principle of Effectivity creates strong incentives for groups to gain control over a territory, by any means available to them, including the killing of rivals and the overthrow of existing governments.

There is one final feature of the international order that contributes to the vulnerability of many people: the fact that it is, to a significant degree, crafted—and often selectively implemented—to further the interests of the most powerful states. The most powerful states play a disproportionate role in determining what is customary international law, because their behavior counts more heavily in evaluating whether the requirement of "state practice" is met in the identification of an emerging customary norm. Likewise, the most powerful states are better able to shape treaty law, either by exerting pressure on weaker states to ratify treaties they favor, or by refraining from ratifying treaties they dislike and thereby limiting their effect. In our world, where the interests of states and global corporations are often aligned—and often at odds with the interests of ordinary people and especially the world's worst off—the disproportionate ability of powerful states to shape the international order, especially in its economic and financial institutions, can be highly destructive.

Taken together, these five flaws are so severe as to make the system morally unjustifiable, unless they can be significantly mitigated. This conclusion requires a qualification: It holds on condition that a modification of the system that mitigated these flaws is feasible. The system of ILHRs has the potential to correct for all of these flaws of the international legal order, with the exception of the last one, or so I shall argue. And the qualifying condition holds: A system of ILHRs already exists, seems to be relatively stable, and does appear to mitigate some of the flaws to some extent.

At least in the case of the first flaw, the virtually unlimited license for states to abuse those under their jurisdiction, the potential has been actualized to some extent. International human rights law has served as the authoritative *lingua franca* for imposing standards on states as to how they may treat those under their jurisdiction, and the institutions of the international legal human rights system have provided an important resource for various parties who strive to hold states to those standards.

Here it is important avoid a common mistake, that of gauging the power of international human rights law by the strength of international institutions. As Beth Simmons, Kathryn Sikkink, and others have documented, most of the enforcement of international human rights occurs through domestic institutions (chiefly courts

---

[26] General Act of the 1885 Conference of Berlin available at http://courses.wcupa.edu/jones/his312/misc/berlin.htm. *Isla de Palmas United States v. Netherlands* (1928).

and legislatures) and the key agents in the process of "mobilizing for human rights" are often domestic groups, operating through domestic civil society institutions and practices.[27]

Although international institutions for implementing it are generally weak, the existence of international human rights law plays a significant role in empowering more capable agents and institutions. One way in which this empowerment occurs is that international human rights law provides a focal point for domestic reform efforts, especially in the case of states that have ratified human rights treaties. Domestic activists can appeal to the international legal obligations their states have undertaken and legitimately appeal to international organizations in their struggle for better compliance.

So far, the Practice has been less successful with respect to modifying the other three norms and mitigating their damaging effects. Apart from including in its major documents the right of individuals to exit their state—the importance of which should not be underestimated—international human rights law has done little to moderate the norm regarding control of immigration, except by encouraging the recognition of a very limited right of sanctuary for victims of political persecution.

With respect to the resource control norm, international human rights law has had some impact so far as it has supported the notion that all people have a right to democratic government and includes a number of rights which, if realized, tend to create the conditions for democratization. To the extent that states become democratic, the accountability of the government to the people lessens the risk that the resource control privilege will be abused. When governments are accountable through democratic processes, they are less able to pillage the country's resources to line their own pockets.

In the case of the borrowing privilege, the prospects are less encouraging. Even where governments are responsive to the public, irresponsible borrowing can and does occur, because the public may be all too willing to impose burdens on future generations. The most promising role for international human rights law and the activism for which it provides a focal point in mitigating the damage of the borrowing privilege norm lies in supporting domestic rights regimes that limit the discrepancy between the interests of government officials and the interests of the public.

If states conscientiously implemented the various social and economic rights that further the welfare purpose of the international legal human rights system—securing for all the conditions for a minimally good or decent life—this would preclude the worst abuses of the resource privilege. Unfortunately, the various domestic, regional, and international agents and institutions of the Practice have been much less successful in holding states accountable for realizing these rights than has been the case with the civil and political rights. Whether this discrepancy can be reduced or eliminated is, of course, one of the greatest challenges for the Practice.

---

[27] Kathryn Sikking, *The Justice Cascade: How Human Rights are Changing World Politics* (New York: WW Norton & Company, 2011); Beth A. Simmons, *Mobilizing for Human Rights: International Law in Domestic Politics* (Cambridge: Cambridge University Press, 2009).

From the standpoint of international human rights law the social and economic rights are not of lesser priority. They are on an equal footing, so far as the law is concerned, with the civil and political rights. Nevertheless, there are two special difficulties in holding states accountable for their realization, and this fact lessens their ability to constrain abuses of the resource control right and the borrowing privilege. First, some states lack the capacity to realize some of the social and economic rights. The doctrine of "progressive realization" is intended to cope with this problem, but makes it more difficult to hold states accountable. Second, as a broad generalization, it may be more difficult for outsiders to determine the extent to which the failure to realize social and economic rights is the result of deficiencies in state policy as opposed to being the consequence of structural features of the international order and in particular of its economic and financial institutions and practices.

A third consideration is often invoked in this context: It is said that the social and economic rights, being "positive" rights, are necessarily more indeterminate or more open-ended than the "negative" civil and political rights and that this fact also makes it harder to hold states accountable for their realization. In my judgment, this last consideration is often over-stated and depends on an exaggerated contrast between civil and political rights and social and economic rights. The realization of civil and political rights involves the fulfillment of extremely demanding "positive" duties and these, too, are necessarily indeterminate. For example, to realize the right to physical security or the right to equal treatment under the law, a state must undertake large-scale, costly social policies, including the training, monitoring, and disciplining of the police and the personnel of penal institutions, supervision of the training of judge and lawyers, and much more. Despite the special problems involved in holding states accountable for the realization of social and economic rights, existing international human rights law has the potential to limit the opportunities for states abusing the borrowing privilege and the right to control resources indirectly, by holding them accountable for realizing social and economic rights, simply because fulfilling these obligations is incompatible with the worst abuses of these aspects of sovereignty.

One way in which progress could be made in this regard would be for international financial institutions such as the International Monetary Fund and the World Bank to alter their lending policies to make them more effective in reducing the risk of damaging borrowing and for the more economically developed states to restrict the ability of corporations based in them to make resource extraction deals with states that are damaging to their populations. Considerable human rights activism is already focused on both of these reforms.

The resources of an international law-based human rights practice for mitigating the ability of the most powerful states to shape the rules of the international order and their implementation in ways that are damaging to others are much more limited. This is not surprising, given that the most basic idea of the human rights enterprise, so far, has been to develop international legal standards for how states treat those under their jurisdiction—not to regulate power relations among states.

It remains to be seen how successful practice that is grounded in appeals to human rights law will ultimately be in mitigating the deleterious effects of the four norms of sovereignty. Be that as it may, the existence of an international legal human rights system is an important resource for making headway on them. If this is the case, then, given the moral necessity of mitigating the negative effects of these norms, one important reason for having such a system is that it is necessary for making the international order justifiable.

The strong powers of sovereignty, and above all the right against intervention in "domestic affairs" that the pre-human rights international order conferred on states, in combination with the morally-undemanding Principle of Effectivity, not only empowered states to abuse their peoples; it also enabled them to ignore or actively suppress efforts on the part of the population to insist that the state perform basic welfare functions, not just provide security and refrain from abuses, such as irresponsible uses of the resource control power, that detract from their welfare. Given the tremendous power the modern state wields over human lives, the robust authority it claims, and the resources at its disposal, it is reasonable for people to expect that the state perform welfare functions, not just provide physical security and refrain from abusing them in doing so.

In other words, in the modern context at least, the state's performance of welfare functions is a necessary condition for its justification. If this is so, and if the international order equips states with powers that they can and sometimes do use to evade their responsibility to perform welfare functions—or to provide basic social and economic benefits only to some but not all of those under their jurisdiction, then the international order is unjustifiable, unless it is modified so as to reduce this risk. A system of international legal human rights that includes rights with correlative duties on the part of states to provide basic social and economic benefits to all those under their jurisdiction is justified, therefore, as a necessary condition for the justifiability of the international order.

Argument 3: The special obligation of states to support the system of international legal human rights

The key premise of this third justificatory argument is that states have a moral obligation to cooperate with one another to remedy the flaws that make the international order morally unjustifiable. The obligation falls on states and their governments for two reasons: They are the chief beneficiaries of the international order in general and in particular of the four dangerous norms discussed earlier; and they are in the best position to correct its flaws because the international order is created and sustained by them. If the international order is morally unjustifiable without a system of international legal human rights and if governments have an obligation to render it justifiable, then they have a special obligation to support the system of international legal human rights. The moral weight of this obligation and the costs which an agent may rightly be expected to bear in discharging it will vary across states, depending on how much power they have to influence the character of the international order and upon the resources at their disposal.

In this section, I have set out three arguments for having an ILHR system similar to the one that exists. Thus, I have taken the first step toward answering what may be the most neglected question in current philosophical theorizing about human rights, the General Justification Question: Why have a system of international legal human rights?

In doing so, I have also provided the initial materials for the first step in answering the Special Justification Question by showing that, to some extent at least, the existing system of international legal human rights performs these valuable functions.

Taken by themselves, the three arguments do not show that having such a system is justified or a good thing, all things considered.[28] To establish that stronger claim, one would have to consider the other side of the ledger: the considerations that count against having such a system. In this chapter, I cannot attempt even to identify the potentially countervailing considerations, much less to assess their weight.[29] Instead, my purpose has been only to begin the task of justifying the system of ILHRs.

VI. Conclusion

I will end this investigation by considering a worry about the justificatory arguments I have advanced. It might be objected that they fall short in this respect: At most they show that having a system of ILHRs rather like the existing one is *one* way to achieve the seven benefits I listed earlier and one way to reduce the risks to individuals and groups that the international legal order's conferral of sovereign powers on states produces. Similarly, it might be argued that supporting the system of ILHRs is only one way for states and governments to discharge the special obligation they have to mitigate these risks. Other kinds of institutional responses might suffice.

This may be true, but it is not damaging to the justificatory case I have made, for several reasons. First, for this objection to have much force, a coherent alternative would have to be spelled out—a fairly determinate alternative institutional practice capable of providing the seven benefits and significantly mitigating the risks entailed by sovereignty as constructed in the existing international legal order would have to be articulated. I, for one, am not confident that this can be done. Second, the alternative arrangement would have to be shown to be feasible, where this involves showing (i) that we can get there from here, (ii) that we can get there from here by a morally acceptable path, (iii) that the benefits of pursuing this alternative arrangement would exceed the costs of pursuing it, and (iv) that the alternative arrangement would be stable. I think it is very likely that it would be a bad bargain to pursue an alternative arrangement at this point, rather than devoting our energies instead to improving the system of ILHRs and the human rights practice that is anchored on it. Even if, were we to start from scratch, there is some alternative arrangement that would satisfy the condition of the three justificatory arguments, given where we are, those arguments still provide strong support for the existing system. In brief, to justify an existing institutional order, one need not show that it is superior to—or even as good as—all alternatives. Considerations of cost-effectiveness, broadly understood, can favor the status quo, even if it is not uniquely good, much less optimal, especially when we take into account the costs and risks of undertaking the transition to an alternative arrangement.[30]

---

[28] Nor does it show that having a system of international legal rights is the *only* way to achieve all of these benefits. That would be an excessively strong requirement for the system being justified.

[29] In *The Heart of Human Rights*, I address this task.

[30] Much of this essay is drawn from Buchanan, *The Heart of Human Rights*, chs. 2, 3, and 4.

14

Human Rights Pragmatism and Human Dignity

David Luban

I. Human Rights Foundationalism and Human Rights Pragmatism

There is a line of argument that I will label *human rights foundationalism* that runs as follows: human rights are, first and foremost, rights that flow from the fact that we are human. Call them, as Allen Buchanan does, "moral human rights."[1] Whatever features of our humanity give rise to moral human rights lie at the foundation of human rights. Therefore, philosophical inquiry into those features is an investigation into the moral and philosophical foundations of human rights. Because people of all nations share their humanity, moral human rights are *universal* human rights, exactly as the title of the Universal Declaration of Human Rights (UDHR) implies. And the reason they are international is straightforward: they're universal.

An important part of human rights foundationalism is the claim that legal human rights should track moral human rights. This is what Buchanan calls the "Mirroring View," which he rejects. According to the Mirroring View, universal human rights flowing from moral rights should be codified in legal human rights instruments; conversely, codified human rights disconnected from moral rights don't belong in the canon. The codifiers got it wrong; they included more rights in their proposals than foundational inquiry can justify. Such overinclusiveness is not harmless error, because rights inflation devalues the currency of human rights.

Buchanan, as I read him, has no objection to philosophical inquiry into universal moral rights. But he rejects the Mirroring View. So do I. Further, Buchanan implicitly disagrees with another important step in the foundationalist argument: the seemingly obvious move from *universal* human rights to *international* human rights. Making human rights international is not simply a recognition of their universality. Buchanan offers several cogent reasons why internationalizing human rights can be an excellent idea whether or not they mirror moral human rights; and their universality (or, as he puts it, their non-parochialism) is only one of the reasons he details. I agree with this point as well.

I would put Buchanan's point this way. Making human rights international is a political decision to make them the business of the international community. It is a *jurisdictional* decision about which institutions will define, codify, monitor, and enforce human rights. It is the international equivalent of the domestic decision to

---

[1] Allen Buchanan, "Why *International Legal* Human Rights?", this volume, ch. 13.

delegate a certain set of rights to the national rather than provincial government in a federal system.

This decision is partly a matter of political–philosophical commitments: localism or globalism? Nationalism or internationalism? Trust or mistrust of "big government" transnational institutions run by elites in New York, Brussels, Strasbourg, The Hague, and Geneva? But it is also a matter of relative institutional competence. As Buchanan notes, domestic protection of constitutional rights often fails. This can result from state incapacity, in weak states or even in strong states with anemic or understaffed rule of law institutions.[2] It can also happen out of state malice, because the state itself is violating the rights.

The fact that domestic rule of law institutions often fail to protect constitutionalized human rights does not by itself show that international institutions will succeed, or even bring about marginal improvements. But they might be able to do so. For example, Buchanan rightly argues that international legal human rights can provide a textual and interpretive template for domestic courts and legislatures to use, in effect a public good that is available off the shelf for states to adopt. International rights can also provide ammunition for local NGOs and activists to organize and pressure their governments, even when outside pressure cannot be brought to bear. Although Buchanan does not mention it, I would add that international human rights institutions and NGOs can and do provide material resources to support human rights in developing states, including rule of law expertise, training, money, monitoring, and networking. Similarly, the fact that legal human rights have been internationalized can provide a legal and political rationale for wealthy states to include material resources for human rights protection in their foreign aid; in some cases donor states' domestic law requires them to condition their foreign aid on human rights improvements.

When I say that internationalizing human rights makes them the business of the "international community," the phrase does not refer only to the collective sentiment of humanity (the "conscience of humanity"), as when we say that some atrocity shocks the international community. Nor does it mean only the society of states, understood as legal persons who are the formal subjects of international law. Rather, the international community is a network of concrete institutions, including states, NGOs, and international organizations. Most important is the UN system, with its many agencies, together with the alphabet soup of spin-offs and quasi-independent bodies created through international treaties: WHO and WTO, UNHCR and ILO and OPCW, the many international tribunals (the International Court of Justice, the criminal

---

[2] Eg, Turkish observers sometimes attribute Turkey's fragile rule of law and human rights environment to the small size and vulnerability of the legal profession. Turkey, notwithstanding its powerful state, has only a third the number of lawyers as the United Kingdom, even though Turkey is larger; furthermore, the Turkish bar has been embattled for political reasons. So too, in 2012 China had only 220,000 licensed lawyers—a third the number of practicing lawyers as the United States—to serve a population more than four times the size of the United States, which itself suffers from unavailability of legal services to low-income people. The ready availability of private legal services is directly connected with the rule of law and therefore to domestic enforcement of human rights. See David Luban, "Existe el derecho humano a un abogado?," in Cristina García Pascual (ed.), *El Buen Jurista. Deontología del Derecho* (Valencia: Editorial Tirant Lo Blanc, 2013), 217–32; an English-language version will appear in the journal *Legal Ethics* as "Is There a Human Right to a Lawyer?".

tribunals, the arbitral tribunals, the WTO appellate body). The international community in this institutional sense also includes leading civil society organizations such as the International Committee of the Red Cross (ICRC) and Amnesty International. Importantly enmeshed in the network constituting the international community are the officially designated human rights institutions: the UN's Human Rights Committee, the European Court of Human Rights, the Inter-American Commission, the African Commission and Court, the ILO (focusing specifically on labor rights), and others.

Although Buchanan does not cast his argument explicitly in these terms, it seems to me that it makes the most sense under this institutional understanding of the international community: he is talking principally about the practical effects of legalizing human rights and making them the institutional business of international institutions.

This takes us to a second key point in Buchanan's argument: the central importance of turning international human rights into legal rights. Buchanan's phrase "international legal human rights" (ILHRs) denotes a proper subset of codified international human rights. Not all international human rights, including rights codified in international instruments, are legal. Recall that the UDHR was specifically designed as a legally non-binding declaration, out of concern that states were not at that point prepared to bind themselves legally to anything so demanding and so ambitious. So the UDHR represents a category of codified international *non-legal* human rights.[3]

Legalizing international human rights is a promising strategy. It makes them more comprehensible to most people, who may not know what a human right is in the abstract, but do know (in a commonsense way) what legal rights are. Legalizing international human rights also places them in the same ontological category as domestic legal and constitutional rights. By doing so, it converts human rights claims into the working currency of judicial and legislative institutions. This, like the decision to internationalize human rights, is a jurisdictional choice about which institutions will make human rights their business. Buchanan's ILHRs are legal rights that are the international community's institutional business, but also the business of domestic courts and legislatures. In effect, by legalizing international human rights the international community deputizes domestic courts and legislatures to help enforce them.[4]

In short, as I read Buchanan's argument, he offers an institutional view of international legal human rights, in place of the Mirroring View. It is a powerful, plausible, and sympathetic argument.

How does all this bear on human rights foundationalism? Viewing matters in this institutional manner decouples ILHRs from their supposed moral foundations, and puts Buchanan in the company of those such as Charles Beitz who deny that international human rights needs any foundation other than the ongoing practice of human

---

[3] Some jurists and publicists believe that the UDHR has now become part of customary international law; others contest this. But even those who think it is part of customary international law would not ground a legal claim against a state solely on the UDHR; rather, the UDHR would be invoked to buttress, and perhaps interpret, some rights claim that is also found in a binding treaty, constitution, or other hard law instrument.

[4] This paragraph represents my own view; Buchanan does not offer these arguments, although I expect he would agree with them.

rights itself.[5] This is a broadly pragmatist approach, in the philosophical sense of the term in which, methodologically, theory answers to practice rather than the other way around. To put it linguistically, the semantics of terms like "human rights" and "international human rights" must answer to their pragmatics, their use. Their meaning is their use, and philosophical theory should limit itself to slight regimentation of the language of human rights practice without pretending that the practice must answer to it.

I agree with this way of proceeding. And I also agree with Buchanan's point that there are cogent practical and moral reasons to legalize and internationalize human rights—reasons independent of the Mirroring View and, more generally, of foundationalist theory. In my view, his paper gets this exactly right, and he significantly enhances our understanding of why human rights should be legalized and internationalized.

In my concluding section, though, I shall resurrect a form of foundationalism within a fundamentally pragmatist framework. As I next argue, without some connection between ILHRs and moral human rights, Buchanan's pragmatist defense of ILHRs will not work.

II. Why Buchanan's Defense of ILHRs Still Requires a Connection with Moral Human Rights

The reason is that without a connection with moral human rights, ILHRs will fail as legal rights. So, even on its own terms, a pragmatist and institutional argument cannot throw ILHRs' theoretical connection with moral rights overboard, as excess baggage. Let us see why. I present the argument in four steps.

Step 1. One perpetual embarrassment that ILHRs have always faced is the lack of effective institutions to enforce them. Sometimes, for jurisdictional or political reasons, international human rights claims cannot be adjudicated. For example, the European Court of Human Rights has held that the European Convention on Human Rights' jurisdiction does not include a military adversary's territory.[6] Sometimes, the adjudicatory bodies have no authority to enforce their decisions and orders. When the United States ratified the International Covenant on Civil and Political Rights (ICCPR), the US Senate attached a reservation declaring that ICCPR's substantive articles are not self-executing, which means that no cause of action can arise under them in US courts unless Congress implements them through legislation (which it has no intention of doing).[7] In addition, the United States declined to join the First Optional

---

[5] Charles R. Beitz, *The Idea of Human Rights* (Oxford: Oxford University Press, 2011). Buchanan's criticism of Beitz for neglecting the General Justification Question is not, I think, a criticism of Beitz's anti-foundationalism, with which Buchanan agrees.

[6] *Banković and Others v. Belgium and 16 Other Contracting States*, 2001-XII Eur. Ct. H.R. 333 (Grand Chamber), 123 ILR 94, §§59–63 (holding that relatives of civilians killed in NATO bombing of a Belgrade television station have no cause of action for violation of human rights under the Convention, because the ECHR's jurisdiction does not extend to the territory of a military adversary that is not party to the Convention).

[7] US reservations, declarations, and understandings, International Covenant on Civil and Political Rights, 138 Cong. Rec. S4781-01 (daily edn, 2 April 1992), available at http://www1.umn.edu/humanrts/usdocs/civilres.html, III(1).

Protocol to the ICCPR, which would authorize the UN's Human Rights Committee to hear complaints against the United States. So, even though the ICCPR is a binding treaty that creates legal rights—unlike the non-binding UDHR—and the United States ratified ICCPR, no judicial body inside or outside the country is empowered to adjudicate complaints about US human rights violations.

For that matter, even if the United States had permitted the Human Rights Committee to accept complaints against it, the Committee lacks enforcement powers: all it can do about complaints is call them to the attention of a state. So too, only twenty of thirty-five American states have accepted the mandatory jurisdiction of the Inter-American Court of Human Rights. The African Court of Human Rights likewise lacks mandatory jurisdiction. Regrettably, the European Court of Human Rights is the only human rights court in the world that actually has robust enforcement powers. Finally, even if international tribunals have the legal authority to order a remedy, they may lack the power to impose their will if a state defies them—consider the current inability of the International Criminal Court (ICC) to arrest its Sudanese suspects.

Call this the problem of *enforcement deficit*.

Step 2. This enforcement deficit makes the ILHRs contained in most of the world's human rights instruments legal rights without legal remedies. Admittedly, legal rights without legal remedies are not conceptually impossible. And they occasionally crop up even in mature and effective domestic legal systems.[8]

I note that legal realists sometimes deny as a conceptual matter that rights without remedies are genuine rights. That is because they equate law with its practical consequences (in Holmes's terms, they view law from the point of view of the Bad Man "who cares only for the material consequences").[9] That this is a weak argument has been recognized since H.L.A. Hart's critique of realism in *The Concept of Law*. But this much of the realist argument seems right: rights without remedies must be the rare exceptions, not the rule, or else it makes little sense to call them *legal* rights. A self-styled legal system in which rights without remedies are common, rather than anomalous, would not do what legal systems do, namely provide a framework for organizing human action. It would be a legal system in name only.[10]

---

[8] A rights violation might occur outside the territorial jurisdiction of any court; or the court may lack the legal authority to order the political branches of government to provide a remedy; or, in the case of treaty-based rights, the violated individual may not be authorized to take a rights infringement to court unless her home state does so on her behalf, which for diplomatic reasons it may decline to do. None of these are imaginary scenarios: all have occurred in recent US practice. In *Maqaleh v. Gates*, 605 F.3d 84 (D.C. Cir. 2010), the court found that it has no jurisdiction over habeas corpus in the US prison camp at Baghram, Afghanistan. The same court found that it lacks authority to order the release of a Guantánamo inmate within US territory even though the detainee had won his habeas case, because the political branches of government, not the courts, have plenary authority over immigration. *Kiyemba v. Obama*, 605 F.3d 1046, 1048 (D.C. Cir. 2010). In an earlier case, that court held that violations of a detainee's Geneva Convention rights are non-justiciable, because the injured party in a treaty breach is not the violated individual but his state. *Hamdan v. Rumsfeld*, 415 F.3d 33 (D.C. Circ. 2005). So too, only states can bring cases to the ICJ, so US breaches of individual consular rights of Mexicans, Paraguayans, and Germans had to be brought by their home states.

[9] Oliver Wendell Holmes, Jr., "The Path of the Law," *Harvard Law Review*, 10 (1897): 459.

[10] In Lon Fuller's terminology, a system-wide failure of congruence between the law in books and the law as it is enforced is simply a failure to make law. Lon L. Fuller, *The Morality of Law*, rev. edn. (New Haven, CT: Yale University Press, 1969), 38–39.

And that spells trouble for the system of international legal human rights, where non-justiciability, legal non-enforceability, or toothless enforceability are no anomaly. They are the rule, not the exception.

Call this the problem of *rights without remedies*.

Step 3. Everyone involved with human rights practice understands that international human rights are frequently under-enforced and unenforceable. The most common response (both in theory and practice) is the argument that the primary enforcer of international human rights, non-legal as well as legal, is the so-called "mobilization of shame."[11] Whether the mobilization comes from the outside world or, as Buchanan rightly emphasizes, from domestic activists using ILHRs as an organizing tool, shame sanctions, bad publicity, and international outrage are the principal remedial scheme that human rights practice has to offer for state violations of ILHRs. Without any such remedial practice, I have argued, there is nothing legal about a system of international human rights—they may be IHRs, but they are not ILHRs.

Call this the problem of *generating international outrage*.

Step 4. How is the mobilization of shame going to come about? Only, it seems to me, if ILHRs matter to people morally, and to a degree that sets ILHRs off from less significant legal rights (say, from the legal right to paint my house yellow). That means ILHRs cannot be decoupled from moral human rights, although they almost certainly can be decoupled from any specific philosophical theory of moral human rights. If legal human rights are just another bit of positive law, then why should anyone invest time and money, let alone risk their lives, to mobilize around ILHRs? Why should state leaders (pretend to) feel ashamed about violating them, any more than they feel ashamed about violating technical regulations about the size and shape of cartons in international shipping?

The moral specialness of human rights is reflected in legal doctrine. Consider this well-known dictum in the European Court of Human Rights' *Soering* decision:

> In interpreting the Convention regard must be had to its special character as a treaty for the collective enforcement of human rights and fundamental freedoms. Thus, the object and purpose of the Convention as an instrument for the protection of individual human beings require that its provisions be interpreted and applied so as to make its safeguards practical and effective.[12]

The Court therefore uses the so-called Principle of Effectiveness to interpret clauses of the Convention broadly rather than literalistically.[13] And it does so because it

---

[11] See Robert F. Drinan, S.J., *The Mobilization of Shame: A World View of Human Rights* (New Haven, CT: Yale University Press, 2001). Drinan borrows the title phrase from Amnesty International. See also Beth A. Simmons, *Mobilizing for Human Rights: International Law in Domestic Politics* (New York: Cambridge University Press, 2009) and Oona Hathaway and Scott J. Shapiro, "Outcasting: Enforcement in Domestic and International Law," *Yale Law Journal*, 121 (2011): 252–349. For an argument that the mobilization of shame is not always the kind of sanctioning suitable for the concept of law, see Joshua Kleinfeld, "Enforcement and the Concept of Law," *Yale Law Journal Online*, 121 (2011), available at http://www.yalelawjournal.org/the-yale-law-journal-pocket-part/international-law/enforcement-and-the-concept-of-law/.

[12] *Soering v. United Kingdom*, 161 Eur. Ct. H.R. 87 (1989), reprinted in 28 I.L.M. 1066, 1091–1092 (1989), para 87.

[13] The principle long pre-dates the European Court; it originates in the old legal maxim "*interpretatio fienda est ut res magis valeat quam pereat*," meaning that an interpretation is to be adopted so that

recognizes that there is something special about human rights and fundamental freedoms, lending special urgency to making them effective, and counseling against narrow, crabbed, or niggling modes of interpretation.

Let me put the point about the moral specialness of human rights another way. Whatever its other infirmities, human rights foundationalism has an answer to the question "why do you call these things '*human* rights'?" The foundationalist answer is that they are moral claims every human being is entitled to make, where the entitlement and the content of the claims flows from our human status itself. But if ILHRs are positive law with no necessary connection with human status, then there is no particular reason to dignify them with the label "human rights." We could delete the word "human" from the label without doing any conceptual damage, because it does no definitional work. Indeed, if Buchanan is right in rejecting the Mirroring View, deleting the word "human" might avoid confusion. We could then give international human rights a more technical name, maybe "transnational legal claim rights," without losing any conceptually definitive feature.

But obviously no organization called Transnational Legal Claim Rights Watch, or Transnational Legal Claim Rights First, will spring into existence to mobilize shame around their violation. And this is not simply a point about the rhetorical force of labels. It is a point about the moral importance of these rights, the fact that we place great moral weight on them, because we think (rightly or wrongly) that they are closely tied to something basic about humanity as such.

What is that something? The UN Charter, the UDHR, the two major human rights covenants, the Helsinki Accords, the American Convention on Human Rights, the African (Banjul) Charter of Human and Peoples' Rights, and the European Charter of Human Rights all call it "human dignity." Without pretending to know what that phrase means—more about that soon—we can say that ILHRs are capable of mobilizing shame because they concern themselves with human dignity, not because they are legal and not because they are international.

Thus, to summarize the argument, the three problems of enforcement deficit, rights without remedies, and the need to generate international outrage require some connection between ILHRs and moral human rights. Otherwise, ILHRs will hardly count as legal rights at all. That connection to morality need not be via the concept of human dignity, but the fact that it is human dignity to which the major human rights instruments refer should recommend it to a human rights pragmatist who derives theory from the proprieties of practice.

I don't for a moment suggest that Buchanan doubts the special moral importance of human rights.[14] On the contrary, his arguments about why internationalizing them is important presuppose that human rights matter immensely. His paper aims to

---

the measure may take effect rather than fail. This has nothing to do with the "Principle of Effectivity" Buchanan mentions in his chapter, which states that whoever exercises de facto effective power over a territory is its ruler. Buchanan's principle has to do with the recognition of governments under international law; the principle of effectiveness used in *Soering* is a maxim for interpreting legal texts.

[14] Indeed, he insists on it in his book *The Heart of Human Rights* (New York: Oxford University Press, 2013). Among other things, this book aims to plug the argumentative gap I identify here, although Buchanan's method for doing so is different from the one I offer here.

provide extra ammunition in the fight to implement human rights, and denying their moral importance is no doubt the furthest thing from his mind. I am likewise not suggesting that Buchanan is dismissive of human dignity.

My point is rather that in rejecting the Mirroring View, and human rights foundationalism more generally, Buchanan's paper leaves a gap in his account of how legalizing (positivizing) and internationalizing human rights is something worth doing. If ILHRs are only accidentally connected with moral human rights, then the phrase "human rights" in "international legal human rights" is merely a homonym of human rights in the moral sense—in which case the mobilization of shame appears to rest on a misunderstanding. Unfortunately, once the misunderstanding is gone, the status of ILHRs as specifically legal rights thins to the vanishing point because of the problems of enforcement deficit, rights without remedies, and generating the mobilization of shame.

And surely Buchanan agrees that the system of ILHRs must have remedies, for this point is crucial to his second argument on behalf of ILHRs: that the existence of a system of ILHRs is essential to the legitimacy of the state system (an argument with which I wholeheartedly agree). A hollow and toothless system of ILHRs cannot legitimize the state system; it can only provide a veneer of legitimacy.

III. An Illustration: Human Rights and IHL

Let me illustrate the phenomenon under discussion with an example drawn from Buchanan's paper: the effect of international legal human rights on the laws of war—international humanitarian law (IHL). Buchanan argues that the development of ILHRs could stimulate progressive development in humanitarian law. I think he is right, and to a degree this has already happened. But the path is not straightforward, and it rests to a great extent not on legal developments but on the mobilization of shame described earlier.

The two bodies of law, IHL and international human rights law, have very different philosophical roots, the former originating in the Benthamite desire to reduce human suffering in war, the latter in a more Kantian notion of respect for individuals and their human dignity (although, as I shall argue later, it is a mistake to tie the notion of human dignity too closely to any philosophical theory including Kant's). The humanitarian impulse to temper war's cruelty is ancient—it can be found in the *Seven Military Classics* of ancient China as well as in Western texts as far back as Cicero and even the *Iliad*. But IHL in its contemporary form did not really launch until the mid-nineteenth century with the formation of the ICRC; international human rights law of course began much later, after the Second World War.

While Buchanan is correct that human rights thinking has very much shaped modern IHL, his chronology is not entirely accurate; modern IHL did not wait on the emergence of human rights law. The Geneva Conventions of 1949 already contain what is rightly called a mini-human rights convention in their common Article 3. Common Article 3 prohibits violence, hostage taking, outrages against personal dignity, and punishments without fair trials against "persons taking no active part in hostilities" in non-international armed conflicts. Protections are even more stringent in the rules governing international armed conflicts. It seems unlikely that the Geneva Conventions in general or common Article 3 in particular were influenced by the UDHR, which was adopted scant months before the text of the Geneva Conventions was completed. But I think it is very likely that the same revulsion against the horrors of the Second World War lay at the root of both the Geneva Conventions and the UDHR—as well as the UN Charter—and there is every reason to call it human rights thinking.

Buchanan is likewise mistaken that "rape was recognized as a violation of international legal human rights long before it was seen to fall within the scope of war crimes." Mass rape, particularly rapes committed in the Nanjing massacres, was a concern of the 1946 Tokyo Tribunal.[15] And the law the allies imposed on occupied Germany, so-called Allied Control Council Law No. 10, explicitly named rape as a crime against humanity.

So it isn't quite right that the regime of international legal human rights pre-dated human rights protection in IHL; but it *is* likely that human rights thinking influenced both. As human rights law continued to develop, its impact on IHL has been unmistakeable. Theodore Meron labels it the "humanization of humanitarian law," and Gabriella Blum calls it the "individualization of war."[16] Both authors mean not only the evolution of ever greater humanitarian protections in IHL, but also a gradual move toward regarding those protections as rights of the protected individuals and not of their states or collectivities. That is a remarkable change, for more than any other human activity, war collectivizes, whereas human rights law individualizes.

Earlier, I mentioned the European Court of Human Rights' *Soering* decision as an example of human rights-oriented legal interpretation—anti-formalist and grounded in the view that human rights are special enough to deserve broad, effectiveness-based reading. A strikingly parallel example in humanitarian law comes from the first major case of the International Criminal Tribunal for the Former Yugoslavia (ICTY), *Tadić*, where the Appeals Chamber resolved a knotty legal issue by resorting to the same interpretive approach as in *Soering*. The judgment explained that one of its conclusions, which has little support in the statutory text,

> is borne out by the entire logic of international humanitarian law. This body of law is not grounded on formalistic postulates...Rather, it is a realistic body of law, grounded on the notion of effectiveness and inspired by the aim of deterring deviation from its standards to the maximum extent possible.[17]

---

[15] See, eg, Kelly Dawn Askin, *War Crimes Against Women: Prosecution in International War Crimes Tribunals* (Leiden: Martinus Nijhoff, 1997), 180–81. Notably, Japanese cabinet minister Koki Hirota was executed for failing to intervene in the government to halt the "rape of Nanjing," a rare example of draconian punishment of a civilian under a theory of command responsibility. Of course, rapes were not the only atrocities committed in Nanjing, but they were salient and notorious.

[16] Theodore Meron, "The Humanization of Humanitarian Law," *American Journal of International Law*, 94 (2000): 239–78; Gabriella Blum, "The Individualization of War: From War to Policing in the Regulation of Armed Conflicts," in Austin Sarat et al. (eds.), *Law and War* (Palo Alto, CA: Stanford University Press, 2014). Meron dates the change to the 1968 Tehran Conference and a pair of 1970 UN Secretary General reports.

[17] *Prosecutor v. Tadić*, Judgment, Case No. IT-94–1-A, Appeals Chamber, 15 July 1999, para 96.

So the "entire logic of international humanitarian law" runs strictly parallel to the logic of human rights law, elevating effectiveness and broad protection over strict interpretation of legal instruments. As the ICTY put it in its *Furundzija* judgment,

> The essence of the whole corpus of international humanitarian law as well as human rights law lies in the protection of the human dignity of every person... The general principle of respect for human dignity is... the very *raison d'être* of international humanitarian law and human rights law; indeed in modern times it has become of such paramount importance as to permeate the whole body of international law.[18]

The humanization of humanitarian law is still very much a work in progress. Unsurprisingly, the human rights orientation of humanitarian law is most prominent in the law of belligerent occupation, where hot combat is the exception and the occupying forces must assume at least limited governance functions.[19] In occupations, the issue of whether the law of war or the law of peace should apply is maximally unclear. The ICJ has held that the "protection of the [ICCPR] does not cease in times of war,"[20] which suggests that human rights law always predominates. But the ICJ adds that the law of war, as *lex specialis* (special law), defines the meaning of human rights in wartime. A killing that would be arbitrary in peacetime might not be so on the battlefield. This means that in practice, human rights protections in wartime can be no broader than the protections in IHL (at least on matters that both of them address). But are belligerent occupations wartime or peacetime events?

Increasingly, the answer has been "peacetime." I noted earlier that the European Court of Human Rights declared that the European Convention on Human Rights does not apply on enemy territory in armed conflict; but in a 2011 opinion, the Court extended its jurisdiction to areas of Iraq under effective control of the British military.[21] Judge Bonello's concurring opinion excoriated the United Kingdom for arguing that applying the Convention in Iraq would be human rights imperialism:

> It ill behooves a State that imposed its military imperialism over another sovereign State without the frailest imprimatur from the international community, to resent the charge of having exported human rights imperialism to the vanquished enemy.[22]

Similarly, the ICJ invoked human rights instruments when it declared Israel's separation barrier illegal.[23]

At the same time, however, militaries and military lawyers have pushed back hard against humanization and individualization in "hot" situations of combat. When the

---

[18] *Prosecutor v. Furundzija*, Judgment, ICTY Case No. IT-95-17/1-T, T.Ch. II, 10 December 1998, para 183.

[19] For an overview, see Eyal E. Benvenisti, *The International Law of Occupation*, 2nd edn. (Oxford: Oxford University Press, 2012).

[20] *Legality of the Threat or Use of Nuclear Weapons, Advisory Opinion, I.C.J. Reports 1996*, 226, para 25.

[21] *Al-Skeini and Others v. United Kingdom*, Application no. 55721/07, Council of Europe: European Court of Human Rights, 7 July 2011, available at: http://www.refworld.org/docid/4e2545502.html (accessed 2 November 2014).

[22] *Al-Skeini and Others v. United Kingdom*, separate opinion of Judge Bonello, para 37. He adds: "At my age, it may no longer be elegant to have dreams. But that of being branded in perpetuity a human rights imperialist, I acknowledge sounds to me particularly seductive" (para 39).

[23] *Legal Consequences of the Construction of a Wall in the Occupied Palestinian Territory*, Advisory Opinion, 2004 I.C.J. 131 (9 July).

ICRC declared that militaries must not kill civilians who directly participate in hostilities if they can be captured—a human rights standard—several military law experts on the ICRC's advisory panel dissented and refused to sign, on the ground that humanitarian law has never prohibited soldiers from killing enemies who have not surrendered.[24] And, notably, the US government has strongly resisted legal arguments that its drone program constitutes extrajudicial assassination—a human rights concept that, the government argues, is wholly inapplicable to targeting enemy combatants in a war.

And yet, in May 2013, the Obama administration issued a policy on drone strikes that includes a preference for capture over killing, and "near certainty that non-combatants will not be injured or killed."[25] In other words, after arguing for years that human rights law does not apply on the battlefield, the US government's declared policy now mirrors the requirements of human rights law. Why?

The answer seems straightforward: the mobilization of shame. International and domestic anger at the US drone strikes has increased dramatically, and seemingly drove US policy in the direction of human rights.

As another example, consider the way the United States has treated *in bello* proportionality. This rule prohibits attacks on legitimate military targets that are anticipated to cause civilian damage excessive in relation to the military advantage—in other words, disproportionate collateral damage. In theory, that standard imposes no upper limit on the number of unintended civilian casualties, if the military advantage of an attack is great enough. And yet in practice the United States reportedly used absolute numerical caps. One former Pentagon official explained that early in the Iraq war "our number was 30. So, for example, Saddam Hussein. If you're gonna kill up to 29 people in a strike against Saddam Hussein, that's not a problem . . . But once you hit that number 30, we actually had to go to either President Bush, or Secretary of Defense Rumsfeld."[26] I have heard military officers saying that a few years later the number was ten; eventually, it approached near zero. Regardless of which number is right, it is conspicuous that no absolute numerical ceiling on civilian casualties makes conceptual sense under a proportionality standard. Clearly, the fixed numerical ceiling reflected a judgment that too many casualties would cause too much outrage, regardless of the importance of the target. The mobilization of shame strikes again. It not only enforces the law of proportionality, but reshapes its pragmatics.

Mightn't the alternative explanation of this phenomenon be more effective law enforcement mechanisms? That seems rather unlikely. The ICC has no jurisdiction over the United States, which is not a member; and the chance of the United States allowing any foreign tribunal to try US forces for war crimes is for all practical purposes zero.[27]

---

[24] For a particularly vituperative response, see W. Hayes Parks, "Part IX of the ICRC 'Direct Participation in Hostilities' Study: No Mandate, No Expertise, and Legally Incorrect," *NYU Journal of International Law & Politics*, 42 (2010): 769–832.

[25] White House Office of the Press Secretary, "Fact Sheet: U.S. Policy Standards and Procedures for the Use of Force in Counterterrorism Operations Outside the United States and Areas of Active Hostilities," available at http://www.whitehouse.gov/the-press-office/2013/05/23/fact-sheet-us-policy-standards-and-procedures-use-force-counterterrorism (accessed 2 November 2014).

[26] CBS News, "Bombing Afghanistan," available at http://www.cbsnews.com/2102-18560_162-3411230.html (last visited 2 November 2014). There has never been an official confirmation of this assertion.

[27] The US Congress enacted legislation authorizing the president to use force to free any US national from ICC custody.

The United States has no genuine fear about international legal accountability; it has substantial concerns about international outrage.

My point in this section is that the humanization of humanitarian law is incomplete as a legal matter, except perhaps in belligerent occupations. But human rights thinking has the power to mobilize shame, and in that sense ILHRs have been effectuated in humanitarian law to a degree far greater than black letter law acknowledges. So, if Buchanan is right that ILHRs stimulate progressive development in humanitarian law, the reason is not institutional law enforcement; it is moral outrage, based on the sense that individual civilians have human rights that must be honored even in wartime.

IV. Human Dignities

If these reflections are correct, Buchanan's argument needs to be supplemented with an explanation of how ILHRs connect with moral human rights. If the Mirroring View is not the answer, what is?

Notice that the ICTY said that the "general principle of respect for human dignity is...the very *raison d'être* of international humanitarian law and human rights law"—as if the two branches of law share a common root in human dignity. I have noted that the major human rights instruments give the same answer: human rights are essential to maintaining human dignity. Precisely because a human rights pragmatist begins with practice rather than theory, the very fact that the promotion of human dignity is the consensus answer embedded in the major human rights instruments makes it the first hypothesis to examine.

Notoriously, though, human dignity is a vague and multiply ambiguous concept, and indeed there has never been a single received analysis of it. For Cicero, who appears to have introduced the term, our dignity comes from our reason, the quality that sets us apart from beasts.[28] In the biblical tradition, human dignity meant being created in God's image and having dominion over nature. In the Renaissance, Pico della Mirandola identified human dignity with free will, which makes man alone a "chameleon" who can "ordain for thyself the limits of thy nature."[29] For Kant, as for the contemporary human rights theory of James Griffin, human dignity lies in autonomy; however, Kant and Griffin may not mean the same thing by autonomy, Kant emphasizing the power of self-legislation and Griffin the power to set one's own ends.[30]

---

[28] Cicero, *De Officiis* 1.30.105–07. For discussion of the Ciceronian origin of the term "human dignity," see Hubert Cancik, "'Dignity of Man' and '*Persona*' in Stoic Anthropology: Some Remarks on Cicero, *De Officiis I* 105–07," in David Kretzmer and Eckhart Klein (eds.), *The Concept of Human Dignity in Human Rights Discourse* (Alphen aan den Rijn: Kluwer Law International, 2002), 19–37. On the other hand, for Cicero "dignity" was reserved entirely to men: "Again, there are two orders of beauty: in the one, loveliness (*venustas*) predominates; in the other, dignity; of these, we ought to regard loveliness as the attribute of woman, and dignity as the attribute of man" *De Officiis*, 1.130, 131–2.

[29] Pico della Mirandola, "Oration on the Dignity of Man," in *The Renaissance Philosophy of Man*, ed. Ernst Cassirer, Paul Oskar Kristeller, John Herman Randall Jr., trans. Elizabeth Livermore Forbes (Chicago: University of Chicago Press, 1948), 225.

[30] I am drawing on Kant's Formula of Autonomy, "So act that your will can regard itself at the same time as making universal law through its maxim," *Foundations of the Metaphysics of Morals*, 4 Ak. 434; James Griffin, *On Human Rights* (Oxford: Oxford University Press, 2008), 33 (defining autonomy as being able "to choose one's own path through life") and 45 (identifying autonomy with human dignity).

To adopt any of these accounts would launch us on a project of human rights foundationalism, committing us to demonstrate how (and which) human rights derive from human dignity as analyzed in the theory. A human rights pragmatist, on the other hand, insists that the meaning of the phrase "human dignity" is not defined by a philosophical theory, but rather determined by its use in human rights practice. In a sense, the pragmatist reverses the order of explanation, defining "human dignity" by its inferential commitments rather than the other way around.

For example, when the German Constitutional Court declared that life sentences without parole (LWOP) are unconstitutional because they violate human dignity,[31] a foundationalist would demand a proof that LWOP interferes with, say, autonomy in a way that a life sentence with the possibility of parole does not. The pragmatist, on the other hand, will take the material inference from the distinctive feature of LWOP (no possibility of parole) to the violation of human dignity as part of the meaning of human dignity. As the German court explained its reasoning, taking away the possibility of parole presumes that atonement and development of the criminal's personality are impossible. So too, when the Israeli Supreme Court declared that interrogating suspects through stress positions violates human dignity, that inference likewise becomes part of the meaning of human dignity.[32]

This is not to say that anything counts as human dignity if human rights adjudicators say it does. Human dignity is not defined by the *ipse dixits* of judges. Declarations like those of the German Constitutional Court and the Israeli Supreme Court need to be accepted and taken up by the relevant communities of discourse before they become part of the public meaning of the phrase; the judicial declarations require retroactive validation through uptake. This phenomenon of retroactive validation may sound mysterious, but in reality it is no different from the familiar path of the common law. Some judicial holdings become part of the common law because subsequent courts and commentators take them to be such, while other holdings do not, either getting explicitly overruled or (more commonly) simply ignored. Here, of course, the relevant community whose acceptance of a conception of human dignity matters is not limited to judges and lawyers, but to all those engaged in human rights practice. But the retroactive validation of a conception by the relevant community is analogous to the path of the common law.[33]

How, then, would a human rights pragmatist understand "human dignity" as it appears in the UDHR and other human rights instruments? Almost certainly, those instruments mean nothing so theoretically and culturally specific as reason, free will, autonomy, the *imago Dei*, or other familiar foundationalist conceptualizations of human dignity. If anything, their drafters deliberately chose to leave the suggestive

---

[31] *Life Imprisonment Case* (1977), 45 BverGE 187, in Donald P. Kommers and Russell A. Miller (eds. and trans.), *The Constitutional Jurisprudence of the Federal Republic of Germany*, 2nd edn. (Durham, NC: Duke University Press, 1997), 308–9.

[32] *Public Committee Against Torture in Israel (PCATI) v. State of Israel*, HCJ 5100/94 (1999), available at http://www.law.yale.edu/documents/pdf/Public_Committee_Against_Torture.pdf (visited 2 November 2014), para 25.

[33] Much of my account of pragmatist meaning-formation comes from Robert B. Brandom, in particular Brandom, *Reason in Philosophy* (Cambridge, MA: Harvard University Press, 2009), ch. 3.

phrase "human dignity" vague and under-theorized in order to avoid getting bogged down in metaphysical and religious debates that would derail the project of attracting worldwide assent to the UDHR.[34] Some delegates at the UDHR drafting sessions wanted to include an explicit declaration that human rights come from God; the reference to "human dignity" was chosen as a less combustible alternative. Different cultures could bring whatever theoretical baggage they wished to the concept of human dignity.

This suggests that the best way of understanding what the UDHR and other human rights instruments mean by "human dignity" is simply by looking at the content of the documents. In effect, the instruments themselves catalogue the material inferences and incompatibilities that define human dignity. The rights to life, liberty, and security (Article 3) are necessary to human dignity, as is the right to personhood before the law (Article 6). But so are labor rights, including rights to rest and leisure, reasonable limitations of working hours, and the much-maligned right to periodic paid holidays (Article 24). (As Buchanan notes, the latter is often cited as a poster child of human rights inflation by foundationalists. Apparently those who so regard it—no doubt they include academic critics writing during their sabbaticals—have not considered seriously what a working life would be like for someone whose day-to-day survival depends on a regular paycheck and who must work at a grinding job fifty-two weeks a year from age fifteen until premature death at fifty.)

It follows, of course, that human dignity cannot underwrite a foundationalist account that derives these particular human rights from the concept of human dignity. Given that the meaning of human dignity is given in significant part by the catalogue of rights, any such derivation would be circular.

One last point about human dignity as the (virtual) foundation of human rights seems important: human dignity, as defined by human rights practice, is context-dependent and may consist of a family of conceptions. In the context of trial rights, for example, the right to participate through counsel focuses on *presumptively having a story to tell* as an aspect of what respect for human dignity means.[35] Voting rights, the right to stand for public office, and the (collective) right of self-determination, understood as an individual right to live in a self-determining political community, focus on our nature as *zoon politikon*, being a political creature, as an aspect of human dignity. Rights as disparate as the right to education and the right not to be subjected to life imprisonment without parole focus on the development of the personality as an aspect of human dignity. The "special care and assistance" owed to "motherhood" (UDHR, Article 25(b)) might plausibly be understood as an assertion that childbearing and caregiving confer—contrary to ancient patriarchal beliefs—a specific form of human dignity. Labor rights assert that even the most menial occupations deserve the respect and solicitude of the larger community, and therefore assert the human dignity of the laborer. Such labor rights, like the very different right not to be subjected

---

[34] See Johannes Morsink, *The Universal Declaration of Human Rights: Origins, Drafting, and Intent* (Philadelphia: University of Pennsylvania Press, 1999), 284–302.

[35] So I have argued in David Luban, *Legal Ethics and Human Dignity* (Cambridge: Cambridge University Press, 2007), ch. 1.

to degrading treatment or punishment, suggest that *non-humiliation* is an important index of human dignity; I have argued that in a great many contexts non-humiliation is a commonsense surrogate for human dignity.[36] And so on; what we confront, therefore, is not a unitary conception of human dignity, but a network of human dignit*ies* bearing family resemblances to each other.

V. Virtual Foundationalism

But anti-foundationalism isn't the whole story. It may still be that human dignity grounds human rights, even as human rights practices teach us concretely what human dignity means. In fact, that human dignity grounds human rights is precisely the essential connection between moral rights and ILHRs—the connection that (I have argued) makes ILHRs possible.

The vocabulary of human rights is one of several moral vocabularies available to us. It seems to me that it has gained dominance in today's conversations because it carries two implications essential to the moral world we inhabit: first, that every human being should count as an object of concern, and second, that no one should have to beg for their rights. The first tells us that no human individual is merely, in Arthur Koestler's phrase, a multitude of one million divided by one million. The individual counts, and indeed all individuals count as individuals.

The second tells us that human rights aren't merely the result of grace, generosity, or charity on the part of the comfortable and powerful, for which the poor and powerless must wheedle and bow and scrape and be forever grateful. A legitimate human rights claim gives the claimant standing to issue a moral writ of mandamus demanding that third parties enforce the claim either through law or through social pressure and shaming. As such, being a bearer of human rights is a badge of self-respect, showing that the claimant is not a vassal or a supplicant.

I think the concept of human dignity brilliantly encapsulates these two foundational commitments of human rights practice. I call them "foundational" not to resurrect the Mirroring View, nor to propose an architectural distinction between basic and derived propositions in ethics, but because it is difficult to see why anyone would engage in human rights practice as we see it today without sharing these commitments. The language of dignity lends itself to those commitments. To talk about dignity is to talk about status and rank—the original semantic field of the concept of "dignity." The two foundational commitments, to individual worth and to rights as justified demands rather than humble beseechings, imply that every human being has high status and rank.[37]

---

[36] Luban, *Legal Ethics and Human Dignity*, ch. 1.

[37] There is a seeming paradox here: if "dignity" is a status-and-rank concept, it presupposes hierarchy and not equality. But contemporary human rights discourse insists not only on human dignity, but on *equal* human dignity. The paradox is only seeming, however. When egalitarianism replaces an earlier rank-and-status, caste, or aristocratic system, societies can either equalize down or equalize up—treating everyone as the lowest were treated in the *ancien régime*, or treating everyone as an aristocrat. The conception of equal human dignity in human rights instruments is a commitment to equalizing up. I take the distinction from James Q. Whitman, *Harsh Justice: Criminal Punishment and the Widening Divide Between Punishment in America and Europe* (New York: Oxford University Press, 2005).

So even if the content of human dignity (that is, the extension of the concept) is intellectually parasitic on human rights practice rather than the other way around, it still makes sense to claim that human dignity is the foundation of human rights. That is because the concept of human dignity condenses and expresses the two foundational commitments of human rights practice.

There is a more subtle point here as well. Wittgenstein once wrote, "The mathematical problems of what is called foundations are no more the foundation of mathematics for us than the painted rock is the support of a painted tower."[38] Wittgenstein means two things by this very canny metaphor. First, of course, is that the painted tower would not fall off the canvas if the painted rock were erased. In that sense, the foundation-relation is an illusion, and Wittgenstein's aphorism is typically read as an anti-foundationalist claim that mathematics needs no foundation beyond the practices of mathematicians. I agree with this reading, which bears a resemblance to what I have been arguing about human rights—and what I take Buchanan to accept as well, inasmuch as he rejects the Mirroring View.

However, Wittgenstein had another point. There is no denying that the picture would look surreal if the tower simply floated Magritte-style in mid-air, and in that sense the painted rock provides necessary verisimilitude—necessary not in the sense that the rock is holding up the tower, but in the sense that without it the picture would portray something quite different. Within the picture, the rock is indeed the foundation for the tower, and the question "What's the tower resting on in Van Gogh's *The Old Tower*?" is perfectly cogent. That, too, I take it, is part of Wittgenstein's point. In the same way, even if human rights practice can exist without a philosophical derivation of human rights from human dignity, human dignity serves as the "virtual" foundation of human rights in the sense that the painted rock is the virtual foundation of the painted tower: those who engage in human rights practice share the foundational commitments captured by the language of human dignity. That connection is the mobilizer of shame and the motor of ILHRs.

---

[38] Ludwig Wittgenstein, *Remarks on the Foundations of Mathematics*, ed. G.H. von Wright et al., trans. G.E.M. Anscombe, rev. edn. (Cambridge, MA: MIT Press, 1978), 171e.

15

Human Rights and Constitutional Law

Patterns of Mutual Validation and Legitimation

*Samantha Besson**

Introduction

When they are approached as legal norms, human rights are primarily guaranteed by domestic law, and usually *qua* constitutional rights and in the form of a constitutional bill of rights. Since 1948, however, human rights have also been protected through international human rights law and the so-called 'international bill of rights'[1]. This dual human rights regime has been famously coined by Gerald Neuman as the 'dual positivization'[2] of human rights in international human rights law (IHRL) and constitutional rights law (CRL).

Interestingly, constitutional lawyers and international human rights lawyers have long been puzzled by the co-existence of those two legal regimes of human rights and wondered about how they ought to relate. Clearly, the reason for this dual human rights regime does not lie in legal *history* or *genealogy* as both types of legal human rights norms as we know them today date back roughly to the same post-1945 era, a time at which or after which the international bill of rights was drafted on the basis of existing domestic bills of rights and at the time at which or after which most existing domestic constitutions were either completely revised or drafted anew on the basis of the international bill of rights. Nowadays, moreover, constitutional rights either pre-exist the adoption of international human rights law or ought to be adopted on the ground of the latter—either in preparation for ratification or as a normative consequence thereof—, thus confirming the synchronic nature of their functions and their co-existence requirement.[3] Nor does the reason for their co-existence lie in the *content* or the *structure* of the human rights protected, as those are held to be, by and large,

* I would like to thank Massimo Renzo, Matthew Liao, and Rowan Cruft for the invitation to contribute to this volume, for their patience and for their feedback, and to Saladin Meckled-Garcia for his comments. Many thanks to Mattias Kumm and Ingolf Pernice for inviting me to present a first draft of this chapter in the Berlin Colloquium *Rethinking Law in a Global Context* on 24 April 2012. Last but not least, many thanks are due to Tancrède Scherf for his assistance with the formal lay-out of the chapter. This chapter was written while on research leave at the Wissenschaftskolleg zu Berlin (2011–12).

[1] See S. Gardbaum, 'Human Rights as International Constitutional Rights', *European Journal of International Law*, 19(4) (2008): 749–68, 750.

[2] G. Neuman, 'Human Rights and Constitutional Rights', *Stanford Law Review*, 55(5) (2003): 1863–900, 1864. See also J. Waldron, 'Rights and the Citation of Foreign Law', in T. Campbell, K.D. Ewing, and A. Tomkins (eds.), *The Legal Protection of Human Rights. Sceptical Essays* (Oxford University Press 2011), 410–27, 424.

[3] See also Gardbaum, 'Human Rights as International Constitutional Rights', 764ff.

similar in practice.[4] International human rights are not there to fill the gaps of domestic law. Nor, finally, does the key to the relationship between domestic and international human rights lie in their *enforcement* mechanisms, as respect for both human rights regimes are owed by domestic institutions, implemented by domestic institutions and monitored in roughly the same way.[5]

So, what could explain that the two regimes are not merely juxtaposed and concurrent, and hence redundant at best? They have, I will argue, distinct albeit complementary *functions*.[6] The present chapter aims at clarifying those respective and complementary functions of international and domestic human rights. So doing, it hopes to shed light on key issues in human rights theory, such as the nature of human rights (moral and/or legal) and the legitimacy of human rights law (domestic and/or international). The complementarity in function of the two human rights regimes reflects indeed what I will refer to as the 'mutual legitimation' of international and domestic human rights,[7] and their corresponding 'mutual positivization' or mutual legal validation.

Surprisingly given the urgency of some of those questions in international and domestic constitutional law, but also for our contemporary human rights practice, human rights theorists have not yet engaged with them thoroughly and systematically, but for a few exceptions.[8] Some human rights scholars have, of course, addressed the question, but their approach to the co-existence of international human rights law and domestic constitutional rights law remains largely descriptive.[9] Most of the time, indeed, their arguments' normative underpinnings remain either unstated or else unargued for. Furthermore, their accounts are usually ones of a static juxtaposition of human rights regimes and of their conflicting authority claims that ought to be managed and reconciled.[10] This is regrettable as the process of dynamic and 'mutual'—as opposed to merely 'dual'—positivization and legitimation of international and domestic human rights law needs to be understood fully. The relationship between international human rights law and constitutional law is actually only the tip of the iceberg of the mutual relationship between international law and domestic law, and of the new concept of 'dual-sourced' sovereignty enacted in 1945.[11] Moreover,

---

[4] Gardbaum, 'Human Rights as International Constitutional Rights', 750–1.

[5] See also R. Dworkin, *Justice for Hedgehogs* (Harvard University Press, 2011), 333–4; K. Hessler, 'Resolving Interpretive Conflicts in International Human Rights Law', *Journal of Political Philosophy*, 13(1) (2005): 29–52, 37.

[6] See also Dworkin, *Justice for Hedgehogs*, 334–5.

[7] See also A. Buchanan, 'Reciprocal Legitimation: Reframing the Problem of International Legitimacy', *Politics, Philosophy & Economics*, 10(1) (2011): 5–19, 15–16.

[8] See, eg, A. Buchanan and R. Powell, 'Constitutional Democracy and the Rule of International Law: Are they Compatible?', *The Journal of Political Philosophy*, 16(3) (2008): 326–49; S. Benhabib, 'The Legitimacy of Human Rights', *Daedalus*, 137(3) (2008): 94–104; S. Benhabib, 'Claiming Rights across Borders: International Human Rights and Democratic Sovereignty', *American Political Science Review*, 103(4) (2009): 691–704; Gardbaum, 'Human Rights as International Constitutional Rights'; C. Wellman, *The Moral Dimension of Human Rights* (Oxford University Press, 2011).

[9] See, eg, Neuman, 'Human Rights and Constitutional Rights'.

[10] See Neuman, 'Human Rights and Constitutional Rights', 1873–4, 1900.

[11] See, eg, S. Besson, 'Sovereignty', in R. Wolfrum et al. (eds.), *Max Planck Encyclopedia of Public International Law* (Oxford University Press 2012), online edition, http://www.mpepil.com; S. Besson, 'Sovereignty, International Law and Democracy: A Reply to Waldron', *European Journal of International Law*, 22 (2011): 373–87; J.L. Cohen, 'Rethinking Human Rights, Democracy, and Sovereignty in the Age of Globalization', *Political Theory*, 36(4) (2008): 578–606.

human rights scholars' perspective is usually that of either international or domestic human rights law, but rarely both at the same time and in their mutual relationship, most probably because of the remaining separation between international and constitutional lawyers on the human rights issue. Finally, existing legal accounts are usually made with a specific domestic legal order in mind, for example, from a US constitutional law perspective[12] or a European one, and this limits their generalization potential.

Importantly, this chapter also pertains to understanding the relationship between human rights and constitutional law more generally. As Stephen Gardbaum argues, 'there is undoubtedly something inherently constitutional in the very nature and subject-matter of international human rights law'.[13] And this arguably calls for a broader assessment of both the constitutional dimensions of human rights and of the human rights dimensions of constitutional law. After a discussion of the underlying understanding of human rights, and in particular of their legal nature and relationship to moral rights (section I), the chapter sets out to look at the constitutional dimension of human rights in three constellations: first of all, their guarantees as *domestic constitutional rights* and their relation to international legal human rights (section II); secondly, their relationship to other *domestic constitutional law* norms (section III); and, finally, their role in the *constitutionalization of international law* itself (section IV).

I. Human Rights between Morality and Law

Human rights are best understood as a legally recognized and enforceable subset of universal moral rights.[14] The proposed understanding of the moral (section I.A) *and* legal (section I.B) nature of human rights and how those dimensions relate underpins much of the proposed argument about their relationship to constitutional law and constitutional rights. It differs from other accounts of human rights that work from the premise of the independent moral existence of human rights, on the one hand, and of their legal recognition or so-called 'positivization' as domestic constitutional or legislative rights and/or as international rights, on the other.[15] Neither of them explains the moral justification

---

[12] See, eg, Neuman, 'Human Rights and Constitutional Rights'; D. Golove, 'Human Rights Treaties and the US Constitution', *DePaul Law Review*, 52 (2002): 579–626; M. Kumm, 'Constitutional Law Encounters International Law: Terms of Engagement', in S. Choudhry (ed.), *The Migration of Constitutional Ideas* (Cambridge University Press, 2006), 256–93. On those debates, see V. Jackson, 'Transnational Constitutional Values and Democratic Challenges', *International Journal of Constitutional Law*, 8 (2010): 517–62; Buchanan and Powell, 'Constitutional Democracy and the Rule of International Law'.

[13] Gardbaum, 'Human Rights as International Constitutional Rights', 752.

[14] See S. Besson, 'Human Rights—Ethical, Political...or Legal? First Steps in a Legal Theory of Human Rights', in D. Childress (ed.), *The Role of Ethics in International Law* (Cambridge University Press 2011), 211–45; S. Besson, 'European Human Rights, Democracy and Supranational Judicial Review—Thinking outside the Judicial Box', in P. Popelier., P. van Nuffel, and C. van de Heyning (eds.), *Human Rights Protection in the European Legal Order: Interaction between European Courts and National Courts* (Intersentia 2011), 97–145; J. Raz, 'Human Rights without Foundations', in S. Besson and J. Tasioulas (eds.), *The Philosophy of International Law* (Oxford University Press 2010), 321–37.

[15] This chapters differs from Buchanan, in this volume (ch. 13), who assesses the relationship between 'moral human rights' and 'international legal human rights'; from Buchanan and Powell, 'Constitutional Democracy and the Rule of International Law', who assess the compatibility between 'international human rights' and 'constitutional law'; from Wellman, *The Moral Dimension of Human Rights*, 138, who assesses the relationship between 'moral human rights' positivized into 'international legal human

for the *legal* positivization of human rights, on the one hand, and for their *dual* positivization in both international human rights law and domestic human rights law, on the other.

A. Human rights as moral rights

Human rights are a subset of universal moral rights (i) that protect fundamental and general human interests (ii) against action or omission of (national, regional or international) public institutions that exercise jurisdiction (iii).[16]

First of all, a human right exists *qua* moral *right* when an interest is a sufficient ground or reason to hold another agent (the duty-bearer) under a duty to respect that interest against certain general albeit reasonable or standard threats vis-a-vis the right-holder.[17] For a right to be recognized, an objective interest must be identified and weighed against other interests and other considerations. Its duties will be determined in each concrete case by reference to the specific circumstances and potential duty-bearers. Rights are, on this account, intermediaries between interests and duties.[18]

Secondly, *human* rights are universal and general moral rights of a special intensity that belong to all human beings by virtue of their humanity. Human rights are *universal* moral rights, on the one hand, because the interests they protect belong to all human beings. *Qua general* moral rights, on the other, they protect fundamental human interests that human beings have by virtue of their humanity and not of a given status or circumstance (unlike special rights). Those interests constitute part of a person's well-being in an objective sense; they are the objective interests that, when guaranteed, make for a decent or minimally good individual life.

Of course, there has to be a threshold of importance at which a given interest is regarded as sufficiently fundamental to give rise to duties and hence to a right. While interests are trans-historical, the sufficiently fundamental nature of the protected interests and hence the existence of the corresponding human rights have to be determined by reference to a context and time rather than established once and for all. What makes it the case that a given individual interest is regarded as sufficiently fundamental or important to generate a duty and that, in other words, the threshold of importance and point of passage from a general and fundamental interest to a human right is reached, may be found in the normative status of each individual *qua* equal member of the moral–political community. This is also what one may refer to as their

---

rights' and, indirectly via the former, 'constitutional rights'; or from Neuman, 'Human Rights and Constitutional Rights', who assesses the relationship between 'international legal human rights' and 'constitutional rights' and the ways in which both regimes positivize 'moral human rights'.

[16] See for a full-length argument on the moral/legal nature of human rights: Besson, 'Human Rights—Ethical, Political…or Legal?; on the egalitarian dimension of human rights: S. Besson, 'The Egalitarian Dimension of Human Rights', *Archiv für Rechts- und Sozialphilosophie Beiheft*, 136 (2013) 19–52; on human rights' duties and their allocation: S. Besson, 'The Allocation of Anti-poverty Rights Duties—Our Rights, but Whose Duties?', in K. Nadakavukaren Schefer (ed.), *Poverty and the International Legal System* (Cambridge University Press 2013), 408–31.

[17] J. Raz, 'On the Nature of Rights', *Mind*, 93(370) (1984): 194–214, 195.

[18] Raz, 'On the Nature of Rights', 208.

political equality or equal political status.[19] Only those interests that are recognized as socio-comparatively equally important by members of the community can be recognized as sufficiently fundamental to give rise to duties and hence as equal human rights. A person's interests deserve equal protection in virtue of her status as member of the community and of her mutual relations to other members in the community. The recognition of human rights is done mutually and not simply vertically and top-down, and, as a result, human rights are not externally promulgated but mutually granted by members of a given political community.[20] This is particularly important as it allows for the mutual assessment of the general and standard threats on certain interests that deserve protection, on the one hand, and of the feasibility of the burdens and costs of the recognition of the corresponding rights and duties, on the other.

As a matter of fact, human rights are not merely a consequence of individuals' equal moral–political status, but also a way of earning that equal status and consolidating it; they are constitutive of that status. Without human rights, moral–political equality would remain an abstract guarantee; through mutual human rights, individuals become actors of their own equality and members of their political community.[21] Borrowing Arendt's words: 'we are not born equal; we become equal as members of a group on the strength of our decision to guarantee ourselves mutually equal rights'.[22]

This brings me to the third element in the definition of human rights: human rights are entitlements against (national, regional or international) *public institutions* that have jurisdiction. Human rights are rights all individuals have against all other individuals in the political community, ie, against themselves collectively. For practical reasons, but also for reasons of political equality in the allocation of the burden and cost of human rights' duties and of democratic legitimacy of the corresponding procedures, those duties should be mediated institutionally. They generate duties on the part of public authorities not only to protect equal individual interests, but also individuals' political status *qua* equal political actors. Of course, other individuals may violate the interests protected by human rights and ought to be prevented from doing so by public institutions as part of their positive human rights' duties, and in particular through legal means.

B. Human rights as legal rights

Just as moral rights are moral propositions and sources of moral duties, legal rights are legal propositions and sources of legal duties. They are moral interests recognized by

---

[19] See R. Forst, 'The Justification of Human Rights and the Basic Right to Justification. A Reflexive Approach', *Ethics*, 120(4) (2010): 711–40; R. Forst, 'The Basic Right to Justification: Toward a Constructivist Conception of Human Rights', *Constellations*, 6(1) (1999): 35–60, 48; T. Christiano, *The Constitution of Equality* (Oxford University Press 2008), 138, 156.

[20] See J.L. Cohen, 'Minimalism about Human Rights: The Most We Can Hope For?', *The Journal of Political Philosophy*, 12(2) (2004): 190–213, 197–8; Forst, 'The Justification of Human Rights'; K. Baynes, 'Towards a Political Conception of Human Rights', *Philosophy and Social Criticism*, 35(4) (2009): 371–90, 382.

[21] See Cohen, 'Minimalism about Human Rights'; Cohen, 'Rethinking', 585–6.

[22] H. Arendt, 'The Decline of the Nation-state and the End of the Rights of Man', in *The Origins of Totalitarianism* (Penguin 1951), 147–82.

the law as sufficiently important to generate moral duties.[23] The same may be said of legal human rights: legal human rights are fundamental and general moral interests recognized by the law as sufficiently important to generate moral duties.

Generally speaking, moral rights can exist independently from legal rights, but legal rights recognize, modify or create moral rights by recognizing moral interests as sufficiently important to generate moral duties. Of course, there may be ways of protecting moral interests or even independent moral rights legally without recognizing them as legal 'rights'. Nor should all moral rights be recognized and protected legally. Respect for them should be a matter of individual conscience in priority. Conversely, some legal rights may not actually protect pre-existing moral rights or create moral rights, thus only bearing the name of 'rights' and generating legal duties at the most.[24] The same cannot be said of human rights more specifically, however.

First of all, not all universal moral rights ought to be legally recognized as legal rights, but human rights should. Not all universal moral rights have been or are recognized as legal human rights. Some are even expressly recognized as universal moral rights by the law even though they are not made into legal rights or modulated by the law.[25] A distinct question is whether they ought to be legalized and hence protected by law. Again, respect for universal moral rights ought to be voluntary in priority, and this independently from any institutional involvement. However, for the reasons mentioned before, the universal moral rights that are (equal) human rights create moral duties for institutions, and hence for the law as well, to recognize and protect human rights.[26] In the moral–political account of human rights presented previously, the law provides the best and maybe the only way of mutually recognizing the socio-comparative importance of those interests in a political community of equals.[27] It enables the weighing of those interests against each other and the identification of the general and standard threats to those interests, and hence the drawing of the political equality threshold or comparative line. Further, the law provides the institutional framework in which the necessary pre-human rights recognition assessment of the abstract feasibility of human rights can take place, and in particular the abstract assessment of a feasible identification and egalitarian allocation of human rights duties and duty-bearers.

In short, the law turns universal moral rights into human rights, just as politics turn equal moral status into political equality. As a result, in the moral–political account of human rights propounded here, the legal recognition of a fundamental human interest as a human right, in conditions of political equality, is part of the creation of a moral–political human right. In other words, while being independently justified morally and having a universal and general scope, human rights *qua* subset of universal

---

[23] J. Raz, 'Legal Rights', *Oxford Journal of Legal Studies*, 4(1) (1984): 1–21, 12; J. Raz, 'Human Rights in the New World Order', *Transnational Legal Theory*, 1(1) (2010): 31–47.

[24] See also Dworkin, *Justice for Hedgehogs*, 331. Contra: Wellman, *The Moral Dimension of Human Rights*.

[25] One may think here of the moral rights mentioned by the 9th Amendment of the US Constitution.

[26] See Raz, 'New World Order'.

[27] See eg Cohen, 'Rethinking', 599–600; Forst, 'Justification of Human Rights'; Forst, 'Basic Right', 48–50.

moral rights are also of an inherently legal nature. To quote Jürgen Habermas, 'they are conceptually oriented towards positive enactment by legislative bodies'.[28]

Secondly, and this follows, legal rights may or may not pre-exist as independent moral rights, but human rights are at once moral and legal and hence do not pre-exist as universal moral rights but become such through legal recognition. Most legal rights are legally recognized moral rights,[29] but others are legally created or legally specified moral rights.[30] Human rights, however, do not pre-exist as independent universal moral rights, but, once recognized, become a subset of those rights. The inherently moral–political nature of human rights and the role the law plays in recognizing given interests as sufficiently important in a group as to generate duties and hence human rights, make it the case that the law recognizes universal moral rights by making them human rights. The law may also specify and modulate moral human interests when recognizing them as legal human rights. One may even imagine certain political interests whose moral–political significance stems from the very moral–political circumstances of life in a polity.

II. Human Rights and Domestic Constitutional Rights

The first constitutional constellation in which the human rights issue arises is their recognition as rights within a domestic constitutional legal order. In this section, I argue, first, that human rights ought to be protected by both domestic and international law at the same time (section II.A) and, second, more specifically as domestic constitutional rights (section II.B). A third section addresses the controversial question of how to solve conflicts between international human rights and domestic constitutional rights (section II.C).

A. Human rights between domestic and international law

The first question pertains to the political community that ought to be recognizing the existence of human rights legally and whose members' political equality is in the making, and hence to the level of legalization of those rights.[31] Here, it is important to understand how international human rights law protects the right to have rights (section II.A.i), before explaining how both the domestic and international levels of legalization but also of legitimation of human rights are mutually reinforcing in practice (section II.A.ii).

---

[28] J. Habermas, 'Die Legitimation durch Menschenrechte', in *Die postnationale Konstellation. Politische Essays* (Suhrkamp, 1998), 170–92, 183. See also J. Habermas, *Faktizität und Geltung. Beiträge zur Diskurstheorie des Rechts und des demokratischen Rechtsstaats* (Suhrkamp 1998), 310–12; J. Habermas, 'The Concept of Human Dignity and the Realistic Utopia of Human Rights', *Metaphilosophy*, 41(4) (2010): 464–80, 470; J. Habermas, *Zur Verfassung Europas. Ein Essay* (Suhrkamp 2011), fn 19.

[29] See eg B. Cali and S. Meckled-Garcia, 'Lost in Translation: The Human Rights Ideal and International Human Rights Law', in S. Meckled-Garcia and B. Cali (eds.), *The Legalization of Human Rights, Multidisciplinary Perspectives on Human Rights and Human Rights Law* (Routledge, 2006), 11–31.

[30] See Raz, 'Legal Rights', 16–17; Raz, 'New World Order'.

[31] See also Besson, 'Human Rights'; S. Besson, 'Human Rights and Democracy in a Global Context—Decoupling and Recoupling', *Ethics and Global Politics*, 4(1) (2011): 19–50.

i. International human rights and the right to have rights

The legalization of human rights could take place either at the domestic or at the international level. Prima facie, of course, international law offers the universal scope that matches that of universal moral rights, and would seem to be the privileged locus of legalization of human rights. Given what was said about the interdependence between human rights, political equality and democracy, however, the political process through which their legalization takes place ought to be egalitarian and public, and include all those whose rights are affected and whose equality is at stake. As a result, using international law as the main instrument to recognize fundamental and general human interests as sufficiently important to generate state duties at the domestic level would not be democratically legitimate.[32]

To solve the riddle of the democratic legitimacy of human rights and succeed in recoupling human rights and democracy across levels of governance, it is important to distinguish between two categories of rights: rights that pertain to the access to membership in a political community (rights to membership) and those that pertain to actual membership in the political community (membership rights). Interestingly, this distinction corresponds to two competing readings of Hannah Arendt's idea of the 'right to have rights' depending on whether one understands them as being moral or legal rights, first, and as being domestic or international rights, second.[33]

Starting with the first category, rights to equal political membership contribute to the constitution of equal political status, as opposed to the second category of rights that protect that very equal political status once it is in existence.[34]

Moral and legal rights to membership cannot be guaranteed exclusively from within a given political community since they work as constraints on democratic sovereignty and self-determination. This is why they are usually protected from the outside and through international human rights law.[35] Of course, to be democratically legitimate, they have to be recognized legally through inclusive and deliberative processes. This may prove difficult in the current circumstances of international law, but processes of that kind are incrementally developed in international law making. Importantly, the legalization of international human rights is a two-way street that is not limited to a top-down reception of international law in domestic law, but is bottom-up. The recognition and existence of those rights *qua* international human rights that constrain domestic politics ought indeed to be based on democratic practises recognized domestically. Their content derives from the outcome of democratic human rights' interpretations. Thus, only those polities that respect international human rights and are democratic are then deemed legitimate in specifying the content of those rights,

---

[32] See eg T. Christiano, 'Democratic Legitimacy and International Institutions', in S. Besson and J. Tasioulas (eds.), *The Philosophy of International Law* (Oxford University Press 2010), 119–37. See also Cohen, 'Rethinking', 599–600; S. Besson, 'The Legitimate Authority of International Human Rights', in A. Follesdal, J. Karlsson Schaffer, and G. Ulfstein (eds.), *The Legitimacy of International Human Rights Regimes* (Cambridge University Press 2013), 32–83.

[33] Arendt, 'Decline', 177–8. See S. Besson, 'The Right to have Rights—From Human Rights to Citizens' Rights and Back', in M. Goldoni and C. McCorquodale (eds.), *Arendt and the Law* (Hart Publishing, 2012), 335–56.

[34] See Cohen, 'Rethinking', 587.   [35] See also Dworkin, *Justice for Hedgehogs*, 335–9.

and hence in contributing to the further recognition and existence of those rights *qua* international human rights that will constrain them in return.[36] This dynamic phenomenon is what Allen Buchanan refers to as the mutual legitimation of domestic and international law.[37]

In short, rights to membership correspond to a first and main reading of Arendt's right to have rights: those universal moral rights, and potentially also international legal rights to membership, are rights that guarantee the ulterior benefit of human rights within each political community.[38] Those universal moral rights to have human rights are constitutive of one's equal moral status and amount, in political circumstances where the conditions of political equality are given, to a right to equal political membership and participation.

The second group of rights that guarantee membership in the political community, ie, most human rights, can at least be regarded as legally protected universal moral rights and most of the time as legal rights as well. However, unless they refer to and correspond to existing domestic (moral–political and legal) human rights, they cannot (yet) be regarded as human rights for lack of an international moral–political community.

Qua legal rights, those international human rights norms guarantee rights to individuals under a given state's jurisdiction, on the one hand, and to other states (or arguably international organizations [IOs]) (international human rights are usually guaranteed *erga omnes*), on the other, to have those rights guaranteed as 'human rights' within a given domestic community. They correspond to states' (and/or arguably IOs') duties to secure and ensure respect for those rights as 'human rights' within their own jurisdiction.[39] In that sense, international human rights duties are second-order duties for states (and/or arguably IOs) to generate first-order human rights duties for themselves under domestic law, ie, international duties to have domestic duties. What those international human rights norms do, in other words, is protect legally the universal moral right to have rights discussed as a first kind of human rights, ie, the right to equal membership in a moral–political community with all the other human rights this status implies.

Unlike most readings of Arendt's right to have rights,[40] this reading understands rights in the second category, ie, membership rights, as universal moral rights which may also be protected as international legal rights. Their underlying nature as universal moral rights actually explains their *erga omnes* effects. They are not human rights

---

[36] See Hessler, 'Resolving Interpretive Conflicts', 48ff.

[37] See A. Buchanan, *Justice, Legitimacy and Self-determination: Moral Foundations for International Law* (Oxford University Press, 2004), 187–9; Buchanan, 'Reciprocal Legitimation'; Buchanan and Powell, 'Constitutional Democracy and the Rule of International Law', 348–9.

[38] See eg Cohen, 'Rethinking'; S. Benhabib, '"The Right to have Rights": Hannah Arendt on the Contradictions of the Nation-state', in S. Benhabib, *The Rights of Others: Aliens, Residents, and Citizens* (Cambridge University Press 2004), 56–61.

[39] See O. O'Neill, 'The Dark Side of Human Rights', *International Affairs*, 81(2) (2005): 427–39, 433.

[40] See eg Benhabib, '"The Right to have Rights"'; S. Gosepath, 'Hannah Arendts Kritik der Menschenrechte und ihr 'Recht, Rechte zu haben', in H. Böll-Stiftung (ed.), *Hannah Arendt: Verborgene Tradition—Unzeitgemäße Aktualität?* (Akademie Verlag 2007), 253–62.

yet, but are rights to have human rights, the latter being at once moral and legal rights and not only positive legal rights.

In sum, there are two groups of rights among the rights usually referred to as 'international human rights': the first group (rights to membership) to be legalized at the international level, while rights belonging to the second group (membership rights) have to be legalized both internationally and domestically in a given political community before they can also be recognized as human rights under international law. In the meantime, international law's human rights norms that protect rights in the latter category guarantee rights to have human rights protected under domestic law.

ii. From international human rights to domestic constitutional human rights and back

Interestingly, those normative considerations about the complementary locus of legalization and legitimation of human rights are reflected in our current human rights legal practice.

International human rights law secures the external protection of the right to have domestic human rights in the political community in which one is a member. That externalized human rights regime works on three dimensions domestically and has three distinct albeit complementary functions accordingly: (i) a *substantive* one: it requires the protection of the minimal and abstract content of those rights against domestic levelling-down, and works therefore as a form of back-up;[41] (ii) a *personal* one: it requires the inclusion of all those subjected to domestic jurisdiction, territorially and extra-territorially and whether they are nationals or not, in the scope of those rights;[42] and (iii) a *procedural* one: it requires the introduction of both internal and external institutional mechanisms of monitoring and enforcement of those rights.

Thus, it is through the relationship of mutual reinforcement between domestic human rights and international human rights and the productive tension between external guarantees and internal ones that human rights law has consolidated at both domestic and international levels.[43] International human rights are specified as domestic human rights, but domestic human rights progressively consolidate into international human rights in return.

This virtuous circle can actually be exemplified by the sources of international human rights law. Historically, much of the content of international human rights treaties was actually drawn from domestic bills of rights, and many of the latter were then revised post-1945 to be in line with the former. International human rights law also finds its sources in general principles of international law, but arguably also in customary international law. Both sets of sources derive international norms from

---

[41] See Buchanan, 'Reciprocal Legitimation', 11; Gardbaum, 'Human Rights as International Constitutional Rights', 764.

[42] See Buchanan, 'Reciprocal Legitimation', 12–13; Gardbaum, 'Human Rights as International Constitutional Rights', 765–6, 767.

[43] See Besson, 'Decoupling and Recoupling'; Habermas, 'Concept of Human Dignity', 478; Benhabib, 'Claiming Rights'; S. Benhabib, *Dignity in Adversity: Human Rights in Troubled Times* (Polity Press, 2011), 16 and 126; Habermas, 'Zur Verfassung', 31–2, 36–8.

domestic ones.[44] In return, the mutual validation of international and domestic human rights law may also be observed from the way in which international human rights norms are inserted within the domestic legal order.[45] Unlike other international law norms, international human rights law claims, and is usually granted immediate validity and direct effect in domestic legal orders. This occurs in many cases through the joint and largely indiscriminate application of international and constitutional human rights by domestic authorities, and in particular domestic courts.

B. Human rights as domestic constitutional rights

The next question pertains to the way in which human rights should be legalized within the domestic legal order, and in particular whether they should take the form of constitutional rights.[46]

In international human rights law, states are required to 'secure' or 'recognize' (for example, ECHR, Article 1, in English and in French) the international human rights they have committed to respect. This implies a positive duty to legalize those rights as legal rights under domestic law and to implement them legally so as to grant them full effectivity. There is no obligation, however, to legalize them as constitutional rights. Not all states have written constitutions to date, and some do not even have bills of rights.

In practice, human rights may be recognized legally through various sources and hence at different formal ranks in the legal order: they may be guaranteed either as constitutional rights or as any other legal rights. The question then is whether human rights *should* also be legalized as constitutional rights.

Depending on the political organization corresponding to the domestic legal order, various arguments in favour[47] and against[48] their constitutionalization may be mentioned. First of all, the constitutionalization of human rights contributes to their democratic legitimation to the extent that the constitutional law-making process is usually the most inclusive and deliberative of all. Secondly, constitutional law has a fundamental constitutive function and the inclusion of human rights within the fundamental norms of the legal order confirms their fundamental character. Thirdly, the constitutionalization of human rights guarantees their uniform application across the legal order at all legislative levels. Fourthly, constitutional protection of abstract human rights allows for variations in the legislative specifications of the human rights

---

[44] See S. Besson, 'General Principles in International Law—Whose Principles?', in S. Besson and P. Pichonnaz (eds.), *Les principes en droit européen—Principles in European Law* (Schulthess, 2011), 21–68.

[45] See Neuman, 'Human Rights and Constitutional Rights', 1890–5.

[46] It is very important not to conflate the inherent legality of human rights and their legalization with the question of how to implement human rights most effectively (contra J. Tasioulas, 'The Moral Reality of Human Rights', in T. Pogge (ed.), *Freedom from Poverty as a Human Right: Who Owes What to the Very Poor* (Oxford University Press, 2007), 75–101; J. Nickel, *Making Sense of Human Rights*, 2nd edn. (Blackwell, 2007), 28–33). See also Besson, 'Human Rights'; Raz, 'New World Order'.

[47] See eg R. Alexy, 'Die Institutionalisierung der Menschenrechte im demokratischen Verfassungsstaat', in S. Gosepath and G. Lohmann (eds.), *Philosophie der Menschenrechte* (Suhrkamp, 1998), 244–64, 258–4; Wellman, *The Moral Dimension of Human Rights*, 128ff.

[48] See eg J. Waldron, *The Dignity of Legislation* (Cambridge University Press, 1999); J. Waldron, *Disagreement and the Law* (Oxford University Press, 1999), 211–31.

duties, but without questioning their abstract guarantees. This constitutes a minimal albeit incompletely theorized agreement on certain interests being deemed sufficiently important to give rise to rights and then to duties, and protects them against being balanced and outweighed by other interests and moral considerations in case of conflict. Finally, human rights' constitutionalization secures the priority of their corresponding duties over other legal norms and obligations stemming from the legal order.

Of course, the constitutional entrenchment of human rights comes in degrees. Further, judicial scrutiny may also vary. As a result, the mere constitutionalization of human rights need not be equated with rigid constitutional entrenchment nor with strong judicial review. There are arguments in favour of the latter, but also against them in democratic theory.[49] In short, it is important to understand that the risks of constitutional rigidity and of democratic precommitment may be put to rest by a soft form of constitutional entrenchment where revision by popular vote is possible and no constitutional judicial review exists.[50]

C. Conflicts between international human rights and domestic constitutional rights

Even though international and domestic human rights are complementary and their legal regimes mutually validating and legitimating, conflicts may arise. This is the so-called 'divergence question', and it is usually described as a conflict between incompatible claims to authority stemming from domestic and international human rights law.[51]

Interestingly, the question is posed in a misleading fashion and needs to be re-formulated. The same domestic and international human rights norms cannot enter into conflict as they share the same abstract content (ie, the protection of the same interests against the same standard threats) and this independently from their international or domestic sources—even though their duties may, of course, enter into conflict, but again this is independent from their respective sources. Rather, it is their interpretations and the specifications of the corresponding duties in concrete local circumstances by international and domestic institutions that may diverge and hence conflict with each other.

Once re-formulated, the question then is how one should handle conflicts of interpretation and specification of human rights' duties between international and domestic human rights institutions.[52] This means identifying which institution is legitimate or justified in its claim to final authority over the issue.[53]

There are various arguments for the priority of domestic human rights institutions in the interpretation and specification of human rights.[54] First of all, domestic human

---

[49] See eg Waldron, 'Dignity'; Waldron, 'Disagreement', 211–31; J. Waldron, 'Judges as Moral Reasoners', *International Journal of Constitutional Law*, 7(1) (2009): 2–24. See also S. Besson, *The Morality of Conflict: Reasonable Disagreement and the Law* (Hart Publishing, 2005), 287–336.

[50] See eg Besson, *The Morality of Conflict*.

[51] Neuman, 'Human Rights and Constitutional Rights', 1873–4 and 1874ff.

[52] See eg Hessler, 'Resolving Interpretive Conflicts', 32–3.

[53] See Besson, 'Democratic Authority'.

[54] See Hessler, 'Resolving Interpretive Conflicts', 42ff. See also Besson, 'European Human Rights'.

rights institutions are the institutions of the democratic polity whose members' rights are affected and whose members' duties need to be allocated. The egalitarian dimension of human rights ties them closely to political and, more specifically, democratic procedures in the specification and allocation of human rights duties. Secondly, domestic institutions have the institutional capacity to allocate the burden of duties fairly in view of the resources available in the political community and the knowledge of the concrete threats on the protected interests. The concrete dimension of human rights duties makes their identification and distribution a necessarily situated matter and the same applies to the resolution of conflicts of human rights duties or to the justification of the restrictions to human rights duties.

Importantly, however, the parallel existence of international human rights institutions with a claim to final and legitimate authority, despite being situated outside the democratic polity whose members' human rights and duties are concerned, does not mean that it should be perceived as a juxtaposed and competing monitoring system and hence as a threat. International and domestic human rights institutions' claims to legitimate authority are not in competition and mutually exclusive the way they would if they belonged to different political communities and corresponding legal orders.[55] Their respective claims to legitimate authority are not distinctly justified on different bases and in an exclusive fashion, but on the contrary share a mutually reinforcing democratic justification.[56] Thus, it is the international human rights' institutions' potential contribution to democratic processes or compensation for the lack thereof domestically that helps justify its legitimate authority in the cases in which they impose certain human rights interpretations on domestic authorities.[57] Just as international human rights contribute to protecting the right to democratic membership and the right to have human rights in a democratic polity, international human rights institutions protect democratic institutions and guarantee their ability to respect human rights.

Because international and domestic human rights law complement each other and are in productive tension, their interpreting institutions should be understood as situated in a joint albeit complementary interpretive endeavour and not as mutually exclusive interpretive authorities. As a matter of fact, historically international institutional and procedural standards for the implementation and monitoring of human rights have been developed internally in cooperation among democratic states, transnationalized and internationalized bottom-up and then imposed top-down again as external constraints on domestic institutions and procedures.

This normative account of the mutual interpretive authority of domestic and international human rights institutions actually fits current human rights practice, especially that of the European Convention on Human Rights, and the ways in which potential interpretive conflicts are handled.[58] It finds a clear confirmation in the principle of *subsidiarity* that characterizes that practice.[59] International human rights institutions only

---

[55] See eg Neuman, 'Human Rights and Constitutional Rights', 1873–4.
[56] See Buchanan, 'Reciprocal Legitimation'; Buchanan and Powell, 'Constitutional Democracy and the Rule of International Law', 348–9.
[57] See also Hessler, 'Resolving Interpretive Conflicts', 45ff; Buchanan, 'Reciprocal Legitimation'.
[58] See Neuman, 'Human Rights and Constitutional Rights', 1880ff.
[59] See L.R. Helfer, 'Redesigning the European Court of Human Rights: Embeddedness as a Deep Structural Principle of the European Human Rights Regime', *European Journal of International Law*, 19

have jurisdiction once domestic remedies have been exhausted and domestic authorities have had a chance to specify, allocate, and interpret human rights duties in context. This may be referred to as procedural or jurisdictional subsidiarity. Further, they are usually very reluctant to question domestic institutions' interpretations and specifications of human rights in the respective political context. They respect domestic institutions' 'margin of appreciation' in most cases.[60] This may be referred to as material or substantive subsidiarity. Finally, international human rights institutions usually impose obligations of results through judgement or decision, but leave the choice of means to domestic authorities. One may refer to it as remedial subsidiarity.

The only limit on international human rights institutions' subsidiarity, however, is the existence of a *consensus* among most democratic states going another direction than the one chosen by a given state.[61] The joint interpretive endeavour of all democratic domestic authorities leads indeed to the gradual constitution of a transnational interpretation and specification of a given human right, albeit a minimal and abstract one. Once there is such a consensual minimal interpretation among most domestic authorities, it may be recognized by international human rights institutions themselves and thus be consolidated at the international level. The evolutive nature of this joint interpretive process is sometimes referred to as 'dynamic interpretation' of international human rights law. And the joint and mutual process of human rights interpretation between domestic and international human rights institutions is often referred to as 'judicial dialogue'.[62] Once identified, that minimal human rights interpretation can then be re-imposed on domestic authorities. This is what is often referred to as the interpretive authority or *erga omnes* effect of an international human rights interpretation or decision.[63]

Importantly, however, those minimal international interpretations can only be more protective and never less protective than the conflicting domestic ones; they entrench interpretations to prevent a levelling-down but never a levelling-up. This is the point of so-called *saving clauses* in many international human rights instruments.[64] Of course, a domestic institution may still object to the argument that some international interpretation provides a better protection of a given human right than a domestic one.[65] Here, the judicial nature of the interpretive authority of international

---

(2008): 125–59; S. Besson, 'The *Erga Omnes* Effect of ECtHR's Judgements—What's in a Name?', in *The European Court of Human Rights after Protocol 14—First Assessment and Perspectives*, Collection Forum de droit européen (Schulthess, 2011), 125–75.

[60] See C. van de Heyning, 'No Place like Home: Discretionary Space for the Domestic Protection of Fundamental Rights', in P. Popelier, C. van de Heyning, and P. Van Nuffel (eds.), *Human Rights Protection in the European Legal Order: Interaction between European Courts and National Courts* (Intersentia, 2011), 65–96, 87–91.

[61] See also Neuman, 'Human Rights and Constitutional Rights', 1884.

[62] See eg N. Krisch, 'The Open Architecture of European Human Rights Law', in N. Krisch, *Beyond Constitutionalism: The Pluralist Structure of Postnational Law* (Oxford University Press, 2010), 109–52, 126ff.

[63] See eg Besson, 'The *Erga Omnes* Effect of ECtHR's Judgements'; J. Christoffersen, 'Individual and Constitutional Justice: Can the Power of Adjudication Balance be Reversed?', in J. Christoffersen and M. Rask Madsen (eds.), *The European Court of Human Rights between Law and Politics* (Oxford University Press, 2011), 181–203; L. Wildhaber, 'Rethinking the European Court of Human Rights', in Christoffersen and Rask Madsen (eds.), *The European Court of Human Rights between Law and Politics*, 204–29.

[64] See Neuman, 'Human Rights and Constitutional Rights', 1886–7.

[65] See Besson, 'Human Rights'; Buchanan, 'Justice, Legitimacy', 180–6.

human rights' decisions implies that judicial distinction and overruling may always be possible provided judicial reasoning across institutional levels leads to that result.[66] Thus, nothing prevents a new transnational consensus from lowering the level of protection reached before, even though the latter was internationalized through international judicial interpretation as a result. Of course, some of those international judicial interpretations may be vested with stronger authority than others to mark the difficulty of reversing them in the future. Furthermore, domestic courts may invoke a change in the transnational interpretive consensus itself. Thus, international human rights institutions' interpretive authority ought to evolve hand in hand with states' margin of appreciation as a two-way street and not against it, as some may fear.[67] Moreover, restrictions to human rights may always be justified on important grounds and provided the conditions of democratic necessity are fulfilled. Finally, if saving clauses and judicial dialogue seem too risky a perspective in view of certain potential structural violations of human rights, states have the possibility of devising interpretive declarations or even *reservations* to certain human rights and their established interpretations when acceding to a human rights instrument.[68] Importantly, however, those may not be devised later on once new interpretations of those human rights have arisen.

III. Human Rights and Domestic Constitutional Law

The second set of issues pertains to the relationship between human rights and constitutional law more generally. The question is particularly sensitive in constitutional democracies where there are no or few constitutional limits on the revision of constitutional law, and not even human rights-related ones, but where international human rights law, or rather their international interpretations, are said to take priority over constitutional law. To see more clearly through those difficult issues, it is important to explore, first, how international human rights may conflict with domestic constitutional law (section III.A). A second step in the argument broaches the question of the relationship between human rights and constitutional democracy (section III.B).

A. Human rights in domestic constitutional law

The question of the potential conflict between international human rights and domestic constitutional law is better understood as one between domestic human rights and domestic constitutional law. Given the mutual relationship and complementarity between international and domestic human rights, what matters here is that there are other constitutional norms that protect important interests that may conflict with human rights whether the latter finds their source in domestic or international law.

---

[66] See eg Besson, 'European Human Rights'. See also Van de Heyning, 'No Place like Home', 91–4; Christoffersen, 'Individual and Constitutional Justice', 198–200.
[67] See Wildhaber, 'Rethinking', 215–17.
[68] See Neuman, 'Human Rights and Constitutional Rights', 1888–90.

Re-formulated in this way, the question actually pertains to the justification of human rights' restrictions, and in particular to the kind of moral considerations that may justify restrictions to human rights duties and under which procedural conditions. Scope precludes fully addressing the question here, but it is interesting to focus on the role of other constitutional norms in this context. One may indeed argue that the fact that certain moral considerations are constitutionally entrenched may provide enhanced justification for a human right's restriction. It certainly makes the argument of democratic necessity that is the main justification for human rights restrictions under the ECHR, for instance, more plausible. The egalitarian dimension or threshold underlying all human rights that protect interests that are deemed sufficiently socio-comparatively important calls for egalitarian justifications to human rights restrictions. The requirement is that all human rights duties are restricted in an egalitarian way by reference to public interests.[69] This implies, for instance, paying attention to the distributive consequences of any human right restriction: the losers should not always be on the same side. In institutional terms, this egalitarian requirement of human rights restrictions means that democratic procedures are the adequate procedures in which to justify human rights restrictions. Given the democratic qualities of constitutional procedures, constitutional interests or principles conflicting with concrete human rights duties may thus be presumed to be more justified than others in restricting the latter.

Of course, in case interpretations about the justification of constitution law-based restrictions to human rights differ between democratic and international human rights institutions, the model proposed in the previous section could apply. The fact that those international human rights' interpretations conflict with domestic constitutional norms may not in any case vindicate the priority of domestic constitutional law merely because it is constitutional law. Constitutional law, even democratic, may be restricted just as human rights may, whether the latter's sources are international or domestic.

B. Human rights and constitutional democracy

More generally, the relationship between human rights and constitutional law raises the question of the relationship between human rights and constitutional democracy, ie, the way the constitution determines the structure and organization of democracy and hence the way a democratic polity self-determines or self-constitutes itself. What is at stake here, in other words, is the relationship between constitutional self-determination and international human rights law: some fear indeed that the latter may gradually erode constitutional self-determination.

Of course, the question of the relationship between human rights and democracy is an old chestnut. Human rights both constrain and enable democracy, and vice versa. With the internationalization of human rights, however, the debate has sharpened.[70]

---

[69] See Besson, 'The Egalitarian Dimension of Human Rights'.
[70] See Buchanan and Powell, 'Constitutional Democracy and the Rule of International Law', 326–7, 336ff.

Examples of potential erosion through the pressure of international human rights guarantees are, for instance, the development of judicial review domestically, the de-parliamentarization of domestic political regimes or the centralization of previously federal regimes.

The opposition between domestic democratic self-determination and international human rights protection is exaggerated, however.[71] Since 1945, international law has protected the self-determination of people as much as the individual rights of their members: the former through sovereignty and the latter through human rights. Importantly, therefore, state sovereignty under international law protects a collective entity of individuals—a people—and not individual human beings per se. Of course, their fates are connected, the way democracy and human rights are correlated domestically. But sovereignty, and sovereign equality in particular, protects democratic autonomy in a state's external affairs and remains justified for this separately from international human rights law. If the answer to the classical challenge domestically is that human rights and democracy are mutually required by reference to their egalitarian dimension, then that argument also holds once both elements have been externalized in their guarantees. Importantly, this means that the debate has moved one step outside the domestic legal order and is not that imbalanced after all in favour of human rights, but has only gained in complexity due to its relevant external dimensions. We should no longer be asked to discuss the constitutional democracy issue independently from the external guarantees of democracy one finds in international law the way some constitutional lawyers would like it.

International law standards of democracy contribute to the consolidation of domestic democracy, but they also constrain it. International human rights are an example in point, of course, but one should also mention international law norms on the protection of minorities or on election standards.[72] The question then is how to democratically legitimize them as external standards of democracy.

Interestingly, the issues that arise with the legitimation and validation of international democratic standards without an international democratic polity come very close to the ones discussed before, ie the legitimation and validation of international human rights without an international democratic polity. Unless one opts for global democracy and the corresponding idea of international constitutional law, which is neither normatively desirable nor realistic, the solution should come very close to the one proposed in the human rights context: mutual validation and legitimation through the mutually reinforcing mechanisms of internalization and externalization of standards between domestic and international law-making processes and institutional interpretations. This is also what one may refer to as the development of transnational and mutual democratic standards.

The key then would be to develop a constitutional theory for these transnational legal processes that are captured neither by constitutional legal theory nor by international legal theory as they currently stand. That transnational constitutional theory would have to account for the criteria and procedures for the development of shared

---

[71] See Besson, 'Democratic Authority'.

[72] See Buchanan and Powell, 'Constitutional Democracy and the Rule of International Law', 330ff.

democratic standards across democratic polities without those standards and procedures being themselves democratic in the absence of a transnational democratic polity. No comparisons could be made in this context with secession theory,[73] however; secession theory pertains indeed to the democratic criteria and procedures applicable to the renunciation to self-determination in one democratic entity to join another democratic entity. Self-determination within the boundaries of some kind of democratic polity, whether national or regional, has to remain the ultimate limit on transnational processes, as a result. This is, of course, an indeterminate constraint, but an absolute one from the perspective of democratic theory.

IV. Human Rights and International and Transnational Constitutional Law

A third concern raised by human rights in a constitutional context is whether human rights can be said to be part of a constitutionalization process in international law. A first question pertains to their relation to international constitutional law (section IV.A). This question also relates closely to a second one, however: that of human rights *qua* transnational constitutional law (section IV.B).

A. Human rights and international constitutional law

The relationship between human rights and international constitutional law may be framed as both one of constitutionalization of international law through human rights and as one of constitutionalization of human rights within the international legal order.[74]

With respect to the first question, it should be clear that although human rights belong, in domestic circumstances, to materially constitutional law norms, they do not suffice in themselves to vest a formally constitutional character on a legal order. The other elements of constitutional law are still missing on the international level. For instance, there is at present no democratic subject constituting itself on the international plane. Constituting such a global democratic subject would not be normatively desirable in any case.[75] The second question pertains to the constitutionalization of human rights within international law. Besides lacking a formal subject, the arguments to the existence of such a constitutionalization process fail to convince. International human rights are legalized in many different sources of international law. Besides, those are of equal rank and none of them are being entrenched against legal change.

It is important to remember that international human rights' function as an external guarantee and pressure on domestic law would be lost if they were too readily identified with the domestic human rights law of the international legal order, ie, as global domestic human rights law.[76] There is even a danger they might turn into a maximal

---

[73] Contra Buchanan and Powell, 'Constitutional Democracy and the Rule of International Law', 345.
[74] See Gardbaum, 'Human Rights as International Constitutional Rights', 752.
[75] See S. Besson, 'Whose Constitution(s)? International Law, Constitutionalism and Democracy', in J. Dunoff and J. Trachtman (eds.), *Ruling the World? Constitutionalism, International Law and Global Governance* (Cambridge University Press, 2009), 381–407.
[76] See Besson, 'Human Rights'.

threshold of human rights protection domestically, if they are treated as international constitutional rights and interpretations thereof.[77] The international constitutionalization discourse blinds to one of the key features of the international law order post-1945: the mutual relationship between democratic constitutional legal systems and the international legal order.

B. Human rights and transnational constitutional law

The consolidated corpus of international and domestic human rights may also be referred to as transnational human rights law[78] or even transnational constitutional law.[79] This idea of a transnational set of constitutional rights corresponds to the way in which international human rights apply in priority in the domestic legal order and bind domestic institutions *qua* constitutional rights, albeit in all domestic legal orders at the same time. As I argued before, the process of mutual validation and legitimation of domestic and international human rights requires a certain amount of democratic states through which the process of internalization and externalization can take place. It is the scope of that process that is clearly transnational.

Evidence of that transnational process in practice abounds, as I argued before. Its contours, however, remain curiously undertheorized. One key question that arises is whether this transnational process of mutual validation gives comparative constitutional law, and more particularly combined foreign law, a particular claim to legitimate authority besides its informative and persuasive authority.

Scope precludes rehearsing all the arguments here. It suffices to mention that, among the most serious critiques usually uttered against the legitimate authority of comparative human rights law, one finds the democratic one. It is generally argued indeed that using human rights' interpretations stemming from other domestic institutions than one's own country's would be a clear violation of the democratic principle.[80] It follows from this chapter's argument about the bottom-up legalization and legitimation of international human rights standards and their constraining domestic institutions in return, however, that comparative constitutional law may not only provide the best way to grasp the interpretive content of the transnational human rights practice at stake,[81] but also that transnational human rights may be vested with some indirect democratic legitimation through the respective democratic processes by which they have gradually been recognized.

The proposal made here should not be conflated, however, with a one-to-one use of comparative constitutional law between domestic human rights institutions (for

---

[77] See eg S. Besson, 'The Reception of the ECHR in the United Kingdom and Ireland', in H. Keller and A. Stone Sweet (eds.), *A Europe of Rights. The Reception of the European Convention on Human Rights* (Oxford University Press, 2008).

[78] See also Hessler, 'Resolving Interpretive Conflicts', 37; C. McCrudden, 'A Common Law of Human Rights: Transnational Judicial Conversations on Human Rights', *Oxford Journal of Legal Studies*, 20(4) (2000): 499–532, 530; Waldron, 'Citation of Foreign Law', 423.

[79] For that expression: McCrudden, 'A Common Law of Human Rights'.

[80] See McCrudden, 'A Common Law of Human Rights', 501ff, 529ff; Waldron, 'Citation of Foreign Law', 412ff.

[81] See also Buchanan, 'Justice, Legitimacy', 189.

example, based on Article 39, paragraph 1 of the South African Constitution). The present argument refers, on the contrary, to an international interpretation of a given international human right based on comparative or transnational constitutional law.

Of course, there are distinct arguments for the use of comparative constitutional law and the reference to 'foreign consensus' within domestic constitutional adjudication itself, including, most importantly, its contribution to conceptual clarification.[82] Importantly, however, if the mutual democratic legitimation of human rights law proposed in this chapter holds, there should, first be an external and international institution interpreting human rights on the basis of the existing transnational consensus and imposing it on domestic institutions in return, and, second, internal and domestic institutions should be focusing on their local political circumstances. Of course, local circumstances may be comparable and domestic human rights interpretations could be consciously 'boiler-plated',[83] to borrow Jeremy Waldron's terms, in real time as it were and before being constrained by international interpretations based on their transnational consensus. However, they need not. Nor should they be for the purpose of the proposed model. One important reason to refer to foreign interpretations of human rights, however, may be for a domestic institution to make an argument of change with respect to the transnational interpretive consensus of a given human right and to hope to trigger a judicial dialogue with international institutions and maybe bring about a new international interpretation of that right, as I argued before. In any case, one should note a third distinction of relevance here: whereas the one-to-one use of comparative constitutional law by domestic human rights institutions is usually said to have persuasive authority at the most,[84] the kind of transnational human rights law concerned in the consolidation of a human rights consensus is regarded here as having binding authority on the international human rights institutions at stake.

In practice, it is comparative constitutional law that is used to assess whether a general principle of international law may readily be identified among domestic constitutional traditions,[85] or whether there is a European consensus on a given human rights interpretation. Of course, the practice is largely irregular.[86] International human rights institutions lack resources and the time necessary to devote themselves rigorously to comparative human rights law studies. Criteria fail, moreover, as to what comparative evidence may amount to.[87]

The time has come therefore to propose the development of the transnational constitutional theory mentioned at the end of the previous section. One should start by articulating potential constraints on the consolidation process for transnational human rights and democratic standards. First of all, it is important for the domestic standards selected to have been submitted to public constitutional deliberation and vote domestically, and not just to judicial deliberation. Secondly, the international

---

[82] See eg Waldron, 'Citation of Foreign Law', 411, 418, 420ff; J. Waldron, 'Foreign Law and the Modern Ius Gentium', *Harvard Law Review*, 119 (2005): 129–47; McCrudden, 'A Common Law of Human Rights'.
[83] Waldron, 'Citation of Foreign Law', 423.
[84] See McCrudden, 'A Common Law of Human Rights', 513.
[85] See Besson, 'General Principles'.
[86] See McCrudden, 'A Common Law of Human Rights', 510ff.
[87] See McCrudden, 'A Common Law of Human Rights', 522, 532.

processes through which those standards are being recognized abstractly should be as inclusive as possible and their outcome approved through public constitutional deliberation and vote domestically. Thirdly, the international institutions interpreting them should be composed of members democratically elected domestically. Finally, the ultimate constraint on the authority of international interpretations of human rights and other democratic standards should be democratic self-determination. Of course, these are just some of the criteria one could think of.[88]

Conclusions

The main claim in this chapter was that, in the context of human rights, the relationship between international and domestic law differs from other areas. International human rights and domestic constitutional rights are situated in a relationship of mutual validation and legitimation. Their sources are interrelated, in other words, and so are their grounds of legitimacy. Gradually, this process has also led to the development of transnational human rights law and, arguably, of transnational constitutional law more broadly. It is this integrated and dynamic body of human rights norms and institutions, and their mechanisms of mutual interpretation and consolidation, whether at the regional level or on a more universal scale, and their democratic legitimacy, that are now calling for urgent attention.

[88] See eg Jackson, 'Transnational Constitutional Values and Democratic Challenges'.

16

Specifying Human Rights

Saladin Meckled-Garcia

Human rights are typically identified under specific headings: the right to life, to security of person, to freedom of expression, to freedom from slavery, to due process, and so forth. But beyond those headings, notoriously, the trouble starts. What normative content the rights have, what they *mean*, for the right-holder and for others in terms of obligations and burdens, is a matter of specification. One could treat this specification as a legal question, the interpretation of legal provisions in statutes, prior decisions, or practices. But there is a question in morality that should influence that legal specification: what is the *morally* justified content of any human right? What can holders of such rights legitimately claim from others and, correspondingly, what morally justified burdens does this imply for those others? One school of thought, call it the *democratic specification* tradition, holds that at least in part the specified moral content of human rights, not just the content of legal rights, must be what a democratic political community decides it to be. Specified human rights as moral rights, then, are hybrids: inherently moral in the abstract but inherently political in their specification.[1]

In what follows I challenge the cogency of the key theses of democratic specificationism on human rights, which I take to be two:

(1) Weight-of-Interests thesis: to justify the existence of a *moral right* a person must have an interest that is sufficiently important so as to imply obligations for others to secure that interest, and that means interests must be weighed against each other to establish their relative importance.

(2) Specification thesis: Which interests have the requisite degree of importance to become *human rights* by implying obligations for others is a question that must be settled by democratic decision making, where the relative importance of different interests (and corresponding costs and burdens) is weighed.

Not all views committed to the specification thesis are explicit about the weight-of-interests thesis.[2] However, that thesis is necessary to give the specification thesis enough structure to frame an argument. I will explore, and challenge, both.

[1] S. Besson, 'Human Rights and Constitutional Law: Patterns of Mutual Validation and Legitimation', (this volume, ch. 15); S. Benhabib, *Dignity in Adversity* (Cambridge: Polity, 2011). Benhabib takes specification to be a fundamentally political–legal question: universal claims are specified as different 'normatively defensible' (80) legal entitlements, deriving their content and legitimacy from the democratic nature of political orders (73ff).

[2] Eg, Besson, in this volume, holds the first (282) and second theses (282). Benhabib argues that abstract human rights can only acquire a concrete content through a process of democratic deliberation, Benhabib, *Dignity in Adversity*, 73ff. However, while she states that human rights justification must presuppose a conception of human needs (65), her argument for democratic specification of moral rights

The principal argument offered for the specification thesis is what I shall call 'contextualism'. This is the idea that whether an interest is sufficiently important so as to ground specific duties, and so rights with some normative content, is a matter sensitive to features of a social context. Democratic specification theorists take the central feature to be the way that members of a democratic society collectively weigh the importance of an interest against the burdens required to secure it.[3]

But there are two possible understandings of contextualism here, objective and subjective. The objective version appeals to different objective features of a context, such as scarcity, to justify the need for a different weighing exercise in each different context. But that kind of contextualism in fact relies on clear, pre-contextual, principles to establish the priority of any interest. Whether a given tax burden should be borne by fellow citizens, for example, in conditions of scarcity will depend on what constitutes a fair distribution of benefits and burdens. That in turn depends on what counts as a plausible moral principle of fairness, which is not itself a context-sensitive question. The views of the political community are not relevant to which, if any, principle is justified and applies. Objective contextualism, then, does not support the specification thesis and in fact undermines it. The subjective version of Contextualism offers a moral reason for taking the democratic decisions of the political community to be decisive in establishing the relative weight, or importance, of interests. The equal status of citizens entitles them to an equal say in that rights-specifying question, and that is a reason to take a democratic decision to be decisive. The problem with this argument, however, is that it runs together the separate questions of what constitutes political legitimacy and what justifies moral rights. What counts as an authoritative decision for a political community, a basis for valid law for example, is a wholly different question to what is the *morally* valuable way to prioritize interests. That latter question concerns the intrinsic merits of one scheme of priority over another. Moreover, a plausible role for human rights standards is to define the limits of acceptable political authority—when, for example, even a collective political decision can be judged wrongful enough to fail to have legitimacy.

In the last part of the paper I also question the weighing-of-interests thesis and the whole weighing metaphor as appropriate for justifying rights, given their special role in practical reason.

I. Interests and Well-being

Before considering the two theses just identified, I will clarify some essential terminology. The version of the view on which I am focusing is articulated in terms of interests and their importance in specifying what a right requires.

An interest, here, is a component of a person's well-being that can be advanced or thwarted, where well-being is understood as the degree to which one successfully pursues

---

is not explicitly articulated in terms of weighing interests. See also S. Meckled-Garcia, 'Which Comes First, Democracy or Human Rights?' *Critical Review of International Social and Political Philosophy*, 17(6) (2014): 681–8.

[3] Besson, 'Human Rights and Constitutional Law', 283.

one's plan of life or conception of the personal good.[4] There are conditions under which one can better pursue one's chosen plan of life or one's conception of the good, which is to say conditions under which one enjoys the securing of certain interests. Rights, in interest-based views of this kind, represent people's valid claims to having such conditions secured for specific interests. Enjoying an above survival state of nutrition can be seen as a component of a life plan and plausibly improves people's well-being. A right to nutrition would be a valid claim to having certain conditions in place where one can achieve some such level of nutrition. It is important to note that burdens corresponding to securing an interest also engage interests for the person shouldering the burdens. That person could use the effort, time, and resources her burden implies towards pursuing her own interests and well-being. A burden or a cost, then, is effectively a thwarted interest. So when I go on to discuss weighing of interests, this will often be shorthand for weighing the importance of interests secured versus the importance of the thwarted interests for those shouldering the burdens.

Specifying a right, for the purposes of this paper, means specifying which agents have obligations to act so as to secure the conditions associated with a right and which burdens they and others must bear. Elsewhere I have argued for a distinction between burdens associated with a right and the obligations corresponding to a right.[5] Obligations are just one type of burden or cost corresponding to a specified right. Other examples include the opportunity costs that satisfying someone's claim will imply. Burdens of whichever kind must nevertheless be justified if we are to justify the specification of a right.

So, if Jane has a right to have a promise kept, then the specification of the right provides a means by which one can identify who must act and what burdens others (including those who are obliged) must *justifiably* shoulder. It is sufficient for specifying a right that it specifies a type-description of the relevant features that pick out duty-bearers. 'The person that has made a promise' picks out promise-based duty-bearers, and 'anyone in a position to officially punish me' might pick out those against whom my right to due process is held. By joining together such descriptions with facts (Joe made the promise to babysit) we can judge that the right is held against Joe, and so that Joe has an obligation to babysit for Jane, and it is justifiable that others forego babysitting services from Joe (shouldering those opportunity costs), because his time is justifiably occupied babysitting for Jane. However, the specification that matters for a theory of rights, and that concerns democratic specification views, is clearly the deriving of justified duty-bearer type, duty type, and burden type, *descriptions*. After all, a concern with weighing interests is motivated by the need for an account of which burdens are justified and when rather than predicting for whom

---

[4] Raz, eg, defines well-being as consisting in 'a wholehearted and successful pursuit of valuable relationships and goals', J. Raz, 'The Role of Wellbeing', *Philosophical Perspectives*, 18(1) (2004): 269–94, 269. A variety of views exist on what constitutes well-being, ranging across accounts based on sensations like happiness, desire satisfaction, informed desire satisfaction, needs satisfaction, and 'objective list' accounts, J. Griffin, *Well-being* (Oxford: Oxford University Press, 1986). What is important to note is that different degrees of well-being can be had on all of them, depending on what degree of the relevant object (sensations, satisfactions, and objectively listed goods) one achieves.

[5] S. Meckled-Garcia, 'Giving up the Goods: Rethinking the Human Right to Subsistence, Institutional Justice, and Imperfect Duties', *Journal of Applied Philosophy*, 30(1) (2013): 73–87, 79.

they will be justified. So, the names and addresses of those on whom the obligations will fall, as a result of applying such descriptions, is not a question of moral theory but rather of its application.

For the purposes of this paper also, I will not consider what makes something into a right, as opposed to merely a duty, say.[6] Instead I focus on the 'justification conditions' for any claim specified as a set of burdens for others. That is, how does one show that a given rights claim can justify a set of corresponding duties and duty-bearer descriptions from which we might derive concrete judgements? Call that the *normative content* of a right.

By *democratic* specification, in what follows, I will not necessarily mean there has to be a full democratic legislative process for every specifying decision. So long as legal institutions, including courts, are validated as part of a democratic constitutional order their decisions can count as the decisions of a democratic political community. Nothing in the following argument turns on whether a demos or a judge decides how a right should be specified.

So to restate the democratic specification view, human rights cannot be adequately specified such that we know their normative content for a specific social context unless we can decide how to 'weigh' or 'balance' interests, so as to decide which interests reach the threshold of 'sufficient importance' necessary to imply obligations for others. Only a democratic political community can do that, which is to say that whilst human rights must be moral rights imposing moral duties, their specification must be the result of a political–legal process. Prior to such a democratic process, the content of such rights cannot be adequately specified, and so cannot be said to exist as concrete entitlements.[7] For that reason human rights are inherently moral but also inherently political or legal.

It is worth noting how this contrasts with an interest-based view. Tasioulas, for example, concedes that the specification necessary for a right to be 'claimable' might require a democratic decision or even negotiation.[8] However, he rejects the idea that the right does not really exist in the absence of such a specification. This is because he takes it that we can know an interest to be important enough to justify a right, given our knowledge of certain practical considerations ('the constraints set by human capacities, available resources, and general features of social life').[9] Specification is needed simply because there are various ways to protect or further an interest, and choices have to be made.[10] The democratic specification view, on the other hand, holds that whether interests are sufficiently important to justify rights is itself a matter to

---

[6] That is a conceptual question about the meaning of the term 'right'. 'Interest theories' have been offered as identifying (categorizing) what is distinctive about rights versus duties say, but in this paper I am concerned with views that take rights to be grounded in the weighing of interests, and more specifically the weighing of interests by a democratic political community.

[7] Besson, 'Human Rights and Constitutional Law', 284–5.

[8] It is 'an important issue, one to be addressed through further moral and empirical investigation and possibly even negotiation or formal determination within the context of democratic politics or judicial reasoning', J. Tasioulas, 'The Moral Reality of Human Rights', in T. Pogge (ed.), *Freedom from Poverty as a Human Right* (Oxford: Oxford University Press, 2007), 94.

[9] Tasioulas, 'The Moral Reality of Human Rights', 92.

[10] Tasioulas, 'The Moral Reality of Human Rights', 94.

be settled by democratic institutions. It is unclear how one can know that an interest is important enough to justify a right without knowing the normative content of the right, given that 'important enough' must mean important enough to justify the specific burdens the right will imply for others. Tasioulas assumes that satisfying the practical constraints is enough, but without an account of how the specific burdens would be justified for those carrying them it is unclear that a claimed right has any justified normative content.[11] The two views overlap in accepting that (in at least some cases for Tasioulas) the normative content of a moral right can be settled by democratic decisions.[12]

II. Contextualism

The democratic specification view, as I am construing it, accepts that there are universal moral rights, and holds that these are based on interests sufficiently important to ground moral duties for others. A universal moral right of this kind can be justifiably claimed regardless of a person's institutional membership, as corresponding moral obligations can be specified independently of institutional membership. The right to have promises kept, for example, is a plausible moral right with corresponding obligations clearly falling on those who have made promises. By contrast, human rights are, on this view, inherently institutional moral rights. That is, they do not exist until they have been appropriately 'recognized' in a legal order as implying public institutional duties.[13] When they do exist, however, these duties of public institutions are moral duties. The institutional nature of human rights is due to the fact that specifying the content of a human right necessarily requires resolving the question of which interests are of sufficient importance, or fundamental enough, to justify imposing burdens on others to secure their enjoyment. On the version of the democratic specification view I am considering, that question can only legitimately be decided democratically. Members of a political community must decide the threshold of importance by weighing interests against each other (burdens, or thwarted interests, included), and deciding what constitutes a standard threat from which interests must be protected, and what is feasible in securing those interests.[14]

This would contrast with a view that says human rights can be specified through working out a clear moral theory with principles for assigning burdens. On that kind of view specification occurs at the level of theory, and is independent of institutional decisions. The argument for this view rests on the idea that any specification of human rights must be sensitive to a given social context.[15]

---

[11] Similarly Raz says 'one may know of the existence of a right and of the reasons for it without knowing who is bound by duties based on it or what precisely are these duties', J. Raz, *The Morality of Freedom*, 184, yet he does think that there are principles of responsibility for working this out.

[12] See also appeals to democratic deliberation to settle the content of human rights in J. Griffin, *On Human Rights* (Cambridge: Cambridge University Press, 2008), 128 and 171.

[13] Besson, 'Human Rights and Constitutional Law', 283–4; Benhabib, *Dignity in Adversity*, 65 and 74.

[14] Besson, 'Human Rights and Constitutional Law', 282–3.

[15] Benhabib, *Dignity in Adversity*, 73, 74, 80, 125, 130; Besson, 'Human Rights and Constitutional Law', 282.

Let me spell this argument out. In order to apply a right in a given context, one must be able to specify that right. In order to specify a right, one must adjudicate between the competing interests present in that context, available agents to act as duty-bearers, and feasibility conditions. That is, one must be sensitive to features of this context. This means deciding when an interest is sufficiently important so as to justify others carrying duties (for example, institutionally imposed duties to pay taxes). This raises questions of cost to those carrying the burdens. The view rightly observes that to ground a duty for others, one must also take into account the burdens and costs of that duty.[16]

So, the view stresses, interests can be general and important but the kind of importance that creates moral duties must take into account features of the context. That is because the ground for giving rights a clear normative content must be context sensitive.[17] The right way to ensure that, on this view, is if collective institutions in a democratic order make decisions on the relative importance of interests and create legal rights that codify this.

On the democratic specification view, then, the correct response to the need for contextual sensitivity is to leave that specification to political and legal processes. Resolution comes through collective deliberation, decision making, and legality. In fact, human rights on such a view do not really have any meaningful normative content at all without this kind of specification.[18] So, the moral nature of human rights is partly supplied by considering people's interests and partly by a democratic political order. Human rights are not, then, simply pre-legal moral rights that can be enforced through positive law. They are hybrid standards, part moral and part legal, in their specification but fully moral in their demands.

There is however a problem with an approach that passes the specification buck, as it were, to the political community. The contextualism in question can be understood as either objective or subjective. On the objective version, discernible and objective features of specific social conditions shape people's entitlements because they determine which agents and which burdens are in play. What is relevant are the facts about social circumstances that make a moral difference, such as who is in a position to take on the burdens, including the duties, and whether it is justifiable that people in that kind of position do so. Discerning what matters enough and what kind of burdens can be justly imposed requires a principle that, applied in different contexts and together with the facts, will tell us which agent types should bear responsibility and why. On the subjective version of Contextualism, on the other hand, how interests are compared and weighed to decide whether they ground obligations is a matter decided by subjective features: the views of members of the political community.[19] This is the core contextual feature according to which human rights must be specified and made

---

[16] Besson, 'Human Rights and Constitutional Law', 282ff.

[17] Besson says interests are 'trans-historical' but 'sufficient' importance and the 'fundamental' nature of some interests has to be determined by reference to a context, Besson, 'Human Rights and Constitutional Law', 282.

[18] Besson, 'Human Rights and Constitutional Law', 282–3.

[19] Besson calls this 'socio-comparative' recognition of interest importance, 'Human Rights and Constitutional Law', 283 and 284 and 294.

real.[20] The only relevant moral principle, then, would be one that says 'if the political community decides to prioritize interests over burdens in a certain way, that is the content of human rights'.

The problem is that neither version of Contextualism gives adequate support to democratic specificationism. The objective version does not because it actually implies appeal to moral principles that are right independently of the decisions of political communities and can be used to judge those decisions. It is on the basis of those principles that we identify objective features of a social context that matter when judging what burdens are justified—ie, when specifying the normative content of human rights. Whether an interest is important in the right way so that a right should protect it will depend on applying principles to the objective facts in a judgement.

Whether a burden is justified, and for whom it is justified, will depend on discernible features about those who might shoulder it, such as being a member of a political community capable of treating its members fairly in terms of personal security. Those features themselves must be identifiable by reference to principles of justified burden for securing others' interests. On an objective reading of Contextualism, then, decisions of the political community might get it right or wrong as to what the relevant objective features are, and what duties are justified. They might wrongly prioritize Joe's interests in quashing Jane's views. This is because they do not define what is justified, the principles do. On the subjective version, on the other hand, the relevant features of a given context are decisions of the political community about how to prioritize securing interests versus costs to others. I begin by discussion the objective version and turn to the subjective version late.

Objective contextualism

Consider an interest such as the interest in nutrition. Should people in a given political community have rights to be provided with nutrition? This will depend on what securing that interest might mean for others. Securing the conditions for nutrition of any degree will imply that others must take on the burdens, such as contributing to the nutrition of those who cannot secure it for themselves. It will imply duties on agents in a position of authority to allocate burdens, such as allocating tax burdens, and duties on productive individuals to contribute through the tax burdens allocated to them. It will also imply costs incurred by others resulting from these duties, such as reduced opportunities to engage in financial exchanges with those who have been taxed or reduced opportunities in their family group when the breadwinners have increased allocated tax burdens. Whether these costs are justified by the pressing importance of the interests will depend on whether there is a suitable moral principle for justifying the allocation of burdens and benefits.

Political theorists have developed theories of distribution for allocating benefits and burdens in a society based on concepts of fair distribution or equal opportunities.[21]

---

[20] Besson, 'Human Rights and Constitutional Law'—'Only those interests…recognized as socio-comparatively equally important by members…can…give rise to duties' (283); Benhabib, *Dignity in Adversity*, 64 and 74.

[21] S. Meckled-Garcia, 'Giving up the Goods', 75–6.

Such principles indicate when interests are to be prioritized so much that others must carry obligations to respond to them. For example, Rawls' difference principle indicates that persons capable of obtaining unequal advantages should only be socially guaranteed those unequal advantages that are necessary for, or coincide with, improving the position of the least advantaged in society. An alternative view in the literature holds that people are entitled to equality of resources, even if ultimately their choices lead to different achievements.[22] On these views a right like the claim to nutrition will imply obligations because of values like fairness and equal concern in a society. Fairness might indicate that the advantages of nourished people over un-nourished are socially unfair if the nourished can contribute to improving the condition of those at the bottom. Their tax burdens in doing so are justified burdens. Equal concern might tell us that others' nutrition must be paid for, say if it is not their choice to be under-nourished (as it might be for a person seeking weight loss) but due to society's arbitrary distribution of resources.

The point is that when it comes to deciding on whether interests are to be advanced, or burdens shouldered, according to objective features of a social context, we need guidance. That guidance, if we are to give a morally satisfactory answer, must take the form of a moral principle indicating which interests have the characteristics making them important in the right way: rendering the burdens corresponding to securing them justified. Which means the objective features of a social context that help us in specifying people's rights have to be features picked out by moral judgements and moral principles. Consider whether Jane Doe's interest in freedom of movement should matter more than an interest Joe Doe might have in constraining her. Consider a principle prescribing that interests in controlling others' movement for the purpose of disadvantaging religious minorities do not count as morally relevant considerations. On that principle Joe's interest would be ruled irrelevant as a basis for deciding whether to constrain Jane's movements. On the other hand, if Joe's interest is in having his life protected from assault will represent a sufficiently high priority for constraining Jane's movements when she aims to assault him. Consider the political community's tax burdens in resourcing protection, of Joe from Jane. So long as the burdens are fair, on a reasonable account of fairness, Joe's interests in protection are fairly treated by being prioritized. In each case the objectively justified principle will indicate the order of priority. What a political community decides is the right balance between benefits and burdens, interests and the duties to secure them, is beside the point. If it concurs with the objectively right principle the polity gets it right. If it does not, it gets it wrong.

It is important at this juncture to further clarify the notion of specification. One might say that there are a variety of ways to skin a cat, and similarly a variety of arrangements that might prioritize general and fundamental interests. Which social arrangements are feasible, and out of the feasible ones which are to be selected and, given that different arrangements will fall on different shoulders, on whose shoulders should they fall? These are all specification questions. Yet, those questions cannot be decided by moral principles given moral principles can only indicate what kinds of

---

[22] R. Dworkin, *Sovereign Virtue* (Cambridge, MA: Harvard University Press, 2002), 65ff.

interests should be prioritized. They do not indicate how to operationalize securing those interests.[23] For example, securing people's interests in being free from slavery may have priority over the costs to the political community of doing so. But whether the police, a special institution, or a militia should do the securing will depend on circumstances and feasibility.

These questions of policy are rightly questions that a political community must decide. However, they have nothing to do with the *moral* specification of human rights. Whether a given police action, a tax scheme to pay for it, or a state's actions in requiring such actions (or all of these) are appropriate specifications of the right to be free from slavery will nevertheless depend on principles directing us as to how to prioritise the claims of greater security over claims not to have higher tax burdens. Which officers are available will depend on morally appropriate contractual conditions in working for the police service. Whether more officers can be employed will depend on available tax revenues, and that will depend on the productiveness of a given social set up, and what is morally justified in terms of production and the fair distribution of its benefits and burdens.

For some aspects of a right, such as the imperative not to enslave others, or not to enact legislation permitting such acts, the prioritization will not vary with resources, as they are straightforward prohibitions. For others, such as the imperative for a political community to protect its members from enslavement, the degree of protection will be sensitive to principles for prioritizing different demands, principles of fairness in what burdens citizens can be expected to shoulder for example. But in specifying the kind of agent that must carry the duty and the kind of duties they must carry, appeal to such principles is unavoidable. Whilst their specific application depends on objective contextual facts, the correct content of the principles does not. Nor does it depend on collective political decisions.

The reason why principled grounds for specification may seem a tall order is that human rights theorists have been inattentive to specification. Theorists have sought to base their views of justified human rights claims on identifying important interests. They have interpreted the relevant sense of importance of interests as detachable from showing over which burdens an interest has priority, and thus avoided supplying clear principles for interest prioritisation, and so for justifying burdens. This is partly due to a commonly held view that identifying human rights and specifying their corresponding duties are separate enterprises.[24] But identifying principles of priority or legitimate burden is nevertheless a problem that demands a solution in *moral* theory, and so one that cannot be avoided in offering a theory of human rights with a discernible practical content. In that enterprise there is no reason to think that a democratic community is uniquely positioned to ascertain the right principles, as there is no reason to think a democratic community uniquely gets moral theory right. The crux question is what reasons there are *on the merits* for adopting one principle and its

---

[23] Cf Tasioulas, 'The Moral Reality of Human Rights' 92, 94 ff..

[24] Viz. M. Nussbaum, *Frontiers of Justice* (Cambridge, MA: Belknap Press, 2006), 277ff; Tasioulas, 'The Moral Reality of Human Rights', 93 and 99; A. Gewirth, *Human Rights: Essays on Justification and Application* (Chicago: University of Chicago Press, 1982), 15; Griffin, *On Human Rights*, 97 and 103.

prioritizing of interests over another. For objective contextualism, then, passing the buck to the collective is misconceived.

I am of course assuming here that democratic specification views are not motivated by scepticism about moral principles and about moral arguments generally. After all, the view seems to presuppose that some elements of human rights decision making, such as the selection of relevant interests for weighing which protections are necessary in providing the moral conditions for democracy, are not moral questions we should be sceptical about.[25] So moving from morality about interests to scepticism about how to balance them lacks coherence. An argument would have to be offered why in this special case there could be no morally justified theory of priority. Without that argument, the sceptical blade that cuts against moral principles would also cut against the moral value of having democracy and the point of engaging in balancing interests at all. Democratic decisions or the judgement of a court would then amount to coin-flipping exercises, with no special moral warrant for their outcomes.

There is a problematic position in the literature that has been highly influential and may lie behind this sceptical approach to specification. This originates in a branch of German constitutional scholarship.[26] It says that constitutional rights (which the view does not adequately distinguish from human rights) are not clear principles for imposing obligations, but rather instructions to optimise specific interests. Each interest represents a heading for a right (life, security of person, freedom from torture, freedom from slavery, and so forth). In the context of any one political community, however, the optimization of these interests for any one person will at times clash with the optimization for others, and with the collective interests of the political community.[27] That is why contextual judgement is needed to settle the content of what people are entitled to have on a case-by-case basis. Favouring this kind of judgement grants courts the authority to balance, and optimize, interests. On one reading of the view, there are no moral principles for prioritizing interests, which is the sceptical position I mentioned earlier. But as I have said, without a special argument to prevent such scepticism infecting all moral appraisals, including our appraisal of democracy

---

[25] Besson, 'Human Rights and Constitutional Law', 282; Benhabib, *Dignity in Adversity*, 60 and 65.

[26] Alexy takes constitutional rights to be instructions to optimize interests under their headings, and the role of judges in a constitutional democracy to solve the problem of how to optimize in conditions where these rights conflict (where a decision on what gets optimized must be taken), R. Alexy, *A Theory of Constitutional Rights* (Oxford: Oxford University Press, 2002); R. Alexy, 'Constitutional Rights, Balancing and Rationality', *Ratio Juris*, 16 (2003): 131–40. See also K. Moller, 'Balancing and the Structure of Constitutional Rights', *International Journal of Constitutional Law*, 5(3) (2007): 453–68; M. Kumm, 'Constitutional Rights as Principles: On the Structure and Domain of Constitutional Justice', *International Journal of Constitutional Law*, 2 (2004): 574–96. Often the balancing metaphor accompanies a conception of 'proportionality' as optimizing different interests (especially where collective interests are also in play), see: M. Kumm, 'Political Liberalism and the Structures of Rights: On the Place and Limits of the Proportionality Requirement', in S. Paulson and G. Pavlakos (eds.), *Law, Rights, Discourse: Themes from the Work of Robert Alexy* (Portland, Oregon: Hart Publishing, 2007); K. Moller, 'Proportionality: Challenging the Critics', *Oxford Journal of Legal Studies*, 10(3) (2012): 709–31. For a critique of the balancing conception of proportionality, see G. Letsas, this volume, ch. 17. Democratic specification views are clearly influenced by the idea of legal institutions balancing (or proportionately optimizing) interests.

[27] Whether or not the collective interests of a political community can reduce to the interests of each of its members is a question I shall leave open here.

itself, that position would be self-defeating. Another reading of this position is to take optimization to mean a principle requiring we maximize important interest protections, and I will return to that in section III. Now I turn to the subjective version of contextualism.

Subjective contextualism

One might also think that in conditions where people disagree over what the right principles might be, then there is moral warrant for the answer to be settled democratically.[28] This is a moral argument for democratic deliberation. That takes us to the subjective version of contextualism, which offers a moral argument in favour of settling interest-weighing disputes by democratic deliberation. This view effectively hones in on decisions of the political community as the relevant features of the context that decide how interests should be prioritized. For this to count as relevant, then, we need a moral argument for making such deliberations decisive. But, as I will show, the most plausible moral argument for the decisiveness of democratic deliberation can only make it decisive for a different purpose. It can tell us which interpretation of human rights a society should adopt for enforcement purposes, *all things considered*; it cannot decide the morally right specification of the normative content of human rights.

The moral argument, as offered by democratic specification theorists, is that in a democratic context, people are given an equal say in the rights and burdens to be socially enforced. This equal say both recognizes that they have interests worthy of protection and accords them an *equal* memberships status in the community.[29] Recognition means giving each an equal say in assessing what that status means, what burdens are justifiably imposed in securing each other's interests.[30] The moral value behind this idea is the expression of political equality and what this means for distributing rights to political *participation*.

But there is a difference between what counts as a legitimate procedure for deciding which rights should get socially or legally *enforced* and the right basis for deciding the *moral* content of human rights. There may indeed be morally good reasons to accept collective decisions on what socially guaranteed rights members of a political community are to enjoy, even decisions that get it wrong within reasonable limits. Where there is pervasive moral disagreement in a pluralist society we might need to reasonably resolve some debates over society's rules as a practical necessity, even if those debates have not been resolved intellectually, and even if there are some moral questions for which no one has developed clear and definitive answers. Out of the available decision-making processes to move on practically some respect the equal status of citizens more than others: democracy respects equal deliberation and input whereas

---

[28] Viz. 'Philosophical differences will still persist in articulating the content of such recognition', Benhabib, *Dignity in Adversity*, 65.

[29] Benhabib, *Dignity in Adversity*, 74; Besson, 'Human Rights and Constitutional Law', 282–3, 286, 287, 291.

[30] 'The recognition of human rights is done mutually and not simply vertically and top-down, and…human rights are not externally promulgated but mutually granted by members of a given political community'; 'it allows for the mutual assessment…of the recognition of the corresponding rights and duties…', both Besson, 'Human Rights and Constitutional Law', (283).

authoritarianisms do not. Public legal institutions complement this form of respect, as they provide a transparent decision-making forum on how legislative decisions should be interpreted and their consequences adjudicated. But this is all justifiable as legitimate on the basis of citizen equality (not itself justified by democratic decisions). It is, on those grounds a very different project to answering the *normative* question of what moral rights people can legitimately claim regardless of their fellow citizens' practically constrained decisions.

It is important to note what is at stake here. Without a special argument shielding some rights from having their content democratically decided, the democratic specification view implies every right, and every element of every right, must be subject to interest priority-orderings decided by a political community. There is no exception, because any possible practical content that any right could have requires prioritizing some interests over others. Even something as straightforward as the prohibition on slavery implies a priority ordering in terms of the interests of those enslaved versus those who might benefit from it.[31] As I argued earlier, claiming *all* moral decisions should be subject to democratic practical decisions in this way is self-defeating. It implies we have no moral reason to even accept the basic rights that make democracy itself possible, giving it some moral warrant. Democratic rights, after all, imply prioritizing some interests over others. Note that the version of democratic specificationism I have been discussing is indeed committed to a value basis—equal status— that justifies the democratic process.[32] So, moving to subjective contextualism cannot, on this view, be justified by adopting general scepticism about specifying moral rights.

The (non-sceptical) democratic specification solution, then, only makes sense if it serves some *value* that is also part of the initial impetus to develop an account of human rights. As I have shown, one such value is giving people an equal say and an equal status in their collective institutions, to thereby respect their equal moral status.[33] That value is perfectly well served by accepting a fundamental role for democratic institutions, plus judicial propriety, in *practical* decision making. However, as also argued, what makes a correct form of *practical* decision making is not the same as what makes a correct moral decision, otherwise democratic decisions could not themselves have any moral warrant. Correct practical decision making is simply morally justified decision making under specific constraints, such as having processes that respect all members of the political community equally.

The same candidate value is also an excellent candidate for underpinning a view about the right way to prioritise interests. This is the value of treating people in a way that shows equal respect for their status and equal concern for the way their lives will fare in the face of non-optional collective institutions. But if that is the point of the enterprise, it is not well served by claiming the morally justified content of the values,

---

[31] For those uncomfortable with describing a preference for torture, either instrumental or intrinsic, as just another interest in a priority ordering this section can be phrased in terms of preferences that should be discounted. We still need a principle that sets out criteria for which those are.

[32] See n 30.

[33] Viz. '…the threshold of importance and point of passage from a general and fundamental interest to a human right…may be found in the normative status of each individual qua equal member of the moral-political community', Besson, 'Human Rights and Constitutional Law', 282.

of equal respect and concern, is a matter for practical decision-making procedures. That value must inform us in determining which practical decision-making procedures are legitimate and the extent, and the limits of, their legitimacy. That is why slavery, even if it were underwritten through a majoritarian 'democratic' process could never represent a rightful prioritizing of interests, nor could absence of due process, or general suppression of dissenting political speech and associations. Which is to say that some decisions can be so wrong that they are illegitimate regardless of the constraints under which they are made, even if it is normally reasonable to decide matters democratically under such constraints. For other rights, such as those seeking to best express equal mutual concern for members of a political community, there might be leeway under these constraints to allow us to implement what is not the morally right solution on the merits, but the right on the merits of the decision-making procedure.

Of course, democratic specificationism is motivated by a desire to establish which interests should be prioritized and the apparent difficulty in pure moral theory of doing so. One reason that apparent difficulty is the *kind* of moral theory such views appeal to in trying to explain moral rights—interest-based accounts looking to establish the priority of interests by 'weighing' how important their fulfilment is for each person's well-being. There are inherent problems with that theoretical framework that underpin specification problems, as I show in section III.

III. Weight-of-interests

The weighing-of-interests component of the view, as I have construed it here, is not specific to democratic specification theories. However, it gives some structure to the democratic specification argument.[34] Nevertheless, the view that rights must be justified by reference to the relative importance (weight) of interests is a widely held view. There are, however, two possible readings of the idea that an interest has 'sufficient importance' (is of sufficient weight) such that it grounds obligations. The reading that the democratic specification approach needs, however, is the less plausible of the two.

On the first reading, the importance of an interest is in terms of its importance for a person's well-being. For example it is usually highly important for a person to enjoy even minimal well-being that such interests as water, food, freedom from attack, and so forth, are secured. On the second understanding of importance, securing an interest is important by reference to some moral value, such that prioritizing this interest realizes that value and failing to prioritize it does not, or even runs counter to it. So, equal pay for equal work is more in line with the value of fairness than random pay for equal work. The additional pay a person in the random pay system might get in the equal pay system might be of marginal importance to her well-being, given her life aims. More pay may not alter the well-being of someone whose life satisfaction is focused on her work. Yet the distribution is hugely important for fairness.

The democratic specification view needs the first sense of importance. The view says a political community must deliberate under conditions of equality in order to weigh

---

[34] 'Of course, there has to be a threshold of importance at which a given interest is regarded as sufficiently fundamental to give rise to duties and hence to a right', Besson, 'Human Rights and Constitutional Law,' 282.

how important, or fundamental, interests are. That weighing (or 'balancing') results in decisions as to the importance of interests and what the threshold of importance is for grounding duties. If an interest in increased personal security for Paul has sufficiently greater weight than Peter's interest in avoiding increased taxation, this will justify duties to pay more taxes. But for any scheme proposing decisions about obligations on the basis of weighing the importance of interests, there has to be a common currency of importance in terms of which the interests are compared.

I am assuming the only relevant common currency here is the importance of interests to people's well-being. Yet, however important an interest is in that sense, that fact is not even a prima facie ground for moral obligations. That is because grounding duties for others requires an account of when, and why, those others must prioritize Paul's interest over their own in pursuing their own lives as they wish. In other words it requires a third factor: an account of when an interest is of overriding importance: when it demands that we override the interests others have in not being burdened.

For any two interests, if they are interests of the same person it makes perfect sense that, when deciding which she has reason to act to secure, she has most reason to choose the interest that matters to her the most in the scheme of her aims and overall conception of the good. That is a key aspect of well-being and its value—the degree to which someone gets to pursue her conception of the good. But things are different if these interests belong to different persons. While an interest might be of high importance to Paul, that is not by itself a reason for Peter to prioritize securing that interest, given securing his own interests will be important for him too. Peter needs a reason to prioritize securing Paul's interest over those of his interests thwarted by taking on these burdens. But the fact that Paul's interest is important to his well-being is not the right kind of reason.

What is needed is a value-based reason: a reason for Peter to value prioritizing the securing of another's interest over his own. And that reason must guide Peter as to how much priority he should give the interests of others, given he has interests of his own. The same structure of reasoning applies to the social case as using social resources such as taxes implies tax burdens for people and so calls for a justification for prioritizing others' interest over our own burdens. This is why human rights theorists often appeal to moral values such as dignity or minimal decency, to justify placing priority on securing a minimal list of interests. One could also appeal to values like fairness, which on one view means the interests of the least advantaged are prioritized over those of the most advantaged. It is fair that those inequalities enjoyed by those who can achieve them because of social cooperation are taxed for the sake of those not otherwise in a position to benefit so much from that cooperation.

So the first reading of importance, as simply importance for a person's well-being, will not get us to human rights (moral reasons to act in ways that are beneficial to some and burdensome to others). We need a moral value, perhaps expressed as a moral principle, like fairness or respect, and that is the second reading of the notion of importance.

On this reading, importance is priority in terms of serving a moral value. But note that this priority is not of the kind involved in balancing and weighing. A right, as a type of practical reason, must be able to *silence* some considerations, including other interests. Consider a version of the earlier example where someone's conception of the good involves dedication to a discriminatory religious view. A worshipper might have an interest, as a result of pursing a life of dedication, in discriminating against other religions. The holder of such a view might claim a right to discriminate. The correct response to such a claim is not that non-discrimination is sufficiently important to others, in terms of some value like fairness or dignity, that it outweighs the importance of the devotee's interest in discriminating in terms of fairness or dignity.[35] Rather, the correct response is that her interest does not even count as a relevant consideration. It automatically gets a weighting of zero in all equations. The moral priority of rights, then, is a more complex form than the weight-of-interest-importance view suggests.

There is one candidate for a moral value that would seem to instruct us to look at how much securing interests contributes to a person's well-being. That is any moral view that values actions maximizing well-being, because more protected well-being is better than less.[36] An example of this would be a kind of 'interest calculus' where securing an interest is prioritized if it produces an overall gain in well-being.[37] On that kind of view, we are indeed required to weigh interests against each other in terms of their contribution to well-being, but we must then consider them in the aggregate to decide what duties they ground. An interest deserves securing on this view if it contributes to a higher sum of secured interests. Whilst this is indeed a candidate for the second interpretation of importance, it is unfortunately retrogressive as an account of human rights. It implies that individual-centred concerns are beside the point, and an individual's plight only matters enough to ground rights when it contributes to the common good. If not fully a utilitarian view, this is open to similar objections to such views, based on the intrinsic importance and value of individual destinies.

In summary, there are significant problems with the weight-of-interests view that frames the prioritization problem to which the democratic specification approach is supposed to resolve. A challenge to that framework is the idea that we sometimes prioritise some interests over others, and impose some burdens as a result, not because of their respective contributions to well-being but because doing so serves a moral value such as equal respect. I sketch the beginnings of such a view elsewhere.[38]

---

[35] I am here emphasizing the capacity of rights to block other considerations or 'reasons'. Other authors have stressed this characteristic of moral rights, see R. Dworkin, 'Taking Rights Seriously', in his *Taking Rights Seriously* (Cambridge, MA: Harvard University Press, 1978); J. Waldron, 'Pildes on Dworkin's Theory of Rights', *The Journal of Legal Studies*, 29(1) (2000): 301–207, 305; Meckled-Garcia, 'Giving up the Goods', 83ff.

[36] This will include different views on maximization, such as straight aggregate increase and pareto improvement.

[37] Another example, proposed by Marmor, is an 'interest calculus' (a 'cost-benefit analysis') to decide what burdens are justified in terms of maximizing overall interest protection, A. Marmor, 'On the Limits of Rights', *Law and Philosophy*, 16(1) (1997): 1–18, 10ff, yet he eschews the idea that this implies any kind of utilitarian calculus, because utilitarian calculi require 'quantitative commensurability' of interests. Whether that is sufficient to separate this form of aggregation from utilitarianism, I shall leave aside here. It is nevertheless a consequentialist view of rights, given what is required as a matter of right is decided by its consequences for the interest calculus (although I note that Marmor claims his view is not consequentialist, 'On the Limits of Rights', 14).

[38] Meckled-Garcia, 'Giving up the Goods'.

IV. Conclusion

In conclusion I have offered some reasons for doubting the cogency of the specification thesis and the weighing-of-interests thesis. This challenges versions of democratic specification subscribing to either or both theses. I hope also to have given some general reasons to re-consider the idea that human rights can be grounded in the weighing of interest, in terms of their importance for well-being. This is not a sceptical challenge to human rights, as there are candidate accounts of human rights that do not suffer from the problems of well-being-based accounts.

17

Rescuing Proportionality

George Letsas*

I. Introduction

What human rights people have is a contested and complex philosophical issue. It involves many different questions about the nature of rights, about when some right is a *human* right, as well as institutional questions about when particular human rights courts should enforce individual claims. Not all rights are enforceable and not all rights are human rights. Gratuitous promises create moral rights and duties between the promisor and the promisee but these are neither human nor enforceable. Not all rights enforceable in law moreover are human rights. In English law, the seller of a property has the right to use the buyer's deposit, between exchange of contracts and completion, in order to purchase another property. The seller's right is an enforceable legal right in English law but we would hardly call it a human right. On the other hand, many rights are proclaimed as human without necessarily being enforceable. Socio-economic rights to health, education, or shelter are nowadays considered to be human rights, but their enforceability is the exception, not the norm.

In Europe and other parts of the world, courts use the doctrine of proportionality as a test in order to determine whether someone's human rights have been violated. Proportionality is hailed as a universal criterion of constitutionality.[1] According to the orthodox understanding of this legal doctrine, state interference with non-absolute human rights (such as privacy, freedom of religion or expression) is lawful, if it is proportionate to a legitimate aim in pursuit of which the state acted. In its standard form the test consists of two main stages. First, courts will ask whether there has been an interference with a liberty or interest that falls within the scope of a right protected in the relevant convention or constitution (the *scope or definitional* stage). Second, the court will ask whether that interference was justified or 'necessary in a democratic society' (the *justification or limitation* stage). The limitation will be deemed justified, if it was prescribed by law and was proportionate to a legitimate aim in pursuit of which the government acted. On their face, the labels suggest that the first stage of the

* I have benefited enormously from discussions with Dimitrios Kyritsis, Stuart Lakin, Virginia Mantouvalou Prince Saprai, Nicos Stavropoulos, Robert Stevens and from their comments on earlier drafts. A version of this paper was presented at the UCL Colloquium in Legal & Social Philosophy in February 2013. I am grateful to the audience for their questions and to my two commentators, John Tasioulas and Jeff King, for their extremely valuable comments, corrections, and suggestions. I am much indebted to the editor, Massimo Renzo, who helped me enormously to clarify the main arguments of the paper and to address its main weaknesses.
[1] David M Beatty, *The Ultimate Rule of Law* (Oxford University Press, 2004), 162.

orthodox test is about what rights we have and the second stage is about the conditions under which they can be limited.

The doctrine of proportionality adds another layer of complexity to philosophical questions about the nature of human rights. Does proportionality determine what *constitutes* a right? Does it determine what makes a right, a *human* right? Or does it determine what makes one's human right, all things considered, *enforceable*?

The difference between these questions is not terminological. It is of practical, as well as philosophical, significance. Consider the European Court of Human Rights case of *Hatton v. United Kingdom*.[2] Ms Ruth Hatton lived next to Heathrow airport in London. She complained that the night flight scheme of Heathrow airport violated her human right to private life. The European Court held that the government's flight scheme had interfered with the applicant's private life, but that the interference was proportionate to advancing the economic well-being of the United Kingdom, which is a legitimate state aim under the European Convention on Human Rights (ECHR). The Court decided that the applicant had no enforceable right under the ECHR to be free from that interference. Now, saying that the applicant in *Hatton* had a human right, which was justifiably violated, has practical consequences. Looking backwards, we should regret that the government had to violate the applicant's human rights and feel for the victim. Looking forward, we should seek to prevent it from happening again and from happening to others. If, on the other hand, we say that the applicant in *Hatton* had no right—or no *human* right—to be free from noise interference, then we let the British government off an important moral hook; this is because human rights are typically thought to be standards of high moral stringency. If the government did not violate Ms Hatton's rights then it has no human-rights-based reason not to interfere with people's private life in similar ways in the future, say by expanding the night flight scheme to other airports in the country. In either case, we are subjecting the result in *Hatton* to moral scrutiny and making assumptions about the moral value of human rights and the justifiability of governmental action.

What it is that proportionality is supposed to determine has also philosophical significance. If we count the applicant's claim in *Hatton* as constituting a genuine human right (albeit defeated in the circumstances) then we have to explain what property it has in common with other rights that we consider human, and in virtue of which they are *all* human rights. Suppose, for example, that we take the view that what makes torture a human right is the fact that it is an assault on one's agency. We now have to show the sense in which allowing night flights assaulted the agency of the applicant in *Hatton*. If we cannot show this, then we should revise either our philosophical theory of human rights or our view about *Hatton*. Likewise, if we dismiss the applicant's claim in *Hatton* as bogus, not constituting a real human right, then we have to explain what it is that the claim lacks and real human rights have. Suppose for example that we endorse a theory of human rights, according to which what makes something a human right is the fact that it protects important and universal interests of human beings. We now have to show why freedom from loud noise is not an important interest, or why it

---

[2] *Hatton v. United Kingdom* (2003) 37 EHRR 611.

is not a universal one. If we cannot show this, then we should revise either our philosophical theory of human rights or our view about *Hatton*.

So thinking about proportionality is a complex equation that also includes moral rights, human rights, and legally enforceable rights. Philosophers have written a great deal about moral and legal rights but only recently turned their attention to human rights. Proportionality has attracted even less philosophical attention, though it has received extensive doctrinal treatment by European constitutional theorists and lawyers. It is, I suspect, too lawyerly a concept to attract philosophical interest, particularly if its role is to tell us what a human rights court should enforce in given circumstances. It is tempting to view it as a 'practicality',[3] to do with various contingencies regarding the implementation of human rights norms. The approach of the courts does not help either, since their reasoning under the heading of proportionality is often scant and conclusory, as is typical in civil law jurisdictions.[4]

In this paper I engage in the familiar philosophical task of seeking to make sense of proportionality, as it figures in human rights doctrine. By 'sense' I mean nothing more (and nothing less) than *moral* sense. I am interested in the very possibility that the doctrine of proportionality picks out a moral principle that is capable of justifying human rights or limits to them. It is of course possible that human rights courts appeal to proportionality as a ground of justification whereas they ought not to. It is also possible that courts misapply or mischaracterize what is otherwise a valid moral principle. Finally, it is possible that some principle justifies the outcomes in cases where 'proportionality' figures in the reasoning of the courts, but that that principle bears no connection—semantic or otherwise—to the concept of proportionality. I want to leave all these possibilities open and address them only after we have a good sense of the moral dimension of proportionality, if it has any. So I should like to begin by moving away from the jargon of legal doctrine, so far as it is possible to do so, and explore first what proportionality means in non-legal contexts. If some moral concern underlies proportionality, it should have a life outside of legal doctrine.

II. Four Senses of Proportionality

We should begin by assigning some preliminary content to the concept of proportionality with a view to fix which of the many possible uses of the word is of relevance to human rights. The word figures in ordinary language in many different contexts and it is important to distinguish between them.

In mathematics and physics, we use the notion of proportionality to mean that there is a fixed ratio between two variable quantities, such that a change in one quantity always co-relates to a change in the other. In mathematics, what fixes the constant ratio between two quantities is the truth of some theorem or axiom. Consider for

---

[3] This is Griffin's term for how particular human rights play out in different institutional contexts. See James Griffin, *On Human Rights* (Oxford University Press, 2009), 37.

[4] On the differences between common law and civil law reasoning about rights see George Letsas, 'Judge Rozakis's Separate Opinions and the Strasbourg Dilemma', in Dean Spielmann et al., *The European Convention on Human Rights: A Living and Dynamic Instrument—Liber Amicorum in Honour of Judge Rozakis* (Bruylant, 2011).

example Thales's basic proportionality theorem. If you draw a line within a triangle parallel to one of its sides, then it will divide the other two sides in exactly the same ratio. Whatever is the ratio in which the drawn line will divide one side, it will be exactly the same for the other side. We can prove the truth of this theorem in a mathematical form, given what a triangle and a parallel line are. In physics on the other hand, what fixes the constant ratio between two variable quantities is the truth of some law of nature. For example, Newton's law of universal gravitation tells us that the force by which two objects attract each other is directly proportionate to their mass and indirectly proportionate to the distance between them. The bigger the objects, the more they attract each other. And the longer the distance between them, the less they attract each other. Newton's law is an empirical fact about the world. Knowing it helps us build bridges that hold up and fly planes that don't crash.

We can call this notion of proportionality *descriptive*, since it figures in statements that tell us that two things in the world co-relate. It can be contrasted with *normative* uses or proportionality, which tell us that two variables *ought* to co-relate. These uses are no less familiar. Many people around the world believe in the system of proportional representation, which advocates a particular co-relation between votes and seats in parliament. In its simple form, proportional representation requires that the share of seats each political party has in parliament be the same as its share of the popular electoral vote. Proportional representation is not meant to express a law of physics or a mathematical theorem. It is an action-guiding normative statement about how we *ought* to conduct our politics, design our electoral process, and allocate legislative power. It is a statement moreover whose truth depends, not on some empirical fact, but on a moral ideal, that of democracy. The normative dimension of the principle of proportional representation should not be obscured by how simple its application is. If correct, the principle requires us to assign seats in proportion to popular vote. Applying this in practice requires no more than basic mathematics. All we have to do to find out how many seats a party is entitled to have following an election, is to multiply the number of votes it got by the total number of available seats and then divide the product by the total number of voters. The application of proportionality here is easy because we are dealing with arithmetic percentages of quantifiable variables (votes and seats). But just because the application of proportionality here involves no moral reasoning, that is not to say that it has no moral basis. It is democracy, on the proposed hypothesis, that requires us to assign seats following the mathematical model of 1:1 ratio between the share of the votes and the share of seats.

Sometimes the concept of proportionality can be normative in a more direct way, requiring no resort to mathematical reasoning. Consider the familiar moral injunction that punishment must fit the crime. We shouldn't sentence someone to life imprisonment for a traffic violation and we shouldn't impose a small fine to someone who has committed murder. The severity of punishment one receives must be proportionate to the gravity of the crime she has committed. This statement, like that of proportional representation, is an action-guiding statement about how we ought to arrange our institutions. Its truth depends, not on some empirical fact, but on some moral fact about the nature of punishment and of crime. But unlike proportional representation, the principle that punishment must be proportionate to the crime has a direct moral appeal. Most of us would assert it intuitively without much thought and we would be very surprised to be told that morality allows us to sentence someone to life imprisonment for violating a speed limit.[5] Moreover, we find punishment disproportionate not only when it fails to match the gravity of the wrongness but also when it fails to match the circumstances of the wrongdoer. For example, it would be disproportionate to sentence a minor to a life sentence, even if he has committed murder. The wrongdoer's age is a consideration that the state authorities ought to take into account. But it is also a consideration a parent should take into account in disciplining his child. Proportionality, in its normative sense, can track a variety of moral reasons and applies to a variety of moral practices. Its semantic content is subservient to the moral value that governs the domain in question (for example, democracy or desert in punishment). I shall take this to be the central sense of proportionality and the only one that is of interest to the discussion of moral rights, including human rights.

Apart from proportionality it its descriptive sense, proportionality as a normative notion must be distinguished from two further senses. The first is the one which figures in Lord Diplock's oft-quoted phrase: 'you must not use a steam hammer to crack a nut, if a nutcracker would do'.[6] We can call this notion *proportionality as instrumental rationality*. The idea here is that the means one employs to achieve a certain end that he has, must be proportionate to that end. There are several layers to this instrumental notion of proportionality, each of which relates to the rationality of choosing means in order to advance one's ends. First, one is to employ means that are suitable for one's purpose, ie, that are capable of bringing about the intended outcome. You should not waste your time trying to crack a nut with a toothpick. You would be irrational if you were to do so. Second, given the choice of various alternatives, each of which suffices to bring about the intended outcome, one is to employ the least costly or onerous one. Why spend time and money to get a steam hammer to crack a nut, when you have a nutcracker right there? Assuming you have reason to save time and money, then you would be irrational using a steam hammer over a nutcracker. Third, the overall cost of taking the means to achieve the intended outcome should not be greater than the benefit that outcome will confer. You would be acting irrationally spending hours of your valuable time trying to crack a bunch of tough nuts, time which you could be using to make an income, when you can easily go out and get shelled nuts at a price much lower than the financial value of your work.

Proportionality as instrumental rationality is action-guiding, but hardly in a moral sense. Though it has an intuitive appeal, it lacks a moral dimension. There is nothing morally untoward in employing means for achieving one's goals that are ineffective or sub-optimal. I may be irrational trying to crack a nut with a toothpick or a steam hammer, but I do not violate anyone's moral rights. Likewise, I am acting irrationally paying a costly gym subscription every month, rather than pay per visit, given that

---

[5] This is not to say of course that the principle of proportionate punishment cannot and should not be given a moral justification. One way to justify it is under a retributive theory according to which the point of punishment is to give wrongdoers what they *deserve*. Since they deserve to suffer for the wrong they committed, the severity of their punishment must be proportionate to the gravity of their wrongdoing. Punishing someone more severely than he deserves is punishing him for a crime that he did not commit.

[6] *Regina v. Goldstein* (1983) WLR 151, HL.

I very rarely use it. This makes me foolish and spendthrift, not to mention poorer, but not a wrongdoer. The fact that an action is disproportionate, *qua* irrational, does not make it wrongful.

Of course, my spendthrift habits *can* interfere with someone's rights if someone has a moral right to a share of my income. For example, if a parent is struggling to pay for his children's school fees or his mortgage, then we may say that he is wrong to spend a disproportionate amount of money for a gym subscription that he rarely uses. But the notion of proportionality employed here has nothing to do with instrumental rationality, but rather with the presence of moral rights on the part of others and the demand for just distribution, just like in proportionate representation: the parent has a duty to distribute his disposable income in proportion to the needs of his family. His children have a right to a share of his income of which he may be depriving them, by paying a costly gym subscription. Notice here that the direction of the argument is *from* the fact that the parent has distributive responsibilities *to* what counts as him spending disproportionately. What is morally relevant is not the fact that having a gym subscription is not a rational means to promote his ends; it is that it prevents him from carrying out his distributive duties towards his family. Absent distributive duties to others, his profligacy would be morally innocuous.

So the fact that the means one takes to pursue one's goal are irrational is not, in itself, wrongful. The other side, or I should say downside, of *proportionality as instrumental rationality* is this: the fact that an action is rationally connected to one's aim doesn't make it rightful. This is because the moral character of an action depends on the aim that the agent seeks to achieve. If the aim is morally improper, then it matters little that one employs cost-effective means to bring it about. An extortionist who has read Lord Diplock's quote, and uses the most cost-effective means to break his victim's fingers, acts proportionately to his aim, but wrongly nevertheless. There is no such thing as proportionate extortion or proportionate torture.

Finally, we should distinguish cost-effectiveness, as a non-moralized standard of instrumental rationality, from a moral idea which is too familiar an idea in law and philosophy, namely that an action is morally right if it maximizes the total sum of expected *societal* benefits minus the costs; it is wrongful if it fails to do so. Utilitarianism, in its many variants, makes this particular kind of cost-effectiveness, ie, maximizing utility, the only standard of rightness and wrongness. I doubt however whether the idea of proportionality can be used to express an overtly utilitarian moral outlook. On this outlook, punishing an innocent person would be proportionate if it maximizes utility; having a dictator would be a proportionate distribution of legislative power if it maximizes utility,[7] and so on and so forth. No doubt, the avowed utilitarian will try to offer an indirect utilitarian justification for non-utilitarian rules of ordinary morality. He will argue for example, as Bentham himself claimed,[8] that proportionate punishing is morally justified because, in the long run, it is more likely to

---

[7] On the idea that representative democracy need not be an effective way to maximize utility see Jeremy Waldron, *Liberal Rights* (Cambridge University Press, 1993), ch. 16.

[8] Jeremy Bentham, *An Introduction to the Principles of Morals and Legislation*, edited by J. H. Burns and H. L. A. Hart (Oxford University Press, 1996), ch. 14 ('Of the Proportion between Punishment and Offences').

maximize utility. Appealing to ways in which rules or decision procedures can indirectly maximize utility is a familiar manoeuvre in the history of utilitarian thought that need not, however, distract us here. It suffices to say that direct utilitarianism has difficulty accounting for standard uses of the principle of proportionality, as found in ordinary moral discourse. Punishing someone who commits a traffic offence—let alone an innocent person—with life imprisonment is wrong, regardless of the contribution that doing so makes to social utility. Indirect forms of utilitarianism could try to account for these judgments of proportionality, but then again such forms of utilitarianism can try, by reverse engineering, to account for *anything* we take to be a moral right. Whatever form such attempts take, they will always get the order of explanation wrong: one has a right not to be subjected to punishment disproportionate to his crime, regardless of whether it maximizes utility to punish him more severely than he deserves.

III. The Vacuous Orthodoxy and its Critics

In the previous section I identified four ways in which the concept of proportionality is used: first, in descriptive judgments about the way the physical world is (for example, Newton's law); second in moral judgments about what rights people have according to some value (for example, democracy or retribution); third, as a norm of instrumental, 'means-ends', rationality; and fourth as a utilitarian principle of maximizing utility. Now, which of these four senses figures in the legal practice of human rights?

The orthodox understanding of proportionality amongst constitutional scholars and judges includes elements from both the third and the fourth sense above, and at first glance appears morally objectionable. As mentioned earlier, proportionality is described as a judicial test whose aim is to determine the conditions under which governmental measures may justifiably infringe constitutional or human rights (the 'limitation stage'). Courts tend to devote little time to the first stage of rights-based review which is about what falls within the protect scope of a human right ('the scope stage'), moving quickly to the limitation stage. In German constitutional theory, the test of proportionality is said to have three prongs:

(i) Is the impugned measure rationally connected to the pursuit of a legitimate aim (the *'suitability'* test)?

(ii) Is the measure necessary for the pursuit of that aim (the *'necessity'* test)?

(iii) Is the seriousness of the interference with the applicant's right proportionate to the benefits gained in pursuit of the legitimate aim in question ('proportionality in the *narrow sense*', or *'balancing'*)?

The first two prongs echo norms of instrumental rationality, as they figure in Lord Diplock's nutcracker quote, discussed earlier. Without the third prong, they reflect ordinary judicial tests that are used outside the context of human rights review, such as the English test of Wednesbury unreasonableness,[9] and that are not considered

---

[9] *Associated Provincial Picture Houses Ltd v. Wednesbury Corporation* [1948] 1 KB 223.

to be very stringent. The addition of the third prong (proportionality *stricto sensu*) is what is supposed to make the judicial test of proportionality more stringent. It requires an analysis of the costs and benefits of infringing someone's right *across* persons, not just from the point of view of the right-holder, and hence bears close resemblance to utilitarian calculations. Here is how judge Aharon Barak, a former judge of the Israeli Supreme Court, describes this part of the orthodox test in a recent book on proportionality:

> The last test of proportionality is the 'proportional result' or 'proportionality *stricto sensu*' (*Verhaltnismassigkeit im engeren Sinne*)…[A]ccording to proportionality stricto sensu, in order to justify a limitation on a constitutional right, a proper relation ('proportional in the narrow sense of the term'), should exist between the benefits gained by fulfilling the purpose and the harm caused to the constitutional right from obtaining that purpose. This test requires a balancing of the benefits gained by the public and the harm caused to the constitutional right through the use of the means selected by law to obtain the proper purpose. Accordingly, this is a test balancing benefits and harm.[10]

So we can say that the orthodox view of proportionality consists in two main claims:

(1) Proportionality *stricto sensu* ('balancing') is a test that speaks to the limitation, rather than the content of rights (*the Balancing Orthodoxy*).

(2) Rights may justifiably be limited if the overall societal benefits of limiting them exceeds the cost of the harm done to the person whose right it is (*the Maximizing Orthodoxy*).

As evidenced by the label (*Verhaltnismassigkeit im engeren Sinne*), this orthodoxy originated in German constitutional theory and has received theoretical support in the work of the German constitutional scholar, Robert Alexy.[11] It has been very influential in many jurisdictions (Europe, Canada, Israel, South Africa), becoming Germany's biggest exporting legal doctrine, the BMW of constitutional theory. According to the orthodoxy, proportionality does not offer an account of what rights you have; rather, it offers an account of how they can be taken *away* from you. Moreover, the orthodoxy offers a specific account of when rights may be justifiably limited: If the cost of interfering with someone's right is minor and the benefits to the collective good are huge, then the right may be infringed. But if the cost of interference is high and the benefits to the collective good are minor, then the right should be upheld.

The idea that the conditions for justifiably limiting constitutional or human rights are imposed by the need to maximize some good figures prominently in the work of Robert Alexy, though it is less clear what he takes the *maximand* to be. Alexy argues

---

[10] Aharon Barak, *Proportionality* (Cambridge University Press, 2012), 340.
[11] See Robert Alexy, *A Theory of Constitutional Rights* (Oxford University Press, 2002); Robert Alexy, 'Constitutional Rights, Balancing and Rationality', *Ratio Juris*, 16 (2003): 131; See also Mattias Kumm, 'Institutionalizing Socratic Contestation, The Rationalist Human Rights Paradigm, Legitimate Authority and the Point of Judicial Review', *European Journal of Legal Studies*, 1 (December 2007).

that many constitutional rights in the German Constitution are principles, rather than rules, and that principles are *optimization* requirements. He writes:

> Principles are optimization requirements relative to what is legally and factually possible. The *principle of proportionality in its narrow sense*, that is, the requirement of balancing, derives from its relation to the *legally* possible... [T]he *principle of proportionality in its narrow sense* follows from the fact that principles are optimization requirements relative to what is legally possible.[12]

Alexy's optimization requirement is constrained by a proviso about what is 'legally possible'. But this proviso is ambiguous. Understood to mean what is legally *permissible*, it is either question-begging or clearly wrong. If it means legally permissible as matter of *human rights law*, then the proviso is circular. Proportionality is meant to determine what human rights law permits and we cannot define it in terms of what human rights law permits. If, on the other hand, Alexy's proviso means what is permissible under other areas of law (say criminal law, or administrative law, or tort law) then it is clearly wrong: human rights law is used to judge the constitutionality (or lawfulness) of other areas of law and we cannot assume that what these areas require is lawful. Suppose that a human rights challenge is launched against a criminal statute that prohibits blasphemous remarks made about the dominant religion. Is the task of optimizing free speech constrained by what criminal law requires, such that there is, automatically, no free speech right to blaspheme? This cannot be right and it is not clear to me what else Alexy could mean by 'legally possible'.

Be that as it may, the orthodox understanding of proportionality has made it very unpopular amongst scholars who reject utilitarianism and defend rights as resistant to utilitarian calculations. Some commentators have equated proportionality with this orthodoxy, then equated the orthodoxy with utilitarianism, and then concluded that proportionality is the enemy of rights.[13] This criticism is valid, insofar as it is directed against utilitarian or consequentialist approaches to rights. Surely, my right to criticize the government or practice my religion shouldn't depend on a cost–benefit calculation of how important it is to me to have this right compared to how important it is to others that I do not have it. Surely, it is not even *relevant* whether others prefer it if I don't practice my religion or don't express my political views. So the orthodoxy is deeply mistaken to the extent that it advocates cost–benefit analysis that takes the form of maximization of preference satisfaction or optimization of interests. But we should be charitable here. The *Maximizing Orthodoxy* is just a piece of unsophisticated doctrinal jargon about legal rights. It is an attempt to reconstruct what courts say when adjudicating rights, rather than an essay in the philosophy of rights. We shouldn't read too much into it, out of some excessive liberal preoccupation with the moral defects of utilitarianism. In particular, we should avoid making two unwarranted equations: first to equate balancing with utilitarian reasoning. And second, to equate judicial tests courts use to decide cases (which is an *epistemic* or heuristic task),

---

[12] Alexy (2002), 67.

[13] See, eg, Stavros Tsakyrakis, 'Proportionality: an Assault on Human Rights?', *International Journal of Constitutional Law*, 7 (2009): 468.

with a theory of what human rights we have (which is a *constitutive* moral question). Let me discuss these two unwarranted equations in turn.

We should begin by observing that only the second orthodox claim (the *Maximizing Orthodoxy*) is tied to an overtly utilitarian outlook. The first orthodox claim—ie, that proportionality speaks to the balancing and limitation of rights—need not be premised on utilitarian grounds. One can accept that pro tanto moral rights may sometimes be balanced against other considerations and be justifiably infringed, while rejecting that it is ever permissible to do so merely in order to maximize overall utility. This is not an incoherent view. For example, it could be argued that it is morally justified to break a promise to meet someone for lunch on the basis that one has to take his child to the doctor. But it is not justified to break the promise on the basis that the aggregated happiness of the promisor and others (for example, that of his child and his child's friends whom the promisor decides to takes to the park instead of keeping his promise) exceeds the unhappiness caused to the promisee by the breach. Believing that pro tanto rights may sometimes be justifiably infringed does not commit one to the view that the conditions for infringement consist in the maximization of some good across persons, let alone the maximization of *happiness* or *preference-satisfaction*. In other words, balancing (or trade-offs) needn't be *utilitarian*, seeking to maximize things like happiness or preference satisfaction.[14] The *Balancing Orthodoxy* is independent from the *Maximising Orthodoxy*.

Second, the *Balancing Orthodoxy* may in practice have little to do with real balancing. This is because it needn't be an accurate description of what human rights courts actually do. Human rights courts may speak of 'balancing' the cost to the right of the individual against the benefit to the public, while ending up routinely upholding rights that a utilitarian would not. Contrary to the unsophisticated orthodoxy, we should be mainly concerned with what courts *do*, not what they *say*. Consider for example the European Court of Human Rights. Looking at its case law, one finds numerous cases in which upholding an individual right goes against the preferences of the majority. Just to offer a few examples, the Court has recognized the right of juveniles not to be subjected to corporal punishment,[15] the right of children born out of wedlock to be treated on equal terms with children born in wedlock,[16] the right of homosexuals to engage in sexual activities free from criminal prosecution,[17] the right of post-operation transsexuals to have their new gender recognized by law,[18] the right of religious minorities to practice their religion free from criminal persecution,[19] the right of homosexuals to be eligible for single-parent adoption on equal terms with heterosexuals,[20] the right of prisoners not to lose the right to vote indiscriminately and automatically upon conviction.[21] These judicial outcomes are hardly compatible with an overtly utilitarian conception of proportionality. They recognize rights of minority

---

[14] On how trade-offs operate within deontological moral frameworks see Judith Jarvis Thomson, *The Realm of Rights* (Harvard University Press, 1992), ch. 6.
[15] *Tyrer v. United Kingdom* (1978) 2 EHRR 1.   [16] *Marckx v. Belgium* (1979) 2 EHRR 330.
[17] *Dudgeon v. United Kingdom* (1982) 4 EHRR 149; *Modinos v. Cyprus* (1993) 16 EHRR 485.
[18] *Goodwin v. UK* (1996) 22 EHRR 123.   [19] *Kokkinakis v. Greece* (1994) 17 EHRR 397.
[20] *E.B. v. France* (2008), Application No 43546/02.
[21] *Hirst v. United Kingdom* (2005) ECHR 681.

groups (juveniles, children born out of wedlock, religious minorities, homosexuals, foreigners, transsexuals, prisoners) to exercise certain liberties, or enjoy some benefit, despite the fact that the majority has a preference against the minority doing so. If the effect of the test of proportionality *stricto sensu* (balancing) were to lead the Court to seek to maximize happiness or preference satisfaction for the greatest number of people, then we would not have such results. Yet not only has the Court upheld rights of minority groups against majoritarian preferences, but it has also done so without assigning much weight to the fact that such majoritarian preferences exist within the applicant's state, and without requiring an explicit consensus amongst most contracting states to recognize such rights.[22] Notice moreover that in these cases the Court's language was one of 'balancing' the right of the applicant against some public interest. If what went on there had been real balancing then the result would have been very different.

It follows that when courts talk of 'balancing' rights against other considerations, what they often mean is that they are considering (which is an *epistemic* task) the effect of a measure upon the interests of both applicant and society at large, with a view to discover what moral rights people have (which is a *constitutive* task). But considering something is not the same as assigning normative weight to it. One way to read these anti-majoritarian judgments is that the court considered ('balanced' in its own language) the negative effect of legalizing an activity (such as homosexual acts) on the preferences of the majority and found it *irrelevant*. Of course, moral philosophers would know better than to use the word 'balancing' to describe the epistemic task of considering. For from a normative point of view, only considerations with real moral weight can be balanced. But judges and constitutional lawyers are not moral philosophers and we should be charitable towards what they say.

Nor can it be argued that human rights courts should *never* consider the effect of a state measure on the majority's interests. For that effect can sometimes be morally relevant with respect to what moral rights one has, even on a non-utilitarian view. Consider for example Ronald Dworkin's principle that one should not suffer severe restrictions on his interests for the sake of marginal or speculative gains to the interests of others.[23] On Dworkin's view, there is no moral right to any specific liberty or interest but there is a moral right not to be deprived of a liberty on the basis of certain considerations, including on the basis that the restriction produces marginal or speculative gains to the interests of others. For example, it is wrong to prohibit pornography if it has only a speculative effect on increasing violence against women. So to discover what moral rights we have, an inquiry into the effect of a measure on the interests of others may be relevant. Courts and constitutional lawyers might mischaracterize this inquiry as the task of 'balancing' rights against societal gains. This is a mischaracterization because, to use the same example, it is not the case that one has a pro tanto moral right to consume pornography *simpliciter*, ie, independently of the effects on the interests of others. Nor is it the case that the right not to be deprived of

---

[22] I have argued that this is the case in George Letsas, 'The ECHR as a Living Instrument: its Meaning and Legitimacy', in Andreas Follesdal et al. (eds.), *Constituting Europe* (Cambridge University Press, 2013).

[23] Ronald Dworkin, *Taking Rights Seriously* (Duckworth, 1977), 269.

the liberty to consume pornography on the basis of a mere speculation about the effect on the interests of women is to be balanced against *anything*—let alone against the majority's (or women's) distaste of pornography. But so long as courts uphold the right to consume pornography in the absence of clear evidence of immediate harm, as they in fact do, then the difference is terminological.

To be sure, the language of balancing also figures in cases where the Court assigned weight to factors that are either morally irrelevant or morally impermissible to consider. For example, the European Court has failed to uphold the right of someone to engage in non-harmful activities that others find blasphemous (such as publish books,[24] screen movies,[25] exhibit art,[26] or place radio advertisements),[27] citing how much the activity offends the majority. The outcome in these cases has been morally indefensible from a non-utilitarian liberal perspective, depriving the applicants of fundamental rights of free speech and freedom of religion. And the Court's reasoning there looks a lot like a direct utilitarian calculation. But it is questionable whether the orthodox language of balancing rights against societal benefits is to blame for these unjustified outcomes. After all, this language has not prevented the reaching of correct outcomes in the other cases mentioned earlier. Whether a different test, lacking the balancing connotations, would have produced more correct results is an empirical question that may vary from jurisdiction to jurisdiction. Judicial tests employed by human rights courts are diagnostic institutional tools that help the courts reach outcomes.[28] It is a mistake to equate them directly with theories of what rights people have. Like with any diagnostic test, part of what makes the use of a judicial test morally defensible is how many false negatives and false positives it produces compared to alternative tests.[29] Whether the language of balancing, as used in Europe and elsewhere, produces worse results than possible alternatives (say the test of strict scrutiny of the US Supreme Court) is an empirical question which cannot be settled by armchair reflection.

In sum, the problem with the orthodox account of proportionality is not so much that it has utilitarian connotations or that it encourages utilitarian thinking. Rather, the problem is that it is a misleadingly vacuous metaphor. All that it really says, charitably interpreted, is that courts should consider the effect of an impugned measure on the interests of others, as well as on the interests of the applicant. This is not a moral principle, nor is it an account of what moral rights we have and when they can be overridden. Considering something is not the same as assigning normative weight on it. The content of some moral rights may sometimes, constitutively, turn on the effect of a measure on the interests of others. The orthodox test allows courts to consider such effects but it does not specify which effects and interests count and under which conditions. Whether courts will assign normative weight to the wrong effects (for example, the prejudices and bias of the majority) and ignore the morally relevant ones depends

---

[24] *I.A. v. Turkey* (2007) 45 EHRR 967.
[25] *Otto-Preminger Institute v. Austria* (1995) 19 EHRR 34.
[26] *Muller and others v. Switzerland* (1991) 13 EHRR 212.
[27] *Murphy v. Ireland* (2004) 38 EHRR 212.
[28] For a more detailed defense of this view see George Letsas, 'The Scope and Balancing of Rights: Diagnostic or Constitutive?', in Janneke Gerards and Eva Brems (eds.), *Shaping Rights in the ECHR* (Cambridge University Press, 2013).
[29] Letsas, 'The Scope and Balancing of Rights'.

on how good the court in question is. Criticizing the orthodox test on the basis that it gets the nature of human rights wrong makes the mistake of elevating the orthodox test to a level that it does not deserve. It makes the mistake of treating the test as a constitutive theory of rights. But the orthodox doctrinal view that we have a human right to pretty much everything, which is to be balanced against pretty much everything, is so daftly implausible as a theory of rights that it is not even worth criticizing. We do better to ignore the vacuous orthodoxy and analyze judicial outcomes in the light of first-order normative arguments about the nature of human rights as moral rights.

IV. Proportionality Beyond the Orthodoxy: Two Views

In the previous section I argued that the orthodox understanding of proportionality is vacuous. It is not a utilitarian calculation (at least not necessarily so), nor is it a theory of what rights we have and when they can be overridden. The two orthodox claims (the *Balancing Orthodoxy* and the *Maximizing Orthodoxy*), found in legal doctrine and the academic literature, are not to be taken at face value. The two-stage approach of the judicial test (scope-balancing), and the language of balancing rights and public interest, is merely a rough conceptual framework that courts use in order to discover what rights litigants have. The framework has not precluded courts from recognizing and upholding strong anti-majoritarian moral rights.

Still, we have to give an account of what it is that courts actually do when they adjudicate on rights. Even if the orthodox view of proportionality is vacuous, having little or no moral substance, we still need to give a normative explanation of the nature of the courts' task. Suppose that there were no history of rights-based judicial review. What is it that courts *should* be doing, were we to institute one now? It is unlikely that what courts actually do departs radically from what they should be doing, from the point of view of ideal morality. In this respect, we should be able to explain the popularity and pervasiveness of the doctrinal test courts use (scope and balancing), rough and loose as it may be, as an imperfect attempt to capture the moral nature of human rights. And we should recall that the second sense of proportionality I identified in the second section of the paper links it to moral values (such as democracy or retribution) that determine constitutively what rights people have. Any attempt to reconstruct what courts do under the heading of proportionality should therefore begin with normative arguments about the nature of human rights as moral rights made *independently* of legal practice. The best reconstruction of the legal doctrine of proportionality is one that begins outside the four corners of courts' judgments. Two options are open in this regard.

The first is to take a popular view about the moral nature of human rights that is teleological. Rights protect objective interests of individual well-being that are important enough to impose duties on others.[30] To have an interest is a necessary but not

---

[30] Joseph Raz, *The Morality of Freedom* (Clarendon Press, 1986). Interestingly, Raz's view about human rights is that they denote a narrower set of rights, those whose violation warrants some kind of external interference with the sovereignty of the infringing state. See his 'Human Rights Without Foundations' in Samantha Besson and John Tasioulas (eds.), *Philosophical Foundations of International Law* (Oxford University Press, 2010).

sufficient for the existence of a right. The conditions for when an interest generates a right depend on factors such as the nature of the interest and how demanding it is to impose a duty on others to respect or promote it.[31] On the interest-based view of rights, the test of proportionality can be seen as an umbrella term that encompasses an inquiry into whether the applicant's claim relates to an objective interest of well-being which is such that it imposes duties on the government (or private individuals). For example, in the case of *Hatton*, the test of proportionality would on this view be about whether the interest to sleep at night free from loud noise is important enough to impose a duty on the government to ban night flights, taking into account also what burdens this entails for others. Interestingly, whether the imposition of a duty on others to serve someone's interest entails heavy burdens on them would always be relevant for determining what human rights people have on this theory of rights. This means that a type of cost–benefit analysis would be part and parcel of what courts would have to do to discover what human rights we have, albeit of a cost–benefit analysis of non-utilitarian kind. According to the teleological theory of rights, costs and benefits are moralized notions, viewed from the objective standpoint of the importance of different interests for our well-being and without being committed to the need to maximize the serving of those interests.

The second option is a non-teleological theory that denies that the point of rights is to protect interests of individual well-being. Rather, it insists that the most fundamental moral right individuals have against the government, from which more specific requirements follow, is the right to be treated with equal respect and concern, in Ronald Dworkin's famous formulation. This conception of rights is known as a reason-blocking theory:[32] rights tell us which facts do not constitute valid reasons for depriving someone of a liberty or an opportunity or for imposing a risk on him. For example, the fact that the majority dislikes pornography or homosexuality is not a valid reason for banning these activities. The reason-blocking theory is often misunderstood as a claim solely about the motivation of the acting agent. It is then objected that certain actions (say torture or censorship of political speech) are violations of rights, regardless of the motives of the acting agent. The objection is based on a misunderstanding of the word 'reason'. The reason-blocking theory uses the concept of a reason in a normative, not a motivating sense. The theory argues that certain empirical facts are not normative reasons for action in virtue of the value of equal respect and concern and the status of individuals as beings with inherent dignity.[33] On the reason-blocking theory of rights, the judicial test of proportionality is an inquiry into whether the government offended the status of the applicant as an equal member of his political community whose dignity matters. Consider *Hatton* for example. Under the reason-blocking theory the question would be this: did the UK's scheme of night flights violate the applicant's right to be treated with equal respect and concern? This is not a question about whether Ms Hatton's interest in sleep is strong enough to stop

---

[31] See John Tasioulas, this volume, ch. 1.

[32] See George Letsas, *A Theory of Interpretation of the European Convention on Human Rights* (Oxford University Press, 2009), ch. 5.

[33] Ronald Dworkin, *Justice for Hedgehogs* (Harvard University Press, 2011).

the rest of us from flying during the night. Rather, it is a question about the fairness of the scheme of night flights and whether the scheme showed contempt for the equal status of the applicant.

It is beyond the scope of this paper to defend, at the moral level, the reason-blocking theory of rights over its rival, the interest-based theory. I do however wish to argue, in the remainder of this paper, that the reason-blocking theory captures better than its rival a very large part of what courts decide under the heading of proportionality. This is not, by itself, an argument in favour of the reason-blocking theory. It does suggest however that proportionality can be understood not merely as a heuristic device for determining what rights we have but also as denoting a moral value (equal respect and concern) that partly *constitutes* what rights we have against the government.

There are at least two areas of human rights cases in which the right to equal respect and concern plays a constitutive role in determining the moral rights of the applicant against the government. The first category includes cases in which the government has employed a blanket or indiscriminate measure that prevents it from taking into account morally relevant considerations. The second category includes cases in which the government has taken into account considerations that are normally irrelevant to what equal respect and concern requires of government in its core functions. These include so-called suspect grounds, such as one's race, religion, and sexual orientation. But they also include a number of other considerations such as one's political or philosophical beliefs, one's conception of the good life, one's lifestyle choices, one's traits of character, one's looks, one's genetic or biological condition, one's immigration status, and many others. Absent special circumstances (for example, affirmative action programs), governmental action is wrongful when grounded on such considerations.

V. Proportionality as the Right to Equal Respect and Concern I: Indiscriminate Measures

In 2001, Mr Michael Marper was arrested and charged with harassing his partner. The police took his fingerprints and a sample of his DNA. Soon after, he was reconciled with his partner who pressed no charges. A few months later the Crown Prosecution Service dropped the charges against him. The same year another person, Mr S., was arrested and charged with attempted robbery. The police took his fingerprints and a sample of his DNA. He was at the time eleven years old. Within less than a year, he was tried and found innocent of the crime of which he was accused. After the end of their respective run-ins with the authorities, both Mr Marper and Mr S. asked the police to destroy their fingerprints and DNA samples from their database. The police refused. Section 64 of the Police and Criminal Evidence Act (PACE) had changed the previous position of English law, which required the police to destroy DNA samples of unconvicted suspects. Mr S. and Mr Marper applied for judicial review seeking a judicial order to have their samples destroyed. They invoked Article 8 ECHR, as incorporated by the Human Rights Act 1998 (HRA), which protects the right to private life. The Administrative Court decided to reject their request and the Court of Appeal upheld the decision. The case reached the House of Lords on appeal.

Lord Steyn gave the leading speech in the House of Lords. He applied the standard two-stage doctrinal test of proportionality. Regarding the first stage (the *definitional* or *scope* stage), Lord Steyn found that the retention of DNA samples either does not interfere at all with private life or does so in a very minor way. Regarding the second stage (the *limitation* stage), he found that the interference—insofar as there was one—promoted a legitimate aim: keeping a database of DNA samples helps the authorities to solve and prosecute serious crimes and to exculpate the innocent. He also found that the interference was proportionate to the aim pursued, on the basis that it confers enormous advantages in the fight against serious crime. Indeed, Lord Steyn gave examples of cases where, if DNA samples had been destroyed, the authorities would not have been able to detect serious crimes. According to the statistics he gave, approximately 6,000 DNA samples that would have been destroyed under the previous, more restrictive, legal regime were linked to crime-scene stains. These included fifty-five murders, thirty-three attempted murders, and ninety-four rapes.

We can see in Lord Steyn's approach the lingering infection of the orthodox view about proportionality. Lord Steyn balanced the cost to the appellants' right to private life against the benefit to the public interest. Given how many serious crimes we can solve by retaining DNA samples and given how minor the interference is with the suspects' private life, proportionality—thus understood—requires finding no violation. The idea of proportionality as cost-effectiveness looms large in this approach: minor costs, major benefits, *ergo* no human rights violation. Baroness Hale dissented, holding that there was a violation of the appellants' human right to private life. She did not however dispute the cost–benefit character of the test of proportionality that Lord Steyn applied. Rather, she thought that the cost to the appellants' right to private life was substantial, because in her view few things, if anything, are more private than knowing and controlling one's own genetic make-up.

In 2004, Mr S. and Mr Marper took their cases to the European Court of Human Rights claiming that their right to private life under Article 8 ECHR had been violated.[34] In its judgment, the European Court had no difficulty acknowledging the importance of DNA samples and profiles in detecting and prosecuting serious crimes. It also accepted the UK government's submission that keeping the DNA of unconvicted suspects has contributed to the detection and prevention of crime.[35] It nevertheless decided that the interference with the applicants' private life was *disproportionate*, amounting to a violation of their human rights.

How could the Court justify this decision? The Court accepted that retaining the DNA samples of unconvicted suspects secures a substantial societal advantage in the fight against crime. Unlike Baroness Hale on the other hand, it did not place emphasis on the interest people have to keep information about their genetic make-up private. Besides, whatever value that interest has, it is the same whether or not one has been convicted of a crime. And the question that interested the Court was not whether, in general, it is permissible for the government to retain DNA samples. The question was whether it was permissible to retain the DNA of *unconvicted* persons. We

---

[34] *S. and Marper v. United Kingdom* (2009) 48 EHRR 1169.
[35] *S. and Marper v. United Kingdom*, para 117.

cannot assume that unconvicted persons have less of an interest in keeping their genetic make-up private. If the policy of retention were impermissible solely in virtue of the importance of that interest, then it would be impermissible for *both* convicted and unconvicted persons. From the point of view of the interest in privacy, we would be unable to distinguish between the two classes. Nor could we distinguish between them on the basis of the benefit to the public interest (fighting crime). For there was no evidence that the DNA of convicted persons matched crime scenes more often than that of unconvicted persons. If proportionality were supposed to govern the relationship between the cost to one's interest in privacy on one hand and the benefit to public interest on the other, then retaining the DNA of the applicants in *S. and Marper* would be as proportionate as retaining the DNA of a convicted murderer. We would have to conclude, with Lord Steyn and against the European Court that the UK did not violate the human rights of Mr S. and Mr Marper.

But of course, that is exactly the reason why proportionality does *not*, contrary to the orthodoxy, mean *cost-effectiveness*. The outcome in *S. and Marper* is perfectly justified if we understand it, as I propose: *proportionality as the right to equal respect and concern*. To see this we should unpack the Court's dictum that it was 'struck by the blanket and indiscriminate nature of the power of retention in England and Wales'.[36] To say that the policy is indiscriminate is to say that it fails to discriminate between people who have a moral *right* to be treated differently based on their circumstances. What were these circumstances?

To begin with, the applicants were never convicted of the crimes of which they were accused. Moreover, they were accused of crimes that, compared to rape or murder, were of minor gravity: harassment of one's partner and attempted robbery by a minor. When they were arrested, at t^1, the fact that they were reasonably suspected of a crime was a valid ground for the authorities to take their DNA material. But at t^2, when they were acquitted (or the charges were dropped) that ground ceased to exist. So at t^2, the authorities had no valid justification for keeping the applicants' DNA and they ought to have destroyed it. Just like the visitor to your house whom you invited and now you ask to leave, they ought to do it as soon as possible. Now contrast their circumstances to those of a convicted murderer. The convicted murderer doesn't get to t^2. The fact that he was convicted of a serious crime gives the authorities a valid justification to retain his DNA. The convicted murderer is liable to be treated like that because his circumstances are different: he was proven to be guilty of a very serious wrong.[37] Though not a form of punishment, indefinite retention of his DNA is justified given the gravity of his wrong. He is fairly treated. This is the territory of proportionality as a normative notion, determining moral rights and duties: the nature and intensity of our reaction to someone's wrong ought to co-relate with the gravity of their wrong. By retaining however the DNA of unconvicted persons, we treat them the same way as we treat people convicted of serious crimes and that is unfair. We fail to take into account a very important aspect of their circumstances. Here is how the Court put it:

---

[36] *S. and Marper v United Kingdom*, para 119.
[37] I am grateful to Massimo Renzo for suggesting to me that the normative position of suspects and wrongdoers is one of liability rather than desert.

... [t]he Court must bear in mind that the right of every person under the Convention to be presumed innocent includes the general rule that no suspicion regarding an accused's innocence may be voiced after his acquittal. It is true that the retention of the applicants' private data cannot be equated with the voicing of suspicions. Nonetheless, their perception that they are not being treated as innocent is heightened by the fact that their data are retained indefinitely in the same way as the data of convicted persons, while the data of those who have never been suspected of an offence are required to be destroyed.

The point here is not that the applicants suffered an emotional harm, feeling that they were being stigmatized as wrongdoers or prone to crime. They may or may not have felt like that. The point is that they had a *reason* to feel aggrieved because they were treated unjustly. They were treated like murderers. Whether or not this actually bothered them is neither here nor there, in the same way that it is neither here nor there whether it bothers me that my guest refuses to leave my house upon my request. I am being wronged regardless of my emotional reaction. Note moreover that the wrong the applicants suffered would not disappear if the authorities decided to retain *everyone*'s DNA indefinitely. Doing so would simply amount to wronging everyone except those convicted of serious crimes. For only those people are liable to this kind of treatment.

Another dimension of the government's policy is worth mentioning here. Placing *anyone*'s DNA details in a database that is used to match future crime-scene evidence, exposes him to a certain risk: it increases one's chances of being unjustly implicated in a future crime, either by mistake (your DNA was in the vicinity of a crime but you had nothing to do with it) or because of police abuse (they are known to plant evidence to 'solve' crimes). Those who are convicted of a serious crime are liable to be exposed to this risk, given what they have done, just like they are liable to receive punishment. Though not in itself a form of punishment, exposing convicted wrongdoers to this risk is an appropriate reaction to what they have done (and have been proved to have done). By contrast, those who are innocent should not be liable to be exposed to this serious risk, just like they should not be liable to receive punishment. Retaining indefinitely the DNA of suspects who were never convicted is treating them *as if* they have committed a serious crime. The government apportions a risk in an unjust way.

Note moreover that the distinction between convicted and unconvicted persons was not the only relevant one that the government's policy, being blanket, was unable to take into account. It is also relevant if a particular defendant is a minor, if he is accused of a minor '*malum prohibitum*' crime, if there is no indication that he will re-offend, and so on and so forth. Hence, the blanket character of the UK government's scheme was bound to offend justice. Here is how the Court put it:

The material may be retained irrespective of the nature or gravity of the offence with which the individual was originally suspected or of the age of the suspected offender; fingerprints and samples may be taken— and retained—from a person of any age, arrested in connection with a recordable offence, which includes minor or non-imprisonable offences.

The *S. and Marper* case illustrates that *proportionality as the right to equal respect and concern* is an ingredient of the moral right applicants have in human rights cases. To put it precisely: the applicants in *S. and Marper* had a moral right that their DNA material be treated justly, ie, in a way that was sensitive to their circumstances: the fact that they were never convicted, the fact that they were charged with minor wrongs (harassment of one's partner and attempted robbery by a minor), the age of Mr S., and others. The government's blanket scheme violated this right by treating the applicants in the same way as someone who had committed a very serious crime: they put their DNA in the database indefinitely, which is not an appropriate response given the applicants' circumstances.

The above normative explanation of the outcome in *S. and Marper* bears all the features of *proportionality as the right to equal respect and concern*. First, it is moral judgment about how the authorities ought to have treated the applicants in the light of their actions and circumstances. Second, it grounds a moral right that the applicants had, even if society would benefit substantially by not respecting this right. Recall that the Court accepted that retaining the DNA of unconvicted persons contributed significantly to the detection and prevention of crime. Yet for the Court, that was neither here nor there. Third, the applicants were wronged regardless of whether their privacy interest was harmed.

Note further that this normative justification has nothing to do with balancing rights. It is not the case that the applicants had a right to keep their DNA private, which was then balanced against the need to fight crime and was found to be weightier. The justification I propose makes no reference to an alleged right to keep one's DNA private, whatever that means. On the contrary, it assumes no such right and it finds no rights issue—let alone a violation—in the case of a convicted murderer whose DNA material is kept in the database indefinitely; he is liable to be treated in this way just like he is liable to be sentenced to life imprisonment. Neither treatment violates any of his rights. It is important here to set aside another misconception that often underlies the orthodox obsession with balancing. It is the idea that there is a general right to liberty. This idea is presented as a valid legal statement in the context of German constitutional law, encompassing the alleged right to feed pigeons in a public park.[38] As a moral statement however this idea has been discredited.[39] Dworkin gives the example of the government that makes a street one-way, restricting people's liberty to drive both ways; this restriction does not interfere with anyone's rights.[40] Nor are my rights violated when the government takes away the liberty to murder, torture or rape without criminal sanctions.

I should finally stress that I have chosen *S. and Marper* as just one out of the numerous cases in which the European Court of Human Rights has found state measures disproportionate *qua* indiscriminate and blanket. The public's perception of these cases is often led astray by being told that the Court recognized a right to the resource to which the indiscriminate measures relates. For example, in the controversial case

[38] See Alexy, *A Theory of Constitutional Rights*, ch. 8.
[39] Dworkin, *Taking Rights Seriously*, ch. 12.
[40] Dworkin's example, Dworkin, *Taking Rights Seriously*, ch. 12.

of *Hirst v. United Kingdom*, the public was told that the Court recognized the human rights of prisoners to vote. But of course, that it is an inaccurate description of the ratio of the judgment. All that the Court said is that the ban on prisoners' voting cannot be blanket and indiscriminate, applying automatically upon receiving a prison sentence and regardless of the duration of that sentence or the nature of the offence. And of course that's the only thing that the Court *could* have justifiably decided. For if I am right, all that the applicants had a right to was to an egalitarian scheme of crime prevention, not to any specific object of that scheme.

VI. Proportionality as the Right to Equal Respect and Concern II: Irrelevant Factors

In December 1985 a man identifying himself as Klaus Wegner sent a letter to Judge Miosga of the Freising District Court in Germany. The letter was signed on behalf of the *Freiburg Bunte Liste* ('Multi-colored Group'), a local political party. It contained a strong, anti-clerical, criticism of criminal proceedings pending before Judge Miosga against a man described as 'Mr J.'. Mr J., an atheist, had refused on ethical grounds to pay church tax for his employees. The authorities charged him with the criminal offence of 'insulting behavior'. The letter accused Judge Miosga of abusing his office in order to 'try—by means which give a warning and a reminder of the darkest chapters of German legal history—to break the backbone of an unloved opponent of the Church'. In January 1986 the authorities charged the author of the letter, Klaus Wegner, with a criminal offence (the same as that used against Mr J.), but were unable to establish his real identity. Six months later the authorities obtained a warrant to search the office of a man called Gottfried Niemietz. Niemietz was a practising lawyer who had been chairman of the *Freiburg Bunte Liste* for some years. The authorities searched his law office thoroughly, going through all his files, but found no documents pointing to the identity of Klaus Wegner. Niemietz told them that he had 'already destroyed them'. Niemietz later challenged the lawfulness of the search before the German courts, claiming that his constitutional rights had been violated. His claim was rejected. The President of the Munich District Court said that the search was *proportionate* because the letter constituted a serious interference with a pending case. In 1988, Niemietz took his case to the European Court of Human Rights, complaining that the German authorities had violated his human rights to 'private life, home and correspondence' under Article 8 ECHR.

In its judgment, the Court formally followed the two-stage orthodox test. It first examined whether the search amounted to an interference with the rights protected under Article 8 ECHR (the *scope* stage). It rejected the respondent state's submission that the search of business premises falls outside the scope of Article 8, offering a number of different arguments: first, that it is in the course of their professional activities that people have the opportunity to develop relationships of private nature with others. Second, that it is not always easy in modern societies to distinguish between one's professional and one's private life. Third, that the essential object and purpose of Article 8 ECHR is to 'protect the individual against arbitrary interference by the public authorities'. And fourth, that the text of Article 8 ECHR does not limit correspondence to *private* correspondence and hence the scope of the right also includes professional correspondence of the kind that existed in the applicant's business premises when it was searched. On the basis of the above arguments, the Court concluded that the respondent state had interfered with the applicant's right under Article 8 ECHR.

Having found that there was an interference with the rights protected under Article 8 ECHR, the Court turned to the question of whether the interference was justified as 'necessary in a democratic society' (the *limitation* stage). It held that the restriction to the applicant's right to private life and correspondence was disproportionate to the aims of preventing crime and protecting the honor of Judge Miosga. The Court based its decision on a number of considerations: that the warrant had been drawn in broad terms; that German law did not impose any special procedural safeguards on searches (such as the presence of independent observers); that the search impinged on the applicant's professional secrecy (lawyer–client confidentiality) which in turn may affect fair trial rights under Article 6 ECHR; finally, that the publicity surrounding the search could potentially harm Mr Niemietz's professional reputation. It concluded that the applicant's rights under Article 8 ECHR had been violated.

How do we best explain what made the actions of the German authorities disproportionate? If the question was whether the benefit to solving crimes was higher than the cost of the interference with the applicant's privacy, then the German courts would have been right to find the search proportionate. It was the only way to determine who the author of the letter was and it had little impact on the applicant's privacy (this was his office, not his home). But if the question was whether being an atheist who criticizes church tax is *relevant* to how authorities should use their power to search people's property (homes or offices), then the answer is different. One's philosophical or political beliefs are not relevant to how the state should apportion the search of people's premises. It was clear from the facts of the case that the authorities were using their powers of criminal law (prosecution for insulting behavior, investigation, searches) with a view to persecute those who held a particular political view. The search was disproportionate because one's political and philosophical beliefs are *not* a reason to subject him to criminal sanctions. Just like in *S. and Marper* moreover, the injustice done to Mr Niemietz had nothing to do with harm to his privacy interest. The Court did *not* say that the action of the German authorities were disproportionate because the harm to the applicant's privacy was greater than the benefit to the cause of fighting crime. How much Mr Niemietz's privacy interests were affected was neither here nor there.[41]

It may be objected here that the principle of proportionality is ill-suited to capture the wrongness that Mr Niemietz suffered. On the proposed normative explanation, the problem was that the government pursued an impermissible end (persecuting

---

[41] The *rationale* that justifies the outcome in *Niemietz* also applies to numerous other judgments of the European Court. The case of *Redfearn v. United Kingdom* concerned the dismissal of a private employee who was a member of the British National Party. English employment law did not allow the applicant to challenge his dismissal as discriminatory on the basis of political belief or political association. The European Court found a violation of Article 11 ECHR (freedom of association). The case of *Sidabras and Dziautas v. Lithuania* concerned a ten-year ban on former KGB agents from both private and public employment. The Court found a violation of Article 8 (right to private life).

atheists) rather than a disproportionate means to achieve a permissible end, as in the case of *S. and Marper* (preventing crime).[42] There are two responses to this objection. The first is pragmatic: this is simply what courts do; they use the language of proportionality even when, as in the case of *Niemietz,* the wrongness of the government's action appears to lie in the ends, not the means. It is of little practical significance whether, from a philosophical point of view, such action is best described as wrongful in its ends rather than disproportionate in its means. What matters is that courts carry out this investigation as a fundamental part of their task of upholding rights. Often the presence of considerations that are irrelevant (and hence make state action unjust) is difficult to surmise, as an evidentiary matter. In *Niemietz* it was clear, from the facts of the case, that the authorities used the applicant's political beliefs as the basis for using their criminal law powers. But in other cases there may be evidentiary difficulties.[43] And these difficulties are of greater significance in the case of suspect grounds such as race, religion, and sexual orientation. It is part of the role of courts to seek to 'smoke out' such illicit motives, a task whose label varies across jurisdictions.[44]

The second response to the objection supplies a philosophical justification for why courts are inclined to resort to the language of proportionality in cases like *Niemietz.* In most cases to do with qualified rights (for example, private life, expression, religion, association) the action of government could in principle be permissible. Unlike an act of torture, it is possible that actions like searching people's offices, taking their DNA or sentencing them to life imprisonment do not violate anyone's rights. Such actions normally form part of pursuing the legitimate aims of government, such as promoting safety and security via the enforcement of criminal law. Absent full epistemic access to the facts of each case that might reveal the presence of impermissible reasons, the action of government is prima facie justified as pursuing a legitimate aim. This is why, pending full investigation into the facts of each case, courts have normative reason to take the action of government as pursuing the legitimate aim that it invokes. They take the government's word at face value and then proceed to investigate whether, on the facts of the case, it acted on an irrelevant consideration (for example, the fact it persecuted the applicant's philosophical beliefs in *Niemietz*). Since courts will have already granted that the government's aim is in principle legitimate, they present the finding of any irrelevant (and hence impermissible) considerations as a disproportionate measure in pursuit of a legitimate aim. Are courts conceptually confused? Should they

---

[42] I am grateful to Massimo Renzo for raising this objection.

[43] A good example is the case of *E.B. v. France.* The applicant was a lesbian who was refused authorization to adopt by the French authorities. French law allowed single persons to apply for authorization to adopt and granted discretion to authorities to examine individual applications. The applicant was refused on two grounds: first, because of the lack of a paternal referent in the household of the applicant, and second, because of the attitude of the applicant's homosexual partner who expressed no commitment to the adoption plans. The Grand Chamber of the European Court however held that though these two grounds are legitimate in principle, the first ground was used, *in the circumstances of the case,* as a pretext and that it was the applicant's homosexuality that served, implicitly, as a decisive factor leading to the decision of the French authorities to refuse her authorization to adopt.

[44] The idea of smoking out illicit motives figures prominently in US constitutional theory. Richard Fallon has argued that it underlies both the test of strict scrutiny of the US Supreme Court and the test of proportionality as applied in Europe and elsewhere, arguing that the test is in effect the same. See Richard Fallon, 'Strict Judicial Scrutiny' 54 *UCLA Law Review,* 1267 (2007).

instead conclude that the action of government turned out *not* to be in pursuit of legitimate aim, as they had originally granted? Hardly. Recall that the normative notion of proportionality is subservient to whatever moral principle governs the practice in question.[45] In human rights law, its conceptual meaning is fixed by the moral value governing the egalitarian duties of government. If proportionality properly captures the wrongness of failing to take into account what are relevant considerations given the duties of government (as in *Marper*), then it also captures the wrongness of taking into account irrelevant considerations (as in *Niemietz*). The former is the flip side of the latter. There is little point resisting the use of the label of proportionality here on the basis of some fixed semantic content of the concept.

VII. The Moral Merits of the Scope Test

According to the reading of the cases that I propose, the effect of the government's action on the applicants' interests is not constitutive of their right under the ECHR. For example, in *S. and Marper*, the ratio that I propose does not draw on the applicants' interest to keep their DNA private, let alone assume that this interest was balanced against something else. Recall that the importance of this interest was in Baroness Hale's view what was the relevant human rights issue in this case. I argued earlier that the risk to which one is exposed by having his DNA included in the database is not the risk of suffering harm to one's privacy. It is the risk of being unjustly accused and convicted. To be sure, having one's DNA included on the police database does normally mean that one worries about it. But notice the direction of this worry: one has *reason* to worry because he is exposed to a higher risk of being implicated in a crime that he has not committed. What matters is not that the applicants worried about their DNA material but that the government had given them normative *reason* to worry, whether or not they did worry.[46] And the problem with the government's action was not that it gave them reason to worry, but that it *unjustly* gave them reason to worry. For government is fully justified in giving precisely this reason to convicted murderers.[47]

I am emphasizing the absence of a privacy interest here in order to challenge another part of the orthodox test. Recall that according to this test we should first ask whether there was an interference with a liberty or interest that falls within the protected scope of the relevant right (the *definitional* or *scope* stage), before we ask whether that interference was justified. But in *S. and Marper* it was not the case that the policy of retaining the applicants' DNA was wrong *because* it harmed their privacy interest. Rather,

---

[45] The set of considerations that the principle of proportionality tracks will therefore differ depending on the moral practice in question and the role of the acting agent. Not all action against reason is disproportionate and not all reasons that apply to an acting agent are proportionality-apt. In this sense, proportionality is not a reductive notion. It signals the existence of distinctive moral domains and obligations of role.

[46] This is how I think we should read the Court's remark that 'the mere retention and storing of personal data by public authorities, however obtained, are to be regarded as having direct impact on the private-life interest of an individual concerned, irrespective of whether subsequent use is made of the data'.

[47] 'Reason' here should be understood in its normative, not motivating sense. It is about what normatively counts as a consideration in favor an action not about what were the considerations in the light of which one acted. On this distinction, see Dancy, *Practical Reality* (Oxford University Press, 2002).

it was wrong because it treated them unjustly given their circumstances. Whether or not their privacy interest was in fact harmed was irrelevant. In this respect, Lord Steyn was right to think that the policy of retention did not interfere with the applicants' private life. But just because there has been no harm to one's interests, it doesn't mean that there has been no wrong. For example, I wrong you when I trespass on your land even if I make you no worse off (you didn't mind or you hardly noticed) and even if I make you better off (I watered your plants).[48] And vice versa: just because one's interests have been harmed, does not mean that there has been a wrong. You do not wrong me when you open a shop next to mine and drive me out of business, nor when you make my partner fall in love with you.

The preceding remarks cast doubt on the moral merits of the first stage of the orthodox test. Insofar as the first stage is testing for harm (*damnum*) to one's interests, it can lead to error. It can pre-empt the examination of a possible rights violation, either because the applicant's interests in general were not harmed or because the specific interest protected by the relevant Convention right was not harmed.[49] It is in my view no surprise that the European Court of Human Rights does not bother any more with the first stage of the orthodox test. If I am right about proportionality that is exactly what it should do. And it is no surprise either that it has been criticized by European scholars for doing so, on the ground that it departs from the orthodox understanding of the test of proportionality.[50] To be sure, the European Court still sometimes talks the talk of the orthodoxy. It says for instance, in order to justify examining complaints in accordance with the two-stage orthodox test, that privacy is a wide notion encompassing a number of things: controlling information about one's DNA (*S. and Marper*), search of one's office (*Niemietz*), prohibition from employment (*Sidabras and Dziautas*), dismissal from employment (*Redfearn*), applications for authorization to adopt (*E.B.*), and many others.[51] My argument has been that privacy interests, important as they may be, do not play a constitutive role in justifying the outcome in the cases. Proportionality as the right to equal respect and concern does.

---

[48] Robert Stevens reminds us, drawing on the Romans, that *damnum* is not the same as *injuria*. See his attack on conflating harms and wrongs in Stevens, 'Rights and Other Things', in Andrew Robertson and Donal Nolan (eds.), *Rights and Private Law* (Hart Publishing, 2011).

[49] A good example of the second error is the Court of Appeal case of *X v. Y* [2004] EWCA Civ 662. The appellant was an employee working for a charity that promoted the general development of young offenders. While off-duty he was arrested having sex in a public toilet with another man. He admitted the offence and was cautioned. When his employer found out, he dismissed him and the employment tribunal upheld this dismissal as lawful. The appellant raised a complaint under the right to private life of the HRA but the Court of Appeal rejected in on the ground that his actions were not private, having taken place in a public toilet.

[50] See the extensive criticism of the Court in Janneke Gerards and Hanneke Senden, 'The Structure of Fundamental Rights and the European Court of Human Rights', *International Journal of Constitutional Law*, 7 (2009): 619–53.

[51] For the view that the Court's approach is based on a non-spatial conception of privacy see Virginia Mantouvalou, 'Human Rights and Unfair Dismissal: Private Acts in Public Spaces', *Modern Law Review*, 71 (2008): 912–39; Virginia Mantouvalou, 'Work and Private Life: *Sidabras and Dziautas v Lithuania*', *European Law Review*, 30 (2005): 573–85.

VIII. Conclusion

The language of proportionality figures routinely in non-legal contexts. It has a life outside law, and it can be used to express genuine moral concerns about what various values (for example, democracy or punishment) require. By contrast, the orthodox understanding of proportionality as a human rights doctrine is vacuous. At best, it is a heuristic device that courts use to decide cases that makes little or no normative assumptions about the nature of rights. At worst, it is a rough approximation of what indirect forms of utilitarianism would require. I have argued that the best reconstruction of what courts actually do under the heading of proportionality must begin with normative assumptions about the nature of rights, made at the level of moral theory. At that level, I distinguished between a teleological, interest-based theory of rights and an equality-based, reason-blocking theory of rights. The latter seems to me to capture better the nature of human rights as rights against the state. This is because it links human rights to the responsibility the government has to treat those under its coercive power with equal respect and concern. The responsibility consists in the stringent duty to take into account morally relevant aspects of people's circumstances and to ignore morally irrelevant aspects. Proportionality as the right to equal respect and concern captures the moral rights we have correlative to that stringent duty.

In the second part of the paper, I aimed to show that proportionality, understood as denoting egalitarian rights against one's government, fits and justifies central elements of human rights cases. The European Court of Human Rights finds disproportionate those government policies that are unable to take into account morally *relevant* aspects of people's circumstances (indiscriminate measures), as well as those policies that take into account morally *irrelevant* aspects of their circumstances. I have also argued that proportionality, understood in its moral dimension, has nothing to do with its orthodox doctrinal understanding. Proportionality is neither about means–ends rationality, nor about cost–benefit calculations, nor about balancing moral rights with other moral considerations. Proportionality, properly understood, can be rescued from the vices of the doctrinal orthodoxy if we see it as denoting a subset of normative reasons of political morality, to do with the right to be treated with equal respect and concern by one's government.

18

Rescuing Human Rights from Proportionality

Guglielmo Verdirame*

Proportionality has become a staple of adjudication on fundamental rights in international and domestic courts. It has been embraced by civil and common law judges alike, and described as the "principle of principles" and the "ultimate rule of law".[1] Unsurprisingly, legal scholars are turning their attention to it.

Most studies of proportionality have been doctrinal but even these approaches cannot ignore the philosophical foundations of proportionality. George Letsas's main claim is that proportionality, as developed by international and constitutional courts and "understood as denoting egalitarian rights against one's government",[2] can be part of a moral theory of human rights. Proportionality—he argues—need not take us where many of us, him included, do not wish to be taken: utilitarianism. Although he acknowledges that the application of proportionality by courts has at times been utilitarian, he thinks the blame does not lie with the idea of proportionality itself.

It is true that not in all cases where proportionality was at least nominally applied a utilitarian approach followed, but is this enough to let proportionality off the hook?

I begin where Letsas does—with a classification of the different uses of the term proportionality, although my taxonomy differs from Letsas's in some important respects. I then proceed to address a question that should be at the heart of both explanatory and normative accounts of proportionality: what is the justification for proportionality in the different contexts in which it is applied? By looking at different uses of proportionality in a systematic fashion, I challenge the idea that there is an overarching canon of proportionality stretching from geometry to aesthetics of which legal proportionality is just an instantiation. The next question I address is whether the application of proportionality to fundamental rights can be based on anything other than a consequentialist idea of rights. Letsas maintains that we can make *moral* sense of proportionality outside utilitarianism.[3] Although Letsas's efforts have much to be commended, I remain of the view that an approach to human

* King's College London. I am grateful to the Templeton Foundation for supporting a research initiative on the theory and practice of human rights for which Jacob Mchangama, Dr Aaron Rhodes and I were the principal investigators. I am also indebted to the comments of the editors of this collection, and of Joseph Raz, Larry Siedentop, John Tasioulas, Leif Wenar, and the participants in a seminar on the idea of human rights held in London on 8–9 May 2013 as part of the Templeton project.

[1] Imer Flores, "Proportionality in Constitutional and Human Rights Interpretation", *Problema: Anuario de Filosofía y Teoría del Derecho*, 7 (2013): 87 and 113; David Betty, *The Ultimate Rule of Law* (Oxford University Press, 2004) esp. 159ff.

[2] Letsas, "Rescuing Proportionality", this volume, ch. 17.

[3] Letsas, "Rescuing Proportionality", 318.

rights that is centred on proportionality cannot be reconciled with non-utilitarian conceptions of human rights.

I. Meanings of Proportionality

Letsas identifies "four ways in which the concept of proportionality is used":[4] first, in statements that describe physical features of the world; second, in "moral judgments about what rights people have according to some value (for example, democracy or retribution)";[5] third, as a tool of instrumental rationality; and fourth as a principle of utility. While the first notion of proportionality is descriptive, the others—he maintains—are normative. According to Letsas, the "orthodox understanding of proportionality amongst constitutional scholars and judges" combines instrumental rationality and utility. I will return to this "orthodox understanding" in the next section, but first let us consider the different meanings of proportionality.

Proportionality is in origin a mathematical idea. It describes the ratio between two variables which may be arithmetic (for example, in the Fibonacci sequence) or geometric (for example, in Pythagoras's theorem). The variables may also be physical forces, as in Netwon's law of gravity. In some cases proportionality between physical elements will reflect a law of physics (again, in the example of gravity); in others it will reflect a value judgment (for instance, a recipe which prescribes ratios between different ingredients).

Proportionality can also be a standard of aesthetics. The correlation between aesthetic ideas, such as beauty and harmony, and proportions has been a feature of Western thought at least since the Pythagoreans. A classic illustration is Leonardo's *Vitruvian Man*. In aesthetics the boundary between descriptive and prescriptive proportionality is sometimes blurred. Aesthetic proportionality is not always decoupled from mathematical or physical proportionality. For the proportions which generate beauty may also be considered true in a natural sense, albeit probably in that peculiar Greek sense of truth as "un-hiddenness" (ἀλήθεια):[6] the idea, for example, that a golden ratio governs proportions in art and architecture has often been regarded as a hidden mathematical truth about the physical world capable of generating, among other things, a perception of beauty.[7]

Proportionality has traditionally been an important canon of both distributive and retributive justice. This is the case in Aristotle's theory of distributive justice which culminates with the judgment that "[t]he just is...the proportionate, and the unjust is that which is contrary to the proportionate".[8] The notion that punishment should

---

[4] Letsas, "Rescuing Proportionality", 322.   [5] Letsas, "Rescuing Proportionality", 322.

[6] On the relationship between the idea of truth and concealment see Heidegger's essay "On the Essence of Truth", in Martin Heidegger, *Pathmarks* (Cambridge University Press, ed. Wlliam McNeill, 1998) esp. 148ff.

[7] In Plato's aesthetics, proportions are idealistic and art is conceived as approximation, or imitation (μίμησις), of these perfect proportions. A later example of this idealization of proportions is the classic work of Renaissance aesthetics, *De divina proportione* (1509) by Luca Pacioli.

[8] *Nicomachean Ethics*, 1130b (V.iv.3) This is my translation based on the Greek text in the *Loeb Classical Library* (1926). I have been aided by the H. Rackham translation in *Loeb* as well as the R. Crisp translation in the Cambridge University Press edition (2000) of *Nicomachean Ethics*. Aristotle uses the

have some correlation to the offence is at the heart of most philosophies of retribution, the *lex talionis* being an example. Also connected to the theory of justice is the use of proportionality in arguments about desert.[9]

Proportionality is often invoked in practical reason—or, more accurately, in that particular type of practical reason that governs judgments about instrumentality. This kind of proportionality is relevant to certain areas of the law, for example when deciding on the requirement in the law of self-defence that we use only such force as is, in the circumstances, necessary and proportionate.

Finally, proportionality has been developed by courts as a juridical doctrine in cases on the limitation of constitutionally or internationally protected fundamental rights. Proportionality only applies to rights that are subject to express or implied limitation.[10] German public lawyers, who are credited with first developing the concept of proportionality, understand proportionality to include "three sub-principles": the rational connection between the measure limiting rights and the legitimate aim it purports to pursue (*suitability*); the absence of alternative measures which would not violate the fundamental right or would do so to a lesser extent (*necessity*); and the balance between the detriment to the fundamental right and the satisfaction of the legitimate aim for which that right is being limited (proportionality *stricto sensu*).[11]

---

word ἀναλογία for proportionality. He draws a further distinction between geometric proportionality (ἀναλογία ἐκείνη) and arithmetic proportionality (ἀναλογία ἀριθμητική)—*Nichomachean Ethics* 1132a (V.iv.3). The former applies to distributive justice and the latter to corrective justice. On the use of the term ἀναλογία in Aristotle, see Carl Huffman, *Archytas of Tarentum: Pythagorean, Philosopher and Mathematician King* (Cambridge University Press, 2005), 179–81. In Greek philosophy and mathematics a third type of proportionality was also discussed (subcontrary or harmonious proportionality)—see the fragment from Porphyry attributed to Archytas (Huffman, *Archytas of Tarentum*, 162–4 and 168–70).

The reason why different kinds of proportionality apply to distributive and corrective justice may elude the modern reader. The cue is in the fact that, according to Aristotle, for distribution to be just the same ratio must apply to the shares that are being distributed from the common stock as to the persons to whom those shares are assigned, because "if the persons are not equal, they will not receive equal shares" (*Nichomachean Ethics* 1131a (V.iii.6)). The premise of this argument is natural inequality. By contrast, in corrective justice, the natural inequality of the individuals is irrelevant "[f]or it makes no difference whether a good man has defrauded a bad man or a bad one a good one" (*Nichomachean Ethics* 1132a, (V.iv.3). On the transition from natural inequality to natural equality in Western thought see Larry Siedentop, *Inventing the Individual* (Allen Lane, 2014).

[9] This is also already evident in the *Nichomachean Ethics* 1131a (V.iii.7). See also the discussion of the ratio view of desert in S. Kagan, "Comparative Desert" in Serena Olsaretti (ed.), *Desert and Justice* (Oxford University Press, 2007), 100–3.

[10] In the European Convention on Human Rights (ECHR), a right is typically guaranteed in the first sub-section of a provision (eg, Article 8(1): "Everyone has the right to respect for his private and family life, his home and his correspondence"), and subject to limitation in the second sub-section (eg, Article 8(2): "There shall be no interference by a public authority with the exercise of this right except such as is in accordance with the law and is necessary in a democratic society in the interests of national security, public safety or the economic well-being of the country, for the prevention of disorder or crime, for the protection of health or morals, or for the protection of the rights and freedoms of others"). On implied limitations see Aharon Barak, *Proportionality: Constitutional Rights and Their Limitations* (Cambridge University Press, 2012), 134–9.

[11] Robert Alexy, "Constitutional Rights, Balancing, and Rationality", *Ratio Juris*, 16 (2003): 131, 135–6 and Letsas, "Rescuing Proportionality", 9.

This understanding of proportionality is no longer exclusive to German public law. Aharon Barak, former President of the Israeli Supreme Court (one of the many courts to embrace proportionality over the last decades), gives the following account of proportionality *stricto sensu*:

> ...the required balance is between the marginal social importance of the benefit in fulfilling the law's proper purpose, and the marginal social importance in preventing the harm to the constitutional right. This therefore concerns the relative notion of social importance found on each side of the scale.[12]

An important question is whether these different uses of proportionality—from mathematics to physics, from aesthetics to practical reason, from retributive to distributive justice, and so on—share any common feature. Each case is said to be about balancing. But this does not tell us very much. First, there is a difference between the balancing that requires a judgment of *suitability* (for example, whether the means are appropriate to meet the ends) and the balancing that requires a judgment of *comparability* (for example, whether a certain social benefit is weightier than another). Secondly, the terms involved in these various balancing exercises differ. In retributive justice, they are the gravity of the offence and the severity of the punishment. In distributive justice, those terms are the scope of an individual's entitlement, and the portion of the common stock to which he is laying claim. In proportionality as an adjudicative principle on the limitation of fundamental rights, the terms that are being balanced seem to be two types of benefits to society—one deriving from the protection of the fundamental right and the other from a competing public interest.

Understanding at the outset that the different senses in which proportionality is used have little in common by way of justification is important because, as we are about to see, there is a tendency to present proportionality as a kind of self-evident principle requiring no justification. The different uses of proportionality must instead each be justified on its own terms: there is no meta-justification of proportionality capable of accommodating all of them.

II. Justifications of Proportionality

In the first meaning of proportionality discussed earlier, the justification may be found in principles of mathematics or in the laws of nature. However, if proportionality is used to prescribe a particular ratio between, for example, ingredients in a recipe or cocktail, the justification will be different: taste or flavour. In aesthetic judgments, the justification for proportionality is found in an underlying idea of beauty or harmony: proportions are simply attributes or manifestations of that idea.

In its uses in distributive and retributive justice, proportionality also gives effect to an underlying idea. The principles that wealth must be distributed among different persons or that a guilty person must be punished in proportion with the offence he has committed

---

[12] Barak, *Proportionality*, 11.

derive from particular conceptions of justice and desert. In both of those cases, proportionality is the method, not the basis, for justice.[13]

The notion that there should be proportionality between means and ends is justified by practical reason. If I use a crane to lift a shopping bag, I am doing something which, on any view of instrumental rationality, is irrational. This failure of rational judgment does not however always entail a failure of moral judgment, for instrumental rationality does not tell me whether I should in the first place pick up the shopping bag or not, and if so at what cost and with which means.

In proportionality in self-defence, a moral principle is engaged. If I kill a person for slapping me in the face, my action would be considered disproportionate *and* immoral. But this is not because there is a moral imperative of proportionality that is being violated, rather because I have exceeded the bounds of what the moral law of self-preservation allows me to do. Under that moral law, I have a right to do things that would otherwise be wrong in order to preserve my life or my bodily integrity but only to the extent necessary to that preservation. This law requires me to apply instrumental reasoning. If I choose means which, all circumstances considered, instrumental rationality cannot justify, the immunity which the moral law of self-preservation has accorded me will cease to apply.

Each of these uses of proportionality must therefore find a justification outside proportionality. Proportionality does not possess any intrinsic moral value. Moreover, the use of proportionality in one context cannot justify its uses in other contexts. Even if I am able to show that physical beauty must respect ideal proportions, it does not follow that distributive justice should also do so.

What is then the principled basis for applying proportionality to fundamental rights? In judgments by international human rights bodies and domestic courts, little is said on this topic. For perfectly good reasons courts are not in the habit of justifying their rulings by reference to first principles. Judges are not philosophers. Moreover, since proportionality is now part of the *jurisprudence constante* in many legal systems, courts can justify proportionality simply by reference to precedent. Yet, it is noteworthy that the legal instruments which are being applied—for example, the Bill of Rights in Germany's Basic Law; the ECHR; Israel's Basic Laws; or the Canadian Charter of Rights and Freedoms—contain no mention of proportionality. So how did courts justify proportionality when they *first* applied it?

As mentioned, the consensus among scholars is that proportionality was first developed in German public law, and migrated from there to European law and beyond.[14] To the extent that a principled basis was at all identified when proportionality was first introduced into these legal systems, that basis may have often included references to the use of proportionality in other areas. It is telling that Judge Barak introduces his analysis of the historical evolution of proportionality in constitutional jurisprudence

---

[13] Letsas cites democratic representation and punishment as examples of ways in which proportionality "can be used to express genuine moral concerns about what various values require" (Letsas, "Rescuing Proportionality", 340), but I do not see what the case for proportional representation (PR) in elections has in common with the argument that punishment should be proportionate to the offence.

[14] Barak, *Proportionality*, 175ff.

with the heading *"Proportionality: In Life and in the Law"*.[15] One of the early decisions where the Israeli Supreme Court applied proportionality employs even more revealing language:

> The notion of "balancing" controls us and everything that is around us. Planet Earth revolves around the sun "to balance" between the gravitational forces pushing it towards the sun and the gravitational forces pulling it back to outer space. Each and every one of us is a kind of "balance" between their father and mother and their respective families. The same is true for every living organism. The same is true of the legal universe... [16]

Pythagorean echoes reverberate through this passage: the proportionality that exists between physical forces becomes a principle that governs both the macro- and the microcosm, and is then invoked to justify proportionality in law. But, as is often the case when the metaphors are rich, the reasoning is poor. Why should gravitational balancing provide a justification for rights balancing? As for the ECHR, in the first case where it applied proportionality, it did not even attempt to coax with metaphor. It simply stated that it would apply this principle.[17]

Some legal scholars have tried to come up with more sophisticated justifications for proportionality. According to one of its main defenders, Robert Alexy, proportionality "logically follows from the nature of principles; it can be deduced from them".[18] The background to this position is Alexy's view that principles, including constitutional rights, are "optimisation requirements".[19] Some scholars seek to enlist Ronald Dworkin in support of the case for proportionality, citing his distinction between rules and principles.[20] It is true that principles, as understood by Dworkin, have "the dimension of weight and importance", and that conflicts between principles may be resolved by taking into account the relative weight of each principle.[21] Nonetheless, for Dworkin the distinction between principles and rules is analytical—not normative. In his theory, principles, as "propositions that describe rights", may still include absolute rights;[22] in his later writings, a number of political rights and human rights are clearly regarded as absolute trumps.[23] Dworkin may have agreed with the idea that proportionality plays *some* role in the limitation of non-absolute rights, but not with the notion that proportionality inheres to fundamental rights in any *logical* sense. Moreover—and crucially—there is a fundamental difference between saying that principles (or values or interests) have different moral weight and saying that their moral weight depends on their ability to optimize. This is a point which will become clear later.

---

[15] Barak, *"Proportionality"*. Letsas also refers to the fact that proportionality has a life outside the law ("Rescuing Proportionality, 30).

[16] *Ganimat v. State of Israel* [1995] IsrSC 49(3) 355, 397 (cited in Barak, *Proportionality*, 345).

[17] "Every 'formality', 'condition', 'restriction or penalty imposed in this sphere must be proportionate to the legitimate aim pursued" (*Handyside v. United Kingdom*, Application no. 5493/72, Judgment of 7 December 1976, para 47). A critical analysis of the ECHR's approach to proportionality is found in S. Tsakyrakis, "Proportionality: An Assault on Human Rights", *International Journal of Constitutional Law*, 3 (2009): 468.

[18] Robert Alexy, *A Theory of Constitutional Rights* (Oxford University Press, 2002), 66.

[19] Alexy, "Constitutional Rights", 135.   [20] See Flores "Proportionality", 86ff.

[21] Ronald Dworkin, *Taking Rights Seriously* (Duckworth, 1997), 26.

[22] Dworkin, *Taking Rights Seriously*, 90 and 92.   [23] Dworkin, *Justice for Hedgehogs*, 327–39.

III. Human Rights and their Limits

Some bills of rights contain no express limitation clauses. This is the case of the US Bill of Rights and of the Universal Declaration of Human Rights (UDHR). Had the US State Department had its way, the same model would have been followed by the ECHR.[24] Hersch Lauterpacht's proposal for an International Bill of Rights also avoided express limitation clauses.[25]

As for express limitations, they come in two types exemplified by the following provisions:

Article 5(2), Germany's Basic Law
These rights [of free expression] *find their limit* [*finden ihre Schranken*] in the provisions of the general laws, in statutory provisions for the protection of the youth and in the right to personal honour. [*emphasis added*]

Article 10(2), European Convention on Human Rights
The exercise of these freedoms [of expression], since it carries with it duties and responsibilities, *may be subject to such formalities, conditions, restrictions or penalties as are* prescribed by law and are necessary in a democratic society, in the interests of national security, territorial integrity or public safety, for the prevention of disorder or crime, for the protection of health or morals, for the protection of the reputation or the rights of others, for preventing the disclosure of information received in confidence, or for maintaining the authority and impartiality of the judiciary. [*emphasis added*]

Rights in the first example are *limited rights*, while those in the second example are more aptly described as *qualified rights* or *limitable rights*. My interest here is not to discuss the judicial interpretation of these two different ways of limiting rights. I will not therefore undertake a comprehensive analysis of jurisprudence with a view to establishing if the distinction that I am about to draw is borne out by judicial practice. Rather, what I want to find out is if the difference between limited and limitable rights is a matter of mere terminology, or whether it contains a subtler conceptual distinction which can cast light on the relationship between proportionality and rights.

---

[24] Brian Simpson, *Human Rights and the End of Empire* (Oxford University Press, 2004), 467. The Charter of Fundamental Rights of the European Union follows a different model. The provisions creating individual rights do not normally contain express limitations, but a general limitation clause is found in Article 52(1) which provides:

> Any limitation on the exercise of the rights and freedoms recognised by this Charter must be provided for by law and respect the essence of those rights and freedoms. Subject to the principle of proportionality, limitations may be made only if they are necessary and genuinely meet objectives of general interest recognised by the Union or the need to protect the rights and freedoms of others.

The principle that "the essence" of the rights and freedoms cannot be subject to limitation is an important one. It mirrors the German constitutional jurisprudence that excludes dignity from proportionality. For a critique of the ECHR model of limiting rights as compared with these other models, see Andrew Williams, "The European Convention on Human Rights, the EU and the UK: Confronting a Heresy", *European Journal of International Law*, 24 (2013): 1157, 1169–71.

[25] Hersch Lauterpacht, *An International Bill of the Rights of Man* (Columbia University Press, 1945, *reprinted* by Oxford University Press, 2013, with an introduction by Philippe Sands).

To understand how these two types of limitations exist in principle (as opposed to how courts have applied them), it may help to think of rights as allotments of land and of their limits as fences. I should emphasize that this metaphor is not premised on an exclusively individualistic conception of rights: ownership of land may still be connected to the idea of a common good—aesthetic or environmental for example.

Now, if I own a piece of land limited by a fence, within the fence I am, so to speak, sovereign; uncertainty as to the exact position of the fence may make my ownership of the contested spaces less secure but it will not change the overall sense of a strong title. If, instead, the position of the fence depends on the balancing of my interests with those of my neighbours, the quality of my ownership will be different: I may still describe myself as the owner of the land, but it will be ownership in a precarious, weaker and essentially indeterminate sense. Human rights that are limitable through proportionality are *weak rights*. By contrast, human rights that are limited, but not limitable, are still *strong rights* in terms of the nature of the entitlement they bestow upon us.

Doctrinal theories on the nature of balancing do not change this assessment. There are two views on the characterization of the effects of balancing. According to one view, the result of balancing is "a derivative constitutional rights norm in the form of a rule" which becomes a constitutional limit to the right.[26] According to another view, the new rule that is formed does not operate on the constitutional level, but only on the sub-constitutional level.[27] For the purposes of the distinction between limited rights as strong rights and limitable rights as weak rights, not much turns on these debates: whether each exercise of proportionality results in a constitutional rule or not, the right that is subject to open-ended limitation through proportionality still creates a weaker and more uncertain entitlement.

I have said that the exercise of limited rights is not subject to a general principle of balancing. To say that my right is limited is to say that it does not extend beyond a specified area: no question of balancing arises as long as I stay within the limits of the right. The areas excluded from the scope of the right may be defined teleologically, in which case a means-end review will be called for. A case in point is the right to free expression in Germany's Basic Law which, as we saw earlier, finds a limit in "laws for the protection of youth". If a state enacted a draconian law banning all unauthorized conversations between adults and minors, that law would have to be subjected to a means-end review in order to establish if it is really protecting minors. To do so, we would need to develop an appropriate legal test requiring, for example, a rational or suitable connection between the means (ie, the law) and the end (ie, the protection of minors). Applying a suitability test to this legislation, we would conclude that the outright ban is unlikely to have general positive effects on the protection of children, and probably has many negative ones. Because my right of free expression *finds a limit* only in those laws that do protect minors, if I choose to speak with a child without authorization, I would still be within my constitutional right.

The above example includes an assessment of consequences. The legal reason for this assessment is that the right is limited in terms that require such an assessment. But, even where a right is limited in this way, it remains qualitatively different from a

---

[26] Alexy, *A Theory of Constitutional Rights*, 56.   [27] Barak, *Proportionality*, 39–42.

limitable right. There is a difference between consequences as grounds for qualifying rights and consequences as the basis for justifying rights.[28] As the following analysis will show, rights that are generally limitable through proportionality can find justification only in consequentialism, whereas rights that are subject to a specific limit, for the identification of which consequences are relevant, are still consistent with non-consequentialist theories of rights.[29]

IV. Proportionality and the Idea of Human Rights

My main contention here is that rights subject to limitation under a general proportionality test should be viewed with suspicion across the wide spectrum of liberal theories of fundamental rights that reject consequentialism. In this sense, the distinction between limited and limitable rights is not merely analytical. It also has a normative dimension.

The theoretical foundations of human rights have been explored extensively by others in this collection and elsewhere; I do not propose to do so again here. But in order to justify my contention that proportionality offends more than one theory of fundamental rights, let me take as a starting point the distinction between status-based and instrumental theories of human rights.[30] According to the proponents of this distinction, status-based theories view human rights as "a non-derivative and fundamental element of morality. They embody a form of recognition of each individual's value which supplements and differs in kind from the form that leads us to value the overall increase of human happiness and the eradication of misery."[31] On this account, instrumental theories are instead those which consider "rights [to be] morally derivative from other, more fundamental values".[32]

I will return to the theories labelled as instrumental later. For now let us consider how a status-based account of human rights would view rights limitable through

---

[28] On this point see L. Wenar, "The Value of Rights", in M. O' Rourke, *Law and Social Justice* (MIT, 2005), 181. Letsas also appears to subscribe to the view that "balancing and limitation of rights need not be premised on utilitarian grounds" ("Rescuing Proportionality", 325), but his attempt to rescue proportionality does afford consequences a peculiar role. He maintains that balancing includes both epistemic and constitutive tasks: "when courts talk of 'balancing' rights against other considerations, what they often mean is that they are considering (which is an epistemic task) the effect of a measure upon the interests of both applicant and society at large, with a view to discover what moral rights people have (which is a constitutive task)" (p. 326). But if consequences are needed in order to discover what rights people have, do they not become the basis for justifying rights? This approach may not be the same as the kind of consequentialism where the primary factor is majoritarian utility, but it is still consequentialist in a fundamental sense.

[29] This is where Letsas and I disagree. Letsas accepts that criticism of proportionality "is valid, insofar as it is directed against utilitarian or consequentialist approaches to rights" but, in my view, fails to see that rights limitable through general proportionality entail a consequentialist foundation. Letsas, "Rescuing Proportionality", 324.

[30] This distinction is challenged by many, among others John Tasioulas (see his "On the Foundations of Human Rights", this volume, ch. 1, and "Human Dignity as a Foundation for Human Rights", in C McCrudden (ed.), *Understanding Human Dignity* (Oxford University Press, 2013), 291–312).

[31] T. Nagel, "Personal Rights and Public Space", *Philosophy & Public Affairs*, 24 (1995): 83, 87. See also: F.M. Kamm, "Non-consequentialism, the Person as an End-in-Itself, and the Significance of Status", *Philosophy and Public Affairs*, 21 (1992): 381.

[32] Nagel, "Personal Rights and Public Space", 86.

proportionality. A passage from Jürgen Habermas's *Between Fact and Norm* offers a good starting point:

> As soon as rights are transformed into goods and values in any individual case, each must compete with the others at the same level of priority. Every value is inherently just as particular as every other, whereas norms owe their validity to a universalization test…Because norms and principles, in virtue of their deontological character, can claim to be *universally binding* and not just *specially preferred*, they possess a greater justificatory force than values. Values must be brought into a transitive order with other values from case to case. Because there are no rational standards for this, weighing takes place either arbitrarily or unreflectively…[33]

Habermas maintains that the enforcement of a right is different from the enforcement of a value—an analytical distinction which few would find problematic although whether a moral distinction also corresponds to it is a different matter. Habermas continues:

> An adjudication oriented by principles has to decide which claim and which action in a given conflict is right—and not how to balance interests or relate values…The legal validity of the judgment has the deontological character of a command, and not the teleological character of a desirable good that we can achieve to a certain degree under the given circumstances and within the horizon of our preferences.[34]

One criticism which status-based theorists would move against proportionality is that it produces a transformation in the deontology associated with human rights: "we no longer ask what is right or wrong in a human rights case but, instead, try to investigate whether something is appropriate, adequate, intensive, or far-reaching".[35]

Let us now turn to the positions described before as instrumentalist. Some of the theories which pass as instrumentalist cannot be characterised as consequentialist in any meaningful sense of that term. Take for example Joseph Raz's well-known theory of fundamental rights in *The Morality of Freedom*. Raz rejects the status-based accounts, and proposes a theory of fundamental rights that is grounded in important individual interests as well as in "the promotion and protection of a certain public culture…valued for its contribution to the well-being of members of the community".[36] Interest-based theories of rights—and Raz's theory is an example, although, as we have seen, other considerations are also part of his account—need not entail the "premise that the moral logic appropriate to interests is exclusively one of aggregation";[37] nor do they entail the idea of balancing competeting social benefits. An interest may, for example, be considered so fundamental as to be inviolable. The difference between an inviolable interest to free expression, to which an absolute right of free expression would correspond, and an inviolable right of free expression representing an intrinsic moral quality may not be all that substantial. The distinction between interest-based and status-based theories acquires normative significance when the interests which

---

[33] Habermas, *Between Fact and Norm*, 259.   [34] Habermas, *Between Fact and Norm*, 261.
[35] Tsakyrakis, "Proportionality", 487.
[36] Joseph Raz, *The Morality of Freedom* (Clarendon Press, 1986), 256.
[37] Tasioulas, "Human Dignity", 300.

rights are meant to serve are based on collective interests and disconnected from any individual dimension: it is one thing to justify free expression as an important individual interest (or as an important individual interest which also serves the common good); it is another to justify it because it produces positive social consequences (for example, it makes our society better by strengthening public argument or it supports democratic debate).

The idea of incommensurability also plays an important role.[38] Insofar as the interests or values on which human rights are grounded include incommensurables, there can be no room for balancing. This is not to say that all incommensurables are absolutes, but the process by which we may end up determining that an incommensurable has to give way to some other principle need not be governed by proportionality and balancing. Nor does incommensurability exclude, to use Raz's words, "pockets of commensurability" within which optimization may be possible.[39] There is a difference between an approach to the limitation of rights that admits of the occasional resort to consequentialist assessments in defined circumstances, and one that consists of a generalized system of consequentialist assessments aimed at the optimisation of social benefits.[40]

There is of course much more to say about the theory of rights, but what I have outlined here enables us to reach two conclusions on the relationship between proportionality and the idea of human rights. The first one is that limitable rights are, in an analytical sense, weaker than absolute or limited rights. This analytical weakness will have a bearing on the kind of duties that these rights can generate. The second conclusion is that rights that are generally limitable through proportionality do not sit comfortably with liberal theories of fundamental rights. They are difficult to reconcile with both status-based theories of human rights, and most interest-based accounts. Limitable rights through general proportionality are difficult to accept for those who think that human rights have intrinsic moral value, as well as for those who think that they derive from individual interests endowed with intrinsic moral value or that they are connected to some idea of the good.

Might there not be a mid-road solution? For example, how about having two classes of human rights, one for those human rights which we think ought to be absolute or limited only in specific and narrow ways (ie, deserving protection as strong rights), and another for those human rights which we think should be subject to general proportionality (ie, deserving protection merely as weak rights)? Is there any principled reason that tells us that *only* strong rights should be characterized as fundamental rights?

---

[38] It is a central part of Raz's argument (see *The Morality of Freedom*, 321ff).

[39] Raz, *The Morality of Freedom*, 358.

[40] The importance of incommensurability may be related to the fact that "all of the familiar instrumental theories of rights rest at the deepest level on status-based rights" (Wenar, "The Value of Rights", 209). A non-inferential moral judgment about the inherent worth of the individual and of human life is common to all liberal theories of human rights. For the purposes of understanding the extent to which proportionality can be accommodated within a particular theory of rights, this commonality may actually be more significant than any difference based on the instrumentalist/non-instrumentalist classification.

Whether a particular entitlement should be protected as a strong or weak right will depend on our moral and political views. For example, a classical liberal view would consider freedom of expression to be deserving of strong right protection—limited only in specific and narrow ways, rather than limitable in a general and open-ended sense. By contrast, utilitarians would approve of freedom of expression as a limitable right, and make its enjoyment dependent on whether the right is producing concrete social advantages and offers the greater utility when balanced against competing benefits.

But what if we reject the view that the starting point for a theory of human rights should be an argument about their moral foundations? "Political" conceptions of human rights do precisely this, and suggest instead that the theory of human rights should be grounded in their practice, not least because a foundational moral theory—elusive as it already is in the domestic constitutional sphere—is not appropriate for international human rights which are intended to cover the entire globe.[41] The protection of human rights in the weak limitable form does however pose a problem even in this practical-political perspective.

The crucial consideration is that the practice of human rights rests on a series of foundational claims which provide a yardstick against which subsequent developments in the practice should be assessed. These claims are normally included in the preambles of international human rights treaties. There we find various passages intended to impress upon us that human rights differ in some fundamental sense from other entitlements which the law may confer upon us. Human rights are described as the "foundation of justice and peace in the world" (preamble to the ECHR); they "derive from the inherent dignity of the human person" (preamble to the International Covenant of Civil and Political Rights (ICCPR)); failure to respect them may compel us "to have recourse, as a last resort, to rebellion", while "disregard and contempt for human rights have resulted in barbarous acts which have outraged the conscience of mankind" (preamble to the UDHR). These statements may not amount to a comprehensive moral theory of human rights in a philosophical sense; nor were they designed to be one. But they are not there for nothing. They occupy a special position in the practice of human rights for they identify a raison d'être.

This matters because it shows that the recognition of rights which are weak, uncertain and indeterminate as human rights is not merely an error of designation. It creates an inconsistency in the practice judged on its own standards of political justification. Those standards tell us that these rights are so fundamental that respect for them is what separates us from barbarism and war. If that is true, how can we justify making the enjoyment of some of these rights uncertain, vague and weak?

The coherence of the idea of human rights thus requires that all human rights be conceived and guaranteed as strong rights. True, on most liberal understandings of human rights, some rights, like freedom of speech or the right to free assembly, may need to "find limits" while others, like freedom from torture, should be unlimited. But, as explained earlier, both absolute and limited rights are strong rights.

---

[41] See Joseph Raz, "Human Rights Without Foundations", in S. Besson and J. Tasioulas (eds.), *The Philosophy of International Law* (Oxford University Press, 2010), 321–37.

This is not to say that our laws—domestic and perhaps international ones too—should never establish weak rights. Our social and political arrangements are complex. The relationship between the individual and the state should take different juridical forms, some putting the individual in a stronger position of entitlement than others. In the legal systems of most countries, for example, a basic distinction is drawn between fundamental rights entrenched under the constitution and statutory rights created under ordinary legislation.[42]

Some important individual interests are protected merely as statutory rather than constitutional rights. For example, many countries have introduced freedom of information legislation granting individuals access to government databases. This legislation rests on important principles of good governance, such as accountability and transparency. But, judged by the high moral and political standards of justification for human rights referred to before, denial of access to government information would normally fail to reach the threshold required for recognition as a human right. Important though it certainly is, access to government information is not a foundation of peace and justice; it does not derive from the inherent dignity of the individual; and disregard for it does not usually produce outrageous acts of barbarism. There may be situations, for example East Germany under the Stasi, where the collection and use of information about individuals by a government offends something more fundamental because it puts into effect a totalitarian system of social control. In these cases the sphere of fundamental rights, the right to privacy in particular, will be engaged. But, outside these exceptional circumstances, the ordinary interest of the individual in accessing government information is adequately protected as a limitable right, subject to extensive qualifications of both a general and specific nature. In the UK, for example, the specific limits are to the effect of exempting categories of information and government departments from the duty of disclosure, while the general limits are expressed in terms of proportionality and reasonableness.[43]

From the perspective of non-consequentialist theories, rights generally limitable through proportionality are a category error. Either they should be downgraded to ordinary statutory rights (rather than constitutional rights or international human

---

[42] Throughout this chapter, I have treated international human rights as cognate to fundamental constitutional rights. It may be objected that entrenchment makes constitutional rights different from international human rights. There is no doubt that there are important differences between human rights contained in treaties and those found in constitutions although, in a legal system like the British one, that difference is blurred by the fact that the domestic bill of rights (ie, the Human Rights Act (HRA)) incorporates a set of international human rights *verbatim*. Even beyond the British example, however, the difference between international human rights and constitutional rights thins out when one considers their political justification: expressions very similar to those I have mentioned earlier can be found in the preambles of national constitutions. Moreover, although not entrenched in a constitutional sense, the protection of a fundamental right in an international treaty also provides an entrenchment of sort: it too seeks to protect "the basic political culture of a society" (the expression is used by Raz, *The Morality of Freedom*, 260), and does so by connecting it to a system of binding international obligations which are in practice even more difficult to amend than constitutional bills of rights.

[43] See Freedom of Information Act 2000. It is also noteworthy that in some countries public and administrative law contemplates a third position, in addition to constitutional rights and statutory rights. In Italian law individual interests which are not guaranteed as constitutional or ordinary rights are described as legitimate interests, and may still attract some legal protection.

rights) or they should be upgraded to absolute or limited rights. A right that is balanceable and negotiable cannot be fundamental. These points will acquire greater force and clarity once we consider the implications that the recognition of weak limitable rights as human rights has for our public culture of rights and liberty.

V. Proportionality and our Public Culture of Rights and Liberty

To advance an argument—as I am about to—on what proportionality does to our public culture of rights and liberty does not entail acceptance of a consequentialist theory of rights. The juxtaposition of liberalism and communitarianism in contemporary Anglo–American political theory has contributed to the impression that a liberal theory of human rights is by necessity predominantly or even entirely individualistic.[44] It is true that some liberal theories of fundamental rights have these features, Locke's theory being an example. But a number of important thinkers spanning different liberal traditions have also linked the ideal of liberty, and the protection of basic rights which derives from it, to some version of the common good. Examples range from nineteenth-century French liberalism (for instance, Alexis de Tocqueville) to Joseph Raz's theory of freedom.

In order to understand what proportionality means for our public culture of rights and liberty, let us for a moment return to the two different ways of limiting rights discussed earlier: the *limited* right to free expression in Article 5(2) of Germany's Basic Law and the *limitable* right to free expression in Article 10(2) ECHR. Under the approach to freedom of expression as a limited right in Germany's Basic Law (albeit not necessarily as interpreted by the German Constitutional Court), a person has, for example, no right to publish paedophiliac pornography, because his right to free speech *finds a limit* there. The right terminates before that point. Under the ECHR approach to limitation, a person may have such a right *in the abstract*, but his exercise of that right will be restricted under the limitation clause.

This comparison tells us something else about the difference between limited and limitable rights, and about proportionality. Before proportionality is applied to them, limitable rights may actually be wider in scope than limited rights. This is because limitable rights begin with a wide assertion of principle (for example, "Everyone has the right to freedom of expression"), and it is only their *enjoyment* that is limited through proportionality. This two-pronged approach thus distinguishes "between the scope of the constitutional right and the extent of the right's realisation".[45] A consequence of this way of formulating human rights is that their scope is, at first, generously defined in the knowledge that the exercise of the right can subsequently be restricted. Unsurprisingly, fundamental rights defined, interpreted and applied in this way become, as Alexy has written, "ubiquitous".[46] But is it good for human rights to be ubiquitous?

---

[44] For a criticism of the predominant view see Will Kymlicka, *Liberalism, Community and Culture* (Clarendon Press, 1989, *reprinted* 2010).

[45] See, eg, Barak, *Proportionality*, 45ff.

[46] Alexy, "Constitutional Rights, Balancing and Rationality", 133.

If human rights are a good thing, one might think their ubiquity can be nothing other than good. But this superficially attractive position is problematic. First, ubiquity inflates and dilutes human rights.[47] Individuals have many rights, but their rights are subject to the Damocles' sword of proportionality. To be entitled to these ubiquitous human rights is a bit like owning a big house burdened by a huge mortgage. It is a big asset, but it is not fully ours and can be re-possessed by the bank.

Secondly, human rights ubiquity risks generating an unhealthy public culture of rights and liberty characterized by a sequence of entitlement and disappointment: we are first told we have rights but then asked to surrender them to some competing value on the basis of a vague calculus of social benefits. Not all rights are absolute and some measure of disappointment may be necessary, but because of its centrality in human rights adjudication proportionality has generalized entitlement followed by disappointment. No less insidious is the notion of progressive realization which has acquired particular importance in the context of economic and social rights. Like balancing, progressive realization undermines the idea of human rights. On the one hand, human rights are characterized as fundamental, with disregard and contempt for them even blamed—as we have seen—for "barbarous acts which have outraged the conscience of mankind"; on the other hand, the bearers of these rights are told that their full realization can be postponed. It is tantamount to saying that something which is morally necessary is still impossible today: the state is obliged to do something of the gravest importance but it cannot yet do it. Regardless of the theoretical justifications which may be advanced to account for this incongruity between "ought" and "can",[48] the public culture that results from it will be one of insatiability, disenchantment, and even cynicism.

As mentioned, human rights do not pertain exclusively to the realm of adjudication. More broadly, and perhaps even more significantly, they should be central to public argument. An approach that first inflates human rights and then limits their exercise risks bringing democratic institutions into disrepute: parliaments and governments are presumed to be abusers of rights which are initially very widely defined, although the liberty that derives from these broad definitions is neither deep nor strong.

Thirdly, the ubiquity of human rights marginalizes or suppresses other political, legal, and moral understandings of the relationships between individual, society, and state. Take an example which continues to generate controversy in the UK: prisoner voting rights. One may disagree with the predominant view in British society that a convicted criminal has for a time severed his social contract and should be punished

---

[47] The problem of human rights proliferation is obviously related to that of their ubiquity. A study of the Freedom Rights Project counted at least 1,377 human rights provisions in 64 core human rights treaties concluded under the UN and the Council of Europe. Because of their central political and moral role, human rights should be susceptible to succinct articulation and capable of being grasped and owned by everyone, rather than only by a technocratic elite. See: Freedom Rights Projects, "Human Rights Inflation" at http://www.freedomrights.info/activities/new-frp-report-1377-human-rights/; and J. Mchangama and G. Verdirame, "The Danger of Human Rights Proliferation", *Foreign Affairs*, 24 July 2013 at http://www.foreignaffairs.com/articles/139598/jacob-mchangama-and-guglielmo-verdirame/the-danger-of-human-rights-proliferation.

[48] See Jeremy Waldron's discussion of the "ought"-implies-"can" question in "Rights in Conflict", *Ethics*, 99(3) (1989): 506–7. See also Tasioulas's discussion of the "threshold of possibility" (Tasioulas, "Human Dignity", 296ff).

not only with a loss of personal liberty but also with a temporary deprivation of his political rights. There may be good non-human rights arguments in support of prisoner voting rights—for example, their exercise contributes to the civic education of individuals whom society is punishing now but will one day have to reintegrate—but the articulation of the case in human rights terms has a "crowding out effect" on these arguments; or, to use more familiar language, it trumps them and, by doing so, it impoverishes public argument on this issue. Here too there is a risk of a dangerous disconnect between the law of human rights, and widespread social understandings of them.[49]

The idea of proportionality, as developed by courts and by its enthusiastic supporters among legal scholars, is at the heart of the problems about human rights which I have set out in this chapter. In particular, it is because they know that balancing is around the corner that judges and lawyers have been prepared to recognize an ever wider range of situations as engaging fundamental human rights. In this process both legal and public argument about rights has often become sloppy and simplistic.[50] Here I differ from Letsas in that my view is that doctrinal writings, even when "vacuous" and "unsophisticated",[51] may still matter a great deal, as they both reflect and shape the application of the law by the courts. At its best, legal doctrine acts as a bridge between legal theory and judicial practice. At its worst it corrupts both. In this context, it is worth mentioning in passing a recent but related trend that has emerged in the jurisprudence of the European Court of Human Rights: the doctrine of "dividing and tailoring" the rights protected under the Convention when they are applied extra-territorially in an armed conflict.[52] The contours of this doctrine are still undefined: it is not clear on what basis and for what reasons human rights should be divided and tailored. But this idea, in its generality and vagueness, echoes proportionality and might perhaps take it to an even more dangerous level.

---

[49] On this point, see eg Justice O' Connor's dissenting opinion in *Roper v. Simmons*, 543 U.S. 551 (2005). The issue was whether the Court should overrule its precedents and develop a new interpretation of the Eighth Amendment to the effect that it prohibits the imposition of the death penalty on seventeen-year old murderers. Justice O' Connor explained that she "would demand a clearer showing that our society truly has set its face against this practice before reading the Eighth Amendment categorically to forbid it."

[50] An admittedly extreme example of such sloppiness in argument is a debate which took place at the end of 2013 in Britain on the question of how universities should respond to an external speaker requesting that male and female members of the audience be seated separately. The organization which represents British Universities, Universities UK, adopted its guidance on this issue after going through extensive internal consultations and after obtaining a legal opinion from a QC. The legal advice was that the case involved a conflict between the speaker's rights to freedom of expression and religious belief, and the right to freedom of association "of those who do not wish to be segregated while hearing a particular speaker," and that the issue was one of balancing these competing interests (See the Opinion of Fenella Morris QC, http://www.universitiesuk.ac.uk/highereducation/Documents/2013/ExternalSpeakersLegalOpinion.pdf). This Opinion obviously confused the liberty to manifest religious beliefs or express opinions, and the power to impose restrictions on others. A guest speaker is entitled to believe that women should sit separately or dress modestly. But only a perverse understanding of human rights would justify the view that a speaker's rights would potentially be violated by a university which refuses to enforce his beliefs on others.

[51] Letsas, "Rescuing Proportionality", 324ff.

[52] *Al-Skeini and others v. the United Kingdom*, para 137, cited with approval by the UK Supreme Court in *Smith and Others (FC) v. The Ministry of Defence*, 2013 UKSC 41, para 45.

VI. Conclusion

One notable exception to the success of proportionality is the United States. There the idea of balancing was "tested in the context of a powerful right—freedom of speech—and was found problematic as a method of adjudication".[53] This is not to say that US law has no place whatsoever for proportionality but crucially—and notwithstanding growing support among some academics and also among judges (like Justice Bryer)—proportionality has not been adopted by the US Supreme Court "as a constitutional concept which can stand on its own and which applies in different fields of the Bill of Rights".[54]

Outside the US the spread of proportionality seems almost irresistible. It has been argued that proportionality may be a code-word for something else—for example, a right to equal respect and concern in dealings with the public authorities.[55] However, the principle of equal respect and concern in dealings with the public authorities is covered by other principles like equality and non-discrimination. I do not see what, descriptively or prescriptively, proportionality can add.

In conclusion, I do not think there is anything to rescue in the doctrine of proportionality. Proportionality has an important role to play in many areas of public and administrative law, but the idea of fundamental rights is to protect, as far as possible, a select group of entitlements from other considerations—be they utility, convenience or public interest. There will be exceptional circumstances where fundamental rights will have to give way to these considerations. But if we allow them to encroach upon fundamental rights in an almost open-ended way, we will have downgraded fundamental rights to a different status. As we have seen, there may be pockets of proportionality even in the application of fundamental rights, but general proportionality is a different matter.

The only reason I can see for attempting to rescue proportionality is tactical. A doctrine which has so successfully penetrated the legal universe is not likely to vanish any time soon. The force of precedent counts. Moreover, as far as the ECHR is concerned, we are stuck with regrettable formulations which protect some of the most important rights only in a weak way and subject to wide-ranging consequentialist limitations: a case for abridging rights will often be at least arguable under those provisions. The Convention was, in other words, infected with utilitarianism even before judges began to interpret it. As far as legal doctrine goes, there may thus be a case for seeking to infuse a better spirit into proportionality. But, as far as a normative theory of rights and our public culture of rights are concerned, we are much better off without it.

---

[53] Tsakyrakis, "Proportionality", 7ff.
[54] Barak, *Proportionality*, 207. See also E.T. Sullivan and R. S. Frase, *Proportionality Principles in American Law: Controlling Excessive Government Actions* (Oxford University Press, 2009).
[55] See Letsas, "Rescuing Porportionality", 311ff.

PART III

CANONICAL AND CONTESTED
HUMAN RIGHTS

19

Free Speech as an Inverted Right and Democratic Persuasion*

Corey Brettschneider

According to Elizabeth Anderson and Richard Pildes, rights should be understood, not as based on the interests of the individual, but rather as delineated by the expressive capacities of the state.[1] The Establishment Clause of the First Amendment of the United States Constitution for example, which bars "endorsement" of religion by the state can be best understood in terms of what the state should or should not express. By this account, a cross in a public school classroom is problematic because it suggests that the state is endorsing Christianity. According to the "expressivist" view, it is a mistake to think that we should understand why the cross would be problematic by looking to the interests of the students. None of these students are coerced directly, nor are their interests obviously affected. They may, for instance, simply ignore the cross. Instead, displaying the cross in a public school classroom is problematic for the expressivists because it violates what Anderson and Pildes regard as the state's fundamental identity; it implies that the state is Christian. Anderson and Pildes helpfully demonstrate that issues concerning religious establishment are linked to what the state should or should not say when it "speaks." Inevitably, the state will express a message in many circumstances. It is unrealistic that classrooms, for instance, could entirely avoid conveying any state message. Rather the issue, as expressivists demonstrate, is what the state should say, given that it will unavoidably express itself.

I do not wish to dispute Anderson's and Pildes' influential account of the Establishment Clause here. Instead I want to discuss a kind of problem that can arise in the tension between state expression and the protection of negative rights against coercive intervention. This problem is distinct from Anderson's and Pildes' focus on direct state expression relevant to the Establishment Clause, so it is not surprising that their theory does not address it.[2] The right to be free from state coercion in matters of individual expression requires a distinct kind of expressivist theory, because the way that the state conveys its message in protecting free speech is inevitably more ambiguous than in the Establishment Clause context. What is distinctive about the

---

* Part of this essay reprises verbatim selections from my book, *When the State Speaks, What Should it Say? How Democracies can Protect Expression and Promote Equality* (Princeton, 2012) and my article 'Born Free, But Not Indifferent', published at http://foreignpolicy.com.

[1] Elizabeth Anderson and Richard Pildes, "Expressive Theories of Law: A General Restatement," *University of Pennsylvania Law Review*, 148 (2000): 1503–75.

[2] My focus is on the right to free speech, but a similar analysis might be given of other negative rights like the right to privacy.

jurisprudence of the rights related to the Establishment Clause is that it concerns direct limits on what the state can say. To the extent that citizens have a right against the establishment of religion, they possess a right against the state endorsing a particular religion. In the Establishment context, the relationship between state expression and rights is perfectly congruent: the citizen's right against establishment of religion correlates with the state's duty not to establish a religion.

Rights to freedom of expression, however, differ in a key sense. In the free speech context, I argue, state expression can at times seem to be "inverted" when rights are used to protect speech that opposes the reasons for the right to free expression itself. For example, the state's protection of free speech rights for hate groups might appear to suggest that there should be no judgment about the racist content of the protected expression. In this sense, there is a possible tension between the implicit message of speech protections and the reasons that are rightly understood to underlie those protections. Given the possible confusion that inverted rights present for the successful promulgation of the reasons for rights, any workable theory of free expression should explain how the state might overcome this challenge.

I also suggest that my account of democracy, which I call "value democracy," offers an original answer to the challenge of inverted rights. It argues that the state should protect rights against coercion in a neutral manner, but that it should not be neutral regarding the values expressed by hateful viewpoints. The state needs to clarify its democratic values due to the risk that state protection of hateful viewpoints might be seen as condoning them. In other words, there is a risk that in protecting the right to express hateful viewpoints the liberal democratic state will be viewed as complicit in these viewpoints. Value democracy's solution to the problem of inverted rights then is for the state to protect the right to free speech in regard to coercion, while at the same time criticizing hateful or discriminatory viewpoints in its various non-coercive expressive capacities. The state should engage in democratic persuasion, criticizing hate speech, and promulgating the reasons for rights. Democratic persuasion thus solves the problem of inverted rights by pronouncing the state's criticism of protected but hateful viewpoints. In this way, democratic persuasion serves as a necessary complement to the rights protected under the doctrine of viewpoint neutrality.

I. The Inverted Structure of Hate Speech Protections

Some theorists of free speech think that government condemnation of actions requires outlawing such actions. Such theories have appeal because the structure of viewpoint neutral free speech protections permits acts of expression at odds with the reasons for free speech in the first place. This has seemed to some an untenable paradox where free speech seems to allow for the flourishing of views that would undermine liberal democracy in the first place. This is the thought behind the adage that liberals are people who "can't take their own side in an argument." In this section I begin by examining how such theories suggest that inverted rights are untenable. I then explain how value democracy and my account of democratic persuasion offer a way to clarify inverted rights without government coercion.

I begin with the view of critical race theorist Charles Lawrence, who in turn draws on the work of Richard Delgado. Lawrence believes that the state is always acting in its expressive capacities because all state action, including coercive action, is backed by reasons and value judgments. For instance, Lawrence views the decisions to desegregate lunch counters and to prohibit signs barring entry to African Americans as themselves expressions of the state's support for the values of equal citizenship.[3] Lawrence takes this approach to argue that the state should use criminal law to limit hate speech and prosecute hate groups. He points out, as have I, that hate groups directly threaten the basic values of a free society and that the state must therefore clearly condemn these groups. Lawrence's approach, however, differs from my own in suggesting that the state should express its condemnation of hate groups through criminal law. Lawrence, like Catherine MacKinnon, rejects the doctrine of viewpoint neutrality in favor of a balancing approach to issues of equal protection and civil rights.[4]

The problem with Lawrence's account is that it does not recognize the distinction between the type of values expressed when the state acts in its expressive capacities and the type of values expressed when the state protects the speech of citizens and groups within society. For instance, when the state bans murder in criminal law, it is clearly expressing the idea that murder violates the rules of a legitimate society. Anti-discrimination law functions similarly; it expresses disapproval of the inegalitarian treatment of citizens. But not all decisions about coercion are similar. If the state protects a Klansman's right not to be murdered, it does not express support for the Klan's values, nor is it neutral about the Klan's beliefs. On the contrary, the state that protects the Klansman from murder is acknowledging that citizens are entitled to rights in virtue of their being citizens, even when their viewpoints are deeply illiberal. Thus it does not follow from the state's protection of the lives of Klan members that the state endorses the viewpoints of these speakers. Similarly, the state protects the Klan members' right to expression for reasons related to respect for the liberal principles of freedom, although these values are rejected in the content of the Klan members' speech.

Lawrence's critique, despite its inability to differentiate between the types of values expressed when the state acts in its two distinct capacities, is nevertheless helpful in forcing liberal theory to clarify its reasons for refusing to regulate illiberal expression. When the state refrains from regulating illiberal viewpoints, it is essential that it also use its expressive capacities to clarify that it is not expressing support for the viewpoints themselves. The state is instead guaranteeing an entitlement that stems from the need to respect all citizens as free and equal. In my account, the state can clarify the relationship between the rights and the reasons behind rights by clearly condemning hateful political viewpoints while protecting them from coercive law.

Without this clarification, there is a significant risk that the real meaning of the protection of free expression will be inverted. Because free speech rights often protect

---

[3] Charles Lawrence, "If He Hollers Let Him Go: Racist Speech on Campus," in Mari J. Matsuda and Charles R. Lawrence, III (eds.), *Words That Wound: Critical Race Theory, Assaultive Speech, And The First Amendment* (New York: Westview Press, 1993), 53–88.

[4] Catharine MacKinnon, *Only Words* (Cambridge, MA: Harvard University Press, 1993), see in particular ch. 3, "Equality and Speech."

messages at odds with the liberal democrat state's own foundational values, there is a risk that the state might be seen to endorse or to be indifferent to messages that challenge its very foundation. For Lawrence and others this potentially self-contradictory message is untenable. Thus free speech rights must be limited to disallow messages that are at odds with the expression of the state's own core values.

Consider the Court's opinion in *Virginia v. Black*.[5] In this case, the Court held that cross-burning was protected during a rally in which no member of the targeted class was singled out. Although the Court allowed for the possibility of an exception to the requirement of content neutrality in the instance of a threat to particular individuals, it did not think that the rally constituted such a threat. The Court invoked its doctrine of content neutrality, which includes but is not limited to the doctrine of viewpoint neutrality. The important point for our purposes is that the protected "speech" in this case—the burning of the cross—clearly opposes the normative reasons that underlie its legality in the first place. The Klan's message, as the Court pointed out, is in opposition, for instance, to the ideal of equality under law enshrined in the Equal Protection Clause of the Fourteenth Amendment.

To bring into clearer relief the idea of inverted rights, it is helpful to further develop the ways that the viewpoint of protected speech might conflict with the underlying "reasons for rights" that undergird the doctrines of viewpoint and content neutrality. To illustrate, consider how John Rawls, Ronald Dworkin, and Alexander Meiklejohn connect viewpoint neutrality with a wider set of values that are required for political legitimacy, in particular what I refer to as the value of free and equal citizenship.

In developing this argument it is helpful to begin with the value-based defenses of viewpoint neutrality developed by Rawls, Dworkin, and Meiklejohn. According to Rawls, political equality requires a respect for the "two moral powers" of all citizens to develop and exercise what he calls a "capacity for a sense of justice" and a "capacity for a conception of the good."[6] Citizens must be free from coercive threat as they develop their own notion of justice and the good. Otherwise, they would not be able to affirm and choose their own ideas about the most fundamental matters of politics (the just) and what constitutes, in their view, a valuable life (the good). Rawls' argument could be interpreted to support viewpoint neutrality, because the value of equality would be violated if some but not all citizens were free to develop their moral powers. Government discrimination or non-neutrality among viewpoints would make respect for the exercise of the moral powers unequal and would deny political freedom to the coerced citizens. Non-neutrality would undermine the equal treatment, not only of the citizens whose viewpoints were banned, but also of the citizens who otherwise could have listened to and argued with those viewpoints. The state would undermine equal treatment by failing to respect the capacity of citizens to make the free decision to accept or reject any viewpoint. Viewpoint neutrality is therefore necessary for the full and equal exercise of the two moral powers of citizens.[7]

---

[5] 538 US 343 (2003).

[6] John Rawls, *Political Liberalism*, rev. edn. (New York: Columbia University Press, 2005) lecture 8, esp. 302, 332, 334–5.

[7] Rawls endorses viewpoint neutrality in *Political Liberalism*, 336: "So long as the advocacy of revolutionary and even seditious doctrines is fully protected, as it should be, there is no restriction on the content of political speech, but only regulations as to time and place, and the means used to express it." However,

A similar line of egalitarian justification for this doctrine can be found in the work of Dworkin and Meiklejohn. These thinkers can be seen as defending viewpoint neutrality in the right of free expression, even for the hateful viewpoints held by the Nazis and the Klan, because neutrality is required to respect the democratic autonomy of citizens to develop their own political opinions.[8] Meiklejohn famously employs the metaphor of a town meeting to argue that all viewpoints must be protected in a democracy. On his view, while the moderator of a town meeting could limit speakers based on relevance and time constraints, censorship based on the content would compromise the meeting's democratic aims. Such censorship would prevent participants from hearing a variety of arguments for and against the measure under consideration, and would constrain their ability to express their own views. This kind of censorship would impede the ability of citizens to be the source of their own democratic decisions and would therefore undermine the democratic ideal.

Like Rawls, Meiklejohn argues that any attempt to discriminate based on the content of a particular viewpoint would threaten a regime's democratic credentials, even if the viewpoint in question were deeply undemocratic. Coercively limiting or banning an illiberal viewpoint would prevent citizens from actively affirming the core values of democracy. According to this argument, we must have the option to consider and reject all values, even democratic ones, in order to be truly free to affirm them. As Ronald Dworkin puts it, "a majority decision is not fair unless everyone has had a fair opportunity to express his or her attitudes or opinions or fears or tastes or presuppositions or prejudices or ideals, not just in the hope of influencing others, though that hope is crucially important, but also just to confirm his or her standing as a responsible agent in, rather than a passive victim of, collective action."[9] In short, the right to hear and make political arguments is a fundamental component of equal citizenship. Viewpoint neutrality should therefore not be confused with a justification for free speech; it is rather a doctrine that offers guidance regarding whether it is appropriate to limit coercion.

One might ask, however, whether it is empirically necessary for citizens to have the option to choose inegalitarian principles to develop Rawls' two moral powers or to deliberate about policy. Perhaps individuals living under censorship would select the same policy views and conceptions of justice and the good that they would choose living under freedom. However, I do not read the defenders of viewpoint neutrality as making an empirical argument, but rather as presenting a claim about what it means to respect citizens as free and equal. It is not that the protection of all viewpoints is empirically necessary to develop the two moral powers or the capacities for democratic citizenship. Rather, such protection from hateful viewpoints would disrespect the independent judgment of free and equal citizens, regarded as having the two moral powers, if the state were to restrict their options. Even if citizens ought not to choose views that are at odds with an ideal of equal citizenship, it is essential to the

the literature on Rawls is divided over whether viewpoint neutrality extends to hate speech, since he does not address the issue explicitly in his work. See Samuel Freeman, *Rawls* (New York: Routledge, 2007), 72.

[8] This view of democratic autonomy corresponds with one of Rawls' moral powers, the capacity for a sense of justice.

[9] Dworkin, "A New Map of Censorship," *Index on Censorship*, 35 (February 2006): 131.

legitimacy of value democracy that they *could* choose to embrace inegalitarian principles and policies.[10]

Much of my emphasis, and that of the familiar free speech tradition following John Stuart Mill, is on the problems posed by coercive or criminal bans on speech. Such bans are blunt instruments with harmful effects. As Mill reminds us, coercive bans risk the loss of partial truths that might, as part of public discourse, serve to enlighten, despite being couched in arguments that are generally wrong.[11] Coercive sanction merely tries to bury opinion and therefore misses the grievances that might be held legitimately even by those with deeply racist views.[12] Mill reminds us, too, that coercive sanction denies citizens the opportunity to clarify what is wrong with hateful views.[13] As Nancy Rosenblum argues, it also has the potential to force these views underground.[14] It would be better for hateful viewpoints to be publicly seen, tracked, and refuted.

I have sought to emphasize why value democracy's defense of viewpoint neutrality should be couched in a wider non-value neutral concern to protect the core values of freedom and equality, which a legitimate society must respect. It follows from the grounding of viewpoint neutrality in a wider non-neutral theory that the legitimate state can and should protect some views that are at odds with its own core values. A ban on certain viewpoints would disrespect the moral powers of free and equal citizens because it would, through threat of punishment, force people to come to particular conclusions about politics.

However, there is a tension between hateful viewpoints and the democratic values that form the core structure of free speech as an inverted right that requires protecting those viewpoints. For instance, as I noted in the preceding discussion, the Klan has been devoted since its inception to opposing racial equality under law. Indeed, its founding ambition in the nineteenth century was to oppose precisely the kind of guarantees that the Equal Protection Clause of the Fourteenth Amendment provides. The Equal Protection Clause is the clearest constitutional guarantee of the ideal of equal status, an ideal that also serves as a basis of the freedom of speech.[15]

The question of whether to protect the Klan's right peaceably to articulate its viewpoint therefore offers a clear illustration of a possible tension between the doctrine of viewpoint neutrality as a means of limiting state coercion and the values and reasons

---

[10] In *Democratic Rights: The Substance of Self-Government* (Princeton, NJ: Princeton University Press, 2007), I defend the idea that respect for free and equal status requires a respect not only for democratic rights of participation, but also a respect for other substantive rights protections.

[11] See John Stuart Mill, *On Liberty* in *The Collected Works of John Stuart Mill, Volume XVIII—Essays on Politics and Society, Part I*, ed. John M. Robson (Toronto: University of Toronto Press, 1977), 252. As Mill writes: "Such being the partial character of prevailing opinions, even when resting on a true foundation, every opinion which embodies somewhat of the portion of truth which the common opinion omits, ought to be considered precious, with whatever amount of error and confusion that truth may be blended."

[12] Steven Shiffrin, "Racist Speech, Outsider Jurisprudence, and the Meaning of America," *Cornell Law Review*, 80 (1994): 43–103.

[13] Mill, *On Liberty*, 229: "If the opinion is right, they are deprived of the opportunity of exchanging error for truth: if wrong, they lose, what is almost as great a benefit, the clearer perception and livelier impression of truth, produced by its collision with error."

[14] Nancy Rosenblum, especially in *Membership and Morals: The Personal Uses of Pluralism in America* (Princeton, NJ: Princeton University Press, 2000).

[15] See in particular the discussion of the founding of the Klan in *Virginia v. Black*.

underlying that doctrine. There is a clear conflict between the viewpoint of the Klan, which is a protected by a right to free speech, and the reasons to protect that viewpoint in the first place. In short, the Klan opposes the values of political equality and autonomy for all persons subject to the law, and these values are the very basis for the protection of its rights.

In sum, I want to concede that those like Lawrence, who offer an expressive justification for banning free speech, have identified a distinct structure of free speech jurisprudence that embraces viewpoint neutrality. Such a doctrine protects speech at odds with the reasons for free speech in the first place. Although, the protection of undemocratic viewpoints might be confused with endorsement of such viewpoints, I believe protection and endorsement are importantly distinct. Accordingly, I argue in the next section that "democratic persuasion," the state's active defense of its own values through its expressive capacities, has the potential to create a role for inverted free speech rights in a liberal democracy.

II. Democratic Persuasion as a Solution to the Problem of Inverted Rights

On my view, it is important to retain a doctrine of viewpoint neutrality, but also to give expression to the reasons that underlie that doctrine. Thus, the state should protect the rights of hate groups, while also criticizing their discriminatory views. To see why there is an interest in both protecting and criticizing the Klan's viewpoint, for instance, it is important to consider three perspectives that reflect the different interests related to free speech: those of the speaker, the listener, and the democratic polity as a whole.

Dworkin describes the interest of citizens as *speakers* in being able to say whatever they wish. If citizens want to articulate a view that is at odds with the basis for the state's legitimacy, coercively preventing them from doing so would directly limit their autonomy. Denying speakers the ability to say what they want restricts one of the most basic capacities of citizens to decide and express their own political positions. Dworkin therefore emphasizes the importance of the citizen *qua* speaker in his defense of viewpoint neutrality. His view clearly articulates why the affirmative value of autonomy requires respect and protection of all viewpoints.

In addition to the interest of speakers, a second interest at stake in free speech rights is that of *listeners*, as Meiklejohn points out in his account of viewpoint neutrality. To fully exercise their right to autonomously form their own opinions, citizens in a democracy must be free to hear and consider any viewpoint they wish, free from government intrusion. Indeed, this interest of the listener might be held by citizens who are critical of hateful viewpoints. For instance, if I want to argue against a hateful viewpoint, I should be free to seek it out, understand it, and then criticize it.

Finally, a third perspective, according to Charles Beitz and T.M. Scanlon, is that of the citizenry as an *audience* in a democratic polity.[16] The interest of citizens as an audience is distinct from their interest as listeners. The perspective of citizens as listeners is

---

[16] Charles Beitz, *Political Equality* (Princeton, NJ: Princeton University Press, 1989) and T.M. Scanlon, "Freedom of Expression and Categories of Expression," *University of Pittsburgh Law Review*, 40 (1979): 519–50.

an individual one, whereas the perspective of citizens as an audience regards them as a collective and emphasizes the importance of the whole democratic polity. Citizens as a democratic audience have interests at stake in deciding what beliefs should prevail in their democracy. In particular, they have an interest in seeing that democratic values thrive in the polity as a whole, so that the right to vote and other procedural and substantive democratic rights are preserved for all citizens.

However, if these institutions are to be preserved, the democratic values that support them must also be defended. Some viewpoints, such as the Klan's, oppose the values of free and equal citizenship and are hostile to the values that underlie democratic institutions. On my view, the appropriate state response to this conflict is to protect the free speech rights of citizens to make all arguments as speakers and to hear all arguments as listeners. At the same time, the state should criticize antidemocratic and discriminatory viewpoints to uphold the interests of citizens as an audience in preserving democracy.

It might be objected that my view is unfair to discriminatory viewpoints because it does not allow them the equal chance to spread. However, this objection rests on a mistaken conception of fairness. Respect is owed not to specific viewpoints per se, but to individual citizens. Viewpoint neutrality requires that the state not coercively limit the free speech rights of citizens, but it does not oblige the state to be neutral when it comes to the expression and defense of the values central to its own legitimacy. Viewpoint neutrality does not mean value neutrality. On my account, the state should protect the right to freely express all viewpoints, but it should not be neutral in its own expression or endorsement of values. The state and its citizens should promote the democratic values of free and equal citizenship, while at the same time criticizing hateful or discriminatory values.

It would be implausible to interpret neutrality as guaranteeing equal success for all viewpoints. This misguided interpretation of neutrality would commit the state to bolstering viewpoints that seek to deny the rights of some citizens. Consider, for instance, whether the state should seek to revive Nazi ideology. If neutrality were interpreted as a state obligation to guarantee the equal success of all viewpoints, it would require the state affirmatively to promote Nazi ideology and other racist beliefs that are contrary to its most basic democratic values. The state's promotion of racism would contradict citizens' interest as an audience in preserving the institutions and entitlements of democracy and in ensuring that the democratic values of freedom and equality are widely shared and endorsed. Thus, the proper interpretation of viewpoint neutrality and the state's obligation to protect the right of free expression does not imply that everyone has an entitlement for the state to ensure that their own views prevail. On the contrary, the state has no obligation to ensure the equal success of hateful viewpoints, but instead has an interest on behalf of the democratic citizenry as an audience in seeing that the viewpoints consistent with the values of free and equal citizenship succeed while those inimical to these values fail. Furthermore, some viewpoints should not be promoted by the state and should be criticized by it.

I have outlined the tension between two sets of interests: the interest of speakers and listeners in viewpoint neutral protections and the interest of the citizenry as a whole in ensuring that democratic values have a prominent place in public discourse and that hateful viewpoints are combated. One way to resolve this tension is to simply go the way of militant democrats and ban the hateful speech. Indeed, Jeremy Waldron has argued in his recent work that there would be no loss in legitimacy from banning racist ideological viewpoints, such as those of the Klan.[17] Waldron asks whether societies that do ban the expression of hateful viewpoints have less legitimate law, and he argues that they do not. Waldron's position would suggest, for instance, that in countries where hateful viewpoints are banned, the power to tax or to enforce the law is no less legitimate.

I agree with Waldron that some viewpoints risk undermining and challenging the equal status of all citizens. As I have emphasized, no viewpoint is entitled to success. I also agree with Waldron that it would go too far to claim that a society that lacks a doctrine of viewpoint neutrality would lack legitimacy in all its laws. But in my view, there would be an increase in the *degree* of democratic legitimacy in a society if it could counter hateful viewpoints while still maintaining viewpoint neutrality when it comes to protecting speakers from being punished for expressing their views.

To determine whether protecting free speech for hateful viewpoints would enhance legitimacy, we would do well to consider whether there is a difference between a society that has free speech and few hateful viewpoints and a society that limits free speech and has an equal number of hateful viewpoints, all else being equal.[18] If it is possible to counter hateful viewpoints while protecting free speech, there would be an overall gain in the degree of democratic legitimacy. Specifically, the gain would come from preserving the entitlement of individuals to make and hear any opinion they wish. Such guarantees would enhance legitimacy by respecting the autonomy of citizens as speakers and listeners. It would also avoid the limits on autonomy that would come from coercively punishing some speakers. A society that offers this kind of viewpoint neutral protection of free speech would also realize political equality to a greater degree because it would extend free speech protections to all citizens. Given the greater legitimacy lent by free speech, the task is to devise a way for the state to protect the entitlements of citizens as speakers and listeners to say and listen to whatever they desire, while at the same time enabling it to combat hateful viewpoints that seek to undermine the values of free and equal citizenship. In short, the aim is to ensure that the interests of the speakers, listeners, and audience of the democratic citizenry as a whole are all respected and realized.

In my account of value democracy, we can both protect the rights of autonomous citizens and counter the discriminatory messages of hate groups. We can accomplish this by distinguishing between the state's expressive capacities and its coercive capacities. When acting in its coercive capacities, the state has an obligation to respect

---

[17] Jeremy Waldron, "Dignity and Defamation: The Visibility of Hate," *Harvard Law Review*, 123 (May 2010): 1596–657 and Jeremy Waldron, "Free Speech and the Menace of Hysteria," *New York Review of Books*, 55 (29 May 2008). <http://www.nybooks.com/articles/archives/2008/may/29/free-speech-the-menace-of-hysteria/>. Waldron's article is a review of Anthony Lewis, *Freedom for the Thought that We Hate* (New York: Basic Books, 2007). See too Jeremy Waldron, *The Harm in Hate Speech* (Cambridge, MA: Harvard University Press, 2012).

[18] See Frank Michelman, "Legitimacy and Autonomy: Values of the Speaking State" for a discussion of my account of legitimacy in *Brooklyn Law Review* 79 (2014): 985–1004.

viewpoint neutrality by not coercing any speakers or listeners on the basis of their viewpoint. When the state acts in its expressive capacities, on the other hand, it must clarify why some protected viewpoints are at odds with the reasons for free expression in the first place. In this role, the state should both protect and criticize deeply inegalitarian viewpoints. These dual duties follow from the recognition that it is important not only for legitimate law to be justified, but also for the reasons behind the law be promulgated.

It is often thought that the state should promulgate the content of the law. Indeed laws passed in secret and never publicized are rightly thought to be a paradigm of illegitimacy,[19] and the content of laws must be publicized so that citizens can predict when their actions might be sanctioned. But citizens should not only know their rights and the rules that are set out by law, but also the *reasons* for these rights and rules. The key issue is how the state might find a way to express the reasons underlying rights, given that the state must also protect citizens' expression of hateful viewpoints that oppose those reasons. One place to look for expression of the reasons for rights is within the decisions of the Court. The Court is ideally an "exemplar" of public reason in the sense that it protects democratic values by striking down unconstitutional laws, like those constraining free expression.[20] In my view, however, the Court acts as an exemplar of public reason in a second sense as well by promulgating the reasons for rights. Namely, it acts as a model for the wider citizenry, including public officials who deliberate about and make the law, when it explains why certain laws are legitimate or illegitimate, and when it speaks in defense of the values of free and equal citizenship. The Court's audience extends to all citizens who are concerned to think and deliberate publicly about law making. This second notion of the Court as an exemplar of public reason is an instance of the state relying on its expressive capacity to promulgate the reasons for rights. Ideally, the Court should clarify to the citizenry that the state's protection of hateful viewpoints does not imply its approval of these viewpoints, as it has in fact done on some occasions.[21] In other words, the Court should affirm the importance of rights such as free speech, while giving reasons to criticize discriminatory views.

Although the doctrine of viewpoint neutrality does call for a certain kind of humility when it comes to coercive action, the Court should not avoid articulating the values that underlie the doctrine. For instance, in *Virginia v. Black*, Justice O'Connor gives evidence that could be used to criticize the Klan's racist views, although she emphasizes the importance of protecting the group when it is expressing a viewpoint.[22] In particular, O'Connor underscores that the Klan was founded to oppose basic legal

---

[19] Lon L. Fuller, *The Morality of Law* (New Haven, CT: Yale University Press, 1964), 39.

[20] Rawls terms the Supreme Court an "exemplar" of public reason. It is clear he means to do so in my first sense, but it is unclear whether he would agree with my extension of this term to the second sense, that the Court should be an example for the wider citizenry. See Rawls, *Political Liberalism*, 231.

[21] *Snyder v. Phelps*, 131 S. Ct. 1207, 1220 (2011). In this case, while protecting the Westboro Baptist Church's right to demonstrate on public sidewalks, the Court repeatedly referred to the Westboro Baptist Church's activities as "hurtful."

[22] *Virginia v. Black*. Eg, while defending the Klan's expressive rights, Justice O'Connor argues that "the history of cross-burning in this country shows that cross burning is often intimidating, intended to create a pervasive fear in victims that they are a target of violence."

protections of equality under law.[23] This history highlights why the Klan should be viewed as clearly opposing the ideals of free and equal citizenship. On my account, the Klan and other organizations with a discriminatory message should have the right, under the doctrine of viewpoint neutrality, to speak and hold their views, but they do not have the right to be free from criticism by the state in its expressive capacity. Although the state should be restrained in its coercive capacity so that it respects citizens' autonomy to make their own decisions, the state should be free to explain why it protects rights of free speech. Indeed, a robust role for the state in defending the values that underlie free speech is another way of honoring these values.

I take the idea of promulgating the reasons for rights to be the first step in what I call "democratic persuasion," which is a central feature of value democracy. Although the state should act in a viewpoint neutral manner when exercising its coercive capacity, it has a corresponding obligation to explain why it respects viewpoint neutrality in the first place. The state should use democratic persuasion, promulgating or publicly offering the reasons for rights, in an attempt to convince citizens that its reasons are good reasons. Democratic persuasion encourages citizens to engage in reflective revision, with the aim of respecting and incorporating the public values of equal citizenship in their own lives, families, and civic associations. But the state must be careful to make reasoning central and to avoid force when pursuing democratic persuasion.

Part of the Court's audience in the *Black* case is legislatures considering passing coercive laws that would ban hateful viewpoints short of direct threats. These state actors should be reminded of why such laws violate the ideals of free and equal citizenship. But a second audience for Court opinions is the Klan itself and other hate groups in the marketplace of ideas. To these citizens, the Court is saying that, while their right to free expression is protected, the content of their hateful views conflicts with the reasons for those rights protections. In addressing these citizens, the Court acts as an exemplar of public reason in the first and second senses described previously—it is both protecting a right and promulgating the reasons for that right.

Value democracy argues that the reasons for rights are not just intended to be expressed publicly; they are also meant to be persuasive. The arguments offered as part of democratic persuasion are intended to challenge and change the minds of those who do not appreciate the importance of free and equal citizenship in a legitimate society. Of course, hate groups including the Klan might not listen to reason or be persuaded, but in those cases, it is important to convince third parties and the population at large of the values of free and equal citizenship. Part of the task here is clarifying that the state is not neutral in regard to groups like the Klan, and that the state instead affirms the freedom and equality of all citizens. In short, the legitimate state should employ democratic persuasion to convince the citizenry as a whole that its reasons for protecting the rights of all citizens are good reasons.

As I have suggested, one example of democratic persuasion is Supreme Court opinions. However, these Court opinions on their own may not be effective in changing the minds of hate groups that oppose the ideal of equal citizenship. The early

---

[23] See *Virginia v. Black*, at 352. O'Connor writes, "The Klan fought Reconstruction and the corresponding drive to allow freed blacks to participate in the political process."

Klan membership of Justice Hugo Black aside, I assume that most members of hate groups are not thinking analytically about the nuances of First Amendment doctrine. Although they still have an important expressive purpose, we must acknowledge that Court opinions alone will not effectively persuade the citizenry at large of the reasons for rights. No single institution of government has an exclusive monopoly on the reasons that underlie rights. Other state actors in addition to the Court should also appeal to these reasons. These institutions should be concerned with the question of how to express the *reasons* for coercion and its limits.

When the state attempts to promulgate the reasons for rights without violating freedom of expression, it is essential that it observe two limits: means-based and substance-based. The first, *means-based limit* of democratic persuasion requires that the state must not pursue the transformation of citizens' views through any method that violates fundamental rights like freedom of expression, conscience, and association. For example, the state cannot use criminal sanctions to prohibit Klan meetings on the grounds that Klan members reject the reasons for freedom of expression. However, it would be appropriate for the state and its public officials to articulate why the Klan's views are inconsistent with the reasons for freedom of expression. In my view, the state can avoid crossing the means-based limit by confining its method of communicating its message to its expressive rather than its coercive capacity. For example, public officials and citizens engaged in public discussion may make arguments that seek to transform hateful viewpoints. In addition, I will suggest in the next section that there is a wide role for educators and the state more broadly to teach the importance of the ideal of equal citizenship. The challenge for value democracy, however, lies in simultaneously protecting rights to expression against coercive interference, while criticizing inegalitarian beliefs protected by these rights.

As I suggested earlier, the criticism involved depends on the degree to which the beliefs oppose free and equal citizenship. Hate groups like the Klan should be condemned by the state, as their very mission is to undermine democratic values like the equal protection of all citizens under law. However, in many instances, it is the specific discriminatory beliefs of citizens that the state should criticize, and in these cases, the state should make it clear that it is not condemning their entire belief set.

Since the notion of coercion is central to the means-based limit, it is worth elaborating on how I will use this term. Drawing on Robert Nozick's work on this subject, I define coercion as the state threat to impose a sanction or punishment on an individual or group of individuals with the aim of prohibiting a particular action, expression, or belief.[24] Coercion, by this definition, need not be carried out; indeed some people might resist the state's threats. But the mere fact that a state action is coercive does not imply, as some have inferred, that the action is unjustifiable.[25] On the contrary, there

---

[24] Robert Nozick, "Coercion," in Nozick, *Socratic Puzzles* (Cambridge, MA: Harvard University Press, 1997), 15–44.

[25] I do not, therefore, rely on a moralized conception of coercion. In a moralized conception, an act counts as coercion only if it is not fully justified. For the moralized conception, see Alan Wertheimer, *Coercion* (Princeton, NJ: Princeton University Press, 1990). However, my definition differs from the moralized conception in that it acknowledges that certain acts can be morally justified and yet coercive. Eg, imprisoning murderers is coercive in my definition, but morally justified. My definition uses the

are certainly justifiable cases of state coercion. For example, it is justifiable for the state to employ coercive criminal law in an attempt to stop citizens from committing acts of violence like murder, rape, and assault. The means-based limit, however, suggests that the state should not use coercion to prohibit expression. Coercive threats would deny the ability of persons to decide for themselves what kinds of policy beliefs to express. This denial would fail to respect the entitlement of citizens to develop and exercise their moral powers. In particular, coercively banning viewpoints would impair the ability of citizens to determine autonomously which beliefs they wish to hold and defend.

It should be emphasized, however, that a state's attempt to change people's minds by expressing certain beliefs does not constitute coercion, since the state does not seek to prohibit citizens from holding conflicting beliefs. To the contrary, it is central to the idea of expression and, more specifically, to the expression and defense of the core values of freedom and equality that citizens remain free to reject it. Although I argue that the state should seek to persuade citizens to endorse democratic values, it is essential to the values of freedom and equality that the state not attempt to force acceptance. On the contrary, citizens should be free to reject the state's defenses of the core values of free and equal citizenship. For similar reasons, the state should avoid manipulating citizens into accepting the values of free and equal citizenship by intentionally misleading them or by subliminally trying to change their minds. To respect autonomy, the means-based limit suggests that democratic persuasion must be transparent. But the requirement that democratic persuasion include explicit reasons does not mean that it must avoid emotion or rhetorical persuasiveness. Indeed as Sharon Krause has pointed out, there is nothing about the appeal to emotion that need be inconsistent with reasoning.[26]

In addition to being subject to a means-based limit, democratic persuasion is also subject to a second, *substance-based limit*. This substance-based limit restricts the kinds of beliefs that the state is obligated to seek to transform through its expressive capacity as well as the circumstances under which the state is justified in exercising that capacity. It is necessary for the state to use its expressive capacity to challenge only those beliefs that violate the ideals of free and equal citizenship. In particular, the state should not seek to transform all inegalitarian beliefs, but only those that challenge the ideals of free and equal citizenship.

It is essential to clarify here that equal citizenship constitutes a political ideal; it is not the equivalent to equality in every sense. For instance, if I always neglect to pay the check at dinner with my friend, I might violate the ideal of an equal friendship, but in doing so I do not violate the ideal of equal citizenship. In sum, the substance-based limit of democratic persuasion requires the state to criticize only views incompatible with the ideals of free and equal citizenship and not views that are incompatible with morality per se.

---

non-moral but normative criterion that acts count as coercion when they attempt to deny a choice. For discussion on this point, I thank Eric Beerbohm and Daniel Viehoff.

[26] See Sharon R. Krause, *Civil Passions: Moral Sentiment and Democratic Deliberation* (Princeton, NJ: Princeton University Press, 2008).

Of course, there will be easy and hard cases—it is not always obvious whether a belief is incompatible with the ideal of equal citizenship and therefore subject to criticism by the state. It is only views that are openly hostile to the ideal of equal citizenship or implausibly compatible with it that the state has an obligation to criticize, according to the substance-based limit. For example, the views of hate groups are paradigmatic of views that are openly hostile to democratic values or implausibly disguised in a language of equality.[27] However, groups or citizens who hold opinions that might be plausible interpretations of equal citizenship, although there may be controversy over them, should not be subject to disapproval by the state in its expressive capacities. For instance, while some may think an ideal of equality requires affirmative action, other citizens who disapprove of this policy are not expressing opinions that are necessarily hostile to or implausibly connected to the ideal of equal citizenship. They may oppose affirmative action on grounds that may be plausibly interpreted as consistent with equal citizenship, like an ideal of colorblindness in the college admissions process. The disagreement would be reasonable in that case and not subject to democratic persuasion. The substance-based limit therefore makes the state use of democratic persuasion more limited than the principle of public relevance. The principle of public relevance identifies conflicts generally between free and equal citizenship and individual beliefs and suggests the importance of making these beliefs consistent with democratic values. The substance-based limit, on the other hand, further narrows the instances when the state should engage in democratic persuasion. According to the substance-based limit, the state should use democratic persuasion only when individuals hold or advance ideas that clearly conflict or are implausibly claimed to be consistent with the ideals of free and equal citizenship.

The substance-based limit of democratic persuasion concerns the content of what the state is obligated to say on behalf of its own values. At times, the state articulates these values and their justifying reasons through state actors, and in these cases the substance-based limit should then be followed. But this limit certainly does not entail that state actors cannot articulate opinions on controversial matters when speaking in their own capacities. Particular citizens, politicians, or state actors may have their own opinions on questions about which there is reasonable disagreement, including questions about conflicting interpretations of equal citizenship. Moreover, although my focus is on instances in which the state is obligated to promote the ideals of free and equal citizenship and to criticize viewpoints at odds with it, I hold open the possibility that other kinds of state speech might be neither obligatory nor prohibited. Pronouncements in favor of public health, like warnings about smoking or trans-fat, do not violate an ideal of equal citizenship, but neither are they required to clarify the meaning of equal citizenship. Such pronouncements might be permissible on grounds that are distinct from the ones I explore.

---

[27] I am thinking, for instance, of the case of former Klan Grand Wizard David Duke. His National Association for the Advancement of White People masks clearly inegalitarian views in the language of equality. The Association makes the misleading claim on its website that it "campaigns merely for the equal treatment of all races." See http://www.davidduke.com/general/what-is-racism_32.html.

In sum, democratic persuasion is an attempt by the legitimate state to express the reasons and values that underlie rights. In some instances, democratic persuasion requires challenging viewpoints that are protected by rights, especially when the viewpoints are hateful. But the point of democratic persuasion is not merely to express the values of equal citizenship as a philosophical exercise. It is ideally an attempt to change the minds both of the members of hate groups and of citizens more generally, and to keep the hate group's influence from spreading. Given the choice between expressing the values of freedom and equality in a non-persuasive or a persuasive manner, all else being equal, the state should opt for forms of persuasion that are more convincing. If the reasons and values that underlie rights are central to the legitimacy of the state, it follows that the state has a role in defending them, especially when they are under attack. Part of defending democratic values is making persuasive arguments on their behalf.[28]

I have argued so far that an account of free expression should both defend the free-speech rights of individuals against state coercion, and allow the state to promote the values that underlie these rights. I have also maintained that the state must respect both the *substance-based* and *means-based* limits of democratic persuasion when it promotes the ideal of free and equal citizenship through its expressive capacity. I now turn to explore how the state might fulfill these duties. The contemporary state can "speak" in favor of its own values—and against those who deny the freedom and equality of citizens—in a variety of ways, ranging from the direct statements of politicians to the establishment of monuments and public holidays. Martin Luther King Day and Black History Month exemplify official endorsement of the Civil Rights Movement's struggle for equality. Public officials do not shy away from political viewpoints when they celebrate and commemorate these official holidays. Rather, they articulate the ideal of equal status and celebrate those citizens who have promoted it. Far from being viewpoint neutral about Southern segregation or groups like the Klan, the state promotes a particular viewpoint in defense of equal protection. Of course, citizens have the right to dissent from such expression. But here the state and its citizens should stand together to express disapproval of those who defend segregation in our society or who, more subtly, lament the end of "states' rights" that would protect segregation.

Another way to frame state expression in defense of these values is through the state's action as an educator. When state standards require that the history of civil rights and the struggle against groups like the Klan be taught in schools, for instance, these matters are not taught in a viewpoint neutral way. The movement and its victories

---

[28] Democratic persuasion allows for certain forms of rhetoric to further the democratic values that underlie rights, provided that the rhetoric is truthful and combined with the promulgation of reasons. My aim, however, is not to provide a roadmap detailing how such rhetoric might be employed, but to justify and describe the state's role as it engages in democratic persuasion. A model for the rhetoric of democratic persuasion might be found in what Simone Chambers and others have called a "deliberative rhetoric," in which effective communication is tied together with public reasoning, as opposed to a "plebiscitary rhetoric," which tries to change people's minds without explaining the underlying reasons or principles. An account of deliberative rhetoric can help to show that democratic persuasion can effectively promote the ideals of free and equal citizenship. See Simone Chambers, "Rhetoric and the Public Sphere: Has Deliberative Democracy Abandoned Mass Democracy?" *Political Theory*, 37(3) (2009), 323–50.

are rightly taught as part of the American effort to live up to our proclaimed values of equality. The hope of public educators in teaching the lessons of Martin Luther King Day and Black History Month is that, regardless of what they are taught at home, students will learn the value of equal status for all citizens.

III. An Urgent Example of Inverted Rights: The International Furor Over an Anti-Islam Video

"Innocence of Muslims" is a video made by a Coptic Christian resident of California. When a preview for the video was uploaded to YouTube, much of the Muslim world reacted with protests and in some cases riots. The video depicted the Prophet Mohammed and the Muslim people as child molesters. In a homophobic vein, too, the video indicated that widespread homosexuality was also inherent to Islam.

Reactions to the protection of the video under American free speech law have been divided on two familiar lines that separate the United States from most other nations in the world. "Prohibitionists" called for free speech to be limited in the face of blasphemous or hateful expression, while "neutralists," the most vocal defenders of free speech, have argued that the government should express no opinion about hate speech. For example, the conservative press reacted to President Obama's condemnation of the video by calling it an apology for our rights of free expression.

Lost in these two familiar reactions, however, is the third way of envisioning free speech that I have outlined and that lacks the flaws of prohibitionist bans and neutralist refusals to condemn even the worst hate speech. Value democracy would protect all viewpoints, even racist and anti-religious ones, from coercion. But in my view, the protection of free speech must be combined with a strong defense of the value of equal respect. The state should use its status as an influential speaker to defend democratic values and to argue against hateful viewpoints. It is essential that the state criticize hate speech to avoid the misperception that protection means indifference or endorsement. This kind of misperception is endemic in the inverted structure of free speech rights based on viewpoint neutrality, which protect all viewpoints.

The State Department and the President appropriately used this third approach in their public statements and advertisements run on Pakistani television. Far from being a flawed "apology," as conservative media charged, the advertisements released by the State Department suggested how we might appeal to democratic values to condemn hate speech. This approach allows American foreign policy to articulate and explain our uniquely robust free speech tradition. The policy avoids the blunt instrument of prohibiting hate speech as well as the anemic refusal to condemn it.

A viewpoint neutral right to free speech protects the freedom to express "blasphemous" viewpoints that may be seen as defaming or disparaging fundamental religious tenets. Included in this right is the freedom to assert the truth of one religion's beliefs and to disparage assertions of another religion. The anti-Muslim video is also protected by this standard. The video is meant to cause offense in its depictions of the Prophet Mohammed as a child molester. It combines homophobia and anti-Muslim animus in asserting that homosexuality is fundamental to Islam. In the United States, however, attempts to ban this work would be restricted on free speech grounds.

But the fact that the video is protected on free speech grounds has been confused throughout the world with the endorsement of the content of the video or at least the refusal to condemn it. This misperception that the state's protection of an anti-Islamic video means that it endorses the video has sparked riots throughout the world. One widely circulated clip that is typical of these denunciations uses the video to suggest that democracy is inherently disrespectful to Islam, because it allows hateful anti-Islamic speech to be expressed without punishment. An impassioned critic goes so far as to suggest that disrespect of Islam is "what democracy is all about."

The confusion of protection and approval is deeply linked to the structure of our rule of viewpoint neutrality. If the government wants to condemn a message, it often does so through a ban. For instance, the government sends the message that murder is wrong by punishing murderers. Conversely, the protection of an act is often thought to signal indifference to it. For instance, the state does not ban interracial marriage, and the lack of a ban is often interpreted as a lack of state disapproval. So it is not surprising that protection of the video might be wrongly thought to signal that the state condones or even approves of it. This example therefore serves to clearly illustrate why free speech has an "inverted structure," in that the right of free expression can protect viewpoints that are hostile to the very reasons for protecting rights. We protect Nazi speech, even though Nazism would deny free speech protection to others and even though it stands in deep opposition to the democratic value of equal respect that underlies our free speech protection. Although the conflation between protection and approval is understandable given the inverted structure of free speech, it is a mistake to think that free speech entails government indifference to hate speech.

The need to clarify that robust free speech commitments are compatible with the condemnation of hateful viewpoints is evident domestically, but it is also important abroad. When the state "speaks" in its public diplomacy, it is essential that it explains the values that underlie free speech. Confusion about the meaning of the United States' commitment to free speech has drastic consequences. Rioters in Pakistan appeared to believe that the American government was neutral toward or even approving of the hateful views expressed in the video. The nation and its representatives need to explain to the world that the United States does not protect free speech out of indifference to the content of those who abuse it. We can clarify that the United States protects all viewpoints, but that it condemns those viewpoints that violate the democratic value of equal respect.

It is essential to clarify what kinds of viewpoints are rightly subject to criticism if the United States is successfully to deliver to the international community the subtle message that it protects the right to express hateful viewpoints but criticizes their content. What precisely merits government criticism in the video? One option is to criticize the video as blasphemous. But blasphemy is the wrong frame of criticism, as it would violate the substance-based limit on democratic persuasion. The state in a liberal democracy should not take a position on which religions are false and which are true. Since blasphemy takes a side in disputes between religions, it is not a perspective to endorse. Citizens must not only be free from coercion but also free from state criticism if they assert the truth of one religion and the falsity of others.

The content of "Innocence of Muslims" is not merely about asserting the "falsity" of Islam and the truth of another religion. Instead, it is filled with hostility toward the

Muslim people as child molesters. It is analogous to the famous blood libel, myths about Jewish ritual used to slander Jews. The blood libel is anti-Semitic hate speech masked as criticism of religious practice. Similarly, "Innocence of Muslims" claims to criticize religious practice, but it actually aims to disparage the Muslim people. The video should thus be regarded as a form of hate speech against Muslims.

The United States government should articulate why our tradition of free speech and religious freedom is founded upon an ideal of equal respect. That ideal is violated by the anti-Muslim video. The government has a duty to articulate why the right to free speech is protected in the case of the video, even though it condemns the video's message. This can clarify for an international audience that the state's protection of hateful expression does not imply approval of the content of that expression. The State Department adopted this response when it aired ads in Pakistan to quell riots there. The videos show President Obama and Secretary of State Hillary Clinton giving an official defense of our free speech traditions while condemning the video. They took neither a neutralist nor a prohibitionist approach to hate speech, but a third approach: democratic persuasion. They defended free speech protection for the videos, yet made use of state speech to clarify that protection does not imply approval or indifference. Instead, they articulated that protection of the right of free speech was based on the value of equal respect. They clarified that the same values that lead us to protect hate speech can also lead us to condemn it.

With the lens of this third view of democratic persuasion, we can see the State Department ads as a principled defense of democratic values, not an apology or a pragmatic concession to the need to quell the riots. Of course the violence abroad provided an impetus for these advertisements. But rightly understood, the aim to protect and criticize hate speech should be a broader part of United States public diplomacy beyond the specific commercials run in Pakistan. Such a policy of democratic persuasion would articulate why we defend free speech, while at the same time condemning hateful expression.

IV. Conclusion

Critics of viewpoint neutral speech protections have argued that state protection of hate speech would render states incapable of expressing disapproval of hate speech. This argument has led these critics to recommend banning hate speech. But I have argued that these critics help to elucidate a distinct structure of viewpoint neutral protections: They are inverted in that they protect speech at odds with the foundational values that ground free speech in the first place.

The inverted structure of free speech therefore carries with it a duty to explain that some protected speech may be at odds with the state's own viewpoint. To make this clarification, the state should engage in democratic persuasion, condemning anti-democratic protected speech.

Nowhere is the confusion regarding the inverted structure of free speech more clear than in the case of the international reaction to "Innocence of Muslims." I have defended the State Department's condemnation of the video as a kind of democratic persuasion, necessary to explain the inverted structure of free speech rights.

20

Free Speech and "Democratic Persuasion"

A Response to Brettschneider

Larry Alexander

I. The Paradox of Liberalism

Liberalism's hallmark is its endorsement of certain basic freedoms: freedom of speech, freedom of religion, and freedom of association. Yet the content of some speech, religious doctrines, and criteria of association are inconsistent with liberalism's tenets. Speech might advocate restrictions on speech as well as the abolition of democracy, the expulsion of religious and racial groups, and so forth. So might religious doctrines. And associations might require various "illiberal" conditions for membership and might seek to advance various "illiberal" goals. I shall refer to illiberal speech, religion, and association as "illiberalism" for short.

What should be the liberal state's response to illiberalism? If it outlaws illiberalism, its credentials as a liberal state appear to be undermined. If it permits illiberalism, it licenses Robert Frost's derogatory quip that liberalism can't take its own side in an argument. Either way, liberalism appears self-contradictory and incoherent. It must either betray its principles or betray itself (and thereby betray its principles). Liberalism both appears to be possible—we've seen it done—and impossible (it can't be done).

That is, in brief, the paradox of liberalism. Elsewhere, I have diagnosed the problem as one that stems from the impossible-to-realize idea of evaluative neutrality that defines the liberal freedoms.[1] I there argued that the paradox was real and insoluble.

II. The Brettschneider Solution: Paradox Lost

Corey Brettschneider, in his contribution to this book (see chapter 19) and in his monograph, *When the State Speaks, What Should It Say? How Democracies Can Protect Expression and Promote Equality*,[2] believes he can cut the Gordian Knot of this paradox. Although his focus is on freedom of speech, his approach has obvious applications to religion and association as well. My discussion, like his, will be focused on freedom of speech. What I say about his approach in that context will, however, apply to that approach in the religion and association contexts as well.

[1] Larry Alexander, *Is There a Right of Freedom of Expression?* (New York: Cambridge University Press, 2005).

[2] Corey Brettschneider, *When the State Speaks, What Should It Say? How Democracies Can Protect Expression and Promote Equality* (Princeton, NJ: Princeton University Press, 2012).

Brettschneider's solution to the paradox is to distinguish between government coercion and government persuasion. Coercing illiberal speech by punishing it would be an illiberal government response. On the other hand, countering illiberal speech by publicly arguing for liberalism and its fundamental tenets—the free and equal citizenship of all—is perfectly consistent with liberalism. And although this argument is prominent in Brettschneider's book but not in his contribution here, there he contends that government is also permitted to refuse to subsidize illiberal speech, religions, and associations on an equal basis with speech, religions, and associations that are not illiberal. For refusals to subsidize are not coercive. So the government *can* take its own side in an argument so long as it is doing so non-coercively, as when it speaks and subsidizes on behalf of liberalism. Paradox solved!

III. Paradox Regained

Although I believe Brettschneider has made a valiant attempt at solving the paradox of liberalism, the sword he has wielded has left the knot that is the paradox intact. Indeed, Brettschneider's sword is, I believe, more dangerous to liberalism in today's world than the illiberalisms that generate the paradox.

A. Just hate speech and hate groups?

Brettschneider writes as if the major illiberal threats were hate speech and hate groups. Although he isn't clear on this point, I take Brettschneider to view the threat of hate speech to stem from the possibility that unless it is countered, enough others might be persuaded by it to eventually abandon the key values of liberalism and deny equal rights to the targets of hate speech. I do not take his principal worry to be that hate speech might offend its targets and cause them emotional upset. Although the emotional upset caused by offense is undoubtedly painful, that is not the harm that concerns Brettschneider. Plenty of speech that he would protect can cause emotional pain.

Brettschneider's examples are typically Nazis, the Klan, the producer of an anti-Muslim video, and (in his book) Bob Jones University, a small college that banned interracial dating. In all truth, the purveyors of hate that Brettschneider identifies are realistically no threat to anyone's status as a free and equal citizen. They are beyond marginal. (The only substantial group Brettschneider attacks as a hate group is the Boy Scouts because of their exclusion of gays—but not because of their exclusion of girls, or the Girl Scouts for their exclusion of boys.)

The real threats to liberalism and to the free and equal citizenship of all come not from hate speech, and surely not from the marginal characters Brettschneider identifies. The real threats are more likely the advocacy of policies that will threaten national bankruptcy or persistent high unemployment, or that force major religious groups to bend to governmental demands they oppose in conscience. Economic stagnation and decline might usher in wholesale scapegoating of certain groups. It might lead to a coup and autocracy. Think about Weimar Germany or Argentina in the 1930s. Measures opposed by religions with a significant number of devout adherents might likewise threaten to bring down liberal democracy.

Indeed, it could plausibly be argued that racist and sexist speech, Brettschneider's villains, is far less likely a threat to free and equal citizenship than the current millet regime of preferences for various groups. The latter fosters an unhealthy identity politics that balkanizes the populace and pits groups against one another in a competition over scarce benefits. My guess is that these group preferences are a far greater threat to free and equal citizenship than the tiny number of Nazis, Klansmen, and their sympathizers.

If this is a correct diagnosis of where the real threats to free and equal citizenship reside, what would Brettschneider urge the government to do—assuming, of course, that it is the opposition, not the government in power itself, that is advocating these dangerous (to liberalism) policies? Speak out against monetary and fiscal excesses? Speak out against intruding too much on religious conscience? Speak out against group preferences? Refuse to subsidize groups that advocate imprudent spending measures, measures vehemently opposed by some religions, or group preferences? Do we really want government *qua* government, as opposed to politicians and citizens, to enter these battles over policy? The outcomes of these battles, however, and not the kinds of hate speech and hate groups that Brettschneider identifies, are likely the truly consequential ones for the future of free and equal citizenship.

B. Will government be effective?

If illiberal policies have gained enough popular support to truly threaten free and equal citizenship, will the non-coercive measures Brettschneider proposes be successful in preventing the eventual success of those policies? Perhaps, though there is reason to doubt that they will. Government speech, as opposed to speech by particular members of the government, will be viewed by many as bureaucratically generated propaganda. (Imagine, if you will, government public service announcements on radio and television telling people "Don't believe the Klan; blacks should be regarded as equals." Would these persuade people who would otherwise have been persuaded by the Klan? Or would they on balance bring more attention to the Klan's message than the Klan could have garnered on its own? Often, the most effective repudiation of an idea in terms of effect on the public is for its expression to be "loudly" ignored.)

The threat to withdraw or withhold various subsidies is likely to be more effective in modifying behavior than is government speech. Brettschneider distinguishes between coercive measures, which he believes are illiberal, and refusals to subsidize, which he believes are not illiberal. I shall raise doubts about his distinction in sections III.C, III.E, and III.F of this chapter.

C. Whose liberalism?

The core of liberalism for Brettschneider, underlying the freedoms of speech, religion, and association as well as democracy, is the notion of free and equal citizenship. That notion, however, can either be regarded as a "thin" one or a "thick" one. Regarded as a "thin" notion, free and equal citizenship would be consistent with libertarianism, the welfare state, luck egalitarianism, thoroughgoing egalitarianism, perfectionist liberalism, and a number of other versions of liberalism. The "thin" notion is analogous to the Rawlsian overlapping consensus among reasonable views of the Good.

Free and equal citizenship might, however, be regarded as a thick notion, with definite implications for the choice among liberalisms. My own view, which I shall merely state but not defend here, is that thin views are philosophical cop-outs. "Free and equal," to be defensible, should have thick normative implications. And if it does, then much more speech will be illiberal than will be on a thin notion.

Moreover, if free and equal is a thick notion, but there is disagreement over *which* particular thick notion it is, then when government speaks out against illiberal speech and religion, its speech will reflect the partisan views of whoever has managed to take control of propaganda. If those who are currently in control of the government believe, say, that "free and equal" entails luck egalitarianism, they will deem advocacy of libertarianism and thoroughgoing egalitarianism to be illiberal speech. On Brettschneider's view, then, government should speak out against those views and refuse to subsidize groups that promote those views. When those with a different conception of "free and equal" ascend to power however, the tables will be turned, and the luck egalitarians will have their government subsidies withdrawn and their views publicly denounced.

One can see why Brettschneider would prefer a thin conception of free and equal citizenship, as it makes his endorsements of government counter-speech and withdrawals of subsidies more palatable.[3] Only "unreasonable" views, those outside the liberal overlapping consensus, would be the targets of governmental speech and subsidy policies. But whether "free and equal" can be given a coherent and non-arbitrary thin reading is, as I said, a matter about which I have a serious doubt.

Here is a related point. Just when does speech qualify as hate speech even on the "thin" conception of free and equal? What if someone speaks out against gays, not because he denies their equal worth, but because he believes gay *sex* is immoral? Or what if he believes gay men serving as boy scout leaders or as infantry men, being sexually attracted to persons of the same sex, will be more prone to improper or disruptive sexual liaisons than heterosexual men? If he speaks out on these subjects, has he engaged in hate speech? Or what if one urges that Muslims not be hired by the CIA, not because he denies their equal worth, but because he believes their beliefs make them security risks? Or what if one urges discrimination against blacks or women based on statistical predictions rather than bigotry? Hate speech?

D. Whose hate speech?

Even on a thin conception of free and equal citizenship, however, Brettschneider seems to lack the courage of his convictions. As I said, the principal purveyors of hate speech that he mentions are anti-black and anti-Semitic groups like the Klan and the Nazis.

---

[3] Indeed, Brettschneider makes it clear that advocacy of libertarianism is not a denial of free and equal citizenship even though it is obviously not Brettschneider's own conception of liberalism. Brettschneider, *When the State Speaks*, 36. Thus, he favors the "thin" notion of free and equal citizenship. Brettschneider, *When the State Speaks*, 14, 19–21, 53–5.

And in his book, the one example of withdrawal of a subsidy that serves as his model for a proper subsidy policy is the Internal Revenue Service's denial of tax exempt status to Bob Jones University because of its rule against interracial dating.[4]

To repeat, the Nazis, the Klan, and Bob Jones University are truly fringe groups. What is curious is why Brettschneider singles out them rather than much more significant groups. For example, he never mentions the virulent anti-white and anti-Semitic views of Black Muslims or the New Black Panthers, nor the anti-gay and misogynistic views of elements of Islam. Nor does he mention the homophobic views heard in many black churches. And while he endorses the withdrawal of the subsidies for Bob Jones University for its religiously motivated policy of racial segregation in dating, he gives a pass to the sex discrimination of the Catholic Church and the sex segregation in Orthodox Judaism.[5]

Brettschneider's arguments for not withholding subsidies and tax exempt status from the Catholic Church and Orthodox Judaism, and for not urging the government to publicly gainsay the tenets of Catholicism and Orthodox Judaism, are quite strained.[6] He distinguishes between a church's theological doctrines that have implications only for matters within the church and those that implicate statuses in the wider society. The Catholic Church's ban on women priests and opposition to gay marriage, and Orthodox Judaism's similar distinctions between men and women and straights and gays, surely spill over into public policy positions, particularly with respect to gay marriage. Moreover, Brettschneider's position regarding Catholicism and Orthodox Judaism seems flagrantly inconsistent with what he says about the Christian Legal Society (CLS), the group that lost its suit for recognition as an officially recognized student group at Hastings Law School.[7] The CLS did not deny anyone membership and only banned from leadership positions persons who had engaged in extramarital sex. (Because gay marriage was not available at the time, the rule against extramarital sex impacted gays more severely than others; but non-gays were also excluded, and gays who were chaste were not.) Brettschneider incredibly dismisses the distinction between status and conduct with the offhand remark that "such an attempted distinction between status and choice of behavior is inconsistent with the ideal of free and equal citizenship."[8] I call that remark incredible because it would imply that any organization that requires particular conduct or forbearance from particular conduct as a condition for membership, particularly if it advocates that conduct or forbearance as a public ideal, has engaged in hate speech, inimical to free and equal citizenship. Thus, if one's organization takes a stand against adulterers or polygamists, not to mention murderers and rapists, it should be publicly denounced and denied tax exempt status! (Is condemning adultery hate speech directed at adulterers because of their status? Can we not hate the sin but love the sinner?) I find it hard to believe

[4] *Bob Jones University v. United States*, 461 U.S. 574 (1983).
[5] See Brettschneider, *When the State Speaks*, 134–6.
[6] Brettschneider, *When the State Speaks*, 134–6.
[7] Brettschneider, *When the State Speaks*, 117–20. The case is *Christian Legal Society v. Martinez*, 561 U.S. 661 (2010).
[8] Brettschneider, *When the State Speaks*, 119–20.

Brettschneider really believes that condemning conduct is condemning status, but what he says about the CLS surely suggests that he does.

Nor does Brettschneider mention the satirizing of Mormonism in the Broadway musical, *The Book of Mormon*, even though I suspect he would have condemned as hate speech a similar satire of blacks or Muslims—indeed, he mentions the anti-Muslim video as an example of hate speech. There's much more than a whiff of political correctness in this. It is far more palatable to pick on the Klan, the CLS, and Bob Jones than on Catholics and Orthodox Jews, Black Panthers and Black Muslims, or successful Broadway musicals.[9]

My point here is that identifying hate speech that government *qua* government should, according to Brettschneider, publicly condemn, will likely turn out to be much more partisan a matter than Brettschneider imagines. Experience on campuses with speech codes should alert one to this danger. And the worry is only amplified by Brettschneider's remarkably selective application of his own theory.

E. What's a subsidy?

Brettschneider approves of the government's not subsidizing illiberal groups even if otherwise comparable groups are receiving government subsidies. In the *Bob Jones* case, the subsidy at issue was the tax exempt status granted to charitable and educational institutions. On Brettschneider's view, tax exempt status is government largesse and equivalent to a monetary grant. For him, treating illiberal groups unequally with other groups with respect to such largesse is perfectly acceptable and indeed commendable.

To determine whether some benefit is a subsidy, however, we need to know what the baseline is. If the baseline is that charitable and educational organizations pay taxes on the donations they receive, and the donors get no tax deductions, then Bob Jones University did suffer the withdrawal of a subsidy, as Brettschneider contends. Perhaps the proper baseline for determining subsidies, which would explain the Bob Jones outcome, is that it is the worst condition in which the government could constitutionally place the organization. If the government could deny tax exempt status and charitable deductions across the board, then the baseline for Bob Jones University is no tax exempt status. That status was a subsidy, which has now been withdrawn.

Suppose, however, that Bob Jones University needs a level of fire and police protection, the cost of which exceeds the share of its taxes that goes to pay for fire and police services. If the government provides Bob Jones with the fire and police protection it needs, is it thereby subsidizing Bob Jones? Could it then withdraw police and fire protection beyond the amount Bob Jones's taxes pay for as a withdrawal or withholding of a "subsidy"?

---

[9] Hillary Clinton, too, denounced the anti-Muslim video, but she attended, apparently enjoyed, and surely did not denounce *The Book of Mormon*. Nor did she condemn Andres Serrano's Piss Christ, featuring a crucifix immersed in the "artist's" urine, which was originally exhibited with the support of federal money. Was that "hate speech" on a par with the anti-Muslim video, and if not, why not?

My point here is only that if certain groups because of their views or practices need not be subsidized by government, we need to know when they are being subsidized. And it will not be an uncontroversial matter whether a group denied some governmental benefit or service is having a subsidy withdrawn or withheld or is instead being penalized for its illiberal views.

F. Regulatory subsidies

We might imagine that subsidies exclusively consist of monetary benefits, such as cash, services, or exemption from taxation. However, there are other forms subsidies can take. For example, in *Police Department of City of Chicago v. Mosely*,[10] the teachers' unions were exempted from a regulation banning picketing near a school in session. The Supreme Court held that the exemption unconstitutionally treated some speakers (the teachers' unions) better than others (everyone else). The Court in another contemporaneous case (*Grayned v. City of Rockford*)[11] had approved of a complete ban on demonstrations, such as picketing, near schools. So if the latter decision was correct, the unions in *Mosely* were receiving a subsidy, one that the Court thought illegitimate. For exemption from regulations that comparable others are subject to *is* a subsidy, albeit a regulatory rather than a monetary one.

It follows from this that on Brettschneider's view of *Bob Jones*, illiberal groups could be singled out for regulations that did not apply to any other groups—so long, that is, that it would have been permissible to subject everyone to such regulations. If all groups of comparable income could be taxed at a 95 percent rate, then illiberal groups could be taxed at that rate even if other comparable groups were not taxed at all. Once we know the extent of the permissible regulatory regime, we can subject illiberal groups to its full extent while regulating all other groups with a much lighter hand. For we are "subsidizing" the latter groups rather than penalizing the former.

In his book, Brettschneider attempts to allay this concern. He argues there that hate groups have a right, not just to advocate their views, but to have the resources necessary for such advocacy. If, for example, other groups are allowed to hold rallies under conditions that impose costs on the public, hate groups must also be allowed to do so.[12] I think Brettschneider is being inconsistent here. If the costs to the public are such that all groups could have been denied the right to hold rallies at the times and places in question, then the groups that are allowed to do so are receiving a regulatory subsidy, which the hate groups can, by hypothesis, be denied.

G. Is government speech coercive?

The principal axiom on which Brettschneider relies for his claim to have solved the paradox of liberalism is that government speech and government subsidies of speakers it favors do not coerce the disfavored speakers. Their speech is not banned nor penalized. It is merely subjected to governmental counterspeech and not subsidized.

---

[10] 408 U.S. 92 (1972).   [11] 408 U.S. 104 (1972).
[12] Brettschneider, *When the State Speaks*, 113–14.

Now I have already noted the difficulty of determining whether a group is being penalized or is only not being subsidized. As I said, if the proper baseline for determining what is a subsidy is the maximum scope of the government's coercive reach, then groups engaging in hate speech can be treated quite harshly without being coerced. If government could permissibly ban most demonstrations, signage, and public speeches because of non-message related concerns, then denying only hate groups these avenues for expression would only be denying them "subsidies."

Beyond the problem of defining subsidies is the reality that government counter-speech uses resources that are in part extracted coercively from those whose speech is countered. That is, government speech costs money, money forcibly extracted from taxpayers, many of whom may object to government's message. As I pointed out in my book on freedom of expression, government speech and monetary subsidies, which are paid for in part by taxpayers who object to government's messages, leave those taxpayers with fewer resources for advocating their opposing views.[13] Depending upon how much the government speaks and how much it subsidizes groups other than the illiberal groups—and this could be a substantial amount depending upon what the baseline for deeming something a "subsidy" is[14]—the resource loss for those opposing the government's message might be crippling.

Moreover, the Supreme Court has been quite tough on schemes that force some to pay for others' speech with which they disagree. In a series of cases it has held such schemes to be violations of the freedom of speech of the dissenters.[15] And it has also held violative of freedom of speech laws that penalize speech beyond a certain amount by funding opposing speech.[16]

Brettschneider might believe those cases were wrongly decided. However, even he, I suspect, would object to a government speech campaign on behalf of, say, classical liberalism, with government urging support of classical liberal candidates and subsidizing classical liberal groups but not more redistributionist liberal groups.

Of course, he will reply that government should only oppose hate groups and support a thin version of liberalism. I have already discussed that point. The point here, however, is that if Brettschneider thinks it wrong and violative of his right of free speech for government to be partisan on behalf of liberal principles that he opposes, it must be because he believes such government partisanship is akin to a penalty on those who oppose it. And members of hate groups would feel no differently about governmental opposition in the form of speech or discriminatory subsidies.

In short, it is a mistake to think that Brettschneider's speech and subsidy approach to hate groups is not coercive. It does not, it is true, send people to jail for voicing illiberal views. But it does coercively extract resources from them to support views they oppose, leaving them with fewer resources with which to advance their views.

---

[13] See Alexander, *Is There a Right of Freedom of Expression?*, 101–2.   [14] See section III.E.
[15] See, eg, *Abood v. Detroit Board of Education*, 431 U.S. 209 (1977); *Keller v. State Bar of California*, 496 U.S. 1 (1990); *Harris v. Quinn*, 134 S. Ct. 2618 (2014).
[16] See *Arizona Free Enterprise Club's Freedom Club PAC v. Bennett*, 131 S. Ct. 2806 (2011).

IV. Conclusion

So what have I shown in my criticisms of Brettschneider's views? I have not shown that government speech opposing hate groups is necessarily wrongheaded or a violation of anyone's rights. Nor have I shown that withdrawing "subsidies" from hate groups is necessarily wrongheaded or a violation of rights. All I have shown is that these policies, which are the policies Brettschneider advocates, do not escape the paradox of liberalism. They exemplify instead one side of that paradox—liberalism acting illiberally towards illiberal groups. Because the paradox is inescapable, however, the policies Brettschneider advocates cannot be faulted for not escaping it.

To say that these policies are not necessarily wrongheaded is not to say that they are wise. Indeed, they may be quite unwise, even dangerous. As I argued, "thin" versions of liberalism are philosophically unsatisfying. Because of that, there will be an everpresent temptation for those in power to translate the thin values of liberty and equality into the thick versions of liberalism they happen to favor. And a likely, if not strictly necessary, consequence of enforcing a thick version of liberalism will be a tendency to see those who oppose that thick version on behalf of a different thick version as themselves illiberal hate groups. Thin liberalism easily evolves into thick, and thick liberalism easily evolves into illiberalism.

There is plenty of evidence that this is not armchair hysteria. Colleges have labeled those opposing affirmative action as racists and in some cases subjected them to hate speech prosecutions. The same is true of mandated diversity sensitivity training. Indeed, Brettschneider himself unwittingly exposes this tendency in both his selectivity about whom to label as hate groups and in his comments about the CLS. It is just far too easy for those in power to convince themselves that those who oppose their policies are, despite their rhetoric, really illiberal haters.

Liberalism, and its central liberties of freedom of expression, religion, and association, is a theoretical contradiction. Its successes are instead pragmatic ones. And from my armchair, I have more pragmatic worries about Brettschneider's prescriptions than about the problems for which he offers them.

21

Freedom of Religion in a Secular World

Lorenzo Zucca

I. Introduction

In February 313, now 1,700 years ago, the Emperor Constantine signed the edict of Milan, that put an end to the persecution of Christians in the Empire. It was the first official proclamation of freedom of religion. To be more precise, since Constantine was himself Christian, and actively promoted the respect of the Christian religion in the Empire, it came to be regarded as the union between power and religion. Religion, that is Christian religion, was not only free in the Empire but came to dominate the whole moral and political space. One paradoxical effect was the denial of religious freedom for dissenters. This paved the way for religious schisms, and in fact promoted brutal confrontations between Christians. Many Christians persecuted by their fellow brothers left Europe to establish a polity with a greater freedom for differing religious views. Those who remained decided to gradually distance themselves from an understanding of religion too deeply involved in politics. The modern secular state was born out of the necessity of creating a distance between power and religion. The obvious risk that religious people run is to be persecuted again by the secular state. The right to freedom of religion is a local response against the possibility of new persecution.

The human right to freedom of religion is interpreted in radically different ways in the West. Some insist that religious people should be protected from external interferences, other insist that non-religious people should be protected from the interference of religion in public affairs. Perhaps the problem is that it is impossible to accurately define the human right to freedom of religion (HRFR). The human right to freedom of religion features in most international human rights documents. The Universal Declaration of Human Rights (UDHR), for example, encapsulates it in Article 18. The question here is not whether the HRFR is recognized as such, but rather what its status is in an international system of human rights.

The HRFR, more importantly, is not equally recognized in western secular states. Some constitutions give it a prominent place (the United States), others a very limited position: the French Declaration of the Rights of Man and of the Citizen (DRMC), for example, contains a very limited recognition.[1] The first amendment of the American Constitution gives a much more generous place to freedom of religion and attaches to

---

[1] Article X: 'No one shall be disquieted on account of his opinions, including his religious views, provided their manifestation does not disturb the public order established by law.'

Article XI: 'The free communication of ideas and opinions is one of the most precious of the rights of man. Every citizen may, accordingly, speak, write, and print with freedom, but shall be responsible for such abuses of this freedom as shall be defined by law.'

it a very articulated protection.[2] While the American Bill of Rights carves out a clear place for religion in the constitution, the French Declaration laconically acknowledges that opinions, even religious ones, benefit from protection against prosecution. And it is only by way of analogy that we can infer that freedom of expression of thought and opinion also covers religious people. It is important to stress that this freedom of opinion is very important but in no way amounts to an independent HRFR.

How is it possible, or indeed is it possible, to distill from those disparate understandings of freedom of religion one that is common for everyone at the international level? The question is not merely theoretical, but it is of very great practical significance since a common understanding of the HRFR could be the basis for intervention in domestic affairs of national sovereign states in case of major violations at least. However, I find it difficult to pin down a sufficiently precise meaning of the HRFR; and as a consequence my suggestion is that the HRFR has a very limited role to play at the international level.

There are several reasons for this. To begin with the nature of freedom of religion depends heavily on historical contingencies at the domestic level (section II). Moreover, the practice of freedom of religion shows that the scope and strength of the right can only be determined in relation to the local understanding of religion and what it means to be free for a religion. As a result, supranational institutions adjudicate on these issues by displaying a great deference to national institutions that are better positioned to evaluate local practices (section III). One has to add to that that at the international level, lacking an institutional system that can resolve disputes, the role of human rights in general, and that of the HRFR more specifically, is limited and has to take into account respect for national sovereignty, which is very important in practice. The way in which national sovereignty is limited depends on the way religious freedom is conceived, but it might be impossible to conceive of it at the international level without imposing a unilateral understanding of what religion amounts to (section IV). It is therefore concluded that even if the HRFR is emphatically declared at the international level, it has a very limited status in practice.

II. The Nature of Freedom of Religion

Few dispute the status of freedom of speech, and everyone can see why it is important to let everyone express herself in a democracy, even if we don't know exactly where the protection of free speech ends. With religion things are different because people disagree as to whether religion deserves special protection, and nobody agrees on what exactly religion covers. In other words the questions *'why that freedom?'* and *'freedom of what?'* remain highly contested. To those questions one can add *'freedom for whom?'* Is it freedom for religious people in general or is it freedom of religion for neglected minorities? The fourth question is *'what kind of freedom?'*: is it freedom

---

[2] 'Congress shall make no law respecting an establishment of religion, or prohibiting the free exercise thereof; or abridging the freedom of speech, or of the press; or the right of the people peaceably to assemble, and to petition the Government for a redress of grievances.'

from religion—to protect the state from interference, or is it freedom for religion—to help religion maintain a place and role within society?

Theories of freedom of religion attempt to answer all those questions. Those theories attempt to give an account of the status of freedom of religion in a state.[3] The answers to those questions depend on highly contingent factors such as the outlook of the society and the precise constitutional history of a country. It is difficult to distill from local experiences a theory of freedom of religion that could suit the international community at large. Philosophical sophistication and abstraction do not cut much ice in this area since freedom of religion poses fundamental questions that are fraught with contingent assumptions concerning the nature of religion and the cognitive realm of theology. In this section I will explore to what extent freedom of religion is dependent on contingent factors which put into doubt the possibility of a human right to freedom of religion at the international level.

A. Society

The status of freedom of religion in a state closely depends on the way in which religion is perceived and practiced in the relevant society. The American and French human rights movements were coming from deeply different societies from a religious viewpoint. American pilgrims were fleeing Europe because of its religious persecutions. There was there a germ of a plural religious society. France was trying to break from the ties of the *Ancien Regime*, which had entrenched one religion as part of its own aristocracy. Thus in a religious society, the special status of freedom of religion is simply assumed, whereas it is deeply contested in a society that wants to break free from the domination of one religion. In the United States, freedom of religion is paramount, while it is at best secondary in France.

One thing is clear, though. Freedom of religion is not a central preoccupation of theocratic regimes. It was not a central preoccupation for absolutist France nor for Britain in the seventeenth century. When the state supports one religion, it also tries to demote other religions; at best other religions will be tolerated, at worst they will be banned. And it is not a central preoccupation of modern theocracies such as Iran. So for example, the Iranian Constitution entrenches immutable establishment of Islam (Article 12),[4] and only recognizes a handful of other religions as official minorities who have a qualified freedom to perform their rites and ceremonies (Article 13).[5] Interestingly, the Iranian Constitution recognizes that other non-Muslims are owed respect for their human rights (Article 14).[6] But if you read Articles 13 and 14 together,

---

[3] C. Laborde, 'Equal Liberty, Non-establishment and Religious Freedom,' *Legal Theory* 20(1), March 2014: 52–77.
[4] Article 12: 'The official religion of Iran is Islam and the Twelver Ja'fari school [in usual al-Din and fiqh], and this principle will remain eternally immutable....'
[5] Article 13: 'Zoroastrian, Jewish, and Christian Iranians are the only recognized religious minorities, who, within the limits of the law, are free to perform their religious rites and ceremonies, and to act according to their own canon in matters of personal affairs and religious education.'
[6] Article 14: 'In accordance with the sacred verse; ('God does not forbid you to deal kindly and justly with those who have not fought against you because of your religion and who have not expelled you from your homes' [60:8]), the government of the Islamic Republic of Iran and all Muslims are duty-bound to

you can conclude that only few official religious minorities have a qualified freedom of religion. Other non-Muslims may see their human rights respected, but amongst those human rights, we have to infer that the HRFR has at best a very limited place.

Freedom of religion has, for a long time, been a Euro–Atlantic preoccupation; there is however a crucial difference between Europe and the United States: in Europe, the presence of religion in a society has traditionally being organized along the lines drawn by the treaty of Westphalia, which engineered religiously homogeneous societies with a dominant religion. Where one religion was dominant, all the others were at best tolerated. This artificial device led to a slow but progressive secularization of societies, which became disaffected from the one dominant religion. Freedom of religion was just a dormant concern from the past, which was rekindled only very recently because of the presence of new religious minorities. In the United States, the society aspires to be religiously plural, albeit not perfectly so. The point of religious freedom is to protect and promote a plurality of religious faiths in the society, while keeping the state free from the interference of any one religion in particular.

It is only recently that Europe has had to reconsider the status of freedom of religion, precisely because of major social changes due to massive immigration. Thus, each European state has had to grapple with various claims from diverse minorities from North Africa, South America, the Middle East, and Asia. When minorities do not integrate into the mainstream society, they are highly motivated to use religious identity as an explanation of diversity. Freedom of religion thus becomes the individual right through which religious minorities claim autonomy from what they perceive as a highly secularized mainstream society.

Despite the differences between the American and the European models, what is clear is that freedom of religion is relevant when the society displays great religious plurality. In these pluralistic societies, the status of freedom of religion is assumed to be important rather than being fully justified. There is no real attempt to answer the four questions I sketched earlier (freedom of what/why that freedom/freedom for whom/what kind of freedom), since answers to those questions depend on contingent societal factors and on constitutional practice.

B. Religious freedom and constitutional assumptions

The American constitutional experiment is the first attempt to separate religion from politics, not with the intent of removing religion from society, but on the contrary with the intent of protecting freedom of conscience for every individual.[7] In contrast with that project, France has attempted to separate religion from politics in order to free the whole society from religious influence in the public sphere.[8] Thus, we have two

---

treat non-Muslims in conformity with ethical norms and the principles of Islamic justice and equity, and to respect their human rights. This principle applies to all who refrain from engaging in conspiracy or activity against Islam and the Islamic Republic of Iran.'

[7] M. Nussbaum, *Liberty of Conscience—In Defense of America's Tradition of Religious Equality* (Basic Books, 2008).

[8] C. Laborde, *Critical Republicanism—The Hijab Controversy and Political Philosophy* (Oxford University Press, 2008).

different models of separation: one is bilateral separation with the intent of preserving religion from the corruption of politics (the United States). The other is unilateral, with the intent of preserving the state from the corruption of religion (France). Within the first model, freedom of religion is dominant. Within the second model, freedom of religion is residual. The way in which freedom of religion is conceived depends on the complex relation between societies and politics on one hand, and church and state on the other.

The separation between state and church is chiefly an historical doctrine but one which happens to have major consequences. First of all, the idea of separation implies the existence of two separate cognitive domains working independently one from the other. To recognize the existence of an independent domain is tantamount to acknowledging that that domain is important and worthy of special consideration. Moreover, the religious domain determines its own identity and scope. So here's a paradoxical consequence of any form of separation: the state does not know the religious reasons, but respects them as such, refraining from interference.[9]

Constitutional theories of freedom of religion do not address our four questions directly, but only do so implicitly.[10] To begin with, the mere fact of mentioning freedom of religion in a constitutional text assumes that freedom of religion is special and important—in US constitutional history not only is freedom of religion mentioned but it is in the first amendment, supporting the belief that it is amongst the most important freedoms. Unfortunately, the text does not explain why religion deserves special protection by comparison to other human activities. Moreover, the text does not say what amounts to religion, so the only way of working that out is by looking at constitutional practice, in particular adjudication. This point corroborates the idea that freedom of religion is highly dependent on contingent factors and is quite difficult to export. Finally, the way in which constitutional practice works is coherentist rather than critical. This means that constitutional actors and theorists try to make sense of past decisions with an eye to preserving and explaining the values that constitute society from the beginning and that are typically declared in constitutions. So the mere fact that freedom of religion features in the constitutional text is a reason strong enough to consider it as special and important from the constitutional viewpoint.

Thus in practice, judges often treat freedom of religion in a special way without knowing what religion is about and without asking why it is special.[11] If you show that your claim is religious, then you have a pro tanto reason to have your claim protected. The main way to establish what amounts to a religious claim as opposed to any other claim is by way of analogy with mainstream conceptions of religion within a society. Freedom of religion is especially important but its nature cannot be investigated.

Some constitutional theories of freedom of religion attempt to challenge the paradigm of freedom of religion as an individual human right that provides pro tanto reasons to defeat governmental policies.[12] They argue instead that freedom of religion

---

[9] See R. Audi, *Democratic Authority and the Separation of Church and State* (Oxford University Press, 2011).

[10] C. Eisgruber and L. Sager, *Religious Freedom and the Constitution* (Harvard University Press, 2007).

[11] Laborde, 'Equal Liberty, Non-establishment and Religious Freedom'.

[12] Eisgruber and Sager, *Religious Freedom and the Constitution*.

should be understood as an equal liberty of conscience, that is to say that whoever has a strong enough claim of conscience—be they religious or non-religious people—should have a defense against discrimination on the basis of their beliefs. In this case you don't have to show that your claim is religious, but that your claim is deep enough or is vulnerable.[13] The problem with these constitutional theories is that they merely displace the burden of assumptions concerning the nature and role of religion.[14] Indeed, practice shows that there is an assumption that religious people have deep and vulnerable claims, whereas non-religious people will have to show why that is the case.

Constitutional theories deal, implicitly or explicitly, with two separate and inescapable queries: first, is religion special? Second, what kind of treatment does it deserve? There is no answer to the first question; it is simply assumed that freedom of religion is in some way special since it is mentioned in most constitutions. This of course informs its treatment, which amounts at times to qualified privilege and at others to qualified burden.

C. The ontology and epistemology of religion

Philosophical explanations of freedom of religion seem to suffer from the same problem as constitutional theories. They are not capable of distilling one definition of religion that explains in non-religious terms the special importance of religion for the sake of its protection. Indeed many believe that we ought not delve into the trap of defining religion since a definition could always be under- or over-inclusive. Many attempts have been made but with very limited success: it is in fact common to suggest that no definition is possible.[15] In fact most lawyers and philosophers agree that a definition of religion is a thankless exercise. Instead they propose criteria or paradigmatic cases to use in analogical fashion. By doing this, they also implicitly accept that religion should be apprehended on a case-by-case basis and with an eye to the local contingencies that shape practice.

Brian Leiter is nearly unique in his effort at providing a simple straightforward definition of religion that aims to capture any possible religious phenomena. The ambition is to provide a universally valid, and simple, definition of religion.[16] Leiter offers two elements, which he regards as central: categoricity of belief and insulation from evidence.[17] Categoricity refers to the stringency of beliefs in guiding behavior. Insulation from evidence addresses the way in which religion relates to the knowledge of the world that we have on the basis of common sense or science. Religion, being based on faith, is not responsive to reason, Leiter argues, and this insulates religion from the requirement of evidential proofs.

---

[13] The claim is deep when it is part of a worldview that the individual follows in a consistent way. It is vulnerable when it is held by minorities that do not have an easy access to mainstream society.

[14] Laborde, 'Equal Liberty, Non-establishment and Religious Freedom'.

[15] W.F. Sullivan, *The Impossibility of Religious Freedom* (Princeton University Press, 2007).

[16] B. Leiter, *Why Tolerate Religion?* (Princeton University Press, 2012). This began as a reply to Martha Nussbaum's avowedly local, *Liberty of Conscience*.

[17] Leiter, *Why Tolerate Religion?*, 27.

There is no space here to address this view critically, but a few comments are in order. Leiter assesses religion from the viewpoint of an exclusively naturalistic world-view, which presupposes a conflict between science and religion. To assess the cogency of this conflict one would have to provide an accurate account of the naturalistic worldview,[18] that is a view according to which the world described by scientific laws is all there is to know. This assumption creates a fundamental problem for Leiter's definition as it presents faith as necessarily fallible, as if there was scientific evidence to prove that claim. In Leiter's account, faith is the source of unwarranted beliefs, as they cannot be supported by scientific evidence, indeed they are insulated from it. But this assumes too much, namely that all the beliefs we hold on the basis of faith are incompatible with scientific evidence. This cannot be true, in particular in relation to moral beliefs that are inherited from religious convictions. It also assumes wrongly that those religious beliefs that are incompatible with scientific evidence cannot be revised or put aside. But again people of faith and religious institutions are prepared, albeit at times reluctantly, to change their beliefs on the strength of contrary scientific evidence.

I also note that Leiter's definition is consistent with the idea of separation between theology and other domains of knowledge. In other words, Leiter's definition preserves an epistemic integrity to the domain of religion, by isolating faith as the source of religious knowledge. Epistemic integrity postulates a distinction between public reason and religious reason.[19] Integrity thus conceived cuts both ways. On the one hand, it excludes religion from participation in the discussion of public policies. On the other, it recognizes the dignity of religious reasons as being different in nature from public reasons.

Since religious reasons are sovereign in their domain according to this perspective, it follows that philosophy has a very limited role to play in providing a definition of a practice that defines itself. Moreover, the question: 'what is religion?' for the purpose of determining the right-holders and the content of the right is an altogether different question from 'what is speech?' Secular institutions are notoriously ill equipped to answer the former question. Partly this is because secular institutions do not have the theological training required to examine the problem. Partly it is because secular law encapsulates an understanding of evidence that is not compatible with the proofs that religious people may put forward in order to establish the genuineness of their beliefs. On top of all that the question: 'what is religion?' can be broken down into many difficult quandaries. The broadest underlying problem concerns the kind of object that religion is, that is its nature, or ontology, so to speak.

But even assuming that domestic secular institutions can come up with a working definition of religion so as to guarantee respect for freedom of religion, that definition is based on local contingencies that militate against the possibility of a universal definition of religion. These brief considerations highlight the puzzles that one necessarily

---

[18] A. Plantinga, *Where the Conflict Really Lies—Science, Religion, and Naturalism* (Oxford University Press, 2012. Plantinga, eg, shows that the conflict as presented by holders of a naturalistic worldview is only apparent and not real, after careful examination.

[19] Laborde, 'Equal Liberty, Non-establishment and Religious Freedom'.

faces when trying to pin down the meaning of the HRFR in Western states. This is not to mention the difficulties related to non-Western states, difficulties that are even greater.

When a policy maker has to grapple with problems of religious freedom, she is bound to face two extraordinarily complicated problems:

(1) What is the nature of the right to freedom of religion?

(2) How does one know what counts as religion across the world if one begins with one's own local conception of religion?

The practice of the human right to freedom of religion highlights that each legal political system has in-built assumptions that depend on historical contingencies. Moreover, as will be seen in the next section, that is a reason for supranational and international institutions to display a great degree of caution in matters that have to do with the domestic treatment of freedom of religion.

III. The Practice of Freedom of Religion

What emerges so far is that freedom of religion is characterized by a very strong local contingency. This is a central consideration when we attempt to pin down the meaning of the international human right to freedom of religion. The practice of freedom of religion also shows that domestic institutions are reluctant to enter into theological debates as to the nature of religion, for obvious reasons. They prefer instead to use sociological and anthropological criteria to address the question.[20] The practice of freedom of religion also clearly shows that supranational and international judges adopt a very deferential stance toward domestic religious litigations.

Freedom of religion is not an absolute right at the national level, even when it has pride of place like in the US Constitution. Even so, its treatment in practice displays a number of legal problems with which policy makers and the judiciary are confronted. In general, the legal treatment of freedom of religion presents three distinct puzzles that contribute to its limitation in practice. One has to determine the scope, the strength, and the way to deal with conflicts between freedom of religion and other rights.

A. Scope

To determine the scope of protection afforded by a human right one has to engage in several different steps. First, one has to translate the broad statement of principle into deontic modalities (prohibitions/permissions/obligations).[21] So, for example, the US Constitution prohibits on the one hand the making of laws that establish one religion, and on the other the making of laws prohibiting the free exercise of one's own religion (here the prohibition of a prohibition must be read as a broad permission).

Secondly, one has to establish the correlative duty imposed on other people by virtue of the existence of a right.[22] At the constitutional level, generally speaking a liberty

---

[20] *R (on the application of E) v. Governing Body of JFS and the Admissions Appeal Panel of JFS.*

[21] G.H. von Wright, 'Deontic Logic', *Mind*, New Series, 60(237) (January 1951): 1–15.

[22] W.N. Hohfeld, *Fundamental Legal Conceptions* (Aldershot, 2001).

protected by claim rights is correlated with the absence of a right on the part of other persons. This means very blandly that if I have a right to exercise my religion in the private sphere, nobody has a right to curtail my right by violating my private space. Surely the HRFR also implies a more general immunity on the part of the right-holder which corresponds with a disability on the part of the state. For example, the American legislator is prime duty-bearer of the HRFR, and this entails a constitutional disability to make laws that prohibit free exercise of religion.

Thirdly, and much more controversially, in order to decide the actual scope of pro-hibitions and the extent to which the legislator is disabled one has to work out what kind of beliefs and behaviours are to be classified as religious. Looking at both the US and French texts, we can readily see that there is great difference as to the religiously inspired behavior that is covered by constitutional articles. In the United States, free exercise forms the core of the protection, while in France what is protected is religious belief. If we compare the two, there is a striking difference between protection of reli-gious thought and protection of acts based on religious thinking. So the distinction between speech and act is an important dividing line between the regime of protec-tion in America and in France.

Another possible dividing line, perhaps even more important, is between free-dom of religion understood as an individual or as a group right. The idea of free exer-cise has been interpreted as leaning towards the protection of individual conscience rather than the protection of religious groups. In fact, on this point it is clear that the American state attempts to avoid supporting any religious group as far as possible, even if they obviously have the freedom to gather together to celebrate religious ritu-als. But the basis of religious assembly can still be found in the individual act of con-science rather than being derivative from a special status of religious organizations. Thus in the United States, religious conscience is the basic element for the recognition and protection of some religious beliefs and acts.

In revolutionary France, the text only mentions religious opinions. In both cases, there seems to be an accent on the individual experience but we have to draw an important distinction between conscience on one side, and thought and opinion on the other. Conscience clearly covers both belief and action, while opin-ions can hardly be stretched to cover actions. There is a big difference between conscience and thought; the former functions like a sword, whereas thought (or opinion) is more of a shield. In other words, once the existence of religious claims of conscience can be established it seems as if an exemption from ordi-nary law might be requested. In the case of religious opinion, the only concern seems to create a private space shielded from the interference of ordinary law, but in no way does religious opinion seem to be entitled to claim an exemption from ordinary law.

It is only with more recent human rights treaties that the scope of the right to free-dom of religion covers a collective aspect. In particular the European Convention of Human Rights (ECHR), Article 9 states:

1. Everyone has the right to freedom of thought, conscience *and religion*; this right includes freedom to change his religion or belief and freedom, either alone or in

community with others and in public or private to manifest his religion or belief, in worship, teaching, practice and observance [emphasis added].

The European formulation goes well beyond conscience and thought and spans from that individual dimension to a much more collective one. It also moves beyond the private sphere to cover the public aspect of religion.

B. Strength

In determining the strength of the HRFR, one has to compare the strength of other rights *in abstracto*; it is also necessary to single out the importance of religious practices within a society; and finally one has to compare the freedom of different religious groups between themselves.

Some American commentators see a paradoxical treatment of religion.[23] Free exercise receives special protection, and thus religious conscience has special force in comparison to other claims of conscience, whereas establishment is the object of special burdens, and therefore religion as a collective enterprise has lesser strength than other collective activities. In France, according to the DRMC, religious opinions are protected at the same level as other opinions, but certainly not more so. So in this sense, religious opinions receive equal treatment. As far as religious groups are concerned, France allows itself the possibility to interfere with them whenever it deems it suitable. In both cases we talk about separation between church and state, but in fact in America it is bilateral separation while in France it is unilateral separation.

The ECHR admits of systems of separation and establishment, so the strength of the interest protected by freedom of religion should be evaluated *in different contexts*. But it is important to note one thing at the outset: if one religion is established *de jure* then it goes without saying that there is a presumption of more favorable treatment of that religion over others. Establishment does not promote equality between religions, and can easily undermine the freedom of all other religions.

So another interesting problem is the following: when a state establishes one religion, it may very well undermine the freedom of other religions. *Kokkinakis*, the first case to reach the Strasbourg court, is precisely about asserting the freedom of religion of Jehovah's witnesses in Greece, where the Orthodox Church is constitutionally established and, in this specific case, one side effect of that establishment is a prohibition on proselytism resulting in a criminal offence.[24]

De jure establishment, however, does not automatically mean that only one religion enjoys the benefit of constitutional protection. In the United Kingdom, *de jure* establishment goes hand in hand with a constant concern to offer equal benefits to a vast array of other religions.[25] Conversely, *de jure* separation does not prevent altogether the possibility of *de facto* establishment or at least a strict collaboration

---

[23] Eisgruber and Sager, *Religious Freedom and the Constitution*.

[24] *Kokkinakis v. Greece*, Application No. 14307/88, Judgement of 25 May 1993.

[25] J. Rivers, *The Law of Organized Religion. Between Establishment and Secularism* (Oxford University Press, 2010).

between state and one church, as is the case in Italy between the state and the Vatican. This means that one religion enjoys very special benefits, while other may be treated comparatively much less favorably. For example, freedom of religion for Muslims in Italy does not meet with great legal protection nor with public enthusiasm, which results in a series of administrative burdens to prevent them from building religious places of worship.[26]

An important concern one faces when determining the strength of the interest protected by religious freedom is the issue of whether or not we are talking about equal freedom for all religions or whether one religion is treated better than others.[27] The main concern, though, is about the strength of the interest of religious freedom within a system of plural rights. Religious freedom in the United States seems at first glance a central concern of the Constitution since it is placed at the very front of the bill of rights and is the object of an elaborated set of norms. In the French DRMC, there is no article devoted to religious freedom and religion is only mentioned in passing so it is clear that its status, and the strength of the interest resulting from it, is much less important.

In the ECHR, freedom of religion has an independent place amongst derogable rights. So we know that other rights such as freedom from torture, and the right to life have a greater strength at least insofar that they are to be considered non-derogable, that is to say there is no interest that can prevail over them. *A contrario*, it is clear that there may be a number of interests that can prevail over the interest protected by freedom of religion and paragraph 2 of Article 9 ECHR is there to confirm this.

> 2. Freedom to manifest one's religion or beliefs shall be subject only to such limitations as are prescribed by law and are necessary in a democratic society in the interests of public safety, for the protection of public order, health or morals, or for the protection of the rights and freedoms of others.

Freedom of religion as embedded in the ECHR has a very broad scope, since it covers thought, conscience, and religion. Thus, it covers both individual and collective beliefs and behavior based on those beliefs. However, the strength of the right is limited and limitable on the ground of paragraph 2 of the same Article 9. The strength of the interest protected by freedom of religion can be limited on the basis of interests of public safety, for the protection of public order, health or morals, and finally—last but not least—for the protection of the rights and freedom of others. Also it is important to note at this stage that scope and strength are linked in a relationship of inverse proportionality: the wider the scope of protection, the lesser the strength, and vice versa. If the scope was very narrow, then one could always argue that it was a matter of preserving the very core of the right. See Table 21.1.

---

[26] The European Court of Human Rights is set to hear the Swiss case on the administrative prohibition to build minarets in the near future.

[27] Eisgruber and Sager, *Religious Freedom and the Constitution*.

Table 21.1 Summary of various possible combinations showing the protean nature of freedom of religion

Strength/scope	Individual	Collective
High strength	Conscience (eg US)	Group Right (ECHR, Art 9, para 1)
Low strength	Thought (DRMC (France))	Group Right with limitations (ECHR, Art 9, para 2)

C. Conflicts

The most difficult cases of limitations are those of conflicts between the right to freedom of religion and other rights. As pointed out earlier, and as a matter of law, freedom of religion can be limited in order to guarantee the promotion and protection of other rights. Examples of such conflicts are multiple, but we cannot discuss them all. Here we can only sketch the contours of the problem.

Freedom of religion can conflict with other freedoms, such as for example freedom of expression. It may be argued that in plural democratic societies, people are free to express negative judgments about religious practices, including judgments that are offensive. After all, if protected expression was only positive expression, then there wouldn't be any need to proclaim such freedom. But it can also be argued that offensive opinion concerning religious minorities can undermine the respect of the whole community towards religious minorities as well as undermining the status of that minority within a wider society. In other words, offensive speech can easily polarize societies and create huge social tension within and outside the national territory. A common example of this scenario is the Muhammad cartoon saga.

This issue is, I think, all the more exacerbated if we look at the European Court of Human Rights' *Otto Preminger* case, where the artistic expression of a movie director was limited on the ground that the movie could offend the religious majority in the Tyrol region.[28] The Court reasoned that the interference with the applicant association's freedom of expression was proscribed by law but the seizure and forfeiture of the film were aimed at 'the protection of the rights of others', namely the right to respect for one's religious feelings, and at ensuring religious peace. The Court assessed the conflicting interests of the exercise of two fundamental freedoms guaranteed under the Convention and concluded that the Austrian authorities had not overstepped their margin of discretion. It is not clear whether the same protection would be afforded to religious feelings of a minority as in the case of Mohammed cartoons.

In any event, what matters here is to highlight that we have two specific problems: first, one has to determine whether the right to respect for one's religious feelings is within the scope of freedom of religion. Secondly, whether that right is strong enough to prevail over freedom of expression. Both questions are determined by the judge who takes the conflict of rights as an instance of a very hard case which justifies

---

[28] *Otto-Preminger-Institut v. Austria* (13470/87) [1994] ECHR 26 (20 September 1994).

an increased power to decide the case on the basis of her own assumptions about the nature and value of religion.

Another set of conflicts concerns more closely the very nature of freedom of religion. At issue is whether religion, as an established societal practice of institutions, can discriminate against some categories of people that are normally protected against discrimination. The abstract conflict is between equality and liberty.

This conflict is particularly difficult as it may put a great pressure on religions to adapt to societal standards that religion is desperately trying to resist. The conflict takes place in different settings, however the workplace is a perfect example of a domain where the fight against discrimination has been strong recently, at least in Europe.[29] So if religion enters the workplace, the tension between non-discrimination and liberty of religion is more visible.

There are in fact various tensions. The employer may be secular, and employees may wish to wear religious symbols;[30] in this case the discrimination is against religious people. The employer may also be the state or a public authority, and the employee may be in a situation in which she refuses to carry out basic public functions that are at odds with some religious precepts that are discriminatory.[31] Or the employer may be religious and dismiss the employee who does not meet some religious standards.[32] Assuming that churches can employ whomever they want, is it possible to fire people who don't meet some religious precepts that would normally be seen as discriminatory?

In other words, when religion engages in a secular employment contract, does that make the religious workplace free from the constraints applicable to the non-religious workplace? Again we have a problem of scope: to what extent does freedom of religion color the activities in which religion engages? And a problem of strength: to what extent does the special protection of freedom of religion prevail over other constitutionally entrenched interests such as non-discrimination? The answers to these questions are not written in stone, and depend heavily on very contingent and local understandings of the nature and value of religion in a discrete society. This simple fact must caution us against the temptation of acting abroad in the name of our own contingent and local convictions about the human right to freedom of religion, and also explains the cautious attitude of supranational courts that display a great deference when it comes to freedom of religion.

---

[29] In the US, the doctrine of ministerial exception bars the possibility of applying anti-discrimination laws.

[30] The case of Eweida and Chaplin (*Eweida and Others v. the United Kingdom* Application no. 59842/10, 15 January 2013) deals with the restriction on wearing Christian crosses in the working environment.

[31] The case of Ladele (grouped with Eweida and others) deals with the dismissal of Ladele following her refusal to register civil unions for homosexual people.

[32] Several cases have reached the European Court of Human Rights in the last five years. Eg, *Lombardi Vallauri*, Application No. 39128/05 (20 October 2009), which concerned a professor of legal philosophy whose employment contract at the Catholic University of Milan was terminated on the ground that the Congregation of Catholic Education refused its approval after the professor had been employed there for 20 years.

D. Margin of appreciation

The upshot of the previous discussion is that international institutions that adjudicate on matters of religious freedom face considerable problems that derive from the contingent and local nature of that freedom. It is clear that domestic institutions are seen as being better positioned to evaluate the attitude that the state should take vis-a-vis religion. Even when there is an established regional system of protection of human rights, the human right to freedom of religion seems to be one of the most controversial issues. European states accept interference to a limited extent. The European Court of Human Rights began to make use of Article 9 only in 1993, that is, in the last two decades. All other rights have been adjudicated upon since the very creation of the Court. It can be argued that the Court is attempting to set up a marketplace of religions by countering obvious obstacles to religious pluralism, as might have been the case in *Kokkinakis* (1993) where the Greek Constitution prohibited any form of proselytism. Strasbourg intervened to lift the ban in order for other religions not to be restricted in their freedom.

The point of the marketplace of religion is to lessen the monopolistic hegemony of one religion, especially when domination is exercised in a coercive way, ie, through criminalization. But it certainly does not involve the promotion of equal liberty in the sense of protecting all religions at the same level. To do so, it would have to engineer a profound change of society, which cannot possibly be done through law. The example of Turkey shows that even when the constitution attempts to engineer a secular change, a religious backlash is always possible.

The latest decision seems to recognize a great freedom on the part of the state to decide to what extent its identity is dependent on religious symbols.[33] If anything the European Court of Human Rights has taken a very deferential stance towards national sovereignty: the core principle is that the national state is sovereign when it comes to the definition of its symbols of identity. The human right to freedom of religion is in practice very limited at the supranational level. Given this very clear stance, it is hard to square this position with the idea of having a very aggressive foreign policy in the name of freedom of religion. If that was not the case, it would amount to another double standard according to which the European nations can see their sovereignty respected while non-European nations can be the object of intrusive interventions in the moralizing name of the human right to freedom of religion.

IV. The Status of the Human Right to Freedom of Religion

We have learned so far that: (1) the definition of the HRFR is deeply local and contingent, and (2) international judicial institutions display deference on matters of freedom of religion at best and at worst there is no centralized institution that has the power to interpret that right so as to apply it in the international context. Moreover,

---

[33] Grand Chamber *Lautsi v Italy*, Application no. 30814/06.

any reason for intervention grounded on the HRFR must be weighed against the interest of any state to the respect of its national sovereignty. In light of this we can try to
make sense of the fact that the HRFR is the object of many international declarations,
but in practice makes very little difference. In other words, its status amongst other
human rights is limited as a matter of practice.

A. Freedom of religion as an international human right

Freedom of religion features prominently in international documents. The UDHR
makes it one of the core rights in Article 18: 'Everyone has the right to freedom of
thought, conscience and religion; this right includes freedom to change his religion or
belief, and freedom, either alone or in community with others and in public or private,
to manifest his religion or belief in teaching, practice, worship and observance.' The
UDHR is followed by a plethora of international documents that deal with freedom
of religion. The International Covenant on Civil and Political Rights 1966 (ICCPR)
reiterates the same formula used in the UDHR and adds other dispositions that cover
prohibition against discrimination on religious grounds and the right of parents to
control the religious education of their children. The Covenant also offers a catch-all
definition of freedom of religion that includes theistic and non-theistic religions, and
it is obviously largely over-inclusive since any form of conviction can pass muster.

Perhaps the most lavish text on freedom of religion is the United Nations
Declaration on the Elimination of all Forms of Intolerance and of Discrimination
Based on Religion or Belief 1981. Articles 1 and 6 protect a great panoply of actions of
worship and religious behavior that are too long to report in detail.[34] Finally the 1989
concluding document encapsulates recommendations from the UDHR, the ICCPR,
and the 1981 Declaration. There is hardly another human right that receives more textual recognition.

However, it must be very clear that all those documents are not legally binding
on states unless they are formally incorporated into domestic law. The United States,
for example, has not made them legally binding. These texts have at best the moral
force of persuasion but no legal sanction is attached. Moreover, it is hard to pin down
exactly the force of the moral argument since religion is defined very broadly in the
ICCPR and is not defined at all in the 1981 Declaration, which brings us back to square
one: domestic states have considerable freedom in managing the way in which they
understand and treat religion. Indeed practice shows that religious people are still very
much the object of all forms of discrimination in many countries.

We saw that in some states freedom of religion is central to the constitutional project, while it is clearly not in other states. It is therefore impossible to claim that freedom of religion is universally recognized as a strong right at the national level; it follows
that it is impossible to claim that the HRFR should be regarded as fundamental to the

---

[34] See for a useful guide D. Davis, 'The Evolution of Religious Freedom as a Universal Human
Right: Examining the Role of the 1981 United Nations Declaration on the Elimination of All Forms of
Intolerance and of Discrimination Based on Religion or Belief,' BYULR (2002): 217–35.

international project of human rights and for this reason can hardly be regarded as a strong ground of intervention at the international level.

International human rights are a widely used currency, but they only apply in a limited way. When we try to make sense of the fast-developing practice of human rights, it is possible to distinguish between human rights that have an impact on national sovereignty and those that are only a matter of noble declaration without serious sanctions or precise moral pressure attached to it. The HRFR falls into the second category: the panoply of texts and good intentions is not followed by an international regime of protection that is capable of identifying with precision instances in which the right should be protected and sanctions attached to its violation.

B. Foundations

The relationship between international human rights and religion is ambivalent. Starting with the grounding of human rights: there seem to be two broad families of theories that attempt to ground human rights—one is secular and the other religious. In order to make a difference both theories must provide reasons that are strong enough to outweigh arguments from national sovereignty, and this implies that the ethical conception of human rights should provide a minimum threshold beyond which intervention is justified.[35] The problem with ethical conceptions is that they are not substantive enough to provide a clear, applicable, understanding of what that minimum threshold is.[36] Ethical conceptions of human rights may point to what it is impermissible to do to religious people but they never give a full account of what kind of violations of the HRFR warrant the limitation of national sovereignty.

So for example, a theocratic regime may not be compatible with the HRFR, but this is hardly an argument for intervention at the international level. Respect for national sovereignty is compatible with the idea of having a theocratic regime. If democracy means anything, then the people of one nation can surely decide to have their decisions vetted by religious leaders. This is not to say that it is a desirable thing, but it is compatible with what people can choose.

Religious theories of human rights start from similar premises and argue that we have to be protected simply in virtue of being human beings because we have been made in the image of god. But these theories often fail to account for the fact that some human beings have lost their god-like image and therefore are not worthy of being right-holders any more.[37] Other candidates are offered: Religion claims to provide a universal ethical foundation to human rights in the name of the love of god. Others claim that an ethical religious foundation can coincide with a secular one,

---

[35] J. Raz, 'Human Rights Without Foundations', in S. Besson and J. Tasioulas (eds.), *Philosophy of International Law* (Oxford University Press, 2010).

[36] Even at the national level human rights do not usher in a conclusive ethical worldview. If anything, they bracket it out of the picture. So it is not possible to claim that human rights are important because they have—or they provide—a strong ethical foundation. The protection of the HRFR in each society is a political question, not an ethical one, and this is all the more true at the international level.

[37] N. Wolterstorff, *Understanding Liberal Democracy—Essays in Political Philosophy* (Oxford University Press, 2012).

such as for example brotherhood.[38] However, the problem does not lie with the difference between secular and religious foundations; the problem lies with the very idea of there being an ethical foundation that is universal and that explains all human rights in a univocal way. As we pointed out earlier, ethical foundations are unlikely to explain the emerging practice of human rights and they also seem to lack a necessary critical punch to help improve on the practice as it evolves.

Besides secular and religious foundational theories of human rights that attempt to ground human rights in a secular or religious argument, there are theories that deny the need for foundations, which I find more promising at this level of debate and practice.[39] These theories do not deny that there may be ethical foundations to human rights. Rather, they claim that given the present practice of human rights, it is not possible to spell out one precise ethical foundation that illuminates the practice or provides a helpful critical standard.[40] The practice of human rights is evolving at a fast pace and does not point to any conclusive argument as to the moral status of human rights. Human rights protect important interests that receive legal protection to the extent that they are not limited by other more important interests. Human rights have two levels, one which is domestic, and the other which is international.

The HRFR is more stringent at the national level for all the reasons advanced earlier in this chapter. To a large extent the meaning of freedom of religion is deeply dependent on the social role of religion at the national level. It is therefore a deeply contingent relationship between a society and its state, and cannot be evaluated fairly from an external standpoint. In addition to that, I agree with Raz that human rights themselves are very much dependent 'on the contingencies of the current system of international relations.'[41] It is in this sense that human rights lack a foundation, that is, their practice cannot be described as being grounded in a fundamental moral concern.

If you put together the contingency with regard to the relation between religion and society in every state, with the contingency due to the place of human rights in international relations, then what emerges is a very fragile picture of the human rights to freedom of religion. To which one has to add that religion as an object can hardly be defined in a way that is universal in any meaningful way. Religion seems to escape any definition, and when it does not that definition relies on very specific assumptions.

C. Freedom of religion and foreign policy

Western states often justify military intervention on the ground of human rights breaches without acknowledging that the understanding of a human right may be very much dependent on contingent presuppositions. There is a difference between the human right not to be tortured and the human right to freedom of religion. The former can be defined and nobody would object to the need to remove that violation. The latter is not objectively definable and not all violations are likely to be a ground strong

---

[38] M. Perry, *The Morality and Law of International Human Rights* (Routledge, forthcoming).
[39] C. Beitz, *The Idea of Human Rights* (Oxford University Press, 2011).
[40] Raz, 'Human Rights Without Foundations'.
[41] Raz, 'Human Rights Without Foundations', 336.

enough for intervention. That is very much the view of international judicial bodies that, as we saw, give considerable margin of appreciation to national authorities.

Moreover, more serious violations such as persecution and killing are covered by less controversial human rights such as the right to life or the right to freedom of expression. The point is that unless the HRFR is precisely defined in scope and strength, it cannot add very much either at the moral or at the legal level. And in addition to that, a biased conception of the HRFR has many risks, starting from the highly polarizing politicization of the role of religion in politics. The European Union is hardly capable of managing religious diversity within its territory; it is really unthinkable that it would erect itself as a promoter of freedom of religion in the world.

Regional and international systems of protection of human rights present differences as to the way in which national sovereignty is respected. The organized system of European human rights allows for the intervention of the European Court of Human Rights as a means of sanctioning member states. Human rights in general are those rights that can justify international intervention against violators.[42] But what is fundamentally flawed is the attempt to launch a foreign policy that attempts to promote a skewed understanding of freedom of religion—something that rides roughshod over local understanding and practices.

However, the United States and Europe are often very keen to use freedom of religion as a ground for intervention in foreign policy. Since the Constantinian union between the church and state in 313, religion has been used for various political endeavors and in particular to give a moral aspect to the intervention of the Empire. Colonialist intervention has often been justified on those grounds, and examples can be multiplied: think of the military intervention in Mali to counter the religious extremists. Colonial powers have supported the worst dictators in the name of freedom of religion. The Assad family, Sadam Hussein, Mubarak, and Gaddafi have all been supported by the West because they could guarantee more or less secular regimes that would fight against the alleged threat of religious extremists. The United States has tried to play a strong role in the area of religious freedom as a matter of international policy. The most obvious problem is that action is guided not by an international—universal—understanding of the HRFR but by a very domestic one. The obvious result is that foreign policies and international relations based on very local and contingent understanding of human rights are likely to divide rather than to unite.

V. Conclusion

The HRFR has a limited place within a system of international human rights for several reasons. First, the meaning of religious freedom is deeply dependent on contingent factors, such as constitutional history, the social outlook of the society, and the presence of religious minorities. Secondly, judicial actors at the supranational level are keen to show deference to national institutions when faced with complex issues

---

[42] I agree with Raz ('Human Rights Without Foundations') that a violation of human rights justifies international intervention of various types and not necessarily armed intervention.

regarding freedom of religion. Thirdly, any international actor will have to factor in a strong requirement of national sovereignty when deciding whether or not to intervene on the basis of the HRFR.

There is no easy way to understand the role of religion in other societies, and there is no steadfast definition of religion for that purpose. The way in which each state comes up with a cocktail of these different factors is a matter of its own national sovereignty that can hardly be interfered with without suspicion of new imperialism. The HRFR is not a strong concern in the system of international human rights, even if some would like to present it as such. It is just one human right amongst many others, and it must always be weighed against many other considerations.

It may be that the practice of human rights will come to resemble something altogether different one day. For the moment, it is not desirable to claim that human rights stand for a univocal set of moral demands at the international level. They are rights against national sovereignty; for this reason they have to be used with great caution, in order to avoid the worst suspicions of a new imperialism. This is particularly the case for the human right to freedom of religion, which is for the moment a limited right in the system of international human rights.

22

Religious Liberty Conceived as a Human Right

Robert Audi

Rights are better than gold. Their value is incalculably great; they cannot be lost by theft; and—in principle—they protect us from myriad harms. At the national level, the rights backed by government constitute deontic capital whose value is incommensurable with its gold reserves, and their protection is more important than gross national product. But rights are also harder to identify than gold; their quality is not measurable in any straightforward way; and the rights possessed by others automatically affect ours. The notion of a religion is perhaps no easier to clarify than that of a right. The question, then, of whether there is a human right to religious liberty is doubly difficult. That question is central for Lorenzo Zucca in "Freedom of Religion in a Secular World"[1] and it will also be central in this paper, which explores his highly informative essay at several important points.

I. A Broad Conception of Rights

My concern here is mainly moral rights, but legal rights, which commonly align with them—often by resting on a different ground supporting the same content—will also figure in the discussion. On any conception of rights, moral, legal, or more narrowly institutional, they are the sorts of things that may be (among other things) claimed, asserted, respected, violated, and forfeited. Human rights such as the right to free speech, can be claimed on a moral basis even if not under law. Presumably some rights, such as the right not to be enslaved, are "inalienable" and hence cannot be transferred; some, such as the right not to be punished for a deed one has not done, may also be plausibly held to be incapable of forfeit.

A. Sketch of a conception of rights

It is difficult to find a clear unifying notion of a right. Perhaps the most we can hope for is to identify a core idea that, interpreted broadly, provides the basis for account. On my view—which I sketch to clarify the discussion to follow—a right, in what seems the most basic sense, is (roughly and in very broad terms) a defeasible normative protection from a certain kind of coercive conduct, such as suppression of free speech.[2]

---

[1] This volume, ch. 21, 388. All subsequent references to ch. 21 appear parenthetically in the text.
[2] The overall account of rights in this section is based in large part on the sketch of rights presented in Robert Audi, *The Good in the Right: A Theory of Intuition and Intrinsic Value* (Princeton and Oxford: Princeton University Press, 2004), ch. 5 and developed in "Wrongs within Rights".

I do not claim that every notion of a right is reducible to this one; but the sense roughly characterized here is at least most relevant for our topic.

Three qualifications are essential. The first concerns the scope of "coercive conduct". To include the rights not to be killed or harmed in certain other ways that do not compel one to *do* anything, we must take killing and such harms as temporarily drugging someone as limiting cases of coercive conduct. They forcibly *prevent* doing anything even if they compel no *act*. What they may be said to compel, then, is omissions. Secondly, *normative* protection is understood broadly to encompass legal norms: as a (defeasible) justification for prohibiting the acts in question—morally prohibiting them where the right is moral, legally doing so if it is legal—and of course the same range of acts might be prohibited or required under both a moral and a legal right, which might bear the same name. Although my concern is not legal rights but rather moral and human rights, I am particularly interested in legal rights, such as the right to hold religious services, because they protect human rights.

The third qualification concerns rights sometimes called *entitlements*. To see these in relation to the basic conception just sketched, we must conceive coercive acts broadly enough to bear appropriately on rights to have promises to one kept and rights not to be lied to (promissory and veracity obligations represent major bases of entitlements). In part, the idea is that such violations tend to limit our choices. There may be no particular thing we must do; but we may well be forced to do things we otherwise would not have had to do. To be sure, where the right is to have a promise honored, the protection from coercion does have this specificity: we are protected from being forced to relinquish our claim or forbear from asserting it. This leaves open, however, what, if anything, we must do *given* that forcible relinquishment.

My broad notion of protection from coercive conduct applies most clearly to rights *to do certain things,* by contrast with rights *against having certain things done to oneself.* But the notion is nonetheless clarifying, particularly if, as I assume here, rights are above all (though not entirely) a kind of protection of agency.[3] Physical harms tend to impair agency and thereby to force us to perform compensatory actions and forgo others. A rights violation need not compel the victim to do a particular thing, but they do characteristically force one either to choose among options that, from the moral point of view, are inappropriately limited or at least to do something in a way that, given the right, is morally objectionable. Thus, lies might put desirable options out of reach; and (to illustrate the second case) a broken promise might force one to undertake something without the promised help, even if one can still manage it. Similarly, privacy violations might force me to listen to loud music or the blare of bell ringing that calls people to prayer. This last case also shows that a rights violation need not

---

[3] My view is similar in some ways to James Griffin's in *On Human Rights* (Oxford: Oxford University Press, 2008). For him, human rights "can be seen as protections of our human standing…our personhood" (33), to which agency is central: one can break down the notion of personhood into clearer components by breaking down the notion of agency" (33). Moreover, human rights can also be *grounded* in personhood (33–7)…Space does not permit comparison here, but a detailed and informative discussion of Griffin's view, including its relation to the notion of dignity, is provided by Charles R. Beitz in *The Idea of Human Rights* (Oxford: Oxford University Press, 2009), 60–8.

cause what is ordinarily considered harm, except insofar as reducing one's options is itself a kind of harm.

B. The specification of rights

Regardless of our theory of what it is to have a right, to specify to what a given right amounts we must indicate at least four kinds of information. One or more of these are often unclear in discussions of rights.

First, it must be clear who has the right, the *possessor*: whoever is protected by it, say all human beings, and may also justifiedly claim it (or have it claimed by proxy). By extension, groups of people and even organizations can possess rights. Secondly, the *addressee*—the person(s) against whom a right is held—must be specified for full clarification of a right, though they may never be mentioned in describing the conduct within the scope of the right, including, for instance, free religious expression. Thirdly the *content* of the right—the conduct it protects (or prohibits) and concerning which the addressee (and possibly others) owe the possessor(s) non-interference—must be indicated. This is normally specifiable behaviorally: say *to* vote for representatives in one's government or *not to* be incarcerated without charges. Rights are commonly named using just nouns, as with the "right to life." Such nominal specification enhances the difficulty of seeing what their possession entails. Infinitival specification makes it easier to see that they are not closed under entailment. A right to remove an appendix does not entail a right to do *either* that or euthanize the patient.[4] Fourth, understanding a right requires knowing its *domain*, say moral or legal—the normative realm in which criticism or sanctions are (prima facie) in order for non-performance of the relevant conduct. Applying these points to our topic, a right to religious liberty would be *possessed* by anyone who can do religious deeds or engage in religious expression; *addressed* to anyone who might restrict such action, especially governments and organizations; in *content* as comprehensive as the religious actions in question (to be described in Section III); and (arguably), in *domain*, intrinsically moral and hence a prima facie candidate for legal status as well.

C. The defeasibility of rights

The suggested conception of rights is akin to a Rossian conception of prima facie duties. I have argued elsewhere[5] that—*given* their grounds—these duties are ineradicable, hence cannot be deprived of all normative significance. But they remain defeasible, as where a right to send text messages is overridable by others' rights not to be endangered by distracted driving and where religious freedom to make sacrifices may be restricted by the right not to be killed. For certain ascriptions of rights, say a general right to freedom of speech, it is arguable, as it is for certain principles of prima facie

---

[4] There are many technical difficulties concerning the content, individuation, and entailment relations among rights, but I am suggesting that their content be specifiable in a fine-grained way appropriate to relation to intentions to perform the acts crucial for their exercise.

[5] In Audi, *The Good in the Right*, eg ch. 1, 23–4, where there is much discussion of W. D. Ross's now classic *The Right and the Good* (Oxford: Oxford University Press, 1930).

duty, that these ascriptions are self-evident. As in the case of duties, this self-evidence does not preclude rights' being grounded (or at least groundable) in something else, including principles. I take the self-evident to be knowable without epistemic reliance on independent evidence, but this does not entail that there can *be* no such evidence.[6]

Given the number of rights that fall under the conception presented here, one might think all possible human action is in their *scope*, in the sense that for any person, P, and act-type, A, either P has a right to A or someone has a right against P that precludes P's A-ing. But there are possible deeds, such as taking a bracelet glistening in the sun on a deserted beach, that none of us has a right to do or a right to prevent others from doing.[7] There *is* a right not to be prevented *by force* as one attempts to pick up the bracelet; but this is a special case of some other right, such as the right to freedom of action. This is not a right to be protected from others taking it if they get to it first.

The case illustrates that there are permissible acts that are neither protected by rights nor forbidden by rights. This may be a special case of the point that moral obligation does not cover all acts—in the sense that all come under a moral *ought* or *ought not*. Having some coffee at an airport is discretionary, hence permissible in the sense that it is not wrong: though I do not have a right to have it on demand, no one has a right to prevent me from having some (if I ask and pay), and I am neither obligated to have it nor obligated not to have it. Some religious acts, such as burning celebratory incense, are similarly discretionary.

The partial sketch of rights is meant to supply a conception that, though incomplete, is adequate to the normative purpose of the paper: to support the view that there is a human right to religious liberty (even if it derives from some broader right); to clarify that right in a way that indicates how it may be plausibly regarded as special; and to indicate some of the conditions under which it is overriddable.

II. Some Contrasting Conceptions of Human Rights

Against this background, we can learn much from considering Zucca's concern with *human* rights. The notion of a human right has become increasingly important since the UN's Universal Declaration of Human Rights (UDHR) (adopted in 1948), but I have found no single conceptual characterization that is both clear and widely accepted. Its Article 1 begins "All human beings are born free and equal in dignity and rights." With that and other elements of the Declaration and later documents in mind, one might take human rights to be natural rights—roughly, those we have by virtue of human nature: consequentially upon being human. On this view, *basic* human rights would be a subset of natural rights.[8] Given the breadth of the Declaration, however,

---

[6] This conception of the self-evident is clarified and defended in Audi, *The Good in the Right*, ch. 2 (where the conception is contrasted with that of Moore and Ross).

[7] In the terminology of Wesley Hohfeld, this might be called a privilege or a "no-right," where (in line with my point in the text) the *absence* of a right is on the part of the other party. For a lucid brief discussion of the Hohfeldian conception of rights, see William A. Edmundson, *An Introduction to Rights* (Cambridge: Cambridge University Press, 2004), esp. 88–95.

[8] This volume, ch. 21, 403.

one is inclined to conclude that the category of human rights is wider than this implies. Let me elaborate.

Might the category of human rights be that of *general moral rights*? That of *dignity-based rights*, or *flourishing-based rights*? These all entail protections from coercion, and they include, by the kind of extension described earlier, certain entitlements. The acts that lie within the content of these rights are taken to be crucial for maintaining dignity or achieving flourishing (or both). Both dignity and flourishing conceptions might be suggested by Article 22:

> Everyone, as a member of society, has the right to social security and is entitled to realization, through national effort and international co-operation and in accordance with the organization and resources of each State, of the economic, social and cultural rights indispensable for his dignity and the free development of his personality.

Other articles of the Declaration suggest that human rights include what might be called *nation-based*, or, more broadly, *governmental-community-based*, rights, roughly those that are or should be recognized wherever people fall under laws, as is suggested by Article 6, which says simply "Everyone has the right to recognition everywhere as a person before the law." Perhaps "institutionally-based" would cover both nation-based and governmental-community based cases, on the assumptions that (1) if a community has laws, then it has some institutional framework even if not a government proper and (2) institutions might have rules that confer rights even if the institutions are not governmental and the rights have sufficiently wide and strong support, as could be the case with certain international institutions. The relation of any of these conceptions to that of a natural right is complex. There are no laws in a state of nature; but arguably natural rights imply such *conditional* rights as to be treated equally before laws *if* one is subject to them, as in a nation or a community, such as a provincial or even tribal government, with law-making authority. The same would hold for institutional rules with coercive authority (or perhaps simply moral authority), even if those rules are not strictly speaking laws.[9]

To be sure, at least some human rights could be included in the kind of special rights *conferred* by human actions. One would be the right to have governmental promises to us kept. This in turn may imply an entitlement right to be given health care. This is of course not a natural right. The theoretical point here is that a right *implied by* a natural right, say to have promises to one kept, together with contingent facts, say that a government promises health care, need not itself be a natural right. Human rights, then, can have natural rights as their foundation (or their normative core) even if some are quite different in kind, say in content, from natural rights.

---

[9] The kind of protectiveness conception of rights I have sketched is broad enough to accommodate these conceptions of human rights, even if it cannot be stretched to include all the individual rights called human rights in one or another document. The conception also incorporates rationales commonly associated with two different theories of the basis of rights: the "interest theory," on which rights function to protect their holder's interests, and "choice theory," on which rights function to protect their holder's freedom of choice. For critical discussion of these two conceptions, see Edmundson, *An Introduction to Rights*, 120–32, and John Tasioulas, "Human Rights, Universality and the Values of Personhood: Retracing Griffin's Steps," *European Journal of Philosophy*, 10(1) (2002): 79–100.

There is, however, still another way to conceive human rights: as those that are internationally recognized as normative protections of the kinds described earlier. The idea of natural rights is likely a major element in shaping such consensus as there is on the international scene; but, as our discussion will suggest, the two approaches are quite different, and we might speculate that the former is more likely to anchor philosophical discussion of human rights and the latter is more likely to anchor legal discussion of them.

This difference in anchoring conceptions is easy to overlook because many human rights, conceived in the first way, are protected by law in most legal systems; this implies an identity of scope between pairs of rights in question, which often bear the same name, say 'a right to freedom of religion'. But we should not take that to imply equivalence of the rights. The grounds are different, and in the legal case there is an at least implicit protection-enforcement structure not entailed by the existence of human rights. One might take human rights to be a subset of natural rights, but this is far from being uncontroversial.[10] By contrast with my conception of human rights as, on any plausible conception, supported at least by conditional moral rights, Zucca's may be quasi-legal or otherwise in some way institutional. In neither case do I see any reason to take him to imply *reducibility* of human rights to either legal ones or to any other institutional notions, but I would like more clarity on whether he takes it to be a necessary condition for a human right that it be in a certain way institutionally described and defended. He says, for example,

> I find it difficult to pin down a precise enough meaning of the HRFR [human right to freedom of religion]; and as a consequence my suggestion is that the HRFR has a very limited role to play at the international level.
>
> There are several reasons for this. To begin with the nature of freedom of religion heavily depends on historical contingencies at the domestic level (section 2). Moreover, the practice of freedom of religion shows that the scope and strength of the right can only be determined in relation to the local understanding of religion and what it means to be free for a religion. As a result, supranational institutions adjudicate on these issues by displaying a great deference to national institutions that are better positioned to evaluate local practices" (389)

In the same vein, he later says, "I agree with Raz that human rights are themselves very much dependent 'on the contingencies of the current system of international relations'. It is in this sense that human rights lack a foundation, that is, their practice cannot be described as being grounded in a fundamental moral concern" (404).

One important question here is whether the focus is on human rights conceived as (in the basic cases) natural and—I take it—therefore a normative basis for sound law making, or on legal rights. Surely, if we conceive human rights as possessed by human

---

[10] It seems at odds with the approach of those who see human (and moral) rights as grounded in dignity, at least where that notion is associated with the Kantian tradition or indeed with the idea that possessors of dignity have *intrinsic value*. For a view that makes use of socio-cultural elements in describing dignity, see Jeremy Waldron's *Dignity, Rank, and Rights* (Oxford: Oxford University Press, 2012), Lecture 1. Informative discussion of the relation between dignity and rights is also provided in the works cited earlier by Beitz and Griffin. See too Jeremy Waldron, "Is Dignity the Foundation of Human Rights?" this volume, ch. 5 and Pablo Gilabert, "Human Rights, Human Dignity, and Power," this volume, ch. 10.

beings *as such,* then they do not depend "on the contingencies of the current system of international relations." Their *protection* might so depend. Even their recognition might. But I do not think Zucca intends to treat human rights in general as grounded only in conventions or other contingencies. Perhaps, to be sure, he would conceive some of them as a special case of these, say one in which the protections in question are universally agreed to be warranted. But this does not seem to be his meaning, especially given his emphasis on lack of consensus on normative questions.

A weaker condition would be that human rights must possess a certain kind of *institutionalizability.* This would go with both the idea that such rights should be *claimable* in a governmental framework—or an institutional non-governmental one such as that of the UN—and with Zucca's idea (following Raz perhaps) that they depend on the contingencies of international relations. My preference is to take the practicability of citing human rights in various documents or statutes to have this dependence but (as Zucca might agree) to take their basis to be non-contingent facts about the normative status of human beings. The idea that we have normative status may or may not be taken to entail (or depend on) our having natural rights.

Another important question is whether the frequent variant local understandings of religion Zucca refers to imply that "the HRFR has a very limited role to play at the international level." To be sure, we must distinguish, as Zucca does, between an international role in justifying *intervention* and one justifying only non-military kinds of support. In suggesting that a human right to religious liberty might play an international role, I am leaving aside the complicated question of when rights violations rise to the level of justifying intervention. One point bearing on the question of whether there is *any* kind of religious liberty right is that understandings can vary around a core of agreement, as where, for most candidates for the category of religion, virtually everyone (who has the relevant concepts) agrees on whether to include them as religion, but, on peripheral cases, there is widespread disagreement among the same people. A further point is that people can have general ethical and political conceptions that dispose them to accept certain carefully formulated statements of religious liberty rights, even if they begin with different ideas of what these should be. Actual beliefs may be a poor indication of the potential for agreement given a good statement of a position that has universal plausibility or can be made plausible in different terms for different cultures or particular people.

III. Religion as a Multiple-Criterion Concept

These considerations raise the question whether we should seek or try to construct a definition of "religion" that might help to sustain a case for a human right to freedom of religion—or at least to clarify its scope, ie, the behaviors it protects. The definitions of "religion" I am acquainted with seem to be inadequate, but rather than discuss them I will propose a *conception* of religion and a strategy for discussing religious freedom in the light of it. The conception derives from the idea, perhaps initially given detailed development by Wittgenstein, that some concepts are such that we understand them in terms of a number of criteria no one of which is individually necessary or sufficient.

Here are nine criteria that apparently determine whether a social practice (or even a practice by an individual) constitutes a religion. In calling them *criteria*, I am implying that each is conceptually relevant to, even if not strictly necessary for, a social institution's constituting a religion or (as applied to individuals) to an individual's having a religion. In part, this is to say that to fail to see the relevance of any one of them to the applicability of the concept of a religion implies at least some lack of understanding of the concept. Here are the criteria: (1) appropriately internalized belief in one or more supernatural beings (gods); (2) observance of a distinction between sacred and profane objects; (3) ritual acts focused on those objects; (4) a moral code believed to be sanctioned by the god(s); (5) religious feelings (awe, mystery, etc.) that tend to be aroused by the sacred objects and during rituals; (6) prayer and other communicative forms concerning the god(s); (7) a worldview according the individual a significant place in the universe; (8) a more or less comprehensive organization of life based on the worldview; and (9) a social organization bound together by (1)–(8).[11]

This characterization is very broad, but that may be desirable for our topic. For instance, it leaves open whether the social practice in question has votaries, or enough to be de facto *social*; it is neutral concerning whether the ethical element implies a divine command theory of morality; and, even apart from rituals concerning sacred objects, it leaves open there being right and wrong ways to treat such objects. This breadth is desirable. It is better to avoid too narrow a conception of religion than to err on the side of excessively restricting the notion. To be sure, there are dangers of an overboard definition. One might overextend privileges that may burden society in certain ways, such as tax exemptions for churches and legal permissions to use certain drugs in religious rituals. Definitional breadth, however, tends to be preferable for a free society, and certainly for a liberal democracy, over an unduly narrow conception of religion, since that breadth means protecting liberty and equality more widely than would be likely on too narrow a conception.

If this approach to understanding the concept of religion is taken, do we then have an explanation of why, as Zucca holds, "people disagree as to whether religion deserves special protection, and nobody agrees on what exactly religion covers" (389)? The approach can certainly help to explain these phenomena, but it also leads to caution about exaggerating the amount of disagreement there is *on concrete cases*. There is no reason to expect even near universal agreement on a definition, provided I am correct in thinking that no conventional definition will suffice—and, in any case, people tend to be very poor at framing (or even assessing) definitions that capture their own usage. And if the reference is to the thesis that "religion deserves

---

[11] These features are stressed by William P. Alston in *Philosophy of Language* (Englewood Cliffs, NJ: Prentice-Hall, 1964), 88 (I have abbreviated and slightly revised his list). This characterization does not entail that religions must be theistic, but even in non-theistic religions, the relevant moral code tends to be given a somewhat similar privileged status in relation to other items on this list, such as the sacred and profane, and certain rituals. It is noteworthy that in *United States v. Seeger*, 380 US 163 (1965), the Supreme Court ruled that religious belief need not be theistic; but theistic religions raise the most important church–state issues at least for many societies.

special protection," again there is too much abstractness to expect full convergence among thoughtful people.

Let us be more concrete. Is there *reasonable* disagreement about whether government should protect people's right to participate in religious activities peacefully and in buildings properly maintained for the purpose and to form voluntary associations with the same civil rights possessed by secular associations, such as trade unions and political parties? I doubt that there is such disagreement, at least in "advanced" countries not under totalitarian rule. It should also be pointed out that similar problems arise for the matter of *political* liberty. The vagueness of our unavoidable descriptive language is a challenge to sound law making and plausible theorizing, but neither activity is thereby rendered impossible.

Three further clarifications are needed. First, on these criteria, a person can be religious without belonging to an institutional religion. Secondly, secularity is no easier to characterize than religion and has similar vagueness. It is clarifying, however, to note that secularity in individuals is compatible with their being *spiritual*, for instance sensitive to what lies beyond appearances, temperamentally meditative, and not "materialistic" in their pursuits and values. Spirituality, then, is compatible not only with being non-religious but with *secularism*, which, taken in the strongest common sense of the term, is a position both calling for strong separation of church and state and implying opposition to religious worldviews as, for instance, not rational or politically divisive. Secularity in a person is thus compatible with, but does not entail, secularism.

The third clarification appropriate here concerns a contrast between the view I am proposing on the "definition problem" regarding religion, and one which Zucca takes to be significant, though he does not endorse it. He says,

> [Brian] Leiter offers two elements, which he regards as central: categoricity of belief and insulation from evidence. Categoricity refers to the stringency of beliefs in guiding behavior. Insulation from evidence addresses the way in which religion relates to the knowledge of the world that we have on the basis of common sense or science. Religion, being based on faith, is not responsive to reason, Leiter argues, and this insulates religion from the requirement of evidential proofs (393).

In a critical vein, Zucca says,

> Leiter assesses religion from the viewpoint of an exclusive naturalistic worldview, which presupposes a conflict between science and religion…faith is the source of unwarranted beliefs, as they cannot be supported by scientific evidence, indeed they are insulated from it. But this assumes too much, namely that all the beliefs we hold on the basis of faith are incompatible with scientific evidence. This cannot be true, in particular in relation to moral beliefs that are inherited from religious convictions. It also wrongly assumes that those religious beliefs that are incompatible with scientific evidence cannot be revised or put aside…people of faith and religious institutions are prepared, albeit sometimes reluctantly, to change their beliefs on the strength of contrary scientific evidence (394).

Here I largely agree with Zucca and want to clarify and amplify his points. We may differ on whether religious beliefs are all "held on the basis of faith," though Zucca does not explicitly affirm this and might recognize that such philosophers of religion as Richard Swinburne are at once scientifically oriented and armed with arguments for theistic conclusions.[12] One should also recall here the Thomistic tradition and other philosophical approaches in which natural facts are taken to entail God's existence or, as with the argument from design, render it highly probable. On the matter of moral beliefs, Zucca is right to treat these as different in kind from scientific beliefs: *nonscientific* but not *unscientific*, as I would put it. He is also correct in noting that many religious people are prepared to given up certain religious beliefs in the light of scientific evidence. Many have qualified beliefs drawn from scripture in the light of the theory of evolution.

A general point I would make here (with which I think Zucca and many others can agree) is that science is not fundamentally metaphysical. If so, scientific practice and, more broadly, a scientific habit of mind, do not commit one to philosophical naturalism, the kind Leiter apparently presupposes, as distinct from methodological naturalism.[13] Theism as a metaphysical view, then, as opposed to various claims made by theists that they consider religious, is not in conflict with scientific findings and theories.

One further point essential here is perhaps implicit in what Zucca says and certainly consistent with it. I refer to the need to qualify Leiter's claim that religion is in part defined by categoricity: "Categoricity refers to the stringency of beliefs in guiding behavior."[14] This is not an element in all religion. Indeed, the very idea is philosophical and not found in any scripture I am aware of. One might think it is implied by such commandments as "Thou shalt love thy God with all thy heart..." But first, love alone does not imply any such privileging of the pronouncements made by the beloved; and, secondly, there is the matter of a religious person's criteria of identity for a genuine divine pronouncement. One might think God infallible but still not take any pronouncement, at least any by a human being or even a high-ranking cleric or a revered scripture, to be categorical in the relevant sense. Indeed, one might have an ethical view on which any pronouncement that goes against, say, protection of human rights, is to be attributed to a source other than God. Even absolute love might be guided by a sense of the moral character of the beloved. The conviction that God is loving and just could in practice far outweigh the conviction that an apparently divine command requires hatred, or injustice. Morality can influence theological interpretation quite as much as theology can influence the sense of moral obligation.

Suppose that religion does not require of its adherents either indifference to evidence or unswerving obedience to religiously endorsed injunctions. Zucca can grant

---

[12] See, e.g., Richard Swinburne, *The Existence of God* (Oxford: Oxford University Press, 2004). Zucca himself cites Alvin Plantinga, who, though avowedly committed to the view that theistic belief does not *require* arguments based on evidence, offers many arguments from non-religious facts to theistic conclusions.

[13] This view, and the constituent notions of naturalism are clarified in Robert Audi, *Rationality and Religious Commitment* (Oxford: Clarendon Press, 2011), ch. 10.

[14] Brian Leiter, *Why Tolerate Religion* (Princeton: Princeton University Press, 2012) 33–7.

this and still be quite properly concerned with the vagueness of the notion of religion. But how much clarity about it is needed for an ethical theory of religious liberty rights or even a theory of the relation between governmental and other institutions and religion? And in particular, is *greater* clarity required than we need for an adequate theory of freedom of expression independent of subject-matter?

We must also be careful not to underestimate the clarity that comes with a good understanding of paradigms. Take Christianity, Judaism, and Islam. A conception of religion that does justice to these three will include many other cases and will usefully guide much normative reflection on the right to religious expression. Moreover, even apart from the extent to which we can understand the notion of religion in terms of a study of these world religions, if we have a theory of the relation between church and state that deals adequately with these, we have something of great value.

IV. Religious Liberty in the Context of the Defeasibility of Freedom Rights

So far, my aim has been to argue that the notions of rights and of religion itself are not vague in a way that precludes the possibility of articulating a plausible account of the nature (though not the strength) of a human right to religious liberty. But there is a third concept needing attention here: that of freedom. It may be instructive to begin with John Stuart Mill's famous pronouncement in his *On Liberty*:

> The object of this Essay is to assert one very simple principle, as entitled to govern absolutely the dealings of society with the individual in the way of compulsion and control…That principle is, that the sole end for which mankind are warranted, individually or collectively, in interfering with the liberty of action of any of their number, is self-protection…to prevent harm to others.[15]

This "harm principle" raises the question what constitutes self-protection. Presumably it is protection from harm, but that notion is contestable. I hope there can be wide agreement that the criteria for its application in legal cases should be secular, as, arguably, they are even for the notion as it figures in general ethics. (Mill would of course have defined harm in terms of causing pain or suffering or at least reducing pleasure in certain ways.)[16] The appropriate scope of liberty has been extensively discussed, and here I will simply record sympathy with the idea, defended in *On Liberty* and a multitude of

---

[15] John Stuart Mill, *On Liberty* (Indianapolis: Hackett, 1978), 9–10. Mill is strongly opposed to parentalism and (for competent adults) excludes harm to oneself as a ground for interference. See esp. 10ff. The notion of harm is seriously vague, and both in connection with damaging the environment and in relation to such economic behavior as purchasing goods manufactured by sweatshop labor, questions have arisen regarding just how free we ought to be even if the harm principle is sound so far as it goes. Instructive recent studies of the scope of moral responsibility and, especially of the strength of the obligation not to harm in comparison with that of the obligation to render aid, see Garrett Cullity, *The Moral Demands of Affluence* (Oxford: Oxford University Press, 2004) and Judith Lichtenberg, "Negative Duties, Positive Duties, and the 'New Harms'," *Ethics*, 120 (2010): 557–78.

[16] It is noteworthy that Bernard Gert's widely known system of moral rules includes among the basic ones "Do not deprive of pleasure," which is the fifth of his system of ten. See *Common Morality* (Oxford: Oxford University Press, 2004), 20. Gert argues plausibly, and in ways relevant here, for widespread agreement on such rules.

later writings, that justification of restrictions of liberty must come from adequate evidence that non-restriction will be significantly harmful to persons—though I would add that harm to animals or the environment should also be taken to be a potentially adequate ground for restricting liberty.

If liberty rights are limited by a conception of what is required to prevent harm, and that conception is religiously neutral, it is natural to ask why religious freedom should be singled out, as it is in the United States and other countries, as special, at least in deserving emphasis in constitutions and in statements of human rights. In providing a partial answer to this question I want to restrict my attention to democratic societies and simply to assume that governments in morally sound democracies seek to protect the people and to do at least something toward their flourishing. I am conceiving democratic government as "of, by, and for the people." I have in mind a principle applicable to church and state alike:

> *The principle of protection of identity*: the deeper a set of commitments is in a person, and the closer it comes to determining that person's sense of identity, the stronger the case for protecting the expression of those commitments.[17]

This principle is religiously neutral in content; but, as a matter of historical fact and perhaps of human psychology as well, religious commitments tend to be important for people in both ways: in depth and in determining the sense of identity. This is especially apparent where religious people satisfy all of the criteria described above for having a religion. Secular commitments can be comparably deep, in a sense implying that the persons in question cannot easily give them up and tend to protect them even at great cost to their well-being; this principle does not discriminate against those other commitments. But few if any non-religious kinds of commitment combine the depth and contribution to the sense of identity that go with many (though by no means all) religious commitments. I would not go so far as to say that restrictions of the free exercise of religion are necessarily a kind of harm, though in fact they may constitute or at least cause harm; but to those in whom religion is deep, they tend to be *felt* as such and as threats to one's sense of identity or at least to one's expression of it.

Earlier I suggested there is a human right to religious liberty. The main point of bringing the harm principle and the protection of identity principle into this paper is to indicate how religious liberty might be so conceived. The right to liberty, including free expression of various kinds, is implicit in the harm principle; and what the protection of identity principle shows is that religious liberty is (for most religious people) one kind of liberty having great importance for the sense of identity. Given its role in the sense of identity of many religious people, religious liberty may be, for them, relative to the subjective sense of well-being, *contingently basic*. If so, this provides a sense in which religion (though not necessarily only religion) is "special."[18] But even apart from this point, the practice of religion is so widespread—and so visible and controversial—that, if only for pragmatic reasons, it is useful to single out a right

---

[17] Robert Audi, *Democratic Authority and the Separation of Church and State* (Oxford: Oxford University Press, 2011), 42.

[18] This view contrasts with Zucca's comment that to the question whether religion is special "There is no answer" (this volume, ch. 21, 393).

to these rather than simply treat the relevant acts as protected (within the limits of a sound harm principle) as exercises of liberty. Indefeasibility is of course not entailed by the kind of importance I have suggested the right to religious liberty is to most people who reflect on it, including many who are religious. Among the defeaters of any right are conflicts with other rights, such as the right not to be harmed. If a religion calls for human sacrifice or even major kinds of mutilation of children, neither morality not a sound account of human rights will countenance such practices.[19]

V. The Limits of the Free Exercise of Religion

If I have been right in thinking that some version of the harm principle is crucial for determining the proper legal scope of religious liberty, and also right in taking the protection of identity principle to be a constitutive standard for guiding policy, then from the point of view of political philosophy, religious liberty is only contingently special, however important it may be historically or for particular individuals or cultures. I do not see that Zucca need disagree with this conclusion. The difference between us may concern my greater optimism about clarifying the issues and my sense of the importance of protecting the sense of identity when threats to it come from restrictions of religious freedom.

I include under religious liberty the right to leave a religion (whether for secularity or another religion). I see nothing in Zucca's paper that would preclude his agreeing that given the coercive pressures this may generate in some religious groups, governments and international organizations should take pains to defend such liberties of departure. Indeed, a case might be made that the liberty of departure is as important a human right as the liberty of religious exercise.

Given the framework assumptions of this paper—in particular that our concern is democratic societies and, on the international scene, democratically structured institutions, whether governmental or not—it is appropriate to indicate how democratic societies may justifiedly limit religious freedom in ways that go beyond the ordinary kinds of protection that require, for instance, prohibiting human sacrifice and mutilation of children. In particular, I would argue that a sound democracy should separate church and state even if a majority of the population would prefer that it not do so. To be sure, if a large enough majority in a democracy wishes to have, say, an established church, then this will be instituted. But a constitutional democracy can at least require a supermajority for amendments, which might prevent any simple majority's establishing a church; and my point concerns what is constitutionally appropriate, roughly

---

[19] Genital mutilation of female children is an example (though where practiced it may be culturally rather than religiously endorsed); male circumcision is not in my view major mutilation, but it is being debated as a practice that autonomy rights might preclude, in the sense that the child's right (ultimately) to control what is done to its body outweighs the religious imperative to circumcise. A related matter is raised in a recent *New York Times* report describing controversy over the legal propriety of (in Hebrew) *metzitzah b'peh*, in which the officiant (the *mohel*) removes blood from the infant's wound by mouth. The case has pitted city health officials, who attribute spread of the herpes simplex virus and (since 2000) two infant deaths to the practice, against defenders of the practice as covered by a right to religious liberty.

in the sense of being (defeasibly) part of the basic legal structure of the governmental entity in question.

Why should democracies separate church and state, given that a country with an established church can respect religious liberty? So far, I have not mentioned basic political equality as, together with liberty, a constitutive normative requirement for a morally sound democracy. It is true that establishment is consistent with a very high level of civil liberty; but if I am not a member of the established church, one thing I am not free to do is compete for any official positions its members occupy in government. These may of course be minor; but plainly the established religion and its members will be privileged in a way that is inconsistent with equal treatment of citizens.

A related standard is governmental religious neutrality: not only should government not include an established church; it should also not give preference to the religious as such over the non-religious. Thus, such privileges as conscientious objector status should not be available only on religious grounds, as has been the case historically. Here some citizens' moral objections to killing may be as much a part of their sense of identity as other citizens' religious objections to it. The neutrality principle also applies to legal definitions, for instance of health care and indeed of religious freedom itself. The human right to religious liberty should not be keyed to a definition of religious liberty that is peculiar to any one religion. Here, as in other cases, the multiple-criterion conception of religion, applied within a reasonable theory of liberty rights in general, provides a good combination of latitude and determinacy.

VI. Religious Freedom and the Status of Animals

In discussing human rights we may easily forget that animals may have rights as well. To be sure, we can, as Kant did, make good sense of the notion of acting wrongly toward animals whether they have rights or not. I propose to leave open whether animals have rights. First, they clearly can suffer and can experience pleasure. We may thus speak of their *welfare* or their well-being or its opposite. Secondly, human beings can do wrongs toward animals, be morally responsible for them, and have attitudes toward them that are morally appropriate or inappropriate, and this need not depend on *any* rights being violated, whether of the animals or of anyone else. It is, for instance, prima facie morally wrong to cause a dog pain, especially if the pain is severe and extended, as with torture; and it is a prima facie morally good thing to cure a dog of a debilitating disease. Such deeds count toward good and bad character in the sense in which 'character' is a moral term. The language of virtue and vice also applies to treatment of dogs, horses, and many other kinds of animals.

The special relevance of this for our topic here is that some religions (or at least some sects within them), such as Judaism and Islam, call for animal sacrifice. To be sure, killing in itself need cause no pain, but in a good animal life it is at least a deprivation of pleasure.[20] Suppose that a lamb is to be sacrificed by putting it directly on a hot fire. This is a kind of torture, and it seems reasonable to consider a governmental

---

[20] In Gert's moral theory, as noted earlier, deprivation of pleasure is a major category of ethical prohibition, and I see no reason not to apply it to the treatment of animals as well as human beings.

prohibition of it justified, even if it is religiously enjoined. To be sure, illegalization is one thing; the extent, say in length of sentence, and kind of punishment, for instance in imprisonment or fines, is another. Each society should discuss such matters, but I cannot see that causing animal suffering should be permissible simply by virtue of being required by an exercise of religious liberty. (Here matters of the degree of suffering and the importance of the religious liberty much be taken into account.) Whether the legal sanction is a fine rather than a more serious deprivation or punishment is a further matter.

A useful analogy here might be destruction of property. Preventing that may justify some restrictions of religious liberty. Now there are people who would rather lose a car or even a residence rather than allow the death of a pet—especially if it is by fire. This is surely reason to think that preventing animal suffering also justifies certain restrictions of religious liberty. Not only does this point not depend on any appeal to animals' rights; there is also no a priori principle to the effect that good ethics always gives priority to rights over principles in a case of conflict. If the would-be sacrificial animal has no rights, the principle that we ought not to subject animals to torture may still take priority over rights of free exercise of religion that would protect the torture. Here, as in other cases, we can see that moral obligation does not depend on its addressees or beneficiaries having a right which its non-fulfillment violates.

Part of the point of bringing up the moral status of animals is to indicate both the breadth, and the difficulty of fully understanding the scope, of the human right to religious liberty. Even if one takes religious expression to be close to the sense of identity of those who have internalized the relevant religion, it does not follow that all the actions that go with that expression should be legally protected against other interests or in violation of principles that may concern pain and pleasure and apply to beings capable of those but not assumed to have rights. This point is compatible with distinguishing, as Mill did, qualities of pleasure. A plausible theory of the differential value of pleasures—and indeed of pains—is quite consonant with taking very seriously the simple pains and pleasures of animals. Indeed, as different as we are from domestic animals in the far greater variety of our pleasures, in our most excruciating pains we seem to be very much like them. When this is taken together with the point that, other things equal, ethics gives greater weight to reducing or preventing pain than to enhancing or achieving pleasure, the problem of comparing rights of religious freedom and, related to this, property rights regarding animals, to what might be called the justified claims of animals becomes both clearer and more difficult.

On the account of rights suggested in this paper, it is plausible to conclude that there is a human right to religious liberty—indeed a double-barreled right encompassing both exercise and departure: the practice of religion or the leaving of it. Conceived as moral, this human right may be considered a special case of a natural right to liberty. If human rights are, in the basic cases, the natural rights of human beings, then there is a human right to religious liberty if there is a natural right to liberty whose scope encompasses religious practice. If, however, human rights are a kind of internationally recognized status, then a right to religious liberty is a contingent and variable matter. I prefer the former, broadly moral-connectedness conception of human rights; but on either conception, liberty rights are defeasible. Zucca, I think, is free to work with either conception or, as he perhaps does, with one or the other depending on the demands of the context of discussion. In any case, if religious liberty seems to many political thinkers especially worth protecting, that may be not just because of historically memorable threats to it but also because it is deep in the sense of identity of many people. Just how far it goes however, and the extent to which governments should protect it, is a matter for both moral and political reflection and national and international policy.[21]

---

[21] This paper has benefitted from comments by Massimo Renzo and from discussion with Lorenzo Zucca and the audience for presentation of an earlier version at King's College London.

23

The Right to Security

Liora Lazarus

Introduction

The right to security is enshrined in international human rights treaties and constitutions globally. In many of these provisions, the right is articulated alongside the right to liberty from the state. In others, the right is linked to freedom from violence or bodily invasion from non-state actors. These rights give rise to correlative duties which can at times appear diametrically opposed. One right calls for protection from the state, while the other calls for state protection. These opposing dimensions give rise to different philosophical justifications for why security ought to be regarded as a human right.

At first blush, both aspects of the right to security seem axiomatically a good thing. All people share the ambition to live free from fear of attack, loss of life, arbitrary arrest, detention or coercive interrogation. This chapter explores the theoretical arguments that support the recognition of that ambition as a right worthy of legal and moral protection. Section I identifies competing conceptions of security in the theories of Hobbes and Locke. Section II discusses the philosophical justifications for the right to security in the work of Blackstone, Shue, Fredman, Powell, and Ramsay. Section III exposes the problems associated with broad conceptions of security as a meta-right, and argues in favour of a specific and narrow conception of the right.

I. Competing Conceptions of Security

Before embarking on this analysis it is worth our setting out some key distinctions. There is a difference between recognizing the 'good' of security, and recognizing whether specific actions taken in its pursuit constitute a social good. There is also a difference between recognizing the social good of security, and deciding that we ought to recognize and protect an individual's right to security. Finally, there is a difference between recognizing a right to security in principle, and determining the scope of the correlative obligations it places upon states and the weight it holds relative to other rights.

What makes security a good? Loader and Walker argue that security is a '"thick" public good', a 'great civilizing force', and a 'necessary and virtuous component of the good society'.[1] Their arguments are not without key antecedents, for Hobbes and Locke thought carefully about security too.

---

[1] Ian Loader and Neil Walker, *Civilizing Security* (Cambridge University Press, 2007).

A. Hobbes and the primacy of peace

Ever since Hobbes' *Leviathan*, security has been identified as the primary benefit of political community, and the good against which we trade off our natural liberty. The rationale of the Hobbesian state, and the foundation of its legitimacy, rest on its assurance of the security of its citizens. Hobbes' social contract is the route through which mankind averts the social conditions whereby 'every man is enemy to every man' and 'men live without other security'.[2] In this condition of 'war', Hobbes was convinced that no civilization, no self-realization, nothing good about being human, could be achieved and life would be 'solitary, poor, nasty, brutish, and short'.[3] Humanity's transition from a state of nature to a political community is thus motivated by the promise of security, which in turn provides conditions in which our lives can become meaningful, and culturally and socially expressive.

Little to dispute thus far. But Hobbes went on to give security such primacy that no one in his society can contest the power of the provider of peace: the sovereign power constituted by the mutual consent of those inside a commonwealth. Hobbes' social contract was a bargain between individuals to cede their liberty—or 'right to do every thing'—to the extent necessary to avoid war.[4] In so doing, they agreed to afford the sovereign—which he referred to as the 'Mortal God'—unlimited power.[5] Security, then, for Hobbes, was both the rationale for the existence of the state, and the justification for unlimited sovereign power over the subjects within it. The sovereign 'may use the strength and means of them all, as he shall think expedient, for their peace and common defence'.[6]

Hobbes drew a stark distinction between peace (or bare security) assured by the absolute power of the sovereign, and war where such power is limited, divided or infringed. Because individuals contract with one another to mutually obey the sovereign in return for security, the sovereign cannot be held to account for breach of that contract.[7] The powers which constituted the 'essence of sovereignty' were indivisible.[8] It mattered not whether sovereignty was vested in a monarch or a democratically elected power, but whether that power was capable of eliminating war and the threat of war between men in his society.

This concern for peace was by no means abstract. Writing at the end of the English Civil War, Hobbes was evidently motivated by an immediate and concrete concern with peace and security in his time. Making sovereign powers divisible, in the sense of constitutionally accountable, had been the route to failure in the past.[9] While well aware that there would be complaints about the sovereign, Hobbes thought the good of security too valuable to be threatened by civil dispute. Individual grievances with the actions of the sovereign could never be compared with 'the miseries, and horrible calamities, that accompany a civil war; or that dissolute condition of masterless men, without subjection to laws, and a coercive power to tie their hands from rapine and

---

[2] Thomas Hobbes, *Leviathan*, ch. XIII, §9.   [3] Hobbes, *Leviathan*, ch. XIII, §9.
[4] Hobbes, *Leviathan*, ch. XIII, §4.   [5] Hobbes, *Leviathan*, ch. XVII, §13.
[6] Hobbes, *Leviathan*, ch. XVII, §13.   [7] Hobbes, *Leviathan*, ch. XVIII, §4.
[8] Hobbes, *Leviathan*, ch. XVIII, §16.   [9] Hobbes, *Leviathan*, ch. XVIII, §16.

revenge'.[10] Averting this condition was Hobbes' persuasive mission, as he was convinced that men were incapable of knowing what was in their own interests: 'for all men are by nature provided of notable multiplying glasses...but are destitute of those prospective glasses, (namely moral and civil science,) to see afar off the miseries that hang over them...'.[11]

But looking with our retrospective 'glasses' over the last three centuries, it is easier to disagree with Hobbes about what is in our interests. Hobbes' account is instructive insofar as it highlights the value of security and its intimate connection to political power. Further, his understanding of the way that the good of security allows human flourishing and social and cultural development is seminal. But the primacy Hobbes affords to the assurance of security, and the power he gives to the sovereign in its pursuit, is less persuasive, as he fails to appreciate how the state itself might pose a threat to individual security. Notwithstanding, Hobbes' recognition of the value of security as a prerequisite to the realization of other individual and social goods has echoes in contemporary justifications for security as a meta-right.

Hobbes' account is also instructive in another way. It is the paradigmatic example of the way that fear of war, and an immediate sense of insecurity, can forge an inextricable logic towards a security state. The immediacy of insecurity, and the strength of our fear of harm, can lead us to prioritize security at the cost of corroding other social goods. Centuries after Hobbes, liberals generally agree that security has to be balanced with other goods, and that its attainment at the expense of all liberty, and all capacity to challenge political power, is a step too far. So for liberals, some conceptions of security, and their resultant implications for the ordering of political life, can in themselves constitute the wrong kind of society or even the wrong kind of security.

B. Locke's conception of liberty as security

It is imperative therefore to craft a conception of security that is good, not just for security's sake, but for the social arrangements that flow from its pursuit. For Locke, Hobbes' society threatened the security of citizens themselves. He believed that individuals were equal to each other in their enjoyment of their natural rights to life, liberty, and property, which he referred to collectively as 'property'. He also believed that individuals had in equal measure the natural right to 'self-preservation'. This right included each individual's executive power to punish and police invasions of their 'property'. While Locke agreed with Hobbes that 'Safety and Security' were the 'end for which [individuals] are in Society',[12] he was clear that individuals yielded up their power to others on the 'express or tacit Trust, that it shall be employed for their good'.[13]

Unlike Hobbes' agreement between 'subjects' to cede their liberty to an unrestricted sovereign power, Locke's social contract imposed reciprocal obligations on the state which had to be liberty regarding. For Locke, the point of entering into a political community was precisely to optimize the enjoyment of one's liberty and property. In

---

[10] Hobbes, *Leviathan*, ch. XVIII, §20. [11] Hobbes, *Leviathan*, ch. XVIII, §20.
[12] John Locke, *Two Treatises of Government* (1689), §222.
[13] Locke, *Two Treatises of Government*, §171.

entering into society from the state of nature, men give up certain freedoms, but they do so 'only with an intention in every one the better to preserve himself his Liberty and Property', because 'no rational Creature can be supposed to change his condition with an intention to be worse.'[14]

Locke did not share Hobbes' view of the state of nature as a state of war, nor of the benefits of an absolute monarchy to preserve against such a condition. He brought sovereign power down from Hobbes' pedestal. Rather than viewing the sovereign as a 'mortal God',[15] Locke argued that *absolute Monarchs are but Men*' and favoured limits upon their power.[16] In opposition to Hobbes, Locke viewed 'absolute power' as the greatest threat to the security of individuals. Absolute power was, in his view, both a declaration of war against the people and an act of enslavement. As a consequence, Locke argued, 'to be free from such force is the only security of my Preservation'[17] and that the '*Freedom* from Absolute, Arbitrary Power, is so necessary to, and closely joined with a Man's Preservation, that he cannot part with it, but by what forfeits his Preservation and Life together'.[18]

For Locke the power vested in the state or Sovereign can therefore have no other 'end or measure... but to preserve the Members of that Society in their Lives, Liberties, and Possessions'.[19] Where this end was not fulfilled, and where those in power 'endeavour to grasp themselves or put into the hands of any other an Absolute Power over the Lives, Liberties, and Estates of the People; By this breach of Trust they forfeit the power, the People had put into their hands, for quite contrary ends, and it devolves to the People, who have a Right to resume their original Liberty'.[20]

If arbitrary power constituted the greatest threat to the security and preservation of individuals, then its antithesis constituted the greatest source of security for Locke. This meant that power must be constrained by law. Locke called this 'security within the limits of law'. He argued that men simply 'would not quit the freedom of the State of Nature' if what they stood to gain was government subject to 'Absolute Arbitrary Power, or Governing without settled standing Laws'.[21] Since the power of the government was 'only for the good of the Society', then 'so it ought to be exercised by established and promulgated Laws'.[22] This would mean 'that both the People may know their Duty, and be safe and secure within the limits of the Law, and the Rulers too kept within their due bounds'.[23]

Locke's conception of security thus differed greatly from that of Hobbes. He agreed that security underpinned meaningful human existence, and constituted the object of civic or political community. However, Locke's ideal of security was a rich conception embedded in the enjoyment of basic rights to liberty, life, and property. It was the law's capacity to protect these rights and the law's limits on sovereign power that kept individuals 'safe and secure within the limits of the Law'.[24] Thus, while Locke himself did not expressly articulate a right to security, his theory forms the foundation of a

---

[14] Locke, *Two Treatises of Government*, §131.
[16] Locke, *Two Treatises of Government*, §13.
[18] Locke, *Two Treatises of Government*, §23.
[20] Locke, *Two Treatises of Government*, §222.
[22] Locke, *Two Treatises of Government*, §137.
[24] Locke, *Two Treatises of Government*, §137.

[15] Hobbes, *Leviathan*, ch. XVII, §13.
[17] Locke, *Two Treatises of Government*, §17.
[19] Locke, *Two Treatises of Government*, §171.
[21] Locke, *Two Treatises of Government*, §137.
[23] Locke, *Two Treatises of Government*, §137.

liberal conception of the right to security grounded in the protection of liberty, life, and property.

Our choice between Hobbes and Locke therefore rests on a choice about the ordering of values in a good society. Either we believe, as Hobbes did, that peace (or bare security) was a value so important as to supersede other goods in a political community, or we believe, like Locke, that a rich conception of security is inseparable from the enjoyment of the liberties and property that is naturally ours to enjoy. Locke certainly found favour with political thinkers of his time. Benjamin Franklin echoed his sentiments in his famous words, 'they who can give up essential liberty to obtain a little temporary safety, deserve neither liberty nor safety'.[25] But the balance between liberty and security remains a perennial debate in liberal theory, and is certainly no less contested now than it was in Locke's time. We shall see in section III that the choice of whether security or liberty 'comes first'[26] is a key element of our understanding of what the right to security should protect, the weight it should hold relative to other rights, and whether we believe this right should constitute a meta-right—the right of rights.

II. The Right to Security

The theories of Hobbes and Locke laid the foundations for our competing conceptions of security and the social ordering that is consequent upon its pursuit. But neither of them ever spoke explicitly about a right to security. Section II of this chapter explores the theories that explicitly develop such a right. Here we make the transition from theories identifying security as the rationale of political community and a valuable social good, to theories of security as an individual and subjective right. This transition was first made in Blackstone's *Commentaries on the Laws of England*.[27]

A. Blackstone and the right to personal security

Blackstone was a jurist, and not a political philosopher like Hobbes or Locke. His *Commentaries* were a systematic treatise offering explanatory structure to the common law in the eighteenth century, and identifying rights and principles from existing legal doctrine. Like Hobbes and Locke, Blackstone identified security as the prize of entering into social and political community: 'for no man, that considers a moment, would wish to retain the absolute and uncontrolled power of doing whatever he pleases: the consequence of which is, that every other man would also have the same power; and then there would be no security to individuals in any of the enjoyments of life'.[28]

---

[25] Benjamin Franklin and William Temple Franklin, *Memoirs of the Life and Writings of Benjamin Franklin* (Henry Colborn, 1818), 260.

[26] Amitai Etzioni, *Security First* (Yale University Press, 2007).

[27] William Blackstone, *Commentaries on the Laws of England* (1753) (hereinafter 'Blackstone's *Commentaries*').

[28] Blackstone's *Commentaries*, 125.

Blackstone identified a 'right to personal security' as the first of the three absolute and natural rights of man. He argued that the rights of man could be 'reduced to three principal or primary articles; the right of personal security, the right of personal liberty, and the right of private property'.[29] By absolute rights, Blackstone meant those 'primary' rights which belong 'to persons merely in a state of nature, and which every man is entitled to enjoy, whether out of society or in it'.[30] The law's primary goal was the enforcement and balancing of these rights: 'the first and primary end of human laws is to maintain and regulate these absolute rights of individuals'.[31]

Blackstone's right to personal security included rights to protection from the state as well as rights to resources. As the right to personal security protected natural life, the 'immediate donation of the great creator'[32] it placed considerable restrictions on the state's use of capital punishment, which he viewed as a central limitation on an accountable state.[33] Consequently, English law ensured that no that 'no man shall be put to death, without being brought to answer by due process of law'.[34] Blackstone also saw the right to personal security as the source of the common law prohibition of murder, the basis of the right to 'necessary self defence' and the foundation of the prohibition of abortion.[35] Interestingly, Blackstone also identified a legal right to the resources necessary to sustain life: 'the law not only regards life and member, and protects every man in the enjoyment of them, but also furnishes him with every thing necessary for their support. For there is no man so indigent or wretched, but he may demand a supply sufficient for all the necessities of life from the more opulent part of the community, by means of the several statutes enacted for the relief of the poor, of which in their proper places'.[36]

Blackstone's conception of the right to personal security went beyond protecting life. It also included protection against injury of 'those limbs and members that may be necessary to a man, in order to defend himself or annoy his enemy'.[37] He went on to argue that the right to security included protection against insult or injury, as a 'person or body is also entitled, by the same natural right, to security from the corporal insults of menaces, assaults, beating, and wounding; though such insults amount not to destruction of life or member'.[38] Finally, Blackstone believed the right to security prompted the law to protect against risks to health, and even damage to reputation. In his words the law protected 'the preservation of a man's health from such practices as may prejudice or annoy it, and ... the security of his reputation or good name from the arts of detraction and slander'.[39]

Blackstone's right to security was the first extensive account of security as a personal and legal right vested in individuals. While Hobbes thought security was the primary rationale for the sacrifice of absolute liberty, his account was so inimical to the idea of personal or civic rights that the notion of a right to security did not feature. For Hobbes, security was the inverse of liberty. While Locke included the right to life

---

[29] Blackstone's *Commentaries*, 129.
[30] Blackstone's *Commentaries*, 124.
[31] Blackstone's *Commentaries*, 124.
[32] Blackstone's *Commentaries*, 133.
[33] Blackstone's *Commentaries*, 133.
[34] Blackstone's *Commentaries*, 133.
[35] Blackstone's *Commentaries*, 133.
[36] Blackstone's *Commentaries*, 131.
[37] Blackstone's *Commentaries*, 133.
[38] Blackstone's *Commentaries*, 133.
[39] Blackstone's *Commentaries*, 134.

amongst his list of natural rights, he did not extend this into a broader right to personal security within a political community. Blackstone identified the right to security as a natural right expressed in the content of the law in his time. An important dimension of Blackstone's account of the right to personal security was his inclusion of the right to resources necessary to sustain life. This anticipated later accounts of the socio-economic aspects of security, and gives lie to the idea that civil and political rights were initially and exclusively conceived as constraints upon the state. Moreover, it is noteworthy that Blackstone gave the right to personal security a broader remit than mere protection of life, including in its remit the protection of health, reputation, and bodily integrity.

However, Blackstone's account offers little guidance on the balance between the absolute rights he views it as the law's job to regulate. While the balance between security and liberty is a continuing discussion in political theory, the issues are even sharper when we introduce the notion of a basic right to security. Rights bring with them immediate demands for indications of weight and of relative balance. They introduce correlative duties on the state to act in certain ways. Without clear guidance on where to place the right to security in the hierarchy of rights, states may face irreconcilable legal duties. So the definition of the right to security matters in more immediate ways than many philosophers realise. Blackstone presents a starting point in recognising the primacy of the right to security, and by setting it alongside in equal measure to liberty and property. But it is the thornier question of the relative balance between these rights with which section III of this chapter is concerned.

B. Shue and the basic right to security

We skip now to the latter part of the twentieth century, when Henry Shue's book—*Basic Rights*—marked a turning point in Anglo–American rights theory. Shue viewed basic rights as specifying 'the line beneath which no one is to be allowed to sink', providing 'some minimal protection against utter helplessness to those too weak to protect themselves'.[40] Rights are 'basic' if and when 'enjoyment of them is essential to the enjoyment of all other rights.'[41] He took the instrumental view that 'whether a right is basic is independent of whether its enjoyment is also valuable in itself'.[42]

Like Blackstone, Shue identified security as one of the three basic rights, alongside 'liberty' and 'subsistence'. For Shue, security is therefore a right of utmost importance, a meta-right which acts as a precondition to the enjoyment of all other rights. This is a novel claim regarding the right to security. Unlike Blackstone, Shue does not draw the foundation of his argument from the moral claim that basic rights are intrinsic to our human nature, and basic because of their intrinsic value. Rather, Shue makes an instrumental and pre-conditional argument that security constitutes a basic right because the enjoyment of all other enumerated rights would be impossible without it. Indeed, for Shue security is a 'constituent part of the enjoyment of every other right'.[43]

---

[40] Henry Shue, *Basic Rights: Subsistence, Affluence, and US Foreign Policy*, 2nd edn. (Princeton University Press, 1996), 18.
[41] Shue, *Basic Rights*, 19.   [42] Shue, *Basic Rights*, 20.   [43] Shue, *Basic Rights*, 67.

Shue defines the right to security as the right 'not to be subjected to murder, torture, mayhem, rape or assault'.[44] He argues that at the very least 'if there are any rights (basic or not basic) at all, there are basic rights to physical security'.[45] This is because:

> no one can fully enjoy any right that is supposedly protected by society if someone can credibly threaten him or her with murder, rape, beating, etc., when he or she tries to enjoy the alleged right. Such threats to physical security are among the most serious and—in much of the world—the most widespread hindrances to the enjoyment of any right. If any right is to be exercised except at great risk, physical security must be protected. In the absence of physical security people are unable to use any other rights that society may be said to be protecting without being liable to encounter many of the worst dangers they would encounter if society were not protecting the rights. A right to full physical security belongs, then, among the more basic rights—not because the enjoyment of it would be more satisfying to someone who was also enjoying a full range of other rights, but because its absence would leave available extremely effective means for others, including the government, to interfere with or prevent the actual exercise of any other rights that were supposedly protected. Regardless of whether the enjoyment of physical security is also desirable for its own sake, it is desirable as part of the enjoyment of every other right. No rights other than a right to physical security can in fact be enjoyed if a right to physical security is not protected. Being physically secure is a necessary condition for the exercise of any other right, and guaranteeing physical security must be part of guaranteeing anything else as a right.[46]

The scope of Shue's right to security is broad, not because the dangers against which it protects are necessarily diffuse, but because the duties that flow from it are potentially wide ranging. He enumerates three duties that correlate to the existence of a basic right to security:

  I. Duties not to eliminate a person's security—duties to *avoid* depriving.
  II. Duties to protect people against deprivation of security by other people—duties to *protect* from deprivation.
  III. Duties to provide for the security of those unable to provide their own—duties to *aid* the deprived.[47]

The state's correlative duties to act are a key insight into the scope of Shue's right to security. Without the state fulfilling these duties, the enjoyment of all other rights (of which security forms a constitutive part) is impossible.

Shue leaves unresolved the relationship between security and liberty, and the trade-offs that might have to be made between them. For Shue, in order for liberty to attain the same *basic* status as the rights to security and subsistence, it has to be constitutive of the enjoyment of other rights. In this constitutive sense, Shue sees a smaller role for liberty than he does for 'security' and 'subsistence'. While he argues that the basic rights to security, subsistence, and liberty are mutually dependent, he nevertheless admits 'that the dependence is not completely symmetrical: the enjoyment of rights

---

[44] Shue, *Basic Rights*, 20.   [45] Shue, *Basic Rights*, 21.   [46] Shue, *Basic Rights*, 21–2.
[47] Shue, *Basic Rights*, 52.

to *every liberty* is dependent upon the enjoyment of security and subsistence, but the enjoyment of rights to security and rights to subsistence is dependent upon the enjoyment of *only some liberties*.[48] Consequently, Shue goes on to identify those aspects of liberty which constitute essential elements of the enjoyment of other rights: namely rights to participation and rights to freedom of movement.[49] His account of liberty as a basic right is thus a thinner rendition of the kind of liberty Locke viewed as intrinsically valuable.

When viewed from the perspective of the correlative duties flowing from Shue's right to security, the right to liberty certainly appears more limited than the right to security. Shue is vague on the practical forms that the correlative duties might take. He is clearly aware of the coercive potential of duties to protect, and the deleterious effects that overblown coercive powers can have on society:

> [R]eliance on duties to protect rather than duties to avoid would constitute heavy reliance on something like national police power rather than self-restraint by individuals...and would involve obvious disadvantages if—probably, especially if—the police power were adequate actually to enforce duties to avoid upon a generally reluctant society...What division of labor is established by one's account of duties between self-restraint and restraint by others, such as police forces, will obviously have an enormous effect upon the quality of life of those living in the social system in question.[50]

As a consequence, Shue suggests that the appropriate way to fulfil such protective duties is to build organizations and society in a way that encourages self-restraint, rather than bolstering the coercive duties of state agents over individuals. In this way, he hopes to mitigate against the risk of coercive overreach:

> The duty to protect ought not to be understood only in terms of the maintenance of law-enforcement, regulatory, and other closely related agencies. A major and more constructive part of the duty to protect is the duty to design social institutions that do not exceed the capacity of individuals and organizations, including private and public corporations, to restrain themselves. Not only the kinds of acute threats of deprivation that police can prevent, but the kinds of chronic threats that require imaginative legislation and sometimes, long term planning fall under the duty to protect.[51]

Notwithstanding Shue's worthy intentions, section III argues that the potential for the state's coercive overreach is shaped by the environment in which the right to security—and its attendant duties—is articulated. States seeking to legitimate extensive security measures may draw on the notion of security as a basic right in more pernicious ways. Shue's account of broad state duties to mitigate threats to personal security, coupled with his thin conception of liberty, provides more ammunition to proponents of the security state than he might have anticipated.

---

[48] Shue, *Basic Rights*, 70.   [49] Shue, *Basic Rights*, 71–82.   [50] Shue, *Basic Rights*, 61.
[51] Shue, *Basic Rights*, 62.

C. Fredman, Powell, and the capabilities approach

Sandra Fredman's expansive conception of the right to security is grounded in her broader theory of socio-economic rights. She argues that 'protection against hunger, want and other material deprivations that threaten a person's existence are ... as much part of the right to personal security as protection against assaults by the state or others'.[52] Her emphasis is on the social aspect of the right, viewing it as 'arising directly from the need to co-operate'.[53]

Like Shue, Fredman identifies security as an essential prerequisite to the exercise of liberty. Liberty is conceived in the positive sense of 'autonomy and genuine freedom of choice, rather than freedom from interference'.[54] Once we view autonomy in this way, Fredman argues that socio-economic 'constraints' on individual choice become the focus of 'the right to security from want'.[55]

Fredman comes to this conclusion via Sen and Nussbaum's theory of human agency.[56] They believe that a human being must have certain 'capabilities' protected in order to allow them to actualise their autonomy and freedom of choice. Autonomy can thus only flourish when key social conditions are in place: 'economic opportunities, political liberties, social powers and the enabling conditions of good health, basic education, and the encouragement and cultivation of initiatives'.[57] This requires a view of constraints that go beyond those associated with the 'tyrannical' or 'repressive state', to one that includes economic deprivation. For Fredman, freedom from economic deprivation is as essential to 'security' as freedom from 'state repression'.

Powell also relies on capabilities theory when addressing her conception of 'the right to security of person', but for different reasons and ends. She argues that 'security' is nothing more than a referent to the goods, attributes and things we want to secure and 'thus, [it] represents the endurance of certain valuable interests without threat'.[58] For Powell, security is inherently a relational concept, and it requires a set of referents to give it meaningful content. As a consequence, one must ask the questions: (1) security for whom (an agent or patient), (2) security of what (the 'referent object' or an interest or value to be protected), (3) security against/from what (a risk or threat), and (4) who or what will provide protection.[59]

Security thus describes the relation between these four factors and derives its meaning, in any particular context, from them. Crucially, for Powell the 'referent object' of 'the right to security of person' is, without question, 'the person'. Hence, the meaning of the right will depend crucially on the meaning attributed to 'personhood': a concept

---

[52] Sandra Fredman, 'The Positive Right to Security', in B.J. Goold and L. Lazarus (eds.), *Security and Human Rights* (Hart Publishing, 2007), 307–24, 308.

[53] Fredman, 'The Positive Right to Security', 309.

[54] Fredman, 'The Positive Right to Security'.   [55] Fredman, 'The Positive Right to Security'.

[56] Amartya Sen, *Development as Freedom* (Oxford University Press, 1999); Martha Nussbaum, *Women and Human Development: The Capabilities Approach* (Cambridge University Press, 2000).

[57] Fredman, 'The Positive Right to Security'.

[58] Rhonda Powell, *The Relational Concept of Security* (DPhil Dissertation, University of Oxford, 2006), 73.

[59] Powell, *The Relational Concept of Security*, 79.

which itself invites normative discussion, and to which the attachment of the word 'security' adds little clarification.

Powell develops a theory of 'personhood' in order to give meaning to the right to security. Like Fredman, she invokes capabilities theory to identify the interests protected by the right. For Powell, a theory of the right to security which doesn't engage with material conditions risks being lopsided, and preferencing a particular political agenda. Hence:

> [T]o not recognize capabilities as relevant to security of person amounts to retaining the bias in the policy agenda whereby freedom from fear is automatically privileged over freedom from want. In other words, not to recognize these issues as security issues only protects a limited part of what is essential to 'the person'. Conceptions of security of person, which assume a particular content (for example freedom from arbitrary detention or freedom from violence), import a bias into the analysis. These are the questions for legitimate political debate.[60]

Fredman and Powell's use of capabilities theory thus provides justification for both the positive and negative aspects of the right to security. They particularly emphasize the material provisions required to facilitate the development of capabilities. This echoes Blackstone's original conception of the right, where he identified the material context of the right. Section III will explain however that there are grounds for caution in deploying the right to security to support other concrete socio-economic rights such as the right to subsistence, food, health, and housing.

D. Ramsay, the right to security, and vulnerable autonomy

Peter Ramsay offers the most recent formulation of a right to security, which he grounds in his broader theory of 'vulnerable autonomy'.[61] He locates the right to security in the individual's subjective need to be free from the fear of crime, which itself is a precondition to the exercise of autonomy. For Ramsay, autonomy requires 'self-respect, self-esteem and self-trust', and these fragile preconditions demand protection as a matter of social justice. Drawing on Anderson and Honneth, and in a similar vein to capabilities theory, Ramsay argues that individuals depend on 'supportive and recognitional' social institutions to exercise their autonomy.[62]

One aspect of the citizen's sense of self-esteem is her experience of 'ontological security'—an individual's subjective sense of security.[63] Ontological security is achieved through a reflexive process of mutual reassurance and trust between individuals.[64]

---

[60] Powell, *The Relational Concept of Security*, 145.

[61] Peter Ramsay, *The Insecurity State: Vulnerable Autonomy and the Right to Security in the Criminal Law* (Oxford University Press, 2012), 84–112. See also Peter Ramsay, 'The Theory of Vulnerable Autonomy and the Legitimacy of the Civil Preventative Order', London School of Economics Legal Studies Working Paper No. 1/2008.

[62] Joel H. Anderson and Axel Honneth, 'Autonomy, Vulnerability, Recognition and Justice', in John Philip Christman and Joel Anderson (eds.), *Autonomy and the Challenges to Liberalism: New Essays* (Cambridge University Press, 2005), 127–49.

[63] Ramsay, *The Insecurity State*, 90. Quoting A. Giddens, *Modernity and Self-Identity* (Polity, 1991), 40.

[64] Ramsay, *The Insecurity State*.

Ramsay explains the preventive provisions of the criminal law as a consequence of a citizen's vulnerable autonomy and their duties of mutual reassurance. On this view, failure to reassure others justifies imposing liability through preventative criminal law means, such as Anti-Social Behaviour Orders and their successors. This is because the 'responsibility to protect the vulnerability of others is the reflex of those others' right to be free from the fear of crime, which is to say their *right to security*'.[65]

Ramsay argues not only that his conception of the right to security is implicit in mainstream political theories,[66] but also that it is fundamental to the European Convention on Human Rights (ECHR). Although the right appears only obliquely in Article 5 ECHR, Ramsay correctly notes that security constitutes a ground for legitimate rights limitations in a range of qualified Convention provisions. Hence, he argues that an 'individual has no cause for complaint if their human rights are interfered with when the interference is necessary to uphold another's right to security'. From this he derives the novel, and rather questionable, legal conclusion that 'the right to security is enforced by means of a liability for failure to reassure others, and this liability implies a positive obligation to be aware of what will cause others insecurity.[67]

Ramsay's broad-ranging theory seeks to provide a coherent normative foundation for the emerging paradigm of prevention within the criminal law. In his search for this underlying paradigm he develops the broadest possible conception of the right to security, stretching it to include subjective feelings of insecurity, and applying a rather unique interpretation of human rights law. Section III of this chapter takes issue with this conception and with Ramsay's argument for it to be 'legitimated in the language of human rights'.[68]

III. Securitizing Rights

This chapter has discussed the arguments supporting the moral and political claim to a human right to security. Blackstone views the right as the consequence of a social contract in which the state gives security to individuals in return for restrictions of their natural liberty. Shue sees the right as basic, as without it all other rights would be incapable of realization. Fredman draws on capabilities theory to justify the right as essential to the exercise of autonomy and self-realization. Powell uses capabilities theory to give content to the idea of personhood, which she views as the key interpretive stem of the right to security of person. Ramsay grounds the right to security in his theory of 'vulnerable autonomy' and an elaborate view of the ECHR. But Shue, Fredman, Powell, and Ramsay do not take sufficient account of the potential for the right to security to legitimate the state's coercive overreach. My own view, closer to Locke, is that the state's political and moral duty to secure individuals must always be clearly constrained. If there is a right to security correlative upon the state's broader duty of security, it must be balanced within a hierarchy of rights which places liberty, dignity, and equality firmly at its apex.

---

[65] Ramsay, *The Insecurity State*, 112–13.   [66] Ramsay, *The Insecurity State*, 113.
[67] Ramsay, *The Insecurity State*, 120.   [68] Ramsay, *The Insecurity State*, 113.

The remainder of this chapter thus explores how the right to security has been shaped in the practice of the law and contemporary politics. While Blackstone and Ramsay both identify legal material that 'regulates' or 'expresses' the right to security as they see it, there is little concrete discussion of a posited right to security that must operate and have meaning within the law. The final part of this chapter examines the legal material and political rhetoric on the right to security. It concludes with some reflections on the difficulties of aspiring to a meta-right to security.

A. The right to security in law

Certain consequences flow when we transfer a moral claim to a legal claim. Legal claims engage a set of social institutions and institutional activities that have potentially far reaching effects. When courts afford remedies for violations of legal rights, a range of tangible institutional consequences follow. This institutional force gives the claim a different character in social life to the rhetorical statements of politicians or the well-reasoned arguments of philosophers.

Further, legal claims must be intelligible to those who invoke them, argue against, and adjudicate upon them. Human rights claims may not always meet the standard of formal specificity that some lawyers would like, but they must at least be capable of giving rise to plausible legal arguments. Citizens, lawyers, legislators, and others must be able to discern the scope of the right, what its weight is relative to other rights, what duties it gives rise to, and what interests are protected under the right.

A brief comparative examination suggests that the core legal meaning of the right to security is unsettled. This is despite textual similarity between some of the relevant provisions. In a number of these, the right is linked closely to 'liberty', or 'freedom', and often with 'life'. The 'security' and 'liberty' nexus is present in the constitutions of Canada, South Africa, and Hungary, as well as the Universal Declaration of Human Rights (UDHR) and the ECHR.[69] In the South African Constitution and the Northern Irish Draft Bill of Human Rights, in contrast, the right is expressed as a 'positive' right and protects explicitly against threats to security or violence from non-state actors.[70]

These more recently drafted documents also express the ordering of the right in contrasting ways. The South African Constitution has a specific right to be 'free from violence whether from public or private sources.'[71] It also uses the right to personal security as an overarching title for a cluster of other rights such as 'freedom from torture and cruel, inhuman or degrading treatment or punishment, and the right to bodily and psychological integrity'.[72] The Northern Irish Draft

---

[69] Article 5 ECHR states that 'everyone has the right to liberty and security of person'. Article 3 UDHR states 'Everyone has the right to life, liberty and security of person'. Section 7 of the Canadian Charter of Rights and Freedoms provides that 'everyone has the right to life, liberty, and security of the person'. Section 55(1) of the Constitution of Hungary declares that 'everyone has the right to freedom and personal security'. Section 12 of the South African Constitution provides that 'everyone has the right to freedom and security of the person'.

[70] Northern Ireland Human Rights Commission, 'Progressing a Bill of Rights for Northern Ireland: An Update', April 2004.

[71] Constitution of the Republic of South Africa, s. 12(1)(c).

[72] Constitution of the Republic of South Africa, s. 12.

Bill articulates the right to security as a self-standing preambular principle: 'everyone has the right to live free from violence, fear, oppression and intimidation, with differences to be resolved through exclusively democratic means without the use of threat or force'. However, the right to be protected against violence is also expressly grounded in the 'right to dignity and physical integrity' under section 6 of the Draft Bill.

These legal provisions are subject to varying judicial interpretations even where they share similar wording.[73] In Canada, the right to security is understood very broadly, to include 'personal autonomy', 'control over one's physical and psychological integrity' and 'basic human dignity'.[74] In contrast, the European Court of Human Rights sees no additional role for the term 'security' in Article 5 ECHR beyond that which liberty already protects.[75] Where the legal norms themselves are broadly and positively expressed, as in South Africa, the courts have taken a narrow and restrictive view of the specific positive obligations imposed on the state.[76] The broadest conception of all may be that found in the United Nations World Summit notion of human security, encompassing a range of existing human rights including dignity, the right to subsistence, and freedom from fear.[77] While this norm is non-justiciable, it has clear normative weight within the United Nations (UN), and has very recently been reaffirmed by the UN General Assembly.[78] It is evidently influenced by the capabilities approach.

From this rather brief and sweeping legal summary it is evident that the right to security is now seen to protect dignity, equality, liberty, physical and psychological autonomy, freedom from fear and freedom from want. This extensive range of interests has prompted me to conclude previously that the 'right to security can be deployed to protect most things that we want in life'.[79] The breadth and opacity of the right to security gives rise to rule of law concerns about clarity and transparency, but it also gives rise to another concern about the legal legitimation of coercive action by the state. Coercive state action looks very different when it is cast as the exercise of a correlative duty flowing from the right to security, and politicians are only too well aware of this.

---

[73] See further, Liora Lazarus, 'Mapping the Right to Security', in Liora Lazarus and Benjamin Goold (eds.), *Security and Human Rights* (Hart Publishing, 2006) and Liora Lazarus, 'The Right to Security: Securing Rights or Securitizing Rights?' in Rob Dickinson (ed.), *Examining Critical Perspectives on Human Rights* (Cambridge University Press, 2012).

[74] *Rodriquez v. British Columbia (Attorney General)* [1993] 3 SCR 519.

[75] Richard Clayton and Hugh Tomlinson (eds.), *The Law of Human Rights*, 2nd edn. (Oxford University Press, 2009), 628.

[76] This is justified by reference to reasonableness, resource constraints, and the proximity of the state to the harm done to the individual complainant. See *Rail Commuters Action Group and Others v. Transnet Ltd* 2005 (4) *BCLR* 301 (CC).

[77] Article 143 of the 2005 World Summit Outcome Document provides: 'We stress the right of people to live in freedom and dignity, free from poverty and despair. We recognize that all individuals, in particular vulnerable people, are entitled to freedom from fear and freedom from want, with an equal opportunity to enjoy all their rights and fully develop their human potential. To this end, we commit ourselves to discussing and defining the notion of human security in the General Assembly.

[78] United Nations General Assembly Resolution 66/290. Follow up to paragraph 143 on human security of the 2005 World Summit Outcome (A/RES/66/290).

[79] Lazarus, 'The Right to Security', 95.

B. The right to security in political rhetoric

An analysis of the use of the term 'right to security' in global political rhetoric since 9/11 indicates that the right has become a popular means to legitimate security measures.[80] The term is most frequently used regarding the Middle East and North Korea, and it is commonly engaged when justifying counter-terrorist measures or military invasion in the name of the war on terror.[81] Most leading politicians will have engaged the term at some stage in one of these contexts. Importantly, politicians are claiming that the 'right to security' is 'the basic right on which all others are based'.[82] They used this premise to argue that negative rights ought to be 'rebalanced' in favour of the right to security and to legitimate strong coercive measures. On only one occasion, out of the 400 examples examined, has a politician invoked the right to security in its negative sense as a 'right to security against the power of the state'.[83] This growing tendency to invoke the right to security as a means to extend the state's coercive or military reach is a process I have previously called 'righting security'.

Politicians can hardly be blamed for picking up on this rhetoric, when the UN and a number of leading domestic courts are doing the same. They have found themselves inadvertently bolstered by strange bed fellows within the human rights and development community. Both of these communities have found the language of the right to security to be an effective means to shore up the interests they are most concerned to promote. In the face of the initial onslaught on rights that came with early counter-terror strategy for example, Amnesty International was quick to claim that 'the right to security is a basic human right'.[84] Moreover, the development community has clearly been a key part of the human security movement, presumably because the animating purchase of the concept of security is more powerful than invoking the language of the rights to subsistence, food or health on their own.[85]

So in short, the broad and inclusive capabilities approach to the right to security, and other philosophers' arguments for the meta-right to security have become a staple of international institutions and NGOs. Why should we care if they deploy strategically effective language for increasing human happiness? The problem is that a subtle shift is taking place that may be more pernicious than any well-meaning human rights activist might recognize. This lies in the securitization of rights.

C. Securing rights or securitizing rights?

Given the potentially sharp coercive consequences of assertions of the right to security, and the current political context in which many of these claims are made, viewing

---

[80] This analysis was conducted in 2011 and is discussed in Lazarus, 'The Right to Security'.

[81] Lazarus, 'The Right to Security', 95–8.

[82] Full text of speech reported by BBC News 'Reid Urges Human Rights Shake Up',12 May 2007, available at http://news.bbc.co.uk/2/hi/uk_news/politics/6648849.stm, accessed 17 March 2012.

[83] Speech made by Sir Menzies Campbell in the House of Commons debates into extending the limits of pre-charge detention, 25 July 2007, HC Deb., vol. 463, col. 851.

[84] William Schulz, *Safer or Scared? Impact of the War on Terror*—CNN, 28 May 2003.

[85] Lazarus, 'The Right to Security', 95–8.

the right to security too broadly carries some unsettling implications. The problems are various, but the most urgent is a subtle transformation of the ordering of human rights. I term this process the 'securitization' of rights.

In order to explore these objections, we need to recapitulate the argument in favour of security as a basic right. For Shue, security is such a right because its enjoyment is the 'necessary condition' of the enjoyment of any other right.[86] The right to security is thus the 'right to secure rights'.[87] But when we think of this in terms of meaningful obligations that might be imposed on a duty-bearer, what does this actually amount to? These claims regarding a broad and meta-right to security can be reformulated as follows: the right to security gives rise to correlative duties for states to create the conditions in which objective risks of future threats which might reasonably cause subjective feelings of apprehension or insecurity, are minimized to a degree that allows the enjoyment of other rights.[88] In other words, the right to security imposes a 'protective' duty on the state to anticipate and mitigate the risks that militate against the enjoyment of all other rights.

There is a range of objections to this broad conception of the right. Two of these are chiefly issues of legal practicality: indeterminability and redundancy. The remainder are broader normative concerns: the argument concerning the weakness of the precondition, and the risk of securitization.

The first objection—vagueness—raises classic rule of law concerns. A right conceived of in this way is simply too broad to be legally workable. This is not only because it lacks specificity as such, but rather because its substance is connected to perceptions of future risk which are notoriously opaque. Potentially, there is no end to the kinds of risks that would have to be averted. Equally, our definition says nothing about how foreseeable the risks have to be in order to establish a breach of the right. How much risk can we tolerate in order to exercise our other rights? There is as a consequence little plausible legal material in the statement that the right to security constitutes a meta-right. We would need far more clarification for this norm to be legally workable, and that is exactly what the courts have found themselves doing when they have to explain the specific obligations flowing from the right.

In any event, we might argue, the idea of a meta-right is nothing more than a rhetorical flourish. The meta-right merely duplicates other rights, or to put it another way, the component parts of the meta-right to security are made up of the enjoyment of other rights. Could it be that the meta-right to security is nothing more than an illusion or a hologram? Or perhaps it is not a thing (or a right) in itself? At the very least, there is no plausible reason to introduce a legally redundant norm. In this formulation at least, it serves little legal function.

At best then, conceptions of the legal right to security as a meta-right amount to rhetorical claims of the importance of security as a value or good. A right so conceived is either so indeterminate as to defy implementation, or simply redundant, adding nothing of substance to the exercise of other rights. The real 'meat' of the legal right therefore consists in the specific obligations and duties which the courts are forced to

---

[86] Shue, *Basic Rights*, 21–2.   [87] Lazarus, 'The Right to Security', 100.
[88] Lazarus, 'The Right to Security, 100.

develop when confronted with motherhood statements about security as a meta-right. Beyond the mere impracticality or redundancy of transposing a meta-conception of the right to security into a legal setting, however, there are deeper normative and practical reasons to resist this approach.

The first of these normative objections is pursued by Jeremy Waldron who questions whether security is always a necessary precondition to the exercise of all other rights. Because 'security is not an all-or-nothing matter, but a matter of more or less'[89] it may be possible to exercise rights in conditions of insecurity. Certainly, this is the case in many fragile states today where citizens exercise a range of rights and freedoms in conditions of severely compromised security. It may even be that in more secure environments the same is true. I might exercise freedom of expression one day, and have my home burgled the next. This patchy experience of security doesn't always correlate to the negation of all human rights.

Waldron alerts us to a further risk that focusing on the precondition to the exercise of all rights might steer us away from the meaningful enjoyment of other rights. Because security is a 'voracious ideal',[90] we might skew the balance between security and other important rights in damaging ways. Waldron highlights this problem of balance when security is viewed as the right from which all other rights flow.

> Many people think we would be safer if we were to abandon some of our rights or at least cut back on some of our more aggressive claims about the extent and importance of our civil liberties. Or maybe the trade-off should go in the other direction. Many people think we should be a little braver and risk a bit more in the way of security to uphold our precious rights. After all, security is not the be-all and the end-all; our rights are what really matter. But this alternative line will not work if it turns out that our security is valuable, not just for its own sake, but for the sake of our rights. What if the enjoyment of our rights is possible only when we are already secure against various forms of violent attack? If rights are worth nothing without security, then the brave alternative that I alluded to is misconceived.[91]

This brings us to the core of the problem. Without a specific and distinctive conception of the right to security—one which has meaningful content and limits—we do not know what it is we are balancing. What we do know is that the amorphous right to security can be used to legitimate measures in political rhetoric that threaten the other rights that security is meant to be 'securing'. We must urgently delimit the right to security in the political imagination; otherwise, the other human rights which security is meant to be serving are under more threat than we might want to acknowledge.

This brings us to the final objection. The argument that security constitutes a meta-right overlooks the distinction between foundational rights (the value-based claim) and pre-conditional rights (a factual claim). To argue that a right is foundational is more than arguing that rights can be enjoyed only in certain factual circumstances. Rather, a foundational right provides the broader value from which more specific rights can be derived. When we say someone has the right to dignity and

---

[89] Jeremy Waldron, *Torture, Terror and Trade-Offs: Philosophy for the White House* (Oxford University Press 2010), 177.
[90] Waldron, 'Security as a Basic Right'.   [91] Waldron, 'Security as a Basic Right', 166.

therefore they must not be tortured, we are making a value statement that we believe must be respected for basic human existence to be meaningful. This isn't a question of the factual conditions, but a question of the values which guide the way we live and treat others. But the pre-condition argument presented by Shue is not doing the same thing. His argument is self-admittedly instrumental. The intrinsic value of security is less important to him than the purpose it serves to the exercise of other rights.

The puzzle then is whether security represents a non-instrumental value in its own terms, as Fredman and Powell claim. Security might be foundational because of the intrinsic value of its enjoyment, and because of the value-based platform it provides for the derivation of other more specific rights. In my view this is unsuccessful because, as Powell herself argues, security is an empty vessel which only attains meaning through attachment to other goods and interests. Powell's attempt to resolve the opacity of the right to security by reference to the notion of personhood doesn't entirely resolve this problem.

One way of demonstrating my point is to imagine a world in which security is achieved but in which the values of dignity, equality, and liberty are absent. What other specific and distinctive rights would the right to security afford? While we could at least say that the absence of threat to life or limb would be valuable in and of itself, life would have very little meaning beyond the bare fact of survival. And in any event, we could arrive at the same place by protecting the right to life, without importing all sorts of other open-ended interests through the hazy concept of security.

My objections are not purely theoretical however, as the confusion between the instrumental and non-instrumental value of security risks securitizing other rights, particularly when we move beyond the pages of philosophical texts to popular and political rhetoric. Securitization, simply put, is a sociological term used to describe a 'speech act' which results in security becoming the prism through which more and more social issues and categories are viewed.[92] Loader and Walker have shown convincingly that securitization occurs when security is 'elevated to an unhealthy hegemonic category and comes to mean the unreflexive, parochial and anxious cleaving to a security-driven conception of a risk free society'.[93]

When politicians argue, as they have, that 'the right to security, to the protection of life and liberty, is and should be the basic right on which all others are based' they are in effect performing a securitizing act. They mean something a lot less comforting than Shue, Fredman, Powell or Ramsay would like to believe. Rather, by subsuming liberty into security, we can observe a subtle reordering of the value of liberty relative to security. It is reminiscent of a claim far closer to Etzioni's proposition that 'security comes first'.[94] But liberty means something different to the anxious avoidance of risk. If it is seen as the subset of the right to security, then it becomes a lot less adventurous. When security is its root, liberty risks being reduced to a single dimension—its complexity and richness removed. Liberty may even mean the right to take risks.[95]

---

[92] Lucia Zedner, *Security* (Routledge, 2009), 23–5.
[93] Loader and Walker, *Civilizing Security*, 168.   [94] Etzioni, *Security First*.
[95] Mark Neoclaus, *Critique of Security* (Edinburgh University Press, 2008), 24f.

Perhaps the starkest way to emphasize the dangers of securitization therefore, is to promote a *right to insecurity*. As I have argued elsewhere,[96] such a right could be used to protect a life of self-creation, the value of unknowns and surprises, the importance of improvization and innovation, and most importantly, of freedom. For if we are to live in a society where the right to security becomes the meta-right upon which we legitimate claims to all other social values, we will, inevitably undermine the freedom which we hold dear. The point, is 'with freedom comes risk and insecurity, it is a necessary concomitant of the liberal society'. [97] For those who think that arguing for a right to insecurity is frivolous at dangerous times like these, we ought at the very least to argue for restraint in the deployment of the right to security. If there is to be such a right, we must find a way to distinguish it sharply from the right to be secure.[98]

Conclusion

If there is a right to security, it should be meaningful on its own terms: we cannot resolve its opacity by reference to personhood or capabilities or all other rights. The right to security should be distinctive: it ought to protect those essential interests which other rights cannot plausibly be interpreted to protect. The right to security should not detract or distract from other rights: if security constitutes such an essential element of all other rights, then let us secure those rights in the first instance, instead of deploying the language of security to arrive at their protection. The right to security needs to be specific: it should correlate to clear and meaningful obligations and duties, rather than empty rhetorical statements. The right to security must be narrow: a right that is meaningful in law, that cannot be so easily deployed to legitimate the state's coercive overreach in a politics of security.

In short, we need to examine far more closely why the right to security or 'human security' has become such an animating language in human rights discourse today. We need to reflect on the reason why organisations like the World Justice Project single this right out in their Rule of Law index, over all other rights.[99] We need to understand why invoking the basic rights to dignity, equality, and liberty isn't quite enough to spur institutional and political action nowadays. Finally, we need to resist the tendency to deploy the right to security as the means through which all other human interests are protected. If we don't, we risk colluding in a subtle reordering of the hierarchy of rights.

---

[96] Liora Lazarus, 'Inspecting the Tail of the Dog', in M. McCarthy (ed.), *Incarceration and Human Rights* (Manchester University Press, 2010), 45.
[97] Lazarus, 'Inspecting the Tail of the Dog'.
[98] Fredman, 'The Positive Right to Security'.
[99] World Justice Project, *Rule of Law Index* 2012–13, 9.

24

Rights and Security for Human Rights Sceptics

*Victor Tadros**

It may seem that the central question to ask when considering the human right to security is: Is there a human right to security, and if so what is its source and content? This question, though, is unhelpfully unspecific for two reasons. First, until the object of security is clarified, the scope of the question is unclear. The main focus of the right to security has been on security from serious criminal offending. But we ought also to be interested in security from state wrongdoing and security from natural disasters. Hence, in a discussion of the right to security, we could include food security, water security, security from disease, security of accommodation, and so on.

Secondly, and more importantly, what the question asks depends on our conception of human rights. Many think that human rights are rights that we have in virtue of our status as human. Some think that human rights are distinctive in being rights held against states. Some think that human rights are distinctive in that international interference with sovereign states is permitted to enforce only these rights. Theories of human rights differ about which of these features are essential features of human rights. For reasons outlined later, I think that there is no good way of adjudicating these disputes, and that even if there was there would be no point in doing so. We should abandon the philosophy of human rights.

For this reason, I will not aim to answer the question with which I began. Nevertheless, making progress on the ethical questions that some of the discussion of the human right to security has been concerned with is important. I aim to make modest progress with these questions by distinguishing between different kinds of rights. That will help to structure our thinking about the relationship between rights and duties with respect to security at national and international levels.

As Liora Lazarus notes, the right to security has been understood as both a negative and a positive right.[1] On this understanding it grounds both negative duties not to harm or affect others in various ways and positive duties to protect others from being harmed or affected. I think that the right to security is better understood solely as a positive right—the correlate of the right is a set of positive duties of protection. Understood as a negative right, the right to security is simply an umbrella term for a range of more specific rights, such as the right not to be killed or the right

* I am grateful to participants at a workshop on human rights at Worcester College, Oxford, and especially to Cécile Fabre and Massimo Renzo.
[1] See Liora Lazarus, 'The Right to Security', this volume, ch. 23.

to bodily integrity. Even understood as a positive right, the right to security is prob-lematically umbrella-like given the range of threats that people may face. But at least in evaluating the right to security as a positive right we focus on a distinctive moral question: to what extent are there positive duties of protection against threats, and how are they related to duties and permissions on states and on the international community?

Debate about the right to security can usefully be structured by answering these four broad questions:

(1) Are there any enforceable positive duties to protect others?

(2) To what extent do these duties fall on states?

(3) Under what circumstances and in what way should the right to security be enshrined in a state's constitution?

(4) In what circumstances is the international community permitted or required to interfere with sovereign states to enforce duties of security, or to provide security directly?

Obviously, I will not make much progress in answering these questions, but I hope at least to illuminate the questions by identifying some difficult issues that need address-ing if they are to be answered.

I. The Philosophy of Human Rights: Forget it!

There has recently been extensive philosophical discussion about the nature of human rights. I think that philosophers should not continue this debate—they lack the tools to make progress with it, and the debate is in itself unimportant.

The language of human rights has great currency in international politics and law, and for that reason it should not be abandoned by activists, politicians, and lawyers: in politics and law precision is less important than results. Abandoning the language of human rights would probably set back the ability of activists to prevent injustice, pro-tect others from harm, and so on. Retaining a poor discourse is a small price to pay in the face of these ambitions. There is little point, though, in philosophical reflection on political and legal discourses to work out what conception of human rights fits the practice best. Here are two reasons why.

A. Which discourse? Who cares?

First, the question 'what is a human right?' has a non-stipulative answer only if there is a dominant discourse of human rights with a certain degree of coherence in its use of the concept of a human right. I suspect that there is no single dominant discourse. The features that are treated as essential for a right to be a human right are likely to differ across discourses (and perhaps within them). Even if I am wrong about these things, philosophers have not done the work necessary to establish what the dominant discourse of human rights is, or what features of a right make it a human right in that discourse. And they lack the skills to do that. Finally, even if they could do that, there would be little point in doing it. For the way in which we draw the distinction between human rights and other rights lacks normative implications.

I agree with Joseph Raz that a theory of human rights should have the following ambitions '(a) to establish the essential features which contemporary human rights practice attributes to the rights it acknowledges to be human rights; and (b) to identify the moral standards which qualify anything to be so acknowledged.'[2] Before carrying out the normative project of determining what we have human rights to, in other words, we ought to do the interpretative work of establishing what people mean when they refer to human rights.

Unlike Raz, I think the interpretative project is unpromising. The language of human rights has been used and developed in various different ways in different contexts, for different political goals, and by agents with different roles and responsibilities. Different conceptions of human rights will tend to further different political projects in different ways, resulting in significant variation in the way the term is used.

There are many disputes about the concept of a human right that we could focus on. Let me focus only on the following claim:

> *International Enforcement*: D has a human right to *x* only if states or international organizations ought to be permitted to interfere with sovereign states to protect D's right to *x*.

Whether *International Enforcement* is true is a matter of dispute. How should this dispute be resolved?

John Rawls and Joseph Raz are prominent defenders of *International Enforcement*.[3] Raz argues for this view as follows: 'the dominant trend in human rights practice is to take the fact that a right is a human right as a defeasibly sufficient ground for taking action against violators in the international arena'.[4] I agree with Raz that in order to understand the concept of human rights, if it is possible to do so, we should identify the dominant trend in human rights practice. How successful is Raz's argument for *International Enforcement* in the light of this?

One problem is that Raz's argument is far too vague to be assessable. What is 'dominant trend of human rights practice'? What is 'the international arena'? And, perhaps most importantly, what 'actions' are governed by human rights? Actions might include war, trade sanctions, public condemnation, decisions to prefer other trading partners, decisions to enter certain political arrangements (for example, accession to the European Union depends on human rights compliance), and so on. On which kinds of interference does the existence of human rights depend?[5]

---

[2] J. Raz, 'Human Rights Without Foundations', in S. Besson and J. Tasioulas (eds.), *The Philosophy of International Law* (Oxford: Oxford University Press, 2010). For more on this methodological constraint, see J. Tasioulas, 'Human Rights', in A. Marmor (ed.), *The Routledge Companion to Philosophy of Law* (New York: Routledge, 2011), 350–1.

[3] J. Rawls, *The Law of Peoples* (Cambridge, MA: Harvard University Press, 1999), esp. 78–81; Raz, 'Human Rights Without Foundations'.

[4] Raz, 'Human Rights Without Foundations', 328.

[5] Rawls' list of human rights is extremely limited in part because he thought that human rights violations were grounds for war. He provides no evidence for his unlikely view that this is the way in which human rights have been conceived of in the international arena since the Second World War. See Rawls,

Let us suppose that Raz's argument has been specified in some way or another. However it is specified, others, such as James Griffin,[6] Amartya Sen,[7] and John Tasioulas,[8] disagree with Rawls and Raz. They think that the idea of human rights includes very important rights regardless of whether international actors have a permission to intervene in sovereign states to protect these rights. Who is right?

Given Raz's first ambition for a theory of human rights, this depends on the answer to an empirical question—which account best tracks the ordinary discourse of human rights. Raz provides no evidence to support *International Enforcement*. His opponents mostly fail to provide any real evidence against it.[9] They sometimes point to the fact that people make human rights claims without recognizing the restriction advocated by Rawls and Raz. But this fact is hardly decisive—people often misuse language, and, as we will see in a moment, there are powerful reasons to use the language of human rights even where that language might not be apt.

What theorists of human rights require, then, is a convincing account of what the dominant discourse of human rights is, and an empirical investigation of the conception of human rights in this discourse. I suspect, though, that little progress can be made in this investigation. I suspect there is no dominant discourse of human rights, but rather a lot of vague and conflicted human rights talk, developed in different ways in different social, political, and institutional contexts.

Here is why my suspicion is likely well founded. Human rights language is a very powerful tool. It is used by those who develop and interpret legal and political instruments, in the course of political argument in both the domestic and international arena, by activists in furthering their causes, and so on. There is little reason to think that people in all of these different contexts understand the concept in the same way. Some, perhaps mainly those working in the international arena, are concerned to ensure that certain legal instruments are acceptable to a range of people with different ethical views and cultural heritages. For others, for example activists fighting for a cause within their own community, this issue is unimportant. For some, the discourse of human rights is developed in particular national or international legal contexts, where questions of legitimacy and enforcement naturally arise. Others discuss human rights independently of these contexts.

The Law of Peoples, 79, and for criticism, J. Griffin, *On Human Rights* (Oxford: Oxford University Press, 2008), 24 (though Griffin's own views seem no better defended than Rawls').

[6] Griffin, *On Human Rights*.

[7] A. Sen, 'Elements of a Theory of Human Rights', *Philosophy and Public Affairs*, 32 (2004): 315.

[8] Tasioulas, 'Human Rights'.

[9] Eg, James Griffin claims that his 'bottom up' approach 'starts with human rights as used in our actual social life by politicians, lawyers, social campaigners, as well as theorists of various sorts, and then sees what higher principles one must resort to in order to explain their moral weight, when one thinks they have it, and to resolve conflicts between them' (*On Human Rights*, 29). But he does almost nothing to investigate how politicians, lawyers, or social campaigners use the language of human rights in ordinary discourse. Similarly, Charles Beitz, in *The Idea of Human Rights* (Oxford: Oxford University Press, 2009), claims to explore the practice of human rights in depth, but provides almost no evidence for his neutralist account of human rights. He relies mostly on claims about the intentions of those who framed significant human rights documents post-Second World War, who aimed for international agreement on basic standards. But even if Beitz is right about these intentions (and he provides very little evidence for his claim) it is difficult to see why these intentions are decisive, given that others have taken up the language of human rights with other ambitions, and without a concern for international agreement.

Even within different groups, there is likely to be little uniformity in the way in which the concept is understood. Human rights activists aim to achieve a variety of goals. These include ensuring that states comply with duties they have not to wrong their citizens, but also ensuring that powerful international actors are restricted in the power that they have. Activists focused on the first ambition will tend not to be focused on *International Enforcement*. Activists focused on the second ambition will take *International Enforcement* much more seriously. The discourse of neither activist seems dominant. Hence, the question whether *International Enforcement* is true is inapt. It is true in some important human rights discourses but not in others.

To illustrate the point, consider the right to security. Activists fighting for their state to protect some of its citizens against serious violence when the state is allowing them to be harmed will claim that the human rights of their citizens are being violated. As the language of human rights has a great deal of power, couching their claims in the language of human rights helps to secure their goals. These activists will be uninterested, in mounting this challenge to their states, in the question of international interference. Furthermore, it would surely be inadequate for the state in question to respond to these activists by denying that it is violating the human rights of its citizens on the grounds that international interference to compel the state adequately to protect its citizens would be unwarranted. This response would be inappropriate even if it had arguments to support the view that international interference would indeed be unwarranted. The question of international interference, in this context, is irrelevant.

Other activists are concerned about the over-zealous pursuit of security by their states, and international pressure to achieve security. They have powerful reasons to resist or limit the use of the language of a human right to security. For if there is an unrestricted human right to security, states will have greater ability to secure their security driven and authoritarian ends by claiming that they are advancing human rights. And national and international institutions and agents will be more likely to pressure states into pursuing security at the cost of other rights. For example, international recognition of a right of security may lead to rights against state interference being balanced against this right. And international pressure to improve security may further erode the legal rights of individuals against their states. Activists in this context thus have reasons to limit the use of human rights language by endorsing *International Enforcement*.

We should expect, then, that different discourses of security and human rights will come apart with respect to their use of the concept of a human right. As neither discourse just identified seems dominant, there is no reason to favour or to reject *International Enforcement*.

Perhaps someone will make a real advance in this debate by providing an argument that there is a dominant discourse of human rights, and by doing the empirical work that one must do to establish what that discourse implies about the concept of human rights. Frankly, I find it hard to see why anyone would bother to do this. Whether *International Enforcement* is true has no important normative implications. The truth or falsity of *International Enforcement* cannot tell us about the importance of a right, how that right should be protected, what its moral foundations are, or anything else of any interest. It can tell us only whether we should call that right a human right, and there really isn't much reason to care about that. The best answer to the conceptual question will not even provide a powerful reason to influence the discourse of human rights lawyers and activists. Where people might help to secure justice with respect to torture, free speech, fair trials and so on, who cares whether they are abusing language?

When it comes to normative philosophical work, we are better avoiding the difficult and probably unanswerable question of the best conception of human rights. As moral and political philosophers, assuming that we have little or no influence over real world events, or that our influence is very difficult to predict, we can do so at little expected cost. We can then move more directly to the normative issues that should provide our primary focus.

B. What's so special about being human?

A second reason to abandon the philosophy of human rights is that the term 'human rights' wrongly implies that it is in virtue of being human that we have the rights that we have. I doubt that we have any of the rights that we have in virtue of being human, and even if we do, being human is not the property that we have that is most fundamental in explaining why we have these rights.

Many theories of human rights begin with an attempt to establish what is essential about human life that gives human life or activity its value, importance or moral significance. Tasioulas summarizes this basic idea, which is pervasive in the literature, as follows:

> Human rights are distinguished from other moral rights because we possess them not due to any personal achievement, social status or transaction, nor because they are conferred upon us by a positive legal order, but simply in virtue of our standing as human beings.[10]

I doubt we have *any* rights in virtue of our standing as human beings. It is the properties that typical humans have that ground their rights rather than the fact that they are humans. Non-humans that have these properties have the same rights. Some, but only some, of these properties are exclusive to humans. And not all humans have all right-grounding properties.

It may be objected to this that humans who lack the relevant properties nevertheless retain rights that are grounded in properties that are exclusive to humans. Compare individual humans and individual non-human animals that have the same degree of intelligence, end setting power, and so on. Do they not have different rights? Perhaps. It might be argued to follow that these humans have some rights in virtue of being human. Again, perhaps.

The argument seems to rest on the following idea. Suppose that an individual, X, is a member of a species, S. Typical members of S have certain properties that ground

---

[10] Tasioulas, 'Human Rights', 348.

certain duties that are owed to those members. If so, these duties are also owed to X even if X lacks the properties just identified. There are different variations on this idea. On a narrower view, only those who are also members of S owe the relevant duties to X. On a broader view, anyone owes the relevant duties to X. The broader view strikes me as more plausible—if human beings owe special duties to humans who lack significant agential capacities, so do non-human intelligent aliens.

The general view that species membership is morally significant in this way is difficult to defend. Why should it matter, in determining what rights one has, whether typical members of one's species have certain properties if one lacks those properties? The rights that are distinctive to humans are held by humans in virtue of the special agential capacities that humans have. If that is so, why should it not also be true that whether a particular human has these rights depends on whether that human has these agential capacities?

Furthermore, the view that species membership matters has counterintuitive implications. Suppose that due to some ecological disaster, most human beings were born without the relevant properties. Would these human beings then lack human rights? Suppose, in contrast, that many dolphins suddenly acquire the relevant properties. Does that mean that all dolphins suddenly acquire more rights? Why should the respective rights of particular humans or dolphins depend on how many other humans or dolphins have the agential properties that are required to ground certain rights?

Even if being human is sufficient to give rise to certain special rights, though, the rights that all humans have are held in virtue of other properties that humans typically have, such as their agential capacities. It is not because humanness is itself especially important that all humans have these rights. Were most dolphins to gain the relevant agential capacities, and species membership is morally significant, all dolphins would also acquire these rights.

Perhaps the human species is the only species that has any members that have the properties that ground certain rights. Perhaps these rights are the most important rights. I certainly agree that the special properties that most humans have makes them especially important, and grounds certain rights that non-human animals all lack. I doubt that this is good enough reason to restrict our focus to them. Even if non-human animals lack some of the most important rights that humans have, they nevertheless have very important rights.

We even lack a good reason to focus exclusively on humans if we restrict our attention to those rights that can be enforced internationally. International interference is surely permitted, and perhaps required, in order to enforce duties owed by state officials to non-human animals, at least in the form of international condemnation and monetary sanctions. It follows from this that the right to security extends to non-human animals. It is permissible for international organizations to condemn, and perhaps sanction, states that offer insufficient protection to non-human animals against being wronged by citizens of those states. As state officials have positive duties to non-human animals to protect them against being harmed severely, non-human animals have a right to security. The right to security is thus also not best conceived of as a distinctively human right.

II. Important Rights

In the light of these doubts I will focus on important rights rather than on human rights. Humans and non-human animals may hold some of these rights. Here are some distinctions between important rights that will help to focus our discussion:

Important Rights: Rights that there are powerful reasons to respect in virtue of the moral importance of the right holder.

Important Rights to State Action: Important rights that ground duties on state officials, or duties to take certain actions by developing or utilizing state institutions.

Important Constitutional Rights: Important rights that grounds duties that ought (under some conditions, and in some way) to be enshrined in the state's constitution.

Important International Rights: An important right that grounds a permission or duty of international interference, in some ways to be specified.

Let us first focus on the intentionally vague definition of important rights.

A. Interpreting the right

The fact that a subject, X, has a right to p does not derive simply from the fact that it is important to X that p.[11] X has a right to p only if someone has (or perhaps someone will or may have) a duty to ensure that p. A right is important if it is important that the duty is fulfilled.

For a right to be important, in the sense that I intend, the importance of fulfilling the duty must be in virtue of the moral importance of the right-holder. There may be duties that it is important to fulfill for other reasons—for example, the integrity of the duty-holder or the interests of those other than the right-holder. The fact that fulfilling the duty is important for these reasons does not render the right important in the intended sense.

I have not outlined what makes fulfilling duties important. Some people—interest theorists—think (roughly) that rights are grounded in interests. They will claim that the importance of a right is normally a function of the importance of the interest which grounds it. Others—will theorists—think (roughly) that rights are grounded in the provision of choices to people. They will claim that the importance of a right is normally a function of the importance of the right holder having these choices. I think that different rights are grounded in different ways—some are grounded in interests, others are grounded in respect for autonomy.[12] Hence, I think that different rights may be important for different reasons.

---

[11]   See, further, Raz, 'Human Rights Without Foundations', 326.

[12]   To understand why, see V. Tadros, 'Harm, Sovereignty and Prohibition', *Legal Theory*, 17 (2001): 35.

B. Shue's thesis

In the light of these clarifications, how important is the right to security? Henry Shue believes that there is an important distinction between the rights that protect things that we require to make any other rights worth having—what he calls basic rights—and the rights that protect things that are not valuable in this way.[13] Because enjoying other rights depends on the enjoyment of the right of security, Shue thinks, the right to security is basic. Basic rights, Shue claims, take priority over non-basic rights.

I doubt that Shue is right. A right may be very important even if no other rights depend on it. For Shue, my right to security is basic because being murdered, raped, and beaten prevents me enjoying any of my other rights. But the moral significance of my right against being murdered, raped, and beaten does not depend on whether my enjoyment of other rights depends on my not being murdered, raped, and beaten. Being treated in these ways may affect my enjoyment of my other rights, but that is not the most significant reason why these rights are important.[14]

Furthermore, Shue relies on the following more general claim:

Shue's Thesis: If everyone has a right to y, and the enjoyment of x is necessary for the enjoyment of y, everyone has a right to x.[15]

One concern with *Shue's Thesis* is that it is difficult to know what Shue means by the 'enjoyment' of a right. Shue explains that he means that a person enjoys the thing that the right protects whilst being conscious that it is protected as a right.[16] However, rights, or the things that rights protect, are not important primarily because having them is enjoyable, so Shue cannot mean 'enjoyment' literally. But if that is not what is meant, what is meant?

Perhaps a person enjoys a right, for Shue, if the good that the right protects is in fact realized. But this wrongly treats the normative significance of rights exclusively in the goods that rights protect. The falsity of this view is demonstrated by the fact that I have a right to sacrifice myself for the sake of others, and a right that others don't interfere with me to prevent me from doing so. The importance of my right to sacrifice myself for the sake of others is not that self-sacrifice is good for me. Without a clearer indication of what enjoyment means, Shue's claim is difficult to assess.

Shue's Thesis also seems too demanding (as Shue himself is aware). Suppose that I am about to be killed by natural causes and nothing can be done about that. It seems false that I have a right to be protected from this disaster given that nothing can be done about it. And *Shue's Thesis* seems to offer too little protection against interference

---

[13] H. Shue, *Basic Rights: Subsistence, Affluence, and US Foreign Policy*, 2nd edn. (Princeton: Princeton University Press, 1996), 19.

[14] Shue also fails to recognize that even the most basic rights protect goods that come in degrees, and hence a degree of protection may be sacrificed for the sake of other less basic rights. See, further, J. Waldron 'Security as a Basic Right (After 9/11)', in *Global Basic Rights* (Oxford: Oxford University Press, 2009).

[15] Shue, *Basic Rights*, 32.   [16] Shue, *Basic Rights*, 15.

to those who cannot enjoy rights. Suppose that I am about to be killed by a natural disaster. Another person kills me at just that time. This person violates my rights. But in killing me he does not deprive me of enjoyment of any of my rights, for I was about to be killed anyway.

There are various non-trivial variations on Shue's thesis that are worth considering. For example:

> *Shue's Thesis (Equivalence)*: If everyone has a right to *y*, grounding a duty on others not to *v*, and the enjoyment of *x* is necessary for the enjoyment of *y*, everyone has a duty to provide *x* that is as stringent as the duty not to *v*.

This thesis is non-trivial and not *obviously* false. It is, nevertheless, false. It is false because negative duties are typically more stringent than positive duties.

First, let me specify what I mean by stringency. The stringency of a duty depends on the costs that the duty holder must bear to ensure that he complies with the duty, or that are sufficient to vitiate the duty. For example, I have a duty to rescue others at some cost to myself. The stringency of the duty depends on the costs that are sufficient to vitiate the duty. Compare:

> *Weak Demand*: X, an innocent bystander, has a duty to rescue Y, an innocent person who is threatened with harm, if in doing so X will not be harmed, or will be harmed to a degree significantly less severe than the harm that he will prevent Y from suffering.

> *Strong Demand*: X, an innocent bystander, has a duty to rescue Y, an innocent person who is threatened with harm, if in doing so X will not be harmed, or will be harmed to a degree that is less severe than the harm that he will prevent Y from suffering.

Those who endorse *Weak Demand* believe that the duty of rescue is less stringent than those who endorse *Strong Demand*.

Stringency and importance are different dimensions of rights, and they must not be confused. The stringency of a duty is a function of the costs on the duty-bearer that must be borne to fulfill the duty. The importance of a duty is a function of the value that will be set back if the duty is not fulfilled. The duty to rescue a person from a lethal threat is not very stringent. But it is very important. The duty not to break a person's arm is very stringent, but may be less important.

To see this, notice how difficult it is to justify breaking an arm—one is justified in doing this only if one will bear a significantly greater cost if one does not do so. In contrast, one is permitted to refrain from saving a life if doing so will impose on one some much lesser cost, perhaps less than a broken arm. In contrast, however, it is much more important that the duty to rescue a person from a lethal threat is performed than the duty not to break a person's arm. If a third party could ensure that only one of these duties is fulfilled, he ought to ensure that the duty to rescue a person from a lethal threat is fulfilled.

One explanation for Shue's error in roughly equating positive and negative duties is his failure to distinguish the importance of a duty from its stringency. He believes that those who strongly contrast negative and positive duties are making claims about the relative importance of these duties. Were that true, his objection would be valid.

However, the contrast may not be in virtue of the importance of these duties but rather in virtue of their stringency.[17]

In other words *Shue's Thesis (Equivalence)* implies the falsity of important non-consequentialist principles such as the *Doctrine of Doing and Allowing* (DDA) and the *Means Principle* (MP). The DDA holds that the duty against harming others is more stringent than the duty to prevent others from being harmed. MP holds that there is an especially stringent duty not to use people as a means to the greater good. If DDA and MP are stringent principles, *Shue's Thesis* is false.

If MP is valid, it is wrong to torture one person as a means of preventing two other people from being tortured. It does not follow, though, that the duty to ensure that others will not be tortured is very stringent. Although the duty not to torture is very stringent, MP does not imply that there are especially strong reasons to prevent torture. For failing to prevent the torture occurring does not itself use the person tortured as a means. It may be wrong to fail to prevent the torture occurring in order that the torture will have good consequences—that would wrongly treat the one person as a means.[18] But it would not be wrong to fail to prevent the torture occurring in order to save two innocent people, unconnected to the torture, from being killed.

Even if MP is accepted, it might be argued that there are especially strong reasons to prevent rights being violated—much stronger reasons than there are to prevent people being harmed. Hence, in my earlier example, there would be a duty to prevent the torture even if two other innocent people could be saved if these other people are saved from natural disaster rather than wrongdoing. Shue rejects this view, and I think that he is right to do so.

Consider:

HIV: There is a queue of children who have been infected with HIV. Only some of these children can receive retroviral drugs to prevent the development of AIDS. Some have been intentionally infected in order to kill them. Others have been infected as a result of the unjust policies of their state, which fails to provide them with contraception. Others have been infected by chance, and not as a result of injustice.

If there were a significantly stronger reason to prevent rights violations than there is to prevent killing by natural disaster, there would be a strong reason to push those who have wrongfully been infected to the front of the queue. Doing so would prevent the right to life of these children being violated. But it is unintuitive that there is any strong reason of this kind. Any such reason seems insufficiently powerful to provide those who have wrongfully been infected with a greater chance of survival than those who were infected by chance.[19] This, though, does not show that there is no important

---

[17] He is somewhat unclear about the Doctrine of Doing and Allowing (DDA)—he appears to recognize that it might be important, notes that it cuts across security from wrongdoing and subsistence, but then fails to draw conclusions about whether positive and negative duties on the state are equally stringent. See Shue, *Basic Rights*, 35–40.

[18] See, also, the *Guinea Pig* case, in which one person is allowed to die of a disease so that more can people can later be cured of it, discussed in W. Quinn, 'Actions, Intentions and Consequences: The Doctrine of Double Effect', in *Morality and Action* (Cambridge: Cambridge University Press, 1993), 177.

[19] See, further, J. McMahan, 'Humanitarian Intervention, Consent, and Proportionality' and P. Singer, 'Bystanders to Poverty', both in N.A. Davis, R. Keshen, and J. McMahan (eds.), *Ethics and Humanity: Themes from the Philosophy of Jonathan Glover* (Oxford: Oxford University Press, 2010) and

difference in the stringency between negative and positive duties, only that our positive duties to protect people against negative duties being violated are no more important than our positive duties to protect people against being harmed.

III. State Security

A further question is whether duties of security are enforceable, and if so by whom. It seems clear that some positive duties are enforceable. The enforceability of a duty, I think, depends primarily on its importance rather than on its stringency. The fact that some will die or suffer serious injuries if duties of security are not fulfilled supports the claim that they are enforceable.

Libertarians doubt this. Some deny that there are positive duties. Others deny that positive duties are enforceable. Neither view is at all plausible. Consider an extreme case. Suppose that you could prevent very many people from being killed by a nuclear weapon simply by pressing a button. Pressing the button will cost you nothing. Obviously, you have a duty to press the button. Obviously, also, it would not be wrong for me to force you to do this if I could do so at little cost to anyone else. In fact, I am surely required to force you to do this.

What role does the state have with respect to duties of security? Some claim that a distinctive property of a human right is that it is a right held against a state. Charles Beitz, for example, claims that 'states have the primary or "first level" responsibility to ensure the satisfaction of the human rights of their own residents.'[20] This idea is reflected in human rights law—cases before the European Court of Human Rights designate states as the duty-holders.

Beitz's view relies on the idea that states can be duty-holders. We might doubt this idea. One reason to doubt it is that only responsible agents can be duty-holders, and states are not agents. It seems difficult to resist the claim that only responsible agents can be duty-holders. Perhaps it is easier to resist the claim that states are not responsible agents. Some may claim that states are collective agents, and perhaps collective agents can be responsible agents. It is not completely clear to me when a state meets the conditions of collective agency, if ever. Perhaps some do. I doubt that all do.

If not all states are collective agents the view that human rights are rights against states has absurd implications. Suppose, as is likely, that some states are too chaotic and disorganized to meet the conditions of responsible collective agency. These states are amongst those that are most likely to harbour officials who perpetrate very serious moral wrongs against their citizens in carrying out state functions. As these states are not responsible collective agents, they cannot be duty-holders. Hence, the view that human rights are rights held against states implies that citizens of these states lack human rights. Hence, the view that human rights are rights held against states implies that the human rights of citizens who are subject to serious wrongdoing by officials

---

V. Tadros, *The Ends of Harm: The Moral Foundations of Criminal Law* (Oxford: Oxford University Press, 2011), ch. 5.

[20] Beitz, *The Idea of Human Rights*, 114.

are not being violated. Even if we should retain philosophical interest in human rights, this implication is unwelcome.

This brief argument also supports the more general conclusion that we should not distinguish rights on the basis of whether they are held against states—if the state–citizen relationship is important, its importance does not depend on whether the state is a responsible collective agent. We should replace the idea that citizens have special rights against states with a better idea: citizens have a distinctive right against certain individuals, grounding certain duties, where fulfilling these duties is to be done in the name of the state, and through certain state institutions or mechanisms. The phrase 'a duty of the state to provide its citizens with security' is better understood as a set of duties that citizens owe to each other both in their private and their official capacities that can best be realized by developing, sustaining and utilizing state institutions, capacities, techniques, and so on.

I won't examine the sources of these duties in any detail. There is a duty of easy rescue that citizens owe to each other simply in virtue of the fact that there is a duty of easy rescue that all people owe to all others. One way to satisfy that duty is to fund state activities that ensure high levels of security, including education, policing, a decent physical environment, and so on. It may be that citizens have stronger duties than this to each other in virtue of shared citizenship, the collective production of resources, and so on. These facts may enhance the stringency of the right to security. But there is a powerful right to security held against the state regardless of citizenship that is grounded in the duty to rescue.

A further question concerns the stringency and importance of the special state duties that I identified earlier. Are they different in kind, stringency, and importance when compared with duties that individuals owe to each other, other things being equal? Do familiar non-consequentialist principles, such as DDA and MP, apply equally to state officials working in their official capacities as they do to individuals acting privately?

If the DDA and MP are valid, I believe that they are also valid for state officials acting in their official capacities. Whilst some doubt it,[21] there is little reason to believe that there is some kind of 'moral magic' of the state that renders these principles invalid with respect to state action. That is also the intuitive view. For example, suppose that if one state official, Officer X, tortures A to get information another official, Officer Y will refrain from wrongly torturing B and C to get the same information. Overall, fewer tortures will occur if Officer X acts. Furthermore, fewer tortures will have been committed in the name of the state if X acts. Yet it seems wrong for X to torture A.[22] This is so even though Officer Y will also be acting in the name of the state, and hence that the state will have violated fewer rights if Officer X tortures A than if he does not.

---

[21] Some people believe that the DDA and MP, even if they are valid, do not apply to states. See, eg, C. Sunstein and A. Vermeule, 'Is Capital Punishment Morally Required? Acts, Omissions, and Life-Life Tradeoffs', *Stanford Law Review*, 58 (2005): 703 and D. Enoch, 'Intending, Foreseeing, and the State', *Legal Theory*, 13 (2007): 69. This is clearly false, though explaining why is beyond the scope of this paper. For rebuttals of various arguments concerning the DDA, see A.O. Hosein, 'Doing, Allowing, and the State', *Law and Philosophy*, 33 (2014): 235.

[22] Things are different if A will also be tortured by Officer Y. In that case, the harm to A is overdetermined.

Here is another issue. Suppose that Officer X could either prevent Officer Y from torturing A or prevent a private citizen, Z, from torturing B. The tortures will be identical in seriousness and will be done for identical reasons with identical results. Does Officer X have a more important duty to prevent the torture by Officer Y than the torture by Z? Perhaps the latter duty is somewhat less important than the former. I doubt that this difference is very profound. Again, it seems that the fact that some act will be conducted in the name of the state does not affect its moral significance in any profound way.

Some may doubt this on the grounds that it is worse for a person to be harmed by a person who has a duty to protect her.[23] Others may doubt it on the grounds that there are much stronger reasons to prevent torture in the name of the state, and especially in the name of the state of which one is a state official, than there are to prevent torture by private citizens. I agree that there is some force in these ideas. But I think that their force is insufficient to justify a duty to protect A rather B. We will return to the implications of this idea for obligations of international actors later.

To summarize: there is an enforceable right of security that is held between individuals. It is grounded in the duty to rescue, and perhaps it has other sources in the special duties of protection that citizens owe against each other. The duties of officials to protect people against wrongdoing by officials acting in their official capacities are not much more important than the duties of officials to protect people against wrongdoing by private citizens.

IV. Constitutionalizing the Right to Security

Let us now focus on the constitutional question, which is Liora Lazarus's main focus. As there are many different ways in which a right may be 'constitutionalized' the idea of an important constitutional right admits many variations. There are many different ways of dividing labour for the scrutiny and legal protection of important rights. Rights might form part of the written constitution of a particular state. Alternatively, they may form part of an international agreement, such as the Universal Declaration of Human Rights (UDHR), or the European Convention of Human Rights (ECHR), that states are signatories to. And there are different roles that courts (national and cross national) and legislatures might be given in ensuring that these rights are adhered to.

In some jurisdictions, such as the United States, courts are given the power to strike down legislation that is deemed incompatible with constitutional arrangements. In others, such as the United Kingdom, courts only have interpretative and declaratory powers. There might also be constitutional arrangements that articulate what important rights citizens have, but which give no role to courts in enforcing these rights.

Jeremy Waldron dissents from the last claim. He thinks it inevitable that courts lead the way in shaping constitutional rights.[24] Waldron, though, is guilty of a lack

---

[23] See J. Gardner, 'Criminals in Uniform', in R.A. Duff, L. Farmer, S.E. Marshall, M. Renzo, and V. Tadros (eds.), *The Constitution of the Criminal Law* (Oxford: Oxford University Press, 2013).

[24] J. Waldron, 'A Right-Based Critique of Constitutional Rights', *Oxford Journal of Legal Studies*, 13 (1993): 18, 41–6.

of institutional imagination. It is perfectly feasible for a body such as the United Kingdom's Joint Committee for Human Rights to scrutinize constitutional rights compliance and report to the legislature without the involvement of courts. Reports by non-judicial bodies might be important only in guiding and structuring debate by legislatures. Some may claim that this will inevitably result in weak protection of rights. I doubt that this is inevitable. Constitutional rights compliance depends as much on political culture as it does on institutional arrangements.

In defending claims about the proper constitutional arrangement to protect rights, we must attend both to empirical and principled questions. One important question concerns the rights that citizens have to shape their own institutions and laws. More important is the question of which institutional arrangement will best protect important rights that citizens have that are less closely connected to democracy, such as the right to life, or the right to a family life. Because the instrumental question is largely empirical I will not aim to make progress with it here. Again, much will depend on the particular qualities that legislatures have and the possibility of improving them when compared with other institutional arrangements including court scrutiny of legislation.

With respect to the right to security, I tend to think that instrumental considerations are paramount. In assessing the rightness of any action that is at some risk of seriously affecting others, including the action of law making, we must attend to the consequences of the action to determine whether it is justified and proportionate. That will turn on the relationship between the values that we are pursuing and the harms that we will do and prevent in pursuing those values. It will typically be disproportionate to do or allow violations of important rights such as the right against being tortured, killed, raped, wrongfully imprisoned, in order to adhere to less important democratic rights.

I am very skeptical about a constitutional right to security in the light of this concern, at least in the UK context. And I suspect that the same concern is valid for other developed countries. The skepticism stems from a concern that I share with Lazarus and many others. The risk of modern developed countries being insufficiently zealous in providing security to their citizens in order to protect civil liberties is remote. A constitutional right to security will almost certainly enhance the overzealous response to threats from offending, and especially the threat of terrorism. A constitutional right to security will, in this way, do less well in promoting security—security from the state will be eroded with little advance in security from criminal wrongdoing. For this reason, I am glad that the right to security is not given an important role in the ECHR—not because the right to security is less important than other rights, but because of the detrimental effects of giving the right a more significant constitutional status in practice.

Perhaps things are different in other contexts where states are poor at providing security to many of their citizens. In those contexts, it might be argued, whilst there may still be risks that a constitutional right to security will be used to erode civil liberties, if the right constitutional arrangements are in place a right to security might also be used by the vulnerable to enhance the state protection to which they are entitled. Again, everything depends on answers to empirical questions that I am ill placed to provide, but Lazarus's chapter has reinforced my skepticism about the constitutionalization of the right to security in these contexts as well.

V. International Interference: Ought Implies Can, not Will

To what extent should other states and international organizations have the power to enforce the right to security against the wishes of the duty holding state officials? We can ask this question about the here and now: to what extent, under current imbalances of power in the international arena, ought states, through their officials, to be permitted to interfere with decisions of other states in order to secure important rights? Or we can ask it in a more idealistic way. Suppose that there was a more ideal set of international institutions. To what extent should such institutions be used to enforce important human rights?

As I noted earlier, Raz endorses *International Enforcement*. His version of *International Enforcement*, though, is especially problematic. He claims:

(1) 'Human rights are those regarding which sovereignty-limiting measures are justified';[25] and

(2) The moral limits of state sovereignty 'are determined not merely by the moral limits to the authority of states but also by the possibility of morally sound interference'.[26]

On this view, the extent to which a person has human rights is sensitive to fact that we wish to restrict the power of international organizations. Raz puts it like this: 'When the international situation is one in which it is clear that international measures will not be implied impartially, that they will be used to increase the domination of a super-power over its rivals, or over its client states, etc. the moral principles setting limits to sovereignty will tend to be more protective of sovereignty.'[27]

Raz's view thus has the following unappealing implication.

(3) Given (2), the worse the dispositions and tendencies of international actors, the more limited the permission to interfere with state sovereignty.

(4) Given (1) and (3), the worse the dispositions and tendencies of international actors, the fewer human rights people have.

The implication that our human rights depend on the bad dispositions of others cannot be accepted. The fact that international actors cannot be trusted with the task of protecting rights because of their colonial or exploitative ambitions cannot render these rights non-existent. The ordinary discourse of human rights may be incoherent, but no one thinks *that*.

To illustrate the problem, suppose that some state, X, can interfere with some other state, Y, in a way that would protect the citizens of Y against serious violations of their rights. This will be at little cost to the citizens of X, or anyone else. However, if X does

---

[25] Raz, 'Human Rights Without Foundations', 329.
[26] Raz, 'Human Rights Without Foundations', 331.
[27] Raz, 'Human Rights Without Foundations', 331–2.

this it will overthrow the government of Y and perpetrate greater violations against the rights of Y's citizens.

There is a sense in which X ought not to interfere with Y's affairs. *Relative to the fact that X will perpetrate greater rights violations against Y's citizens*, X ought not to interfere. But this fact cannot vitiate the rights of the citizens of Y to be protected by X, nor can it vitiate any duty on X to protect Y's citizens. Our moral duties, and the rights to which these duties are related, are not held relative to whether we will tend to go wrong if others have these rights. It vitiates my duty to do something, and hence the right that another person has that it be done, if I *cannot* do that thing. It does not vitiate my duty to do something, and hence the right that another person has that it be done, that I *will* not do it.

Similarly, the fact that states will tend to go wrong if they interfere in the affairs of other states cannot vitiate their duties to do this, nor can it affect the rights of the citizens of those states. For this reason, when we focus on important international rights, we ought to idealize the international order. The right question to ask, in determining whether people have certain rights against the international community, is not what we expect states to do if we give them the power to interfere. That is a question that we should ask when determining the law, but it is not relevant to determining the moral obligations of officials of a state to the citizens of other states, nor can it affect their rights. The question to ask when determining the rights and duties of citizens to be provided with security is what states *could* do for each other, not what they will in fact do.[28]

Conclusion

I have only provided a sketch of an exploration of the right to security in the light of a framework for evaluating rights. Whilst many people, like Lazarus, are rightly sceptical about the constitutionalization of the right to security, this should not distract us from the range of important and interesting questions that such a right raises. Although the academic insistence that security from private wrongdoing may come at the expense of security from the state is worth emphasizing and repeating, it ought not to swamp an investigation into the range of other questions that we might ask about the right to security, questions only to be asked when government officials aren't listening.

---

[28] See, further, V. Tadros 'A Human Right to a Fair Criminal Law?' in J. Chalmers, L. Farmer, and F. Leverick (eds.), *Essays in Honour of Sir Gerald Gordon* (Edinburgh: Edinburgh University Press, 2010).

25

Self-determination and the Human Right to Democracy

Thomas Christiano

Collective self-determination and democracy seem to have very similar grounds and yet they are sometimes thought to conflict. In particular, some have argued that the human right to democracy conflicts with the right of collective self-determination of peoples. Some have argued that one must decide which of these two rights must be accepted in the international arena.[1] The potential for conflict seems to arise in a number of different ways. Some have argued that the idea of equality at the root of democracy is a controversial notion and that in some societies equality has little or no resonance as a principle for regulating political life. If these societies are capable of legitimate self-determination then the principle of self-determination seems to conflict with the egalitarianism of democracy. And so one might think that one must decide that either a people should be able to organize themselves in accordance with non-egalitarian principles or that they must not have such a right because each must treat all the others as equals.

The idea of self-determination may seem to conflict with the idea of democracy in yet a different way. One might think that the human right to democracy implies a permission on the part of the members of the international community to intervene militarily or by means of highly coercive sanctions on behalf of democracy in non-democratic states. The idea of self-determination, in this case, is a moral barrier to such intervention and so it seems to defeat the duties that are supposedly correlative with the right to democracy and thus defeat the idea that there is a right to democracy.

In this paper I will defend the idea that democracy is at the core of the self-determination of peoples, but that this does not imply that only democratic societies can be self-determining. I shall argue that there can be fully self-determining, non-democratic societies with rights to collective self-determination. And I will argue that the human right to democracy is at the core of the right of collective self-determination of peoples even though the right may protect some non-democratic societies. In my view the right to democracy and the right to self-determination are not in conflict in a deep conceptual way. Certainly a universal demand for democracy will conflict with the right of collective self-determination but such a demand

---

[1] See Joshua Cohen, "Is There a Human Right to Democracy?" in Cohen, *The Arc of the Moral Universe and Other Essays* (Cambridge, MA: Harvard University Press, 2009) and Charles Beitz, *The Idea of Human Rights* (Oxford: Oxford University Press, 2009), ch. 7 for accounts of this kind of argument. Both are inspired by John Rawls's idea that there can be decent non-liberal societies in a just society of peoples, Rawls, *Law of Peoples* (Cambridge, MA: Harvard University Press, 1999).

does not follow logically from the human right to democracy. Nevertheless the human right to democracy imposes severe constraints on the possibility of a legitimate non-democratic exercise of self-determination. Indeed, these constraints may be so severe that legitimate, non-democratic self-determination may be practically all but impossible in the modern world. I will argue for these claims in what follows.

I will lay out the conception of the human right to democracy and a very brief account of the different grounds of this right that I have defended elsewhere. Then I will lay out the concept of collective self-determination and the associated rights that are particularly prominent in contemporary thinking. I will then argue that the human right to democracy, understood in a richer way than it is usually conceived of, is the ground of the right of collective self-determination of peoples. And I will show how this enriched conception of the human right to democracy can yield a right to collective self-determination in some non-democratic societies. Finally I will discuss the context and the particular manner in which democracy and self-determination can actually come into conflict.

I. The Human Right to Democracy: Conceptual Preliminaries

In this paper, I will defend a set of jointly sufficient conditions for asserting that there is a moral human right to x, which are particularly salient for my argument. These are conditions for a moral human right to democracy and not merely a legal human right. Two jointly sufficient formal conditions for a moral human right to x are: (1) there is strong moral justification for any state to establish, respect, protect, and promote a legal or conventional right to x (or a set of legal and conventional rights that can be usefully summarized as a right to x) and (2) there is moral justification for the international community to respect, protect, and promote the above legal or conventional right to x in all persons. By "international community" I mean states other than the one in question, international non-governmental organizations (NGOs), and international organizations.

The institutional structure that effectively implements and enforces the conventional or legal rights has a strong moral justification when it is *normally* minimally necessary and sufficient for realizing very urgent moral goods.[2] Without it, it is very unlikely that the very urgent moral goods will be realized; with it, it is very likely that the very urgent moral goods will be realized. When I say that the institution is normally necessary and sufficient to realize the urgent goods, I mean more than that the institution is statistically connected with the realization; I mean, in addition, that the normal functioning of the institution explains the realization of the urgent goods. This is compatible with the existence of statistical outliers. An institution or action has

---

[2] See L.W. Sumner, *The Moral Foundation of Rights* (Oxford: Oxford University Press, 1987), 144–5 for the distinction between weak and strong moral justification of a convention. This account is close to Joseph Raz's interest theory of rights though it broadens the possible grounds of a right to include other morally very urgent goods that can be possessed by the right-holder. See his *The Morality of Freedom* (Oxford: Oxford University Press, 1986), ch. 7.

a moral justification when it is morally desirable that it be constructed or undertaken in order to realize morally urgent goods.

I will not settle here for a definitive list or a basic account of the very urgent moral goods. Very urgent moral goods can include the protection of human dignity, the satisfaction of fundamental interests, the protection of natural rights or the good of not being treated as a moral inferior. Here I will rely on the very urgent moral goods that constitute the basis for a traditional ground for democracy as well as the basic interests that are enshrined in the most important human rights treaties. These are the basic interests that ground democracy and the equality of persons.

To be clear, this account does not require the existence of states or international institutions recognizing the right in question. In the absence of an international institution or even of a functioning state, one may still say that the human right to x exists since one is saying that the construction of institutions that include a conventional right to x is strongly morally justified. And I think one may even say that the right is violated or infringed by those who block the construction of these institutions, interfere with the proper functioning of those institutions or simply fail to comply with the core rules of those institutions.

The human right to democracy I argue for asserts that there is a strong moral justification for states to adopt or maintain the institutions of minimally egalitarian democracy and it is morally justified for the international community to respect, protect, and promote the right of each person to participate in minimally egalitarian democratic decision making concerning their society. By "minimally egalitarian democracy" I mean a democracy that has an effective formal or informal constitutional structure that ensures that persons are able to participate as equals in the collective decision making of their political society. A paradigm instance of it can be more precisely characterized in terms of the following three conditions. (1) Persons have formally equal votes that are effective in the aggregate in determining who is in power, the normal result of which is a high level of participation of the populace in the electoral process. (2) Persons have equal opportunities to run for office, to determine the agenda of decision making and equal opportunities to influence the processes of deliberation. Individuals are free to organize political parties and interest group associations without legal impediment or fear of serious violence and they are free to abandon their previous political associations and join new ones. They have freedom of expression at least regarding political matters. In such a society there is normally robust competition among parties so that a variety of political parties have a significant presence in the legislature. (3) Such a society also acts in accordance with the rule of law and supports an independent judiciary that acts as a check on executive power. This cluster of rights can be characterized simply as a right to participate as an equal in the collective decision making of one's political society. I will refer to it from now on as a right to democracy.[3]

---

[3] I use the expression "paradigm instance of democracy" here because, though I think representative democracy is the main instance of what I have in mind, I want to leave room for some forms of democracy that are not representative but that are recognizably egalitarian. See Jeremy Webber, "The Grammar of Customary Law," *McGill Law Journal*, 54 (2009): 579–626.

Such a society need not be fully just by any means nor need it live up fully to the ideals of democracy. For that reason I call it minimally egalitarian. Such a society may in effect limit some opportunities to participate due to inequalities of wealth. It might have a suboptimal system of representation. It need not be fully liberal since it may restrict non-political activities and violate liberal rights that are not connected to the democratic process. But it is not merely majoritarian with universal suffrage and elections. Minorities must have the protections of the rule of law, free association, and expression as well as equal opportunities for organizing politically effective groups and there must be free and fair competition for power among a variety of groups that compete on an equal footing. Normally this will result in minorities having a significant place in the legislature.

This conception of a human right to x as entailing a strong moral justification for a legal or conventional right to x first at the state level and then a moral justification to protect and promote those rights at the international level is supported by four considerations. One, it implies that we are talking about rights because it supports a legal or conventional right to x in order to protect and promote the very urgent moral goods. The very urgent moral goods are sufficient to ground duties in each to protect the minimally egalitarian democratic rights of each. And the protection of the urgent moral goods justifies putting a brake on the pursuit of the common good. Two, the proposed conception implies that we are talking about universally held rights. Three, the rights are pre-institutional in the sense that they do not depend for their existence on actual institutions. Four, the moral structures of these rights correspond to the structure of moral justification that is common for many if not most of the human rights we observe in contemporary international human rights practice. Contemporary moral justifications of human rights law impose upon states the moral duties to realize certain fundamental moral goods by instituting and protecting various legal rights and they impose on the international community the duties to help states do this.[4] If we can successfully show that there is strong moral justification for states to be minimally democratic and that the international community is morally justified in promoting and protecting democracy then we have an argument for a human right to democracy that fits within the mainstream concept of human rights.

II. The Two Grounds of the Human Right to Democracy

I will briefly sketch here two arguments for a human right to democracy that I have made in more detail elsewhere. Each of these arguments makes use of the basic schema for a human right that I elaborated earlier. Each is composed of two sub-arguments: one for the domestic level and the other for the international level. I call these two arguments the instrumental argument and the egalitarian argument for a human right to democracy.

---

[4] See Beitz, *The Idea of Human Rights*, ch. 5 for a defense of this conception. Unlike Beitz, I do not insist that these conditions are necessary for human rights and I do not insist on an interest theory of human rights.

The *instrumental argument* proceeds from the premise that democracy in the sense I have described it here is normally necessary and reliable in protecting basic human rights of an uncontroversial kind: the human rights not to be tortured, not to be killed by the state, not to be disappeared by the state, and not to be arbitrarily imprisoned by the state. The protections of these rights to physical intergrity are the morally very urgent goods for which democracy is normally necessary and reliable.

There is a very large body of data and statistical analysis that supports this contention.[5] The normal necessity claim is supported by statistical analyses of data that support the idea that societies that are not very democratic or not democratic at all normally do not protect these rights and societies that meet the criteria of minimally egalitarian democracy normally protect these rights quite well. There is indeed a threshold effect here that supports the strong differentiation between minimally egalitarian democracies and other kinds of societies. This threshold effect shows up using different measures of democracy, so it is robust. And it shows up in correlation studies as well as multivariate regression analyses that control for other variables. Moreover there is strong support for the thesis that democracy is the cause of the protections since the onset of minimally egalitarian democracy seems to precede by a number of years the full realization of the protections. Furthermore, we have a reasonable model for explaining how democracy can protect these rights. That is, democracy protects these rights because citizens, even if they are only mildly concerned with the human rights of others, tend to vote out officials who are clearly responsible for the violation of these rights.[6]

As with any instrumental argument, we must be modest in our claims. I think the evidence above gives us good reason to think that democracy is normally necessary and reliable in protecting the basic human rights of physical integrity. It allows for outliers and it is possible that the reasoning will be defeated at some time in the future, but for the moment we can claim with justification that democracy has these remarkable effects.

The international dimension of the human right to democracy is established first on the grounds that if the international community is morally justified in attempting to protect the human rights to physical integrity, then it is morally justified in promoting, protecting, and respecting those institutions that are normally necessary and reliable for protecting those rights. Moreover the international community has a number of related reasons for promoting, protecting, and respecting democracy in contemporary political societies. First, the democratic peace argument establishes that democracies do not go to war with one another and war is one of the chief causes of the violations

---

[5] See Christian Davenport and David A. Armstrong, II, "Democracy and the Violation of Human Rights: A Statistical Analysis from 1976 to 1996," *American Journal of Political Science*, 48(3) (July 2004): 538–54. See also, Bruce Bueno de Mesquita, G.W. Downs, A. Smith, and F.M. Cherif, "Thinking Inside the Box: A Closer Look at Democracy and Human Rights," *International Studies Quarterly*, 49(3) (2005): 439–57. For a fuller discussion, see Christian Davenport, *State Repression and the Domestic Democratic Peace* (Cambridge: Cambridge University Press, 2007).

[6] The evidence we have gives us good reason to think that hierarchical regimes normally do not protect basic human rights. My argument implies that what John Rawls calls a decent hierarchical society is at best an anomaly that is highly unlikely to be stable over time. See Rawls, *The Law of Peoples*, 71–85 for a discussion of decent hierarchical societies.

of human rights to physical integrity.[7] Second, democratic states tend to comply with international law to a significantly greater extent than do non-democratic states.[8] To the extent that peace and the development of international institutions are morally important aims, the international community has an important moral justification for promoting, protecting, and respecting democratic states.

These two arguments support the thesis that there is a strong moral justification for states to be democratic and that there is a moral justification for the international community to promote, protect, and respect democracy in contemporary political societies. Hence, they support the thesis that there is a human right to democracy.[9]

The *egalitarian argument* for a human right to democracy proceeds from premises that support the standard defenses of the intrinsic value of democracy. I will invoke my own account of these premises but I do not think it is necessary to the argument. Other accounts can work here as well.

The basic principle from which my argument here starts is the idea that it is a requirement for establishing justice in a society that the society publicly realize the equal advancement of the interests of the members of society. The fundamental argument for democracy at the domestic level is that it is necessary to the public realization of the equal advancement of the interests of the members of society. Persons have fundamental political interests in shaping the society they live in. They have interests in correcting for the cognitive biases of others in determining how to shape the society. They have interests in being at home in the world they live. And they have interests in being recognized and affirmed as equals. Against the background of conflict of interest, disagreement, cognitive bias, and fallibility on how best to organize society, the only public way of realizing the equality of persons in a society is to give each an equal say in how to shape the society. The idea, in brief, is that each person can see, once she acknowledges the facts of disagreement and conflict and the interests involved, that the only way to realize the equal advancement of interests in a society in a way that every other person (who also acknowledges these facts and interests) can agree on, is to make collective decisions democratically.[10] Hence, democracy is a public realization of equality.

---

[7] For a recent survey of the evidence, see Jack S. Levy and William R. Thompson, *Causes of War* (Malden, MA: Wiley-Blackwell, 2010), 108.

[8] See Beth A. Simmons, "Compliance with International Agreements," *Ann. Rev. Pol. Sci.*, 1 (1998): 75, 77, 83–5.

[9] For a more complete elaboration of this argument and an account of the empirical evidence for all these claims, see my "An Instrumental Argument for a Human Right to Democracy," *Philosophy and Public Affairs*, 39(2) (Spring 2011): 142–76.

[10] One might worry, with Andrew Altman and Christopher Wellman (in *A Liberal Theory of International Justice* (Oxford: Oxford University Press, 2009), ch. 2), that the principle of equality cannot support democracy in the way I have suggested here because equality is compatible with lack of publicity and it is compatible with no one having power (while outsiders impose their will). Aside from the fact that imposition by outsiders is a clear violation of equality, this misses an essential feature of the principle of equality that I have defended. The principle is welfarist and thus is opposed to leveling down. In other words, it is contrary to the principle of equality as I understand it, to prefer, morally speaking, a situation in which everyone is worse off but equally so to one in which everyone is better off even if there are inequalities. The reason for this rejection of leveling down, I claim, is that there is an internal connection between the value and point of equality and the promotion of the good that is equalized. If the promotion of the good to be equalized were not important, there would be no significance to equalizing it. For this argument, see Thomas Christiano and Will Braynen, "Inequality, Injustice and Leveling

To allow a society to be shaped by a certain group of elites or by an obviously ine-galitarian process favoring elites is to set back the fundamental interests above in a publicly clear way. Others, with all their cognitive biases, can be expected to shape the society in accordance with their own interests even if they do not intend this. They will likely make the world a home for themselves and make the world an alien place for others. And this will clearly undermine the public recognition of persons as equals.

The public equality at stake here is necessary to the realization of equality in a society, though it may not be sufficient since the protection of basic liberal rights is also necessary. Because of the facts of fallibility, disagreement, conflict, and cogni-tive bias, any attempt to achieve equality in some substantive way by a small elite in non-democratic ways will have the necessary consequence that the fundamental interests of many described earlier will be set back in a publicly clear way. Because of the facts just enumerated the only public way to realize equality is to ensure that persons have equal opportunities to shape the society in accordance with their judg-ments. This is not to say that the other substantive forms of equality are not important but it is to say that they cannot achieve the public realization of equality under the normal circumstances of political societies if the democratic realization is not present. Democracy is indispensable for this. Thus the right to democracy normally and reli-ably secures the very urgent moral good of treating persons publicly as equals. Hence there is a strong moral justification of democracy at the domestic level.[11]

The argument for the thesis that there is a moral justification for the international community to concern itself with democracy at the domestic level of each society pro-ceeds from the increasing influence of global processes of pollution, trade, communi-cation, finance and investment for the interests of persons throughout the world and the increasing significance of international law in regulating these. To the extent that international law is impinging on persons' lives either directly or through require-ments to make domestic law conform to international law, and to the extent that the increasingly important global processes need to be regulated by international law, per-sons have interests in having a say in the making of international law. These interests are the same as those that ground the concern with domestic democracy. Indeed the interests in many ways may be more strongly at stake given the greater degree of disa-greement at the international level, which results from the diversity of types of socie-ties, cultures, and histories that exist in the global arena.

To the extent that the global arena cannot now be ruled by globally democratic institutions, international law will for now and the foreseeable future be made by states or the international institutions they create on a fairly short leash.[12] Hence, the process of making international agreements will have to satisfy democratic norms to

Down," *Ratio*, XXI(4) (December 2008): 392–420. The defense of publicity in my work is grounded in equality and an account of the particular fundamental interests persons have in society. See Thomas Christiano, *The Constitution of Equality: Democratic Authority and Its Limits* (Oxford: Oxford University Press, 2008), ch. 2.

[11] See Christiano, *The Constitution of Equality*, chs 2–3, for a fuller elaboration of this argument.

[12] For the arguments for this claim, see Thomas Christiano, "Democratic Legitimacy and International Institutions," in Samantha Besson and John Tasioulas (eds.), *The Philosophy of International Law* (Oxford: Oxford University Press, 2011).

the greatest extent possible. In my view this can only be achieved through a process of fair negotiation among democratic states. So in order for international law to gain any kind of reasonable democratic credentials it is necessary for the states that create international law to be democratic. Of course, this is not sufficient; it must also be the case that the process of treaty making be one that is done through fair compromise among the different states. But democracy does seem to be a necessary condition for the whole process to treat persons publicly as equals.

We can see now that the urgent moral good of treating persons publicly as equals gives strong moral justification for a state to be democratic but it also provides a moral justification for the international community to promote, protect, and respect democracy in particular societies. Only then can international agreement making satisfy democratic norms. Hence we have a second argument for the human right to democracy.[13]

These arguments for a human right to democracy are independent and complementary. The first, instrumental argument points to the effect democracy has on protecting basic rights and the second, more intrinsic argument points to the importance of democracy in the process of making ordinary legislation in domestic societies and in international society.

III. Collective Self-Determination

Here, I want to define the notion of collective self-determination that I will be working with. It is meant to capture important values within the international system, but it is not meant to capture all the uses of the term self-determination that are in play. First I lay out the conception of collective self-determination and the associated rights of collective self-determination. Then I will contrast this notion of the right to collective self-determination with a notion that establishes the right of a people to an independent territory.

The basic notion of collective self-determination I will work with is the freedom of a community to organize itself politically as it sees fit. Many thinkers have thought that this implies democratic decision making since they see this seems to be the main interpretation of the idea of a community organizing itself.[14] While this is not an implausible way of elaborating the idea of a collectively self-determining community, I don't think it is conceptually necessary. And this is why there is a potential for conflict between the human right to democracy and a right to collective self-determination.

I will interpret the idea of a community organizing itself politically as it sees fit in an individualistic manner. The fundamental idea is that the community is self-determining to the extent that its members see it as organized politically in accord with basic political norms they genuinely accept. In cases where there is not unanimous agreement on the basic political norms, there is either a strong reason for

---

[13] See Thomas Christiano, "An Egalitarian Argument for a Human Right to Democracy," in Cindy Holder and David Reidy (eds.), *Human Rights: The Hard Questions* (Cambridge: Cambridge University Press, 2013), 301–25 for a more complete discussion of this argument.

[14] See, for instance, Antonio Cassese, *Self-Determination of Peoples: A Legal Reappraisal* (Cambridge: Cambridge University Press, 1999).

breaking up the community or it must be democratically ruled. Another way of putting this is that a community is self-determining if it is democratically ruled unless there is unanimous agreement on some non-democratic form of governance, which is then exercised by the members of the community.

Before I defend the democratic default condition I want to discuss two elements that are potentially worrisome in this account. One is the question of membership and community. What is the community of persons referred to? This is where the boundary problem of democracy and the territorial notion of self-determination come in. In this paper, I am working with a notion of collective self-determination that assumes a well-defined group with a territory over which it has jurisdiction.

The second worry is the issue of genuine acceptance. Under what conditions do we say that a person has genuinely accepted a set of norms? People often say that genuinely to accept a set of norms requires that there be some alternative that can be implemented. But, in my view, though this is often a plausible empirical test of genuineness it cannot be a conceptual requirement. This is because such a test would preclude the genuine acceptance on the part of individuals of the basic norms of a society, whether democratic or non-democratic. It is simply beyond the capacities of individuals to be able to transform the basic norms of their societies. And this holds whether the society is democratic or non-democratic. The basic political norms of a society are deep coordination points that require the simultaneous conformity of large numbers of persons to maintain. They also require the simultaneous coordination of large numbers of people to change. No one, at least normally, is in a position to change such coordination points on his or her own or even with a group of like-minded persons.

But it does seem plausible to think that people can genuinely affirm and accept the basic norms of their society. And this is a feature of their attitudes toward the society. As long as the basic norms of the society are approved of by a person on the basis of reasoned reflection (including reflection on alternatives) and not on the basis of fear of reprisals or ignorance of the alternatives one can say that a person genuinely accepts the basic norms of the society. The genuine acceptance of political norms does not require that the norms are fully or even adequately justified to the possessor of the attitudes. And it certainly does not require that the norms are morally valid norms. But they do require that the norms have satisfied some kind of test of reasoned reflection on alternatives. No doubt some civil and political rights are normally empirically necessary to achieve such genuine acceptance, but I am not convinced that they are conceptually necessary.

If all of this is correct, one can see that a group of people can be self-determining even if it is not democratic. The members of the group can accept a set of basic political norms that are non-democratic and the group can thereby constitute itself in accordance with the norms. It is essential here that not only do the members of the group accept the non-democratic norms but the members' acceptance plays a significant role in explaining the fact that the society is so constituted.

Strictly speaking, I think a group can constitute itself in many different ways if it accepts the basic norms and still be self-determining. Some, however, require the further condition that at least all the members of the society do participate in some way in the processes of collective decision making.[15] John Rawls's conception of a consultation hierarchy involves not only the genuine acceptance of all the members but the ongoing participation of all the members in the collective decision-making processes. Their participation is not on an equal basis in Rawls's conception so it is not democratic but there is universal inclusion and participation.[16] I am not sure I see the necessity of this further condition on self-determination but I will take no stance on it since the difficulties raised are similar for the more expansive notion of self-determination as for the narrower conception.

IV. The Rights of Collective Self-determination

The right to collective self-determination possessed by a group protects a group's self-determination. There are two classes of rights of self-determination. The first is a right of non-interference of other communities in the affairs of the self-determining community. This is a right against military intervention. It may also be a right against highly coercive economic sanctions. It protects the community from other communities. It is a right against those other communities.

The second class of rights is the class of rights of inclusion in the activities of the international community. This involves minimally a right to recognition by other states and the international community. It involves a right to participate voluntarily in treaty making in all of its complexity (as specified for example in the Vienna Convention on Treaties) as well as a right to register persistent objections to evolving rules of customary international law. It involves a right to participate in international institutions such as the Committees and Councils of the United Nations, the World Trade Organisation (WTO), International Monetary Fund (IMF), and the World Bank. It can involve the right to be included without reservation in international trade and cooperation. And it can involve the rights to be treated as members in good standing for the purposes of receiving loans and other forms of non-essential assistance from the international community.

To say that there is a full collective right to self-determination in the international community is to say that there is a strong moral justification for the international community to accord legal or conventional rights of non-interference and inclusion to collectively self-determining communities and that there is no such strong moral justification for non self-determining communities.

One can define weaker rights of collective self-determination in terms of the possession of just a right of non-interference or that right plus just a few others of the rights of inclusion.

The right of self-determination as I have defined it does not include rights of self-determination in the sense of the right of a people to a territory that they do not currently have jurisdiction over. The right I am describing refers exclusively to actually existing political communities. I do not mean to say that it is illegitimate to use the term "collective self-determination" for the right of a group of persons to form a

---

[15] Cohen, "Is There a Human Right to Democracy?" and Beitz, *The Idea of Human Rights*, ch. 7.
[16] See Rawls, *The Law of Peoples*, 72–8.

state with territory and jurisdiction of its own or even to form an autonomous political community within a larger state. These are important rights within the international community but I do not discuss them here.[17] My discussion may have implications for how to structure these rights insofar as the fact of self-determination I have described may be relevant to the formation of new communities.

V. The Grounds of the Rights of Collective Self-determination

The strong moral justification for the extension of these rights derives from the fundamental interests of persons normally protected by the right of self-determination. And I want to argue that the interests that are normally protected by this right are the very same interests, though modified in some important ways, as those that underpin the right to democracy. This similarity of interests is crucial for understanding my claims about the nature of the rights of collective self-determination.

It is important to note at the outset that we are looking at these rights from the standpoint of political communities in relation to each other and not from the standpoint of individuals within the political community. Recall the facts of fallibility, disagreement, conflict of interest, and cognitive bias, but think of them now in the context of an international political society. Now we can think of them as characterizing relations between persons across political societies. People can disagree with each other about what political system is best and there may be some degree of cognitive bias towards their own interests in these disagreements.

At the same time we can see that the interests in correcting for cognitive bias, in being at home in the world and in being recognized and affirmed as an equal can apply in the case of the structure of political decision making as well as other issues. And we can see that these interests can attach to persons in part as members of particular political communities and can be threatened by other political communities. So individuals in different societies can have interests in correcting for the cognitive biases of others in the contexts of these disagreements. The interests of those who have lived and developed under democratic institutions and the ideals of equality that characterize them could be distinct in a variety of ways from those who are educated in non-democratic societies and who internalize non-democratic norms. As a consequence the imposition of democratic modes of organizing the political society on a people that is non-democratic comes with costs that may not be fully visible to members of the democratic society. Furthermore, the interest in being at home in the world is at stake here as well. Insofar as a non-democratic mode of organization is familiar and makes sense to a people, the democratic norms may engender a feeling of alienation and disorientation in persons who are members of the non-democratic society. The interest in being at home in the world can be set back. Finally the interest in being

---

[17] I develop a partial account of rights to territory in Thomas Christiano, "A Democratic Theory of Territory and Some Puzzles about Global Democracy," *Journal of Social Philosophy*, 37 (2006): 81–107. My account extends the basic remedial right account offered by Allen Buchanan in *Justice, Legitimacy and Self-Determination* (Oxford: Oxford University Press, 2004), ch. 8.

recognized and affirmed as an equal is at stake here as well. To be sure, the people in question do not look upon each other as equals, but they nevertheless have an interest in having their community and the people in it recognized and affirmed as equals vis-a-vis other communities and the members of other communities and in the international community as a whole.

Recall that one can have interests in having one's judgment respected even in those cases where one's judgment is mistaken. Here we have already argued that there is a right to democracy so we must think that the views of those who prefer non-democracy are mistaken but we can nevertheless have an attitude of respect for those persons and the judgments that they reflectively endorse.

The idea then is that there is a collective right of self-determination to the extent that there are important interests that are protected by the right to self-determination within the international political community. There can be a strong moral justification for establishing a legal or conventional right of self-determination within the international community. The right against intervention or coercive economic sanctions protects a community and its members from the imposition of alien forms of political organization. The right to inclusion protects it ability to flourish in the international environment without compromising its character and it enables the society to shape the international environment in which it must develop in such a way that conforms to the interests of its members.

VI. A Qualification to the Right of Collective Self-determination of Non-democratic Peoples

There is nevertheless a weakness in the idea of a non-democratic people having a right of collective self-determination. This weakness can be appreciated by comparing the rights of self-determination of non-democratic peoples with the toleration of the intolerant in a liberal society. For the most part, the intolerant in a liberal society are extended the same liberal rights as the tolerant. They are extended the same equal rights to expression, association, conscience, and private pursuits that others are. This is despite the fact that they reject certain norms that are taken as justified in a liberal society. Indeed they reject the very norms that are the basis of their freedom and equality. In part because of this there is a certain weakness in the rights they possess. This weakness is expressed in the following ways. First, the state does no wrong in expressing publicly its disapproval of their views and even in giving support to more egalitarian groups that oppose them.[18] This is in contrast to the normally appropriate restraint of the state regarding the disparate views on the good life of those who do accept the freedom and equality of their fellow citizens. Second, while a liberal society permits expression and association by these persons, it does not permit them to realize their aims in collective decision making. A society may permit ultra right wing militias to exist and even flourish but it imposes constitutional constraints that prohibit

---

[18] See Corey Brettschneider, *When the State Speaks, What Should It Say? How Democracies Can Protect Expression and Promote Equality* (Princeton: Princeton University Press, 2012), and 'Free Speech as an Inverted Right and Democratic Persuasion', this volume, ch. 19, for a fuller discussion of this point.

the legislative imposition of the ultra right wing norms on the rest of society. Third, a democratic society properly tends to accept a lower degree of risk of harm from these groups. It is appropriate for such a society to keep a watch on these groups in case they might act in ways that threaten the society. In some respects, the attitude towards these groups in a liberal society is one of cautious, sometimes apprehensive, toleration.

I think the weakness in their rights can be explained in part by a weakness in the interests that these persons have. The interests in correcting for cognitive bias are real but they are weaker than those of others because a significant part of the particular views that are protected by their rights are regarded as false from a public standpoint in the society, that is from a standpoint that is meant by its nature to correct for cognitive bias.[19] The interest in being at home in the world is weaker as well to the extent that it is an interest in being at home in an unjust world. There are genuine interests present here because there are concomitant interests that are associated with, but not entirely tainted by, the desire for an unjustly organized society. Those concomitant interests may not themselves involve injustice even though they are part of what makes the unjust world a home for these persons.[20] And the interest in being recognized and affirmed as an equal is obviously a weakened interest for the intolerant because, by hypothesis, the intolerant does not recognize the equality of persons. This weakness in the interests of the intolerant are part of what play a role in explaining the diminished and somewhat hedged versions of the liberal rights that they possess.

I think there may be something similar in the case of the right of collective self-determination of non-democratic societies. The interests in participating in such a society and in non-interference as well as inclusion will be somewhat weakened in strength for roughly the same reasons in the case of the intolerant as in the case of non-democratic societies. If we take democratic forms of organization as minimally just, then we must view the genuine acceptance of non-democratic organizations as mistaken and thus, though many of the interests that are bound up with such mistakes can be real interests, they are not as robust as the interests that conform with justice.

VII. The Nature of the Right of Collective Self-determination

With these observations in mind, I now want to say what I think the collective right of self-determination is. My thesis is that the right of collective self-determination is derived from the human right to democracy. But it comes with an interesting complication in order to deal with the special case of a society of persons who genuinely prefer non-democratic modes of decision making to democratic ones.

---

[19] The public standpoint is not merely the view of the majority in the society. It is the standpoint that each person occupies once she takes into account the facts of disagreement, cognitive bias, conflict of interests, and fallibility and she considers, in the light of these facts, what everyone can agree on as a way of realizing equal advancement of interests in the light of these facts. The thesis is that democracy, equal basic liberal rights, and a basic minimum are the basic conditions under which people can see that they are being treated as equals under the epistemic and moral conditions I describe. Hence the public standpoint is a standpoint every conscientious, informed, and egalitarian person occupies.

[20] Interests are qualified when they involve wrongs or bads. I have argued that all interests, being parts of a person's well-being, are states of a person in which they have a genuine appreciation of a good. The injustice of a situation detracts from its goodness. See Christiano, *The Constitution of Equality*, ch. 1.

The basic idea is that a people have the full rights to collective self-determination when the human rights to democracy of its members are fulfilled. Thus the international community has a strong moral justification for extending legal or conventional rights of non-interference and inclusion to societies that respect the human rights to democracy of their members. Thus minimally egalitarian democracies have collective rights of self-determination.

A further specification of the human right to democracy must be introduced in order to accommodate the possibility that non-democratic peoples can have rights to self-determination. The idea is that the human right to democracy includes a moral power on the part of each person to waive the right to democracy. The power to waive is a common feature of many rights, though I do not insist that it is a feature of all rights. Thus a person may waive a right to receive a promised obligation. A person may waive at least some aspects of his rights to liberty and to avoid harm. These are powers that persons have that put them in command in part of the kinds of obligations others hold towards them.

Normally it is only one's own right that one may waive. One may not waive others' rights. For example, if one shares with another in the right to receive some treatment from a third person, one cannot waive the obligation of the third person to the other person in the arrangement. Let us call this the restriction to self-regarding waivers.

Taking the observations about the grounds of a right to self-determination from the previous section, I think it makes sense to think that there is a power to waive one's right to democracy because this power can be grounded in the same interests in asserting control over one's political world that the claim right to democracy is grounded in. That is, a person may decide that she is not at home in a democratic world, say, because the principle of equality has no resonance for her, and that such a world reflects the interests of others and not her own. And respect for the power to do this may express respect for the interests of the power-holder. But one cannot waive one's claim right to democracy just on one's own (except in the special case of exiting a society). The reason for this is that one's waiver can actually have adverse effects on the equal rights of others in a quite direct way.

This may depend on the character of the waiver. If I simply choose not to vote in elections, the exercise of others' rights need not be affected. On the other hand if I agree to waive my right to vote in favor of another, by transferring it to someone who now acquires my right, this may affect other people's equal vote. For example, vote selling is usually forbidden in democratic countries. Essentially it involves not only one person giving up their right to vote in a particular election, it also involves another person (the one to whom the vote is sold) having more than an equal vote. This exchange has the external effect on third party voters of making their votes less than equal to the votes of the vote buyer. Thus the third party's right to participate as an equal is diminished by the seller's waiver. The same can happen in single member district representation schemes. Single member districts are supposed to be of equal size so that in elections for representatives, the principle of one person, one vote is satisfied. If a substantial number of the voters in a particular district give up their votes or transfer them to one person in that district, the system will lose the character of one person, one vote and the rights of persons in other districts to equal participation will be violated. We will see that cases like these have relevance later in the paper.

To see how the right to collective self-determination is connected to the human right to democracy in the particular case of non-democratic peoples, we should first envision an isolated society the members of which genuinely accept the non-democratic political form they have. These persons have, we have argued, human rights to democracy. Now let us remember that these persons genuinely accept some non-democratic form of collective decision making and they express this acceptance in their compliance with the decisions of the authorities in the society and their expressed opinions.

One question is whether this acceptance-expressing compliance is a real waiver of the democratic claim right. Strictly speaking, there is no mention of such a waiver. The persons involved may not think of themselves as having a right to democracy, though they have, by hypothesis, thought about a democratic form of political organization and reflectively prefer the one they have. And it is the case that if one asks them if they waive a (legal) right to democracy they would actually say yes. There is still something puzzling about saying that they have waived their rights, when they have not done anything and do not even believe they have the right in question.

I want to say that there is something like, or analogous to, waiver here and that this has the same moral effect. What we see here has the most important earmarks of a waiver since the actions express a reflective preference for non-democracy and may genuinely express the kinds of interests that are usually expressed by a waiver, or interests in asserting a kind of control over their social world. If we were to try to promote democracy in their country, we would be interfering with something they are committed to on the basis of something they oppose.

Consider an example. Suppose that I have promised you that I will come over and paint some part of your house for you. You have a right that I do this. But you have since forgotten about this and have developed new and incompatible plans for the redecoration of your house. At the moment when I must fulfill my promise to paint your house, you are nowhere to be found, though your new incompatible plans are plainly in evidence. Now I have to decide what to do. If I do as I promised, I directly disrupt your plans for your house. Yet, you have not done anything that signals your waiver of your right that I paint your house. I reflect that you would waive the right were you asked. Or you might say that if you had the right you would waive it. I want to say that in this case, you have done something like waived your right with the same moral effect of such a waiver. This is because I would directly disrupt your current plans in a way that is obvious to both you and me if I fulfilled my promise to you. Even though you have not said anything to me, I must assume that you have done something to waive your right.

I think the presence of a genuinely accepted political structure that is preferred over democracy by a people, and clearly incompatible with it, can have the same effect of waiving the claim right of those persons to democracy in much the same way that your incompatible plans for your house waive your right that I paint it.[21] So I want to

---

[21] I thank Massimo Renzo for pressing me on how to justify this notion of a waiver.

conclude that the actions of compliance that express genuine acceptance can stand for an exercise of the power to waive the claim right to democracy.

So here we can see the full conception of the right to collective self-determination. The idea is that a society has the rights to non-interference and inclusion when it is democratically organized or when its members have collectively waived the right to democracy in favor of some other form of organization that they genuinely accept.

The primacy of democracy in this conception of the nature and grounds of the right to collective self-determination is based on the arguments for the human right to democracy. Democracy is shown by these to be a form of political organization that is uniquely capable of protecting certain basic rights as a consequence of the participation of its members in collective decision making. Democracy also uniquely enables citizens to advance their interests in shaping the social world they live in and thus uniquely serves the purposes of the right to collective self-determination. A democratic form of organization is uniquely designed to enable citizens to advance their interests in shaping the social world while protecting their fundamental rights. Democracy enables citizens to pursue their interests in shaping the social world while at the same time ensuring the citizens are treated publicly as equals in the process of collective decision making, which we have supposed here to be a fundamental principle of justice.

A minimally egalitarian democratic society is not a fully just society; it need not even live up fully to the ideals of democracy. It satisfies a minimum standard only. The satisfaction of the standard of minimally egalitarian democracy is compatible with many different forms of democracy. And the processes of collective decision making in democracies bring about very different legal and social structures in different societies as a consequence of the different views and interests of the citizens in those societies.

One might wonder why the minimal egalitarianism of democracy is in effect the default position for the international community. Why not simply require that the collective decision making be merely inclusive in the case of collective self-determination? Drawing on the arguments for the human right to democracy, there are two considerations that suggest that equality is the appropriate default. One, the instrumental argument for the human right to democracy suggests that the minimally egalitarian character of democracy is normally necessary and reliable for the protection of the basic human rights of physical integrity, which are generally accepted throughout the international community (though not generally respected). The evidence gives us good reason to think that what Rawls has called a consultation hierarchy normally does not protect basic human rights. The egalitarianism of democracy has a special place for this reason alone. It is at least the default instance of the right to collective self-determination.

Second, the egalitarian argument for a human right to democracy suggests another argument. I think we can take it as a given that the international community is committed to regarding persons from different societies as equals. Mere inclusion would not be acceptable from the standpoint of international society. If the international community tended to protect the human rights of persons from one proper subset of countries in the international community with greater effort than those of the members of another distinct proper subset of countries in the international community and this discriminatory tendency were intentional, the international community would be in for severe criticism.[22] If the response were that all were included though not equally so, I do not think the criticism would be much dulled. Equality of persons across societies is a generally accepted norm of the international community, however poorly this norm is respected. But if this is so, then consistency demands that the international community regard persons generally, at least initially, as equals within each society. The reasoning is simple. If the international community must regard individuals from different societies as equals, then any member x in country A must be regarded as the equal of any member y in society B. But if some member y in society B is regarded as the moral superior of some other member z in society B, then either x in A is the superior to z in B or y in B is the superior to x in A. Both of these possibilities are inconsistent with our initial, widely accepted premise. Hence the international community must regard any members z and y in any society as equals.

Now, it may be that z and y have the power to change this relationship at least toward each other, but the starting point at least from the international vantage point must be equality. Hence I think we can say that equality is the default principle from the standpoint of the international community. Therefore, I think we have another reason for thinking that democracy must be the default position with regard to the right to collective self-determination.

These reflections show that a democratic society is the primary case of a self-determining society. This explains the intuition that democracy and self-determination are very closely associated.

Now that we have established the primacy of democracy in a conception of the nature and grounds of self-determination we need to say more about a society that waives the democratic rights. We are supposing here that the society is a hierarchical society of some sort. It is important to see that the waiver of the democratic claim right is a kind of grant of authority to a non-democratic way of making decisions. But if this is so, it is important that all or at least nearly all the persons in the society waive their democratic rights. If some minority does not waive their democratic rights, the consequence of the others waiving their democratic rights will be that they undermine the democratic rights of those who do not waive their rights. This will be the case because the waivers of the majority will transfer authority to a non-democratic group and they will consequently have more power than the members of the minority, thus undermining the right to equal participation.

This is not just a conflict of interests between the majority and the minority. Democracy has primacy with respect to self-determination because it is a minimally just way in which citizens can advance their interests in shaping their social world together while protecting certain basic rights. The waiver provides an escape hatch from such a system for those who cannot find a home in it. The escape hatch makes sense because it is based on interests of a similar kind to those that are advanced by democracy though they are significantly weaker. Though it legitimizes the

---

[22] Indeed, this is precisely the criticism often made of the international community because of its failure to intervene in Rwanda while it intervened in Yugoslavia.

non-democratic form, it cannot make it just. Thus if one person's waiver undermines the rights of others who do not wish to waive their democratic rights, the waiver cannot be permitted.

Therefore because of the interdependence of the rights in collective decision making among members, the only kind of waiver that can be permissible is one that is exercised by the whole community together.

In sum I have argued for a conception of the grounds of the right of collective self-determination and for a conception of the basic structure of the right. The right of collective self-determination can be seen as grounded in the individual right to democracy. At the same time the right to collective self-determination leaves room for the possibility that a non-democratic society whose non-democratic character is genuinely accepted by its members can possess this right. And the right to collective self-determination is not, strictly speaking, an individual right, it is a right of a community to non-interference from the international community and to inclusion in the activities of the international community. It is nevertheless based on the human right to democracy and a power that each possessor of the right has to waive the right as long as the possessor does not waive the rights of others. Given the interdependence of the individual rights to democracy, the power to waive can only be legitimately exercised by all the members of the community together.

To be clear here, I do not think of the waiver of the democratic right as a waiver in perpetuity. It can be revoked. A person may be alienated from democratic decision making for a period but then come to see that she should reclaim the right. This, I think, is necessary if the interests in the possession of the right and the attendant power are to be respected over time. A person cannot reasonably foreclose forever the possibility of a fundamental change of attitude and of the attendant interests. And thus it would be perverse if a person, who has come to see upon reflection that she wishes to exercise the democratic claim right (say, as a consequence of now coming to see her fundamental equality with her fellow members of society), could now not exercise that right.

VIII. A Tension between the Right to Democracy and the Right to Self-determination

Conceptually, at least, we have a reconciliation of the human right to democracy with the right of collective self-determination of non-democratic political communities. But there is a potential for conflict in the account I have given, though it is a practical conflict. And we need to explore this difficulty.

The problem arises from the combination of the interdependence of political communities in the modern international community and the self-regarding waiver principle. Recall that the right of collective self-determination of a non-democratic people can arise when all the members of the people waive their rights to democracy collectively. The unanimity is necessary because of the self-regarding waiver principle. But we have observed that the international system is an interdependent system of states. These states interact with each other, in many cases, to pursue morally mandatory aims such as the reduction of globally threatening pollution, a decent system of international trade, the maintenance of peace and the protection of human rights. And states have long embedded themselves in a system of international institutions, international trade and communications. The international system pursues these aims through the negotiation and bargaining involved in creating treaties.

But here's the rub. First, negotiation and treaty making between democratic and non-democratic societies make the democratic societies partly complicit in the non-democratic decision making of the other societies. Second, it also partly compromises the democratic decision making of the democratic societies.

To illustrate with a highly simplified example, suppose a democratic society is negotiating with an autocratic society of roughly the same size and wealth. They negotiate to create treaties that will then have the force of law in each society. Complicity with non-democratic rule arises because in effect democratic citizens collude with the autocrat to impose law on the members of the non-democratic society. Even if the members of the non-democratic society have waived their rights, complicity with the autocrat in imposing law on the other members of the non-democratic society is problematic because the basis of the exercise of the waiver of the right to democracy is a set of convictions that democratic citizens regard as mistaken. Though the members of the non-democratic society have, by hypothesis, genuinely accepted the non-democratic norms, there is still something problematic for democratic citizens in dealing with them. They seem to be treating the members as unequals themselves, even though they have not agreed that the members are unequals. The problem is that the members can agree to treat each other as unequals, but can they make it permissible for others, who do not agree, to treat them as unequals? It is not clear to me that they can.

The more serious and straightforward problem is that compromise of democratic principles occurs in much the same way as in the cases of vote selling in the earlier discussion. The compromise of democratic principles occurs because the autocrat in effect has more power than the democratic citizens over the creation of the law that is to go into force in the democratic society. The autocrat has a kind of veto over the treaty making and the democratic citizens have a veto over the treaty, but only collectively. So, with regard to the domestically enforceable law in the democratic society that derives from the treaty, the autocrat exercises much more power than any of the citizens. The non-democrats' waivers of their democratic rights has in effect undermined the right to participate as equals of democratic citizens in the making of law that governs them. In effect, the non-democrats' waiver has subordinated the democratic citizens in part to the autocrat. It thus has the external effect of undermining the equal right to participation of democratic citizens in the making of the law that governs them. Hence it looks like the exercise of the waiver on the part of the non-democratic citizens is no longer merely self-regarding. Hence it may not be permissible.

To be sure, we could say that the democratic society is voluntarily engaged in treaty making with the autocratic society, and so the citizens have chosen to do this and they didn't have to do it. But the situation is more complex than this insofar as we recognize the deep interdependence of societies in the international system and we recognize that there are important morally mandatory aims that must be pursued through interstate cooperation. The association is not entirely voluntary; and in some cases it is required. This implies that the inegalitarian decision making is not avoidable or at least can be avoided only at great cost. It still seems to undermine the equal participation of the democratic citizens.

So we have a situation in which we must choose between the self-determination of non-democratic peoples and the rights to democracy of democratic citizens. I have argued that there is an asymmetry between these considerations in that the democratic rights have primacy. And that is reflected in the self-regarding waiver principle attached to the human right to democracy. Hence these observations suggest that in fact non-democratic societies cannot legitimately waive their rights to democracy because in doing so they compromise the rights of others who do not wish to waive their rights, at least under the modern conditions of interdependence in the international arena.

It seems to me that here it makes sense to think that the rights of inclusion that are involved in the right to collective self-determination are precisely the ones that will come into question in the case of non-democratic societies. Those societies threaten the democratic character of the democratic societies when they interact with them. Thus it makes sense to say that the democratic societies have rights to curtail the degree to which non-democratic societies are included in the international community. Democratic societies are legitimately acting in defense of the human rights of their members in doing so. For democratic societies to have duties to include non-democratic societies under these circumstances, which would follow from a full right of collective self-determination, would be for them not to take seriously the human rights to democracy of their own citizens.

But there is a complication here. The democratic rights that are compromised are limited to treaty making, which is still a relatively limited source of domestic law. The right of self-determination of non-democratic peoples that is being denied is more comprehensive. Hence, the interests in the power to waive of the non-democratic societies appear to be more comprehensive than the interests at stake of the democratic citizens in equal participation in this instance. There is something worrisome in denying the non-democratic peoples their power to waive and requiring that they retain their democratic rights when we have acknowledged the interests involved in waiving and when we see that the reason for not waiving is based in the interests of the democratic citizens.

However, a theoretical solution does exist to this problem. A compromise can be made in which the non-democratic society must be organized democratically when it comes to treaty making while it may retain its non-democratic organization when it is concerned with purely domestic law. I do not know to what extent such a division of collective decision making can be achieved in a society. It seems to require a rather complex political status for each person and it is hard to see how that can be maintained. And I certainly do not know how plausible it is to think that any society would be willing to divide up decision making in this way. This is a highly artificial and theoretical solution, but it does suggest that there is some kind of middle way between denial of democratic rights and denial of rights of self-determination.

There is one other worry raised by the foregoing considerations. The last worry derives from the first argument for the human right to democracy. It states that democracies are normally necessary and reliable in protecting basic rights of physical integrity. These rights are commonly accepted and have a particularly central place in the human rights system. If non-democratic societies normally violate these rights, can they still have rights to collective self-determination? One way we could go about thinking about this question is by asking if members can waive their rights not to be tortured or not to be killed or disappeared by the state. I don't know how to answer this question definitively. But it is useful to note here at least that the considerations that made it reasonable to append a self-regarding power to waive to the democratic rights don't seem to hold as straightforwardly in this case. In the democratic case, we noted that the interests in the power to waive were the same kind of interests as the interests in the democratic right. But the interests in not being tortured, killed, disappeared or arbitrarily imprisoned are not entirely of the same nature as the political interests in democracy. They are fundamental interests in the physical integrity and the dignity of the person. It may be that the rights protecting these urgent goods cannot be waived.

If this is true, we could still try to answer this question by saying that only those societies that do protect the rights of physical integrity can have a right of collective self-determination. This would limit the rights of collective self-determination of non-democratic states to the statistical outliers to the claim that democracies are normally necessary in protecting the rights of physical integrity. The extent of legitimate protection of non-democratic societies would be very limited indeed if this were the case. I will leave the discussion at this point, though I want to note here that the conflict that I have been discussing in these last paragraphs is one between the collective self-determination of non-democratic peoples and the basic rights of physical integrity.

IX. Conclusion

We have arrived at a point where there appears to be conceptual space for the possibility of a right of collective self determination for non-democratic societies even when there is a human right to democracy. But the actual practical space for such a right seems quite limited because of the morally necessary interdependence of states in the international system and because of the fact that non-democratic states normally do not protect basic human rights. This problem does not arise because there is a direct moral incompatibility between the human right to democracy and the right of collective self-determination of non-democratic peoples. But it is nevertheless the case that the scope for such self-determination is very limited.

I want to close the discussion on a softer note. Even though normally non-democratic peoples will not have a full right to collective self-determination in the sense of rights to non-interference and full inclusion, they will usually still be in possession of rights to non-interference from democratic states. The right against non-interference can be sustained even if the rights to full inclusion cannot be. Aside from all the worries that arise merely from considering the terrible effects of war on a society, a basic reason for the right against non-interference is grounded in essentially democratic principles. One basic problem with one society intervening militarily against another is that the intervening society is not politically accountable to the society and the people for whom intervention is intended. That is, there are no political mechanisms for ensuring that the society that is supposedly being helped actually has some voice in the decision making of the intervening power during the intervention and during the subsequent occupation. Since the intervening power has its own interests and is politically accountable to its own people and not to those for whom intervention is intended, the interests of the supposed beneficiaries are likely to be forgotten or mis-understood in the process. Only in the most egregious cases of widespread internal human rights abuses, can this worry be overcome in favor of intervention. But in the cases of collectively self-determining, non-democratic societies these violations may not normally rise to this magnitude. So they do possess a weaker right of collective self-determination even if not the full rights.[23]

---

[23] I want to thank Massimo Renzo, Carol Gould, Andrew Williams, Alistair Macleod, Allen Buchanan, Kristen Hessler, and Gopal Sreenivasan for very helpful comments on previous drafts of this paper.

26

A Human Right to Democracy?

Fabienne Peter

I. Introduction

There is something counterintuitive about imposing democracy on peoples.[1] In the recent debate in political and legal philosophy, many have argued against the human right to democracy, often on grounds of its conflict with another right, the right to self-determination.[2] The thought is that the human right to self-determination, which allows peoples to choose their own constitution and development, would be undermined by the human right to democracy, which requires a specific constitution and thus restricts developmental choices.

Thomas Christiano, in his contribution to this volume ("Self-determination and the Human Right to Democracy", this volume, chapter 25; all subsequent references to ch. 25 appear parenthetically in the text), challenges this line of thought. He argues that, properly understood, the right to self-determination presupposes the right to democracy. Christiano's argument reverses the order of priority between the two rights. He aims to show that the right to democracy has priority over the right to self-determination. But he also wants to argue that affirming the priority of democracy need not imply reserving the right to self-determination to democratic peoples. The innovative core of his paper consists in his proposal for how the right to democracy can be made compatible with the right to self-determination even for peoples that are not democratic.

Christiano's argument involves the following main steps. He first defends the human right to democracy, both on instrumental and on intrinsic grounds. He then moves on to the right to self-determination and offers an interpretation of this right as grounded in the protection of the same interests as the right to democracy. This step aims to establish that there is no necessary conflict between the two rights.[3] The final step of the argument covers the case of the right to self-determination of undemocratic states. Christiano handles this through the introduction of a power to waive the right to democracy. He writes: "it makes sense to think that there is a power to

[1] I greatly benefitted from a series of workshops on human rights that Rowan Cruft and others organized at the University of Stirling. I'm also very grateful for comments I've received from Tom Christiano and Massimo Renzo.
[2] See eg Joshua Cohen, "Is There a Right to Democracy?" in C. Sypnowich (ed.), *The Egalitarian Conscience* (Oxford: Oxford University Press, 2006); Matthew Lister, "There is No Human Right to Democracy. But May We Promote It Anyway?" *Stanford Journal of International Law*, 48 (2012): 257–76; and David Reidy, "On the Human Right to Democracy: Searching for Sense without Stilts," *Journal of Social Philosophy*, 43 (2012): 177–203.
[3] Carol Gould, *Globalizing Democracy and Human Rights* (Cambridge: Cambridge University Press, 2006) and Andrew Altman and Christopher H. Wellman, *A Liberal Theory of International Justice* (Oxford: Oxford University Press, 2009) have also offered interpretations of the right to self-determination as requiring democracy.

waive one's right to democracy because this power can be grounded in the same inter-ests in asserting control over one's political world that the claim right to democracy is grounded in" (472). While the right to self-determination is thus contingent on the right to democracy, since the right to democracy, like many other rights, is one that can be waived, self-determination is possible even for certain non-democratic states.

Christiano's argument for the priority of democracy is intertwined with an interest-based, moral conception of human rights. On this interpretation, the case for the human right to democracy rests on the moral goods that democracy protects. And the case for the compatibility between the human right to democracy and the human right to self-determination rests, similarly, on the fact that the two rights protect the same moral goods. Both the right to democracy and the right to self-determination are defended as minimal requirements of justice.

Those who reject the human right to democracy tend to reject the sufficiency of such justice-based arguments for establishing a human right. They tend to argue that human rights are and should be distinct from moral rights based on justice—because of what human rights are and/or because of how human rights are justified. They don't deny that there is a connection between justice and democracy for some societies. But they deny that this connection is sufficient to underpin the human right to democracy.

There are two main ways in which the case can be made.[4] The first focuses on the nature of human rights. It stresses the functional role of human rights, for exam-ple with regard to the justification of third-party interventions or the exclusion from the international community. The second focuses on the justification of human rights and appeals to non-parochial normative foundations for human rights. In John Rawls' treatment of human rights, as well as in some other approaches, the two aspects are not sharply distinguished but are jointly invoked in support of a political conception of human rights that can underpin international legitimacy.

In this comment, I shall side with those who reject the justice-based case for the human right to democracy, focusing on the justificatory challenge that human rights face.[5] My sympathies are with the political conception of human rights. I think it is a mistake to think about human rights in straightforwardly moral terms, as discovered rights that explicate certain universal moral facts. This strikes me as empirically and historically inadequate. It also obscures the significance of the achievement of con-temporary human rights practice, namely that the practice has created a standard for international political legitimacy. Human rights apply to national, international, and global politics. This standard is not set in stone, of course: human rights are a work in progress and as such subject to both negative criticism—focusing on problems of the current set of standards—and positive criticism—proposals for what should be included. But while the achievement may be fragile, this does not lessen the normative significance of the political project, it seems to me. Vice versa, the attempt to overcome

---

[4] I am using a distinction drawn by John Tasioulas, "Are Human Rights Essentially Triggers for Intervention?" *Philosophy Compass*, 4 (2009): 938–50.

[5] It is based on ideas that I've developed more fully in Fabienne Peter, "The Human Right to Political Participation," *Journal of Ethics and Social Philosophy*, 7 (2013): 1–16.

this fragility by providing moral foundations to this project risks being too parochial to be successful.

I think Christiano's argument for the human right to democracy fails because it doesn't sufficiently address the justificatory challenge. My comment doesn't focus on the conflict between democracy and self-determination, however. I think Christiano is right to question the priority of the right to self-determination. Instead, I shall contrast the justice-based argument for a human right to democracy with a legitimacy-based argument for a human right to political participation—I understand the right to political participation in a weaker sense than the right to democracy. But I will discuss the implications of this right to political participation for self-determination in the final section.[6]

II. Two Conceptions of Human Rights

Christiano provides a moral defense of the human right to democracy. The defense rests on two claims: (i) that human rights are best interpreted as minimal norms of justice and (ii) that minimal justice requires democracy. Let me discuss them in turn, starting with the conception of human rights.

The normative commitment at the core of Christiano's moral defense of the human right to democracy is that each person's interests deserve equal consideration. This normative commitment explains both the significance of human rights and the value of democracy. Adapting a Millian thought, human rights are moral rights grounded in the protection of important individual interests. A moral right to x is a human right when the interests are such that there is "a strong moral justification for any state to respect, protect, and promote a legal or conventional right to x in all persons" (460). Not all moral rights will pass this test and so not all moral rights are necessarily human rights.

This conception of human rights follows the orthodox pattern. The orthodox conception contrasts with a political conception of human rights with regard to both the nature of human rights and the justification of rights. On the orthodox conception, human rights are moral rights that all human beings have qua salient features of their humanity. Salient features may relate to fundamental interests or basic aspects of human agency.[7] On the political conception, human rights are a set of special rights that have their origins in salient features of contemporary human rights practice. Different conceptions identify different features of this practice as salient.[8]

---

[6] I shall follow Christiano by focusing only on political participation in the domestic context. In Peter, "The Human Right to Political Participation," I've commented on the possibility of broadening the right to political participation in the international and global context.

[7] On the link to fundamental interests, see Joseph Raz, *The Morality of Freedom* (Oxford: Oxford University Press, 1986) and on the link to human agency, see James Griffin, *On Human Rights* (Oxford: Oxford University Press, 2008).

[8] The most fully developed account is found in Charles Beitz, *The Idea of Human Rights*. (Oxford: Oxford University Press, 2009). Note that in addition to these pure forms of the traditional and the political conception of human rights, some writers have recently proposed mixed conceptions. Joseph Raz is, I think, best understood as defending a mixed conception. See his "Human Rights Without Foundations," in Samantha Besson and John Tasioulas (eds.), *The Philosophy of International Law* (Oxford: Oxford University Press, 2007), 321–37 and "Human Rights in the Emerging World Order," *Transnational Legal Theory*, 1 (2010): 31–47. He accepts the political conception with regard to the first dimension—with

With regard to the question of what justifies human rights, defenders of the orthodox conception typically maintain that ordinary moral reasoning is necessary and sufficient to establish what should count as a human right. Defenders of the political conception, by contrast, typically maintain that human rights are based on political norms and established by some form of public reason or public reasoning.

There are important objections to the orthodox conception of human rights. One concerns the justification of human rights. If human rights are to function as a standard of international political legitimacy, they need a non-parochial justification. The objection against the orthodox conception is that ordinary moral reasoning produces disagreement and as such cannot justify human rights.

I don't think Christiano has a good answer to this objection. He may claim that while moral disagreement is indeed common, it will be less common with regard to the minimal requirements of justice on which his account of the human right to democracy rests. That may or may not be so; it's an empirical question. But my point is that when disagreements do occur about how societies should be organized, the orthodox account doesn't have a strategy to confront them. Instead, it merely asserts one blueprint for how society should be organized.

When Rawls originally came up with the idea of a political conception of justice for the domestic case of liberal democracies, he proposed to circumvent controversies about the morality of justice by developing a conception of justice based on fundamental political values embodied in democracy.[9] The thought was that while we might disagree about the good, we can agree that we live in a democracy and that a democracy is based on certain values. Defenders of a political conception of human rights are drawn to the same thought: while we are likely to disagree about what makes a life go well and what people need to make their lives go well, we can agree—and that's the achievement of the contemporary human rights practice—that there is such a thing as a human rights practice and that this practice is associated with certain political norms and values. Reference to salient features of the contemporary practice offers a way of settling disagreements that are likely to arise about human needs and interests.

A second important objection to the orthodox conception is that it has the wrong account of what human rights are. This objection comes in several versions. One focuses on the account of universality that the orthodox conception gives rise to. With regard to basic human rights at least, the orthodox conception appears to be committed to a timelessness about human rights that doesn't sit well with human rights practices. Human rights are not timeless, but that doesn't mean that they are not universal. As Raz has convincingly argued in "Human Rights in the Emerging World Order", human rights are best understood as committed to synchronic universality—as rights all human beings alive today have. The political conception can easily accommodate synchronic universality.

---

regard to the question of what human rights are. But he combines this with the view that what justifies human rights is ordinary moral reasoning. Rainer Forst, "The Justification of Human Rights and the Basic Right to Justification: A Reflexive Approach," *Ethics*, 120 (2010): 711–40 is drawn to the opposite move: he defines human rights on the basis of salient features of human agency, but answers the question of how they are justified by invoking an account of public reasoning.

[9] See John Rawls, *Political Liberalism* (New York: Columbia University Press, 1993).

With regard to the human right to democracy, I think that it is not plausible to claim timeless universality. Democracy is a political institution—or, more accurately, a family of sets of political institutions—that has evolved over time and, who knows, that may further evolve in the future or even disappear completely. So if there is to be a human right to democracy at all, it can only be a right that is relative to specific historical circumstances. But once this point is accepted, the question whether the relevant historical circumstances currently obtain internationally is once again wide open. The moral case for a human right to democracy thus doesn't seem to achieve that much.

A related version of the objection states that human rights are a set of explicitly political norms that only make sense in certain institutional contexts.[10] Human rights get their distinctive content not from essential features of humanity as such, but from institutionalized relations between individuals and their governments and other political agents. The political conception of human rights is better equipped to capture this aspect of human rights practice than the traditional conception. Many have argued that this objection fails, however, as the orthodox conception of human rights can incorporate the institutional specificity of human rights. Indeed, as we saw, Christiano's version of the orthodox conception also emphasizes the role of the international community and of international law for human rights.

Still, the relationship between human rights and the institutional context that Christiano postulates rests on a set of fundamental interests that he identifies as essential features of humanity to which a conception of justice responds. As such, Christiano offers a particular moral interpretation of the political project that human rights stand for. But I don't think that a moral interpretation best furthers the human rights project; it's too divisive. This gets me back to the problem of justifying human rights. The political conception of human rights can deal with the specifically political project that human rights are more directly and already factors in the justificatory problem.

III. Justice, Legitimacy, and the Human Right to Democracy

Is it possible for Christiano to argue that because of the special way in which his approach emphasizes the link between justice and democracy, the objection from disagreement and the problem of justifying human rights are taken into account? I don't think he can and that's because I don't think his argument for the human right to democracy works.

Christiano defends democracy on both instrumental and intrinsic grounds. The instrumental argument is based on the empirical claim that democracies better protect a range of human rights than non-democracies.[11] There are some questions about this argument.[12] One is whether the correlation is actually with democracy or whether

---

[10] See Beitz, *The Idea of Human Rights.*

[11] The instrumental argument is more fully developed in Thomas Christiano, "An Instrumental Argument for a Human Right to Democracy," *Philosophy & Public Affairs*, 39 (2011): 142–76.

[12] See the discussions in Lister, "There is No Human Right to Democracy" and Reidy, "On the Human Right to Democracy".

it is instead with observance of the rule of law. If the correlation is with democracy, another question is whether democracy is strictly necessary for the protection of the other human rights or merely often associated with it. Rawls, for example, captured the possibility of peoples that are non-democratic yet not human rights violating, through his category of "decent societies".[13] I shall leave these worries about the instrumental defense of democracy to the side.

The intrinsic argument is based on democracy's egalitarianism and is developed more fully in *The Constitution of Equality*. It starts from the normative commitment that each person's interests matter equally. According to this "egalitarian" argument, democracy is distinctive because it is the only political regime that publicly affirms equality. Here is what Christiano has to say in support of the relationship between democracy and justice understood as the public affirmation of equality:

> The fundamental argument for democracy at the domestic level is that it is necessary to the public realization of the equal advancement of the interests of the members of society. Persons have fundamental political interests in shaping the society they live in. They have interests in correcting for the cognitive biases of others in determining how to shape the society. They have interests in being at home in the world they live. And they have interests in being recognized and affirmed as equals. Against the background of conflict of interest, disagreement, cognitive bias and fallibility on how best to organize society, the only public way of realizing the equality of persons in a society is to give each an equal say in how to shape the society (464).

The demand for democracy is supported by three considerations, situated in a context of four main facts about our judgments about how the world should be organized. The four facts are: (i) conflict of interest, (ii) cognitive bias, (iii) fallibility, and, presumably as a consequence of the first three, (iv) extensive disagreement. The considerations supporting democracy are (i) the interest in correcting the cognitive bias of others, (ii) the interest in being at home in the world, and (iii) the interest to be recognized and respected. The main idea uniting them is that there is value in the connection between people's judgments about how the world should be organized and how the world is actually organized. And only democracy can deliver the right kind of connection between the two, Christiano argues:

> the only public way to realize equality is to ensure that persons have equal opportunities to shape the society in accordance with their judgments. This is not to say that the other substantive forms of equality are not important but it is to say that they cannot achieve the public realization of equality under the normal circumstances of political societies if the democratic realization is not present. Democracy is indispensable for this (465).

I want to ask two main questions about this intrinsic argument. First, is the intrinsic argument a good argument for democracy? And, second, does it support a human right to democracy?

---

[13] John Rawls, *Law of Peoples* (Cambridge: Harvard University Press, 1999), 4.

I am very much in sympathy with Christiano's characterization of the background conditions that shape political decisions and the evaluation of political institutions. I also think he's right to emphasize the significance of political participation as such and not just its outcomes. But I'm not convinced by his justice-based argument for why political participation is significant and as a result I'm not convinced by his argument for democracy.

As others have also pointed out, Christiano's argument for democracy faces an epistemic challenge.[14] The challenge is: why assume that democracy performs better than alternative political regimes in securing the "public realization of the equal advancement of the interests of the members of society"? Or, to put the same point slightly differently, what is the link between equality as a constraint on the decision-making procedure and equality as a constraint on the results? As we saw, Christiano's "egalitarian" argument aims to show that given the background conditions of politics, only democracy can secure (i) the interest in correcting the cognitive bias of others, (ii) the interest in being at home in the world, and (iii) the interest to be recognized and respected.

But, surely, even if we accept Christiano's moral theory, it's too strong to claim we each value our own political participation in order to secure these interests. I may have an interest that the cognitive bias of others is corrected—by me or by someone else. If someone else is able to correct others' cognitive biases on my behalf, that must be sufficient. Similarly, I may have an interest in seeing a connection between my judgment about how the world should be organized and how the world is organized. But that doesn't imply that I necessarily have an interest in expressing my judgment. Finally, the interest to be recognized and respected need also not have its prime expression through political participation—it may be possible for me to be recognized and respected in other ways that are more important. If we grant these limitations on the moral value of the collective decision-making procedure, however, then the necessary link to democracy is lost. It then becomes possible that non-democratic decision-making procedures are better suited than democracy to achieve a certain desirable outcome.

To argue for democracy, I think it is necessary to combine an argument for political equality with an epistemic argument. One way to do that is by focusing on how democracy performs and by defending it on grounds of its potential to achieve just outcomes. David Estlund has adopted this epistemic instrumentalist approach.[15] But I don't think that it is successful either. Instead, I think democracy is best defended on grounds of the procedural epistemic values that it embodies, values that become significant in circumstances where a collective cannot establish what the correct decision would be.[16]

---

[14] See David Estlund, "Debate: On Christiano's *The Constitution of Equality*," *Journal of Political Philosophy*, 17 (2009): 241–52.

[15] David Estlund, *Democratic Authority* (Princeton: Princeton University Press, 2008).

[16] I've argued for this view in Fabienne Peter, *Democratic Legitimacy* (New York: Routledge, 2009) and "The Epistemic Circumstances of Democracy," in Michael Brady and Miranda Fricker (eds.), *The Epistemic Life of Groups* (Oxford: Oxford University Press, forthcoming).

While the epistemic instrumentalist option, if it were successful, would retain the link between justice and democracy, the epistemic proceduralist alternative that I favor distinguishes more sharply between the legitimacy of democratic decision making and the justice of its outcomes. The idea is not that democracy is legitimate because it tends to produce just outcomes. It is, rather, that legitimacy is a normative concept in its own right, significant in circumstances where more comprehensive moral assessments fail—because of value pluralism, for example. The reason why I favor the epistemic proceduralist approach is because I think that democracy has its natural space in situations where there is no access to a privileged position from which to make valid assertions about which decision should be made and where democratic procedures are themselves epistemically valuable. When it is possible to make valid factual or moral claims about how society should be organized, there is less scope for democracy.

This epistemic argument undermines the justice-based case for democracy even for the domestic context of liberal democracies. Meanwhile, many societies do not currently have political institutions that resemble a democracy. What are the implications of a legitimacy-based argument for a human right to democracy for those societies? I don't think that there is a clear legitimacy-based case for a human right to democracy. I shall focus on the ideal itself, leaving aside problems that would arise with implementing a particular set of democratic institutions.[17]

Can political institutions that are not fully democratic—whatever exactly that is supposed to mean—produce legitimate decisions? The dominant view in democratic theory and democratization research has been that political institutions that are not fully democratic are seen as deficient and in need of correction in direction of full democracy. This so-called transitional paradigm is challenged in the literature on democratization, however.[18] Based on research on new forms of political participation both in Western liberal democracies and in countries with other political regimes, an alternative paradigm in democratization research is emerging that focuses on the possibility of a stable coexistence of elements from different regime types—democratic and authoritarian—and examines the diversity of channels of political participation beyond traditional democratic electoral politics.[19] The transitional paradigm suggests a false dualism between politically legitimate democracies and illegitimate non-democracies. The dualism is false because it obscures the many ways in which even established liberal democracies contain authoritarian elements and, vice versa, how there can be multiple forms of political participation beyond those narrowly associated with a human right to democracy. If the transitional paradigm is rejected in favor of a more pluralist model of political regimes, however, the legitimacy-based case for a human right to democracy crumbles.

This said, I find it very plausible that some political participation must be possible in light of the background conditions of politics that Christiano lists: cognitive bias, fallibility, conflict of interest, and disagreement. Nothing in what I have said so

---

[17] See Beitz, *The Idea of Human Rights* for a further discussion of this issue.
[18] See Thomas Carothers, "The End of the Transition Paradigm," *Journal of Democracy*, 13 (2002): 5–21.
[19] See Pippa Norris, *The Democratic Phoenix: Reinventing Political Activism* (Cambridge: Cambridge University Press, 2002).

far, however, forces me to deny that there is a right to political participation as recognized by the United Nations Universal Declaration of Human Rights (UDHR) and the International Covenant on Civil and Political Rights (ICCPR). And that is because the right to political participation, while it is frequently interpreted as a right to democracy, can be interpreted in weaker terms. Henry Steiner argues that human rights conventions encourage full-fledged democratic participation as a programmatic ideal, but they do not require it.[20] The right to political participation has two parts: an "election clause" and a "take part" clause. The take part clause is too vague to require any particular political system and would be satisfied by a right to participate in deliberative political processes. The elections clause is more specific, but it, too, can be satisfied by political systems other than democratic self-government as modelled, say, on modern Western democracies. Both clauses can thus be interpreted in ways that do not require democracy. The right to political participation, understood in this way, neither presupposes democratic institutions nor does it demand that they be imposed where they are absent.

IV. Political Participation and Self-determination

In this final part of my comment I want to return to my starting-point, the relationship between a right to democracy and a right to self-determination. The ICCPR recognizes both a right to self-determination (Article 1) and a right to political participation (Article 25). The official comment on Article 25 explicitly addresses its relationship to Article 1 and emphasizes that the two rights are not in tension. It explains that while the right to self-determination is a right of peoples, the right to political participation is a right of individuals. The right to political participation, as mentioned, is the right of individuals to take part in political affairs, including in some form of elections. According to the right to self-determination, peoples should be free to choose their constitution and their "economic, social, and cultural development". This article also formulates an obligation on all peoples to foster and respect the self-determination of other peoples.

To point to the distinction between a right of individuals and a right of peoples doesn't seem sufficient to rule out conflict, however. It is entirely possible that a particular right of peoples has implications that are in tension with some rights of individuals and, vice versa, that rights of individuals have implications for the decision-making of peoples. I thus think that Christiano is right to probe deeper. As mentioned, his paper attempts to dispel conflict by de-prioritizing the right to self-determination and providing an account of the right to self-determination that rests on the right to democracy. According to Christiano, there is no right to self-determination that is compatible with the denial of the right to democracy. Self-determination, properly understood, just is the expression of the collective exercise of the right to democracy or, as an added twist, of the collective waiver—not denial—of the right to democracy.

---

[20] Henry Steiner, "Political Participation as a Human Right," *Harvard Human Rights Journal*, 1 (1988): 77–134. See also Lister, "There is No Human Right to Democracy" for a recent argument in favor of treating democracy as an aspirational ideal, but not as a human right.

The right to self-determination protects both the collective exercise of the right to democracy and the collective waiver of this right.

While this solution is very elegant, I'm not convinced by its normative appeal. And that is because I don't believe that the moral case for a human right to democracy is successful. As I've argued in the previous section, I think we should pursue a legitimacy-based approach and that this approach can only support a human right to political participation, not a right to democracy. But if there is no case for a human right to democracy, then the interpretation of the right to self-determination as based on the right to democracy also fails. And if we reject that interpretation, then the tension resurfaces: while the right to democracy implies that a particular constitution should be imposed on peoples, the right to self-determination implies greater choice in this regard.

Still, I think Christiano is right that we should question the priority of an unqualified right to self-determination. Is it possible to endorse the priority of the right to political participation and reconcile it with the right to self-determination? I think this is possible, along the lines of what the comment on Article 25 suggests. If the right to political participation is interpreted in a weaker sense than the right to democracy, it does not presuppose a blueprint for how society should be organized. As such, it can, more plausibly than the right to democracy, be interpreted in individualistic terms, as a right to be heard in processes of public reasoning. Beyond that, it leaves it to peoples to determine what set of institutions they want to adopt.

Is that proposal unappealing because it is too undemanding? I don't think so. Note, first, that human rights don't fully determine political legitimacy—additional domestic constraints would apply. In addition, the human right to political participation is only one element, albeit an important one, of the minimal requirements of legitimacy. But, more positively, there is a sense in which a human right to political participation in the weak sense is more empowering than the human right to democracy, precisely because it does not presuppose any particular set of institutions. It puts the choice of political institutions more directly in people's hands than a version of this right that is constrained by a particular moral blueprint.

27

The Content of the Human Right to Health

Jonathan Wolff

The human right to health is attracting increasing attention from philosophers, and a range of questions has been asked. The most fundamental one, no doubt, is whether there are good reasons for believing that there is any such thing. I have directly addressed that question elsewhere,[1] but here my concern is somewhat different, and I address the fundamental question only in more indirect fashion. My aim is to consider a type of criticism that has the conclusion that there could not be—or perhaps should not be—a human right to health. The core of that objection is that there are insuperable difficulties in attempting to specify the content of the human right to health. This type of objection splits into two. One is conceptual; that the content of the human right to health cannot be coherently specified. The second is of a more practical nature: when specified the human right to health leads to unattractive, or at least sub-optimal, health policies. Answering these objections is the task of this paper, and in fact I will argue that the two objections need to be answered together. Understanding the conceptual core is necessary to answer the practical challenge and dealing with the practical challenge helps to specify the conceptual core. If I am successful this would show only that there could be a human right to health. Other arguments would be needed to establish that, in fact, there is one.

In international law the human right to health makes a relatively subdued appearance in the Universal Declaration of Human Rights (UDHR). Human beings are declared to have a right to a standard of living adequate to health, and, insightfully, a right to various other underlying determinants of health, such as food, clothing, and housing, but also medical care. However, the drafters of the later International Covenant on Economic, Social and Cultural Rights (ICESCR) went much further, declaring a universal right to the highest attainable standard of physical and mental health. In doing this one has to admit that they did not make things easy for their defenders. For, as Onora O'Neill has pressed, what is to be made of the idea of the 'highest attainable standard of health'? Consider a low resource environment such as rural India or sub-Saharan Africa. If we mean the globally highest attainable standard then we are setting a utopian standard. If we mean the locally highest attainable standard are

---

[1] Jonathan Wolff, 'The Human Right to Health', in S. Benatar and G. Brock, *Global Health and Global Health Ethics* (Cambridge: Cambridge University Press, 2011); Jonathan Wolff, 'Global Justice and Health: The Basis of the Global Health Duty', in J. Millum and E. Emanuel (eds.), *Global Justice and Bioethics* (New York: Oxford University Press, 2012); Jonathan Wolff, *The Human Right to Health* (New York: Norton, 2012); Jonathan Wolff, 'The Demands of the Human Right to Health', *Proceedings of the Aristotelian Society: Supplementary Volume* 86 (2012).

we not setting our target far too low?[2] A related difficulty is pointed out by Joseph Raz, although overall he is much more sympathetic to the human right to health than O'Neill. He points out that the notion of the 'highest attainable' standard does not specify whether it is the 'highest attainable' or 'highest attainable, given proper weight to all other considerations, including other moral rights and worth-while goals' (this volume, chapter 11, 230). Conceptually, there seems to be much work to be done.

How is progress to be made in specifying a determinate content for the human right to health? The United Nations has not stood still, and among several initiatives, in 2000 the Committee on Economic, Social and Cultural Rights issued what is known as 'General Comment 14' (hereinafter GC14), which sets out to clarify the 'normative content' (Section 6) of the right to the highest attainable standard of health. GC14 makes some useful observations, such as 'The right to health is not to be understood as a right to be healthy' (Section 8) for biological factors make it impossible to ensure everyone's health. Consequently some theorists may be tempted to retreat to the more modest right to medical care, which was mentioned in the UDHR. However, this is too narrow: the right to medical care was listed as only one of several determinants of health, alongside clean water and a safe environment, among other things. But perhaps just as importantly, supposing that the right to health can be restricted to the right to health care opens the way to some of the alleged practical difficulties that we will explore later. Thus we must conclude that the right to health lies somewhere between the right to be healthy and the right to health care. But where, exactly? Is it an agglomeration of rights to the determinants of health (but then how do we know which ones, as so many things can affect health?), or does it have a determinate conceptual core?

GC14 tries to address this gap. It sets out some very general guidelines. So, for example, it famously says that the right to health contains the elements of availability, accessibility, acceptability, and quality (Section 12) and expands on the particular examples given in ICESCR Article 12.2, such as 'the right to maternal, child and reproductive health'. There is no doubt that in reading through GC14 one can get a 'feel' for the idea of the human right to health, and the duties it generates, or at least correlates with. Nevertheless, one comes away from the General Comment with a suspicion that to some degree it has avoided the main question. And that question can be put like this: when is failure to supply medical care or other determinants of health nevertheless not a human rights failure?[3] Human right to health litigation has, in the vast majority of cases, concerned the claim for medical treatment in the form of drugs, surgery or equipment that has not been supplied by the litigant's country.[4] Presumably in almost

---

[2] See Onora O'Neill, 'The Dark Side of Human Rights', *International Affairs*, 81 (2005): 427–39. Note, though, in many low resource settings the local elite achieve a level of health comparable to the global elite. Hence the locally highest attainable level is far higher than that commonly achieved. I owe this observation to Paula Braverman.

[3] It could be said that this is a question not about the content of the human right to health, but the scope of the right. However, I take it that the two issues are very closely connected: generally the content will determine the scope. Arguably, though, GC14 provides a good account of the content of the human right to health, but leaves the scope indeterminate. Whichever way one puts the issue, the central and urgent question remains the same: when is a failure to provide health-improving services or resources nevertheless not a violation of the human right to health?

[4] Alicia E. Yamin and Siri Gloppin, (eds.), *Litigating Health Rights* (Cambridge MA: Harvard University Press, 2011).

all cases there is a good chance that meeting the claim would have improved the litigant's health to some degree. But if courts are at least sometimes to turn down such suits then they need to have an answer to our question: when is it acceptable not to supply something that would be likely to improve health? If we were to take the idea of 'highest attainable standard of health' as our benchmark, then withholding anything that is clinically effective would be a violation. But in practice this would mean a huge diversion of resources to the health sector even when the health benefits, though real, are small. It is no wonder, then, that the right to health is often accused as being contrary to cost-effective health planning, or what Albert Weale calls 'beneficial design' of health systems.[5]

It is not the case that GC14 is entirely silent on the question of how to understand the idea of the 'highest attainable standard of health'. The authors well understood that in low resource settings there are severe limits to what is attainable. Indeed the document early on strikes a rather melancholy note: 'The Committee is aware that, for millions of people throughout the world, the full enjoyment of the right to health still remains a distant goal. Moreover, in many cases, especially for those living in poverty, this goal is becoming increasingly remote' (Section 5).

Clearly GC14 takes the plight of those living in poverty as a central concern. Rather than providing further analysis of the idea of the 'highest attainable standard' the document somewhat finesses the problem by implicitly suggesting that while, indeed, everyone does have a right to the highest attainable standard of health, it is not the case that all countries have the duty to supply their citizens with what would fulfil this right.[6] We can see this in one of two ways. One would be to say that there is a gap between the right—which is to the highest attainable standard of health—and the duties it generates, which vary in the circumstances. This would be the most literal reading of the General Comment. Alternatively one could make a distinction between a fully fledged aspirational right to the highest attainable standard of health, and what we might call 'human rights in the circumstances', which again vary. Perhaps which route we go is a question of language, but the inescapable point is that whether or not individuals have the right to the highest attainable standard of health, GC14 does not assign to all countries the duty that all their citizens should achieve the highest attainable standard of health.

In order to deal with apparent non-compliance GC14 appeals to two important concepts: progressive realization (Sections 30–31) and core obligations (Sections 43–45). The idea of progressive realization is that it is unrealistic to expect poor countries to be able to offer the level of medical care and health protection available in wealthy countries, but it would be wrong to accuse them of violating the human rights of their people simply in virtue of this comparison. Hence it is vital to give countries a justification for not meeting the globally highest standard if their resources do not permit this. However this is not to be conceived of as a licence to neglect health. First,

---

[5] Albert Weale, 'The Right to Health Versus Good Medical Care?', *Critical Review of International Social and Political Philosophy*, 15 (2012): 473–93.

[6] The role of external state parties in GC14 is interesting. Several sections set out 'international obligations' (38–42), with special reference to the effect of the policies of international financial institutions, as well as humanitarian and disaster assistance and treatment of infectious disease, but it seems clear that the duties of external states are regarded as less demanding than the duties of the citizen's own state.

countries need to take 'deliberate, concrete and targeted [steps] towards the full realization of the right to health' (Section 30). And second, they nevertheless have certain 'core obligations' such as an obligation not to discriminate, and to supply a basic package of primary health services, as well as food, shelter, and essential drugs, and to adopt and implement a national public health strategy (Section 43), relying on international cooperation where necessary (Section 45).

We can see, then, that the task of setting out the content of the human right to health really comes down, now, to the issue of setting out an account of the duties of governments and other actors, whether national or international, in relation to health. And GC14 does this by way of setting out a list of duties, albeit at a certain level of abstraction. While sensible, indeed defensible, there remains something unsatisfactory about defining rights and duties by a list when hard cases will occur. The right to health is a protection against certain types of neglect, but, perhaps, not all.

How can we go further? GC14, as we noted, expands on details, yet without giving enough to know how to decide what is in and what is out. Yet there is a clue in the General Comment about how to develop the approach. In Section 33 we are told that the right to health, like all rights, entails a tri-partite structure of duties: duties to respect, protect, and fulfil. It has been argued that the source of this account of duties is, in fact, Henry Shue's book *Basic Rights*, as modified by others.[7] As a way of overcoming what he regarded as a misleading and simplistic division of rights into 'negative' requiring duties of non-intervention, and 'positive' requiring duties of active assistance, Shue pointed out that the rights he was interested in—to liberty, security, and subsistence—generate duties to 'avoid' certain types of behaviour, to 'protect' individuals from violations by others, and to 'aid' some individuals in achieving their rights.[8] These duties do not have to be held by the same party, although often they will be. Even 'negative' rights, such as the right to security, require positive action by governments, such as the provision of a police force. Shue's insight has been generalized to all human rights by the United Nations, and therefore, has had extraordinary influence in the development of United Nations human rights doctrine over the whole range of rights.

My thought is that there is more to learn from Shue than has been taken up by the United Nations so far. For the problem we are considering in relation to the right to health is simply a more explicitly formulated problem that afflicts all human rights doctrine. Shue himself is concerned with the 'basic' human rights to liberty, security, and subsistence. To see the problem let us take one of Shue's basic rights: the right to security. Suppose I am attacked on my way home from work. Can I say that the government has in some manner failed in relation to my human right to security?

Now, there are some cases in which such an attack could be conceived as a violation of a human right to security. For example, if it were the government itself that organized the attack. Here the government would have clearly failed in its duty to respect my right to security and much else. Or if the police knew it was going to happen but did not try to prevent it, because they don't like me or people of my kind. Obviously the duty to protect would have been breached. Or if such things happen on a very regular

---

[7] D.E. Reeve, *Global Poverty, Human Rights and Development*, PhD Thesis, University College London, 2013.

[8] Henry Shue, *Basic Rights*, 2nd edn (Princeton NJ: Princeton University Press, 1996), 51–5.

basis and the police and other government authorities have not helped to reduce their incidence by means that they have at their disposal. Here the government would have failed in its duty to fulfil. Yet a one-off, unpredictable attack by another private citizen, although a violation of my individual rights, could not generally be construed as a failure by the government to secure my human right to security.[9] As Shue remarks, he is 'not suggesting the absurd standard that a right has been fulfilled only if it is impossible for anyone to be deprived of it or only if no one is ever deprived of it. The standard can only be some reasonable level of guarantee'.[10]

But what is a reasonable level? Naturally it would be too much to expect a formula. Yet Shue does provide us with some important insight, and it is this I would like to try to develop. Human rights, he says, require social guarantees against 'standard threats'. This immediately provides some clarification. The government cannot be expected to protect us against everything. Standard, here, contrasts with 'exotic', and, perhaps 'rare' and 'new'; although all of these ideas need to be treated with caution, as an exotic, rare, and new threat can very easily become mundane, common, and familiar.

Shue's own analysis of the idea of a standard threat is that it must be 'ordinary,[11] and serious, but remediable'.[12] This, perhaps draws together different ideas: the ordinary nature of a threat makes it standard; the serious nature makes it worthy of attention; but only if it remediable is the failure to remedy it a breach of human rights (although the failure to research how to remedy a non-remediable ordinary and serious threat could be a human rights failure, which is especially important in the area of health).

Each of these terms—ordinary, serious, and remediable—are context dependent. Shue himself notes 'Precisely what those [typical major] threats are, and which it is feasible to counter, are of course largely empirical questions, and the answers to both questions will change as the situation changes'.[13] So, for example, Shue notes that what is eradicable changes over time. 'Today, we have very little excuse for allowing so many poor people to die of malaria and more excuse probably for allowing people to die of cancer. Later perhaps we will have equally little excuse to allow deaths by many kinds of cancer, or perhaps not'.[14]

The example of variability over time that Shue points to is a difficulty only on a very pedantic understanding of human rights. Human rights, it is generally thought, are universal, but, so the criticism runs, if they are variable over time how can they be universal? One response to this problem is to point out that the required universality is 'synchronic universality' (Raz, this volume, chapter 12). It may well be that some human rights are universal through time, but the general claim is that if one person

---

[9] Note that I am not arguing that one-off, unpredictable events can never be a violation of a person's human rights. As Matthew Liao pointed out to me, the *Fritzl* case in Austria, where Joseph Fritzl kept his daughter Elizabeth imprisoned and subject to sexual abuse for over twenty years, is clearly a violation of her human rights. However my claim is that the Austrian government's failure to protect Elizabeth Fritzl from her father is not a human rights failing by the government. If, however, such imprisonments started to become more common (eg as kidnappings have become in some countries) and the government did not take steps to try to protect its population then it is much more likely that the government's failure to protect is a human rights failure.

[10] Shue, *Basic Rights*, 17.

[11] Sometimes Shue uses the terms 'common' (32) or 'predictable' (33) or 'typical' (33) or 'pervasive' (fn 191) in place of 'ordinary'.

[12] Shue, *Basic Rights*, 32.   [13] Shue, *Basic Rights*, 33.   [14] Shue, *Basic Rights*, 33.

has a human right then, generally speaking, all people currently alive have the same rights, if they are in a position to benefit from them (for example men cannot have rights to a particular type of maternal care).

However, a more troubling variability—and an apparent denial of synchronic universality[15]—enters in through the other two parts of the idea of a standard threat: 'common' and 'serious'. Shue addresses this only in a footnote, stating 'Although this admission opens a theoretical door to a certain amount of "relativism", I suspect the actual differences across societies to the standard preventable threats are much less than they conceivably might be. Compare Barrington Moore's thesis that although differences in conceptions of happiness are great and important, virtually everyone agrees upon the "miseries"' (fn 190). Note, though, that even if Barrington Moore is correct this would mean only that empirically there is little variation on what is to count as serious. And 'little variation' is not the same as 'no variation'; it seems sufficient to refute synchronic universality.

Even worse is the variability of what is common. And in the field of health, on an ordinary understanding of the word 'common', there is huge variability in common threats to health in different parts of the world. The global pattern of infectious diseases, contrasted with the pattern of non-infectious 'life-style' diseases makes this point plain, even if it is true that conditions such as diabetes and lung cancer are becoming more prevalent in the developing world.

For such reasons, Beitz and Goodin remark:[16]

> The idea of rights only protecting against 'standard threats' is difficult to state precisely—more so, perhaps, than Shue himself may recognize. Still, as a start, we might say that 'standard threats' are those 'ordinary and serious but remediable' potential interferences that can reasonably be expected to arise in the normal circumstances of human social life.... The significance of this is to register a kind of non-arbitrary variability within the concept of a basic right: what counts as an 'ordinary and serious' potential interference to any particular type of action may be different in one society or at one historical moment rather than another. As a result, basic rights may have different institutional requirements in different social contexts.

In the light of these comments, it does seem possible to save synchronic universality as long as the content of the right is specified in very general terms: a right to be protected against common, serious, and remediable threats, where it is accepted that what is common and serious differs from place to place, and what is to count as remediable must also take resource constraints into account.[17]

Shue's account, then, has the advantage of moderating the human right to health so that it does not generate impossible duties in difficult times, and thus is consonant with the approach in GC14, providing the much needed theoretical unity to the

---

[15] Raz notes that cultural variability in health conflicts with synchronic universality. He does not appear to say how this is to be dealt with (this volume, ch. 12, 230).

[16] Charles Beitz and Robert Goodin, 'Introduction: *Basic Rights* and Beyond', in Beitz and Goodin (eds.), *Global Basic Rights* (Oxford: Oxford University Press, 2009), 10.

[17] For a similar distinction, framed as the distinction between the 'aim' and the 'object' of a right, see S. Matthew Liao and Adam Etinson, 'Political and Naturalistic Conceptions of Human Rights: A False Premise?', *Journal of Moral Philosophy*, 9(3) (2012): 327-52. See too Liao, this volume, ch. 3.

account. Indeed, Shue's position has a further advantage, which also picks out a major theme in GC14. Noting that human rights protect against standard threats suggests that a government's duty will, in the first instance, be a duty to create effective institutions to provide a reasonable guarantee of a reasonable level.[18] Sometimes a reasonable level is an absolute level—consider the example of torture—but this is not universally so. The main point is that human rights, so understood, generally in the first instance call on the government to put effective institutions in place—rather like a Rawlsian basic structure—rather than to meet the particular needs of particular individuals.[19] Of course where there is institutional failure individuals may well pursue their own complaints, and one such failure may be where a government in its actions has failed to *respect* an individual's rights, by, for example, engaging in violent or arbitrary acts against an individual. But where a government has failed to *protect* individuals against threats, or to *fulfil* a right, an individual claim should have something of the character of a test case or implicit class action. That is, in the general case the suit should only succeed if it is an example of something that happens on a larger scale, and the government ought, by way of remedy, to change its practices rather than (or in addition to) providing individual compensation. What this means in relation to health, it seems, is that failure to protect and, especially, fulfil should primarily be *condition-based* (or non-condition group based, such as ethnicity) rather than *person-based*. (Failure to respect, in contrast, could easily take any form.)

However, when we turn to human rights practice as it takes place in the law courts of the world (as distinct, perhaps, from more general human rights activism), we see very many individual cases being brought, for people seeking particular treatments, which apparently cuts against the point I have derived from Shue's argument that fulfilling human rights duties generally requires institutional change rather than individual action. This leads us to the practical difficulty. Even if we can satisfy ourselves that the conceptual difficulties can be met, in practice the human right to health leads to very unsatisfactory legal judgments that disrupt efficient planning in the health sector.

Consider the following remarks from Albert Weale:[20]

A good example of the untoward possibilities of constitutionalizing a right to health is provided by Rueda's (2010) account of the changing jurisprudence of the Colombian Constitutional Court during the 1990s. The 1991 constitution had strengthened the mechanisms of judicial review and created a writ for the protection of fundamental constitutional rights known as the tutela. According to Rueda's analysis, this resulted in a 'top-down' extension of social rights to the poor and the marginalized deriving from the Court's use of the concept of minimo vital between 1992 and 1998. However, when economic crisis hit Colombia in the late 1990s, the middle classes were able to use those same legal powers to protect their economic and social rights, including the right to healthcare in a way that the poor were not. The constitutional

---

[18] Shue, *Basic Rights*, 17.

[19] This is not to say that the government will never have the duty in the first instance to protect individuals: in cases of emergency and rescue then, as Matthew Liao pointed out to me, the government should help individuals before putting protective institutions in place. But of course emergencies remain the exception.

[20] Weale, 'The Right to Health Versus Good Medical Care?', 475.

provisions thus worked as a device for maintaining social inequalities and economic privileges, not ending them. The example illustrates how in practice the language of rights may be deployed by different groups of actors for politically incompatible ends.

Similar comments could be made about Brazil and other South and Central American countries, and an impressive amount of scholarship now exists regarding health right litigation.[21] While some are celebrating the development of worldwide right to health litigation, others look on in horror as it turns the courts into arbitrary or biased health resource priority setting mechanisms, and thus distorts rational health planning (which is especially ironic as designing and implementing a health plan is a human right to health obligation on governments).

Yet we need to treat these examples with caution. At the present time it is not possible to bring a case under the ICESCR, and it will not be possible to do so until the Optional Protocol of the Covenant has been ratified, which may still be some way off. Hence the cases discussed by Weale and others are *constitutional right to health* cases, as distinct from *human right to health* cases. Even if it is true, as has been claimed, that domestic courts refer to the international human rights instruments,[22] it should not be taken for granted that the courts are authentic or definitive interpreters of what the human right to health demands. Indeed, when appropriated in constitutional law, the right to health may well serve a subtly different purpose than it does in international law.

What, then, is the difference between a human right and a constitutional right? My understanding of human rights relies on two main ideas, from Charles Beitz and Joseph Raz. Beitz suggests that the institutionalization of human rights is a response to a defect in the world system which has left each individual under the authority of a particular state, and hence liable to the exercise of arbitrary power: power that even a constitution may not be able to check.[23] Recall that the drafting of the UDHR took place in the shadow of Nazi Germany. If a government persecutes its citizens, or treats them in certain other ways (something we will return to) those citizens should have the opportunity to turn to the world community for support. Raz makes the point by suggesting that human rights seek to protect interests that are so fundamental that a government's failure to respect, protect or fulfil is a matter for concern for the society of states, to which it must be held accountable. Where a human right is concerned a state cannot claim that whether it observes a particular duty to its citizens is a matter of state sovereignty and thus the business of no other country. Human rights trump the 'none of your business' response.[24] This is not to say that human rights are entirely constituted, or defined by, their role in international law, but rather that they pick up on a set of individual rights that are so important that, at the least, they place limits on state sovereignty.

---

[21] Yamin and Gloppin, *Litigating Health Rights*.

[22] Yamin and Gloppin, *Litigating Health Rights*, 5.

[23] Charles Beitz, *The Idea of Human Rights* (Oxford: Oxford University Press, 2009).

[24] Joseph Raz, 'Human Rights without Foundation', in Samantha Besson and John Tasiolous (eds.), *The Philosophy of International Law* (Oxford: Oxford University Press, 2010).

What, then, is a constitutional right? A conventional understanding is that it protects individuals against 'the tyranny of the majority'. To put the point parallel to the Beitz/Raz reflections upon human rights, a constitutional right is presumably a right so fundamental that no incumbent government should be permitted to change it at least without going to a great deal of trouble. (This is a 'mark' of a constitutional right rather than a definition that somehow reveals its essence.) The purpose of a constitutional right, presumably, is to protect individuals from the vagaries of party politics in the form of political expediency, populism, and arbitrary spending cuts, as well as the tyranny of the majority. Critically, then, the purpose of constitutional rights is not the same as human rights, and it is quite possible that human rights will be less demanding than constitutional rights.

The right to health cases that Weale mentions, and others have discussed and documented in great detail, seem to me to raise serious problems for the way the constitutional right to heath has played out in some countries. Yet from the contents of this chapter, it should be clear that their bearing on the human right to health requires further consideration. For is it obvious that the sorts of issues that have come up in the courts are always the sorts of things that are serious enough to allow one country to take a legitimate interest in the internal affairs of another? In at least one class of cases the Colombian courts have indeed called for institutional reform, which fits well with Shue's analysis.[25] Yet in other cases 'The Court has also approved...post-mastectomy breast implants [and] the provision of growth hormones'.[26] Undeniably important as these concerns are, and perhaps worthy of inclusion as constitutional rights, depending on the history, traditions, and resources of the country, it is hard to see the case for making these issues human rights: is the threat to health so serious as to make it a matter of international concern? Raising these questions helps us address one of the issues left hanging by Shue's analysis of 'standard threats': how serious is 'serious'? One answer, albeit not a complete solution, is that it must be serious enough that its neglect should be a matter of concern for the international community.

To make further progress it will be helpful to think through the ways in which a state may fail to meet its responsibilities. Or to put in another way, inspired by Beitz's thinking, if part of the point of human rights is to protect us from the misfortune of being born into a territory run by the 'wrong kind' of state, what do we mean by 'wrong kind'? Although there are many ways in which one may classify moral failures by government, it may be helpful to contrast:

1. Those states that victimize a group within their territory, normally an unpopular minority (unjust states).

2. Those that are institutionally too weak to act effectively (incompetent states).

3. Those that lack the resources to act effectively (impoverished states).

---

[25] Alicia E. Yamin, O. Parra-Vera, and C. Gianella, 'Colombia: Judicial Protection of the Right to Health: An Elusive Promise?, in Alicia E. Yamin and Siri Gloppin (eds.), *Litigating Health Rights* (Cambridge MA: Harvard University Press, 2011).

[26] Yamin et al., 'Colombia: Judicial Protection of the Right to Health', 111.

4. Those that have the capacity to act effectively but use it to the advantage of those who rule (corrupt states).

5. Those where the national interest is pursued to the neglect and detriment of some of its citizens (reckless states).

Of course a given state may fail in several ways, and it may not always be possible to put a failure in a particular category, but each of these failures gives rise to possible human rights abuses, and also to possible human right to health failures.

Reading GC14 in the light of these distinctions is a useful exercise, although what I say will be illustrative rather than exhaustive. Where a state is unjust, it is very likely that there will be numerous violations regarding the unpopular or minority group that it neglects or persecutes. This may include other forms of discrimination, such as access to law, and treatment with respect to welfare services and within the criminal justice system. In relation to health the many references in GC14 to the importance of non-discrimination (Sections 3, 12(b), 12(c), 19, 20–27, 34, 35) and perhaps the right to be free from torture and non-consensual medical treatment and experimentation (Section 8) could fall under this head, as well as under several others. Reference to gender difference (Section 10) picks up on injustice, whether 'overt' or not, to use the language of Section 19. Section 12(b) lists a range of groups that could suffer discrimination including older people and people with disabilities, as well as ethnic minorities. Some of these violations will be violations of the duty to respect (Section 50) such as 'the denial of access to health facilities, goods and services, to particular individuals as a result of de jure or de facto discrimination.' But failure of duties to protect, for example failing to protect women against violence (Section 51) are also possible, as well as failures to fulfil by discriminatory allocation practices (Section 52).

To take another example, recklessness (in the sense of pursuing national interests to the detriment of people) may be covered by references to such things as the duty to provide 'healthy occupational and environmental conditions' (Section 11) which could easily be neglected by a rapidly developing country. The prevention of exposure to radiation and harmful chemicals is mentioned in Section 15, which could be relevant at all levels of development, as could the degree to which other rights can be limited for the sake of public health, which is discussed in Sections 28 and 29, guarding against over-intrusive or disproportionate limitations on individual freedoms. Recklessness can include failures to respect, for example 'the failure of the State to take into account its legal obligations regarding the right to health when entering into bilateral or multilateral agreements with other States, international organizations and other entities' (Section 50) or 'the failure to enact or enforce laws to prevent the pollution of water, air and soil by extractive and manufacturing industries' (Section 51).

The check on what I have called 'incompetence' in the General Comment is, it seems, reflected through several mentions of 'the adoption and implementation [of] a national public health strategy and plan of action'. A state that fails to set out a plan, as well as neglecting the health of its citizens, is in deep violation. Planning is a test of competence, and a failure to plan will, presumably, be a matter of international concern. Distinctly, as Section 47 recognizes, it is possible for a state to be willing, but unable to fulfil its obligations through what I referred to as impoverishment. It may have a plan but be very limited in its ability to carry it out. Here considerations about progressive realization enter in, as discussed earlier.

Where does this leave us with the question of whether the human right to health comes into conflict with rational design and planning? GC14's emphasis on planning would superficially suggest the two things should be complementary, but of course the challenge comes not from the incompatibility with the treatises, but litigation. I have suggested that in several cases there is a good argument that a constitutional right to health can lead to distortions in health care allocation. But I want to emphasize that this alone does not make the case against the human right to health.

Indeed, although the human right to health mandates high levels of vigilance in the duty to respect and protect, in the case of the duty to fulfil it is arguable that the human right to health requires a level of provision below that currently offered in many wealthy societies: ie, in many cases wealthy countries presently exceed many of their human right to health obligations. Consequently, although there are always difficulties in withdrawing benefits, it may not be a violation of the human right to health to withdraw some medical services from the standard package offered to all citizens in a country (as we have seen with dental services, for example, in the United Kingdom). The argument for this is derived from reflection on the purpose of human rights and the further consequences of such a purpose in the realm of health. In this respect it is unfortunate that the drafters used the phrase 'the highest attainable standard of health': the language of 'fully adequate' may well have been better.

In conclusion, I have addressed two problems that turn out to be closely related: how to understand the conceptual core of the human right to health; and the practical limits of that right in terms of the health-related services it does not or should not cover especially in relation to cases pursued in constitutional courts around the world. The paper takes the purpose of human rights as central, combining ideas from Beitz (human rights are needed because of a defect in the world structure which would otherwise leave individuals at the mercy of the state that governs the territory in which they happen to live); from Raz (that human rights give, or at least mark, a licence for one state to express concerns about what is happening within the borders of another); and from Shue (that rights provide social guarantees against common, serious, and remediable threats). The link is provided through understanding that serious threats are those that give one state a licence to take an interest in the affairs of another. Not everything pursued in constitutional courts has such a high level of seriousness. Hence on this understanding we cannot assume that all constitutionally protected rights are human rights, strictly understood, and hence criticisms of what happens within a particular national court system cannot be assumed automatically to apply to the human right to health. The conceptual core and practical implications of the human right to health are, in combination, clarified.[27]

[27] My thanks to Matthew Liao for very helpful comments on the penultimate draft of this paper.

28

Do We Have a Human Right to the Political Determinants of Health?

Kimberley Brownlee[1]

Introduction

The human right to health necessarily lies somewhere between the too-demanding idea of a right to be *healthy* and the too-limited idea of a right merely to *health care*. The problem, as Jonathan Wolff points out in his contribution to this collection (chapter 27), is to figure out where exactly the human right lies. International agreements such as the Universal Declaration of Human Rights (UDHR) state that human beings have both a right to a standard of living adequate to health and, equally importantly, a right to various other underlying determinants of health, such as food, clothing, and housing as well as medical care.[2] The question, as Wolff notes, is whether the human right to health is simply an agglomeration of rights to underlying determinants of health or whether it has a more determinate conceptual core. If it is an agglomeration of rights, then how do we know which underlying determinants of health are parts of that agglomeration since so many things can affect health?

This is an important question, and it frames my discussion in what follows. Some of the things that centrally affect health are not often explicitly examined in relation to a right to health. The most notable of these are human-generated threats to physical and mental health such as chronic physical insecurity, constant fear of attack, and chronic stress as well as actual attacks, abuse, mistreatment, and discrimination, which compound the effects of insecurity and stress. Protection from such threats counts among what I shall call the *underlying political determinants of health*. These determinants of health can be divided into two broad categories. The first category concerns protecting people from direct or indirect discrimination in their access to health services. The

[1] I thank Thomas Parr for his helpful feedback and research assistance on this paper. I thank Matthew Liao for helpful comments on this paper.
[2] UDHR Article 25 states: '(1) Everyone has the right to a standard of living adequate for the health and well-being of himself and of his family, including food, clothing, housing and medical care and necessary social services, and the right to security in the event of unemployment, sickness, disability, widowhood, old age or other lack of livelihood in circumstances beyond his control.' The International Covenant on Economic, Social, and Cultural Rights (ICESCR) goes further. Article 12 states: '1. The States Parties to the present Covenant recognize the right of everyone to the enjoyment of the highest attainable standard of physical and mental health. 2. The steps to be taken by the States Parties to the present Covenant to achieve the full realization of this right shall include those necessary for: (a) The provision for the reduction of the stillbirth-rate and of infant mortality and for the healthy development of the child; (b) The improvement of all aspects of environmental and industrial hygiene; (c) The prevention, treatment and control of epidemic, endemic, occupational and other diseases; (d) The creation of conditions which would assure to all medical service and medical attention in the event of sickness.'

second concerns protecting people from the more general disadvantages, mistreatment, discrimination, abuse, and stress that go with vulnerability and persecution, and which render people more likely either to be injured or become unwell or to die early. In what follows, I explore the nature of these two types of political determinants of health, and consider reasons for and against including all of them, particularly those of the second type, in an agglomeration of rights comprising the human right to health.

I. Political Determinants of Health

Human-generated threats to mental and physical health are the life experiences of persecuted peoples. They are the life experiences, for example, of women and girls who live in societies where there is a persistent, credible threat of physical assault, sexual assault, rape, and domestic abuse as well as threats of social ostracism and material deprivation if they are raped, and few, if any, legal avenues for redress. In Afghanistan, for instance, several hundred women are presently in prison for the 'moral crime' of being raped.[3] Psychology studies indicate that victims of physical and sexual violence experience distress that sometimes fails to resolve and instead develops into a chronic, though heterogeneous, symptom pattern whose core features include fear/avoidance, affective constriction, disturbance of self-concept, and sexual disturbance.[4] These features are consistent with the criteria for post-traumatic stress disorder (PTSD), which is associated with a variety of anxiety-related symptoms such as sleep disturbance, avoidance of any stimuli associated with the trauma, and intensification of anxiety when confronted with reminders of the trauma. Mary Koss states that, 'Even when evaluated many years after the assault, victims were significantly more likely than nonvictims to qualify for psychiatric diagnoses that included major depression, alcohol abuse/dependence, drug abuse/dependence, generalized anxiety, obsessive–compulsive disorder, and posttraumatic stress disorder.'[5]

Similarly, human-generated threats to health are the life experiences of children who grow up in brutal environments, who face a constant, credible risk of mistreatment, and for whom there are few effective legal, social, and political mechanisms for their protection. In times of war, for example, as the United Nations Office of the Special Representative of the Secretary General for Children and Armed Conflict notes, 'girls are raped and suffer from other forms of sexual violence with detrimental effect on their physical and mental health. When associated with an armed group, girls might be forced into marriage and early pregnancy.' And, even when conflicts end and armed groups make commitments to release children, they sometimes refuse to give up the girls, who continue to be held captive as 'wives'.[6]

---

[3] See Jeremy Kelly, 'Afghan Woman to be Freed from Jail after Agreeing to Marry Rapist' *The Guardian*, 1 December 2011: http://www.guardian.co.uk/world/2011/dec/01/afghan-woman-freed-marry-rapist?newsfeed=true.

[4] Mary Koss states that '…some experts consider female sexual abuse and assault victims to be the largest single group of PTSD sufferers'. See Mary Koss, 'The Women's Mental Health Research Agenda: Violence Against Women', *American Psychologist*, 45(3) (1990): 375.

[5] Koss, 'The Women's Mental Health Research Agenda', 376.

[6] 'Girl Child', United Nations Office of the Special Representative of the Secretary General for Children and Armed Conflict: http://childrenandarmedconflict.un.org/effects-of-conflict/girl-child/.

Such threats to mental and physical health are also the life experiences of persecuted cultural minorities, persecuted people with impairments, persecuted elderly people, and people living in war torn countries. The stress and fear that pervade their lives as well as the actual mistreatments they suffer have similar psychological and physiological effects as chronic hunger and thirst in setting off a chain of anxiety inducing reactions, known as the 'fight or flight' response, that are associated with high blood pressure, increased risk of heart attack, stroke, and depression, and more rapid ageing. Studies indicate that the changes in the morphology and chemistry of brain regions, such as the hippocampus, prefrontal cortex, and amygdala, in response to acute and chronic stress are largely reversible if the chronic stress lasts only for weeks, but that it is unclear whether prolonged stress for months or years can have irreversible effects on the brain.[7]

Human-generated threats to physical and mental health are exacerbated when people experience a clustering, or joint frequency, of multiple disadvantages. As Wolff argues in his book, *Disadvantage*, co-authored with Avner de Shalit, typically, people who are vulnerable to one type of disadvantage such as unemployment are often also vulnerable to other disadvantages that can accumulate over time, such as homelessness, loss of social networks, and severe illness. The people who are at risk of poverty are also often the people who are vulnerable to abuse, have little political voice, and are less socially integrated, less well educated, and less healthy. The effects of each of these individual disadvantages are compounded by the agglomeration of disadvantage.[8] In addition, as Wolff and de Shalit observe, some disadvantages are corrosive in that their presence leads to further disadvantages.[9] A lack of education is corrosive, for example, as it undermines a variety of further capabilities including caring, nursing, and health-related capabilities.

Human-generated threats to physical and mental health in vulnerable populations are further exacerbated in financially difficult times. For instance, a 2013 report from Plan International and the Overseas Development Institute states that the 'brunt of the recent global economic recession has been borne by women and girls: this demographic is more likely to be poor, to drop out of school, and to die sooner.'[10] The report finds that family poverty has a greater impact on girls' survival than on boys' survival, where a 1 percent fall in GDP increases infant mortality by 7.4 deaths per 1,000 births for girls versus 1.5 deaths for boys. The report also finds that maternal mortality, which disproportionately affects adolescent mothers, increases during times of

---

[7] Bruce S. McEwen, 'Central Effects of Stress Hormones in Health and Disease: Understanding the Protective and Damaging Effects of Stress and Stress Mediators', *European Journal of Pharmacology*, 583 (2008): 174–85.

[8] Jonathan Wolff and Avner de Shalit, *Disadvantage* (Oxford: Oxford University Press, 2007) ch. 7, 120ff.

[9] Wolff and de Shalit, *Disadvantage*, 10, 121.

[10] Jessica Prois, 'Global Economic Recession Causing More Poverty, Deaths For Females Than Males: Report', in *Huffington Post*, 23 January 2013: http://www.huffingtonpost.com/2013/01/23/global-economic-recession-females_n_2534912.html. Prois quotes Nigel Chapman, CEO of Plan International, who says that: 'It is little surprise that the most vulnerable suffer more in times of austerity but to see the impact in higher mortality rates, reduced life expectancy, less opportunities and greater risks for girls and boys is stark…'

economic crisis as cuts are made to health care budgets.[11] Between 1990 and 2008, the number of women's deaths in childbirth doubled in both the United States and Canada, a statistic that is worrying irrespective of whether it can be attributed in part to economic difficulties.[12]

Undoubtedly, economic constraints hinder governments in their efforts to honour the duties generated by the right to health.[13] In this regard, Wolff cites the UN Committee on Economic, Social, and Cultural Rights's General Comments, which address substantive issues arising from the implementation of the ICESCR. General Comment No. 14 (2000) (hereinafter GC14) explicitly addresses the human right to health (ICESCR Article 12), and, amongst other things, observes that poor countries may find it hard to discharge the duties generated by the right to health due to their lack of resources. The GC14 draws a distinction that Wolff endorses between the *progressive realization* of the right to health and the *core obligations* of the right to health. The latter refer to obligations that have immediate effect, such as:

> ...the guarantee that the right will be exercised without discrimination of any kind (art. 2.2) and the obligation to take steps (art. 2.1) towards the full realization of article 12. Such steps must be deliberate, concrete and targeted towards the full realization of the right to health.[14]

The idea of progressive realization acknowledges that it is unrealistic, as Wolff puts it, to expect poor states to be able to offer the level of medical care and health protection available in wealthy states, and it would be wrong to accuse them of violating the human rights of their people simply in virtue of this comparison.[15]

This claim about poor states is certainly valid, but there are two points to note about economic constraints. The first is captured by the GC14's examples of core obligations, which highlight that resource constraints should not allow for incidental or intentional discrimination in health services against a particular demographic, such as women and girls. Governments facing economic constraints must make concerted efforts to ensure that the brunt of economic difficulties is not borne by a particular

---

[11] Currently, pregnancy is a leading cause of death for 14–19 year-old girls. Maria Stavropoulou and Nicola Jones, 'Off the Balance Sheet: The Impact of the Economic Crisis on Girls and Young Women', *Plan International and Overseas Development Institute Report* (2013): https://plan-international.org/files/global/publications/economics/off-the-balance-sheet-english.

[12] Lizzie Malcolm, 'International Women's Day: Political Rights Around the World Mapped', *The Guardian*, 8 March 2013: http://www.guardian.co.uk/world/datablog/interactive/2013/mar/08/international-womens-day-political-rights.

[13] In related work, Wolff observes that '...some states are unwilling or unable to act, while others that may be willing are hobbled by the power of globalizing forces that inhibit their release from sustained poverty. Nevertheless, we can still say that in the first instance the duty falls on the state of which the person is a citizen; if that is problematic then the country of residence; and as a last resort the international community'. See Jonathan Wolff, 'The Human Right to Health', in S. Benatar and G. Brock (eds.), *Global Health and Global Health Ethics* (Cambridge: Cambridge University Press, 2011), 111.

[14] Committee on Economic, Social and Cultural Rights (2000), GC14, August 2000.

[15] The GC14 explicitly states that well-off states have a special responsibility and interest to assist poor states in giving priority to the provision of medical aid, distribution and management of resources, such as safe and potable water, food and medical supplies, and financial aid should be given to the most vulnerable or marginalized groups of the population.

demographic, and especially not by a demographic that is already disadvantaged and vulnerable.[16]

Second, for many vulnerable groups, such as women and girls, it is not only in poor countries that governments fail to honour their duties to attend to these persons' health needs including the underlying political determinants of their health. For instance, some of the countries that rank among the worst places in the world to be a woman are not poor countries. Industrialized nations such as Saudi Arabia and, perhaps, India cannot claim that they lack the resources to secure either women's and girls' basic medical needs or the underlying political determinants of their health.

In Saudi Arabia, there is little protection of either direct or indirect political determinants of women's and girls' health. Concerning direct determinants of health, there are, for example, no laws against domestic violence and marital rape. The law also prevents a woman from being admitted to a government hospital unless accompanied by a male relative. Additionally, male relatives may prohibit a woman from being treated by a male gynaecologist or obstetrician even in an emergency and only male relatives may sign the consent forms for an urgent, invasive, medical procedure.[17]

Concerning indirect determinants of health, women do not have the right to vote and hence have few legal and political channels through which to push for greater political and legal equality (though it has been announced that they will be allowed to vote in the 2015 municipal elections).[18] Also, women and girls are not allowed to travel, study, or work without permission from their male guardians, and the country has a *de facto* ban on women driving, all of which exacerbates the stress of extreme dependency, and makes women and girls vulnerable both to corrosive disadvantages and to clusterings of disadvantage.[19] Although some steps have been taken to improve conditions for women and girls, these steps are modest. Is the political impotence in Saudi Arabia to remedy the situation of women and girls on a par, morally, with having few economic resources? This would be a convenient excuse for inactivity.

Similarly, in India, which has seen rapid economic growth in recent years, there is no law against marital rape, and reports indicate that crimes against women in India are on the rise. According to the National Crime Records Bureau, there was a 7.1 percent rise in recorded crimes against women between 2010 and 2011 with the biggest

---

[16] The GC14 remarks on the 'highest attainable standard' stated in the ICESCR, noting that in low resource settings, there are severe limits to what is attainable. This is certainly true since low resource settings face the threats of no water, little food, poor shelter, poor medicine, and so on. But, high stress settings also pose severe limits on what is attainable, and high stress settings do not inevitably coincide with low resources or vice versa. We need not take anything like the 'highest attainable standard of health' to see the extent to which the right to health depends on protection from chronic stress and threatening environments.

[17] A.E.H. Mobaraki and B. Söderfeldt, 'Gender Inequity in Saudi Arabia and Its Role in Public Health', *Eastern Mediterranean Health Journal*, 16(1) (2010): 113–18. See this review article for additional references on forced marriage, underage marriage, female illiteracy, maternal mortality, restrictions on abortion and contraception, and male polygamy in Saudi Arabia.

[18] Human Rights Watch, *World Report 2012: Saudi Arabia*: http://www.hrw.org/world-report-2012/world-report-2012-saudi-arabia.

[19] Human Rights Watch, *World Report 2012*.

rise being in cases that fall under the Dowry Prohibition Act (up 27.7 percent), cases of kidnapping and abduction (up 19.4 percent year on year) and cases of rape (up 9.2 percent).[20] Concerning women's health care in India, only 47 percent of women receive skilled assistance during childbirth.[21] Between 1990 and 2008, the number of women who died in childbirth more than halved, from 570 per 500,000 births to 230 per 500,000 births, which is encouraging, but 230 deaths is still 20 times the figure in other G20 countries such as Canada and the United Kingdom.[22] And, currently, the child-sex ratio in India is 914 girls for every 1,000 boys, a figure that is at its worst in the history of independent India.[23]

The question to ask is whether the failures of countries, be they affluent or not, to attend to the underlying political determinants of health of women, girls, and other vulnerable groups are principally (1) failures to honour the *core obligations* of the human right to health, (2) failures to commit to the long-term *progressive realization* of the right to health, or, indeed, (3) no failure at all in relation to the right to health, but instead failures to honour other human rights. The point made earlier about avoiding discrimination in access to health services signals that there must be *some* political rights in any credible agglomeration of rights comprising the human right to health. The first type of political determinant of health noted at the outset of this paper—non-discrimination in access to health services—is uncontroversially part of a right to health (and the debate then must centre on what 'non-discriminatory access' requires). But, are *all* political determinants of health parts of such an agglomeration?[24] The second type of political determinant—legal equality and protection from mistreatment and chronic stress—is much more contentious as a part of a right to health. I shall therefore explore, first, some reasons to think that political determinants of this second type are parts of the human right to health, and then some reasons to think they are not, one of which I take to be decisive.

---

[20] Helen Pidd, 'Why is India So Bad for Women?', *The Guardian*, 23 July 2012: http://www.guardian.co.uk/world/2012/jul/23/why-india-bad-for-women.

[21] Malcolm, 'International Women's Day'.   [22] Malcolm, 'International Women's Day'.

[23] Sruthi Gottipati, 'Is it a Good Time to Be a Girl in India?' *The New York Times*, 11 October 2012: http://india.blogs.nytimes.com/2012/10/11/is-it-a-good-time-to-be-a-girl-in-india/. The *Global Gender Gap Report 2012* gives a slightly worse gender ratio for India of 0.89, which apparently has not changed over the past year, Ricardo Hausmann, Laura Tyson, and Saadia Zahidi, *The Global Gender Gap Report 2012*. Geneva: World Economic Forum, 27: http://www.weforum.org/reports/global-gender-gap-report-2012.

[24] The general lack of attention to political determinants of health is reflected in the GC14's efforts to specify the location of the right to health between healthiness and mere health care by highlighting four features of the right to health: 1) availability, 2) accessibility, 3) acceptability, and 4) quality. All four of these features clearly connote provision of medical care as well as, perhaps, water, food, clothing, and housing. They do not align well with the kinds of political determinants of health I have discussed. I agree with Wolff that one comes away from the GC14 with a sense that it has avoided the main question, which is: When is a failure to supply medical care or other determinants of health nevertheless *not* a human rights failure? The narrowness of the GC14's lens is regrettable. And, Wolff buys into this narrowness when he talks about courts' efforts to make sense of the right to health. His use of the language of 'supply', and his attention to the most common claims, which are for medical treatment in the form of drugs, surgery or equipment, feeds into the narrow, and intuitively physicalist, view of human health reflected in the GC14.

II. Reasons to Include All Political Determinants in the Right to Health

Wolff gives a nod to what I am calling the 'underlying political determinants of health' in his explication of different ways for governments to fail in their duties to respect, to protect, and to fulfil the human right to health:[25]

> Where a state is unjust...it is very likely that there will be numerous violations regarding the unpopular or minority group[s] that it neglects or persecutes. This may include other forms of discrimination, such as access to law, and treatment with respect to welfare services and within the criminal justice system. In relation to health the many references in GC14 to the importance of non-discrimination (Sections 3, 12(b), 12(c), 19, 20–27, 34, 35) and perhaps the right to be free from torture and non-consensual medical treatment and experimentation (Section 8) could fall under this head, as well as under several others. Reference to gender difference (Section 10) picks up on injustice, whether 'overt' or not, to use the language of Section 19. Section 12(b) lists a range of groups that could suffer discrimination including older people and people with disabilities, as well as ethnic minorities. Some of these violations will be violations of the duty to respect (Section 50) such as 'the denial of access to health facilities, goods and services, to particular individuals as a result of de jure or de facto discrimination.' But failure of duties to protect, for example failing to protect women against violence (Section 51) are also possible, as well as failures to fulfil by discriminatory allocation practices (Section 52).

Although Wolff does not pursue this thought further, or consider whether some particular political determinants of health fall outside the human right to health, nevertheless his treatment of these issues inspired the observations I am making about the importance of attending to human-generated threats to health in general, and political determinants of health in particular.

Amongst other things, Wolff says that the task of setting out the content of the human right to health really comes down to setting out an account of the duties that governments and other actors, whether national or international, have in relation to health. And, the right to health, he says, is a protection against certain types of neglect and mistreatment (though, perhaps, not all). From these points, we can derive the first reason to include *all* political determinants in the right to health. Briefly, if we are truly committed to the human right to health, then a paramount objective must be to sort out the legal inequality, moral inequality, neglect, and abuse of disadvantaged groups that not only impair their access to health resources, but also expose them to chronic stress and mistreatment that impair their health. Put differently, appreciating the central impact that chronic stress and mistreatment have on health should prompt us to put the focus as much on securing non-threatening, low-stress environments as on securing drugs and surgery.

A related, instrumental reason to include all political determinants of health in the right to health concerns preventative medicine. Given the exacerbating effects that

---

[25] Wolff, this volume, ch. 27, 500.

stress has on health, focusing on securing non-stressful environments is undeniably useful, and may do as much good for persons as focusing on curative medicine, drugs, and surgery.

A further related reason not only to include, but to emphasize political determinants of health in the right to health is that it might lessen Wolff's practical worry about the implementation of health rights in the courts, by putting the focus on legal and political measures rather than on comprehensive health care rights beyond minimal, preventative care and the guarantees of food, shelter, water, basic medicines, and physical and mental security.[26]

A final, pragmatic reason to emphasize political determinants is that the right to health is a potentially powerful tool. First, a lot of other rights and goods are dependent on its protection for their realization.[27] Second, it is less contentious than some other socio-economic human rights such as the right to be free from poverty. Including political determinants of health under the banner of the human right to health may make it more likely that they will be taken seriously than if they are not put under that banner.

In contrast with these reasons, there are at least three reasons to doubt that the second type of political determinants of health noted here are part of the human right to health. The first two reasons are mistaken, but the third is compelling. Briefly, the first reason says that political determinants of health such as legal equality and protection from mistreatment do not meet the stringent conditions for human rights status, namely, the conditions of *standard recurrent threats* to health (in combination with other features). The second reason says that rights to political determinants of health are conceptually redundant and, hence, unnecessary in a specification of the human right to health. The third says that the duties that governments and other individuals have to guarantee the political determinants of health are indeed human-rights-based duties, but they are not *health*-rights-based duties because the arguments for health rights are principally instrumental and the arguments for equal recognition and adequate protection are not. Let me take these three reasons in turn.

III. Reasons Against Political Determinants as Part of the Right to Health

A. Standard recurrent threats

Political determinants of health such as legal equality and protection from mistreatment are not part of the human right to health, so this argument goes, because they do not satisfy the requisite conditions to warrant human rights status. The conditions for human rights status are those of standard recurrent threats, to use James

---

[26] Certainly, proper attention to the health rights of a vulnerable group, such as women and girls, will require some expensive provisions such as ensuring, at the very least, that all women have access to skilled assistance at childbirth, but this does not make such provisions 'non-minimal'.

[27] Using Wolff and de Shalit's language, we might say that the human right to health is *fertile*. Fertile functionings are those functionings 'which spread their good effects over several categories, either directly or by reducing risk to other functionings', Wolff and de Shalit, *Disadvantage*, 122.

Nickel's phrase, or common, serious, remediable threats, to use Henry Shue's phrase. A threat is common if it is ordinary or standard. A threat is sufficiently serious according to Wolff (which I will not dispute) if its neglect should be a matter of concern for the international community. A threat is remediable if it can be practically addressed. However, Wolff notes correctly that 'the failure to research how to remedy a non-remediable ordinary and serious threat could be a human rights failure, which is especially important in the area of health'.[28]

The claim that legal inequality and vulnerability to mistreatment are not common, serious, and remediable threats is unpersuasive. First, on commonness, the data cited earlier on vulnerable groups such as women and girls make plain that the political determinants of health I have discussed pass the commonness test. For such people, political threats to their physical and mental health are pervasive experiences in their lives. These threats are not unique to a small subset of persons within these groups, and they are not isolated to one-off instances of abuse, neglect, or discrimination.

Second, concerning seriousness, political threats to vulnerable people's mental and physical health are sufficiently serious to warrant human rights status because protection from chronic stress, abuse, and mistreatment are no less pressing than other things that more transparently fit under the heading of 'underlying determinants of health' such as food, clothing, housing, and medical care. The abuse of girls who are held captive by armed groups, the neglect of women in childbirth, and the practice of female infanticide are cases in point.

However, we might look at seriousness in a different way and argue that, in politically fraught contexts, persons' *health* is a secondary issue and not the truly *serious* issue. For example, when a paramilitary group recruits child soldiers (typically through brutal means), the threats this poses to the children's *health* seem secondary. To say that such treatment is a human rights failure because it robs children of their right to health seems to put the focus in the wrong place. Similarly, when women face a persistent, credible threat of being raped, to say that this is a human rights failure because it threatens their right to health again seems to put the focus in the wrong place. In both cases, undeniably the mistreatment does threaten health, but something more fundamental than health is at stake, which can broadly go under the heading of basic respect. These observations lay the foundation for a credible reason to hold that many political determinants of health are not part of the right to health, which I turn to later.

Finally, concerning remediability, I have doubts about the credibility of this condition for human rights protection, but, if we accept it, then the answer to whether political determinants satisfy it is contingent on various facts and assumptions. Presumably, only certain barriers to remediability should be taken seriously. A state that is under siege, attacked in war, or suffering from a natural disaster faces barriers to human rights protections that may indeed be irremediable. No state can avoid all of the stress and risks that go with such crises. But other stressful environments, such as those experienced by women and girls in Saudi Arabia, can be avoided. Wealthy countries like Saudi Arabia should not be able to plead that the threats faced by women

---

[28] Wolff, this volume, ch. 27, 495.

and girls are (at least presently) irremediable because there is not the political will to improve their condition and redress violence, mistreatment, and discrimination against them. Women and girls have human rights against the health-impairing effects of their disadvantaged condition in Saudi Arabia even though remedying that condition is presently politically difficult. The stress of their extreme dependency and their vulnerability to attack as well as the lack of redress and the knowledge that there is no option for redress are all things that the government can seek to remedy even if the efforts may be, for the present, largely ineffective.

The duties that governments fail to honour by not attending to political determinants of health can be specified according to the taxonomy of duties that Wolff discusses, namely, duties to respect, to protect, and to fulfil the right to health. First, if government officials such as police and soldiers rape women and girls as control mechanisms, punishments, or interrogation techniques, then they fail in their duty to *respect* women's and girls' mental health, physical security, and much else. Second, if government officials or police know that assaults and rapes regularly occur and they fail to intervene, then they fail to *protect* women and girls from violations of their mental and physical health by others. And, finally, if the government does not prosecute private parties who abuse or assault women and girls, or does not even have laws on the books that prohibit acts such as marital rape, then it fails to *fulfil* women's and girls' rights to physical security as an underlying determinant of mental and physical health. That said, the fact that governments' failures to honour women's and girls' rights to mental and physical security *can* be framed in relation to the right to health does not mean that ultimately this is the best way to think about such failures, as I argue later.

Together, these observations show that the standard-recurrent-threats objection against including all political determinants of health in the human right to health is not compelling.

B. Conceptual redundancy

A second reason not to incorporate all political determinants of health into the human right to health is conceptual redundancy. The argument here is not so much that political determinants of health such as legal equality and protection from mistreatment are not part of the right to health, but that it is not necessary to identify them as part of that right since guarantees of legal equality and protection from mistreatment are necessary pre-conditions for the right to health to exist at all. The right to health cannot be either achieved or fully maintained without these guarantees.

In response, even if political determinants of health were conceptually redundant, subsuming them under other things in an agglomeration of health rights could distract us from the distinctive health-related problems that political threats pose. And, not subsuming them under other rights could enable us to recognize the distinctive political dimensions of our health needs. In short, there is practical value in identifying political determinants of health as distinctive health-related concerns.

That said, there is a cost in incorporating political claims against mistreatment and legal inequality within an account of the right to health. It is that our political claims are not purely, or even principally, health-based. Acknowledging the significance of our political claims is part of respecting each other as persons. It is in this thought that the real reason lies not to incorporate all political determinants of health within the right to health.

C. Instrumental value and intrinsic value

The most credible reason to exclude the second type of political determinants from the human right to health turns on the grounds for protecting health in the first place.

The right to health is analogous to the right to education in that the principal arguments for its protection are instrumental. Undeniably, the right to health, like the right to education, protects something that is valuable in itself. The experience of becoming fit, alert, and healthy, like the experience of learning, is typically an intrinsically valuable experience, and the state of being healthy, like that of being educated, is typically an intrinsically valuable state. Nevertheless, the central arguments for securing and enforcing a human right to health, like those for a human right to education, are instrumental. They include, first, the instrumental benefits of each person having the capacity to lead her life and to contribute meaningfully to the human community, as well as, second, the benefits of protecting health in general within and across societies, and, third, through that, the benefits of promoting global ideals and values for the maintenance of peace. In addition to these community-oriented instrumental values, there is, as Joseph Raz notes, a more personal instrumental value in health, which is that health greatly increases a person's prospects of having a rewarding life: 'If not all, at least many forms of ill-health—involving as it does pain, suffering and disability—make fulfilling and satisfying life much harder to achieve, or even impossible.'[29]

Raz thinks, as I do, that it is principally the instrumental value of health, and not its intrinsic value, that grounds the human right to health. But, his argument for that view is an odd one. He says that, absent special relations, no one has a duty to secure for any other person a feeling of physical (or mental) well-being, but they may have a duty to secure for people the *opportunity* to have a fulfilling life.[30] This is right, but since, as noted at the outset (and indeed as Raz himself notes), the right to health is not a right to be *healthy*, there is no proposal on the table that the duties the right to health generates would include a duty for anyone to *secure* for anyone else a feeling of physical or mental well-being.[31]

My own argument for the instrumental basis of the right to health is that governments and individual persons have a duty to ensure that we are able to contribute meaningfully to our communities, that our health and opportunities to lead a full life are not unnecessarily put at risk by the unhealthiness of others, and that the ideals and

---

[29] Joseph Raz, 'Human Rights in the Emerging World Order', this volume, ch. 11, 229.

[30] Raz, 'Human Rights in the Emerging World Order', 229.

[31] Raz observes that '...it would be silly to think that people really have a right to be healthy, a right which is violated every time they are not healthy' Raz, 'Human Rights in the Emerging World Order', 229.

values of international cooperation and peace are furthered through the cultivation of safety and well-being including emphasis on preventative medicine and decent care.

In this idea that the grounds for the right to health are instrumental, we find a way to distinguish the determinants of health that should be protected as part of that right from the determinants that should not be, because the grounds for the latter determinants do not lie in the instrumental benefits of health. We would be acting on the wrong reason if we were, for example, to protect women from rape and children from brutal environments because physical and mental security are underlying determinants of health and hence are instrumentally valuable. Certainly, they have this value. But the real reason to protect women and children in these ways is that it respects them as people. The core reasons are hence non-instrumental. Therefore, although protecting the legal and political claims of vulnerable groups is an underlying determinant of their health, we should not view governments' *health*-related duties as including this task.

Saying that the principal reasons to protect the political claims of women, girls, and other vulnerable groups are non-instrumental does not prevent us from favouring a government policy that has, in addition, the side-benefit of good instrumental effects for those groups. If, for example, a government can choose between two policies that will reduce the frequency of rape by identical amounts, but only one of those policies will have beneficial, health-related instrument effects, the government may, of course, favour that policy.[32]

Briefly, by way of conclusion, denying that the second type of political determinants are part of the right to health has an advantage when it comes to the degree of protection. One challenge for health-related guarantees is to determine how much protection is a reasonable amount of protection. Wolff notes that, in relation to the right to health, *sometimes* a reasonable guarantee of a reasonable level of protection against a standard threat is actually an absolute level of protection—the example of torture is a case in point. But, Wolff acknowledges, this is not universally so:[33]

> The main point is that human rights, so understood, generally in the first instance call on the government to put effective institutions in place—rather like a Rawlsian basic structure—rather than to meet the particular needs of particular individuals. Of course where there is institutional failure individuals may well pursue their own complaints, and one such failure may be where a government in its actions has failed to *respect* an individual's rights, by, for example, engaging in violent or arbitrary acts against an individual. But where a government has failed to *protect* individuals against threats, or to *fulfil* a right, an individual claim should have something of the character of a test case or implicit class action. That is, in the general case the suit should only succeed if it is an example of something that happens on a larger scale, and the government ought, by way of remedy, [to] change its practices rather than (or in addition to) providing individual compensation.

---

[32] I thank Thomas Parr for prompting me to consider this point.
[33] Wolff, this volume, ch. 27, 497.

What this seems to mean in relation to health, Wolff says, is that 'failure to protect and, especially, fulfil should primarily be *condition-based* (or non-condition group based, such as ethnicity) rather than *person-based*. (Failure to respect, in contrast, could easily take any form.).'[34]

Now, if we were to incorporate all political determinants of health into the right to health, this would not secure an absolute guarantee against many forms of mistreatment that should be absolutely prohibited. Protection from rape, for example, like protection from torture, should be an absolute guarantee. If we follow Wolff's reasoning, then when private parties perpetrate individual acts of rape, this would signal a government's failure to *protect* persons and perhaps failure to *fulfil* their claims to physical security, and thus should succeed as a human rights lawsuit only if it is an example of something that happens on a larger scale. And, to remedy it, the government ought to change its practices rather than (or in addition to) providing individual compensation. By contrast, if we approach human rights to legal equality and protection from mistreatment independently of their impact on health, then we can more easily take a categorical stand against political risks and say that only an absolute guarantee is a reasonable amount of protection.

---

[34] Wolff, this volume, ch. 27, 497.

29

A Moral Inconsistency Argument for a Basic Human Right to Subsistence

Elizabeth Ashford

There is a long-standing debate over whether or not it is possible to enjoy traditional negative human rights against harmful or coercive treatment without enjoying some minimal degree of economic security. [1] At issue is the plausibility of the view that the only genuine human rights are negative rights against interference by other agents, such as the right not to be tortured. (For ease of exposition I will refer to this as "the libertarian position" since it is at the core of libertarianism, although it is of course shared by many who do not accept other aspects of libertarianism. Indeed, as I discuss in the last section, the standard response to violations of certain rights against harmful treatment to which the destitute are vulnerable has much in common with the libertarian position.) A central critique of this view is that negative rights cannot be adequately enjoyed by those who do not enjoy the right to subsistence.

There are two ways in which this critique may be formulated. The first is that those who do not enjoy the right to subsistence cannot adequately enjoy their negative rights in the sense that they cannot derive maximum advantage from those rights. On this argument, lack of economic means affects the value to the right-holder of their liberty rights. It does not, though, undermine the liberty rights themselves.

Thus Isaiah Berlin, for example, while emphasizing that liberty rights may not be very valuable to those who lack adequate subsistence, argues that lack of means affects the worth of liberty, not liberty itself.[2] Similarly, Rawls draws a distinction between a liberty itself and the worth of that liberty, and argues that lack of means is not to be counted among the constraints definitive of liberty. He takes a liberty to be a socially protected option, and the worth of that liberty to be the value a person can derive from the exercise of the option.[3]

This first argument has the important implication that if we take seriously the values that make the possession of liberty rights important to the right-holder we ought to take seriously the right to subsistence. Nevertheless, it is still open to the libertarian to respond that there is no obligation to ensure that right-holders derive the full

---

[1] I am grateful to Charles Beitz, Sarah Conly, Rowan Cruft, Anthony Duff, Pablo Gilabert, Robert Goodin, David Miller, Quentin Skinner, Henry Shue, and Leif Wenar for their extremely helpful comments on previous drafts.
[2] Isaiah Berlin, "Two Concepts of Liberty", in Isaiah Berlin, *Four Essays on Liberty* (London: Oxford University Press, 1969).
[3] John Rawls, *A Theory of Justice*, rev. edn. (Cambridge, MA: Harvard University Press, 1999), see esp. 179.

advantage from their rights. Accordingly, she can argue that it is perfectly coherent to affirm the existence of negative human rights without affirming the existence of a human right to subsistence.

There is, however, a second, stronger version of the critique. This is the claim that those who do not enjoy the right to subsistence cannot be held to adequately enjoy negative human rights in the sense that the duties imposed by those other rights cannot be held to have been adequately fulfilled. I should emphasize that the claim is not that actually enjoying the object of the right to subsistence is a physical precondition for enjoying the *object* of other negative human rights; the claim, rather, is that fulfilling the duties imposed by the right to subsistence is a precondition for adequately fulfilling the *duties* imposed by negative human rights. The claim therefore does not have the implausible implication that a right cannot be enjoyed unless the preconditions for actually enjoying the object of that right are enjoyed.[4]

If enjoyment of the right to subsistence is essential to enjoyment of negative human rights in this second sense of the term "enjoyment", then in affirming a negative human right we are thereby committed to affirming the right to subsistence. Core human rights are claim rights, which conceptually entail the existence of corresponding duties. Therefore, acknowledging a claim right entails acknowledging its corresponding duties. If fulfilling the duties imposed by negative human rights requires realizing right-holders' right to subsistence, then acknowledging the negative right entails acknowledging a human right to subsistence.

An especially famous and influential version of this argument has been put forward by Henry Shue.[5] He contends that moral rights are, by definition, claims that actual enjoyment of the substance of the right be socially protected against standard threats. They therefore impose a corresponding duty to implement social guarantees against such threats. Shue then claims that not enjoying the right to subsistence is itself a standard threat to the enjoyment of the substance of any other right. His principal argument for this claim is that the destitute are highly vulnerable to being coerced into forgoing their other rights.

Shue concludes that enjoying the right to subsistence is "necessary for enjoying any other right", where the term "necessary" is to be interpreted "in the restricted sense of 'made essential by the very concept of a right'".[6] Accordingly, it is logically inconsistent to acknowledge any right without also acknowledging a right to subsistence. It is also practically inconsistent, given that enjoying the right to subsistence is indispensible to the enjoyment of every other right.

---

[4] A precondition for actually enjoying the object of a liberty right to take a certain journey is that the route not be blocked by freak weather conditions, but clearly such weather conditions do not undermine enjoyment of the right. Thomas Pogge takes Henry Shue's argument for a basic human right to subsistence, on one interpretation of it, to be based on such an assumption. (I have defended Henry Shue's argument against this and some other aspects of Pogge's critique in "In What Sense is the Right to Subsistence a Basic Right?", *Journal of Social Philosophy*, 40(4) (December 2009), special issue on "Human Rights: Normative Requirements and Institutional Constraints", eds. Andreas Follesdal, Thomas Pogge, and Carol Gould.)

[5] Henry Shue, *Basic Rights: Subsistence, Affluence, and U.S. Foreign Policy*, 2nd edn. (Princeton: Princeton University Press, 1996).

[6] Shue, *Basic Rights*, 31.

In recent years, however, it has been widely argued (even among advocates of the claim that there is a human right to subsistence) that Shue's claim that enjoyment of the right to subsistence is necessary to the enjoyment of every other human right is too strong.[7] One objection that has been raised to Shue's argument is that he fails to establish that inadequate enjoyment of the right to subsistence is a severe threat to the enjoyment of other human rights.[8] A second objection is that he fails to establish that it is a standard threat.[9] Third, it has been argued that the threat can in any case be addressed without securing the right to subsistence, simply by banning the coercive contracts to which the destitute are vulnerable.[10]

But a further objection to Shue's argument concerns the concept of moral rights on which it is based. It has been objected that his argument relies on a contentious definition of rights that a libertarian will simply reject. Therefore, it is argued, Shue begs the question by building into his definition of moral rights substantive assumptions that cannot be settled by conceptual fiat, and that underlie his conclusion that the right to subsistence is a basic right.[11]

Shue is assuming that acknowledging a right entails acknowledging a duty to ensure that right-holders are protected against standard threats to their enjoyment of the substance of the right. However, the libertarian can deny this. The libertarian will argue that the right not to be tortured, for example, can be fully respected by agents' merely refraining from torturing anyone else. It should be emphasized that libertarians do also acknowledge a (secondary) duty to enforce a ban on acts of torture.[12] However, they do not acknowledge a duty of justice to protect right-holders against all standard threats to freedom from torture. Therefore even if the libertarian accepts that not enjoying the right to subsistence is a standard threat to the enjoyment of negative human rights, it does not follow that in affirming the negative human rights she is thereby committed to affirming a human right to subsistence.

---

[7] See, eg, James Nickel, *Making Sense of Human Rights*, 2nd edn. (Oxford: Blackwell, 2007), 88–9 and 144–5, and "Rethinking Indivisibility: Towards A Theory of Supporting Relations between Human Rights", *Human Rights Quarterly*, 30 (2008): 984–1001; Thomas Pogge, "Shue on Rights and Duties", in Charles Beitz and Robert Goodin (eds.), *Global Basic Rights* (Oxford: Oxford University Press, 2009); Simon Caney, *Justice Beyond Borders* (Oxford: Oxford University Press, 2005), 119–20.

[8] James Nickel and Lizbeth Hasse, Review article on *Basic Rights*, *California Law Review*, 69(5) (September 1981): 1569–96.

[9] Pogge, "Shue on Rights and Duties", 121; Nickel and Hasse, Review article.

[10] Andrew I. Cohen, "Must Rights Impose Enforceable Positive Duties?", *Journal of Social Philosophy*, 35 (2004): 264–76.

[11] See, eg, Michael Goodhard, "None So Poor That He is Compelled to Sell Himself", in Shareen Hertel and Lanse Minkler (eds.), *Economic Rights: Conceptual, Measurement, and Policy Issues* (New York: Cambridge University Press, 2007), 94–114, 100. For an incisive analysis of this aspect of Shue's argument, see Beitz and Goodin, *Global Basic Rights*, Introduction, 7–8.

[12] The claim that the right not to be tortured can be adequately respected by refraining from torturing draws a distinction between the primary and secondary duties imposed by a right, where the primary duties are the correlative duties, violation of which constitutes the violation of the right. Shue argues against the claim that rights can be divided into positive and negative rights, on the ground that both kinds of rights impose both positive and negative duties (Shue, *Basic Rights*, ch. 2). The libertarian, however, can reply that negative rights are those that impose only negative duties as their *primary* duties. Thus, the right against torture imposes only a negative primary duty not to torture, and a secondary (positive) duty to enforce a ban on torture.

In short, this worry with Shue's argument is that it collapses into the first line of argument. The absence of social guarantees against standard threats to enjoyment of the substance of negative rights means that such rights will be less effective. They will therefore be of less worth to the right-holder. Once more, though, the libertarian can deny that we have any positive duty to ensure that others' negative rights are effective (beyond enforcing a ban on violations of the rights).

On behalf of Shue, it should be emphasized that the threat to the enjoyment of other rights on which his argument primarily focuses is that of vulnerability to coercion. While libertarians do not acknowledge a positive duty to protect right-holders against all standard threats to their enjoyment of human rights, they do acknowledge a positive duty to protect right-holders against being coerced into forgoing such rights; they accept that if right-holders are coerced into forgoing the object of a right, this undermines their enjoyment of the right, and they acknowledge a duty to enforce a ban on such coercion.

Nevertheless, the problem reemerges with the account of coercion on which Shue's argument is based. Libertarians conceive of coercion as a form of wrongful interference, involving reducing the victims' range of options by threatening to harm them if they fail to comply with the coercer's demand. Shue's first example of the kind of coercion to which the destitute are vulnerable uncontroversially constitutes extreme coercion. He points out that the threat of destroying persons' means of subsistence is just as effective as the threat of assault in coercing people into not exercising, say, their right to peaceful assembly. However, this justifies only some aspects of the human right to subsistence, as it is generally understood and as Shue understands it. It justifies a claim against being actively deprived of one's means of obtaining a subsistence income. It does not, though, justify a claim to assistance if one is unable to obtain for oneself a subsistence income and if the obstacles to one's doing so have not been wrongfully created by other agents. Establishing a human right to subsistence that incorporates this second claim requires showing that destitution in itself undermines adequate enjoyment of other rights.

Shue's argument therefore relies on his claim that those who are already destitute are also vulnerable to being coerced into forgoing their negative human rights in exchange for subsistence.[13] I will call contracts of this second kind "subsistence exchange contracts" (and will shortly argue that they are in fact far from exotic). However, given that subsistence exchange contracts do not involve the threat of harm, but rather increase right-holders' range of options, libertarians are liable to deny that they constitute coercion. Moreover, while neither Shue nor his critics have distinguished his two examples of coercion, what I will call the torture contract example—a subsistence exchange contract in my sense—has been the target of most of the criticism of his argument.[14]

---

[13] Shue, *Basic Rights*, 184–7. Thus, although his discussion of this comes only in a footnote, it is crucial to his argument.

[14] Thus, Nickel and Hasse argue that the torture contract is not a severe threat to enjoyment of the right against torture; Nickel and Pogge argue that it is not a standard threat to the enjoyment of the right against torture; and Andrew I. Cohn argues that the right against torture could be secured against the threat to it posed by the torture contracts by banning the torture contracts (for references see nn. 7 and 8).

I offer here a development of Shue's argument. I will argue that an analysis of the *difference* between subsistence exchange contracts and standard coercion implies that the failure to acknowledge a human right to subsistence is inconsistent with the substantive values that underlie acknowledgement of uncontroversial negative human rights, on any plausible account of such values. My argument, then, unlike the second line of argument against the libertarian, appeals directly to the substantive values that underlie acknowledgement of negative human rights, rather than to the very concept of such rights. However, my argument goes beyond the first line of argument in response to the libertarian, that taking seriously such values implies that we ought to take seriously the right to subsistence. I aim to show that failing to acknowledge a human right to subsistence is *inconsistent* with the values that underlie the acknowledgement of negative human rights.

In section I, I analyse the nature of subsistence exchange contracts and the way in which they differ from standard coercion. I argue that regardless of whether or not subsistence exchange contracts are classified as coercion, the threat they pose to the enjoyment of negative rights is just as severe as that posed by extreme standard coercion. This enables an argument to be made for the moral significance of subsistence exchange contracts that avoids the contentious assumption that they constitute coercion.

In section II, I further analyse what underlies the threat that subsistence exchange contracts pose to the enjoyment of other human rights. On the basis of this analysis I then argue, in section III, that this threat is common, and in fact liable to be pervasive. Indeed, an increasingly prevalent form of widely recognized violations of negative rights against harmful treatment actually consist in subsistence exchange contracts. (Examples include child labor, sweat-shop labor, and human smuggling.) It is widely accepted (including by libertarians) that acknowledgement of rights against such harmful treatment entails acknowledging both a primary duty not to inflict it and a secondary duty to enforce a ban on it. Accordingly, the standard response to child labor and so on is to enforce an immediate ban. However, as I argue in section IV, another implication of the way in which subsistence exchange contracts differ from standard coercion is that enforcement of a ban on them without securing right-holders' right to subsistence is systemically severely detrimental to right-holders' overall interests and range of options. Thus, enforcing a ban on these violations of uncontroversial negative human rights, without securing the right-holders' right to subsistence, is not just of little value to the right-holder, it is actually severely disvaluable to the right-holder. This is inconsistent with taking the acknowledgement of the right to be for the sake of the right-holder. In section V I further analyse the nature of this moral inconsistency.

I. The Nature of Subsistence Exchange Contracts

Subsistence exchange contracts, in which a destitute individual agrees to severely harmful treatment in exchange for subsistence, have one important similarity with standard coercion, which I now discuss, and two important differences (which I discuss in sections II and III, respectively). As I now argue, the threat they pose to the enjoyment of other rights is just as severe as that posed by standard coercion. I begin with an analysis of Shue's torture contract example.

A. The torture contract

Shue's argument that subsistence exchange contracts constitute coercion is based on the claim that the choice of accepting the contract is just as non-voluntary as in cases of severe standard coercion. Shue points out that a common form of coercion in prisons involves the guards' threatening to withhold food from the prisoners unless the prisoners agree to the guards' demands. This is an uncontroversial example of extreme coercion, given that the guards are responsible for deliberately and wrongfully introducing the prisoners' restricted choice situation. It is equally uncontroversial that the prisoners' choice of complying with the guards' demand in order to avoid the threat of inadequate food is non-voluntary. Shue argues that in just the same way, destitute individuals are vulnerable to being coerced into forgoing another right in exchange for subsistence. Shue's example of this kind of coercion is a torture contract a destitute individual enters into with a sadistic millionaire, in which he forgoes his right against torture in exchange for subsistence.[15] Shue contends that since the destitute individual agrees to the contract only because the alternative is not eating adequately, his choice is just as non-voluntary as the prisoners' choice to comply with the guards' demands. Shue infers that the contract should be classified as coercion, rather than as a contract in which the destitute individual is voluntarily waiving his right against torture:

> If one's only hope of eating adequately is to submit to torture, one is being coerced into submitting to torture, not renouncing one's right not to be tortured.[16]

Shue is here appealing to a widely assumed moralized conception of non-voluntary choice, according to which non-voluntary choice is intrinsically morally problematic, and its morally problematic nature is to be equated with its being is coerced.[17] Shue's reasoning is that since the destitute individual's choice is driven by the fact that the only alternative is inadequate subsistence, which is not a sustainable option, it should be classified as non-voluntary in just the same way as the prisoners' choice to comply with the prison guards' demands. He concludes from this that it ought to be classified as coercion. Along similar lines, O'Neill argues that the hallmark of a coercive proposal is that it is one the victim "cannot refuse", so that agreeing to it is not a genuine "expression of agency".[18]

---

[15] Shue, *Basic Rights*, 184–7.   [16] Shue, *Basic Rights*, 186.

[17] Alan Wertheimer, in his classic book on coercion, defends such a moralized conception of voluntary choice; *Coercion* (Princeton, NJ: Princeton University Press, 1987), 201. He contends that "there are no structural features of an individual's 'choice conditions' that are of much moral interest"; rather, the moral significance of a restricted choice situation depends on whether it wrongfully arose. He then offers an analysis of non-voluntary choice in terms of choice that is coerced. I take him to be assuming that non-voluntary choice is an intrinsically morally significant concept. If the structural features of an agent's restricted choice situation are of no moral significance then an analysis of non-voluntary choice, if it is to capture its moral significance, cannot be based only on those structural features themselves. Non-voluntary choice therefore has to be analysed as choice made in a restricted choice situation that has been wrongfully introduced by the coercer.

[18] Onora O'Neill, "Which are the Offers You Can't Refuse?", in O'Neill, *Bounds of Justice* (Cambridge: Cambridge University Press, 2000), 81–96, 89.

Again, coercion is conceived in terms of whether or not the choice to accept the proposal is voluntary (which O'Neill understands in terms of whether or not the choice is a genuine "expression of agency").

However, advocates of the position Shue opposes, that draws a sharp distinction between positive and negative duties and rights,[19] are liable to deny that subsistence exchange contracts constitute coercion precisely because the proposer is not wrongfully introducing the recipient's restricted choice situation. The proposer is, rather, increasing the recipient's range of options. Given the assumption that a non-voluntary choice is one that is coerced, then if, as the libertarian claims, the torture contract is not coercive, it follows that the destitute individual's choice of accepting it is voluntary.

The libertarian will therefore describe the contract as one in which the destitute individual *exercises* his right against torture by voluntarily choosing to waive it in exchange for subsistence, rather than as one in which he is forced to forgo it. On this view, then, the torture contract should not be described as a threat to the destitute individual's right against torture, but as an exercise of that right.

The difference between the torture contract and standard coercion is presumably what underlies James Nickel and Lizbeth Hasse's objection that the torture contract is not in fact a *severe* threat to the enjoyment of the right against torture:

> Even if a person chooses to waive his right not to be tortured by accepting torture in exchange for food, the person could still be said to have in some sense enjoyed the right not to be tortured. By choosing to waive his right not to be tortured, the person was able to receive something of value, namely food, in exchange.[20]

Their reasoning here seems to be that since the contract differs from standard coercion in that the destitute individual agrees to it because he gets something out of it, it should be characterized as one in which he exercises and thereby (at least "in some sense") enjoys his right against torture.

Thus, if non-voluntary choice is equated with choice that is coerced, then whether or not the choice to accept the contract is voluntary depends on what account of coercion is accepted. Shue argues that the choice is non-voluntary and that the contract therefore constitutes coercion. The libertarian, conversely, will argue that the contract does not constitute coercion, because the agent's restricted choice situation has not been wrongfully introduced by the coercer. The libertarian will conclude that the choice to agree to the contract is voluntary.

If the choice to agree to the torture contract is not voluntary, the contract is a threat to the enjoyment of the right against torture, since the destitute individual is forced to forgo her right against torture. If, on the other hand, the choice is voluntary, it constitutes the destitute individual's exercising her right against torture by voluntarily choosing to waive it.

Thus, Shue's appeal to the claim that the torture contract (to which destitute individuals are vulnerable) constitutes coercion, in defence of the claim that destitution

---

[19] For a general critique of this distinction, see Elizabeth Ashford, "The Alleged Dichotomy Between Positive and Negative Rights and Duties", in Beitz and Goodin, *Global Basic Rights*, 92–112.

[20] Nickel and Hasse, Review article, 1576.

poses a severe threat to the enjoyment of negative human rights, relies on an account of coercion that many, libertarians among them, will dispute. It is therefore in tension with his general strategy of showing that the right to subsistence constitutes a basic right by appeal to uncontentious premises that the libertarian accepts, in order to show that in affirming only negative rights the libertarian is thereby committed to affirming a human right to subsistence.

I will now offer a non-moralized analysis of the nature of non-voluntary choice, which separates the nature of the threat to voluntary choice itself from the question of whether the agent's choice should be classified as one that is coerced.[21] I shall analyse non-voluntary choice in terms of the way in which the structural features of the agent's restricted choice situation affect the agent's will. These structural features themselves are independent of the way in which the restricted choice situation arose. They can therefore be assessed independently of the question of whether or not the agent's choice situation was wrongfully introduced by a coercer.[22]

I aim to show, on the one hand, that Shue is right to claim that the destitute individual's choice to accept the torture contract is non-voluntary. The contract should indeed be described as constituting a severe threat to the enjoyment of the right against torture, rather than as an instance of the right-holder's voluntarily choosing to waive her right against torture.

On the other hand, I also contend that classifying the torture contract as coercion is unhelpful and liable to be misleading. It is unhelpful, insofar as it begs the question against the libertarian. An advantage of the non-moralized analysis of the nature of voluntary choice is that it can ground the argument that subsistence exchange contracts pose a severe threat to the enjoyment of negative human rights, while avoiding the contentious assumption, which the libertarian will reject, that the contracts constitute coercion.

The reason that classifying subsistence exchange contracts as "coercion" is liable to be misleading is because it may lead us to put the moral focus on the wrongfulness of the behavior of the people offering the subsistence exchange contracts, by labeling them as coercers. Insofar as the label is appropriate it is because, in common with standard coercers, agents offering subsistence exchange contracts may be subjugating the victim to their own will. The torture contract is a salient example of this. The torture contract overrides the destitute individual's enormously strong aversion to torture, and could not have been reasonably agreed to unless the option of refusing were completely unsustainable. Moreover, sadistic desire is premised on the awareness of such aversion. The torture contract is therefore an extreme case of a person's being

---

[21] Along similar lines, Serena Olsaretti offers a non-moralized account of voluntary choice; *Liberty, Desert and the Market* (Cambridge: Cambridge University Press, 2004), 140.

[22] I should emphasize that a non-moralized analysis of the nature of non-voluntary choice is compatible with acknowledging that the *term* "non-voluntary" is generally used in a moralized sense. Moreover, in cases of minor coercion, the moral significance of the agent's mildly restricted choice situation is likely to be entirely exhausted by the fact that the victim's restricted choice situation has been wrongfully introduced by the coercer. In such cases, we would normally describe the choice as non-voluntary only because it has been coerced; we would not normally apply the term "non-voluntary" to a choice made in a structurally identical choice situation in which the restriction to the agent's options had not been wrongfully introduced by the coercer.

used as a mere means to another's ends. It is worth emphasizing, then, that although the torture contract does not conform to the libertarian account of coercion, it instantiates the feature that Hayek and other libertarians identify as what is particularly morally troubling about coercion: that it "eliminates an individual as a thinking and valuing person and makes him a bare tool in the achievement of the ends of another".[23]

Nonetheless, in all cases of subsistence exchange contracts, focusing on the wrongfulness of the proposer's behavior is too narrow, because the core threat to the right-holder's range of options is independent of the proposer. As I argue in section III, it is for this reason that the threat that subsistence exchange contracts pose to the enjoyment of other rights is so common and pervasive. And, as I argue in section IV, it is for this reason that addressing subsistence exchange contracts by simply enforcing a ban on them—which is the appropriate response for cases of standard coercion—is deeply problematic from the point of view of the right-holder.

For these reasons, I contend, a non-moralized account of non-voluntary choice, that does not identify such choice with choice that is coerced, enables a clearer analysis of the moral implications of the threat that subsistence exchange contracts pose to other human rights. I now turn to such an account.

B. A non-moralized analysis of non-voluntary choice

In order to develop an account of non-voluntary choice that does not appeal to contentious intuitions about what constitutes coercion, I will examine cases that are uncontroversial examples of standard coercion. It is generally accepted that coerced choices are non-voluntary. I will identify the key features of non-voluntary choice in cases of classic coercion, and will then argue that these features are shared by subsistence exchange contracts.

i. *What makes coerced choices non-voluntary?*

In cases of standard coercion, the coercer threatens to harm the victim unless the victim complies with the coercer's demand. The coercer thereby renders ineligible every option other than that of complying with the demand, on the ground that all these other options involve suffering the threatened harm. By "ineligible" options, I mean ones that are not choice-worthy. Thus the way coercion operates is to ensure that the victim has no eligible choice but to accept the proposal.

It is widely acknowledged that some forms of coercion are more severe than others, and the obvious explanation for this is the severity of the threatened harm, on an objective conception of well-being. In cases of minor coercion, a fairly trivial threat of harm renders the option of refusing the proposal an ineligible choice *in comparison with* the other available options. For example, the threat of vandalizing one of a millionaire's many luxury yachts unless she agrees to pay out a small fraction of her wealth as "protection money" could be sufficient to bring it about that she judges the option of refusing the demand to be an ineligible choice relative to the alternative

---

[23] *The Constitution of Liberty* (London: Routledge & Kegan Paul, 1960), 21.

available options.[24] Clearly, the threatened harm could not be plausibly held to be one that would, in Herman's phrase, "gravely diminish her life."[25]

By contrast, in cases of extreme coercion, the cost of refusing the coercer's demand is so severe that the option of refusing the demand is ineligible not just in the sense of being non-choiceworthy *relative* to the available alternatives, but in the sense of being intrinsically unacceptable, on an objective conception of well-being. In the most extreme cases of coercion, the threatened harm is so severe as to be unsustainable—not in the sense that it is beyond human capacity to endure, but in the sense that anyone would have a desperate and ever-pressing desire to avoid it. (Even here, then, *pace* O'Neill, it is not the case that the coercer's demand is an option the victim literally "cannot refuse." As O'Neill herself points out, some people do.)[26]

Examples of extreme coercion include the threat to murder or torture the victim, or the victim's family members. The murder of the victim's child would significantly undermine their well-being so as to mar their life, in large part because it would undermine one of their most central ends, of raising a flourishing child and protecting their child from harm. Shue's example of prison guards' threatening prisoners with inadequate food is another example of extreme coercion, given that not eating adequately is an unsustainable option. This kind of severe coercion is, as Shue points out, a common and very effective way of pressuring right-holders into refraining from exercising a certain right.

It should be emphasized that the sense in which coerced choices are non-voluntary is perfectly compatible with their being based on a reasoned assessment of the value of the alternatives. Indeed, even in cases of extreme coercion in which the coercer threatens to kill the victim's child unless the victim complies with the coercer's demand, the victim's choice of complying is an expression of one of his most fundamental values, as a parent. In one important sense, then, coerced choices are a deeply important "expression of agency", also *pace* O'Neill (I return to the significance of this in the final section).

Rather, the sense in which a coerced choice is non-voluntary is that it is made only because of the ineligibility of the alternative options. In cases of extreme coercion, the threatened harm is so severe that the option of refusing is unacceptable on an objective conception of well-being, to the point of being unsustainable. In such cases, the choice to comply with the demand is non-voluntary in the sense that it is made only because the alternative is unsustainable.

---

[24] This is an example in which the moral significance of the mild threat to voluntary choice posed by the agent's somewhat restricted choice situation is entirely exhausted by its having been wrongfully introduced by the coercer. Given that, as I mentioned earlier (see n. 22), the term "non-voluntary" is generally used in a moralized sense, as referring only to contexts in which the threat to voluntary choice is morally significant, we would describe her choice to pay the "protection" money as non-voluntary only because her restricted choice situation has been wrongfully introduced by the coercer. If she were to choose to pay the same sum of money to prevent naturally occurring damage to the yacht, we would not normally describe this choice as non-voluntary.

[25] Herman, "Mutual Aid and Respect for Persons", 71.
[26] O'Neill, "Which are the Offers You Can't Refuse?", 91.

ii. Why subsistence exchange contracts are equally non-voluntary

If, as I have argued, what makes the prisoners' acceptance of the guards' demands non-voluntary is that the option of refusing is unsustainable, then the destitute individual's acceptance of the torture contract is just as non-voluntary. In just the same way as the coerced prisoner, the destitute individual agrees to the subsistence exchange contract only because the only available alternative is inadequate subsistence, which is unsustainable.

The core difference between the two cases is that in the first case, the threat to the victim's basic interests posed by inadequate subsistence is wrongfully introduced by the coercer in order to ensure the victim's compliance. In the second case, the threat to the victim's basic interests posed by inadequate subsistence is already in place, prior to the contract. In both cases, however, the choice to agree to the contract is made only because the cost of refusing the contract is inadequate subsistence, which is unsustainable. It makes no difference to the nature of the choice itself whether or not the person offering him the proposal is responsible for having wrongfully introduced the victim's severely restricted choice situation.

Thus, on this analysis, voluntariness or non-voluntariness is a property of the choice itself. The nature of the choice depends on how the structural features of the agent's choice situation affect the agent's will, and this is unaffected by how that choice situation arose. In the case of the coerced prisoner and the destitute individual agreeing to the torture contract, the restricted choice situation is identical, and affects the agent's will in the same way: in both cases the agents make the choice they do only because the alternative is inadequate subsistence, which is unsustainable. Thus, both choices are non-voluntary in the same respect: they are made only because the option of refusing is unsustainable. (I should emphasize once more that choices that are non-voluntary in this sense may be deeply important expressions of agency.)

I contend, then, that Shue is right that the destitute individual's agreeing to the torture contract is non-voluntary, in just the same way as extreme standard coercion; the threat to the right-holder's voluntary choice itself is the same in both cases. The destitute individual can no more plausibly be held to be voluntarily waiving his right against torture in exchange for food than is the prisoner voluntarily waiving other rights in exchange for subsistence. Rather, the torture contract should be classified as a case in which the destitute individual non-voluntarily forgoes his right against torture, in just the same way as the coerced prisoner. I conclude that subsistence exchange contracts pose a threat to the enjoyment of other rights that is just as severe as the threat posed by extreme standard coercion.

This brings us to the question of whether the threat is also a standard one. A central aspect of Shue's argument is that inadequate enjoyment of the right to subsistence poses a standard threat to the enjoyment of other rights. On Shue's account of rights, to recall, rights impose a duty to implement social guarantees against standard threats to their enjoyment of other rights. If not enjoying the right to subsistence is a standard threat to enjoying negative human rights, then those negative human rights impose a duty to fulfill the right to subsistence.

However, a second core objection to Shue's argument is that the torture contract, far from being a standard threat to the right against torture, is an "exotic threat."[27] Thomas Pogge argues moreover that contracts in which a destitute individual forgoes another human right in exchange for subsistence might be unavailable, in which case the link that Shue draws between destitution and inadequate enjoyment of other human rights is altogether severed.

I now give a fuller analysis of the nature of the threat to enjoyment of other rights posed by inadequate subsistence, and of the way in which this threat differs from that posed by standard coercion. I then argue that in virtue of this difference, the threat subsistence contracts pose to the enjoyment of other rights is liable to be more pervasive than that posed by standard coercion.

II. The Nature of the Threat that Subsistence Exchange Contracts Pose to the Enjoyment of Human Rights

The core threat that destitution poses to the enjoyment of other rights is grounded in the severity of the threat to persons' basic interests and most important ends posed by inadequate subsistence. The severity of this threat has two central implications. First, inadequate subsistence is unsustainable. Second, it is liable to be even worse than the option of forgoing any other right. It follows that whenever forgoing another right is the only available opportunity for obtaining adequate subsistence, the right-holder is liable to be driven to forgo that right, because continuing inadequate subsistence is liable to be the most unsustainable option of all.

Human rights against harmful and coercive treatment are identified as such (at least in large part) because of the severity of the harm they inflict on persons' basic interests and the threat they pose to agents' pursuit of their own ends. However, the threat to persons' basic interests and core ends posed by inadequate subsistence is so severe that it is liable to outweigh even the harm posed by forgoing negative human rights.

The torture contract case vividly illustrates this. The right against torture is one of the most urgent negative human rights, given the severity of the harm it causes, relative to an uncontroversial moral baseline of harm, and the undermining it is liable to cause of victims' capacity to adhere to their core commitments and ends.[28] The option of agreeing to torture is itself unsustainable. Torture constitutes deliberately inflicted unbearable pain that the victim has an urgent and continually pressing desire to end. Nevertheless, we can well imagine a destitute individual agreeing to a torture contract (in order to be able to feed her child, for example). This is because her interest in subsistence is so urgent that it is liable to outweigh her interest in the object of even the right against torture. Given that the interest in subsistence is liable to outweigh the interest in the object of any other human right, this is a potential threat to the enjoyment of any other human right.

---

[27] Nickel and Hasse, Review article, 1569–86.
[28] For a powerful analysis of this second aspect of torture, see David Sussman, 'What's Wrong with Torture?', *Philosophy & Public Affairs*, 33 (2005): 1–33.

In cases of standard coercion, the threat that the coercion poses to enjoyment of other rights arises from the coercer's posing a specific threat of harm to the victim unless the victim agrees to forgo another right. By contrast, the threat that destitution poses to the enjoyment of other rights lies with the fact that the existing plight of the destitute is already completely unsustainable. If forgoing another right is the only available opportunity for obtaining subsistence, then the choice not to forgo the right, which will lead to the continuation of the status quo, is an unsustainable option.

This can be expressed in terms of Robert Nozick's distinction between moral and empirical baselines of harm. In his analysis of coercion, he argues that the coercer's threat of harm can be characterized relative to a moral or empirical baseline.[29] Relative to the empirical baseline, a threat of harm is characterized as a proposal to make someone worse off than she would otherwise expect to be in the normal course of events. Relative to the moral baseline, by contrast, a threat is characterized as a proposal to make someone worse off than she morally ought to be. Nozick illustrates the way in which these two baselines can come apart with an example of a slave-owner who normally beats his slave each morning but on one occasion says that he will refrain from beating the slave if the slave performs a certain action. Relative to the empirical baseline, this is an offer to make the slave better off than he would normally expect to be. However, relative to the moral baseline it is a threat to beat the slave and thereby make the slave worse off than he morally ought to be unless he complies with his master's demand. The core threat that destitution poses to the enjoyment of other rights lies with the fact that the plight of continuing destitution is unsustainable to the point that even treatment that is severely harmful, relative to an uncontroversial moral baseline of harm, is liable to make the right-holder significantly better off than she would otherwise be, relative to the empirical baseline of continuing destitution, and is liable to significantly increase her range of options.

Thus, what underlies the threat that destitution poses to the enjoyment of other human rights is that for those who are destitute, their existing plight is already completely unsustainable. Furthermore, their interest in obtaining subsistence is so urgent that it is liable to outweigh their interest in the object of *any* other human right (even the right against torture), whenever forgoing that other right is the only available opportunity for obtaining subsistence. I now argue that one crucial implication of this is that the threat that subsistence exchange contracts pose to the enjoyment of other rights is common, and indeed liable to be pervasive.

III. The Commonness and Pervasiveness of the Threat Subsistence Exchange Contracts Pose to the Enjoyment of Other Human Rights

In cases of standard coercion, the threat such coercion poses to the enjoyment of other rights arises from the coercer's posing a specific threat of harm to the victim unless the

---

[29] Robert Nozick, "Coercion", in Sidney Morgenbesser et al. (eds.), *Philosophy, Science and Method* (New York: St. Martin's, 1969), 447–50.

victim agrees not to exercise another right. Such threats are generally short-term and episodic. By contrast, as we have seen, the threat that destitution poses to the enjoyment of other rights lies with the fact that the existing plight of the destitute individual is already completely unsustainable. Inadequate subsistence poses a threat to the destitute individual's most basic interests that is just as severe as the threat posed by the most extreme standard coercion. But unlike with cases of standard coercion, in which the coercer poses a specific and generally short-term threat of harm to the victim, the threat to right-holders' basic interests posed by destitution is ongoing, and indeed likely to be life-long. Thus the option that is liable to be the most unsustainable of all is also the status quo and the default option, unless the individual finds some way of avoiding it.

For this reason, destitute individuals are continually desperate to find opportunities to obtain a subsistence income. However, given the drastic shortage of economic opportunities available to them, doing so is liable to involve having to forgo another right in exchange for subsistence. And given that inadequate subsistence is liable to be even worse than forgoing the substance of any other right, then *whenever* forgoing another right is the only way of obtaining subsistence, the right-holder is liable to be driven to forgo that other right in order to avoid the most unsustainable option of all, that of continuing destitution.

As Shue points out, it is widely recognized that prisoners are highly vulnerable to coercion by prison guards, through the threat of withholding their subsistence. The reason for this is that they are entirely dependent on the prison guards for subsistence. We may have a recalcitrant intuition that unless we are in prison, we are not dependent in this way.[30] But when persons lack any realistic opportunity to earn for themselves a subsistence income, their choice situation is just as restricted as that of the prisoners. They are just as dependent for subsistence on anyone offering them an opportunity that would be otherwise unavailable for obtaining it, and are just as vulnerable to having no sustainable alternative but to forgo another right in exchange for subsistence.

This can be illustrated first by considering the torture contract itself. Although explicit torture contracts are indeed rather rare (though not so rare as to be "exotic"),[31] exchanges in which individuals whose access to subsistence is insecure accept severely physically cruel treatment, because it is the only way of obtaining subsistence, are indeed common. One common example is severe domestic violence.[32] If women who are experiencing such violence have no realistic opportunity to earn for themselves a subsistence income, they are vulnerable to not being in a position to exercise their right against the violence (by leaving the relationship, for example), because they are likely

---

[30] This point was suggested to me by Sarah Conly.

[31] Eg, prostitutes who accept the job because it is the only available opportunity for being able to obtain a subsistence income for themselves and their children are especially vulnerable to being forced to accept a high risk of sadistic abuse as inherent to their job.

[32] The treatment I am referring to consists in the deliberate infliction of extreme pain, motivated by cruelty and often a desire to subordinate and control the victim, and often causing permanent physical harm. Even if the classification of this treatment as torture is rejected, it is comparably serious and is widely held to be a human rights violation.

to be entirely dependent on their husbands for subsistence. Leaving the relationship is therefore liable to jeopardize their access to subsistence. Since this cost is unsustainable, the choice of taking up their right against the violence is not one that is genuinely available to them. Until the right to subsistence has been secured, one important threat to the enjoyment of the right against domestic violence will remain: that the option of taking up the right is unsustainable, and therefore not genuinely available, because it conflicts with obtaining adequate subsistence. This is a common threat to the enjoyment of the right against domestic violence, and the threat is likely to be at least as real and severe as that posed by legal impediments to prosecuting or separating from violent partners.

Similarly, severely poor domestic workers are highly vulnerable to being forced to accept abusive treatment because of fear of their own or their children's starvation if they leave the employment. Destitute child laborers are also extremely vulnerable to severe and sadistic abuse. As Debra Satz puts it, "Millions of children are beaten, raped... and abused, suggesting that more than economic motives are driving employers... Indeed, children's lives might be much better if only the bloodless impersonal economic motives of an ideal market were at issue".[33] Thus the destitute are highly vulnerable to being forced to accept extreme abuse in exchange for subsistence.

It should also be noted that another implication of the nature of the threat that destitution poses to the enjoyment of other rights is that it need not involve the individual's agreeing to a contract at all, either implicit or explicit. Thomas Pogge points out that a contract in which a destitute individual forgoes a certain human right in exchange for subsistence might not be on offer at all. Pogge gives the example of a kidnap victim, who is being starved and assaulted by his kidnappers.[34] Pogge argues that the victim does not enjoy the right to subsistence (or to physical security), but that this does not plausibly undermine his enjoyment of, say, the right not to be arbitrarily deprived of a nationality, because a contract in which he forgoes such a right in exchange for subsistence is of no interest to his kidnappers.

However, as I have argued, the underlying threat to the enjoyment of other rights is posed by the fact that whenever enjoying a right comes into conflict with obtaining subsistence, the choice of enjoying the right is unsustainable. Subsistence exchange contracts are not the only context in which this conflict is likely to occur. Therefore, while Pogge is right that coercive contracts in which the right-holder forgoes a certain right in exchange for subsistence may not actually be of interest to would-be coercers and so may not be on offer, this does not entail that the threat to other rights posed by insecure access to subsistence is not in place.

This can be illustrated with Pogge's own example of the kidnap victim who is being starved by his kidnappers, but is not being coerced by them into forgoing his right to a nationality. If we take the core threat to this right to be posed by the ineligibility of continuing to lack subsistence, then it is much broader than the threat posed by

---

[33] Debra Satz, "Child Labor: A Normative Perspective", *World Bank Economic Review*, 17(2) (2003): 297–309, fn 10, 304. For a further discussion of child labor, see Debra Satz, *Why Some Things Should Not Be for Sale: The Moral Limits of Markets* (Oxford: Oxford University Press, 2010).

[34] Pogge, "Shue on Rights and Duties", 121.

coercive contracts. While contracts in which people forgo their right to a nationality in exchange for subsistence may be rare, conflicts between obtaining adequate subsistence and enjoying the right to a nationality are far from rare. One way in which this conflict arises is that of illegal immigrants, who are forced to leave their own country because of the lack of opportunities to earn a subsistence income. Given restrictive immigration policies, applying for citizenship in the new country is highly likely to lead to deportation and to a return to the destitution from which they were fleeing, and so is not a sustainable option. These individuals therefore do not effectively enjoy the right to citizenship in the new country, and are in turn highly vulnerable to violations of the rights conferred by such citizenship, such as the right to decent working conditions. Destitution does therefore pose a standard threat to actual enjoyment of the right to a nationality.

I contend, then, that subsistence exchange contracts are indeed common. Moreover, the threat that inadequate subsistence poses to the enjoyment of other rights is liable to be much more pervasive than that posed by standard coercion. In cases of extreme standard coercion, the coercer poses a severe threat of harm in virtue of which the option of refusing to comply with the coercer's demand is rendered unsustainable. By contrast, those who are destitute face an ongoing severe threat to their most basic interests in virtue of which the existing status quo for them is completely unsustainable. Treatment that is harmful relative to an uncontroversial moral baseline (such as torture), is liable to make them significantly better off than they would otherwise be, relative to the empirical baseline of the continuation of the status quo, whenever accepting such treatment provides the only available opportunity for obtaining subsistence.

Evidence for the frequent nature of subsistence exchange contracts is the fact that an increasingly common class of violations of widely recognized negative human rights against harmful treatment actually take the form of subsistence exchange contracts, in which people accept the harmful treatment in exchange for the opportunity to earn a subsistence income. Examples include sweatshop labor, child labor, and human smuggling. These are cases in which forgoing the right against the harmful treatment does constitute the only available opportunity for obtaining subsistence.

These subsistence exchange contracts are standardly classified as violations of negative human rights against harm. This is because they involve treatment at the hands of other agents that is severely harmful relative to an uncontroversial moral baseline. Child labor is standardly classified as a human rights violation in large part because of the severely detrimental impact it is liable to have on children's developmental interests; it is therefore held to make them much worse off than they morally ought to be. Sweat-shop labor is also widely classified as a human rights violation, on the grounds that the unhygienic, unsafe, and exhausting working conditions endemic to sweat-shop labor are morally unacceptable. Human smuggling is widely classified as a human rights violation on the ground that people ought not be subject to an extremely high risk of death during the journey, as a result of travelling in a poorly ventilated lorry, for example.

They are also commonly classified as coercion. As I have argued, regardless of how they are classified they share two key features in common with standard coercion.

First, the destitute individuals' choice of accepting the contract is non-voluntary. Second, the contracts often involve subjugation.

As I now argue, another core implication of the way in which the threat to other human rights posed by subsistence exchange contracts differs from the threat posed by standard coercion is that enforcing a ban on subsistence exchange contracts, without securing the right-holders' right to subsistence, is systemically severely detrimental to the right-holders' overall interests and range of options. This detrimental impact on the right-holder of bans on subsistence exchange contracts is illustrated particularly vividly by considering the standard response to human rights violations that actually take the form of subsistence exchange contracts.

IV. The Moral Inconsistency Involved in Banning Subsistence Exchange Contracts Without Securing Right-holders' Right to Subsistence

Many subsistence exchange contracts are widely recognized as violations of negative human rights against harm, on the ground that they involve treatment at the hands of other agents that is harmful relative to an uncontroversial moral baseline. Since the right to subsistence is, by contrast, widely held to be merely progressively realizable, the ban on these negative rights violations is generally enforced without addressing the severe poverty associated with the prevalence of such contracts. They are also widely held to constitute coercion. Accordingly, the standard response to child labor, sweat-shop labor, and so on is to seek to enforce an immediate ban without securing the victims' right to subsistence. This response is in line with the libertarian view that the only genuine human rights are negative human rights, and that these impose a secondary duty to enforce a ban on violations of them.[35] But as the commonness of this response indicates, this aspect of libertarianism is widely reflected in current human rights practice. While violations of negative human rights against harmful treatment are taken to demand an immediate ban, the duty to secure right-holders' right to subsistence is generally treated as far less urgent.

[35] Article 2.2 of the International Covenant on Economic, Social and Political Rights (ICESPR) stipulates that each state party will take "a view to achieving progressively" the rights in the Covenant in accordance with "the maximum of its available resources". This takes right-holders' own governments to be the primary addressees of the right to subsistence, responsible for fulfilling the primary positive duty to respect the right (for the distinction between the primary and secondary duties imposed by human rights, see n 12). Even where right-holders' own governments lack adequate resources to fulfill the primary positive duties imposed by the right to subsistence towards all their citizens, responsibility for fulfilling these primary duties is not held to fall on other nations. Foreign governments are held to be only under *secondary* duties "to encourage and assist countries in their efforts to respect and uphold human rights, to pressure governments that violate rights to cease doing so, and to assist the victims of rights violations" (James Nickel, "How Human Rights Generate Duties to Protect and Provide", *Human Rights Quarterly*, 15 (1993): 77–86, 85). Yet if the right to subsistence is held to be a universal human right, the relevant level of current resources should be that of global resources rather than the level of resources internal to poor countries themselves, and the relevant social institutions should be feasible global, as well as domestic, social institutions. For further defence of this, see Elizabeth Ashford, "The Duties Imposed by the Human Right to Basic Necessities", in T. Pogge (ed.), *Freedom From Poverty as a Human Right* (Oxford: Oxford University Press, 2007), 183–218, and Pablo Gilabert, "Humanist and Political Perspectives on Human Rights", *Political Theory*, 39 (2011): 439–67.

This response overlooks the fact that the reason destitute individuals agree to subsistence exchange contracts is that they reasonably judge the continuation of the status quo—ongoing destitution—to be the most unsustainable option of all. Thus, while the contracts are agreed to non-voluntarily (in the sense that the choice is driven by the fact that every other option is unsustainable), and the treatment is harmful relative to an uncontroversial moral baseline, the contracts also significantly improve the right-holders' overall interests and range of options. It follows that simply banning the subsistence exchange contracts without securing the right-holders' right to subsistence is systemically detrimental both to those right-holders' overall interests and to their range of options.

Let us consider first the way in which the ban impacts on right-holders' range of options. Right-holders are liable to agree to a subsistence exchange contract because it may, for example, provide an opportunity that would otherwise be unavailable for a destitute individual to afford to prevent his child from dying through lack of subsistence. Therefore coercive enforcement of a ban on the contract, without ensuring the right-holder has another realistic opportunity to earn a subsistence income, may remove his only realistic opportunity to save his child. As I argued in section II, choices that are non-voluntary in the sense that they are driven by the fact that the option of refusing is unsustainable may nevertheless be a deeply important expression of agency. Removing persons' only available opportunity to save their child's life without securing an alternative opportunity to do so is an extremely severe further restriction on their range of options, which undermines their pursuit of what they may reasonably judge to be their most important end.

The ban in some respects resembles the kind of paternalistic intervention that libertarians in particular find deeply objectionable; it is a form of intervention in the lives of right-holders that severely restricts their range of options, and is taken to be motivated by concern for the interests of the individual. However, unlike genuine paternalism, it is also systematically severely detrimental to the right-holders' overall interests.

Similarly, deaths as a result of human smuggling rightly evoke outrage. This outrage generally leads to a call to tighten up a ban on the smuggling, independently of securing the right to subsistence. However, those who pay the smugglers may be doing so because even an extremely risky attempt to escape destitution will significantly improve their chances of survival. In such cases, implementing a ban without addressing the destitution removes what may be their best available opportunity to feed themselves and their children, and is liable to substantially further reduce their chances of survival.

The impact on children of immediate bans on child labor, without addressing the background destitution, has been especially well documented. It has often led to the children's starvation, or to their being driven to a worse way of earning a subsistence income, such as prostitution.[36]

In common with standard violations of liberty rights against coercion and harmful treatment, the contracts are agreed to non-voluntarily and often involve subjugation,

---

[36] See, eg, Kaushik Basu and Zafiris Tzannatos, "The Global Child Labor Problem: What Do We Know and What Can We Do?", *World Bank Economic Review*, 17(2) (2003): 147–73.

and they involve treatment at the hands of other agents that is severely harmful relative to an uncontroversial moral baseline. Nevertheless, enforcing a ban without securing right-holders' right to subsistence, far from protecting the right-holders, systemically further undermines their range of options and overall interests. This is incompatible with taking the implementation of the rights to be for the sake of the right-holder. On any plausible account of human rights, however, they are positions of normative advantage, the implementation of which must be for the sake of the right-holder. This response, therefore, is morally inconsistent.

What underlies this inconsistency is, once more, the fact that for those who are destitute, the moral and empirical baselines of harm systemically diverge. Responding to the harmful and coercive treatment by simply enforcing a ban on it puts the moral focus on the wrongfulness of the behavior of the agent inflicting such treatment, and on protecting the right-holder against such treatment. The assumption that the appropriate response to such treatment is simply to enforce a ban on it is based on the implicit assumption that the status quo is (at least minimally) acceptable. Violations of negative rights against harmful treatment are conceived as discrete harmful actions, where the harm is measured against a baseline implicitly assumed to be acceptable. The violation therefore makes the victim worse off relative to both the moral and the empirical baselines of harm. Enforcing a ban thus protects the victim against the threat to their interests posed by the would-be violator. Violations of negative rights against coercion are conceived as threats to the victims' voluntary choice and freedom from subjugation, and enforcing a ban protects right-holders against such threats.

However, the assumption that the status quo is minimally acceptable does not apply to those who are destitute. For these individuals, the moral and empirical baselines of harm systemically diverge, so that they are made significantly better off than they would otherwise be (relative to the empirical baseline) by treatment that is severely harmful relative to an uncontroversial moral baseline, whenever accepting such treatment is the only opportunity for obtaining subsistence. Therefore enforcing a ban on the treatment without ensuring an alternative opportunity to earn a subsistence income is systemically liable to be more detrimental to the right-holder's overall interests than the treatment against which they would be "protected". And although subsistence exchange contracts are very similar to standard coercion, in that acceptance of them is equally non-voluntary and they are liable to involve subjugation, the threat to the victims' interests that renders refusing the contract an unsustainable option is posed not by the agent labeled the coercer but by the victims' ongoing destitution. Enforcing a ban on the contract does not protect the right-holder against the threat to their range of options posed by the agent labeled the coercer, but significantly further reduces the right-holder's range of options.

To sum up, I have argued that while subsistence exchange contracts significantly differ from standard coercion, the choice of accepting them is just as non-voluntary as in the most extreme cases of standard coercion. In both cases, the right-holder's choice is driven by the fact that every other option is unsustainable. The interest in subsistence is so urgent that, first, inadequate subsistence is unsustainable, and, second, it is liable to outweigh the interest in the object of *any* other right—even the right against torture. Subsistence exchange contracts therefore constitute a potential threat to the enjoyment of every other human right. Given that what underlies the threat is that for those who are destitute their existing status quo is unsustainable, the threat is liable to be common, and more pervasive than that posed by standard coercion; and responding to it by simply banning the subsistence exchange contract, without fulfilling the right-holders' right to subsistence, is liable to be systemically severely detrimental to their overall interests and range of options.

Human rights are universal moral claims held by every person. It follows that whatever human rights there are must be held by the destitute as much as anyone else. However, unless the right to subsistence is universally fulfilled, there will be one group of right-holders—the destitute—for whom the continuation of the status quo, of ongoing destitution, is liable to be worse than accepting treatment in exchange for subsistence that is severely harmful relative to an uncontroversial moral baseline, and that shares with the most extreme standard coercion the fact that agreeing to it is non-voluntary and is liable to involve subjugation.

30

The Force of Subsistence Rights

Charles R. Beitz

Elizabeth Ashford observes that those whose access to the means of subsistence is under continuous and unavoidable threat are in a situation of existential vulnerability: they can be induced by offers of subsistence to put other urgent interests in jeopardy.[1] This is because, in circumstances of extreme deprivation, it may be rational to trade away most any other interest in order to gain access to the means of subsistence. Ashford notes that such bargains ("subsistence exchange contracts") are not esoteric: child labor, sweatshop labor, and human smuggling are instances. Although we might hesitate to classify the offer of such a bargain as a form of coercion, it has two features in common with ordinary coercion: its acceptance is in a certain sense non-voluntary (because the alternative is unsustainable) and the consequences are likely to be harmful to the vulnerable party. At the same time, the offer and acceptance of such a bargain differs from ordinary coercion in the important respect that it leaves the vulnerable party better off, all-things-considered, than her condition ex ante, notwithstanding the harm done.

Ashford argues for two conclusions, both of which draw on the analysis of the subsistence exchange relationship. First, the position of those who would prohibit subsistence exchange contracts in order to protect the vulnerable from harm is insupportable. Banning these contracts would in fact make the vulnerable worse off overall by denying them an option they have reason to want. Those who favor doing so should also support social guarantees of access to the means of subsistence in order to eliminate the vulnerability that makes subsistence exchange contracts advantageous. Second, the position of those who accept that there is a human right against coercive interference with individual liberty and security ("libertarians," in her terms)[2] yet dispute that there is a right to the means of subsistence is also unsupportable. The prospect of subsistence exchange contracts shows that persistent deprivation of access to the means of subsistence is an obstacle to enjoyment of the substance of the right against coercive interference with liberty and security. Those who hold that there is a human right to protection of liberty and security should accept that there is also a human right of access to the means of subsistence.

This is a severely compressed précis of a complex analysis. One of its aims is to vindicate Henry Shue's well-known argument for "basic rights" against an objection to

---

[1] Elizabeth Ashford, "A Moral Inconsistency Argument for a Basic Human Right to Subsistence," this volume, ch. 29.

[2] She understands this position as characterized by the view that only "negative" rights (rights against interference) are genuine human rights. Ashford, this volume, ch. 29, 515.

which it is sometimes thought susceptible. Shue conceives of a moral right as the basis of a claim that enjoyment of the substance of the right be socially guaranteed against predictable ("standard") threats. He argues that if there are any moral rights at all, then there must be "basic" rights to security and subsistence, because without such rights there could be no secure expectation of enjoyment of the substance of whichever other rights we suppose people to have.[3] Some have objected, however, that this argument trades on an esoteric conception of a right (or perhaps of "enjoyment" of a right). They hold that as rights are ordinarily understood, there are some rights that can be enjoyed even if security or subsistence are not guaranteed. It does not seem a stretch, for example, to say that there could be an effective right against torture if social institutions were to prohibit torture and enforce the prohibition, even if there were no effective guarantee of subsistence. But if this is correct, then there is no "basic right" to subsistence, because a guarantee of access to the means of subsistence is not necessary to guarantee enjoyment of the substance of all other rights.

Ashford's analysis of subsistence exchange contracts is a response to this objection. The strategy of the response is to enlist a "libertarian" commitment to protection of interests in liberty and security in the service of protection of subsistence interests. She takes the former commitment as given and holds that, because severe poverty is a standing invitation to the kind of exploitation manifested by subsistence exchange contracts, the protection of subsistence interests is necessary for the protection of liberty and security interests. In this way she seeks to avoid the appeal to "positive" duties that evokes the libertarian challenge. I am not sure that libertarians will be satisfied—much depends on whether they agree that acceptance of a subsistence exchange contract is nonvoluntary in a morally significant way. However, I shall not try to formulate the libertarian rejoinder. I am interested instead in a form of skepticism about subsistence rights that might survive even if the essentials of the argument against the libertarian were granted. It arises when we take the perspective of those who may be called upon to contribute to the relief of deprivations of the means of subsistence rather than that of those who suffer the deprivations. Skepticism is at its sharpest when we assume the perspective of potential contributors beyond the boundaries of the society in which the deprivations occur. I shall rehearse the skeptical view and discuss what might be said in response to it, relying in part on arguments I have made before.[4] This moves beyond the central concern of Ashford's paper, but I believe the view set forth here is complementary.

I. Skeptical Doubts

I begin with a preliminary comment about the subject-matter of human rights. Shue takes "basic rights" to be a species of moral rights. But there is no mistaking that his book aims to contribute to discourse about *human* rights understood roughly as they

---

[3] Henry Shue, *Basic Rights*, 2nd edn. (Princeton: Princeton University Press, 1996), ch. 1. Ashford's idea of a subsistence exchange contract elaborates Shue's idea of a "torture contract" (Shue, *Basic Rights*, 185).

[4] Charles R. Beitz, *The Idea of Human Rights* ((New York: Oxford University Press, 2009) (hereinafter *IHR*), particularly sections 18 and 25).

are within the international practice that originated after the Second World War with the framing of the Universal Declaration of Human Rights (UDHR) and the covenants on Civil and Political Rights (ICCPR) and on Economic, Social and Cultural Rights (ICESCR). At the time Shue wrote, most philosophers tended to regard the rights catalogued in the international documents as moral rights of a more-or-less ordinary kind—that is, individual claim-rights to which correlative duties are attached. This identification has caused trouble in the discourse of the international practice, in which human rights are usually presented as standards for institutions whose implications for the conduct of individual and collective agents can be uncertain.[5] One of the important contributions of Shue's book was to concentrate attention on the variety of duties that might plausibly be thought to attach to basic (and other) rights. But the question whether it is best to interpret international human rights as a species of individual moral rights as familiarly understood rather than as a *sui generis* class of norms was left unexplored. As a result, it may be ambiguous what practical conclusions would follow for various types of agents from our agreeing that the right to subsistence should be "universally fulfilled."[6]

The skeptical view arises from pressing on this ambiguity. Because human rights present themselves as grounds of claims, reflection about their basis is naturally directed towards the interests of potential claim-makers—that is, the beneficiaries of these rights. As Ashford's analysis of the similarities and differences of rights to security and to subsistence illustrates, when we think about the significance of these rights for their beneficiaries, it can seem incontrovertible that enjoyment of the substance of the rights is of great urgency—perhaps even a condition of living any kind of decent life. But the satisfaction[7] of these rights will normally impose burdens on other agents—as we might say, on contributors as distinct from beneficiaries. The skeptical view proceeds from the perspective of potential contributors and denies that recognition of the significance of the rights in question for their beneficiaries is enough, by itself, to explain why potential contributors should regard themselves as under an obligation to contribute to their satisfaction.

My aim is not to persuade anyone that the skeptical view is finally persuasive so I will not develop it in detail. I imagine the view only to call attention to the independent importance of considering subsistence rights from the perspective of potential contributors both within and beyond the society in which enjoyment of the substance of the rights might be threatened. As I imagine it, the skeptical view draws on two kinds of doubt to which an explanation of the responsibilities of potential contributors should respond. One is conceptual. It holds that, for any authentic human right, there should be a criterion or process for assigning responsibilities to potential contributors such that, if these responsibilities were to be carried out, the right would be satisfied for everyone. The skeptic argues that, for subsistence rights, there is no feasible

---

[5] For discussion see Thomas Pogge, *World Poverty and Human Rights*, 2nd edn. (Cambridge: Polity, 2008), 64–9.

[6] Ashford, this volume, ch. 29, 534. I mean this as an observation, not a criticism. Shue considers the institutional aspect of basic rights in the Afterword to the 1996 edition of *Basic Rights*, 153–80.

[7] "Satisfaction" is an awkward term, though it seems to be common in the discourse of human rights.

assignment of responsibilities under which this would be the case. The other skeptical doubt is normative and, although easily conflated with the first, is distinct from it. This second doubt holds that the demands for action associated with subsistence rights, taken in aggregate, require unreasonably much of those on whom these rights profess to impose responsibilities to act. In contrast to the first source of doubt, the claim is not that there is no practicable assignment of responsibilities that would result in the satisfaction of the right for all. Instead, the position is that the burdens imposed by any assignment of responsibilities would be greater than their assignees might reasonably be expected to bear. To put it differently and perhaps more clearly, the second doubt is that, however the responsibilities are assigned, their assignees would not, in general, have sufficient reason to act on them.

I believe that both of these doubts miss their target. They gain their grip by invoking an idea of human rights as a species of moral claim-right of the kind that holds between individual persons. This idea does not register the fact that human rights, as we find them in international doctrine, are in the first instance conditions for institutions rather than for individual persons taken seriatim. And it misses the significance of the fact that international human rights constitute a global practice in which human rights claims serve distinctive political purposes. Once we understand the role played by claims of right within this public practice, we can see that the doubts I have mentioned are not in any straightforward way grounds for skepticism that subsistence rights have normative force. And we shall be better able to appreciate the reasons for action available to those in a position to act in favor of satisfying these rights.[8]

II. Human Rights in the Global Practice

If I were to say that there is a human right to do or to have something, what, exactly, would I be saying? There are several ways to answer this question. A common approach among philosophers is to adopt a conception of a right from some other context and to interpret the notion of a human right in light of this adopted conception. One might, for example, look to the history of thought about "natural" or "fundamental" rights in the hope of finding a model to which the idea of a human right could be assimilated. Alternatively, we might look to the practice itself and try to work up a conception of human rights from the role the idea plays within it.

In *The Idea of Human Rights* I argue that we should resist the first approach in favor of the second.[9] If our interest in human rights is motivated by a desire to make sense of the existing international practice, then it is hard to resist the thought that we should frame a conception of the idea of a human right by looking to the way the idea is understood by competent participants in the practice. Roughly the picture is this. We have on hand an international doctrine whose authoritative statements include subsistence rights. We are confronted with skeptical claims holding that the inclusion

---

[8] I discussed subsistence rights within the practice in an earlier paper ("Human Rights and *The Law of Peoples*," in Deen Chatterjee (ed.), *The Ethics of Assistance: Morality and the Distant Needy* (Cambridge: Cambridge University Press, 2004), 193–214). Here and in *IHR* I characterize the practice differently and advance a different view about the force of these rights.

[9] See *IHR*, chs. 3 and 5.

of these rights in international human rights doctrine is the result of a conceptual or a normative error. To decide if we should agree with the skeptical claims, we need a grasp of the idea of a human right as it is found in international doctrine and in the public practice in which it is embedded.

To say this, of course, is to suppose that there is such a thing as an international practice of human rights. I doubt that readers of this volume will need to be persuaded that this is true, but it is worth saying quickly what I mean by it. The practice of human rights is normative and discursive. It consists of a series of norms for the regulation of behavior together with various forms of legal and political action for which the norms are taken by participants in the practice to provide reasons. People appeal to these norms to justify claims on various agents and to appraise their conduct. This practice has developed on several fronts since the end of the Second World War, when its doctrinal foundations were laid in the UDHR and subsequently in two international covenants and various other international agreements. It has grown since the Helsinki Accords of 1975 and the end of the Cold War around 1990. We see elements of the practice expressed in international law, in the monitoring and reporting activities of global and regional institutions devoted to human rights, in the policies of other international organizations, in the conduct of foreign policy by states, and in the activities of a diverse assortment of non-governmental organizations. Notwithstanding its evolved complexity, we must regard the practice as emergent, because it lacks important features found in more mature normative practices. For example, levels of compliance are uneven and the practice lacks authoritative institutions for interpreting and enforcing its norms.

We arrive at a "practical" conception of human rights by exploring the role played by the idea of a human right in the discourse of this practice. Human rights claims are supposed to provide reasons to a range of agents for various kinds of political action. In order to understand the concept of a human right as it operates within the practice we ask for what kinds of actions, by which kinds of agents, and in which kinds of circumstances human rights claims are typically understood to give reasons.

The working out of a practical conception of human rights would therefore require an analysis of the history of the contemporary human rights system and of its political dynamics. Since I cannot do this here,[10] I will simply stipulate what I call a "two-level model" that I believe describes the idea of a human right as we find it in the practice today. Like any model, this is both an idealization and a simplification but I believe the main elements are observable in the contemporary legal and political culture of human rights (though I would not claim that the model accommodates all of the uses of the idea of human rights found in contemporary practice).

The two-level model expresses a division of labor between states as the bearers of the primary responsibilities to respect and protect human rights and agents of the international community as bearers of responsibilities to act when states default. There are three main elements.[11]

---

[10] I have tried to do it, briefly, in *IHR*, ch. 2.

[11] For the main ideas I am indebted to Shue, *Basic Rights*, ch. 1 and the 1996 Afterword, and James W. Nickel, *Making Sense of Human Rights*, 2nd edn. (Oxford: Blackwell Publishers, 2006), chs. 1–4. For more detail about the two-level model see *IHR*, ch. 5.

First: Human rights are requirements whose object is to protect urgent individual interests against predictable threats to which they are vulnerable under the general circumstances of life typical in what we might roughly describe as the modern world. They cannot plausibly be regarded as pertaining to all times and places.

Second: Human rights apply in the first instance to the political institutions of states, including their constitutions, laws, and public policies. Each state is responsible for protecting the human rights of its citizens and others residing in its territory. The nature of the protection called for will vary with the content of the right and the social and political context, but as a general matter, human rights may impose at least three kinds of requirements on states and their agents: to respect the underlying interests in its laws and policies, to protect these interests against threats from other agents, and to help those who are non-voluntarily victims of deprivation.[12]

Third: A state's failure to protect the human rights of its members may be a source of reasons for action for agents outside the state. Human rights are distinctively matters of international concern. The international community has a general responsibility to hold states accountable for respecting their people's human rights and to act when states fail egregiously to do so. Moreover, states and non-state agents with the means to act effectively have pro tanto reasons to assist an individual state to satisfy human rights standards in cases in which the state itself lacks the capacity to do so. These importantly include reasons to remove externally imposed conditions that obstruct or undermine the state's capacity to act.

For the most part I will have to leave the elaboration and defense of this model to my readers' imaginations, but let me call attention to four features that have special relevance for subsistence rights. The first involves the idea of a violation of human rights, which we must understand more broadly than we would if we were to think of human rights as individual moral claim-rights. Human rights, in the first instance, are requirements for institutions. As I have observed, they may impose several types of requirement (both "negative" and "positive"). A "violation" may be said to occur when a protected interest is set back as a result of a government's failure to satisfy these requirements, whether through lack of capacity or of will. This means that a government might be said to have violated a human right even when there is no intention to do so (for example, through a lack of capacity or poor policy planning) and when the proximate cause of the deprivation is something other than government action (for example, when a government fails to take the appropriate preventative or remedial steps). This clearly stretches the ordinary idea of a "violation" but it seems to me to be faithful to the discourse.

Second, according to the model, human rights violations are reason-giving for external agents. A state's default on its responsibility to protect the human rights of its people supplies pro tanto reasons for outside agents to act. Pro tanto reasons, of course, are not necessarily conclusory. However, as we shall see in the case of subsistence rights, the reasons for action facing external agents are often likely to be weighty. In some cases (for example, when what is required is the removal of an obstructing

---

[12] This typology of duties is due to Shue. As he observes, these combine what are conventionally classified as "negative" and "positive" requirements. *Basic Rights*, ch. 3.

condition) a failure to accord them due weight and to act appropriately might itself be considered a form of violation.

Third, in contemporary international practice human rights violations supply reasons for many kinds of international or transnational political action. It is natural to think of military intervention as the paradigm, but this is artificially narrow.[13] The array of means available to states to promote and protect human rights in other states also includes nonviolent forms of coercive interference (for example, economic sanctions), the imposition of conditions on participation in international cooperative activities, the offering of other kinds of political and economic incentives, and the provision of consensual economic and political assistance. These are in addition to the forms of action carried out within the UN human rights system itself, with its procedures for monitoring and reporting. Finally, and of increasing salience, human rights violations supply reasons for assorted forms of contestation by non-state actors, ranging from reporting and advocacy to transnational political organizing.

Fourth, the features I have listed, taken together, characterize human rights as the constitutive elements of a public political practice that aims to regulate relations among states and other international agents. Human rights are publicly available norms to which appeal can be made to justify political action. This fact has two corollaries. First, as public standards, human rights need not presuppose the general acceptance of any particular philosophical or religious view about their moral basis (though of course they are not equally accessible from every such view). As the early interpreters of international human rights doctrine recognized, human rights are open to a variety of justifications.[14] Second and relatedly, human rights are norms crafted to apply to whole classes of cases whose empirical characteristics are likely to be quite diverse. The weights to be attached to the reasons for action arising from actual or potential violations in any particular case, and the array of possibly conflicting reasons that might be at play in that case, will vary with the empirical background. The application of norms to cases will therefore require judgment, and one should not be surprised to discover that these judgments might be controversial. As Joshua Cohen puts it, human rights define a "terrain of deliberation and argument" rather than a set of fixed points for law and policy.[15] That they do so ought not to be regarded as a deficiency; it is part of the nature of a public, normative practice.

III. The Conceptual Challenge

One source of skepticism about subsistence rights is conceptual. It holds that once we understand what it is for something to be a right, we shall see that there cannot be

---

[13] The thought might be encouraged by the conception of human rights set forth by John Rawls in *The Law of Peoples* (Cambridge, MA: Harvard University Press, 1999), section 10. I believe he is right to conceptualize human rights in terms of the types of political action their violation might justify. But it distorts contemporary practice to fix on coercive intervention as the modal type.

[14] Eg, Jacques Maritain, "Introduction," in UNESCO, *Human Rights: Comments and Interpretations* (London: Allan Wingate, 1949), 10.

[15] Joshua Cohen, "Minimalism about Human Rights: The Most We Can Hope For?" *Journal of Political Philosophy*, 12 (2004): 195.

subsistence human rights. They are ruled out for lack of one or more essential features of rights.[16]

Many people have held this view in one or another form.[17] Consider, for example, the version advanced by Onora O'Neill.[18] She distinguishes between "normative" and "aspirational" views of rights and argues that a value cannot count as a right, on a "normative" view, unless it can be seen as the ground of a claim that specifically identifiable other agents have obligations to act or refrain from acting in ways that would result in the claimant's having or being able to enjoy the value. Values not satisfying this complex condition are better conceived of as "aspirations:" they describe goods that their beneficiaries have reason to want but do not identify any agent as having an obligation to provide them. O'Neill thinks it obvious that the familiar "rights of man" to freedom, property, and security can count as rights on a "normative" view because the inferences to be drawn from claims of right about the deontic situations of other agents are clear: these are rights against interference that everybody has a duty to respect. She believes that the same cannot be said about rights to goods and services such as food and health care. Without more, rights to goods, as opposed to rights against interference, do not generate obligations for specific agents, the performance of which would result in enjoyment of the substance of the rights. When somebody's "right" to food or health care is unsatisfied, we have no way of saying who is responsible. We must regard rights of this latter kind as merely aspirational; since they do not serve to guide the actions of any agent, they are without normative force.[19]

Joel Feinberg took what might appear to be a similar position when he described economic rights as "manifesto rights." Such rights, in his view, "are not necessarily correlated with the duties of any assignable persons" because "under widely prevalent conditions of scarcity and conflict, [they may] be impossible for *anyone* to discharge."[20] Feinberg seems to have believed, as an empirical matter, that there is no feasible assignment of duties such that their performance would result in the satisfaction of everyone's subsistence rights. Today, of course, this is very likely false. But leave the empirical question aside for the moment. The important point for our purposes is that in Feinberg's view, even if a "manifesto right" cannot be satisfied in the present, it might still be action guiding. He thought we should understand the assertion of "manifesto rights" as "expressing the conviction that they ought to be recognized by states as potential rights and consequently as determinants of present aspirations and guides to present policies."[21] Feinberg did not disparage "manifesto rights" as normatively inert. He held that they can guide action even if they are not correlated with duties to see to the satisfaction of the right for any particular person in need. They do so by establishing as a priority goal of political action the creation of conditions in

---

[16] Parts of this section restate an argument from *IHR*, 120–1 and 164–6.

[17] Eg, Maurice Cranston, *What Are Human Rights?* (London: Bodley Head, 1973), 65–71; Bernard Williams, "Human Rights and Relativism," in Bernard Williams, *In the Beginning Was the Deed* (Princeton, NJ: Princeton University Press, 2005), 63–5.

[18] Onora O'Neill, "The Dark Side of Human Rights," *International Affairs*, 81 (2005): 427–39.

[19] O'Neill, "The Dark Side of Human Rights," 428.

[20] Joel Feinberg, *Social Philosophy* (Englewood Cliffs, NJ: Prentice-Hall, 1973), 94 (emphasis in original).

[21] Feinberg, *Social Philosophy*, 67.

which it would be possible to satisfy the right, and hence to assign duties to see to its satisfaction.

Here is another way to put the point. A government's failure to prevent or remediate a deprivation can give rise to two types of reasons for action. "Direct" reasons are reasons to act in ways whose success would bring about enjoyment of the substance of the right for those deprived. Reasons of this type can call for various kinds of action—for example, ceasing activities that bring about or contribute to the deprivation, offering protection against threats of deprivation by other agents or by natural forces, or providing aid that would offset or compensate for the effects of the deprivation. "Indirect" reasons are those that count in favor of actions by which an agent can help establish conditions in which those deprived could enjoy the substance of the right in the future. A particularly important indirect reason is the reason one may have to contribute to the establishment and operation of institutions and practices designed to undertake such actions. An agent's situation would be analogous to what it might be in an unjust society: although there would be no duty to comply with the rules that would apply if the society's institutions were just, one might have a duty to help establish just arrangements with which one would have a duty to comply once they were established, at least when this could be done without excessive sacrifice.[22] What the idea of a "manifesto right" shows is that although circumstances may be such that there are no direct reasons for action available (perhaps, as Feinberg thought, because resources are scarce, or perhaps, as O'Neill suggests, because there is no institutional mechanism for assigning obligations to act), there may nevertheless be indirect reasons.

There is a further point. Let us continue to suppose, (again) most likely counterfactually but as Feinberg appears to have believed, that there is no feasible assignment of duties under which everyone's subsistence rights would be satisfied. This still would not mean that nobody has any direct reasons to act. Even if it were not possible to satisfy everyone's subsistence rights in the present, it might be possible to satisfy the rights of some, or to increase the level of satisfaction of the rights of all. Possibilities like these may be what is intended by the idea of "progressive realization."[23] These possibilities are capable of supplying reasons for action in the present even if there were no feasible sequence of actions that could be taken now that would result in enjoyment of the substance of subsistence rights by all those presently deprived.

To return to the skeptical view, we can now see that the distinction between the "normative" and the "aspirational" is incomplete. It does not follow from the (supposed) fact that there is no assignment of obligations under which everyone's enjoyment of the substance of the right would be secured that such a right cannot generate reasons for action. There may be direct reasons to help some people, even if it is not possible to help all. And there may be indirect reasons to help create more favorable conditions. The distinction between "normative" and "aspirational" interpretations of

---

[22] I adapt John Rawls's formulation of the natural duty of justice. *A Theory of Justice*, rev. edn. (Cambridge, MA: Harvard University Press, 1999), section 19.

[23] Each state shall "take steps...to the maximum of its available resources, with a view to achieving progressively the full realization of the rights recognized in the present Covenant by all appropriate means." ICESCR, Article 2.

subsistence rights obscures these ways that subsistence rights can be action-guiding. It has the effect of ruling out an interpretation of subsistence rights more in keeping with a practical conception of human rights than either of these alternatives.

It is a further question whether and why anyone, and in particular prospective donors, should care about violations of subsistence rights, even if they are not conceptually suspect. This is a normative question and, on the view I have sketched, we cannot avoid it. Reflection about this question suggests a second skeptical doubt.

IV. The Normative Challenge

Our second skeptical view differs from the first in accepting that subsistence rights might count as bona fide human rights even if they do not serve as grounds of assignable obligations whose successful performance would result in satisfaction of the interests the rights are meant to protect. The view arises in response to the fact that, within the practice, human rights violations are supposed to generate reasons for action for agents in a position to prevent or remediate the violations, particularly those outside the society in which the violations occur. It holds that any candidate for recognition as a human right should satisfy what we might call the "sufficient reason" condition: a government's persistent failure to prevent or remediate violations should generate reasons that would be sufficient to justify action by (some) outside agents under reasonably foreseeable circumstances. The normative challenge holds that in typical cases in which subsistence interests are threatened, the sufficient reason condition is not likely to be satisfied.[24]

Since the urgency of subsistence interests is beyond question, we might begin by asking how the normative challenge gets off the ground. In response, we should recall what I observed earlier: that the actions for which violations of subsistence rights might provide reasons, although aimed at protecting and satisfying the interests of their beneficiaries, are likely to be burdensome for their prospective agents. It can always be asked why this or that agent should incur a cost in order to contribute to protecting or advancing the interests of others. In certain circumstances it may be enough to reply that the interest is urgent and the prospective agent is in a position to satisfy or protect it without significant cost or risk. But as a general matter, considerations of urgency, capacity, and cost will not be enough to determine whether potential agents have sufficient reason to act to protect or satisfy subsistence interests, particularly when they are considered on a large scale and threats to them are understood to be consequences of complex and deep-seated natural and social facts. Typically more needs to be said—for example, about the causes of the likely threats, the nature of the historical and contemporary relationships between those deprived and the potential agents, and the consequences for third parties of protecting the interests or allowing them to go unprotected.

The normative challenge arises from doubt that enough more *can* be said. The doubt can have various sources. One, of course, is a more general alienation from morality

---

[24] Parts of this section restate the argument in *IHR*, 168–73.

(doubt, that is, that arises from skepticism that we can ever owe each other anything), but I leave that aside. Someone can take moral considerations seriously yet still believe that under the circumstances to be expected the considerations at hand are not likely to be strong enough to command action. This is the kind of doubt that interests me. It consists of the belief that in the typical case in which subsistence interests are threatened on a large scale, the reasons for action likely to be available to any prospective external agent are not strong or weighty enough to offset the other reasons for action (in other realms) likely to be in competition for that agent's adherence.

Suppose, for example, that one accepts the following two sets of beliefs. One might believe, first, that although severe poverty is always an occasion for beneficence, reasons of beneficence can exercise only limited command over our lives and resources. This is not only because there are some goods and commitments we reasonably judge to be too important or too central to the conduct of our own lives to be given up.[25] It is also because, in living our lives, we regularly find ourselves having to resolve conflicts between reasons of beneficence and (other-regarding) reasons of various other kinds—for example, to take care of dependants, to contribute to cooperative schemes from which we benefit, to pay our debts, and so forth. One might think that those other kinds of reasons would typically be weightier. Second, one might believe that severe poverty, at least when it occurs in another society, is not usually an occasion for any particular other kind of reason for action. Perhaps one thinks the sources of severe poverty are so diverse that it is impossible to generalize in ways that would enable responsibility for ameliorative action to be fixed in any agent or set of agents. Poverty may be brought about or sustained by features of the local culture and political traditions; it may be a legacy of historical injustice; or it may be imposed or sustained by patterns of exploitative international economic transactions or the exercise of unequal bargaining power by other societies. If one grants that (some of) an agent's reasons to act in response to a threat to someone else's urgent interests depend on the agent's relationship to the threat, then it may seem that no single account can explain why and to what extent severe poverty, wherever it occurs, should provide a reason for potential agents in other societies to bear the costs of its alleviation. The conjunction of these beliefs produces the conclusion that, in the general case, the violation of subsistence rights does not provide a distinctive reason for action to external agents. There is always beneficence, but in a world with limited resources and multiple demands, much of the time reasons of beneficence will be trumped by other reasons. If this is right, then in typical cases of violation, subsistence rights may not satisfy the "sufficient reason" condition.

One thing that might be said in response is that the challenge depends on a faulty judgment about the weight of considerations of beneficence as they apply to cases of severe material deprivation. I believe there is much to be said for this line of response. Subsistence interests are indeed urgent and the costs to the affluent countries of taking

---

[25] This point is emphasized in T.M. Scanlon's remarks on reasons to give aid in *What We Owe to Each Other* (Cambridge, MA: Harvard University Press, 1999), 224. For a discussion of this aspect of Scanlon's view, see Elizabeth Ashford, "The Demandingness of Scanlon's Contractualism," *Ethics*, 13 (2003): 273–302.

steps that could produce a significant improvement in satisfaction are modest relative to their economic capacities.[26] To this we should add the familiar observation that the idea that reasons of beneficence can only exercise limited command over our lives and resources applies differently to whole societies than to individuals. One reason we are inclined to accept this idea, at the level of interpersonal morality, is the perception that by contributing to the satisfaction of the interests of third parties under circumstances in which others cannot be expected to do the same, one sets oneself at a relative disadvantage. But matters look different when we think of human rights as institutional rather than interpersonal standards. When a local government is unable to prevent or remediate deprivations of subsistence rights, the international agents who have reasons for action are collective agents—other states, international organizations, private non-governmental organizations, and the like. Most such agents have a capacity to manage problems of individual relative disadvantage by distributing the cost of acting across whole populations. So considerations of beneficence may command a larger contribution when the actions they support are taken or coordinated by institutional agents than when the same considerations are acted on seriatim by individuals. The tendency to think of human rights as individual claim-rights obscures this fact.

These points are important. However, I want to concentrate on a more basic aspect of the normative challenge. The challenge seems plausible due to a background belief that the only reason for action that we can be sure will arise for external agents in cases of severe poverty is a reason of beneficence. As I have stated it, however, this is ambiguous. One interpretation—the "no single reason" view—holds that, beneficence aside, there is no one reason or kind of reason for action that will arise for external agents throughout the range of what I have called standard cases of severe poverty. A different interpretation—the "no reason at all" view—holds that, beneficence aside, in most cases of severe poverty no other reason for action, of any kind, will arise for external agents.

The "no single reason" view is suggested by a thought I mentioned earlier: that the causes of poverty are too diverse to allow for generalizations that would enable responsibility to be placed. Perhaps there is no persuasive general reply to the question whether poverty tends to be generated or sustained by natural facts or contingent internal forces or, instead, is imposed or aggravated by aspects of the global political–economic order. If this is true, then we cannot say that severe poverty, wherever it occurs, typically gives rise to the same distinctive reason for action. Different cases must be treated differently. If any particular type of human rights claim must be interpreted as always demanding action for the same distinctive kind of reason, then there may be trouble ahead for subsistence rights.

But it is hardly obvious that we should accept the "no single reason" view. Human rights, as I have said, is a public normative practice. Within the practice, specific rights operate in the same way that middle-level principles operate in other practical

---

[26] There is no non-controversial way to evaluate these costs. Jeffrey Sachs reports a range of estimates, with varying assumptions as to the kind and extent of investments required, between 0.5% and 0.7% of the GDP of the rich countries. *The End of Poverty: Economic Possibilities for Our Time* (New York: Penguin Press, 2005), ch. 15. See also Paul Collier, *The Bottom Billion: Why the Poorest Countries Are Failing and What Can Be Done About It* (New York: Oxford University Press, 2007), esp. ch. 11.

domains. We typically expect practical principles to rest on some deeper level of reasoning in which a variety of basic ethical concerns are brought together with facts about the world in a way that shows the principles to be reliable guides to action in the range of circumstances we are likely to confront. So, for example, the principle of freedom of expression might be thought to summarize and bring into focus an array of underlying ethical and practical considerations lying at a more fundamental level of practical reasoning.[27] It is not an objection that the circumstances to which the principle will have to apply may vary in their morally significant features or that, as a result, different elements of the principle's justification will be significant in different circumstances. This is just how practical principles function.

It is the same for human rights. As the constitutive norms of a public doctrine, human rights should afford reasons for action across a wide range of more-or-less likely circumstances ("typical" or "standard" cases). But we have no more reason here than in other domains to require that the same reason or weighted set of reasons motivate the application of a human right to every set of circumstances to which it applies.

So the question we should care about is not whether a single analysis of the sources of poverty applies to all standard cases, so that, in all such cases, external agents would face the same kind of reason to act. The question is whether, for each type of case in the central range, we can discern some reason or set of reasons, in addition to considerations of beneficence, that would be sufficient to require external agents to act in some foreseeable circumstances. It need not be the same kind of reason in every case.

Here I can only offer this as a conjecture, but I believe the answer is yes. To see why this might be plausible one must consider the patterns of interaction that might exist between societies containing substantial amounts of severe poverty and more affluent societies with which they interact and ask in each case what kinds of reasons for action would be available to external agents.[28] The possibilities begin with two limiting cases. One is autarchy; here, by hypothesis, there are no reasons other than those of beneficence in play. The other is symmetrical interdependence, in which poor and non-poor societies cooperate as equals. The most important reasons in this case have to do with the fairness of individual transactions and of whatever cooperative practices and institutions organize them. These polar cases are, however, not very interesting for our purposes. There are several intermediate and, on the whole, more likely possibilities which I hope can be suggested with descriptive labels: for example, harmful interaction, historical injustice, mutually beneficial exploitation, and political dependence. Each pattern evokes a different kind of reason for action: for example, not to cause harm, to compensate for the results of harm done earlier, not to exploit one's bargaining advantage, to respect the interest in collective self-determination. This does not exhaust the possibilities but it will illustrate the point. The relationships that characterize the various dyads of interacting poor and affluent societies are diverse, not only in the patterns of interaction they instantiate but also in the reasons

---

[27] Consider, eg, Mill's argument for liberty of thought and discussion in "On Liberty" [1859], in *Essays on Politics and Society I* [*Collected Works of John Stuart Mill*, vol. 18], ed. J. M. Robson (Toronto: University of Toronto Press, 1977), 213–310.

[28] Compare A.J. Julius, "Nagel's Atlas," *Philosophy & Public Affairs*, 34 (2006): 189–90.

why these patterns are morally salient. But it seems plausible that most such dyads are characterized by one or more of these or similarly salient patterns. Except for autarchy, each pattern suggests a different reason for action that would arise for the rich country from poverty in the poor one. If this is right, then members of affluent societies are likely to have some reason to act to reduce poverty or to mitigate its effects in most poor societies with which they actually interact, but these reasons will vary in strength and perhaps in the forms of action they call for.

Two further considerations reinforce this conjecture. The first concerns uncertainty. There is reasonable disagreement about the causes of societal poverty and wealth. The disagreement manifests itself at the aggregate level and in connection with many, and perhaps even most, individual cases.[29] In any dyadic relationship it may not be known to what extent the parties' present or past interactions contribute or contributed to the affluence of one or the poverty of the other. A workable public practice of human rights must abstract from these uncertainties. The parties' asymmetrical vulnerability to error supplies a reason to resolve the uncertainty in favor of the more vulnerable party.[30]

The other consideration concerns the international structure. I presented the diversity of reasons for action as arising from a range of patterns of dyadic interaction among individual agents, but in practice, of course, these patterns are frequently organized and facilitated by international property law and the international institutions that regulate trade and finance. To the extent that features of the international structure enable or facilitate patterns of interaction that are objectionable in one of the ways we have distinguished, those in a position to benefit may come under pressure from an additional kind of reason for action, one requiring them to reform the structure or compensate for its undesirable effects on those who cannot avoid them at reasonable cost.[31]

All of this suggests that, if we accept the two-level model's characterization of a human right, then the "sufficient reason" condition does not rule out subsistence rights as human rights. Consider again the analogy with freedom of expression. When one invokes the principle of free speech, one is saying, among other things, that we have reasons to want institutions to offer some reliable form of protection against various interferences with expression that might be anticipated in a society's general circumstances. Different kinds of interferences might be objectionable for different of these reasons and might call for different kinds of protection. The nature and strength of the reasons, and the kind of protection required, are matters to be worked out, so to speak, at the "point of application." Similarly, when one asserts a human right, say, to an adequate standard of living, one is saying, among other things, that external agents have reasons to act when domestic governments either fail or are unable to provide

---

[29] One way to see this is to consider the difficulties in devising a theory of economic growth capable of explaining inter-country differences in growth rates in sufficiently specific terms to guide policy. There is an instructive survey in Dani Rodrik, *One Economics, Many Recipes: Globalization, Institutions, and Economic Growth* (Princeton, NJ: Princeton University Press, 2007), ch. 1.

[30] Thanks to Thomas Pogge for this observation.

[31] For an exploration of the moral considerations associated with the structure and norms of the global trade regime, see Aaron James, *Fairness in Practice* (New York: Oxford University Press, 2012).

the protections such a right calls for. Since I cannot argue it here, I have proposed as a conjecture that we are likely to have good grounds for believing that in many and probably most cases of severe poverty, there will be reasons for action available of significant weight. The details of these reasons and the nature and extent of required action depend on features of the individual case.

V. Objections

I have argued that two sources of skepticism about the justification for counting subsistence rights as human rights will be less troubling if we adopt a conception of human rights in keeping with the contemporary practice. In responding to the second skeptical view, I have also pointed to a range of potentially relevant reasons for action that may arise for agents in a position to contribute to the satisfaction of subsistence rights where they are most severely threatened. With the exception of reasons of beneficence, these considerations pertain to the nature of the relationships between potential contributors to and beneficiaries of subsistence guarantees, and so they complement the beneficiary-oriented considerations that motivate Ashford's moral inconsistency argument.

I would like to conclude by commenting about two objections that may be provoked by the view I have taken here. The first is this. A practice-based approach takes its understanding of the nature and role of human rights from the discursive practice as we observe it. But regarded from a moral point of view, this might lead to excessively conservative conclusions. According to the two-level model, the governments of states have the primary responsibilities to satisfy human rights and external agents have secondary responsibilities to act when states fail or default. This is in accord with the authoritative documents of international human rights, but one might regard it as too narrow. Why should not human rights requirements apply directly ("in the first instance") to agents other than states—to international institutions, for instance, or to multinational firms? After all, these types of agents are capable of setting back the interests protected by human rights in many of the same ways as the governments of states. It is sometimes said, for example, that enforcement of the intellectual property provisions of world trade law leads to avoidable deprivations of life-saving medications in poor countries. If this is true, why should we not say that these provisions violate subsistence rights? And that, if the two-level model denies the propriety of making such a claim, so much the worse for the model?[32]

I believe the best response to this objection is to deny its premise. International institutions such as the trade regime are creatures of states. They are the outcomes of international negotiations and exercise whatever authority they possess as agents of their members. A state that adheres to an agreement whose enforcement results in deprivations of the interests protected by a human right for its own people violates that right. And the prospect of violation supplies a reason for other states to refrain from adhering themselves or insisting on adherence by others, or perhaps to revise the

---

[32] I am grateful to Thomas Pogge for pressing this question. A similar question is raised by O'Neill, "The Dark Side of Human Rights," 434–5.

terms. This suggests that there may be nothing one might want to say about the bearing of human rights standards on international institutions that would be foreclosed by accepting the two-level model.

Things are more complicated in the cases of multinational firms and other non-state actors that cannot be regarded as the agents of states. It is true that business firms are usually chartered by one or another state and that their operations fall within the jurisdictions of states. States that fail to regulate their conduct in ways aimed at avoiding deprivations of interests protected by human rights might therefore be said to be violators. And perhaps business firms, like non-governmental organizations, can be counted among the external agents that can acquire secondary obligations to act when the governments of states default. But it would require an artificial stretch to say, within the terms of the two-level model, that multinational firms can be primary violators of human rights. The question is what to make of this fact. It does not count against the two-level view as a model of contemporary human rights practice; the practice, by design, primarily regulates the conduct of states. One might well conclude, however, after considering the effectiveness of the practice, that the limitation of human rights enforcement to states is ineffective against certain kinds of threats and that the practice is in need of reform. The reformist argument would have to be that the regulative aims of the practice are frustrated by its own existing limitations. I have some sympathy for this argument but it is beyond my scope to pursue it here. All I mean to suggest is that a practical approach to human rights does not foreclose criticism of the structure of the practice.

Let me turn now to a second objection. A consequence of thinking about human rights in the way I have suggested is that human rights claims may often leave more to be worked out at the "point of application" than one might wish. This is because the grounds and force of a claim will vary with the context in which it is made, and because the reasons supporting the claim will have to be reconciled with whatever conflicting reasons exist under the circumstances. This picture of human rights as privileged but not necessarily decisive norms of action stands in contrast to another picture of human rights that people sometimes entertain. In that alternative picture, human rights claims are expected to be conclusively action-guiding: that is, as if, once it is established that an assertion of right is warranted under the circumstances, no more needs to be said about whether action is required. If torture or genocide or political repression are going on, they should stop. What else might there be to say? But human rights as the two-level model characterizes them may not operate this way. On this characterization, human rights claims serve two related purposes: they call attention to the likelihood that without some form of legal or political action, urgent human interests are likely to be set back, and they recall that in most such cases, at least some agents who are in a position to take action are likely to have relatively strong reasons to do so. But from a perspective that regards human rights as the most important of political values this may seem anemic.

The justification for adopting this characterization is that this is, in fact, how human rights often seem to function in the discursive practice of contemporary global political life. The cases mentioned earlier—torture, genocide, political repression—are special; the threatened interests are uncontroversially urgent and given plausible assumptions about the empirical background, there are unlikely to be offsetting reasons that would argue against acting to eliminate or contain the threats to these interests. But many of the human rights of international practice are not like this. Subsistence rights, in particular, protect against complicated threats whose lasting containment or elimination pose a complex challenge to public policy and may never be fully achieved.

It is tempting to describe human rights as the language of global justice.[33] But this would be excessive: human rights are not the whole of justice, even of global justice. They state a partial standard, limited primarily to what are plausibly regarded as expectations to which it is reasonable for the international community to hold domestic-level governments. What seems correct in that description is the suggestion that human rights have come to occupy a privileged place in the discourse of global political life. They are public standards for domestic-level institutions to which appeal can be made in claims for external help. Their privileged place is based on the urgency of the underlying interests and the likelihood that various external agents will have good reasons to act when domestic-level governments fail egregiously to protect these interests against predictable threats. The combination of the normative ambition of human rights doctrine taken as a whole and the diversity of situation among the world's societies makes it inevitable that these standards will exhibit a substantial amount of open texture. So it would be unrealistic, even if it were not a mistake for other reasons, to expect even well-founded assertions of human rights to determine decisions about who should act and in which ways. Yet if I am right about the nature of the practice, this is no reason to disparage the normative force of human rights in general or of subsistence rights in particular.

[33] I have been tempted myself, eg, in "Human Rights as a Common Concern," *American Political Science Review*, 95 (2001): 269.

PART IV

HUMAN RIGHTS: CONCERNS AND ALTERNATIVES

31

The Relativity and Ethnocentricity
of Human Rights*

James Griffin

I. Ethical Relativity

Ethical relativism, as I shall understand it, makes two claims: first, that ethical judgements are made within a framework of basic evaluations, which may take the form of beliefs, preferences, sentiments, and so on; and, second, that there are divergent frameworks for judgements on the same matter, no one framework being most authoritative.[1] We can then specify the framework further case by case—the basic evaluations of individual persons, of social groups, of cultures, and so on.

Ethical relativism, as most commonly expressed, is universal: *all* ethical judgements are relative to a framework. Its contradictory is therefore particular negative: some are not. I have already argued[2] that some ethical judgements—namely, judgements about basic human interests—are objective, where 'objective' means dependent not upon a person's subjective states but upon considerations that would lead all successfully rational persons to the same conclusion. So universal ethical relativism is, I conclude, false. But philosophers tend to treat values as if they were uniform: all are objective, or none is; all are a matter of knowledge, or none is; all are relative to a framework, or none is. But I have also questioned this assumption of uniformity.[3] Some complex moral norms, such as 'Don't deliberately kill the innocent', have an element of policy to them, and so lack empirical truth-value, whereas the judgements that a particular human interest is or is not met have one.

Relativism need not take a universal form. Consider relativity to the evaluative framework of individuals, based on their different desires and sentiments. Value beliefs can be subjected to criticism by facts[4] and by logic.[5] Many ethical beliefs are shaped by a person's understanding, often misunderstanding, of the empirical world: of the consequences of our acts, of what the objects of our desires are really like, and so on. Once one's desires and attitudes have been corrected, one may come to change them; over time they may increasingly converge with the desires and attitudes of others. What a relativist must maintain, however, is that some divergent beliefs will remain, and

* This chapter first appeared in James Griffin, *On Human Rights* (Oxford: Oxford University Press, 2008).

[1] I have already said something about ethical relativism in discussing John Rawls' views about ethnocentrism, see Griffin, *On Human Rights*, section 1.5.

[2] Griffin, *On Human Rights*, ch. 6   [3] Griffin, *On Human Rights*, ch. 6.

[4] See David Hume, 'Of the Standard of Taste', in various collections of his essays.

[5] See Richard Brandt, *A Theory of the Good and the Right* (Oxford: Clarendon Press, 1979), 10.

remain for the reasons relativists give. In any case, our interest here is human rights. Are *they* relative to a framework?

How can one make a case for ethical relativism? The commonest way is to cite, with little in the way of argument, certain examples of particularly stubborn ethical disagreement, which are meant to leave one thinking that the best explanation of the disagreement is the relativist's. This is, of course, an extremely weak form of argument. Establishing the best explanation of stubborn ethical disagreements requires understanding all the possible origins of these conflicting beliefs and all the possible resources that might resolve the conflict—no quick or easy job. That the job is so difficult leaves many relativists, despite its inadequacy, doing no more than citing examples. Let me give a brief sampler of the examples that they have offered.

Some societies regard theft as a serious crime; others do not even have the concept of private property, on which the idea of 'theft' depends.[6] It is hardly obvious that relativism provides the best explanation of this difference. If one lives where food is plentiful without cultivation, there may be no pressure to develop an institution of private property. But if one's survival depends upon clearing land and shouldering the burdens of growing one's own food, some form of control over the land and the crop is highly likely to emerge. The best explanation may be difference not in ethical framework but in material conditions.

Some societies have tolerated infanticide; others condemn it.[7] But consider the extreme case of life-threatening poverty. Tolerance of infanticide is an adaptation that most of us would make if forced to it by the direst poverty: say, if one were faced with the awful choice between the survival of one's newborn baby or one's young child. A plausible explanation of the disagreement over infanticide between a society of such abject poverty and one better off may not be a difference in evaluative frameworks but, again, a difference in material conditions.

Many people are committed to preserving the environment; others see no objection to exploiting it.[8] This is a conflict that does indeed look irresolvable. To my mind, we can coherently talk about the value of the environment not just when changes in the environment affect human beings, say our health or enjoyment, but also apart from any effect on sentient life. The environment has a value in itself. The idea of the environment's being intrinsically valuable rests, I believe, on an idea of appropriateness of attitude. The only appropriate response to, say, the enormous age, biological complexity, and beauty of the Great Barrier Reef is wonder and awe. And wonder and awe prompt respect. There is something lacking in a person who does not have some such response. The wanton destruction of the Great Barrier Reef would be a monstrous act. Ethics, I should say, is broad enough to encompass standards not just of *right* and *wrong* but also of *appropriate* and *inappropriate*. Now, if the natives on an island in the Great Barrier Reef decide to improve their quality of life by mining, and

---

[6] This is one of Gilbert Harman's examples of relativity to an ethical framework; see his 'Moral Relativism', in Gilbert Harman and Judith Jarvis Thomson, *Moral Relativism and Moral Objectivity* (Oxford: Blackwell, 1996), 9.

[7] Also Gilbert Harman's example: Harman and Thomson, *Moral Relativism and Moral Objectivity*, 8–9.

[8] For the citation of incommensurable values as an example of moral relativity, see Maria Baghramian, *Relativism* (London: Routledge, 2004), ch. 9.

thereby destroying, the Reef, the apparent rational resolution of the conflict between the preservationists and the exploiters would be to weigh the costs and benefits to sentient creatures against the intrinsic value of the Reef. But that, I suspect, is a piece of weighing we cannot do. We must remember that some values may be incommensurable, in this sense of the term: two values are incommensurable if and only if they cannot be ranked against one another as 'greater than', 'less than', 'equal to', or 'roughly equal to'.[9] For a pair of values to be commensurable in this sense, there must be a bridging notion in terms of which the comparison between them can be made. For example, most, perhaps all, human interests, I should say, lend themselves to comparison. They do, not because there is a substantive super-value behind them, but because there is a formal value notion in terms of which we can, and regularly do, compare them: for example, 'prudential value', 'quality of life', or 'human interest' itself. We thus have the conceptual materials to judge that 'this would enhance the quality of my life more than that', 'this is a more major human interest than that', and so on. But sometimes—not often, I believe—two competing values are so different in nature from one another that there is no bridging notion available. In this conflict over the environment, for example, there is no bridging notion; comparison breaks down. This is indeed an intractable difference, but it does not derive from difference in ethical framework but from incommensurably different values. There is even a possible resolution of this disagreement: bringing both parties to see that the values they purport to commensurate are incommensurable.

A last example. Many of us think that abortion is prohibited; many others think that it is permitted.[10] Most often a person who holds that abortion is forbidden also holds background religious beliefs. But then is this, after all, an example of ethical relativity? Virtually all of us would accept that abortion is prohibited if we believed that an all-good, all-wise God had told us so. But with such a background, this intractable disagreement seems to have arisen not from different ethical frameworks but from different metaphysical beliefs. Perhaps, though, this just means that we should reconsider our definition of ethical relativism as relativity to a framework of basic *evaluations*. Evaluations cannot be sharply divided from empirical and metaphysical beliefs; our basic evaluations are what they are in part because of non-ethical beliefs. But if this truth is to support the relativity of a belief about the morality of abortion, it must be because of the further relativity of facts or of metaphysical conceptual schemes. Ethical relativity would then not stand alone. Although these further relativities seem much shakier than ethical relativity, perhaps that impression is mistaken.

Still, not all ethical disagreements about abortion arise from differences over religion. When they do not, what best explains the stubbornness of the divergence? No doubt, many different things. But one explanation that is hard to make plausible is that there are two different frameworks of fairly well-articulated and well-defined ethical

---

[9] For fuller treatment, see James Griffin, 'Mixing Values', *Proceedings of the Aristotelian Society*, suppl. vol. 65 (1991): 101–18; and James Griffin, 'Incommensurability: What's the Problem?', in Ruth Chang (ed.), *Incommensurability, Incomparability, and Practical Reason* (Cambridge, MA: Harvard University Press, 1997), 35–51.

[10] David B. Wong offers this as an example of what he would regard as ethical relativism; see his *Moral Relativity* (Berkeley: University of California Press, 1984), ch. 12, section 5.

beliefs producing this disagreement. That would make thought at this level far clearer and more inferential than it is. What might these ethical beliefs be? Nor is it plausible that these divergent beliefs about abortion are themselves basic ethical beliefs. They do not have quite that depth; they need justification themselves. What is more plausible, I should say, is that the framework for each of these conflicting views is a complex mix of ethical beliefs, factual beliefs, and sentiments. They might be beliefs such as 'A foetus is already a fully biologically formed potential person, as much so as a new-born baby' or 'An early foetus is too biologically primitive to be a person'. Or they might be sentiments such as revulsion at the very thought of killing a foetus or, on the contrary, equanimity in the face of it. But these beliefs are vague, and their implications for action by no means clear. And we should have to decide what weight to attach to these sentiments of revulsion or equanimity. What authority do they have?

My discussion of each of the four examples I have given is, I admit, inconclusive—neither decisively for nor against their relativity. But that is my point. One would have to dig much deeper before one could reach a satisfactory conclusion. Merely citing an example is no case at all. Let me now try to dig somewhat deeper in the example that primarily concerns us: human rights.

II. The Relativity of Human Rights

Human rights are suspected—by Westerners as much as by Easterners—of being relative to Western culture. Human rights are undoubtedly a Western product: introduced by Christians in the late Middle Ages and further developed there in the early modern period and in the seventeenth and eighteenth centuries.[11] They were part of the growth in individualism in that particular time and place; they were part of a new sense in Europe and the Americas of 'the dignity of man' and the great value of human autonomy and liberty.

But why think that human rights are, as well as a product of the West, also relative to the values of the West? One argument might be that the values from which human rights are derived—most prominently autonomy and liberty—are themselves peculiarly Western values. Some societies, it is true, value autonomy highly, seeing in it the peculiar dignity of the human person, while other societies value autonomy much less, seeing in it the threat of social atomism and the loss of solidarity and fraternity and of the harmony that comes from our all serving the same values. But anyone who thinks seriously about the value of our status as normative agents and the benefits of living in a cohesive fraternal community will recognize that both are highly important. And they will recognize the same about both others' having to respect our individuality and our having duties of concern and care for others. It may be that realizing certain of the values of individualism is incompatible with realizing certain of the values of community. But incompatibility of values is not their relativity. Besides, the frequency of the incompatibility is exaggerated. Not all forms of autonomy are the autonomy to which we attach great value.[12] I would display more autonomy, in one

---

[11] See Griffin, *On Human Rights*, sections 1.1 and 2.2.
[12] See Griffin, *On Human Rights*, sections 8.2 and 8.3.

correct use of the word, if I calculated my own income tax each year and decided for myself the plausibility of the Big Bang, instead of relying on the expertise of others. But neither of those is the autonomy to which we attach great value. What we attach great value to is the autonomy that is a constituent of normative agency, and relying on a tax accountant or an astrophysicist does not derogate in the least from one's normative agency. And the form of solidarity to which we attach such great value does not require surrendering our normative agency, though it may require greater trust in one another and greater convergence in public standards. The form of solidarity that is of great value is a joint commitment to the members of one's community and to the community's successful working. The plausible explanation of the fact that different societies rank autonomy and solidarity differently is not that they are rankings of the relativist sort. Everyone, on pain of mistake, has to admit that autonomy and solidarity are both highly valuable. No one would maintain that any loss in autonomy is worse than any loss in solidarity, or vice versa. And the more specific a choice between the two becomes—a certain loss of autonomy, say, to achieve a certain gain in solidarity—the more convergence in choice one will expect there to be. We do seem able, if only roughly, to compare these competing values.

A second argument for the relativity of human rights—indeed, an argument arising from my own account—is this. We have seen how certain moral judgements—for example, 'That's cruel'—could be derived from judgements about human interests—for example, 'That's painful'.[13]

The judgement 'That's cruel' goes so little beyond claims about pain, cause, and intention that it inherits the metaphysical and epistemic standing they have—standing as natural facts, I proposed. This suggests—merely suggests—that a human right (a moral standard) might similarly be derived from a certain human interest (a prudential value), again inheriting from it a sort of objectivity that would defeat the claim of relativity. Take the derivation of autonomy (the human right) from autonomy (the prudential value). But I also admitted that the derivation of still other human rights from human interests was less simple—for example, the right to life, which has an element of policy to it. The norm 'Don't deliberately kill the innocent', which is one of the correlative duties of the right to life, in part expresses a policy, and different societies might adopt different policies. Some human rights thus have a clear conventional element. Do they thereby have an element of relativity?

Take the right to autonomy. Once one recognizes the value of autonomy, one recognizes also a reason to be autonomous oneself and a reason not to deny other people their autonomy. Human rights are protections of one's personhood, and so protections of, among other things, one's capacity for and exercise of autonomy. Is the objective epistemic status of the judgement that autonomy is prudentially valuable transferred to the judgement that autonomy is a human right? We should ask: What more comes into the second judgement than is already present in the first? The obvious answer is: the first is a prudential judgement, the second a moral judgement. I find it very hard to understand the nature of the transition from prudence to morality, but, despite my uncertainty, I think that at least there is a kind of rationality to it. It is tempting

---

[13] See Griffin, *On Human Rights*, section 6.4.

to treat the reason-generating consideration that moves me when my autonomy is at stake as different from the one that moves me when yours is at stake. The obvious difference between these two cases is that in the one it is *my* autonomy, and in the other it is *yours*. But the most plausible understanding of the engine of these two judgements is *autonomy: because a person's quality of life is importantly at stake*. The *my* and *your* are not part of the reason-generating consideration. The clause *because a person's quality of life is importantly at stake* lacks reference to me or to you, but it lacks nothing of what we understand the reason to be. To try to deny 'autonomy' its status as a reason for action unless it is attached to 'my' would mean giving up our grasp on how 'autonomy' works as a reason for action.

Return now to my question: What more is present in the second judgement than is already contained in the first? There is, of course, whatever is added by calling autonomy a 'human right'. Many philosophers say that the judgement that something is a human right carries with it a claim that it has a particular moral importance: for example, it has the status of a 'trump' or a 'side-constraint'. But I have already argued several times against this characterization of human rights. They are neither trumps nor side constraints. They are not even the most important of rights. Autonomy—or, more generally, personhood—is not necessarily the most important human interest. Human rights make only an overrideable claim that a person's autonomy be given due respect—that is, the respect due to the sort of autonomy at stake in any particular case. And that much follows simply from autonomy's being a prudential value. It is true that to know that autonomy is a prudential value is also to know how valuable it is: that it is generally highly valuable to us, valuable enough to attract, as it has, special protection, but of varying value from case to case, and overrideable by other important values.

When I speak here of the 'derivation' of the human right to autonomy, I do not mean an entailment. I mean only that a reasonable person who recognizes the prudential value of autonomy will also recognize the respect that it is due. And the reasonableness of that transition is enough to deny a relativist a foothold here.

Another important qualification. The transition from prudence to morality is, of course, too complicated a matter to be dealt with as briskly as I have just done—so complicated that there is no point in my embarking on a few more brisk comments. I have discussed the subject more fully elsewhere, and will fall back on that.[14] So let me leave my brief sketch of the kind of rationality involved in the transition from prudence to morality as a kind of marker: I need a fuller argument at this point, but so too would a relativist who wants to resist the objective tendency of my line of thought.

Let me turn to the second example I mentioned: the human right to life. Does a relativist find a foothold at least here? There is, I said, an element of policy in this right. Such policies are, it is true, social artefacts. All that we can say, though, is that a different society might choose a *somewhat* different policy. There are strong constraints on the policies that can be chosen. The non-arbitrary determinants of the content of the policy are the prudential value of human life, facts about human nature, and facts about how societies work. The great value of life would lead nearly all societies to adopt severe restrictions on deliberately taking an innocent person's life, the severity

---

[14] James Griffin, *Value Judgement: Improving Our Ethical Beliefs* (Oxford: Clarendon Press, 1996), ch. V.

manifesting itself in reluctance to recognize many exceptions, especially, given what people are like, exceptions that cannot themselves be clearly enough limited or that have to rely on agent's being capable of highly subtle distinctions. Some societies may, even so, turn out to be relatively liberal about the restrictions, while others are relatively conservative. But that fact offers no appreciable support for relativity. If the convention adopted by one society could be seen to be working rather better than the convention of another, then there is strong rational ground for the second to adopt the convention of the first. If, as is common, we cannot tell whether any one convention is working better than the others, then no society would have good reason to resist an obvious solution to the divergence: agreement on a common convention. This sort of difference between societies represents not a different framework of basic evaluations but merely a highly constrained difference in a rational opting.

What may we conclude? I have carried my discussion both of the metaphysics of human rights and of their relativity only so far. I have not argued for the reality of prudential values, but only for their factuality: judgements about human interests, I concluded, can be true or false in the way that judgements about an ointment's being soothing can be. Here, I want to conclude that judgements about human interests and about human rights do not offer appreciably more scope for relativism than do judgements about natural facts. But I have already acknowledged[15] that one can be a relativist about natural facts—for example, the sort of comprehensive relativism that Wittgenstein is sometimes thought to hold: relativity to a form of life. The assessment of this radical form of relativism I again leave to others.[16]

III. What is the Problem of Ethnocentricity?

There are those who maintain that, even if ethical relativism were false, the problem of ethnocentricity would remain.[17]

What exactly *is* the problem of ethnocentricity? Perhaps it is this.[18] Human rights are, or are widely held to be, universally applicable. But if the only available justification for them is in Western terms, then they are not universally authoritative. If this were the problem, it would be overcome by establishing an objective justification of human rights authoritative for all rational beings. An objective justification of this sort would be sufficient, but perhaps not necessary. Certain forms of intersubjective justification might also do.

Still, if such an objective or intersubjective justification were forthcoming, a problem of ethnocentricity might even then remain. Such justification may be a long way

---

[15] See Griffin, *On Human Rights*, section 6.3.

[16] For a good recent assessment see Paul Boghossian, *Fear of Knowledge: Against Relativism and Constructivism* (New York: Oxford University Press, 2006).

[17] For Rawls on the need to avoid ethnocentrism, see his *The Law of Peoples* (hereinafter *LP*) (Cambridge, MA: Harvard University Press, 1999), section 17. 1, 'Law of Peoples not Ethnocentric'; also 68: 'To argue in these ways [ie largely the ways of the Enlightenment] would involve religious or philosophical doctrines that many decent hierarchical peoples might reject as liberal or democratic, or as in some way distinctive of Western political tradition and prejudicial to other cultures.'

[18] John Tasioulas adopts this interpretation in his 'International Law and the Limits of Fairness', *European Journal of International Law*, 13 (2002): 993–1023, section 2.

off, or may take some societies a long time to come around to, and the language of human rights is something that we use now and have reason to go on wanting to use now. Perhaps we need a case for human rights, or even a variety of cases, not made in what for many are alien Western terms. Perhaps we must still aim to avoid ethnocentricity.

But this does not follow. Hundreds of thousands of Westerners have adopted Asian religions, and not because they have managed to find Western metaphysical and ethical counterparts for these often culturally remote Asian beliefs, but, on the contrary, because they have looked into these religions on their own terms and been attracted by what they found. No one regards their Eastern origin as, in itself, an unscalable barrier. The alien can be baffling, but if this problem can be overcome by Westerners in the case of Eastern religions, why not Easterners in the case of the much more accessible Western human rights?

Full, definitive rational justification aside, there seem to me, as I said earlier,[19] to be two ways to bring about unforced agreement on human rights. One would be to put the case for human rights as best we can construct it from resources of the Western tradition, and hope that non-Westerners will look into the case and be attracted by what they find. The other would be to search the ethical beliefs of various non-Western societies for indigenous ideas that might provide a local case for human rights, or for something not unlike them. This search is a valuable component of the current debate about Asian values, and many writers have helpfully explored the conceptual resources of Islam, Buddhism, Confucianism, and so on to that end. At first glance it will seem that this second approach (let me call it the less ethnocentric approach) is clearly the better one simply because less ethnocentric. But on a longer look the first approach (let me call it the more ethnocentric approach) is, I want to propose, on balance, preferable.

We now, in these cosmopolitan times, tend to exaggerate the differences between societies; societies change faster than foreigners' pictures of them.[20] It is true that different parts of the world have sometimes had radically different histories, which still exert an influence on their vocabularies, their ways of thinking, their religions, their values. But the influences on the members of virtually all societies are now much more a mix of local and global than they were even a hundred years ago. Since then there has been a massive increase in global communication, convergence on economic structures, homogenization of ways of life due to growing prosperity, and widespread travel and study abroad precisely by the persons most likely to be influential in their society. Too many contemporary writers merely echo Rawls's belief that a pervasive and ineradicable feature of international life is a radical inter-society pluralism of conceptions of justice and the good. But Rawls's reasons for regarding these differences as ineradicable are difficult to find. We exaggerate, in particular, the disagreement between societies over human rights. Several Asian governments emphatically affirmed human rights in the Bangkok Declaration of 1993, though, it is true, also insisting that 'while human rights are universal in nature, they must be considered in

---

[19] See Griffin, *On Human Rights*, section 1.5.
[20] I discuss this more fully in Griffin, *On Human Rights*, sections 1.5 and 13.4.

the context of a dynamic and evolving process of international norm-setting, bearing in mind the significance of national and regional particularities and various historic, cultural and religious backgrounds'.[21] To declare that human rights are 'universal' but qualified by 'particularities' makes one alarmed about what that qualification will be used to justify. Still, there are loopholes in human rights themselves; no human right is absolute. Westerners themselves often contribute to the exaggeration of differences between East and West by exaggerating the strictness of the Western conception of human rights. Much of the flexibility and qualification in the Eastern conception is there, too, in theWestern conception, on an accurate account of it. There is a wide variety of conditions that outweigh or qualify human rights: for example, if the very survival of a good government is at stake, or if a large number of lives can be saved from terrorist attack.[22] And there is a great difference between possessing a freedom and its possession's being of value. This raises the question, also prompted by the Bangkok Declaration, whether social and economic rights have priority over civil and political rights. I myself think that the arguments go heavily against such a priority,[23] but these are all legitimate questions, as the United Nations Universal Declaration of Human Rights (UDHR) (1948) perhaps too amply acknowledged,[24] and they deserve serious answers. Still, these legitimate questions are raised by the 'particularities' not of Asian societies but of any society in certain circumstances of emergency, or at certain stages of development, or in facing certain ethical choices that we all face (for example, between the values of individualism and the values of community).

How might the less ethnocentric approach go today? An obvious move would be for members of each society to look for their own local understanding of what, according to the United Nations, is the ground of human rights—'the dignity of the human person'. One's local explanation of that idea need not repeat my explanation: namely, autonomy, liberty, and minimum provision. It might also include, for example, forms of justice and fairness and well-being that my account does not.[25] But there is a problem for this whole strategy for reducing ethnocentricity.

The less ethnocentric approach, on the present interpretation, would come down to finding local values similar to the Enlightenment values of autonomy, liberty, justice, fairness, and so on. It would look for local counterparts of whatever Western values back human rights. It would then have to rely on the indigenous population's seeing how valuable these values or close counterparts of them are, and how they can serve as the ground of human rights. But this is virtually what the more ethnocentric approach does. The less ethnocentric approach might, of course, aim for greater independence of the Western approach to human rights. It might look, not for local counterparts of Enlightenment values, but for possibly non-equivalent indigenous values that can serve as that society's own peculiar ground for human rights. The Western ground and various non-Western grounds might turn out to support pretty much the same list of human rights. The advantage, it might be thought, in indigenous

---

[21] Bangkok Declaration (1993), preamble and Articles 1, 8.

[22] See Griffin, *On Human Rights*, section 3.2.

[23.] For reasons given by, eg, Partha Dasgupta, *An Enquiry into Well-Being and Destitution* (Oxford: Clarendon Press, 1993), ch. 5.

[24] UDHR, Article 29.2.   [25] See Griffin, *On Human Rights*, section 2.9.

societies' aiming for independence of Western ideas, would be that they would then accept human rights discourse more readily. Global conversation in terms of human rights could start straightaway. The drawback, however, is that the conversation would be likely to break down early. A useful human rights discourse is not made possible just by agreeing on the *names* of the various rights, which is all that agreement on the list secures. We need also to be able to determine a fair amount of their content to know how to settle some of the conflicts between them. Think of how the international law of human rights would be constrained if it knew only their names. To know their content and ways to resolve their conflicts requires knowing what the values are that ground human rights and to reach some measure of agreement on them. That is, international law requires such knowledge if, as I shall argue later, international law aspires, and should aspire, to incorporate basic human rights with ethical weight. It is hard to tell how well the international community could scrape along, agreeing only on the names of human rights; perhaps we are not far from that position now, and the discourse of human rights has, none the less, had some undeniably good results. But we should be much better off if we could agree on the contents of human rights and how to resolve their conflicts. And that constitutes a strong case for favouring the more ethnocentric approach, if it were found feasible.

And it is feasible. The deepest cultural divide in history is not between the West and China (for example, Confucianism, leaving Buddhism aside as an Indian import), and certainly not the West and Islam (Islam is an Abrahamic religion), but the West and India (Hinduism and Buddhist). The West aims at progress, at the growing achievement of the goods of human life; Hinduism at timeless, changeless being. Westerners see understanding as largely analytic—breaking things down into parts and discovering their interaction; for Hindu metaphysicians knowledge is an intuition of an indivisible whole, and differences between things are illusory. Westerners regard knowledge, in large part, as knowledge of the behaviour of external objects, as in paradigmatically that largely Western achievement, the natural sciences; in contrast, Hindus regard reality as a distinctionless, entirely static *nirvana*. And so on.[26]

But this deep cultural difference is not evidence of a serious current 'problem of ethnocentricity'. It is perfectly proper to use the word 'culture' in this context. The differences between the West and India go far back: the European idea of human rights goes back to the late Middle Ages, and the idea that human beings are made in God's image goes back to Genesis 1: 27. The Buddha was born about 563; Hinduism emerged centuries before that. Each of these religions developed at a time when Europe and India were sufficiently isolated for there to be criteria of identity for their 'cultures'. But our problem of ethnocentricity, we must take account of where each of us is *now*.

Also, the ultimate religious ideals are usually considerably different from, and far less influential in ordinary life than, the rules for everyday conduct that they also teach. Buddhism tells us to extinguish the self, but it also has rules for the whole pack of squabbling, thieving, lying ordinary people. Buddhism has its Five Precepts: do not kill, do not steal, do not lie, do not be unchaste, do not drink intoxicants. Jesus

---

[26] These contrasts are more fully drawn out by Archie J. Bahm, *Comparative Philosophy: Western, Indian and Chinese Philosophies Compared* (Albuquerque: World Books, revised 1995), esp. ch. III.

set unattainable standards: be ye therefore perfect; love thy neighbour as thyself. But Christianity never abandoned the down-to-earth Jewish Ten Commandments: thou shalt not steal, nor commit adultery, etc. So, though Indians may have heard occasionally about ultimate goals and ultimate reality, most of them, like most of the rest of humanity, lived their lives well this side of the 'ultimate'.

The picture of India as spiritual, mystical, anti-rational, in sharp contrast to a West of science, rationality, and progress, is a gross oversimplification. It became, none the less, the dominant European picture of India, not least because it was a self-serving picture for European colonists in need of a justification for their presumptuous civilizing mission. But, as Amartya Sen and others have shown, India has a long tradition of secular rationality, scientific investigation, and freedom of thought. It goes back at least to Ashoka, Buddhist Emperor of India in the third century BC, and to the late medieval and early modern period—a striking example given by Sen is the liberal thought of Akbar, the late sixteenth-century Mughal emperor of India.[27] And these rational, liberal ideas spread widely among a middle-class elite during the nineteenth and twentieth centuries.

When Indians came in contact with the development of the natural sciences of the West, they had no trouble whatever, despite reality's being unchanging, understanding and contributing to the laws of its change. Similarly, when Indians campaigned for their independence from Britain, they had no trouble at all, despite autonomy's and liberty's being illusions, articulating what their aims were. When they were told by the British that they were not yet ready for self-government, that they would make mistakes, Gandhi replied: 'Freedom is not worth having if it does not include the freedom to make mistakes.'[28] It may well be the case that the Hindu tradition, with its caste structure as the source of rights and privileges, contains no concept of the rights one has simply in virtue of being human.[29] It may also be the case that the Buddhist tradition, with its focus on perfecting the individual through meditation and insight rather than on improving society, also lacks the concept.[30] But this does not matter. The Hindus (and Muslims) who made up India at Independence seem to have had no trouble grasping the values of liberty and autonomy, and their Constitution (1950) puts beyond doubt that they had no trouble handling the language of human rights.[31]

---

[27] Amartya Sen, *The Argumentative Indian: Writings on Indian History, Culture, and Identity* (Harmondsworth: Allen Lane, The Penguin Press, 2005), esp. chs. 1, 4, 13.

[28] http://www.quotationspage.com, *sub* Mahatma Gandhi.

[29] Jack Donnelly thinks so; see his article 'Traditional Values and Universal Human Rights: Caste in India', in Claude E. Welch Jr. and Virginia A. Leary (eds.), *Asian Perspective on Human Rights* (Boulder, CO: Westview Press, 1990). This question is discussed by Harold Coward, *The Hindu Tradition*, vol. 4 of William H. Brackney (series ed.), *Human Rights and the World's Major Religions* (Westport, CT: Praeger, 2005).

[30] Robert E. Florida thinks so; see his book *The Buddhist Tradition*, vol. 5 of Brackney (series ed.), *Human Rights and the World's Major Religions*, see 9, 205ff.

[31] Part III of the Constitution is devoted to 'fundamental rights', which include guarantees of equality before the law (Article 14), no discrimination on grounds of religion, race, caste, sex, or place or birth (Article 15), freedom of speech and expression, assembly, association, movement, and residence (Article 19), freedom of religion (Articles 25–28), and rights to life, personal liberty (Article 21), and due process (Article 22). What is more, the Indian drafters took Western constitutional practice as a model. See Pratap Kumar Ghosh, *The Constitution of India: How It Has Been Framed* (Calcutta: World Press, 1966), 70: 'The framers of our [Indian] Constitution shared the American view [viz. Jefferson's view that a democratic constitution should include a bill of rights] and, therefore, incorporated in our Constitution a

And Aung San Suu Kyi, the determined human rights advocate in next-door Burma, regards human rights as consistent with and as developing Buddhist teaching.[32]

The case of India and the West reveals no serious, present-day divergence in understanding what human rights are and why they are important.[33]

IV. Tolerance

I have already discussed John Rawls's views on human rights.[34] I want now to look at what he says about tolerance between peoples. There may be 'decent' peoples, as Rawls calls them,[35] who reject some of the items on the Enlightenment list of human rights.

---

list of fundamental rights'; also M. V. Pylee, *India's Constitution* (Bombay: Asia Publishing House, 1962), 3: 'The makers of the Indian Constitution draw much from the American Constitution though not its brevity…Thus the Constitution of India is the result of considerable imitation and adaptation…'.

[32] See Florida, *Buddhist Tradition*, 209.

[33] Nor, I believe, does the case of Islam and the West. In cultural terms Islam is very much closer to the Jewish–Christian West than is India. Islam accepts the Old and New Testaments as among its own holy scriptures, and the prophets, including Jesus, as its prophets, too. In philosophy, Islam was deeply influenced by the writings of Classical Greece and Rome. In mathematics and the natural sciences, Islam was often well ahead of Europe during the Middle Ages. In social thought, Muhammad, by being more detailed than Jesus in his moral teaching and more specific about the desired social order, was in many ways also more explicitly egalitarian. The Koran prescribes a Poor Due, a two-and-a-half per cent tax on the rich to aid the poor. This may look meagre alongside the tithe of Jews and Christians, but the two taxes are quite different: the tithe was devoted more to the maintenance of religious institutions than, as with the Poor Due, to direct help for the poor, and the two-and-a-half per cent was levied not just on one's income but also on one's holdings. (See Huston Smith, *The World's Religions* (San Francisco: Harper, 1991), 246, 250.) And there was often more freedom of religion in Islam than in the West. 'Let there be no compulsion in religion', says the Koran (2: 257; see also 5: 48). When the Catholics conquered Andalusia, where the Muslims had for long tolerated Jews and Christians, they expelled, slaughtered, or forced Muslims and Jews to convert. When the Muslims conquered Constantinople, they allowed the Eastern Catholic Church to carry on much as before, and Constantinople (Istanbul) is still today its seat. On Muslim tolerance of other religions, see Bernard Lewis, *The Crisis of Islam* (New York: Random House, 2004), xxix–xxx. I go through this recital so quickly because the facts are familiar. One would have no more trouble discussing autonomy, liberty, and minimum provision with many modern Muslims than one would with many modern Indians. Not with all Muslims, admittedly; not clearly, eg, with the Taliban of Afghanistan. Different Muslims draw very different lessons from the Koran. The Koran seems to teach very different lessons, from rare tolerance of non-believers, as above, to bloodthirsty intolerance, as in the famous 'verse of the sword': 'Fight and slay the pagans wherever you find them: seize them, beleaguer them, and lie in wait for them in every stratagem.' But differences within a cultural group are not, of course, differences between cultural groups. The term 'fundamentalism' acquired its present sense used of conservative Protestant evangelicals in the United States in the 1920s, and its contemporary Eastern and Western versions probably have causes in common: perhaps a desperation resulting from a fear that the modern world is inexorably leaving them behind. (See Malise Ruthven, *Fundamentalism: The Search for Meaning* (Oxford: Oxford University Press, 2004), 10–15.) But there are, no doubt, causes special to Islam: a history of colonial exploitation, poverty, lack of education, the legacy of the Crusades and of the Ottoman penetration into Europe culminating in the second siege of Vienna in the late seventeenth century. And part of the explanation of the tension between the West and Muslim Middle East must be simply that they are next-door neighbours—geographical proximity rather than cultural distance. Think of the Protestants and Catholics in Ulster. The record of democracy in the Islamic world is varied, encompassing as it does North and Middle Africa, Turkey, the Middle East, the Indian sub-continent, South-East Asia, and Indonesia. But much the same political variation can be found in Latin America, where the explanation is unlikely to be cultural difference from Europe. Economic structures must play an important part in explaining the political structures of both Islam and Latin America. All that I want to deny is that cultural differences between Islam and the West are largely responsible for their political differences. They play a role, but so does much else.

[34] See Griffin, *On Human Rights*, section 1.5.   [35] *LP*, 61–7.

Some rights may be contrary to deep, sincerely held commitments of theirs—religious beliefs, say, about the role of women. So long as a people counts as 'decent', however, it deserves our tolerance. 'To tolerate', Rawls says, 'means not only to refrain from exercising political sanctions...to make a people change its ways', but also 'to recognize these non-liberal societies as equal participating members in good standing of the Society of Peoples.'[36] Granting decent, non-liberal peoples this form of respect may encourage them to reform themselves, or at least not discourage reform, while denying them respect might well do so.[37] But there is also a non-instrumental reason to grant them respect: it is their due.

Rawls takes as his example of a decent, non-liberal people an imaginary hierarchical Islamic society, Kazanistan.[38] He attributes the difference in political structure between Kazanistan and a Western liberal country largely to their cultural, particularly religious, differences. For the reasons just given, this seems to me highly doubtful. Rawls's question about tolerance, though, need not be motivated by cultural differences. A decent hierarchical people, according to Rawls, has two defining properties. One is that such a people does not have aggressive aims. The other is that its system of law secures human rights for all, imposes genuine moral obligations upon its members, and its legal officials sincerely and not unreasonably believe that the law is guided by a common good conception of justice.[39] Recall, though, that Rawls substantially shortens the list of human rights and reduces their function.[40] His list omits such typical human rights as freedom of expression, freedom of association (except for the limited form needed for freedom of conscience and religious observance), the right to democratic political participation, and any economic rights that go beyond mere subsistence. And he reduces human rights to two functions: fixing both the rules of war and the grounds for international intervention.

A great obstacle to our accepting Rawls's shortened list of human rights—especially if, like Rawls, we want a list with a realistic chance of being adopted—is that it would never be accepted by the international community. The United Nations' list of human rights is too deeply entrenched for it to be changed quite so greatly. It could no doubt be amended here and there, but not subjected to Rawls's radical surgery at its very heart. The international community would firmly resist the reduction of the discourse of human rights to Rawls's two functions only; it would carry on using human rights to assess the behaviour of a single nation and institutions within a nation; and many of us, I believe, would go on using them to assess even the conduct of individual persons. Rawls, it is true, does not deny that the rights he drops from the list could appear among a people's 'fundamental' or 'international' rights. They are not, though, human rights proper, he says; they are merely 'liberal aspirations'.[41] But this is a radical demotion in their status, and it is this demotion that would be resisted. That raises a question about a strong, unexamined assumption of Rawls's. 'I leave aside', he says, 'the many difficulties of interpreting...rights and limits, and take their general meaning and tendency as clear enough.'[42] There is, of course, some clarity to them; they are not nonsense. But my first chapter was devoted to arguing that there is an intolerable

---

[36] *LP*, 59.   [37] *LP*, 62.   [38] *LP*, 5, 75–8.   [39] *LP*, 64–7.
[40] See Griffin, *On Human Rights*, section 1.5.   [41] *LP*, 80 fn 23.   [42] *LP*, 27.

degree of indeterminacy of sense in what a human right is—an indeterminacy that leaves unclear the criteria both for what should be on the list of human rights and, even more worryingly, what the contents of the individual rights are. This applies also to all the rights on Rawls's own shortened list: for example, the rights to life, liberty, health, and welfare, each of which I shall come to later.[43] We can make our understanding of these rights adequate for our own thought only with the addition of some further substantive value. It need not be my addition, only *some* addition. Once the value is added, however, it will determine which human rights there are, and they can then be restricted in the arbitrary way that Rawls chooses to do.

There is another worry. There are grounds for intervention that are not violations of human rights. I argued earlier that the domains of human rights and of justice overlap, but are not congruent.[44] Some matters of justice—for example, certain forms of retributive and distributive justice—are not matters of human rights. Imagine, for instance, a country structured socially so that nearly all of its great prosperity goes to a small white colonial elite, leaving the mass of the black native population just at subsistence level. If this gross injustice were also likely to persist for some time, diplomatic or economic sanctions might well be justified. Think of a country somewhat like South Africa under apartheid, but with a decent consultation hierarchy that works well enough to raise the poor to subsistence level but not higher. So far as his theory goes, Rawls is free to amend it to say that serious violation of human rights is sufficient, but not necessary, to justify intervention, and that certain violations of justice (and perhaps yet more) are also sufficient. Actually, Rawls treats observance of human rights as definitive of a decent hierarchical society, without mention of retributive or distributive justice.[45] Admittedly, he does mention as also definitive the possession of 'a common good conception of justice',[46] but it is doubtful that this requires acceptance of a principle for distribution of welfare at fairly high levels.[47] Rawls cannot believe that a common good conception requires a society to raise its members above subsistence level, because a decent hierarchical society need not do more than that. My example of the South Africa-like country raises doubts that subsistence level is high enough. A satisfactory case that the level must be higher than subsistence is likely to make appeal to something especially valuable about human status that will not be protected by mere subsistence, and once that special value starts generating rights, no arbitrary stopping points are allowable.

The serious weakness in Rawls's functional explanation of human rights is that it leaves the content of his shortened list—the content both of the list itself and of each individual right—unworkably obscure. How do we determine, for example, the minimum of welfare required by human rights? If one has a further substantive value to appeal to—say, the value attaching to normative agency—then the minimum would be the somewhat more generous provision of what is necessary to function effectively as a normative agent. But it looks as if Rawls could, if he wanted, avail himself of an altogether different approach to fix the minimum. He could ask: at what level of welfare would its neglect start to provide prima facie justification for intervention by

---

[43] See Griffin, *On Human Rights*, chs 8, 9, 11.   [44] See Griffin, *On Human Rights*, section 2.6.
[45] *LP*, 65–7.   [46] *LP*, 65.   [47] *LP*, 88.

other peoples? But confronted with that question, we would not know how to answer. We should need help from some further substantive ethical thought. We might, for instance, appeal to the idea of 'the dignity of the human person', but that suffers badly from vagueness. We should lose the dignity of our normative agency, for instance, before we sank as low as mere subsistence. Subsistence that forced us to labour all our waking hours just to scratch out an existence from the earth, without leisure, reflection, or hope, brutalized by our conditions, would lack the dignity of normative agency. So, if this were our line of thought, we should still need to determine what sort of 'dignity' is at work in human rights. In any case, Rawls does not seem to avail himself of this approach. Instead, as we have just seen, he assumes that 'the general meaning and tendency' of human rights are already 'clear enough'. But, as I have argued, they are not.

I am not trying here to make a contribution of my own to the understanding of tolerance, important though that matter is. My interest now is human rights, and my conclusion negative. We should not follow Rawls's lead in commandeering the language of human rights to explain intervention. The language that he can provide is too indeterminate in sense to do so, and, once its sense is made more satisfactorily determinate, it will contain what is needed to justify the ampler list of human rights that, for so long, the tradition has championed.

32

Human Needs, Human Rights*

Massimo Renzo

I. Human Rights: Naturalistic and Political Conceptions

The language of human rights has become the main currency in which all the most important issues of international justice are normally cashed out. The need to protect human rights is invoked, among other things, to defend the legitimacy of military intervention, to justify the institution of international courts and tribunals, and to assess the eligibility of countries to be part of international agreements or to receive aid they desperately need. The role played by human rights at the domestic level tends to get less attention, but is equally significant. All of the most important human rights are embodied in domestic law, and states bear primary responsibility for their protection and their enforcement. Indeed, according to many, it is precisely the task of protecting and enforcing human rights that ultimately justifies whatever authority states have.[1]

A notion that plays such a pervasive role both at the domestic and at the international level is in need of justification, and to this task philosophers have turned in recent years. Initially, the obvious move in explaining what human rights are and what justifies their existence has been to look at the natural law tradition, and in particular at the notion of natural rights: rights that all human beings possess simply in virtue of their human nature.[2] The crucial element of this "naturalistic" approach, whose root can be found in the thought of Grotius, Pufendorf, and Locke, is the claim that human rights are entitlements that every human being has against every other human being, independently of the existence of institutional arrangements or specific practices.

Although the specific form that human rights will take in different socio-historical contexts might change depending on the institutional background within which they are invoked (which explains why, for example, the human right to education in Ancient Greece takes a different form than the human right to education in Britain today), there is a set of abstractly defined human rights (for example, the human right

* I am grateful to Simon Caney, Rowan Cruft, Luara Ferracioli, Simon Hope, Matthew Liao, Saladin Meckled-Garcia, and Matthew Noah-Smith for very helpful comments, Thanks also to audiences at CAPPE, King's College London, Oxford, Warwick and the 2013 *Priority in Practice* conference at UCL for stimulating discussions.

¹ Allen Buchanan, *Justice, Legitimacy, and Self-Determination: Moral Foundations for International Law* (New York: Oxford University Press, 2007); Andrew Altman and Christopher Heath Wellman, *A Liberal Theory of International Justice* (Oxford: Oxford University Press, 2011).

² Thomas Pogge, *World Poverty and Human Rights: Cosmopolitan Responsibilities and Reforms* (Cambridge; Malden, MA: Polity, 2002), 60–5; John Tasioulas, "On the Nature of Human Rights," in G. Ernst and J.-C. Heilinger (eds.), *The Philosophy of Human Rights: Contemporary Controversies* (Berlin/Boston: de Gruyter, 2012), 17–59.

to education) that all human beings have independently of their being part of any institution or of their being involved in particular social practices.[3]

The naturalistic view, however, has been criticized for two reasons: first, the view is said to ignore the political dimension of human rights. In recent years, many have argued that human rights are primarily claims that we have against officials and members of particular institutional structures, in virtue of the fact that we are subject to their authority. These rights do not exist outside of this institutional context. Indeed, their function according to some of the defenders of this view (often referred to as the "political conception of human rights"), is precisely to mark the limits of political authorities by setting the conditions of their internal legitimacy (ie, states' right to impose obligations on their subjects) or external legitimacy (ie, states' right against interference with their sovereignty).[4]

The second problem with the naturalistic conception of human rights is that it invites the objection that human rights are parochial constructions, insofar as they seem to ultimately rely on controversial metaphysical and moral assumptions about human nature that are not acceptable to non-Western cultures. This worry has accompanied the debate on human rights since its very beginning. The year before the adoption of the Universal Declaration of Human Rights (UDHR), a "Statement on Human Rights" was prepared by the American Anthropological Association for the UN Commission on Human Rights, which was drafting the Declaration. One of the questions raised in the Statement was: "How can the proposed Declaration be applicable to all human beings, and not be a statement of rights conceived only in terms of the values prevalent in the countries of Western Europe and America?"[5] The problems encountered by naturalistic conceptions in answering this question are one of the reasons why some philosophers have moved toward a political account of human rights.[6]

The first objection can, I think, be resisted quite easily. It is not clear why naturalistic conceptions would have a problem in acknowledging the important political functions that human rights play as triggers for international intervention or standards of political legitimacy. The question, however, is *why* we should think that human rights perform such a role: Why should we think that those states that violate or fail to fulfil human rights, lose their right to rule, or at least their right against being interfered with by other states? This is something that political conceptions of human rights simply postulate, but that naturalistic conceptions can actually explain. It is because human rights constitute important normative protections we are endowed

---

[3] James Griffin, *On Human Rights* (Oxford: Oxford University Press, 2008), 149; Carl Wellman, *The Moral Dimensions of Human Rights* (New York: Oxford University Press, 2011), 28; but see Tasioulas, "On the Nature of Human Rights," pp. 31–6, for a criticism of this way to understand the idea that human rights are natural.

[4] John Rawls, *The Law of Peoples* (Cambridge, Mass.: Harvard Univ. Press, 2002); Charles R. Beitz, *The Idea of Human Rights* (New York: Oxford University Press, 2009); Joshua Cohen, *The Arc of the Moral Universe and Other Essays* (Cambridge, MA: Harvard University Press, 2010), chs. 9–10; Joseph Raz, "Human Rights without Foundations," in Samantha Besson and John Tasioulas (eds.), *The Philosophy of International Law* (Oxford: Oxford University Press, 2010), 321–38, and "Human Rights in the Emerging World Order," this volume, ch. 11. I borrow the distinction between "naturalistic" and "political" conceptions of human rights from Beitz.

[5] "Statement on Human Rights," *American Anthropologist*, 49 [1947]: 53.

[6] Rawls, *The Law of Peoples*, 68.

with independently of our membership in political or social institutions, that they can constrain the way in which political institutions operate in the way indicated by the political conception.[7]

Whereas other claims of justice can be made only against the backdrop of the existence of particular institutions, human rights constitute claims that we are entitled to insist upon regardless of any institutional membership. These claims are not created by states, but pre-exist them. And it is because they do so that they contribute to establishing the legitimacy of states by specifying the limits within which states can operate if they are to retain their authority.

Naturalistic conceptions however, have their own problems. To begin with, they need to provide a convincing account of the features of human beings that justify the existence of human rights. If they fail to do so, the move toward a political justification seems more compelling. Moreover, naturalistic conceptions should provide an account of the features of human beings that justify human rights while resisting the second objection raised earlier, namely that of being parochial constructions. For one feature of human rights that is taken to be uncontroversial is their universality, and we could not account for this feature if human rights turned out to be tied to a specific moral or cultural point of view.[8]

The aim of this paper is to outline an account that meets these two desiderata, ie, a naturalistic conception of human rights that is capable of resisting the objection of parochialism. I start by considering James Griffin's attempt to ground human rights in normative agency. I raise two objections against his view and argue that we should abandon it in favour of a needs-based justification of human rights. I then articulate what I call the "basic needs approach" to the justification of human rights, and show how this approach can address the parochialism objection.

II. Human Rights and Normative Agency

One of the strengths of naturalistic approaches is that they are better placed than political approaches to make sense of the link between human rights and human dignity, a link that is explicitly affirmed in many of the most important human rights documents. For example, the preamble of the UDHR refers to the "inherent dignity and…equal and inalienable rights of all members of the human family" and to the fact that "[a]ll human beings are born free and equal in dignity and rights." The International Covenant on Civil and Political Rights (ICCPR) and the International Covenant on Economic, Social and Cultural Rights (ICESCR) go further and explicitly acknowledge that human rights "*derive* from the inherent dignity of the human person,"[9] as does the Vienna Declaration.[10]

These formulations seem to ground the existence of human rights in human dignity, where the latter is understood as something that belongs to all and only human

---

[7] I develop this argument in Massimo Renzo, "Human Rights and the Priority of the Moral," *Social Philosophy and Policy*, forthcoming.

[8] Rawls, *The Law of Peoples*, 68.   [9] Emphasis added.

[10] The preamble of the Vienna Declaration states that "all human rights derive from the dignity and worth inherent in the human person."

beings in virtue of certain features they possess (their being human or, as the UDHR puts it, their belonging to "the human family"). Moreover, the preamble of the UDHR explicitly acknowledges the existence of pre-existing moral rights that all human beings have, *qua* human beings. The function of the Declaration is to "recognize" these rights and "promote [their] respect."

Historical accounts of the drafting of the UDHR seem to confirm this picture. Johannes Morsink's influential reconstruction, for example, stresses that the drafters took themselves as formulating a list of moral rights possessed by human beings as such, to which legal recognition would have to be given in the future.[11] Maritain's famous remark that the drafters could agree on the rights only "on condition no one asks us why" is sometimes quoted in support of the view that human rights cannot be justified by appealing to the sort of moral rights invoked by naturalistic accounts, but this is a mistake. The fact that the drafters decided not to appeal to a particular moral justification of human rights in drafting the Declaration does not mean that they did not think such justification was available and that it was ultimately this justification that validated the list of human rights on which they converged. Maritain himself, while advocating the need to pursue practical agreement on the rights to be included in the declaration, firmly believed that human rights were ultimately grounded in what he considered to be inalienable natural rights.[12]

The mere appeal to the notion of "human dignity," however, is too vague to do any substantive justificatory work, unless we explain in what sense human rights protect human dignity. Griffin's theory does this by invoking the idea of "personhood" or "normative agency." His argument is straightforward: in order to find out what the distinctive features of humanity are, we need to look at those features that distinguish human life from the life of non-human animals. These features, according to Griffin, have to do with our capacity to form pictures of what a good life is and to pursue the conception of the good life that we have chosen for ourselves. Thus, it is in these terms that we should understand the notion of human dignity. Having human dignity is having the capacity to choose what to do with our life and to successfully pursue the plan of life we have chosen. Human rights protect this capacity, because whatever threatens this capacity threatens the very possibility to live a "human" life.[13]

The capacity to have a human life for Griffin is thus tied to our capacity to act as autonomous moral agents. In particular, three conditions must be fulfilled for us to qualify as normative agents: first, we must be able to choose what to do with our life; second, we must have sufficient resources available to pursue the path that we have chosen; third, we must not be prevented from pursuing the path we have chosen. The protection afforded to us by human rights serves the function of favouring the fulfilment of these conditions for all human beings.

Griffin's view has been extremely influential and much has been written about each of these components.[14] For the purposes of this paper I want to focus on the first one,

---

[11] Johannes Morsink, *The Universal Declaration of Human Rights: Origins, Drafting, and Intent* (Philadelphia: University of Pennsylvania Press, 1999).

[12] Jaques Maritain, "On the Philosophy of Human Rights," in *Human Rights, Comments and Interpretations*, ed. UNESCO (New York: A. Wingate, 1949).

[13] Griffin, *On Human Rights*, 31–3.

[14] John Tasioulas, "Human Rights, Universality and the Values of Personhood: Retracing Griffin's Steps," *European Journal of Philosophy*, 10(1) (2002): 79–100; John Gardner, "'Simply in Virtue of Being

as it is here that the link between human dignity and the capacity to act as autonomous agents is made. Should we follow Griffin in using this link as a ground for the justification of human rights? One problem with this view is that it has the unappealing implication that children, the severely mentally disabled, and individuals suffering from advanced dementia cannot be said to have human rights. Given that these subjects do not have the capacity for normative agency, they cannot enjoy those rights whose justification consists in protecting normative agency.[15]

At first sight this might sound like a *reductio* of Griffin's view, but we should be careful not to overstate the force of this objection. Saying that children, the severely mentally disabled or individuals suffering from dementia do not have a human right, say, not to be tortured is not saying that there would be nothing wrong with torturing them. In fact, it's not even to say that they don't have a *moral* right not to be tortured. As Griffin correctly points out, we should resist the temptation to turn every important moral consideration into a consideration of human rights. The capacity of children or the severely mentally disabled to suffer imposes on us a powerful obligation to refrain from torturing them, and possibly also grounds a moral right on their part not to be tortured. Griffin's point is simply that these subjects do not have a *human* right not to be tortured, since a human right not to be tortured, like all human rights, protects our capacity to exercise normative agency, which children and the severely mentally disabled do not possess.[16]

But even so qualified, Griffin's position seems unpalatable. There certainly is a sense in which the wrong committed when we murder or torture someone capable of rational agency is different from the wrong committed when we torture or murder someone who is not. In the former case we are thwarting the capacity of the victim to set ends for herself and plan how to achieve those ends, whereas in the latter we are not. And yet it seems that when we say that this sort of behaviour is incompatible with the respect that we owe the victim *qua* human being, we are not referring to this. When we say that murdering or torturing someone is incompatible with the respect that we owe the victim *qua* human being we are referring to a sort of disrespect that does not depend on whether our conduct will thwart her capacity to act as a normative agent. The sort of disrespect for our common humanity that we are invoking when we blame the torturer is the same, whether his victim is a fully rational agent, a child or someone in the advanced stage of senile dementia. If we think that this reaction is appropriate, we should reject Griffin's view, despite its ability to accommodate the thought that we are under an obligation not to torture or murder children or the severely mentally disabled. For this is not enough to bring his view in line with our considered judgment about who the bearers of human rights are.

Notice that this objection does not challenge Griffin's view only at its margins. The problem is not whether and how his view can accommodate some non-central cases. The objection goes right to the heart of Griffin's account, in that it challenges the claim

---

Human': The Whos and Whys of Human Rights," *Journal of Ethics and Social Philosophy*, 2 (2008): 1–22; Roger Crisp (ed.), *Griffin On Human Rights*, forthcoming. See also the "Symposium on James Griffin's *On Human Rights*," *Ethics*, 120 (2010), with papers by John Tasioulas, Allen Buchanan, and Rainer Forst, and a response by Griffin.

[15] Griffin, *On Human Rights*, ch. 4.

[16] Griffin, *On Human Rights*, 85. I should make clear that Griffin does not commit to the claim that children or the severely mentally disabled have moral rights. I am simply noticing that his argument leaves this option available to him.

that normative agency is the right notion to invoke in order to explain what it is to have human dignity. If we think that the relevant sense in which someone's humanity is disrespected when she is tortured, murdered or raped is the same in the case of children or the mentally disabled as well as in the case of rational agents, we have reasons to look for a different conception of humanity on which to ground the notion of human rights. Particularly so if, like Griffin, we believe that in constructing an adequate account of human rights we need to aim not only at correctness but also at achieving a substantive and durable agreement. Griffin plausibly introduces this condition as necessary in order to produce a theory of human rights that will have a "fighting chance" to be adopted and make a practical difference.[17] A theory that excludes children, the mentally disabled, and people affected by senile dementia from the class of human rights bearer does not seem to have such a chance.

More generally, the objection here is that Griffin's view fails to account for the widely shared idea that human rights are universal, in the sense that they are possessed by all *human beings*.[18] What his view vindicates is rather the different claim that human rights are possessed only by a subset of the group of human beings: the group of *persons* (or rational agents). To the extent that universality is an important feature of an adequate account of human rights, we should resist theories that fail to account for it.

In the next section I suggest that a better candidate for grounding our conception of humanity is the notion of human needs. Before I do that however, let me introduce a second problem for Griffin's view, namely the difficulties it encounters in resisting the objection of parochialism. Grounding the notion of humanity in the capacity to act as autonomous agents makes Griffin's theory particularly appealing to members of liberal societies, whose social and political structures are largely organized around the importance of this value, but inevitably exposes the theory to the objection of being founded on a particular conception of the good, one that members of non-liberal societies could reasonably reject. If so, it looks as if human rights cannot be defended as universal moral standards and can be criticized as the expression of a particular set of values and impugned as a manifestation of a form of "Western cultural imperialism."

Griffin's main reply to this objection seems to be that any morality that does not acknowledge the importance of moral autonomy should be rejected, since "[a]nyone who thinks seriously about the value of our status as normative agents...will recognize that...[it is] highly important."[19] But even if we were to grant this, his view would still be problematic insofar as it commits us to the conclusion that those who lead their lives according to non-liberal moralities do not have a properly *human* life. This is because to the extent that these individuals follow moralities that are structured around the authority of tradition or the value of certain forms of community, rather than around the importance of moral autonomy, they fail to have the sort of agency that, according to Griffin, is necessary to have a properly human life. But

---

[17] James Griffin, "Human Rights: Questions of Aim and Approach," *Ethics*, 120 (2010): 746, 749–50.

[18] At least all human beings living within the same historical context (Raz, "Human Rights in the Emerging World Order," this volume, ch. 11).

[19] Griffin, *On Human Rights*, 133.

this view seems implausible. Even if we think that there are reasons to reject these moralities, surely saying that those who fail to do so lack a properly human life goes too far.[20]

III. Human Needs, Human Rights

Human rights are particularly strong normative protections. In fact, they are probably the strongest normative protections afforded within our current moral and political frameworks. Although they are not absolute (we can imagine situations in which competing normative concerns are sufficiently weighty to justify their violation), human rights are nonetheless so strong that they can be overridden only by particularly weighty considerations. This is why a plausible naturalistic account of human rights will have to ground them in especially important human interests.

Our interest in acting as autonomous agents might at first seem like a plausible candidate, but should ultimately be rejected because autonomy-based theories of human rights fail to meet the two desiderata identified earlier, ie, providing a convincing account of the features of human beings that justify human rights, while resisting the parochialism objection. Autonomy-based theories fail to meet the first desideratum because our considered judgment does not seem to tie the possession of human rights to the capacity to act as autonomous agents. They fail to meet the second because the value of autonomy depends on the adoption of a conception of the good that can be reasonably rejected by non-liberal moralities.[21]

An adequate theory of human rights will thus have to provide a more inclusive account, one capable of accommodating our considered judgment that children, the severely mentally disabled, and individuals suffering from advanced dementia also possess human rights, while at the same time relying on some feature of humanity whose value cannot be reasonably rejected by non-liberal moralities. The best candidate, I will suggest, is the idea of human needs.[22]

---

[20] A second argument Griffin offers against the parochialism objection is based on the idea that prudential judgments about human welfare presuppose the existence of a shared conceptual scheme that ultimately must rely on a list of shared values (Griffin, *On Human Rights*, chs. 6–7). Whilst more sophisticated than the argument I discuss in the text, this argument is also unconvincing. However, I will not be able to address it here for reasons of space. For a sympathetic, although ultimately critical, discussion, see Simon Hope, "Common Humanity as a Justification for Human Rights Claims," in Gerhard Ernst and Jan-Christoph Heilinger (eds.), *The Philosophy of Human Rights Contemporary Controversies* (Berlin: De Gruyter, 2012), 219–24.

[21] Although I have focused here on Griffin's account, similar objections can be raised against other autonomy-based theories of human rights, such as the one defended by Alan Gewirth, *Human Rights: Essays on Justification and Applications* (Chicago: University of Chicago Press, 1982).

[22] The idea that human rights can be grounded in human needs is defended by David Miller (*National Responsibility and Global Justice* (Oxford: Oxford University Press, 2007), ch. 7; "Grounding Human Rights," *Critical Review of International Social and Political Philosophy*, 15 (2012): 407–27) and Thomas Pogge (*World Poverty and Human Rights.*). The view overlaps to some extent with the capabilities approach defended by Martha Nussbaum (*Women and Human Development: The Capabilities Approach* (Cambridge: Cambridge University Press, 2000); *Creating Capabilities: The Human Development Approach* (Cambridge, MA: Belknap Press of Harvard University Press, 2011) and Amartya Sen ("Elements of a Theory of Human Rights," *Philosophy & Public Affairs*, 32 (2004): 315–56).

At first sight, the idea of needs might seem like a bad candidate for grounding human rights. After all, the needs we have typically depend on certain aims or goals that we have adopted. If I want to drive a car, I need to get a licence. If I want to be a tennis player, I need to learn how to play a backhand. Those who don't want to drive a car don't need to get a licence. Those who don't want to be a tennis players don't need to learn how to play a backhand. However, there seems to be a class of needs that we have simply *qua* human beings, independently of specific goals that we have adopted for ourselves. In order to function as human beings we need things like food, air, water, shelter, a minimum level of health, and a minimal level of social interaction. When we are deprived of the opportunity to fulfil these needs to a significant extent, our capacity to lead a minimally decent human life is compromised. Call these *basic human needs*. It is on this notion that a plausible justification of human rights can be founded.

Using the idea of basic human needs, rather than autonomy, as the ground for the justification of human rights has the obvious advantage of accounting for the fact that children, the severely mentally disabled, and individuals suffering from advanced dementia have human rights. For while the individuals falling into these three classes do not have the capacity for normative agency, they certainly have basic human needs. However, the basic needs account incurs a number of other objections. In this section, I consider two objections raised by Griffin; in the next one, I raise and address two further problems; in section V, I show how the basic needs account can address the parochialism objection.

Griffin briefly considers the possibility of grounding human rights in something like basic needs but rejects it because the idea of a "normal functioning" seems to him too narrow to provide an account of human rights. For in what way am I malfunctioning if, say, I am denied freedom of religion? As Griffin puts it,

> [t]hat puts the malfunction in the wrong place. What is functioning badly is my society. The idea of health, mental and physical, may be central to a useful notion of basic needs, but it is the wrong place to be looking for an explanation of human rights. It is too narrow.[23]

Griffin is certainly right in saying that a society that denies freedom of religion to some of its members would be malfunctioning, but why would it be implausible to also claim that those who are denied freedom of religion cannot have the sort of spiritual life and social recognition that play a fundamental role in a minimally decent human life? One problem with Griffin's objection is that the idea of a minimally decent human life is reduced by him to the idea of a healthy biological and psychological life. This however, is an unduly restrictive way of understanding the notion of human life. The way in which the notion is understood within the basic needs account is richer, as it encompasses a number of social needs that must be met in order to have a minimally decent life: at the very least, needs for a minimum degree of social interaction and for a minimum level of recognition. In fact, it is arguably the presence of these needs which have a social dimension that marks the difference between a properly human life and a

---

[23] Griffin, *On Human Rights*, 89.

sub-human, or animal one, where the latter is conceived as aiming primarily at fulfilling a number of physiological needs.[24] And once we pay attention to the importance of these social needs, the idea that freedom of religion, or something like it, must be guaranteed in order to have a minimally decent life does not seems problematic at all.

A second objection raised by Griffin to the basic needs account is that if human rights were grounded in the need to avoid ailment and malfunctioning then they would be implausibly lavish, as we could invoke them to claim protection against any form of ailment or malfunctioning, no matter how slight. "But nearly everyone accepts that, on the contrary, there comes a point where aliments and malfunctions become minor enough that they do not create by right, a demand upon others to remedy them."[25] This, however, is a thought that the basic needs account can easily accommodate. Malfunctions that are minor enough not to impair our capacity to live a minimally decent life (Griffin's example are colds and minor psychological hang-ups) do not ground human rights because they fall outside the scope of the notion of *basic* needs, ie, needs that must be met in order to lead a minimally decent human life.

It is important here to distinguish between using the notion of needs as the foundation of a theory of human rights and using it as the foundation of a broader theory of morality (or perhaps political morality). Griffin intends to reject the former, but ends up discussing the latter instead. This is confirmed by the fact that he concludes his argument by claiming that "if a society were well off and a cold or . . . minor hang-ups would be cured by a cheap pill, then the National Health Service ought to provide it. It is hard to find in the need account resources to draw the line we want here."[26] This is a problem that defenders of needs-based account of morality acknowledge. David Braybrooke, for example, admits that medical demands constitute a "breakdown in the concept of needs" because there is no way out of acknowledging that nothing already present in the concept of needs saves the need for medical care from becoming a "bottomless pit."[27] But while grounding morality on the moral imperative to meet needs does indeed raise the problem of why we should stop short of meeting trivial medical needs such as those discussed by Griffin, a theory of human rights that focuses on the basic needs that must be met in order to have a minimally decent life does not have the same problem.

Although some discussion is required as to where to draw the line, it seems obvious enough that the sort of medical issues brought up by Griffin do not compromise our capacity to have a minimally decent life as human beings. This means that even if a society were well-off and could provide anti-colds and anti-minor-hang-ups pills for everyone, this should not be addressed as a matter of human rights. This is not to say that the society in question should not provide the pills, if this could be done at a reasonable cost. Perhaps it should. But this moral requirement, if it exists, would fall

---

[24] For further elaboration of this point, see section V.   [25] Griffin, *On Human Rights*, 89.
[26] Griffin, *On Human Rights*, 89.
[27] David Braybrooke, *Meeting Needs* (Princeton: Princeton University Press, 1987), 299, 301. Needs-based moral theories are also defended by David Wiggins, Garrett Thomson, and Gillian Brock; see David Wiggins, *Needs, Values, Truth: Essays in the Philosophy of Value* (Oxford: Basil Blackwell, 1987); Garrett Thomson, *Needs* (London: Routledge & Kegan Paul, 1987); Gillian Brock, "Morally Important Needs," *Philosophia*, 26 (1998): 165–78.

outside the scope of the basic needs justification of human rights, insofar as it would be grounded on needs that are not basic. Needs that are not basic do not contribute to the justification of human rights, because meeting those needs is not necessary in order to have a minimally decent human life. We can have a life of dignity, of the sort required by the basic needs account, even if those needs are not met.[28]

IV. The Idea of a "Minimally Decent Human Life"

In the previous section I introduced the idea of basic human needs, ie, needs that must be met in order to have a minimally decent life, and I suggested that human rights are grounded in our interest in having these basic needs met. The aim of this section is to further refine this idea. To begin with, it's worth stressing that a minimally decent life is something less than a minimally happy or flourishing life. A flourishing life is one in which I develop and exercise the capacities that are important to me. But, the capacities that are important to me and make my life flourish are different from those that are important to you and make your life flourish (unless we operate with an implausibly restrictive conception of the good life, whereby there is only one set of valuable choices that equally applies to everyone). The idea of a minimally decent life, by contrast, is the same for everyone, because it includes the pre-conditions that need to be secured in order to achieve whatever further goals we intend to pursue in light of our own conception of the good.[29]

While we all have different needs to the extent that we have different goals and pursue different conceptions of the good, basic needs are the same for everyone because they do not depend on what we require in order to pursue specific goals or conceptions of the good. They only depend on what it takes to live a minimally decent human life—a life that needs to be secured independently of what our specific plans and goals are. In this sense the notion of basic needs seems particularly well-suited to ground an account of human rights, as the point of human rights, as many have noticed, is to set minimum standards: "the lower limits on tolerable human conduct," rather than "great aspirations and exalted ideals."[30]

At the same time, grounding human rights in the conditions for a minimally decent human life seems to create a number of problems. The first is that we normally think

---

[28] Notice that while the basic needs account relies on the idea that respecting human dignity requires guaranteeing the conditions for a minimally decent life, I haven't said anything here about how the notion of human dignity is to be understood. In this paper I want to be as ecumenical as possible about this. The basic needs account does not depend for its validity on the adoption of a specific account of human dignity, and can be combined with several different accounts. (See, eg, Michael Rosen, *Dignity: Its History and Meaning* (Cambridge, MA: Harvard University Press, 2012); Christopher McCrudden (ed.), *Understanding Human Dignity* (Oxford: Oxford University Press, 2013); Jeremy Waldron, "Is Dignity the Foundation of Human Rights?," this volume, ch. 5.) Of course, depending on how we understand human dignity, we will have different answers to the question of why guaranteeing the conditions for a minimally decent life is necessary to respect human dignity.

[29] Miller, *National Responsibility and Global Justice*, 181. A similar line is pursued by the primary goods account defended by S. Matthew Liao, "Human Rights as Fundamental Conditions for a Good Life," this volume, ch. 3).

[30] Henry Shue, *Basic Rights: Subsistence, Affluence, and U.S. Foreign Policy* (Princeton: Princeton University Press, 1996), xi.

that we can choose not to have some of these needs fulfilled, without thereby failing to have a minimally decent human life. For example, if I choose not to eat or not to move freely as part of a political protest or as part of a religious practice, we would not say that my life is not minimally decent. It is only when I am forcibly prevented from having those needs met that we would say that. This suggests that what is required in order to have a minimally decent life is not that the needs are in fact met, but that we have the opportunity to meet them. Thus, human rights protect the conditions for a minimally decent life by providing us with the opportunity to have our basic needs met. It is the lack of such opportunity that would prevent us from having a minimally decent life.[31]

The second problem is more serious. We might challenge the basic needs approach, even once reformulated as protecting the opportunity to have our needs met, along the following lines. Consider the case of someone who has been tortured or raped. Should we say that this person's life is not minimally decent, not a *human* life, since her human rights have been violated? This would be implausible. Certainly it is possible for victims of rape or torture to have a minimally decent life, a properly human life, despite the wrongful harm they have suffered. But if so, it looks as if we'll have to give up the gist of the basic needs account. For if the life of someone whose human rights have been violated can be minimally decent, then it is not true that the point of human rights is to secure the conditions for a minimally decent life in the sense that we cannot have a minimally decent life unless we have the opportunity to have our basic needs met. Victims of torture or rape were deprived of this opportunity (as opposed to monks or protesters, who voluntarily choose to deprive themselves of the opportunity to have certain basic needs met), and yet we want to say that their life can be minimally decent. [32]

This seems to me the most important challenge for any naturalistic account that grounds human rights in the conditions necessary for a "minimally decent human life." If we want this idea to be more than a mere piece of rhetoric, we need to explain how it is possible to say that human rights protect the conditions necessary for a minimally decent human life, without having to accept at the same time the view that whoever has been the victim of torture or rape (or any other human rights violation) cannot be said to have a minimally decent human life.

We might think that one way to answer this question is to bite the bullet and argue that once we consider the lasting damaging effects produced by human rights violations such as torture and rape, the view that the victims of these violations do not have a minimally decent life is not so implausible after all. Jim Nickel, for example, argues that rape is degrading because "it treats a person as a mere sexual resource to be used without consent, or because in many cultures it destroys one's social standing as a virtuous and pure person," and that "degradation may deprive a person of the respect of

---

[31] This distinction is particularly important within the capability approach. See Amartya Sen's discussion of the distinction between fasting and starving in his *Development as Freedom* (Oxford: Oxford University Press, 1999), 76, and Nussbaum, *Creating Capabilities: The Human Development Approach*, 25. See also Miller, "Grounding Human Rights," 414.

[32] For a helpful discussion of this problem, see Rowan Cruft, "From a Good Life to Human Rights: Some Complications," this volume, ch. 4.

self and others."[33] However, this won't do. Not because similar effects are never produced, but because (fortunately) they are not always produced. Only in a limited number of cases would we consider saying that the damaging effects of rape or torture are such that the life of the victim is not minimally decent. Typically these effects will be produced only when some important human right is repeatedly violated, or when its violation takes place in the context of a large number of other human rights violations suffered by the victim.

A better answer is, I think, this: the point is not that someone who has been tortured or raped cannot have a minimally decent life. The point is that a life in which we don't have strong normative protections against human rights violations such as torture or rape is not a minimally decent one. All that the basic needs account must show in order to conclude that we have a human right not to be tortured is that if we did not have such a right, we would not be able to have a minimally decent life. The basic needs account is not required to show that our human right not to be tortured can be derived from the fact that if we are tortured, our life is not minimally decent. In fact, the basic needs account is not committed to this further claim.

Although this answer is an improvement over the one offered by Nickel, it is insufficient, I think, to rescue the basic needs account. For it is not clear that a life in which we lacked human rights against being tortured would fail to be minimally decent, given that others would still have a duty not to torture us. The main difference between a world in which we have a right not to be tortured and a world in which there is an obligation not to torture, but this obligation lacks a correlative right, is this: in the second world, although torturers would be acting wrongly, their victims would not be wronged by their actions.[34] This difference is certainly significant, but it is not clear that someone's life would fail to be minimally decent in the second world, if it is minimally decent in the first one (assuming that the two worlds are similar in all other respects).

The basic needs view here shows its limits if understood as an instrumental account of human rights. The view, as I have presented it so far, is instrumental because it starts by identifying a valuable state of affairs, ie, having a minimally decent life, and then ascribes human rights to individuals insofar as doing so is necessary to realize, or at least significantly contributes to the realization of, such a state of affairs.[35] But once it becomes clear that our capacity to have a minimally decent life is not significantly affected by the fact that we lack rights that protect the opportunity to meet basic needs, the claim that human rights can be justified by appealing to the importance of protecting such opportunity seems less plausible. If the justification of human rights rests on their capacity to protect the conditions for a minimally decent life, and if we can have a minimally decent life despite the fact that we lack rights that protect the opportunity to have our basic needs met, appealing to the importance of meeting such needs (or of having the opportunity to meet these needs) cannot provide a justification for human rights.

---

[33] James W. Nickel, *Making Sense of Human Rights* (Malden, MA; Oxford: Blackwell, 2007), 65.

[34] Joel Feinberg, "The Nature and Value of Rights," *The Journal of Value Inquiry*, 4 (1970): 247.

[35] This is how the view is understood by prominent defenders such as David Miller and Thomas Pogge. Views that are in the vicinity of the need based one (those that grounds human rights on capabilities or primary goods) are also typically presented as instrumental accounts of human rights.

However, I don't think that the basic needs view should be constructed exclusively in instrumental terms. In addition to being instrumentally valuable, human rights also have non-instrumental value, and this non-instrumental value contributes to their justification. What does it mean to claim that human rights have non-instrumental value? The idea is that these rights express the worth that human beings have as ends in themselves. Instead of deriving their value from their capacity to realize some fundamental interests we have, human rights express our nature as beings of a certain sort: beings "whose interests are worth protecting. [These rights] express the *worth of the person* rather than the *worth of what is in the interests of that person.*"[36]

According to the non-instrumental approach, human rights should not be ascribed to individuals only insofar as they are necessary to realize the more fundamental valuable state of affairs of having a minimally decent life. Rather, human rights "express a particular conception of the kind of place that should be occupied by individuals in a moral system—how their lives, actions, and interests should be recognized by the system of justification and authorization that constitute morality...They embody a form of recognition of the value of each individual."[37] Thus, when human rights are violated, according to the non-instrumental approach the problem is not that the conditions for a minimally decent life will be compromised to such an extent that the victim cannot be said to have a properly human life. Rather, the problem is primarily that with their conduct, those who violate human rights fail to acknowledge the status that human beings possess simply in virtue of their being human.

Jean Hampton has suggested that there are actions that "morally injure" their victim, in the sense that the victim is treated in a way which is precluded by her value.[38] These actions represent the value of the victim as less than the value that she possesses, as they deny the entitlements which are generated by that value. This is what violations of human rights do (in addition to whatever harm they cause): they deny that the victim has the status of human being, in that they treat the victim as if she did not have those basic protections that all human beings possess simply in virtue of their being human.[39] In doing so, they fail to acknowledge the dignity of the victim.

Here it might be objected that to the extent that human rights are justified in non-instrumental terms, the basic needs account I have offered is redundant. If human rights are justified as the expression of the intrinsic value that human beings possess, it looks as if any appeal to needs can be dispensed with at the level of justification. This however, would be a mistake. To begin with, adopting a non-instrumental account of human rights is perfectly compatible with also adopting an instrumental account.

---

[36] F.M. Kamm, *Intricate Ethics: Rights, Responsibilities, and Permissible Harm* (New York: Oxford University Press, 2007), 271.

[37] Thomas Nagel, "Personal Rights and Public Space," in *Concealment and Exposure: And Other Essays* (New York: Oxford University Press, 2002), 33–4. In addition to Kamm and Nagel, non-instrumental accounts of human rights are also defended by Warren Quinn, "Actions, Intentions and Consequences: The Doctrine of Doing and Allowing," in *Morality and Action* (Cambridge: Cambridge University Press, 1993), 149–74, and Rowan Cruft, "On the Non-Instrumental Value of Basic Rights," *Journal of Moral Philosophy*, 7 (2010): 441–61.

[38] Jean Hampton, *The Intrinsic Worth of Persons: Contractarianism in Moral and Political Philosophy*, ed. Daniel Farnham (New York: Cambridge University Press, 2007).

[39] I originally suggested this view in Massimo Renzo, "Crimes Against Humanity and the Limits of International Criminal Law," *Law and Philosophy*, 31(4) (2012): 443–76.

Indeed, a plausible justification of human rights is likely to be one that acknowledges the important role that both justifications play.

We have seen that there will be cases in which it is possible for someone to have a minimally decent human life despite the fact that some of her human rights have been violated. But if too many human rights are violated, or if some important human rights are violated too often, the idea that the life of the victim will fall below the threshold of what we would consider a minimally decent life becomes more plausible. This is the contribution that the instrumental reading of the basic needs account makes to the justification of human rights.

However, the notion of basic needs also figures within the non-instrumental account of human rights I intend to defend. For basic needs are precisely what identify the sort of protections that if disrespected, produce the relevant type of moral injury to our status as human beings described by Kamm and Nagel. It is by failing to acknowledge that individuals have strong normative protections that guarantee their option of having basic needs met, that we fall short of treating them with the respect owed to them *qua* human beings. Thus, far from being in tension with each other, the instrumental and the non-instrumental accounts of basic needs can work in tandem to provide what seems to me the most promising justification of human rights.[40]

More needs to be said, of course, to develop the basic needs account. For reasons of space, this task will have to wait. In the next section I will assess whether the account has the resources to address the parochialism objection. As we have seen, the incapacity of naturalistic approaches to provide a convincing answer to this objection is one of the main reasons that has motivated some philosophers to adopt a political account of human rights. Thus, it is important to show whether and how the basic needs account can deal with it.

V. Human Rights and Parochialism

In assessing the capacity of the basic needs account to address the parochialism objection, we can start by noticing that the account is better equipped to do so than other formulations of the naturalistic conception, such as Griffin's. While theories that ground human rights in distinctively liberal values such as autonomy or liberty can be more easily criticized as manifestations of "Western cultural imperialism," it's hard to see how the same objection could be moved against a theory that appeals to the notion of basic needs. For basic needs do not depend on a specific conception of the good, but rather on what it takes to function as human beings, whichever conception of the good we hold. Even if we grant that different conceptions of the good are authoritative in

---

[40] Leif Wenar and Rowan Cruft also argue that instrumental and non-instrumental justifications of rights can co-exist, although they offer different accounts of how the two justifications can be reconciled (Leif Wenar, "The Value of Rights," in Joseph K. Campbell, Michael O'Rourke, and David Shier (eds.), *Law and Social Justice* (Cambridge, MA: MIT Press, 2005), 179–209; Cruft, "On the Non-Instrumental Value of Basic Rights"). Nagel also seems open to the idea (Nagel, "Personal Rights and Public Space," 34, 42), although his arguments mainly seem to support the non-instrumental justification. For a powerful defense of the idea that we should adopt a pluralistic approach to the justification of human rights, see John Tasioulas' contribution to this volume. Tasioulas also acknowledges that an adequate justification for human rights should encompass both instrumental and non-instrumental considerations (though he avoids these labels).

different cultural contexts, this cannot weaken the claim that basic human needs will have to be protected, as the very possibility of pursuing a conception of the good, be it a liberal or a non-liberal one, requires that basic needs be met.

Of course this is not to say that there can be no disagreement about basic needs, or about how the relationship between basic needs and human rights should be conceived. Three sources of disagreement, in particular, should be considered. First, different basic needs will take different forms in different social contexts, because although the point of basic needs considerations is to guarantee a minimally decent human life, there is some margin for reasonable disagreement about what counts as a minimally decent human life, as well as about the best way to guarantee it. Different cultures will have different views as to what the best way to meet basic needs is and as to when these needs can be said to be met. (Consider for example how different cultures will look at the question of how to meet the need for a minimal level of social interaction.)[41] Second, different cultures will disagree about *why* meeting basic needs is morally mandatory, thereby disagreeing about the moral reasons that ultimately justify human rights. This might be worrisome because having different views about which moral considerations ultimately justify human rights might be thought to lead to significant disagreement as to which human rights we have, as well as to what their limits are and who can be said to have them. Third, members of different cultures might disagree about the relative urgency of different needs, thereby reaching different conclusions about the relative importance of different human rights and about how trade-offs between them should be conducted.

These three sources of disagreement are certainly important, but I will argue that they do not pose significant problems for a theory of human rights founded on basic needs. I consider them in turn. The idea that the same basic needs will be conceived in relatively different ways in light of different social contexts should come as no surprise. After all, we have already seen that basic human needs consist not only of biological or material needs, but also of social needs (such as the need for a minimum degree of social interaction and for a minimum level of recognition).[42] There is a deeper point to be made here however, namely that all of our basic needs, including those connected to purely material functions (such as eating or drinking), are inevitably embedded in a particular social context which specifies the way in which they are to be fulfilled in order to be fully met.

Marx saw this when he wrote that "eating, drinking, procreating, etc., are...genuinely human functions. But taken abstractly, separated from the sphere of all other human activity and turned into sole and ultimate ends, they are animal functions."[43] Thus, the point here is not only that human needs include social needs in addition to material needs that are shared by non-human subjects. The point is also that human needs necessarily have a social dimension, even when they are primarily connected to biological functioning.[44] It is only to be expected that this social dimension will

---

[41] See Miller's distinction between "basic needs" and "societal needs," *National Responsibility and Global Justice*, 182–3.

[42] See earlier, section III.

[43] Karl Marx, "'Economic and Philosophical Manuscripts of 1844,'" in Jon Elster (ed.), *Karl Marx: A Reader* (Cambridge: Cambridge University Press, 1986), 40.

[44] Nussbaum is particularly sensitive to this dimension of the problem. See, eg, *Frontiers of Justice: Disability, Nationality, Species Membership* (Cambridge, MA: Harvard University Press, 2006).

significantly vary across different cultures and that, because of this, different societies will be organized in very different, and sometimes conflicting, ways. Nonetheless, there seems to be a number of common elements that can be found in each of them.

Human societies are typically structured around small social units, often founded on something like the notion of the family; they provide for some form of education and upbringing of children; they have rules about how access to resources should be regulated and about when resort to violence and coercion is justified. This claim is a descriptive claim as much as a normative one. Not only are we likely to find the presence of these elements, or closely related ones, in all societies that have ever existed. But a society that failed to include one of these core elements is one that would challenge the very notion of a *human* society.

The second source of disagreement might seem more worrisome. Disagreeing about why meeting basic needs is morally mandatory is ultimately disagreeing about the underlying moral considerations to be invoked in justifying human rights, and we might worry that this is likely to lead to disagreement about what these rights are and about what they require. In fact, the opposite is true. One of the reasons why human rights are so valuable is precisely that they enable us to address important practical concerns without having to resort to questions of ultimate value about which people holding different conceptions of the good will inevitably disagree, *including* the question of why we should meet the basic needs upon which the justification of human rights rests.

You might believe, for example, that human dignity should be protected because we have been made in the image of God, whereas I might have a secular understanding of its value. The point of invoking the language of human rights is to bypass our disagreement about this more fundamental issue and converge on the claims that human dignity must be protected by guaranteeing the conditions for a minimally decent life and that this requires fulfilling a set of basic human needs. As long as we do that, there is much we can agree upon in relation to what these rights are and what they require.

This is not a special feature of human rights, but a feature of all moral rights. As Joseph Raz puts it,

> [a]ssertions of rights are typically intermediate conclusions in arguments from ultimate values to duties...Such intermediate conclusions are used and referred to as if they are themselves complete reasons. The fact that practical arguments proceed through the mediation of intermediate stages so that not every time a practical question arises does one refer to ultimate values for an answer is...of crucial importance in making social life possible, not only because it saves time and tediousness, but primarily because it enables a common culture to be formed round shared intermediate conclusions, in spite of a great degree of haziness and disagreement concerning ultimate values.[45]

I now turn to what seems to me the most serious source of disagreement, namely, the one about the urgency of different human needs. This source of disagreement is particularly worrisome because disagreeing about the urgency of different needs is

---

[45] Joseph Raz, *The Morality of Freedom* (Oxford: Clarendon Press, 1986), 181.

likely to lead to different ways of assessing the relative importance of specific human rights, which might be considered a problem to the extent that different cultures will then be likely to disagree about how to trade-off between particular human rights.

After all, the conflicts produced by disagreement about human rights are not typically determined by the fact that certain cultures believe that there is a human right to X while others don't, but rather by disagreement as to how important the human right to X is in comparison to other human rights—for example, how important the right to physical integrity is in comparison to religious or cultural rights (the debate on female genital mutilation is an obvious example). If so, it looks as if a theory of human rights will not be able to neutralize the parochialism objection by pointing at the existence of certain basic needs that must be met in all societies, because the problem of having to mediate between different conceptions of the good will be replicated when it comes to assessing the way in which different cultures value different needs.

Two points should be made in addressing this worry. One is that the relationship between human rights and the fundamental interests protected by them is not a one-to-one relationship, but rather a relationship between a set of fundamental human needs that ought to be protected and a set of fundamental human rights that protects them. Some human rights may directly map onto specific human needs, but normally particular needs will support a range of different rights (for example, the need for physical integrity will support rights such as the right to life and security, the right against torture and cruel punishment, and the right to an adequate standard for health and well-being). At the same time, a given human right might be grounded in a number of different human needs (for example, our right to freedom of conscience will be grounded, among other things, in our need for psychological health and our need for social interaction).[46] This means that disagreeing about the urgency of certain needs will not immediately lead to disagreeing about the importance the rights protecting those needs. Since the same human right will be grounded in a plurality of basic needs, different cultures are likely not to disagree about its importance as long as they converge on the urgency of a sufficient number of needs protected by that right, although not all of them.

The second point I intend to make is more general. In dealing with the question of how conflicts between the demands imposed by different cultures should be handled, it's important that we get clearer about what we should expect from a theory of human rights. The point of invoking the language of human rights cannot be to completely eliminate such conflicts. If that was the case, we should indeed conclude that the language of human rights ultimately does constitute a form of "moral imperialism." The point of invoking the language of human rights is rather to make sure that certain minimum standards are guaranteed, while respecting as much as possible the particular cultural and moral values adopted in different political and legal contexts.

---

[46] For an excellent analysis of this point and it implications for the question of how to deal with conflicts of human rights, see Miller, "Grounding Human Rights," 416–19. See also Allen Buchanan's discussion of the "mirroring view" in his contribution to this volume, ch. 13 ("Why *International Legal* Human Rights?").

This is why whereas general international law obligations are normally implemented uniformly across these different contexts, international human rights law obligations are not. The European Court of Human Rights, for example, recognizes the existence of a "margin of appreciation," which gives local authorities some leeway in determining how international human rights law should be implemented domestically. The main justification for this provision is precisely that when it comes to controversial issues such as sexual ethics, bioethics or the place of religion in society, local cultural and moral values should be allowed to play some role in determining how human rights are to be understood and enforced.

Thus, we should not be worried too much by the fact that the basic needs account cannot completely neutralize cultural divergences concerning how human rights should be interpreted and about their relative weight. The important thing is that there is a substantive agreement about the heart of the matter: the existence of norms that protect our status as human beings by imposing powerful obligations whose function is to provide us with the opportunity to fulfil certain needs we have simply *qua* human beings. In other words, instead of conceiving human rights as something to which different cultures and societies should somehow adapt, we should conceive them as providing us with a common ground within which disagreements and conflicts between societies about how basic needs should be met can be addressed. So understood, far from being a manifestation of moral imperialism, human rights become a powerful tool to constrain moral imperialism. They ensure that interference with a particular society's autonomy is justified *only* when the protection of basic needs is at stake; and that even in this case, interference should be sensitive to the way in which these needs are understood in the society in question.

VI. Conclusion

A minimally decent life is one in which we have the option to fulfil a core group of socially embedded biological and psychological needs, as well as social needs. I have suggested that this notion can be used to provide a convincing justification for human rights. Human rights protect the conditions for a minimally decent life by providing us with the opportunity to meet such needs and by expressing the value we have *qua* human beings.

The basic needs account is to be preferred to the most prominent alternative naturalistic account of human rights, namely Griffin's autonomy-based view, for two reasons. First, it accommodates our considered judgment that children, the severely mentally disabled, and individuals suffering from advanced dementia possess human rights; second, it has the resources to address the parochialism objection. Obviously, more work is required to develop this account. The aim of this paper was simply to show that it is a promising framework within which to think about the justification of human rights.

33

Liberty Rights and the Limits of Liberal Democracy

Jiwei Ci

Liberty rights are first among human rights, both in order of invention and in importance usually ascribed. They begin life (or their first life) as liberal rights, rights enjoyed by members of liberal societies, and come to be treated as human rights through extension to the international arena. Thus liberty rights have a double identity and are doubly ambitious: as liberal rights, they create, legitimate, and intensify the desire characteristic of members of liberal societies for nothing less than some form of self-determination; as human rights, they generalize what originally was a culturally particular desire into a universal human aspiration worthy of the strongest protection. As a committed and precisely for this reason uneasy believer in liberty rights or, more precisely, in many of the things liberty rights are supposed to make possible, I want to see how well liberty rights live up to these two ambitions and what lessons we can draw if they fall short. By considering liberty rights in their double identity, I hope especially to arrive at a critical appraisal of liberty rights as human rights that would be difficult to reach by attending to liberty rights as human rights alone.

I. Liberty Rights as Human Rights

It seems appropriate to start from what strikes me as a deep contradiction in the concept of human rights, especially liberty rights as a subset of human rights. The contradiction lies between the universalism and supposed minimalism of human rights, on the one hand, and the fact that human rights—again I have in mind liberty rights in particular—are not necessary conditions for human beings to live what is normally and reasonably recognized as a human life, on the other. I call the latter a fact because people in different times and places have led humanly meaningful and worthwhile lives without anything like liberty rights. I am not denying (nor at this point affirming) that a human life without the protection of liberty rights is one that would become better with such protection, but only saying that liberty rights impose on human life a standard that goes beyond what human beings strictly need in order to live a humanly meaningful and worthwhile life. In this significant sense, it is a mistake to consider the concept of human rights minimalist, at least when it comes to liberty rights, and to regard liberty rights as rights that human beings have simply by virtue of being human. Whatever reasons may justify liberty rights, it cannot be that these reasons are such that they must be made good if human beings are to live a human life. Liberty rights, no matter how justified, cannot be justified as human rights on any minimalist conception.

This is no terminological quibble. Once a minimalist justification is shown not to work for liberty rights, we can no longer use the concept of human rights as applied to liberty rights. The only way to be precise and upfront about what we mean by liberty rights would be to say that liberty rights are the rights that human beings have when being human is conceived *in a particular way*. This particular way requires a spelling out and a justification in which one must be aware of one's political or ideological position and put one's cards on the table. Since the task at hand is that of the clarification and justification of a *particular* conception of being human and of the rights that follow from this conception, one must steer clear of all talk of rights that human beings have simply by virtue of being human. We are thus led, once again, to see a contradiction in the very concept of human rights as applied to liberty rights.

It is characteristic of philosophical treatments of human rights that, when human rights are understood as the rights that human beings have simply by virtue of being human, being human (in "by virtue of being human") is in turn understood in terms of agency. There is nothing wrong with this second step, for agency is indeed what is fundamental to human being. What is problematic is a further step that is at least implicit in so much philosophical theorizing about human rights: the understanding of human agency on the model of a particular (liberal) configuration of human agency. The problem here does not lie in configuring human agency in a particular (liberal) way but in treating human agency as disclosed by *any* particular configuration as if it is human agency as such.

What do I mean by human agency *as such*? Human beings act in human ways, and it is in so acting that they become and remain all that is distinctively and variously human. What is at stake in human action is not only self-preservation, individually and collectively, but also, for each individual, the acquisition of a certain identity as a specific kind of human being embedded in various significant human groups, and, for each group, the construction of a collective identity embedded in turn in an yet larger, social setting, and so on. All human action requires a certain amount of room—objective freedom in a generic (as distinct from a liberal) sense. This room could be all that is needed for self-preservation. But what makes human action distinctively human is the other stake in it, that which involves self-making, where the self may be individual or collective on various scales. For self-making to be accomplished, whatever the self in the making happens to be like and to whatever degree this self may lack initiative or self-consciousness, the self has to participate with a significant degree of willingness—subjective freedom in a generic sense—if not initial voluntariness. One cannot acquire a self or an identity, with all its meaning and spirit, without some active and willing involvement of oneself, and, of course, this involvement in turn requires room. This involvement is a matter of degree, just as the room available is a matter of degree, but no one can altogether do without either. Thus, given its goals and stakes, human action needs both more or less room and more or less willingness of participation. We need a much more complex account than I can provide here in order to understand how these needs are negotiated, contested, and constantly reshaped. But one thing already seems quite clear: room for action and willingness of participation are the only necessary conditions of human agency as such, as distinct from any particular, culturally specific configuration of agency, and they are jointly sufficient for human agency.[1]

It is worth emphasizing that I have spoken of the room for action as *objective freedom* and of the willingness of participation as *subjective freedom*, and of both as *generic freedom*, as distinct from freedom in a liberal sense. There is a world of difference between generic freedom and liberal freedom: no human being can survive for long as a human being, and no human society as a human society, without a significant degree of generic freedom. But liberal freedom is largely a modern invention, and it has served as part of the configuration of agency, and hence as a necessary condition of agency, only for that minority of the world's population which inhabits liberal or liberal democratic societies. Liberal freedom consists in carving out a certain amount of space for generic freedom explicitly in the name of the right to *individual freedom* of various types of action, and in creating and maintaining a special kind of willingness of participation that is conceived in terms of *individual autonomy*.

It is characteristic of proponents of liberal freedom that they mistake their conception of liberal freedom for one of generic freedom. "Out of the notion of personhood," writes James Griffin, meaning by personhood the status of a normative agent,

> we can generate most of the conventional list of human rights. We have a right to life (without it, personhood is impossible), to security of person (for the same reason), to a voice in political decision (a key exercise of autonomy), to free expression, to assembly, and to a free press (without them exercise of autonomy would be hollow), to worship (a key exercise of what one takes to be the point of life).[2]

Is a voice in political decision really essential for human status as distinct from human flourishing, a distinction on which Griffin himself insists?[3] And is free expression really essential to meet the modest standard of human status? In both cases, hardly. These, and other things such as free assembly and a free press, may be regarded as necessary conditions for a good human life, on one understanding of such a life. But mere human status does not require so much. What is needed for human status must be sufficiently general and undemanding to allow all kinds of societies other than liberal ones to qualify as human societies, that is, as societies whose members under ordinary circumstances live a life compatible with human status.

Rather than treating members of non-liberal societies as being denied the necessary conditions for human agency, then, it would be more accurate, and more consistent with the spirit of liberalism itself, to say that members of liberal societies live a distinctive kind of human life for which liberal freedom, in the shape of liberty rights, serves as a necessary condition. This does not mean that liberals cannot reasonably fault non-liberal societies, but they can do so only on the grounds that the latter fail to provide sufficient generic freedom as distinct from liberal freedom. Nor does it mean that liberals cannot reasonably argue for the superiority of the liberal way of life, but

---

[1] For a more substantial account, see Jiwei Ci, "Evaluating Agency: A Fundamental Question for Social and Political Philosophy," *Metaphilosophy*, 42(3) (April 2011): 261–81.

[2] James Griffin, *On Human Rights* (New York: Oxford University Press, 2008), 33.

[3] See Griffin, *On Human Rights*, 34.

they can do so only by trying to show that a liberal society offers the prospect of a better human life rather than the only acceptable form of life for human beings as agents. It follows that in neither case is it reasonable for liberals to invoke the idea of liberty rights as human rights.

II. Liberty Rights as Liberal Rights

To say that liberty rights are too strong as *human* rights is not to imply that they are unproblematic as *liberal* rights. There is, I believe, a lot to be said for liberty rights in principle. But I also believe that liberty rights as understood in the standard way are *too weak* as liberal rights, and this is shown by a contradiction within the liberal approach to liberty rights in a liberal society. Within this approach, liberty rights are pitched at an awe-inspiringly high level of ambition, as allowing individuals to be nothing less than the architects of their own lives and the authors of their own identities: sovereign individuals, according to one familiar way of putting it. This applies not only to determining what life one wants to lead and what kind of self one wants to be (autonomy) but also to choosing how one goes about putting such self-determination into effect (liberty).[4] Liberty thus understood is relatively straightforward, at least in broad outline, subject as it is only to some harm principle and to certain not too stringent considerations of justice and social efficiency. Autonomy, on the other hand, is an altogether more complicated matter.

It is in the very nature of the human form of life that individual self-determination can take place only in a social setting that individuals cannot determine remotely in the same way or to the same degree that they can determine their own lives *within* it. This social setting draws a line, a fuzzy and mobile yet (at any given time) firm line, separating more or less real possibilities for acting and being from near impossibilities and as yet unimagined possibilities, and thus opening up a space of actual freedoms as distinct from unfreedoms as well as undreamed-of freedoms. And it is of varying levels, from specific practices through broad institutions to a whole social system, an entire way of life, and, at its all-encompassing and most elusive, the "mood" or "spirit" of an age. The higher the level, the more profound if less tangible will be its effect on all those living under its spell and sway, and yet the more powerless individuals are in their ability to determine it as they determine their own lives within its confines. The highest level recedes beyond the power and cognitive grasp of most, and more often than not into sheer invisibility.

Yet every social setting, however large and complex, is humanly made—the corrigible result of struggles for survival and dominance. The struggles themselves get ever more complicated as later struggles take place in an environment created by earlier struggles, all too often difficult or impossible to reverse, and are complicated further still by the fact that all struggles are informed by and conducted in the name of values,

---

[4] See Griffin, *On Human Rights*, 33, 149 for the distinction between autonomy and liberty. Clearly, Griffin's notion of autonomy is different from and less stringent than Kant's. Since this is the notion of autonomy that is invoked in the human rights discourse in general, for easily understandable reasons, I will follow Griffin's usage, with a corresponding adjustment to the meaning of heteronomy.

which in turn have a tendency to take on a life of their own, though never in complete independence from the reality which they help shape. None of this can be consciously planned and executed in a liberal social setting, of course, least of all in its entirety. But because social settings are determined by struggles for power, with interests and values on the line, there are bound to be winners and losers. The most important difference between winners and losers in our world today is that between the "movers and shakers"—the "Davos Men," for example[5]—on the one hand and the helpless multitude on the other. The latter have no say in how the social setting—the dominant games and their rules—is determined and are left to exercise their individual autonomy in an environment that is entirely of other people's making. This state of affairs is well captured by John Dunn:

> A world at last fit for capitalism will be a world in which those whose talents, good fortune and energy equip them to trade profitably profit handsomely, irrespective of where they happen to have been born. It will be a world in which property rights are highly secure, but other human claims have force only insofar as they fit comfortably with the security of property rights. In this sense, it will be a world of increasingly pure power, where the strong take what they can get and the weak endure what they have to.[6]

Despite this, the weak are no less autonomous than the strong: in a liberal society the weak and the strong enjoy strictly equal autonomy *within* the given social setting. Where the weak are relatively inferior to the strong is in their ability to use their autonomy (and liberty) to get what they want. What matters even more is that the weak are absolutely inferior to the strong in their ability to shape the social setting for individual autonomy. It is true even of the most accomplished form of liberal democracy, and hence of any global arrangement made in its image, that the strong not only "take what they can get" but also, with infinitely greater audacity and consequence, determine what there is to take and is worth getting. And this means that what the weak have to "endure" is not only a much smaller share of whatever they can use their autonomy (and liberty) to get but also, at a deeper level that may elude their conscious awareness, the fact that they are little more than an inert multitude when it comes to shaping the social setting that frames and constrains their exercise of autonomy.

In the face of the great disparity in power to determine the social setting for individual autonomy, it would be a very inadequate response to say that this setting is by nature heteronomously determined and to leave it at that. It is undoubtedly the case that no individual *qua* individual can autonomously determine the social setting for his or her exercise of autonomy. In this sense, all individual autonomy is heteronomously determined. It does not follow, however, that individuals cannot, as participants in a social setting, have a say in shaping it: a greater say is more autonomous or less heteronomous. Thus, while the basic fact of the heteronomous determination of the social setting for individual autonomy cannot be changed, it can be redeemed, as it

---

[5] See Richard Sennett, *The Corrosion of Character: The Personal Consequences of Work in the New Capitalism* (New York: W. W. Norton, 1998), 61.
[6] John Dunn, *The Cunning of Unreason* (New York: Basic Books, 2000), 332.

were, or rendered largely free of domination, by making the participation of individuals in this determination as autonomous, perhaps as equally autonomous, as humanly possible. In this regard, what is commonly called democracy is of no help, since such democracy takes place within a more or less fixed and unexamined social setting as much as individual autonomy does.

What is heteronomously determined, moreover, is not just the social setting in which individual autonomy is exercised. When individuals reach a point at which they are able, and can be trusted, to exercise their autonomy, they have already been shaped in a particular way—down to their innermost being, including their desire for individual autonomy and their probable lack of willingness and ability to look beyond such autonomy to the social setting that constrains it. It is a basic fact of the human form of life that individuals are determined before they can come to determine themselves, and how they determine themselves cannot but bear the inerasable imprint of the prior determination from the outside. Thus, the heteronomy that makes autonomy possible extends, beyond the determination of the social setting for individual autonomy, to the very constitution of the subjects of individual autonomy.

With regard to this second kind of heteronomy, it is obvious that the strong and the weak are in the same boat. Nothing can be done about this heteronomy directly: no matter how autonomous we can come to be, our very status as autonomous subjects is determined from the outside in the first place. For this reason, the way in which the first kind of heteronomous determination can be redeemed does not quite apply here—though not completely, as we shall see. What must be done instead to redeem this second kind of heteronomy is something with which those among us with a thoroughly postmetaphysical outlook may feel very uncomfortable, as we have no choice but to ask and attempt to answer a question that takes our focus away from the form of autonomy to its content. The question is this: whether, in any given case, the actual heteronomous determination of autonomous subjects is *ethically* good in terms of the kind of things that such subjects are disposed to do and the kind of persons they are disposed to be rather than whether they do such things or come to be such persons autonomously.

While so-called autonomous subjects cannot but be heteronomously determined, they can be so determined in *substantively different* ways. Accordingly, although members even of a fully liberal society cannot reasonably hope each to create their own individual autonomy instead of only exercising it, they can reflect on the kind of individual autonomy they have been disposed by their society to develop, and decide for themselves whether it is worthy of endorsement after the fact. Such reflection will not be easy, of course, as properly socialized subjects, however autonomous, are disposed not to seriously challenge the determinants of the actual shape of their autonomy. Moreover, such reflection, however critical, will tend to draw on resources that are made available by the very society that is placed under reflection. But experience shows that reflective endorsement is a possible way of redeeming the heteronomous determination of autonomous subjects in a liberal society. Indeed, the exercise of reflection accompanied by the power to give or withhold endorsement is itself a form of autonomy.

To complicate the picture slightly, it is possible to apply to the first fact of heteronomy the consideration that presents itself more naturally in the case of the second, and vice versa. In other words, we can ask of the social setting for individual autonomy whether it is conducive to choosing and living a good life, and ask of the socialization of individuals into autonomous subjects whether the process itself, though essentially heteronomous, cannot be made less resistant to individual revision and hence more compatible with individual autonomy. But in the main, as I have said, the heteronomous determination of the social setting for individual autonomy calls for redemption in terms of more equal participation, while the heteronomous determination of autonomous subjects cannot be fully redeemed without ethical reflection on what is done with autonomy.

When I say that liberty rights are too weak as liberal rights, what I mean is that proponents of liberty rights for a liberal society fail to confront the two facts of the heteronomous determination of individual autonomy and therefore miss the opportunity to make liberty rights stronger in the light of these facts. They miss the opportunity to make liberty rights stronger, first, by failing to reflect on the *political* question of whether one should regard individual autonomy as seriously compromised if the social setting for individual autonomy is shaped by grossly unequal relations of power. They miss the opportunity to make liberty rights stronger, second, by failing to consider the *ethical* question of how one should assess the good of individual autonomy if the social setting that determines the socialization of autonomous subjects is stacked against the choice and pursuit of worthwhile conceptions of the good life capable of withstanding a suitable degree of critical reflection. Since proponents of liberty rights do not raise these questions, they give the impression that liberal societies are immune to problems suggested by them. But this impression is mistaken.

Regarding the political question, a hint will suffice. Nowhere is this question more manifest and pressing than in the impact of global capitalism on our social world. One cannot read Leo Panitch and Sam Gindin, Sheldon Wolin, Gary Cross, John Gray, and Zygmunt Baumann, to name a somewhat random assortment of the many plausible writers on the subject, without forming the hypothesis that the exercise of individual autonomy is warped, compromised, and even undermined when it is framed by a social setting increasingly dominated by global capital.[7] And one does not have to be persuaded by all or even most of what these authors have to say on the subject to see the initial plausibility of such a hypothesis.

This hypothesis finds strong theoretical and historical underpinnings in Karl Polanyi's classic work, *The Great Transformation*, which can be read, among other things, as an account of highly compulsive attempts by the forces of capital to disembed

---

[7] See Leo Panitch and Sam Gindin, *The Making of Global Capitalism: The Political Economy of American Empire* (London: Verso, 2012); Sheldon Wolin, *Democracy Incorporated: Managed Democracy and the Specter of Inverted Totalitarianism* (Princeton: Princeton University Press, 2008); Gary Cross, *An All-Consuming Century: Why Commercialism Won in Modern America* (New York: Columbia University Press, 2000); John Gray, *False Dawn: The Delusions of Global Capitalism* (New York: New Press, 1998); and Zygmunt Bauman, *Does Ethics Have a Chance in a World of Consumers?* (Cambridge, MA: Harvard University Press, 2008).

the economy from society and to run society as an "adjunct to the market."[8] Although such disembedding is impossible to achieve fully in reality, as Polanyi shows, and thus the idea is a fiction, there is little doubt that the very making of such attempts has left a deep mark on the whole organization of modern society, including the practice of individual autonomy, as no other social force has done. Thus Polanyi is able to concentrate his strictures against nineteenth-century capitalism into the single most important charge that "The congenital weakness of nineteenth-century society was not that it was industrial but that it was a *market society*" (as distinct from a mere market economy).[9] What was true of nineteenth-century capitalism is no less true of the increasingly global capitalism for which the ascendancy of neoliberalism has provided the most obvious impetus and ideology. This global version of the Great Transformation, which Polanyi did not live to see, has effectively reversed an earlier process remarked with a note of optimism by Polanyi "under which the economic system ceases to lay down the law to society and the primacy of society over that system is secured."[10] The pendulum has decidedly swung back in favor of the fiction and partial reality of a market society, this time on a global scale, and there is little evidence to suggest that the reaction to the first Great Transformation for much of the twentieth century is about to repeat itself. The power of capital to shape society and human life has never been as wide and deep as it is now.

Polanyi's thesis of the Great Transformation is not undisputed, to be sure, and the same is true of the views of authors, including those I have referred to, who have charted the course of the Great Transformation in its recent, global phase under the auspices of neoliberalism. But these authors, between them, clearly help cast reasonable doubt on the legitimacy of the liberal democratic social setting for individual autonomy when that setting is so powerfully shaped by global capital. This reasonable doubt is all we need to take proponents of liberty rights to task for failing to respond to it.

More complicated is the ethical question. As we have seen, the question of *how* the social setting for individual autonomy (and for the socialization of autonomous subjects) is determined is distinct from the question of *what* that social setting is like (and what the autonomous subjects are like). The latter question has to do with what choices of life, considered severally or as a range, autonomous individuals are able and likely to make within a given social setting and whether the autonomous choices enabled and constrained by such a setting are conducive to the good life. The two questions are distinct and largely independent, and it is impossible to say which is more important. But it is not difficult to argue that, when one has serious (political) reservations about how the social setting for individual autonomy is determined, those reservations are compounded if one also separately comes to the (ethical) judgment that the social setting thus determined happens to present serious and unnecessary obstacles to the good life. And it is not difficult to arrive at the further thought, in the spirit of

---

[8] Karl Polanyi, *The Great Transformation: The Political and Economic Origins of Our Time* (Boston: Beacon Press, 2nd Beacon pbk. edn., 2001), 60.

[9] Polanyi, *The Great Transformation*, 258; the entire sentence is italicized in the original.

[10] Polanyi, *The Great Transformation*, 259. On this reversal, see Gray, *False Dawn*.

a hypothesis, that the wrong "how" and the bad "what" are related in a way that is not accidental. Such, I believe, is the case with the undermining of individual autonomy by global capital: the social setting for individual autonomy is overwhelmingly shaped by global capital, and, furthermore, it is shaped in such a way as to make choosing and pursuing the good life an increasingly uphill struggle. Having made the first, political argument briefly, I want next to say something more substantial about the second, ethical argument.

Since this is a complex issue that does not permit comprehensive treatment here, I will illustrate my argument by looking at what people tend to do with their liberty rights under the familiar principle of equal opportunity in a competitive capitalist social setting. There is no reason to see obstacles to the good life in competitive activities simply in virtue of their competitiveness. A sensible appraisal depends on the kind of things people compete for in such activities, how they compete for them, and with what effects on themselves and their fellows and on their social and natural environment. The notion of a practice as elucidated by Alasdair MacIntyre is very helpful for pinpointing what is amiss with the sort of competitive activities that liberty rights typically entitle people to join under the principle of equal opportunity.[11] What we see in liberal democratic societies, with their distinctive kind of competitiveness and social mobility, is the gradual breakdown of practices with a corresponding corrosion of character (to use Sennett's phrase). As more and more people are drawn into the competitive activities that make up the social domain,[12] they compete more and more for external instead of internal goods. This opening up of the social domain to all is informed by the liberal principle of equal opportunity while the displacement of internal by external goods is driven by the need of capital to expand consumption and profit. With the eclipse of internal by external goods, people also come to compete more and more for the same things, for all external goods find their measure and common denominator in money (power being beyond the reach of most) and what money can buy and symbolize. In this process of externalization and homogenization, practices break down in two senses.

The first has to do with the very nature of a practice. Since a practice is defined by the internal goods achievable in it, it loses its character as a practice the moment when the pursuit of its internal, constitutive goods gives way to the desire to acquire the external goods that are only contingently related to the practice. What is left is only the shell of a practice, as its internal goods are hollowed out and members of the practice engage in it exclusively or chiefly for the external goods which they could in principle secure from any other activity. When people lose the desire to pursue the internal goods of a practice, they also lose the motivation to cultivate and practice the virtues internal to that practice or, as MacIntyre shows, to *any* practice, for the virtues such as justice, courage, and honesty are nothing but firm dispositions conducive to the pursuit of internal goods. This is the second sense in which a practice can break down

---

[11] Alasdair MacIntyre, *After Virtue*, 2nd edn. (Notre Dame, IN: University of Notre Dame Press, 1984), esp. ch. 14.

[12] For a particularly illuminating analysis of what the "social" means, see Hannah Arendt on "the rise of the social" in *The Human Condition* (Chicago: University of Chicago Press, 1958), ch. 2.

and it is continuous with the first. What gets lost with the erosion of the virtues is a certain attitude to work and life. It is the attitude of someone who knows the distinction between the internal and external goods of a practice, who places internal ahead of external goods, who cultivates and practices the virtues as an intrinsic part of the pursuit of the internal goods, who on the strength of these virtues has an internally engendered motivation to refrain from adopting certain means even when he or she also takes a reasonable interest in acquiring the external goods available, who maintains a certain solidarity with fellow members of the practice despite the competitiveness of the practice or even in part because of its specific kind of competitiveness, and who, all in all, is capable of achieving a life that is as good as it is autonomous.

What is especially disturbing about the breakdown of practices is not so much the nearly exclusive competition for external goods as the fact that what is chiefly at stake in this competition is the relative value of individual identities. The competition for external goods is at bottom a competition for symbolic carriers of socially valorized individual identities. It is this fact that gives a particular character both to the competition and to the kind of self that emerges from it. Take away the internal goods and the virtues, and what is left is only a competitive quest for more highly valued individual identities through the struggle for larger shares of external goods. Insofar as individuals constitute themselves through such a quest, they cannot but develop identities that are marked by two general features. On the one hand, individual identities formed in the competition for external goods are hollow and spiritless since no one can really put one's heart and soul into activities aimed at acquiring external goods. Yet, on the other hand, such identities have something fiercely competitive about them, in that, in the absence of internal goods and the related virtues, people find their worth only through comparison with others and at the expense of others. This combination makes for a regime of self-constitution in which people acquire what is most important for themselves through efforts directed at the most unsuitable objects and in the least auspicious manner.

It is necessary to place this general account under a more differentiated historical perspective, as this will allow us to see that the process comprising the breakdown of practices and the atrophy of the virtues has greatly accelerated in the past few decades. In this context, Richard Sennett can be seen as providing a sociological fleshing out of MacIntyre's philosophical sketch of the breakdown of practices, and, just as important, as picking up where MacIntyre leaves off by reflecting on the more recent developments in such a breakdown in the braver newer world of global capitalism. What Sennett gives us is a picture of a new "ideal man or woman" who is at home in the new capitalism and is indeed a product of "the culture of the new capitalism." This is a "self oriented to the short term, focused on potential ability, [and] willing to abandon past experience"[13]—in other words, a self (or semblance of self) willing and able to reinvent itself constantly and in any way called for in an ever more flexible workplace in return for maximum gain in external goods as markers of individual worth. Just as in MacIntyre's general account, so in Sennett's more specific one, this kind of seeker of external goods may be as autonomous as one could wish, provided that one

---

[13] Richard Sennett, *The Culture of the New Capitalism* (New Haven: Yale University Press, 2006), 5.

does not call into question the social setting in which he or she is disposed to exercise individual autonomy. The quest for external goods and for individual identity in terms of external goods is perfectly compatible with individual autonomy. Indeed, it is the typical way in which members of liberal societies today exercise their individual autonomy, with the "ideal man or woman" depicted by Sennett as the latest version of the autonomous individual.[14]

To me this "ideal man or woman" represents anything but a truly autonomous individual capable of leading a good life. If proponents of liberty rights share this judgment, it should seriously worry them that the good life fails to materialize and yet the so-called individual autonomy is left intact as long as the individuals involved do not feel imposed upon by being socialized in the image of this ideal. What makes matters worse is that "Most people are not like this [the ideal man or woman]; they need a sustaining life narrative, they take pride in being good at something specific, and they value the experiences they've lived through. The cultural ideal required in new institutions thus damages many of the people who inhabit them."[15] The claim here, translated into MacIntyre's vocabulary, is that most people can lead what for them is a good life only in the context of well-functioning practices. It is only in such a context that they can "take pride in being good at something specific," and this pride rests on the achievement of internal goods and the development of the virtues. As MacIntyre makes clear,[16] and Sennett implies, practices presuppose, in turn, what MacIntyre calls the narrative unity of a human life ("a sustaining life narrative," as Sennett calls it) and the presence of a tradition (that is why people "value the experiences they've lived through," in Sennett's words).

If Sennett is correct, a more serious charge must be leveled at "the culture of the new capitalism" for building into the social setting for individual autonomy and the socialization of autonomous subjects a model of an "ideal man or woman" that goes against the nature of "most people." It is not just that people are made autonomous to live a kind of life *others* may have reason to find ethically wanting; it is rather that they are forced to be autonomous in a way to which they themselves would take exception given the opportunity. This is domination in the guise of autonomy, or autonomy created in the spirit of domination. That this is true of "most people" but not necessarily of all only confirms that the social setting for individual autonomy is determined, in the liberal societies covered by Sennett's generalization, by grossly unequal relations of power. Those at the receiving end of such unequal heteronomous determination—"most people"—naturally suffer damage as capitalism's new cultural ideal is burned into the very conditions and conditioning of their individual autonomy.

Speculative as it may sound, Sennett's claim, made in the context of an empirical study of the culture of the new capitalism, is well worth the attention of all those who truly care about individual autonomy. Complementing those authors who alert us to the corporate determination of the social setting for individual autonomy, Sennett succeeds at least in casting reasonable doubt on the ethical failings of that setting.

---

[14] See Sennett, *The Culture of the New Capitalism*, 12 for his claim that this cutting-edge or as yet minority phenomenon is a basis for "inferring the culture of the whole."

[15] Sennett, *The Culture of the New Capitalism*, 5.　　[16] See MacIntyre, *After Virtue*, ch. 15.

III. Griffin on Liberty Rights

I have argued that liberty rights are too strong as human rights, and that they are too weak as liberal rights. With regard to the first claim, it will be helpful to supplement my general argument with a specific example of the kind of view at which this argument is directed. With regard to the second claim, it will be helpful to illustrate, again with a specific example, what I have in mind by liberalism's failure to take up the challenge of redeeming individual autonomy. To both ends, we can hardly do better than examine James Griffin's widely respected treatment of liberty rights.

Griffin finds the basis for human rights in the notion of normative agency. According to him, there are three necessary conditions for normative agency, namely, autonomy, liberty, and minimum provision (or welfare), and thus the protection of these conditions requires three "highest-level human rights."[17] Of these, the rights that cater respectively to autonomy and liberty make up what are commonly lumped together as liberty rights.[18]

Griffin readily acknowledges that the "human" in "human rights" is not a straightforward statement of fact about human beings, and he does so in order to preempt the charge of deriving "ought" from "is" statements. Rather, "my notions of 'human nature' and 'human agent' are already well within the normative circle, and there is no obvious fallacy involved in deriving rights from notions as evaluatively rich as they are" (35). This immediately prompts a question about the basis and provenance of such evaluatively rich notions. As one might expect, the basis and provenance of these notions, and thus the notions themselves, cannot but belong to a *particular* conception of what it means to be "human." This becomes obvious when Griffin defines agency as a matter of "deliberating, assessing, choosing, and acting to make what we see as a good life for ourselves" (32). As anyone familiar with the moral universe of modern liberalism will recognize, the language of deliberation and choice already builds the liberal preference for a particular kind of individualism and autonomy into what should be a more open, elastic, and hence more generally applicable notion of human agency as required by any unprejudiced concept of human rights. The notion of human agency couched in this liberal vocabulary is a gloss not on being "human" but on *being "human" in a particular way*.

It is precisely the attempt to specify being "human" in a particular way that makes unavoidable what Griffin calls an "evaluatively substantive" account (174). It can be readily inferred from this account that the correct or best (particular) way of being "human" is the liberal way. In fact, Griffin comes close to saying as much when he speaks of the "spread of the largely *Western-inspired* discourse of human rights that we have witnessed over the last sixty years" (26, emphasis added) and explicitly traces this discourse in turn to the Enlightenment (1–2). In the process of defending this Western-inspired view, Griffin is quite right to mention "a sense in which persecution can even enhance agency," in that "when Alexander Solzhenitsyn was sent to a gulag,

---

[17] Griffin, *On Human Rights*, 149. Hereinafter cited parenthetically by page number only.
[18] Throughout I use "liberty rights" as a general term that covers what Griffin distinguishes as autonomy and liberty.

he seems to have become a more focused and determined agent than ever," and then immediately to reject this as a reason for concluding that agency needs no protection. But he is surely mistaken to treat this as following simply from a larger notion of agency: "My somewhat *ampler* picture is of a self-decider (ie, someone autonomous) who, within limits, is not blocked from pursuing his or her conception of a worthwhile life (ie, someone also at liberty). If either autonomy or liberty is missing, one's agency, on this *ampler* interpretation, is deficient" (46, emphasis added). It seems to me that if we cannot draw any conclusion in favor of persecution from the case of Solzhenitsyn, it is because there is no evidence that persecution *generally* enhances agency or *generally* promotes better and more intense forms of agency than is possible without persecution. Were the facts of the matter otherwise, we would do well to think again.

We should be worried if normative agency already means, substantively, a kind of agency that rules out whatever agency happens to be enhanced, for however few or many people, by persecution. For this would be to equate human agency with a *particular* kind of human agency. There is, of course, nothing at all amiss with advancing a particular conception of normative agency—with operating from the very beginning, as Griffin puts it, "well within the normative circle" (35). The only thing one cannot hope to accomplish within such a normative circle, which is by nature particular, is a set of rights general or universal enough to be properly *human* rights. Just as being "human" in a particular way fails, as we saw earlier, to properly capture what is "human" in "human rights," so a particular kind of normative agency cannot serve as a suitable foundation for such rights as the rights indispensable to all human agents.

Although Griffin discusses liberty rights as human rights, he does so in the context of trying to provide a theoretical foundation for such rights, and there is no reason to think that this *foundation* for liberty rights as human rights would, for Griffin, be any different from a foundation for liberty rights as liberal rights. Aside from the question of whether liberty rights are fit to be human rights, liberty rights themselves need an adequate spelling out so that we can understand how strong liberty rights need to be if they are to make good the rationale that gives them their special meaning and importance. In this spirit it is worth considering whether liberty rights as conceived by Griffin are strong enough as liberal rights.

One is initially encouraged by Griffin's avowed aim to find "the notion of human rights that fits into the best ethics that we can establish" (2) and by his correspondingly unequivocal desire to have his proposal assessed "ultimately, by deciding whether it gives us human rights that fit into the best ethics overall" (4). When Griffin proceeds to place the dignity of the human person at the center of this ethics and to understand this dignity in terms of normative agency, however, what we get is a veritable reduction of ethics to autonomy. It comes to me as a surprise, I must confess, that Griffin's notion of normative agency is so undemanding as to be almost *ethically* empty: it is just "the agency involved in living a worthwhile life" (45), where what counts as a worthwhile life is left almost entirely open and unrestricted, and this not due to oversight but as a matter of principle. As Griffin typically puts it, "What we attach value to, what we regard as giving dignity to human life, is our capacity to choose and to pursue our conception of a worthwhile life" (44). It is because nothing substantive is required of what is called a worthwhile life that Griffin is able to say, with little need for argument, that "Normative agency is the typical human condition" (45).[19]

Griffin seems to be suggesting that what is normative in normative agency is entirely a matter of having and exercising the capacity to choose and pursue what a human agent considers a worthwhile life, within the enormously wide range of what is permissible. There are no further conditions to be satisfied beyond this largely formal requirement, and hence no conditions regarding either the content of a worthwhile life or the conduct of such a life in terms of the virtues. If it is nevertheless possible to accept this characterization as one of *normative* agency, it is difficult to see how normative agency so thinly and undemandingly conceived can support the weighty burden of dignity. Surely, for normative agents to have dignity, they must live in ways that carry dignity over and above the mere fact that they have chosen to live thus.[20]

If Griffin is almost entirely permissive with regard to the content of autonomous choices, he is very demanding, and rightly so, with regard to what autonomy as sheer self-direction involves. This is most explicit in Griffin's explanation of the distinction between autonomy and liberty in terms of their different enemies:

> Autonomy and liberty are different values. And their enemies are different. The enemies of autonomy are indoctrination, brain-washing, domination, manipulation, conformity, conventionality, false consciousness, certain forms of immaturity...One can be at liberty but not autonomous—say, so conventionally raised that, without thought, one falls in with society's values, but is free to pursue them as one wishes (151).

What we find here is an unusually perspicacious appreciation of what autonomy, to be worthy of its name, must require and how difficult it is for individuals to live up to its requirements and for a society to provide an environment free of excessive obstacles to meeting them. Griffin seems even to imply a distinction not unlike mine between individual autonomy and its social setting.

By the standard implicit in the quoted passage, most members of any liberal society are free but not autonomous. Since socialization not of one's own choosing is a condition of subjecthood, some "indoctrination" or "brain-washing" is unavoidable as a precondition of all subjects, even the most autonomous. The question therefore is not whether "indoctrination" is present but what kind of "indoctrination" is acceptable, or, in other words, how well the unavoidable "indoctrination" is redeemed politically and ethically. If we examine what happens in liberal societies, however, we shall find that the "indoctrination" that is part of the very creation of autonomous subjects and of the social setting for individual autonomy is not redeemed but rather made largely invisible. It is a sign of the successful production of this invisibility that most people

---

[19] It is worth noting, though obvious, that Griffin's view is widely shared among contemporary liberal philosophers, most notably John Rawls. See, eg, Rawls's discussion of "the basis of equality" in *A Theory of Justice*, rev. edn. (Cambridge, MA: Harvard University Press, 1999), section 77.

[20] It does not follow, of course, that in the absence of such dignity human agents cannot be entitled to autonomy and liberty on other grounds. One such ground, refreshingly honest though not particularly uplifting, is available in what John Skorupski labels "populism." See his *Ethical Explorations* (New York: Oxford University Press, 1999), 194.

learn to conform and do so with such ease that they think of themselves as acting of their own free will rather than in accordance with the conventional values and preferences which they have picked up with little reflection. Lulled to sleep by the invisibility of the "enemies of autonomy," we sink into the comfortable illusion that a society can be free of indoctrination altogether and a liberal society, despite its imperfections, is close to being such a society. And so we forget that all individual autonomy and autonomous subjectivity have their necessary antecedents in "indoctrination," and that therefore "indoctrination" is something that cannot be eliminated but must instead be redeemed. Without conscientious and continual efforts at such redemption, along with the vigilance required by such efforts, liberal societies make short shrift of the value of individual autonomy.

Such a conclusion is unavoidable if we take seriously Griffin's rightly stringent understanding of autonomy; why else would one invoke this value and call it autonomy in the first place? As it turns out, however, Griffin names "the enemies of autonomy" only to set a very low standard for their elimination in his subsequent discussion:

> What human rights guarantee is that one be able to live the life of a normative agent. In a society with an ample range of options, if one cannot realize one conception, there are others: other lives that one can also value and that can become fully worthwhile lives for one to live…And generally one can find fulfillment in various sorts of lives. For the many of whom this is true, there is equality of opportunity on a more general level: not equal opportunity to achieve any particular conception of a worthwhile life that one might choose, but equal opportunity to make a good life for oneself. *So long as the various ground floors guaranteed by human rights are in place, the obstacles to making a good life are likely to be deep inside oneself,* beyond the reach of others (163, emphasis added).

What human rights patently cannot guarantee, as we have seen, are the right kind of social setting for individual autonomy and the good kind of autonomous subject. Think of the workplace as it has evolved in what Sennett calls "the culture of the new capitalism." Is it at all obvious that one has only oneself to blame in such a setting if one fails to make a good life for oneself, as long as one's human rights are not violated, and as long as "the culture of the new capitalism" does not entail such violation (as it clearly does not)? Is it not more plausible to think, rather, that the social setting for individual autonomy and the socialization of autonomous subjects that have led to the "corrosion of character" are increasingly preventing ordinary men and women of "character" from living a worthwhile life as they reasonably see it?

I am not sure if Griffin is responding to the state of affairs addressed by these questions when he writes: "Liberty is not a right to a worthwhile life itself, but merely a right to pursue it with *no more impediments than those imposed by mother nature,* including, prominently, human nature" (168, emphasis added), or when he writes: "In general, *we must simply accept, and build our lives from, the range of options with which fortune has endowed us.* Society cannot do much to alter it, and the life of a normative agent does not require more than this" (163, emphasis added). What is missing in these remarks is the crucial distinction between "the range of options with which fortune has endowed us" and the range of options that is the result of groups of human beings each trying to shape the structure and ethos of their society in one way rather than another through never-ending struggles for the preservation and preeminence of their kind. The dominant form of society in the world today—liberal democratic capitalism—is one such result. There will be something deeply deficient about liberty rights, by liberalism's own standard, if such rights can do little to redress those limits to options of the good life that are imposed in this way, unless liberals are ready to admit (and this would be a very significant admission indeed) that their attachment to the value of individual autonomy does not extend to the determination of the social setting in which this value is exercised. In this light, Griffin's caution against asking too much of liberty rights would make good sense only on the understanding that the heteronomous production of the antecedent conditions and subjects of individual autonomy has been properly redeemed.[21]

I have taken issue, then, with Griffin's notion of normative agency for being a *particular*, liberal conception of human agency and for being overly *permissive* with regard to ethics. I should now explain how the particularity and the permissiveness come together, and what this seemingly odd combination signifies. It is useful to begin by noting that the concept of what Marx would call "egoistic man" (as the subject of "the rights of man") is replaced in our prevailing, liberal understanding of civil society or the private sphere by that of a moral agent who, as Rawls puts it, pursues the interest of a self which need not be an interest in oneself. All the same, the conceptual possibility of genuine engagement with interests much wider than one's own which is left open by Rawls's distinction is severely limited if not foreclosed by the historical process in which, to use Marx's terminology, the political state came to be separated from civil society. This is a process in which, as Marx puts it, "the bonds which [in the feudal order] had restrained the egoistic spirit of civil society were removed along with the political yoke." The upshot of this process comprises at once the "consummation of the idealism of the state," in the shape of what we now call democracy, and the "consummation of the materialism of civil society," in the shape of the rights of individuals to pursue their private interests as they see fit.[22] It is no accident that the abstract interest of a self has turned out to be, for the most part, a concrete interest in one's own atomistic self, in property, security, and individual happiness, and thus ethical permissiveness is constitutive of a particular conception of the good life.

When we speak of human rights today, then, the rights in question are not the rights of the human being as such but the rights of the human being as shaped in a particular way by a particular historical process. It is this *particular* human being who is the bearer of what we call human rights. If this is so, then the rise of human rights and the function and meaning of such rights must be understood as part of this historical process. This is not changed in any way by the fact that human rights are meant

---

[21] To see to such redemption, not only do we need an account of rights, human or liberal, that fits into the best ethics available, we also need an ethics that fits into the best understanding of the most important features and patterns of development of a liberal democratic society. This is why I have found it necessary to go beyond philosophy's typical abstract normative theorizing and seek help from the work of scholars who tell us what our societies are like.

[22] Karl Marx, "On the Jewish Question," in Robert C. Tucker (ed.), *The Marx–Engels Reader*, 2nd edn. (New York: W. W. Norton, 1978), 45.

to be available to every human being on an equal footing, that indeed the language of human rights is the language of equality. Rather, this fact reminds us to ask the question of "equality among what kind of human beings," a deeper question than "equality of what."[23] Just as there is no human being as such, so there is no equality as such. The same historical process that has resulted in the formation of a particular kind of human being, the modern possessive and increasingly consuming individual, has also given rise to a particular value of equality that is applicable to such beings. Thus it is ultimately for such individuals that equality has come to be what Ronald Dworkin calls the sovereign virtue of our modern world.[24] It is such individuals who are of equal importance and who are the bearers of special responsibility each for himself or herself.

IV. Liberty Rights beyond Liberal Democracy

If I am roughly correct about liberty rights being too strong as human rights and too weak as liberal rights, a satisfactory explanation for this strange awkwardness is bound to tell us something important about liberty rights. Liberty rights, as we have seen, fall considerably short of the ambition of self-determination that informs them, and this is true even in the most liberal of liberal societies. Small wonder, then, that when liberty rights are transplanted from a liberal society to the international arena as human rights, they must suffer a further weakening, since human rights are meant to apply to all human beings and must therefore have a minimalist character.[25] What is at work in both cases is a liberal moral vision that stands in the way of the full working out of liberal rights. This liberal moral vision has as its outer limits a comprehensive ordering of human life in which prominently figures the capitalist organization of production and consumption and, given the central importance of both, in effect of society as a whole.

These outer limits of the liberal moral vision are responsible both for the mistake of propagating liberty rights as human rights and for the largely opposite mistake of stopping well short of the potential of liberty rights when treated as liberal rights. The latter mistake, as we have seen, involves attaching great importance to individual autonomy without taking the logical next step of attaching equal importance to the determination of the social setting for, and of the subjects of, individual autonomy. Given how obvious this mistake is and yet how commonly it is made, I am inclined to think of it as a motivated blind spot: if you set great store by the value of autonomy and yet, in spelling out what it means and requires, do not follow its inner logic to its proper conclusion, with no explanation of why you stop short in this way, this gives one reason to think that you are not motivated to go all the way. Why not? Because you have no problem with the way in which the social setting for, and the subjects of,

---

[23] A particularly incisive treatment of this question can be found in Christoph Menke, *Reflections of Equality*, trans. Howard Rouse and Andrei Denejkine (Stanford: Stanford University Press, 2006), 22–33.

[24] See Ronald Dworkin, *Sovereign Virtue: The Theory and Practice of Equality* (Cambridge, MA: Harvard University Press, 2000).

[25] On the rationale for the minimalist character to human rights, see Griffin, *On Human Rights*, 34, 45, 156.

individual autonomy are actually determined. You have no problem, that is, with the determination of individual autonomy by the capitalist order. You value autonomy, to be sure, and value it greatly, but you are happy or at least prepared to exercise autonomy and have others exercise autonomy under constraints imposed by the capitalist organization of economic and social life. That is why you are not interested in following the inner logic of autonomy to its proper conclusion.[26] When we understand liberty rights, whether as liberal or human rights, as being informed by the moral vision of liberal democracy, then, we must in turn understand liberal democracy itself as standing in a relationship of mutual accommodation and transformation with capitalism. And thus we must understand liberty rights as advancing the cause of human well-being within limits set by the capitalist order.[27]

It is liberty rights thus determined and constrained that serve as the prototype of liberty rights as human rights. As I have tried to show, it is a mistake to treat liberty rights as human rights: if liberty rights as typically understood in the context of a liberal democratic society are too weak, they are too strong as human rights. This mistake has its explanation in the same liberal moral vision that is responsible for the opposite mistake, with only one additional and very important factor to be mentioned, namely, the liberal attempt to extend a duly extenuated version of its moral vision to the international arena especially in the post-Cold War era of global capitalism. I believe Samuel Moyn is entirely correct in characterizing the human rights movement in terms of "the last utopia."[28] This utopia envisions a vastly better *world* than we have now—*one* world, in that all societies in it respect and protect human rights. But rather than being truly responsive to the diverse conditions and traditions in different parts of the world, this vision rests on the conviction that the combination of liberal democracy and capitalism represents the best available organization of economic, political, and social life *everywhere*. If this did not seem so unequivocally the case in the immediate aftermath of the Second World War, there can be little doubt now, given how the Cold War ended with the economic and ideological triumph of liberal democratic capitalism. Since the end of the Cold War, capitalist

---

[26] The inner logic of autonomy is, in this context, social or political, not metaphysical, and one can therefore steer clear of the question of free will versus determinism in the way, say, Philip Pettit does in *A Theory of Freedom: From the Psychology to the Politics of Agency* (New York: Oxford University Press, 2001). Thus understood, "autonomy" is the name of a humanly constructed way of life, with its distinctive practices of self-constitution, in which individuals are allowed, indeed compelled, to determine their own lives. To follow the inner logic of autonomy to its proper conclusion is thus to make it possible for individuals to determine their own lives as much as is humanly possible and meaningful, not on the basis of any metaphysical belief in libertarian free will but according to the social or political value of autonomy itself. By the same token, compatibilism cannot provide any reason to care about determining one's own life within a given social setting but not to care about taking a humanly possible and meaningful part in co-determining that setting.

[27] To say of the human rights movement that it operates largely within the parameters of the capitalist order is not to suggest, however, that what this movement helps to achieve is something that can be taken for granted as the natural outcome of the capitalist system. The capitalist system must be pushed, and pushed very hard, to turn into reality what is otherwise merely structurally possible within it. The human rights movement, especially when it fights simultaneously for liberty rights and welfare rights, is a very important part of that hard pushing. As such, it is the human face—the conscience—of (global) capitalism.

[28] Samuel Moyn, *The Last Utopia: Human Rights in History* (Cambridge, MA: Harvard University Press, 2010).

globalization has assumed an altogether new momentum and scale, and this has made necessary and seemingly natural, in the realm of values, the new moral universalism and political internationalism as embodied in the concept of human rights. The significance of the minimalist character of human rights in this context may be less immediately apparent, but this much is obvious enough, that moral universalism and political internationalism already dictate a certain minimalism, aided by an ideological climate in which the demise of communism has caused all but the tiniest minority to avoid like plague any form of moral maximalism. Thus, when liberty rights once again enter the international arena as human rights, it is entirely predictable that they will largely retain their shape and meaning as liberal rights, so that any society that effectively introduces such rights will become more like a liberal society. And it follows from this, and from the already compromised status of liberty rights in a liberal society, that liberty rights as human rights must suffer the double incoherence of being both too weak (by the measure of their rationale) and too strong (thanks to their misguided universality).

To take issue with liberty rights in the way I have done throughout is not to argue against liberty rights. It is rather to suggest that, to be coherent and true to their own rationale, liberty rights must be made stronger by redeeming the heteronomous determination of the social setting for, and the subjects of, individual autonomy. With this step duly accomplished, we may go a step further and allow liberty rights to re-enter the international arena, as part of a perfectly legitimate proposal for making the world a better place, but no longer as human rights as we now understand them, for no plausible conception of objectively minimal requirements for human status can treat liberty rights as necessary conditions. For these two steps to be taken, liberal democratic societies as we now find them will have to undergo a major transformation, as the conditions for individual autonomy will have to cease to be determined by a capitalist mode of production together with which liberal democracy has so far formed a comprehensive economic, political, and social arrangement. It is only after such a transformation that liberty rights will no longer figure in any dubious project of changing the world in the image of the liberal democratic capitalist order.

This is a very tall order indeed, something we can only approach in the spirit of a new utopia. There is nothing in human nature that need render such a utopia implausible; whether it is realistic (to use Rawls's term), given the way the world has come to be and its sedimentation in human "second" nature, is another matter. If this utopia of genuine autonomy is implausible, or so we believe, then we must own up to the incoherence of the liberal ambition of a society (and world) made up of autonomous agents and to the hopelessness of trying to realize such an ambition. We must own up, that is, to the fact that the autonomy we cherish is no more than a certain room for individual maneuver whose range of choices and outer limits are determined by a capitalist order that has no concern for individual autonomy, or for any other human good for that matter, unless it is instrumental to the profitability and expansion of capital. If this is what we mean by autonomy, we should, in the interest of accuracy and honesty, consider dropping this term—or else spell out the qualifications every time we use it.

More importantly, we will be well advised to reconsider the very rationale for individual autonomy thus determined and compromised. Nothing is more difficult, and more fraught with ideological traps and temptations, than an attempt to fix the level of liberty rights, whether as liberal rights or human rights. And nothing is more revealing or symptomatic than how one settles on a particular level or minimum and how one goes about justifying it—the more so as the attempt is actually doomed to incoherence from the start. If we really care about liberty, we should care about autonomy, and if we really care about autonomy rather than its mere semblance, then we just cannot rest content with the exercise of individual autonomy without bothering to examine the determination—insofar as such determination is carried out by human beings, in however complex a manner, and its outcome could be otherwise—of the social setting for, and of the subjects of, individual autonomy. It is a slippery slope, so to speak, and there is no natural stopping-place until we follow the inner logic of the value of autonomy to its proper conclusion. To stop before we reach this proper conclusion is to stop for reasons other than autonomy. In that case, we might as well settle for less than what we mistakenly regard as autonomy. At least we will have no moral vantage point from which to take issue with those who do if they themselves feel comfortable with it—and most definitely no such vantage point afforded by professed belief in autonomy.

In the end, I believe that liberty rights are among the truly indispensable inventions of the modern moral and political imagination—indispensable not for living but for flourishing under modern conditions of life. But I believe with equal conviction that the rationale and full potential of liberty rights can be made good only if we look beyond the exercise of individual autonomy to its social determination. I labor under no illusions as to the enormity of the task of redeeming the heteronomy of such determination. But all my realism cannot persuade me that philosophers who rightly set such great store by liberty rights, especially autonomy, are not at least intellectually obligated to spell out the inner logic of autonomy and pursue that logic to its proper conclusion before they can speak with reasonable confidence about liberty rights as liberal rights or with respect to the international arena.

34

Human Rights Without the Human Good?

A Reply to Jiwei Ci

Simon Hope

Bernard Williams, in his magisterial discussion of Ancient Greek attitudes to slavery, observes that

> [i]n many comparisons between the ancient and the modern world it is assumed that in the ancient world social roles were understood to be rooted in nature. Indeed, it is often thought to be a special mark of modern societies, distinguishing them from earlier ones, that they have lost this idea...A central feature of modern liberal conceptions of social justice can indeed be expressed by saying that they altogether deny the existence of necessary social identities.[1]

Williams is undoubtedly correct about this; as he is about the fact that the 'intellectual machinery' by which the point can be expressed is itself distinctly modern, and about the need to guard against making this contrast the sole lynchpin on which our understanding of distant social moralities hangs. Williams's point makes it well worth asking: what has the history of liberal thought proposed to replace notions of necessary social identity with, and how do those proposals relate to other elements of modern liberalism?

For Jiwei Ci, answers to these questions expose some crippling deficiencies in our thinking about human rights. Ci's specific target is liberty rights, about which he advances two critical theses:

1. '[l]iberty rights, no matter how justified, cannot be justified as human rights.'[2]
2. 'liberty rights as understood in the standard way are *too weak* as liberal rights, and this is shown by a contradiction within the liberal approach to liberty rights in a liberal society.'[3]

In the first half (roughly speaking) of this paper I shall argue that neither of these theses should be accepted. Nonetheless—and this forms my paper's second half—there may be serious tensions in the way that modern global justice theorists assemble the deliverances of the liberal tradition when vindicating human rights. These tensions centre on the liberal conception of the human good, and I shall suggest that we would

---

[1] Williams, *Shame and Necessity* (Berkeley: University of California Press, 1993), 126–7.
[2] Ci, 'Liberty Rights and the Limits of Liberal Democracy', this volume, ch. 33, 588–9.
[3] Ci, this volume, ch. 33, 591.

do much better, when vindicating human rights, to draw on strands of liberalism which do not invoke any conception of the human good.

I. Against Ci's Two Theses

I begin with Ci's iconoclastic claim that liberty rights, as liberals standardly conceive of such rights, cannot be human rights. Ci's reasoning is as follows: 'because people in different times and places have led humanly meaningful and worthwhile lives with-out anything like liberty rights', it is mistaken 'to regard liberty rights as rights that human beings have simply by virtue of being human.'[4] Rather, the standard liberal understanding of liberty rights denotes a set of freedoms associated with a *particular way* of being human, where human agency is fundamentally determined by lib-eral social forms. The mistake, Ci claims, occurs when global justice theorists treat the peculiarly liberal way of configuring human agency 'as if it were human agency as such'.

I find this argument deeply flawed. For one thing, it is too quick. Liberal global justice theorists will be unperturbed by Ci's objection if they hold that the particular configuration of agency that liberty rights protect is the true or correct configuration of human agency. Thus, to give one example, Darrel Moellendorf defends an expan-sive account of human rights centred on the Rawlsian conception of the person, on the grounds that the Rawlsian conception of the person is true, and so 'the fact that the conception of persons originates in the democratic tradition cannot be a reason not to apply it elsewhere.'[5] Here, Moellendorf seems to take the liberal rejection of any nec-essary social identity as allowing the claim that the liberal (or rather, Rawls's) concep-tion of the person strikes bedrock.

I suspect Ci does not contemplate this counter-argument because he assumes we already have in view a bedrock understanding of common humanity that is not con-clusively liberal. Ci employs the phrase 'the human form of life' repeatedly in his essay, and the Wittgensteinian resonance[6] of that phrase suggests that a certain set of prac-tices which could shape one's life mark, when manifest, that life as *non-defectively human*. Ci is at any rate committed to such a notion: his objection to seeing liberty rights as human rights depends on the assumption that the appropriate 'minimal-ist justification' for human rights must appeal to what is involved in living 'a human life' or 'humanly meaningful' life.[7] This sort of talk is common enough in the philo-sophical literature on human rights, but—like talk of the *unnaturalness* of nuclear power—complex philosophical commitments are necessary if the atypically nar-row scope given to the classificatory term is to make sense. In judgments that some blighted lives are less than fully *human* the commitment in question must be that reflection on human nature reveals a singularly human form of life. While what Ci

---

[4] Ci, this volume, ch. 33, 588.

[5] Darrel Moellendorf, *Cosmopolitan Justice* (Boulder: Westview, 2002), 18–23; quotation from 23.

[6] Wittgenstein, *Philosophical Investigations*, trans. G.E.M. Anscombe (Oxford: Blackwell, 1976), I, §241; II, 226e. Compare Michael Thompson, *Life and Action* (Cambridge, MA: Harvard University Press, 2008), 207–8.

[7] Ci, this volume, ch. 33, 589.

takes this form of life to involve is opaque, it seems to be characterized by 'generic freedom': roughly, that the shape of one's life passes some test of individual and collective reflective endorsement, and lives that do not pass this test are not fully human. Generic freedom is not liberal freedom (the latter involves a distinctive conception of autonomy that the former lacks), and, armed with this understanding of *the* human form of life, Ci cannot entertain the notion that a distinctively liberal understanding of agency hits bedrock.

Yet matters cannot be so straightforward. If 'the human form of life' is to be specified in sufficiently generic terms that the objection Ci presses against liberty rights as human rights does not apply to it, then the notion of 'the human form of life' ends up vacuously empty. Many societies certainly have forced some human beings into lives that do not pass, from the inside, the relevant test of reflective endorsement. But if Ci is to say, of slave-holding societies, etc., that they are not *human* societies, then his notion of 'the human form of life' is in the relevant respects just as limited as the liberal understanding: it is associated with a particular set of historically and culturally contingent social practices, alternatives to which humans have found meaningful.[8]

An even more urgent question concerns the coherence of the very idea of *the* human form of life. I do not think it plausible to speak of such a thing. The only way to see human behaviour in terms of the forces that animate it is to keep in view the remarkable diversity of human mores and conventions, social moralities, forms of life, and conceptions of ourselves; all the diverse patterns of conduct through which particular constellations of concepts, beliefs, and values are combined into reflective experiences of the world. One must *also* keep in view the complex tides and eddies of thought created by individuals' intellectual engagement with the particular constellations of concepts and beliefs they have inherited in particular times and places, so that any appropriately historical view of all this is a decidedly kaleidoscopic one. I hope the reader will excuse the mangled metaphors, but this is the clearest and most accurate way I know of to characterize what human nature and human reasoning is. And because all that anyone's reasoned reflection, anywhere, has to go on is an ensemble of culturally inherited and historically contingent notions, it is not plausible to think that there is a distinctively *human* form of life characterized by the exercise of human reason. There are, in Clifford Geertz's marvelous phrase, only 'the forms human life has locally taken'.[9]

None of this stops us reflecting on the features of the sort of creature that inhabits these diverse forms of life. Nor is there an obvious reason to rule out tying the justification for human rights to those elements of human *beings* which are morally significant enough to ground rights, rather than to a singularly human *way* (form) of life.

---

[8] Compare Raymond Geuss, *The Idea of a Critical Theory* (Cambridge: Cambridge University Press, 1981), 66: 'I find it quite hard to burden pre-dynastic Egyptians, 9th century French serfs, or early 20th century Yanomamö tribesmen with the view that they are acting correctly if their action is based on a norm on which there would be universal consensus in an ideal speech situation.' Or, for that matter, on Ci's understanding of generic freedom.

[9] Clifford Geertz, *Local Knowledge* (New York: Basic Books, 1983), 16. See also Richard Schweder, *Thinking Through Cultures* (Cambridge MA: Harvard University Press, 1991); and Michael Jackson, *Life Within Limits* (Durham, NC: Duke University Press, 2011).

What then matters is whether liberty rights protect those morally significant features of human beings, and the question of which forms of life liberty rights are appropriate to becomes uninteresting: human beings have basic rights in virtue of the kind of creature a human being is, and these rights determine which forms of life are morally acceptable.

Just how a liberal argument along the above lines might unfold is a very complex question. If we are to attribute weighty moral significance to some notion of what it is to be human, we must acknowledge that the contours of the concept 'human being' we appeal to are shaped by more than the properties of the *natural kind* 'human being' as a biologist might understand it. Any understanding of 'human being' that could bear the required philosophical weight will be a deliverance of our second nature: of a particular shaping of our brute biological capacities for reason, speech, and sociability that one acquired in becoming habituated into a culturally and historically particular form of life.[10] I am allowing my language to become McDowellian here to register the point that the sorts of notions of 'human being' one must use to vindicate moral claims are themselves products of particular, historically contingent, social moralities. We should not readily assume that just because we all are human beings any rational convergence on the sort of understanding of our life-form that could ground human rights is obvious or to be expected.[11] As Geertz observes,

> the Western conception of the person as a bounded, unique, more or less integrated motivational and cognitive universe, a dynamic centre of awareness, emotion, judgment, and action organised into a distinctive whole and set contrastively both against other wholes and against its social and natural background is, however incorrigible it may seem to us, a rather peculiar idea within the context of the world's cultures.[12]

This does not mean we cannot, in justifying human rights, appeal to such a conception. I think it does show that we would do very well to avoid blithe assertions of the truth of the liberal conception of our life-form, and to focus instead on the very hard question of how we might adduce considerations for seeing things our way that are accessible to others who see things differently.[13]

Other difficulties also intrude. There is a complex question, which I shall not address here, over the work a conception of human life-form can do in our thinking about moral obligation.[14] There is also a question, to which I will return, of the extent

---

[10] John McDowell, 'Two Sorts of Naturalism', in R. Hursthouse, G. Lawrence, and W. Quinn (eds.), *Virtues and Reasons* (Oxford: Clarendon Press, 1995), 149–79); compare Simon Hope, 'Neo-Aristotelian Justice: An Unsolved Question', *Res Publica*, 19(2) (2013): 157–72.

[11] As, eg, Martha Nussbaum seems to: 'We [meaning, apparently, all reasonable souls] can accept without profound metaphysics the idea that human life has a characteristic shape and form'. *Frontiers of Justice* (Cambridge, MA: Belknap, 2006), 186; compare Martha Nussbaum, *Women and Human Development* (Cambridge: Cambridge University Press, 2000), 72–3.

[12] Geertz, *Local Knowledge*, 59.

[13] This is a very controversial point, which I cannot adequately defend here, but nothing I go on to say depends upon this view of the task of moral philosophy.

[14] Compare G.E.M. Anscombe, 'Modern Moral Philosophy', 38 (in *Collected Papers* vol. III, Oxford: Basil Blackwell, 1981), speaking of the sense in which the possession of certain capacities/virtues is the norm for mankind: 'in *this* sense "norm" has ceased to be roughly equivalent to "law"'. See also the concerted attempt by Thompson, *Life and Action*, to overcome Anscombe's doubt.

to which defenders of human rights slip between appeals to what a human being *is* and appeals to a 'truly human' form of *life*. But the point I wish to register here is that Ci's claim that liberty rights cannot be human rights depends on the assumption that human rights are grounded in a distinctively human *form of life*. There is no reason for liberal defenders of human rights to accept that assumption; indeed, we should reject it.

I turn now to Ci's second critical claim: that the liberal understanding of liberty rights is too weak. Ci's criticism is motivated by the belief that contemporary liberal thinkers ignore the extent to which their favoured conception of agency is determined by the institutions of global capitalism. What is missed is that the autonomy liberty rights protect is 'autonomy under constraints imposed by the capitalist organization of economic and social life...thus we must understand liberty rights as advancing the cause of human well-being within limits set by the capitalist order.'[15] This fact, Ci claims, cripples liberty rights as liberal rights, because the institutions of global capitalism fatally undermine autonomy.

Ci seeks to vindicate this criticism via a complex argument. Ci sensibly observes that autonomous agents can only determine themselves through inherited understandings they did not initially choose.[16] But Ci goes on to describe certain liberal moral aims, such as individuals' access to the various mechanisms within local forms of life through which changes in social practices may be effected, and the attainment of moral goods, as *grounded* in the need to 'redeem' autonomy from our unchosen second nature. This grounding I find much less obvious, both as a description of liberalism and as a sensible idea.[17]

Ci offers two arguments to show that the social forms of modern capitalism are in direct conflict with these moral aims. The first is to observe that under market institutions 'the weak are absolutely inferior to the strong in their ability to shape the social setting for individual autonomy'.[18] Given that free market institutions offer no corrective for inequalities in bargaining power that individuals bring into the market, this is an accurate criticism of libertarian versions of liberalism that only acknowledge rights against interference. But there are plenty of alternative liberal conceptions of liberty rights where liberty rights and welfare rights must be taken together,[19] and Ci's point does not show that *those* conceptions are too weak.

Ci's second argument is more ambitious. As Ci puts it, 'the exercise of individual autonomy is warped, compromised, and even undermined when it is framed by a social setting increasingly dominated by global capital...shaped in such a way as to make

---

[15] Ci, this volume, ch. 33, 605.   [16] Ci, this volume, ch.33, 592–3.

[17] I struggle to see how 'redemption' is at all a plausible idea. That individuals only acquire the capacities for interaction under *any* complex social forms in virtue of having been habituated into an historically and culturally particular form of life is simply a part of our finitude. Saying that this fact requires *redemption* betrays a dubious wishful thinking, identifying human finitude as a source of regret for human beings. I cannot see why we should take such a thought seriously: it is akin to genuine regret that one lacks x-ray vision or the ability to freeze time.

[18] Ci, this volume, ch. 33, 592.

[19] Eg, Henry Shue, *Basic Rights*, 2nd edn. (Princeton: Princeton University Press, 1980), 31; Elizabeth Ashford, 'The Alleged Dichotomy Between Positive Rights and Negative Duties', in C. Beitz and R. Goodin (eds.), *Global Basic Rights* (New York: Oxford University Press, 2009), 94–100.

choosing and pursuing the good life an increasingly uphill struggle.'[20] Here, the argument is that the liberal conception of liberty rights is consistent with social forms that undermine our attainment of ethical goods. Ci develops the argument via a detailed meditation on Alasdair MacIntyre's jeremiad on the atomizing, hollow nature of modern liberal social forms—a social world fit for aesthetes, managers, and therapists but one entirely unsuited to the attainment of meaningful virtues and lives[21]—and the related sociological work of Richard Sennett. The lesson Ci draws is that the liberal conception of liberty rights 'makes for a regime of self-constitution in which people acquire what is most important for themselves [individual identities] through efforts directed at the most unsuitable objects [external goods] and in the least auspicious manner [sheer competitiveness].'[22]

Social forces promoting success in terms of ultimately meaningless baubles achieved at the expense of one's fellows are undoubtedly at work in liberal societies, but the connection to *liberty* rights may not be immediately apparent. As Brian Barry once remarked, a properly liberal society 'provides alcohol, tranquilizers, wrestling on the television, astrology, psychoanalysis, and so on, endlessly' for those who do not wish to take the opportunity liberty rights provide for taking responsibility and control over their own lives.[23] But for Barry, nothing about the basic structure of liberal society *entails*, rather than merely makes possible, the dominance of the hollow, atomized, and morally debased lives MacIntyre and Ci lament. Why, then, does Ci think liberty rights are too weak when conceived of as liberal rights, rather than holding that not all individuals may prove strong enough to make the most of their liberty?

Ci's answer, if I understand him, is that one cannot isolate the liberal conception of liberty rights from the atomising social forces in modern liberal societies. 'This liberal moral vision' Ci writes, 'has as its outer limits a comprehensive ordering of human life in which prominently figures the capitalist organization of production and consumption'.[24] Ci's appeal to the close historical connection between liberalism and capitalism is what makes his essay so interesting and potentially powerful. But I do not think the MacIntyrean jeremiad is at all helpful in making sense of how, if at all, the close historical connection between liberalism and capitalism renders liberal conceptions of liberty rights problematic.

For one thing, there is something unfortunate about the one-sided MacIntyrean contrast between the hollow, atomized, and morally debased liberal form of life and some rich, interconnected, non-liberal alternative in which lives have meaningful narratives. The non-liberal alternative in such comparisons is invariably presented in a remarkably idealized fashion, applying notions of 'community' or 'narrative structure' solely to favoured instances of such. 'It is', Stephen Holmes has penetratingly remarked, 'as if "the dental" referred exclusively to healthy teeth'.[25] In this light, Ci's own avowedly utopian vision of a post-liberal alternative can scarcely be encouraging.

---

[20] Ci, this volume, ch. 33, 594 and 596.
[21] Alasdair MacIntyre, *After Virtue*, 2nd edn. (London: Duckworth, 1985).
[22] Ci, this volume, ch. 33, 597.
[23] Brian Barry, *The Liberal Theory of Justice* (Oxford: Oxford University Press, 1973), 127.
[24] Ci, this volume, ch. 33, 604.
[25] Stephen Holmes, 'The Permanent Structure of Anti-Liberal Thought', in N. Rosenblum (ed.), *Liberalism and the Moral Life* (Cambridge, MA: Harvard University Press, 1989), 232.

One also wishes for a more nuanced picture of liberal social forms. Consider, for example, Ajume Wingo's comparison between Ghanaian life and the life of one of his American students:

> A responsive government makes it possible for persons to lead isolated, even eccentric, lifestyles. While in communalistic parts of Ghana it takes a village to raise a child, in my student's hometown, it takes a daycare centre. Whereas one can fish, hunt, and farm at Whole Foods for far more food than is needed to survive, in rural Ghana, one must trek long distances in order to *literally* fish, hunt, and farm. Whereas extended family is central to the survival of the individual in Ghana, in my student's homeland, an extended family can be ignored without peril. For him, and Americans more generally, value is measured in dollars. But for an average African who lives with (or perhaps in spite of) her non-responsive, dysfunctional government, a familial network is a far surer measure of wealth, guarantor of survival, and protector of freedom than is a government-issued currency.[26]

Ghanaian life as Wingo describes it is much less atomized, and this has advantages: Wingo observes that something like the Kitty Genovese tragedy would be extremely unlikely in a Ghanaian community. But Wingo is also sensitive to the fact that atomized modes of life can only arise under stable, effective, generally responsive—although by no means perfectly just—social institutions. Seen in this light, there is considerable force to Judith Shklar's observation that any hankering for more extensive communal or individual identities is the luxury of a privileged liberal society.[27]

The one-sidedness of the MacIntyrean jeremiad Ci deploys also obscures the fact that there is more room for thinking through the connections between liberalism and capitalism than Ci allows. At this point, it becomes necessary to pin down precisely what I take 'liberalism' to be. 'Liberalism' is a contested notion, with various restrictive definitions stipulated for specific purposes: thus Philip Pettit (for the purpose of too-sharply separating liberalism from republicanism) treats liberalism as a nineteenth-century invention; thus Sam Freeman (for purposes unclear to me) seeks to distance libertarian views from the liberal tradition.[28] These are just two examples among many, but if one is to get a proper grip on liberalism a broader characterization is needed. The following seems accurate to me: to borrow a phrase from John Pocock, liberalism is fundamentally concerned with the 'separation and recombination' of individual liberty and political authority,[29] and it holds that the appropriate separation and recombination must be justifiable to all citizens as individuals. I think it is also fair to say that capitalist thinking is entwined with liberalism from the very outset: the seventeenth-century originators of liberalism saw

---

[26] Ajume Wingo, 'The Odyssey of Human Rights', *Transition*, 102(1) (2010): 120–38; quotation from 121. Compare Jackson, *Life Within Limits*.

[27] Judith Shklar, 'The Liberalism of Fear', in N. Rosenblum, *Liberalism and the Moral Life*, 35–6.

[28] Philip Pettit, 'Liberalism and Republicanism', *Australian Journal of Political Science*, 28(4) (1993): 163; Philip Pettit, *Republicanism* (Oxford: Oxford University Press, 1997), 8; Samuel Freeman, 'Illiberal Libertarians: Why Libertarianism is Not a Liberal View', *Philosophy and Public Affairs*, 30(2) (2001): 105–51.

[29] J.G.A. Pocock, *Virtue, Commerce, and History* (Cambridge: Cambridge University Press, 1985), 44.

inviolable property rights as the best way of achieving and securing the correct separation and recombination of liberty and authority.[30] By the eighteenth century the nascent institutions of global commerce quickly came to be seen as the best means of subjugating both mankind's anti-social interests and the political pursuit of glory, thereby ensuring a world in which the liberal separation and recombination was stable.[31]

Grasping the initial links between liberalism and capitalism enables us to reject Ci's claim that liberals effectively lack the philosophical materials to think of human nature in terms other than unencumbered, atomized, self-interest.[32] The early liberals embraced a much richer and more plausible conception of human nature, and it was precisely a concern with the darker human tendencies that linked liberalism and capitalism. As Albert Hirschman notes,

> capitalism was precisely expected and supposed to repress certain human drives and proclivities and to fashion a less multifaceted, less unpredictable, and more 'one-dimensional' human personality. This position, which seems so strange today, arose from extreme anguish over the clear and present dangers of a certain historical period, from concern over the destructive forces unleashed by the human passions with the only exception, so it seemed at the time, of 'innocuous' avarice.[33]

The idea that human nature is accurately described in terms of unencumbered egoism is one contingent possibility within liberal thought, and it rose in influence only by exploiting the use—by earlier liberal arguments for capitalism—of the term 'interest' to denote innocuous passions, in such a way as to break with those arguments' richer conceptions of human nature. To the earlier liberal writers, the idea that commerce harnessed the deepest human drives in a way that *naturally transformed* (via invisible hands, and so on) discord into concord was seen as wishful thinking based on a misguidedly narrow understanding of human nature. The context in which the early liberals thought of human nature is one in which a belief in the universality of human nature was increasingly thought to be feasible only if narrowly reductive accounts of human nature were avoided,[34] and by the end of the eighteenth century some thinkers were convinced that diversity was *so* great that commercial interaction offered the only hope of understanding other cultures.[35] The point here is that whatever is lost to us from 18th-century accounts of human

---

[30] Pocock, *Virtue, Commerce, and History*, Part I; Joyce Appleby, *Liberalism and Republicanism in the Historical Imagination* (Cambridge, MA: Harvard University Press, 1992), chs. 1–3.

[31] Albert Hirschman, *The Passions and the Interests* (Princeton: Princeton University Press, 1977); see also Istvan Hont, 'Free Trade and the Economic Limits to National Politics', in J. Dunn (ed.), *The Economic Limits of Modern Politics* (Cambridge: Cambridge University Press, 1992).

[32] Ci, this volume, ch. 33, 605, formulates the point as follows: while certain modern liberals do not outrightly endorse atomized self-interest, the fundamentally capitalist nature of the liberal moral vision excludes the real possibility of an alternative. See also MacIntyre, *After Virtue*, 34.

[33] Hirschman, *The Passions and the Interests*, 132.

[34] For an excellent account of this context see Aaron Garrett, 'Human Nature', in Knud Haakonssen (ed.), *The Cambridge History of 18th Century Philosophy*, vol. I (Cambridge: Cambridge University Press, 2011), 160–233.

[35] See Anthony Pagden, *European Encounters With the New World* (Yale: Yale University Press, 1994), ch. 5.

nature, the rejection of simplistically reductive accounts is still an option for us, and it has always been a part of the liberal tradition's materials for thinking through connections with capitalism.

A similar point can be made with respect to virtue and character, which both MacIntyre and Ci assert are eroded by capitalism. Early liberals were profoundly concerned that the separation and recombination of liberty and authority must be *institutionally protected*: they came to see that conceiving of good government and society through the mode of civic virtue was inadequate. Such a mode appeared to them not only to be unable to address the institutional complexities of liberty, but also to hopelessly idealize away aspects of our nature.[36] But the liberal ambivalence towards civic virtue does not necessitate a blindness to character. Whereas older traditions of thinking through the virtues located character within a religious or natural scheme that specified the variety of roles through which man's social nature was understood,[37] the liberal rejection of any necessary social identity made appeal to such schemes unavailable. In its place, a distinctively liberal strand of thinking about character attempted to make do with the imperfect elements of human nature as such, playing humanity's negative tendencies off one another in order to negate their effects.[38]

The initial intertwining of liberal and capitalist thought emerges as part of the solution to the problem of man's inhumanity to man; a problem which is very much still with us, although of course not to be understood now in quite the same way it was then. The early liberals' solution had to render stable the liberal separation and recombination of individual liberty and political authority, and at that point the nascent institutions of capitalism become instrumentally implicated in the solution. In light of all this, Ci's complaint that liberty rights are too weak as liberal rights must appear implausible. This is not to say that the tendencies of modern life that so concern MacIntyre and Ci are entirely untroubling. What I am trying to say is that even if those concerns are a problem created by the liberal vision of liberty rights, *those concerns cannot show that the liberal conception of liberty rights is too weak*. If I am right there is a venerable, and clearly liberal, way of conceiving of liberty rights that does not attempt to do any more than secure the basic institutional conditions for the legitimate use of political authority. Ci has not shown that liberty rights, as standardly conceived, are too weak for *that* task.

---

[36] See Steve Pincus, 'Neither Machiavellian Moment nor Possessive Individualism', *American Historical Review* (June 1998): 705–36, 729–32. Pincus deals with the seventeenth-century English context, and see Herbert Storing, *What the Anti-Federalists Were For* (Chicago: University of Chicago Press, 1981), 71–3, for the eighteenth-century American context.

[37] Think, eg, of the efforts the Roman of good character would go to in order to display proper masculinity, moderating their gait and vocal resonance: see Peter Brown, *The Body and Society*, 2nd edn. (New York: Columbia University Press, 2008), 9–12. Greek attitudes are not much different in these respects: Williams, *Shame and Necessity*, 117–23; Julia Annas, 'Plato's *Republic* and Feminism', *Philosophy*, 51(197): 307–21.

[38] Judith Shklar, *Ordinary Vices* (Cambridge, MA: Belknap, 1984). See also Hirschman, *The Passions and the Interests*.

II. The Liberal Good Life and the Institutions of Global Capitalism

So we ought to reject both of Ci's theses about liberty rights. Yet there is more to be said about human rights generally, for there is more than one way of pressing the objection that, in Katrin Flikschuh's words, 'the currently evolving liberal morality may be labouring under its own historically engendered economic and political constraints' in a way that undermines certain liberal accounts of human rights.[39] Flikschuh herself, in pressing this objection, differs from Ci on at least two points. First, whereas Ci focuses on the attainment of ethical goods *within* liberal societies, Flikschuh focuses on whether liberalism can achieve *globally* the political and economic aspirations that it holds to be universally valid. The worry, which Flikschuh advances only tentatively, is that societies may only secure liberal moral commitments domestically via political and economic institutions that sustain inequalities at the global level; inequalities which necessarily undermine liberalism's universal commitments.[40] But—and this is the second important difference between Flikschuh and Ci—Flikschuh is careful not to portray the issue in broadly Marxist terms as a contradiction *inherent* in the *very idea* of liberalism. Everything depends on how liberals understand the universal commitments captured by justice and human rights, and only some strands of liberal thought are open to the charge that the standards of universal justice they promulgate are intermeshed with inequalities at the global level that prevent the realisation of those standards for all.

Making sense of Flikschuh's point calls for a second excursion into the history of liberalism. Flikschuh emphasizes two distinct strands of liberal thought. One—older, reaching back to liberalism's seventeenth-century origins—is deontological, understanding the demands of universal morality as a set of constraints on permissible ways of going on. The second strand—venerable but more recent, originating in utilitarian thinking—is fundamentally teleological in outlook, deriving the demands of universal morality from an account of the good human life. For Flikschuh, the problem liberal global justice theorists face lies in the influence in contemporary thinking of this second strand. Whereas the older, deontological, strand of liberalism was fundamentally oriented around questions of political legitimacy, 'liberalism's teleological strand...took questions of political legitimacy as settled and considered the question of individual wellbeing entirely from within the institutional and conceptual framework of the individual state'. And precisely because the earlier questions of legitimacy had been settled in ways that vindicated the nascent capitalist international order, the liberal good life 'presupposes the presence of a competitive free market economy as well as a strong conception of liberal sovereign statehood that deploys political power with an eye to achieving maximal economic advantage'.[41]

---

[39] Katrin Flikschuh, 'The Limits of Liberal Cosmopolitanism', *Res Publica*, 10(2) (2004): 190.
[40] Flikschuh, 'The Limits of Liberal Cosmopolitanism', 186.
[41] Flikschuh, 'The Limits of Liberal Cosmopolitanism', 189.

The deontological strand was certainly not eclipsed by the later teleological strand;[42] the two persist contemporaneously, as two contingent paths via which liberal thought develops and adapts, and liberal theorists assemble the deliverances of either or both strands in a wide variety of ways. This point may make the historical argument Flikschuh offers appear entirely unconvincing: that a strand of liberal thought developed in a certain way hardly implies that liberal thinking has to stay that way, and the teleological strand of liberal thought certainly does not lack the philosophical resources to give an account of political legitimacy rather than simply taking the issue as settled. Yet I think Flikschuh's point can be both strengthened and deepened, in a way that exposes this rebuttal as too simplistic, by further reflection on what the conception of the good that forms the liberal *telos* requires of an institutional scheme.

Any plausibly liberal conception of the good life will reflect the abiding concern of liberal thought with the separation and recombination of individual liberty and political authority. For this reason, the liberal good life is the life of *personal autonomy*: the liberal conception of flourishing is one where the shape of one's own life is, to a significant degree, under one's control. In Stephen Wall's words:

> Personal autonomy is the ideal of people charting their own course through life, fashioning their character by self-consciously choosing projects and taking up commitments from a wide range of eligible alternatives, and making something out of their lives according to their own understanding of what is valuable and worth doing.[43]

All of this will be very familiar to any reader of contemporary political philosophy, and I shall not dwell on the details of differing philosophical accounts. What I want to emphasize is that significant, or at least sufficient, control over the shape of one's life, as it is understood in liberal conceptions of the good life, is a complex matter requiring social institutions to secure for individuals a considerable array of capabilities.

To see this it is necessary to interrogate further what it *is* to 'make',[44] or 'shape',[45] or chart the course of, one's own life. It is consistently held to involve an array of meaningful options, although the width of that array is often left unclear.[46] Yet it should be possible to say more. According to Martha Nussbaum, to live a sufficiently autonomous life requires (among other things) that one attains a decent basic level of education; exercising one's creative choice according to one's own lights; control over one's body and the ability to form mutually consensual sexual relationships according to one's tastes and orientation; an informed view of the world and politics that one has

---

[42] To give one example of the deontological strand's persistence, although there is a common tendency now to think that liberalism has always opposed slavery as a monstrous enemy of human flourishing and dignity, one of the most powerful nineteenth century anti-slavery arguments—Abraham Lincoln's, among many others—made no such appeal to flourishing, and decried slavery solely in (libertarian) terms of the evil of denying a man the fruit of his own labour. See Garry Wills, 'Lincoln's Black History', *NYRB*, LVI(10) (2009): 52–5. That is a recognizably liberal argument, even if not everyone (including Lincoln) who made it held uniformly liberal views on race.

[43] Stephen Wall, *Liberalism, Perfectionism, and Restraint* (Cambridge: Cambridge University Press, 2007), 203.

[44] Joseph Raz, *The Morality of Freedom* (Oxford: Oxford University Press, 1986), 375.

[45] Nussbaum, *Women and Human Development*, 72.

[46] Raz, *The Morality of Freedom*, 204; Joseph Raz, *Ethics in the Public Domain* (Oxford: Clarendon Press, 1995), 4–5; Wall, *Liberalism, Perfectionism, and Restraint*, 188–9.

been able to assemble oneself in the market-place of ideas; freedom of movement; the ability to form personal attachments with others and to engage in the pursuits through which those attachments play out; the secure ownership of property; a significant degree of social and workplace mobility; and the economic, political, legal, and physical resources to be able to do all these things without sacrificing or rendering insecure (to an objectionable degree) any basic needs.[47] My punctuation is here intended to convey the breathlessness one may be left with when confronted by Nussbaum's list. Yet it is difficult to see how someone could have sufficiently authored/made their life if control with respect to one of Nussbaum's items is denied them (their sexual relations; their possessions, etc.). Something fundamentally similar to this list must, then, be entailed by the liberal conception of the good life as a life that is, to the requisite degree, 'made', 'shaped', 'authored', or 'charted' by oneself.

Anything close, if not identical, to Nussbaum's list will require a very complex constellation of capabilities involving a considerable array of options in a very wide number of spheres of life. These options are not of course limitless—Nozick's remark[48] about being able to leave my knife where I like, but not in your chest applies to all this too—but they must be considerable. Defenders of the liberal good life typically take this to be a strength of their conception of the human good: it is not a culturally specific conception, and can be lived within a wide variety of local forms of life.[49] I am not so sure. What this conception of the good life involves is the option to pursue whichever cultural values one chooses to under one's own terms *within the context of a basic structure of institutions that secure the long list of capabilities and options that the good life requires.*

In fact, very few sorts of institutional structure will be able to secure the constellation of capabilities and options that constitute the conditions for the liberal good life. It is very hard to see how the requisite institutional structure could be anything other than fundamentally market-based, both because of the range of options required, and because a considerable degree of freedom not only to expend but also to generate one's wealth seems a fundamental part of this constellation of capabilities and options. This is not to say that what is required is the completely unfettered market that libertarians dream of.[50] What it is to say is that the conditions for the attainment of the liberal good life seem perfectly suited to, and so far as anyone has managed seem only achievable under, the socio-economic institutions of global market capitalism, constrained by—but also, importantly, constraining in turn—the domestic forms of liberal democracy. Given that the prosperity that enables liberal societies to secure (should they choose to) the liberal good life for all their members has only been furnished by global socio-economic institutions that systematically deny that prosperity to others elsewhere,[51] I find the following disquieting suggestion entirely plausible: the

---

[47] Nussbaum, *Frontiers of Justice*, 77–8.

[48] Robert Nozick, *Anarchy, State, and Utopia* (New York: Basic Books, 1974), 171.

[49] Nussbaum, *Frontiers of Justice*, 296–7; Raz, *Ethics in the Public Domain*, 24.

[50] Compare Joseph Heath, 'Liberal Autonomy and Consumer Sovereignty', in John Christman and Joel Anderson (eds.), *Autonomy and the Challenges to Liberalism* (Cambridge: Cambridge University Press, 2005), 204–25.

[51] See, eg, the compelling condemnation of global institutions in Thomas Pogge, *World Poverty and Human Rights*, 2nd edn. (New York: Polity, 2008).

liberal good life is not one that can be universally attained. It cannot be, because the institutional structures that create the conditions for the attainment of the good life within liberal societies are inextricably intertwined with systemic economic inequalities at the global level that prevent all from attaining it.

At this point I would like to bring back into view the question of what liberal thought replaces the notion of necessary social identities with. John Tasioulas has recently insisted that to uncover a philosophically robust conception of human rights one must focus on 'the human good and the special protection it merits'.[52] Many, many liberal defenders of human rights follow this route of argument. In doing so, they locate a conception of common humanity devoid of any necessary social roles or stratification by defining it through an account of (what is taken to be) a *truly human* life. And that conception of the good life has to be the liberal life marked by autonomy. Here is a reliably representative (if unusually explicit concerning the slip between human *being* and human *life*) example:

> [T]he core idea is that of the human being as a dignified and free being who shapes his or her own life in cooperation and reciprocity with others, rather than being passively shaped or pushed around by the world in the manner of a 'flock' or 'herd' animal. A life that is really human is shaped throughout by [the] twin human powers of practical reason and sociability.[53]

Insofar as defenders of human rights follow this line, it is hard to see how their conception of human rights avoids the contradiction of setting universal entitlements for all that are intermeshed with global economic institutions that prevent the universal fulfilment of those entitlements.

In reply, defenders of human rights within liberalism's teleological strand might argue that while the content of human rights must be grounded in the liberal conception of human flourishing, the derivation could fall well short of the array of capabilities and options that are intermeshed with capitalist socio-economic forms. Thus Thomas Pogge has insisted that human rights be understood 'largely in terms of the unspecific means to, rather than components of, human flourishing', and Pogge is careful to select a narrow list of means that fall far short of the complex constellation of capabilities and options one would need to sufficiently shape or author one's life.[54] Or one might hold that connecting the liberal good life to human rights itself introduces a deontological constraint: the *very idea* of human rights as held by all human beings entails that the conception of the human good that gives such rights content is one simultaneously achievable by all human beings.[55]

But the coherence of either sort of rebuttal is far from clear. As Thomas Hurka correctly observes, *if* we think that the criteria of justice are fundamentally concerned

---

[52] John Tasioulas, 'The Moral Reality of Human Rights', in T. Pogge (ed.), *Freedom from Poverty as a Human Right* (New York: Oxford University Press, 2007), 75–102, 100.

[53] Nussbaum, *Women and Human Development*, 72. Compare Griffin's understanding of common humanity through shared prudential judgments about well-being: James Griffin, *On Human Rights* (Oxford: Oxford University Press, 2008), 113–25.

[54] Pogge, *World Poverty and Human Rights*, 42.

[55] Nussbaum seems to follow this line at *Frontiers of Justice*, 285–6.

with the human good, then we cannot 'first select principles of right and then just slot an account of the good into them, as if the latter made no difference to the former. The good does matter to the right: structural principles that might be plausible given one account of value may not be plausible given another.'[56] Hurka's point should be very well taken: if human rights matter because they protect the human good, it is not at all clear how such rights can justifiably fall short of entailing the institutional structures through which that good is to be achieved.[57]

To be clear, the conclusion I have been arguing for in this section is just that the close connection between liberalism and capitalism *only* creates a contradiction when human rights are defined and justified through the teleological strand of liberal thinking. Liberal thought, understood in broader terms, contains the intellectual machinery to support an array of acute and persuasive criticisms of the unjust effects of the institutions of global capitalism. But if liberals are to offer such criticisms, it is by no means clear that they can coherently do so by appealing to the liberal conception of the human good. And they would be well-advised not to do so: the familiar slip in liberal accounts of the good from 'human being' to 'human life' exposes such accounts to the same objection I pressed against Ci earlier: it is not plausible to speak of *the* distinctively *human* form of life. A robust defence of human rights would do much better to draw on the resources of other strands of the liberal tradition.

This point can, however, be very hard to see because of the striking dominance of the teleological strand in liberal political philosophy in the era of human rights. Should anyone wish to dispute this remark by pointing out that the single most influential liberal thinker of our current period, John Rawls, consistently defended the idea that criteria of justice could be detached from any conception of the human good, I would make two related observations. The first is that if one looks at the initial reception of *A Theory of Justice*, even very sympathetic reviewers—Thomas Nagel and Brian Barry among them—insisted that what was missing from Rawls's account was a conception of the good.[58] Here one catches a glimpse of the orthodoxy of the teleological strand. The second observation is that while a number of liberals (including Nagel and Barry) came around to Rawls's view, the notion that one cannot talk of the basic rights and duties of justice in isolation from considerations of the human good is still so central to contemporary liberal theorising that there is an unfortunately common tendency to assume that the *only* way one can try to detach criteria of justice from a conception of the good is to be a Rawlsian 'political liberal'.[59] That many global justice theorists do indeed echo Tasioulas's claim that the human good grounds human rights is a manifestation of the dominance of the teleological strand. So, too, is Ci's own erroneous equation of *the very idea* of liberalism with a conception of the human good.

---

[56] Thomas Hurka, 'Capability, Functioning, and Perfectionism', *Aperion*, 35(4) (2002): 137–6, 161.

[57] Although see Rowan Cruft, 'From a Good Life to Human Rights: Some Complications', this volume, ch. 4, for a fascinating account of the complexities here.

[58] Thomas Nagel, 'Rawls's Theory of Justice', *Philosophical Review*, 82(2) (1973): 220–34; Barry, *The Liberal Theory of Justice*, esp. 126–7.

[59] A typical example: Jonathan Quong, *Liberalism Without Perfection* (New York: Oxford University Press, 2011), 16. One wonders what Quong, who is particularly sure of this assumption, would make of Kant's political philosophy—would he really claim Kant was a 'political liberal'?

One thing all this has obscured is a very different deontological strand of liberal thinking, which eschews any of the cumbersome Rawlsian apparatus of 'political' liberalism. I know of no better description of this strand of liberalism than the words of the late Tony Judt:

> Liberalism... is necessarily indeterminate. It is not about some sort of liberal project for society; it is about a society in which the messiness and openness of politics precludes the application of large-scale projects, however rational and ideal—especially, indeed, if they are rational and ideal.[60]

Although obscured, this strand of liberal thinking is not lost: it has modern defenders with cosmopolitan vision in the likes of, for example, Judith Shklar, Bernard Williams, and Onora O'Neill.[61] I shall not here try to trace out all its main features or the divergences among its adherents. Suffice to say that this liberalism is indeterminate, insofar as it is, in virtue of the fact that it understands social moralities not as artefacts of academic contemplation, but as constellations of reason-giving concepts embodied in the mores and conventions of historically and culturally contingent forms of life. Accordingly, reasoning about what social justice requires is to be understood from the point of view of historically located individuals.[62] It is argued that inclusive reasoning among a diverse domain of agents must necessarily focus on the principles such a domain *cannot* adopt; criteria of social justice are then embodied in a set of constraints against acting on such principles, and questions of *telos* or human good left entirely indeterminate.

The key point I wish to register is that this strand of liberalism, in rejecting the notion of any necessary social identity, puts in its place a conception of human nature understood in terms of the finitude of vulnerable, interdependent beings. It does not equate this conception with a distinctively or 'truly' *human form of life*. Rather, it seeks to identify features of human finitude that the mores and conventions of any local form of life must register. The moral significance of these aspects of human finitude is not assumed to be intuitive to bearers of all diverse local forms of life;[63] nor need it even be claimed that there are any intrinsically valuable properties of human beings.[64] Instead, the fact that social moralities are embedded in lived conventions that must register the nature of our finitude is taken to render accessible, to the bearers of diverse

---

[60] Tony Judt, *Past Imperfect* (New York: New York University Press, 2011), 315.

[61] Shklar, 'The Liberalism of Fear'; Bernard Williams, *In the Beginning Was the Deed* (Princeton: Princeton University Press, 2007); Onora O'Neill, *Towards Justice and Virtue* (Cambridge: Cambridge University Press, 1996).

[62] Compare O'Neill, *Towards Justice and Virtue*, ch. 2 (esp. 58: 'Reasoning is defective when reasoners misjudge or misrepresent what others can follow'), with Bernard Williams, 'Saint-Just's Illusion', in his *Making Sense of Humanity* (Cambridge: Cambridge University Press, 1995). See also Onora O'Neill, *Faces of Hunger* (London: Harper Collins, 1986), 32; Williams, *In the Beginning was the Deed*, 50–1.

[63] This is certainly true of O'Neill and Williams; Shklar may be more optimistic: see 'The Liberalism of Fear', 30.

[64] This is especially true of a certain Kantian line: see, for the complexities, Oliver Sensen, 'Dignity and the Formula of Humanity (*ad* IV 429, IV 435)', in Jens Timmermann (ed.), *Kant's 'Groundwork of the Metaphysics of Morals': A Critical Guide* (Cambridge: Cambridge University Press, 2010), 102–18. Compare O'Neill, *Towards Justice and Virtue*, 91–7.

forms of life, the justification for institutions which systematically limit vulnerability and foreclose possibilities for exploitation.

To spell all this out in a philosophically robust way would require far more room than I have here. All I can hope to make clear is the mere suggestion that this sub-strand of deontological liberalism offers something potentially very useful to our thinking about human rights. What it offers is a way of grounding the basic obligations mankind owes to all mankind in a conception of common humanity opposed to any necessary social identity which does not slip into implausible talk of *the human* form of life, and does not implicate the problematic liberal conception of the good. To my mind, this deontological substrand therefore represents a much more promising strand of liberalism to work with when thinking through the relationship between human rights and the socio-economic institutions of global capitalism. It may well be that adopting this deontological substrand involves philosophical costs regarding the standard understanding of human rights: it is doubtless much easier to vindicate *welfare* rights by appeal to the human good than it is within the indeterminate liberalism I am putting forward as an alternative. But exactly how duties concerning others' welfare might feature within such an approach is a debate for another day.[65]

I want to conclude by returning to where I began: my title. My title asks a question: human rights without the human good? I have not tried to answer that question here, only to raise it. Ci is correct to ask defenders of human rights to reflect more carefully than many have done on the interconnections between liberalism and capitalist institutions, and if what I have said is plausible such reflection should undermine the plausibility of grounding human rights in the liberal conception of the human good. But—although it is hard to see at times in the current literature—the broad liberal tradition leaves open many paths for conceiving of human rights *without* appeal to the human good, and it is well worth investigating whether human rights would ultimately be better served by attending to such paths.

[65] For further discussion within a Kantian version of this indeterminate strand, see Simon Hope, 'Subsistence Needs, Human Rights, and Imperfect Duties', *Journal of Applied Philosophy*, 30(1) (2013): 88–100; Simon Hope, 'Kantian Imperfect Duties and Modern Debates over Human Rights', *Journal of Political Philosophy*, 22(4) (2014): 396–415

35

Care and Human Rights

Virginia Held

Human rights have made remarkable progress in the last half-century. As Joseph Raz, a foremost contemporary legal theorist, notes, "This is a good time for human rights."[1] At the start of this period, realism in foreign policy, and in thought about international issues and political theory, was so dominant that moral considerations were widely dismissed as pointless, and considerations of human rights were seen as belonging to the realm of ignorable moral exhortation. There were only a handful of books on morality and international affairs.[2] Human rights, as little more than moral goals, were taken seriously by only rather a few practitioners and theorists.

Human rights still have a long way to go in becoming enforceable claims. But there is no doubt that they are taken very seriously not only by many theorists but by activists pressing governments to improve all sorts of conditions, and by courts deciding cases. They are taken seriously by governments around the world. Charges of human rights violations have weight, can notably cut reputations and influence, and actually affect actions and policies. They are widely recognized as an actual part of the world's actual international law.[3]

This progress illustrates well the "normative pull of law" that is so much of what makes law potentially more effective than it is, and capable of significant improvement. Spelling out the arguments for every person's fundamental rights, and how we ought to respect persons and their rights, gradually persuades more and more people to pay attention to such rights and to shame those who disregard them. We have seen the process at work and should not fail to appreciate it.

At the same time, we can recognize the limitations and fragilities of this progress. Millions and millions of persons in the world continue to die of hunger and preventable illnesses, to be crushed by poverty, felled by violence, and blocked by ignorance. "About half of all human beings live in severe poverty," Thomas Pogge reminds us, "and about a quarter live in extreme or life-threatening poverty...About one third of all human deaths, 18 million each year, are due to poverty-related causes."[4] How

---

[1] Joseph Raz, "Human Rights Without Foundations," in Samantha Besson and John Tasioulas (eds.), *The Philosophy of International Law* (New York: Oxford University Press, 2010), 321.

[2] See, for instance, Richard Falk, *Legal Order in a Violent World* (Princeton, NJ: Princeton Univerersity Press, 1968); Virginia Held, Sidney Morgenbesser, and Thomas Nagel (eds.), *Philosophy, Morality, and International Affairs* (New York: Oxford University Press, 1974); Charles Beitz, *Political Theory and International Relations* (Princeton, NJ: Princeton University Press, 1979); and Stanley Hoffman, *Duties Beyond Borders: On the Limits and Possibilities of Ethical International Politics* (Syracuse, NY: Syracuse University Press, 1981).

[3] See, eg, Besson and Tasioulas, *The Philosophy of International Law.*

[4] Thomas Pogge, "Are We Violating the Human Rights of the World's Poor?" *Yale Human Rights and Development Law Journal*, 14(2) (2011): 1–33, 21.

much is achieved by declaring that all persons have rights to adequate food and health care and security and education is unclear. So much of what is needed cannot be best addressed by progress in the law and legal processes.

I. Rights and Human Rights

Rights are elements of law. Of morality also, along with all sorts of values and virtues, norms and judgments. But when we think of human rights as moral rights we think of them as rights that ought to be enforceable legal rights. As we try to make delineations of rights that are no more than moral into rights that can be effective in the cruel world, we try to translate moral rights into legal ones. For instance, when a moral right to freedom of expression is recognized within a given legal system as an enforceable legal claim, we can judge that the relevant human right is respected. And when the human right to freedom of expression is invoked to criticize and perhaps sanction an actual government that fails to respect it, what we are criticizing is that government's failure to provide or protect the relevant legal right. As Pogge expresses it, "human rights are not merely part of the law but also moral standards that all law ought to meet and a standard that is not yet met by much existing law in many countries."[5]

We ought also to consider, however, how *rights* may not be the best focus to give to the moral considerations with which we have started. It may be that it was the dominant moral theories at the time Declarations of Human Rights were developed that led to the concentration on rights and justice at the expense of many other moral approaches. With different emphases in moral thinking, we might be thinking more about other ways than those of rights and law to address various moral concerns. And that is what I am exploring in this chapter. I do not intend my inquiry here to be a critique of human rights, which I see as highly justified in their appropriate domain. What I question is the nearly exclusive focus of attention on the approach of justice through law and rights. Rights and law belong to a limited domain within the social, which must be composed of relations that are at least somewhat caring. At this level, caring is weak, but essential nevertheless. Without enough of us caring that our fellow members of society are treated decently there will not be sufficient trust and support to enable a legal or political system, or the implementation of human rights, to function. An approach that focuses on care rather than rights might be a promising alternative, at least for various problems.

In the half-century considered that has led to such progress in the development of human rights, a major new approach to morality has been developed by feminist theorists interested in the ethics of care. And from this perspective, the emphasis on rights appears limited at best. Alternative approaches are in need of development and may be highly important.

Fiona Robinson considers the way issues of morality in international affairs have, in standard discussions, emphasized the rights of states and individuals, and their corresponding duties. "Analysis of the ethical dimension of international relations,"

---

[5] Pogge, "Are We Violating the Human Rights of the World's Poor?", 7.

she writes, "is dominated overwhelmingly by the liberal–contractualist language of rights."[6] She explores how different the issues would look from the perspective of a critical ethics of care. I agree, and will suggest some ways, for various issues.

Consider the definition of a human right offered by Joseph Raz. He writes that he takes human rights to be "rights which set limits to the sovereignty of states, in that their actual or anticipated violation is a (defeasible) reason for taking action against the violator in the international arena" even when doing so would otherwise infringe on such a state's sovereignty.[7] Now consider applying such a conception of violating human rights to an impoverished state dealing with violence between its ethnic groups whose government cannot possibly provide for the basic necessities of each person within its borders. It may be a government so corrupt that it intentionally or just carelessly violates the human rights of its inhabitants on a massive scale, but it may be a government simply unable to respect their rights. Such a government may request outside aid, but intervention against the will of such a state, intervention that violated its sovereignty, would hardly be called for.

Traditionally, rights, including early understandings of human rights, were developed as negative rights against governments and other persons, assuring that persons would essentially be left alone, free from attack and interference. The history of notions of human rights heavily emphasized rights to be free from interference by governments and other persons as we live our lives, pursue our interests, accumulate wealth, and express our views. Such conceptions led to the familiar lists of civil and political rights such as rights to freedom of expression, to a fair trial, and to participate in a government based on the will of the people. More recently it has been acknowledged throughout most of the world, although not in the US legal system, that persons have positive rights to basic necessities, to what they need to live and act. To the traditional lists of civil and political rights have in recent decades been added the lists of economic and social rights that reflect the awareness that if we lack the basic resources of food, shelter, health, and the like, we will be unable to be an agent of any kind, free or unfree.

Those of us writing on morality and concerned with such problems as poverty and health care have argued for decades that conceptions of rights are badly inadequate unless they include what we think of as welfare rights. It is hardly satisfactory to imagine that a person's human rights are respected if they are merely left alone without the food or resources needed to live their lives and pursue their interests.[8] Traditional and dominant liberal conceptions of the already self-sufficient individual need revision. It was vindication of the views of those who insisted that rights include welfare rights that, however resistant to them the US legal system remained, lists of economic and social rights became part of the conceptions of human rights recognized

---

[6] Fiona Robinson, *Globalizing Care: Ethics, Feminist Theory, and International Affairs* (Boulder, CO: Westview Press, 1999), 148.

[7] Raz, "Human Rights Without Foundations," 328.

[8] See, eg, Henry Shue, *Basic Rights* (Princeton: Princeton University Press, 1980); Virginia Held, *Rights and Goods: Justifying Social Action* (Chicago: University of Chicago Press, 1984); and James W. Nickel, *Making Sense of Human Rights* (Berkeley: University of California Press, 1987).

in international law in such documents as the International Covenant on Economic, Social, and Cultural Rights (ICESCR).[9]

These rights have never become firmly established even in the human rights discourse. While they may be suitable and important to argue for in the context of adequate social welfare programs in developed countries that can well afford them, they are awkwardly invoked in the context of massive global poverty. They only become meaningful as rights when we have some clarity about how and by whom they are to be fulfilled, and some way to assure that progress toward achieving this will be made. Seen as Kantian imperfect duties, questions about their fulfillment are left so vague as to be of dubious use. And discussion of Kantian obligations to alleviate global poverty, Fiona Robinson writes, "end up faltering on the question of motivation."[10] For much of what human rights are used to argue for in the global context, other moral notions may often be more suitable.

How to implement positive rights to food, shelter, basic medical care, and the like in a global context has been and continues to be thoroughly controversial. Doing so would seem to require enormous restructurings of economic arrangements, of governmental policies, of cultural recognitions of the interests of various groups. Much that would be needed reaches far beyond the legal systems of individual states and beyond their governments. Even when conceptions of rights are expanded to include group rights along with individual rights,[11] many of the relevant issues seem to fit awkwardly within the purview of rights rather than of other moral considerations. Not all that we do or want or think we ought to aim at can possibly be captured within the essentially legal notion of right or human right. Even with the moral theories that emphasize the moral right as distinct from the moral good, we know that to do what is right is not at all the same as to have a right, and the former is far wider than the latter.

Thomas Pogge holds that the global economic order is responsible for the massive violation of human rights constituted by the annual deaths of many millions of persons from hunger and preventable disease.[12] Persistent global poverty results, he claims, from the enforceable legal order of trade and property law. Robert Howse and Ruti Teitel in the same volume doubt that blame can be assigned so clearly, but note that even if it could, it is unclear what respecting human rights would prescribe for the reform of the global economic order.[13] Pogge points to the morally deplorable practice of corrupt regimes that enter into commercial arrangements whereby they are accorded large loans they can squander on themselves, while their successors and their impoverished populations are left with the legally enforceable bills to be paid. But interpreting what respect for the human rights of such citizens would

---

[9] United Nations, 1966.   [10] Robinson, *Globalizing Care*, 152.

[11] See, eg, S. James Anaya, *Indigenous Peoples in International Law* (New York: Oxford University Press, 2004).

[12] Thomas Pogge, "The Role of International Law in Reproducing Massive Poverty," in Besson and Tasioulas, *The Philosophy of International Law*. See also Pogge, "Are We Violating the Human Rights of the World's Poor?".

[13] Robert Howse and Ruti Teitel, "Global Justice, Poverty, and the International Economic Order," in Besson and Tasioulas, *The Philosophy of International Law*.

require in the way of changing such practices is hard to discern. As Howse and Teitel point out, it might entail serious costs and questionable benefits to have more responsible successor governments repudiate such state obligations. Undoing the legal foundation that *pacta sunt servanda* (states are to keep their agreements) might be dangerous indeed.

Recognizing the way negative duties are theoretically more compelling than positive ones, Pogge has recently formulated our obligations to the world's poor as a negative requirement that we stop collaborating "in the imposition of unjust institutional arrangements" on the world's poor.[14] But when he outlines some concrete measures to be taken to do this, similar doubts arise.

Many of our most important relations are not legal ones except in the most peripheral sense approached by the misleading claim that law covers "everything" because whatever it does not forbid, it allows. Our relations with family and friends only become legal in a significant way when disputes arise, as about custody or unpaid loans. When we interact with our neighbors we seldom need to invoke the law. Even when cities cooperate with other cities around the world to solve various problems, law and legal enforcement and the legal institutions of states often remain in the background.[15] Most of the time the rich patterns of connection and relatedness, and dependency and mutual pursuit of mutual interests proceed without the intervention of the law. And yet they are often guided by moral considerations. When we attend to the kind of morality suitable for these sorts of relations, we see how they are not especially focused on rights and their corresponding duties. They concern themselves far more with sensitivity to the needs of others, with responding to actual needs, and with trust and mutuality. It is persuasive to argue that rights *can* protect our fundamental needs. But their focus on individuals is not always appropriate, nor is the focus on law that they require, and it is clear that they often *do* not protect even the most basic needs of millions of people.

Women and members of minorities understand how limited is the reach of law when bias is exercised in offering opportunities or in evaluating performance. Only the most blatant of cases or egregious of practices can be addressed by law and legal remedies. Certainly legal rights to equal treatment are highly important, but in advancing equality much more than law is needed. Cultural change must precede and accompany and go beyond legal enactments of rights. The experience of the gay rights movement offers much evidence. So too with many human rights.

Perhaps a focus on the moral approaches of care would be suitable for dealing with many of the most serious problems facing the globe's inhabitants. They might supplement or strengthen or perhaps even be more effective than the approach of human rights.

---

[14] Pogge, "Are We Violating the Human Rights of the World's Poor?", 20. See also Thomas Pogge, "Severe Poverty as a Violation of Negative Duties," *Ethics and International Affairs*, 55 (2005): 80–3.

[15] See Benjamin R. Barber, *If Mayors Ruled the World: Why They Should And How They Already Do* (New Haven: Yale University Press, 2013).

II. The Ethics of Care

In the half-century during which the human rights agenda has moved from vague moral goal to somewhat effective influence, a significant development has occurred within the domain of moral theory. The previously dominant theories of Kantian morality and utilitarian ethics have been joined by the new feminist approach of the ethics of care.

The ethics of care is an important strand of feminist thought, though many feminists are not advocates of the ethics of care. Almost all feminists want to revise existing conceptions of justice and human rights to better assure the rights of women.[16] Feminists have examined the issues of global gender justice, showing how "women everywhere are disproportionately vulnerable to poverty, abuse, and political marginalization."[17] They want to add requirements for women's equality and protections against violence to lists that fail to provide for them. Alison Jaggar considers whether the definition of genocide should be "expanded to include female infanticide, the systematic withholding of food, medical care, and education from girls, and the battery, starvation, mutilation, and even murder of adult women," and rights against genocide understood accordingly.[18]

Many feminists want to go further and to reconceptualize moral theory itself, recognizing the bias in the approaches of the dominant theories.[19] A major way in which this has been done is in the development of the ethics of care.[20]

The ethics of care has been built on the acknowledgment of the enormous amount of valuable and unrecognized labor involved in care, especially the care of children, without which there would be no persons to fit the traditional images of those for whom morality is devised. The ethics of care starts not with the fully formed individual agent considering how he ought to act, but with the basic recognition that human beings are dependent on other human beings and are essentially vulnerable and in need of care for substantial parts of their lives.

It is remarkable how much the concept of 'liberal individual' at the heart of the dominant moral theories still rests on the Lockean image of a man going off into unoccupied territory (Locke said he could always go to America), clearing the land, tilling the soil, and acquiring property through his own labor. Now, few of us even

---

[16] Eg, Carol C. Gould, *Globalizing Democracy and Human Rights* (Cambridge: Cambridge University Press, 2004); and Alison M. Jaggar (ed.), *Global Gender Justice*. Special issue of *Philosophical Topics*, 37(2) (Fall 2009): 33–52.

[17] Alison M. Jaggar, "Transnational Cycles of Gendered Vulnerability," in Jaggar, *Global Gender Justice*, 33.

[18] Alison M. Jaggar, "The Philosophical Challenges of Global Gender Justice," in Jaggar, *Global Gender Justice*, 11.

[19] See Virginia Held, *Feminist Morality: Transforming Culture, Society, and Politics* (Chicago: University of Chicago Press, 1993).

[20] See, eg, Virginia Held, *The Ethics of Care: Personal, Political, and Global* (New York: Oxford University Press, 2006); Joan C. Tronto, *Moral Boundaries: A Political Argument for an Ethic of Care* (New York: Routledge, 1993); Peta Bowden, *Caring: Gender-Sensitive Ethics* (London: Routledge, 1997); Eva Feder Kittay, *Love's Labor: Essays on Women, Equality, and Dependency* (New York: Routledge, 1999); and Michael Slote, *The Ethics of Care and Empathy* (New York: Routledge, 2007).

grow our own food, let alone make our own possessions. As any number of Marxists have reminded us repeatedly, we are all highly interdependent.

The ethics of care rests on a conception of persons as relational and interdependent, and on an appreciation of the values of care embedded in practices of care. Although existing practices are usually structured by social arrangements in need of reform, especially in the way women are pressed into providing the overwhelming proportion of care, we can discern the values in existing practices and even more satisfactorily in such practices as they ought to be.

The ethics of care has developed care as a value of at least as much importance as justice. And perhaps it is even more fundamental. Persons can exist without justice but they cannot exist without the value-laden care essential for every child to live. Attending to care and its practices brings to the fore such values as empathetic understanding, sensitivity to the needs of others and especially, responsiveness to such needs. It calls especially for trust between care givers and recipients, and for understanding the relations between them as much from the point of view of the recipient of care as of the provider.[21] This offers the moral resources for good relations of care, and it is caring relations that are especially valued.

The ethics of care is not a kind of consequentialism, evaluating actions only in terms of their consequences, although attention to the effectiveness of any given activities involved in the practice of care is important in evaluating those activities. But the activities can also be valued on more deontological grounds in terms of the caring intentions and motives they express. Care seeks to meet effectively, and with sensitivity and respect, the actual needs of embodied persons located in actual contexts. It appreciates and relies on the caring emotions and rejects the view of the dominant theories that morality must be based only on ideal, abstract, impartial principles recognizable by reason.

Care is based especially on experience. Without care, no human person would survive into adulthood to become the rational individual of traditional moral theories. Every person has received care that has incorporated moral values, and every person can reflect on his or her experience of practices of care. Many such practices are inadequate, paternalistic, domineering, insensitive, and should be reformed. Those who provide care often fail to provide good care, but they and the recipients of such care can reflect on how it should be improved. The ethics of care has no need for the religious foundations of many other moral theories, foundations that are divisive and unpersuasive to those not sharing the religion of such foundations. The ethics of care is based on experience that truly is universal: the experience of care. Care is both practice and value.

Marian Barnes, who writes on the practice of care in the social services, describes the emphasis of care ethics on lived experience. "A key argument of an ethic of care," she writes, "is that care as practice and as moral and political value cannot be understood in the abstract. We need to consider the lived experience of giving and receiving

---

[21] For discussion of practices that might adequately bring the perspectives of recipients of care into the making of policies, and provision and delivery of social services, see Marian Barnes, *Care In Everyday Life: An Ethic of Care in Practice* (Bristol, UK: The Policy Press, 2012).

care, and how context, conflicts and power impact the difficult moral decisions as well as the practical tasks of care."[22]

The care alternative started with feminist attention to the vast area of experience provided by caring work performed mostly by women and almost completely ignored by dominant moral theorists. This area was largely written off by moral theorists as belonging to "nature" rather than morality or the distinctively human. It was seen as "governed by natural instinct" and as irrelevant to morality. As David Heyd wrote, in a comment typical of the time, a mother's sacrifice for her child need not be thought relevant to morality or contrary to assumptions about persons acting on self-interest because it belongs to "the sphere of natural relationships and instinctive feelings (*which lie outside morality*)."[23]

To feminists, it gradually became clear that the care in which we engaged was infused with moral considerations, presented endless moral problems and possibilities, and was clearly relevant to what we thought about morality. It was clear that emotion had value, not only in carrying out the dictates of reason but in discerning what ought to be done and in acting morally. The emotion of caring was not to be dismissed as irrational or threatening to morality, or simply instinctive, but to be appreciated. Moral action in this context was not simply based on what was an empirically given natural tendency. Nor was it based purely on impartial principles recognized by reason, or on rational self-interest, or on a calculation of maximizing preference satisfaction, as the dominant moral theories would have to construe it to be to fit their assumptions.

Care should not be understood as self-sacrifice. Egoism versus altruism is the wrong way to interpret the issues. Yes, the interests of care giver and care receiver will sometimes conflict, but for the most part we do not pit our own interests against those of others in this context. We want what will be good for both or all of us together. We want our children and others we care for to do well along with ourselves, and for the relations between us to be good ones. If we are the recipients of care we want our care givers to do well along with us. The whole framework of self *versus* other needs to be revised for this context, and then perhaps for others.

The beginnings of the ethics of care can be traced to the work of Sara Ruddick on the thinking involved in the practice of mothering,[24] and the work of Nel Noddings in examining the phenomenology of care work.[25] The initial delineation of care in contrast with justice emerged with the psychological inquiries of Carol Gilligan, who found differences in the ways most men and boys on the one hand, and many women and girls on the other, interpreted moral problems.[26] The men and boys studied tended to construe the problems presented as calling for the application of abstract moral

[22] Barnes, *Care In Everyday Life*, 40.

[23] David Heyd, *Supererogation: Its Status in Ethical Theory* (New York: Cambridge University Press, 1982), 134 (emphasis added).

[24] Sara Ruddick, "Maternal Thinking," *Feminist Studies*, 6 (Summer 1980): 342–67; and Sara Ruddick, *Maternal Thinking: Toward a Politics of Peace* (Boston: Beacon Press, 1989).

[25] Nel Noddings, *Caring: A Feminine Approach to Ethics and Moral Education* (Berkeley: University of California Press, 1984).

[26] Carol Gilligan, *In A Different Voice: Psychological Theory and Woman's Development* (Cambridge, MA: Harvard University Press, 1982).

principles, such as principles of justice, to situations of conflicting rights. Many of the women and girls studied interpreted the problems as particular and concrete, as problems of maintaining human relationships and meeting the actual needs of those for whom they felt responsible. The "different voice" of care was thus distinguished from the more traditional moral approaches. And in subsequent decades the ethics of care was further developed by feminist moral philosophers and contrasted with the ethics of justice of the dominant Kantian and utilitarian approaches.

There are affinities between care theory and virtue theories but there are important differences.[27] The ethics of care values caring relations rather than the mere virtuous dispositions of individuals—to be compassionate for instance. Some elements of the moralities of the British sentimentalists and especially of Hume's ethics can be noted and built upon in care theory.[28] But the ethics of care sees persons as relational, not the independent individuals of the British moralists. More importantly, the ethics of care is a feminist moral outlook and approach built on experience that has not been the focus of previous moral theories.

As feminists have developed the alternative moral approach of the ethics of care, they have been able to see its potential for more and more of what morality is called on to do: to guide and motivate actions that ought to be taken and lives that ought to be led. It is easiest to see how the approach of care is appropriate for the more personal contexts of families and friendship, where the awkwardness of the dominant rationalistic and universalistic moralities are most clear: we do not play with our children out of respect for the moral law, yet playing with our children is part of good care, care that has moral value. We do not offer sympathy to our friends who are ill because of a calculation that it would produce the greatest good of the greatest number, but because we care for them.

When the inclination flags to do what caring calls for, as often happens when there is too much to do and too many demands on one, one may look to duty for instructions on the most stringent requirements of care. No matter how otherwise busy one may be, one must keep one's child safe and in health if possible. At the same time, one can recognize the superiority of the motive of caring rather than obligation in contexts of care, and recognize that the motivation underlying our performance of duty is our caring.

As the ethics of care has flourished, its relevance to political and social and global issues has been made more and more evident.[29] Instead of entrenching the division between "public" and "private" supported by traditional moralities, the ethics of care breaks down the division and shows the relevance of the personal to the political.

---

[27] See Slote, *The Ethics of Care and Empathy*; Margaret A. McLaren, "Feminist Ethics: Care as a Virtue," in Peggy DesAutels and Joanne Waugh (eds.), *Feminists Doing Ethics* (Lanham, MD: Rowman & Littlefield, 2001); and Maureen Saunder-Staudt, "The Unhappy Marriage of Care Ethics and Virtue Ethics," *Hypatia*, 21(4) (Fall 2006): 21–39.

[28] See Annette Baier, *Moral Prejudices: Essays on Ethics* (Cambridge, MA: Harvard University Press, 1994); and Tronto, *Moral Boundaries*.

[29] See esp. Held, *The Ethics of Care*; Tronto, *Moral Boundaries*; Selma Sevenhuijsen, *Citizenship and the Ethics of Care: Feminist Considerations on Justice, Morality and Politics* (London: Routledge, 1998); Robinson, *Globalizing Care*; and Daniel Engster, *The Heart of Justice: Care Ethics and Political Theory* (New York: Oxford University Press, 2007).

Instead of resembling a contract voluntarily entered into between independent, equal, and self-interested individuals, or autonomous and rational individuals making laws for themselves and all others, the ethics of care starts with interdependent embodied persons in actual historical and social and personal circumstances. It applies to persons of highly unequal power in relationships that they often did not choose. Parents have vast power over their helpless infants and morality calls on them not to misuse it. None of us can choose our parents yet morality is heavily involved in how we deal with them. We only become the independent autonomous individuals of dominant moral theories with the enormous help of the many other persons with whom we are interdependent.

The strength of applying the ethics of care to issues such as global poverty and deprivation can be envisioned. Theorists have tried to deal with these problems in terms of human rights, with very limited success. The use of the ethics of care might be more promising and effective.

It may be thought that an advantage of conceptualizing these issues in terms of the rights of the poor is that this avoids the paternalism and imperialism of traditional efforts of charity, benevolence, and humanitarian aid. But care theory is to be based on the experience of care receivers as fully as of care providers. It calls for the relations between them to especially avoid being paternalistic and imperialistic and to be, instead, trusting, considerate, and characterized by mutuality.

Fiona Robinson argues that "practices of care are the basic substance of morality," and recognition of our responsibilities should lead to "sustained attention to people not as autonomous rights-bearers but as relational subjects who are both givers and receivers of care."[30] While rights and interests are important to care, "they must always be understood as embedded in and realized through existing social and political arrangements."[31] A critical ethics of care, Robinson emphasizes, must pay attention to the ongoing and everyday global relations that so seriously fail to meet peoples' needs. In contrast to the way international relations discussion usually deals with "moral issues" by focusing on moments of crisis, attention to care could "form the basis for a new international political theory." It would challenge "our conventional views of which individuals, groups or states are 'dependent' on which others, and how."[32] The increasing dependence of the global North on the global South for the provision of care work is one example. More familiarly, one can recall the dependence of the well-off on the workers who produce value, and the dependence of those who govern on the support of those who are governed. Interdependence surrounds us.

The ethics of care has been shown to be relevant to and promising for the quest for peace and the reduction of violence in international affairs.[33] It can be shown that the

---

[30] Fiona Robinson, "After Liberalism in World Politics? Towards an International Political Theory," *Ethics and Social Welfare*, 4(2) (July 2010): 130–44, 139.

[31] Robinson, "After Liberalism in World Politics?" 140.

[32] Robinson, "After Liberalism in World Politics?" 140.

[33] See, eg, Ruddick, *Maternal Thinking*; Robinson, *Globalizing Care*; Joan C. Tronto, "Is Peace Keeping Care Work?" in Rebecca Whisnant and Peggy DesAutels (eds.), *Global Feminist Ethics* (Lanham, MD: Rowman & Littlefield, 2008); Virginia Held, *How Terrorism is Wrong: Morality and Political Violence* (New York: Oxford University Press, 2008) and Virginia Held, "Can the Ethics of Care Handle Violence?" *Ethics and Social Welfare*, 4(2) (July 2010): 115–29.

ethics of care would lead to respect for international law in the short term, because of the contributions international law can make to peace and civility and mutual benefit among states and groups.[34] At the same time, we can speculate that as care became more influential, there would be in the longer term a reduction in the need for and reliance on law, both within states and among them.

The ethics of care calls for the transformation of the different domains within society, as, for instance, it asks that the institutions of the law or of health care be more caring. But it also and especially asks for the transformation of the relations between these domains.[35] In a caring society, the state and the economy would not be aimed above all at military prowess and economic dominance, while child care and much health care were left at the margins for people to deal with on their own as best they could. A caring society would enable many forms of care, education, non-commercial cultural expression, and economic activity that actually served real needs to be at the center of attention. As the institutions and practices of care would become more satisfactory, the need for law and it enforcements would diminish.

As the values of care were extended to a global level, the building of more caring approaches to global connectedness would increase. If global problems were addressed more fundamentally in ways called for by the ethics of care, the need for and appeal to law would become less likely. Addressing global poverty and deprivation would be a leading example of the kind of urgent problem that is not primarily an issue of law. It does not have the kind of remedy that legal institutions can well address. It might be more promising to think that it should be addressed not only because it violates human rights, which it certainly does, but more urgently because care demands it.

III. Rights and Care

The foundations of human rights have clearly been the dominant political theories of the liberal–contractualist tradition and the rationalist moral theories of Kantian ethics and utilitarianism in contrast with which the ethics of care developed.

Feminists influenced by the ethics of care may well have reservations about the human rights agenda. Not that it is misguided, but that it may not emphasize what is most important or most needed in many actual situations. Or that appeals to human rights may count for too little without the underlying emotions of caring that needs are met and rights are respected.

Rights and human rights attach to individuals conceptualized as separable entities in a way that is often misleading. The ethics of care works with conceptions of persons as relational, dependent, interdependent. Such a view is much more appropriate for populations dying of hunger and easily preventable disease.

In trying to bring morality into the arena of international relations, human rights, along with the laws of war, have been by far the major focus. This focus diverts our

---

[34] See Virginia Held, "Morality, Care, and International Law," *Ethics and Global Politics*, 4(3) (2011): 173–94. Open Access journal.
[35] See Held, *The Ethics of Care*.

attention from relational issues, where we recognize the dependency of human beings on others and on their environments.

Rights are tied to justice, and the ethics of care can be seen as contrasting with moralities of justice. It is persuasive to think of the dominant moralities of justice—Kantian ethics and utilitarianism—as generalizations to the whole of morality of moral approaches suitable for law and government but much more questionable as moralities for contexts of family and friendship where care and its values would seem, once we pay attention to these neglected contexts, to have priority. We can then see how relevant care is to social and global concerns as well.

Human rights are tied to liberal conceptions of persons as independent, self-sufficient, autonomous. This disregards the vulnerability, the need for care, the interdependency of actual persons. Rights are primarily *against* others: governments, and other persons. Care focuses especially on *mutual* interests. When we care for another person we do not construe our situation primarily as one of conflicting interests where your gain is my loss and my gain is your loss. As parents, we *want* our children to thrive and to do well. As children grow and become more independent, they want their frail and aged parents to be well cared for. We want what will be good for us together, mutually. The approach of care recognizes the fantastical and distorted picture of human reality in the "state of nature," on which notions of human rights are importantly based.

Economic and social rights are much closer to the concerns of care, but they are still individualized, whereas care understands how often the issues concern groups, collectivities, and relations between persons.

From the perspective of the ethics of care, there would certainly be agreement with Pogge that the advanced countries of the world have a moral obligation to rapidly reduce the hunger and deprivation that afflicts so many millions of people in the poor countries. It is an obvious and outrageous affront to the values of care that in a world that can easily afford it, millions of children die from hunger and preventable diseases. But the basis for the argument would be the care that needs to underlie respect for persons, to motivate assurance of rights, and to guide efforts to meet the needs of the suffering.

Fiona Robinson writes that a critical ethics of care would focus our attention on "the permanent background of those decisions which must be taken in times of crisis. From this perspective, ethics in international relations is concerned...with the nature and quality of existing social relations."[36] The ethics of care would demand that we attend more to global poverty and the way "normative international relations theory has systematically obscured the extent to which the everyday processes, practices, and social relations in international relations often lead to devastating levels of human suffering."[37]

Discussion of poverty has focused on rights within a liberal–contractualist framework, but "rights-based ethics," Robinson writes, "exalts the value of individual autonomy."[38] What is needed instead, she argues, is a "restructuring of political action in such a way that enduring relationships can flourish and agents can focus their moral

---

[36] Robinson, *Globalizing Care*, 144. [37] Robinson, *Globalizing Care*, 146–7.
[38] Robinson, *Globalizing Care*, 148.

attention and, ultimately, act with the virtues of care—attentiveness, responsiveness, and responsibility."[39] It is our "feelings of connection and responsibility in our personal and social relations" that actually motivate us, Robinson writes.[40] To motivate those in rich countries to do what respect for the rights of the poor would require, we need to build the social relations that "encourage agents to be attentive and responsive and to recognize shared responsibilities..."[41]

Sarah Clark Miller examines the "justice-dominated discourse" apparent in dealing with the global problems that morality ought to address. "Cosmopolitan theories of justice," she writes, "have dominated contemporary philosophical discussions of global responsibility."[42] In her book, *The Ethics of Need: Agency, Dignity, and Obligation*, she argues instead for "cosmopolitan care." She considers the shortcomings of the dominance of justice and rights in cosmopolitan thinking about global moral issues. These shortcomings are their "hyper-individualism, idealization, abstraction, and acontextuality."[43]

She delineates instead a feminist ethical outlook based on views of persons as relational, interconnected, interdependent, vulnerable, and located in actual contexts. "Persons," from this perspective, are "vulnerable moral agents with inevitable needs. As embodied and finite, humans share a susceptibility to suffering and needing."[44] Hence she aims to respond to the shortcomings of the emphasis on justice in thinking about global moral problems with a "relational, nonidealized, contextual oppression-informed account of feminist global responsibility."[45]

She shows how an emphasis on "human interdependence, vulnerability, need, and care might transform the current justice-dominated discourse of global responsibility."[46] In her view it would lead to recognition of a global "duty to care." She concludes that we should understand care as a "practice of taking responsibility for others' well-being in the context of dependency relations, of responding to their needs," and of "acknowledging and fostering moral atunement to the vicissitudes of their lives." We would then, she thinks, recognize how care ethics is relevant to intimate spheres and also "to ethical, social, and political spheres at the national and international level."[47]

In her book, *Care for the World: Fear, Responsibility and Justice*, Elena Pulcini shows how inadequate justice is when it is a merely rational principle.[48] Building in part on the recent discourse of care, she argues that justice needs the emotions of indignation at injustice to motivate acting to overcome failures of justice. As we survey the extraordinary deprivations and suffering of millions of people in the poor countries of the globe, we can agree that merely recognizing rights is painfully insufficient. From the point of view of care, we could say that we need to practice care, to care that rights

---

[39] Robinson, *Globalizing Care*, 154.   [40] Robinson, *Globalizing Care*, 157.

[41] Robinson, *Globalizing Care*, 145.

[42] Sarah Clark Miller, *The Ethics of Need: Agency, Dignity, and Obligation* (New York: Routledge, 2012), 121.

[43] Clark Miller, *The Ethics of Need*, 126.   [44] Clark Miller, *The Ethics of Need*, 124.

[45] Clark Miller, *The Ethics of Need*, 126.   [46] Clark Miller, *The Ethics of Need*, 127.

[47] Clark Miller, *The Ethics of Need*, 128.

[48] Elena Pulcini, *Care for the World: Fear, Responsibility and Justice* (Dordrecht: Springer, 2013).

are respected and implemented, and to engage in the caring that will actually meet the goals of morality.

Using the example of the way states deal with asylum seekers, Elizabeth Porter argues that compassion is both possible and necessary in politics. Influenced by the ethics of care, she examines the appropriateness of emotions in political life: anger at injustice, shame at callous governmental decisions, frustration at promises unkept. "Feminists have come to see," she writes, "compassionate empathy as 'the essence of morality'..." not only in personal relationships but importantly in political life.[49]

One of the strengths of the ethics of care is that it deals with the world as it is. It thus avoids some of the problems of ideal conceptions of justice that only awkwardly connect or fail to connect with the actual world.

One can and should agree with human rights theorists, and cosmopolitan justice theorists, that every person has a human right to the basic necessities that they need to live and to be an agent. But this is still a statement of a moral ideal. In the world as it is, this right is not being assured to vast numbers of persons, or even addressed at a reasonable level of effectiveness even by those who recognize the validity of the claims that all have such rights. The numbers of children under five in the world who die of hunger or preventable disease has in recent years been cut to 7 million.[50] But it is still 7 million! From the perspective of care this is so outrageous as to be unbelievable. How can responsible human beings be letting this happen? As Pogge points out, only a little more than *half* of what the richest one-twentieth of the world's population have *gained* in the past decades of globalization would have enabled the world's poor to attain an adequate standard of living.[51]

One moral recommendation that follows from recognizing the rights of all is that we ought to work to increase the implementation of these rights, and we can agree that we ought to do that. But for the foreseeable future there will be many times and places where many of these rights are not being assured. And there will always be emergency cases—natural disasters for instance, and increasingly, weather disasters induced by climate change—where they cannot be.

Trying to deal with situations of dire deprivation in terms of rights will always have limited utility. As David Hume pointed out, justice applies to situations of moderate scarcity. In situations of extreme scarcity, justice breaks down and in cases of complete abundance, there is no need for justice.[52]

In dire circumstances, we do not want to say that child A has more of a right to limited aid than child B. Both have rights to what they desperately need. But the world as it exists is full of triage and lifeboat-like situations. The ethics of care can handle these where the framework of rights breaks down. We do want to care for both child A and child B, but if we only have the resources to care for one, we should use those resources in the ways that will do the most good. Yes, they both have equal rights, and fairness might require something like a lottery. But in the real desperation of humanitarian

---

[49] Elisabeth Porter, "Can Politics Practice Compassion?" *Hypatia*, 21(4) (Fall 2006): 97–123.
[50] See, eg, http://www.un.org/milleniumgoals.
[51] Pogge, "Are We Violating the Human Rights of the World's Poor?", 23.
[52] David Hume, *An Inquiry Concerning the Principles of Morals*. ed. Charles W. Hendel (New York: Liberal Arts Press, 1957), Section III, Part I.

assistance, this might not be the best policy. It is morally legitimate to consider how the constraints of acting rapidly may be more important than the demands of fairness. Those guided by the values of care understand these moral considerations where those looking to the legalistic framework of rights and justice are left with the conclusion that morality breaks down in these situations.

It is certainly true that we ought to work to reduce the occurrence of lifeboat situations. We ought to move towards recognizing the human rights, including rights to what they need to live, of all. Justice requires it and the ethics of care will agree. But we also need moral guidance for when assurance of such rights is no more than a distant goal, and for all the situations when it is impossible to assure them.

The ethics of care starts with actual, dependent, often helpless, vulnerable human beings: for example, a child. Care responds to the needs of such beings. Good care, morally recommended care, does so with sensitivity, effectiveness, intelligence, and good will. It reflects the experience and points of view of recipients as well as providers of care. And it does not give up or break down even when law is ineffective. It recognizes the urgency of need and moves us to respond. And in contrast with views that recommend versions of Pareto optimality and primarily counsel gradualism, care has ways to demand that we respond to urgent problems urgently.

The distinction between positive and negative rights and duties that creates such difficulties for rights-based efforts to deal with global poverty is much less of a problem for the ethics of care: of course you ought to not bludgeon your child, but above all you should feed her; as elderly and infirm, of course you want to not be assaulted, but you especially want to be able to eat. As Fiona Robinson notes, starting with our "contextual, situated experience," as we would from the perspective of care, the goals of impartiality and universality would "recede into the background."[53]

IV. Care, Migration, and Climate Change

Other global problems for which the conceptual framework of justice and rights may be inadequate include the vast migrations of care workers currently taking place. In recent years, massive numbers of workers have been migrating from poor countries to developed ones to engage in care work.[54] Economic pressures lead them to leave their own families in the global South to provide care work in the global North. Often they have been trained as nurses or teachers in their own countries, but they can earn more as domestics or in the ill-paid positions of health or elder care institutions in rich countries than if they worked at their professions in their home countries. This causes a shortage of trained care workers in the poor countries where they are most needed. Frequently, migrants headed for care work become pressed into sex work or are the victims of sex

---

[53] Robinson, *Globalizing Care*, 145.

[54] Barbara Ehrenreich and Arlie Hochschild (eds.), *Global Woman: Nannies, Maids, and Sex Workers in the New Economy* (New York: Metropolitan Books, 2003); Rianne Mahon and Fiona Robinson (eds.), *Feminist Ethics and Social Policy: Towards a New Global Political Economy of Care* (Vancouver: University of British Columbia Press, 2011).

trafficking and then unable to send funds to the families they left out of concern for their welfare.[55]

Defenders of markets and globalization accept these developments without serious objection. Care work has been increasingly commodified, bought and sold in the market, for many years. As more women in the developed world enter the labor market, there are opportunities for others to replace them in their previously unpaid care work. Migrant care workers are usually not overtly coerced. They and their families benefit from the additional earnings the migrants receive. Often their home countries support these migrations because their economies benefit from the remittances sent home. And yet there are other factors to consider than market ones.

Eva Kittay tries to articulate the harm involved when mothers in poor countries leave their own children in the care of relatives to do care work in households and nursing homes and hospitals in the developed countries. Because the distances are great and the costs of travel high, they may not see their own children for many years at a time. Kittay asserts that "there is an important harm to the migrant women's central relationships."[56] It is a harm not just to the individual woman but to the whole transnational family, and the issues are not easily addressed, she finds, in the traditional theories from which challenges and defenses are usually drawn.

Kittay notes that "because caring relationships and the right to nurture these (a right to give care) are so critical to one's self-respect…the injury to the migrant careworker is also an injury to her self-respect…"[57] Using conceptions derived from the ethics of care, she argues that "among the most serious harms people experience are the fracturing of central relationships."[58] Care workers suffer a grievous injustice in having to choose between caring for their own families or migrating for remittances because of unjust global and national basic institutions. Kittay argues for a right to provide care as well as a right to receive the care one needs. Fiona Robinson asks that attention be paid "to the ways in which parents themselves may be empowered to care adequately for their own children."[59]

Kittay thus tries to deal with the issues involved in migrant care labor by revising the conceptions of rights and justice of traditional theories such as Rawls'. Others examining the transnational "care chains" that have developed conclude that the traditional language and concepts of rights and justice are not satisfactory for understanding and evaluating the issues. As Rianne Mahon and Fiona Robinson write, "traditional concepts of rights, justice, and citizenship may be inadequate to address the contemporary challenge of care and well-being at the transnational scale… [A]n ethics of care is best suited to illuminate these issues… Care ethics can serve as a lens through which to focus and organize our thinking about the ways in which care is delivered…"[60] And Yasmeen Abu-Laban concludes that the ethics of care, better than

---

[55] Olena Hankivsky, "The Dark Side of Care: The Push Factor in Human Trafficking," in Mahon and Robinson, *Feminist Ethics and Social Policy.*

[56] Eva Feder Kittay, "The Moral Harm of Migrant Carework: Realizing a Global Right to Care," in Jaggar, *Global Gender Justice*, 55.

[57] Kittay, "The Moral Harm of Migrant Carework."

[58] Kittay, "The Moral Harm of Migrant Carework."

[59] Robinson, *Globalizing Care*, 154.

[60] Mahon and Robinson, *Feminist Ethics and Social Policy*, 13–16.

the dominant cosmopolitan approaches, allows us to deal with problems at a global level.[61] It is attuned to the relationality of persons and to power differences. It may allow us to move from the "world of strangers" of traditional moral and political theories to the "world of relationships" that exists and is involved in such issues as migration. Care ethics, Abu-Laban writes, has great potential for re-envisioning policy.[62]

We seem to need to move beyond our established understandings of justice and rights to deal with and to evaluate such developments as the migrations of care workers. We also may need to do so with issues concerning the environment and climate change. Our obligations are to future generations and perhaps to the environment itself. Such obligations can only metaphorically be thought of as based on the human rights of persons who do not yet exist. The moral issues may be more fruitfully handled in terms of care for future persons and groups, and care for the environment.

When considering environmental issues, it is entirely unsatisfactory to think that the moral problems involved reduce to questions of human rights. Then, when we move beyond the domain of the human, it may be more satisfactory to think in terms of the values of species rather than the rights of individual members, and, in turn, of ecosystems rather than of individual species.[63] This does not suggest, however, that we should be indifferent to the non-human individuals involved. Caring about their well-being is appropriate, as is caring for the environment. It is also important to understand the role of gender in how traditional views of "man and nature" have been construed.[64] Configuring moral problems in terms of the rights of man, and then belatedly adding women to the category of rights-holders, hardly addresses most environmental issues.

Problems such as that of climate change, like the problems of global poverty and of migration, will require serious and fundamental changes in our economic arrangements. The ethics of care would have the normative resources to guide the restructuring of economic orders so that economic activity really would meet the needs of all, instead of primarily enriching the already advantaged. The ethics of care would recommend limits on markets in ways that ethics of justice and rights have not.[65] It would comprehend the relations, relations of power and dependence and attachment and interdependence, within which and with which economic activity is conducted.

V. Law, Society, and Care

Legal systems are created and exist within societies. Societies are much more than their legal systems. A collection of liberal individuals all pursuing their own interests,

---

[61] Yasmeen Abu-Laban, "A World of Strangers or a World of Relationships? The Value of Care Ethics in Migration Research and Policy," in Will Kymlicka and Kathryn Walker (eds.), *Rooted Cosmopolitanism: Canada and the World* (Vancouver: University of British Columbia Press, 2012).

[62] Abu-Laban, "A World of Strangers or a World of Relationships?"

[63] See, eg, Holmes Rolston III, "Environmental Ethics: Values in and Duties to the Natural World," in Lori Gruen and Dale Jamieson (eds.), *Reflecting on Nature: Readings in Environmental Philosophy* (New York: Oxford University Press, 1994).

[64] See, eg, Marti Kheel, *Nature Ethics: An Ecofeminist Perspective* (Lanham, MD: Rowman and Littlefield, 2008).

[65] See Held, *The Ethics of Care*, ch. 7.

or rationally contracting with each other to agree on the rules within which they will do so, but with nothing to hold them together, do not make a state or a society, or a world willing to respect the human rights of all.

There has been in recent years a large and welcome growth of appreciation for the importance of civil society. The members of civil society may find other institutions than legal ones appropriate for any number of the purposes with which they interact. When persons come together to play sports, engage in artistic productions, share interests in religion or intellectual activities, these engagements of civil society are not primarily legal ones. And for the rights of law to be upheld, the members of society must care enough about their fellow members to care that they are.

Before democracy can work well or legal systems of rights and obligations function adequately, the connections and interactions of civil society must be sufficiently developed.[66] Social bonds are needed to hold the foundations of law and political institutions together. For law to uphold rights and assure the fulfillment of obligations, civil society must provide sufficient trust and practice at cooperative interactions for there to be functioning legal institutions.

The most useful way for us to think of the social connections of civil society, with its associations and clubs and groups and congregations and leagues, is, I have argued, in terms of caring relations.[67] These are not the strong caring relations of family and friendship, but they are a long way from the indifference at the heart of the leading theories of justice.[68]

Before people can agree on the political principles underlying their legal institutions, they need to understand who are included among those between whom agreement is to be imagined or sought. Political theories standardly assume rather than confront these problems of boundaries and membership. We have begun to see the large-scale development of civil society organizations at the global level.[69] Increasingly, it can be hoped that all persons everywhere in the world can agree on human rights, including rights to basic necessities. But to have institutions that can make such rights more than very distant moral goals, people everywhere would need to have sufficient trust and mutuality and responsiveness to the needs of all to make such institutions work. Even Pogge says that "if citizens of Western states cared about the avoidance of [global] poverty, then so would their politicians," and action would be taken.[70]

The priority of social ties is an empirical condition for the relevant institutions. It is also a normative priority since moral recommendations must have sufficient moral force for persons to care whether morality is honored or not. The ethics of care is capable of providing such normative force and is suitable for doing so.

---

[66] See Robert D. Putnam, *Making Democracy Work* (Princeton, NJ: Princeton University Press, 1994); John Keane, *Civil Society: Old Images, New Visions* (Stanford, CA: Stanford University Press, 1998), and John Keane, *Global Civil Society?* (Cambridge: Cambridge University Press, 2003).

[67] See Held, *The Ethics of Care*, chs. 8 and 10.

[68] John Rawls included among his assumptions, about the hypothetical rational contractors seeking principles of justice on which they agree, that "they are conceived as not taking an interest in one another's interests" (John Rawls, *A Theory of Justice* (Cambridge, MA: Harvard University Press, 1971), 13.

[69] Keane, *Global Civil Society?*

[70] Pogge, "Are We Violating the Human Rights of the World's Poor?", 31.

36

Care and Human Rights

A Reply to Virginia Held

Susan Mendus

Virginia Held begins her thoughtful and engaging chapter by drawing attention to the progress which human rights have made in the last half century.[1] She quotes Joseph Raz's claim—'this is a good time for human rights'—and she notes that human rights are now taken 'very seriously not only by many theorists, but by activists pressing governments to improve all sorts of conditions, and by courts deciding cases'. 'Charges of human rights violations have weight' Held notes. They are taken seriously by governments around the world; they can 'cut reputations and influence, and actually affect actions and policies'. In short, human rights claims are very weighty and human rights violations are very serious.

However, despite these positive opening comments, Held is, in the end, doubtful about the value of human rights as a way of addressing the most serious and pressing problems of the modern world. She notes the fragility of our alleged progress, particularly in the area of social and economic (positive) rights, and asks 'how much is achieved by declaring that all persons have rights to adequate food and health care and security and education'.[2] More generally, she is concerned that an emphasis on rights and justice may come at the expense of other moral approaches, and she suggests that 'a focus on the moral approaches of care would be suitable for dealing with many of the most serious problems facing the globe's inhabitants. They might' she says, 'supplement or strengthen or perhaps even be more effective than the approach of human rights'.[3] So, despite her initial acknowledgement of the importance of human rights, Held is, in the end, deeply doubtful about their power to assist us. On the negative side, she wonders whether they can adequately respond to our most serious global problems and, on the positive side, she suggests that an adequate response to those problems may be found in the appeal to care.

Held's reservations about human rights seem to me to be both important and well-grounded. Indeed, there is a long tradition of philosophical scepticism about human rights, and Held's chapter is an eloquent contribution to that tradition. However, I am less convinced that the appropriate response to those concerns is to invoke the language of care. In this reply, therefore, I will try to indicate the reasons for and extent of my support for Held's concerns about rights, and I will then go on to offer some reasons for thinking that those concerns, important though they are, need

---

[1] Virginia Held, 'Care and Human Rights', this volume, ch. 35, 624.
[2] Held, 'Care and Human Rights', 624–5.   [3] Held, 'Care and Human Rights', 628.

not (and should not) lead us to place undue emphasis on the concept of care. In short, and *pace* Held, I believe that the concept of care is of very limited use in dealing with the most significant and pressing problems of the modern world.

My paper is divided into three sections: in the first section I will outline what I take to be Held's main reservations about human rights. In section II, I will raise some queries about her position—in particular I will ask whether the motivational problems associated with rights might be addressed in ways other than by an appeal to care. Finally, in section III, I will offer some reasons for being cautious about deploying an ethic of care in the way Held suggests. First, however, some reservations about rights.

I. Reservations about Rights

Scepticism about human rights has a long and distinguished history. As long ago as 1843 both Jeremy Bentham, in *Anarchical Fallacies*, and Karl Marx, in *On the Jewish Question*, expressed grave doubts about such rights: Bentham denied that we have any reason to believe in the existence of them, and (notoriously) he referred to talk of them as 'nonsense, and nonsense upon stilts'.[4] Karl Marx's scepticism, meanwhile, had a slightly different character. Marx's concern was not so much with the ontological status of human rights as with the moral values which they seemed to reflect. He wrote: 'none of the so-called rights of man goes beyond egoistic man, man as he is in civil society namely an individual withdrawn behind his private interests and whims and separated from the community'.[5] Here, the question is not whether rights exist, but rather what moral attitude an appeal to them evinces. Either way, though, questions arise about the legitimacy and value of human rights, and the passing of time has done little to dispel the reservations expressed by these philosophers. Writing nearly 150 years after Bentham and Marx, Alasdair MacIntyre declared: 'There are no [human] rights and belief in them is one with belief in unicorns and witches',[6] while Milan Kundera announced, frustratedly, 'the more the fight for human rights gains in popularity, the more it loses in concrete content, becoming a kind of universal stance of everyone towards everything, a kind of energy that turns all human desires into rights'.[7]

Running through these quotations we can see a variety of objections to, or reservations about, human rights. Some, like Bentham and MacIntyre, focus on the (allegedly dubious) ontological status of human rights; others, like Marx and Kundera, are more concerned with the moral values which talk of rights reflects or implies. Held's concerns seem to fall firmly into the latter category. She is not especially concerned about how we know that rights exist. Rather, her focus is on the extent to which we can expect an appeal to human rights to help us in our response to the very serious social, political and economic problems of the modern world and, more generally, she doubts whether the values which are implied by human rights are the ones which will

[4] Jeremy Bentham, *Anarchical Fallacies*, as printed in Jeremy Waldron (ed.), *Nonsense Upon Stilts: Bentham, Burke and Marx on the Rights of Man* (London: Methuen, 1987), 53.
[5] Marx, 'On the Jewish Question', as printed in Waldron, *Nonsense Upon Stilts*, 147.
[6] Alasdair MacIntyre, *After Virtue* (London: Duckworth, 1981), 67.
[7] Milan Kundera, *Immortality* (London: Faber, 1991), 153.

prove to be most efficacious in our struggle against these problems—problems such as inequality, poverty, and hunger. Held writes:

> Millions and millions of persons in the world continue to die of hunger and preventable illnesses, to be crushed by poverty, felled by violence, and blocked by ignorance. "About half of all human beings live in severe poverty", Thomas Pogge reminds us, "and about a quarter live in extreme or life-threatening poverty…About one third of all human deaths, 18 million each year, are due to poverty-related causes". How much is achieved by declaring that all persons have rights to adequate food and health care and security and education is unclear. So much of what is needed cannot be best addressed by progress in the law and legal processes.[8]

In this quotation from Held's chapter we find, in fact, not one, but three distinct concerns about human rights. These are: first, a concern about the status and legitimacy of positive, as distinct from negative, rights; second, a motivational concern; and third, a concern about the significance of law and justice vis-a-vis morality more widely construed. I will discuss these reservations in turn, but before joining the ranks of human rights sceptics, it is perhaps worth reminding ourselves of some of the things which can be said in favour of rights, and some of the reasons why both philosophers and activists have been reluctant to abandon them.

A. In defence of rights

In his 1991 book, *Modern Political Thought*, Raymond Plant draws attention to the political power and importance of appeals to human rights. 'Fundamental human rights' he tells us 'are supposed to answer the question of how *any* human being ought to be treated and what kinds of actions can legitimately be enforced by the state to ensure that persons are treated in this proper manner'.[9] Additionally, they 'serve to remind us that the boundaries of nations are not the boundaries of our moral concern'. So the fact that slavery, for example, was legally sanctioned in some states of the United States does not make it any less a violation of human rights, nor any less a matter of concern for the rest of us. In short, human rights are an expression of our views about how people—all people—*ought* to be treated independently of how they are in fact treated. They serve to set minimum standards by which all should abide and to provide a common framework within which all must operate.

In emphasizing this, one of Plant's main aims is to remind us that laws and governments do not stand above criticism, and the fact that something is sanctioned by the laws of a given society does not itself vindicate the practice. Additionally, in a world where culture, religion, and community are taken very seriously, and where there are frequent calls for the recognition of different cultural practices, appeals to human rights remind us that there are nonetheless limits to what can legitimately be endorsed in the name of culture or religion. So whatever doubts we may have about the power of an appeal to human rights, we should note that such rights can serve to remind us

---

[8] Held, 'Care and Human Rights', 624–5.
[9] Raymond Plant, *Modern Political Thought* (Oxford: Blackwell, 1991), 255.

that governments are not self-legitimizing, that not everything is culturally dependent, and that some values transcend the boundaries of nations, of cultures, and of religions.

Additionally, an appeal to human rights can serve to remind us of the importance of offering, not only *a* reason, but *the right* reason for taking a particular moral stance. In some of his very earliest writings, John Rawls pointed out that we should be wary of appealing to utilitarian arguments when opposing slavery because utilitarianism can furnish us with pragmatic reasons only, whereas our opposition to slavery is (or should be) principled. In his discussion of Rawls and Utilitarianism, Richard Arneson puts the point this way:

> Perhaps the animating philosophical idea in *A Theory of Justice* is that utilitarianism does not take rights seriously, that not taking rights seriously is a grave defect, and so we need a theory of justice that better fits our core convictions about ways that people must not be treated. Slavery is morally wrong because it violates fundamental moral rights of the persons who are enslaved.[10]

And in similar vein Joel Feinberg, in 'The Nature and Value of Rights' notes that one of the most conspicuous defects of a world without rights is that it is also a world in which the notion of claiming has no place. To remove talk of rights is to remove the possibility of a claim against others, and the possibility of claiming is, says Feinberg, a significant factor in self-respect. Thus:

> To have a right is to have a claim against someone whose recognition as valid is called for by some set of governing rules or moral principles. To have a *claim* in turn, is to have a case meriting consideration, that is, to have reasons or grounds that put one in a position to engage in performative and propositional claiming. The activity of claiming, finally, as much as any other thing, makes for self-respect and respect for others, [and] gives a sense to the notion of personal dignity.[11]

Taken together, these considerations suggest that, even though human rights have certainly not expunged the ills of inequality, hunger, and poverty, it may nonetheless be important to retain them in our analysis of the wrongs and shortcomings of our world. After all, if we are to provide solutions to our problems, we first need to be clear about the precise nature of those problems, and here human rights may be very significant.

I shall return to some of these points at the end of the paper. For now, however, I simply want to note that, even though Held is surely right to draw attention to the fact that 'progress' in human rights has not brought an end to inequality, poverty or hunger, she may nonetheless be premature in her suggestion that rights be supplemented by, or rejected in favour of, an appeal to care.

With these preliminary considerations in place, therefore, I now turn to the three reservations which Held expresses about human rights. To recall, these are: a reservation about the value of positive rights; a concern about motivation; and a query about the status and ubiquity of law and justice.

---

[10] Richard Arneson, 'Rawls versus Utilitarianism in the Light of Political Liberalism', in V. Davion and C. Wolf (eds.), *The Idea of a Political Liberalism: Essays on Rawls* (Lanham: Rowman and Littlefield, 2000), 232.
[11] Joel Feinberg, 'The Nature and Value of Rights', in Joel Feinberg, *Rights, Justice and the Bounds of Liberty* (Princeton: Princeton University Press, 1980), 155.

B. Positive rights

In the quotation given earlier, Held tells us that it is unclear 'how much is achieved by declaring that all persons have rights to adequate food and health care and security and education'. In saying this, she could be saying one of several things: she could, for instance, be doubting whether an appeal to rights is doing any work above and beyond the simple statement that these people are suffering and that we ought to do something about it. If we know that millions of people go to bed hungry each night, and if we deplore that state of affairs, what do we add by insisting that they have a *right* to food? Or a *right* to education? Or a *right* to a decent standard of living? If this is Held's question, then it is a question about, so to speak, the 'value-added' of rights talk, and it is reminiscent of Milan Kundera's concern that rights talk rapidly becomes a 'kind of universal stance of everyone towards everything'.

However, another possibility is that Held is casting doubt on the appeal to so-called 'positive' rights. In the literature on rights, a distinction is often drawn between positive and negative rights, where negative rights are rights to be left alone, or rights not to be interfered with. Thus, a right to life, negatively construed, is a right not to be killed, and other people can respect my right to life in this sense simply by doing nothing.

However, negative rights have been thought to stand in need of supplementing, and this has led to an appeal to positive rights or, as they are sometimes known, social and economic rights. These rights are not simply rights to be left alone, but rights to be given what one needs. In the specific example of the right to life, they are rights to be provided with the food that is necessary to keep starvation at bay, or rights to be given the kind of education that will enable one to escape poverty and destitution, or rights to be provided with the medical care needed to ensure continued existence. Of course the problem with rights of this kind is that, unlike negative rights, they make heavy demands on other people and may even put others under conflicting and incompatible obligations. If my right to life is construed simply as a right not to be killed, then it is a very simple matter for others to respect that right. They may respect my right to life, and indeed the right to life of millions of people across the entire globe, simply by sitting at home and doing nothing. If, however, the right to life is a right to be given what is needed for continued existence, then that will be extremely demanding on others, who may even find that it is straightforwardly impossible to meet all the rights claims made by the poor. If this happens, then the question (Held's question) 'how much is achieved by declaring that all persons have rights to adequate food and health care and security and education?' may be a question about the gap between what is demanded and what is possible.

Either way, though, positive rights are problematic: on the first interpretation it is not clear what is gained by invoking rights, rather than simply saying that we ought to do more.[12] And on the second interpretation, it *is* clear that an appeal to rights may be a demand to do what cannot (logically) be done.

---

[12] Of course, to say this is to presuppose a particular answer to the challenge set by Feinberg, Rawls, Arneson, and others. It is to suppose that the language of rights does not assist in the identification of the real wrong inherent in poverty, eg, or hunger.

C. The motivational problem

A second concern which Held expresses in the quotation given earlier, is a concern about the motivational power of human rights. Even if we suppose that it is (somehow) possible to satisfy all positive rights claims, there remains the fact that, in our world, people are inadequately motivated to do so, and it might therefore be thought that the real problem is not a problem about rights at all, but a problem about motivation.

This concern is very eloquently expressed by Thomas Pogge in his Introduction to *World Poverty and Human Rights*, where he asks two questions:

1. How can severe poverty of half of humankind continue despite enormous economic and technological progress and despite the enlightened moral norms and values of our heavily dominant Western civilization? And
2. Why do we citizens of affluent Western states not find it morally troubling, at least, that a world heavily dominated by us and our values gives such very deficient and inferior starting positions and opportunities to so many people?[13]

What troubles Pogge is the fact that we, in the affluent West, could do much to alleviate poverty and suffering, but we do very little, and it therefore seems likely that we are, at root, unconcerned about, or indifferent to, the plight of others and about their fate.

And similar anxieties are voiced by Samuel Scheffler when he writes:

The task of defending moderate cosmopolitanism should not be thought of as a narrowly philosophical undertaking. In other words, it is not just a matter of producing cogent arguments in support of some abstract formulation of the view. Instead, moderate cosmopolitanism about justice will be a compelling position only if it proves possible to devise human institutions, practices and ways of life that take seriously the equal worth of persons without undermining people's capacity to sustain their special loyalties and attachments.[14]

Both Pogge and Scheffler identify a motivational gap, and both see this gap as a major impediment to improving the lot of the poor. Held's concerns, as reflected in the passage quoted earlier, are very similar.

D. Justice, law, and morality

The third concern which Held expresses is the concern that there is more to morality than mere justice, and that it is a mistake to suppose that the most serious problems in our world will be solved by focusing on law and justice. She emphasizes this point

---

[13] Thomas Pogge, *World Poverty and Human Rights* (Cambridge: Polity Press, 2002), 3.
[14] Samuel Scheffler, 'Conceptions of Cosmopolitanism', in Samuel Scheffler, *Boundaries and Allegiances* (Oxford: Oxford University Press, 2001), 129.

a number of times in the earlier parts of her chapter, noting that 'not all that we do or want or think we ought to aim at can possibly be captured within the essentially legal notion of right or human right'.[15] And again 'many of our most important relations are not legal ones except in the most peripheral sense approached by the misleading claim that law covers "everything" because whatever it does not forbid, it allows'.[16] And finally, 'certainly legal rights to equal treatment are highly important, but in advancing equality much more than law is needed. Cultural change must precede and accompany and go beyond legal enactments of rights. The experience of the gay rights movement offers much evidence. So too with many human rights'.[17] So her concern is that the focus on law and justice which is inherent in rights talk is a focus on the wrong kind of thing.

Taken together, Held's three concerns about human rights are: first, that where human rights are understood as positive rights (rights to receive support and not merely rights not to be interfered with), they are too demanding and not always simultaneously satisfiable; second, that talk of rights disguises, or deflects attention from, the real problem, which is our lack of motivation to help others; and third that the appeal to the language of rights and of justice supposes what is not true—namely, that we should look to the law for a resolution of our most serious problems.

As I noted at the outset, I share some of Held's concerns about human rights. In particular, I share her concern about the motivational problems associated with positive rights. She is surely correct to wonder what is gained by invoking rights in cases where we know that there is little if any motivation to take the actions which would secure the things which the rights dictate. As she pointedly asks, 'What is achieved by declaring that all people have rights to food and health care and security and education?' Since we know that in much of the world these things are not provided, the appeal to a right to them seems at best wishful thinking, at worst a culpable disregard for the realities of others' lives.

Nonetheless, there is a considerable gap between the acknowledgement of these problems about human rights and the move to a morality of care which Held urges upon us. We might agree that there are problems with an appeal to human rights while denying that the solution to those problems lies in a morality of care. This, indeed, is the argument I now wish to advance and my main focus will be on the shortcomings in the morality of care. So although I agree with Held that rights are problematic, I do not agree with her claim that care is the solution to the problem. My reasons for this will be given in the third, and final, section of the paper. First, however, some alternative responses to the problems with human rights.

II. Human Rights and Motivation

I have already noted the wide variety of ways in which and reasons for which rights have been thought to be problematic, and I have also noted that Held's concerns about rights centre on their alleged motivational shortcomings. She is not alone in noting these shortcomings. Over a long period of time Onora O'Neill has also expressed

---

¹⁵ Held, 'Care and Human Rights', 627.   ¹⁶ Held, 'Care and Human Rights', 628.
¹⁷ Held, 'Care and Human Rights', 628.

concern about the motivational power of appeals to human rights and has argued eloquently for the superiority of a theory of obligation over a theory of rights. Moreover, one of O'Neill's main reasons for invoking obligations rather than rights is that the latter are, as she puts it, motivationally inert. She writes:

> Claims about rights need only assert what rights-holders are entitled to; only the curmudgeonly will object. Others may be animated and have their hopes raised. But claims about obligations have to specify not only what is to be accorded, but which obligation-bearers are going to have to do what for whom and at what cost. This is a much less charming topic. Unsurprisingly the rhetoric of obligations and duties has an unsavoury reputation, and those on whom burdens fall may often object.[18]

For O'Neill, the crucial question is not 'who has the rights?' but 'who is obliged to meet those rights?' Like Held, she is concerned about the motivational gap, but unlike Held she believes the best way of bridging it is by appealing to obligation, not by appealing to the morality of care. And her main reason for making this move is her conviction that a focus on obligations will draw attention to the need for claims to be met *by someone*, for rights to be recognized *by someone*, and for entitlements to be guaranteed *by someone*.

Of course, there may be disagreement about who exactly has these obligations, and in the most serious cases—cases of world poverty and inequality—the 'someone' on whom the obligation falls is likely to be a government rather than an individual. Where extensive poverty, suffering, and inequality are concerned, there is often very little individuals can do by themselves, and obligations must therefore fall upon governments or other institutional actors to ensure that appropriate and effective structures are in place to alleviate the suffering and reduce the inequalities. Nonetheless, the prioritization of obligations rather than rights highlights the fact that, in order to fill the gap between a claim of right and an action in fulfilment of that right, we need to identify who it is who is obligated, and of course this is especially true in the case of positive, or social and economic, rights. As O'Neill notes:

> A violation of a right not to be raped or of a right not to be tortured may be clear enough, and the perpetrator may even be identifiable, even when the institutions for enforcement are lamentably weak. But the correspondence of universal rights to goods and services to obligations *to provide or deliver* remains entirely amorphous when institutions are missing or weak. Somebody who receives no maternity care may no doubt *assert* that her rights have been violated, but unless obligations to deliver that care have been established and distributed, she will not know where to press her claim, and it will be systematically obscure whether there is any perpetrator, or who has neglected or violated her rights.[19]

So the appeal to care is only one possible strategy open to those who are concerned about the motivational gap. There is also the possibility of an appeal to obligation. Why might this be thought preferable to an appeal to care? It is this question which I will address in the next, and final, section of the paper.

---

[18] Onora O'Neill, 'Women's Rights: Whose Obligations?', in Onora O'Neill, *Bounds of Justice* (Cambridge: Cambridge University Press, 2000), 100.

[19] O'Neill, 'Women's Rights: Whose Obligations?', 105.

III. Concerns about Care

I have already identified what I take to be Held's main reservations about rights, and I have noted that, even where we share these reservations, we should be cautious about moving directly to an endorsement of care. Care may not be the best response to the motivational problem inherent in rights, and it is certainly not the only response. But why should we be concerned about the move to a morality of care? What is the precise nature of that move and what are the problems inherent in it? In this, final, section I will focus on two problems with the morality of care, both of which are associated with the motivational gap which Held identifies in her critique of rights.

The first problem arises from the fact that an ethics of care is rooted in our experience of individual, personal relationships. Carol Gilligan's initial work on the ethics of care took its inspiration from differences in the ways men and women respond to small-scale, face-to-face situations. 'The moral imperative for women' Gilligan wrote 'is an injunction to care, a responsibility to discern and alleviate the "real and recognisable trouble" of this world…The standard of moral judgement that informs [women's] assessment of the self is a standard of relationship, an ethic of nurturance, responsibility and care'.[20] And Held concurs with this understanding of the ethics of care when she writes: 'care is based especially on experience. Without care, no human person would survive into adulthood to become the rational individual of traditional moral theories. Every person has received care that has incorporated moral values, and every person can reflect on his or her experience of practices of care'.[21] And again:

> Attending to care and its practices brings to the fore such values as empathetic understanding, sensitivity to the needs of others and especially, responsiveness to such needs. It calls especially for trust between care givers and recipients, and for understanding the relations between them as much from the point of view of the recipient of care as of the provider.[22]

In short, it is actual relationships between actual people which inspire an ethics of care and which lend it its persuasive power. But there is a real question about whether and why we might expect the insights derived from these individual cases to transfer to the wider world and inform our responses to global issues of poverty, inequality, and hunger.

To see what is at stake here, consider two problems associated with the transition from the personal to the global. First, and as a number of commentators have pointed out, there are considerable psychological problems with the transition: the care we have for our friends and family is, by its nature, particular, and is not easily extended to unknown others, or to the wider world generally. Michael Ignatieff puts the point this way:

> We recognize our humanity in our differences, in our individuality, our history, in the faithful discharge of our particular culture of obligation. There is no identity we

[20] Carol Gilligan, *In a Different Voice* (Cambridge, MA: Harvard University Press, 1982), 159–60.
[21] Held, 'Care and Human rights', 630.   [22] Held, 'Care and Human Rights', 630.

can recognize in our universality. There is no such thing as love of the human race, only love of this person for that, in this time and not in any other.[23]

So it is not clear that the care which arises in individual, face-to-face relationships can (psychologically) be extended to unknown others, or to humanity as a whole.

Additionally, and even if care could be extended in this way, we might find that it is transformed in the process and becomes a vice rather than a virtue. The care which operates at the individual level and which is an admirable character trait may cease to be admirable if it is translated into a policy for society as a whole. To see how this may be, we need to focus less on the perspective of the carer, and more on the perspective of the recipient of care. Proponents of the ethics of care tend to focus their attention on those who provide care—on women as those who nurture, support, and provide succour to the needy and vulnerable.

All this is admirable, but it can take on a slightly different quality if viewed from the perspective of the recipient of care: to receive care and nurture from those whom we love is indeed highly desirable, but when the ethics of care is extended to society more widely it implies the provision of care to unknown others and, from their point of view, to be the recipient of care is, potentially, humiliating and degrading. Put simply, the care and compassion which we embrace at the individual level may become patronizing at the political level. Here, what is desired is not sympathy from those who are better off than ourselves, but rather a recognition of our claims of need as claims of justice, not as requests for compassion or sympathy. The substitution of compassion for justice at the political level was, in part, responsible for the some of the most morally disreputable aspects of Victorian Poor Law in England, and this should serve as a warning against unbridled enthusiasm for the extension of care to the wider political world.

This first concern—that the ethics of care may be transformed when applied to society as a whole—leads to a second, which is that a focus on care, far from supplementing considerations of justice, as Held hopes, may in fact drive them out and thus reduce what are properly claims of right to pleas for generosity. Indeed it is this possibility that informs Joel Feinberg's defence of rights, and his anxiety that a world in which there are no rights is a world in which there are no claims and therefore, ultimately, no dignity or self-respect. To recall, Feinberg writes:

> To have a right is to have a claim against someone whose recognition as valid is called for by some set of governing rules or moral principles. To have a *claim* in turn, is to have a case meriting consideration, that is, to have reasons or grounds that put one in a position to engage in performative and propositional claiming. The activity of claiming, finally, as much as any other thing, makes for self-respect and respect for others, [and] gives a sense to the notion of personal dignity.[24]

So, despite its many advantages, the ethics of care does not speak to the importance of claiming and to its role in human dignity, since care, by definition, is not something to which we can lay claim. Moreover, the rejection of rights, and the claims that are a

---

[23] Michael Ignatieff, *The Needs of Strangers* (London: Hogarth, 1984), 42.
[24] Feinberg, 'The Nature and Value of Rights', 155.

concomitant of them, is a very dangerous strategy for women in particular. Many, if not most, of the achievements of early feminism were gained through appeals to rights and justice, so to reject or minimize these is to embark on a dangerous journey. Anne Phillips puts the point this way:

> Compassion cannot substitute for the impartiality of justice and equality, for compassion is potentially limited to those we can understand—and hence those who are most like ourselves. For feminists, in particular, this would be a risky road to pursue, and it was precisely the demand for equality across seemingly impassable barriers of incomprehension and difference that gave birth to the feminist tradition.[25]

There are, then reasons for endorsing Held's critique of human rights and for sharing her concern about the motivational gap which exists between claims of rights and the actions required to meet those rights. However, her appeal to the ethics of care may be both premature and problematic: premature because there are other responses to the problem of motivation—notably, but not uniquely, Onora O'Neill's appeals to obligation; problematic because it is difficult to see how care can be extended to unknown others while retaining its character as a virtue rather than a vice, and also risky to relinquish the rights-based appeals which have done so much to improve the position of many people—including women—both politically and socially.

It would, however, be wrong to end on a negative note. Held's article is rich, engaging, and philosophically sophisticated. She sees many, if not all, the problems I have identified here and she tackles them with imagination and skill. My criticisms should therefore be read as different 'judgement calls' about the amount of weight we, as feminists, should accord to the claims of justice vis-a-vis the morality of care, and as a slightly less optimistic analysis of the political promise inherent in the ethics of care. Certainly they are not reasons to reject the ethics of care wholesale, nor are they reasons to forget the very significant contribution to moral theory which has been made by care theorists in general and by Virginia Held in particular. For this insightful and thought-provoking chapter, and for much else, we owe her our thanks.

---

[25] Anne Phillips, 'So What's Wrong with the Individual?', in Peter Osborne (ed.), *Socialism and the Limits of Liberalism* (London: Verso, 1991), 147.

37

Human Rights in Kantian Mode

A Sketch

Katrin Flikschuh

I. Reservations about Human Rights

Many legal and political theorists think the idea of human rights intuitive and their moral and political importance self-evident. Others worry that the concept is badly delimited and human rights' moral and political appeal overrated. In current human rights relevant debates, the latter are the reservations of a dwindling minority. Philosophical discussions about global poverty alleviation, about state legitimacy, about international law and humanitarian intervention make ubiquitous appeal to human rights: the idea plays an increasingly central conceptual and justificatory role in these and related debates.

In general, recurrent appeal to a single concept as solvent to a diverse range of theoretical and practical problems should be treated with caution. The increasingly routine appeal to human rights in global justice debates is particularly disconcerting given that debate's acknowledged state of flux following nearly five hundred years of sophisticated political theorizing firmly *within* the boundaries of the self-contained territorial state. Under conditions of such comprehensive change and uncertainty appeal to all-too-readily available practical or theoretical remedies seems ill-advised. The very allure of human rights theorizing here counsels circumspection with regard to their possible illusionary quality as quick fixes to complex global problems we confront.[1]

Since my brief here concerns human rights, I shall not simply set them aside. Still, everything I say here should be read in the light of the reservations just noted. I have a strong sense of my *lack* of grasp of the concept: whenever I try to think it, I overwhelmingly sense my confusion. Admittedly, one cannot easily call to mind concepts 'as such'—in abstraction, that is, from their discursive employment in some context. My confusion in trying to think the concept may merely reflect my bewilderment over its currently ubiquitous usage. Still, insofar as a concept's use at least partly determines its meaning, confusion about use may be indicative of confusion about meaning.[2]

Following Henry Allison's sketch of Kant's notion of a concept in general, I shall here think of a concept as consisting of 'a set of marks (themselves concepts), which

---

[1] cf Onora O'Neill, 'The Dark Side of Human Rights', *International Affairs*, 81 (2005): 427–39; Samuel Moyn, *The Last Utopia: Human Rights in History* (Harvard University Press, 2010).
[2] Contrast Charles Beitz, *The Idea of Human Rights* (Oxford University Press, 2009) who believes that a coherent theoretical conception of human rights can be derived from observing and interpreting current human rights practice.

are thought together in an "analytic unity" and which can serve as a ground for the recognition of objects. These marks collectively constitute the intension of a concept. One concept is "contained in another" if and only if it is itself either a mark of the concept or a mark of a mark'.[3] On this sketch, which Allison offers in the wider context of his discussion of Kantian analyticity, a concept is a cognitive construct made up of a plurality of other concepts that together specify the concept's semantic content, delimiting it from other, neighbouring concepts.[4] Concepts, on this account, are neither ready-made 'thought entities' nor abstractions from empirically perceived objects—they are conclusions, rather, of subjects' cognitive judgements of sensible intuitions as objects of experience in accordance with certain rules of cognition.[5] As such, any given concept consists of (or 'contains') that which it is *thought* to contain by the judging subject in accordance with specified rules of judgement or cognition. Assuming human knowers' finite cognitive capacities and fallibility in judgement in general, concepts as cognitive constructs can have varying levels of semantic determination. We may not always be wholly confident as to which marks we take a given concept to contain. We think of the boundaries of some concepts as more fuzzily delimited (or delimitable) than those of others.[6] Precisely what we take to be 'contained in' a given concept may shift with different usage over time. My claim is not that the concept of human rights can or must be rendered fully perspicacious;[7] my claim is merely that we must acknowledge the concept's necessary boundedness. No concept, if it is to be intelligibly employed in some contexts is intelligibly employable in all contexts, and no concept the set of constitutive marks of which serves to delimit it from neighbouring concepts can accommodate an infinite number of such marks.

Some of a concept's constituent marks may be taken to specify its core meaning. Other marks are less central but lie nonetheless comfortably within the concept's boundary. Yet others are peripheral, lying at or beyond a concept's boundary. Take the concept of a chair: its constitutive marks include 'four-legged structure', 'raised

---

[3] Henry Allison, *Kant's Transcendental Idealism. An Interpretation and Defense* (Yale University Press, 1983), 76.

[4] Allison goes on to suggest that what he calls Kant's 'thoroughly intensional' conception of analyticity, 'depends on the fixity of a concept', ie, on 'the thesis that the marks of a concept can be sufficiently determined (even without an explicit definition) for the purpose of analysis.' In this, he concurs with Lewis White Beck's earlier study of Kantian analyticity in 'Can Kant's synthetic judgements be made analytic?', *Kant-Studien* (1956). I am not myself persuaded that Kant *is* committed to the 'fixity thesis'—the view that he is seems to me to depend on the rejection of what Allison and Beck call Kant's 'phenomenological' criterion of analyticity, according to which judgements of conceptual containment are based on mere introspection: 'we reflect on what is "actually thought" in a given concept'. The subjectivist connotations of the phenomenological reading lead both Allison and Beck to favour what they take to be an alternative 'logical' criterion of analyticity—ie, the principle of contradiction. My own view is that the two criteria are not mutually exclusive: the phenomenological criterion tells against the 'fixity thesis' and in conjunction with the logical criterion implies a conception of analyticity as objectively rule governed though substantively fallible human judgement.

[5] cf Alison, *Kant's Transcendental Idealism*, esp. 63–130. See also Beatrice Longuenesse, *Kant and the Capacity to Judge* (Princeton University Press, 2000), esp. 81–130.

[6] cf Kant, *Critique of Pure Reason*, 'The knowledge of appearances in their complete determination, which is possible only through the understanding, demands an *endless progress in the specification of our concepts*, and an advance to *yet further remaining differences...*' (A656 / B684, emphasis added).

[7] Contrast James Griffin, 'First Steps in an Account of Human Rights', *European Journal of Philosophy*, 9 (2001): 306–27.

seating surface', 'back rest', and so on. If we take 'raised seating surface' to specify its core meaning, we may think of 'back rest' as occupying a less central but still non-marginal position. By contrast, 'armrests' lies at or outside the concept's boundary. One can meaningfully debate whether or not a given object with a raised seating surface, a back-rest and armrests can legitimately count as an instance of the concept of a chair. However, such boundary disputes make sense only on the presumption of concepts' boundedness in general.

In contrast to empirical concepts, practical concepts (including moral concepts) are not restricted to the constraints of the physical world. This may make them more liable to conceptual contestation. The practical concept of happiness, for example, may or may not be taken to contain semantic marks like 'heightened emotional well-being', 'a feeling of personal contentment', 'at-one-ness with the world'. Each is a plausible candidate for either inclusion or exclusion—if included, each is liable to being arrayed either more towards the core or towards the boundary of the concept. Again, however, there has to be some boundary and hence some *exclusions*—if only to differentiate 'happiness' from neighbouring concepts, such as 'pleasure' or 'joy'.

The practical concept of human rights appears at times to be treated as infinitely capacious and capable of accommodating a wide array of psycho–physiological, value-based, and deontological marks, including marks relating to physical and psychological features of personhood, marks that pick out particular values, such as agential autonomy or individual well-being, and marks that specify interpersonal constraints, such as human dignity or respect for personhood. In confessing my confusion when trying to 'think the concept' I mean that I find it difficult mentally to represent this diversity of constitutive marks in the unity of a single concept.

If pressed, I would place some marks closer to the concept's core than others: deontological marks associated with negative rights language over the value marks of positive rights language. Granted, the negative / positive distinction is itself contested; growing numbers of theorists make the case for the equal inclusion of negative and positive rights;[8] some perhaps even prioritize positive over negative rights.[9] Still, most human rights advocates who invoke what they take to be central features of Kant's moral philosophy as the justificatory basis of their favoured human rights conceptions—human dignity, respect for the humanity in persons, capacity for moral autonomy—acknowledge that these features' deontological orientation tends to support negative rather than positive rights conceptions.

I do not believe that Kant himself possessed the concept of a human right.[10] If we nonetheless *must* have a Kantian conception of contemporary human rights—and

---

[8] Most notably by Henry Shue, *Basic Rights: Subsistence, Affluence, and US Foreign Policy* (Princeton University Press, 1980). See also Elizabeth Ashford, 'The Duties Imposed by the Human Right to Basic Necessities', in Thomas Pogge (ed.), *Freedom from Poverty as a Human Right* (Oxford University Press, 2007), 183–218. Likewise, one might add, with the traditional distinction between deontological and teleological morality, to which I shall nonetheless simply help myself here. But see Barbara Herman, 'Leaving Deontology Behind', in her *The Practice of Moral Judgment* (Harvard University Press 1994), 208–42.

[9] As Simon Hope has pointed out to me, this may be especially true of virtue–ethical human rights accounts. See, eg, Martha Nussbaum, 'Capabilities and Human Rights', *Fordham Law Review*, 66 (1997): 273–300.

[10] Kant does invoke terms such as 'das Recht der Menschheit', or das 'Recht der Menschen'. However, he does not deploy these terms consistently or systematically, and he nowhere develops an explicit theory

I am not myself persuaded that we must—we should seek to develop one that is plausibly consistent with the general contours of Kant's philosophical thinking. In what follows, I sketch what I call a *transcendent* human rights conception, the distinguishing feature of which I take to be its acknowledgement of human cognitive and moral fallibility. On the transcendent human rights conception I propose, to invoke the idea of human rights is to acknowledge the limits of human moral understanding and political authority: from a Kantian perspective, the idea is humbling rather than empowering.[11]

I build my case for a transcendent human rights conception indirectly, ie, by rejecting as a plausible interpretive basis Kant's obscure though increasingly popular juridical category of innate right in his *Doctrine of Right*. In an ironic twist of philosophical fate, the innate right of each is coming to be treated by many as a proto-natural right that serves Kant as 'foundational pillar' for his theory of positive rights: Kant, the erstwhile constructivist is fast coming to be transformed in contemporary normative debates as Kant, the rights-foundationalist.[12] This new interpretative trend makes it tempting to go one step further and to gloss the foundationally interpreted innate right to freedom as a pre-legal human right. I believe we should resist this temptation: partly because it is so obviously inconsistent with Kant's philosophical

---

of human rights. In general, Kant's invocation of notions such as 'das Recht der Menschheit' tends to have collective, not individualistic connotations and is better translated as a 'right of humanity' rather than as 'a human right'.

[11] In the *Critique of Pure Reason*, Kant refers to what I here call 'transcendent concepts' as 'transcendental ideas': these are 'empty' thought constructs, which are generated through the 'problematic extension' of pure concepts (categories) of the understanding beyond the sensibly given conditions of their application. In the Transcendental Dialectic of the first *Critique*, Kant argues that the human tendency to extend the categories of the understanding beyond sensibly given conditions of experience is indicative of the search for first causes, ie, of the search for the unconditioned first ground of all conditional knowledge. Though Kant critiques this tendency and rejects the attendant rationalist metaphysics, which he thinks the search for an unconditioned first cause gives rise to, he eventually assigns transcendent(al) ideas a critical, reflective status according to which they do not constitute legitimate knowledge claims as such but may guide our wider reflections on the systematizing form and teleological orientation of human experience. Kant's use of his terminology is not, however, consistent; what is more, the term 'transcendental' is often, in contemporary debates, invoked rather loosely to refer to anything mind-dependent. I have here decided to stick with the terms 'transcendent' in part because I prefer to reserve the term 'transcendental' for Kantian categories of the understanding; unlike the latter, transcendent ideas of reason are not necessary conditions of the possibility of human cognitive experience. In contrast to 'transcendental', 'transcendent' retains the connotations of a mind-independent, supersensible order of things. Although Kant unambiguously rejects our possible knowledge of such an order and of the items it may or may not contain, he nonetheless defends the thought of the possibility of such an order. In retaining the notion of 'transcendence' I want to draw attention to the Kantian thought of the possibility of such an order, though not thereby endorsing any unKantian assumptions about its knowability.

[12] See, eg, Louis-Philippe Hodgson, 'Kant on the Right to Freedom: A Defense', *Ethics*, 120 (2010): 791–819; also Anna Stilz, 'Nations, States, and Territory', *Ethics*, 121 (2011): 572–601. The general trend towards the casual attribution of rights-foundationalism to Kant is exemplified in the contributions to a recent book symposium on Arthur Ripstein's *Force and Freedom* in the *European Journal of Philosophy*, 20 (2012). In her contribution, Laura Valentini asserts the innate right as the 'pillar' of Kant's *Doctrine of Right*; Andrea Sangiovanni speaks of the innate right as the 'load-bearing foundation' of Kant's property argument. See also Ripstein's understandable terse response, though in fairness to his commentators, Ripstein's own somewhat ambivalent treatment of innate right in *Force and Freedom* does invite foundationalist interpretations of it. For some reservations in this regard, see Katrin Flikschuh, 'A Regime of Equal Private Freedom? Individual Rights and Public Law in Ripstein's *Force and Freedom*', in Sari Kisilevsky and Martin Stone (eds.), *Freedom and Force: Essays on Kant's Legal Philosophy* (Hart Publishing, forthcoming).

non-foundationalism; partly because it fails to tell us anything about human rights that we could not just as easily derive from Lockean rights premises instead.

I begin by setting out Kant's division of the domain of ordinary morality in general, treating his systematic approach as emblematic of his general philosophical non-foundationalism. I then sketch a non-foundationalist interpretation of innate Right before turning to the idea of human rights as a critically transcendent idea of pure practical (moral) reasoning. I close with some remarks on what I take to be distinctive about the proposed transcendent human rights conception.

II. Structuring the Field of Morality in General

When Kantians consider the concept of human rights, they usually incline towards a negative rights conception: rights as some sort of side-constraints on others' actions.[13] This does not make them closet libertarians. Kantians generally regard duties as conceptually prior to rights. While for libertarians (and for most liberal egalitarians, too), rights *entail* corresponding duties, Kantians generally think of rights as *grounded* in duties.[14] The current emphasis on the 'second-personal' or 'relational' structure of Kantian moral reasoning is a gloss on the justificatory priority of the concept of duty over the concept of a right.[15] Kant's property argument, for example, construes a person's right to a particular object of her choice as grounded in another's duty to refrain from using the object without her consent.[16] Insofar as rights are grounded in duties there can be no *natural* rights for Kant—not, if by 'natural' one means the predication of innate powers or entitlements to persons independently of their coexistence with others. From a Kantian perspective, to say that a person's rights are side-constraints on others' actions is not to say that persons are endowed with innate powers that give others reason to abstain from certain types of action against them. It is to say, rather, that others have (coercible) duties of restraint in action towards them.

Rights specify only one type of duty. Kant distinguishes between juridical and ethical duties.[17] The former are sometimes glossed as 'perfect' and the latter as 'imperfect'—although there is growing doubt about the felicity of superimposing the earlier perfect / imperfect distinction upon the later distinction between juridical and ethical duties.[18] One reason for thinking of juridical as perfect duties may be that Kant takes juridical duties to hold without exception. However, under at least one description of 'exception-less validity'—unconditional validity—he evidently assumes the same of

---

[13] cf Robert Nozick, *Anarchy, State, and Utopia* (Blackwell Publishers, 1975).

[14] The precise contours of the derivation of rights from duties remains obscure; rights may ultimately be grounded in duties towards the self. cf Bernd Ludwig, 'Die Einteilung der Metaphysik der Sitten im Allgemeinen und die der Tugendlehre im Besonderen', in A. Trempton, O. Sensen, and J. Timmermann (eds.), *Kants Tugendlehre* (Berlin: de Gruyter 2103), 59–84.

[15] cf Stephen Darwall, *The Second Person Standpoint. Morality, Respect and Accountability* (Harvard University Press, 2006); Arthur Ripstein, *Force and Freedom. Kant's Legal and Political Philosophy* (Harvard University Press, 2009).

[16] This (*a priori*) presupposition morally necessitates common entrance into the civil condition. cf Katrin Flikschuh, *Kant and Modern Political Philosophy* (Cambridge University Press, 2000), 113–43.

[17] See Kant's table of duties in the *Metaphysics of Morals*, 6: 240.

[18] cf Marcus Willaschek, 'Why the Doctrine of Right does not Belong in a Metaphysics of Morals: On some Basic Distinctions in Kant's Moral Philosophy', *Jahrbuch für Recht und Ethik*, 5 (1997): 205–27.

ethical duties. Perhaps more pertinently, juridical duties, unlike ethical duties, leave no room for discretion in individual judgement but must be determined 'with mathematical exactitude'.[19] Relatedly, juridical duties impose constraints on persons' actions without requiring the adoption of moral ends. By contrast, ethical duties prescribe the adoption of particular moral ends, including the furtherance of others' happiness. Ethical duties allow for latitude in judgement *because* furtherance of others' happiness requires resources of the requisite kind; it requires an adequate understanding of relevant others' happiness conceptions and, correspondingly, judgements about one's ability and indeed one's moral authority to assist particular others.[20]

Although many non-Kantians find it hard to resist the thought that perfect duties of right are somehow more stringent than imperfect duties of virtue, this in fact makes little sense: all duties are unconditionally binding; juridical and ethical duties merely bind in different ways. Duties of justice are externally binding; duties of virtue bind internally. Internal bindingness is related to the adoption of moral ends. To adopt a moral end is to make it one's maxim to act in furtherance of this end: it requires one to *will* the end in question. Since no one can compel another autonomously to will a moral end, duties of virtue are not externally enforceable. Yet the mere fact that one cannot be externally compelled to adopt a moral end hardly makes duties of virtue less weighty. To the contrary, self-binding of the requisite kind—autonomous willing—is in many respects *more* demanding of the agent than is conformity with duties of right, for which mere outward conformity of action is sufficient.

The external enforceability of juridical duties is a function in turn not of their greater intrinsic weightiness but of the reciprocal structure of Kantian rights relations. Rights are reciprocally valid claims to the legitimate restriction of one another's 'power of choice': I cannot by rights bind you to more than you can bind me in turn. The problem with reciprocally valid rights claims is their mutual non-enforceability. While the validity of my rights claim against you depends on my reciprocal acknowledgement of your equally valid rights claim against me, my acknowledgement of your equally valid rights claim against me renders illegitimate my unilateral restriction of your power of choice by mine (and vice versa). This stalemate is resolvable only through common entrance into the civil condition, including submission under a public coercive authority with the power externally to constrain the capacity for choice of all in accordance with universal law.

In the present context, the important point to note is the fact *that* Kantian morality is structured into these two distinct but coeval and complementary domains of duty. Neither domain is either logically or morally prior to the other—a Kantian agent can be virtuous in the pre-civil condition (which is a condition devoid of justice); he can be just though non-virtuous in the civil condition (as virtue is non-coercible). Deficiencies in the one domain cannot be compensated for by greater exertion in the other: excess in virtue cannot make up for lack of justice.[21] The two domains are systematically

---

[19] Kant, *The Metaphysics of Morals*, 6:233.

[20] On the non-reducibility of Kantian ethical duties to Kantian juridical duties, see Onora O'Neill, *Towards Justice and Virtue. A Constructive Account of Practical Reasoning* (Cambridge University Press, 1996), esp. 154–212.

[21] For more extensive discussion, see Katrin Flikschuh. 'Justice without Virtue', in Lara Denis (ed.), *Kant's Metaphysics of Morals. A Critical Guide* (Cambridge University Press, 2010), 51–70.

delimited from each other but relate horizontally rather hierarchically to one another. Of course, the distinction between justice and virtue does not originate with Kant. Nonetheless, the systematic nature of Kant's division of ordinary morality into these two coeval, complementary, yet conceptually distinct domains has counterintuitive implications that routinely cause consternation. The strictly reciprocal structure of rights relations prevents Kantians from according rights to children, for example. The exclusion of substantive ends from the juridical domain lends his philosophy of Right a seemingly 'libertarian' character (though Kant is hardly a 'minimalist' about the state!). The characterization of ethical as imperfect duties is suggestive of a kind of moral voluntarism that places them in the neighbourhood of supererogation. And so on. Kant's systematizing penchant is frequently seen as preventing us from following our moral intuitions where they should naturally lead us. For many, these counterintuitive implications are evidence of Kant's moral rigorism.[22]

It is not, however, Kant's moral rigorism so much as his philosophical non-foundationalism that constrains Kant to proceed systematically.[23] His philosophical strategy invariably begins from uncontested experiential premises and proceeds to a vindication of the necessary grounds of their possibility. The deduction of the categories of the understanding in the first *Critique*, which begins from our experience of objects, is the most prominent example. Yet *Groundwork* in fact adopts a similar strategy, starting from our 'ordinary' concept of duty and regressing from there to its necessary presuppositions before attempting their critical vindication. The structure of the *Doctrine of Right* is more obscure. But it, too, begins from the concept of right as employed in ordinary juridical practice and proceeds from there, via the notoriously torturous property argument, to an analysis and vindication of the necessary conditions of its practical possibility.[24]

Note the absence in this critical strategy of foundational premises of either a realist or an empiricist provenance: first-order moral truths, rock-bottom intuitions, generalizable human interests. My contention is that it is the absence of possible reliance on foundationalist premises that leads Kant to the systematization of ordinary moral experience instead. To illustrate briefly, consider a passage in 'What is Orientation in Thinking?' in which Kant draws an analogy with spatial orientation:

> In the dark, I can find my orientation in a familiar room so long as I am able to recall the location of a single object. In determining the location [of remaining objects] I rely solely on a subjective principle of differentiation [ie my subjective sense of left and right]: for I cannot see the objects whose position I seek to determine. If, to play a trick on me, someone had re-arranged the order of objects, placing to the left what before was to the right, I would be unable to find my orientation in [this] room.[25]

---

[22] A careful (and amusing) dissection and rebuttal of the rigorism charge can be found in Jens Timmermann, 'Alles Halb so Schlimm: Bemerkungen zu Kants ethischem Rigorismus', in Achim Stephan and Klaus Peter Rippe (eds.), *Ethik ohne Dogmen* (Mentis Verlag, 2001), 8–82.

[23] I am much indebted here to Karl Ameriks' nuanced and insightful defense of Kant's 'modest system' in *Kant and the Fate of Autonomy* (Cambridge University Press, 2000), esp. 37–80.

[24] On the distinctiveness of Kant's strategy of philosophical justification in general, see Dieter Henrich's by now classic, 'Kant's Notion of a Deduction and the Methodological Background of the First Critique', in Eckart Foerster (ed.), *Kant's Transcendental Deductions* (Stanford University Press, 1989), 29–46.

[25] Kant, 'What is Orientation in Thinking?', 8: 135, my translation.

Absent objectively given first principles, I must rely on a 'subjective principle of differentiation'—in the case at hand, my subjective bodily awareness of left and right—the fallibility of which I must acknowledge. If by means of it I can locate one object, I can locate the remainder relative to it. The entire reconstruction remains provisional, however—permanently subject to possible error and correction. Philosophical orientation in the field of morality proceeds similarly. Absent foundational premises, it can only begin from subjective moral experience: say, of the concept of duty. It proceeds from there to the determination of neighbouring concepts—the concept of right, say. The determination of the one is relative to that of the other; the absence of an assured objectively fixed starting point entails the permanently provisional nature of philosophical determination. Kant's systematic divisions are not a reflection of his moral rigorism. To the contrary, given his non-foundationalism, he *cannot* appeal to absolute standards of right and wrong. Systematic division is a response to the non-availability of first principles or rock bottom intuitions.[26] Yet to systematize is nonetheless to introduce divisions and distinctions, which impose constraints. If we specify the concept of right as pertaining to a strictly reciprocal relation between persons, this precludes the ascription of rights responsibilities to moral minors. This does not mean that obligations towards moral minors cannot be accommodated elsewhere within our moral system: but they cannot be located within the domain of rights. To systematize is establish order through a process inclusion and exclusion on the basis of specified criteria. Unless this is accepted, systematic division is pointless.[27]

If I were to be asked, in light of the systematic division between right and virtue as outlined, where within this provisionally delimited Kantian system of morals I would locate the concept of human rights, I would locate it somewhere in the domain of juridical duties. A whole slew of Kantian duties—duties of virtue—would by this move alone be rendered out of bounds for human rights reasoning. I am not troubled by this: ethical duties are accommodated elsewhere in Kant's system. But where in the field of juridical duties more precisely would I locate human rights? Somewhere, I think, *beyond* the reach of any possible substantive rights legislation. It is this thought of a right beyond substantively legislated rights that I shall explore over the next two sections, beginning with the innate right to freedom of each.

III. Rights Beyond Legislation: Innate Right

There is mention of one right in the *Doctrine of Right* that may be said to be 'beyond' any positive rights legislation: the innate right to freedom of each. It is tempting to interpret the innate right of each as a foundational freedom right from which all other

---

[26] cf Ameriks, *Kant and the Fate of Autonomy.*

[27] Simon Hope has helpfully pressed the issue of arbitrariness on me in this connection: absent a stated justificatory ground, Kant's specification of rights relations as strictly reciprocal strikes him as arbitrary. Why should rights relation be restricted to moral relations between moral equals? One might offer various justificatory reasons: equal capacity for choice, say, or equal capacity for liability for action. But one might also say—and I am increasingly inclined to say—that the Kantian restriction of rights relations to relations between moral equals is justified by the fact that it (a) picks out a distinctive form of moral relation, and (b) does not preclude the accommodation of other forms of moral relation within neighbouring domains of morality.

rights are derived. It is tempting further to declare Kant's innate right as a foundational human right, moral commitment to which underwrites all subsequently legislated positive rights. My aim in this section is to show that there is good *systematic* reason to resist these temptations. I shall sketch a summary account of a possible, attenuated sense in which innate right may be said to be 'above' or 'beyond' positive rights legislation without therefore being most plausibly dubbed a 'human right'. It will be necessary to engage in some amount of textual footwork, though I shall try to keep it to a minimum.

The Introduction to the *Doctrine of Right* distinguishes between innate and acquired right. The former refers to a class of rights that requires no prior act but that each is said to have 'innately'. In fact, there is only one innate right—the right to freedom of each in accordance with a universal law. By contrast, acquired right refers to a class of rights for the establishment of which an action is required—an act of acquisition, as it turns out. (Kant subsequently goes on to specify three classes of acquired right, but this is immaterial to the present discussion.)

It is by now widely agreed that the moral justification of acquired right depends, for Kant, on the institution of a system of public law-giving. The status of innate right, by contrast, is considerably murkier. Recently, an interpretive trend has begun to establish itself that treats the innate right of each as a quasi-natural right, ie, as an independently given, substantively specifiable freedom premise that serves as 'pillar' or 'load bearing foundation' in relation to Kant's ensuing justification of property rights.[28] The result is a curious interpretive half-way house that combines the assumption of a *foundational* freedom right with the acknowledged *public* right condition of Kant's property argument. The difficulty with such readings is two-fold. First, the assumption of a foundational right within the *Doctrine of Right* is question-begging not just in the usual sense of owing us (rather than supplying) an account of such a right's supposed provenance, but also in the more specific sense of owing us an account of the intelligibility of foundationalist premises of this kind within the methodological constraints of Kant's general philosophical non-foundationalism. Second, though less important in the present context, the dual justification of property rights by means of resort to both foundationalist rights assumptions and public right conditions muddies the waters in any attempt to differentiate clearly between Lockean and Kantian rights justification. For reasons just sketched, my chief concern here is with the first worry, ie, with the foundationalist reading of innate right. I want to block foundationalist readings of innate Right and their likely slide into human rights claims by offering an alternative, non-foundationalist interpretation of innate right, though given the textual work required I can here only sketch my alternative account.[29]

If we do reject rights foundationalism in relation to innate right, we face an interpretive puzzle. The innate right to freedom is explicitly mentioned only once in the text, namely, in the Introduction. The main body of the text is concerned with the

---

[28] See n 12.

[29] The following paragraphs are a highly condensed summary of my interpretation of the status of innate right in Katrin Flikschuh, 'Originally Mine? Innate and Acquired Right in Kant's Doctrine of Right' (manuscript). See also Flikschuh, 'A Regime of Equal Private Freedom?'

moral possibility of property rights. The Introduction sets out a number of preliminaries, including the exposition of the general concept of right, the related universal
principle of right and, finally, the innate right to freedom of each. Thus,

> [t]he concept of right, insofar as it is related to an obligation corresponding to it (i.e.,
> the moral concept of right), has to do, *first*, only with the external and indeed practi-
> cal relation of one person to another…But *second*, it does not signify the relation of
> one's choice to the mere wish of the other, but only in relation to the other's *choice*.
> *Third*, in this reciprocal relation of choice no account at all is taken of the *matter* of
> choice.…All that is in question is the *form* in the relation of choice on the part of
> both…[30]

On this specification, the general concept of right pertains to a formal, external,
strictly reciprocal moral relation between (two or more) persons. From this *moral* concept Kant derives, in conjunction with a universalizing rule, the universal principle of
Right, which sets out the conditions of the moral rightness of actions in general:

> Any action is right if it can coexist with everyone's freedom of each in accordance
> with a universal law, or if on its maxim the freedom of choice of each is consistent
> with the freedom of each in accordance with a universal law.

In conjunction with a distributive rule, the universal principle of Right yields a statement, in the form of innate right, of the formal moral status of each who is subject to it:

> Freedom (independence from being constrained by another's choice), insofar as it
> can coexist with the freedom of every other in accordance with a universal law, is the
> only original right belonging to every man by virtue of his humanity.[31]

The entire Introduction can thus be said to offer an extended *analytic* exposition of
what is implied by the general concept of right conceived as a *moral* concept. Kant
moves from a specification of the form of a rights relation in general to the condition
of its universalizability and from there to a specification of the formal moral status of
each person who is subject to that principle.

Admittedly, Kant is not at all clear about the analytic status of the remarks in the
Introduction.[32] What is more, having introduced the innate right of each, having contrasted it with acquired right, and having listed, in a further dense paragraph, the
'authorizations' said to attach to innate right 'as not really distinct from it',[33] Kant
abruptly announces that the innate right 'can be put in the prolegomena and *the division of the doctrine of right can refer only to what is externally mine or yours*', ie, only
to acquired right. This is a baffling announcement. Given its elaborate introduction in
the Introduction, what justifies the innate right's unceremonious exclusion from the
main text?

---

[30] Kant, *The Metaphysics of Morals*, 6: 230.   [31] Kant, *Metaphysics of Morals*, 6: 230.
[32] cf Allen Wood, 'The Final Form of Kant's Practical Philosophy', in Mark Timmons (ed.), *The
Metaphysics of Morals. Interpretive Essays* (Oxford University Press, 2002), 1–34.
[33] An attentive reader will see that these 'authorizations' essentially set out aspects of person's equality
in formal juridical status: formal equality before the law, the quality of being one's own master, hence of
being legally responsible for one's own actions, the quality of not being held responsible for actions one
did not commit.

Elsewhere I propose a reading according to which the innate right cannot form part of the division of a doctrine of rights because it functions as a formal *a priori* necessary presupposition of any substantive rights doctrine.[34] On this account, the analytic argument in the Introduction sets out the formal moral presuppositions, which the justification of substantive property claims in the main text has indirect recourse to. Given its status as a formal *presupposition* of morally valid substantive rights claims in general, the innate right cannot itself be an object of substantive rights legislation: hence its exclusion from the substantive argument in the main text. Nonetheless, no substantive rights legislation is conceivable that does not acknowledge the formal equality in status (the innate right to freedom) of each as the formal condition of its moral legitimacy.

Consider the innate right's function as formal presupposition of morally valid property claims.[35] Anyone who raises the claim of a property right against others in so doing invokes the general concept of right: he declares all others to be under an obligation henceforth to refrain from further use of the object without his consent. To invoke right as a moral concept is, however, to acknowledge its universal validity as a concept, which if it applies to one, applies to all. Accordingly, anyone who claims a right against others is subject to reciprocal rights constraints in relation to his addressees. The claimant must acknowledge that any rights claims he raises against others are reciprocally binding for him in relation to them. This acknowledgement of rights reciprocity implies in turn that the claimant presupposes the equal status as possible rights bearers of all those against whom he raises his claim. But the innate right of each affirms no more than the equality in formal juridical status of all who are subject to the universal principle of right. Hence persons who raise substantive rights claims against others can justifiably do so under the universal principle of Right only under the presupposition of their reciprocal acknowledgement of others' formal equality in juridical status.

On this account, then, substantive property rights are vindicated by means of recourse to the innate right of each as the formal condition or presupposition of their moral possibility. Note the non-foundationalist relation between innate and acquired right. Neither is self-supporting; innate and acquired right stand in a relation of mutual dependence. The practical reality of the merely formal concept of innate right depends for its indirect empirical instantiation on substantively specifiable property claims. At the same time, the moral validity of substantive property claims depends on the acknowledgement of innate right as their underlying formal presupposition. Phenomenologically substantive property claims precede innate right; justificatorily innate right is prior to acquired right. Crucially, neither can be vindicated independently of appeal to the other. To invoke foundational rights talk in relation to innate right is to fall foul of Kant's well-known non-foundationalist strategy of philosophical justification in general.

---

[34] cf Flikschuh, *Originally Mine?*

[35] Textually, the situation is of course considerably more complicated; I here abstract, eg, from the concept of intelligible possession as the direct object of the justificatory 'deduction' in the main text. cf Kant, *The Metaphysics of Morals*, 6: 249.

IV. Human Rights as a Transcendent Concept

I began this chapter by suggesting that if one must have a distinctively *Kantian* conception of human rights, a plausible approach would be to think of it as a transcendent concept. The argument for such a transcendent human rights conception required some ground-clearing. Over the last two sections I first set out Kant's systematic division of the field of ordinary morality in general: this to counter the widespread implicit assumption of philosophical foundationalism especially in relation to Kant's philosophy of right. I then proceeded to argue against recent interpretations of the innate right to freedom of each as a foundational premise to Kant's property rights argument; in this connection I also rejected re-description of the innate right as a human right. Over both sections my concern was to show that if one does want to develop a *plausible* Kantian human rights conception out of his moral and political thinking, one should respect relevant methodological and systematic constraints.

Consistently with those constraints as I have sketched them, a transcendent concept in the Kantian sense cannot refer to a knowable supersensible object or moral truth. A commitment to transcendence as commitment to knowable final truths would simply mirror a foundationalist commitment to self-evident first principles or rock-bottom intuitions. If we take Kant to reject foundationalism as a defensible philosophical starting point, we should not attribute to him a view according to which philosophical conclusions take the form of supersensible knowledge claims. A transcendent concept of human rights in the Kantian sense of transcendence would instead have to be thought of as an idea of practical reason the substantive content of which is constitutively indeterminable for us: we would have to think ourselves incapable of offering a determinate specification of its conceptual marks. The concept's precise content would thus have to be acknowledged as exceeding our possible understanding in either (or both) of two senses: in the sense either that we are incapable of ever experiencing the object of the clearly formed concept of X, or in the sense that we cannot even form a clear concept of X. The question arises whether concepts without possible objects or simply unclear and indistinct ideas can have any possible function for us. Kant notoriously argues that they can.[36]

The standard Kantian example of a transcendent concept is the idea of God.[37] The marks of that concept include notions such as omniscience, omnipotence, moral perfection. We might think we have a clear and distinct idea of God. Kant denies that the clarity of our idea of God warrants an inference to God's actual existence. Though we can form the relevant concept or idea, we can have no knowledge of its

---

[36] cf Kant, *The Critique of Pure Reason*, A 642-704 / B 670-732. See also Karl Ameriks, 'The Critique of Metaphysics: The Structure and Fate of Kant's Dialectic', in Paul Guyer (ed.), *Kant and Modern Philosophy* (Cambridge University Press, 2006), 269–302. For an excellent analysis of Kant's related distinction between knowledge and faith, see Andrew Chignell, 'Belief in Kant', *Philosophical Review*, 116 (2007): 323-60.

[37] cf Kant, *Critique of Pure Reason*, A 631-A669 / B 659-697; also A 705-831 / B 733-860. Also Kant, *Critique of Practical Reason*, 5:124–48.

object. This acknowledgement in itself may lead us to revise our initial presumption regarding the clarity even of our concept of God. Perhaps our concept of God is in fact less clear and distinct than we initially took it to be. Can we really form a clear *idea* even of what it is to be infinitely wise or powerful? At the end of *Groundwork* Kant speaks of the idea of freedom or the moral law—in that context the two are interchangeable—as one that exceeds all possible understanding for us: we comprehend at best its incomprehensibility. This acknowledgement is a prelude to the second *Critique*'s acceptance of freedom as a non-vindicable (not self-evident!) 'fact of reason'.[38] I take this to amount to acquiesce in our limited knowledge in the second sense specified. We cannot even form a very clear idea of freedom: the very concept 'loses itself in the intelligible realm' (*verliert sich im Intelligiblen*).[39] This does not stop Kant from also declaring the idea of freedom the keystone of the critical philosophy. At the heart of Kant's philosophy is thus (scandalously, if you're a Cartesian) an unclear and indistinct idea—an idea of which we understand that we cannot fully comprehend it.

It is the reflective dimension of Kantian transcendent ideas that warrants their practical employment even despite the strict unknowability of their contents. The transcendent idea of God as supreme moral being or of our freedom as members of an intelligible order has a regulative or reflective function in the domain especially of practical reason. Thus while in the domain of theoretical reason the idea of God enables us, according to the first *Critique*, to order empirical experience in accordance with the idea of a purposively instituted natural order; its principal employment is in the domain of practical reason where critical faith in the possibility of God's existence allows us to hope for the non-futility of our moral agency.[40] The critical warrant for our employment of transcendent concepts of God, or of our freedom as part-noumenal beings, lies in our acknowledgement of these ideas' objective indeterminacy—ie, of our utter lack of knowledge of their possible objects. In that sense they function as a reflective reminder of human frailty and finitude, both epistemologically and morally.

If one were to think of the concept of human rights along these lines, one would think of it as a regulative idea of practical reason the constitutive content of which is indeterminable for us yet the reflective employment of which serves to remind us of our fallibility in the context of the morality of right. As noted, I do not think Kant himself possessed the concept of a human right—transcendent or substantive. Nor am I convinced that his political philosophy requires one. At the very least, I would say that nothing that is affirmed in the *Doctrine of Right* objectively *requires* recourse to the concept of human rights as necessary ground of positive law's practical vindication. In this, the concept of human rights is unlike that of innate right, which *is* indispensible, on my reading, to the moral justifiability of persons' substantive property claims. On the other hand, I concede that there is also nothing in the *Doctrine of Right*

[38] Kant, *Groundwork*, 4: 463; *Critique of Practical Reason*, 5: 42–3, 47–8, 55.
[39] Kant, *Metaphysics of Morals*, 6: 252.
[40] See, eg, Mary-Barbara Zeldin, 'Principles of Reason, Degrees of Judgment, And Kant's Arguments for the Existence of God', *The Monist*, 54 (1970): 285–301. On the difference between subjectively sufficient and objectively sufficient warrant in Kant, see also Andrew Chignell, 'Kant's Concepts of Justification', *Nous*, 41 (2007): 33–63.

that *precludes* conceiving the idea of human rights as a transcendent concept relative to the domain of positive law making. In particular, so long as the idea is not treated as supplying the foundational premise to morally legitimate law making, nothing speaks against its possible status as a subjectively necessary reflective idea that arises from the process of public law making itself.

Recall Kant's discussion of the idea of God in the doctrine of postulates of the second *Critique*. The claim there is that the possibility of morality does not depend on the idea of God but that it is, to the contrary, our acknowledgement of the moral law's validity for us, which leads us to the idea of God. The idea of God is a subjectively necessary postulate of practical reason that arises from our acknowledgement of the moral law. 'Subjective necessity' here contrasts with 'objective sufficiency': despite our acknowledged lack of objectively sufficient theoretical warrant for affirming God's *existence*, we have subjectively sufficient practical warrant for *faith* in God's existence as supreme moral being: a warrant that is grounded in our hope concerning the non-futility of our moral endeavours even in the face of a morally often recalcitrant empirical world.

If the transcendent concept of human rights were to function similarly in the domain of political morality, we would have to think of it as an objectively indeterminate (hence objectively insufficient) yet subjectively necessary, regulative idea of reason that arises from our acknowledgement of the moral imperative to enter with all others into the civil condition, which is a condition of coercively enforced public law making. The place of human rights as reflective idea would be at the end of the lawmaking process, not at its beginning. This is an unusual place to assign human rights relative to public law making. Human rights are more standardly treated as specifying antecedent conditions of morally legitimate public law making. My contrary claim here is that, on the transcendent conception, human rights arise *from* the acknowledged moral necessity of coercive public law making, so cannot be thought of as supplying the conditions *of* law's moral justifiability. Is this not to demean the centrality and importance of the concept? I do not think so: if we were to think of the concept as constituting a mature reflection on the morality of coercive public law making in general, it might even, in a sense, constitute public law's crowning achievement. Consider, in this light, the following remarkable passage in *Perpetual Peace*:

> The exalted epithets often bestowed upon a ruler ('the divinely anointed', 'the administrator of the divine will on earth and its representatives') have frequently been censured as gross and dizzying flattery, but, it seems to me, without grounds. Far from making the rule of a country arrogant, they should rather humble him in his soul, if he is intelligent (as must be assumed) and considers that he has taken on an office far too demanding for any human being—namely, the most sacred office that God has on earth, that of trustee of the right of mankind (*das Recht der Menschheit*)—such that he must always remain concerned about having in some ways offended against this 'apple of God's eye' (8: 353).

The passage is remarkable in part for Kant's critical absorption of traditional, religiously imbued political terminology into his secular philosophy of right. Kant rejects breezy dismissal of the 'exalted epithets' from the doctrine of the divine right to rule on the grounds that their transcendent function survives their secularization. The epithets are to be retained not because belief in divine rule is to be retained, but because their function is to remind the ruler that, strictly speaking, the assumption of public office exceeds human capacities.

Kant's claim that public office is strictly beyond human capacities is not a claim to the effect that, ideally, some supra-human legislator should take up the tasks of public office. Nor, on the other hand, should the reference to the 'right of mankind' be equated with a morally confident declaration of human rights before its time. There is instead a deep connection between the thought of public office as exceeding human capacities and the strictly reciprocally structure of Kantian rights relations. Recall: by rights no person can bind another to more than he can in turn bind her. Reciprocal rights claims demand the institution of a public enforcement authority *because* no one can claim natural (or divinely authorized) moral authority over another. Yet the institution by humans of public office is morally problematic not least in view of the unavoidable institutional elevation it requires of some over others. This is not to say that there is a conceivable alternative to human rule that would better accord with the demands of right. To the contrary: it is *because* an alternative to human rule is not available that the mentioned epithets should be retained. If the ruler *were* divinely appointed, no one would need worry about the possibility of his offending 'the apple of God's eye', for he would then simply be God's mouthpiece and could do not wrong. It is *because* the ruler is a human being who *can* do wrong that the epithets should be retained.

There is thus nothing fanciful about Kant's characterization of humanly instituted public office as 'sacred'. The epithets are a reminder of human moral fallibility—including that of human rulers. The mature legislator will be cognizant of the problematic nature of his occupation of a position of public authority over others; he will be 'humbled' by the thought of having taken on an office that, strictly speaking, exceeds fallible human capacity. The idea of the 'right of mankind' as the 'apple of God's eye' arises for a ruler who reflects, from his position as public office holder, on the morally problematic nature of his legitimate coercive authority over fellow human beings. Note here that the cited passage does appear to address the exalted ruler whom Kant in effect admonishes to approach public office intelligently, ie, with the requisite degree of humility. It is not possible to demand outright or to legislate for such an attitude of humility to public office: plenty of rulers evidently lack it. Whether or not a ruler sees fit to reflect on the moral enormity of public office and authority, and whether or not he or she will feel appropriately humbled is a matter of subjective reflective judgement—there is no guarantee that any particular ruler will possess the requisite degree of reflectiveness or humility. It is not clear to me, though, that the mere fact that we cannot guarantee that all (or any) rulers (and public office holders more generally) will adopt an appropriately reflective attitude regarding the moral hazards of public office warrants discounting the need for subjective reflection on the morally hazardous nature of public office.

V. The Concept of Human Rights: Indeterminacy as Transcendence?

If one did want to offer more than a mere sketch of a possible Kantian human rights conception as transcendent idea one would have to engage in much more detailed textual and interpretive work than I can do here. Certainly, Kant does not himself offer such a conception—a contemporary Kantian human rights conception as transcendent concept would have to be constructed from textual passages, such as the above, in which Kant thematizes fallibility in judgment in relation to public office together with a much more systematic analysis and interpretation of the practically reflective function of transcendent ideas in general. All this quite apart from the question of whether any notion of transcendence—any notion of human cognitive and moral limitations—would be deemed acceptable in an age as insistently upbeat about human powers and capacities as ours.

My aims here have been much more limited. Looking back, they have, I think, been two-fold. One has been an interpretive concern: to rescue Kant's innate right from careless re-description as a semi-natural foundational right from where its ensuing fate as a newly discovered additional human rights premise is all but assured. The second concern has been to take seriously the indeterminate nature of the current concept of human rights, which is being dragged into service in relation to such a wide range of moral and political conundrums that one's mind begins to spin as soon as the concept is mentioned, leading one to suspect that its function must be other than what it is generally taken to be. I don't think these two concerns—one to do with reading Kant, the other to do with the current human rights concept—are wholly unrelated.

One of the reasons why we study the texts of great dead philosophers is in order the better to understand our own philosophical predicaments. Scholarly study is rarely, if ever, antiquitarian.[41] It is nearly always motivated by philosophical concerns that exceed the concerns of the text or thinker studied. For precisely this reason, engagement with these texts has to be serious, detailed, sustained. For one thing, their thoughts are not ours and we obviously want to avoid conflating the two. For another, it is often precisely through appreciating the distance between their thoughts and ours that we gain a critical perspective upon our own. One way of putting it is to say that the serious study of dead thinkers' thoughts can alert us to our own (unavoidable) philosophical parochialism: we come to see that it is possible to think differently than we are wont to do about perennially recurring philosophical problems and ideas (the problem of political power to which human rights may be one possible response is obviously a very old one).

Against the background of these remarks it can be genuinely upsetting—*philosophically*, not psychologically—to see great works in the history of philosophy ransacked for this or that titbit to be used in order to patch up a justificatory gap in some contemporary theory that bears little resemblance to the position from which the item is lifted. I do not venture to declare Kant's *Doctrine of Right* a great work in political philosophy in its own right. But it can, I believe, assume that status when studied through the lens of what unquestioningly are among the greatest philosophical works in the history of modern philosophy—the *Critique of Pure Reason* and *Groundwork*. When read through the lens of Kant's critique of metaphysics in the first *Critique* or through the complex justificatory strategy of *Groundwork* the attribution to Kant of some kind of rights foundationalism in the *Doctrine of Right* verges on the unintelligible. To be clear: my objection here is not to rights foundationalism as such—it may be a plausible or defensible position, at

---

[41] See Allen Wood's excellent, 'What Dead Philosophers Mean', in his *Unsettling Obligations* (CSLI Publications, 2002), 213–44.

least given certain premises. My objection is to underwriting one's independent commitments to rights foundationalism by appeal to a thinker who staked his philosophical
reputation on denying the plausibility of philosophical foundationalism. Importantly,
the injury is to both: both to the thoughts of the dead thinker and to our own thinking.
To hope to find support for rights foundationalism in the *Doctrine of Right* is to understand neither that text nor one's own philosophical commitments.

Let me turn to my second point, which is, I think, related. In this chapter I sketched,
in admittedly highly summary fashion, a non-foundationalist reading of innate right
as constituting nothing more than a formal presupposition of the possibility of a
substantive doctrine of acquired rights. In the present context, my intention was to
block the move from a foundationalist reading of innate right to its re-description as
a human right. The effect of this move was to displace human rights from their usually assigned position as foundational prerequisite to positive law making: at least in
Kant's legal philosophy, that position is on my account occupied by the pre-supposi-
tionally interpreted innate right. The only place left available for a Kantian conception of human rights turned out to be at the *conclusion* of the law-making process—ie,
human rights as a substantively indeterminate if subjectively necessary transcendent
concept. Yet in taking this route I was implicitly guided by my opening remarks on
the current tendency to overburden the concept of human rights: in its current usages
the concept has been made to carry so much content that many of us barely understand any longer what we are to take the concept to mean. But perhaps this is a truth,
of sorts, about the concept: perhaps it is a constitutively indeterminable concept.

The problems of practical and, attendantly, of conceptual overload in relation to
human rights have hardly gone unnoticed among human rights theorists. It is a widely if
not generally recognized tendency of the concept that it comes to be extended across an
ever growing range of moral and political desiderata. Human rights theorists have proposed various ways in which to arrive at a more rigorously delimited concept with a correspondingly tighter range in practical application.[42] In one sense, I have here gone in the
opposite direction. I have in effect conceded that the concept is unspecifiable: its meaning
is constitutively indeterminate. The surprising feature about Kant's philosophy is that it
expressly allows for indeterminate concepts or ideas—concepts which extend themselves
darkly beyond the field of possible human understanding, yet which precisely for that
reason can exert a critical function upon our moral and theoretical thinking.

The human rights concept as we use it today seems to me quite a good possible candidate for characterization as a Kantian transcendent concept. We associate with it
notions such as human dignity, or respect for persons as such—notions of the moral
supremacy of persons merely as persons. We struggle, in truth, clearly to articulate
what precisely we mean by these ideas. Indeed, I would go further: it would arguably
disappoint us to arrive at a final fully perspicacious specification of these notions. This
is not what we want from the concept. The indeterminate concept of human rights

[42] For two radically different attempt to clarify the philosophical concept of human rights contrast
James Griffin, *On Human Rights* (Oxford University Press, 2008) and Beitz, *Idea of Human Rights*. For
a position that denies that the problem of conceptual overload or inflation is a problem in human rights
theorizing, see John Tasioulas, 'The Moral Reality of Human Rights', in T. Pogge (ed.), *Freedom from
Poverty as a Human Right* (New York: Oxford University Press, 2007), 75–102.

allows us, to the contrary, to entertain ideas of human finitude and vulnerability and the idea, more generally, of the extreme fragility of human moral and especially political relations: ideas which, were we to speak of them with great confidence or precision would undermine the point we are trying to express by means of them. If we knew what human dignity really boiled down to it would, I venture to suggest, lose its moral appeal for us. So with human rights: if we really could give a full specification of its meaning and moral significance, it would cease to fulfill its moral function as a reminder, in the political context, of the fragility of humanly instituted legal relations.

So Kant may have room for a particular kind of human rights conception. It would be very different in form and function from the currently prevalent kind, according to which human rights are substantively specifiable desiderata or even enforceable requirements for any morally justifiable system of positive law making. On the view of human rights as a transcendent concept, there are no particular substantive demands we can raise or underwrite on its basis in relation to any given system of positive law making. The concept is far too indeterminate for that: if we cannot know what precisely we mean by it we would be foolish to claim to be able to derive specific substantive demands from it. Instead, the concept would function as a subjective reflective check on the moral quality of public law making in general, reminding legislators of the fallibility of their authority and judgment in relation to those over whom they exert coercive public authority. One may deem this too little in terms of practical pay-off: that is a matter for debate on another occasion. My concluding thought here is merely this: if we take seriously the constraints of Kant's philosophical thinking, we should not simply rush to find a space within it for our own favoured human rights conception about the virtue of which we have in any case long made up our minds. If we desist from thus rushing in and if instead we take the time and make the effort of trying to think within those constraints, surprising philosophical avenues may open themselves up to us, enabling us to think about human rights in ways we had not anticipated. In the case at hand, the surprising and unexpected discovery that Kant may be able to accommodate the indeterminacy of the current concept of human rights. The accommodation carries corresponding constraints, of course: accepting indeterminacy also means accepting the non-substantive function of the idea. I suspect the Kantian conception here proposed will be widely rejected in view of this constraint alone. But this is not to say that it is in itself an implausible human rights conception. Nor is it to say that we can learn nothing about human rights from studying Kant—though we do not, perhaps, learn quite what we had expected.[43]

[43] This essay was written whilst I was a Senior Research Fellow at the Centre of Advanced Studies, Goethe Universität Frankfurt. I would like to thank the Centre for providing an unusually stimulating yet relaxed research environment. I would also like to thank Rowan Cruft, Simon Hope, and Andrea Sangiovanni for excellent and often incisive written comments on an earlier draft.

38

Why there Cannot be a Truly Kantian Theory of Human Rights

Andrea Sangiovanni

Many human rights advocates seek inspiration in Kant, which explains why references to Kant are legion in the literature on human rights. Indeed, it is commonly argued that the most promising foundations on which to construct a secular account of human rights are to be found in Kant. I shall pose a challenge to this idea, arguing that there can be no truly Kantian theory of human rights. Any careful reading of Kant will reveal him to be not just indifferent to human rights claims but actively skeptical of them.

A few preliminaries. First, by 'truly Kantian', I do not mean that there can be no philosophical theory of human rights that has Kantian elements, or that grows out of some part of Kant's opus. What I mean is that there can be no defense of a Kantian theory of human rights that remains faithful to three constituent planks of Kant's practical philosophy, namely, (1) Kant's division between the domain of morality and the domain of right, (2) Kant's arguments for our moral obligation to exit the state of nature, and (3) Kant's arguments for unitary sovereignty. This leaves open, of course, for a less 'truly' Kantian theory of human rights that drops one or more of his arguments for each of these central tenets. But such a theory will not be faithful to Kant, for whom the three tenets stand at the very core of his practical philosophy. In this volume, Katrin Flikschuh writes: 'it can be genuinely upsetting—*philosophically,* not psychologically—to see great works in the history of philosophy ransacked for this or that titbit to be used in order to patch up a justificatory gap in some contemporary theory that bears little resemblance to the position from which the item is lifted'.[1] This strikes me as a useful reminder that, if we are to draw insights from the history of political thought, we had better try to get that history right, rather than to project our own concerns onto it. This is why the question which gives this chapter its purpose is, I believe, an important one to answer.

Second, I also need to say something about what I intend by 'human rights' to avoid misunderstanding. Whatever else they are, human rights are critical moral standards that (a) are 'above politics', (b) track violations of great moral urgency, and (c) (pro tanto) license some form of direct external action or pressure to stop violations from happening or continuing. What I mean by 'above politics' is that they are moral standards that any individual or institutional agent must respect whatever they do, whatever their internal organization, and whatever function they happen to have in political

---

[1] Katrin Flikschuh, 'Human Rights in Kantian Mode: A Sketch', this volume, ch. 37, 668.

and social life. And what I mean by 'direct external action' is that the remedial and protective actions their violation licenses need not be authorized by the state, non-state, or international actor involved in the violation. Pressure of the kind exercised by Amnesty International as well as more coercive forms of international enforcement, for example, could count as (pro tanto) licensed direct and external action in the relevant sense. For our purposes, the definition I am using can be extended to cover the actions of *individuals*, especially though not exclusively actions that have some public significance or impact. The definition also encompasses both 'Orthodox' and 'Political' accounts of the nature of human rights. The critical moral standards that are constitutive of human rights claims can be grounded, that is, in an account of those natural rights that we have in virtue of our humanity (hence the 'Orthodox' reading). Or they can be more general moral standards, not necessarily grounded in natural rights, whose application is restricted to states, and whose violation (pro tanto) justifies either overriding state sovereignty, or pursuing otherwise coercive or non-coercive international action (including, for example, economic and diplomatic sanctions) (hence the 'Political' reading). This very weak definition of human rights is enough for our purposes. If no account of human rights that satisfies the broad conditions I have identified can be 'truly Kantian', then my argument has gone through. There might, of course, be other accounts of human rights (some of which I will mention in passing later) that might still be compatible with truly Kantian practical philosophy, but they will be highly unconventional ones.

The discussion proceeds as follows. In Sections I and II, I reject the hypothesis that the concept of innate right can provide a foundation for a theory of human rights. In Section III, I turn to Kant's argument against the right to revolution, and explore whether the distinction between 'barbarism' and 'despotism' could be used in the service of a theory of human rights. In Section IV, I argue that attempts to ground an account of human right in the Kantian concept of dignity are misguided. Section V concludes.

I

In her contribution to this volume, Flikschuh wonders whether there is a *'plausible Kantian human rights conception'*, by which she means a conception that is faithful to Kant while also remaining interesting in its own right. She ultimately believes there is, though we must find it not in Kant's account of innate right (let alone cosmopolitan right), but in the idea that human right may be a 'transcendent concept' akin to God: substantively unknowable, indeterminate, and incapable of empirical instantiation, but something we must believe in nonetheless. Her reconstruction of such a conception is tentative, because she (rightly) recognizes how difficult it is to shape a full-blown account of human rights in a Kantian mould. I shall argue that Flikschuh should have followed her initial suspicions to a conclusion she seems attracted to but does not ultimately argue for, namely that there can be no truly Kantian conception of human rights.

Flikschuh's reconstruction of a Kantian conception of human rights begins with 'innate right'. According to Kant, innate right is the only right we have merely in virtue of our humanity; all other rights (for example, rights that flow from contract and property) are 'acquired' rights. Innate right gives each human being a right to freedom understood as a kind of independence:

> Freedom (independence from being constrained by another's choice), insofar as it can coexist with the freedom of every other in accordance with a universal law, is the only original right belonging to every man by virtue of his humanity.[2]

This single innate right entails, Kant claims, several further 'authorizations', namely, the right to equal and reciprocal coercion (according to which one cannot be 'bound by others to more than one can in turn bind them'), the right to be one's own master, the right to be 'beyond reproach' (ie, to preserve one's reputation against, for example, libel), and the right to communicate one's thoughts and to make promises (whether insincerely or sincerely). These are all entailed (Kant claims) by the several parts of the initial formulation. The right to equal and reciprocal coercion is entailed by the 'coexistence under universal law' qualification; the right to be beyond reproach by the supposition that no one has yet entered any relations with others and so must be innocent of all charges against their person; and the right to communicate one's thoughts by the fact that no right would be possible without such communication. On Flikschuh's interpretation, innate right and its corollary 'authorizations' cannot be the 'object of any positive law making'; innate right is, as she often puts it, 'beyond legislation'.[3] As a purely formal rather than substantive concept, it sets out a 'necessary presupposition of positive legislated rights', and so of all acquired rights (including contract and property) but doesn't specify their content. This follows, Flikschuh claims, from the structure of Kant's 'non-foundationalist' moral and political theory, and implies that there can be no theory of (substantive) human rights that can be grounded in innate right. Treating innate right as a human right would require us to assign, *contra* Kant, a fully specifiable, pre-political content to innate right that is on a par with the acquired rights (including property rights) we would have in a fully functioning civil condition. Innate right, in sum, is too indeterminate, formal, and relationally dependent to function in the way human rights advocates expect human rights to function, namely, as pre-legal, determinate, and substantive claims on others.

I will argue that Flikschuh endorses the correct conclusion—innate right cannot be a basis for human rights—but for the wrong reasons. My argument begins by showing that Flikschuh's proposed non-foundationalist reading of innate right is not sufficient to establish the impossibility of a human rights theory based on it. Consider that the formal structure of innate right could be used as a higher-order 'test' for generating a list of human rights *even on Flikschuh's non-foundationalist reading*.[4] Flikschuh does not, after all, deny that innate right and the Universal Principle of Right (UPR) can

---

[2] *Doctrine of Right* (hereinafter *DR*), Ak6:237. All translations are from Immanuel Kant, *Practical Philosophy*, ed. M. Gregor (Cambridge: Cambridge University Press, 1999). Hereinafter I shall only refer to the Akademie pagination.

[3] Flikschuh, this volume, ch. 37, 660.

[4] It might do this more explicitly when conjoined with the UPR ('Any action is *right* if it can coexist with everyone's freedom in accordance with a universal law, or if on its maxim the freedom of choice of each can coexist with everyone's freedom in accordance with a universal law').

serve as *constraints* on law making (in the same way, say, the CI can serve as a constraint on permissible maxims in the domain of morality).[5] But if innate right (and the UPR) can function as *constraints* on law making, then they could also surely function as *human rights*. Here's how such a construction might go. We would begin with the idea that innate right sets moral constraints on any possible rightful condition. For example, we know that to be in accordance with innate right, all positive rights must be granted on equal terms to all (such that no one may be bound by others to more than one can in turn bind them), and be consistent with each person's original independence (such that no one be forced, through no choice of their own, to be subject to another's choice—as in, say, feudal relations between lord and serf). From such higher-level implications of innate right, one could then derive a list of (lower-level) human rights. These would be the necessary preconditions that any system of rights must satisfy in order to count as a system of, as Flikschuh puts it, 'strictly reciprocal independence relations'. Some examples might include: All human beings have a right to independence; no human being shall be subject to a feudal order, or be born a slave; all have a right against libel; no human being shall be so economically dependent on another that he is forced to beg; all human beings have a right to a republican constitution[6], etc.[7] Such (Kantian) human rights would be rights that (a) are possessed merely in virtue of our humanity, (b) prescind from any specific division of property or system of contract law, and (c) constitute the limits or outer bounds of any fully rightful legal order. The fact that innate right is 'non-foundationally' justified as the necessary presupposition of any reciprocally rightful condition rather than by appeal to a 'foundational' intuition is not relevant in this context.

The indeterminacy of innate right, similarly, does not constitute a stumbling block for a theory of innate-right based human rights. Flikschuh treats the issue as turning on how 'substantively determinate' or 'empirically instantiable' a human right is, and then concludes that innate right cannot be a human right (or a basis for human rights) because it is a merely formal concept, and hence substantively indeterminate and empirically uninstantiable, whereas human rights, properly understood, must be both substantive and instantiable. But I do not see that there is really any difference between the 'determinability' or 'instantiability' of innate right as against human rights. Like any system of abstract moral rights, human rights standards are just that: standards. No human rights advocate would deny that they require interpretation, and that individuals will reasonably differ regarding what they mandate in any specific case. And, as we saw earlier, we can derive a list of outer bounds or limits that any legitimate legal

---

[5] 'Yet to systematize is nonetheless to introduce divisions and distinctions, which impose constraints' (Flikschuh, this volume, ch. 37, 660).

[6] See, eg, *Perpetual Peace* (hereinafter *PP*): 'the *republican* constitution is the only one that is compatible with the right of human beings' (8:336).

[7] It should be noted that there is some obscurity in Flikschuh's account of the idea that 'innate right' is incapable of 'empirical instantiation'. Surely, innate right rules out certain legal arrangements (such as the ones just mentioned). Why don't such further 'rights' or authorizations count as 'instantiations'? If they aren't possible instantiations of innate right, then what is? We can grant that innate right does not, by itself, stipulate what the content of any specific law or legal right should be, but that does not imply that it can't be 'instantiated' or be the plausible 'object of positive law making'. If my law making is constrained by innate right (or the UPR) then isn't my law making taking innate right as an 'object' in the relevant sense? More on this later.

order must respect directly from the concept of innate right (such as the idea that no human being ought to be born a slave, or all human beings have a right to a republican constitution) just as we can derive a series of lower-level human rights (for example, the right to freedom of the press, or to education) from more abstract moral rights, such as, for example, the right to freedom of expression or to minimal provision (as in James Griffin's account of human rights).[8] The only way to preserve a distinction along this axis would be to deny that one can derive *any* implications from Kant's abstract right to freedom. But then Kant's theory of right would become maximally permissive: any stable and predictable legal order would be compatible with right, even one that enslaved all its inhabitants to a single ruler.[9] Kant's theory of right is (as we will see) fairly permissive, but not *that* permissive.

So why can't innate right form the basis of a truly Kantian theory of human rights? As we have seen, the reason does not have to do with how determinate or instantiable innate right is, or with the non-foundationalist origin of innate right. Rather, I shall argue that innate right cannot be a basis for human rights because human rights must be directly and externally imposeable in a way that innate right (or those rights derived directly from innate right) cannot be. As I mentioned in the introduction to this chapter, for a moral right to count as a human right, it must license direct action to stop violations from happening or continuing. Action is 'direct' when the remedial actions the protection of human rights licenses are not authorized by the state, non-state, or international actor involved in the violation. Put in more Kantian terms, it is constitutive of a human right (in my sense) that its violation licenses *unilateral* action by third parties (whether states, other organizations or even individuals). Such a licence, as we will see in a moment, is straightforwardly denied by Kant's account of the moral obligation to exit the state of nature.

In the state of nature, both our innate right to freedom in our own person and our (provisional) right to external objects are insecure. Because there is no political agent capable of coordinating our wills, and because we cannot know with any certainty others' intentions or designs, we are thereby permitted, Kant says, to 'do what seems right and good to us'.[10] Each one of us is permitted, that is, to protect our person and provisionally acquired property with violence if necessary. So far, Kant is like Hobbes. But for Kant there is a further problem in the state of nature, which creates an enforceable *moral* (rather than merely prudential) obligation to attempt exit from it. The problem is that, in each interpreting for ourselves what the protection of our innate freedom and property requires, we must *unilaterally* impose our will—our view regarding what is within our power by right—on others. I sincerely believe that this particular piece of land is mine and your use of it counts as a trespass; you disagree. I sincerely believe that you have no right to take pictures of me without my

---

[8] See, eg, James Griffin, *On Human Rights* (Oxford: Oxford University Press, 2008), 50.

[9] On some further problems with Kant's conception of innate right, see Andrea Sangiovanni, 'Can the Innate Right to Freedom Alone Ground a System of Public and Private Rights?', *European Journal of Philosophy*, 20 (2012): 460–9; Andrea Sangiovanni, 'Rights and Interests in Ripstein's Kant', in S. Kisilevsky and M. Stone *Freedom and Force: Essays on Kant's Legal Philosophy* (Oxford: Hart Publishing, forthcoming).

[10] *DR*, Ak6:312.

permission; you disagree. Because we are both authoritative interpreters of the (provisional) rights that define the limits of our freedom, the actions we take under our own conception of freedom therefore necessarily subject the choices of others with whom we interact. This would be true even were we to agree with others what Right (or a system of rights) requires of each of us; it would be true, that is, even if our rights were *fully determinate*. Because there is no mechanism available that can assure me that you will continue to comply with the currently agreed distribution of (provisional) rights, there is an important sense in which I still remain subject to your choice to continue supporting the agreement. If you change your mind, and begin acting on a set of (provisional) rights that I believe prejudices my freedom, then I have no recourse.[11] Kant concludes that remaining in the state of nature is therefore 'wrong in the highest degree'.[12] We must set up a rightful civil condition capable of coordinating our wills under a single authority—thus creating an *omnilateral* will from what were merely an aggregate of *unilateral* wills—or continue wronging others.

This argument, at the very heart of Kant's political philosophy, has a very important upshot with respect to the legitimate imposition of human rights norms. Once a civil condition is up and running, the state that protects it acquires a strong right of non-interference. As Kant writes in *Perpetual Peace*, '"No state shall forcibly interfere in the constitution and government of another state." For what can justify it in doing so? Perhaps the scandal that one state gives to the subjects of another state? It can much rather serve as a warning to them, by the example of the great troubles a people has brought upon itself by its lawlessness; and, in general, the bad example that one free person gives another (as *scandalum acceptum*) is no wrong to it'.[13] This makes sense once we understand Kant's argument for the moral obligation to exit the state of nature. Any will that is external to the omnilateral will governing the state—for example, the will of a foreign state or league of foreign states (or indeed the will of a non-state actor such as what we today call an NGO)—must be *unilateral* with respect to it. It would therefore be 'wrong in the highest degree' to impose it on the state concerned. Importantly for our purposes, and as Kant makes clear in the just cited passage, the right to non-interference also binds external actors where the state concerned is *unjust*—where, for example, it violates the innate right of its inhabitants by, say, undermining their independence. As long as the unjust state operates with a unitary legal system that secures a stable and predictable set of (legal) rights—which makes its will omnilateral in the required sense—it retains its claim to non-interference.[14] In sum, innate right cannot provide a basis for a theory of human rights, since the imposition of innate right against the will of foreign states (and the actors within them) would count as unilateral.

To be sure, the fact that states with respect to one another remain in a 'lawless condition'—where each state's will counts as unilateral with respect to all the rest—is also wrong in the highest degree. States, Kant argues, therefore have a duty to exit the *international* state of nature by joining a voluntary federation that will regulate their conduct with respect to one another. Could this be a site for a Kantian theory of

---

[11] *DR*, Ak6:255–7.   [12] *DR*, Ak6:307–8.   [13] *PP*, Ak8:346.
[14] We discuss Kant's closely connected arguments against the right to revolution later.

human rights? Might a Kantian say that the federation must, to be rightful in itself, secure the protection of innate right (and its corollaries) within each of its member states? Could the Kantian mandate the creation of regional human rights organizations flanking the federation (on the model of the European Convention on Human Rights (ECHR))? I shall argue that there is no space within a Kantian theory even for such regionally bounded human rights instruments.

To fix ideas, let us imagine that a group of member states voluntarily creates both a Court with powers to oversee the implementation of innate right within each member state and an executive mechanism for enforcing its judgments. The institution of such a Court would, I shall now argue, divide sovereignty, and so be in violation of Kant's conditions for a rightful condition. This is fairly easy to see. Imagine the Court came to a judgment that a duly enacted member state law was in violation of innate right. And let us say that the member state disagrees with the judgment. Who decides (as a matter of law)? If we assume that the higher-level Court was acting within its powers, and that its judgments are supposed to be ultimately binding on its member states, then clearly the member state should either change its law or leave the union. For a Kantian, if it leaves the union, it would be violating a moral duty. So it must change its law. But, according to Kant's unitary conception of sovereignty, if it changed its law, it would be effectively recognizing that it is no longer sovereign. Having lost the ultimate (normative) power to decide in all cases, it has either dissolved (and hence returned to a state of nature), or simply transferred sovereignty to the higher level. In the latter case, the federal union would now be the relevant 'state', and the former member state merely a subordinate jurisdictional unit within it. With respect to divided constitutions, Kant echoes Hobbes and Bodin:

> Indeed, even the constitution cannot contain any article that would make it possible for there to be some authority in a state[15] to resist the supreme commander in case he should violate the law of the constitution, and so to limit him. For, someone who is to limit the authority in a state must have even more *power* than he whom he limits, or at least as much power as he has; and, as a legitimate commander who directs the subjects to resist, he must also be able to *protect* them and to render a judgment having rightful force in any case that comes up; consequently he has to be able to command resistance publicly. In that case, however, the supreme commander in a state is not the supreme commander; instead, it is the one who can resist him, and this is self-contradictory.[16]

[15] Kant is here thinking of *internally* divided constitutions (such as Britain's, which he discusses at *PP*, 8:303), but the point is still valid with respect to *externally* divided constitutions, in which some part of sovereignty is exercised by a foreign rather than an internal body. This was of course a central issue in the constitutional theory of the time, especially regarding the structure of the Holy Roman Empire. Cf, eg, Pufendorf's attempts to reconcile his theory of sovereignty with the possibility of (regular and irregular) composite states, Samuel Pufendorf, *Of the Law of Nature and Nations*, trans. B. Kennett (London: Walthoe et al., 1729 [1672]), VII.5.15–22, but see also VII.2.22. It is relevant that Pufendorf took himself to be superseding (mainly Aristotelian) theories of mixed government (see, eg, *Law of Nature*, VII.5.19).

[16] See also *DR*, Ak6:320 and *PP*, 8:303.

We might be tempted into thinking that the problem here lies with the 'outdated' view of sovereignty, not with Kant's argument for our obligation to exit the state of nature. Could the Kantian abandon the former while retaining the latter? No. Kant's commitment to a unitary conception of sovereignty follows, I now want to argue, from his account of unilateral imposition.

For a coercing will to be omnilateral with respect to an individual or corporate agent, and hence rightfully binding, it must speak with one voice. If there were two (potentially) contradictory voices, then one of them must be 'external' to the agent. Kant writes:

> The legislative authority can belong only to the united will of the people. For since all right is to proceed from it, it *cannot* do anyone wrong by its law. Now when someone makes arrangements about *another,* it is always possible for him to do the other wrong; but he can never do wrong in what he decides upon with regard to himself (for *volenti non fit iniuria).* Therefore only the concurring and united will of all, insofar as each decides the same thing for all and all for each, and so only the general united will of the people, can be legislative.[17]

This argument presents us with a dilemma. First horn: If our hypothetical Court speaks in the name of the federation, then its will must be *unilateral* with respect to the dissenting member state. It must be unilateral because it is deciding for 'another' (the member state) rather than solely for itself. As the above quoted passage makes clear, within a system of divided sovereignty, it will always be true that at least one of the coordinate bodies must speak with a unilateral voice to the other. Second horn: If we assume, on the contrary, that the hypothetical Court speaks with the *omnilateral* voice of a united people, then the *federation* must be sovereign, and the member state a merely subordinate unit within it. On the first horn of the dilemma, we have unilateral imposition, and on the second, we cease to have a federal league of *states.* This also explains why Kant is very clear that the only matters to be regulated by the *foedus pacificum* are matters necessarily arising *between* states, rather than matters arising only *within* them:

> This league does not look to acquiring any power of a state but only to preserving and securing the *freedom* of a state itself and of other states in league with it, but without there being any need for them to subject themselves to public laws and coercion under them (as people in a state of nature must do).[18]

It is important that, in this passage, Kant speaks of the freedom *of a state* rather than the freedom of *individuals within it.*

One might think that all this argument shows is that states must join a world state in which the human rights of all are respected. Kant clearly rejects this proposal, though it is unclear whether he was consistent in doing so.[19] But we need not decide the dispute. To see why, assume that all current states do indeed have a Kantian duty to enter

---

[17] *DR,* Ak6:313–14.   [18] *PP,* Ak8:356.
[19] '[S]tates…have a rightful constitution internally and hence have outgrown the constraint of others to bring them under a more extended law-governed constitution in accordance with their concepts of right' (*PP,* Ak8:355).

a world state. Would that be a route to a fully fledged Kantian human rights doctrine? No. Once within the state, the only authoritative interpreter of the outer bounds of our innate right (ie, what I have called human rights) would be the world government itself. Because of Kant's arguments against a right of revolution (to which we will turn in the next section), there would no longer exist even the *possibility* (consistent with Right) of an external recourse. By joining a world state, we would be eliminating the very bulwark against illegitimate state action that human rights were meant to secure in the first place! What are human rights for if not to protect against the 'standard threats' posed by the existence of states (which would surely be exacerbated by the existence of a single, all-powerful world state)?

So innate right and its corollaries cannot provide the basis for a regionally authoritative human rights instrument. At most, if we want to remain within the Kantian framework, we might envisage an international body that provides merely advisory opinions. Such a body could issue recommendations to states on how to improve their protection of innate right (and the reciprocal system of equal freedom such right mandates), but it could not impose genuine obligations or demand enforcement of its judgments *in any form*. This is a far cry from the kinds of human rights that contemporary advocates and practitioners see themselves as fighting for.

II

Before turning to two further ways in which a Kantian might try to build a viable theory of human rights (via the distinction between barbarism and despotism and via the idea of dignity), I want (albeit too briefly) to consider Flikschuh's alternative proposal, briefly mentioned earlier. Recall that Flikschuh also comes to the conclusion that innate rights cannot form a basis for human rights. However, as a Kantian, she doesn't give up on human rights altogether. Instead, she reconstructs an account of human rights as a 'transcendent concept': 'On the view of human rights as a transcendent concept, there are no particular substantive demands we can raise or underwrite on its basis in relation to any given system of positive law making.'[20] Innate right (according to Flikschuh) is similarly indeterminate and uninstantiable. The difference, she claims, is that innate right functions as a necessary presupposition for morally legitimate law making. Transcendent concepts don't even do that. They come 'after' morally legitimate law is up and running, and are meant to serve as 'an objectively indeterminate (hence objectively insufficient) yet subjectively necessary, regulative idea of reason'.[21] A good example of a transcendent concept is God. For Kant, God does not provide the objective basis or ground of the moral law. Rather, the idea of God (and the afterlife) is necessary because it makes it subjectively possible for the human agent to seek the 'highest good' (the happiness that ought to follow from a life of virtue) even though they know that the life of virtue will often produce subjective *un*happiness. In the same way, Flikschuh believes that the concept of human rights cannot provide the

---

[20] Flikschuh, this volume, ch. 37, 670.   [21] Flikschuh, this volume, ch. 37, 666.

basis or ground of a legitimate legal order, but a belief in the idea can make it more likely that fallible human beings will secure political relations that are in accordance with Right. On this reading, we could not specify or know what human rights actually *are* (any more than we can know what God is). She writes: '[Like freedom or the moral law, human rights exceed] all possible understanding for us: we comprehend at best [their] incomprehensibility'.[22] I take these and related comments to mean that there are no human rights that we can actively seek to implement. And, indeed, Flikschuh concedes that, on her view, 'there are no particular substantive demands we can raise or underwrite on its basis in relation to any given system of positive law making'.[23] This entails that we cannot say, for example, that states violate the human rights of their subjects when they torture them, or that they violate the human rights of their subjects when they engage in genocide.

So what kind of normative guidance do they offer? At most, she claims, the idea of a 'transcendent' human right can afford the legislator a new perspective on the 'moral enormity of public office'. Their very ineffability, she claims, is meant to alert us to the moral gravity and fragility of ruling others. What they do not do is offer any moral limits to legitimate state governance. The account is so strongly revisionary as to amount, I believe, to changing the subject. While I have no doubt that public officials ought to be more cognizant of the moral enormity of their office, what do we add by calling that mindfulness 'human rights'? The idea of human rights as transcendent takes us too far away from human rights practice. Better to conclude, as I am arguing we should, that there simply is no truly Kantian theory of human rights.

III

Kant famously argues that there is no right to revolution. No matter how unjust a government of a particular state turns out to be, there can be no right withheld by the people (either collectively or individually) to overthrow it. A government has, of course, a duty to seek and protect a fully rightful condition, but no one can force it into doing so.[24] In the essay 'On the Common Saying...', Kant writes:

> [A]ny resistance to the supreme legislative power...is the highest and most punishable crime within a commonwealth, because it destroys its foundation. And this prohibition is *unconditional,* so that even if that power or its agent, the head of state, has gone so far as to violate the original contract and has thereby, according to the subjects' concept, forfeited the right to be legislator inasmuch as he has empowered the government to proceed quite violently (tyrannically), a subject is still not permitted any resistance by way of counteracting force.[25]

---

[22] Flikschuh, this volume, ch. 37, 665.   [23] Flikschuh, this volume, ch. 37, 670.
[24] See, eg, *DR*, Ak6:340f: 'But it must still be possible, if the existing constitution cannot well be reconciled with the idea of the original contract, for the sovereign to change it, so as to allow to continue in existence that form which is essentially required for a people to constitute a state'.
[25] 'On the Common Saying', Ak8:300; see also Ak8:305.

This follows from the same argument that led to the affirmation of unitary sovereignty. Imagine a dispute between a group of private citizens and the government over whether the regime has the legitimacy to carry on enforcing its laws. If there is no higher-level, formally authorized body to resolve the dispute between the people and the government, then the rebellious people are, by their action, effectively claiming a right to re-institute a state of nature, which is (recall) a state 'devoid of justice' and hence 'wrong in the highest degree'. The rebellious would have, by their action, dissolved the single, univocal, omnilateral will required for a fully rightful condition, and left in its place a cacophony of unilateral wills. And in the cacophony of unilateral wills, everyone's right to freedom is necessarily violated: 'a unilateral will cannot serve as a coercive law for everyone...since that would infringe upon freedom in accordance with universal laws'.[26]

But there is, arguably, one exception—an exception that, as we shall see in a moment, might be used to ground a theory of human rights as limits to state legitimacy.[27] At the very end of the *Anthropology*, Kant draws a distinction between *barbarism* and *despotism*, and distinguishes both from a *republic* and *anarchy*:

A. Law and freedom without force (anarchy).

B. Law and force without freedom (despotism).

C. Force without freedom and law (barbarism).

D. Force with freedom and law (republic).[28]

A state of 'despotism' is a defective form of republic, in which there is a lawful condition that is not fully rightful. Kant is clear that we have an obligation to obey such a regime, even if its injustice is evident to all. But what about a state of 'barbarism'? Arthur Ripstein has recently argued that we can understand a state of barbarism not as a defective form of a republic, but as a defective form of the *state of nature*. If a regime rules by force alone, without law and without freedom, then its will cannot count as 'omnilateral'. As a unilateral will imposed on the people it governs, it can be opposed in the same way as any unilateral will in a pure state of nature. Just because a group of people secures a monopoly of force on a territory, in other words, is not sufficient to make it a state. If they don't enforce their rule via the rule of law, then they are no better than gangsters.[29]

This is relevant for our inquiry into a Kantian theory of human rights because one might try to build a conception of the limits of legitimate rule by appeal to Ripstein's reconstruction of Kant's distinction between barbarism and despotism. On this view, human rights would be identified as the standards constitutive of a minimally decent (and hence non-barbaric) regime. Should any of those standards be violated, the government's commands could no longer be considered as securing and protecting the

---

[26] *DR*, Ak6:256.

[27] Ripstein argues for the exception in Arthur Ripstein, *Force and Freedom: Kant's Legal and Political Philosophy* (Cambridge, MA: Harvard University Press, 2009).

[28] *Anthropology*, Ak330-1. Translations are from Immanuel Kant, *Kant: Anthropology from a Pragmatic Point of View*, ed. R.B. Louden (Cambridge: Cambridge University Press, 2006).

[29] See also Sharon Byrd and Joachim Hruschka, *Kant's Doctrine of Right: A Commentary* (Cambridge: Cambridge University Press, 2010), 91, 181.

rule of law; it would then be ruling, that is, by force alone. In that case, those subject to it (as well as international actors not subject to it) would have not only a right to 'rebel' but perhaps also a duty to bring the wrongdoers (and everyone else) into a proper civil condition by rebelling.

As we have seen, we can be in a civil condition that violates the 'original contract' test, namely where there are laws that it would be impossible for a people to give itself, but where we still have a duty to obey. But how do we draw a distinction between a *mere* 'civil condition' and barbarism? Ripstein's answer is the *rule of law*. Because the presence of 'law' distinguishes barbarism from despotism, we can identify a barbaric regime as one that cannot purport to rule by properly legal authority. But the question now arises: What counts as ruling by legal authority for Kant? Ripstein bases his discussion on Kant's definition of a civil condition as a 'condition in which what belongs to each can be secured to him against everyone else'.[30] The constitutive condition of the rule of law is, in short, the existence of a system of mutually consistent public rules in which each person's property and person is secured against others. How restrictive is this condition? Consider that, in Kant's view, it is the state that ultimately determines the division of property rights. In principle, it would be possible (though unjust) for a legal order, through proper legislative channels, to expropriate the holdings of its entire population (though not to strip them of the ability to re-acquire property in the future, on which more later), to prevent them from voting, and to bar them from public office *while still remaining a legal order*.[31] When challenged that it is not protecting each person's property and person, the regime could reply, 'We *are* protecting property and person according to the laws of the land: if you no longer have any property to protect, then that is because of the law that has expropriated you'. The legal order would be unjust, and its subjects would be right in protesting, but it would still remain wrong to resist. The state cannot, however, do just *anything* in a systematic and public way and still remain a legal order. If the state, for example, made its subjects slaves by stripping them not only of their property (as in the previous case) but also their ability to lawfully acquire property in the future, or sought to exterminate them without trial,[32] then it would cease to be a civil condition and descend into barbarism. In such cases, the state cannot claim to be protecting people's person or property, since it is actively seeking to deny their ability to act in

---

[30] Ripstein, *Force and Freedom*, 336.

[31] It is relevant here to remember that Kant infamously believed that women and children ought to have (as a matter of justice[!]) only a status as 'passive' citizens, with no right to vote, and restricted rights over their own labour and freedom of movement, and no rights to represent themselves in civil matters. See, eg, *DR*, 6:314–15.

[32] Though it is important to note that Kant does allow the death penalty for murder and even the enslavement of criminals as not only minimally legitimate but also just. See *DR*, Ak6:333: 'Whoever steals makes the property of everyone else insecure and therefore deprives himself (by the principle of retribution) of security in any possible property. He has nothing and can also acquire nothing; but he still wants to live, and this is now possible only if others provide for him. But since the state will not provide for him free of charge, he must let it have his powers for any kind of work it pleases (in convict or prison labour) and is reduced to the status of a slave for a certain time, or permanently if the state sees fit.—If, however, he has committed murder he must *die*. Here there is no substitute that will satisfy justice'. For the argument pursued in the text, we therefore must imagine a situation in which no one has been convicted of a crime.

the name of either. At that point, its subjects could, Ripstein plausibly argues, resist. The Nazi regime (especially after 1938, the year of Kristallnacht) clearly satisfies this condition for barbarism.[33]

Kant's discussion of the distinction between servants and slaves is useful in seeing the distinction between rule by force alone and rule by law, but also its limitations. In the *Doctrine of Right*, Kant writes,

> Servants are included in what belongs to the head of a household and, as far as the form (the *way of his being in possession)* is concerned, they are his by a right that is like a right to a thing; for if they run away from him he can bring them back in his control by his unilateral choice. But as far as the matter is concerned, that is, what *use* he can make of these members of his household, he can never behave as if he owned them *(dominus servi);* for it is only by a contract that he has brought them under his control, and a contract by which one party would completely renounce its freedom for the other's advantage would be self-contradictory, that is, null and void, since by it one party would cease to be a person and so would have no duty to keep the contract but would recognize only force.[34]

The importance of this passage is twofold. First, Kant is clear that, where people have been entirely stripped of their civil status, the law no longer applies to them *as law*, and the person therefore is under no obligation to obey. Because the relation between a slave and his master is no longer a relation between two (legal) persons, it is characterized, Kant says, 'only by force', and so cannot even purport to be rightful. This is what makes slavery a form of barbarism in Kant's technical sense. Second, the passage also, however, demonstrates the *limits* of Kant's view, since Kant is clear here (and elsewhere) that quite severe restrictions of person and property are compatible not only with a civil condition (and so minimal legitimacy) but also with Right itself. In the passage just cited, Kant imagines a domestic servant renouncing rights to freedom of movement through a contract, but Kant argues that the same limitations are compatible (indeed just) with respect to women without even the need for a contract. In the *Anthropology*, for example, he writes,

> *Children* are naturally immature and their parents are their natural guardians. *Woman* regardless of age is declared to be immature in civil matters; her husband is her natural curator. If she lives with him and keeps her own property, then another person is the curator.—It is true that when it comes to talking, woman by the nature of her sex has enough of a mouth to represent both herself and her husband, even in court (where it concerns mine and thine), and so could literally be declared to be *over-mature*. But just as it does not belong to women to go to war, so women cannot personally defend their rights and pursue civil affairs for themselves, but only by means of a representative.[35]

One might argue that Kant's acceptance of women's (legal) 'immaturity' is a product of his times, or in any case based on false beliefs about women's ability to reason

---

[33] cf Kristen Rundle, 'The Impossibility of an Exterminatory Legality: Law and the Holocaust', *University of Toronto Law Journal*, 59 (2009): 65–125.
[34] *DR*, Ak6:283.   [35] *Anthropology*, Ak209.

and think for themselves.[36] Kant, if he had applied his theory correctly, would have come to the conclusion that it is unjust for women to be subjected in this way. But I see no reason why such restrictions (which, remember, include restrictions on the property-less and on domestic servants as well) could plausibly be regarded as destroying the very basis of a civil condition as Kant himself understands it. Domestic servants and women, for example, can both own property, and are protected by the criminal law. While their dependence may be unjust (correctly understood), it does not dissolve the legal relation existing between them and their 'masters'.

The problem with a theory of human rights grounded in the distinction between barbarism and despotism is that it would be too narrow. While the theory would cover human rights against genocide and enslavement, it would not cover *any* of the other human rights listed in the Universal Declaration of Human Rights (UDHR) or other international covenants. There would be no human rights objection, for example, to the treatment of women, in, say, Saudi Arabia, which is ranked at 130 (out of 134) on the UN Gender Equality Index, or to a denial of any of the civil and political freedoms (including rights of association, marriage, employment, movement, expression, religious worship, etc.). It is arguable whether we would even have a human right against torture, given that torture does not (or need not) undermine our very capacity to own property or to be legal subjects.[37] Torture is the infliction (or threat) of severe pain in order to coerce; if we survive it, there is no sense in which we necessarily cease to be subject to the law. One might argue that this is not a real problem for the theory; at most, it would serve as a problem for any human rights practice that claims to go beyond rights against enslavement and genocide. I leave the reader to decide whether a truly Kantian theory of this kind would be worth defending. We have achieved our goal if we have shown how narrow and constrained a theory of human rights would be within a truly Kantian framework, and how far it would take us from Kant's written text (given how little weight is given to the distinction between barbarism and despotism in Kant's own writings), and from current human rights practice.

IV

One of the most pervasive ideas at the heart of human rights discourse is the idea of human dignity. The UDHR, for example, proclaims the 'inherent dignity' of all human beings, who are declared to be 'equal in dignity and rights'. There is also almost universal agreement that the most prominent exponent of the idea in its secular form is Kant. One might think, as a result, that a truly Kantian theory of human rights can be grounded solely in Kant's conception of the dignity of humanity as an end in itself, thus sidestepping Kant's arguments for unitary sovereignty, for the obligation to exit the state of nature, and against revolution. In this section, I show why this would be a mistake.

The argument is simple. Dignity is, in the Kantian system, a *moral* notion that governs the character of our 'internal' attitudes, reasons, and action. It does not govern

---

[36] See also *Anthropology*, Ak185, 207, 214–15, 303–4, 307. And *DR*, 6:279.
[37] Consider, eg, how permissive Kant's theory of punishment is. See n 32.

the 'external' domain of Right, which sets limits to our actions but remains silent on the character of our reasons or attitudes towards those actions or towards the law governing those actions. It is no surprise, as we shall examine more closely in a moment, that there is *no* systematic use made of the idea of the dignity of humanity as end in itself in all of Kant's political writings, most important of which are the *Doctrine of Right*, but also 'Perpetual Peace', 'Idea of Universal History', 'What is Enlightenment?', and 'On the Common Saying'. This is in contrast to the *Groundwork* and the *Doctrine of Virtue* where use of the concept is pervasive and central.[38] If we accept the division Kant draws between the 'internal' domain of morality and the 'external' domain of Right (which I have classed as one of the central tenets of any truly Kantian account), then dignity cannot ground a theory of human rights, since human rights fall squarely within the domain of Right *simpliciter.*

In the introduction to the *Doctrine of Right*, Kant defines Right as involving only the 'external and indeed practical relation of one person to another, insofar as their actions, as deeds, can have (direct or indirect) influence on each other'.[39] He clarifies that Right has nothing to do with the way one's actions relate to the mere needs or wishes of others, as in 'actions of beneficence or callousness'; it only defines how one's own domain of external freedom interacts with that of others. Where morality commands our 'internal' attitudes towards the law and others, Right is silent. Right does not serve an 'incentive' (or reason or motive) to action; rather it represents merely an 'authorization to coerce'[40] whatever one's incentives. From the point of view of Right, it does not matter if you honor your contract with me solely because it will further your interests, or whether you only refrain from killing yourself because you are frightened of the pain. From the point of view of morality, on the other hand, it does: an action only has 'inner worth' if it is done from the motive of duty alone.[41] Right could be satisfied even among a 'race of devils'; morality could not.[42] As long as a legal order effectively harmonizes our external freedom in such a way as to make our domains of choice mutually consistent (and does so consistently with our innate right to freedom), then, from the point of view of Right, we can have no complaint; while from the point of view of morality, of course, we can.

On which side, 'external' or 'internal', does the idea of the dignity of humanity reside? Put another way, does human dignity govern and delimit the sphere of Right or of morality, or both? I have two arguments supporting the conclusion that dignity solely governs the domain of morality. The first is the argument from the uses of 'dignity' as a term of art. Kant uses the term 'dignity' primarily in two different senses, only the second of which is relevant for our purposes. First, he uses it to refer to designations of civil status and the corresponding rights and duties of office. For example, in 'Perpetual Peace', Kant claims that it would be 'beneath' the 'dignity of a ruler' (or minister) to sign a peace treaty while harboring a mental reservation to break it when

---

[38] It is worth noting that the notion is less central to the *Critique of Practical Reason*, no doubt because, in that work, he sought primarily to reformulate the relation between freedom and the moral law first laid out in Section III of the *Groundwork*, rather than further elucidate the three formulations of the CI. See, eg, Ak5:87–8.

[39] *DR*, Ak6:230.   [40] *DR*, Ak6:231.

[41] See, eg, *Groundwork* (hereinafter *G*), Ak4:397-8; see also *DV*, Ak6:390–1.   [42] *PP*, Ak8:366.

the occasion should prove fruitful.[43] In the *Doctrine of Right*, similarly, he refers to the will of a legislative authority which, regarded in its 'dignity', should be considered irreproachable.[44] Second, he uses it to refer to what has unconditional, absolute worth, and so is 'above all price'. In this second sense, dignity is a property of both humanity and the moral law: 'morality, and humanity insofar as it is capable of morality, is that which alone has dignity'.[45] The second sense is the one that is relevant for a theory of human rights, yet Kant *never uses it in any of his writings on politics or Right*.

It is worth pausing to explain why it would never have occurred to Kant to do so. And this brings us to the second argument for the conclusion that dignity is relevant to morality but not Right. Kant tells that our humanity *qua* rational nature has *dignity*. It is 'above all price', by which he means that its value is both of a higher order and incommensurable with the value of anything else. Why? Kant tells us that our capacity for rational choice raises us above the order of nature. By willing rationally, we make ourselves into law-*makers* rather than merely law-*takers* (in the way the rest of nature is). It is for this reason that we must always treat others as ends in themselves and never merely as means. To treat them as mere means would be to degrade and disrespect the dignity—the unconditional, incommensurable, and absolute value—of their capacity for rational willing. In the *Groundwork*, Kant writes:

> the mere dignity of humanity as rational nature, without any other end or advantage to be attained by it—hence respect for a mere idea—is...to serve as an inflexible precept of the will, and...it is just in this independence of maxims from all such incentives that their sublimity consists, and the worthiness of every rational subject to be a lawgiving member in the kingdom of ends; for otherwise he would have to be represented only as subject to the natural law of his needs.[46]

And, in the *Doctrine of Virtue*, he writes:

> Every human being has a legitimate claim to respect from his fellow human beings and is *in turn* bound to respect every other. Humanity itself is a dignity; for a human being cannot be used merely as a means by any human being (either by others or even by himself) but must always be used at the same time as an end. It is just in this that his dignity (personality) consists, by which he raises himself above all other beings in the world that are not human beings and yet can be used, and so over all *things*.[47]

The dignity of humanity sets limits to how I may permissibly treat not only others but also myself, and commands that in acting, I always respect their and my own capacity for rational choice.

Now imagine that you walk into my store, and I cheerfully tell you how good you look in that shirt. I do so in order to get you to buy the wares that I offer. Say that I have no concern for you, and that I would gladly ignore you were it not for your usefulness in building my business. And say further that it is a blatant lie that you look good in that shirt. In fact, you look awful. Have I respected the dignity of your humanity?

---

[43] *PP*, Ak8:344.   [44] *DR*, Ak6:316; see also *PP*, 8:368; *DR*, 6:317–18; 6:328; 6:329–30.
[45] *G*, Ak4:435, 84.   [46] *G*, Ak4:439.   [47] *DV*, Ak6:462.

According to Kant, plainly not: in lying to you, I have used you as a mere means. And not only have I violated *your* humanity, but I have also degraded *my own*:

> By a lie a human being throws away and, as it were, annihilates his dignity as a human being. A human being who does not himself believe what he tells another…has even less worth than if he were a mere thing; for a thing, because it is something real and given, has the property of being serviceable so that another can put it to some use. But communication of one's thoughts to someone through words that yet (intentionally) contain the contrary of what the speaker thinks on the subject is an end that is directly opposed to the natural purposiveness of the speaker's capacity to communicate his thoughts, and is thus a renunciation by the speaker of his personality, and such a speaker is a mere deceptive appearance of a human being, not a human being himself.[48]

But has what I have done violated any precept of Right? Clearly not. Despite my lie, I have not violated any contract. I may not even have harmed you, if the wares and kind words I offer would do you some good. Kant writes: 'In the doctrine of right an intentional untruth is called a lie only if it violates another's right; but in ethics, where no authorization is derived from harmlessness, it is clear of itself that no intentional untruth in the expression of one's thoughts can refuse this harsh name'.[49] The duty to respect the dignity of humanity is a constraint on internal lawgiving, but no constraint on *external*. But, if this is correct, then dignity can't serve as the sole constraining ground for an account of human rights, which are concerned solely with external freedom.

One might insist that the concept of dignity at the heart of the Formula of Humanity—act in such a way as to treat humanity always as an end and never merely as a means—could be used to derive duties of Right *directly* by telling us which external actions are permissible and which ones are not; on this reading, it could be used to delimit a mutually consistent set of external freedoms, and so a mutually consistent set of *human rights*. By appealing solely to the ethical writings, we could then bypass the arguments for unitary sovereignty, exit from the state of nature, and the strict division between right and ethics. This reading cannot succeed because the CI (including the Formula of Humanity) is, I shall now argue, neither necessary nor sufficient for establishing mutually consistent domains of external freedom. We have just given one example that shows why it is not sufficient: Lying is a violation of another's dignity, yet it is not wrongful from the point of view of Right. How could, then, the CI alone explain this permission? One might think that the CI can be extended by thinking of Right as the application of the CI to a special case, namely, the case of external freedom. But why would the CI not make all instances of lying wrong (given how strongly it prohibits it in the domain of ethics) *also* under principles of Right? Why the 'exception'? We need here some analysis of the domain of Right and its special character before such an argument could go through (of the kind the *Doctrine of Right* aims to provide). Put in terms of human rights, we would need some further argument (not

---

[48] *DV*, Ak6:429.   [49] *DV*, Ak6:429.

provided by the CI or its various justifications) why there is no human right not to be lied to, especially given the fact that lying degrades one's own and others' dignity.

In further support of this point, consider that the UPR is explicitly addressed to a different subject than the CI: 'it cannot be required that this principle [the UPR] of all maxims be itself in turn my maxim, that is, it cannot be required that *I make it the maxim* of my action; for anyone can be free so long as I do not impair his freedom by my *external action,* even though I am quite indifferent to his freedom or would like in my heart to infringe upon it'.[50] Whereas the CI explicitly requires one to make the CI a constraint on one's maxims of action, the UPR does not. The CI cannot, once again, explain why failing to take up respect for someone's external freedom as a as an end (as in the lying example) is *not* wrong. And consider finally that, as Willascheck observes, it is hard to know how the CI could justify the coercion of others entailed by a system of rights, given its strong prohibition on coercion generally. How does the coercion required by public law not treat subjects who do not consent as means to the fulfillment of the state's ends?[51] Furthermore, how could the CI alone ground an entire system of rights, which requires specifying, for example, a set of principles for deriving mutually consistent domains of property? How can the CI alone determine the grounds determining the limits governing what is *meum* and what it *tuum*? The CI alone cannot, I conclude, be sufficient for grounding external domains of freedom without the edifice assembled in the *Doctrine of Right,* which includes the arguments for exit from the state of nature, unitary sovereignty, and the division between right and ethics.

The CI is also not *necessary* for establishing mutually consistent domains of external freedom. All the work can be done by the Universal Principle of Right—'an action is right if it can coexist with everyone's freedom in accordance with a universal law, or if on its maxim the freedom of choice of each can coexist with everyone's freedom in accordance with universal law'. There are two points that can be made in support of this thesis. First, in introducing and expounding the UPR, Kant makes no reference to either to the Formula of Humanity or to the other two representations of the Categorical Imperative. Like 'dignity' in the second sense outlined above, the Formula of Humanity (and its derivative forms) plays *no systematic role* in any of the political writings; no rights are grounded in the idea of using another as a mere means, for example, or of treating each person as end in himself.[52] Indeed, Kant appears to justify

---

[50]   *DR,* Ak6:231.

[51]   See, eg, Marcus Willaschek, 'The Non-Derivability of Kantian Right from the Categorical Imperative: A Response to Nance', *International Journal of Philosophical Studies,* 20 (2012): 557–64, 559.

[52]   With two exceptions, hence my claim that he makes no 'systematic' use. At the end of the Introduction to the *Doctrine of Right,* Kant writes, '*Be an honorable human being (honeste vive). Rightful honor (honestas iuridica)* consists in asserting one's worth as a human being in relation to others, a duty expressed by the saying, "Do not make yourself a mere means for others but be at the same time an end for them." This duty will be explained later as obligation from the right of humanity in our own person *(Lex iusti)*' (Ak6:236). It is not clear in the text where this duty is 'explained' as an obligation from the innate 'right of humanity in our own person', or what work it does in the argument for Right. On the contrary, it seems to refer primarily to a *duty of virtue,* and so to a duty of virtue that is derivable from Right rather than the other way around. Indeed, the passages most relevant to the explanation and extension of the idea of rightful honor (and its relation to humanity) occur in the *Doctrine of Virtue* at Ak6:434–7. The other time he alludes to the 'mere means' formulation is in discussion of why it is wrong to use punishment

the UPR solely from an analysis of Right, where Right is understood as involving the realization of mutually consistent domains of external freedom among embodied beings whose choices can conflict.[53] Second, an increasingly popular reading of the relation between the UPR and the CI has it that the justification of the UPR (and Kant's account of Right more generally) does not presuppose Kant's ethics. While the UPR may be derived from Kant's ethics in conjunction with his analysis of Right, it need not be: neither the validity of the UPR nor its justification depends on the validity or the justification of the CI. This reading has the merit that it would also support and explain the omission of the CI in the *Doctrine of Right*.[54] I cannot further support the reading here (other than what I have already said), but the important point is that, if it is true, then it would provide further evidence that the CI is not necessary for the UPR. I conclude that if Kant's understanding of dignity and the Formula of Humanity are neither necessary nor sufficient for a reconstruction of Kant's theory of Right, then it is not possible to derive a theory of truly Kantian human rights solely on their basis. While someone may reinvent Kant's concept of dignity for other uses, this would take them beyond what a truly Kantian theory can bear.

Conclusion

In this chapter, I have argued that there can be no truly Kantian theory of human rights. There cannot be, that is, a theory of human rights that respects three central (and interconnected) tenets of Kant's practical philosophy, namely (1) Kant's division between the domain of morality and the domain of right, (2) Kant's arguments for our moral obligation to exit the state of nature, and (3) Kant's arguments for unitary sovereignty. The contemporary appropriation of Kant for such purposes should count as one of the great misappropriations in the history of political thought.

---

to benefit society rather than simply to sanction a criminal act; it is wrong because 'a human being can never be treated merely as a means to the purposes of another or be put among the objects of rights to things: his innate personality protects him from this, even though he can be condemned to lose his civil personality' (6:331). I think this is a special case (and so not indicative of any systematic use) because it touches on the criminal law, and hence on the moral character of the criminal act (which is of course relevant in determining 'how much' punishment is deserved on Kant's view). See also the further limitations on punishment as stated in the *Doctrine of Virtue* at 6:463; it is relevant that these passages are in the Doctrine of *Virtue* rather than *Right*. See also Ripstein's useful discussion of the other citations of the CI in the *DR*, Ripstein, *Force and Freedom*, 356 fn 2.

[53] See the way the UPR is introduced at *DR*, 6:230ff.

[54] For more on the supposed independence of Kant's political philosophy from his moral philosophy, see Thomas Pogge, 'Is Kant's *Rechtslehre* a Comprehensive Liberalism?', in M. Timmons (ed.), *Kant's Metaphysics of Morals: Interpretative Essays* (Oxford: Oxford University Press, 2002), 133–59; Ripstein, *Force and Freedom*; Michael Nance, 'Kantian Right and the Categorical Imperative: Response to Willaschek', *International Journal of Philosophical Studies*, 20 (2012): 541–56; Allen W. Wood, 'The Final Form of Kant's Practical Philosophy', in Timmons, *Kant's Metaphysics of Morals: Interpretative Essays*, 1–23; Marcus Willaschek, 'Right and Coercion: Can Kant's Conception of Right Be Derived from His Moral Theory?', *International Journal of Philosophical Studies*, 17 (2009): 49–70. And for some scepticism regarding the idea that the truth and justification of the CI is not necessary for the truth and justification of the UPR, see Paul Guyer, 'Kant's Deductions of the Principle of Right', in Timmons, *Kant's Metaphysics of Morals: Interpretative Essays*, 23–64. Guyer writes: 'Whatever may be analytically "developed" out of the concept of right has no force unless the concept of right itself can be shown to be grounded in the nature and reality of freedom' (32). But here we may wonder: Why isn't the nature and reality of *external* freedom sufficient? Why must it also be *internal*?

Index

absolute rights 351, 352, 354
Abu-Laban, Yasmeen 639–40
accountability 256, 259
acquired rights 662, 663, 669, 673
Afghanistan 503
African (Banjul) Charter on Human and
    Peoples' Rights 269
African Commission on Human and People's
    Rights 265
African Court of Human Rights 267
agency 46, 63–4, 65, 66–8, 69, 115, 116
    conditions for 194–5
    dignity 206, 213
    equal (basic) 186–7, 192
    expression of 520–1, 524
    fundamental aspects 15
    fundamental conditions for a good life 79–80,
        85–90, 100
    instrumental justifications 11–16
    interests 90
    liberty and liberal democracy 589–90,
        599–600, 603, 609
    narrow notion 86
    non-fundamental aspects 15
    non-instrumental justifications 17–18
    religion, freedom of 408–9
    security, right to 432
    social ontology of human rights 178–9, 181,
        182, 185–6, 193, 194
    undermining 88
    wide notion 86
    see also normative agency
agency-in-relations 192
aim and object of a right, distinction between 8,
    30, 96–7, 100
Al-Skeini and Others v. United Kingdom 272n
Alexander, Larry 40
Alexy, Robert 323–4, 346, 354
Allison, Henry 653–4
Alston, William P. 414n
Altman, Andrew 464n
American Anthropological
    Association: Statement on Human
    Rights 571
Amnesty International 437, 672
Anderson, Elizabeth 361
Anderson, Joel H. 433
animals and right-holding status 9
animals, status of and freedom of religion
    420–2
An-Na'im, Abdullahi 21n, 33
Anscombe, G.E.M. 611n
Arab Spring 210
Arendt, Hannah 283, 286–7
Aristotle 13, 342, 343n
Arneson, Richard 645
Ashford, Elizabeth 26n , 27n, 29, 41, 535–7, 549
Audi, Robert 40
Austin, John 134–5

Austria 399
authorizations 662, 673
autonomy 64, 67, 240, 583, 587
    agency 85–6
    dignity 129, 274
    free speech 367, 369
    individual 590, 594–6, 598, 599, 602–6
    internal 99
    liberty rights and liberal democracy 591–3,
        599–601, 605n, 607, 612, 618
    moral 575
    normative agency 573–4, 576
    personal moral desert 153
    relativity and ethnocentricity of human
        rights 558–60, 563, 565
    security, right to 434, 436
    social ontology of human rights 179
    vulnerable 433–4

Bangkok Declaration (1993) 562–3
Bankovic and Others v. Belgium and 16 Other
    Contracting States 266n
Barak, Aharon 344–6
Barnes, Marian 630–1
Barry, Brian 613
Barry, Christian 27
basal/lower-level human rights 8, 30, 675
basic activities 81–2, 103–6, 108–9
    adequate range of fundamental conditions 105,
        107, 110–12, 115–16
basic conditions 194
basic evaluations 557
basic human rights 178, 182, 195, 213
    health, right to 494
    security, right to 434, 450
    self-determination and democracy 463
    social ontology of human rights 181
    subsistence, right to 517, 535–7
basic interests 116, 461
basic needs 11–16, 64n, 116, 572, 577–87
basic norms 467
basis of human rights 207–12
Beck, Lewis White 654n
Beitz, Charles 3, 6–7, 19–20, 26n, 28, 31, 41, 80,
    94–8, 102n, 141, 147–52, 178, 187–8, 190–1,
    202n, 241, 244n, 245n, 247, 265, 367, 408n,
    412n, 445n, 453, 483n, 496, 498–9, 501,
    571n, 653n
beneficence 545–7
Benhabib, S. 300n
Bentham, Jeremy 39–40, 135n, 321, 643
Berlin, Isaiah 181, 515
Besson, Samantha 6, 22, 40, 41n, 244n
bills of rights:
    domestic 250–1, 279, 288–9
    international 279, 347
    see also United States of America
Blackstone, W. 427–9, 433, 434–5
Blum, Gabriella 271

Index

Printed and bound by CPI Group (UK) Ltd, Croydon, CR0 4YY